# Chapter Content

## RECEIVABLES (Chapter 9)

Methods to Account for Uncollectible Accounts

| Direct write-off method | Record bad debts expense when the company determines a particular account to be uncollectible. |
|---|---|
| Allowance methods: Percentage-of-sales | At the end of each period estimate the amount of credit sales uncollectible. Debit Bad Debts Expense and credit Allowance for Doubtful Accounts for this amount. As specific accounts become uncollectible, debit Allowance for Doubtful Accounts and credit Accounts Receivable. |
| Percentage-of-receivables | At the end of each period estimate the amount of uncollectible receivables. Debit Bad Debts Expense and credit Allowance for Doubtful Accounts in an amount that results in a balance in the allowance account equal to the estimate of uncollectibles. As specific accounts become uncollectible, debit Allowance for Doubtful Accounts and credit Accounts Receivable. |

## PLANT ASSETS (Chapter 10)

Presentation

| Tangible Assets | Intangible Assets |
|---|---|
| Property, plant, and equipment | Intangible assets (Patents, copyrights, trademarks, franchises, goodwill) |
| Natural resources | |

Computation of Annual Depreciation Expense

| Straight-line | $\dfrac{\text{Cost} - \text{Salvage value}}{\text{Useful life (in years)}}$ |
|---|---|
| Units-of-activity | $\dfrac{\text{Depreciable cost}}{\text{Useful life (in units)}} \times \text{Units of activity during year}$ |
| Declining-balance | Book value at beginning of year $\times$ Declining balance rate* *Declining-balance rate $= 1 \div$ Useful life (in years) |

*Note:* If depreciation is calculated for partial periods, the straight-line and declining-balance methods must be adjusted for the relevant proportion of the year. Multiply the annual depreciation expense by the number of months expired in the year divided by 12 months.

## BONDS (Chapter 11)

| Premium | Market interest rate < Contractual interest rate |
|---|---|
| Face Value | Market interest rate = Contractual interest rate |
| Discount | Market interest rate > Contractual interest rate |

Computation of Annual Bond Interest Expense

Interest expense = Interest paid (payable) + Amortization of discount
(OR − Amortization of premium)

| Straight-line amortization | $\dfrac{\text{Bond discount (premium)}}{\text{Number of interest periods}}$ | |
|---|---|---|
| Effective-interest amortization (preferred method) | Bond interest expense | Bond interest paid |
| | Carrying value of bonds at beginning of period $\times$ Effective interest rate | Face amount of bonds $\times$ Contractual interest rate |

## STOCKHOLDERS' EQUITY (Chapter 12)

No-Par Value vs. Par Value Stock Journal Entries

| No-Par Value | Par Value |
|---|---|
| Cash    Common Stock | Cash    Common Stock (par value)    Paid-in Capital in Excess of Par Value |

Comparison of Dividend Effects

| | Cash | Common Stock | Retained Earnings |
|---|---|---|---|
| Cash dividend | ↓ | No effect | ↓ |
| Stock dividend | No effect | ↑ | ↓ |
| Stock split | No effect | No effect | No effect |

Debits and Credits to Retained Earnings

| Retained Earnings | |
|---|---|
| Debits (Decreases) | Credits (Increases) |
| 1. Net loss 2. Prior period adjustments for overstatement of net income 3. Cash dividends and stock dividends 4. Some disposals of treasury stock | 1. Net income 2. Prior period adjustments for Understatement of net income |

## INVESTMENTS (Chapter 13)

Comparison of Long-Term Bond Investment and Liability Journal Entries

| Event | Investor | Investee |
|---|---|---|
| Purchase / issue of bonds | Debt Investments    Cash | Cash    Bonds Payable |
| Interest receipt / payment | Cash    Interest Revenue | Interest Expense    Cash |

Comparison of Cost and Equity Methods of Accounting for Long-Term Stock Investments

| Event | Cost | Equity |
|---|---|---|
| Acquisition | Stock Investments    Cash | Stock Investments    Cash |
| Investee reports earnings | No entry | Stock Investments    Investment Revenue |
| Investee pays dividends | Cash    Dividend Revenue | Cash    Stock Investments |

Trading and Available-for-Sale Securities

| Trading | Report at fair value with changes reported in net income. |
|---|---|
| Available-for-sale | Report at fair value with changes reported in the stockholders' equity section. |

**STATEMENT OF CASH FLOWS** (Chapter 14)

Cash flows from operating activities (**indirect method**)
  Net income
  Add:    Losses on disposals of assets                                    $ X
          Amortization and depreciation                                      X
          Decreases in noncash current assets                                X
          Increases in current liabilities                                   X
  Deduct: Gains on disposals of assets                                      (X)
          Increases in noncash current assets                               (X)
          Decreases in current liabilities                                  (X)
  Net cash provided (used) by operating activities                              $ X

Cash flows from operating activities (**direct method**)
  Cash receipts
    (Examples: from sales of goods and services to customers, from receipts
    of interest and dividends on loans and investments)                    $ X
  Cash payments
    (Examples: to suppliers, for operating expenses, for interest, for taxes)   (X)
  Cash provided (used) by operating activities                                 $ X

## PRESENTATION OF NON-TYPICAL ITEMS (Chapter 15)

| | |
|---|---|
| **Prior period adjustments** (Chapter 12) | Statement of retained earnings (adjustment of beginning retained earnings) |
| **Discontinued operations** | Income statement (presented separately after "Income from continuing operations") |
| **Extraordinary items** | Income statement (presented separately after "Income before extraordinary items") |
| **Changes in accounting principle** | In most instances, use the new method in current period and restate previous years results using new method. For changes in depreciation and amortization methods, use the new method in the current period, but do not restate previous periods. |

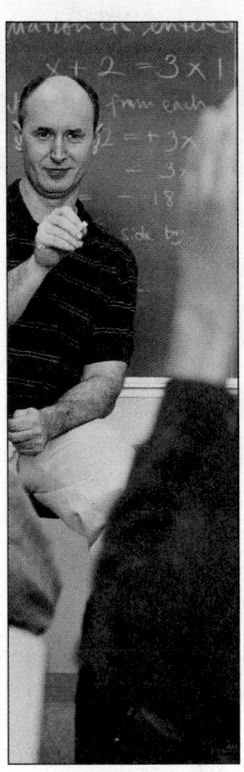

# Success in Accounting is just a click away...

With *WileyPLUS*, students and instructors will experience success in the classroom.

When students succeed—when they stay on-task and make the breakthrough that turns confusion into confidence—they are empowered to realize the possibilities for greatness that lie within each of them. Our goal is to create an environment where students reach their full potential and experience the exhilaration of academic success that will last them a lifetime. *WileyPLUS* can help you reach that goal.

Wiley**PLUS** is an online suite of resources—including the complete text—that will help your students:

- come to class better prepared for your lectures
- get immediate feedback and context-sensitive help on assignments and quizzes
- track progress throughout the course

"I just wanted to say how much this program helped me in studying… I was able to actually see my mistakes and correct them. … I really think that other students should have the chance to use *WileyPLUS*."

Ashlee Krisko, *Oakland University*

www.wileyplus.com

**87%** of students surveyed said it improved their understanding of the material. *

* Based on a fall 2006 survey of 519 accounting student users of *WileyPLUS*

## Prepare & Present

Create outstanding class presentations using a wealth of resources, such as PowerPoint™ slides, interactive simulations, and more. Plus you can easily upload any materials you have created into your course, and combine them with the resources contained in *WileyPLUS*.

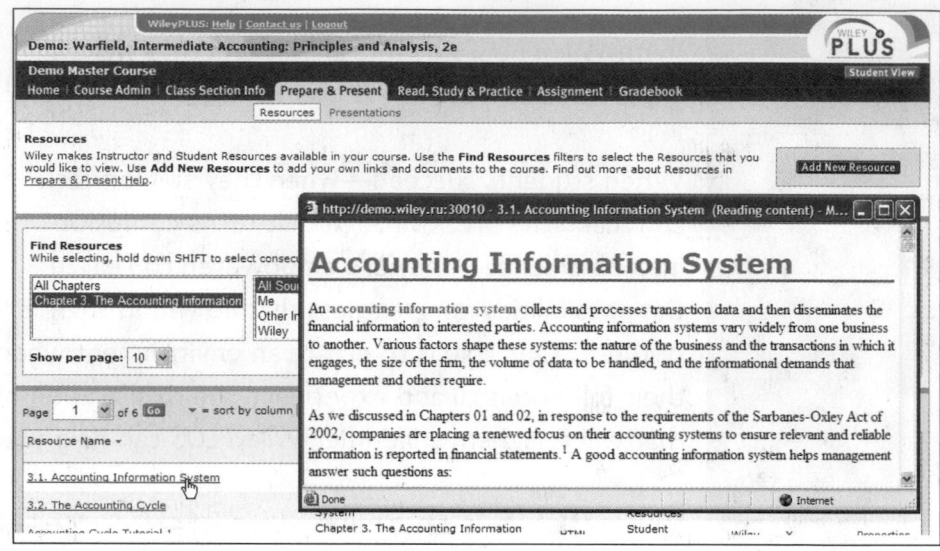

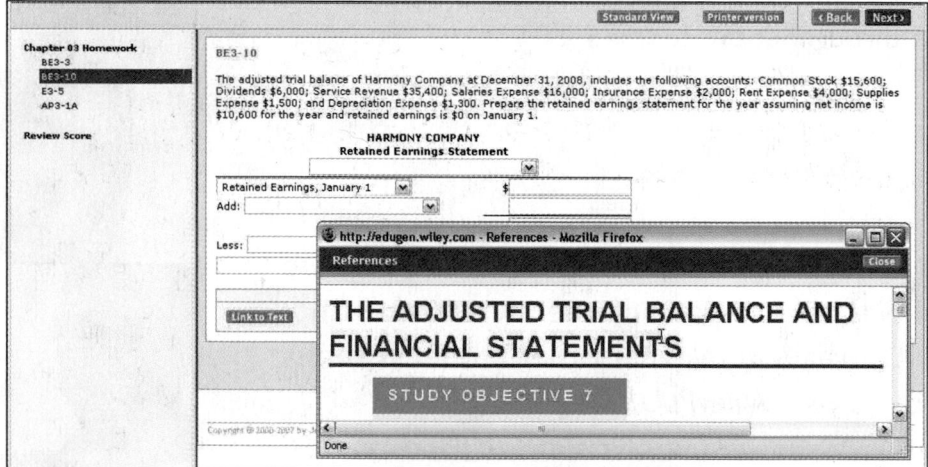

## Create Assignments

Automate the assigning and grading of homework or quizzes by using the provided question banks, or by writing your own. Student results will be automatically graded and recorded in your gradebook. *WileyPLUS* also links homework problems to relevant sections of the online text, hints, or solutions—context-sensitive help where students need it most!

# in your class each day. With Wiley**PLUS** you will:

## Track Student Progress

Keep track of your students' progress via an instructor's gradebook, which allows you to analyze individual and overall class results. This gives you an accurate and realistic assessment of your students' progress and level of understanding.

### Now Available with WebCT and ecollege!

Now you can seamlessly integrate all of the rich content and resources available with *WileyPLUS* with the power and convenience of your WebCT or ecollege course. You and your students get the best of both worlds with single sign-on, an integrated gradebook, list of assignments and roster, and more. If your campus is using another course management system, contact your local Wiley Representative.

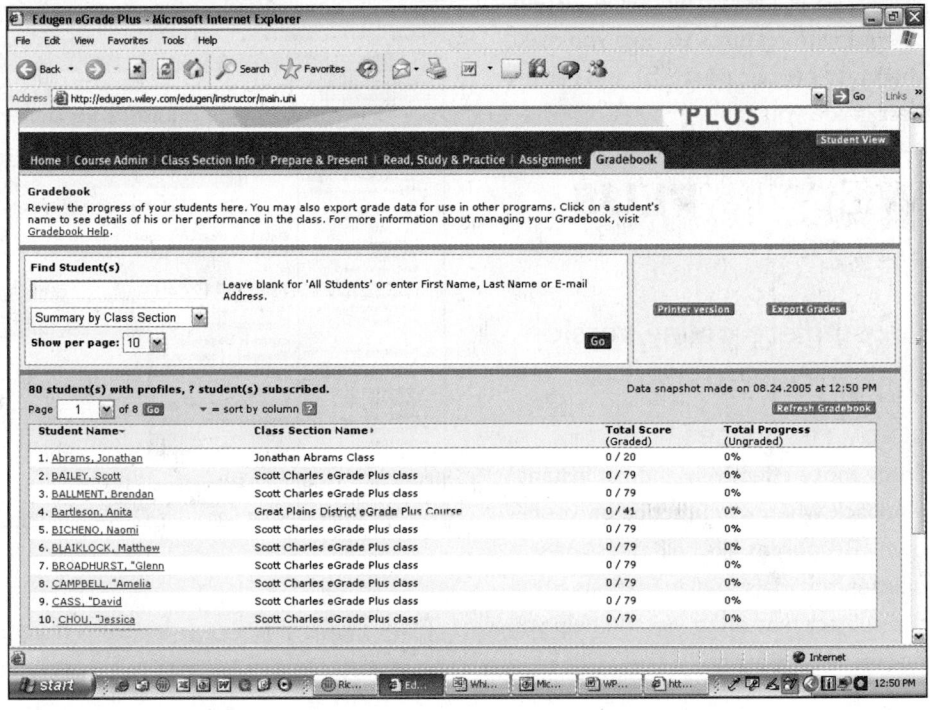

"I studied more for this class than I would have without *WileyPLUS*."

Melissa Lawler, *Western Washington Univ.*

For more information on what *WileyPLUS* can do to help your students reach their potential, please visit

## www.wileyplus.com/experience

# 82% of students surveyed said it made them better prepared for tests. *

*Based on a fall 2006 survey of 519 accounting student users of *WileyPLUS*

## TO THE STUDENT

# You have the potential to make a difference!

*WileyPLUS* is a powerful online system packed with features to help you make the most of your potential, and get the best grade you can!

## With Wiley**PLUS** you get:

### A complete online version of your text and other study resources

Study more effectively and get instant feedback when you practice on your own. Resources like self-assessment quizzes, tutorials, and animations bring the subject matter to life, and help you master the material.

### Problem-solving help, instant grading, and feedback on your homework and quizzes

You can keep all of your assigned work in one location, making it easy for you to stay on task. Plus, many homework problems contain direct links to the relevant portion of your text to help you deal with problem-solving obstacles at the moment they come up.

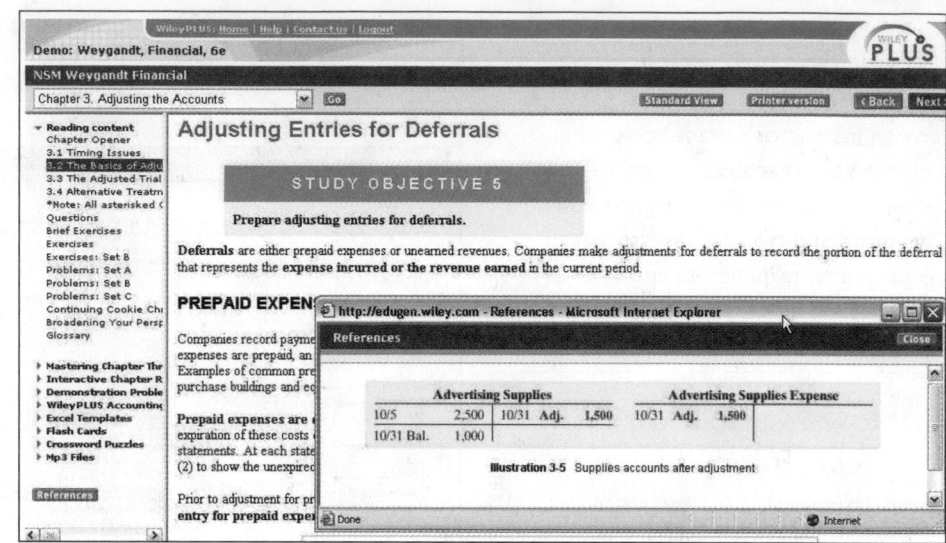

### The ability to track your progress and grades throughout the term.

A personal gradebook allows you to monitor your results from past assignments at any time. You'll always know exactly where you stand.

If your instructor uses *WileyPLUS*, you will receive a URL for your class. If not, your instructor can get more information about *WileyPLUS* by visiting www.wileyplus.com

or

by viewing a *WileyPLUS* demo at www.wileyplus.com/experience

"It has been a great help, and I believe it has helped me to achieve a better grade."

Michael Morris, *Columbia Basin College*

# 74% of students surveyed said it helped them get a better grade. *

**6**th Edition

# Financial
# Accounting

*Jerry J. Weygandt* PhD, CPA

**Arthur Andersen Alumni Professor of Accounting**
University of Wisconsin
Madison, Wisconsin

*Paul D. Kimmel* PhD, CPA

**Associate Professor of Accounting**
University of Wisconsin—Milwaukee
Milwaukee, Wisconsin

*Donald E. Kieso* PhD, CPA

**KPMG Emeritus Professor of Accounting**
Northern Illinois University
DeKalb, Illinois

BICENTENNIAL
1807
WILEY
2007
BICENTENNIAL

**John Wiley & Sons, Inc.**

*Dedicated to*
the **Wiley sales representatives**
*who sell our books and service our adopters*
*in a professional and ethical manner*
*and to*
*Enid, Merlynn, and Donna*

*Executive Publisher*   Donald Fowley
*Executive Editor*   Christopher DeJohn
*Senior Marketing Manager*   Julia Flohr
*Project Editor*   Ed Brislin
*Development Editor*   Ann Torbert
*Production Services Manager*   Dorothy Sinclair
*Associate Editor*   Brian Kamins
*Senior Production Editor*   Valerie Vargas
*Text and Cover Designer*   Madelyn Lesure
*Senior Photo Editor*   Elle Wagner
*Senior Illustration Editor*   Sandra Rigby
*Outside Production Management*   Suzanne Ingrao/Ingrao Associates
*Senior Media Editor*   Allison Morris
*Cover photo*   Pacific Stock/Super Stock
*Editorial Assistant*   Kathryn Fraser

This book was set in Times Ten by *Aptara, Inc.,* and printed and bound by R.R. Donnelley & Sons, Inc.—Jefferson City. The cover was printed by R.R. Donnelley & Sons, Inc.—Jefferson City.

This book is printed on acid-free paper.

The specimen financial statements Appendix A and Appendix B are printed with permission of PepsiCo, Inc. and The Coca-Cola Company.

Pepsi is a registered trademark of PepsiCo, Inc. Used with permission.

To order books or for customer service, please call 1(800)-CALL-WILEY (225-5945).

ISBN 978-0470-12884-8

Printed in the United States of America

10  9  8  7  6  5  4  3  2  1

**Jerry J. Weygandt, PhD, CPA,** is Arthur Andersen Alumni Professor of Accounting at the University of Wisconsin—Madison. He holds a Ph.D. in accounting from the University of Illinois. Articles by Professor Weygandt have appeared in the *Accounting Review, Journal of Accounting Research, Accounting Horizons, Journal of Accountancy,* and other academic and professional journals. These articles have examined such financial reporting issues as accounting for price-level adjustments, pensions, convertible securities, stock option contracts, and interim reports. Professor Weygandt is author of other accounting and financial reporting books and is a member of the American Accounting Association, the American Institute of Certified Public Accountants, and the Wisconsin Society of Certified Public Accountants. He has seved on numerous committees of the American Accounting Association and as a member of the editorial board of the *Accounting Review*; he also has served as President and Secretary-Treasurer of the American Accounting Association. In addition, he has been actively involved with the American Institute of Certified Public Accountants and has been a member of the Accounting Standards Executive Committee (AcSEC) of that organization. He has served on the FASB task force that examined the reporting issues related to accounting for income taxes and served as a trustee of the Financial Accounting Foundation. Professor Weygandt has received the Chancellor's Award for Excellence in Teaching and the Beta Gamma Sigma Dean's Teaching Award. He is on the board of directors of M & I Bank of Southern Wisconsin. He is the recipient of the Wisconsin Institute of CPA's Outstanding Educator's Award and the Lifetime Achievement Award. In 2001 he received the American Accounting Association's Outstanding Accounting Educator Award.

**Paul D. Kimmel, PhD, CPA,** received his bachelor's degree from the University of Minnesota and his doctorate in accounting from the University of Wisconsin. He is an Associate Professor at the University of Wisconsin—Milwaukee, and has public accounting experience with Deloitte & Touche (Minneapolis). He was the recipient of the UWM School of Business Advisory Council Teaching Award, the Reggie Taite Excellence in Teaching Award, and a three-time winner of the Outstanding Teaching Assistant Award at the University of Wisconsin. He is also a recipient of the Elijah Watts Sells Award for Honorary Distinction for his results on the CPA exam. He is a member of the American Accounting Association and the Institute of Management Accountants and has published articles in *Accounting Review, Accounting Horizons, Advances in Management Accounting, Managerial Finance, Issues in Accounting Education, Journal of Accounting Education,* as well as other journals. His research interests include accounting for financial instruments and innovation in accounting education. He has published papers and given numerous talks on incorporating critical thinking into accounting education, and helped prepare a catalog of critical thinking resources for the Federated Schools of Accountancy.

**Donald E. Kieso, PhD, CPA,** received his bachelor's degree from Aurora University and his doctorate in accounting from the University of Illinois. He has served as chairman of the Department of Accountancy and is currently the KPMG Emeritus Professor of Accountancy at Northern Illinois University. He has public accounting experience with Price Waterhouse & Co. (San Francisco and Chicago) and Arthur Andersen & Co. (Chicago) and research experience with the Research Division of the American Institute of Certified Public Accountants (New York). He has done postdoctorate work as a Visiting Scholar at the University of California at Berkeley and is a recipient of NIU's Teaching Excellence Award and four Golden Apple Teaching Awards. Professor Kieso is the author of other accounting and business books and is a member of the American Accounting Association, the American Institute of Certified Public Accountants, and the Illinois CPA Society. He has served as a member of the Board of Directors of the Illinois CPA Society, the AACSB's Accounting Accreditation Committees, the State of Illinois Comptroller's Commission, as Secretary-Treasurer of the Federation of Schools of Accountancy, and as Secretary-Treasurer of the American Accounting Association. Professor Kieso is currently serving on the Board of Trustees and Executive Committee of Aurora University, as a member of the Board of Directors of Kishwaukee Community Hospital, and as Treasurer and Director of Valley West Community Hospital. From 1989 to 1993 he served as a charter member of the national Accounting Education Change Commission. He is the recipient of the Outstanding Accounting Educator Award from the Illinois CPA Society, the FSA's Joseph A. Silvoso Award of Merit, the NIU Foundation's Humanitarian Award for Service to Higher Education, a Distinguished Service Award from the Illinois CPA Society, and in 2003 an honorary doctorate from Aurora University.

In the previous editions of *Financial Accounting*, we sought to create a book about business that made the subject clear and fascinating to beginning students. That is still our passion: to provide a link between accounting principles, student learning, and the real world.

## Student Empowerment and Success

When we ask fellow instructors what is the one student behavior that matters most to success in an accounting class, we hear, overwhelmingly, "Do the work—and especially the homework." Instructors say over and over again that those students who spend more time on the course get a better grade. Also, we've heard again and again that the biggest challenges students face are to become motivated, to learn how to study, and to manage their tasks. Our goal is to give you a book with the *pedagogical tools* and the *technological support* that will so engage students that they spend more "time on task." The result will be more learning and more satisfaction, both for them and for you.

This edition of *Financial Accounting* provides some old tools and some new ones that make accounting interesting and useful to beginning students. One new tool focuses on the skills students will need to succeed in their financial matters, whether it be in business or in their personal lives. Another new tool is a technology that gives students access to numerous online materials that will help them succeed in this course. For more details on both these new tools, read on.

## Goals and Features of the Sixth Edition

The Sixth Edition of *Financial Accounting* improves a teaching and learning package that instructors and students have rated the highest in customer satisfaction. Users and reviewers continue to comment positively on the writing style, the use of real-world examples, pedagogical features, and the fact that the textbook is not only about accounting but also about business. It demonstrates the relevance of accounting to students' future careers. This revision has maintained these successful features and improved on them.

An exciting addition—the first of the new tools referred to above—is titled *All About You.* This high-interest feature links some aspect of the chapter's topic to students' personal lives. Each *All About You* box presents the topic, offers some facts about it, poses a situation for students to think about, and offers alternative answers as a starting place for further discussion. For example, in Chapter 10, we relate the opening story about Rent-a-Wreck maximizing its profitability by buying and renting used cars to the issue of whether a student could maximize economic well-being by buying a used car rather than a new one. As a feedback mechanism at the end of the chapter, we offer our own comments and opinions about the *All About You* situation. The fifteen *All About You* boxes promote financial literacy. They are intended to get students thinking and talking about how accounting issues impact their personal lives.

Linked to the *All About You* boxes is an *"All About You" Activity* (located in the *Broadening Your Perspective* section); it offers further opportunity to explore aspects of the topic in a homework assignment.

The new technology tool is *WileyPLUS.* This online suite of resources offers students "Read, Study, and Practice" tools that can include the entire online textbook, along with interactive feedback and context-sensitive help on assignments and quizzes. An online gradebook enables instructors to maintain student records and students to track their progress. Both students and instructors who have used this technology have raved about its effectiveness. For more on this powerful tool, see the full description of it on page xiii.

In addition, we have kept and improved on some already-successful features of the book: *Accounting Across the Organization* boxes demonstrate use of accounting information by people in *non-accounting functions* (e.g., marketing, finance, management). These boxes provide further evidence of accounting applications throughout an organization. Some of these boxes are new, and some have been adapted from the *Insight* boxes of previous editions. The *Insight* boxes in this edition focus on one of three themes—ethics, investor concerns, and international topics.

Also, to boost student interest and provide more feedback to increase student interaction with content, we have added critical thinking questions at the end of both the *Insight* and the *Accounting Across the Organization* boxes. Guideline answers appear at the end of the chapter.

Further, to give you more choice of homework opportunities, we have added several new assignment features. At the Student Companion website for each chapter are new *B Exercises* and new *C Problems.*

In addition, to further the likelihood of capturing and holding student attention, we have put the text through a rigorous line-edit. The goal of this process was to simplify words and sentences, and to introduce an active voice and conversational style throughout. A new and lively design supports our efforts to freshen the presentation for today's student audience.

This edition was also subject to a comprehensive revision to ensure that it is technically accurate, relevant, and up-to-date. A chapter-by-chapter summary of content changes is provided below. In addition to the specific changes listed there, we also have added three or four additional new exercises per chapter, revised Brief Exercises, Exercises, and Problems in all chapters, and updated the PepsiCo and Coca-Cola Company financial analysis and reporting problems throughout.

## KEY CHANGES, BY CHAPTER

### Chapter 1: Accounting in Action

- New *Feature Story* focuses on the importance of knowing and understanding accounting information.
- Chapter includes brief coverage of *GAAP, relevance* and *reliability*, the *monetary unit assumption*, the *economic entity assumption*, and the *cost principle.*
- Expanded discussion of ethics, including the Sarbanes-Oxley Act.
- Added new discussion of U.S. GAAP and international GAAP (iGAAP) convergence efforts.
- Deleted the section "Why Study Accounting," but heavily revised the appendix on the accounting profession and careers in accounting.
- New *All About You* feature on the ethics of managing personal financial reporting.
- Four new Exercises.
- New *All About You Activity* asks students to analyze ethics of financial aid reporting and corporate reporting.

### Chapter 2: The Recording Process

- New *Accounting Across the Organization* box about links between design and profitability of the Xbox at Microsoft.
- Added accounting equation analyses to transactions-analysis illustrations.
- New *All About You* feature on ethics in reporting one's "personal financial statement"—the résumé.
- Four new Exercises.
- New *All About You Activity* explores short-term career goals and résumé presentation.

### Chapter 3: Adjusting the Accounts

- New *Feature Story* about profit reported at Enron.
- Changed terminology from "prepayments" to "deferrals."
- Four new illustrations highlight the accounting for deferrals and accruals.
- Chapter includes brief coverage of the *time period assumption*, the *revenue recognition principle*, and the *matching principle.*
- Two new Ethics Notes.
- New *Accounting Across the Organization* box on accounting for gift cards.
- New *All About You* feature on environmental liability of old electronic equipment.
- Five new Exercises.

- New *All About You Activity* looks at some alternative situations relating to loan applications.

### Chapter 4: Completing the Accounting Cycle

- Updated all real-company classified balance sheet presentations.
- New *International Insight* about use of International Financial Reporting Standards on Chinese balance sheets.
- Changed worksheets to spreadsheet format.
- New Ethics Note on Sarbanes-Oxley.
- New *All About You* feature about personal balance sheets.
- One new Brief Exercise and eight new Exercises.
- New *All About You Activity* gives students practice preparing a personal balance sheet.

### Chapter 5: Accounting for Merchandising Operations

- New *Feature Story* on Wal-Mart.
- Purchases and sales are now broken out into separate sections.
- Material on freight costs now precedes purchase returns and allowances.
- New subsection, with a T account, summarizing purchase transactions.
- New *Before You Go On* review for purchase transactions.
- Subsection on operating expenses precedes non-operating activities.
- New *Investor Insight* on the effect of accounting-control problems on stock price.
- New *Accounting Across the Organization* box on revenue recognition issues in publishers' return policies.
- New *Ethics Insight* on the amount of detail companies provide about "other gains and losses."
- Two new Ethics Notes.
- New *All About You* feature on channel stuffing.
- Five new Exercises.
- New *All About You Activity* asks students to think through revenue recognition situations related to channel stuffing.

### Chapter 6: Inventories

- New *Feature Story* on accounting for inventory at Caterpillar Inc.
- Chapter now includes brief coverage of *consistency* and *conservatism.*
- New *Accounting Across the Organization* box on use of electronic product codes and RFID technology for inventory control.
- New *Accounting Across the Organization* box on inventory build-up at Samsung Electronics.
- New *All About You* feature on employee theft.
- Four new Exercises.
- New *All About You Activity* has students search the Internet for stories of inventory fraud.

## Chapter 7: Accounting Principles

- Expanded discussion of International Accounting Standards Board and uniformity in standards.
- New *All About You* feature on ethics codes in business and colleges/universities.
- New *All About You Activity* asks students to investigate a code of ethics.

## Chapter 8: Internal Control and Cash

- New section on Sarbanes-Oxley.
- New *Investor Insight* on effects of internal controls on stock price.
- New *Accounting Across the Organization* box on how Sarbanes-Oxley boosts the role of human resources departments.
- Two new Ethics Notes.
- New *All About You* feature on protecting oneself from identity theft.
- One new Brief Exercise.
- Four new Exercises.
- New *All About You Activity* asks students to take a quiz on identity theft.

## Chapter 9: Accounting for Receivables

- New *Feature Story* on receivables at Whitehall-Robins.
- Revised discussion of credit card sales; deleted discussion of credit sales via American Express and Diners Club.
- New *Investor Insight* on signal that a cut in allowance for doubtful accounts should send to investors.
- New *Accounting Across the Organization* box on how credit cards work.
- New *Accounting Across the Organization* box on effect of looser credit terms at Mitsubishi Motors.
- New *All About You* feature on whether students should have credit cards.
- Four new Exercises.
- New *All About You Activity* asks students to evaluate credit card terms.

## Chapter 10: Plant Assets, Natural Resources, and Intangible Assets

- Revised/updated section on intangible assets.
- New *Accounting Across the Organization* box on leasing by U.S. companies.
- New *Accounting Across the Organization* box on the franchise value of Monday Night Football.
- Two new Ethics Notes.
- Now includes brief coverage of the *going concern assumption* and *materiality*.
- Revised appendix on exchange of plant assets.
- New *All About You* feature on whether to buy a used or a new car.
- One new Brief Exercise.
- Four new Exercises.
- New *All About You Activity* tests students' knowledge of famous trade names.

## Chapter 11: Liabilities

- New *Accounting Across the Organization* box on amounts of taxes Americans pay.
- New *Accounting Across the Organization* box on risks of short-term financing.
- New *Accounting Across the Organization* box on shopping for an interest rate.
- New *Accounting Across the Organization* box on debt covenants.
- New *All About You* feature explores how far companies can go in monitoring lifestyle issues.
- New *All About You Activity* has students calculate taxes: state and federal income, property, gasoline, sales, and Social Security.
- Four new Brief Exercises.
- Eight new Exercises.
- New *All About You Activity* asks students to research warning signs of personal-debt trouble.

## Chapter 12: Corporations: Organization, Stock Transactions, Dividends, and Retained Earnings

- *Ethics Insight* now cites Sarbanes-Oxley.
- Section on corporate capital moved; now follows discussion of ownerships rights and stock issue considerations. Section now includes coverage of paid-in capital and retained earnings.
- New Illustration 12-6, comparing owners' equity accounts for proprietorships and corporations.
- New text example on Google's IPO.
- New *Accounting Across the Organization* box on why companies have recently increased dividends.
- New *All About You* feature on home-equity loans.
- Five new Exercises.
- New *All About You Activity* asks students to answer questions about PepsiCo annual report.

## Chapter 13: Investments

- New *Accounting Across the Organization* box on how to report investments.
- New *Accounting Across the Organization* box on valuing securities at fair value.
- New *All About You* feature on the importance of starting a personal savings plan now.
- Four new Exercises.
- New *All About You Activity* sends students to explore the SEC's websites.

## Chapter 14: Statement of Cash Flows

- Significantly revised chapter: shortened coverage of the operating activities section, for both methods, and condensed presentation from two years to one.
- Moved the direct method into an end-of-chapter appendix.
- New *Accounting Across the Organization* box on sales level and cash provided by operations.
- New *All About You* feature on budgeting.

- Four new Exercises.
- New *All About You Activity* asks students to calculate how much to set aside for short-term needs.

### Chapter 15: Financial Statement Analysis

- Replaced Sears with J. C. Penney as featured company throughout.
- Added quality of earnings discussions.
- Shortened section on changes in accounting principle.
- New *Investor Insight* box on effects of large restructuring costs.
- New *All About You* feature on when to begin investing in the stock market.
- One new Self-Study Question, one new Question, and one new Brief Exercise.
- One new Exercise.
- New *All About You Activity* asks students to complete a questionnaire on mutual funds.

### Appendix A: Specimen Financial Statements: PepsiCo, Inc.

### Appendix B: Specimen Financial Statements: The Coca-Cola Company

### Appendix C: Time Value of Money

- Added sections on nature of interest and simple versus compound interest.
- Added section, and related Brief Exercises, on using financial calculators to solve time value of money problems.
- Nine new Brief Exercises.

### Appendix D: Payroll Accounting

- Revised section on federal unemployment taxes, to clarify.
- Updated some illustrations into spreadsheet format.

### Appendix E: Subsidiary Ledgers and Special Journals

- Updated illustrations of ledgers and special journals to spreadsheet format.

### Appendix F: Other Significant Liabilities

- Updated illustration of disclosure of contingent liabilities.

## Proven Pedagogical Framework

In this book we have used many proven pedagogical tools to help students learn accounting concepts and procedures and apply them to the business world. This pedagogical framework emphasizes the processes that students undergo as they learn. Turn to the **Student Owner's Manual** on page xviii to see all of the learning tools in detail. These tools help students learn how to use the textbook, understand the context, learn the material, "put it all together," develop skills through practice, and expand and apply knowledge. Here are a few key features.

### LEARNING HOW TO USE THE TEXTBOOK

- The **Student Owner's Manual**, p. xviii, and **notes in blue** in Chapter 1, explain how to use the text's learning tools to help achieve success in the course.
- A **Learning Styles Quiz**, p. xxvii, includes tips on learning styles and strategies.
- **The Navigator** guides students through each chapter by pulling all the learning tools together into a learning system. **The Navigator** box on the chapter-opening page lays out a study framework throughout the chapter, **Navigator** icons prompt students to use the learning aids and to set priorities as they study.

### UNDERSTANDING THE CONTEXT

- **Study Objectives**, listed at the beginning of each chapter, reappear in the margins and again in the **Summary of Study Objectives.**
- A **Feature Story** helps students picture how the chapter topic relates to the real world of accounting and business and serves as a recurrent example.
- A **Chapter Preview** links the Feature Story to the major topics of the chapter and provides a road map to the chapter.

### LEARNING THE MATERIAL

- Financial statement excerpts emphasize accounting experiences of **real companies throughout.**
- **Business Insight** and **Accounting Across the Organization** boxes give students glimpses into how real companies use accounting in practice. **Accounting Across the Organization** specifically addresses how accounting impacts careers in other areas of business-marketing, management, and finance. Both types of boxes now include critical thinking questions, with guideline answers provided at the end of the chapter.
- **Color illustrations**, including **infographics**, help students visualize and apply accounting concepts to the real world.
- **Before You Go On** sections provide learning checks (**Review It**) and mini demonstration problems (**Do It**). Questions marked with the **PepsiCo** logo send students to find information in PepsiCo's 2005 annual report, excerpts of which are printed in the book as Appendix A.
- **Accounting equation analyses** in the margin next to key journal entries reinforce understanding of the impact of an accounting transaction on the financial statements. They indicate the **stockholders' equity** account that is affected, and also report the **cash effect** of each

transaction to reinforce understanding of the difference between cash effects and accrual accounting.

- **Helpful Hints, Alternative Terminology**, and highlighted **key terms and concepts** help focus students on key concepts as they study the material.
- **Ethics Notes** help sensitize students to some of the ethical issues of accounting.

## PUTTING IT TOGETHER

- The new *All About You* feature links some aspect of the chapter topic to students' personal lives. These high-interest boxes promote financial literacy and are intended to get students thinking and talking about how accounting impacts their personal lives.

At the end of each chapter are several additional features useful for review and reference.

- A **Summary of Study Objectives** reviews the main points of the chapter.
- A **Glossary** of key terms gives definitions with page references to the text.
- A **Demonstration Problem** with an **Action Plan** gives students an opportunity to see a detailed solution to a representative problem before they do homework assignments.

## DEVELOPING SKILLS THROUGH PRACTICE

Each chapter is supported by a full complement of homework material. **Self-Study Questions, Questions, Brief Exercises, two sets of Exercises (one online)**, and three sets of **Problems (one online)** are all keyed to the Study Objectives. Certain exercises and problems, marked with a pencil icon, help students practice business writing skills. *Check figures* for selected Problems appear in the students' textbook. In addition:

- **Comprehensive Problems** in five chapters (Chapter 4, 7, 10, 11, and 13) give students the opportunity to put to use concepts covered across multiple chapters.
- The **Continuing Cookie Chronicle** follows the continuing saga of accounting for a small business.
- Certain Exercises and Problems can be solved using the **Excel templates** that are available to accompany the text and are identified by these icons.

## EXPANDING AND APPLYING KNOWLEDGE

The **Broadening Your Perspective** section at the end of each chapter offers a wealth of resources for those instructors who want to broaden the learning experience by bringing in more real-world decision making, analysis, and critical thinking activities.

- A **Financial Reporting Problem** directs students to study various aspects of the financial statements of PepsiCo, Inc., which are printed in Appendix A.
- A **Comparative Analysis Problem** offers the opportunity to compare and contrast the financial reporting of PepsiCo, with that of a competitor, The Coca-Cola Company, whose financial statements are excerpted in Appendix B.
- **Exploring the Web** exercises guide students to Internet sites from which they can mine and analyze information related to the chapter topic.
- **Decision Making Across the Organization** cases help promote group collaboration and build decision-making and business communication skills by requiring teams of students to evaluate a manager's decision.
- **Communication Activities** provide practice in written communication and presentation, skills much in demand among employers.
- **Ethics Cases** ask students to analyze situations, identify the stakeholders and the ethical issues involved, and decide on an appropriate course of action.
- *All About You* **Activities** offers further opportunities to explore aspects of the *All About You* topic in an activity-based homework assignment. These assignments may involve such matters as evaluating an article, doing research on a subject, answering a series of questions, or stating an opinion and providing rationale.
- Finally, on the last page(s) of the chapter, to give students a way to check their thinking and learning, we provide guideline answers and answer feedback to the following in-chapter items: Answers to Insight and Accounting Across the Organization Questions; Authors' Comments on the *All About You* feature; and answers to the Self-Study Questions.

*Financial Accounting, Sixth Edition*, features a full line of teaching and learning resources. These supplements provide a consistent and well-integrated learning system. This hands-on, real-world package guides *instructors* through the process of active learning and gives them the tools to create an interactive learning environment. With its emphasis on activities, exercises, and the Internet, the package encourages *students* to take an active role in the course and prepares them for decision making in a real-world context.

## WEYGANDT'S INTEGRATED TECHNOLOGY SOLUTIONS HELPING TEACHERS TEACH AND STUDENT LEARN, AT
**www.wiley.com/college/weygandt**

**WileyPLUS—for Instructors.** *WileyPLUS* is an online suite of resources that contains online homework, drill, and practice activities with access to an online version of the text. *WileyPLUS* gives you the technology to create an environment where students reach their full potential and experience academic success. Instructor resources include a wealth of presentation and preparation tools, easy-to-navigate assignment and assessment tools, and a complete system to administer and manage your course exactly as you wish. In addition, *WileyPLUS* includes selected problems powered by new General Ledger Software and Excel Working Papers.

*WileyPLUS* is built around the activities you regularly perform:

- **Prepare and present class presentations** using relevant Wiley resources such as PowerPoint™ slides, image galleries, animations, and other *WileyPLUS* materials. You can also upload your own resources or web pages to use in conjunction with Wiley materials.
- **Create assignments** by choosing from end-of-chapter exercises, problems, and test bank questions organized by chapter, study objective, level of difficulty, and source—or add your own questions. Algorithmic versions are available for each exercise and problems, allowing for additional drill and practice. Also, General Ledger Software (GLS) problems can be assigned as well. *WileyPLUS* automatically grades students' homework and quizzes and records the results in your gradebook.
- **Offer context-sensitive help to students, 24/7.** When you assign homework or quizzes, you decide if and when

students get access to hints, solutions, or answers where appropriate. Or students can be linked to relevant sections of their complete, online text for additional help whenever and wherever they need it most.
- **Track student progress.** You can analyze students' results and assess their level of understanding on an individual and class level using the *WileyPLUS* gradebook, and you can export data to your own personal gradebook.
- Seamlessly integrate all of the rich *WileyPLUS* content and resources with the power and convenience of your **WebCT or Desire2Learn course**—with a single sign-on.

**WileyPLUS—for Students.** *WileyPLUS* for students offers **"Read, Study, and Practice"** resources that include the entire online textbook, select interactive, and end-of-chapter demonstration problems. Additional resources include mastery tutorials, interactive chapter reviews, web-based tutorials, multi-media demo problems, excel templates, and other problem-solving resources.

- **An "Assignment"** area helps students stay "on task" by containing all homework assignments in one location. Many homework problems contain a link to the relevant sections of the ebook, providing students with context-sensitive help that allows them to conquer problem-solving obstacles.
- **A Personal Gradebook** for each student will allow students to view their results from past assignments at any time.

**Book Companion Site—for Instructors.** On this website instructors will find electronic versions of the Solutions Manual, Test Bank, Instructor's Manual, Computerized Test Bank, and other resources.

**Book Companion Site—for Students.** The *Financial Accounting* student website provides a wealth of support materials that will help students develop their conceptual understanding of class material and increase their ability to solve problems. On this website students will find Excel templates, PowerPoint™ presentations, web quizzing, and other resources. In addition, the new B Exercises and C Problems can be accessed at this site. Finally, full versions of the Continuing Cookie Chronicle are included at the student website. Besides showing the data needed to complete these exercises, the website offers Excel templates that encourage completion of the Cookie Chronicle tasks.

## INSTRUCTOR'S ACTIVE-TEACHING AIDS

An extensive support package, including print and technology tools, helps you maximize your teaching effectiveness. We offer useful supplements for instructors with varying levels of experience and different instructional circumstances.

**Wiley Faculty Network.** When it comes to improving the classroom experience, there is no better source of ideas and inspiration than your fellow colleagues. The Wiley Faculty Network connects teachers with technologies, facilitates the exchange of best practices, and helps to enhance instructional efficiency and effectiveness. Faculty Network activities include technology training and tutorials, virtual seminars, peer-to-peer exchanges of experiences and ideas, personal consulting, and sharing of resources. For details, visit *www.wherefacultyconnect.com.*

**Instructor's Resource CD.** The Instructor's Resource CD (IR CD) contains an electronic version of all instructor supplements. The IR CD gives you the flexibility to access and prepare instructional materials based on your individual needs.

**Solutions Manual.** The Solutions Manual contains detailed solutions to all Questions, Brief Exercises, Exercises, and Problems in the textbook as well as suggested answers to the questions and cases. Each chapter includes an *assignment classification table*, an *assignment characteristics table*, and a *Bloom's taxonomy table.* Print is large and bold for easy readability in lecture settings. A team of independent accuracy checkers has carefully verified the Solutions Manual.

**Instructor's Manual.** Included in each chapter are lecture outlines with teaching tips, chapter reviews, illustrations, and review quizzes.

**Solution Transparencies.** The solution transparencies feature detailed solutions to brief exercises, exercises, problems, and Broadening Your Perspectives activities. They feature large, bold type for better projection and easy readability in large classroom settings.

**Teaching Transparencies.** The teaching transparencies are 4-color acetate images of the illustrations found in the Instructor's Manual.

**Test Bank.** With *over 3,000 questions*, the test bank allows instructors to tailor examinations according to study objectives and Bloom's taxonomy. Achievement tests, comprehensive examinations, and a final exam are included.

**Algorithmic Computerized Test Bank.** The algorithmic feature of the new computerized test bank allows instructors to assign different values to a particular question, ensuring each student can receive a different version of the same exam. The computerized test bank also allows instructors to add questions, scramble the order of questions, and scramble the order of possible answers in multiple-choice questions.

**PowerPoint™ Presentation Material.** The new PowerPoint™ presentations contain a combination of key concepts, images, and problems from the textbook. Review exercises and an "All About You" discussion are included in each chapter to encourage classroom participation.

**WebCT and Desire2Learn.** WebCT or Desire2Learn offer an integrated set of course management tools that enable instructors to easily design, develop, and manage Web-based and Web-enhanced courses.

## STUDENT ACTIVE-LEARNING AIDS

**The *Financial Accounting* Website.** The student website at *www.wiley.com/college/weygandt* provides a wealth of support materials that will help students develop their conceptual understanding of course concepts and increase their ability to solve problems. On this website students will find PowerPoint™ presentations, Excel workbook and templates, web quizzing, and other resources.

**Study Guide.** Each study guide chapter contains a detailed chapter review, demonstration problems, true/false, multiple-choice, and matching questions, as well as comprehensive exercises. Solutions are provided.

**Working Papers.** Working Papers are templates for end-of-chapter brief exercises, exercises, problems, and cases. A convenient resource for organizing and completing homework assignments, they demonstrate how to correctly present homework solutions.

**Excel Working Papers.** An electronic version of the print working papers, these Excel-formatted templates help students properly format and present end-of-chapter textbook solutions. Available on a CD or via *WileyPLUS.*

**General Ledger Software.** General Ledger  Software (GLS) allows students to solve select end-of-chapter text problems using a computerized accounting system. Problems available in General Ledger Software are identified by an icon next to end-of-chapter textbook exercises and problems and can be found as assignments within *WileyPLUS*. A networked version is also available.

*Financial Accounting* **Excel Templates.** This online manual and collection of Excel templates

allow students to complete select end-of-chapter exercises and problems identified by a spreadsheet icon in the textbook. They can also be found within *WileyPLUS*.

**Peachtree WorkBook** This stand-alone workbook teaches students how to effectively use Peachtree Complete Accounting software. An accompanying CD contains an educational version of Peachtree softwares of exercise templates.

# ACKNOWLEDGMENTS

In the course of developing *Financial Accounting*, we have benefited greatly from the input of focus group participants, manuscript reviewers, users of the first five editions, ancillary authors, and proofers and problem checkers. We offer our thanks to those many people for their constructive suggestions and innovative ideas. We also are indebted to the following people for their contributions to the most recent editions of the book.

## Reviewers and Focus Group Participants

Sheila Ammons, *Austin Community College*
Matt Anderson, *Michigan State University*
Yvonne Baker, *Cincinnati State Tech Community College*
Peter Battelle, *University of Vermont*
Michael Blackett, *National American University*
David Boyd, *Arkansas State University*
Leon Button, *Scottsdale Community College*
David Carr, *Austin Community College*
Andy Chen, *Northeast Illinois University*
Trudy Chiaravelli, *Lansing Community College*
Edward J. Corcoran, *Community College of Philadelphia*
Kennth Couvillion, *San Joaquin Delta College*
Thomas Davies, *University of South Dakota*
Peggy DeJong, *Kirkwood Community College*
Kevin Dooley, *Kapi'olani Community College*
Edmond Douville, *Indiana University Northwest*
Pamela Druger, *Augustana College*
John Eagan, *Erie Community College*
Jeff Edwards, *Portland Community College*
Richard Ellison, *Middlesex Community College*
Richard Ghio, *San Joaquin Delta College*

Jeannie Harrington, *Middle Tennessee State University*
William Harvey, *Henry Ford Community College*
Zach Holmes, *Oakland Community College*
Paul Holt, *Texas A&M—Kingsville*
Verne Ingram, *Red Rocks Community College*
Mark Johnston, *Washtenaw Community College*
Shirly Kleiner, *Johnson County Community College*
Jo Koehn, *Central Missouri State University*
Doug Laufer, *Metropolitan State College of Denver*
Robert Laycock, *Montgomery College*
James Lukawitz, *University of Memphis*
Maureen McBeth, *College of DuPage*
Janice Mardon, *Green River Community College*
Jerry Martens, *Community College of Aurora*
John Marts, *University of North Carolina—Wilmington*
Shea Mears, *Des Moines Area Community College*
Pam Meyer, *University of Louisiana—Lafayette*
Kathy S. Moffeit, *Southwest Texas State University*
Robin Nelson, *Community College of Southern Nevada*
George Palz, *Erie Community College*
Bill Rencher, *Seminole Community College*
Carla Rich, *Pensacola Junior College*
Renee Rigoni, *Monroe Community College*
Patricia Robinson, *Johnson & Wales University*
Jill Russell, *Camden County College*
Ken Sinclair, *Lehigh University*
Alice Sineath, *Forsyth Tech Community College*
Jeff Slater, *North Shore Community College*
James Smith, *Ivy Tech State College*
Carol Springer, *Georgia State University*
Lynda Thompson, *Massasoit Community College*
Sue Van Boven, *Paradise Valley Community College*
Christian Widmer, *Tidewater Community College*

## Ancillary Authors, Contributors, and Proofers

John Borke, *University of Wisconsin–Platteville:*

Text and Solutions Manual proofer

James M. Emig, *Villanova University:*

Solutions Manual & Test Bank proofer

Larry R. Falcetto, *Emporia State University:*

Instructor's Manual and Check Figures author, Text and Solutions Manual proofer

Douglas W. Kieso, *Aurora University:*

Study Guide author

Laura McNally:

WileyPLUS author and proofer

Lynn Stallworth, *Appalachian State University:*

Test Bank author

Rex Schildhouse, *University of Phoenix, San Diego:*

Excel Workbook & templates author, Peachtree workbook author

We appreciate the exemplary support and commitment given to us by executive editor Chris DeJohn, senior marketing manager Julia Flohr, project editor Ed Brislin, associate editor Brian Kamins, senior media editor Allie Morris, vice president of higher education production and manufacturing Ann Berlin, designer Maddy Lesure, illustration editor Anna Melhorn, photo editor Elle Wagner, development editor Ann Torbert, permissions editor Karyn Morrison, project editor Suzanne Ingrao of Ingrao Associates, indexer Steve Ingle, product manager Jane Shifflet at Aptara, and project manager Kim Nichols at Elm Street Publishing Services. All of these professionals provided innumerable services that helped the book take shape.

Finally, our thanks to Amy Scholz, Susan Elbe, Don Fowley, Joe Heider, Bonnie Lieberman, and Will Pesce, for their support and leadership in Wiley's College Division.

We will appreciate suggestions and comments from users—instructors and students alike. You can send your thoughts and ideas about the book to us via email at: *AccountingAuthors@yahoo.com.*

Jerry J. Weygandt
*Madison, Wisconsin*

Paul D. Kimmel
*Milwaukee, Wisconsin*

Donald E. Kieso
*DeKalb, Illinois*

**Chapter 5**

# Accounting for Merchandising Operations

## STUDY OBJECTIVES

*After studying this chapter, you should be able to:*

1 Identify the differences between service and merchandising companies.
2 Explain the recording of purchases under a perpetual inventory system.
3 Explain the recording of sales revenues under a perpetual inventory system.
4 Explain the steps in the accounting cycle for a merchandising company.
5 Distinguish between a multiple-step and a single-step income statement.
6 Explain the computation and importance of gross profit.
7 Determine cost of goods sold under a periodic inventory system. ✓ *The Navigator*

### ✓ The Navigator

| | |
|---|---|
| Scan **Study Objectives** | ■ |
| Read **Feature Story** | ■ |
| Read **Preview** | ■ |
| Read text and answer **Before You Go On** p. 203 ■ p. 205 ■ p. 208 ■ p. 214 ■ p. 216 ■ | |
| Work **Demonstration Problem** | ■ |
| Review **Summary of Study Objectives** | ■ |
| Answer **Self-Study Questions** | ■ |
| Complete **Assignments** | ■ |

### Feature Story

#### WHO DOESN'T SHOP AT WAL-MART?

In his book *The End of Work*, Jeremy Rifkin notes that until the 20th century the word *consumption* evoked negative images. To be labeled a "consumer" was an insult. In fact, one of the deadliest diseases in history, tuberculosis, was often referred to as "consumption." Twentieth-century merchants realized, however, that in order to prosper, they had to convince people of the need for things not previously needed. For example, General Motors made annual changes in its cars so that people would be discontented with the cars they already owned. Thus began consumerism.

194

person is vastly greater than that of any other country. It appears that we live to shop.

The first great retail giant was Sears, Roebuck and Company. It started as a catalog company enabling people in rural areas to buy things by mail. For decades it was the uncontested merchandising leader.

Today Wal-Mart (*www.walmart.com*) is the undisputed champion provider of basic (and perhaps not-so-basic) human needs. Wal-Mart opened its first store in 1962, and it now has more than 6,000 stores, serving more than 100 million customers every week. A key cause of Wal-Mart's incredible growth is its amazing system of inventory control and distribution. Wal-Mart has a management information system that employs six satellite channels, from which company computers receive 8.4 million updates every minute on what items customers buy and the relationship among items sold to each person.

Measured by sales revenues, Wal-Mart is the largest company in the world. In six years it went from selling almost no groceries to being America's largest grocery retailer.

It would appear that things have never looked better at Wal-Mart. On the other hand, a *Wall Street Journal* article entitled "How to Sell More to Those Who Think It's Cool to Be Frugal" suggests that consumerism as a way of life might be dying. Don't bet your wide-screen TV on it, though.

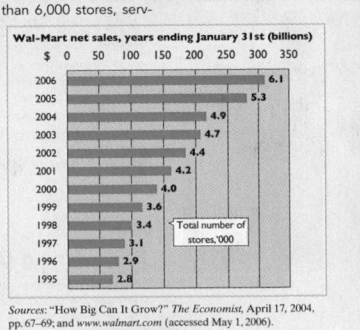

| Wal-Mart net sales, years ending January 31st (billions) |
|---|
| $ 0  50  100  150  200  250  300  350 |
| 2006 — 6.1 |
| 2005 — 5.3 |
| 2004 — 4.9 |
| 2003 — 4.7 |
| 2002 — 4.4 |
| 2001 — 4.2 |
| 2000 — 4.0 |
| 1999 — 3.6 |
| 1998 — 3.4  Total number of stores,'000 |
| 1997 — 3.1 |
| 1996 — 2.9 |
| 1995 — 2.8 |

*Sources:* "How Big Can It Grow?" *The Economist*, April 17, 2004, pp. 67–69; and *www.walmart.com* (accessed May 1, 2006).

✓ *The Navigator*

---

The **Navigator** is a learning system designed to guide you through the chapter and help you succeed in learning the material. It consists of (1) a checklist at the beginning of the chapter, which outlines text features and study aids you will need, and (2) a series of check boxes that prompt you to use the chapter's learning aids and set priorities as you study.

The **Feature Story** helps you picture how the chapter topic relates to the real world of accounting and business. References to the Feature Story throughout the chapter will help you put new ideas in context, organize them, and remember them.

**Study Objectives** at the beginning of each chapter give you a framework for learning the specific concepts in the chapter. Each study objective reappears in the margin where the concept is discussed. You can review the study objectives in the **Summary** at the end of the chapter text.

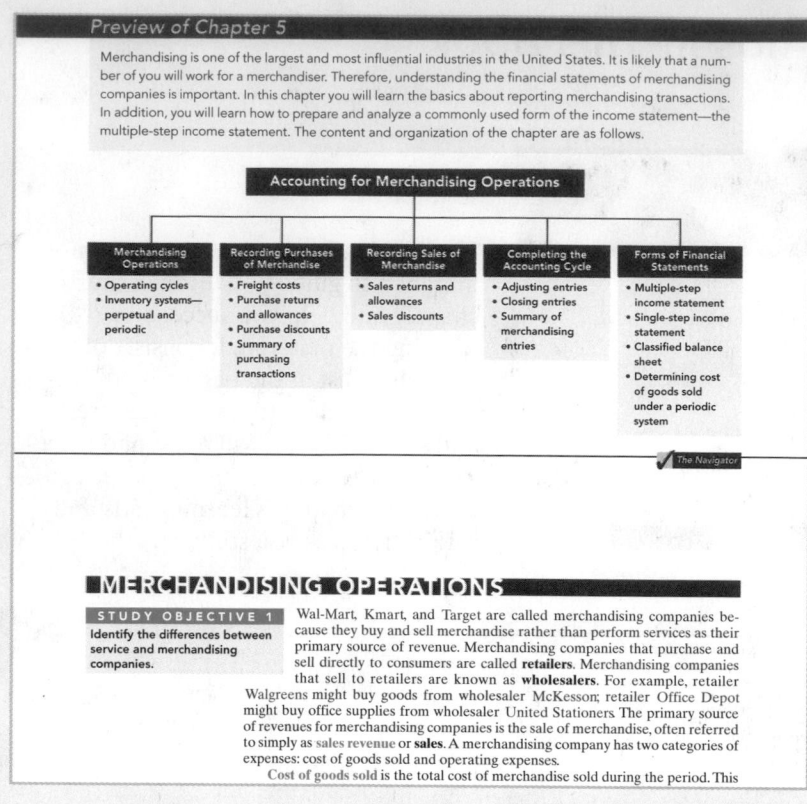

The **Preview** links the Feature Story with the major topics of the chapter and describes the purpose of the chapter.

A **graphic outline** provides a visual preview of the chapter topics. Together, the narrative and visual previews help you organize the information you are learning.

**Study Objectives** reappear in the margins next to the text discussion of the related topic. End-of-chapter assignments are keyed to study objectives.

**Helpful Hints** in the margins further clarify concepts being discussed. They are like having an instructor with you as you read.

**Ethics Notes** point out ethical issues related to the nearby text discussion.

---

204    Chapter 5 Accounting for Merchandising Operations

**HELPFUL HINT**
The merchandiser credits the Sales account only for sales of goods held for resale. Sales of assets not held for resale, such as equipment or land, are credited directly to the asset account.

For internal decision-making purposes, merchandising companies may use more than one sales account. For example, PW Audio Supply may decide to keep separate sales accounts for its sales of TV sets, DVD recorders, and satellite radio receivers. Wal-Mart might use separate accounts for sporting goods, children's clothing, and hardware—or it might have even more narrowly defined accounts. By using separate sales accounts for major product lines, rather than a single combined sales account, company management can more closely monitor sales trends and respond more strategically to changes in sales patterns. For example, if HDTV sales are increasing while DVD-player sales are decreasing, PW Audio Supply might reevaluate both its advertising and pricing policies on these items to ensure they are optimal.

On its income statement presented to outside investors, a merchandising company normally would provide only a single sales figure—the sum of all of its individual sales accounts. This is done for two reasons. First, providing detail on all of its individual sales accounts would add considerable length to its income statement. Second, companies do not want their competitors to know the details of their operating results. However, Microsoft recently expanded its disclosure of revenue from three to five types. The reason: The additional categories will better enable financial statement users to evaluate the growth of the company's consumer and Internet businesses.

**ETHICS NOTE**
Many companies are trying to improve the quality of their financial reporting. For example, General Electric now provides more detail on its revenues and operating profits.

### Sales Returns and Allowances

We now look at the "flipside" of purchase returns and allowances, which the seller records as sales returns and allowances. PW Audio Supply's entries to record credit for returned goods involve (1) an increase in Sales Returns and Allowances and a decrease in Accounts Receivable at the $300 selling price, and (2) an increase in Merchandise Inventory (assume a $140 cost) and a decrease in Cost of Goods Sold

---

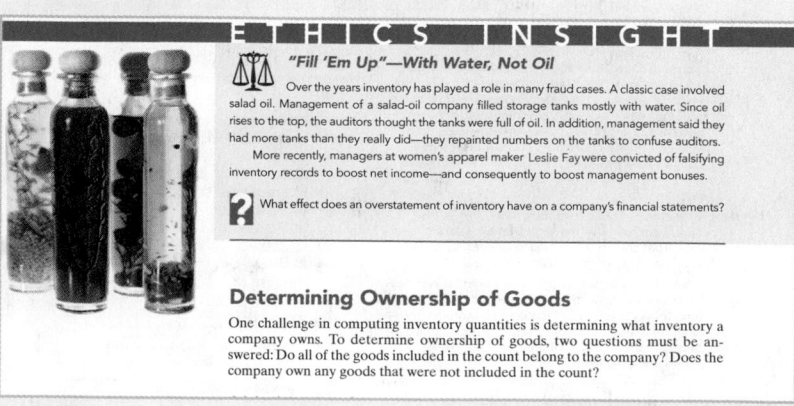

### ETHICS INSIGHT

#### "Fill 'Em Up"—With Water, Not Oil

Over the years inventory has played a role in many fraud cases. A classic case involved salad oil. Management of a salad-oil company filled storage tanks mostly with water. Since oil rises to the top, the auditors thought the tanks were full of oil. In addition, management said they had more tanks than they really did—they repainted numbers on the tanks to confuse auditors.

More recently, managers at women's apparel maker Leslie Fay were convicted of falsifying inventory records to boost net income—and consequently to boost management bonuses.

**?** What effect does an overstatement of inventory have on a company's financial statements?

#### Determining Ownership of Goods

One challenge in computing inventory quantities is determining what inventory a company owns. To determine ownership of goods, two questions must be answered: Do all of the goods included in the count belong to the company? Does the company own any goods that were not included in the count?

*Insight* **examples** give you more glimpses into how actual companies make decisions using accounting information. These high-interest boxes focus on various themes—ethics, international, and investor concerns.

A **critical thinking question** asks you to apply your accounting learning to the story in the example. *Guideline answers* appear at the end of the chapter.

***Accounting Across the Organization*** examples show the use of accounting by people in non-accounting functions—such as finance, marketing, or management.

*Guideline answers* to the critical thinking questions appear at the end of the chapter.

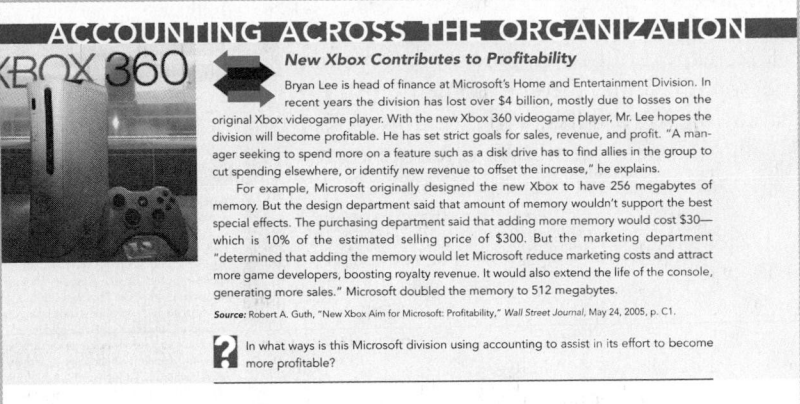

### ACCOUNTING ACROSS THE ORGANIZATION

*New Xbox Contributes to Profitability*

Bryan Lee is head of finance at Microsoft's Home and Entertainment Division. In recent years the division has lost over $4 billion, mostly due to losses on the original Xbox videogame player. With the new Xbox 360 videogame player, Mr. Lee hopes the division will become profitable. He has set strict goals for sales, revenue, and profit. "A manager seeking to spend more on a feature such as a disk drive has to find allies in the group to cut spending elsewhere, or identify new revenue to offset the increase," he explains.

For example, Microsoft originally designed the new Xbox to have 256 megabytes of memory. But the design department said that amount of memory wouldn't support the best special effects. The purchasing department said that adding more memory would cost $30—which is 10% of the estimated selling price of $300. But the marketing department "determined that adding the memory would let Microsoft reduce marketing costs and attract more game developers, boosting royalty revenue. It would also extend the life of the console, generating more sales." Microsoft doubled the memory to 512 megabytes.

*Source:* Robert A. Guth, "New Xbox Aim for Microsoft: Profitability," *Wall Street Journal,* May 24, 2005, p. C1.

In what ways is this Microsoft division using accounting to assist in its effort to become more profitable?

---

**Review It** questions marked with the PepsiCo icon direct you to find information in PepsiCo, Inc.'s 2005 annual report, printed in Appendix A. Answers to these questions appear on the last page of the chapter.

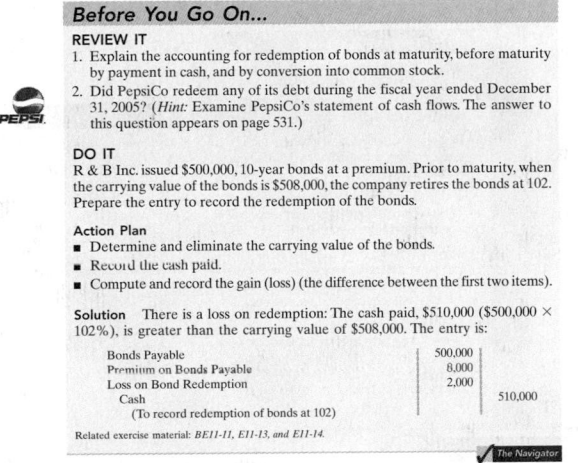

**Before You Go On...**

**REVIEW IT**

1. Explain the accounting for redemption of bonds at maturity, before maturity by payment in cash, and by conversion into common stock.
2. Did PepsiCo redeem any of its debt during the fiscal year ended December 31, 2005? (*Hint:* Examine PepsiCo's statement of cash flows. The answer to this question appears on page 531.)

**DO IT**

R & B Inc. issued $500,000, 10-year bonds at a premium. Prior to maturity, when the carrying value of the bonds is $508,000, the company retires the bonds at 102. Prepare the entry to record the redemption of the bonds.

**Action Plan**

■ Determine and eliminate the carrying value of the bonds.
■ Record the cash paid.
■ Compute and record the gain (loss) (the difference between the first two items).

**Solution** There is a loss on redemption: The cash paid, $510,000 ($500,000 × 102%), is greater than the carrying value of $508,000. The entry is:

| | | |
|---|---|---|
| Bonds Payable | 500,000 | |
| Premium on Bonds Payable | 8,000 | |
| Loss on Bond Redemption | 2,000 | |
| Cash | | 510,000 |
| (To record redemption of bonds at 102) | | |

Related exercise material: *BE11-11, E11-13, and E11-14.*

*The Navigator*

**Before You Go On** sections follow each key topic. **Review It** questions prompt you to stop and review the key points you have just studied. If you cannot answer these questions, you should go back and read the section again.

Brief **Do It** exercises ask you to put to work your newly acquired knowledge. They outline an **Action Plan** necessary to complete the exercise, and they show a **Solution**.

---

**Accounting equation analyses** appear next to key journal entries. They will help you understand the impact of an accounting transaction on the components of the accounting equation, on the stockholders' equity accounts, and on the company's cash flows.

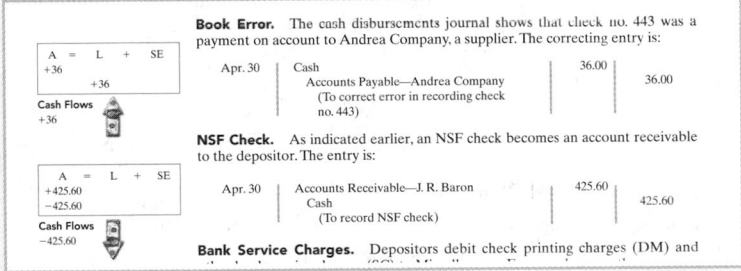

| A | = | L | + | SE |
|---|---|---|---|---|
| +36 | | | | |
| | | | | +36 |

**Cash Flows**
+36

**Book Error.** The cash disbursements journal shows that check no. 443 was a payment on account to Andrea Company, a supplier. The correcting entry is:

| Apr. 30 | Cash | 36.00 | |
|---|---|---|---|
| | Accounts Payable—Andrea Company | | 36.00 |
| | (To correct error in recording check no. 443) | | |

| A | = | L | + | SE |
|---|---|---|---|---|
| +425.60 | | | | |
| −425.60 | | | | |

**Cash Flows**
−425.60

**NSF Check.** As indicated earlier, an NSF check becomes an account receivable to the depositor. The entry is:

| Apr. 30 | Accounts Receivable—J. R. Baron | 425.60 | |
|---|---|---|---|
| | Cash | | 425.60 |
| | (To record NSF check) | | |

**Bank Service Charges.** Depositors debit check printing charges (DM) and

---

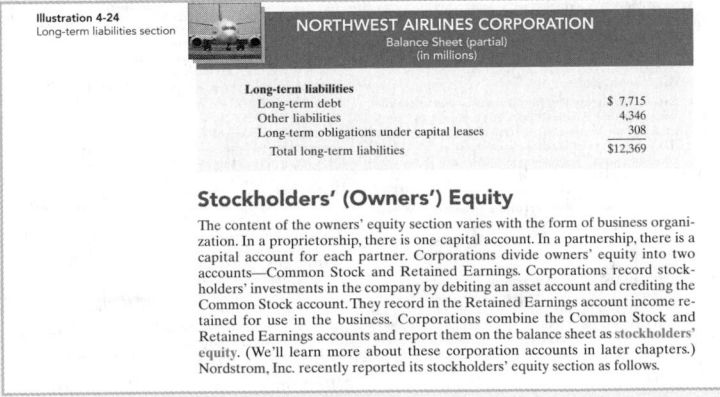

**Illustration 4-24**
Long-term liabilities section

**NORTHWEST AIRLINES CORPORATION**
Balance Sheet (partial)
(in millions)

| **Long-term liabilities** | |
|---|---|
| Long-term debt | $ 7,715 |
| Other liabilities | 4,346 |
| Long-term obligations under capital leases | 308 |
| Total long-term liabilities | $12,369 |

### Stockholders' (Owners') Equity

The content of the owners' equity section varies with the form of business organization. In a proprietorship, there is one capital account. In a partnership, there is a capital account for each partner. Corporations divide owners' equity into two accounts—Common Stock and Retained Earnings. Corporations record stockholders' investments in the company by debiting an asset account and crediting the Common Stock account. They record in the Retained Earnings account income retained for use in the business. Corporations combine the Common Stock and Retained Earnings accounts and report them on the balance sheet as **stockholders' equity.** (We'll learn more about these corporation accounts in later chapters.) Nordstrom, Inc. recently reported its stockholders' equity section as follows.

**Financial statements** appear regularly. Those from actual companies are identified by a company logo or a photo.

An ***All About You* feature** links some aspect of the chapter topic to your personal life, and often to some financial situation you are likely to face now or in the near future. We offer our own *opinions* about the situation near the end of the chapter.

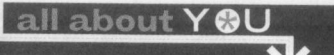

## Should You Be Carrying Plastic?

Smart business people carefully consider their use of credit. They evaluate who they lend to, and how they finance their own operations. They know that getting overextended on credit can destroy their business.

Individuals need to evaluate their personal credit positions using the same thought processes used by business people. Some of you might consider the idea of not having a credit card a ridiculous proposition. But the reality is that the misuse of credit cards brings financial hardship to millions of Americans each year. Credit card companies aggressively market their cards with images of glamour and happiness. But there isn't much glamour in paying an 18% to 21% interest rate, and there is very little happiness to be found in filing for personal bankruptcy.

### ✱ Some Facts

★ About 70% of undergraduates at 4-year colleges carry at least one credit card in their own name. Approximately 22% of college students got their first credit cards in high school.

★ The average monthly debt on a college student's charge account, according to one study, is close to $2,000.

★ In a recent year, Americans charged more than $1 trillion in purchases with their credit cards. That was more than they spent in cash.

★ During one quarter in 2006, the percentage of delinquent credit card payments rose to 5% from 4.3%. Card write-offs increased from 5.6% to 6.4%. Until this year, both numbers were declining.

★ Significant increases in consumer bankruptcy filings occurred in every region of the country. There were 2,043,535 new filings in 2005, up 31.6% from 1,552,967 in 2004—that is, one in every 53 households filed a bankruptcy petition.

### ✪ About the Numbers

Presented below is a chart that shows the major causes of personal financial problems. Note the excessive use of credit, which is cited as the number-one cause. This often translates into addiction to credit cards.

**Causes of Personal Financial Problems**

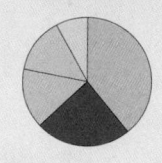

- ☐ Excessive use of credit/Over-obligation 39%
- ■ Reduced income/ Unemployment 24%
- ☐ Poor money management 15%
- ☐ Divorce/ Separation 8%
- ☐ Other 14%

**Source:** Debt Solutions of America, *www.becomedebtfree.com* (accessed May 2006).

### ✪ What Do You Think?

Should you cut up your credit card(s)?

**YES:** Americans are carrying huge personal debt burdens. Credit cards encourage unnecessary, spontaneous expenditures. The interest rates on credit cards are extremely high, which causes debt problems to escalate exponentially.

**NO:** Credit cards are a necessity for transactions in today's economy. In fact, many transactions are difficult or impossible to carry out without a credit card. People should learn to use credit cards responsibly.

**Sources:** Debtsmart, *www.debtsmart.com/pages/debt_stats.html*; Robin Marantz Henig, "Teen Credit Cards Actually Teach Responsibility," *USAToday.com*, July 30, 2001.

---

### Demonstration Problem

Green Thumb Lawn Care Inc. began operating on April 1. At April 30, the trial balance shows the following balances for selected accounts.

| | |
|---|---|
| Prepaid Insurance | $ 3,600 |
| Equipment | 28,000 |
| Notes Payable | 20,000 |
| Unearned Revenue | 4,200 |
| Service Revenue | 1,800 |

Analysis reveals the following additional data.

1. Prepaid insurance is the cost of a 2-year insurance policy, effective April 1.
2. Depreciation on the equipment is $500 per month.
3. The note payable is dated April 1. It is a 6-month, 12% note.
4. Seven customers paid for the company's 6 months' lawn service package of $600 beginning in April. The company performed services for these customers in April.
5. Lawn services provided other customers but not recorded at April 30 totaled $1,500.

### Instructions

Prepare the adjusting entries for the month of April. Show computations.

A **Demonstration Problem** is a review of key concepts and a warm-up before you begin homework. These sample problems provide you with an **Action Plan** in the margin that lists the strategies needed to approach and solve the problem.

The **Solution to the Demonstration Problem** demonstrates both the form and content of complete answers.

### action plan

✓ Note that adjustments are being made for one month.
✓ Make computations carefully.
✓ Select account titles carefully.
✓ Make sure debits are made first and credits are indented.
✓ Check that debits equal credits for each entry.

### Solution

**GENERAL JOURNAL**    **J1**

| Date | Account Titles and Explanation | Ref. | Debit | Credit |
|---|---|---|---|---|
| | **Adjusting Entries** | | | |
| Apr. 30 | Insurance Expense | | 150 | |
| | Prepaid Insurance | | | 150 |
| | (To record insurance expired: $3,600 ÷ 24 = $150 per month) | | | |
| 30 | Depreciation Expense | | | |
| | Accumulated Depreciation—Equipment | | | |
| | (To record monthly depreciation) | | | |
| 30 | Interest Expense | | | |
| | Interest Payable | | | |
| | (To record interest on notes payable: $20,000 × 12% × 1/12 = $200) | | | |
| 30 | Unearned Revenue | | | |

The **Summary of Study Objectives** reviews the main points related to the study objectives. It provides you with an opportunity to review what you have learned and to see how the key topics within the chapter fit together.

## SUMMARY OF STUDY OBJECTIVES

**1 Describe the steps in determining inventory quantities.** The steps are (1) take a physical inventory of goods on hand and (2) determine the ownership of goods in transit or on consignment.

**2 Explain the accounting for inventories and apply the inventory cost flow methods.** The primary basis of accounting for inventories is cost. Cost of goods available for sale includes (a) cost of beginning inventory and (b) cost of goods purchased. The inventory cost flow methods are: specific identification and three assumed cost flow methods—FIFO, LIFO, and average-cost.

**3 Explain the financial effects of the inventory cost flow assumptions.** Companies may allocate the cost of goods available for sale to cost of goods sold and ending inventory by specific identification or by a method based on an assumed cost flow. When prices are rising, the first-in, first-out (FIFO) method results in lower cost of goods sold and higher net income than the other methods. The reverse is true when prices are falling. In the balance sheet, FIFO results in an ending inventory that is closest to current value; inventory under LIFO is the farthest from current value. LIFO results in the lowest income taxes.

**4 Explain the lower-of-cost-or-market basis of accounting for inventories.** Companies may use the lower-of-cost-or-market (LCM) basis when the current replacement cost (market) is less than cost. Under LCM, companies recognize the loss in the period in which the price decline occurs.

**5 Indicate the effects of inventory errors on the financial statements.** *In the income statement of the current year:* (a) An error in beginning inventory will have a reverse effect on net income. (b) An error in ending inventory will have a similar effect on net income. If ending inventory errors are not corrected in the following period, their effect on net income for that period is reversed, and total net income for the two years will be correct.

*In the balance sheet:* Ending inventory errors will have the same effect on total assets and total stockholders' equity and no effect on liabilities.

**6 Compute and interpret the inventory turnover ratio.** The inventory turnover ratio is cost of goods sold divided by average inventory. To convert it to average days in inventory, divide 365 days by the inventory turnover ratio.

## GLOSSARY

**Accounts receivable** Amounts owed by customers on account. (p. 386).

**Accounts receivable turnover ratio** A measure of the liquidity of accounts receivable; computed by dividing net credit sales by average net accounts receivable. (p. 403).

**Aging the accounts receivable** The analysis of customer balances by the length of time they have been unpaid. (p. 393).

**Allowance method** A method of accounting for bad debts that involves estimating uncollectible accounts at the end of each period. (p. 389).

**Average collection period** The average amount of time that a receivable is outstanding; calculated by dividing 365 days by the accounts receivables turnover ratio. (p. 404).

**Bad Debts Expense** An expense account to record uncollectible receivables. (p. 388).

**Cash (net) realizable value** The net amount a company expects to receive in cash. (p. 389).

**Direct write-off method** A method of accounting for bad debts that involves expensing accounts at the time they are determined to be uncollectible. (p. 388).

**Dishonored note** A note that is not paid in full at maturity. (p. 401).

**Factor** A finance company or bank that buys receivables from businesses and then collects the payments directly from the customers. (p. 395).

**Maker** The party in a promissory note who is making the promise to pay. (p. 398).

**Notes receivable** Claims for which formal instruments of credit are issued as proof of the debt. (p. 386).

**Other receivables** Various forms of nontrade receivables, such as interest receivable and income taxes refundable. (p. 386).

**Payee** The party to whom payment of a promissory note is to be made. (p. 398).

**Percentage-of-receivables basis** Management estimates what percentage of receivables will result in losses from uncollectible accounts. (p. 393).

**Percentage-of-sales basis** Management estimates what percentage of credit sales will be uncollectible. (p. 392).

**Promissory note** A written promise to pay a specified amount of money on demand or at a definite time. (p. 398).

**Receivables** Amounts due from individuals and other companies. (p. 386).

**Trade receivables** Notes and accounts receivable that result from sales transactions. (p. 386).

*The **Glossary** defines all the **key terms** and **concepts** introduced in the chapter. Page references help you find any terms you need to study further.*

*The **WileyPLUS icon** here and throughout the end-of-chapter material identifies resources for further reading, study, and practice that can be accessed via WileyPLUS.*

*The **Self-Study Questions** provide a practice test, keyed to study objectives, with which you can check your knowledge of important chapter topics. Answers appear on the last page of the chapter.*

## SELF-STUDY QUESTIONS

*Answers are at the end of the chapter.*

(SO 2) **1.** Buehler Company on June 15 sells merchandise on account to Chaz Co. for $1,000, terms 2/10, n/30. On June 20, Chaz Co. returns merchandise worth $300 to Buehler Company. On June 24, payment is received from Chaz Co. for the balance due. What is the amount of cash received?
   **a.** $700.
   **b.** $680.

percentage-of-sales basis. If the Allowance for Doubtful Accounts has a credit balance of $15,000 before adjustment, what is the balance after adjustment?
   **a.** $15,000.
   **b.** $27,000.
   **c.** $23,000.
   **d.** $31,000.

4. In 2008, Roso Carlson Com

*The **Questions** focus your study on understanding concepts and relationships from the chapter. Use them to help prepare for class discussion and tests.*

## QUESTIONS

**1.** (a)"The steps in the accounting cycle for a merchandising company are different from the accounting cycle for a service company." Do you agree or disagree? (b) Is the measurement of net income for a merchandising company conceptually the same as for a service company? Explain.

**2.** Why is the normal operating cycle for a merchandising company likely to be longer than for a service company?

**3.** (a) How do the components of revenues and expenses differ between merchandising and service companies? (b) Explain the income measurement process in a merchandising company.

**4.** How does income measurement differ between a merchandising and a service company?

**5.** When is cost of goods sold determined in a perpetual inventory system?

goods. Give the journal entry on July 24 to record payment of the balance due within the discount period using a perpetual inventory system.

**9.** Joan Roland believes revenues from credit sales may be earned before they are collected in cash. Do you agree? Explain.

**10.** (a) What is the primary source document for recording (1) cash sales, (2) credit sales. (b) Using XXs for amounts, give the journal entry for each of the transactions in part (a).

**11.** A credit sale is made on July 10 for $900, terms 2/10, n/30. On July 12, $100 of goods are returned for credit. Give the journal entry on July 19 to record the receipt of the balance due within the discount period.

**12.** Explain why the Merchandise Inventory account will usually require adjustment at year-end.

*The **Brief Exercises** focus on one study objective at a time. They help build confidence in your basic skills and knowledge.*

## BRIEF EXERCISES

**BE4-1** The steps in using a worksheet are presented in random order below. List the steps in the proper order by placing numbers 1–5 in the blank spaces.

**(a)** _____ Prepare a trial balance on the worksheet.
**(b)** _____ Enter adjusted balances.
**(c)** _____ Extend adjusted balances to appropriate statement columns.
**(d)** _____ Total the statement columns, compute net income (loss), and complete the worksheet.
**(e)** _____ Enter adjustment data.

*List the steps in preparing a worksheet.*
*(SO 1)*

**BE4-2** The ledger of Ley Company includes the following unadjusted balances: Prepaid Insurance $3,000, Service Revenue $58,000, and Salaries Expense $25,000. Adjusting entries are required for **(a)** expired insurance $1,200; **(b)** services provided $1,100, but unbilled and uncollected; and **(c)** accrued salaries payable $800. Enter the unadjusted balances and adjustments into a worksheet and complete the worksheet for all accounts. Note: You will need to add the following accounts: Accounts Receivable, Salaries Payable, and Insurance Expense.

*Prepare partial worksheet.*
*(SO 1)*

**BE4-3** The following selected accounts appear in the adjusted trial balance columns of the worksheet for Batan Company: Accumulated Depreciation; Depreciation Expense; Common Stock; Dividends; Service Revenue; Supplies; and Accounts Payable. Indicate the financial statement column (income statement Dr., balance sheet Cr., etc.) to which each balance should be extended.

*Identify worksheet columns for selected accounts.*
*(SO 1)*

## EXERCISES

**E2-1** Josh Cephus has prepared the following list of statements about accounts.

**1.** An account is an accounting record of either a specific asset or a specific liability.
**2.** An account shows only increases, not decreases, in the item it relates to.
**3.** Some items, such as Cash and Accounts Receivable, are combined into one account.
**4.** An account has a left, or credit side, and a right, or debit side.
**5.** A simple form of an account consisting of just the account title, the left side, and the right side, is called a T-account.

**Instructions**
Identify each statement as true or false. If false, indicate how to correct the statement.

**E2-2** Selected transactions for D. Reyes, Inc., an interior decorating firm, in its first month of business, are as follows.

Jan. 2  Invested $10,000 cash in the business in exchange for common stock.
    3  Purchased used car for $4,000 cash for use in business.
    9  Purchased supplies on account for $500.
   11  Billed customers $1,800 for services performed.
   16  Paid $200 cash for advertising.
   20  Received $700 cash from customers billed on January 11.
   23  Paid creditor $300 cash on balance owed.
   28  Declared and paid a $1,000 cash dividend.

**Instructions**
For each transaction indicate the following.

**(a)** The basic type of account debited and credited (asset, liability, stockholders' equity).
**(b)** The specific account debited and credited (cash, rent expense, service revenue, etc.).
**(c)** Whether the specific account is increased or decreased.
**(d)** The normal balance of the specific account.

*(SO 1)*

*Identify debits, credits, and normal balances.*
*(SO 2)*

*The **Exercises** are slightly more difficult than Brief Exercises, and may combine two or more study objectives. They help you continue to build confidence in your ability to combine and use the material learned in the chapter.*

## EXERCISES: SET B

Visit the book's website at **www.wiley.com/college/weygandt**, and choose the Student Companion site, to access Exercise Set B.

*A set of **B Exercises**, closely related to the Exercises in the book, appears at the book's companion website, for additional practice.*

Each **Problem** helps you pull together and apply several concepts from the chapter.

An icon identifies **Exercises** and **Problems** that can be solved using Excel templates at the student website.

Selected problems, identified by this icon, can be solved using the **General Ledger Software (GLS)** package.

**Check figures** in the margin provide key numbers to let you know you're on the right track as you work the problems.

---

## PROBLEMS: SET A

*Journalize purchase and sales transactions under a perpetual inventory system.*
(SO 2, 3)

**P5-1A** Sansomite Co. distributes suitcases to retail stores and extends credit terms of 1/10, n/30 to all of its customers. At the end of June, Sansomite's inventory consisted of 40 suitcases purchased at $30 each. During the month of July the following merchandising transactions occurred.

July 1 Purchased 60 suitcases on account for $30 each from Trunk Manufacturers, FOB destination, terms 2/10, n/30. The appropriate party also made a cash payment of $100 for freight on this date.
3 Sold 40 suitcases on account to Satchel World for $50 each.
9 Paid Trunk Manufacturers in full.
12 Received payment in full from Satchel World.
17 Sold 30 suitcases on account to The Going Concern for $50 each.
18 Purchased 60 suitcases on account for $1,700 from Kingman Manufacturers, FOB shipping point, terms 1/10, n/30. The appropriate party also made a cash payment of $100 for freight on this date.
20 Received $300 credit (including freight) for 10 suitcases returned to Kingman Manufacturers.
21 Received payment in full from The Going Concern.
22 Sold 45 suitcases on account to Fly-By-Night for $50 each.
30 Paid Kingman Manufacturers in full.
31 Granted Fly-By-Night $200 credit for 4 suitcases returned costing $120.

Sansomite's chart of accounts includes the following: No. 101 Cash, No. 112 Accounts Receivable, No. 120 Merchandise Inventory, No. 201 Accounts Payable, No. 401 Sales, No. 412 Sales Returns and Allowances, No. 414 Sales Discounts, No. 505 Cost of Goods Sold.

**Instructions**
Journalize the transactions for the month of July for Sansomite using a perpetual inventory system.

*Journalize, post, and prepare a partial income statement.*
(SO 2, 3, 5, 6)

**GLS**

**P5-2A** Olaf Distributing Company completed the following merchandising transactions in the month of April. At the beginning of April, the ledger of Olaf showed Cash of $9,000 and Common Stock of $9,000.

Apr. 2 Purchased merchandise on account from Dakota Supply Co. $6,900, terms 1/10, n/30.
4 Sold merchandise on account $5,500, FOB destination, terms 1/10, n/30. The cost of the merchandise sold was $4,100.
5 Paid $240 freight on April 4 sale.
6 Received credit from Dakota Supply Co. for merchandise returned $500.
11 Paid Dakota Supply Co. in full, less discount.
13 Received collections in full, less discounts, from customers billed on April 4.
14 Purchased merchandise for cash $3,800.
16 Received refund from supplier for returned goods on cash purchase of April 14, $500.
18 Purchased merchandise from Skywalker Distributors $4,500, FOB shipping point, terms 2/10, n/30.
20 Paid freight on April 18 purchase $100.
23 Sold merchandise for cash $6,400. The merchandise sold had a cost of $5,120.
26 Purchased merchandise for cash $2,300.
27 Paid Skywalker Distributors in full, less discount.
29 Made refunds to cash customers for defective merchandise $90. The returned merchandise had a scrap value of $30.
30 Sold merchandise on account $3,700, terms n/30. The cost of the merchandise sold was $2,800.

Olaf Company's chart of accounts includes the following: No. 101 Cash, No. 112 Accounts Receivable, No. 120 Merchandise Inventory, No. 201 Accounts Payable, No. 311 Common Stock, No. 401 Sales, No. 412 Sales Returns and Allowances, No. 414 Sales Discounts, No. 505 Cost of Goods Sold, and No. 644 Freight-out.

**Instructions**
**(a)** Journalize the transactions using a perpetual inventory system.
**(b)** Enter the beginning cash and common stock balances, and post the transactions. (Use J1 for the journal reference.)
**(c)** Prepare the income statement through gross profit for the month of April 2008.

*(c) Gross profit $3,465*

---

In the book, two similar sets of **Problems—A** and **B**—are keyed to the same study objectives.

## PROBLEMS: SET B

*Journalize purchase and sales transactions under a perpetual inventory system.*
(SO 2, 3)

**P5-1B** Sorvino Book Warehouse distributes hardcover books to retail stores and extends credit terms of 2/10, n/30 to all of its customers. At the end of May, Sorvino's inventory consisted of 240 books purchased at $1,200. During the month of June the following merchandising transactions occurred.

June 1 Purchased 180 books on account for $5 each from Atkinson Publishers, FOB destination, terms 2/10, n/30. The appropriate party also made a cash payment of $50 for the freight on this date.
3 Sold 120 books on account to Readers-R-Us for $10 each.
6 Received $50 credit for 10 books returned to Atkinson Publishers.
9 Paid Atkinson Publishers in full, less discount.
15 Received payment in full from Readers-R-Us.
17 Sold 150 books on account to Bargain Books for $10 each.
20 Purchased 120 books on account for $5 each from Bookem Publishers, FOB destination, terms 2/15, n/30. The appropriate party also made a cash payment of $50 for the freight on this date.
24 Received payment in full from Bargain Books.
26 Paid Bookem Publishers in full, less discount.
28 Sold 110 books on account to Read-n-Weep Bookstore for $10 each.
30 Granted Read-n-Weep Bookstore $150 credit for 15 books returned costing $75.

Sorvino Book Warehouse's chart of accounts includes the following: No. 101 Cash, No. 112 Accounts Receivable, No. 120 Merchandise Inventory, No. 201 Accounts Payable, No. 401 Sales, No. 412 Sales Returns and Allowances, No. 414 Sales Discounts, No. 505 Cost of Goods Sold.

**Instructions**
Journalize the transactions for the month of June for Sorvino Book Warehouse using a perpetual inventory system.

---

An additional parallel set of **C Problems** appears at the book's companion site.

## PROBLEMS: SET C

Visit the book's website at **www.wiley.com/college/weygandt**, and choose the Student Companion site, to access Problem Set C.

## COMPREHENSIVE PROBLEM: CHAPTERS 2 TO 4

Julie Molony opened Julie's Maids Cleaning Service Inc. on July 1, 2008. During July, the company completed the following transactions.

July 1 Issued $14,000 of common stock for $14,000 cash.
1 Purchased a used truck for $10,000, paying $3,000 cash and the balance on account.
3 Purchased cleaning supplies for $800 on account.
5 Paid $1,800 on a one-year insurance policy, effective July 1.
12 Billed customers $3,800 for cleaning services.
18 Paid $1,000 of amount owed on truck, and $400 of amount owed on cleaning supplies.
20 Paid $1,600 for employee salaries.
21 Collected $1,400 from customers billed on July 12.
25 Billed customers $1,500 for cleaning services.

Comprehensive **Problems** in six chapters combine concepts covered across multiple chapters.

## CONTINUING COOKIE CHRONICLE

*The Continuing Cookie Chronicle starts in this chapter and continues in every chapter. You also can find this problem at the book's Student Companion site.*

**CCC1** Natalie Koebel spent much of her childhood learning the art of cookie-making from her grandmother. They passed many happy hours mastering every type of cookie imaginable and later creating new recipes that were both healthy and delicious. Now at the start of her second year in college, Natalie is investigating various possibilities for starting her own business as part of the requirements of the entrepreneurship program in which she is enrolled.

A long-time friend insists that Natalie has to somehow include cookies in her business plan. After a series of brainstorming sessions, Natalie settles on the idea of operating a cookie-making school. She will start on a part-time basis and offer her services in people's homes. Now that she has started thinking about it, the possibilities seem endless. During the fall, she will concentrate on holiday cookies. She will offer individual lessons and group sessions (which will probably be more entertainment than education for the participants). Natalie also decides to include children in her target market.

The first difficult decision is coming up with the perfect name for her business. In the end, she settles on "Cookie Creations" and then moves on to more important issues.

**Instructions**
**(a)** What form of business organization—proprietorship, partnership, or corporation—do you recommend that Natalie use for her business? Discuss the benefits and weaknesses of each form and give the reasons for your choice.
**(b)** Will Natalie need accounting information? If yes, what information will she need and why? How often will she need this information?
**(c)** Identify specific asset, liability, and owner's/stockholders' equity accounts that Cookie Creations will likely use to record its business transactions.
**(d)** Should Natalie open a separate bank account for the business? Why or why not?

# BROADENING YOUR PERSPECTIVE

## FINANCIAL REPORTING AND ANALYSIS

### Financial Reporting Problem
#### PepsiCo, Inc.

**BYP1-1** The actual financial statements of PepsiCo, as presented in the company's 2005 Annual Report, are contained in Appendix A (at the back of the textbook).

**Instructions**
Refer to PepsiCo's financial statements and answer the following questions.
**(a)** What were PepsiCo's total assets at December 31, 2005? At December 25, 2004?
**(b)** How much cash (and cash equivalents) did PepsiCo have on December 31, 2005?
**(c)** What amount of accounts payable did PepsiCo report on December 31, 2005? On December 25, 2004?
**(d)** What were PepsiCo's net sales in 2003? In 2004? In 2005?
**(e)** What is the amount of the change in PepsiCo's net income from 2004 to 2005?

### Comparative Analysis Problem
#### PepsiCo, Inc. vs. The Coca-Cola Company

**BYP5-2** PepsiCo's financial statements are presented in Appendix A. Coca-Cola's financial statements are presented in Appendix B.

**Instructions**
**(a)** Based on the information contained in these financial statements, determine each of the following for each company.
  **(1)** Gross profit for 2005.
  **(2)** Gross profit rate for 2005.
  **(3)** Operating income for 2005.
  **(4)** Percent change in operating income from 2004 to 2005.
**(b)** What conclusions concerning the relative profitability of the two companies can you draw from these data?

### Exploring the Web

**BYP5-3** No financial decision maker should ever rely solely on the financial information reported in the annual report to make decisions. It is important to keep abreast of financial news. This activity demonstrates how to search for financial news on the Web.

**Address: biz.yahoo.com/i,** or go to **www.wiley.com/college/weygandt**

**Steps:**
1. Type in either PepsiCo or Coca-Cola.
2. Choose **News**.
3. Select an article that sounds interesting to you.

**Instructions**
**(a)** What was the source of the article? (For example, Reuters, Businesswire, PR Newswire.)
**(b)** Assume that you are a personal financial planner and that one of your clients owns stock in the company. Write a brief memo to your client, summarizing the article and explaining the implications of the article for their investment.

## CRITICAL THINKING

### Decision Making Across the Organization

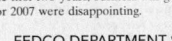

**BYP5-4** Three years ago, Carrie Dungy and her brother-in-law Luke Barber opened FedCo Department Store. For the first two years, business was good, but the following condensed income statement results for 2007 were disappointing.

**FEDCO DEPARTMENT STORE**
Income Statement
For the Year Ended December 31, 2007

| | | |
|---|---:|---:|
| Net sales | | $700,000 |
| Cost of goods sold | | 553,000 |
| Gross profit | | 147,000 |
| Operating expenses | | |
| Selling expenses | $100,000 | |
| Administrative expenses | 20,000 | 120,000 |
| Net income | | $ 27,000 |

### Communication Activity

**BYP8-5** As a new auditor for the CPA firm of Croix, Marais, and Kale, you have been assigned to review the internal controls over mail cash receipts of Manhattan Company. Your review reveals the following: Checks are promptly endorsed "For Deposit Only," but no list of the checks is prepared by the person opening the mail. The mail is opened either by the cashier or by the employee who maintains the accounts receivable records. Mail receipts are deposited in the bank weekly by the cashier.

**Instructions**
Write a letter to Jerry Mays, owner of the Manhattan Company, explaining the weaknesses in internal control and your recommendations for improving the system.

---

The **Continuing Cookie Chronicle** exercise follows the continuing saga of accounting for a small business begun by an entrepreneurial student.

The **Broadening Your Perspective** section helps you pull together concepts from the chapter and apply them to real-world business situations.

The **Financial Reporting Problem** focuses on reading and understanding the financial statements of PepsiCo, Inc., which are printed in Appendix A.

A **Comparative Analysis Problem** compares and contrasts the financial reporting of PepsiCo with its competitor The Coca-Cola Company.

**Exploring the Web** exercises guide you to websites where you can find and analyze information related to the chapter topic.

**Decision Making Across the Organization** cases helps you build decision-making skills by analyzing accounting information in a less structured situation. These cases require teams of students to evaluate a manager's decision or lead to a decision among alternative courses of action.

**Communication Activities** help you build business communication skills by asking you to engage in real-world business situations using writing, speaking, or presentation skills.

**Ethics Cases** ask you to reflect on typical ethical dilemmas, analyze the stakeholders and the issues involved, and decide on an appropriate course of action.

### Ethics Case

**BYP11-6** Sam Farr is the president, founder, and majority owner of Galena Medical Corporation, an emerging medical technology products company. Galena is in dire need of additional capital to keep operating and to bring several promising products to final development, testing, and production. Sam, as owner of 51% of the outstanding stock, manages the company's operations. He places heavy emphasis on research and development and on long-term growth. The other principal stockholder is Jill Hutton who, as a nonemployee investor, owns 40% of the stock. Jill would like to deemphasize the R&D functions and emphasize the marketing function, to maximize short-run sales and profits from existing products. She believes this strategy would raise the market price of Galena's stock.

All of Sam's personal capital and borrowing power is tied up in his 51% stock ownership. He knows that any offering of additional shares of stock will dilute his controlling interest because he won't be able to participate in such an issuance. But, Jill has money and would likely buy enough shares to gain control of Galena. She then would dictate the company's future direction, even if it meant replacing Sam as president and CEO.

The company already has considerable debt. Raising additional debt will be costly, will adversely affect Galena's credit rating, and will increase the company's reported losses due to the growth in interest expense. Jill and the other minority stockholders express opposition to the assumption of additional debt, fearing the company will be pushed to the brink of bankruptcy. Wanting to maintain his control and to preserve the direction of "his" company, Sam is doing everything to avoid a stock issuance. He is contemplating a large issuance of bonds, even if it means the bonds are issued with a high effective-interest rate.

**Instructions**
**(a)** Who are the stakeholders in this situation?
**(b)** What are the ethical issues in this case?
**(c)** What would you do if you were Sam?

The **"All About You" Activity** offers another opportunity to explore the All About You topic in a homework assignment.

###  "All About You" Activity

**BYP11-7** As indicated in the "All About You" feature in this chapter (page 496), medical costs are substantial and rising. But will medical costs be your most substantial expense over your lifetime? Not likely. Will it be housing or food? Again, not likely. The answer is in the *Accounting Across the Organization* box on page 478: taxes. On average, Americans work 79 days to afford their federal taxes. Companies, too, have large tax burdens. They look very hard at tax issues in deciding where to build their plants and where to locate their administrative headquarters.

**Instructions**
**(a)** Determine what your state income taxes are if your taxable income is $60,000 and you file as a single taxpayer in the state in which you live.
**(b)** Assume that you own a home worth $200,000 in your community and the tax rate is 2.1%. Compute the property taxes you would pay.

### Answers to Insight and Accounting Across the Organization Questions

**Be Sure to Read the Fine Print, p. 388**
Q: Why are credit card companies willing to offer relaxed repayment options?
A: *Credit card companies generate their income primarily from interest charges on cardholders' balances. The larger the outstanding balances, the greater the interest income.*

**When Investors Ignore Warning Signs, p. 394**
Q: When would it be appropriate for a company to lower its allowance for doubtful accounts as a percentage of its receivables?
A: *It could do so if the company's collection experience had improved, or was expected to improve, and therefore the company expected lower defaults as a percentage of receivables.*

**How Does a Credit Card Work?, p. 397**
Q: Assume that Nordstrom prepares a bank reconciliation at the end of each month. If some credit card sales have not been processed by the bank, how should Nordstrom treat these transactions on its bank reconciliation?
A: *Nordstrom would treat the credit card receipts as deposits in transit. It has already recorded the receipts as cash. Its bank will increase Nordstrom's cash account when it receives the receipts.*

**Who Gets Credit?, p. 402**
Q: How would reported net income likely differ during the first year of this promotion if Mitsubishi used the direct write-off method versus the allowance method?
A: *Under the direct write-off method, Mitsubishi would not record bad debt expense until a customer defaulted on a loan. Under the allowance method, it would estimate how many of its loans would default rather than waiting until they default. The direct write-off method would have resulted in higher net income during the first year of the promotion.*

### Authors' Comments on *All About You: Should You Be Carrying Plastic?*, p. 405

We aren't going to tell you to cut up your credit card(s). Well, we aren't going to tell *all* of you to do so. Credit cards, when used properly, can serve a very useful purpose. They provide great convenience, are widely accepted, and can be a source of security in an emergency. But too many Americans use credit cards inappropriately. When businesses purchase short-term items such as inventory and supplies, they use short-term credit, which they expect to pay back very quickly. The same should be true of your credit card. When you make purchases of everyday items, you should completely pay off those items within a month or two. If you don't, you are living beyond your means, and you will soon dig yourself a deep financial pit.

Longer-term items should not be purchased with credit cards, since the interest rate is too high. If you currently have a large balance on your credit card(s), we encourage you to cut up your card(s) until you have paid off your balance(s).

**Answers to Insight and Accounting Across the Organization questions** offer guideline answers for questions in the boxed real-world examples.

**Authors' Comments on *All About You*** provide the author's opinions and further discussion about financial literacy topic in the chapter.

The **Answer to PepsiCo Review It Question**, based on the PepsiCo financial statements, appears here.

**Answers to Self-Study Questions** provide feedback on your understanding of the chapter's basic concepts.

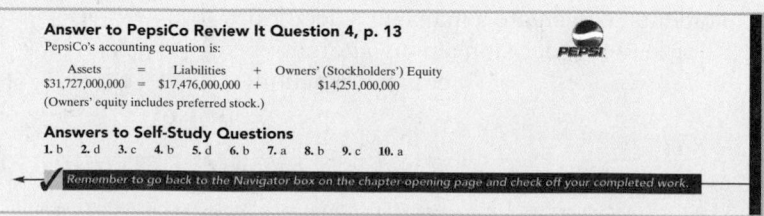

**Answer to PepsiCo Review It Question 4, p. 13**
PepsiCo's accounting equation is:

| Assets | = | Liabilities | + | Owners' (Stockholders') Equity |
|---|---|---|---|---|
| $31,727,000,000 | = | $17,476,000,000 | + | $14,251,000,000 |

(Owners' equity includes preferred stock.)

**Answers to Self-Study Questions**
1. b    2. d    3. c    4. b    5. d    6. b    7. a    8. b    9. c    10. a

✔ *Remember to go back to the Navigator box on the chapter-opening page and check off your completed work.*

After you complete your homework assignments, it's a good idea to go back to **The Navigator** checklist at the start of the chapter to see if you have used all the chapter's study aids.

# SPECIAL STUDENT SUPPLEMENTS

## That Help You Get the Best Grade You Can

**The Financial Accounting Website**

The book's website at **www.wiley.com/college/weygandt** provides a wealth of materials that will help you develop a conceptual understanding and increase your ability to solve problems. For example, you will find PowerPoint™ presentations and web quizzing.

**Working Papers**

Working papers are partially completed accounting forms (templates) for all end-of-chapter brief exercises, exercises, problems, and cases. They are a convenient resource for organizing and completing homework assignments, and they demonstrate how to correctly set up solution formats. The Working Papers are available in various groupings, so take care to order the set that matches the book you are using (check the number of chapters in your book). Also available on CD-ROM or within *WileyPLUS* is an electronic version of the print working papers, which are Excel-formatted templates that will help you learn to properly format and present end-of-chapter textbook solutions.

**Study Guide**

The Study Guide is a comprehensive review of accounting. It guides you through chapter content, tied to study objectives. Each chapter of the Study Guide includes a chapter review (20 to 30 key points); a demonstration problem; and for extra practice, true/false, multiple-choice, and matching questions, and additional exercises, with solutions. The Study Guide is an excellent tool for use on a regular basis during the course and also when preparing for exams.

**General Ledger Software**

GLS The General Ledger Software (GLS) program allows you to use a computerized accounting system to solve the end-of-chapter text problems that are identified by the icon shown here. Your instructor may also assign these problems within *WileyPLUS*.

**Solving Financial Accounting Problems Using Excel**

A manual guides you step-by-step from an introduction to computers and Excel, to completion of preprogrammed spreadsheets, to design of your own spreadsheets. Accompanying spreadsheet templates allow you to complete selected end-of-chapter exercises and problems, identified by the icon shown here.

**Peachtree Complete® Accounting**

A stand-alone workbook and accompanying CD teach you how to use Peachtree Complete® Accounting Software. Selected problems in the book can be solved using this supplementary software package.

For more information on any of these student supplements, check with your professor or bookstore, or go to the Student Companion website at **www.wiley.com/college/weygandt**.

# HOW DO I LEARN BEST?

This questionnaire aims to find out something about your preferences for the way you work with information. You will have a preferred learning style, and one part of that learning style is your preference for the intake and output of ideas and information.

Choose the answer which best explains your preference. You can select more than one response if a single answer does not match your perception. Leave blank any question that does not apply.

1. You are about to give directions to a person who is standing with you. She is staying in a hotel in town and wants to visit your house later. She has a rental car. You would:
   a. draw or provide a map on paper.
   b. tell her the directions.
   c. write down the directions (without a map).
   d. pick her up from the hotel in a car.

2. You are not sure whether a word should be spelled "dependent" or "dependant." You would:
   c. look it up in the dictionary.
   a. see the word in your mind and choose by the way it looks
   b. sound it out in your mind.
   d. write both versions down on paper and choose one.

3. You have just received a copy of your itinerary for a world trip. This is of interest to some friends. You would:
   b. phone, text, or email them and tell them about it.
   c. send them a copy of the printed itinerary.
   a. show them on a map of the world.
   d. describe what you plan to do at each place on the itinerary.

4. You are going to cook something as a special treat for your family. You would:
   d. cook something familiar without the need for instructions.
   a. thumb through the cookbook looking for ideas from the pictures.
   c. refer to a specific cookbook where there is a good recipe.

5. A group of tourists has been assigned to you to find out about wildlife reserves or parks. You would:
   d. drive them to a wildlife reserve or park.
   a. show them slides and photographs.
   c. give them pamphlets or a book on wildlife reserves or parks.
   b. give them a talk on wildlife reserves or parks.

6. You are about to purchase a new CD player. Other than price, what would most influence your decision?
   b. The salesperson telling you what you want to know.
   c. Reading the details about it.
   d. Playing with the controls and listening to it.
   a. It looks really smart and fashionable.

7. Recall a time in your life when you learned how to do something like playing a new board game. Try to avoid choosing a very physical skill, e.g. riding a bike. You learned best by:
   a. visual clues–pictures, diagrams and charts.
   c. written instructions.
   b. listening to somebody explaining it.
   d. doing it or trying it.

8. You have a knee problem. You would prefer that the doctor:
   b. told you what was wrong.
   a. showed you a diagram of what was wrong.
   d. used a model of a knee to show you what was wrong.

9. You are about to learn to use a new program on a computer. You would:
   d. sit down at the keyboard and experiment with the program.
   c. read the manual that came with the program.
   b. telephone or text a friend and ask questions about the program.

10. You are staying in a hotel and have a rental car. You would like to visit friends whose address/location you do not know. You would like them to:
    a. draw you a map on paper or provide a map from the Internet.
    b. tell you the directions.
    c. write down the directions (without a map).
    d. pick you up from the hotel in a car.

11. Apart from the price, what would most influence your decision to buy a particular textbook?
    d. You have used a copy before.
    b. A friend talking about it.
    c. Quickly reading parts of it.
    a. The way it looks is appealing.

12. A new movie has arrived in town. What would most influence your decision to go (or not go)?
    b. You heard a review about it on the radio.
    c. You read a review about it.
    a. You saw a preview of it.

13. You prefer a teacher who likes to use:
    c. a textbook, handouts, and reading.
    a. flow diagrams, charts, and graphs.
    d. field trips, models, laboratories, and practical sessions.
    b. class or email discussion, online chat groups, and guest speakers.

Count your choices:

| a. | b. | c. | d. |
|----|----|----|----|
| ☐ | ☐ | ☐ | ☐ |
| V | A | R | K |

Now match the letter or letters you have recorded most to the same letter or letters in the Learning Styles Chart. You may have more than one learning style preference—many people do. Next to each letter in the chart are suggestions that will refer you to different learning aids throughout this text.

# LEARNING STYLES CHART

| | Intake: To take in the information | To make a study package |
|---|---|---|

## Visual

**Intake:**
- Pay close attention to charts, drawings, and handouts your instructors use.
- Underline.
- Use different colors.
- Use symbols, flow charts, graphs, different arrangements on the page, white spaces.

**To make a study package:**
Convert your lecture notes into "page pictures." To do this:
- Use the "Intake" strategies.
- Reconstruct images in different ways.
- Redraw pages from memory.
- Replace words with symbols and initials.
- Look at your pages.

## Aural

**Intake:**
- Attend lectures and tutorials.
- Discuss topics with students and instructors.
- Explain new ideas to other people.
- Use a tape recorder.
- Leave spaces in your lecture notes for later recall.
- Describe overheads, pictures, and visuals to somebody who was not in class.

**To make a study package:**
You may take poor notes because you prefer to listen. Therefore:
- Expand your notes by talking with others and with information from your textbook.
- Tape-record summarized notes and listen.
- Read summarized notes out loud.
- Explain your notes to another "aural" person.

## Reading/ Writing

**Intake:**
- Use lists and headings.
- Use dictionaries, glossaries, and definitions.
- Read handouts, textbooks, and supplementary library readings.
- Use lecture notes.

**To make a study package:**
- Write out words again and again.
- Reread notes silently.
- Rewrite ideas and principles into other words.
- Turn charts, diagrams, and other illustrations into statements.

## Kinesthetic

K

**Intake:**
- Use all your senses.
- Go to labs, take field trips.
- Listen to real-life examples.
- Pay attention to applications.
- Use hands-on approaches.
- Use trial-and-error methods.

**To make a study package:**
You may take poor notes because topics do not seem concrete or relevant. Therefore:
- Put examples in your summaries.
- Use case studies and applications to help with principles and abstract concepts.
- Talk about your notes with another "kinesthetic" person.
- Use pictures and photographs that illustrate an idea.

| Text features that may help you the most | Output: To do well on exams | |
|---|---|---|
| The Navigator/Feature Story/Preview<br>Infographics/Illustrations<br>Accounting Equation Analyses<br>Highlighted words<br>Graph in *All About You*<br>Demonstration Problem/Action Plan<br>Questions/Exercises/Problems<br>Financial Reporting Problem<br>Comparative Analysis Problem<br>Exploring the Web | • Recall your "page pictures."<br>• Draw diagrams where appropriate.<br>• Practice turning your visuals back into words. | **Visual**<br>**V** |
| Preview<br>Insight Boxes<br>Review It/Do It/Action Plan<br>"What Do You Think?" in *All About You*<br>Summary of Study Objectives<br>Glossary<br>Demonstration Problem/Action Plan<br>Self-Study Questions<br>Questions/Exercises/Problems<br>Financial Reporting Problem<br>Comparative Analysis Problem<br>Exploring the Web<br>Decision Making Across the Organization<br>Communication Activity<br>Ethics Case | • Talk with the instructor.<br>• Spend time in quiet places recalling the ideas.<br>• Practice writing answers to old exam questions.<br>• Say your answers out loud. | **Aural**<br>**A** |
| The Navigator/Feature Story/Study Objectives/Preview<br>Review It/Do It/Action Plan<br>Summary of Study Objectives<br>Glossary/Self-Study Questions<br>Questions/Exercises/Problems<br>Writing Problems<br>Financial Reporting Problem<br>Comparative Analysis Problem<br>"All About You" Activity<br>Exploring the Web<br>Decision Making Across the Organization<br>Communication Activity | • Write exam answers.<br>• Practice with multiple-choice questions.<br>• Write paragraphs, beginnings and endings.<br>• Write your lists in outline form.<br>• Arrange your words into hierarchies and points. | **Reading/ Writing**<br>**R** |
| The Navigator/Feature Story/Preview<br>Infographics/Illustrations<br>Review It/Do It/Action Plan<br>Summary of Study Objectives<br>Demonstration Problem/Action Plan<br>Self-Study Questions<br>Questions/Exercises/Problems<br>Financial Reporting Problem<br>Comparative Analysis Problem<br>Exploring the Web<br>Decision Making Across the Organization<br>Communication Activity<br>"All About You" Activity | • Write practice answers.<br>• Role-play the exam situation. | **Kinesthetic**<br>**K** |

**For all learning styles:** Be sure to use the book's website to enhance your understanding of the concepts and procedures of the text.

# BRIEF CONTENTS

## APPENDIXES

# CONTENTS

The new *"All About You"* features, one in each chapter, promote financial literacy. They are intended to get students thinking and talking about how accounting impacts their personal lives. Students are more likely to understand the accounting concept being made within the textbook when accounting material is linked to a familiar topic. Each All About You box presents a high-interest issue related to the chapter topic, offers facts about it, poses a situation for students to think about, and offers brief opposing answers as a starting place for further discussion. As a feedback mechanism, the authors' comments and opinions about the situation appear at the end of the chapter.

An *"All About You" Activity,* located in the *Broadening Your Perspective* section near the end of the assignment material, offers further opportunity to explore aspects of the topic in a homework assignment.

**CHAPTER 1    Accounting in Action**
## Ethics: Managing Personal Financial Reporting (p. 25)
Compares filing for financial aid, especially the FAFSA form, to corporate financial reporting. Presents facts about student debt loads. Asks whether students should present a negative financial picture to increase the chance of receiving financial aid. *AAY Activity* further examines ethics of financial aid and corporate reporting.

**CHAPTER 2    The Recording Process**
## Your Personal Annual Report (p. 71)
Likens a student's resume to a company's annual report. Presents facts about prominent people with inaccurate résumés. Asks students to consider whether firing Radio Shack's CEO for résumé falsehoods was warranted. *AAY Activity* explores short-term career goals and résumé presentation.

**CHAPTER 3    Adjusting the Accounts**
## Is Your Old Computer a Liability? (p. 115)
Discusses the responsibility for disposing of old electronic equipment and presents facts about the extent of that problem nationally. Asks if companies should consider environmental clean-up costs as liabilities. *AAY Activity* asks students to evaluate different liability-disclosure scenarios.

**CHAPTER 4    Completing the Accounting Cycle**
## Your Personal Balance Sheet (p. 167)
Walks students through identification of personal assets and personal liabilities. Presents facts about Americans' wealth and attitudes toward saving versus spending. Asks if college is a good time to prepare a personal balance sheet. *AAY Activity* gives students practice preparing a personal balance sheet.

**CHAPTER 5    Accounting for Merchandising Operations**
## When Is a Sale Not a Sale? (p. 215)
Discusses channel stuffing as a way to manipulate revenue recognition. Presents facts about companies that improperly recognized revenue and the percentage that restated earnings to correct errors. Asks students to think through what they would do if a boss asked them to engage in channel stuffing. *AAY Activity* presents ethical situations related to revenue recognition.

**CHAPTER 6    Inventories**
## Employee Theft—An Inside Job (p. 263)
Discusses the problem of inventory theft, and how companies keep it in check. Presents facts about inventory theft. Asks for students' opinions on the use of video cameras to reduce theft. *AAY Activity* involves an Internet search for stories on inventory fraud.

**CHAPTER 7    Accounting Principles**
## Corporations Have Governance Structures—Do You? (p. 314)
Discusses the idea of codes of ethics in business and at college. Presents facts about use and abuse of codes of ethics in the workplace, and responses of stockholders. Asks students for opinions on whether schools' codes of ethics serve a useful purpose. *AAY Activity* has students evaluate a code of ethics, and make recommendations to improve it.

**CHAPTER 8    Internal Control and Cash**
## Protecting Yourself from Identity Theft (p. 364)
Likens corporate internal controls to individuals' efforts to protect themselves from identity thieves. Presents facts about how thieves obtain stolen data and how they use it. Asks students about the safety of storing personal financial data on computers. *AAY Activity* asks students to take an online quiz on identity theft.

**CHAPTER 9    Accounting for Receivables**
## Should You Be Carrying Plastic? (p. 405)
Discusses the need for individuals to evaluate their credit positions as thoughtfully as companies do. Presents facts about college-student debt, Americans' use of credit cards, and recent bankruptcy filings. Asks whether students should cut up their credit cards. *AAY Activity* asks students to evaluate credit card terms.

**CHAPTER 10    Plant Assets, Natural Resources, and Intangible Assets**
## Buying a Wreck of Your Own (p. 448)
Presents information about costs and financing of new versus used cars. Asks whether students could improve their economic well-being by buying a used car. The *AAY Activity* tests knowledge of famous trade names.

**CHAPTER 11    Liabilities**
## Your Boss Wants to Know If You Ran Today (p. 496)
Discusses ways to contain cost of health-care benefits. Presents facts on costs and spending on health care. Asks students to consider whose responsibility it is to maintain healthy lifestyles to control health-care costs. *AAYActivity* looks at an employee's other major cost—taxes—and has students calculate various types of taxes.

**CHAPTER 12    Corporations: Organization, Stock Transactions, Dividends, and Retained Earnings**

**Home-Equity Loans (p. 567)**

Compares equity-reducing transactions of companies to use of home-equity loans by individuals. Presents facts about home-equity loans, including tax benefits and variable interest rates. Asks students to assess use of a home-equity loan for a dream vacation. *AAY Activity* asks students to navigate through an annual report like a shareholder would.

**CHAPTER 13    Investments**

**A Good Day to Start Saving (p. 612)**

Lists excuses not to save, and encourages students to begin saving now. Presents facts about U.S. savings rates and the difference made by starting early. Asks students to assess whether to pay off credit cards before contributing to a 401(k). *AAY Activity* sends students to the SEC's websites to define investment terms and for a quiz on investment "smarts."

**CHAPTER 14    Statement of Cash Flows**

**Where Does the Money Go? (p. 656)**

Discusses the need to know how one spends one's cash. Presents facts about college students' spending patterns. Asks students to analyze a personal cash flow statement and decide whether, and where, cuts should be made. *AAY Activity* has students read an article at The Motley Fool site and discuss how much money to set aside for short-term needs.

**CHAPTER 15    Financial Statement Analysis**

**Should I Play the Market Yet? (p. 723)**

Discusses when to begin investing in the stock market. Presents facts about stock ownership in the U.S. Asks students to decide whether a young working person should invest in her employer's stock. *AAY Activity* asks students to complete a questionnaire about appropriate types of mutual fund.

# Financial Accounting

# Accounting in Action

## STUDY OBJECTIVES

*After studying this chapter, you should be able to:*

1 Explain what accounting is.
2 Identify the users and uses of accounting.
3 Understand why ethics is a fundamental business concept.
4 Explain generally accepted accounting principles and the cost principle.
5 Explain the monetary unit assumption and the economic entity assumption.
6 State the accounting equation, and define assets, liabilities, and stockholders' equity.
7 Analyze the effects of business transactions on the accounting equation.
8 Understand the four financial statements and how they are prepared.

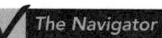

## ✓ The Navigator

| Scan **Study Objectives** | ■ |
| Read **Feature Story** | ■ |
| Read **Preview** | ■ |
| Read text and answer **Before You Go On** p. 7 ■   p. 13 ■   p. 20 ■   p. 24 ■ | |
| Work **Demonstration Problem** | ■ |
| Review **Summary of Study Objectives** | ■ |
| Answer **Self-Study Questions** | ■ |
| Complete **Assignments** | ■ |

*The Navigator is a learning system designed to prompt you to use the learning aids in the chapter and set priorities as you study.*

*Study Objectives give you a framework for learning the specific concepts covered in the chapter.*

## Feature Story

### KNOWING THE NUMBERS

Consider this quote from Harold Geneen, the former chairman of IT&T: "To be good at your business, you have to know the numbers—cold." Success in any business comes back to the numbers. You will rely on them to make decisions, and managers will use them to evaluate your performance. That is true whether your job involves marketing, production, management, or information systems.

In business, accounting and financial statements are the means for communicating the numbers. If you don't know how to read financial statements, you can't really know your business.

When Jack Stack and 11 other managers purchased Springfield ReManufacturing Corporation (SRC) (*www.srcreman.com*) for 10 cents a share, it was a failing

division of International Harvester. Stack had 119 employees who were counting on him for their livelihood, and he knew that the company was on the verge of financial failure.

Stack decided that the company's only chance of survival was to encourage every employee to think like a businessperson and to act like an owner. To accomplish this, all employees at SRC took basic accounting courses and participated in weekly reviews of the company's financial statements. SRC survived, and eventually thrived. To this day, every employee (now numbering more than 1,000) undergoes this same training.

Many other companies have adopted this approach, which is called "open-book management." Even in companies that do not practice open-book management, employers generally assume that managers in all areas of the company are "financially literate."

Taking this course will go a long way to making you financially literate. In this book you will learn how to read and prepare financial statements, and how to use basic tools to evaluate financial results. Appendixes A and B provide real financial statements of two well-known companies, PepsiCo and The Coca-Cola Company. Throughout this textbook we attempt to increase your familiarity with financial reporting by providing numerous references, questions, and exercises that encourage you to explore these financial statements.

*The Feature Story helps you picture how the chapter topic relates to the real world of accounting and business. You will find references to the story throughout the chapter.*

✓ The Navigator

## *Inside Chapter 1*

*"Inside Chapter x" lists boxes in the chapter that should be of special interest to you.*

3

The opening story about Springfield ReManufacturing Corporation highlights the importance of having good financial information to make effective business decisions. Whatever one's pursuits or occupation, the need for financial information is inescapable. You cannot earn a living, spend money, buy on credit, make an investment, or pay taxes without receiving, using, or dispensing financial information. Good decision making depends on good information.

The purpose of this chapter is to show you that accounting is the system used to provide useful financial information. The content and organization of Chapter 1 are as follows.

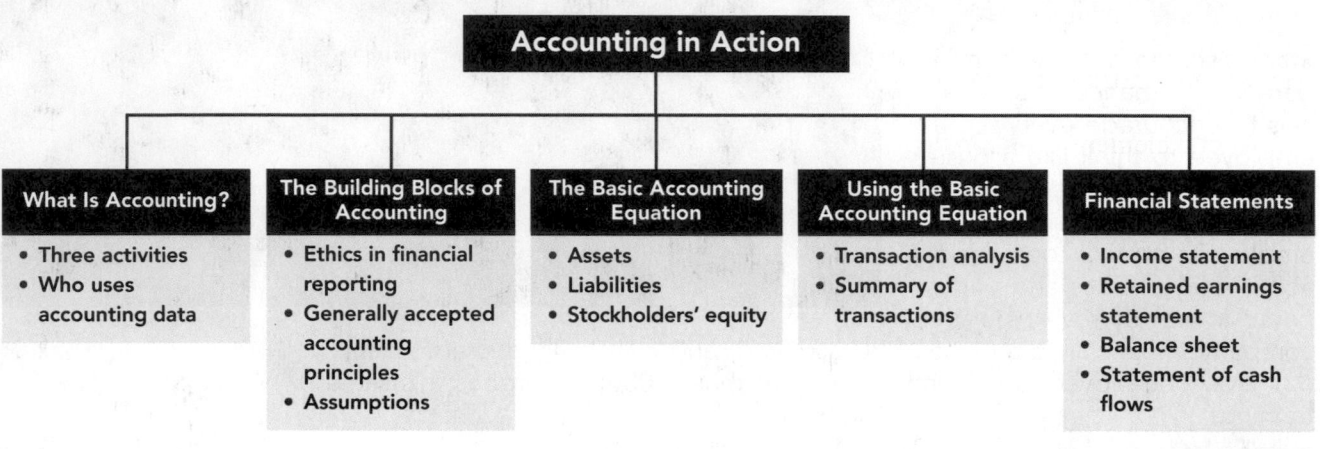

The Navigator

*The **Preview** describes and outlines the major topics and subtopics you will see in the chapter.*

# WHAT IS ACCOUNTING?

**STUDY OBJECTIVE 1**

Explain what accounting is.

Why is accounting so popular? What consistently ranks as one of the top career opportunities in business? What frequently rates among the most popular majors on campus? What was the undergraduate degree chosen by Nike founder Phil Knight, Home Depot co-founder Arthur Blank, former acting director of the Federal Bureau of Investigation (FBI) Thomas Pickard, and numerous members of Congress? Accounting.[1] Why did these people choose accounting? They wanted to understand what was happening financially to their organizations. Accounting is the financial information system that provides these insights. In short, to understand your organization, you have to know the numbers.

**Accounting** consists of three basic activities—it **identifies**, **records**, and **communicates** the economic events of an organization to interested users. Let's take a closer look at these three activities.

## Three Activities

To **identify** economic events, a company selects the **economic events relevant to its business**. Examples of economic events are the sale of snack chips by PepsiCo, providing of telephone services by AT&T, and payment of wages by Ford Motor Company.

---

[1]The appendix to this chapter describes job opportunities for accounting majors and explains why accounting is such a popular major.

Once a company like PepsiCo identifies economic events, it **records** those events in order to provide a history of its financial activities. Recording consists of keeping a **systematic**, **chronological diary of events**, measured in dollars and cents. In recording, PepsiCo also classifies and summarizes economic events.

Finally, PepsiCo **communicates** the collected information to interested users by means of **accounting reports**. The most common of these reports are called **financial statements**. To make the reported financial information meaningful, PepsiCo reports the recorded data in a standardized way. It accumulates information resulting from similar transactions. For example, PepsiCo accumulates all sales transactions over a certain period of time and reports the data as one amount in the company's financial statements. Such data are said to be reported **in the aggregate**. By presenting the recorded data in the aggregate, the accounting process simplifies a multitude of transactions and makes a series of activities understandable and meaningful.

A vital element in communicating economic events is the accountant's ability to **analyze** and **interpret** the reported information. Analysis involves use of ratios, percentages, graphs, and charts to highlight significant financial trends and relationships. Interpretation involves **explaining the uses**, **meaning**, **and limitations of reported data**. Appendix A of this textbook shows the financial statements of PepsiCo, Inc.; Appendix B illustrates the financial statements of The Coca-Cola Company. We refer to these statements at various places throughout the text. At this point, they probably strike you as complex and confusing. By the end of this course, you'll be surprised at your ability to understand, analyze, and interpret them.

Illustration 1-1 summarizes the activities of the accounting process.

**Illustration 1-1**
Accounting process

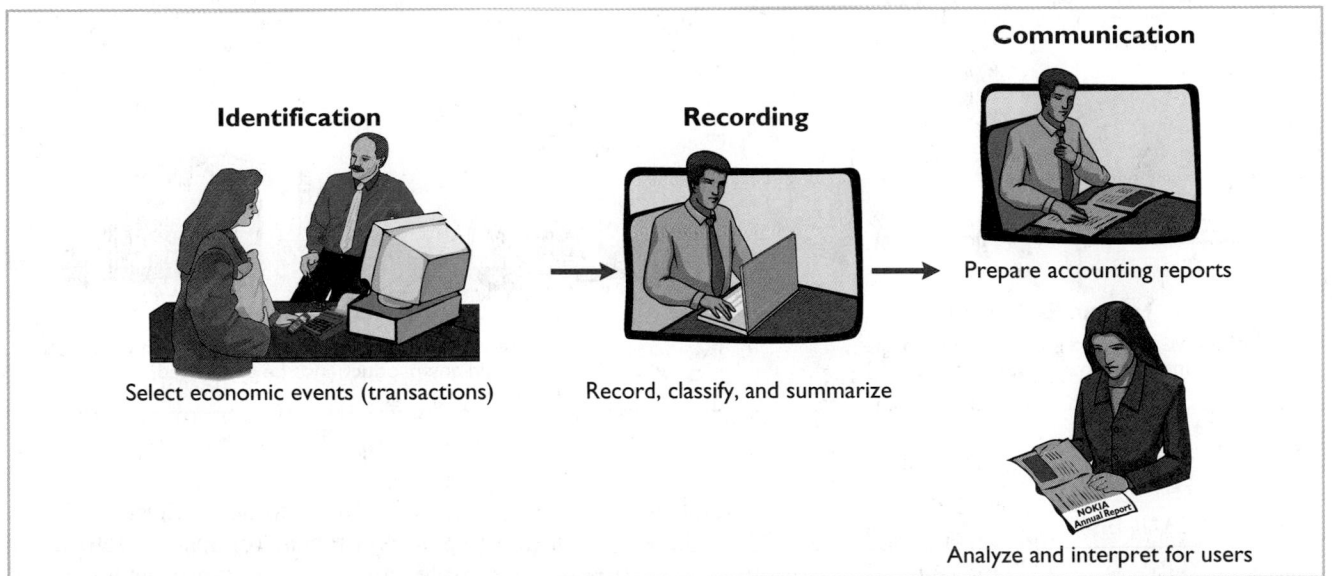

**Identification**

Select economic events (transactions)

**Recording**

Record, classify, and summarize

**Communication**

Prepare accounting reports

Analyze and interpret for users

You should understand that the accounting process **includes** the bookkeeping function. **Bookkeeping** usually involves **only** the recording of economic events. It is therefore just one part of the accounting process. In total, accounting involves **the entire process of identifying, recording, and communicating economic events**.[2]

*Essential terms are printed in blue when they first appear, and are defined in the end-of-chapter glossary.*

---

[2]The origins of accounting are generally attributed to the work of Luca Pacioli, an Italian Renaissance mathematician. Pacioli was a close friend and tutor to Leonardo da Vinci and a contemporary of Christopher Columbus. In his 1494 text *Summa de Arithmetica, Geometria, Proportione et Proportionalite,* Pacioli described a system to ensure that financial information was recorded efficiently and accurately.

# Who Uses Accounting Data?

The information that a user of financial information needs depends upon the kinds of decisions the user makes. There are two broad groups of users of financial information: internal users and external users.

### INTERNAL USERS

**Internal users** of accounting information are those individuals inside a company who plan, organize, and run the business. These include *marketing managers, production supervisors, finance directors, and company officers.* In running a business, internal users must answer many important questions, as shown in Illustration 1-2.

**Illustration 1-2**
Internal users

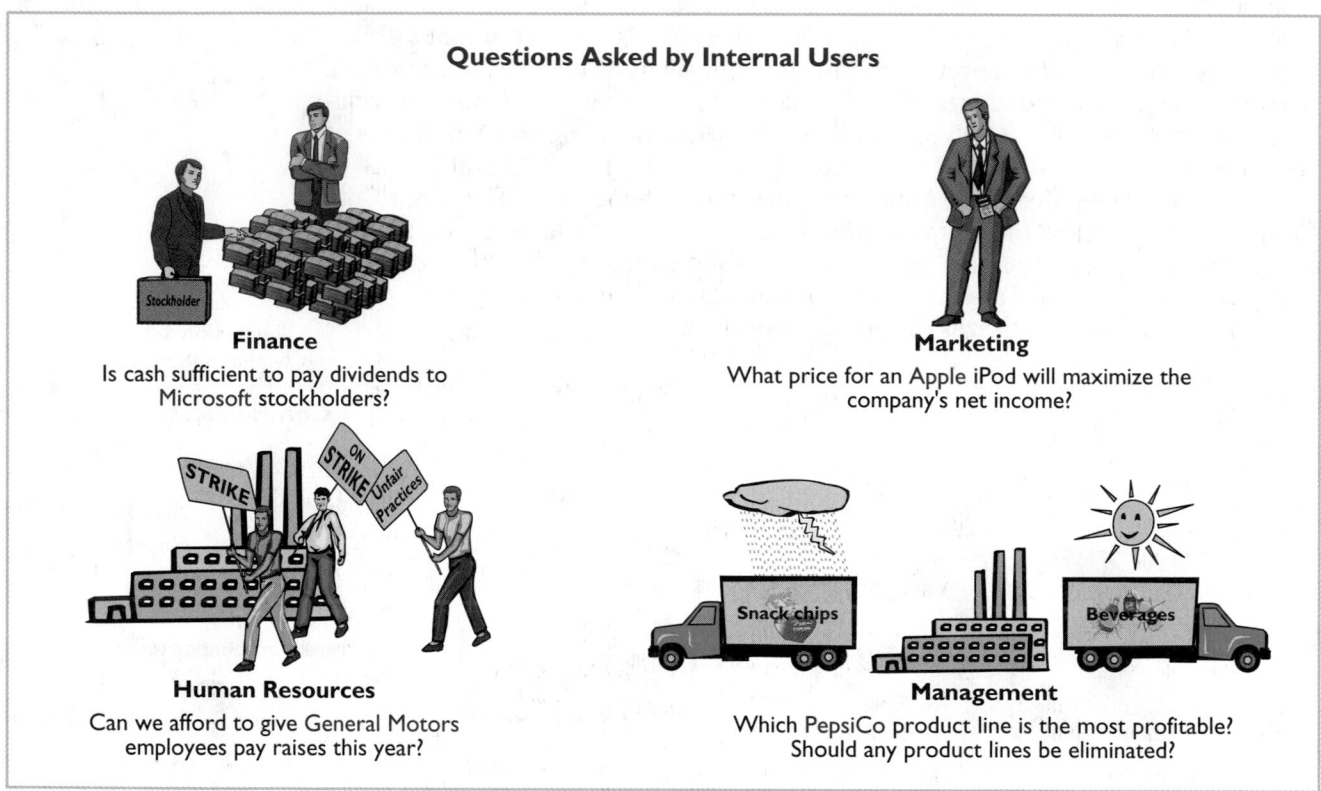

**Questions Asked by Internal Users**

**Finance**
Is cash sufficient to pay dividends to Microsoft stockholders?

**Marketing**
What price for an Apple iPod will maximize the company's net income?

**Human Resources**
Can we afford to give General Motors employees pay raises this year?

**Management**
Which PepsiCo product line is the most profitable? Should any product lines be eliminated?

To answer these and other questions, internal users need detailed information on a timely basis. **Managerial accounting** provides internal reports to help users make decisions about their companies. Examples are financial comparisons of operating alternatives, projections of income from new sales campaigns, and forecasts of cash needs for the next year.

### EXTERNAL USERS

**External users** are individuals and organizations outside a company who want financial information about the company. There are several types of external users. The two most common types of external users are investors and creditors. **Investors** (owners) use accounting information to make decisions to buy, hold, or sell stock. **Creditors** (such as suppliers and bankers) use accounting information to evaluate the risks of granting credit or lending money. Illustration 1-3 shows some questions that may be asked by investors and creditors.

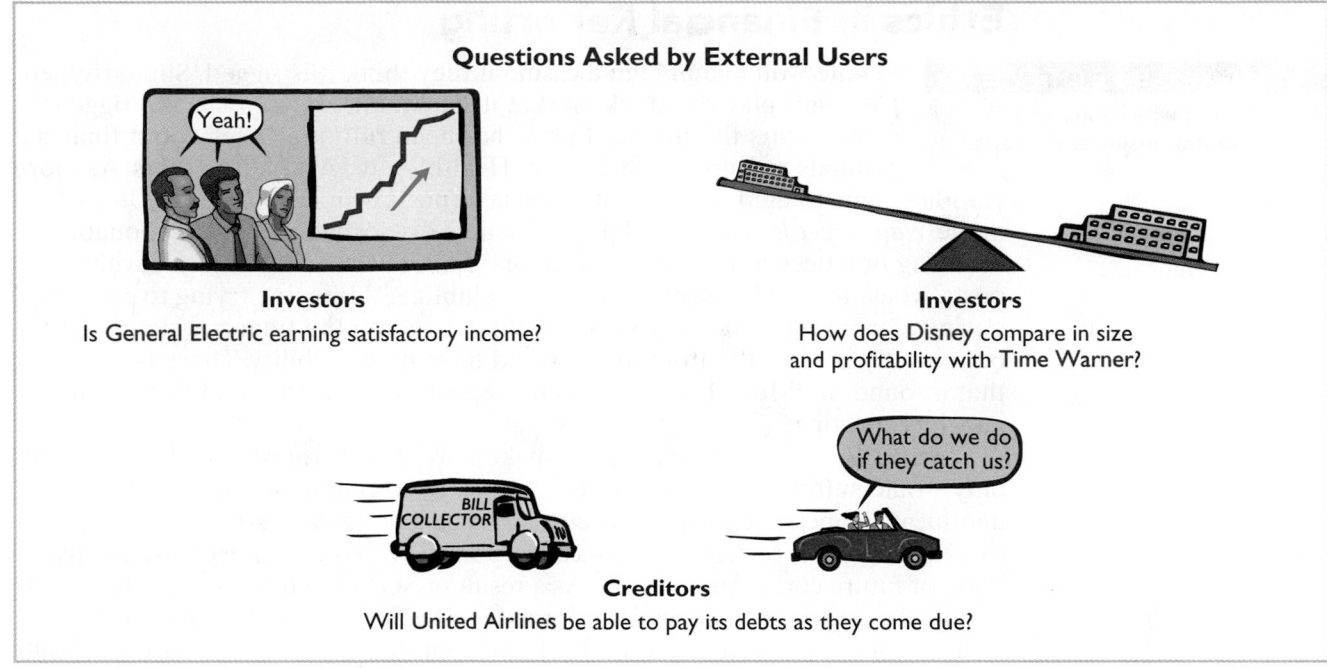

**Illustration 1-3**
External users

*Financial accounting* answers these questions. It provides economic and financial information for investors, creditors, and other external users. The information needs of external users vary considerably. **Taxing authorities** (such as the Internal Revenue Service) want to know whether the company complies with tax laws. **Regulatory agencies**, such as the Securities and Exchange Commission and the Federal Trade Commission, want to know whether the company is operating within prescribed rules. **Customers** are interested in whether a company like General Motors will continue to honor product warranties and support its product lines. **Labor unions** such as the Major League Baseball Players Association want to know whether the owners can pay increased wages and benefits.

*Ethics Notes help sensitize you to some of the ethical issues in accounting.*

**ETHICS NOTE**

The IRS and the SEC require companies to retain records that can be audited.

## Before You Go On...

1. What is accounting?
2. What does it mean to analyze and interpret financial information?
3. What is the difference between bookkeeping and accounting?
4. Identify specific internal and external users of accounting.

The Navigator

# THE BUILDING BLOCKS OF ACCOUNTING

A doctor follows certain standards in treating a patient's illness. An architect follows certain standards in designing a building. An accountant follows certain standards in reporting financial information. For these standards to work, a fundamental business concept must be at work—ethical behavior.

# Ethics in Financial Reporting

STUDY OBJECTIVE 3

Understand why ethics is a fundamental business concept.

People won't gamble in a casino if they think it is rigged. Similarly, people won't play the stock market if they think stock prices are rigged. In recent years the financial press has been full of articles about financial scandals at Enron, WorldCom, HealthSouth, AIG, and others. As more scandals came to light, mistrust of financial reporting in general grew. One article in the *Wall Street Journal* noted that "repeated disclosures about questionable accounting practices have bruised investors' faith in the reliability of earnings reports, which in turn has sent stock prices tumbling."[3] Imagine trying to carry on a business or invest money if you could not depend on the financial statements to be honestly prepared. Information would have no credibility. There is no doubt that a sound, well-functioning economy depends on accurate and dependable financial reporting.

United States regulators and lawmakers were very concerned that the economy would suffer if investors lost confidence in corporate accounting because of unethical financial reporting. Congress passed the **Sarbanes-Oxley Act of 2002** (SOX, or Sarbox) to reduce unethical corporate behavior and decrease the likelihood of future corporate scandals. As a result of SOX, top management must now certify the accuracy of financial information. In addition, top management now faces much more severe penalties for fraudulent financial activity. Also, SOX calls for increased independence of the outside auditors who review the accuracy of corporate financial statements, and increased responsibility of boards of directors in their oversight role.

The standards of conduct by which one's actions are judged as right or wrong, honest or dishonest, fair or not fair, are **ethics**. Effective financial reporting depends on sound ethical behavior. To sensitize you to ethical situations and to give you practice at solving ethical dilemmas, we address ethics in a number of ways in this book: (1) A number of the *Feature Stories* and other parts of the text discuss the central importance of ethical behavior to financial reporting. (2) *Ethics Insight boxes* and *Ethics Notes* highlight ethics situations and issues in actual business settings. (3) Many of the *All About You* boxes (near the chapter Summary) focus on ethical issues you may face in your college and early-career years. (4) At the end of the chapter, an *Ethics Case* simulates a business situation and asks you to put yourself in the position of a decision maker in that case.

When analyzing these various ethics cases, as well as experiences in your own life, it is useful to apply the three steps outlined in Illustration 1-4.

**Illustration 1-4**
Steps in analyzing ethics cases

## Solving an Ethical Dilemma

| **1. Recognize an ethical situation and the ethical issues involved.** | **2. Identify and analyze the principal elements in the situation.** | **3. Identify the alternatives, and weigh the impact of each alternative on various stakeholders.** |
|---|---|---|
| Use your personal ethics to identify ethical situations and issues. Some businesses and professional organizations provide written codes of ethics for guidance in some business situations. | Identify the *stakeholders*—persons or groups who may be harmed or benefited. Ask the question: What are the responsibilities and obligations of the parties involved? | Select the most ethical alternative, considering all the consequences. Sometimes there will be one right answer. Other situations involve more than one right solution; these situations require an evaluation of each and a selection of the best alternative. |

---

[3]"U.S. Share Prices Slump," *Wall Street Journal*, February 21, 2002.

# INTERNATIONAL INSIGHT

**Chinese Investors Lack Confidence in Financial Reports**

Concern over the quality and integrity of financial reporting is not limited to the United States. Recently the Chinese Ministry of Finance reprimanded a large accounting firm for preparing fraudulent financial reports for a number of its publicly traded companies. Afterward, a news agency, run by the Chinese government, noted that investors and analysts actually felt that the punishment of the firm was not adequate. In fact, a recent survey of investors in China found that less than 10% had full confidence in companies' annual reports. As a result of these concerns the Chinese Institute of Certified Public Accountants vowed to strengthen its policing of its members.

**?** What has been done in the United States to improve the quality and integrity of financial reporting and to build investor confidence in financial reports?

*Insight boxes provide examples of business situations from various perspectives—ethics, investor, and international. Guideline answers are provided on the last page of the chapter.*

## Generally Accepted Accounting Principles

The accounting profession has developed standards that are generally accepted and universally practiced. This common set of standards, called **generally accepted accounting principles (GAAP)**, indicate how to report economic events.

The **Securities and Exchange Commission (SEC)** is the agency of the U.S. government that oversees U.S. financial markets and accounting standard-setting bodies. The primary accounting standard-setting body in the United States is the **Financial Accounting Standards Board (FASB)**. Many countries outside of the United States have adopted the accounting standards issued by the **International Accounting Standards Board (IASB)**. In recent years the FASB and IASB have worked closely to try to minimize the differences in their standards.

Most agree that there is a need for one set of international accounting standards. The standards issued by the IASB are often called **iGAAP**. Throughout this text you will find discussions related to international accounting and reporting issues. For example, International Insight Boxes, as shown above, will help you to understand general issues related to international accounting. In addition, Chapter 7 and Appendix G discuss more technical details related to this issue. An encouraging note is that the two standard-setting boards are rapidly eliminating major differences between the two reporting systems.

> **STUDY OBJECTIVE 4**
>
> Explain generally accepted accounting principles and the cost principle.

### COST PRINCIPLE

One important principle is the cost principle. The **cost principle** dictates that companies record assets at their cost. This is true not only at the time the asset is purchased, but also over the time the asset is held. For example, if Best Buy purchases land for $30,000, the company initially reports it on the balance sheet at $30,000. But what does Best Buy do if, by the end of the next year, the land had increased in value to $40,000? Under the cost principle it continues to report the land at $30,000.

Critics contend the cost principle is irrelevant. They argue that market value (the value determined by the market at any particular time) is more useful to financial decision makers. Proponents of the cost principle counter that cost is the best measure. The reason: Cost can be easily verified, whereas market value is often subjective. Recently, the FASB has changed some accounting rules and now requires that certain investment securities be recorded at their market value. In choosing between cost and market value, the FASB weighed the **reliability** of cost figures versus the **relevance** of market value.

*Helpful Hints further clarify concepts being discussed.*

> **HELPFUL HINT**
>
> *Relevance* and *reliability* are two primary qualities that make accounting information useful for decision making.

# Assumptions

Assumptions provide a foundation for the accounting process. Two main assumptions are the **monetary unit assumption** and the **economic entity assumption**.

## MONETARY UNIT ASSUMPTION

The monetary unit assumption requires that companies include in the accounting records only transaction data that can be expressed in terms of money. This assumption enables accounting to quantify (measure) economic events. The monetary unit assumption is vital to applying the cost principle.

This assumption prevents the inclusion of some relevant information in the accounting records. For example, the health of the owner, the quality of service, and the morale of employees are not included. The reason: Companies cannot quantify this information in terms of money. Though this information is important, only events that can be measured in money are recorded.

## ECONOMIC ENTITY ASSUMPTION

**An economic entity can be any organization or unit in society.** It may be a company (such as General Electric Company), a governmental unit (the state of Ohio), a municipality (Seattle), a school district (St. Louis District 48), or a church (Southern Baptist). The economic entity assumption requires that the activities of the entity be kept separate and distinct from the activities of its owner and all other economic entities. To illustrate, Sally Rider, owner of Sally's Boutique, must keep her personal living costs separate from the expenses of the Boutique. Similarly, PepsiCo, Coca-Cola, and Cadbury-Schweppes are segregated into separate economic entities for accounting purposes.

**Proprietorship.** A business owned by one person is generally a **proprietorship**. The owner is often the manager/operator of the business. Small service-type businesses (e.g., plumbing companies, beauty salons, auto repair shops), farms, and small retail stores (e.g., antique shops, used-book stores) are often sole proprietorships. **Usually only a relatively small amount of money (capital) is necessary to start in business as a proprietorship. The owner (proprietor) receives any profits, suffers any losses, and is personally liable for all debts of the business.** There is no legal distinction between the business as an economic unit and the owner, but the accounting records of the business activities are kept separate from the personal records and activities of the owner.

**Partnership.** A business owned by two or more persons associated as partners is a **partnership**. In most respects a partnership is like a proprietorship except that more than one owner is involved. Typically a partnership agreement (written or oral) sets forth such terms as initial investment, duties of each partner, division of net income (or net loss), and settlement upon death or withdrawal of a partner. Each partner generally has unlimited personal liability for the partnership's debts. **Like a proprietorship, for accounting purposes the partnership transactions must be kept separate from the personal activities of the partners.** Partnerships are often used to organize retail and service-type businesses, including professional practices (lawyers, doctors, architects, and certified public accountants).

**Corporation.** A business organized as a separate legal entity under state corporation law and having ownership divided into transferable shares of stock is a **corporation**. The holders of the shares (stockholders) **enjoy limited liability:** they are not personally liable for the debts of the corporate entity. Stockholders **may transfer (sell) all or part of their shares to other investors at any time.** The ease with which ownership can change adds to the attractiveness of investing in a corporation. Because ownership can be transferred without dissolving the corporation, the corporation **enjoys an unlimited life**.

Although the combined number of proprietorships and partnerships in the United States is more than five times the number of corporations, the revenue produced by corporations is eight times greater. Most of the largest enterprises in the United States—for example, ExxonMobil, General Motors, Wal-Mart, Citigroup, and Microsoft—are corporations.

# ACCOUNTING ACROSS THE ORGANIZATION

### How Will Accounting Help Me?

One question that students frequently ask is, "How will the study of accounting help me?" It should help you a great deal, because a working knowledge of accounting is desirable for virtually *every field* of endeavor. Some examples of how accounting is used in other careers include:

**General management:** Imagine running Ford Motors, Massachusetts General Hospital, Northern Virginia Community College, a McDonald's franchise, a Trek bike shop. All general managers need to understand where the enterprise's cash comes from and where it goes in order to make wise business decisions.

**Marketing:** A marketing specialist at a company like Procter & Gamble develops strategies to help the sales force be successful. But making a sale is meaningless unless it is a profitable sale. Marketing people must be sensitive to costs and benefits, which accounting helps them quantify and understand.

**Finance:** Do you want to be a banker for Bank of America, an investment analyst for Goldman Sachs, a stock broker for Merrill Lynch? These fields rely heavily on accounting. In all of them you will regularly examine and analyze financial statements. In fact, it is difficult to get a good finance job without two or three courses in accounting.

**Real estate:** Are you interested in being a real estate broker for Prudential Real Estate? Because a third party—the bank—is almost always involved in financing a real estate transaction, brokers must understand the numbers involved: Can the buyer afford to make the payments to the bank? Does the cash flow from an industrial property justify the purchase price? What are the tax benefits of the purchase?

**?** How might accounting help you?

*Accounting Across the Organization stories demonstrate applications of accounting information in various business functions.*

# THE BASIC ACCOUNTING EQUATION

The two basic elements of a business are what it owns and what it owes. **Assets** are the resources a business owns. For example, The Coca-Cola Company has total assets of approximately $29.5 billion. Liabilities and stockholders' equity are the rights or claims against these resources. Thus, Coca-Cola has $29.4 billion of claims against its $29.5 billion of assets. Claims of those to whom the company owes money (creditors) are called **liabilities**. Claims of owners are called **stockholders' equity**. Coca-Cola has liabilities of $13.1 billion and stockholders' equity of $16.4 billion. We can express the relationship of assets, liabilities, and stockholders' equity as an equation, as follows.

> **STUDY OBJECTIVE 6**
> State the accounting equation, and define assets, liabilities, and stockholders' equity.

| **Assets** | **=** | **Liabilities** | **+** | **Stockholders' Equity** |
|---|---|---|---|---|

**Illustration 1-5**
The basic accounting equation

This relationship is the basic accounting equation. Assets must equal the sum of liabilities and stockholders' equity. Liabilities appear before stockholders' equity in the basic accounting equation because they are paid first if a business is liquidated.

The accounting equation applies to all **economic entities** regardless of size, nature of business, or form of business organization. It applies to a small proprietorship such as a corner grocery store as well as to a giant corporation such as Kellogg. The equation provides the **underlying framework** for recording and summarizing economic events.

Let's look in more detail at the categories in the basic accounting equation.

## Assets

As noted above, assets are resources a business owns. The business uses its assets in carrying out such activities as production and sales. The common characteristic possessed by all assets is the capacity to provide future services or benefits. In a business, that service potential or future economic benefit eventually results in cash inflows (receipts). For example, Campus Pizza owns a delivery truck that provides economic benefits from delivering pizzas. Other assets of Campus Pizza are tables, chairs, jukebox, cash register, oven, tableware, and, of course, cash.

## Liabilities

Liabilities are claims against assets—that is, existing debts and obligations. Businesses of all sizes usually borrow money and purchase merchandise on credit. These economic activities result in payables of various sorts:

> Campus Pizza, for instance, purchases cheese, sausage, flour, and beverages on credit from suppliers. These obligations are called **accounts payable**.

> Campus Pizza also has a **note payable** to First National Bank for the money borrowed to purchase the delivery truck.

> Campus Pizza may also have **wages payable** to employees and **sales and real estate taxes payable** to the local government.

All of these persons or entities to whom Campus Pizza owes money are its **creditors**.

Creditors may legally force the liquidation of a business that does not pay its debts. In that case, the law requires that creditor claims be paid before ownership claims.

## Stockholders' Equity

The ownership claim on total assets is stockholders' equity. It is equal to total assets minus total liabilities. Here is why: The assets of a business are claimed by either creditors or stockholders. To find out what belongs to stockholders, we subtract creditors' claims (the liabilities) from the assets. The remainder is the stockholders' claim on the assets—stockholders' equity. (It is often referred to as **residual equity**—that is, the equity "left over" after creditors' claims are satisfied.)

The stockholders' equity section of a corporation's balance sheet consists of (1) paid-in capital and (2) retained earnings.

### PAID-IN CAPITAL

**Paid-in (contributed) capital** describes the total amount paid in by stockholders. The principal source of paid-in capital is the investment of cash and other assets in the corporation by stockholders in exchange for capital stock. Corporations may issue several classes of stock, but the stock representing ownership interest is common stock.

### RETAINED EARNINGS

The **retained earnings (earned capital)** section of the balance sheet is determined by three items: revenues, expenses, and dividends.

**Revenues.**    Revenues **are the gross increases in stockholders' equity resulting from business activities entered into for the purpose of earning income.** Generally, revenues result from selling merchandise, performing services, renting property, and lending money.

Revenues usually result in an increase in an asset. They may arise from different sources and are called various names depending on the nature of the business. Campus Pizza, for instance, has two categories of sales revenues—pizza sales and beverage sales. Other titles for and sources of revenue common to many businesses are: sales, fees, services, commissions, interest, dividends, royalties, and rent.

**Expenses.**    Expenses are the cost of assets consumed or services used in the process of earning revenue. **They are decreases in stockholders' equity that result from operating the business.** Like revenues, expenses take many forms and are called various names depending on the type of asset consumed or service used. For example, Campus Pizza recognizes the following types of expenses: cost of ingredients (flour, cheese, tomato paste, meat, mushrooms, etc.); cost of beverages; wages expense; utilities expense (electric, gas, and water expense); telephone expense; delivery expense (gasoline, repairs, licenses, etc.); supplies expense (napkins, detergents, aprons, etc.); rent expense; interest expense; and property tax expense.

**Dividends.**    Net income represents an increase in net assets which are then available to distribute to stockholders. The distribution of cash or other assets to stockholders is called a dividend. Dividends reduce retained earnings. However, dividends are **not an expense**. A corporation first determines its revenues and expenses and then computes net income or net loss. If it has net income, and decides it has no better use for that income, a corporation may decide to distribute a dividend to its owners (the stockholders).

In summary, the principal sources (increases) of stockholders' equity are investments by stockholders and revenues from business operations. In contrast, reductions (decreases) in stockholders' equity result from expenses and dividends. These relationships are shown in Illustration 1-6.

**HELPFUL HINT**
The effect of revenues is positive—an increase in stockholders' equity coupled with an increase in assets or a decrease in liabilities.

**HELPFUL HINT**
The effect of expenses is negative—a decrease in stockholders' equity coupled with a decrease in assets or an increase in liabilities.

**Illustration 1-6**
Increases and decreases in stockholders' equity

INCREASES → Investments by stockholders, Revenues → **Stockholders' Equity** → Dividends to stockholders, Expenses ← DECREASES

## Before You Go On...

**REVIEW IT**
1. Why is ethics a fundamental business concept?
2. What are generally accepted accounting principles? Give an example.
3. Explain the monetary unit and the economic entity assumptions.
4. The accounting equation is: Assets = Liabilities + Stockholders' Equity. Replacing the words in that equation with dollar amounts, what is PepsiCo's accounting equation at December 31, 2005? (The answer to this question appears on page 45.)
5. What are assets, liabilities, and stockholders' equity?

*Review It questions encourage you to stop and think about what you have just learned. Sometimes these questions stand alone; other times they are accompanied by practice exercises.*

*Review It questions marked with this icon require that you use PepsiCo's annual report.*

*The **Do It** exercises, like the one here, ask you to put newly acquired knowledge to work. They outline the Action Plan necessary to complete the exercise and show a Solution.*

## DO IT

Classify the following items as issuance of stock (I), dividends (D), revenues (R), or expenses (E). Then indicate whether the following items increase or decrease stockholders' equity: (1) rent expense, (2) service revenue, (3) dividends, and (4) salaries expense.

### Action Plan

- Review the rules for changes in stockholders' equity: Investments and revenues increase stockholders' equity. Expenses and dividends decrease stockholders' equity.
- Understand the sources of revenue: the sale of merchandise, performance of services, rental of property, and lending of money.
- Understand what causes expenses: the consumption of assets or services.
- Recognize that dividends are distributions of cash or other assets to stockholders.

### Solution

1. Rent expense is classified as an expense (E); it decreases stockholders' equity.
2. Service revenue is classified as revenue (R); it increases stockholders' equity.
3. Dividends is classified as dividends (D); it decreases stockholders' equity.
4. Salaries expense is classified as an expense (E); it decreases stockholders' equity.

Related exercise material: *BE1-1, BE1-2, BE1-3, BE1-4, E1-1, E1-2, E1-3, E1-4, E1-5, E1-6, and E1-7.*

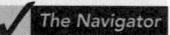 The Navigator

# USING THE BASIC ACCOUNTING EQUATION

**STUDY OBJECTIVE 7**

Analyze the effects of business transactions on the accounting equation.

**Transactions** (business transactions) are a business's economic events recorded by accountants. Transactions may be external or internal. **External transactions** involve economic events between the company and some outside enterprise. For example, Campus Pizza's purchase of cooking equipment from a supplier, payment of monthly rent to the landlord, and sale of pizzas to customers are external transactions. **Internal transactions** are economic events that occur entirely within one company. The use of cooking and cleaning supplies are internal transactions for Campus Pizza.

A company may carry on many activities that do not represent business transactions. Examples are hiring employees, answering the telephone, talking with customers, and placing orders for merchandise. Some of these activities, however, may lead to business transactions: Employees will earn wages, and suppliers will deliver ordered merchandise. The company must analyze each event to find out if it has an effect on the components of the accounting equation. If it does, the company will record the transaction. Illustration 1-7 (page 15) demonstrates the transaction-identification process.

Each transaction must have a dual effect on the accounting equation. For example, if an asset is increased, there must be a corresponding:

1. Decrease in another asset, or
2. Increase in a specific liability, or
3. Increase in stockholders' equity.

Two or more items could be affected when an asset is increased. For example, as one asset is increased $10,000, another asset could decrease $6,000 and a specific liability could increase $4,000. Any change in a liability or ownership claim is subject to similar analysis.

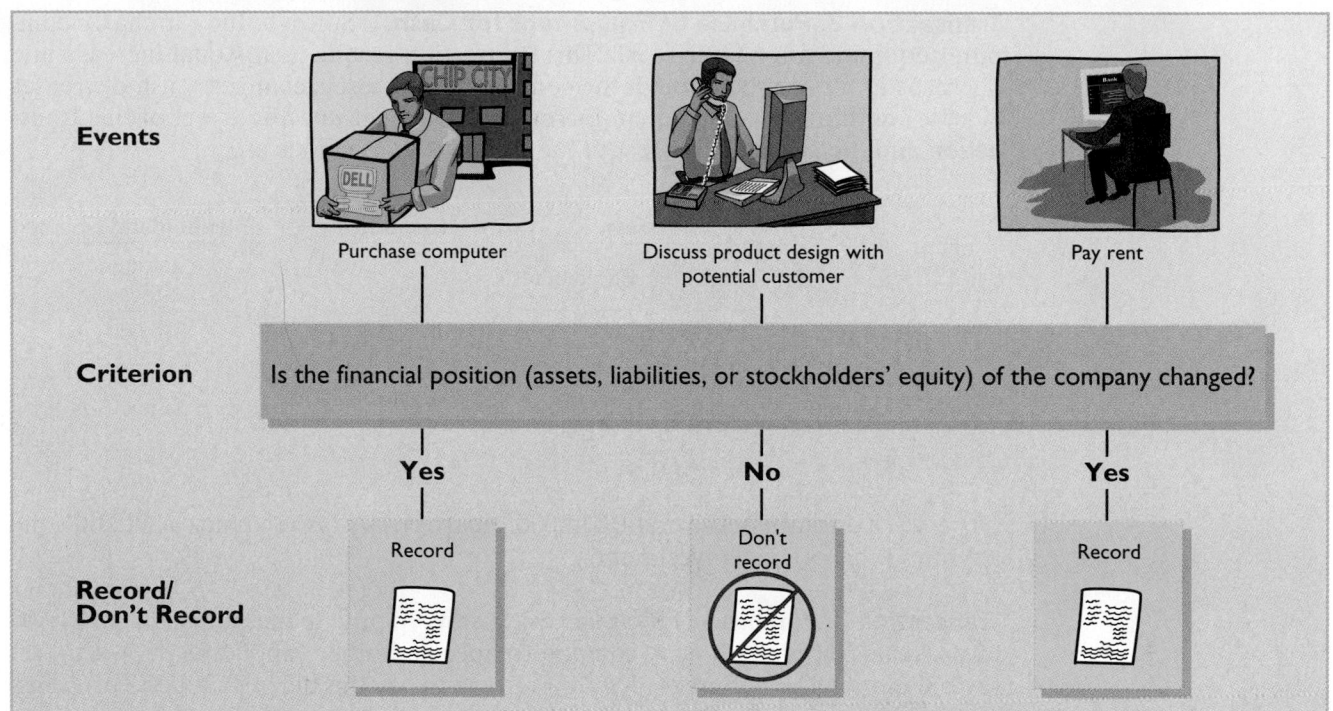

**Illustration 1-7**
Transaction-identification process

## Transaction Analysis

The following examples are business transactions for a computer programming business during its first month of operations. You will want to study these transactions until you are sure you understand them. They are not difficult, but understanding them is important to your success in this course. The ability to analyze transactions in terms of the basic accounting equation is essential in accounting.

**Transaction 1. Investment by Stockholders.**   Ray and Barbara Neal decide to open a computer programming company that they incorporate as Softbyte Inc. On September 1, 2008, they invest $15,000 cash in the business in exchange for $15,000 of common stock. The common stock indicates the ownership interest that the Neals have in Softbyte Inc. This transaction results in an equal increase in both assets and stockholders' equity. In this case, the asset Cash increases $15,000, as does Common Stock. The effect of this transaction on the basic equation is:

|     | **Assets** | **=** | **Liabilities** | **+** | **Stockholders' Equity** |            |
|-----|-----------|-------|-----------------|-------|--------------------------|------------|
|     | Cash      | =     |                 |       | Common Stock             |            |
| (1) | +$15,000  | =     |                 |       | +$15,000                 | Investment |

Observe that the equality of the basic equation has been maintained. Note also that the source of the increase in stockholders' equity (in this case, Investment) is indicated. Why does this matter? Because investments by stockholders do not represent revenues, and they are excluded in determining net income. Therefore, it is necessary to make clear that the increase is an investment rather than revenue from operations. Additional investments (i.e., investments made by stockholders after the corporation has been initially formed) have the same effect on stockholders' equity as the initial investment.

**Transaction 2. Purchase of Equipment for Cash.** Softbyte Inc. purchases computer equipment for $7,000 cash. This transaction results in an equal increase and decrease in total assets, though the composition of assets changes: Cash decreases $7,000, and the asset Equipment increases $7,000. The specific effect of this transaction and the cumulative effect of the first two transactions are:

| | | Assets | | = | Liabilities | + | Stockholders' Equity |
|---|---|---|---|---|---|---|---|
| | | Cash + | Equipment | = | | | Common Stock |
| | Old Bal. | $15,000 | | | | | $15,000 |
| (2) | | −7,000 | +$7,000 | | | | |
| | New Bal. | $ 8,000 | $7,000 | = | | | $15,000 |
| | | $15,000 | | | | | |

Observe that total assets are still $15,000. Neal's equity also remains at $15,000, the amount of his original investment.

**Transaction 3. Purchase of Supplies on Credit.** Softbyte Inc. purchases for $1,600 from Acme Supply Company computer paper and other supplies expected to last several months. Acme agrees to allow Softbyte to pay this bill in October. This transaction is a purchase on account (a credit purchase). Assets increase because of the expected future benefits of using the paper and supplies, and liabilities increase by the amount due Acme Company. The asset Supplies increase $1,600, and the liability Accounts Payable increase by the same amount. The effect on the equation is:

| | | Assets | | | = | Liabilities | + | Stockholders' Equity |
|---|---|---|---|---|---|---|---|---|
| | | Cash + | Supplies + | Equipment | = | Accounts Payable | + | Common Stock |
| | Old Bal. | $8,000 | | $7,000 | | | | $15,000 |
| (3) | | | +$1,600 | | | +$1,600 | | |
| | New Bal. | $8,000 + | $1,600 + | $7,000 | = | $1,600 | + | $15,000 |
| | | | $16,600 | | | $16,600 | | |

Total assets are now $16,600. This total is matched by a $1,600 creditor's claim and a $15,000 ownership claim.

**Transaction 4. Services Provided for Cash.** Softbyte Inc. receives $1,200 cash from customers for programming services it has provided. This transaction represents Softbyte's principal revenue-producing activity. Recall that **revenue increases stockholders' equity**. Both assets and stockholders' equity are, therefore, increased. In this transaction, Cash increases $1,200, and Retained Earnings increases $1,200. The new balances in the equation are:

| | | Assets | | | = | Liabilities | + | Stockholders' Equity | | |
|---|---|---|---|---|---|---|---|---|---|---|
| | | Cash + | Supplies + | Equipment | = | Accounts Payable | + | Common Stock | + | Retained Earnings |
| | Old Bal. | $8,000 | $1,600 | $7,000 | | $1,600 | | $15,000 | | |
| (4) | | +1,200 | | | | | | | | +$1,200 Service Revenue |
| | New Bal. | $9,200 + | $1,600 + | $7,000 | = | $1,600 | + | $15,000 | + | $1,200 |
| | | | $17,800 | | | | | $17,800 | | |

The two sides of the equation balance at $17,800. Note that stockholders' equity increases when revenues are earned. The title Service Revenue indicates the source of the increase in stockholders' equity. Service Revenue is included in determining Softbyte Inc's. net income.

**Transaction 5. Purchase of Advertising on Credit.**   Softbyte Inc. receives a bill for $250 from the *Daily News* for advertising the opening of its business but postpones payment of the bill until a later date. This transaction results in an increase in liabilities and a decrease in stockholders' equity. The specific items involved are Accounts Payable and Retained Earnings. The effect on the equation is:

| | | Assets | | | | = | Liabilities | + | | | Stockholders' Equity | | |
|---|---|---|---|---|---|---|---|---|---|---|---|---|---|
| | | Cash | + Supplies | + Equipment | = | | Accounts Payable | + | Common Stock | + | Retained Earnings | | |
| | Old Bal. | $9,200 | $1,600 | $7,000 | | | $1,600 | | $15,000 | | $1,200 | | |
| (5) | | | | | | | +250 | | | | −250 | Advertising Expense | |
| | New Bal. | $9,200 + | $1,600 + | $7,000 | = | | $1,850 | + | $15,000 | + | $ 950 | | |
| | | | $17,800 | | | | | | $17,800 | | | | |

The two sides of the equation still balance at $17,800. Retained Earnings decreases when Softbyte incurs the expense. In addition, the specific cause of the decrease (advertising expense) is noted. Expenses do not have to be paid in cash at the time they are incurred. When Softbyte pays at a later date, the liability Accounts Payable will decrease and the asset Cash will decrease [see Transaction (8)]. The cost of advertising is an expense (rather than an asset) because Softbyte has used the benefits. Advertising Expense is included in determining net income.

**Transaction 6. Services Rendered for Cash and Credit.**   Softbyte Inc. provides $3,500 of programming services for customers. The company receives cash of $1,500 from customers, and it bills the balance of $2,000 on account. This transaction results in an equal increase in assets and stockholders' equity. Three specific items are affected: Cash increases $1,500; Accounts Receivable increases $2,000; and Retained Earnings increases $3,500. The new balances are as follows.

| | | Assets | | | | = | Liabilities | + | | | Stockholders' Equity | | |
|---|---|---|---|---|---|---|---|---|---|---|---|---|---|
| | | Cash + | Accounts Receivable | + Supplies | + Equipment | = | Accounts Payable | + | Common Stock | + | Retained Earnings | | |
| | Old Bal. | $ 9,200 | | $1,600 | $7,000 | | $1,850 | | $15,000 | | $ 950 | | |
| (6) | | +1,500 | +$2,000 | | | | | | | | +3,500 | Service Revenue | |
| | New Bal. | $10,700 + | $2,000 + | $1,600 + | $7,000 | = | $1,850 | + | $15,000 | + | $4,450 | | |
| | | | $21,300 | | | | | | $21,300 | | | | |

Why increase Retained Earnings by $3,500 when Softbyte has collected only $1,500? We do so because the inflow of assets resulting from the earning of revenues does not have to be in the form of cash. Remember that stockholders' equity increases when revenues are earned. Softbyte's earns revenues when it provides the service. When it later receives collections on account, Softbyte will increase Cash and will decrease Accounts Receivable [see Transaction (9)].

**Transaction 7. Payment of Expenses.**   Softbyte pays the following expenses in cash for September: store rent $600, salaries of employees $900, and utilities $200. These payments result in an equal decrease in assets and stockholders' equity. Cash decreases $1,700 and Retained Earnings decreases by the same amount. The effect of these payments on the equation is:

|  |  | Assets |  |  | = | Liabilities | + |  | Stockholders' Equity |  |
|---|---|---|---|---|---|---|---|---|---|---|
|  | Cash + | Accounts Receivable | + Supplies + | Equipment = | | Accounts Payable | + | Common Stock | + | Retained Earnings |  |
| Old Bal. | $10,700 | $2,000 | $1,600 | $7,000 | | $1,850 | | $15,000 | | $4,450 | |
| (7) | −1,700 | | | | | | | | | −600 | Rent Expense |
| | | | | | | | | | | −900 | Salaries Expense |
| | | | | | | | | | | −200 | Utilities Expense |
| New Bal. | $9,000 + | $2,000 | + $1,600 + | $7,000 | = | $1,850 | + | $15,000 | + | $2,750 | |
| | | | $19,600 | | | | | | $19,600 | | |

The two sides of the equation now balance at $19,600. Three lines are required in the analysis to indicate the different types of expenses that have been incurred.

**Transaction 8. Payment of Accounts Payable.** Softbyte Inc. pays its *Daily News* advertising bill of $250 in cash. The company previously (in Transaction 5) recorded the bill as an increase in Accounts Payable and a decrease in Retained Earnings. This payment "on account" decreases the asset Cash by $250 and also decreases the liability Accounts Payable by $250. The effect of this transaction on the equation is:

|  |  | Assets |  |  | = | Liabilities | + | Stockholders' Equity |  |
|---|---|---|---|---|---|---|---|---|---|
|  | Cash + | Accounts Receivable | + Supplies + | Equipment = | | Accounts Payable | + | Common Stock | + | Retained Earnings |
| Old Bal. | $9,000 | $2,000 | $1,600 | $7,000 | | $1,850 | | $15,000 | | $2,750 |
| (8) | −250 | | | | | −250 | | | | |
| New Bal. | $8,750 + | $2,000 | + $1,600 + | $7,000 | = | $1,600 | + | $15,000 | + | $2,750 |
| | | | $19,350 | | | | | $19,350 | | |

Observe that the payment of a liability related to an expense that has previously been recorded does not affect stockholders' equity. Softbyte recorded the expense in Transaction 5 and should not record it again. Neither Common Stock nor Retained Earnings changes as a result of this transaction.

**Transaction 9. Receipt of Cash on Account.** Softbyte receives the sum of $600 in cash from customers who had previously been billed for services (in Transaction 6). This transaction does not change total assets, but it changes the composition of those assets. Cash increases $600 and Accounts Receivable decreases $600. The new balances are:

|  |  | Assets |  |  | = | Liabilities | + | Stockholders' Equity |  |
|---|---|---|---|---|---|---|---|---|---|
|  | Cash + | Accounts Receivable | + Supplies + | Equipment = | | Accounts Payable | + | Common Stock | + | Retained Earnings |
| Old Bal. | $8,750 | $2,000 | $1,600 | $7,000 | | $1,600 | | $15,000 | | $2,750 |
| (9) | +600 | −600 | | | | | | | | |
| New Bal. | $9,350 + | $1,400 | + $1,600 + | $7,000 | = | $1,600 | + | $15,000 | + | $2,750 |
| | | | $19,350 | | | | | $19,350 | | |

Note that the collection of an account receivable for services previously billed and recorded does not affect stockholders' equity. Softbyte already recorded this revenue in Transaction 6 and should not record it again.

**Transaction 10. Dividends.**   The corporation pays a dividend of $1,300 in cash to Ray and Barbara Neal, the stockholders of Softbyte Inc. This transaction results in an equal decrease in assets and stockholders' equity. Both Cash and Retained Earnings decrease $1,300, as shown below.

|  |  | Cash | + | Accounts Receivable | + Supplies + | Equipment | = | Accounts Payable | + | Common Stock | + | Retained Earnings |  |
|---|---|---|---|---|---|---|---|---|---|---|---|---|---|
|  | Old Bal. | $9,350 |  | $1,400 | $1,600 | $7,000 | = | $1,600 |  | $15,000 |  | $2,750 |  |
| (10) |  | −1,300 |  |  |  |  |  |  |  |  |  | −1,300 | Dividends |
|  | New Bal. | $8,050 | + | $1,400 | + $1,600 + | $7,000 | = | $1,600 | + | $15,000 | + | $1,450 |  |

Assets = Liabilities + Stockholders' Equity

$18,050         $18,050

Note that the dividend reduces retained earnings, which is part of stockholders' equity. **Dividends are not expenses.** Like stockholders' investments, dividends are excluded in determining net income.

## Summary of Transactions

Illustration 1-8 summarizes the transactions of Softbyte, Inc. It shows the transaction number, the specific effects of the transaction, and the balances after each transaction. The illustration demonstrates a number of significant facts:

**Illustration 1-8**

Tabular summary of Softbyte Inc. transactions

| Transaction | Cash | + | Accounts Receivable | + Supplies + | Equipment | = | Accounts Payable | + | Common Stock | + | Retained Earnings |  |
|---|---|---|---|---|---|---|---|---|---|---|---|---|
| (1) | +$15,000 |  |  |  |  | = |  | + | $15,000 |  |  | Investment |
| (2) | −7,000 |  |  |  | +$7,000 |  |  |  |  |  |  |  |
|  | 8,000 |  |  | + | 7,000 | = |  |  | 15,000 |  |  |  |
| (3) |  |  |  | +$1,600 |  |  | +$1,600 |  |  |  |  |  |
|  | 8,000 |  | + | 1,600 + | 7,000 | = | 1,600 | + | 15,000 |  |  |  |
| (4) | +1,200 |  |  |  |  |  |  |  |  | + | 1,200 | Service Revenue |
|  | 9,200 |  | + | 1,600 + | 7,000 | = | 1,600 | + | 15,000 | + | 1,200 |  |
| (5) |  |  |  |  |  |  | +250 |  |  |  | −250 | Advert. Expense |
|  | 9,200 |  | + | 1,600 + | 7,000 | = | 1,850 | + | 15,000 | + | 950 |  |
| (6) | +1,500 | +$2,000 |  |  |  |  |  |  |  |  | +3,500 | Service Revenue |
|  | 10,700 + | 2,000 | + | 1,600 + | 7,000 | = | 1,850 | + | 15,000 | + | 4,450 |  |
| (7) | −1,700 |  |  |  |  |  |  |  |  |  | −600 | Rent Expense |
|  |  |  |  |  |  |  |  |  |  |  | −900 | Salaries Expense |
|  |  |  |  |  |  |  |  |  |  |  | −200 | Utilities Expense |
|  | 9,000 + | 2,000 | + | 1,600 + | 7,000 | = | 1,850 | + | 15,000 | + | 2,750 |  |
| (8) | −250 |  |  |  |  |  | −250 |  |  |  |  |  |
|  | 8,750 + | 2,000 | + | 1,600 + | 7,000 | = | 1,600 | + | 15,000 | + | 2,750 |  |
| (9) | +600 | −600 |  |  |  |  |  |  |  |  |  |  |
|  | 9,350 + | 1,400 | + | 1,600 + | 7,000 | = | 1,600 | + | 15,000 | + | 2,750 |  |
| (10) | −1,300 |  |  |  |  |  |  |  |  |  | −1,300 | Dividends |
|  | $ 8,050 + | $1,400 | + | $1,600 + | $7,000 | = | $1,600 | + | $15,000 | + | $1,450 |  |

Assets = Liabilities + Stockholders' Equity

$18,050         $18,050

1. Each transaction must be analyzed in terms of its effect on:
   (a) the three components of the basic accounting equation.
   (b) specific types (kinds) of items within each component.
2. The two sides of the equation must always be equal.
3. The Common Stock and Retained Earnings columns indicate the causes of each change in the stockholders' claim on assets.

There! You made it through transaction analysis. If you feel a bit shaky on any of the transactions, it might be a good idea at this point to get up, take a short break, and come back again for a brief (10- to 15-minute) review of the transactions, to make sure you understand them before you go on to the next section.

## Before You Go On...

### REVIEW IT
1. What is an example of an external transaction? What is an example of an internal transaction?
2. If an asset increases, what are the three possible effects on the basic accounting equation?

### DO IT
A tabular analysis of the transactions made by Roberta Mendez & Co., a certified public accounting firm, for the month of August is shown below. Each increase and decrease in stockholders' equity is explained.

| | Assets | | = | Liabilities + | | Stockholders' Equity | | |
|---|---|---|---|---|---|---|---|---|
| | Cash + | Office Equipment | = | Accounts Payable | + | Common Stock + | Retained Earnings | |
| 1. | +25,000 | | | | | +25,000 | | Investment |
| 2. | | +7,000 | | +7,000 | | | | |
| 3. | +8,000 | | | | | | +8,000 | Service Revenue |
| 4. | −850 | | | | | | −850 | Rent Expense |

Describe each transaction that occurred for the month.

### Action Plan
- Analyze the tabular analysis to determine the nature and effect of each transaction.
- Keep the accounting equation always in balance.
- Remember that a change in an asset will require a change in another asset, a liability, or in stockholders' equity.

### Solution
1. Stockholders purchased additional shares of stock for $25,000 cash.
2. The company purchased $7,000 of office equipment on credit.
3. The company received $8,000 of cash in exchange for services performed.
4. The company paid $850 for this month's rent.

Related exercise material: *BE1-4, BE1-5, BE1-6, BE1-7, BE1-8, E1-6, E1-7, E1-8, E1-10, and E1-11.*

✓ The Navigator

# FINANCIAL STATEMENTS

Companies prepare, four financial statements from the summarized accounting data:

**STUDY OBJECTIVE 8**

Understand the four financial statements and how they are prepared.

1. An **income statement** presents the revenues and expenses and resulting net income or net loss of a company for a specific period of time.

2. A **retained earnings statement** summarizes the changes in retained earnings for a specific period of time.

3. A **balance sheet** reports the assets, liabilities, and stockholders' equity of a company at a specific date.

4. A **statement of cash flows** summarizes information concerning the cash inflows (receipts) and outflows (payments) for a specific period of time.

Each statement provides relevant financial data for internal and external users.

Illustration 1-9 (page 22) shows the financial statements of Softbyte Inc. Note that the statements are interrelated:

1. Net income of $2,750 shown on the income statement is added to the beginning balance of retained earnings in the retained earnings statement.

2. Retained earnings of $1,450 at the end of the reporting period shown in the retained earnings statement is reported on the balance sheet.

3. Cash of $8,050 on the balance sheet is reported on the statement of cash flows.

Also, explanatory notes and supporting schedules are an integral part of every set of financial statements. We illustrate examples of these notes and schedules in later chapters of this textbook.

Be sure to carefully examine the format and content of each statement in Illustration 1-9. We describe the essential features of each in the following sections.

**HELPFUL HINT**

The income statement, retained earnings statement, and statement of cash flows are all for a *period* of time. The balance sheet is for a *point* in time.

**HELPFUL HINT**

There is only one group of notes for the whole set of financial statements, rather than separate sets of notes for each financial statement.

## Income Statement

The income statement reports the success or profitability of the company's operations over a specific period of time. For example, Softbyte Inc.'s income statement is dated "For the Month Ended September 30, 2008." It is prepared from the data appearing in the retained earnings column of Illustration 1-8. The heading of the statement identifies the company, the type of statement, and the time period covered by the statement.

The income statement lists revenues first, followed by expenses. Finally, the statement shows net income (or net loss). When revenues exceed expenses, **net income** results. When expenses exceed revenues, a **net loss** results.

Although practice varies, we have chosen in our illustrations and homework solutions to list expenses in order of magnitude. (We will consider alternative formats for the income statement in later chapters.)

Note that the income statement does not include investment and dividend transactions between the stockholders and the business in measuring net income. For example, as explained earlier, the cash dividend from Softbyte Inc. was not regarded as a business expense. This type of transaction is considered a reduction of retained earnings, which causes a decrease in stockholders' equity.

**ALTERNATIVE TERMINOLOGY**

The income statement is sometimes referred to as the *statement of operations, earnings statement,* or *profit and loss statement.*

## Retained Earnings Statement

Softbyte Inc.'s retained earnings statement reports the changes in retained earnings for a specific period of time. The time period is the same as that covered by the income statement ("For the Month Ended September 30, 2008"). Data for the

Illustration 1-9
Financial statements and their interrelationships

## SOFTBYTE INC.
### Income Statement
### For the Month Ended September 30, 2008

| Revenues | | |
|---|---|---|
| Service revenue | | $4,700 |
| Expenses | | |
| Salaries expense | $900 | |
| Rent expense | 600 | |
| Advertising expense | 250 | |
| Utilities expense | 200 | |
| Total expenses | | 1,950 |
| Net income | | $2,750 |

## SOFTBYTE INC.
### Retained Earnings Statement
### For the Month Ended September 30, 2008

| | |
|---|---|
| Retained earnings, September 1 | $ 0 |
| Add: Net income | 2,750 |
| | 2,750 |
| Less: Dividends | 1,300 |
| Retained earnings, September 30 | $1,450 |

## SOFTBYTE INC.
### Balance Sheet
### September 30, 2008

#### Assets

| | |
|---|---|
| Cash | $ 8,050 |
| Accounts receivable | 1,400 |
| Supplies | 1,600 |
| Equipment | 7,000 |
| Total assets | $18,050 |

#### Liabilities and Stockholders' Equity

| | | |
|---|---|---|
| Liabilities | | |
| Accounts payable | | $ 1,600 |
| Stockholders' equity | | |
| Common stock | $15,000 | |
| Retained earnings | 1,450 | 16,450 |
| Total liabilities and stockholders' equity | | $18,050 |

## SOFTBYTE INC.
### Statement of Cash Flows
### For the Month Ended September 30, 2008

| | | |
|---|---|---|
| Cash flows from operating activities | | |
| Cash receipts from revenues | | $3,300 |
| Cash payments for expenses | | (1,950) |
| Net cash provided by operating activities | | 1,350 |
| Cash flows from investing activities | | |
| Purchase of equipment | | (7,000) |
| Cash flows from financing activities | | |
| Sale of common stock | $15,000 | |
| Payment of cash dividends | (1,300) | 13,700 |
| Net increase in cash | | 8,050 |
| Cash at the beginning of the period | | 0 |
| Cash at the end of the period | | $8,050 |

preparation of the retained earnings statement come from the retained earnings column of the tabular summary (Illustration 1-8) and from the income statement in Illustration 1-9.

The first line of the statement shows the beginning retained earnings amount. Then come net income and dividends. The retained earnings ending balance is the final amount on the statement. The information provided by this statement indicates the reasons why retained earnings increased or decreased during the period. If there is a net loss, it is deducted with dividends in the retained earnings statement.

## Balance Sheet

Softbyte Inc.'s balance sheet reports the assets, liabilities, and stockholders' equity at a specific date (September 30, 2008). The company prepares the balance sheet from the column headings and the month-end data shown in the last line of the tabular summary (Illustration 1-8).

Observe that the balance sheet lists assets at the top, followed by liabilities and stockholders' equity. Total assets must equal total liabilities and stockholders' equity. Softbyte Inc. reports only one liability, accounts payable, on its balance sheet. In most cases, there will be more than one liability. When two or more liabilities are involved, a customary way of listing is as shown in Illustration 1-10.

|  | **Liabilities** |  |
|---|---|---|
| Notes payable | | $10,000 |
| Accounts payable | | 63,000 |
| Salaries payable | | 18,000 |
| Total liabilities | | $91,000 |

**Illustration 1-10**
Presentation of liabilities

The balance sheet is like a snapshot of the company's financial condition at a specific moment in time (usually the month-end or year-end).

# ACCOUNTING ACROSS THE ORGANIZATION

### What Do Delta Air Lines, Walt Disney, and Dunkin' Donuts Have in Common?

Not every company uses December 31 as the accounting year-end. Why do companies choose the particular year-ends that they do? Many choose to end the accounting year when inventory or operations are at a low. Compiling accounting information requires much time and effort by managers, so companies would rather do it when they aren't as busy operating the business. Also, inventory is easier and less costly to count when it is low. Some companies whose year-ends differ from December 31 are Delta Air Lines, June 30; Walt Disney Productions, September 30; and Dunkin' Donuts Inc., October 31.

 What year-end would you likely use if you owned a ski resort and ski rental business? What if you owned a college bookstore? Why choose those year-ends?

## Statement of Cash Flows

The statement of cash flows provides information on the cash receipts and payments for a specific period of time. The statement of cash flows reports (1) the cash effects of a company's operations during a period, (2) its investing transactions, (3) its financing transactions, (4) the net increase or decrease in cash during the period, and (5) the cash amount at the end of the period.

Reporting the sources, uses, and change in cash is useful because investors, creditors, and others want to know what is happening to a company's most liquid resource. The statement of cash flows provides answers to the following simple but important questions.

1. Where did cash come from during the period?
2. What was cash used for during the period?
3. What was the change in the cash balance during the period?

As shown in Softbyte Inc.'s statement of cash flows in Illustration 1-9, cash increased $8,050 during the period. Net cash flow provided from operating activities increased cash $1,350. Cash flow from investing transactions decreased cash $7,000. And cash flow from financing transactions increased cash $13,700. At this time, you need not be concerned with how these amounts are determined. Chapter 14 will examine in detail how the statement is prepared.

## Before You Go On...

### REVIEW IT
1. What are the income statement, retained earnings statement, balance sheet, and statement of cash flows?
2. How are the financial statements interrelated?

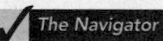 The Navigator

 Be sure to read **ALL ABOUT YOU:** *Ethics: Managing Personal Financial Reporting* on the next page for information on how topics in this chapter apply to you.

# Ethics: Managing Personal Financial Reporting

When companies need money, they go to investors or creditors. Before investors or creditors will give a company cash, they want to know the company's financial position and performance. They want to see the company's financial statements—the balance sheet and the income statement. When students need money for school, they often apply for financial aid. When you apply for financial aid, you must submit your own version of a financial statement—the Free Application for Federal Student Aid (FAFSA) form.

The FAFSA form asks how much you make (based on your federal income tax return) and how much your parents make. The purpose is to find out how much you own and how much you owe. Why do the Department of Education and your school want this information? Simple: They want to know whether you really need the money. Schools and government-loan funds have limited resources, and they want to make sure that the money goes to those who need it the most. The bottom line is: The worse off you look financially, the more likely you are to get money.

The question is: Should you intentionally make yourself look worse off than you are?

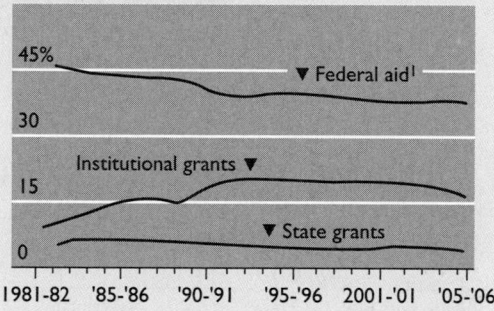

**The federal share of assistance is declining**
Sources of financial aid as a percentage of total aid used to finance postsecondary expenses

**Source for graph:** College Board, *Princeton Review*, as reported in "College Admissions: Is Gate Open or Closed?," *Wall Street Journal*, March 25, 2006, p. A7.

## ✱ Some Facts

* After adjusting for inflation, private-college tuition and fees have increased 37% over the past decade; public-college tuition has risen 54%.

* Two-thirds (65.6%) of undergraduate students graduate with some debt.

* Among graduating seniors, the average debt load is $19,202, according to an analysis of data from the Department of Education's National Postsecondary Student Aid Study. That does not include any debt that their parents might incur.

* Colleges are required to audit the FAFSA forms of at least one-third of their students; some audit 100%. (Compare that to the IRS, which audits a very small percentage of tax returns.) Thus, if you lie on your financial aid forms, there's a very good chance you'll get caught.

Additional information regarding scholarships and loans is available at *www.finaid.org/.* You might find especially interesting the section that discusses how to maximize your chances of obtaining financial aid at *www.finaid.org/fafsa/maximize.phtml.*

## ✱ What Do You Think?

Consider the following and decide what action you would take:

Suppose you have $4,000 in cash and $4,000 in credit card bills. The more cash and other assets that you have, the less likely you are to get financial aid. Also, if you have a lot of consumer debt (credit card bills), schools are not more likely to loan you money. To increase your chances of receiving aid, should you use the cash to pay off your credit card bills, and therefore make yourself look "worse off" to the financial aid decision makers?

**YES:** You are playing within the rules. You are not hiding assets. You are simply restructuring your assets and liabilities to best conform with the preferences that are built into the federal aid formulas.

**NO:** You are engaging in a transaction solely to take advantage of a loophole in the federal aid rules. In doing so, you are potentially depriving someone who is actually worse off than you from receiving aid.

**Sources:** "College Admissions: Is Gate Open or Closed?," *Wall Street Journal*, March 25, 2006, P. A7; *www.finaid.org.*

Legal Services Inc. was incorporated on July 1, 2008. During the first month of operations, the following transactions occurred.

1. Stockholders invested $10,000 in cash in exchange for shares of stock.
2. Paid $800 for July rent on office space.
3. Purchased office equipment on account $3,000.
4. Provided legal services to clients for cash $1,500 (use Service Revenue).
5. Borrowed $700 cash from a bank on a note payable.
6. Performed legal services for client on account $2,000.
7. Paid monthly expenses: salaries $500; utilities $300; and telephone $100.

### Instructions

**(a)** Prepare a tabular summary of the transactions.

**(b)** Prepare the income statement, retained earnings statement, and balance sheet at July 31 for Legal Services Inc.

*Demonstration Problems are a final review of the chapter. The Action Plan (gives tips about how to approach the problem, and the Solution) demonstrates both the form and content of complete answers.*

## action plan

✔ Remember that assets must equal liabilities and stockholders' equity after each transaction.

✔ Investments and revenues increase stockholders' equity.

✔ Dividends and expenses decrease stockholders' equity.

✔ The income statement shows revenues and expenses for a period of time.

✔ The retained earnings statement shows the changes in retained earnings for a period of time.

✔ The balance sheet reports assets, liabilities, and stock- holders' equity at a specific date.

### Solution

**(a)**

| | | | Assets | | | = | Liabilities | | + | Stockholders' Equity | | |
|---|---|---|---|---|---|---|---|---|---|---|---|---|
| Trans- action | Cash | + | Accounts Receivable | + | Equipment | = | Notes Payable | + | Accounts Payable | + | Common Stock | + | Retained Earnings | |
| (1) | +$10,000 | | | | | | | | | | +$10,000 | | | Investment |
| (2) | −800 | | | | | | | | | | | | −$800 | Rent Expense |
| | 9,200 | | | | | = | | | | | 10,000 + | | −800 | |
| (3) | | | | | +$3,000 | | | | +$3,000 | | | | | |
| | 9,200 | + | | | 3,000 | = | | | 3,000 + | | 10,000 + | | −800 | |
| (4) | +1,500 | | | | | | | | | | | | +1,500 | Service Revenue |
| | 10,700 | + | | | 3,000 | = | | | 3,000 + | | 10,000 + | | 700 | |
| (5) | +700 | | | | | | +$700 | | | | | | | |
| | 11,400 | + | | | 3,000 | = | 700 + | | 3,000 + | | 10,000 + | | 700 | |
| (6) | | | +$2,000 | | | | | | | | | | +2,000 | Service Revenue |
| | +11,400 + | | 2,000 | + | 3,000 | = | 700 + | | 3,000 + | | 10,000 + | | 2,700 | |
| (7) | −900 | | | | | | | | | | | | −500 | Salaries Expense |
| | | | | | | | | | | | | | −300 | Utilities Expense |
| | | | | | | | | | | | | | −100 | Telephone Expense |
| | $10,500 + | | $2,000 | + | $3,000 | = | $700 + | | $3,000 + | | $10,000 + | | $1,800 | |

$15,500              $15,500

*This would be a good time to return to the **Student Owner's Manual** at the beginning of the book (or look at it for the first time if you skipped it before), to read about the various types of assignment materials that appear at the end of each chapter. Knowing the purpose of the different assignments will help you appreciate what each contributes to your accounting skills and competencies.*

**(b)**

## LEGAL SERVICES INC.
### Income Statement
#### For the Month Ended July 31, 2008

| | | |
|---|---|---|
| Revenues | | |
|   Service revenue | | $3,500 |
| Expenses | | |
|   Rent expense | $800 | |
|   Salaries expense | 500 | |
|   Utilities expense | 300 | |
|   Telephone expense | 100 | |
|     Total expenses | | 1,700 |
| Net income | | $1,800 |

### LEGAL SERVICES INC.
Retained Earnings Statement
For the Month Ended July 31, 2008

| | |
|---|---:|
| Retained earnings, July 1 | $ –0– |
| Add: Net income | 1,800 |
| Retained earnings, July 31 | $1,800 |

### LEGAL SERVICES INC.
Balance Sheet
July 31, 2008

#### <u>Assets</u>

| | |
|---|---:|
| Cash | $10,500 |
| Accounts receivable | 2,000 |
| Equipment | 3,000 |
| Total assets | $15,500 |

#### <u>Liabilities and Stockholders' Equity</u>

| | | |
|---|---:|---:|
| Liabilities | | |
| Notes payable | | $ 700 |
| Accounts payable | | 3,000 |
| Total liabilities | | 3,700 |
| Stockholders' equity | | |
| Common stock | $10,000 | |
| Retained earnings | 1,800 | 11,800 |
| Total liabilities and stockholders' equity | | $15,500 |

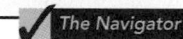 The Navigator

## SUMMARY OF STUDY OBJECTIVES

**1 Explain what accounting is.** Accounting is an information system that identifies, records, and communicates the economic events of an organization to interested users.

**2 Identify the users and uses of accounting.** The major users and uses of accounting are: (a) Management uses accounting information in planning, controlling, and evaluating business operations. (b) Investors (owners) decide whether to buy, hold, or sell their financial interests on the basis of accounting data. (c) Creditors (suppliers and bankers) evaluate the risks of granting credit or lending money on the basis of accounting information. Other groups that use accounting information are taxing authorities, regulatory agencies, customers, labor unions, and economic planners.

**3 Understand why ethics is a fundamental business concept.** Ethics are the standards of conduct by which actions are judged as right or wrong. If you cannot depend on the honesty of the individuals you deal with, effective communication and economic activity would be impossible, and information would have no credibility.

**4 Explain generally accepted accounting principles and the cost principle.** Generally accepted accounting principles are a common set of standards used by accountants. The cost principle states that companies should record assets at their cost.

**5 Explain the monetary unit assumption and the economic entity assumption.** The monetary unit assumption requires that companies include in the accounting records only transaction data that can be expressed in terms of money. The economic entity assumption requires that the activities of each economic entity be kept separate from the activities of its owner and other economic entities.

**6 State the accounting equation, and define assets, liabilities, and owner's equity.** The basic accounting equation is:

$$\text{Assets} = \text{Liabilities} + \text{Stockholders' Equity}$$

Assets are resources owned by a business. Liabilities are creditorship claims on total assets. Stockholders' equity is the ownership claim on total assets.

**7 Analyze the effects of business transactions on the accounting equation.** Each business transaction must have a dual effect on the accounting equation. For example, if an individual asset increases, there must be a corresponding (1) decrease in another asset, or (2) increase in a specific liability, or (3) increase in stockholders' equity.

**8 Understand the four financial statements and how they are prepared.** An income statement presents the revenues and expenses of a company for a specified period

of time. A retained earnings statement summarizes the changes in retained earnings that have occurred for a specific period of time. A balance sheet reports the assets, liabilities, and stockholders' equity of a business at a specific date. A statement of cash flows summarizes information about the cash inflows (receipts) and outflows (payments) for a specific period of time.

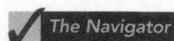 *The Navigator*

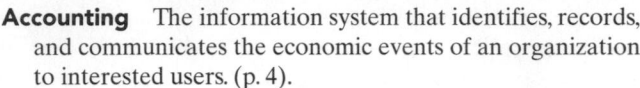 **GLOSSARY**

**Accounting** The information system that identifies, records, and communicates the economic events of an organization to interested users. (p. 4).

**Assets** Resources a business owns. (p. 12).

**Balance sheet** A financial statement that reports the assets, liabilities, and owner's equity at a specific date. (p. 21).

**Basic accounting equation** Assets = Liabilities + Stockholders' Equity. (p. 11).

**Bookkeeping** A part of accounting that involves only the recording of economic events. (p. 5).

**Corporation** A business organized as a separate legal entity under state corporation law, having ownership divided into transferable shares of stock. (p. 10).

**Cost principle** An accounting principle that states that companies should record assets at their cost. (p. 9).

**Dividend** A distribution by a corporation to its stockholders on a pro rata (equal) basis. (p. 13).

**Economic entity assumption** An assumption that requires that the activities of the entity be kept separate and distinct from the activities of its owner and all other economic entities. (p. 10).

**Ethics** The standards of conduct by which one's actions are judged as right or wrong, honest or dishonest, fair or not fair. (p. 8).

**Expenses** The cost of assets consumed or services used in the process of earning revenue. (p. 13).

**Financial accounting** The field of accounting that provides economic and financial information for investors, creditors, and other external users. (p. 7).

**Financial Accounting Standards Board (FASB)** A private organization that establishes generally accepted accounting principles (GAAP). (p. 9).

**Generally accepted accounting principles (GAAP)** Common standards that indicate how to report economic events. (p. 9).

**Income statement** A financial statement that presents the revenues and expenses and resulting net income or net loss of a company for a specific period of time. (p. 21).

**International Accounting Standards Board (IASB)** An accounting standard-setting body that issues standards adopted by many countries outside of the United States. (p. 9).

**Liabilities** Creditor claims on total assets. (p. 12).

**Managerial accounting** The field of accounting that provides internal reports to help users make decisions about their companies. (p. 6).

**Monetary unit assumption** An assumption stating that companies include in the accounting records only transaction data that can be expressed in terms of money. (p. 10).

**Net income** The amount by which revenues exceed expenses. (p. 21).

**Net loss** The amount by which expenses exceed revenues. (p. 21).

**Partnership** A business owned by two or more persons associated as partners. (p. 10).

**Proprietorship** A business owned by one person. (p. 10).

**Retained earnings statement** A financial statement that summarizes the changes in retained earnings for a specific period of time. (p. 21).

**Revenues** The gross increase in owner's equity resulting from business activities entered into for the purpose of earning income. (p. 13).

**Sarbanes-Oxley Act of 2002 (SOX)** Law passed by Congress in 2002 intended to reduce unethical corporate behavior. (p. 8).

**Securities and Exchange Commission (SEC)** A governmental agency that requires companies to file financial reports in accordance with generally accepted accounting principles. (p. 9).

**Statement of cash flows** A financial statement that summarizes information about the cash inflows (receipts) and cash outflows (payments) for a specific period of time. (p. 21).

**Stockholders' equity** The ownership claim on a corporation's total assets. (p. 12)

**Transactions** The economic events of a business that are recorded by accountants. (p. 14).

# APPENDIX **Accounting Career Opportunities**

Why is accounting such a popular major and career choice? First, there are a lot of jobs. In many cities in recent years, the demand for accountants exceeded the supply. Not only are there a lot of jobs, but there are a wide array of opportunities. As observed by one accounting organization, "accounting is one degree with 360 degrees of opportunity."

**STUDY OBJECTIVE 9**

Explain the career opportunities in accounting.

Accounting is also hot because it is obvious that accounting matters. Interest in accounting has increased, ironically, because of the attention caused by the accounting failures of companies such as Enron and WorldCom. These widely publicized scandals revealed the important role that accounting plays in society. Most people want to make a difference, and an accounting career provides many opportunities to contribute to society. Finally, the Sarbanes-Oxley Act of 2002 (see page 8) significantly increased the accounting and internal control requirements for corporations. This dramatically increased demand for professionals with accounting training.

Accountants are in such demand that it is not uncommon for accounting students to have accepted a job offer a year before graduation. As the following discussion reveals, the job options of people with accounting degrees are virtually unlimited.

## Public Accounting

Individuals in **public accounting** offer expert service to the general public, in much the same way that doctors serve patients and lawyers serve clients. A major portion of public accounting involves **auditing**. In auditing, a certified public accountant (CPA) examines company financial statements and provides an opinion as to how accurately the financial statements present the company's results and financial position. Analysts, investors, and creditors rely heavily on these "audit opinions," which CPAs have the exclusive authority to issue.

**Taxation** is another major area of public accounting. The work that tax specialists perform includes tax advice and planning, preparing tax returns, and representing clients before governmental agencies such as the Internal Revenue Service.

A third area in public accounting is **management consulting**. It ranges from installing basic accounting software or highly complex enterprise resource planning systems, to providing support services for major marketing projects or merger and acquisition activities.

Many CPAs are entrepreneurs. They form small- or medium-sized practices that frequently specialize in tax or consulting services.

## Private Accounting

Instead of working in public accounting, you might choose to be an employee of a for-profit company such as Starbucks, Google, or Kellogg. In **private** (or **managerial**) **accounting**, you would be involved in activities such as cost accounting (finding the cost of producing specific products), budgeting, accounting information system design and support, or tax planning and preparation. You might also be a member of your company's internal audit team. In response to SOX, the internal auditors' job of reviewing the company's operations to ensure compliance with company policies and to increase efficiency has taken on increased importance.

Alternatively, many accountants work for not-for-profit organizations such as the Red Cross or the Bill and Melinda Gates Foundation, or for museums, libraries, or performing arts organizations.

## Opportunities in Government

Another option is to pursue one of the many accounting opportunities in governmental agencies. For example, the Internal Revenue Service (IRS), Federal Bureau of Investigation (FBI), and the Securities and Exchange Commission (SEC) all employ accountants. The FBI has a stated goal that at least 15% of its new agents should be CPAs. There is also a very high demand for accounting educators at public colleges and universities and in state and local governments.

## Forensic Accounting

**Forensic accounting** uses accounting, auditing, and investigative skills to conduct investigations into theft and fraud. It is listed among the top 20 career paths of the future. The job of forensic accountants is to catch the perpetrators of the estimated $600 billion per year of theft and fraud occurring at U.S. companies. This includes tracing money-laundering and identity-theft activities as well as tax evasion. Insurance companies hire forensic accountants to detect insurance frauds such as arson, and law offices employ forensic accountants to identify marital assets in divorces.

## "Show Me the Money"

How much can a new accountant make? Salary estimates are constantly changing, and salaries vary considerably across the country. At the time this text was written, the following general information was available from Robert Half and Co.

**Illustration 1A-1**
Salary estimates for jobs in public and corporate accounting

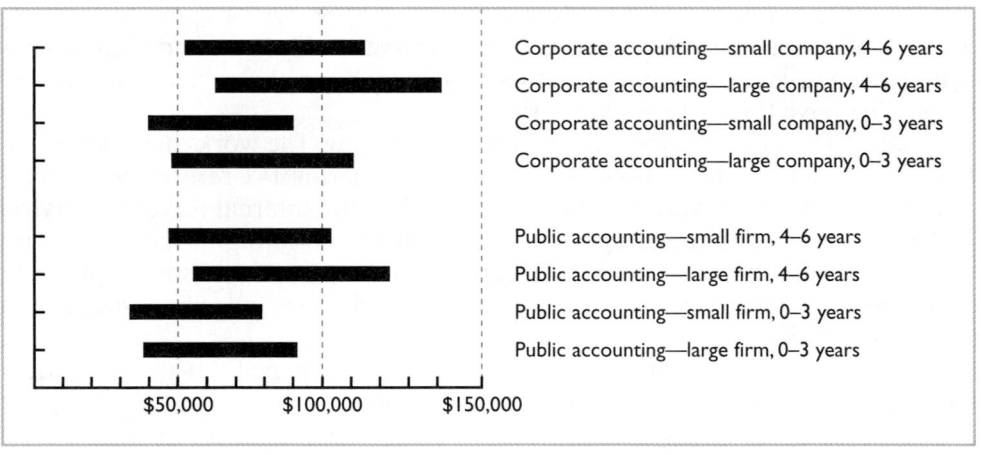

The average salary for a first-year partner in a CPA firm is close to $130,000, with experienced partners often making substantially more. On the corporate side, controllers (the head accountant) can earn $150,000, while chief financial officers can earn as much as $350,000.

For up-to-date salary estimates, as well as a wealth of additional information regarding accounting as a career, check out *www.startheregoplaces.com*.

## SUMMARY OF STUDY OBJECTIVE FOR APPENDIX

**9 Explain the career opportunities in accounting.** Accounting offers many different jobs in fields such as public and private accounting, government, and forensic accounting. Accounting is a popular major because there are many different types of jobs, with unlimited potential for career advancement.

## GLOSSARY FOR APPENDIX

**Auditing**   The examination of financial statements by a certified public accountant in order to express an opinion as to the fairness of presentation. (p. 29).

**Forensic accounting**   An area of accounting that uses accounting, auditing, and investigative skills to conduct investigations into theft and fraud. (p. 30).

**Management consulting**   An area of public accounting ranging from development of accounting and computer systems to support services for marketing projects and merger and acquisition activities. (p. 29).

**Private (or managerial) accounting**   An area of accounting within a company that involves such activities as cost accounting, budgeting, design and support of accounting information systems, and tax planning and preparation. (p. 29).

**Public accounting**   An area of accounting in which the accountant offers expert service to the general public. (p. 29).

**Taxation**   An area of public accounting involving tax advice, tax planning, preparing tax returns, and representing clients before governmental agencies. (p. 29).

## SELF-STUDY QUESTIONS

*Answers are at the end of the chapter.*

(SO 1)   **1.** Which of the following is *not* a step in the accounting process?
 **a.** identification.       **c.** recording.
 **b.** verification.         **d.** communication.

(SO 2)   **2.** Which of the following statements about users of accounting information is *incorrect*?
 **a.** Management is an internal user.
 **b.** Taxing authorities are external users.
 **c.** Present creditors are external users.
 **d.** Regulatory authorities are internal users.

(SO 4)   **3.** The cost principle states that:
 **a.** assets should be initially recorded at cost and adjusted when the market value changes.
 **b.** activities of an entity are to be kept separate and distinct from its owner.
 **c.** assets should be recorded at their cost.
 **d.** only transaction data capable of being expressed in terms of money be included in the accounting records.

(SO 5)   **4.** Which of the following statements about basic assumptions is *correct*?
 **a.** Basic assumptions are the same as accounting principles.
 **b.** The economic entity assumption states that there should be a particular unit of accountability.
 **c.** The monetary unit assumption enables accounting to measure employee morale.
 **d.** Partnerships are not economic entities.

(SO 6)   **5.** Net income will result during a time period when:
 **a.** assets exceed liabilities.
 **b.** assets exceed revenues.
 **c.** expenses exceed revenues.
 **d.** revenues exceed expenses.

(SO 7)   **6.** Performing services on account will have the following effects on the components of the basic accounting equation:
 **a.** increase assets and decrease stockholders' equity.
 **b.** increase assets and increase stockholders' equity.
 **c.** increase assets and increase liabilities.
 **d.** increase liabilities and increase stockholders' equity.

(SO 7)   **7.** As of December 31, 2008, Stoneland Company has assets of $3,500 and stockholders' equity of $2,000. What are the liabilities for Stoneland Company as of December 31, 2008?
 **a.** $1,500.    **b.** $1,000.    **c.** $2,500.    **d.** $2,000.

(SO 8)   **8.** On the last day of the period, Jim Otto Company buys a $900 machine on credit. This transaction will affect the:
 **a.** income statement only.
 **b.** balance sheet only.
 **c.** income statement and retained earnings statement only.
 **d.** income statement, retained earnings statement, and balance sheet.

(SO 8)   **9.** The financial statement that reports assets, liabilities, and stockholders' equity is the:
 **a.** income statement.
 **b.** retained earnings statement.
 **c.** balance sheet.
 **d.** statement of cash flow.

(SO 9)   *****10.** Services provided by a public accountant include:
 **a.** auditing, taxation, and management consulting.
 **b.** auditing, budgeting, and management consulting.
 **c.** auditing, budgeting, and cost accounting.
 **d.** internal auditing, budgeting, and management consulting.

Go to the book's website,
**www.wiley.com/college/weygandt**,
for Additional Self-Study questions.

## QUESTIONS

**1.** "Accounting is ingrained in our society and it is vital to our economic system." Do you agree? Explain.

**2.** Identify and describe the steps in the accounting process.

**3.** (a) Who are internal users of accounting data? (b) How does accounting provide relevant data to these users?

**4.** What uses of financial accounting information are made by (a) investors and (b) creditors?

**5.** "Bookkeeping and accounting are the same." Do you agree? Explain.

6. Karen Sommers Travel Agency purchased land for $90,000 cash on December 10, 2008. At December 31, 2008, the land's value has increased to $93,000. What amount should be reported for land on Karen Sommers's balance sheet at December 31, 2008? Explain.

7. What is the monetary unit assumption?

8. What is the economic entity assumption?

9. What are the three basic forms of business organizations for profit-oriented enterprises?

10. Maria Gonzalez is the owner of a successful printing shop. Recently her business has been increasing, and Maria has been thinking about changing the organization of her business from a proprietorship to a corporation. Discuss some of the advantages Maria would enjoy if she were to incorporate her business.

11. What is the basic accounting equation?

12. **(a)** Define the terms assets, liabilities, and stockholders' equity.
    **(b)** What items affect stockholders' equity?

13. Which of the following items are liabilities of Stanley Jewelry Stores?
    **(a)** Cash.                    **(f)** Equipment.
    **(b)** Accounts payable.        **(g)** Salaries payable.
    **(c)** Dividends.               **(h)** Service revenue.
    **(d)** Accounts receivable.     **(i)** Rent expense.
    **(e)** Supplies.

14. Can a business enter into a transaction in which only the left side of the basic accounting equation is affected? If so, give an example.

15. Are the following events recorded in the accounting records? Explain your answer in each case.
    **(a)** The president of the company dies.
    **(b)** Supplies are purchased on account.
    **(c)** An employee is fired.

16. Indicate how the following business transactions affect the basic accounting equation.
    **(a)** Paid cash for janitorial services.
    **(b)** Purchased equipment for cash.
    **(c)** Invested cash in the business for stock.
    **(d)** Paid accounts payable in full.

17. Listed below are some items found in the financial statements of Alex Greenspan Co. Indicate in which financial statement(s) the following items would appear.
    **(a)** Service revenue.         **(d)** Accounts receivable.
    **(b)** Equipment.               **(e)** Retained earnings.
    **(c)** Advertising expense.     **(f)** Wages payable.

18. In February 2008, Paula King invested an additional $10,000 in Hardy Company. Hardy's accountant, Lance Jones, recorded this receipt as an increase in cash and revenues. Is this treatment appropriate? Why or why not?

19. "A company's net income appears directly on the income statement and the retained earnings statement, and it is included indirectly in the company's balance sheet." Do you agree? Explain.

20. Garcia Enterprises had a stockholders' equity balance of $168,000 at the beginning of the period. At the end of the accounting period, the stockholders' equity balance was $198,000.
    **(a)** Assuming no additional investment or distributions during the period, what is the net income for the period?
    **(b)** Assuming an additional investment of $13,000 but no distributions during the period, what is the net income for the period?

21. Summarized operations for J. R. Ross Co. for the month of July are as follows.

    Revenues earned: for cash $20,000; on account $70,000.

    Expenses incurred: for cash $26,000; on account $40,000.

    Indicate for J. R. Ross Co. (a) the total revenues, (b) the total expenses, and (c) net income for the month of July.

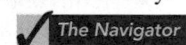

# BRIEF EXERCISES

*Use basic accounting equation.*
(SO 6)

**BE1-1**   Presented below is the basic accounting equation. Determine the missing amounts.

| | Assets | = | Liabilities | + | Stockholders' Equity |
|---|---|---|---|---|---|
| **(a)** | $90,000 | | $50,000 | | ? |
| **(b)** | ? | | $40,000 | | $70,000 |
| **(c)** | $94,000 | | ? | | $60,000 |

*Use basic accounting equation.*
(SO 6)

**BE1-2**   Given the accounting equation, answer each of the following questions.

**(a)** The liabilities of McGlone Company are $120,000 and the stockholders' equity is $232,000. What is the amount of McGlone Company's total assets?

**(b)** The total assets of Company are $190,000 and its stockholders' equity is $80,000. What is the amount of its total liabilities?

**(c)** The total assets of McGlone Co. are $800,000 and its liabilities are equal to one half of its total assets. What is the amount of McGlone Co.'s stockholders' equity?

*Use basic accounting equation.*
(SO 6)

**BE1-3**   At the beginning of the year, Hernandez Company had total assets of $800,000 and total liabilities of $500,000. Answer the following questions.

**(a)** If total assets increased $150,000 during the year and total liabilities decreased $80,000, what is the amount of stockholders' equity at the end of the year?

**(b)** During the year, total liabilities increased $100,000 and stockholders' equity decreased $70,000. What is the amount of total assets at the end of the year?

**(c)** If total assets decreased $80,000 and stockholders' equity increased $120,000 during the year, what is the amount of total liabilities at the end of the year?

**BE1-4**    Indicate whether each of the following items is an asset (A), liability (L), or part of stockholders' equity (SE).

_____(a) Accounts receivable        _____(d) Office supplies

_____(b) Salaries payable            _____(e) Owner's investment

_____(c) Equipment                  _____(f) Notes payable

*Identify assets, liabilities, and stockholders' equity.*

*(SO 6)*

**BE1-5**    Presented below are three business transactions. On a sheet of paper, list the letters (a), (b), (c) with columns for assets, liabilities, and owner's equity. For each column, indicate whether the transactions increased (+), decreased (−), or had no effect (NE) on assets, liabilities, and stockholders' equity.

**(a)** Purchased supplies on account.

**(b)** Received cash for providing a service.

**(c)** Paid expenses in cash.

*Determine effect of transactions on basic accounting equation.*

*(SO 7)*

**BE1-6**    Follow the same format as BE1-5 above. Determine the effect on assets, liabilities, and stockholders' equity of the following three transactions.

**(a)** Invested cash in the business for common stock.

**(b)** Paid a cash dividend.

**(c)** Received cash from a customer who had previously been billed for services provided.

*Determine effect of transactions on basic accounting equation.*

*(SO 7)*

**BE1-7**    Classify each of the following items as dividends (D), revenue (R), or expense (E).

_____(a) Advertising expense        _____(e) Dividends

_____(b) Commission revenue         _____(f) Rent revenue

_____(c) Insurance expense          _____(g) Utilities expense

_____(d) Salaries expense

*Classify items affecting stockholders' equity.*

*(SO 7)*

**BE1-8**    Presented below are three transactions. Mark each transaction as affecting common stock (C), dividends (D), revenue (R), expense (E), or not affecting stockholders' equity (NSE).

_____(a) Received cash for services performed

_____(b) Paid cash to purchase equipment

_____(c) Paid employee salaries.

*Determine effect of transactions on basic stockholders' equity.*

*(SO 7)*

**BE1-9**    In alphabetical order below are balance sheet items for Lopez Company at December 31, 2008. Kim Lopez is the owner of Lopez Company. Prepare a balance sheet, following the format of Illustration 1-9.

| | |
|---|---|
| Accounts payable | $90,000 |
| Accounts receivable | $72,500 |
| Cash | $49,000 |
| Common stock | $31,500 |

*Prepare a balance sheet.*

*(SO 8)*

**BE1-10**    Indicate whether the following items would appear on the income statement (IS), balance sheet (BS), or retained earnings statement (RE).

_____(a) Notes payable            _____(d) Cash

_____(b) Advertising expense      _____(e) Service revenue

_____(c) Common stock            _____(f) Dividends

*Determine where items appear on financial statements.*

*(SO 8)*

# EXERCISES

**E1-1**    Urlacher Company performs the following accounting tasks during the year.

_____Analyzing and interpreting information.

_____Classifying economic events.

_____Explaining uses, meaning, and limitations of data.

_____Keeping a systematic chronological diary of events.

_____Measuring events in dollars and cents.

_____Preparing accounting reports.

*Classify the three activities of accounting.*

*(SO 1)*

_____Reporting information in a standard format.
_____Selecting economic activities relevant to the company.
_____Summarizing economic events.

Accounting is "an information system that **identifies, records,** and **communicates** the economic events of an organization to interested users."

**Instructions**
Categorize the accounting tasks performed by Urlacher as relating to either the identification (I), recording (R), or communication (C) aspects of accounting.

*Identify users of accounting information.*

*(SO 2)*

**E1-2** **(a)** The following are users of financial statements.

| | |
|---|---|
| _____Customers | _____Securities and Exchange Commission |
| _____Internal Revenue Service | _____Store manager |
| _____Labor unions | _____Suppliers |
| _____Marketing manager | _____Vice-president of finance |
| _____Production supervisor | |

**Instructions**
Identify the users as being either **external users** or **internal users**.

**(b)** The following questions could be asked by an internal user or an external user.

_____Can we afford to give our employees a pay raise?
_____Did the company earn a satisfactory income?
_____Do we need to borrow in the near future?
_____How does the company's profitability compare to other companies?
_____What does it cost us to manufacture each unit produced?
_____Which product should we emphasize?
_____Will the company be able to pay its short-term debts?

**Instructions**
Identify each of the questions as being more likely asked by an **internal user** or an **external user**.

*Discuss ethics and the cost principle.*

*(SO 3)*

**E1-3** Larry Smith, president of Smith Company, has instructed Ron Rivera, the head of the accounting department for Smith Company, to report the company's land in the company's accounting reports at its market value of $170,000 instead of its cost of $100,000. Smith says, "Showing the land at $170,000 will make our company look like a better investment when we try to attract new investors next month."

**Instructions**
Explain the ethical situation involved for Ron Rivera, identifying the stakeholders and the alternatives.

*Use accounting concepts.*

*(SO 4, 5)*

**E1-4** The following situations involve accounting principles and assumptions.

1. Grossman Company owns buildings that are worth substantially more than they originally cost. In an effort to provide more relevant information, Grossman reports the buildings at market value in its accounting reports.
2. Jones Company includes in its accounting records only transaction data that can be expressed in terms of money.
3. Caleb Borke, president of Caleb's Cantina, records his personal living costs as expenses of the Cantina.

**Instructions**
For each of the three situations, say if the accounting method used is correct or incorrect. If correct, identify which principle or assumption supports the method used. If incorrect, identify which principle or assumption has been violated.

*Classify accounts as assets, liabilities, and stockholders' equity.*

*(SO 6)*

**E1-5** Meredith Cleaners has the following balance sheet items.

| | |
|---|---|
| Accounts payable | Accounts receivable |
| Cash | Notes payable |
| Cleaning equipment | Salaries payable |
| Cleaning supplies | Common stock |

**Instructions**

Classify each item as an asset, liability, or stockholders' equity.

**E1-6** Selected transactions for Evergreen Lawn Care Company are listed below.

1. Sold common stock for cash to start business.
2. Paid monthly rent.
3. Purchased equipment on account.
4. Billed customers for services performed.
5. Paid dividends.
6. Received cash from customers billed in (4).
7. Incurred advertising expense on account.
8. Purchased additional equipment for cash.
9. Received cash from customers when service was performed.

*Analyze the effect of transactions.*

*(SO 6, 7)*

**Instructions**

List the numbers of the above transactions and describe the effect of each transaction on assets, liabilities, and stockholders' equity. For example, the first answer is: (1) Increase in assets and increase in stockholders' equity.

**E1-7** Brandon Computer Timeshare Company entered into the following transactions during May 2008.

1. Purchased computer terminals for $20,000 from Digital Equipment on account.
2. Paid $4,000 cash for May rent on storage space.
3. Received $15,000 cash from customers for contracts billed in April.
4. Provided computer services to Fisher Construction Company for $3,000 cash.
5. Paid Northern States Power Co. $11,000 cash for energy usage in May.
6. Stockholders invested an additional $32,000 in the business.
7. Paid Digital Equipment for the terminals purchased in (1) above.
8. Incurred advertising expense for May of $1,200 on account.

*Analyze the effect of transactions on assets, liabilities, and stockholders' equity.*

*(SO 6, 7)*

**Instructions**

Indicate with the appropriate letter whether each of the transactions above results in:

**(a)** an increase in assets and a decrease in assets.
**(b)** an increase in assets and an increase in stockholders' equity.
**(c)** an increase in assets and an increase in liabilities.
**(d)** a decrease in assets and a decrease in stockholders' equity.
**(e)** a decrease in assets and a decrease in liabilities.
**(f)** an increase in liabilities and a decrease in stockholders' equity.
**(g)** an increase in stockholders' equity and a decrease in liabilities.

**E1-8** An analysis of the transactions made by S. Moses & Co., a certified public accounting firm, for the month of August is shown below. Each increase and decrease in stockholders' equity is explained.

*Analyze transactions and compute net income.*

*(SO 7)*

| | Cash | + | Accounts Receivable | + | Supplies | + | Office Equipment | = | Accounts Payable | + | Stockholders' Equity | |
|---|---|---|---|---|---|---|---|---|---|---|---|---|
| 1. | +$15,000 | | | | | | | | | | +$15,000 | Investment |
| 2. | −2,000 | | | | | | +$5,000 | | +$3,000 | | | |
| 3. | −750 | | | | +$750 | | | | | | | |
| 4. | +4,600 | | +$3,700 | | | | | | | | +8,300 | Service Revenue |
| 5. | −1,500 | | | | | | | | −1,500 | | | |
| 6. | −2,000 | | | | | | | | | | −2,000 | Dividends |
| 7. | −650 | | | | | | | | | | −650 | Rent Expense |
| 8. | +450 | | −450 | | | | | | | | | |
| 9. | −4,900 | | | | | | | | | | −4,900 | Salaries Expense |
| 10. | | | | | | | | | +500 | | −500 | Utilities Expense |

**Instructions**

**(a)** ▬▬▶ Describe each transaction that occurred for the month.
**(b)** Determine how much stockholders' equity increased for the month.
**(c)** Compute the amount of net income for the month.

*Prepare financial statements.*
(SO 8)

**E1-9**   An analysis of transactions for S. Moses & Co. was presented in E1–8.

**Instructions**
Prepare an income statement and a retained earnings statement for August and a balance sheet at August 31, 2008.

*Determine net income (or loss).*
(SO 7)

**E1-10**   Lily Company had the following assets and liabilities on the dates indicated.

| December 31 | Total Assets | Total Liabilities |
|---|---|---|
| 2007 | $400,000 | $250,000 |
| 2008 | $460,000 | $300,000 |
| 2009 | $590,000 | $400,000 |

Lily began business on January 1, 2007, with an investment of $100,000 from stockholders.

**Instructions**
From an analysis of the change in stockholders' equity during the year, compute the net income (or loss) for:

**(a)** 2007, assuming Lily paid $15,000 in dividends for the year.
**(b)** 2008, assuming stockholders made an additional investment of $50,000 and Lily paid no dividends in 2008.
**(c)** 2009, assuming stockholders made an additional investment of $15,000 and Lily paid dividends of $30,000 in 2009.

*Analyze financial statements items.*
(SO 6, 7)

**E1-11**   Two items are omitted from each of the following summaries of balance sheet and income statement data for two corporations for the year 2008, Craig Cantrel and Mills Enterprises.

| | Craig Cantrel | Mills Enterprises |
|---|---|---|
| Beginning of year: | | |
| Total assets | $ 95,000 | $129,000 |
| Total liabilities | 85,000 | (c) |
| Total stockholders' equity | (a) | 80,000 |
| End of year: | | |
| Total assets | 160,000 | 180,000 |
| Total liabilities | 120,000 | 50,000 |
| Total stockholders' equity | 40,000 | 130,000 |
| Changes during year in stockholders' equity: | | |
| Additional investment | (b) | 25,000 |
| Dividends | 24,000 | (d) |
| Total revenues | 215,000 | 100,000 |
| Total expenses | 175,000 | 55,000 |

**Instructions**
Determine the missing amounts.

*Prepare income statement and retained earnings statement.*
(SO 8)

**E1-12**   The following information relates to Linda Stanley Co. for the year 2008.

| | | | |
|---|---|---|---|
| Retained earnings, January 1, 2008 | $ 48,000 | Advertising expense | $ 1,800 |
| Dividends during 2008 | 6,000 | Rent expense | 10,400 |
| Service revenue | 62,500 | Utilities expense | 3,100 |
| Salaries expense | 30,000 | | |

**Instructions**
After analyzing the data, prepare an income statement and a retained earnings statement for the year ending December 31, 2008.

*Correct an incorrectly prepared balance sheet.*
(SO 8)

**E1-13**   Mary Close is the bookkeeper for Mendez Company. Mary has been trying to get the balance sheet of Mendez Company to balance. Mendez's balance sheet is shown on page 37.

### MENDEZ COMPANY
Balance Sheet
December 31, 2008

| Assets | | Liabilities | |
|---|---|---|---|
| Cash | $15,000 | Accounts payable | $20,000 |
| Supplies | 8,000 | Accounts receivable | (8,500) |
| Equipment | 46,000 | Common stock | 50,000 |
| Dividends | 10,000 | Retained earnings | 17,500 |
| Total assets | $79,000 | Total liabilities and | |
| | | stockholders' equity | $79,000 |

**Instructions**
Prepare a correct balance sheet.

**E1-14**   Deer Park, a public camping ground near the Lake Mead National Recreation Area, has compiled the following financial information as of December 31, 2008.

*Compute net income and prepare a balance sheet.*
*(SO 8)*

| | | | |
|---|---|---|---|
| Revenues during 2008—camping fees | $140,000 | Notes payable | $ 60,000 |
| Revenues during 2008—general store | 50,000 | Expenses during 2008 | 150,000 |
| Accounts payable | 11,000 | Supplies on hand | 2,500 |
| Cash on hand | 23,000 | Common stock | 20,000 |
| Original cost of equipment | 105,500 | Retained earnings | ? |
| Market value of equipment | 140,000 | | |

*R = 190,000*
*E = 150,000*
*NI = 40000*

**Instructions**
**(a)** Determine Deer Park's net income for 2008.
**(b)** Prepare a balance sheet for Deer Park as of December 31, 2008.

**E1-15**   Presented below is financial information related to the 2008 operations of Summers Cruise Company.

*Prepare an income statement.*
*(SO 8)*

| | |
|---|---|
| Maintenance expense | $ 95,000 |
| Property tax expense (on dock facilities) | 10,000 |
| Salaries expense | 142,000 |
| Advertising expense | 3,500 |
| Ticket revenue | 325,000 |

**Instructions**
Prepare the 2008 income statement for Summers Cruise Company.

**E1-16**   Presented below is information related to Kevin and Johnson, Attorneys at Law.

*Prepare a retained earnings statement.*
*(SO 8)*

| | |
|---|---|
| Retained earnings, January 1, 2008 | $ 23,000 |
| Legal service revenue—2008 | 350,000 |
| Total expenses—2008 | 211,000 |
| Assets, January 1, 2008 | 85,000 |
| Liabilities, January 1, 2008 | 62,000 |
| Assets, December 31, 2008 | 168,000 |
| Liabilities, December 31, 2008 | 85,000 |
| Dividends—2008 | 79,000 |

**Instructions**
Prepare the 2008 retained earnings statement for Kevin and Johnson, Attorneys at Law.

# EXERCISES: SET B

Visit the book's website at **www.wiley.com/college/weygandt,** and choose the Student Companion site, to access Exercise Set B.

*Analyze transactions and compute net income.*

(SO 6, 7)

*Check figures next to some Problems give you a key number, to let you know if you are on the right track with your solution.*

(a) Total retained earnings $2,060

(b) Net income $3,060

**P1-1A** Barone's Repair Inc. was started on May 1. A summary of May transactions is presented below.

1. Stockholders invested $10,000 cash to start the repair company.
2. Purchased equipment for $5,000 cash.
3. Paid $400 cash for May office rent.
4. Paid $500 cash for supplies.
5. Incurred $250 of advertising costs in the *Beacon News* on account.
6. Received $5,100 in cash from customers for repair service.
7. Paid dividends of $1,000 cash.
8. Paid part-time employee salaries $2,000.
9. Paid utility bills $140.
10. Provided repair service on account to customers $750.
11. Collected cash of $120 for services billed in transaction (10).

**Instructions**

**(a)** Prepare a tabular analysis of the transactions, using the following column headings: Cash, Accounts Receivable, Supplies, Equipment, Accounts Payable, Common Stock, and Retained Earnings. Revenue is called Service Revenue.

**(b)** From an analysis of the Retained Earnings column, compute the net income or net loss for May.

*Analyze transactions and prepare income statement, retained earnings statement, and balance sheet.*

(SO 6, 7, 8)

**P1-2A** On August 31, the balance sheet of Nashville Veterinary Clinic showed Cash $9,000, Accounts Receivable $1,700, Supplies $600, Office Equipment $6,000, Accounts Payable $3,600, Common Stock $13,000, and Retained Earnings $700. During September the following transactions occurred.

1. Paid $2,900 cash on accounts payable.
2. Collected $1,300 of accounts receivable.
3. Purchased additional office equipment for $2,100, paying $800 in cash and the balance on account.
4. Earned revenue of $8,000, of which $2,500 is paid in cash and the balance is due in October.
5. Paid cash dividends of $1,000.
6. Paid salaries $1,700, rent for September $900, and advertising expense $300.
7. Incurred utilities expense for month on account $170.
8. Received $10,000 from Capital Bank—money borrowed on a note payable.

**Instructions**

(a) Ending retained earnings $4,630

(b) Net income $4,930
Total assets $29,800

**(a)** Prepare a tabular analysis of the September transactions beginning with August 31 balances. The column headings should be as follows: Cash + Accounts Receivable + Supplies + Office Equipment = Notes Payable + Accounts Payable + Common Stock + Retained Earnings.

**(b)** Prepare an income statement for September, a retained earnings statement for September, and a balance sheet at September 30.

*Prepare income statement, retained earnings statement, and balance sheet.*

(SO 8)

**P1-3A** On May 1, Skyline Flying School, a company that provides flying lessons, was started with an investment of $45,000 cash in the business. Following are the assets and liabilities of the company on May 31, 2008, and the revenues and expenses for the month of May.

| | | | |
|---|---|---|---|
| Cash | $ 5,600 | Notes Payable | $30,000 |
| Accounts Receivable | 7,200 | Rent Expense | 1,200 |
| Equipment | 64,000 | Repair Expense | 400 |
| Lesson Revenue | 7,500 | Fuel Expense | 2,500 |
| Advertising Expense | 500 | Insurance Expense | 400 |
| | | Accounts Payable | 800 |

No additional investments were made in May, but the company paid dividends of $1,500 during the month.

**Instructions**

(a) Net income $2,500
Total assets $76,800

**(a)** Prepare an income statement and a retained earnings statement for the month of May and a balance sheet at May 31.

**(b)** Prepare an income statement and a retained earnings statement for May assuming the following data are not included above: (1) $900 of revenue was earned and billed but not collected at May 31, and (2) $1,500 of fuel expense was incurred but not paid.

(b) Net income $1,900

**P1-4A**    Mark Miller started a delivery service, Miller Deliveries, on June 1, 2008. The following transactions occurred during the month of June.

*Analyze transactions and prepare financial statements.*

(SO 6, 7, 8)

June  1  Stockholders invested $10,000 cash in the business.
2  Purchased a used van for deliveries for $12,000. Mark paid $2,000 cash and signed a note payable for the remaining balance.
3  Paid $500 for office rent for the month.
5  Performed $4,400 of services on account.
9  Paid $200 in cash dividends.
12  Purchased supplies for $150 on account.
15  Received a cash payment of $1,250 for services provided on June 5.
17  Purchased gasoline for $100 on account.
20  Received a cash payment of $1,500 for services provided.
23  Made a cash payment of $500 on the note payable.
26  Paid $250 for utilities.
29  Paid for the gasoline purchased on account on June 17.
30  Paid $1,000 for employee salaries.

**Instructions**
**(a)** Show the effects of the previous transactions on the accounting equation using the following format.

(a) Retained earnings $3,850

| Date | Cash | + | Accounts Receivable | + | Supplies | + | Delivery Van | = | Notes Payable | + | Accounts Payable | + | Common Stock | + | Retained Earnings |
|------|------|---|--------|---|----------|---|--------|---|--------|---|--------|---|--------|---|--------|

Assets / Liabilities / Stockholders' Equity

Include explanations for any changes in the Retained Earnings account in your analysis.

**(b)** Prepare an income statement for the month of June.
**(c)** Prepare a balance sheet at June 30, 2008.

(b) Net income $4,050
(c) Cash $8,200

**P1-5A**    Financial statement information about four different companies is as follows.

*Determine financial statement amounts and prepare retained earnings statement.*

(SO 7, 8)

| | Karma Company | Yates Company | McCain Company | Dench Company |
|---|---|---|---|---|
| **January 1, 2008** | | | | |
| Assets | $95,000 | $110,000 | (g) | $170,000 |
| Liabilities | 50,000 | (d) | 75,000 | (j) |
| Stockholders' equity | (a) | 60,000 | 45,000 | 90,000 |
| **December 31, 2008** | | | | |
| Assets | (b) | 137,000 | 200,000 | (k) |
| Liabilities | 55,000 | 75,000 | (h) | 80,000 |
| Stockholders' equity | 60,000 | (e) | 130,000 | 170,000 |
| **Stockholders' equity changes in year** | | | | |
| Additional investment | (c) | 15,000 | 10,000 | 15,000 |
| Dividends | 25,000 | (f) | 14,000 | 20,000 |
| Total revenues | 350,000 | 420,000 | (i) | 520,000 |
| Total expenses | 320,000 | 385,000 | 342,000 | (l) |

**Instructions**
**(a)** Determine the missing amounts. (*Hint:* For example, to solve for (a), Assets − Liabilities = Stockholders' Equity = $45,000.)
**(b)** Prepare the retained earnings statement for Yates Company. Assume beginning retained earnings was $20,000.
**(c)** ▬▬▬▶ Write a memorandum explaining the sequence for preparing financial statements and the interrelationship of the retained earnings statement to the income statement and balance sheet.

*Analyze transactions and compute net income.*

(SO 6, 7)

**P1-1B** On April 1, Jenny Russo established Matrix Travel Agency. The following transactions were completed during the month.

1. Stockholders invested $10,000 cash in exchange for stock.
2. Paid $400 cash for April office rent.
3. Purchased office equipment for $2,500 cash.
4. Incurred $300 of advertising costs in the *Chicago Tribune,* on account.
5. Paid $600 cash for office supplies.
6. Earned $9,500 for services rendered: $3,000 cash is received from customers, and the balance of $6,500 is billed to customers on account.
7. Paid $200 cash dividend.
8. Paid *Chicago Tribune* amount due in transaction 4.
9. Paid employees' salaries $2,200.
10. Received $4,000 in cash from customers who have previously been billed in transaction 6.

**Instructions**

(a) Ending retained earnings $6,400

(a) Prepare a tabular analysis of the transactions using the following column headings: Cash, Accounts Receivable, Supplies, Office Equipment, Accounts Payable, Common Stock, and Retained Earnings.

(b) Net income $6,600

(b) From an analysis of the column Retained Earnings, compute the net income or net loss for April.

*Analyze transactions and prepare income statement, retained earnings statement, and balance sheet.*

(SO 6, 7, 8)

**P1-2B** Cindy Belton opened a law office, Cindy Belton, Attorney at Law, on July 1, 2008. On July 31, the balance sheet showed Cash $4,000, Accounts Receivable $1,500, Supplies $500, Office Equipment $5,000, Accounts Payable $4,200, and Common Stock $6,000, and Retained Earnings $800. During August the following transactions occurred.

1. Collected $1,400 of accounts receivable.
2. Paid $2,700 cash on accounts payable.
3. Earned revenue of $9,000 of which $3,000 is collected in cash and the balance is due in September.
4. Purchased additional office equipment for $1,000, paying $400 in cash and the balance on account.
5. Paid salaries $3,000, rent for August $900, and advertising expenses $350.
6. Paid cash dividend of $750.
7. Received $2,000 from Standard Federal Bank—money borrowed on a note payable.
8. Incurred utility expenses for month on account $250.

**Instructions**

(a) Ending retained earnings $4,550

(a) Prepare a tabular analysis of the August transactions beginning with July 31 balances. The column headings should be as follows: Cash + Accounts Receivable + Supplies + Office Equipment = Notes Payable + Accounts Payable + Common Stock + Retained Earnings.

(b) Net income $4,500
Total assets $14,900

(b) Prepare an income statement for August, a retained earnings statement for August, and a balance sheet at August 31.

*Prepare income statement, retained earnings statement, and balance sheet.*

(SO 8)

**P1-3B** Divine Cosmetics Co., a company that provides individual skin care treatment, was started on June 1 with an investment of $26,200 cash. Following are the assets and liabilities of the company at June 30 and the revenues and expenses for the month of June.

| | | | |
|---|---|---|---|
| Cash | $11,000 | Notes Payable | $13,000 |
| Accounts Receivable | 4,000 | Accounts Payable | 1,200 |
| Service Revenue | 6,000 | Supplies Expense | 1,600 |
| Cosmetic Supplies | 2,000 | Gas and Oil Expense | 800 |
| Advertising Expense | 500 | Utilities Expense | 300 |
| Equipment | 25,000 | | |

Stockholders made no additional investments in June. The company paid a cash dividend of $1,200 during the month.

**Instructions**

(a) Net income $2,800
Total assets $42,000

(a) Prepare an income statement and a retained earnings statement for the month of June and a balance sheet at June 30, 2008.

(b) Net income $3,500

(b) Prepare an income statement and a retained earnings statement for June assuming the following data are not included above: (1) $800 of revenue was earned and billed but not collected at June 30, and (2) $100 of gas and oil expense was incurred but not paid.

**P1-4B**   Laura Geller started a consulting firm, Geller Consulting, on May 1, 2008. The following transactions occurred during the month of May.

*Analyze transactions and prepare financial statements.*

(SO 6, 7, 8)

May  1  Geller invested $8,000 cash in the business in exchange for stock.
    2  Paid $800 for office rent for the month.
    3  Purchased $500 of supplies on account.
    5  Paid $50 to advertise in the *County News.*
    9  Received $3,000 cash for services provided.
   12  Paid a $700 cash dividend.
   15  Performed $5,300 of services on account.
   17  Paid $3,000 for employee salaries.
   20  Paid for the supplies purchased on account on May 3.
   23  Received a cash payment of $3,000 for services provided on account on May 15.
   26  Borrowed $5,000 from the bank on a note payable.
   29  Purchased office equipment for $2,800 on account.
   30  Paid $150 for utilities.

**Instructions**

**(a)** Show the effects of the previous transactions on the accounting equation using the following format.

*(a) Ending retained earnings $3,600*

| | | Assets | | | | Liabilities | | | Stockholders' Equity | |
|---|---|---|---|---|---|---|---|---|---|---|
| Date | Cash + | Accounts Receivable | + Supplies + | Office Equipment | = | Notes Payable | + Accounts Payable | + | Common Stock | + Retained Earnings |

Include explanations for any changes in the Retained Earnings account in your analysis.

**(b)** Prepare an income statement for the month of May.
**(c)** Prepare a balance sheet at May 31, 2008.

*(b) Net income $4,300*
*(c) Cash $13,800*

**P1-5B**   Financial statement information about four different companies is as follows.

*Determine financial statement amounts and prepare retained earnings statement.*

(SO 7, 8)

| | McKane Company | Selara Company | Gordon Company | Hindi Company |
|---|---|---|---|---|
| **January 1, 2008** | | | | |
| Assets | $ 80,000 | $90,000 | (g) | $150,000 |
| Liabilities | 50,000 | (d) | 75,000 | (j) |
| Stockholders' equity | (a) | 50,000 | 49,000 | 100,000 |
| **December 31, 2008** | | | | |
| Assets | (b) | 117,000 | 180,000 | (k) |
| Liabilities | 55,000 | 72,000 | (h) | 80,000 |
| Stockholders' equity | 40,000 | (e) | 100,000 | 145,000 |
| **Stockholders' equity changes in year** | | | | |
| Additional investment | (c) | 8,000 | 10,000 | 15,000 |
| Dividends | 10,000 | (f) | 12,000 | 10,000 |
| Total revenues | 350,000 | 400,000 | (i) | 500,000 |
| Total expenses | 335,000 | 385,000 | 360,000 | (l) |

**Instructions**

**(a)** Determine the missing amounts. (*Hint:* For example, to solve for (a), Assets – Liabilities = Stockholders' Equity = $30,000.)
**(b)** Prepare the retained earnings statement for McKane Company. Assume beginning retained earnings was $0.
**(c)** ▰▰▰▰▰► Write a memorandum explaining the sequence for preparing financial statements and the interrelationship of the retained earnings statement to the income statement and balance sheet.

## PROBLEMS: SET C

## CONTINUING COOKIE CHRONICLE

*The **Continuing Cookie Chronicle** starts in this chapter and continues in every chapter. You also can find this problem at the book's Student Companion site.*

**CCC1** Natalie Koebel spent much of her childhood learning the art of cookie-making from her grandmother. They passed many happy hours mastering every type of cookie imaginable and later creating new recipes that were both healthy and delicious. Now at the start of her second year in college, Natalie is investigating various possibilities for starting her own business as part of the requirements of the entrepreneurship program in which she is enrolled.

A long-time friend insists that Natalie has to somehow include cookies in her business plan. After a series of brainstorming sessions, Natalie settles on the idea of operating a cookie-making school. She will start on a part-time basis and offer her services in people's homes. Now that she has started thinking about it, the possibilities seem endless. During the fall, she will concentrate on holiday cookies. She will offer individual lessons and group sessions (which will probably be more entertainment than education for the participants). Natalie also decides to include children in her target market.

The first difficult decision is coming up with the perfect name for her business. In the end, she settles on "Cookie Creations" and then moves on to more important issues.

**Instructions**
**(a)** What form of business organization—proprietorship, partnership, or corporation—do you recommend that Natalie use for her business? Discuss the benefits and weaknesses of each form and give the reasons for your choice.
**(b)** Will Natalie need accounting information? If yes, what information will she need and why? How often will she need this information?
**(c)** Identify specific asset, liability, and owner's/stockholders' equity accounts that Cookie Creations will likely use to record its business transactions.
**(d)** Should Natalie open a separate bank account for the business? Why or why not?

# BROADENING YOUR PERSPECTIVE

## FINANCIAL REPORTING AND ANALYSIS

## Financial Reporting Problem
### PepsiCo, Inc.

**BYP1-1** The actual financial statements of PepsiCo, as presented in the company's 2005 Annual Report, are contained in Appendix A (at the back of the textbook).

**Instructions**
Refer to PepsiCo's financial statements and answer the following questions.

**(a)** What were PepsiCo's total assets at December 31, 2005? At December 25, 2004?
**(b)** How much cash (and cash equivalents) did PepsiCo have on December 31, 2005?
**(c)** What amount of accounts payable did PepsiCo report on December 31, 2005? On December 25, 2004?
**(d)** What were PepsiCo's net sales in 2003? In 2004? In 2005?
**(e)** What is the amount of the change in PepsiCo's net income from 2004 to 2005?

## Comparative Analysis Problem
### PepsiCo, Inc. vs. The Coca-Cola Company

**BYP1-2** PepsiCo's financial statements are presented in Appendix A. The Coca-Cola Company's financial statements are presented in Appendix B.

**Instructions**
Refer to the financial statements and answer the following questions.

**(a)** Based on the information contained in these financial statements, determine the following for each company.

    (1) Total assets at December 31, 2005, for PepsiCo, and for Coca-Cola at December 31, 2005.
    (2) Accounts (notes) receivable, net at December 31, 2005, for PepsiCo and at December 31, 2005, for Coca-Cola.
    (3) Net sales for year ended in 2005.
    (4) Net income for year ended in 2005.
**(b)** What conclusions concerning the two companies can be drawn from these data?

# Exploring the Web

**BYP1-3**   This exercise will familiarize you with skill requirements, job descriptions, and salaries for accounting careers.

**Address: www.careers-in-accounting.com**, or go to **www.wiley.com/college/weygandt**

**Instructions**
Go to the site shown above. Answer the following questions.

**(a)** What are the three broad areas of accounting (from "Skills and Talents Required")?
**(b)** List eight skills required in accounting.
**(c)** How do the three accounting areas differ in terms of these eight required skills?
**(d)** Explain one of the key job functions in accounting.
**(e)** Based on the *Smart Money* survey, what is the salary range for a junior staff accountant with Deloitte & Touche?

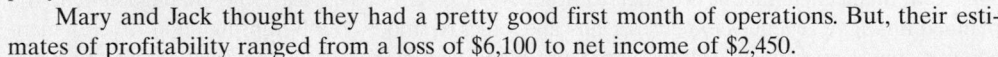

# CRITICAL THINKING

## Decision Making Across the Organization

**BYP1-4**   Mary and Jack Gray, local golf stars, opened the Chip-Shot Driving Range Company on March 1, 2008. They invested $25,000 cash and received common stock in exchange for their investment. A caddy shack was constructed for cash at a cost of $8,000, and $800 was spent on golf balls and golf clubs. The Grays leased five acres of land at a cost of $1,000 per month and paid the first month's rent. During the first month, advertising costs totaled $750, of which $150 was unpaid at March 31, and $400 was paid to members of the high-school golf team for retrieving golf balls. All revenues from customers were deposited in the company's bank account. On March 15, Mary and Jack received a dividend of $1,000. A $100 utility bill was received on March 31 but was not paid. On March 31, the balance in the company's bank account was $18,900.

    Mary and Jack thought they had a pretty good first month of operations. But, their estimates of profitability ranged from a loss of $6,100 to net income of $2,450.

**Instructions**
With the class divided into groups, answer the following.

**(a)** How could the Grays have concluded that the business operated at a loss of $6,100? Was this a valid basis on which to determine net income?
**(b)** How could the Grays have concluded that the business operated at a net income of $2,450? (*Hint:* Prepare a balance sheet at March 31.) Was this a valid basis on which to determine net income?
**(c)** Without preparing an income statement, determine the actual net income for March.
**(d)** What was the revenue earned in March?

## Communication Activity

**BYP1-5**   Lynn Benedict, the bookkeeper for New York Company, has been trying to get the balance sheet to balance. The company's balance sheet is shown on page 44.

| NEW YORK COMPANY | | | |
| --- | --- | --- | --- |
| Balance Sheet | | | |
| For the Month Ended December 31, 2008 | | | |
| **Assets** | | **Liabilities** | |
| Equipment | $25,500 | Common stock | $26,000 |
| Cash | 9,000 | Accounts receivable | (6,000) |
| Supplies | 2,000 | Retained earnings | (2,000) |
| Accounts payable | (8,000) | Notes payable | 10,500 |
| | $28,500 | | $28,500 |

**Instructions**

Explain to Lynn Benedict in a memo why the original balance sheet is incorrect, and what should be done to correct it.

# Ethics Case

**BYP1-6**   After numerous campus interviews, Steve Baden, a senior at Great Northern College, received two office interview invitations from the Baltimore offices of two large firms. Both firms offered to cover his out-of-pocket expenses (travel, hotel, and meals). He scheduled the interviews for both firms on the same day, one in the morning and one in the afternoon. At the conclusion of each interview, he submitted to both firms his total out-of-pocket expenses for the trip to Baltimore: mileage $112 (280 miles at $0.40), hotel $130, meals $36, parking and tolls $18, for a total of $296. He believes this approach is appropriate. If he had made two trips, his cost would have been two times $296. He is also certain that neither firm knew he had visited the other on that same trip. Within ten days Steve received two checks in the mail, each in the amount of $296.

**Instructions**

(a) Who are the stakeholders (affected parties) in this situation?

(b) What are the ethical issues in this case?

(c) What would you do in this situation?

# "All About You" Activity

**BYP1-7**   As discussed in the "All About You" feature in this chapter (p. 25), some people are tempted to make their finances look worse to get financial aid. Companies sometimes also manage their financial numbers in order to accomplish certain goals. Earnings management is the planned timing of revenues, expenses, gains, and losses to smooth out bumps in net income. In managing earnings, companies' actions vary from being within the range of ethical activity, to being both unethical and illegal attempts to mislead investors and creditors.

**Instructions**

Provide responses for each of the following questions.

(a) Discuss whether you think each of the following actions (adapted from *www.finaid.org/ fafsa/maximize.phtml*) to increase the chances of receiving financial aid is ethical.

   (i)   Spend down the student's assets and income first, before spending parents' assets and income.

   (ii)  Accelerate necessary expenses to reduce available cash. For example, if you need a new car, buy it before applying for financial aid.

   (iii) State that a truly financially dependent child is independent.

   (iv)  Have a parent take an unpaid leave of absence for long enough to get below the "threshold" level of income.

(b) What are some reasons why a *company* might want to overstate its earnings?

(c) What are some reasons why a *company* might want to understate its earnings?

(d) Under what circumstances might an otherwise ethical person decide to illegally overstate or understate earnings?

## Answers to Insight and Accounting Across the Organization Questions

**Chinese Investors Lack Confidence in Financial Reports, p. 9**

Q: What has been done in the United States to improve the quality and integrity of financial reporting and to build investor confidence in financial reports?

A: *Congress passed new laws to legislate fair business behavior and accounting and auditing practices. The* Sarbanes-Oxley Act of 2002 *increased the resources for the government to combat fraud and to curb poor reporting practices. It introduced sweeping changes to the structure and practice of the accounting and auditing professions and increased the responsibility of corporate boards and officers.*

**How Will Accounting Help Me?, p. 11**

Q: How might accounting help you?

A: *You will need to understand financial reports in any enterprise with which you are associated. Whether you become a business manager, doctor, lawyer, social worker, teacher, engineer, architect, or entrepreneur, a working knowledge of accounting is relevant.*

**What Do Delta Air Lines, Walt Disney, and Dunkin' Donuts Have in Common?, p. 23**

Q: What year-end would you likely use if you owned a ski resort and ski rental business?

A: *Probable choices for a ski resort would be between May 31 and August 31.*

Q: What if you owned a college bookstore?

A: *For a college bookstore, a likely year-end would be June 30.*

Q: Why choose those year-ends?

A: *The optimum accounting year-end, especially for seasonal businesses, is a point when inventory and activities are lowest.*

## Authors' Comments on *All About You: Ethics: Managing Personal Financial Reporting*, p. 25

In this chapter you saw that there are very specific rules governing the recording of assets, liabilities, revenues, and expenses. However, within these rules there is a lot of room for judgment. It would not be at all unusual for two experienced accountants, when faced with identical situations, to arrive at different results.

Similarly, in reporting your financial situation for financial aid there is a lot of room for judgment. The question is, what kinds of actions are both permissible and ethical, and what kinds of actions are illegal and unethical? It might be argued that paying off your credit card debt to reduce your assets is legal and ethical. It is true that you have intentionally changed the nature of your assets in order to improve your chances of getting aid. You did so, however, through a legitimate transaction. In fact, given the high interest rates charged on credit card bills, it would probably be a good idea to use the cash to pay off your bills even if you aren't applying for aid.

Now, consider an alternative situation. Suppose that you have $10,000 in cash, and you have a sibling who is five years younger than you. Should you "give" the cash to your sibling while you are being considered for financial aid? This would give the appearance of substantially reducing your assets, and thus increase the likelihood that you will receive aid. Most people would argue that this is unethical, and it is probably illegal.

When completing your FAFSA form, don't ignore the following warning on the front of the form: "If you get Federal student aid based on incorrect information, you will have to pay it back; you may also have to pay fines and fees. If you purposely give false or misleading information on your application, you may be fined $20,000, sent to prison, or both."

## Answer to PepsiCo Review It Question 4, p. 13

PepsiCo's accounting equation is:

| Assets | = | Liabilities | + | Owners' (Stockholders') Equity |
|---|---|---|---|---|
| $31,727,000,000 | = | $17,476,000,000 | + | $14,251,000,000 |

(Owners' equity includes preferred stock.)

## Answers to Self-Study Questions

**1.** b  **2.** d  **3.** c  **4.** b  **5.** d  **6.** b  **7.** a  **8.** b  **9.** c  **10.** a

 *Remember to go back to the Navigator box on the chapter-opening page and check off your completed work.*

# Chapter 2

# The Recording Process

## STUDY OBJECTIVES

*After studying this chapter, you should be able to:*

1. Explain what an account is and how it helps in the recording process.
2. Define debits and credits and explain their use in recording business transactions.
3. Identify the basic steps in the recording process.
4. Explain what a journal is and how it helps in the recording process.
5. Explain what a ledger is and how it helps in the recording process.
6. Explain what posting is and how it helps in the recording process.
7. Prepare a trial balance and explain its purposes.

## ✓ The Navigator

| | |
|---|---|
| Scan **Study Objectives** | ■ |
| Read **Feature Story** | ■ |
| Read **Preview** | ■ |
| Read text and answer **Before You Go On** p. 53 ■   p. 56 ■   p. 66 ■   p. 70 ■ | |
| Work **Demonstration Problem** | ■ |
| Review **Summary of Study Objectives** | ■ |
| Answer **Self-Study Questions** | ■ |
| Complete **Assignments** | ■ |

## *Feature Story*

### ACCIDENTS HAPPEN

How organized are you financially? Take a short quiz. Answer *yes* or *no* to each question:

• Does your wallet contain so many cash machine receipts that you've been declared a walking fire hazard?

• Is your wallet such a mess that it is often faster to fish for money in the crack of your car seat than to dig around in your wallet?

• Was LeBron James playing high school basketball the last time you balanced your checkbook?

If you think it is hard to keep track of the many transactions that make up *your* life, imagine what it is like for a major corporation like Fidelity Investments (*www.fidelity.com*). Fidelity is one of the largest mutual fund management firms in the world. If you had your life savings invested at Fidelity Investments, you might be just slightly displeased if, when you called to find out your balance, the representative said, "You know, I kind of remember someone with a name like yours sending us some money—now what did we do with that?"

To ensure the accuracy of your balance and the security of your funds, Fidelity Investments, like all other companies large and small, relies on a sophisticated accounting information system. That's not to say that Fidelity or any other company is error-free. In fact, if you've ever really messed up your checkbook register, you may take some comfort from one accountant's mistake at Fidelity Investments. The accountant failed to include a minus sign while doing a calculation, making what was actually a $1.3 billion loss look like a $1.3 billion gain! Fortunately, like most accounting errors, it was detected before any real harm was done.

No one expects that kind of mistake at a company like Fidelity, which has sophisticated computer systems and top investment managers. In explaining the mistake to shareholders, a spokesperson wrote, "Some people have asked how, in this age of technology, such a mistake could be made. While many of our processes are computerized, accounting systems are complex and dictate that some steps must be handled manually by our managers and accountants, and people can make mistakes."

✔ The Navigator

## *Inside Chapter 2*

In Chapter 1, we analyzed business transactions in terms of the accounting equation, and we presented the cumulative effects of these transactions in tabular form. Imagine a company like Fidelity Investments (as in the Feature Story) using the same tabular format as Softbyte to keep track of its transactions. In a single day, Fidelity engages in thousands of business transactions. To record each transaction this way would be impractical, expensive, and unnecessary. Instead, companies use a set of procedures and records to keep track of transaction data more easily. This chapter introduces and illustrates these basic procedures and records.

The content and organization of Chapter 2 are as follows.

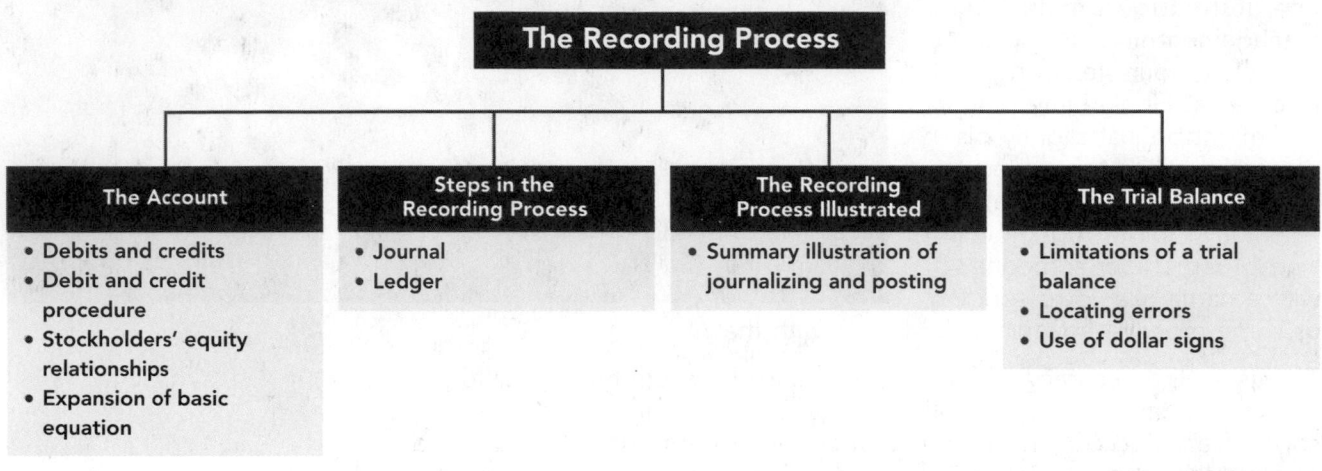

**The Recording Process**

| The Account | Steps in the Recording Process | The Recording Process Illustrated | The Trial Balance |
|---|---|---|---|
| • Debits and credits<br>• Debit and credit procedure<br>• Stockholders' equity relationships<br>• Expansion of basic equation | • Journal<br>• Ledger | • Summary illustration of journalizing and posting | • Limitations of a trial balance<br>• Locating errors<br>• Use of dollar signs |

✔ *The Navigator*

# THE ACCOUNT

**STUDY OBJECTIVE 1**

Explain what an account is and how it helps in the recording process.

An **account** is an accounting record of increases and decreases in a specific asset, liability, or owner's equity item. For example, Softbyte (the company discussed in Chapter 1) would have separate accounts for Cash, Accounts Receivable, Accounts Payable, Service Revenue, and Salaries Expense. In its simplest form, an account consists of three parts: (1) a title, (2) a left or debit side, and (3) a right or credit side. Because the format of an account resembles the letter T, we refer to it as a **T account**. Illustration 2-1 shows the basic form of an account.

**Illustration 2-1**
Basic form of account

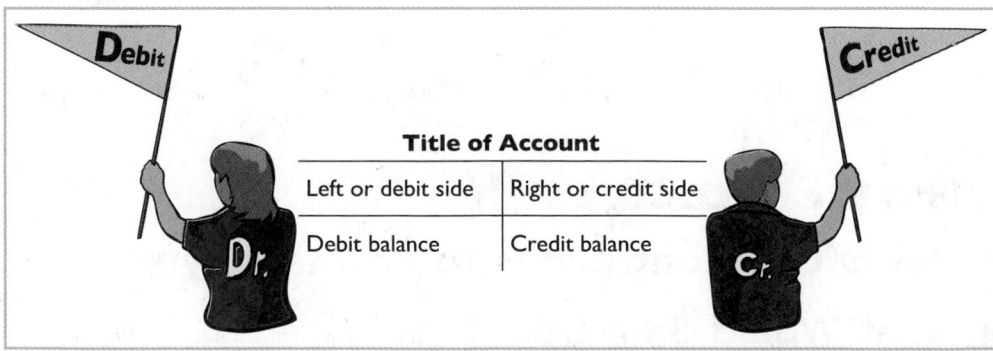

The T account is a standard shorthand in accounting, which helps make clear the effects of transactions on individual accounts. We will use it often throughout this book to explain basic accounting relationships.

# Debits and Credits

The terms debit and credit are directional signals: Debit indicates left, and credit indicates right. They indicate which side of a T account a number will be recorded on. Entering an amount on the left side of an account is called **debiting** the account; making an entry on the right side is **crediting** the account. We commonly abbreviate debit as Dr. and credit as Cr.

Having debits on the left and credits on the right is an accounting custom, or rule, like the custom of driving on the right-hand side of the road in the United States. **This rule applies to all accounts.**

Illustration 2-2 shows the recording of debits and credits in an account for the cash transactions of Softbyte. The data are taken from the cash column of the tabular summary in Illustration 1-8 (from page 19), which is reproduced here.

| Tabular Summary | Account Form | | | |
|---|---|---|---|---|
| **Cash** | **Cash** | | | |
| $15,000 | (Debits) | 15,000 | (Credits) | 7,000 |
| –7,000 | | 1,200 | | 1,700 |
| 1,200 | | 1,500 | | 250 |
| 1,500 | | 600 | | 1,300 |
| –1,700 | Balance | 8,050 | | |
| –250 | (Debit) | | | |
| 600 | | | | |
| –1,300 | | | | |
| $ 8,050 | | | | |

**Illustration 2-2**
Tabular summary compared to account form

In the tabular summary, every positive item represents Softbyte's receipt of cash; every negative amount represents a payment of cash. In the account form we record the increases in cash as debits, and the decreases in cash as credits. Having increases on one side and decreases on the other helps determine the total of each side as well as the overall account balance. The balance, a debit of $8,050, indicates that Softbyte has had $8,050 more increases than decreases in cash.

When the totals of the two sides of an account are compared, an account will have a **debit balance** if the total of the debit amounts exceeds the credits. An account will have a **credit balance** if the credit amounts exceed the debits. The account in Illustration 2-2 has a debit balance.

# Debit and Credit Procedure

In Chapter 1 you learned the effect of a transaction on the basic accounting equation. Remember that each transaction must affect two or more accounts to keep the basic accounting equation in balance. In other words, for each transaction, debits must equal credits in the accounts. The equality of debits and credits provides the basis for the double-entry system of recording transactions.

In the double-entry system the dual (two-sided) effect of each transaction is recorded in appropriate accounts. This system provides a logical method for recording transactions. It also helps ensure the accuracy of the recorded amounts. The sum of all the debits to the accounts must equal the sum of all the credits.

The double-entry system for determining the equality of the accounting equation is much more efficient than the plus/minus procedure used in Chapter 1. On the following pages, we will illustrate debit and credit procedures in the double-entry system.

## ASSETS AND LIABILITIES

Both sides of the accounting equation (Assets = Liabilities + Stockholders' equity) must be equal. It follows, then, that we must record increases and decreases in assets opposite from each other. In Illustration 2-2, Softbyte entered increases in cash—an asset—on the left side, and decreases in cash on the right side. Therefore, we must enter increases in liabilities on the right or credit side, and decreases in liabilities on the left or debit side. Illustration 2-3 summarizes the effects that debits and credits have on assets and liabilities.

**Illustration 2-3**
Debit and credit effects—
assets and liabilities

| Debits | Credits |
|---|---|
| Increase assets | Decrease assets |
| Decrease liabilities | Increase liabilities |

Debits to a specific asset account should exceed the credits to that account. Credits to a liability account should exceed debits to that account. **The normal balance of an account is on the side where an increase in the account is recorded.** Thus, asset accounts normally show debit balances, and liability accounts normally show credit balances. Illustration 2-4 shows the normal balances for assets and liabilities.

**Illustration 2-4**
Normal balances—assets
and liabilities

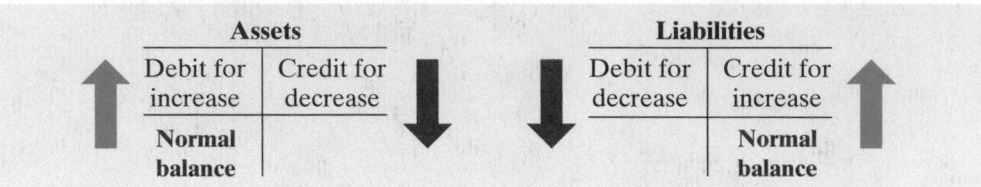

Knowing the normal balance in an account may help you trace errors. For example, a credit balance in an asset account such as Land would indicate a recording error. Similarly, a debit balance in a liability account such as Wages Payable would indicate an error. Occasionally, though, an abnormal balance may be correct. The Cash account, for example, will have a credit balance when a company has overdrawn its bank balance (i.e., written a "bad" check). (Notice that when we are referring to a specific account, we capitalize its name.)

## STOCKHOLDERS' EQUITY

As Chapter 1 indicated, there are five subdivisions of stockholders' equity: common stock, retained earnings, dividends, revenues, and expenses. In a double-entry system, companies keep accounts for each of these subdivisions, as explained below.

**Common Stock.** Companies issue common stock in exchange for the owners' investment paid into the corporation. Credits increase the Common Stock account, and debits decrease it. For example, when an owner invests cash in the business in exchange for shares of the corporation's stock, the company debits (increases) Cash and credits (increases) Common Stock.

Illustration 2-5 shows the rules of debit and credit for the Common Stock account.

**Illustration 2-5**
Debit and credit effects—
common stock

| Debits | Credits |
|---|---|
| Decrease Common Stock | Increase Common Stock |

We can diagram the normal balance in Common Stock as follows.

**Illustration 2-6**
Normal balance—common
stock

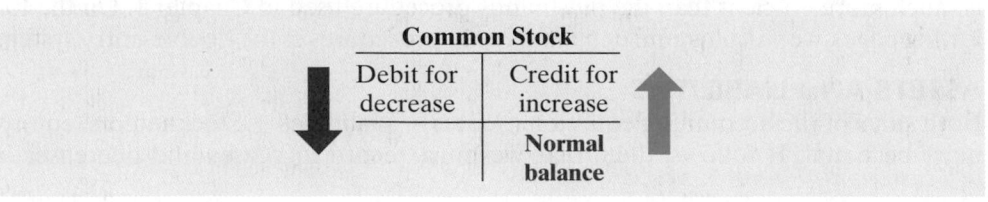

**Retained Earnings.** Retained earnings is net income that is retained in the business. It represents the portion of stockholders' equity that the company has accumulated through the profitable operation of the business. Credits (net income) increases the Retained Earnings account, and debits (dividends or net losses) decrease it, as Illustration 2-7 shows.

**HELPFUL HINT**
The rules for debit and credit and the normal balance of common stock are the same as for liabilities.

**Illustration 2-7**
Debit and credit effects and normal balance—retained earnings

| Retained Earnings | |
|---|---|
| Debit for decrease | Credit for increase |
| | **Normal balance** |

**Dividends.** A dividend is a company's distribution to its stockholders on a pro rata (equal) basis. The most common form of a distribution is a **cash dividend**. Dividends reduce the stockholders' claims on retained earnings. Debits increase the Dividends account, and credits decrease it. Illustration 2-8 shows that this account normally has a debit balance.

**Illustration 2-8**
Debit and credit effect and normal balance—dividends

| Dividends | |
|---|---|
| Debit for increase | Credit for decrease |
| **Normal balance** | |

## REVENUES AND EXPENSES
The purpose of earning revenues is to benefit the stockholders of the business. When a company earns revenues, stockholders' equity increases. Revenues are a subdivision of stockholders' equity that provides information as to **why** stockholders' equity increased. Credits increase revenue accounts and debits decrease them. Therefore, **the effect of debits and credits on revenue accounts is the same as their effect on stockholders' equity**.

Expenses have the opposite effect: expenses decrease stockholders' equity. Since expenses decrease net income, and revenues increase it, it is logical that the increase and decrease sides of expense accounts should be the reverse of revenue accounts. Thus, debits increase expense accounts, and credits decrease them.

Illustration 2-9 shows the effect of debits and credits on revenues and expenses.

**HELPFUL HINT**
Because revenues increase stockholders' equity, a revenue account has the same debit/credit rules as the Common Stock account. Expenses have the opposite effect.

**Illustration 2-9**
Debit and credit effects—revenues and expenses

| **Debits** | **Credits** |
|---|---|
| Decrease revenues | Increase revenues |
| Increase expenses | Decrease expenses |

Credits to revenue accounts should exceed debits. Debits to expense accounts should exceed credits. Thus, revenue accounts normally show credit balances, and expense accounts normally show debit balances. We can diagram the normal balance as follows.

**Illustration 2-10**
Normal balances—revenues and expenses

| Revenues | | Expenses | |
|---|---|---|---|
| Debit for decrease | Credit for increase | Debit for increase | Credit for decrease |
| | **Normal balance** | **Normal balance** | |

## Stockholders' Equity Relationships

As Chapter 1 indicated, companies report common stock and retained earnings in the stockholders' equity section of the balance sheet. They report dividends on the retained earnings statement. And they report revenues and expenses on the income statement. Dividends, revenues, and expenses are eventually transferred to retained earnings at the end of the period. As a result, a change in any one of these three items affects stockholders' equity. Illustration 2-11 shows the relationships related to stockholders' equity.

**Illustration 2-11**
Stockholders' equity relationships

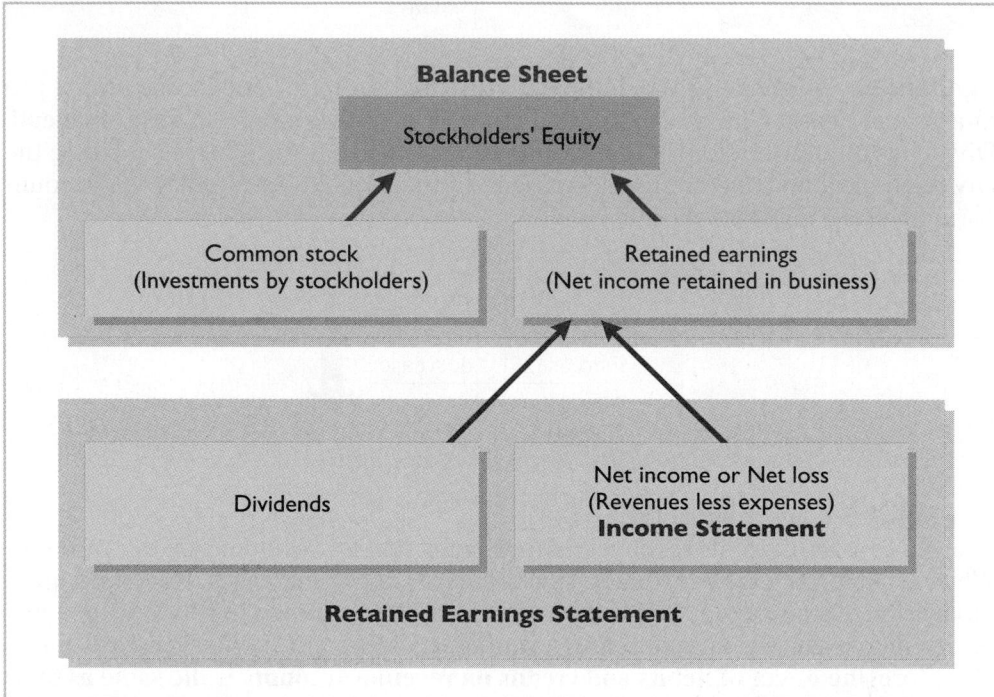

## Expansion of the Basic Equation

You have already learned the basic accounting equation. Illustration 2-12 expands this equation to show the accounts that comprise stockholders' equity. Like the basic equation, the expanded basic equation must be in balance (total debits equal

**Illustration 2-12**
Expanded basic equation and debit/credit rules and effects

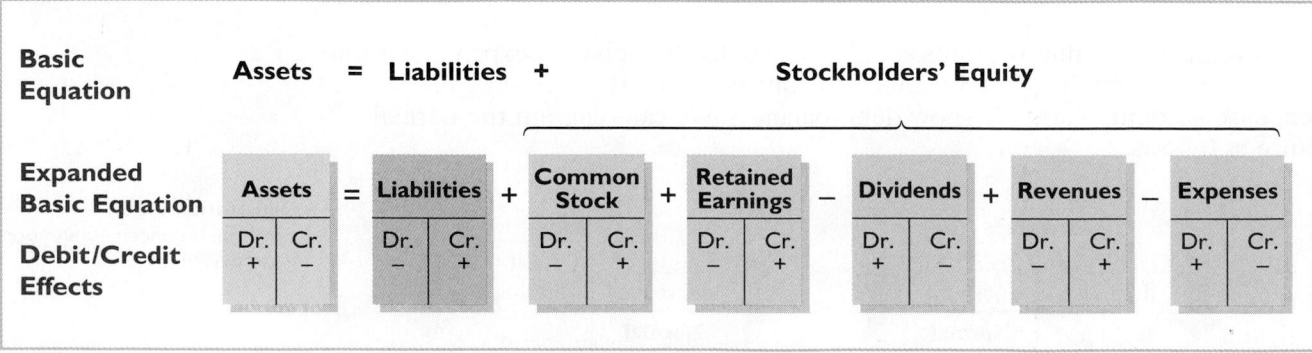

total credits). In addition, it illustrates the debit/credit rules and effects on each type of account. Study this diagram carefully. It will help you understand the fundamentals of the double-entry system.

## Before You Go On...

### REVIEW IT

1. What do the terms *debit* and *credit* mean?
2. What are the debit and credit effects on assets, liabilities, and stockholders' equity?
3. What are the debit and credit effects on revenues, expenses, and dividends?
4. What are the normal balances for PepsiCo's Cash, Accounts Payable, and Interest Expense accounts? (The answer to this question appears on page 90.)

### DO IT

Kate Browne, president of Hair It Is, Inc., has just rented space in a shopping mall in which she will open and operate a beauty salon. A friend has advised Kate to set up a double-entry set of accounting records in which to record all of her business transactions.

Identify the balance sheet accounts that Hair It Is, Inc., will likely need to record the transactions needed to establish and open the business. Also, indicate whether the normal balance of each account is a debit or a credit.

### Action Plan

■ Determine the types of accounts needed: Kate will need asset accounts for each type of asset she invests in the business, and liability accounts for any debts she incurs.

■ Understand the types of stockholders' equity accounts: When Kate begins the business, she will need only Common Stock. Later, she will need other stockholders' equity accounts.

**Solution**    Hair It Is, Inc., would likely need the following accounts to record the transactions needed to ready the beauty salon for opening day:

| | |
|---|---|
| Cash (debit balance) | Equipment (debit balance) |
| Supplies (debit balance) | Accounts Payable (credit balance) |
| Notes Payable (credit balance), if the business borrows money | Common Stock (credit balance) |

Related exercise material: *BE2-1, BE2-2, BE2-5, E2-1, E2-2, and E2-4.*

# STEPS IN THE RECORDING PROCESS

In practically every business, there are three basic steps in the recording process:

**STUDY OBJECTIVE 3**

Identify the basic steps in the recording process.

1. Analyze each transaction for its effects on the accounts.
2. Enter the transaction information in a *journal.*
3. Transfer the journal information to the appropriate accounts in the *ledger.*

Although it is possible to enter transaction information directly into the accounts without using a journal, few businesses do so.

The recording process begins with the transaction. **Business documents**, such as a sales slip, a check, a bill, or a cash register tape, provide evidence of the transaction. The company analyzes this evidence to determine the transaction's effects on specific accounts. The company then enters the transaction in the journal. Finally, it transfers the journal entry to the designated accounts in the ledger. Illustration 2-13 shows the recording process.

**Illustration 2-13**
The recording process

The steps in the recording process occur repeatedly. We illustrated the first step, the analysis of transactions, in Chapter 1, and will give further examples in this and later chapters. The other two steps in the recording process are explained in the next sections.

## The Journal

**STUDY OBJECTIVE 4**

**Explain what a journal is and how it helps in the recording process.**

Companies initially record transactions in chronological order (the order in which they occur). Thus, the **journal** is referred to as the book of original entry. For each transaction the journal shows the debit and credit effects on specific accounts.

Companies may use various kinds of journals, but every company has the most basic form of journal, a **general journal**. Typically, a general journal has spaces for dates, account titles and explanations, references, and two amount columns. See the format of the journal in Illustration 2-14 on page 55. Whenever we use the term "journal" in this textbook without a modifying adjective, we mean the general journal.

The journal makes several significant contributions to the recording process:

1.  It discloses in one place the complete effects of a transaction.
2.  It provides a chronological record of transactions.
3.  It helps to prevent or locate errors because the debit and credit amounts for each entry can be easily compared.

### JOURNALIZING

Entering transaction data in the journal is known as **journalizing**. Companies make separate journal entries for each transaction. A complete entry consists of: (1) the date of the transaction, (2) the accounts and amounts to be debited and credited, and (3) a brief explanation of the transaction.

Illustration 2-14 shows the technique of journalizing, using the first two transactions of Softbyte Inc. On September 1, stockholders invested $15,000 cash in the corporation in exchange for shares of stock, and Softbyte purchased computer equipment for $7,000 cash. The number J1 indicates that the company records these two entries on the first page of the general journal. (The boxed numbers correspond to explanations in the list below the illustration.)

| GENERAL JOURNAL | | | | J1 |
|---|---|---|---|---|
| **Date** | **Account Titles and Explanation** | **Ref.** | **Debit** | **Credit** |
| 2008 | | 5 | | |
| Sept. 1 | 2 Cash | | 15,000 | |
| 1 | 3 Common Stock | | | 15,000 |
| | 4 (Issued shares of stock for cash) | | | |
| 1 | Computer Equipment | | 7,000 | |
| | Cash | | | 7,000 |
| | (Purchase equipment for cash) | | | |

**Illustration 2-14**
Technique of journalizing

1 The date of the transaction is entered in the Date column.

2 The debit account title (that is, the account to be debited) is entered first at the extreme left margin of the column headed "Account Titles and Explanation," and the amount of the debit is recorded in the Debit column.

3 The credit account title (that is, the account to be credited) is indented and entered on the next line in the column headed "Account Titles and Explanation," and the amount of the credit is recorded in the Credit column.

4 A brief explanation of the transaction appears on the line below the credit account title. A space is left between journal entries. The blank space separates individual journal entries and makes the entire journal easier to read.

5 The column titled Ref. (which stands for Reference) is left blank when the journal entry is made. This column is used later when the journal entries are transferred to the ledger accounts.

**It is important to use correct and specific account titles in journalizing.** The main criterion is that each title must appropriately describe the content of the account. For example, a company might use Delivery Equipment, Delivery Trucks, or Trucks as the account title used for the cost of delivery trucks. Once a company chooses the specific title to use, it should record under that account title all later transactions involving the account.[1]

## SIMPLE AND COMPOUND ENTRIES

Some entries involve only two accounts, one debit and one credit. (See, for example, the entries in Illustration 2-14.) An entry like these is considered a **simple entry**. Some transactions, however, require more than two accounts in journalizing. An entry that requires three or more accounts is a **compound entry**. To illustrate,

---

[1]In homework problems, you should use specific account titles when they are given. When account titles are not given, you may select account titles that identify the nature and content of each account. The account titles used in journalizing should not contain explanations such as Cash Paid or Cash Received.

assume that on July 1, Butler Company purchases a delivery truck costing $14,000. It pays $8,000 cash now and agrees to pay the remaining $6,000 on account (to be paid later). The compound entry is as follows.

**Illustration 2-15**
Compound journal entry

| | GENERAL JOURNAL | | | J1 |
|---|---|---|---|---|
| **Date** | **Account Titles and Explanation** | **Ref.** | **Debit** | **Credit** |
| 2008 July 1 | Delivery Equipment | | 14,000 | |
| | Cash | | | 8,000 |
| | Accounts Payable | | | 6,000 |
| | (Purchased truck for cash with balance on account) | | | |

In a compound entry, the standard format requires that all debits be listed before the credits.

# ACCOUNTING ACROSS THE ORGANIZATION

### New Xbox Contributes to Profitability

Bryan Lee is head of finance at Microsoft's Home and Entertainment Division. In recent years the division has lost over $4 billion, mostly due to losses on the original Xbox videogame player. With the new Xbox 360 videogame player, Mr. Lee hopes the division will become profitable. He has set strict goals for sales, revenue, and profit. "A manager seeking to spend more on a feature such as a disk drive has to find allies in the group to cut spending elsewhere, or identify new revenue to offset the increase," he explains.

For example, Microsoft originally designed the new Xbox to have 256 megabytes of memory. But the design department said that amount of memory wouldn't support the best special effects. The purchasing department said that adding more memory would cost $30—which is 10% of the estimated selling price of $300. But the marketing department "determined that adding the memory would let Microsoft reduce marketing costs and attract more game developers, boosting royalty revenue. It would also extend the life of the console, generating more sales." Microsoft doubled the memory to 512 megabytes.

*Source:* Robert A. Guth, "New Xbox Aim for Microsoft: Profitability," *Wall Street Journal*, May 24, 2005, p. C1.

**?** In what ways is this Microsoft division using accounting to assist in its effort to become more profitable?

## Before You Go On...

### REVIEW IT
1. What is the sequence of the steps in the recording process?
2. How does the journal benefit the recording process?
3. What is the standard form and content of a journal entry in the general journal?

**DO IT**

As president and sole stockholder, Kate Browne engaged in the following activities in establishing her beauty salon, Hair It Is, Inc.

1. Opened a bank account in the name of Hair It Is, Inc. and deposited $20,000 of her own money in this accounting exchange for shares of common stock.

2. Purchased equipment on account (to be paid in 30 days) for a total cost of $4,800.

3. Interviewed three applicants for the position of beautician.

In what form (type of record) should Hair It Is, Inc., record these three activities? Prepare the entries to record the transactions.

**Action Plan**

■ Understand which activities need to be recorded and which do not. Any that have economic effects should be recorded in a journal.

■ Analyze the effects of transactions on asset, liability, and stockholder's equity accounts.

**Solution** Each transaction that is recorded is entered in the general journal. The three activities would be recorded as follows.

| | | |
|---|---|---|
| 1. Cash | 20,000 | |
|     Common Stock | | 20,000 |
|       (Issued shares of stock for cash) | | |
| 2. Equipment | 4,800 | |
|     Accounts Payable | | 4,800 |
|       (Purchase equipment on account) | | |
| 3. No entry because no transaction has occurred. | | |

Related exercise material: *BE2-3, BE2-6, E2-3, E2-5, E2-6, and E2-7.*

✔ *The Navigator*

# The Ledger

The entire group of accounts maintained by a company is the **ledger**. The ledger keeps in one place all the information about changes in specific account balances.

Companies may use various kinds of ledgers, but every company has a general ledger. A **general ledger** contains all the asset, liability, and stockholder's equity accounts, as shown in Illustration 2-16. Whenever we use the term "ledger" in this textbook without a modifying adjective, we mean the general ledger.

**STUDY OBJECTIVE 5**

Explain what a ledger is and how it helps in the recording process.

**Illustration 2-16**
The general ledger

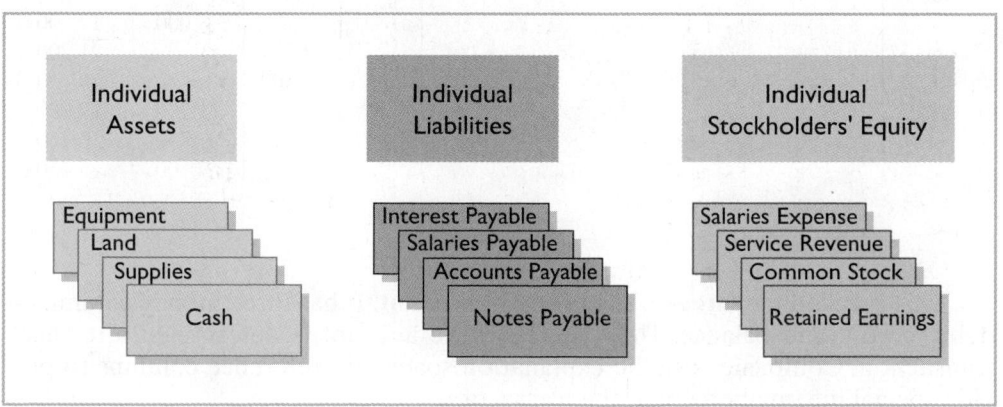

Companies arrange the ledger in the sequence in which they present the accounts in the financial statements, beginning with the balance sheet accounts. First in order are the asset accounts, followed by liability accounts, stockholders' equity accounts, revenues, and expenses. Each account is numbered for easier identification.

The ledger provides the balances in various accounts. For example, the Cash account shows the amount of cash available to meet current obligations. Accounts Receivable shows amounts due from customers. Accounts Payable shows amounts owned to creditors.

# ACCOUNTING ACROSS THE ORGANIZATION

### What Would Sam Do?

In his autobiography Sam Walton described the double-entry accounting system he used when Wal-Mart was just getting started: "We kept a little pigeonhole on the wall for the cash receipts and paperwork of each [Wal-Mart] store. I had a blue binder ledger book for each store. When we added a store, we added a pigeonhole. We did this at least up to twenty stores. Then once a month, the bookkeeper and I would enter the merchandise, enter the sales, enter the cash, and balance it."

**Source:** Sam Walton, *Made in America* (New York: Doubleday, 1992), p. 53.

**?** Why did Sam Walton keep separate pigeonholes and blue binders? Why bother to keep separate records for each store?

## STANDARD FORM OF ACCOUNT

The simple T-account form used in accounting textbooks is often very useful for illustration purposes. However, in practice, the account forms used in ledgers are much more structured. Illustration 2-17 shows a typical form, using assumed data from a cash account.

**Illustration 2-17**
Three-column form of account

| CASH | | | | | NO. 101 |
| --- | --- | --- | --- | --- | --- |
| **Date** | **Explanation** | **Ref.** | **Debit** | **Credit** | **Balance** |
| 2008 | | | | | |
| June  1 | | | 25,000 | | 25,000 |
|       2 | | | | 8,000 | 17,000 |
|       3 | | | 4,200 | | 21,200 |
|       9 | | | 7,500 | | 28,700 |
|      17 | | | | 11,700 | 17,000 |
|      20 | | | | 250 | 16,750 |
|      30 | | | | 7,300 | 9,450 |

This is called the **three-column form of account**. It has three money columns—debit, credit, and balance. The balance in the account is determined after each transaction. Companies use the explanation space and reference columns to provide special information about the transaction.

## POSTING

Transferring journal entries to the ledger accounts is called **posting**. This phase of the recording process accumulates the effects of journalized transactions into the individual accounts. Posting involves the following steps.

1. In the ledger, enter, in the appropriate columns of the account(s) debited, the date, journal page, and debit amount shown in the journal.
2. In the reference column of the journal, write the account number to which the debit amount was posted.
3. In the ledger, enter, in the appropriate columns of the account(s) credited, the date, journal page, and credit amount shown in the journal.
4. In the reference column of the journal, write the account number to which the credit amount was posted.

Illustration 2-18 shows these four steps using Softbyte Inc.'s first journal entry. The boxed numbers indicate the sequence of the steps.

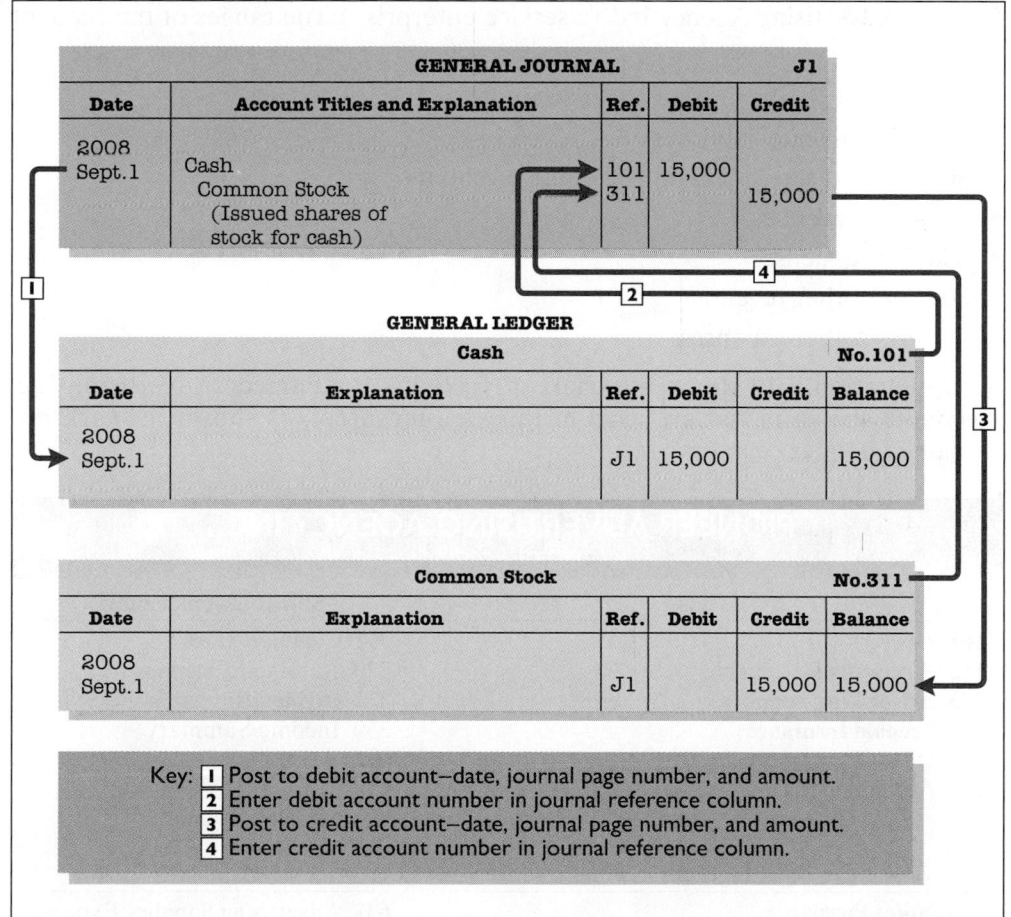

**Illustration 2-18**
Posting a journal entry

Posting should be performed in chronological order. That is, the company should post all the debits and credits of one journal entry before proceeding to the next journal entry. Postings should be made on a timely basis to ensure that the ledger is up to date.[2]

---

[2]In homework problems, you can journalize all transactions before posting any of the journal entries.

The reference column **of a ledger** account indicates the journal page from which the transaction was posted.[3] The explanation space of the ledger account is used infrequently because an explanation already appears in the journal.

## CHART OF ACCOUNTS

The number and type of accounts differ for each company. The number of accounts depends on the amount of detail management desires. For example, the management of one company may want a single account for all types of utility expense. Another may keep separate expense accounts for each type of utility, such as gas, electricity, and water. Similarly, a small company like Softbyte Inc. will have fewer accounts than a corporate giant like Dell. Softbyte may be able to manage and report its activities in twenty to thirty accounts, while Dell may require thousands of accounts to keep track of its worldwide activities.

Most companies have a **chart of accounts**. This chart lists the accounts and the account numbers that identify their location in the ledger. The numbering system that identifies the accounts usually starts with the balance sheet accounts and follows with the income statement accounts.

In this and the next two chapters, we will be explaining the accounting for Pioneer Advertising Agency Inc. (a service enterprise). The ranges of the account numbers are as follows:

- Accounts 101–199 indicate asset accounts
- 200–299 indicate liabilities
- 300–399 indicate stockholder's equity accounts
- 400–499, revenues
- 500–799, expenses
- 800–899, other revenues
- 900–999, other expenses.

Illustration 2-19 shows the chart of accounts for Pioneer Advertising Inc. Accounts shown in red are used in this chapter; accounts shown in black are explained in later chapters.

**Illustration 2-19**
Chart of accounts for Pioneer Advertising Agency Inc.

### PIONEER ADVERTISING AGENCY INC.
#### Chart of Accounts

| Assets | Stockholders' Equity |
|---|---|
| **101 Cash** | **311 Common Stock** |
| 112 Accounts Receivable | 320 Retained Earnings |
| **126 Advertising Supplies** | **332 Dividends** |
| **130 Prepaid Insurance** | 350 Income Summary |
| **157 Office Equipment** | |
| 158 Accumulated Depreciation—Office Equipment | **Revenues** |
| | **400 Service Revenue** |
| **Liabilities** | **Expenses** |
| **200 Notes Payable** | 631 Advertising Supplies Expense |
| **201 Accounts Payable** | 711 Depreciation Expense |
| **209 Unearned Revenue** | 722 Insurance Expense |
| 212 Salaries Payable | **726 Salaries Expense** |
| 230 Interest Payable | **729 Rent Expense** |
| | 905 Interest Expense |

---

[3]After the last entry has been posted, the accountant should scan the reference column **in the journal**, to confirm that all postings have been made.

You will notice that there are gaps in the numbering system of the chart of accounts for Pioneer Advertising. Gaps are left to permit the insertion of new accounts as needed during the life of the business.

# THE RECORDING PROCESS ILLUSTRATED

Illustrations 2-20 through 2-29 show the basic steps in the recording process, using the October transactions of Pioneer Advertising Agency Inc. Pioneer's accounting period is a month. A basic analysis and a debit-credit analysis precede the journalizing and posting of each transaction. For simplicity, we use the T-account form in the illustrations instead of the standard account form.

Study these transaction analyses carefully. **The purpose of transaction analysis is first to identify the type of account involved, and then to determine whether to make a debit or a credit to the account.** You should always perform this type of analysis before preparing a journal entry. Doing so will help you understand the journal entries discussed in this chapter as well as more complex journal entries in later chapters.

In addition, an Accounting Cycle Tutorial at the book's website, **www.wiley.com/college/weygandt**, provides an interactive presentation of the steps in the accounting cycle, using the examples in the illustrations on the following pages.

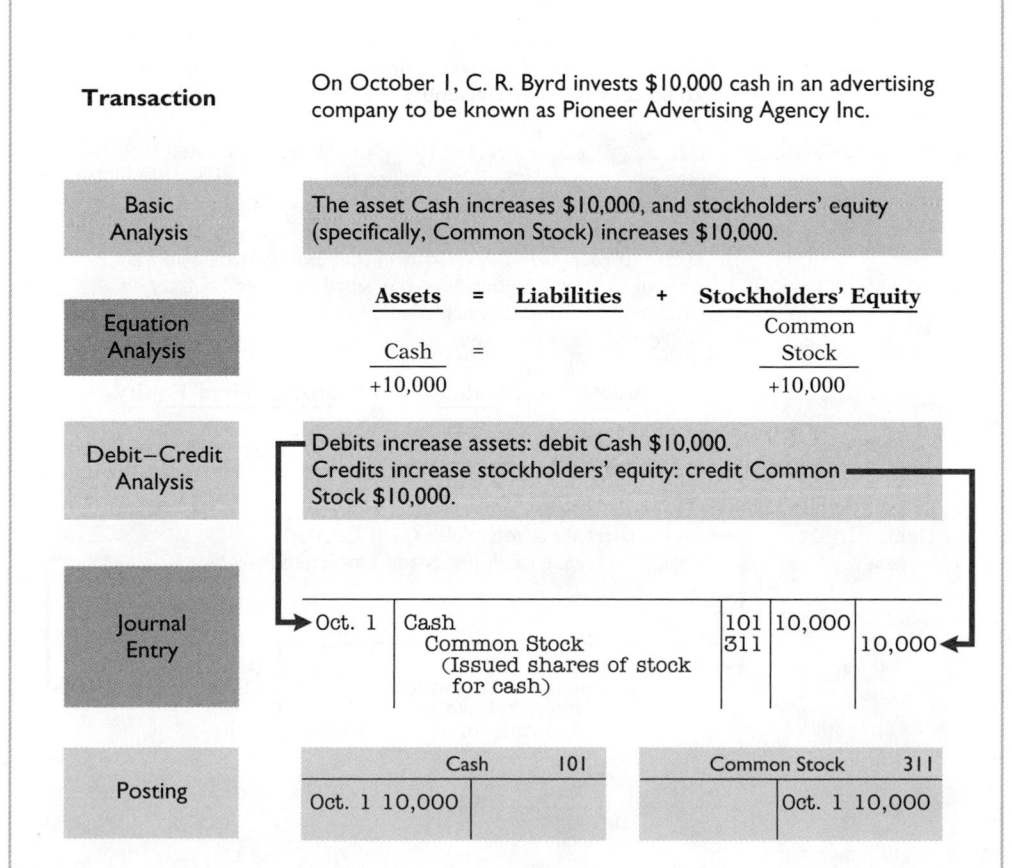

**Illustration 2-20**
Investment of cash by stockholders

**HELPFUL HINT**
Follow these steps:
1. Determine what type of account is involved.
2. Determine what items increased or decreased and by how much.
3. Translate the increases and decreases into debits and credits.

**Illustration 2-21**
Purchase of office equipment

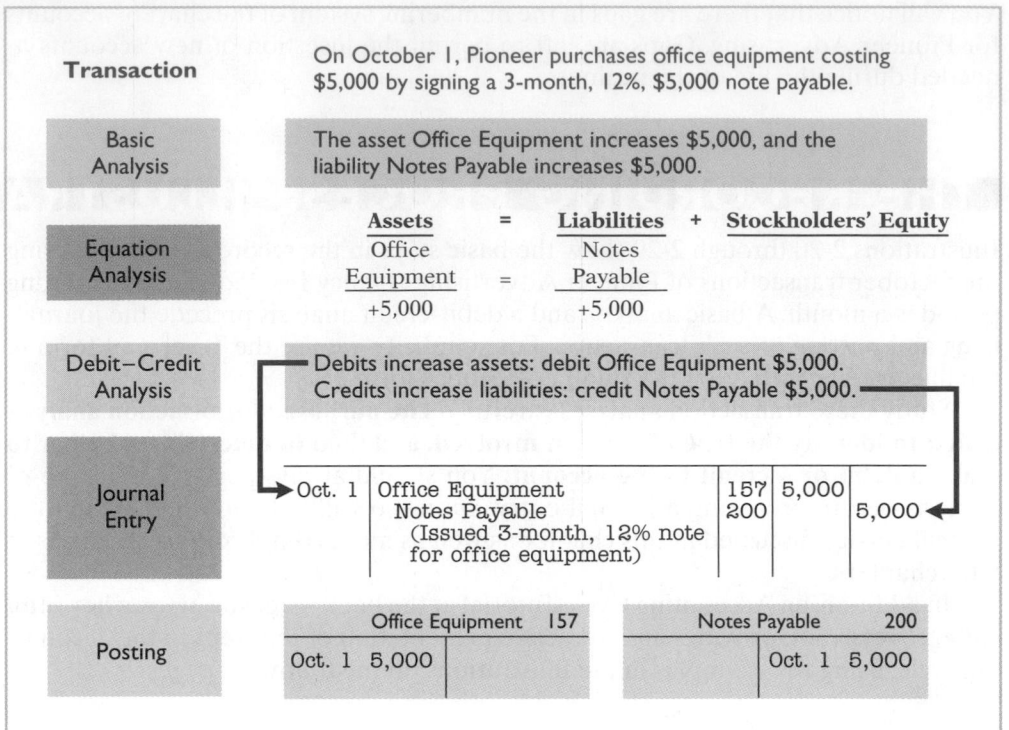

**Illustration 2-22**
Receipt of cash for future service

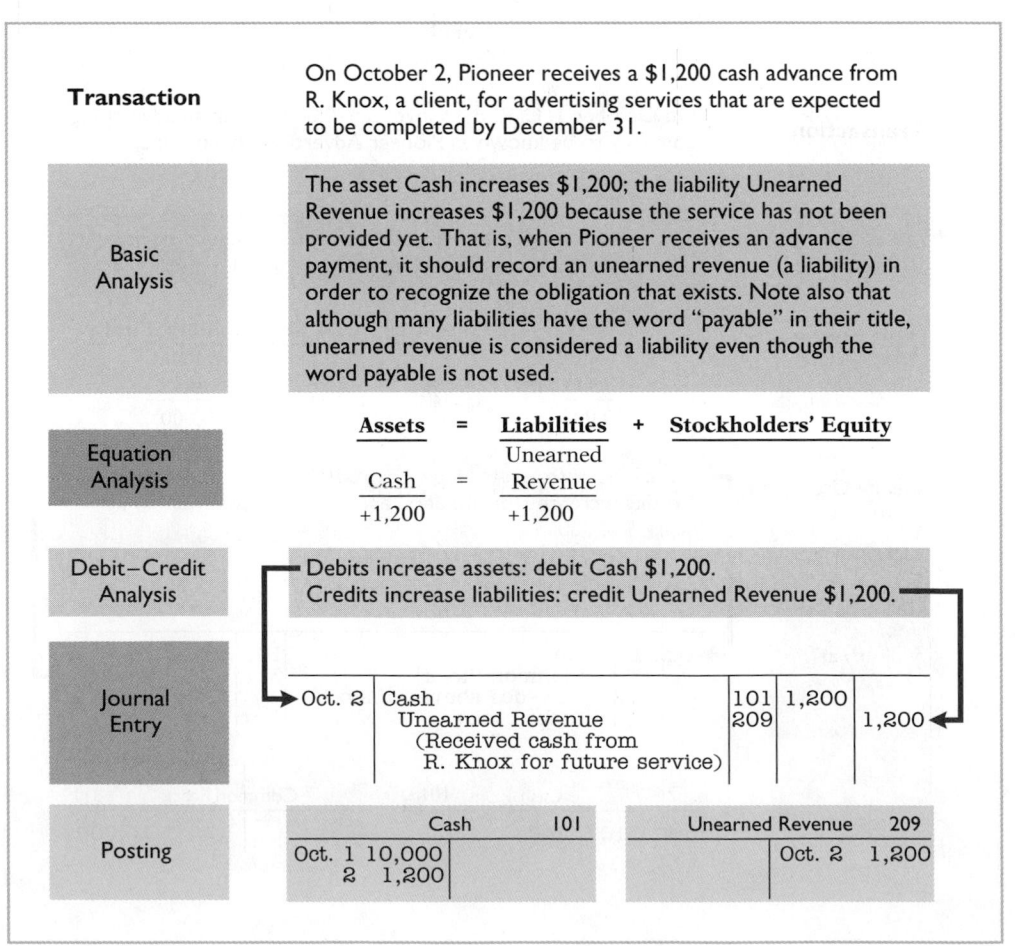

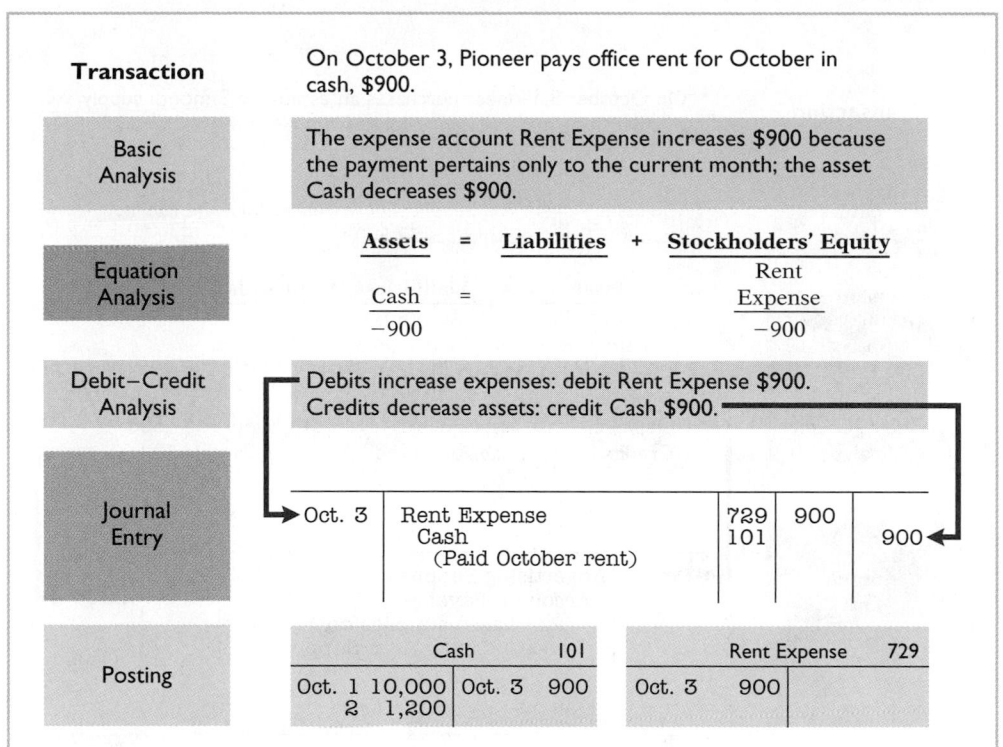

**Illustration 2-23**
Payment of monthly rent

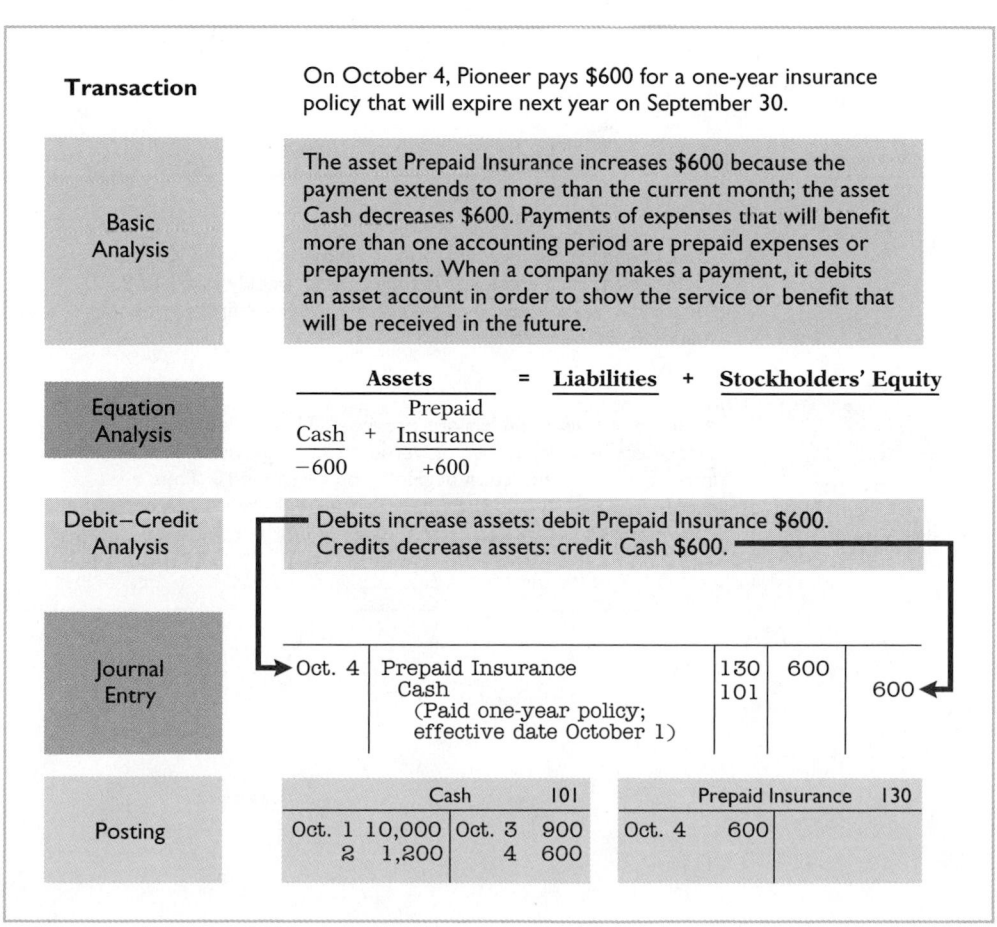

**Illustration 2-24**
Payment for insurance

**Illustration 2-25**
Purchase of supplies on credit

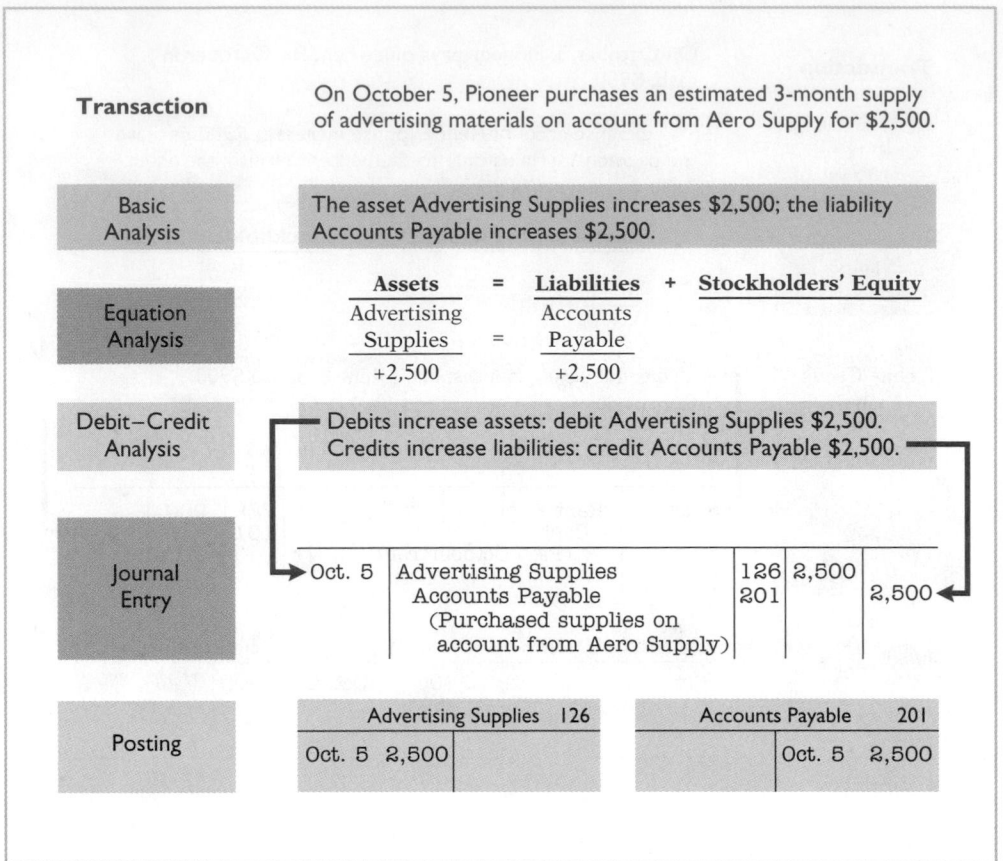

| | |
|---|---|
| **Transaction** | On October 5, Pioneer purchases an estimated 3-month supply of advertising materials on account from Aero Supply for $2,500. |
| Basic Analysis | The asset Advertising Supplies increases $2,500; the liability Accounts Payable increases $2,500. |

**Equation Analysis**

| **Assets** | = | **Liabilities** | + | **Stockholders' Equity** |
|---|---|---|---|---|
| Advertising Supplies | = | Accounts Payable | | |
| +2,500 | | +2,500 | | |

**Debit–Credit Analysis**

Debits increase assets: debit Advertising Supplies $2,500.
Credits increase liabilities: credit Accounts Payable $2,500.

**Journal Entry**

| Oct. 5 | Advertising Supplies | 126 | 2,500 | |
|---|---|---|---|---|
| | Accounts Payable | 201 | | 2,500 |
| | (Purchased supplies on account from Aero Supply) | | | |

**Posting**

| Advertising Supplies 126 | | | Accounts Payable 201 | |
|---|---|---|---|---|
| Oct. 5 2,500 | | | | Oct. 5 2,500 |

**Illustration 2-26**
Hiring of employees

| | |
|---|---|
| **Event** | On October 9, Pioneer hires four employees to begin work on October 15. Each employee is to receive a weekly salary of $500 for a 5-day work week, payable every 2 weeks—first payment made on October 26. |
| Basic Analysis | A business transaction has not occurred. There is only an agreement between the employer and the employees to enter into a business transaction beginning on October 15. Thus, a debit–credit analysis is not needed because there is no accounting entry. (See transaction of October 26 for first entry.) |

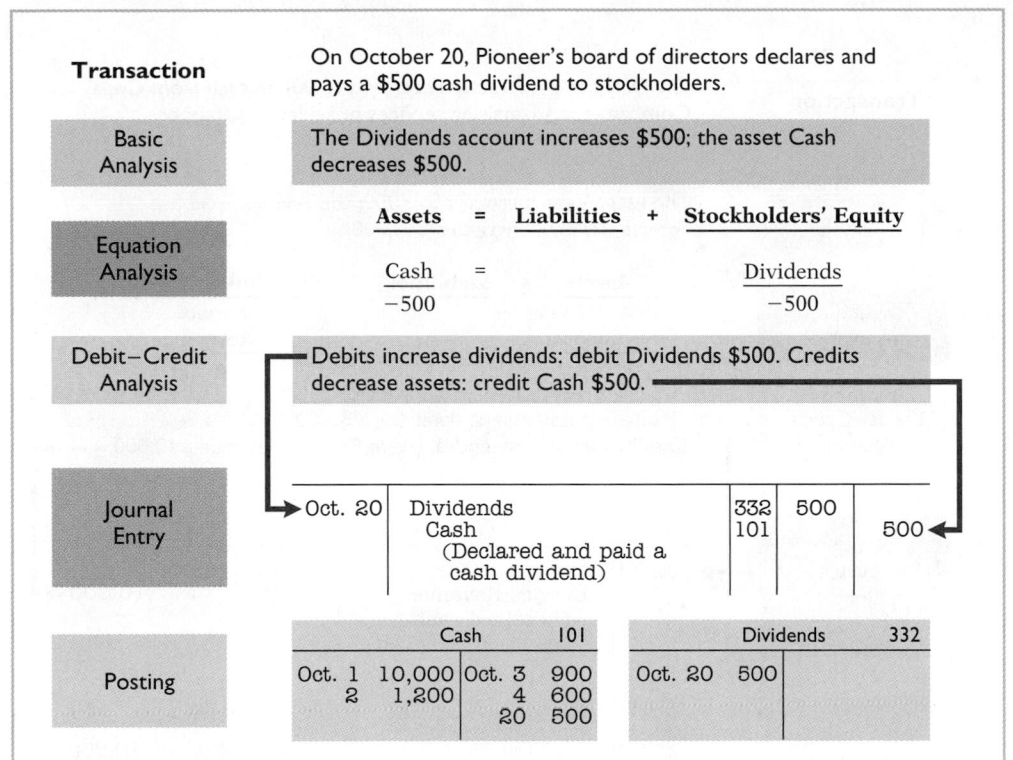

**Illustration 2-27**
Declaration and payment of dividend

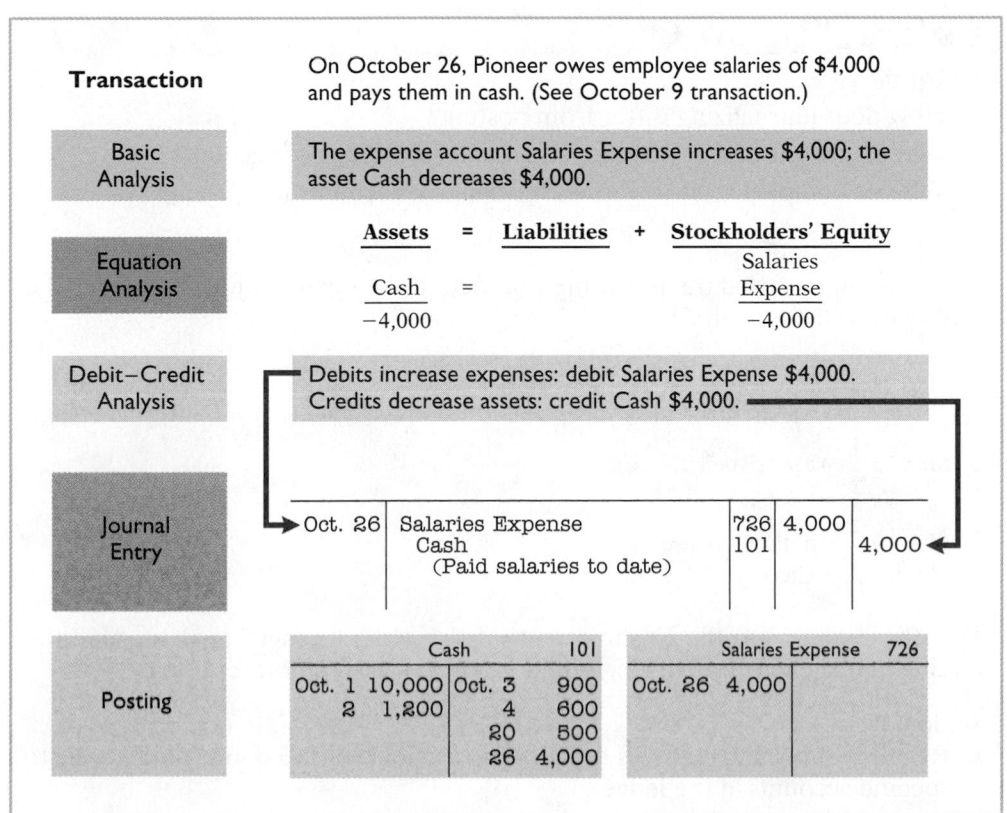

**Illustration 2-28**
Payment of salaries

**Illustration 2-29**
Receipt of cash for services provided

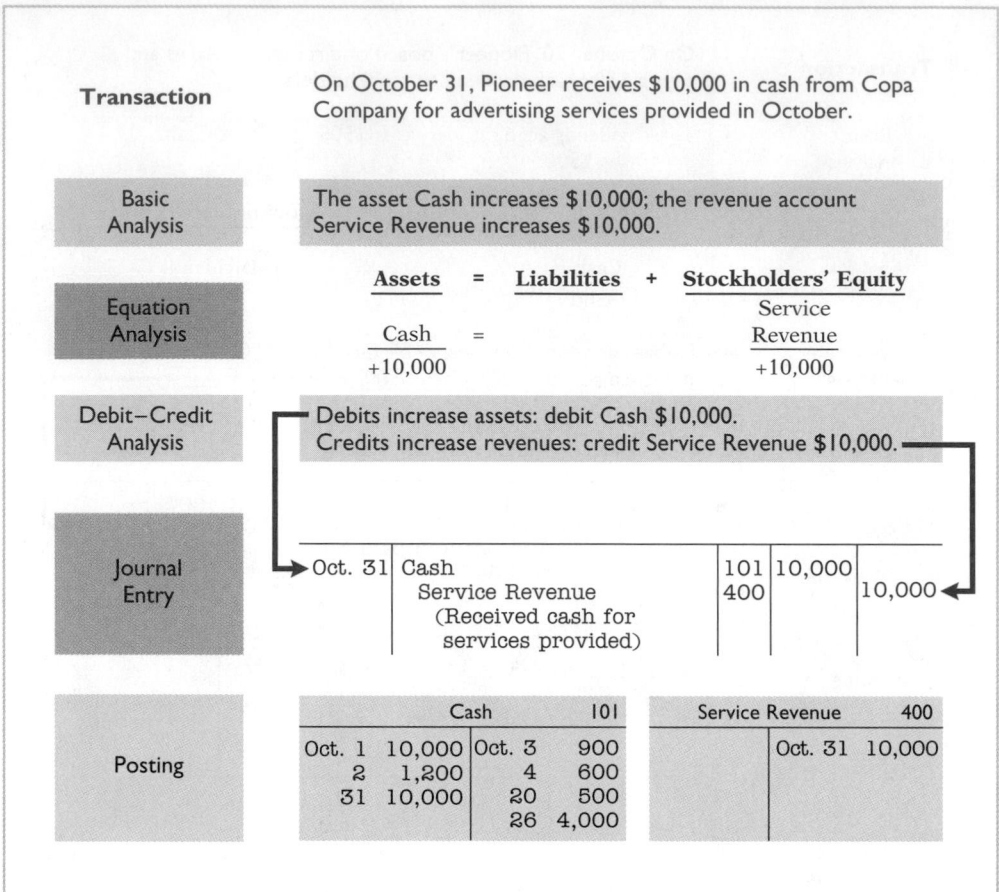

## Before You Go On...

### REVIEW IT

1. How does journalizing differ from posting?
2. What is the purpose of (a) the ledger and (b) a chart of accounts?
3. Why do companies leave gaps in the chart of accounts numbering system?

### DO IT

Kate Brown recorded the following transactions in a general journal during the month of March.

| | | | |
|---|---|---|---|
| Mar. 4 | Cash | 2,280 | |
| | Service Revenue | | 2,280 |
| Mar. 15 | Wages Expense | 400 | |
| | Cash | | 400 |
| Mar. 19 | Utilities Expense | 92 | |
| | Cash | | 92 |

Post these entries to the Cash account of the general ledger to determine the ending balance in cash. The beginning balance in cash on March 1 was $600.

### Action Plan

■ Recall that posting involves transferring the journalized debits and credits to specific accounts in the ledger.

■ Determine the ending balance by netting the total debits and credits.

**Solution**

|  | Cash |  |  |  |  |
|---|---|---|---|---|---|
| 3/1 | 600 | 3/15 | 400 |
| 3/4 | 2,280 | 3/19 | 92 |
| 3/31 Bal. | 2,388 |  |  |

Related exercise material: *BE2-7, BE2-8, E2-8, and E2-12.*

*The Navigator*

# Summary Illustration of Journalizing and Posting

Illustration 2-30 shows the journal for Pioneer Advertising Agency for October. Illustration 2-31, on page 68, shows the ledger, with all balances in color.

| GENERAL JOURNAL | | | | PAGE J1 | |
|---|---|---|---|---|---|
| **Date** | **Account Titles and Explanation** | **Ref.** | **Debit** | **Credit** | |
| 2008 Oct. 1 | Cash | 101 | 10,000 | | |
| | Common Stock | 311 | | 10,000 | |
| | (Issued shares of stock for cash) | | | | |
| 1 | Office Equipment | 157 | 5,000 | | |
| | Notes Payable | 200 | | 5,000 | |
| | (Issued 3-month, 12% note for office equipment) | | | | |
| 2 | Cash | 101 | 1,200 | | |
| | Unearned Revenue | 209 | | 1,200 | |
| | (Received cash from R. Knox for future service) | | | | |
| 3 | Rent Expense | 729 | 900 | | |
| | Cash | 101 | | 900 | |
| | (Paid October rent) | | | | |
| 4 | Prepaid Insurance | 130 | 600 | | |
| | Cash | 101 | | 600 | |
| | (Paid one-year policy; effective date October 1) | | | | |
| 5 | Advertising Supplies | 126 | 2,500 | | |
| | Accounts Payable | 201 | | 2,500 | |
| | (Purchased supplies on account from Aero Supply) | | | | |
| 20 | Dividends | 332 | 500 | | |
| | Cash | 101 | | 500 | |
| | (Declared and paid a cash dividend) | | | | |
| 26 | Salaries Expense | 726 | 4,000 | | |
| | Cash | 101 | | 4,000 | |
| | (Paid salaries to date) | | | | |
| 31 | Cash | 101 | 10,000 | | |
| | Service Revenue | 400 | | 10,000 | |
| | (Received cash for services provided) | | | | |

**Illustration 2-30**
General journal entries

## GENERAL LEDGER

### Cash | | | | | No. 101

| Date | Explanation | Ref. | Debit | Credit | Balance |
|------|-------------|------|-------|--------|---------|
| 2008 | | | | | |
| Oct. 1 | | J1 | 10,000 | | 10,000 |
| 2 | | J1 | 1,200 | | 11,200 |
| 3 | | J1 | | 900 | 10,300 |
| 4 | | J1 | | 600 | 9,700 |
| 20 | | J1 | | 500 | 9,200 |
| 26 | | J1 | | 4,000 | 5,200 |
| 31 | | J1 | 10,000 | | **15,200** |

### Advertising Supplies | | | | | No. 126

| Date | Explanation | Ref. | Debit | Credit | Balance |
|------|-------------|------|-------|--------|---------|
| 2008 | | | | | |
| Oct. 5 | | J1 | 2,500 | | **2,500** |

### Prepaid Insurance | | | | | No. 130

| Date | Explanation | Ref. | Debit | Credit | Balance |
|------|-------------|------|-------|--------|---------|
| 2008 | | | | | |
| Oct. 4 | | J1 | 600 | | **600** |

### Office Equipment | | | | | No. 157

| Date | Explanation | Ref. | Debit | Credit | Balance |
|------|-------------|------|-------|--------|---------|
| 2008 | | | | | |
| Oct. 1 | | J1 | 5,000 | | **5,000** |

### Notes Payable | | | | | No. 200

| Date | Explanation | Ref. | Debit | Credit | Balance |
|------|-------------|------|-------|--------|---------|
| 2008 | | | | | |
| Oct. 1 | | J1 | | 5,000 | **5,000** |

### Accounts Payable | | | | | No. 201

| Date | Explanation | Ref. | Debit | Credit | Balance |
|------|-------------|------|-------|--------|---------|
| 2008 | | | | | |
| Oct. 5 | | J1 | | 2,500 | **2,500** |

### Unearned Revenue | | | | | No. 209

| Date | Explanation | Ref. | Debit | Credit | Balance |
|------|-------------|------|-------|--------|---------|
| 2008 | | | | | |
| Oct. 2 | | J1 | | 1,200 | **1,200** |

### Common Stock | | | | | No. 311

| Date | Explanation | Ref. | Debit | Credit | Balance |
|------|-------------|------|-------|--------|---------|
| 2008 | | | | | |
| Oct. 1 | | J1 | | 10,000 | **10,000** |

### Dividends | | | | | No. 332

| Date | Explanation | Ref. | Debit | Credit | Balance |
|------|-------------|------|-------|--------|---------|
| 2008 | | | | | |
| Oct. 20 | | J1 | 500 | | **500** |

### Service Revenue | | | | | No. 400

| Date | Explanation | Ref. | Debit | Credit | Balance |
|------|-------------|------|-------|--------|---------|
| 2008 | | | | | |
| Oct. 31 | | J1 | | 10,000 | **10,000** |

### Salaries Expense | | | | | No. 726

| Date | Explanation | Ref. | Debit | Credit | Balance |
|------|-------------|------|-------|--------|---------|
| 2008 | | | | | |
| Oct. 26 | | J1 | 4,000 | | **4,000** |

### Rent Expense | | | | | No. 729

| Date | Explanation | Ref. | Debit | Credit | Balance |
|------|-------------|------|-------|--------|---------|
| 2008 | | | | | |
| Oct. 3 | | J1 | 900 | | **900** |

**Illustration 2-31**
General ledger

# THE TRIAL BALANCE

**STUDY OBJECTIVE 7**

Prepare a trial balance and explain its purposes.

A **trial balance** is a list of accounts and their balances at a given time. Customarily, companies prepare a trial balance at the end of an accounting period. They list accounts in the order in which they appear in the ledger. Debit balances appear in the left column and credit balances in the right column.

**The primary purpose of a trial balance is to prove (check) that the debits equal the credits after posting.** The sum of the debit balances in the trial balance should equal the sum of the credit balances. If the debits and credits do not agree, the company can use the trial balance to uncover errors in journalizing and posting. In addition, the trial balance is useful in preparing financial statements, as we will explain in the next two chapters.

The steps for preparing a trial balance are:

1. List the account titles and their balances.
2. Total the debit and credit columns.
3. Prove the equality of the two columns.

Illustration 2-32 shows the trial balance prepared from Pioneer Advertising's ledger. Note that the total debits ($28,700) equal the total credits ($28,700).

| PIONEER ADVERTISING AGENCY INC. Trial Balance October 31, 2008 | | |
| --- | --- | --- |
| | **Debit** | **Credit** |
| Cash | $15,200 | |
| Advertising Supplies | 2,500 | |
| Prepaid Insurance | 600 | |
| Office Equipment | 5,000 | |
| Notes Payable | | $ 5,000 |
| Accounts Payable | | 2,500 |
| Unearned Revenue | | 1,200 |
| Common Stock | | 10,000 |
| Dividends | 500 | |
| Service Revenue | | 10,000 |
| Salaries Expense | 4,000 | |
| Rent Expense | 900 | |
| | **$28,700** | **$28,700** |

**Illustration 2-32**
A trial balance

**HELPFUL HINT**

To sum a column of figures is sometimes referred to as to *foot* the column. The column is then said to be *footed.*

**HELPFUL HINT**

A trial balance is so named because it is a test to see if the sum of the debit balances equals the sum of the credit balances.

A trial balance is a necessary checkpoint for uncovering certain types of errors before you proceed to other steps in the accounting process. For example, if only the debit portion of a journal entry has been posted, the trial balance would bring this error to light.

## Limitations of a Trial Balance

A trial balance does not guarantee freedom from recording errors. Numerous errors may exist even though the trial balance columns agree. For example, the trial balance may balance even when (1) a transaction is not journalized, (2) a correct journal entry is not posted, (3) a journal entry is posted twice, (4) incorrect accounts are used in journalizing or posting, or (5) offsetting errors are made in recording the amount of a transaction. As long as equal debits and credits are posted, even to the wrong account or in the wrong amount, the total debits will equal the total credits. **The trial balance does not prove that the company has recorded all transactions or that the ledger is correct.**

**ETHICS NOTE**

An *error* is the result of an unintentional mistake; it is neither ethical nor unethical. An *irregularity* is an intentional misstatement, which *is* viewed as unethical.

## Locating Errors

Errors in a trial balance generally result from mathematical mistakes, incorrect postings, or simply transcribing data incorrectly. What do you do if you are faced with a trial balance that does not balance? First determine the amount of the difference between the two columns of the trial balance. After this amount is known, the following steps are often helpful:

1.  If the error is $1, $10, $100, or $1,000, re-add the trial balance columns and re-compute the account balances.
2.  If the error is divisible by 2, scan the trial balance to see whether a balance equal to half the error has been entered in the wrong column.
3.  If the error is divisible by 9, retrace the account balances on the trial balance to see whether they are incorrectly copied from the ledger. For example, if a balance was $12 and it was listed as $21, a $9 error has been made. Reversing the order of numbers is called a **transposition error**.
4.  If the error is not divisible by 2 or 9, scan the ledger to see whether an account balance in the amount of the error has been omitted from the trial balance, and scan the journal to see whether a posting of that amount has been omitted.

## Use of Dollar Signs

Note that dollar signs do not appear in journals or ledgers. Dollar signs are typically used only in the trial balance and the financial statements. Generally, a dollar sign is shown only for the first item in the column and for the total of that column. A single line is placed under the column of figures to be added or subtracted; the total amount is double-underlined to indicate the final sum.

# ETHICS INSIGHT

### Sarbanes-Oxley Comes to the Rescue

While most companies record transactions very carefully, the reality is that mistakes still happen: Bank regulators fined Bank One Corporation (now Chase) $1.8 million; they felt that the unreliability of the bank's accounting system caused it to violate regulatory requirements. Also, in recent years Fannie Mae, the government-chartered mortgage association, announced large accounting errors. These announcements caused investors, regulators, and politicians to fear larger, undetected problems. Such problems could spill over into the home-mortgage market, which depends on Fannie Mae to buy hundreds of billions of dollars of mortgages each year. Finally, before a major overhaul of its accounting system, the financial records of Waste Management Company were in such disarray that of the company's 57,000 employees, 10,000 were receiving pay slips that were in error.

The Sarbanes-Oxley Act of 2002 was created to minimize the occurrence of errors like these by increasing every employee's responsibility for accurate financial reporting.

In order for these companies to prepare and issue financial statements, their accounting equations (debits and credits) must have been in balance at year-end. How could these errors or misstatements have occurred?

## Before You Go On...

**REVIEW IT**
1.  What is a trial balance, and what is its primary purpose?
2.  How is a trial balance prepared?
3.  What are the limitations of a trial balance?

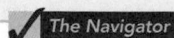

 Be sure to read **ALL ABOUT YOU:** *Your Personal Annual Report* on the next page for information on how topics in this chapter apply to you.

# all about Y✷U

## Your Personal Annual Report

If you haven't already done so, in the not-too-distant future you will prepare a résumé. In some ways your résumé is like a company's annual report. Its purpose is to enable others to evaluate your past, in an effort to predict your future.

A résumé is your opportunity to create a positive first impression. It is important that it be impressive—but it should also be accurate. In order to increase their job prospects, some people are tempted to "inflate" their résumés by overstating the importance of some past accomplishments or positions. In fact, you might even think that "everybody does it" and that if you don't do it, you will be at a disadvantage.

### ✷ Some Facts

Before you turn your résumé into a world-class work of fiction, consider the following:

✷ David Edmondson, the president and CEO of well-known electronics retailer Radio Shack, overstated his accomplishments by claiming that he had earned a bachelor's of science degree, when in fact he had not. Apparently his employer had not done a background check to ensure the accuracy of his résumé.

✷ A chief financial officer of Veritas Software lied about having an M.B.A. from Stanford University.

✷ A former president of the U.S. Olympic Committee, lied about having a Ph.D. from Arizona State University. When the truth was discovered, she resigned.

✷ The University of Notre Dame discovered that its football coach, George O'Leary, lied about his education and football history. He was forced to resign after only five days.

✷ Jeffrey Papows was chairman of Lotus, a $1.4 billion subsidiary of IBM. When it came out that he had made up facts about his life, including a Ph.D. and a black belt in the martial arts, Papows resigned.

✷ Quincy Troupe, former California poet laureate, was well-respected within the California artistic and academic communities—until lies about his college background were exposed.

Tips on resume writing can be found at many websites, such as *http://resume.monster.com/.*

### ✷ About the Numbers

• A survey by Automatic Data Processing reported that 40% of applicants misrepresented their education or employment history.

• A survey by the Society for Human Resource Management of human resource professionals reported the following responses to the question, "*When investigating the backgrounds of job candidates, how important or unimportant is the discovery of inaccuracies in the job candidate's résumé on your decision to extend a job offer?*"

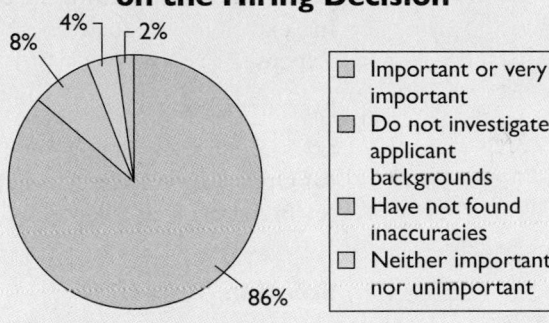

**Importance of Résumé Inaccuracies on the Hiring Decision**

- 8%
- 4%
- 2%
- 86%

□ Important or very important
□ Do not investigate applicant backgrounds
□ Have not found inaccuracies
□ Neither important nor unimportant

**Source:** Society for Human Resource Management, press release, August 31, 2004, *http://www.shrm.org/press/ntu_published/cms_009624.asp.*

### ✷ What Do You Think?

Using Radio Shack as an example, what should the company have done when it learned of the falsehoods on Mr. Edmondson's résumé? Should Radio Shack have fired him?

**NO:** Mr. Edmondson had been a Radio Shack employee for 11 years. He had served the company in a wide variety of positions, and had earned the position of CEO through exceptional performance. While the fact that he lied 11 years earlier on his résumé was unfortunate, his service since then made this past transgression irrelevant. In addition, the company was in the midst of a massive restructuring, which included closing 700 of its 7,000 stores. It could not afford additional upheaval at this time.

**YES:** Radio Shack is a publicly traded company. Investors, creditors, employees, and others doing business with the company will not trust it if its leader is known to have poor integrity. The "tone at the top" is vital to creating an ethical organization.

**Sources:** E. White and T. Herrick, "Ethical Breaches Pose Dilemma for Boards: When to Fire a CEO?" *Wall Street Journal,* February 15, 2006; and T. Hanrahan, "Résumé Trouble," *Wall Street Journal,* March 3, 2006.

## Demonstration Problem

Bob Sample and other student investors opened Campus Laundromat Inc. on September 1, 2008. During the first month of operations the following transactions occurred.

| Sept. | 1 | Stockholders invested $20,000 cash in the business. |
|---|---|---|
| | 2 | Paid $1,000 cash for store rent for the month of September. |
| | 3 | Purchased washers and dryers for $25,000, paying $10,000 in cash and signing a $15,000, 6-month, 12% note payable. |
| | 4 | Paid $1,200 for a one-year accident insurance policy. |
| | 10 | Received a bill from the *Daily News* for advertising the opening of the laundromat $200. |
| | 20 | Declared and paid a cash dividend to stockholders $700. |
| | 30 | Determined that cash receipts for laundry fees for the month were $6,200. |

The chart of accounts for the company is the same as for Pioneer Advertising Agency Inc. except for the following: No. 154 Laundry Equipment and No. 610 Advertising Expense.

### Instructions

**(a)** Journalize the September transactions. (Use **J1** for the journal page number.)
**(b)** Open ledger accounts and post the September transactions.
**(c)** Prepare a trial balance at September 30, 2008.

### action plan

✔ Make separate journal entries for each transaction.

✔ In journalizing, make sure debits equal credits.

✔ In journalizing, use specific account titles taken from the chart of accounts.

✔ Provide appropriate description of journal entry.

✔ Arrange ledger in statement order, beginning with the balance sheet accounts.

✔ Post in chronological order.

✔ Use numbers in the reference column to indicate the amount has been posted.

✔ In the trial balance, list accounts in the order in which they appear in the ledger.

✔ List debit balances in the left column, and credit balances in the right column.

### Solution

**(a)**

| | GENERAL JOURNAL | | | **J1** |
|---|---|---|---|---|

| Date | Account Titles and Explanation | Ref. | Debit | Credit |
|---|---|---|---|---|
| 2008 | | | | |
| Sept. 1 | Cash | 101 | 20,000 | |
| |     Common Stock | 311 | | 20,000 |
| |        (Stockholders investment of cash in business) | | | |
| 2 | Rent Expense | 729 | 1,000 | |
| |     Cash | 101 | | 1,000 |
| |        (Paid September rent) | | | |
| 3 | Laundry Equipment | 154 | 25,000 | |
| |     Cash | 101 | | 10,000 |
| |     Notes Payable | 200 | | 15,000 |
| |        (Purchased laundry equipment for cash and 6-month, 12% note payable) | | | |
| 4 | Prepaid Insurance | 130 | 1,200 | |
| |     Cash | 101 | | 1,200 |
| |        (Paid one-year insurance policy) | | | |
| 10 | Advertising Expense | 610 | 200 | |
| |     Accounts Payable | 201 | | 200 |
| |        (Received bill from *Daily News* for advertising) | | | |
| 20 | Dividends | 332 | 700 | |
| |     Cash | 101 | | 700 |
| |        (Declared and paid a cash dividend) | | | |
| 30 | Cash | 101 | 6,200 | |
| |     Service Revenue | 400 | | 6,200 |
| |        (Received cash for laundry fees earned) | | | |

**(b)**

## GENERAL LEDGER

### Cash     No. 101

| Date | Explanation | Ref. | Debit | Credit | Balance |
|------|-------------|------|-------|--------|---------|
| 2008 |  |  |  |  |  |
| Sept. 1 |  | J1 | 20,000 |  | 20,000 |
| 2 |  | J1 |  | 1,000 | 19,000 |
| 3 |  | J1 |  | 10,000 | 9,000 |
| 4 |  | J1 |  | 1,200 | 7,800 |
| 20 |  | J1 |  | 700 | 7,100 |
| 30 |  | J1 | 6,200 |  | 13,300 |

### Prepaid Insurance     No. 130

| Date | Explanation | Ref. | Debit | Credit | Balance |
|------|-------------|------|-------|--------|---------|
| 2008 |  |  |  |  |  |
| Sept. 4 |  | J1 | 1,200 |  | 1,200 |

### Laundry Equipment     No. 154

| Date | Explanation | Ref. | Debit | Credit | Balance |
|------|-------------|------|-------|--------|---------|
| 2008 |  |  |  |  |  |
| Sept. 3 |  | J1 | 25,000 |  | 25,000 |

### Service Revenue     No. 400

| Date | Explanation | Ref. | Debit | Credit | Balance |
|------|-------------|------|-------|--------|---------|
| 2008 |  |  |  |  |  |
| Sept. 30 |  | J1 |  | 6,200 | 6,200 |

### Notes Payable     No. 200

| Date | Explanation | Ref. | Debit | Credit | Balance |
|------|-------------|------|-------|--------|---------|
| 2008 |  |  |  |  |  |
| Sept. 3 |  | J1 |  | 15,000 | 15,000 |

### Accounts Payable     No. 201

| Date | Explanation | Ref. | Debit | Credit | Balance |
|------|-------------|------|-------|--------|---------|
| 2008 |  |  |  |  |  |
| Sept. 10 |  | J1 |  | 200 | 200 |

### Common Stock     No. 311

| Date | Explanation | Ref. | Debit | Credit | Balance |
|------|-------------|------|-------|--------|---------|
| 2008 |  |  |  |  |  |
| Sept. 1 |  | J1 |  | 20,000 | 20,000 |

### Dividends     No. 332

| Date | Explanation | Ref. | Debit | Credit | Balance |
|------|-------------|------|-------|--------|---------|
| 2008 |  |  |  |  |  |
| Sept. 30 |  | J1 | 700 |  | 700 |

### Advertising Expense     No. 610

| Date | Explanation | Ref. | Debit | Credit | Balance |
|------|-------------|------|-------|--------|---------|
| 2008 |  |  |  |  |  |
| Sept. 10 |  | J1 | 200 |  | 200 |

### Rent Expense     No. 729

| Date | Explanation | Ref. | Debit | Credit | Balance |
|------|-------------|------|-------|--------|---------|
| 2008 |  |  |  |  |  |
| Sept. 2 |  | J1 | 1,000 |  | 1,000 |

**(c)**

### CAMPUS LAUNDROMAT INC.
Trial Balance
September 30, 2008

|  | Debit | Credit |
|--|-------|--------|
| Cash | $13,300 |  |
| Prepaid Insurance | 1,200 |  |
| Laundry Equipment | 25,000 |  |
| Notes Payable |  | $15,000 |
| Accounts Payable |  | 200 |
| Common Stock |  | 20,000 |
| Dividends | 700 |  |
| Service Revenue |  | 6,200 |
| Advertising Expense | 200 |  |
| Rent Expense | 1,000 |  |
|  | $41,400 | $41,400 |

*The Navigator*

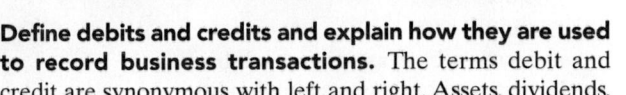

## SUMMARY OF STUDY OBJECTIVES

**1 Explain what an account is and how it helps in the recording process.** An account is a record of increases and decreases in a specific asset, liability, or stockholders' equity item.

**2 Define debits and credits and explain how they are used to record business transactions.** The terms debit and credit are synonymous with left and right. Assets, dividends, and expenses are increased by debits and decreased by credits. Liabilities, common stock, retained earnings, and revenues are increased by credits and decreased by debits.

**3 Identify the basic steps in the recording process.** The basic steps in the recording process are: (a) analyze each transaction for its effects on the accounts, (b) enter the transaction information in a journal, (c) transfer the journal information to the appropriate accounts in the ledger.

**4 Explain what a journal is and how it helps in the recording process.** The initial accounting record of a transaction is entered in a journal before the data are entered in the accounts. A journal (a) discloses in one place the complete effects of a transaction, (b) provides a chronological record of transactions, and (c) prevents or locates errors because the debit and credit amounts for each entry can be easily compared.

**5 Explain what a ledger is and how it helps in the recording process.** The ledger is the entire group of accounts maintained by a company. The ledger keeps in one place all the information about changes in specific account balances.

**6 Explain what posting is and how it helps in the recording process.** Posting is the transfer of journal entries to the ledger accounts. This phase of the recording process accumulates the effects of journalized transactions in the individual accounts.

**7 Prepare a trial balance and explain its purposes.** A trial balance is a list of accounts and their balances at a given time. Its primary purpose is to prove the equality of debits and credits after posting. A trial balance also uncovers errors in journalizing and posting and is useful in preparing financial statements.

*The Navigator*

# GLOSSARY

**Account** A record of increases and decreases in specific asset, liability, or stockholders' equity items. (p. 48).

**Chart of accounts** A list of accounts and the account numbers that identify their location in the ledger. (p. 60).

**Common stock** Issued in exchange for the owners' investment paid in to the corporation. (p. 50).

**Compound entry** A journal entry that involves three or more accounts. (p. 55).

**Credit** The right side of an account. (p. 49).

**Debit** The left side of an account. (p. 49).

**Dividend** A distribution by a corporation to its stockholders on a pro rata (equal) basis. (p. 51).

**Double-entry system** A system that records in appropriate accounts the dual effect of each transaction. (p. 49).

**General journal** The most basic form of journal. (p. 54).

**General ledger** A ledger that contains all asset, liability, and stockholders' equity accounts. (p. 57).

**Journal** An accounting record in which transactions are initially recorded in chronological order. (p. 54).

**Journalizing** The entering of transaction data in the journal. (p. 54).

**Ledger** The entire group of accounts maintained by a company. (p. 57).

**Normal balance** An account balance on the side where an increase in the account is recorded. (p. 50).

**Posting** The transfer of journal entries to the ledger accounts. (p. 59).

**Retained earnings** Net income that is kept (retained) in the business. (p. 51).

**Simple entry** A journal entry that involves only two accounts. (p. 55).

**T account** The basic form of an account. (p. 48).

**Three-column form of account** A form with columns for debit, credit, and balance amounts in an account. (p. 58).

**Trial balance** A list of accounts and their balances at a given time. (p. 68).

# SELF-STUDY QUESTIONS

*Answers are at the end of the chapter.*

(SO 1) **1.** Which of the following statements about an account is true?
  **a.** In its simplest form, an account consists of two parts.
  **b.** An account is an individual accounting record of increases and decreases in specific asset, liability, and owner's equity items.
  **c.** There are separate accounts for specific assets and liabilities but only one account for owner's equity items.
  **d.** The left side of an account is the credit or decrease side.

(SO 2) **2.** Debits:
  **a.** increase both assets and liabilities.
  **b.** decrease both assets and liabilities.
  **c.** increase assets and decrease liabilities.
  **d.** decrease assets and increase liabilities.

**3.** A revenue account: (SO 2)
  **a.** is increased by debits.
  **b.** is decreased by credits.
  **c.** has a normal balance of a debit.
  **d.** is increased by credits.

**4.** Accounts that normally have debit balances are: (SO 2)
  **a.** assets, expenses, and revenues.
  **b.** assets, expenses, and common stock.
  **c.** assets, liabilities, and dividends.
  **d.** assets, dividends, and expenses.

**5.** Which of the following is *not* part of the recording process? (SO 3)
  **a.** Analyzing transactions.
  **b.** Preparing a trial balance.
  **c.** Entering transactions in a journal.
  **d.** Posting transactions.

(SO 4) **6.** Which of the following statements about a journal is *false*?
  **a.** It is not a book of original entry.
  **b.** It provides a chronological record of transactions.
  **c.** It helps to locate errors because the debit and credit amounts for each entry can be readily compared.
  **d.** It discloses in one place the complete effect of a transaction.

(SO 5) **7.** A ledger:
  **a.** contains only asset and liability accounts.
  **b.** should show accounts in alphabetical order.
  **c.** is a collection of the entire group of accounts maintained by a company.
  **d.** is a book of original entry.

(SO 6) **8.** Posting:
  **a.** normally occurs before journalizing.
  **b.** transfers ledger transaction data to the journal.
  **c.** is an optional step in the recording process.
  **d.** transfers journal entries to ledger accounts.

**9.** A trial balance: (SO 7)
  **a.** is a list of accounts with their balances at a given time.
  **b.** proves the mathematical accuracy of journalized transactions.
  **c.** will not balance if a correct journal entry is posted twice.
  **d.** proves that all transactions have been recorded.

**10.** A trial balance will not balance if: (SO 7)
  **a.** a correct journal entry is posted twice.
  **b.** the purchase of supplies on account is debited to Supplies and credited to Cash.
  **c.** a $100 cash withdrawal by the president is debited to Dividends for $1,000 and credited to Cash for $100.
  **d.** a $450 payment on account is debited to Accounts Payable for $45 and credited to Cash for $45.

Go to the book's website,
**www.wiley.com/college/weygandt**,
for Additional Self-Study questions.

 *The Navigator*

# QUESTIONS

**1.** Describe the parts of a T account.

**2.** "The terms *debit* and *credit* mean increase and decrease, respectively." Do you agree? Explain.

**3.** Jeff Hiller, a fellow student, contends that the double-entry system means each transaction must be recorded twice. Is Jeff correct? Explain.

**4.** Maria Alvarez, a beginning accounting student, believes debit balances are favorable and credit balances are unfavorable. Is Maria correct? Discuss.

**5.** State the rules of debit and credit as applied to (a) asset accounts, (b) liability accounts, and (c) the stockholders' equity accounts (revenues, expenses, dividends, common stock, and retained earnings).

**6.** What is the normal balance for each of the following accounts? (a) Accounts Receivable. (b) Cash. (c) Dividends. (d) Accounts Payable. (e) Service Revenue. (f) Salaries Expense. (g) Common Stock.

**7.** Indicate whether each of the following accounts is an asset, a liability, or a stockholders' equity account and whether it has a normal debit or credit balance: (a) Accounts Receivable, (b) Accounts Payable, (c) Equipment, (d) Dividends, (e) Supplies.

**8.** For the following transactions, indicate the account debited and the account credited.
  **(a)** Supplies are purchased on account.
  **(b)** Cash is received on signing a note payable.
  **(c)** Employees are paid salaries in cash.

**9.** Indicate whether the following accounts generally will have (a) debit entries only, (b) credit entries only, or (c) both debit and credit entries.
  **(1)** Cash.
  **(2)** Accounts Receivable.
  **(3)** Dividends.
  **(4)** Accounts Payable.
  **(5)** Salaries Expense.
  **(6)** Service Revenue.

**10.** What are the basic steps in the recording process?

**11.** What are the advantages of using a journal in the recording process?

**12. (a)** When entering a transaction in the journal, should the debit or credit be written first?
  **(b)** Which should be indented, the debit or credit?

**13.** Describe a compound entry, and provide an example.

**14. (a)** Should business transaction debits and credits be recorded directly in the ledger accounts?
  **(b)** What are the advantages of first recording transactions in the journal and then posting to the ledger?

**15.** The account number is entered as the last step in posting the amounts from the journal to the ledger. What is the advantage of this step?

**16.** Journalize the following business transactions.
  **(a)** Hector Molina invests $9,000 cash in the business in exchange for shares of common stock.
  **(b)** Insurance of $800 is paid for the year.
  **(c)** Supplies of $2,000 are purchased on account.
  **(d)** Cash of $7,500 is received for services rendered.

**17. (a)** What is a ledger?
  **(b)** What is a chart of accounts and why is it important?

**18.** What is a trial balance and what are its purposes?

**19.** Jim Benes is confused about how accounting information flows through the accounting system. He believes the flow of information is as follows.
  **(a)** Debits and credits posted to the ledger.
  **(b)** Business transaction occurs.
  **(c)** Information entered in the journal.
  **(d)** Financial statements are prepared.
  **(e)** Trial balance is prepared.
  Is Jim correct? If not, indicate to Jim the proper flow of the information.

**20.** Two students are discussing the use of a trial balance. They wonder whether the following errors, each considered separately, would prevent the trial balance from balancing.

**(a)** The bookkeeper debited Cash for $600 and credited Wages Expense for $600 for payment of wages.

**(b)** Cash collected on account was debited to Cash for $900 and Service Revenue was credited for $90.

What would you tell them?

# BRIEF EXERCISES

*Indicate debit and credit effects and normal balance.*

*(SO 2)*

**BE2-1** For each of the following accounts indicate the effects of (a) a debit or a credit on the accounts and (b) the normal balance of the account.

1. Accounts Payable.
2. Advertising Expense.
3. Service Revenue.
4. Accounts Receivable.
5. Common Stock.
6. Dividends.

*Identify accounts to be debited and credited.*

*(SO 2)*

**BE2-2** Transactions for Kaustav Sen Company, which provides welding services, for the month of June are presented below. Identify the accounts to be debited and credited for each transaction.

June  1 Kaustav Sen invests $4,000 cash in exchange for shares of common stock in a small welding business.

   2 Purchases equipment on account for $900.

   3 Pays $800 cash to landlord for June rent.

   12 Bills J. Kronsnoble $300 for welding work done on account.

*Journalize transactions.*

*(SO 4)*

**BE2-3** Using the data in BE2-2, journalize the transactions. (You may omit explanations.)

*Identify and explain steps in recording process.*

*(SO 3)*

**BE2-4** Tim Weber, a fellow student, is unclear about the basic steps in the recording process. Identify and briefly explain the steps in the order in which they occur.

*Indicate basic and debit-credit analysis.*

*(SO 2)*

**BE2-5** J. A. Motzek Inc. has the following transactions during August of the current year. Indicate (a) the effect on the accounting equation and (b) the debit-credit analysis illustrated on pages 61–66 of the text.

Aug.  1 Opens an office as a financial advisor, investing $5,000 in cash in exchange for common stock.

   4 Pays insurance in advance for 6 months, $1,800 cash.

   16 Receives $800 from clients for services provided.

   27 Pays secretary $1,000 salary.

*Journalize transactions.*

*(SO 4)*

**BE2-6** Using the data in BE2-5, journalize the transactions. (You may omit explanations.)

*Post journal entries to T accounts.*

*(SO 6)*

**BE2-7** Selected transactions for Gilles Company are presented in journal form below. Post the transactions to T accounts. Make one T account for each item and determine each account's ending balance.

J1

| Date | Account Titles and Explanation | Ref. | Debit | Credit |
|------|-------------------------------|------|-------|--------|
| May  5 | Accounts Receivable | | 6,000 | |
| | Service Revenue | | | 6,000 |
| | (Billed for services provided) | | | |
| 12 | Cash | | 2,400 | |
| | Accounts Receivable | | | 2,400 |
| | (Received cash in payment of account) | | | |
| 15 | Cash | | 3,000 | |
| | Service Revenue | | | 3,000 |
| | (Received cash for services provided) | | | |

**BE2-8** Selected journal entries for Gilles Company are presented in BE2-7. Post the transactions using the standard form of account.

*Post journal entries to standard form of account.*
*(SO 6)*

**BE2-9** From the ledger balances given below, prepare a trial balance for P. J. Farve Company at June 30, 2008. List the accounts in the order shown on page 60 of the text. All account balances are normal.

*Prepare a trial balance.*
*(SO 7)*

    Accounts Payable $9,000, Cash $6,800, Common Stock $20,000, Dividends $1,200, Equipment $17,000, Service Revenue $6,000, Accounts Receivable $3,000, Salaries Expense $6,000, and Rent Expense $1,000.

**BE2-10** An inexperienced bookkeeper prepared the following trial balance. Prepare a correct trial balance, assuming all account balances are normal.

*Prepare a correct trial balance.*
*(SO 7)*

## CHENG COMPANY
### Trial Balance
### December 31, 2008

|  | Debit | Credit |
|---|---|---|
| Cash | $16,800 |  |
| Prepaid Insurance |  | $3,500 |
| Accounts Payable |  | 3,000 |
| Unearned Revenue | 4,200 |  |
| Common Stock |  | 13,000 |
| Dividends |  | 4,500 |
| Service Revenue |  | 25,600 |
| Salaries Expense | 18,600 |  |
| Rent Expense |  | 2,400 |
|  | $39,600 | $52,000 |

# EXERCISES

**E2-1** Josh Cephus has prepared the following list of statements about accounts.

*Analyze statements about accounting and the recording process.*
*(SO 1)*

1. An account is an accounting record of either a specific asset or a specific liability.
2. An account shows only increases, not decreases, in the item it relates to.
3. Some items, such as Cash and Accounts Receivable, are combined into one account.
4. An account has a left, or credit side, and a right, or debit side.
5. A simple form of an account consisting of just the account title, the left side, and the right side, is called a T-account.

**Instructions**
Identify each statement as true or false. If false, indicate how to correct the statement.

**E2-2** Selected transactions for D. Reyes, Inc., an interior decorating firm, in its first month of business, are as follows.

*Identify debits, credits, and normal balances.*
*(SO 2)*

Jan. 2 Invested $10,000 cash in the business in exchange for common stock.
   3 Purchased used car for $4,000 cash for use in business.
   9 Purchased supplies on account for $500.
  11 Billed customers $1,800 for services performed.
  16 Paid $200 cash for advertising.
  20 Received $700 cash from customers billed on January 11.
  23 Paid creditor $300 cash on balance owed.
  28 Declared and paid a $1,000 cash dividend.

**Instructions**
For each transaction indicate the following.

**(a)** The basic type of account debited and credited (asset, liability, stockholders' equity).
**(b)** The specific account debited and credited (cash, rent expense, service revenue, etc.).
**(c)** Whether the specific account is increased or decreased.
**(d)** The normal balance of the specific account.

Use the following format, in which the January 2 transaction is given as an example.

| | Account Debited | | | | Account Credited | | | |
|---|---|---|---|---|---|---|---|---|
| | **(a)** | **(b)** | **(c)** | **(d)** | **(a)** | **(b)** | **(c)** | **(d)** |
| | **Basic** | **Specific** | | **Normal** | **Basic** | **Specific** | | **Normal** |
| **Date** | **Type** | **Account** | **Effect** | **Balance** | **Type** | **Account** | **Effect** | **Balance** |
| Jan. 2 | Asset | Cash | Increase | Debit | Stock-holders' Equity | Common Stock | Increase | Credit |

*Journalize transactions.*
*(SO 4)*

**E2-3** Data for D. Reyes, Inc., interior decorating, are presented in E2-2.

**Instructions**
Journalize the transactions using journal page J1. (You may omit explanations.)

*Analyze transactions and determine their effect on accounts.*
*(SO 2)*

**E2-4** Presented below is information related to Hanshew Real Estate Agency.

Oct. 1 Pete Hanshew begins business as a real estate agent with a cash investment of $15,000 in exchange for common stock.
  2 Hires an administrative assistant.
  3 Purchases office furniture for $1,900, on account.
  6 Sells a house and lot for B. Kidman; bills B. Kidman $3,200 for realty services provided.
  27 Pays $700 on the balance related to the transaction of October 3.
  30 Pays the administrative assistant $2,500 in salary for October.

**Instructions**
Prepare the debit-credit analysis for each transaction as illustrated on pages 61–66.

*Journalize transactions.*
*(SO 4)*

**E2-5** Transaction data for Hanshew Real Estate Agency are presented in E2-4.

**Instructions**
Journalize the transactions. (You may omit explanations.)

*Analyze transactions and journalize.*
*(SO 2, 3, 4)*

**E2-6** Konerko Industries had the following transactions.

**1.** Borrowed $5,000 from the bank by signing a note.
**2.** Paid $2,500 cash for a computer.
**3.** Purchased $700 of supplies on account.

**Instructions**
**(a)** Indicate what accounts are increased and decreased by each transaction.
**(b)** Journalize each transaction.

*Analyze transactions and journalize.*
*(SO 2, 3, 4)*

**E2-7** Rowand Enterprises had the following selected transactions.

**1.** Aaron Rowand invested $4,000 cash in the business in exchange for common stock.
**2.** Paid office rent of $1,100.
**3.** Performed consulting services and billed a client $5,200.
**4.** Paid a $700 cash dividend.

**Instructions**
**(a)** Indicate the effect each transaction has on the basic accounting equation
    (Assets = Liabilities + Stockholders' Equity), using plus and minus signs.
**(b)** Journalize each transaction.

*Analyze statements about the ledger.*
*(SO 5)*

**E2-8** Josie Feeney has prepared the following list of statements about the general ledger.

**1.** The general ledger contains all the asset and liability accounts, but no stockholders' equity accounts.
**2.** The general ledger is sometimes referred to as simply the ledger.
**3.** The accounts in the general ledger are arranged in alphabetical order.
**4.** Each account in the general ledger is numbered for easier identification.
**5.** The general ledger is a book of original entry.

**Instructions**
Identify each statement as true or false. If false, indicate how to correct the statement.

**E2-9** Selected transactions from the journal of Teresa Gonzalez, investment broker, are presented below.

*Post journal entries and prepare a trial balance.*
*(SO 6, 7)*

| Date | Account Titles and Explanation | Ref. | Debit | Credit |
|---|---|---|---|---|
| Aug. 1 | Cash | | 5,000 | |
| | Common Stock | | | 5,000 |
| | (Investment of cash for stock) | | | |
| 10 | Cash | | 2,400 | |
| | Service Revenue | | | 2,400 |
| | (Received cash for services provided) | | | |
| 12 | Office Equipment | | 5,000 | |
| | Cash | | | 1,000 |
| | Notes Payable | | | 4,000 |
| | (Purchased office equipment for cash and notes payable) | | | |
| 25 | Accounts Receivable | | 1,600 | |
| | Service Revenue | | | 1,600 |
| | (Billed clients for services provided) | | | |
| 31 | Cash | | 900 | |
| | Accounts Receivable | | | 900 |
| | (Receipt of cash on account) | | | |

**Instructions**
(a) Post the transactions to T accounts.
(b) Prepare a trial balance at August 31, 2008.

**E2-10** The T accounts below summarize the ledger of Simon Landscaping Company at the end of the first month of operations.

*Journalize transactions from account data and prepare a trial balance.*
*(SO 4, 7)*

| Cash | | | No. 101 |
|---|---|---|---|
| 4/1 | 15,000 | 4/15 | 600 |
| 4/12 | 900 | 4/25 | 1,500 |
| 4/29 | 400 | | |
| 4/30 | 1,000 | | |

| Accounts Receivable | | | No. 112 |
|---|---|---|---|
| 4/7 | 3,200 | 4/29 | 400 |

| Supplies | | | No. 126 |
|---|---|---|---|
| 4/4 | 1,800 | | |

| Accounts Payable | | | No. 201 |
|---|---|---|---|
| 4/25 | 1,500 | 4/4 | 1,800 |

| Unearned Revenue | | | No. 205 |
|---|---|---|---|
| | | 4/30 | 1,000 |

| Common Stock | | | No. 311 |
|---|---|---|---|
| | | 4/1 | 15,000 |

| Service Revenue | | | No. 400 |
|---|---|---|---|
| | | 4/7 | 3,200 |
| | | 4/12 | 900 |

| Salaries Expense | | | No. 726 |
|---|---|---|---|
| 4/15 | 600 | | |

**Instructions**
(a) Prepare the complete general journal (including explanations) from which the postings to Cash were made.
(b) Prepare a trial balance at April 30, 2008.

**E2-11** Presented below and on the next page is the ledger for Heerey Co.

*Journalize transactions from account data and prepare a trial balance.*
*(SO 4, 7)*

| Cash | | | No. 101 |
|---|---|---|---|
| 10/1 | 5,000 | 10/4 | 400 |
| 10/10 | 650 | 10/12 | 1,500 |
| 10/10 | 4,000 | 10/15 | 250 |
| 10/20 | 500 | 10/30 | 300 |
| 10/25 | 2,000 | 10/31 | 500 |

| Common Stock | | | No. 311 |
|---|---|---|---|
| | | 10/1 | 5,000 |
| | | 10/25 | 2,000 |

| Dividends | | | No. 332 |
|---|---|---|---|
| 10/30 | 300 | | |

| Accounts Receivable | | | No. 112 |
|---|---|---|---|
| 10/6 | 800 | 10/20 | 500 |
| 10/20 | 940 | | |

| Service Revenue | | No. 407 |
|---|---|---|
| | 10/6 | 800 |
| | 10/10 | 650 |
| | 10/20 | 940 |

| Supplies | | No. 126 |
|---|---|---|
| 10/4 | 400 | |

| Store Wages Expense | | No. 628 |
|---|---|---|
| 10/31 | 500 | |

| Furniture | | No. 149 |
|---|---|---|
| 10/3 | 2,000 | |

| Rent Expense | | No. 729 |
|---|---|---|
| 10/15 | 250 | |

| Notes Payable | | No. 200 |
|---|---|---|
| | 10/10 | 4,000 |

| Accounts Payable | | | No. 201 |
|---|---|---|---|
| 10/12 | 1,500 | 10/3 | 2,000 |

**Instructions**

(a) Reproduce the journal entries for the transactions that occurred on October 1, 10, and 20, and provide explanations for each.

(b) Determine the October 31 balance for each of the accounts above, and prepare a trial balance at October 31, 2008.

*Prepare journal entries and post using standard account form.*

*(SO 4, 6)*

**E2-12** Selected transactions for Tina Cordero Company during its first month in business are presented below.

Sept. 1 Invested $10,000 cash in the business in exchange for common stock.
5 Purchased equipment for $12,000 paying $5,000 in cash and the balance on account.
25 Paid $3,000 cash on balance owed for equipment.
30 Declared and paid a $500 cash dividend.

Cordero's chart of accounts shows: No. 101 Cash, No. 157 Equipment, No. 201 Accounts Payable, No. 311 Common Stock, No. 332 Dividends.

**Instructions**

(a) Journalize the transactions on page J1 of the journal.

(b) Post the transactions using the standard account form.

*Analyze errors and their effects on trial balance.*

*(SO 7)*

**E2-13** The bookkeeper for Sam Kaplin Equipment Repair made a number of errors in journalizing and posting, as described below.

1. A credit posting of $400 to Accounts Receivable was omitted.
2. A debit posting of $750 for Prepaid Insurance was debited to Insurance Expense.
3. A collection from a customer of $100 in payment of its account owed was journalized and posted as a debit to Cash $100 and a credit to Service Revenue $100.
4. A credit posting of $300 to Property Taxes Payable was made twice.
5. A cash purchase of supplies for $250 was journalized and posted as a debit to Supplies $25 and a credit to Cash $25.
6. A debit of $475 to Advertising Expense was posted as $457.

**Instructions**

For each error:

(a) Indicate whether the trial balance will balance.

(b) If the trial balance will not balance, indicate the amount of the difference.

(c) Indicate the trial balance column that will have the larger total.

Consider each error separately. Use the following form, in which error (1) is given as an example.

| Error | (a) In Balance | (b) Difference | (c) Larger Column |
|---|---|---|---|
| (1) | No | $400 | debit |

**E2-14**    The accounts in the ledger of Sanford Delivery Service contain the following balances on July 31, 2008.

*Prepare a trial balance.*

*(SO 2, 7)*

| | | | |
|---|---|---|---|
| Accounts Receivable | $ 7,642 | Prepaid Insurance | $1,968 |
| Accounts Payable | 8,396 | Repair Expense | 961 |
| Cash | ? | Service Revenue | 10,610 |
| Delivery Equipment | 49,360 | Dividends | 700 |
| Gas and Oil Expense | 758 | Common Stock | 40,000 |
| Insurance Expense | 523 | Salaries Expense | 4,428 |
| Notes Payable | 18,450 | Salaries Payable | 815 |
| | | Retained Earnings | 4,636 |

**Instructions**
Prepare a trial balance with the accounts arranged as illustrated in the chapter and fill in the missing amount for Cash.

## EXERCISES: SET B

Visit the book's website at **www.wiley.com/college/weygandt**, and choose the Student Companion site, to access Exercise Set B.

## PROBLEMS: SET A

**P2-1A**    Frontier Park was started on April 1 by C. J. Mendcz and associates. The following selected events and transactions occurred during April.

*Journalize a series of transactions.*

*(SO 2, 4)*

**GLS**

Apr.  1    Stockholders invested $40,000 cash in the business in exchange for common stock.
      4    Purchased land costing $30,000 for cash.
      8    Incurred advertising expense of $1,800 on account.
     11    Paid salaries to employees $1,500.
     12    Hired park manager at a salary of $4,000 per month, effective May 1.
     13    Paid $1,500 cash for a one-year insurance policy.
     17    Declared and paid a  $1,000 cash dividend.
     20    Received $5,700 in cash for admission fees.
     25    Sold 100 coupon books for $25 each. Each book contains 10 coupons that entitle the holder to one admission to the park.
     30    Received $8,900 in cash admission fees.
     30    Paid $900 on balance owed for advertising incurred on April 8.

Mendez uses the following accounts: Cash; Prepaid Insurance; Land; Accounts Payable; Unearned Admission Revenue; Common Stock; Dividends; Admission Revenue; Advertising Expense; and Salaries Expense.

**Instructions**
Journalize the April transactions.

**P2-2A**    Jane Kent is a licensed CPA. During the first month of operations of her business, Jane Kent, Inc., the following events and transactions occurred.

*Journalize transactions, post, and prepare a trial balance.*

*(SO 2, 4, 6, 7)*

**GLS**

May  1    Stockholders invested $25,000 cash in exchange for common stock.
      2    Hired a secretary-receptionist at a salary of $2,000 per month.
      3    Purchased $2,500 of supplies on account from Read Supply Company.
      7    Paid office rent of $900 cash for the month.
     11    Completed a tax assignment and billed client $2,100 for services provided.
     12    Received $3,500 advance on a management consulting engagement.
     17    Received cash of $1,200 for services completed for H. Arnold Co.
     31    Paid secretary-receptionist $2,000 salary for the month.
     31    Paid 40% of balance due Read Supply Company.

Jane uses the following chart of accounts: No. 101 Cash, No. 112 Accounts Receivable, No. 126 Supplies, No. 201 Accounts Payable, No. 205 Unearned Revenue, No. 311 Common Stock, No. 400 Service Revenue, No. 726 Salaries Expense, and No. 729 Rent Expense.

**Instructions**

*Trial balance totals $33,300*

**(a)** Journalize the transactions.

**(b)** Post to the ledger accounts.

**(c)** Prepare a trial balance on May 31, 2008.

*Journalize and post transactions and prepare a trial balance.*

*(SO 2, 4, 6, 7)*

**P2-3A** Jack Shellenkamp owns and manages a computer repair service, which had the following trial balance on December 31, 2007 (the end of its fiscal year).

**BYTE REPAIR SERVICE INC.**
Trial Balance
December 31, 2007

| | | |
|---|---:|---:|
| Cash | $ 8,000 | |
| Accounts Receivable | 15,000 | |
| Parts Inventory | 13,000 | |
| Prepaid Rent | 3,000 | |
| Shop Equipment | 21,000 | |
| Accounts Payable | | $19,000 |
| Common Stock | | 30,000 |
| Retained Earnings | | 11,000 |
| | $60,000 | $60,000 |

Summarized transactions for January 2008 were as follows:

**1.** Advertising costs, paid in cash, $1,000.

**2.** Additional repair parts inventory acquired on account $4,000.

**3.** Miscellaneous expenses, paid in cash, $2,000.

**4.** Cash collected from customers in payment of accounts receivable $14,000.

**5.** Cash paid to creditors for accounts payable due $15,000.

**6.** Repair parts used during January $4,000. (*Hint*: Debit this to Repair Parts Expense.)

**7.** Repair services performed during January: for cash $6,000; on account $9,000.

**8.** Wages for January, paid in cash, $3,000.

**9.** Dividends paid in January were $3,000.

**Instructions**

**(a)** Open T accounts for each of the accounts listed in the trial balance, and enter the opening balances for 2008.

**(b)** Prepare journal entries to record each of the January transactions.

**(c)** Post the journal entries to the accounts in the ledger. (Add accounts as needed.)

*Trial balance totals $64,000*

**(d)** Prepare a trial balance as of January 31, 2008.

*Prepare a correct trial balance.*

*(SO 7)*

**P2-4A** The trial balance of the Sterling Company shown below does not balance.

**STERLING COMPANY**
Trial Balance
May 31, 2008

| | Debit | Credit |
|---|---:|---:|
| Cash | $5,850 | |
| Accounts Receivable | | $2,750 |
| Prepaid Insurance | 700 | |
| Equipment | 8,000 | |
| Accounts Payable | | 4,500 |
| Property Taxes Payable | 560 | |
| Common Stock | | 11,700 |
| Service Revenue | 6,690 | |
| Salaries Expense | 4,200 | |
| Advertising Expense | | 1,100 |
| Property Tax Expense | 800 | |
| | $26,800 | $20,050 |

Your review of the ledger reveals that each account has a normal balance. You also discover the following errors (page 83).

1. The totals of the debit sides of Prepaid Insurance, Accounts Payable, and Property Tax Expense were each understated $100.
2. Transposition errors were made in Accounts Receivable and Service Revenue. Based on postings made, the correct balances were $2,570 and $6,960, respectively.
3. A debit posting to Salaries Expense of $200 was omitted.
4. A $1,000 cash dividend was debited to Common Stock for $1,000 and credited to Cash for $1,000.
5. A $520 purchase of supplies on account was debited to Equipment for $520 and credited to Cash for $520.
6. A cash payment of $450 for advertising was debited to Advertising Expense for $45 and credited to Cash for $45.
7. A collection from a customer for $210 was debited to Cash for $210 and credited to Accounts Payable for $210.

**Instructions**

Prepare a correct trial balance. Note that the chart of accounts includes the following: Dividends, and Supplies. (*Hint:* It helps to prepare the correct journal entry for the transaction described and compare it to the mistake made.)

*Trial balance totals $24,930*

**P2-5A**  The Lake Theater opened on April 1. All facilities were completed on March 31. At this time, the ledger showed: No. 101 Cash $6,000; No. 140 Land $10,000; No. 145 Buildings (concession stand, projection room, ticket booth, and screen) $8,000; No. 157 Equipment $6,000; No. 201 Accounts Payable $2,000; No. 275 Mortgage Payable $8,000; and No. 311 Common Stock $20,000. During April, the following events and transactions occurred.

*Journalize transactions, post, and prepare a trial balance.*

*(SO 2, 4, 6, 7)*

Apr.  2  Paid film rental of $800 on first movie.
     3  Ordered two additional films at $1,000 each.
     9  Received $2,800 cash from admissions.
    10  Made $2,000 payment on mortgage and $1,000 for accounts payable due.
    11  Lake Theater contracted with R. Wynns Company to operate the concession stand. Wynns is to pay 17% of gross concession receipts (payable monthly) for the right to operate the concession stand.
    12  Paid advertising expenses $500.
    20  Received one of the films ordered on April 3 and was billed $1,000. The film will be shown in April.
    25  Received $5,200 cash from admissions.
    29  Paid salaries $2,000.
    30  Received statement from R. Wynns showing gross concession receipts of $1,000 and the balance due to The Lake Theater of $170 ($1,000 × 17%) for April. Wynns paid one-half of the balance due and will remit the remainder on May 5.
    30  Prepaid $900 rental on special film to be run in May.

In addition to the accounts identified above, the chart of accounts shows: No. 112 Accounts Receivable, No. 136 Prepaid Rentals, No. 405 Admission Revenue, No. 406 Concession Revenue, No. 610 Advertising Expense, No. 632 Film Rental Expense, and No. 726 Salaries Expense.

**Instructions**

(a) Enter the beginning balances in the ledger as of April 1. Insert a check mark (✓) in the reference column of the ledger for the beginning balance.

(b) Journalize the April transactions.

(c) Post the April journal entries to the ledger. Assume that all entries are posted from page 1 of the journal.

(d) Prepare a trial balance on April 30, 2008.

*Trial balance totals $36,170*

## ▮PROBLEMS: SET B

**P2-1B**  Surepar Miniature Golf and Driving Range was opened on March 1 by Jerry Glover. The following selected events and transactions occurred during March.

*Journalize a series of transactions.*

*(SO 2, 4)*

Mar.  1  Invested $50,000 cash in the business in exchange for common stock.
      3  Purchased Lee's Golf Land for $38,000 cash. The price consists of land $23,000, building $9,000, and equipment $6,000. (Make one compound entry.)

5 Advertised the opening of the driving range and miniature golf course, paying advertising expenses of $1,600.
6 Paid cash $1,480 for a one-year insurance policy.
10 Purchased golf clubs and other equipment for $2,600 from Palmer Company payable in 30 days.
18 Received $800 in cash for golf fees earned.
19 Sold 100 coupon books for $15 each. Each book contains 10 coupons that enable the holder to play one round of miniature golf or to hit one bucket of golf balls.
25 Declared and paid a $2,000 cash dividend.
30 Paid salaries of $600.
30 Paid Palmer Company in full.
31 Received $500 cash for fees earned.

Jerry Glover uses the following accounts: Cash; Prepaid Insurance; Land; Buildings; Equipment; Accounts Payable; Unearned Revenue; Common Stock; Dividends; Golf Revenue; Advertising Expense; and Salaries Expense.

**Instructions**
Journalize the March transactions.

*Journalize transactions, post, and prepare a trial balance.*

(SO 2, 4, 6, 7)

**P2-2B** Rosa Perez is a licensed architect. During the first month of the operation of her business, the following events and transactions occurred.

April 1 Stockholders invested $30,000 cash in exchange for common stock.
1 Hired a secretary-receptionist at a salary of $500 per week payable monthly.
2 Paid office rent for the month $800.
3 Purchased architectural supplies on account from Halo Company $1,500.
10 Completed blueprints on a carport and billed client $1,200 for services.
11 Received $500 cash advance from R. Welk for the design of a new home.
20 Received $1,500 cash for services completed and delivered to P. Donahue.
30 Paid secretary-receptionist for the month $2,000.
30 Paid $600 to Halo Company for accounts payable due.

Rosa uses the following chart of accounts: No. 101 Cash, No. 112 Accounts Receivable, No. 126 Supplies, No. 201 Accounts Payable, No. 205 Unearned Revenue, No. 311 Common Stock, No. 400 Service Revenue, No. 726 Salaries Expense, and No. 729 Rent Expense.

**Instructions**

*Trial balance totals $34,100*

**(a)** Journalize the transactions.
**(b)** Post to the ledger accounts.
**(c)** Prepare a trial balance on April 30, 2008.

*Journalize transactions, post, and prepare a trial balance.*

(SO 2, 4, 6, 7)

**P2-3B** Slocombe Services was formed on May 1, 2008. The following transactions took place during the first month.

Transactions on May 1:

1. Stockholders invested $100,000 cash in the company in exchange for common stock.
2. Hired two employees to work in the warehouse. They will each be paid a salary of $3,000 per month.
3. Signed a 2-year rental agreement on a warehouse; paid $36,000 cash in advance for the first year.
4. Purchased furniture and equipment costing $60,000. A cash payment of $20,000 was made immediately; the remainder will be paid in 6 months.
5. Paid $3,000 cash for a one-year insurance policy on the furniture and equipment.

Transactions during the remainder of the month:

6. Purchased basic office supplies for $1,000 cash.
7. Purchased more office supplies for $3,000 on account.
8. Total revenues earned were $30,000—$10,000 cash and $20,000 on account.
9. Paid $800 to suppliers for accounts payable due.
10. Received $5,000 from customers in payment of accounts receivable.
11. Received utility bills in the amount of $400, to be paid next month.
12. Paid the monthly salaries of the two employees, totalling $6,000.

**Instructions**

*Trial balance totals $172,600*

**(a)** Prepare journal entries to record each of the events listed.

**(b)** Post the journal entries to T accounts.
**(c)** Prepare a trial balance as of May 31, 2008.

**P2-4B**    The trial balance of Don Kelso Co. shown below does not balance.

*Prepare a correct trial balance.*
(SO 7)

### DON KELSO CO.
Trial Balance
June 30, 2008

|  | Debit | Credit |
|---|---|---|
| Cash |  | $ 2,840 |
| Accounts Receivable | $ 3,231 |  |
| Supplies | 800 |  |
| Equipment | 3,000 |  |
| Accounts Payable |  | 2,666 |
| Unearned Revenue | 1,200 |  |
| Common Stock |  | 9,000 |
| Dividends | 800 |  |
| Service Revenue |  | 2,380 |
| Salaries Expense | 3,400 |  |
| Office Expense | 910 |  |
|  | $13,341 | $16,886 |

Each of the listed accounts has a normal balance per the general ledger. An examination of the ledger and journal reveals the following errors.

1. Cash received from a customer in payment of its account was debited for $470, and Accounts Receivable was credited for the same amount. The actual collection was for $740.
2. The purchase of a printer on account for $340 was recorded as a debit to Supplies for $340 and a credit to Accounts Payable for $340.
3. Services were performed on account for a client for $890. Accounts Receivable was debited for $890, and Service Revenue was credited for $89.
4. A debit posting to Salaries Expense of $600 was omitted.
5. A payment of a balance due for $206 was credited to Cash for $206 and credited to Accounts Payable for $260.
6. The payment of a $500 cash dividend was debited to Salaries Expense for $500 and credited to Cash for $500.

### Instructions
Prepare a correct trial balance. (*Hint:* It helps to prepare the correct journal entry for the transaction described and compare it to the mistake made).

Trial balance totals $15,581

**P2-5B**    The Quinn Theater, owned by Mike Quinn, will begin operations in March. The Quinn will be unique in that it will show only triple features of sequential theme movies. As of March 1, the ledger of Quinn showed: No. 101 Cash $16,000; No. 140 Land $42,000; No. 145 Buildings (concession stand, projection room, ticket booth, and screen) $18,000; No. 157 Equipment $16,000; No. 201 Accounts Payable $12,000; and No. 311 Common Stock $80,000. During the month of March the following events and transactions occurred.

*Journalize transactions, post, and prepare a trial balance.*
(SO 2, 4, 6, 7)

Mar. 2    Rented the three *Star Wars* movies (*Star Wars, The Empire Strikes Back,* and *The Return of the Jedi*) to be shown for the first 3 weeks of March. The film rental was $6,000; $3,000 was paid in cash and $3,000 will be paid on March 10.

3    Ordered the first three *Star Trek* movies to be shown the last 10 days of March. It will cost $300 per night.

9    Received $6,500 cash from admissions.

10    Paid balance due on *Star Wars* movies rental and $4,000 on March 1 accounts payable.

11    Quinn Theater contracted with M. Brewer Company to operate the concession stand. Brewer is to pay 10% of gross concession receipts (payable monthly) for the right to operate the concession stand.

12    Paid advertising expenses $800.

20    Received $7,200 cash from customers for admissions.

20   Received the *Star Trek* movies and paid the rental fee of $3,000.
31   Paid salaries of $4,800.
31   Received statement from M. Brewer showing gross receipts from concessions of $8,000 and the balance due to Quinn Theater of $800 ($8,000 × 10%) for March. Brewer paid one-half the balance due and will remit the remainder on April 5.
31   Received $11,000 cash from customers for admissions.

In addition to the accounts identified above, the chart of accounts includes: No. 112 Accounts Receivable, No. 405 Admission Revenue, No. 406 Concession Revenue, No. 610 Advertising Expense, No. 632 Film Rental Expense, and No. 726 Salaries Expense.

**Instructions**
**(a)** Enter the beginning balances in the ledger. Insert a check mark (✓) in the reference column of the ledger for the beginning balance.
**(b)** Journalize the March transactions.
**(c)** Post the March journal entries to the ledger. Assume that all entries are posted from page 1 of the journal.

*Trial balance totals $113,500*   **(d)** Prepare a trial balance on March 31, 2008.

## PROBLEMS: SET C

Visit the book's website at **www.wiley.com/college/weygandt**, and choose the Student Companion site, to access Problem Set C.

## CONTINUING COOKIE CHRONICLE

(*Note*: This is a continuation of the Cookie Chronicle from Chapter 1.)
**CCC2**   After researching the different forms of business organization, Natalie Koebel decides to operate "Cookie Creations" as a corporation. She then starts the process of getting the business running.

*Go to the book's website,*
**www.wiley.com/college/weygandt,**
*to see the completion of this problem.*

# BROADENING YOUR PERSPECTIVE

## FINANCIAL REPORTING AND ANALYSIS

## Financial Reporting Problem
### PepsiCo, Inc.

**BYP2-1**   The financial statements of PepsiCo are presented in Appendix A. The notes accompanying the statements contain the following selected accounts, stated in millions of dollars.

| | | | |
|---|---|---|---|
| Accounts Payable | $1,799 | Income Taxes Payable | $ 546 |
| Accounts Receivable | 3,261 | Interest Expense | 256 |
| Property, Plant, and Equipment | 8,681 | Inventory | 1,693 |

**Instructions**
**(a)** Answer the following questions.
   **(1)** What is the increase and decrease side for each account?
   **(2)** What is the normal balance for each account?
**(b)** Identify the probable other account in the transaction and the effect on that account when:
   **(1)** Accounts Receivable is decreased.
   **(2)** Accounts Payable is decreased.
   **(3)** Inventory is increased.

**(c)** Identify the other account(s) that ordinarily would be involved when:
  **(1)** Interest Expense is increased.
  **(2)** Property, Plant, and Equipment is increased.

# Comparative Analysis Problem
## PepsiCo, Inc. vs. The Coca-Cola Company

**BYP2-2**   PepsiCo's financial statements are presented in Appendix A. Coca-Cola's financial statements are presented in Appendix B.

**Instructions**
**(a)** Based on the information contained in the financial statements, determine the normal balance of the listed accounts for each company.

| PepsiCo | Coca-Cola |
|---|---|
| **1.** Inventory | **1.** Accounts Receivable |
| **2.** Property, Plant, and Equipment | **2.** Cash and Cash Equivalents |
| **3.** Accounts Payable | **3.** Cost of Goods Sold |
| **4.** Interest Expense | **4.** Sales (revenue) |

**(b)** Identify the other account ordinarily involved when:
  **(1)** Accounts Receivable is increased.
  **(2)** Wages Payable is decreased.
  **(3)** Property, Plant, and Equipment is increased.
  **(4)** Interest Expense is increased.

# Exploring the Web

**BYP2-3**   Much information about specific companies is available on the World Wide Web. Such information includes basic descriptions of the company's location, activities, industry, financial health, and financial performance.

**Address: biz.yahoo.com/i**, or go to **www.wiley.com/college/weygandt**

**Steps**
**1.** Type in a company name, or use index to find company name.
**2.** Choose **Profile**. Perform instructions (a)–(c) below.
**3.** Click on the company's specific industry to identify competitors. Perform instructions (d)–(g) below.

**Instructions**
Answer the following questions.

**(a)** What is the company's industry?
**(b)** What was the company's total sales?
**(c)** What was the company's net income?
**(d)** What are the names of four of the company's competitors?
**(e)** Choose one of these competitors.
**(f)** What is this competitor's name? What were its sales? What was its net income?
**(g)** Which of these two companies is larger by size of sales? Which one reported higher net income?

## CRITICAL THINKING

# Decision Making Across the Organization

**BYP2-4**   Lisa Ortega is president of Ortega Riding Academy, Inc. The academy's primary sources of revenue are riding fees and lesson fees, which are paid on a cash basis. Lisa also boards horses for owners, who are billed monthly for boarding fees. In a few cases, boarders pay in advance of expected use. For its revenue transactions, the academy maintains the following accounts: No. 1 Cash, No. 5 Boarding Accounts Receivable, No. 27 Unearned Boarding Revenue, No. 51 Riding Revenue, No. 52 Lesson Revenue, and No. 53 Boarding Revenue.

The academy owns 10 horses, a stable, a riding corral, riding equipment, and office equipment. These assets are accounted for in accounts No. 11 Horses, No. 12 Building, No. 13 Riding Corral, No. 14 Riding Equipment, and No. 15 Office Equipment.

For its expenses, the academy maintains the following accounts: No. 6 Hay and Feed Supplies, No. 7 Prepaid Insurance, No. 21 Accounts Payable, No. 60 Salaries Expense, No. 61 Advertising Expense, No. 62 Utilities Expense, No. 63 Veterinary Expense, No. 64 Hay and Feed Expense, and No. 65 Insurance Expense.

Ortega makes periodic payments of cash dividends to stockholders. To record stockholders' equity transactions in the business, Ortega maintains three accounts: No. 50 Common Stock, No. 51 Retained Earnings, and No. 52 Dividends.

During the first month of operations an inexperienced bookkeeper was employed. Lisa Ortega asks you to review the following eight entries of the 50 entries made during the month. In each case, the explanation for the entry is correct.

| | | | | |
|---|---|---|---:|---:|
| May 1 | Cash | | 18,000 | |
| | Common Stock | | | 18,000 |
| | (Invested $18,000 cash in exchange for stock) | | | |
| 5 | Cash | | 250 | |
| | Riding Revenue | | | 250 |
| | (Received $250 cash for lessons provided) | | | |
| 7 | Cash | | 300 | |
| | Boarding Revenue | | | 300 |
| | (Received $300 for boarding of horses beginning June 1) | | | |
| 14 | Riding Equipment | | 80 | |
| | Cash | | | 800 |
| | (Purchased desk and other office equipment for $800 cash) | | | |
| 15 | Salaries Expense | | 400 | |
| | Cash | | | 400 |
| | (Issued dividend checks to stockholders) | | | |
| 20 | Cash | | 148 | |
| | Riding Revenue | | | 184 |
| | (Received $184 cash for riding fees) | | | |
| 30 | Veterinary Expense | | 75 | |
| | Accounts Payable | | | 75 |
| | (Received bill of $75 from veterinarian for services rendered) | | | |
| 31 | Hay and Feed Expense | | 1,700 | |
| | Cash | | | 1,700 |
| | (Purchased an estimated 2 months' supply of feed and hay for $1,700 on account) | | | |

**Instructions**

With the class divided into groups, answer the following.

**(a)** Identify each journal entry that is correct. For each journal entry that is incorrect, prepare the entry that should have been made by the bookkeeper.

**(b)** Which of the incorrect entries would prevent the trial balance from balancing?

**(c)** What was the correct net income for May, assuming the bookkeeper reported net income of $4,500 after posting all 50 entries?

**(d)** What was the correct cash balance at May 31, assuming the bookkeeper reported a balance of $12,475 after posting all 50 entries (and the only errors occurred in the items listed above)?

# Communication Activity

**BYP2-5**  Woderson's Maid Company offers home cleaning service. Two recurring transactions for the company are billing customers for services rendered and paying employee salaries. For example, on March 15, bills totaling $6,000 were sent to customers and $2,000 was paid in salaries to employees.

**Instructions**
Write a memo to your instructor that explains and illustrates the steps in the recording process for each of the March 15 transactions. Use the format illustrated in the text under the heading, "The Recording Process Illustrated" (p. 61).

# Ethics Case

**BYP2-6**   Mary Jansen is the assistant chief accountant at Casey Company, a manufacturer of computer chips and cellular phones. The company presently has total sales of $20 million. It is the end of the first quarter. Mary is hurriedly trying to prepare a general ledger trial balance so that quarterly financial statements can be prepared and released to management and the regulatory agencies. The total credits on the trial balance exceed the debits by $1,000. In order to meet the 4 p.m. deadline, Mary decides to force the debits and credits into balance by adding the amount of the difference to the Equipment account. She chose Equipment because it is one of the larger account balances; percentage-wise, it will be the least misstated. Mary "plugs" the difference! She believes that the difference will not affect anyone's decisions. She wishes that she had another few days to find the error but realizes that the financial statements are already late.

**Instructions**
**(a)** Who are the stakeholders in this situation?
**(b)** What are the ethical issues involved in this case?
**(c)** What are Mary's alternatives?

# "All About You" Activity

**BYP2-7**   Every company needs to plan in order to move forward. Its top management must consider where it wants the company to be in three to five years. Like a company, you need to think about where you want to be three to five years from now, and you need to start taking steps now in order to get there. With some forethought, you can help yourself avoid a situation, like those described in the "All About You" feature in this chapter (p. 71), in which your résumé seems to need creative writing.

**Instructions**
Provide responses to each of the following items.

**(a)** Where would you like to be working in three to five years? Describe your plan for getting there by identifying between five and 10 specific steps that you need to take in order to get there.

**(b)** In order to get the job you want, you will need a résumé. Your résumé is the equivalent of a company's annual report. It needs to provide relevant and reliable information about your past accomplishments so that employers can decide whether to "invest" in you. Do a search on the Internet to find a good résumé format. What are the basic elements of a résumé?

**(c)** A company's annual report provides information about a company's accomplishments. In order for investors to use the annual report, the information must be reliable; that is, users must have faith that the information is accurate and believable. How can you provide assurance that the information on your résumé is reliable?

**(d)** Prepare a résumé assuming that you have accomplished the five to 10 specific steps you identified in part (a). Also, provide evidence that would give assurance that the information is reliable.

## Answers to Insight and Accounting Across the Organization Questions

**New Xbox Contributes to Profitability, p. 56**
Q: In what ways is this Microsoft division using accounting to assist in its effort to become more profitable?
A: *The division has used accounting to set very strict sales, revenue, and profit goals. In addition, the division managers use accounting to keep a tight rein on product costs. Also, accounting serves as the basis of communication, so that the marketing managers and product designers can work with production managers, engineers, and accountants to achieve an exciting product within specified cost constraints.*

**What Would Sam Do?, p. 58**

Q: Why did Sam Walton keep separate pigeonholes and blue binders?

A: *Using separate pigeonholes and blue binders for each store enabled Walton to accumulate and track the performance of each individual store easily.*

Q: Why bother to keep separate records for each store?

A: *Keeping separate records for each store provided Walton with more information about performance of individual stores and managers, and greater control. Walton would want and need the same advantages if he were starting his business today. The difference is that he might now use a computerized system for small businesses.*

**Sarbanes-Oxley Comes to the Rescue, p. 70**

Q: In order for these companies to prepare and issue financial statements, their accounting equations (debits and credits) must have been in balance at year-end. How could these errors or misstatements have occurred?

A: *A company's accounting equation (as expressed in its books) can be in balance yet its financial statements have errors or misstatements because of the following: entire transactions were not recorded, transactions were recorded at wrong amounts; transactions were recorded in the wrong accounts; transactions were recorded in the wrong accounting period. Audits of financial statements uncover some, but not all, errors or misstatements.*

## Authors' Comments on *All About You:* Your Personal Annual Report, p. 71

The decision whether to fire Mr. Edmondson was the responsibility of Radio Shack's board of directors, which is elected by the company's shareholders to oversee management. The board initially announced its support for the CEO. After further investigation, the board encouraged Mr. Edmondson to resign, which he did. In contrast, when Bausch and Lomb's CEO offered to resign in a similar situation, the company's board refused to accept his resignation. Board members stated that they felt he was still the best person for the position.

Radio Shack says that although it did a reference check at the time of Mr. Edmondson's hiring, it did not check his educational credentials. Under the Sarbanes-Oxley Act of 2002, companies must now perform thorough background checks as part of a check of internal controls. The bottom line: Your résumé must be a fair and accurate depiction of your past.

## Answer to PepsiCo Review It Question 4, p. 53

Normal balances for PepsiCo (or any company) are: Cash—debit; Accounts Payable—credit; Interest Expense—debit.

## Answers to Self-Study Questions

**1.** b    **2.** c    **3.** d    **4.** d    **5.** b    **6.** a    **7.** c    **8.** d    **9.** a    **10.** c

# Chapter 3

# Adjusting the Accounts

## STUDY OBJECTIVES

*After studying this chapter, you should be able to:*

1 Explain the time period assumption.
2 Explain the accrual basis of accounting.
3 Explain the reasons for adjusting entries.
4 Identify the major types of adjusting entries.
5 Prepare adjusting entries for deferrals.
6 Prepare adjusting entries for accruals.
7 Describe the nature and purpose of an adjusted trial balance.

✓ *The Navigator*

✓ *The Navigator*

Scan **Study Objectives** ■

Read **Feature Story** ■

Read **Preview** ■

Read text and answer **Before You Go On**
p. 97 ■     p. 104 ■     p. 109 ■     p. 114 ■

Work **Demonstration Problem** ■

Review **Summary of Study Objectives** ■

Answer **Self-Study Questions** ■

Complete **Assignments** ■

## Feature Story

**WHAT WAS YOUR PROFIT?**

The accuracy of the financial reporting system depends on answers to a few fundamental questions: At what point has revenue been earned? At what point is the earnings process complete? When have expenses really been incurred?

During the 1990s' boom in the stock prices of dot-com companies, many dot-coms earned most of their revenue from selling advertising space on their websites. To boost reported revenue, some dot-coms began swapping website ad space. Company A would put an ad for its website on company B's website, and company B would put an ad for its website on company A's website. No money changed hands, but each company recorded revenue (for the value of the space that it gave the other company on its site). This practice did little to boost net income, and it resulted in no additional cash flow—but it did boost *reported revenue*. Regulators eventually put an end to this misleading practice.

Another type of transgression results from companies recording revenues or expenses in the wrong year. In fact, shifting revenues and expenses is one of the most common abuses of financial accounting. Xerox, for example, admitted reporting billions of dollars of lease revenue in periods earlier than it should have been reported. And WorldCom stunned the financial markets with its admission that it had boosted net income by billions of dollars by delaying the recognition of expenses until later years.

Unfortunately, revelations such as these have become all too common in the corporate world. It is no wonder that a U.S. Trust survey of affluent Americans reported that 85% of respondents believed that there should be tighter regulation of financial disclosures; 66% said they did not trust the management of publicly traded companies.

Why did so many companies violate basic financial reporting rules and sound ethics? Many speculate that as stock prices climbed, executives were under increasing pressure to meet higher and higher earnings expectations. If actual results weren't as good as hoped for, some gave in to temptation and "adjusted" their numbers to meet market expectations.

✓ The Navigator

## Inside Chapter 3

In Chapter 1 you learned a neat little formula: Net income = Revenues − Expenses. In Chapter 2 you learned some rules for recording revenue and expense transactions. Guess what? Things are not really that nice and neat. In fact, it is often difficult for companies to determine in what time period they should report some revenues and expenses. In other words, in measuring net income, timing is everything.

The content and organization of Chapter 3 are as follows.

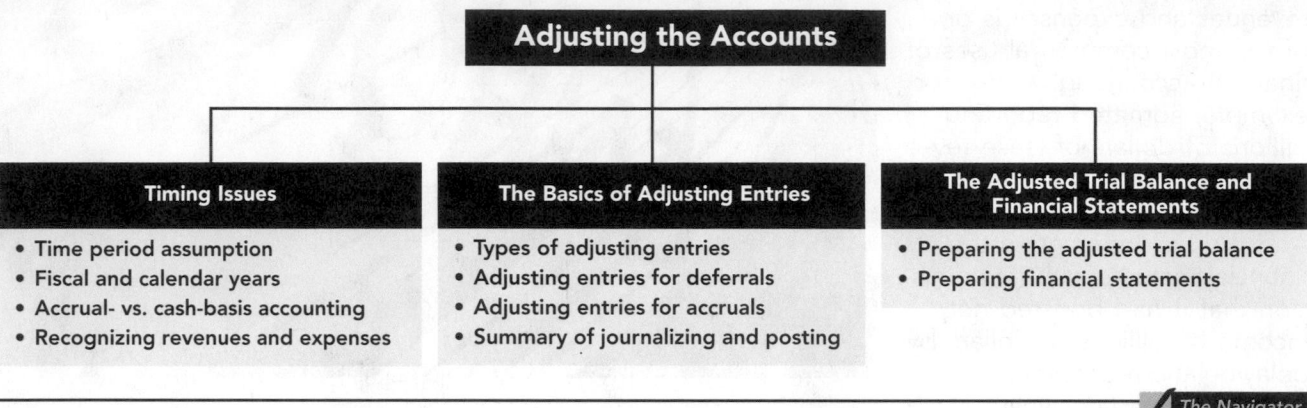

**Adjusting the Accounts**

| **Timing Issues** | **The Basics of Adjusting Entries** | **The Adjusted Trial Balance and Financial Statements** |
|---|---|---|
| • Time period assumption<br>• Fiscal and calendar years<br>• Accrual- vs. cash-basis accounting<br>• Recognizing revenues and expenses | • Types of adjusting entries<br>• Adjusting entries for deferrals<br>• Adjusting entries for accruals<br>• Summary of journalizing and posting | • Preparing the adjusted trial balance<br>• Preparing financial statements |

✔ The Navigator

# TIMING ISSUES

**STUDY OBJECTIVE 1**

Explain the time period assumption.

We would need no adjustments if we could wait to prepare financial statements until a company ended its operations. At that point, we could easily determine its final balance sheet and the amount of lifetime income it earned. The following story illustrates one way to compute lifetime income.

A grocery store owner from the "old country" kept his accounts payable on a spindle, accounts receivable on a note pad, and cash in a cigar box. His daughter, having just passed the CPA exam, chided the father: "I don't understand how you can run your business this way. How do you know what your profits are?"

"Well," the father replied, "when I got off the boat 40 years ago, I had nothing but the pants I was wearing. Today your brother is a doctor, your sister is a college professor, and you are a CPA. Your mother and I have a nice car, a well-furnished house, and a lake home. We have a good business, and everything is paid for. So, you add all that together, subtract the pants, and there's your profit."

**Time Period Assumption**

Year 1 — Year 10

Year 6

**ALTERNATIVE TERMINOLOGY**

The time period assumption is also called the *periodicity assumption*.

## Selecting an Accounting Time Period

Although the old grocer may be correct in his evaluation, it is impractical to wait so long for the results of operations. All companies find it desirable to report the results of their activities on a frequent basis. For example, management usually wants monthly financial statements, and the Internal Revenue Service requires all businesses to file annual tax returns. Therefore, **accountants divide the economic life of a business into artificial time periods**. This convenient assumption is referred to as the **time period assumption**.

Many business transactions affect more than one of these arbitrary time periods. For example, the airplanes purchased by Northwest Air Lines five years ago are still in use today. We must determine the relevance of each business transaction to specific accounting periods. (How much of the cost of an airplane contributed to operations this year?)

## Fiscal and Calendar Years

Both small and large companies prepare financial statements periodically in order to assess their financial condition and results of operations. **Accounting time periods are generally a month, a quarter, or a year.** Monthly and quarterly time periods are called interim periods. Most large companies must prepare both quarterly and annual financial statements.

An accounting time period that is one year in length is a fiscal year. A fiscal year usually begins with the first day of a month and ends twelve months later on the last day of a month. Most businesses use the calendar year (January 1 to December 31) as their accounting period. Some do not. Companies whose fiscal year differs from the calendar year include Delta Air Lines, June 30, and Walt Disney Productions, September 30. Sometimes a company's year-end will vary from year to year. For example, PepsiCo's fiscal year ends on the Friday closest to December 31, which was December 25 in 2004 and December 30 in 2005.

## Accrual- vs. Cash-Basis Accounting

What you will learn in this chapter is accrual-basis accounting. Under the accrual basis, companies record transactions **in the periods in which the events occur.** For example, using the accrual basis to determine net income means companies recognize revenues when earned (rather than when they receive cash). It also means recognizing expenses when incurred (rather than when paid).

An alternative to the accrual basis is the cash basis. Under cash-basis accounting, companies record revenue when they receive cash. They record an expense when they pay out cash. The cash basis seems appealing due to its simplicity, but it often produces misleading financial statements. It fails to record revenue that a company has earned but for which it has not received the cash. Also, it does not match expenses with earned revenues. **Cash-basis accounting is not in accordance with generally accepted accounting principles (GAAP).**

Individuals and some small companies do use cash-basis accounting. The cash basis is justified for small businesses because they often have few receivables and payables. Medium and large companies use accrual-basis accounting.

## Recognizing Revenues and Expenses

It can be difficult to determine the amount of revenues and expenses to report in a given accounting period. Two principles help in this task: the revenue recognition principle and the matching principle.

### REVENUE RECOGNITION PRINCIPLE

The revenue recognition principle dictates that companies recognize revenue in the accounting period in which it is earned. In a service enterprise, revenue is considered to be earned at the time the service is performed. To illustrate, assume that Dave's Dry Cleaning, Inc. cleans clothing on June 30 but customers do not claim and pay for their clothes until the first week of July. Under the revenue recognition principle, Dave's earns revenue in June when it performed the service, rather than in July when it received the cash. At June 30, Dave's would report a receivable on its balance sheet and revenue in its income statement for the service performed.

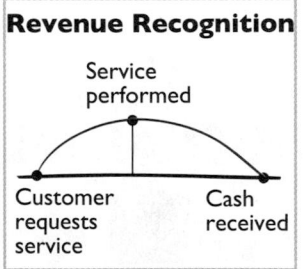

**Revenue Recognition**

Service performed

Customer requests service — Cash received

### MATCHING PRINCIPLE

Accountants follow a simple rule in recognizing expenses: "Let the expenses follow the revenues." That is, expense recognition is tied to revenue recognition. In the dry cleaning example, this principle means that Dave's should report the salary

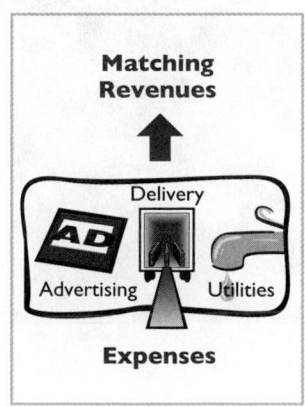

**Matching Revenues**

Delivery

AD

Advertising — Utilities

**Expenses**

expense incurred in performing the June 30 cleaning service in the income statement for the same period in which it recognizes the service revenue. The critical issue in expense recognition is when the expense makes its contribution to revenue. This may or may not be the same period in which the expense is paid. If Dave's does not pay the salary incurred on June 30 until July, it would report salaries payable on its June 30 balance sheet.

This practice of expense recognition is referred to as the **matching principle**. It dictates that efforts (expenses) be matched with accomplishments (revenues). Illustration 3-1 summarizes the revenue and expense recognition principles.

**Illustration 3-1**
GAAP relationships in revenue and expense recognition

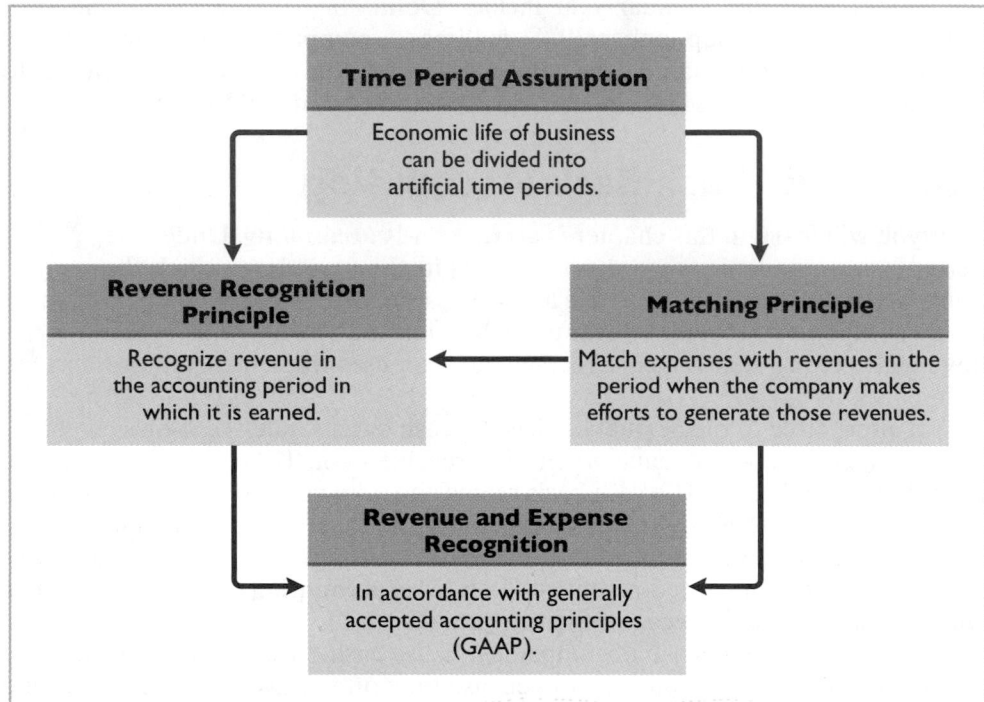

# ACCOUNTING ACROSS THE ORGANIZATION

### How Long Will "The Force" Be with Us?

Suppose you are filmmaker George Lucas and you spent $11 million to produce Twentieth Century Fox's film *Star Wars*. Over what period should the studio expense the cost?

Yes, it should expense the cost over the economic life of the film. But what *is* its economic life? You must estimate how much revenue you will earn from box office sales, video sales, television, and games and toys—a period that could be less than a year or more than 20 years, as is the case for *Star Wars*. Originally released in 1977, and rereleased in 1997, domestic revenues total over $500 million for *Star Wars* and continue to grow.

**?** What accounting principle does this example illustrate? How will financial results be affected if the expenses are recognized over a period that is *less than* that used for revenues? What if the expenses are recognized over a period that is *longer than* that used for revenues?

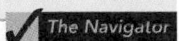
# THE BASICS OF ADJUSTING ENTRIES

In order for revenues and expenses to be reported in the correct period, companies make adjusting entries at the end of the accounting period. **Adjusting entries ensure that the revenue recognition and matching principles are followed.** Adjusting entries make it possible to report correct amounts on the balance sheet and on the income statement.

> **STUDY OBJECTIVE 3**
> Explain the reasons for adjusting entries.

The trial balance—the first summarization of the transaction data—may not contain up-to-date and complete data. This is true for several reasons:

1. Some events are not recorded daily because it is not efficient to do so. For example, companies do not record the daily use of supplies or the earning of wages by employees.

2. Some costs are not recorded during the accounting period because they expire with the passage of time rather than as a result of daily transactions. Examples are rent, insurance, and charges related to the use of equipment.

3. Some items may be unrecorded. An example is a utility bill that the company will not receive until the next accounting period.

**Accounting Cycle Tutorial— Making Adjusting Entries**

**A company must make adjusting entries every time it prepares financial statements.** It analyzes each account in the trial balance to determine whether it is complete and up-to-date. For example, the company may need to make inventory counts of supplies. It may also need to prepare supporting schedules of insurance policies, rental agreements, and other contractual commitments. Because the adjusting and closing process can be time-consuming, companies often prepare adjusting entries after the balance sheet date, but date them as of the balance sheet date.

> **HELPFUL HINT**
> Adjusting entries are needed to enable financial statements to conform to GAAP.

## Types of Adjusting Entries

Adjusting entries are classified as either **deferrals** or **accruals**. As Illustration 3-2 shows, each of these classes has two subcategories.

> **STUDY OBJECTIVE 4**
> Identify the major types of adjusting entries.

**Deferrals**
1. **Prepaid Expenses.** Expenses paid in cash and recorded as assets before they are used or consumed.
2. **Unearned Revenues.** Cash received and recorded as liabilities before revenue is earned.

**Accruals**
1. **Accrued Revenues.** Revenues earned but not yet received in cash or recorded.
2. **Accrued Expenses.** Expenses incurred but not yet paid in cash or recorded.

**Illustration 3-2**
Categories of adjusting entries

The following pages explain each type of adjustment and show examples. Each example is based on the October 31 trial balance of Pioneer Advertising Agency Inc. from Chapter 2 and reproduced in Illustration 3-3.

**Illustration 3-3**
Trial balance

| PIONEER ADVERTISING AGENCY INC. Trial Balance October 31, 2008 | Debit | Credit |
|---|---|---|
| Cash | $15,200 | |
| Advertising Supplies | 2,500 | |
| Prepaid Insurance | 600 | |
| Office Equipment | 5,000 | |
| Notes Payable | | $ 5,000 |
| Accounts Payable | | 2,500 |
| Unearned Revenue | | 1,200 |
| Common Stock | | 10,000 |
| Retained Earnings | | –0– |
| Dividends | 500 | |
| Service Revenue | | 10,000 |
| Salaries Expense | 4,000 | |
| Rent Expense | 900 | |
| | $28,700 | $28,700 |

We assume that Pioneer Advertising uses an accounting period of one month, and thus it makes monthly adjusting entries. The entries are dated October 31.

# Adjusting Entries for Deferrals

**Deferrals** are either prepaid expenses or unearned revenues. Companies make adjustments for deferrals to record the portion of the deferral that represents the **expense incurred or the revenue earned** in the current period.

### PREPAID EXPENSES

Companies record payments of expenses that will benefit more than one accounting period as assets called prepaid expenses or prepayments. When expenses are prepaid, an asset account is increased (debited) to show the service or benefit that the company will receive in the future. Examples of common prepayments are insurance, supplies, advertising, and rent. In addition, companies make prepayments when they purchase buildings and equipment.

**Prepaid expenses are costs that expire either with the passage of time** (e.g., rent and insurance) **or through use** (e.g., supplies). The expiration of these costs does not require daily journal entries. Companies postpone recognizing these costs until they prepare financial statements. At each statement date, they make adjusting entries: (1) to record the expenses that apply to the current accounting period, and (2) to show the unexpired costs in the asset accounts.

Prior to adjustment for prepaid expenses, assets are overstated and expenses are understated. As shown in Illustration 3-4, **an adjusting entry for prepaid expense increases (debits) an expense account and a decreases (credits) an asset account**.

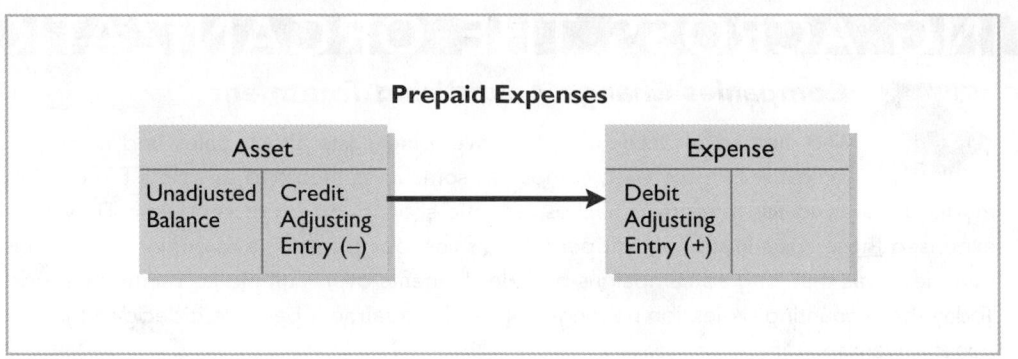

**Illustration 3-4**
Adjusting entries for
prepaid expenses

On the next few pages, we will look in more detail at some specific types of prepaid expenses, beginning with supplies.

**Supplies.**   Businesses use various types of supplies such as paper, envelopes, and printer cartridges. Companies generally debit supplies to an asset account when they acquire them. In the course of operations, supplies are used, but companies postpone recognizing their use until the adjustment process. At the end of the accounting period, a company counts the remaining supplies. The difference between the balance in the Supplies (asset) account and the supplies on hand represents the supplies used (an expense) for the period.

Pioneer Advertising Agency Inc. purchased advertising supplies costing $2,500 on October 5. Pioneer recorded that transaction by increasing (debiting) the asset Advertising Supplies. This account shows a balance of $2,500 in the October 31 trial balance. An inventory count at the close of business on October 31 reveals that $1,000 of supplies are still on hand. Thus, the cost of supplies used is $1,500 ($2,500 − $1,000). Pioneer makes the following adjusting entry.

Supplies

Oct. 5

Supplies purchased;
record asset

Oct. 31
Supplies used;
record supplies expense

| Oct. 31 | Advertising Supplies Expense | 1,500 | |
|---|---|---|---|
| | Advertising Supplies | | 1,500 |
| | (To record supplies used) | | |

| A | = | L | + | SE |
|---|---|---|---|---|
| | | | | −1,500 Exp |
| −1,500 | | | | |

**Cash Flows**
no effect

*Equation analyses* summarize
the effects of the transaction on
the elements of the accounting
equation.

After the adjusting entry is posted, the two supplies accounts show:

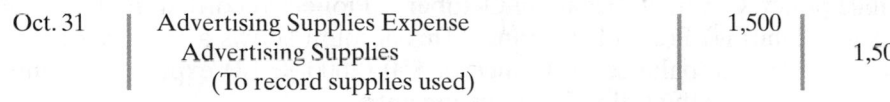

| Advertising Supplies | | | | Advertising Supplies Expense | | |
|---|---|---|---|---|---|---|
| 10/5 | 2,500 | 10/31 **Adj.** | **1,500** | 10/31 **Adj.** | **1,500** | |
| 10/31 Bal. | 1,000 | | | | | |

**Illustration 3-5**
Supplies accounts after
adjustment

The asset account Advertising Supplies now shows a balance of $1,000, which is equal to the cost of supplies on hand at the statement date. In addition, Advertising Supplies Expense shows a balance of $1,500, which equals the cost of supplies used in October. **If Pioneer does not make the adjusting entry, October expenses will be understated and net income overstated by $1,500. Also, both assets and owner's equity will be overstated by $1,500 on the October 31 balance sheet.**

### Companies Change Advertising Treatment

The method of accounting for advertising costs affects sales and marketing executives. In the past, companies sometimes recorded as assets the costs of media advertising for burgers, bleaches, athletic shoes, and other products. They then expensed those costs in subsequent periods as sales took place. The reasoning behind this treatment was that long ad campaigns provided benefits over multiple accounting periods. Today the accounting profession no longer allows this treatment because it decided that the benefits were too difficult to measure.

Instead, companies now must expense advertising costs when the advertising takes place. The issue is important because the outlays for advertising can be substantial. Recent big spenders: The Coca-Cola Company spent $2.2 billion, PepsiCo., Inc. $1.7 billion, Nike, Inc. $1,378 million, and Limited Brands $484 million.

**?** Why might the new accounting method cause companies sometimes to spend less on advertising?

---

## Insurance

**Oct. 4**
Insurance purchased;
record asset

| Insurance Policy | | | |
|---|---|---|---|
| Oct $50 | Nov $50 | Dec $50 | Jan $50 |
| Feb $50 | March $50 | April $50 | May $50 |
| June $50 | July $50 | Aug $50 | Sept $50 |
| I YEAR $600 | | | |

**Oct. 31**
Insurance expired;
record insurance expense

| A | = | L | + | SE |
|---|---|---|---|---|
| | | | | −50 Exp |
| −50 | | | | |

**Cash Flows**
no effect

**Illustration 3-6**
Insurance accounts after adjustment

**Insurance.**    Companies purchase insurance to protect themselves from losses due to fire, theft, and other unforeseen events. Insurance must be paid in advance. Insurance premiums (payments) normally are recorded as an increase (a debit) to the asset account Prepaid Insurance. At the financial statement date companies increase (debit) Insurance Expense and decrease (credit) Prepaid Insurance for the cost that has expired during the period.

On October 4, Pioneer Advertising Agency Inc. paid $600 for a one-year fire insurance policy. Coverage began on October 1. Pioneer recorded the payment by increasing (debiting) Prepaid Insurance. This account shows a balance of $600 in the October 31 trial balance. Insurance of $50 ($600 ÷ 12) expires each month. Thus, Pioneer makes the following adjusting entry.

| Oct. 31 | Insurance Expense | 50 | |
| |     Prepaid Insurance | | 50 |
| |       (To record insurance expired) | | |

After Pioneer posts the adjusting entry, the accounts show:

| Prepaid Insurance | | | | Insurance Expense | | |
|---|---|---|---|---|---|---|
| 10/4 | 600 | 10/31 **Adj.** | 50 | 10/31 **Adj.** | 50 | |
| 10/31 Bal. | 550 | | | | | |

The asset Prepaid Insurance shows a balance of $550. This amount represents the unexpired cost for the remaining 11 months of coverage. The $50 balance in Insurance Expense equals the insurance cost that has expired in October. If Pioneer does not make this adjustment, October expenses will be understated and net income overstated by $50. Also, both assets and stockholders' equity will be overstated by $50 on the October 31 balance sheet.

**Depreciation.** Companies typically own buildings, equipment, and vehicles. These long-lived assets provide service for a number of years. Thus, each is recorded as an asset, rather than an expense, in the year it is acquired. As explained in Chapter 1, companies record such assets **at cost**, as required by the cost principle. The term of service is referred to as the <u>useful life</u>.

According to the matching principle, companies then report a portion of the cost of a long-lived asset as an expense during each period of the asset's useful life. <u>Depreciation</u> is the process of allocating the cost of an asset to expense over its useful life in a rational and systematic manner.

**Depreciation**

Oct. 2

Office equipment purchased; record asset

| Office Equipment | | | |
|---|---|---|---|
| Oct | Nov | Dec | Jan |
| $40 | $40 | $40 | $40 |
| Feb | March | April | May |
| $40 | $40 | $40 | $40 |
| June | July | Aug | Sept |
| $40 | $40 | $40 | $40 |
| Depreciation = $480/year | | | |

Oct. 31
 Depreciation recognized; record depreciation expense

*Need for Depreciation Adjustment.* From an accounting standpoint, acquiring long-lived assets is essentially a long-term prepayment for services. Companies need to make periodic adjusting entries for depreciation, just as they do for other prepaid expenses. These entries recognize the cost that has been used (an expense) during the period and report the unexpired cost (an asset) at the end of the period.

When a company acquires a long-lived asset, it does not know its exact useful life. The asset may be useful for a longer or shorter time than expected, depending on various factors. Thus, **depreciation is an estimate** rather than a factual measurement of expired cost. A common procedure in computing depreciation expense is to divide the cost of the asset by its useful life. For example, if cost is $10,000 and useful life is expected to be 10 years, annual depreciation is $1,000.[1]

Pioneer Advertising estimates depreciation on the office equipment to be $480 a year, or $40 per month. Thus, Pioneer makes the following adjusting entry to record depreciation for October.

| Oct. 31 | Depreciation Expense | 40 | |
|---|---|---|---|
| | Accumulated Depreciation—Office Equipment | | 40 |
| | (To record monthly depreciation) | | |

| A | = | L | + | SE |
|---|---|---|---|---|
| | | | | −40 Exp |
| −40 | | | | |

**Cash Flows**
no effect

After the adjusting entry is posted, the accounts show:

| Office Equipment | |
|---|---|
| 10/1    5,000 | |

| Accumulated Depreciation—Office Equipment | | Depreciation Expense | |
|---|---|---|---|
| | 10/31 **Adj.**    40 | 10/31 **Adj.**    40 | |

**Illustration 3-7**
Accounts after adjustment for depreciation

The balance in the accumulated depreciation account will increase $40 each month. After journalizing and posting the adjusting entry at November 30, the balance will be $80; at December 31, $120; and so on.

*Statement Presentation.* Accumulated Depreciation—Office Equipment is a **contra asset account**. That means that it is offset against an asset account on the balance sheet. This accumulated depreciation account appears just after the account it offsets (in this case, Office Equipment) on the balance sheet. Its normal balance is a credit.

An alternative to using a contra asset account would be to decrease (credit) the asset account (e.g., Office Equipment) directly for the depreciation each month. But use of the contra account is preferable for a simple reason: it discloses *both* the original cost of the equipment *and* the total cost that has expired to date.

**HELPFUL HINT**

All contra accounts have increases, decreases, and normal balances *opposite* to the account to which they relate.

---

[1] Chapter 10 addresses the computation of depreciation expense in detail.

In the balance sheet, Pioneer deducts Accumulated Depreciation—Office Equipment from the related asset account, as follows.

| | | |
|---|---|---|
| Office equipment | $5,000 | |
| Less: Accumulated depreciation—office equipment | 40 | **$4,960** |

The difference between the cost of any depreciable asset and its related accumulated depreciation is its <u>book value</u>. In Illustration 3-8, the book value of the equipment at the balance sheet date is $4,960. The book value of an asset generally differs from its **market value**—the price at which the asset could be sold in the marketplace. Remember that depreciation is a means of cost allocation, not a matter of market valuation.

Depreciation expense identifies that portion of the asset's cost that has expired during the period (in this case, in October). As for other prepaid adjustments, the omission of this adjusting entry would cause total assets, total owner's equity, and net income to be overstated and depreciation expense to be understated.

If the company owns additional long-lived assets, such as store equipment or buildings, it records depreciation expense on each of those items. It also establishes related accumulated depreciation accounts, such as: Accumulated Depreciation—Store Equipment; and Accumulated Depreciation—Buildings.

Illustration 3-9 summarizes the accounting for prepaid expenses.

| | | | |
|---|---|---|---|
| **ACCOUNTING FOR PREPAID EXPENSES** | | | |
| **Examples** | **Reason for Adjustment** | **Accounts Before Adjustment** | **Adjusting Entry** |
| Insurance, supplies, advertising, rent, depreciation. | Prepaid expenses recorded in asset accounts have been used. | Assets overstated. Expenses understated. | Dr. Expenses Cr. Assets |

## UNEARNED REVENUES

Companies record cash received before revenue is earned by increasing a liability account called **unearned revenues**. Examples are rent, magazine subscriptions, and customer deposits for future service. Airlines such as United, American, and Delta, for instance, treat receipts from the sale of tickets as unearned revenue until they provide the flight service. Similarly, colleges consider tuition received prior to the start of a semester as unearned revenue.

Unearned revenues are the opposite of prepaid expenses. Indeed, unearned revenue on the books of one company is likely to be a prepayment on the books of the company that made the advance payment. For example, a landlord will have unearned rent revenue when a tenant has prepaid rent.

When a company receives cash for future services, it increases (credits) an unearned revenue account (a liability) to recognize the liability. Later, the company earns revenues by providing service. It may not be practical to make daily journal entries as the revenue is earned. Instead, we delay recognizing earned revenue until the end of the period. Then the company makes an adjusting entry to record the revenue that has been earned and to show the liability that remains. Typically, prior to adjustment, liabilities are overstated and revenues are understated. Therefore, as shown in Illustration 3-10, the adjusting entry for unearned revenues results in a decrease (a debit) to a liability account and an increase (a credit) to a revenue account.

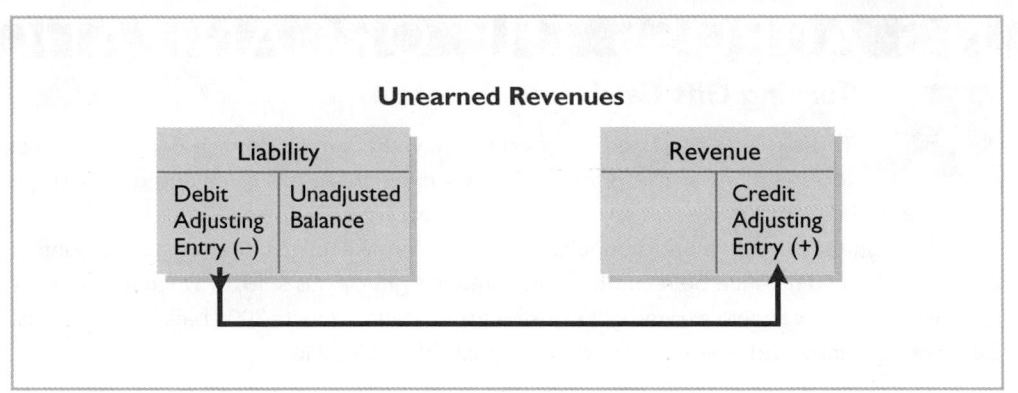

**Illustration 3-10**
Adjusting entries for unearned revenues

Pioneer Advertising Agency Inc. received $1,200 on October 2 from R. Knox for advertising services expected to be completed by December 31. Pioneer credited the payment to Unearned Service Revenue; this account shows a balance of $1,200 in the October 31 trial balance. Analysis reveals that the company earned $400 of those fees in October. Thus, it makes the following adjusting entry.

**ALTERNATIVE TERMINOLOGY**

**Unearned revenue is sometimes referred to as** *deferred revenue.*

| Oct. 31 | Unearned Revenue | 400 | |
| | Service Revenue | | 400 |
| | (To record revenue for services provided) | | |

| A | = | L | + | SE |
|---|---|---|---|---|
| | | −400 | | |
| | | | | +400 Rev |

**Cash Flows**
no effect

After the company posts the adjusting entry, the accounts show:

| **Unearned Revenue** | | | | **Service Revenue** | |
|---|---|---|---|---|---|
| 10/31 **Adj.** 400 | 10/2 | 1,200 | | 10/31 Bal. | 10,000 |
| | 10/31 Bal. | 800 | | 31 **Adj.** | **400** |

**Illustration 3-11**
Revenue accounts after prepayments adjustment

The liability Unearned Revenue now shows a balance of $800. That amount represents the remaining prepaid advertising services to be performed in the future. At the same time, Service Revenue shows total revenue of $10,400 earned in October. Without this adjustment, revenues and net income are understated by $400 in the income statement. Also, liabilities are overstated and stockholders' equity understated by $400 on the October 31 balance sheet.

Illustration 3-12 summarizes the accounting for unearned revenues.

**Illustration 3-12**
Accounting for unearned revenues

| ACCOUNTING FOR UNEARNED REVENUES | | | |
|---|---|---|---|
| **Examples** | **Reason for Adjustment** | **Accounts Before Adjustment** | **Adjusting Entry** |
| Rent, magazine subscriptions, customer deposits for future service. | Unearned revenues recorded in liability accounts have been earned. | Liabilities overstated. Revenues understated. | Dr. Liabilities Cr. Revenues |

# ACCOUNTING ACROSS THE ORGANIZATION

### Turning Gift Cards into Revenue

Those of you interested in marketing know that gift cards are among the hottest tools in merchandising today. Customers purchase gift cards and give them to someone for later use. In a recent year gift-card sales topped $95 billion.

Although these programs are popular with marketing executives, they create accounting questions. Should revenue be recorded at the time the gift card is sold, or when it is used by the customer? How should expired gift cards be accounted for? In its 2004 balance sheet Best Buy reported unearned revenue related to gift cards of $300 million.

*Source:* Robert Berner, "Gift Cards: No Gift to Investors," *Business Week* (March 14, 2005), p. 86.

Suppose that Robert Jones purchases a $100 gift card at Best Buy on December 24, 2007, and gives it to his wife, Devon, on December 25, 2007. On January 3, 2008, Devon uses the card to purchase $100 worth of CDs. When do you think Best Buy should recognize revenue, and why?

## Before You Go On...

### REVIEW IT

1. What are the four types of adjusting entries?
2. What is the effect on assets, stockholders' equity, expenses, and net income if a company does not make a prepaid expense adjusting entry?
3. What is the effect on liabilities, stockholders' equity, revenues, and net income if a company does not make an unearned revenue adjusting entry?
4. Using PepsiCo's Consolidated Statement of Income, what was the amount of depreciation expense for 2005 and 2004? (See Note 4 to the financial statements.) The answer to this question appears on page 140.

### DO IT

The ledger of Hammond, Inc. on March 31, 2008, includes the following selected accounts before adjusting entries.

|  | Debit | Credit |
|---|---|---|
| Prepaid Insurance | 3,600 |  |
| Office Supplies | 2,800 |  |
| Office Equipment | 25,000 |  |
| Accumulated Depreciation—Office Equipment |  | 5,000 |
| Unearned Revenue |  | 9,200 |

An analysis of the accounts shows the following.
1. Insurance expires at the rate of $100 per month.
2. Supplies on hand total $800.
3. The office equipment depreciates $200 a month.
4. One-half of the unearned revenue was earned in March.

Prepare the adjusting entries for the month of March.

### Action Plan
■ Make adjusting entries at the end of the period for revenues earned and expenses incurred in the period.

■ Don't forget to make adjusting entries for prepayments. Failure to adjust for prepayments leads to overstatement of the asset or liability and related understatement of the expense or revenue.

**Solution**

| | | | |
|---|---|---:|---:|
| 1. | Insurance Expense | 100 | |
| |     Prepaid Insurance | | 100 |
| |         (To record insurance expired) | | |
| 2. | Office Supplies Expense | 2,000 | |
| |     Office Supplies | | 2,000 |
| |         (To record supplies used) | | |
| 3. | Depreciation Expense | 200 | |
| |     Accumulated Depreciation—Office Equipment | | 200 |
| |         (To record monthly depreciation) | | |
| 4. | Unearned Revenue | 4,600 | |
| |     Service Revenue | | 4,600 |
| |         (To record revenue for services provided) | | |

Related exercise material: *BE3-3, BE3-4, BE3-5, and BE3-6.*

*The Navigator*

# Adjusting Entries for Accruals

The second category of adjusting entries is **accruals**. Companies make adjusting entries for accruals to record revenues earned and expenses incurred in the current accounting period that have not been recognized through daily entries.

## ACCRUED REVENUES

Revenues earned but not yet recorded at the statement date are accrued revenues. Accrued revenues may accumulate (accrue) with the passing of time, as in the case of interest revenue and rent revenue. Or they may result from services that have been performed but are neither billed nor collected. The former are unrecorded because the earning process (e.g., of interest and rent) does not involve daily transactions. The latter may be unrecorded because the company has provided only a portion of the total service.

An adjusting entry for accrued revenues serves two purposes: (1) It shows the receivable that exists at the balance sheet date, and (2) it records the revenues earned during the period. Prior to adjustment, both assets and revenues are understated. Therefore, as Illustration 3-13 shows, **an adjusting entry for accrued revenues increases (debits) an asset account and increases (credits) a revenue account.**

**Accrued Revenues**

Oct. 31

*My fee is $200*

Revenue and receivable are recorded for unbilled services

Nov. 10

Cash is received; receivable is reduced

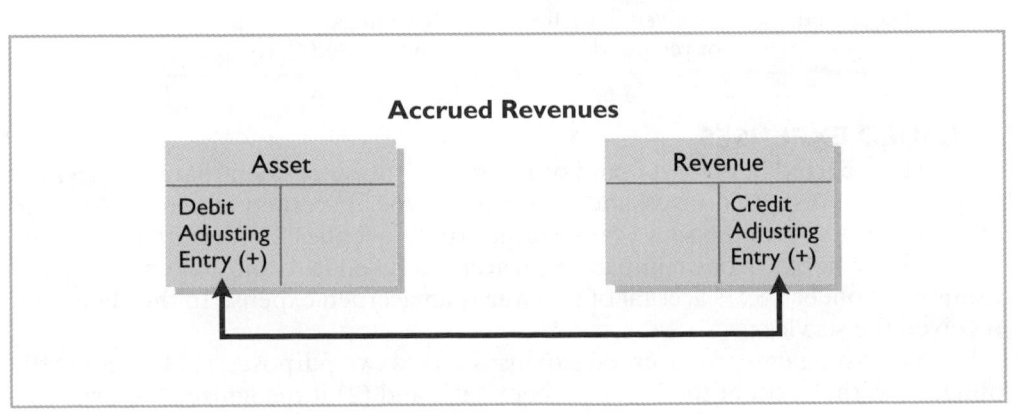

**Accrued Revenues**

| Asset | | Revenue | |
|---|---|---|---|
| Debit Adjusting Entry (+) | | | Credit Adjusting Entry (+) |

**Illustration 3-13**
Adjusting entries for accrued revenues

In October Pioneer Advertising Agency Inc. earned $200 for advertising services that have not been recorded. Pioneer makes the following adjusting entry on October 31.

| A | = | L | + | SE |
|---|---|---|---|---|
| +200 | | | | |
| | | | | +200 Rev |

**Cash Flows**
no effect

| Oct. 31 | Accounts Receivable | 200 | |
| | Service Revenue | | 200 |
| | (To record revenue for services provided) | | |

After Pioneer posts the adjusting entry, the accounts show:

**Illustration 3-14**
Receivable and revenue accounts after accrual adjustment

| Accounts Receivable | | Service Revenue | |
|---|---|---|---|
| 10/31 **Adj.** 200 | | 10/31 | 10,000 |
| | | 31 | 400 |
| | | 31 **Adj.** | **200** |
| | | 10/31 Bal. | 10,600 |

The asset Accounts Receivable indicates that clients owe $200 at the balance sheet date. The balance of $10,600 in Service Revenue represents the total revenue Pioneer earned during the month ($10,000 + $400 + $200). Without the adjusting entry, assets and stockholders' equity on the balance sheet, and revenues and net income on the income statement, are understated.

On November 10, Pioneer receives cash of $200 for the services performed in October and makes the following entry.

| A | = | L | + | SE |
|---|---|---|---|---|
| +200 | | | | |
| −200 | | | | |

**Cash Flows**
+200

| Nov. 10 | Cash | 200 | |
| | Accounts Receivable | | 200 |
| | (To record cash collected on account) | | |

The company records collection of cash on account with a debit (increase) to Cash and a credit (decrease) to Accounts Receivable.

Illustration 3-15 summarizes the accounting for accrued revenues.

**Illustration 3-15**
Accounting for accrued revenues

| | ACCOUNTING FOR ACCRUED REVENUES | | |
|---|---|---|---|
| **Examples** | **Reason for Adjustment** | **Accounts Before Adjustment** | **Adjusting Entry** |
| Interest, rent, services performed but not collected. | Revenues have been earned but not yet received in cash or recorded. | Assets understated. Revenues understated. | Dr. Assets Cr. Revenues |

**ACCRUED EXPENSES**

Expenses incurred but not yet paid or recorded at the statement date are **accrued expenses.** Interest, rent, taxes, and salaries are typical accrued expenses. Accrued expenses result from the same causes as accrued revenues. In fact, an accrued expense on the books of one company is an accrued revenue to another company. For example, Pioneer's $200 accrual of revenue is an accrued expense to the client that received the service.

An adjusting entry for accrued expenses serves two purposes: (1) It records the obligations that exist at the balance sheet date, and (2) it recognizes the expenses of the current accounting period. Prior to adjustment, both liabilities and expenses are understated. Therefore, as Illustration 3-16 shows, **an adjusting entry for accrued expenses increases (debits) an expense account and increases (credits) a liability account**.

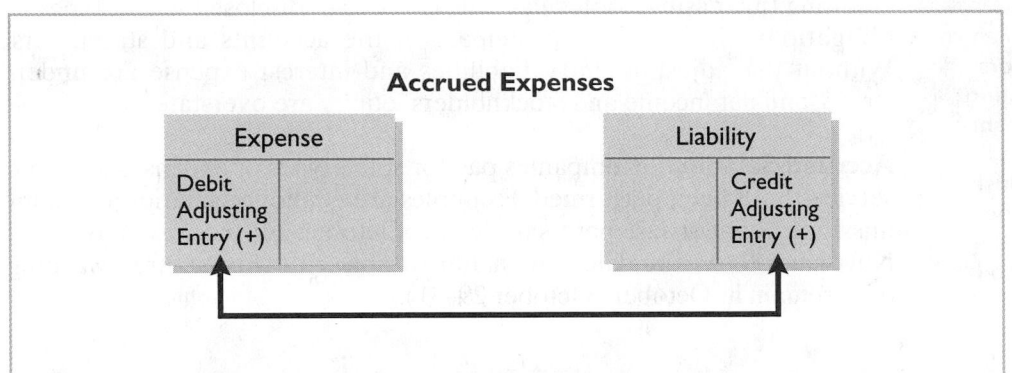

**Illustration 3-16**
Adjusting entries for accrued expenses

On the next few pages, we will look in more detail at some specific types of accrued expenses, beginning with accrued interest.

**Accrued Interest.** Pioneer Advertising Agency Inc. signed a $5,000, 3-month note payable on October 1. The note requires Pioneer to pay interest at an annual rate of 12%.

Three factors determine the amount of interest accumulation: (1) the face value of the note, (2) the interest rate, which is always expressed as an annual rate, and (3) the length of time the note is outstanding. For Pioneer, the total interest due on the note at its due date is $150 ($5,000 face value × 12% interest rate × 3/12 time period). The interest is thus $50 per month. Illustration 3-17 shows the formula for computing interest and its application to Pioneer Advertising Agency Inc. for the month of October.[2] Note that the time period is expressed as a fraction of a year.

**HELPFUL HINT**
Interest is a cost of borrowing money that accumulates with the passage of time.

| Face Value of Note | × | Annual Interest Rate | × | Time in Terms of One Year | = | Interest |
|---|---|---|---|---|---|---|
| $5,000 | × | 12% | × | 1/12 | = | **$50** |

**Illustration 3-17**
Formula for computing interest

Pioneer makes the following accrued expense adjusting entry on October 31.

| Oct. 31 | Interest Expense | 50 | |
| | Interest Payable | | 50 |
| | (To record interest on notes payable) | | |

| A | = | L | + | SE |
|---|---|---|---|---|
| | | | | −50 Exp |
| | | +50 | | |

**Cash Flows**
no effect

After the company posts this adjusting entry, the accounts show:

| Interest Expense | | Interest Payable | |
|---|---|---|---|
| 10/31 **Adj.** 50 | | | 10/31 **Adj.** 50 |

**Illustration 3-18**
Interest accounts after adjustment

---

[2]We will consider the computation of interest in more depth in later chapters.

Interest Expense shows the interest charges for the month of October. Interest Payable shows the amount of interest owed at the statement date. (As of October 31, they are the same because October is the first month of the note payable.) Pioneer will not pay the interest until the note comes due at the end of three months. Companies use the Interest Payable account, instead of crediting (increasing) Notes Payable, in order to disclose the two types of obligations—interest and principal—in the accounts and statements. Without this adjusting entry, liabilities and interest expense are understated, and net income and stockholders' equity are overstated.

**Accrued Salaries.** Companies pay for some types of expenses after the services have been performed. Examples are employee salaries and commissions. Pioneer last paid salaries on October 26; the next payday is November 9. As the calendar in Illustration 3-19 shows, three working days remain in October (October 29–31).

**Illustration 3-19**
Calendar showing Pioneer's pay periods

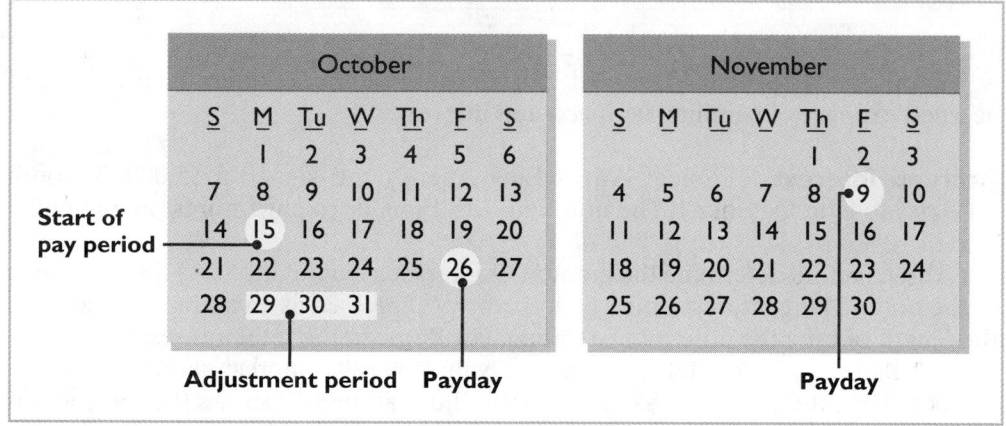

At October 31, the salaries for the last three days of the month represent an accrued expense and a related liability. The employees receive total salaries of $2,000 for a five-day work week, or $400 per day. Thus, accrued salaries at October 31 are $1,200 ($400 × 3). Pioneer makes the following adjusting entry:

```
A  =  L  +  SE
            −1,200 Exp
   +1,200
```

**Cash Flows**
no effect

| Oct. 31 | Salaries Expense | 1,200 | |
| | Salaries Payable | | 1,200 |
| | (To record accrued salaries) | | |

After the company posts this adjusting entry, the accounts show:

**Illustration 3-20**
Salary accounts after adjustment

| | Salaries Expense | | | Salaries Payable | |
|---|---|---|---|---|---|
| 10/26 | 4,000 | | | 10/31 **Adj.** | **1,200** |
| 31 **Adj.** | **1,200** | | | | |
| 10/31 **Bal.** | **5,200** | | | | |

After this adjustment, the balance in Salaries Expense of $5,200 (13 days × $400) is the actual salary expense for October. The balance in Salaries Payable of $1,200 is the amount of the liability for salaries Pioneer owes as of October 31. Without the $1,200 adjustment for salaries, Pioneer's expenses are understated $1,200, and its liabilities are understated $1,200.

Pioneer Advertising pays salaries every two weeks. The next payday is November 9, when the company will again pay total salaries of $4,000. The payment will consist of $1,200 of salaries payable at October 31 plus $2,800 of salaries expense for November (7 working days as shown in the November calendar × $400). Therefore, Pioneer makes the following entry on November 9.

| Nov. 9 | Salaries Payable | 1,200 | |
|--------|------------------|-------|-------|
| | Salaries Expense | 2,800 | |
| |     Cash | | 4,000 |
| |     (To record November 9 payroll) | | |

```
A  =   L   +  SE
      −1,200
                −2,800 Exp
−4,000
```

**Cash Flows**
−4,000

This entry eliminates the liability for Salaries Payable that Pioneer recorded in the October 31 adjusting entry. It also records the proper amount of Salaries Expense for the period between November 1 and November 9.

Illustration 3-21 summarizes the accounting for accrued expenses.

| ACCOUNTING FOR ACCRUED EXPENSES | | | |
|---|---|---|---|
| **Examples** | **Reason for Adjustment** | **Accounts Before Adjustment** | **Adjusting Entry** |
| Interest, rent, salaries | Expenses have been incurred but not yet paid in cash or recorded. | Expenses understated. Liabilities understated. | Dr. Expenses   Cr. Liabilities |

**Illustration 3-21**
Accounting for accrued expenses

## Before You Go On. . .

### REVIEW IT

1. If an accrued revenue adjusting entry is not made, what is the effect on assets, stockholders' equity, revenues, and net income?
2. If an accrued expense adjusting entry is not made, what is the effect on liabilities, stockholders' equity, expenses, and net income?

### DO IT

Calvin and Hobbs are the new owners of Micro Computer Services Inc. At the end of August 2008, their first month of ownership, Calvin and Hobbs are trying to prepare monthly financial statements. They have the following information for the month.

1. At August 31, Micro Computer owed employees $800 in salaries that will be paid on September 1.
2. On August 1, Micro Computer borrowed $30,000 from a local bank on a 15-year note. The annual interest rate is 10%.
3. Service revenue unrecorded in August totaled $1,100.

Prepare the adjusting entries needed at August 31, 2008.

### Action Plan

■ Make adjusting entries at the end of the period for revenues earned and expenses incurred in the period.

■ Don't forget to make adjusting entries for accruals. Adjusting entries for accruals will increase both a balance sheet and an income statement account.

**Solution**

| | | | |
|---|---|---:|---:|
| 1. | Salaries Expense | 800 | |
| |     Salaries Payable | | 800 |
| |       (To record accrued salaries) | | |
| 2. | Interest Expense | 250 | |
| |     Interest Payable | | 250 |
| |       (To record interest) | | |
| |       ($30,000 × 10% × 1/12 = $250) | | |
| 3. | Accounts Receivable | 1,100 | |
| |     Service Revenue | | 1,100 |
| |       (To record revenue for services provided) | | |

Related exercise material: *BE3-7, E3-5, E3-6, E3-7, E3-8, E3-9, E3-10, E3-11, E3-12, and E3-13.*

✓ The Navigator

# Summary of Journalizing and Posting

Illustrations 3-22 and 3-23 show the journalizing and posting of adjusting entries for Pioneer Advertising Agency Inc. on October 31. The ledger identifies all adjustments by the reference J2 because they have been recorded on page 2 of the general journal. The company may insert a center caption "Adjusting Entries" between the last transaction entry and the first adjusting entry in the journal. When you review the general ledger in Illustration 3-23, note that the entries highlighted in color are the adjustments.

**Illustration 3-22**
General journal showing adjusting entries

| | GENERAL JOURNAL | | | J2 |
|---|---|---|---|---|
| **Date** | **Account Titles and Explanation** | **Ref.** | **Debit** | **Credit** |
| 2008 | **Adjusting Entries** | | | |
| Oct. 31 | Advertising Supplies Expense | 631 | 1,500 | |
| |     Advertising Supplies | 126 | | 1,500 |
| |       (To record supplies used) | | | |
| 31 | Insurance Expense | 722 | 50 | |
| |     Prepaid Insurance | 130 | | 50 |
| |       (To record insurance expired) | | | |
| 31 | Depreciation Expense | 711 | 40 | |
| |     Accumulated Depreciation—Office Equipment | 158 | | 40 |
| |       (To record monthly depreciation) | | | |
| 31 | Unearned Revenue | 209 | 400 | |
| |     Service Revenue | 400 | | 400 |
| |       (To record revenue for services provided) | | | |
| 31 | Accounts Receivable | 112 | 200 | |
| |     Service Revenue | 400 | | 200 |
| |       (To record revenue for services provided) | | | |
| 31 | Interest Expense | 905 | 50 | |
| |     Interest Payable | 230 | | 50 |
| |       (To record interest on notes payable) | | | |
| 31 | Salaries Expense | 726 | 1,200 | |
| |     Salaries Payable | 212 | | 1,200 |
| |       (To record accrued salaries) | | | |

**HELPFUL HINT**

(1) Adjusting entries should not involve debits or credits to cash.
(2) Evaluate whether the adjustment makes sense. For example, an adjustment to recognize supplies used should increase supplies expense.
(3) Double-check all computations.
(4) Each adjusting entry affects one balance sheet account and one income statement account.

**Cash**      No. 101

| Date | Explanation | Ref. | Debit | Credit | Balance |
|---|---|---|---|---|---|
| 2008 | | | | | |
| Oct. 1 | | J1 | 10,000 | | 10,000 |
| 2 | | J1 | 1,200 | | 11,200 |
| 3 | | J1 | | 900 | 10,300 |
| 4 | | J1 | | 600 | 9,700 |
| 20 | | J1 | | 500 | 9,200 |
| 26 | | J1 | | 4,000 | 5,200 |
| 31 | | J1 | 10,000 | | 15,200 |

**Accounts Receivable**      No. 112

| Date | Explanation | Ref. | Debit | Credit | Balance |
|---|---|---|---|---|---|
| 2008 | | | | | |
| Oct. 31 | Adj. entry | J2 | 200 | | 200 |

**Advertising Supplies**      No. 126

| Date | Explanation | Ref. | Debit | Credit | Balance |
|---|---|---|---|---|---|
| 2008 | | | | | |
| Oct. 5 | | J1 | 2,500 | | 2,500 |
| 31 | Adj. entry | J2 | | 1,500 | 1,000 |

**Prepaid Insurance**      No. 130

| Date | Explanation | Ref. | Debit | Credit | Balance |
|---|---|---|---|---|---|
| 2008 | | | | | |
| Oct. 4 | | J1 | 600 | | 600 |
| 31 | Adj. entry | J2 | | 50 | 550 |

**Office Equipment**      No. 157

| Date | Explanation | Ref. | Debit | Credit | Balance |
|---|---|---|---|---|---|
| 2008 | | | | | |
| Oct. 1 | | J1 | 5,000 | | 5,000 |

**Accumulated Depreciation—Office Equipment**      No. 158

| Date | Explanation | Ref. | Debit | Credit | Balance |
|---|---|---|---|---|---|
| 2008 | | | | | |
| Oct. 31 | Adj. entry | J2 | | 40 | 40 |

**Notes Payable**      No. 200

| Date | Explanation | Ref. | Debit | Credit | Balance |
|---|---|---|---|---|---|
| 2008 | | | | | |
| Oct. 1 | | J1 | | 5,000 | 5,000 |

**Accounts Payable**      No. 201

| Date | Explanation | Ref. | Debit | Credit | Balance |
|---|---|---|---|---|---|
| 2008 | | | | | |
| Oct. 5 | | J1 | | 2,500 | 2,500 |

**Unearned Revenue**      No. 209

| Date | Explanation | Ref. | Debit | Credit | Balance |
|---|---|---|---|---|---|
| 2008 | | | | | |
| Oct. 2 | | J1 | | 1,200 | 1,200 |
| 31 | Adj. entry | J2 | 400 | | 800 |

**Salaries Payable**      No. 212

| Date | Explanation | Ref. | Debit | Credit | Balance |
|---|---|---|---|---|---|
| 2008 | | | | | |
| Oct. 31 | Adj. entry | J2 | | 1,200 | 1,200 |

**Interest Payable**      No. 230

| Date | Explanation | Ref. | Debit | Credit | Balance |
|---|---|---|---|---|---|
| 2008 | | | | | |
| Oct. 31 | Adj. entry | J2 | | 50 | 50 |

**Common Stock**      No. 311

| Date | Explanation | Ref. | Debit | Credit | Balance |
|---|---|---|---|---|---|
| 2008 | | | | | |
| Oct. 1 | | J1 | | 10,000 | 10,000 |

**Retained Earnings**      No. 320

| Date | Explanation | Ref. | Debit | Credit | Balance |
|---|---|---|---|---|---|
| 2008 | | | | | |

**Dividends**      No. 332

| Date | Explanation | Ref. | Debit | Credit | Balance |
|---|---|---|---|---|---|
| 2008 | | | | | |
| Oct. 20 | | J1 | 500 | | 500 |

**Service Revenue**      No. 400

| Date | Explanation | Ref. | Debit | Credit | Balance |
|---|---|---|---|---|---|
| 2008 | | | | | |
| Oct. 31 | | J1 | | 10,000 | 10,000 |
| 31 | Adj. entry | J2 | | 400 | 10,400 |
| 31 | Adj. entry | J2 | | 200 | 10,600 |

**Advertising Supplies Expense**      No. 631

| Date | Explanation | Ref. | Debit | Credit | Balance |
|---|---|---|---|---|---|
| 2008 | | | | | |
| Oct. 31 | Adj. entry | J2 | 1,500 | | 1,500 |

**Depreciation Expense**      No. 711

| Date | Explanation | Ref. | Debit | Credit | Balance |
|---|---|---|---|---|---|
| 2008 | | | | | |
| Oct. 31 | Adj. entry | J2 | 40 | | 40 |

**Insurance Expense**      No. 722

| Date | Explanation | Ref. | Debit | Credit | Balance |
|---|---|---|---|---|---|
| 2008 | | | | | |
| Oct. 31 | Adj. entry | J2 | 50 | | 50 |

**Salaries Expense**      No. 726

| Date | Explanation | Ref. | Debit | Credit | Balance |
|---|---|---|---|---|---|
| 2008 | | | | | |
| Oct. 26 | | J1 | 4,000 | | 4,000 |
| 31 | Adj. entry | J2 | 1,200 | | 5,200 |

**Rent Expense**      No. 729

| Date | Explanation | Ref. | Debit | Credit | Balance |
|---|---|---|---|---|---|
| 2008 | | | | | |
| Oct. 3 | | J1 | 900 | | 900 |

**Interest Expense**      No. 905

| Date | Explanation | Ref. | Debit | Credit | Balance |
|---|---|---|---|---|---|
| 2008 | | | | | |
| Oct. 31 | Adj. entry | J2 | 50 | | 50 |

Illustration 3-23
General ledger after adjustment

# THE ADJUSTED TRIAL BALANCE AND FINANCIAL STATEMENTS

STUDY OBJECTIVE 7

Describe the nature and purpose of an adjusted trial balance.

The company has journalized and posted all adjusting entries. Next it prepares another trial balance from the ledger accounts. This is called an **adjusted trial balance**. Its purpose is to **prove the equality** of the total debit balances and the total credit balances in the ledger after all adjustments. The accounts in the adjusted trial balance contain all data that the company needs to prepare financial statements.

## Preparing the Adjusted Trial Balance

Illustration 3-24 presents the adjusted trial balance for Pioneer Advertising Agency Inc., prepared from the ledger accounts in Illustration 3-23. The amounts highlighted in color are those affected by the adjusting entries. Compare these amounts to those in the unadjusted trial balance in Illustration 3-3 on page 98.

**Illustration 3-24**
Adjusted trial balance

### PIONEER ADVERTISING AGENCY INC.
#### Adjusted Trial Balance
#### October 31, 2008

|  | Dr. | Cr. |
|---|---|---|
| Cash | $15,200 | |
| Accounts Receivable | 200 | |
| Advertising Supplies | 1,000 | |
| Prepaid Insurance | 550 | |
| Office Equipment | 5,000 | |
| Accumulated Depreciation—Office Equipment | | $    40 |
| Notes Payable | | 5,000 |
| Accounts Payable | | 2,500 |
| Unearned Revenue | | 800 |
| Salaries Payable | | 1,200 |
| Interest Payable | | 50 |
| Common Stock | | 10,000 |
| Retained Earnings | | –0– |
| Dividends | 500 | |
| Service Revenue | | 10,600 |
| Salaries Expense | 5,200 | |
| Advertising Supplies Expense | 1,500 | |
| Rent Expense | 900 | |
| Insurance Expense | 50 | |
| Interest Expense | 50 | |
| Depreciation Expense | 40 | |
|  | $30,190 | $30,190 |

# Preparing Financial Statements

**Companies can prepare financial statements directly from the adjusted trial balance.** Illustrations 3-25 and 3-26 show the interrelationships of data in the adjusted trial balance and the financial statements.

As Illustration 3-25 shows, companies first prepare the income statement from the revenue and expense accounts. Next, they use the Retained Earnings and Dividends accounts and the net income (or net loss) from the income statement to prepare the retained earnings statement. As Illustration 3-26 shows, companies then prepare the balance sheet from the asset and liability accounts, the common stock account, and the ending retained earnings balance as reported in the retained earnings statement.

**Illustration 3-25**
Preparation of the income statement and retained earnings statement from the adjusted trial balance

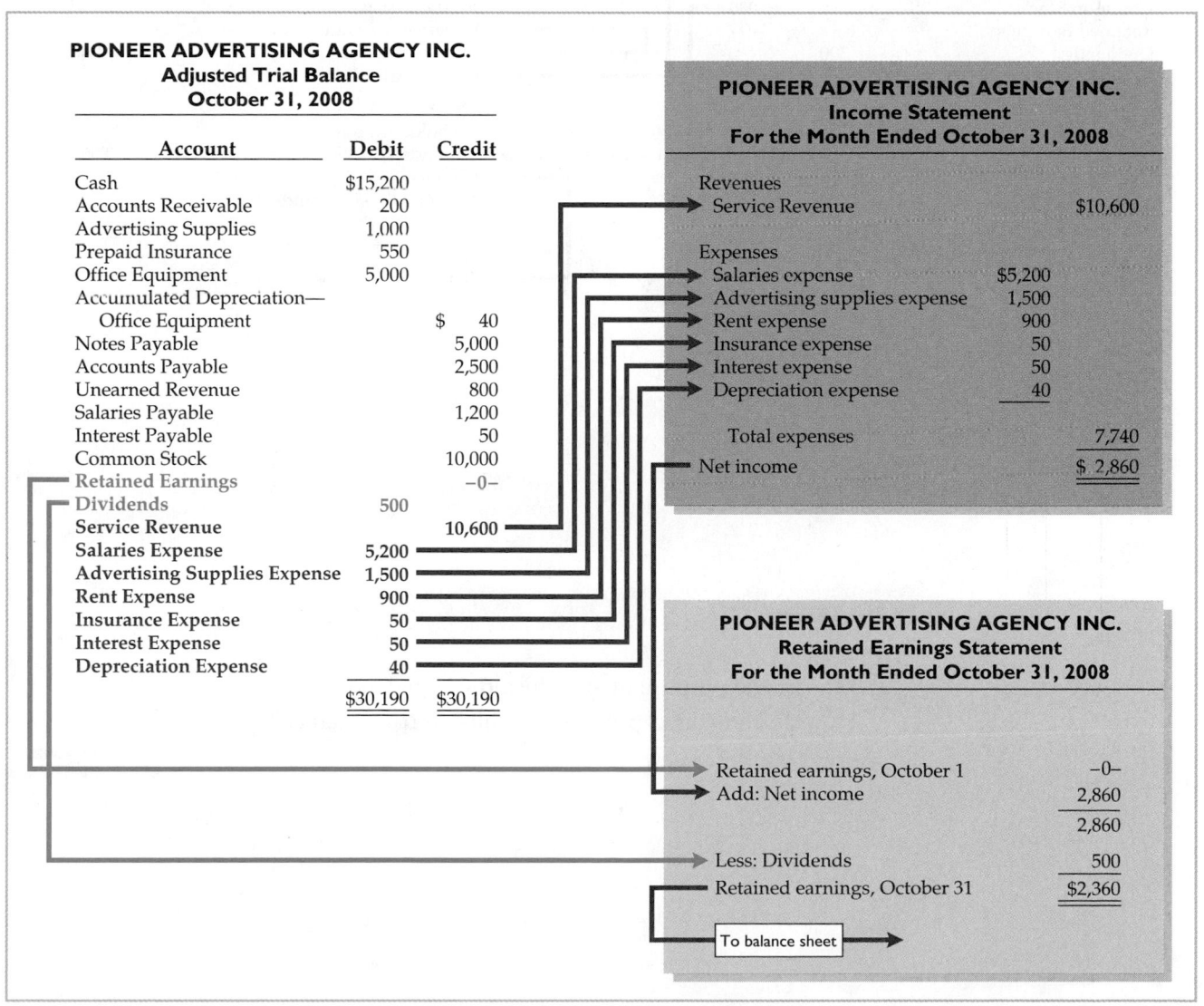

**PIONEER ADVERTISING AGENCY INC.**
**Adjusted Trial Balance**
**October 31, 2008**

| Account | Debit | Credit |
|---|---|---|
| Cash | $15,200 | |
| Accounts Receivable | 200 | |
| Advertising Supplies | 1,000 | |
| Prepaid Insurance | 550 | |
| Office Equipment | 5,000 | |
| Accumulated Depreciation— | | |
| Office Equipment | | $ 40 |
| Notes Payable | | 5,000 |
| Accounts Payable | | 2,500 |
| Unearned Revenue | | 800 |
| Salaries Payable | | 1,200 |
| Interest Payable | | 50 |
| Common Stock | | 10,000 |
| Retained Earnings | | –0– |
| Dividends | 500 | |
| Service Revenue | | 10,600 |
| Salaries Expense | 5,200 | |
| Advertising Supplies Expense | 1,500 | |
| Rent Expense | 900 | |
| Insurance Expense | 50 | |
| Interest Expense | 50 | |
| Depreciation Expense | 40 | |
| | $30,190 | $30,190 |

**PIONEER ADVERTISING AGENCY INC.**
**Income Statement**
**For the Month Ended October 31, 2008**

| Revenues | | |
|---|---|---|
| Service Revenue | | $10,600 |
| Expenses | | |
| Salaries expense | $5,200 | |
| Advertising supplies expense | 1,500 | |
| Rent expense | 900 | |
| Insurance expense | 50 | |
| Interest expense | 50 | |
| Depreciation expense | 40 | |
| Total expenses | | 7,740 |
| Net income | | $ 2,860 |

**PIONEER ADVERTISING AGENCY INC.**
**Retained Earnings Statement**
**For the Month Ended October 31, 2008**

| | | |
|---|---|---|
| Retained earnings, October 1 | | –0– |
| Add: Net income | | 2,860 |
| | | 2,860 |
| Less: Dividends | | 500 |
| Retained earnings, October 31 | | $2,360 |

To balance sheet

**PIONEER ADVERTISING AGENCY INC.**
**Adjusted Trial Balance**
**October 31, 2008**

| Account | Debit | Credit |
|---|---|---|
| Cash | $15,200 | |
| Accounts Receivable | 200 | |
| Advertising Supplies | 1,000 | |
| Prepaid Insurance | 550 | |
| Office Equipment | 5,000 | |
| Accumulated Depreciation— Office Equipment | | $ 40 |
| Notes Payable | | 5,000 |
| Accounts Payable | | 2,500 |
| Unearned Revenue | | 800 |
| Salaries Payable | | 1,200 |
| Interest Payable | | 50 |
| Common Stock | | 10,000 |
| Retained Earnings | | –0– |
| Dividends | 500 | |
| Service Revenue | | 10,600 |
| Salaries Expense | 5,200 | |
| Advertising Supplies Expense | 1,500 | |
| Rent Expense | 900 | |
| Insurance Expense | 50 | |
| Interest Expense | 50 | |
| Depreciation Expense | 40 | |
| | $30,190 | $30,190 |

**PIONEER ADVERTISING AGENCY INC.**
**Balance Sheet**
**October 31, 2008**

| Assets | | |
|---|---|---|
| Cash | | $15,200 |
| Accounts receivable | | 200 |
| Advertising supplies | | 1,000 |
| Prepaid insurance | | 550 |
| Office equipment | $5,000 | |
| Less: Accumulated depreciation | 40 | 4,960 |
| Total assets | | $21,910 |

| Liabilities and Stockholders' Equity | | |
|---|---|---|
| Liabilities | | |
| Notes payable | | $ 5,000 |
| Accounts payable | | 2,500 |
| Unearned revenue | | 800 |
| Salaries payable | | 1,200 |
| Interest payable | | 50 |
| Total liabilities | | 9,550 |
| Stockholders' equity | | |
| Common stock | | 10,000 |
| Retained earnings | | 2,360 |
| Total liabilities and stockholders' equity | | $21,910 |

Balance at Oct. 31 from Retained Earnings Statement in Illustration 3-25

**Illustration 3-26**
Preparation of the balance sheet from the adjusted trial balance

## Before You Go On...

**REVIEW IT**
1. What is the purpose of an adjusted trial balance?
2. How do companies prepare an adjusted trial balance?

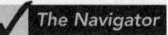 The Navigator

 Be sure to read **ALL ABOUT YOU:** *Is Your Old Computer a Liability?* on the next page for information on how topics in this chapter apply to you.

# Is Your Old Computer a Liability?

Do you have an old computer or two in your garage? How about an old TV that needs replacing? Many people do. Approximately 163,000 computers and televisions become obsolete *each day*. Yet, in a recent year, only 11% of computers were recycled. It is estimated that 75% of all computers ever sold are sitting in storage somewhere, waiting to be disposed of. Each of these old TVs and computers is loaded with lead, cadmium, mercury, and other toxic chemicals. If you have one these electronic gadgets, you have a responsibility, and a probable cost, for disposing of it.

What about companies? Many have potential pollution or environmental-disposal problems—not only for electronic gadgets, but also for the lead paint or asbestos they sold. How do we fit these issues into the accounting equation? Are these costs and related liabilities that companies should report?

In the past, two arguments were made for excluding pollution and environmental costs from the financial statements of product manufacturers. First, companies argued that pollution wasn't their responsibility. If it wasn't their responsibility, then there was no liability. Second, even if there was a liability, companies argued that they could not easily estimate its amount.

These arguments may be as out-of-date as last year's cell phone model. Increasingly, states are putting environmental liabilities into the accounting equation by passing laws that hold companies responsible for the toxic waste from their discarded products. Also, courts are levying steep fines for environmental cleanup caused by product waste.

## ✱ Some Facts

* California adds $6 to $10 of sales tax to the cost of computers and televisions to fund recycling programs.

* Each cathode ray tube (CRT) monitor contains 4–6 pounds of lead. Consumer electronic products account for about 40% of the lead found in landfills.

* Environmental groups put a resolution on Apple Computer's 2006 shareholder meeting agenda requiring the company to study how it can increase recycling.

* The average household has two to three old computers in its garage or storage area.

## ✱ About the Numbers

The nearby chart shows the amount of electronic products, in millions of tons, in storage, now being recycled, and in landfills.

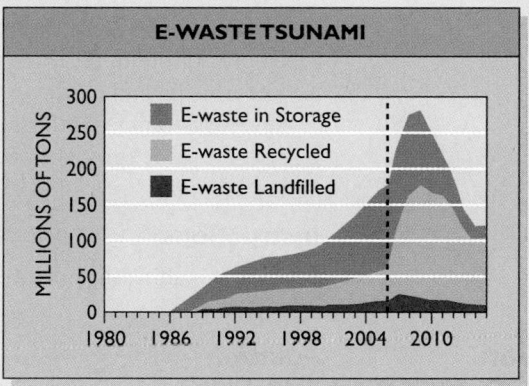

**E-WASTE TSUNAMI**

Legend:
- E-waste in Storage
- E-waste Recycled
- E-waste Landfilled

Y-axis: MILLIONS OF TONS (0, 50, 100, 150, 200, 250, 300)
X-axis: 1980, 1986, 1992, 1998, 2004, 2010

**Source for graph:** Silicon Valley Toxics Coalition, "Poison PCs and Toxic TVs," *www.svtc.org/cleancc/pubs/ppcttv2004.pdf*, p. 5.

## ✱ What Do You Think?

Should companies accrue for environmental clean-up costs as liabilities on their financial statements?

**YES:** As more states impose laws holding companies responsible, and as more courts levy pollution-related fines, it becomes increasingly likely that companies will have to pay large amounts in the future.

**NO:** The amounts still are too difficult to estimate. Putting inaccurate estimates on the financial statements reduces their usefulness. Instead, why not charge the costs later, when the actual environmental clean-up or disposal occurs, at which time the company knows the actual cost?

**Sources:** Lorraine Woellert, "HP Wants Your Old PCs Back," *Business Week*, April 10, 2006, pp. 82-83; "Poison PCs and Toxic TVs: E-waste Tsunami to Roll Across the U.S.: Are We Prepared?" 2004 report of the Silicon Valley Toxics Coalition.

Green Thumb Lawn Care Inc. began operating on April 1. At April 30, the trial balance shows the following balances for selected accounts.

| | |
|---|---|
| Prepaid Insurance | $ 3,600 |
| Equipment | 28,000 |
| Notes Payable | 20,000 |
| Unearned Revenue | 4,200 |
| Service Revenue | 1,800 |

Analysis reveals the following additional data.

1. Prepaid insurance is the cost of a 2-year insurance policy, effective April 1.
2. Depreciation on the equipment is $500 per month.
3. The note payable is dated April 1. It is a 6-month, 12% note.
4. Seven customers paid for the company's 6 months' lawn service package of $600 beginning in April. The company performed services for these customers in April.
5. Lawn services provided other customers but not recorded at April 30 totaled $1,500.

### Instructions

Prepare the adjusting entries for the month of April. Show computations.

## action plan

✔ Note that adjustments are being made for one month.

✔ Make computations carefully.

✔ Select account titles carefully.

✔ Make sure debits are made first and credits are indented.

✔ Check that debits equal credits for each entry.

### Solution

**GENERAL JOURNAL**                                   **J1**

| Date | Account Titles and Explanation | Ref. | Debit | Credit |
|---|---|---|---|---|
| | **Adjusting Entries** | | | |
| Apr. 30 | Insurance Expense | | 150 | |
| |    Prepaid Insurance | | | 150 |
| |      (To record insurance expired: | | | |
| |      $3,600 ÷ 24 = $150 per month) | | | |
| 30 | Depreciation Expense | | 500 | |
| |    Accumulated Depreciation—Equipment | | | 500 |
| |      (To record monthly depreciation) | | | |
| 30 | Interest Expense | | 200 | |
| |    Interest Payable | | | 200 |
| |      (To record interest on notes payable: | | | |
| |      $20,000 × 12% × 1/12 = $200) | | | |
| 30 | Unearned Revenue | | 700 | |
| |    Service Revenue | | | 700 |
| |      (To record service revenue: $600 ÷ 6 = $100; | | | |
| |      $100 per month × 7 = $700) | | | |
| 30 | Accounts Receivable | | 1,500 | |
| |    Service Revenue | | | 1,500 |
| |      (To record revenue for services provided) | | | |

✔ *The Navigator*

# SUMMARY OF STUDY OBJECTIVES

**1 Explain the time period assumption.** The time period assumption assumes that the economic life of a business is divided into artificial time periods.

**2 Explain the accrual basis of accounting.** Accrual-basis accounting means that companies record events that change a company's financial statements in the periods in which those events occur, rather than in the periods in which the company receives or pays cash.

**3 Explain the reasons for adjusting entries.** Companies make adjusting entries at the end of an accounting period.

Such entries ensure that companies record revenues in the period in which they are earned and that they recognize expenses in the period in which they are incurred.

4  **Identify the major types of adjusting entries.** The major types of adjusting entries are deferrals (prepaid expenses and unearned revenues), and accruals (accrued revenues and accrued expenses).

5  **Prepare adjusting entries for deferrals.** Deferrals are either prepaid expenses or unearned revenues. Companies make adjusting entries for deferrals to record the portion of the prepayment that represents the expense incurred or the revenue earned in the current accounting period.

6  **Prepare adjusting entries for accruals.** Accruals are either accrued revenues or accrued expenses. Companies make adjusting entries for accruals to record revenues earned and expenses incurred in the current accounting period that have not been recognized through daily entries.

7  **Describe the nature and purpose of an adjusted trial balance.** An adjusted trial balance shows the balances of all accounts, including those that have been adjusted, at the end of an accounting period. Its purpose is to prove the equality of the total debit balances and total credit balances in the ledger after all adjustments.

The Navigator

# GLOSSARY

WILEY PLUS

**Accrual-basis accounting**  Accounting basis in which companies record transactions that change a company's financial statements in the periods in which the events occur. (p. 95).

**Accruals**  Adjusting entries for either accrued revenues or accrued expenses. (p. 97).

**Accrued expenses**  Expenses incurred but not yet paid in cash or recorded. (p. 106).

**Accrued revenues**  Revenues earned but not yet received in cash or recorded. (p. 105).

**Adjusted trial balance**  A list of accounts and their balances after the company has made all adjustments. (p. 112).

**Adjusting entries**  Entries made at the end of an accounting period to ensure that companies follow the revenue recognition and matching principles. (p. 97).

**Book value**  The difference between the cost of a depreciable asset and its related accumulated depreciation. (p. 102).

**Calendar year**  An accounting period that extends from January 1 to December 31. (p. 95).

**Cash-basis accounting**  Accounting basis in which companies record revenue when they receive cash and an expense when they pay cash. (p. 95).

**Contra asset account**  An account offset against an asset account on the balance sheet. (p. 101).

**Deferrals**  Adjusting entries for either prepaid expenses or unearned revenues. (p. 97).

**Depreciation**  The allocation of the cost of an asset to expense over its useful life in a rational and systematic manner. (p. 101).

**Fiscal year**  An accounting period that is one year in length. (p. 95).

**Interim periods**  Monthly or quarterly accounting time periods. (p. 95).

**Matching principle**  The principle that companies match efforts (expenses) with accomplishments (revenues). (p. 96).

**Prepaid expenses**  Expenses paid in cash that benefit more than one accounting period and that are recorded as assets. (p. 98).

**Revenue recognition principle**  The principle that companies recognize revenue in the accounting period in which it is earned. (p. 95).

**Time period assumption**  An assumption that accountants can divide the economic life of a business into artificial time periods. (p. 94).

**Unearned revenues**  Cash received and recorded as liabilities before revenue is earned. (p. 102).

**Useful life**  The length of service of a productive facility. (p. 101).

# APPENDIX  Alternative Treatment of Prepaid Expenses and Unearned Revenues

In discussing adjusting entries for prepaid expenses and unearned revenues, we illustrated transactions for which companies made the initial entries to balance sheet accounts. In the case of prepaid expenses, the company debited the prepayment to an asset account. In the case of unearned revenue, the company credited a liability account to record the cash received.

Some companies use an alternative treatment: (1) When a company prepays an expense, it debits that amount to an expense account. (2) When it receives payment for future services, it credits the amount to a revenue account. In this appendix, we describe the circumstances that justify such entries and the different adjusting

**STUDY OBJECTIVE 8**

Prepare adjusting entries for the alternative treatment of deferrals.

entries that may be required. This alternative treatment of prepaid expenses and unearned revenues has the same effect on the financial statements as the procedures described in the chapter.

## Prepaid Expenses

Prepaid expenses become expired costs either through the passage of time (e.g., insurance) or through consumption (e.g., advertising supplies). If, at the time of purchase, the company expects to consume the supplies before the next financial statement date, **it may choose to debit (increase) an expense account rather than an asset account**. This alternative treatment is simply more convenient.

Assume that Pioneer Advertising Agency Inc. expects that it will use before the end of the month all of the supplies purchased on October 5. A debit of $2,500 to Advertising Supplies Expense (rather than to the asset account Advertising Supplies) on October 5 will eliminate the need for an adjusting entry on October 31. At October 31, the Advertising Supplies Expense account will show a balance of $2,500, which is the cost of supplies used between October 5 and October 31.

But what if the company does not use all the supplies? For example, what if an inventory of $1,000 of advertising supplies remains on October 31? Obviously, the company would need to make an adjusting entry. Prior to adjustment, the expense account Advertising Supplies Expense is overstated $1,000, and the asset account Advertising Supplies is understated $1,000. Thus Pioneer makes the following adjusting entry.

| A | = | L | + | SE |
|---|---|---|---|---|
| +1,000 | | | | |
| | | | | +1,000 Exp |

**Cash Flows**
no effect

| Oct. 31 | Advertising Supplies | 1,000 | |
| | Advertising Supplies Expense | | 1,000 |
| | (To record supplies inventory) | | |

After the company posts the adjusting entry, the accounts show:

**Illustration 3A-1**
Prepaid expenses accounts after adjustment

| Advertising Supplies | | Advertising Supplies Expense | |
|---|---|---|---|
| 10/31 **Adj.** **1,000** | | 10/5 2,500 | 10/31 **Adj.** **1,000** |
| | | 10/31 **Bal.** **1,500** | |

After adjustment, the asset account Advertising Supplies shows a balance of $1,000, which is equal to the cost of supplies on hand at October 31. In addition, Advertising Supplies Expense shows a balance of $1,500. This is equal to the cost of supplies used between October 5 and October 31. Without the adjusting entry expenses are overstated and net income is understated by $1,000 in the October income statement. Also, both assets and stockholders' equity are understated by $1,000 on the October 31 balance sheet.

Illustration 3A-2 compares the entries and accounts for advertising supplies in the two adjustment approaches.

**Illustration 3A-2**
Adjustment approaches—a comparison

| Prepayment Initially Debited to Asset Account (per chapter) | | | Prepayment Initially Debited to Expense Account (per appendix) | | |
|---|---|---|---|---|---|
| Oct. 5 | Advertising Supplies | 2,500 | Oct. 5 | Advertising Supplies | |
| | Accounts Payable | 2,500 | | Expense | 2,500 |
| | | | | Accounts Payable | 2,500 |
| Oct. 31 | Advertising Supplies | | Oct. 31 | Advertising Supplies | 1,000 |
| | Expense | 1,500 | | Advertising Supplies | |
| | Advertising Supplies | 1,500 | | Expense | 1,000 |

After Pioneer posts the entries, the accounts appear as follows.

Illustration 3A-3
Comparison of accounts

| (per chapter) Advertising Supplies | | | | (per appendix) Advertising Supplies | | |
|---|---|---|---|---|---|---|
| 10/5 | 2,500 | 10/31 **Adj.** | 1,500 | 10/31 **Adj.** | 1,000 | |
| 10/31 **Bal.** | 1,000 | | | | | |

| Advertising Supplies Expense | | | Advertising Supplies Expense | | |
|---|---|---|---|---|---|
| 10/31 **Adj.** | 1,500 | | 10/5 | 2,500 | 10/31 **Adj.** 1,000 |
| | | | 10/31 **Bal.** | 1,500 | |

Note that the account balances under each alternative are the same at October 31: Advertising Supplies $1,000, and Advertising Supplies Expense $1,500.

## Unearned Revenues

Unearned revenues become earned either through the passage of time (e.g., unearned rent) or through providing the service (e.g., unearned fees). Similar to the case for prepaid expenses, companies may credit (increase) a revenue account when they receive cash for future services.

To illustrate, assume that Pioneer Advertising Agency Inc. received $1,200 for future services on October 2. Pioneer expects to perform the services before October 31.[3] In such a case, the company credits Service Revenue. If it in fact earns the revenue before October 31, no adjustment is needed.

However, if at the statement date Pioneer has not performed $800 of the services, it would make an adjusting entry. Without the entry, the revenue account Service Revenue is overstated $800, and the liability account Unearned Revenue is understated $800. Thus, Pioneer makes the following adjusting entry.

**HELPFUL HINT**

The required adjusted balances here are Service Revenue $400 and Unearned Revenue $800.

| Oct. 31 | Service Revenue | | 800 | |
|---|---|---|---|---|
| | Unearned Revenue | | | 800 |
| | (To record unearned revenue) | | | |

| A | = | L | + | SE |
|---|---|---|---|---|
| | | | | −800 Rev |
| | | +800 | | |

**Cash Flows**
no effect

After Pioneer posts the adjusting entry, the accounts show:

Illustration 3A-4
Unearned revenue accounts after adjustment

| Unearned Revenue | | Service Revenue | | |
|---|---|---|---|---|
| | 10/31 **Adj.** 800 | 10/31 **Adj.** 800 | 10/2 | 1,200 |
| | | | 10/31 **Bal.** | 400 |

The liability account Unearned Revenue shows a balance of $800. This equals the services that will be provided in the future. In addition, the balance in Service Revenue equals the services provided in October. Without the adjusting entry, both revenues and net income are overstated by $800 in the October income statement. Also, liabilities are understated by $800, and stockholders' equity is overstated by $800 on the October 31 balance sheet.

Illustration 3A-5 compares the entries and accounts for service revenue earned and unearned in the two adjustment approaches.

---

[3]This example focuses only on the alternative treatment of unearned revenues. In the interest of simplicity, we have ignored the entries to Service Revenue pertaining to the immediate earning of revenue ($10,000) and the adjusting entry for accrued revenue ($200).

**Illustration 3A-5**
Adjustment approaches—a comparison

|  | Unearned Revenue Initially Credited to Liability Account (per chapter) | | | | Unearned Revenue Initially Credited to Revenue Account (per appendix) | | |
|---|---|---|---|---|---|---|---|
| Oct. 2 | Cash | 1,200 | | Oct. 2 | Cash | 1,200 | |
| | Unearned Revenue | | 1,200 | | Service Revenue | | 1,200 |
| Oct. 31 | Unearned Revenue | 400 | | Oct. 31 | Service Revenue | 800 | |
| | Service Revenue | | 400 | | Unearned Revenue | | 800 |

After Pioneer posts the entries, the accounts appear as follows.

**Illustration 3A-6**
Comparison of accounts

| | (per chapter) Unearned Revenue | | | | (per appendix) Unearned Revenue | |
|---|---|---|---|---|---|---|
| 10/31 **Adj.** 400 | 10/2 1,200 | | | | 10/31 **Adj.** 800 | |
| | 10/31 **Bal.** 800 | | | | | |

| | Service Revenue | | | | Service Revenue | |
|---|---|---|---|---|---|---|
| | 10/31 **Adj.** 400 | | | 10/31 **Adj.** 800 | 10/2 1,200 | |
| | | | | | 10/31 **Bal.** 400 | |

Note that the balances in the accounts are the same under the two alternatives: Unearned Revenue $800, and Service Revenue $400.

# Summary of Additional Adjustment Relationships

**Illustration 3A-7**
Summary of basic relationships for deferrals

Illustration 3A-7 provides a summary of basic relationships for deferrals.

| Type of Adjustment | Reason for Adjustment | Account Balances before Adjustment | Adjusting Entry |
|---|---|---|---|
| 1. Prepaid expenses | (a) Prepaid expenses initially recorded in asset accounts have been used. | Assets overstated Expenses understated | Dr. Expenses Cr. Assets |
| | (b) **Prepaid expenses initially recorded in expense accounts have not been used.** | **Assets understated Expenses overstated** | **Dr. Assets Cr. Expenses** |
| 2. Unearned revenues | (a) Unearned revenues initially recorded in liability accounts have been earned. | Liabilities overstated Revenues understated | Dr. Liabilities Cr. Revenues |
| | (b) **Unearned revenues initially recorded in revenue accounts have not been earned.** | **Liabilities understated Revenues overstated** | **Dr. Revenues Cr. Liabilities** |

Alternative adjusting entries **do not apply** to accrued revenues and accrued expenses because **no entries occur before companies make these types of adjusting entries**.

## SUMMARY OF STUDY OBJECTIVE FOR APPENDIX

**8 Prepare adjusting entries for the alternative treatment of deferrals.** Companies may initially debit prepayments to an expense account. Likewise, they may credit unearned revenues to a revenue account. At the end of the period, these accounts may be overstated. The adjusting entries for prepaid expenses are a debit to an asset account and a credit to an expense account. Adjusting entries for unearned revenues are a debit to a revenue account and a credit to a liability account.

*Note: All asterisked Questions, Exercises, and Problems relate to material in the appendix to the chapter.

## SELF-STUDY QUESTIONS

*Answers are at the end of the chapter.*

(SO 1)  **1.** The time period assumption states that:
   **a.** revenue should be recognized in the accounting period in which it is earned.
   **b.** expenses should be matched with revenues.
   **c.** the economic life of a business can be divided into artificial time periods.
   **d.** the fiscal year should correspond with the calendar year.

(SO 2)  **2.** The principle or assumption dictating that efforts (expenses) be matched with accomplishments (revenues) is the:
   **a.** matching principle.
   **b.** cost assumption.
   **c.** periodicity principle.
   **d.** revenue recognition principle.

(SO 2)  **3.** One of the following statements about the accrual basis of accounting is *false*. That statement is:
   **a.** Events that change a company's financial statements are recorded in the periods in which the events occur.
   **b.** Revenue is recognized in the period in which it is earned.
   **c.** This basis is in accord with generally accepted accounting principles.
   **d.** Revenue is recorded only when cash is received, and expense is recorded only when cash is paid.

(SO 3)  **4.** Adjusting entries are made to ensure that:
   **a.** expenses are recognized in the period in which they are incurred.
   **b.** revenues are recorded in the period in which they are earned.
   **c.** balance sheet and income statement accounts have correct balances at the end of an accounting period.
   **d.** all of the above.

(SO 4)  **5.** Each of the following is a major type (or category) of adjusting entries *except:*
   **a.** prepaid expenses.
   **b.** accrued revenues.
   **c.** accrued expenses.
   **d.** earned revenues.

(SO 5)  **6.** The trial balance shows Supplies $1,350 and Supplies Expense $0. If $600 of supplies are on hand at the end of the period, the adjusting entry is:

| **a.** Supplies | 600 | |
|---|---|---|
|    Supplies Expense | | 600 |
| **b.** Supplies | 750 | |
|    Supplies Expense | | 750 |

| **c.** Supplies Expense | 750 | |
|---|---|---|
|    Supplies | | 750 |
| **d.** Supplies Expense | 600 | |
|    Supplies | | 600 |

(SO 5)  **7.** Adjustments for unearned revenues:
   **a.** decrease liabilities and increase revenues.
   **b.** have an assets and revenues account relationship.
   **c.** increase assets and increase revenues.
   **d.** decrease revenues and decrease assets.

(SO 6)  **8.** Adjustments for accrued revenues:
   **a.** have a liabilities and revenues account relationship.
   **b.** have an assets and revenues account relationship.
   **c.** decrease assets and revenues.
   **d.** decrease liabilities and increase revenues.

(SO 6)  **9.** Kathy Siska earned a salary of $400 for the last week of September. She will be paid on October 1. The adjusting entry for Kathy's employer at September 30 is:
   **a.** No entry is required.

| **b.** Salaries Expense | 400 | |
|---|---|---|
|    Salaries Payable | | 400 |
| **c.** Salaries Expense | 400 | |
|    Cash | | 400 |
| **d.** Salaries Payable | 400 | |
|    Cash | | 400 |

(SO 7)  **10.** Which of the following statements is *incorrect* concerning the adjusted trial balance?
   **a.** An adjusted trial balance proves the equality of the total debit balances and the total credit balances in the ledger after all adjustments are made.
   **b.** The adjusted trial balance provides the primary basis for the preparation of financial statements.
   **c.** The adjusted trial balance lists the account balances segregated by assets and liabilities.
   **d.** The adjusted trial balance is prepared after the adjusting entries have been journalized and posted.

(SO 8)  *11. The trial balance shows Supplies $0 and Supplies Expense $1,500. If $800 of supplies are on hand at the end of the period, the adjusting entry is:
   **a.** Debit Supplies $800 and credit Supplies Expense $800.
   **b.** Debit Supplies Expense $800 and credit Supplies $800.
   **c.** Debit Supplies $700 and credit Supplies Expense $700.
   **d.** Debit Supplies Expense $700 and credit Supplies $700.

Go to the book's website,
**www.wiley.com/college/weygandt**,
for Additional Self-Study questions.

## QUESTIONS

**1. (a)** How does the time period assumption affect an accountant's analysis of business transactions?

   **(b)** Explain the terms *fiscal year, calendar year*, and *interim periods*.

**2.** State two generally accepted accounting principles that relate to adjusting the accounts.

**3.** Rick Marsh, a lawyer, accepts a legal engagement in March, performs the work in April, and is paid in May. If Marsh's law firm prepares monthly financial statements, when should it recognize revenue from this engagement? Why?

4. Why do accrual-basis financial statements provide more useful information than cash-basis statements?

5. In completing the engagement in question 3, Marsh pays no costs in March, $2,000 in April, and $2,500 in May (incurred in April). How much expense should the firm deduct from revenues in the month when it recognizes the revenue? Why?

6. "Adjusting entries are required by the cost principle of accounting." Do you agree? Explain.

7. Why may a trial balance not contain up-to-date and complete financial information?

8. Distinguish between the two categories of adjusting entries, and identify the types of adjustments applicable to each category.

9. What is the debit/credit effect of a prepaid expense adjusting entry?

10. "Depreciation is a valuation process that results in the reporting of the fair market value of the asset." Do you agree? Explain.

11. Explain the differences between depreciation expense and accumulated depreciation.

12. Shinn Company purchased equipment for $18,000. By the current balance sheet date, $6,000 had been depreciated. Indicate the balance sheet presentation of the data.

13. What is the debit/credit effect of an unearned revenue adjusting entry?

14. A company fails to recognize revenue earned but not yet received. Which of the following accounts are involved in the adjusting entry: (a) asset, (b) liability, (c) revenue, or (d) expense? For the accounts selected, indicate whether they would be debited or credited in the entry.

15. A company fails to recognize an expense incurred but not paid. Indicate which of the following accounts is debited and which is credited in the adjusting entry: (a) asset, (b) liability, (c) revenue, or (d) expense.

16. A company makes an accrued revenue adjusting entry for $900 and an accrued expense adjusting entry for $700. How much was net income understated prior to these entries? Explain.

17. On January 9, a company pays $5,000 for salaries, of which $2,000 was reported as Salaries Payable on December 31. Give the entry to record the payment.

18. For each of the following items before adjustment, indicate the type of adjusting entry (prepaid expense, unearned revenue, accrued revenue, and accrued expense) that is needed to correct the misstatement. If an item could result in more than one type of adjusting entry, indicate each of the types.
    (a) Assets are understated.
    (b) Liabilities are overstated.
    (c) Liabilities are understated.
    (d) Expenses are understated.
    (e) Assets are overstated.
    (f) Revenue is understated.

19. One-half of the adjusting entry is given below. Indicate the account title for the other half of the entry.
    (a) Salaries Expense is debited.
    (b) Depreciation Expense is debited.
    (c) Interest Payable is credited.
    (d) Supplies is credited.
    (e) Accounts Receivable is debited.
    (f) Unearned Service Revenue is debited.

20. "An adjusting entry may affect more than one balance sheet or income statement account." Do you agree? Why or why not?

21. Why is it possible to prepare financial statements directly from an adjusted trial balance?

*22. Adel Company debits Supplies Expense for all purchases of supplies and credits Rent Revenue for all advanced rentals. For each type of adjustment, give the adjusting entry.

## BRIEF EXERCISES

*Indicate why adjusting entries are needed.*

(SO 3)

**BE3-1**   The ledger of Dey Company includes the following accounts. Explain why each account may require adjustment.
   (a) Prepaid Insurance        (c) Unearned Revenue
   (b) Depreciation Expense     (d) Interest Payable

*Identify the major types of adjusting entries.*

(SO 4)

**BE3-2**   Nunez Company accumulates the following adjustment data at December 31. Indicate (a) the type of adjustment (prepaid expense, accrued revenues and so on), and (b) the status of accounts before adjustment (overstated or understated).
   1. Supplies of $100 are on hand.
   2. Services provided but not recorded total $900.
   3. Interest of $200 has accumulated on a note payable.
   4. Rent collected in advance totaling $800 has been earned.

*Prepare adjusting entry for supplies.*

(SO 5)

**BE3-3**   Windsor Advertising Company's trial balance at December 31 shows Advertising Supplies $6,700 and Advertising Supplies Expense $0. On December 31, there are $2,700 of supplies on hand. Prepare the adjusting entry at December 31, and using T accounts, enter the balances in the accounts, post the adjusting entry, and indicate the adjusted balance in each account.

**BE3-4**  At the end of its first year, the trial balance of Denton Company shows Equipment $30,000 and zero balances in Accumulated Depreciation—Equipment and Depreciation Expense. Depreciation for the year is estimated to be $5,000. Prepare the adjusting entry for depreciation at December 31, post the adjustments to T accounts, and indicate the balance sheet presentation of the equipment at December 31.

*Prepare adjusting entry for depreciation.*

*(SO 5)*

**BE3-5**  On July 1, 2008, Spahn Co. pays $18,000 to Randle Insurance Co. for a 3-year insurance contract. Both companies have fiscal years ending December 31. For Spahn Co., journalize and post the entry on July 1 and the adjusting entry on December 31.

*Prepare adjusting entry for prepaid expense.*

*(SO 5)*

**BE3-6**  Using the data in BE3-5, journalize and post the entry on July 1 and the adjusting entry on December 31 for Randle Insurance Co. Randle uses the accounts Unearned Insurance Revenue and Insurance Revenue.

*Prepare adjusting entry for unearned revenue.*

*(SO 5)*

**BE3-7**  The bookkeeper for Oglesby Company asks you to prepare the following accrued adjusting entries at December 31.

*Prepare adjusting entries for accruals.*

*(SO 6)*

1. Interest on notes payable of $400 is accrued.
2. Services provided but not recorded total $1,500.
3. Salaries earned by employees of $900 have not been recorded.

Use the following account titles: Service Revenue, Accounts Receivable, Interest Expense, Interest Payable, Salaries Expense, and Salaries Payable.

**BE3-8**  The trial balance of Bair Company includes the following balance sheet accounts. Identify the accounts that may require adjustment. For each account that requires adjustment, indicate **(a)** the type of adjusting entry (prepaid expenses, unearned revenues, accrued revenues, and accrued expenses) and **(b)** the related account in the adjusting entry.

*Analyze accounts in an unadjusted trial balance.*

*(SO 4)*

Accounts Receivable                          Interest Payable
Prepaid Insurance                             Unearned Service Revenue
Accumulated Depreciation—Equipment

**BE3-9**  The adjusted trial balance of Harmony Company, Inc. at December 31, 2008, includes the following accounts: Common Stock $15,600; Dividends $6,000; Service Revenue $35,400; Salaries Expense $16,000; Insurance Expense $2,000; Rent Expense $4,000; Supplies Expense $1,500; and Depreciation Expense $1,300. Prepare an income statement for the year.

*Prepare an income statement from an adjusted trial balance.*

*(SO 7)*

**BE3-10**  Partial adjusted trial balance data for Harmony Company, Inc. is presented in BE3-9. The balance in Common Stock is the balance as of January 1. Prepare a retained earnings statement for the year assuming net income is $10,600 for the year and retained earnings is $0 on January 1.

*Prepare a retained earnings statement from an adjusted trial balance.*

*(SO 7)*

**\*BE3-11**  Duncan Company records all prepayments in income statement accounts. At April 30, the trial balance shows Supplies Expense $2,800, Service Revenue $9,200, and zero balances in related balance sheet accounts. Prepare the adjusting entries at April 30 assuming **(a)** $1,000 of supplies on hand and **(b)** $3,000 of service revenue should be reported as unearned.

*Prepare adjusting entries under alternative treatment of deferrals.*

*(SO 8)*

## EXERCISES

**E3-1**  Jo Seacat has prepared the following list of statements about the time period assumption.

*Explain the time period assumption.*

*(SO 1)*

1. Adjusting entries would not be necessary if a company's life were not divided into artificial time periods.
2. The IRS requires companies to file annual tax returns.
3. Accountants divide the economic life of a business into artificial time periods, but each transaction affects only one of these periods.
4. Accounting time periods are generally a month, a quarter, or a year.
5. A time period lasting one year is called an interim period.
6. All fiscal years are calendar years, but not all calendar years are fiscal years.

**Instructions**

Identify each statement as true or false. If false, indicate how to correct the statement.

**E3-2**  On numerous occasions, proposals have surfaced to put the federal government on the accrual basis of accounting. This is no small issue. If this basis were used, it would mean that billions in unrecorded liabilities would have to be booked, and the federal deficit would increase substantially.

*Distinguish between cash and accrual basis of accounting.*

*(SO 2)*

**Instructions** ◀━━

(a) What is the difference between accrual-basis accounting and cash-basis accounting?

(b) Why would politicians prefer the cash basis over the accrual basis?

(c) Write a letter to your senator explaining why the federal government should adopt the accrual basis of accounting.

*Compute cash and accrual accounting income.*

*(SO 2)*

**E3-3** Conan Industries collected $100,000 from customers in 2008. Of the amount collected, $25,000 was from revenue earned on account in 2007. In addition, Conan earned $40,000 of revenue in 2008, which will not be collected until 2009.

Conan Industries also paid $70,000 for expenses in 2008. Of the amount paid, $30,000 was for expenses incurred on account in 2007. In addition, Conan incurred $42,000 of expenses in 2008, which will not be paid until 2009.

**Instructions**

(a) Compute 2008 cash-basis net income.

(b) Compute 2008 accrual-basis net income.

*Identify the type of adjusting entry needed.*

*(SO 4)*

**E3-4** Emeril Corporation encounters the following situations:

1. Emeril collects $1,000 from a customer in 2008 for services to be performed in 2009.
2. Emeril incurs utility expense which is not yet paid in cash or recorded.
3. Emeril's employees worked 3 days in 2008, but will not be paid until 2009.
4. Emeril earned service revenue but has not yet received cash or recorded the transaction.
5. Emeril paid $2,000 rent on December 1 for the 4 months starting December 1.
6. Emeril received cash for future services and recorded a liability until the revenue was earned.
7. Emeril performed consulting services for a client in December 2008. On December 31, it billed the client $1,200.
8. Emeril paid cash for an expense and recorded an asset until the item was used up.
9. Emeril purchased $900 of supplies in 2008; at year-end, $400 of supplies remain unused.
10. Emeril purchased equipment on January 1, 2008; the equipment will be used for 5 years.
11. Emeril borrowed $10,000 on October 1, 2008, signing an 8% one-year note payable.

**Instructions**

Identify what type of adjusting entry (prepaid expense, unearned revenue, accrued expense, accrued revenue) is needed in each situation, at December 31, 2008.

*Prepare adjusting entries from selected data.*

*(SO 5, 6)*

**E3-5** Drew Carey Company has the following balances in selected accounts on December 31, 2008.

| | |
|---|---|
| Accounts Receivable | $ -0- |
| Accumulated Depreciation—Equipment | -0- |
| Equipment | 7,000 |
| Interest Payable | -0- |
| Notes Payable | 10,000 |
| Prepaid Insurance | 2,100 |
| Salaries Payable | -0- |
| Supplies | 2,450 |
| Unearned Consulting Revenue | 40,000 |

All the accounts have normal balances. The information below has been gathered at December 31, 2008.

1. Drew Carey Company borrowed $10,000 by signing a 12%, one-year note on September 1, 2008.
2. A count of supplies on December 31, 2008, indicates that supplies of $800 are on hand.
3. Depreciation on the equipment for 2008 is $1,000.
4. Drew Carey Company paid $2,100 for 12 months of insurance coverage on June 1, 2008.
5. On December 1, 2008, Drew Carey collected $40,000 for consulting services to be performed from December 1, 2008, through March 31, 2009.
6. Drew Carey performed consulting services for a client in December 2008. The client will be billed $4,200.
7. Drew Carey Company pays its employees total salaries of $9,000 every Monday for the preceding 5-day week (Monday through Friday). On Monday, December 29, employees were paid for the week ending December 26. All employees worked the last 3 days of 2008.

**Instructions**

Prepare adjusting entries for the seven items described on page 124.

**E3-6**    Affleck Company accumulates the following adjustment data at December 31.

1. Services provided but not recorded total $750.
2. Store supplies of $300 have been used.
3. Utility expenses of $225 are unpaid.
4. Unearned revenue of $260 has been earned.
5. Salaries of $900 are unpaid.
6. Prepaid insurance totaling $350 has expired.

*Identify types of adjustments and account relationships.*

*(SO 4, 5, 6)*

**Instructions**

For each of the above items indicate the following.

**(a)** The type of adjustment (prepaid expense, unearned revenue, accrued revenue, or accrued expense).

**(b)** The status of accounts before adjustment (overstatement or understatement).

**E3-7**    The ledger of Piper Rental Agency on March 31 of the current year includes the following selected accounts before adjusting entries have been prepared.

*Prepare adjusting entries from selected account data.*

*(SO 5, 6)*

|  | Debit | Credit |
|---|---|---|
| Prepaid Insurance | $ 3,600 | |
| Supplies | 2,800 | |
| Equipment | 25,000 | |
| Accumulated | | |
|    Depreciation—Equipment | | $ 8,400 |
| Notes Payable | | 20,000 |
| Unearned Rent | | 9,900 |
| Rent Revenue | | 60,000 |
| Interest Expense | –0– | |
| Wages Expense | 14,000 | |

An analysis of the accounts shows the following.

1. The equipment depreciates $400 per month.
2. One-third of the unearned rent was earned during the quarter.
3. Interest of $500 is accrued on the notes payable.
4. Supplies on hand total $700.
5. Insurance expires at the rate of $200 per month.

**Instructions**

Prepare the adjusting entries at March 31, assuming that adjusting entries are made **quarterly**. Additional accounts are: Depreciation Expense, Insurance Expense, Interest Payable, and Supplies Expense.

**E3-8**    Andy Wright, D.D.S., opened a dental practice on January 1, 2008. During the first month of operations the following transactions occurred.

*Prepare adjusting entries.*

*(SO 5, 6)*

1. Performed services for patients who had dental plan insurance. At January 31, $875 of such services was earned but not yet recorded.
2. Utility expenses incurred but not paid prior to January 31 totaled $520.
3. Purchased dental equipment on January 1 for $80,000, paying $20,000 in cash and signing a $60,000, 3-year note payable. The equipment depreciates $400 per month. Interest is $500 per month.
4. Purchased a one-year malpractice insurance policy on January 1 for $12,000.
5. Purchased $1,600 of dental supplies. On January 31, determined that $400 of supplies were on hand.

**Instructions**

Prepare the adjusting entries on January 31. Account titles are: Accumulated Depreciation—Dental Equipment, Depreciation Expense, Service Revenue, Accounts Receivable, Insurance Expense, Interest Expense, Interest Payable, Prepaid Insurance, Supplies, Supplies Expense, Utilities Expense, and Utilities Payable.

*Prepare adjusting entries.*
(SO 5, 6)

**E3-9** The trial balance for Pioneer Advertising Agency is shown in Illustration 3-3, p. 98. In lieu of the adjusting entries shown in the text at October 31, assume the following adjustment data.

1. Advertising supplies on hand at October 31 total $500.
2. Expired insurance for the month is $100.
3. Depreciation for the month is $50.
4. Unearned revenue earned in October totals $600.
5. Services provided but not recorded at October 31 are $300.
6. Interest accrued at October 31 is $70.
7. Accrued salaries at October 31 are $1,500.

**Instructions**
Prepare the adjusting entries for the items above.

*Prepare correct income statement.*
(SO 5, 6)

**E3-10** The income statement of Benning Co. for the month of July shows net income of $1,400 based on Service Revenue $5,500, Wages Expense $2,300, Supplies Expense $1,200, and Utilities Expense $600. In reviewing the statement, you discover the following.

1. Insurance expired during July of $400 was omitted.
2. Supplies expense includes $200 of supplies that are still on hand at July 31.
3. Depreciation on equipment of $150 was omitted.
4. Accrued but unpaid wages at July 31 of $300 were not included.
5. Services provided but unrecorded totaled $500.

**Instructions**
Prepare a correct income statement for July 2008.

*Analyze adjusted data.*
(SO 4, 5, 6, 7)

**E3-11** A partial adjusted trial balance of Sila Company at January 31, 2008, shows the following.

### SILA COMPANY
Adjusted Trial Balance
January 31, 2008

|  | **Debit** | **Credit** |
|---|---|---|
| Supplies | $ 850 | |
| Prepaid Insurance | 2,400 | |
| Salaries Payable | | $ 800 |
| Unearned Revenue | | 750 |
| Supplies Expense | 950 | |
| Insurance Expense | 400 | |
| Salaries Expense | 1,800 | |
| Service Revenue | | 2,000 |

**Instructions**
Answer the following questions, assuming the year begins January 1.

**(a)** If the amount in Supplies Expense is the January 31 adjusting entry, and $500 of supplies was purchased in January, what was the balance in Supplies on January 1?

**(b)** If the amount in Insurance Expense is the January 31 adjusting entry, and the original insurance premium was for one year, what was the total premium and when was the policy purchased?

**(c)** If $3,500 of salaries was paid in January, what was the balance in Salaries Payable at December 31, 2007?

**(d)** If $1,600 was received in January for services performed in January, what was the balance in Unearned Revenue at December 31, 2007?

*Journalize basic transactions and adjusting entries.*
(SO 5, 6)

**E3-12** Selected accounts of Tabor Company are shown below and on page 127.

| **Supplies Expense** | |
|---|---|
| 7/31 | 800 |

| **Supplies** | | | | **Salaries Payable** | |
|---|---|---|---|---|---|
| 7/1 Bal. | 1,100 | 7/31 | 800 | 7/31 | 1,200 |
| 7/10 | 400 | | | | |

| Accounts Receivable | | | Unearned Revenue | | |
|---|---|---|---|---|---|
| 7/31 | 500 | | 7/31 | 900 | 7/1 Bal.  1,500 |
| | | | | | 7/20  1,000 |

| Salaries Expense | | | Service Revenue | | |
|---|---|---|---|---|---|
| 7/15 | 1,200 | | | | 7/14  2,000 |
| 7/31 | 1,200 | | | | 7/31  900 |
| | | | | | 7/31  500 |

**Instructions**

After analyzing the accounts, journalize **(a)** the July transactions and **(b)** the adjusting entries that were made on July 31. (*Hint:* July transactions were for cash.)

**E3-13** The trial balances before and after adjustment for Garcia Company at the end of its fiscal year are presented below.

*Prepare adjusting entries from analysis of trial balances.*

(SO 5, 6, 7)

## GARCIA COMPANY
### Trial Balance
### August 31, 2008

| | Before Adjustment | | After Adjustment | |
|---|---|---|---|---|
| | **Dr.** | **Cr.** | **Dr.** | **Cr.** |
| Cash | $10,400 | | $10,400 | |
| Accounts Receivable | 8,800 | | 9,800 | |
| Office Supplies | 2,300 | | 700 | |
| Prepaid Insurance | 4,000 | | 2,500 | |
| Office Equipment | 14,000 | | 14,000 | |
| Accumulated Depreciation—Office Equipment | | $ 3,600 | | $ 4,500 |
| Accounts Payable | | 5,800 | | 5,800 |
| Salaries Payable | | –0– | | 1,100 |
| Unearned Rent | | 1,500 | | 600 |
| Common Stock | | 10,000 | | 10,000 |
| Retained Earnings | | 5,600 | | 5,600 |
| Service Revenue | | 34,000 | | 35,000 |
| Rent Revenue | | 11,000 | | 11,900 |
| Salaries Expense | 17,000 | | 18,100 | |
| Office Supplies Expense | –0– | | 1,600 | |
| Rent Expense | 15,000 | | 15,000 | |
| Insurance Expense | –0– | | 1,500 | |
| Depreciation Expense | –0– | | 900 | |
| | $71,500 | $71,500 | $74,500 | $74,500 |

**Instructions**

Prepare the adjusting entries that were made.

**E3-14** The adjusted trial balance for Garcia Company is given in E3-13.

*Prepare financial statements from adjusted trial balance.*

(SO 7)

**Instructions**

Prepare the income statement and a retained earnings statement for the year and the balance sheet at August 31.

**E3-15** The following data are taken from the comparative balance sheets of Girard Billiards Club, which prepares its financial statements using the accrual basis of accounting.

*Record transactions on accrual basis; convert revenue to cash receipts.*

(SO 5, 6)

| December 31 | 2008 | 2007 |
|---|---|---|
| Fees receivable from members | $14,000 | $ 9,000 |
| Unearned fees revenue | 17,000 | 25,000 |

Fees are billed to members based upon their use of the club's facilities. Unearned fees arise from the sale of gift certificates, which members can apply to their future use of club facilities.

The 2008 income statement for the club showed that fees revenue of $153,000 was earned during the year.

**Instructions**

(*Hint:* You will probably find it helpful to use T accounts to analyze these data.)

(a) Prepare journal entries for each of the following events that took place during 2008.
  (1) Fees receivable from 2007 were all collected.
  (2) Gift certificates outstanding at the end of 2007 were all redeemed.
  (3) An additional $35,000 worth of gift certificates were sold during 2008. A portion of these was used by the recipients during the year; the remainder was still outstanding at the end of 2008.
  (4) Fees for 2008 for services provided to members were billed to members.
  (5) Fees receivable for 2008 (i.e., those billed in item [4] above) were partially collected.

(b) Determine the amount of cash received by the club, with respect to fees, during 2008.

*Journalize adjusting entries.*
(SO 8)

**\*E3-16**  Colin Mochrie Company has the following balances in selected accounts on December 31, 2008.

| | |
|---|---|
| Consulting Revenue | $40,000 |
| Insurance Expense | 2,100 |
| Supplies Expense | 2,450 |

All the accounts have normal balances. Colin Mochrie Company debits prepayments to expense accounts when paid, and credits unearned revenues to revenue accounts when received. The following information below has been gathered at December 31, 2008.

1. Colin Mochrie Company paid $2,100 for 12 months of insurance coverage on June 1, 2008.
2. On December 1, 2008, Colin Mochrie Company collected $40,000 for consulting services to be performed from December 1, 2008, through March 31, 2009.
3. A count of supplies on December 31, 2008, indicates that supplies of $800 are on hand.

**Instructions**

Prepare the adjusting entries needed at December 31, 2008.

*Journalize transactions and adjusting entries.*
(SO 8)

**\*E3-17**  At Natasha Company, prepayments are debited to expense when paid, and unearned revenues are credited to revenue when received. During January of the current year, the following transactions occurred.

Jan.  2  Paid $1,800 for fire insurance protection for the year.
   10  Paid $1,700 for supplies.
   15  Received $6,100 for services to be performed in the future.

On January 31, it is determined that $2,500 of the services fees have been earned and that there are $800 of supplies on hand.

**Instructions**

(a) Journalize and post the January transactions. (Use T accounts.)
(b) Journalize and post the adjusting entries at January 31.
(c) Determine the ending balance in each of the accounts.

# EXERCISES: SET B

Visit the book's website at **www.wiley.com/college/weygandt**, and choose the Student Companion site, to access Exercise Set B.

# PROBLEMS: SET A

*Prepare adjusting entries, post to ledger accounts, and prepare adjusted trial balance.*
(SO 5, 6, 7)

**P3-1A**  Tony Masasi started his own consulting firm, Masasi Company, Inc., on June 1, 2008. The trial balance at June 30 is shown on page 129.

## MASASI COMPANY, INC.
Trial Balance
June 30, 2008

| Account Number | | Debit | Credit |
|---|---|---|---|
| 101 | Cash | $ 7,150 | |
| 112 | Accounts Receivable | 6,000 | |
| 126 | Supplies | 2,000 | |
| 130 | Prepaid Insurance | 3,000 | |
| 157 | Office Equipment | 15,000 | |
| 201 | Accounts Payable | | $ 4,500 |
| 209 | Unearned Service Revenue | | 4,000 |
| 311 | Common Stock | | 21,750 |
| 400 | Service Revenue | | 7,900 |
| 726 | Salaries Expense | 4,000 | |
| 729 | Rent Expense | 1,000 | |
| | | $38,150 | $38,150 |

In addition to those accounts listed on the trial balance, the chart of accounts for Masasi Company, Inc. also contains the following accounts and account numbers: No. 158 Accumulated Depreciation—Office Equipment, No. 212 Salaries Payable, No. 244 Utilities Payable, No. 631 Supplies Expense, No. 711 Depreciation Expense, No. 722 Insurance Expense, and No. 732 Utilities Expense.

Other data:

1. Supplies on hand at June 30 are $600.
2. A utility bill for $150 has not been recorded and will not be paid until next month.
3. The insurance policy is for a year.
4. $2,500 of unearned service revenue has been earned at the end of the month.
5. Salaries of $2,000 are accrued at June 30.
6. The office equipment has a 5-year life with no salvage value. It is being depreciated at $250 per month for 60 months.
7. Invoices representing $1,000 of services performed during the month have not been recorded as of June 30.

### Instructions
**(a)** Prepare the adjusting entries for the month of June. Use J3 as the page number for your journal.
**(b)** Post the adjusting entries to the ledger accounts. Enter the totals from the trial balance as beginning account balances and place a check mark in the posting reference column.
**(c)** Prepare an adjusted trial balance at June 30, 2008.

(c) Adj. trial balance $41,550

**P3-2A** Neosho River Resort, Inc. opened for business on June 1 with eight air-conditioned units. Its trial balance before adjustment on August 31 is as follows.

*Prepare adjusting entries, post, and prepare adjusted trial balance, and financial statements.*
(SO 5, 6, 7)

## NEOSHO RIVER RESORT, INC.
Trial Balance
August 31, 2008

| Account Number | | Debit | Credit |
|---|---|---|---|
| 101 | Cash | $ 19,600 | |
| 126 | Supplies | 3,300 | |
| 130 | Prepaid Insurance | 6,000 | |
| 140 | Land | 25,000 | |
| 143 | Cottages | 125,000 | |
| 149 | Furniture | 26,000 | |
| 201 | Accounts Payable | | $ 6,500 |
| 208 | Unearned Rent | | 7,400 |
| 275 | Mortgage Payable | | 80,000 |
| 311 | Common Stock | | 100,000 |
| 332 | Dividends | 5,000 | |
| 429 | Rent Revenue | | 80,000 |
| 622 | Repair Expense | 3,600 | |
| 726 | Salaries Expense | 51,000 | |
| 732 | Utilities Expense | 9,400 | |
| | | $273,900 | $273,900 |

In addition to those accounts listed on the trial balance, the chart of accounts for Neosho River Resort also contains the following accounts and account numbers: No. 112 Accounts Receivable, No. 144 Accumulated Depreciation—Cottages, No. 150 Accumulated Depreciation—Furniture, No. 212 Salaries Payable, No. 230 Interest Payable, No. 320 Retained Earnings, No. 620 Depreciation Expense—Cottages, No. 621 Depreciation Expense—Furniture, No. 631 Supplies Expense, No. 718 Interest Expense, and No. 722 Insurance Expense.

Other data:

1. Insurance expires at the rate of $400 per month.
2. A count on August 31 shows $600 of supplies on hand.
3. Annual depreciation is $6,000 on cottages and $2,400 on furniture.
4. Unearned rent of $4,100 was earned prior to August 31.
5. Salaries of $400 were unpaid at August 31.
6. Rentals of $1,000 were due from tenants at August 31. (Use Accounts Receivable.)
7. The mortgage interest rate is 9% per year. (The mortgage was taken out on August 1.)

**Instructions**

(c) Adj. trial balance $278,000

(d) Net income $14,100
   Ending retained
   earnings $9,100
   Total assets $199,900

(a) Journalize the adjusting entries on August 31 for the 3-month period June 1–August 31.
(b) Prepare a ledger using the three-column form of account. Enter the trial balance amounts and post the adjusting entries. (Use J1 as the posting reference.)
(c) Prepare an adjusted trial balance on August 31.
(d) Prepare an income statement and a retained earnings statement for the 3 months ending August 31 and a balance sheet as of August 31.

*Prepare adjusting entries and financial statements.*

(SO **5**, 6, 7)

**P3-3A** Fernetti Advertising Agency, Inc. was founded by John Fernetti in January of 2007. Presented below are both the adjusted and unadjusted trial balances as of December 31, 2008.

## FERNETTI ADVERTISING AGENCY, INC.
### Trial Balance
### December 31, 2008

|  | Unadjusted | | Adjusted | |
| --- | --- | --- | --- | --- |
|  | **Dr.** | **Cr.** | **Dr.** | **Cr.** |
| Cash | $ 11,000 |  | $ 11,000 |  |
| Accounts Receivable | 20,000 |  | 22,500 |  |
| Art Supplies | 8,600 |  | 5,000 |  |
| Prepaid Insurance | 3,350 |  | 2,500 |  |
| Printing Equipment | 60,000 |  | 60,000 |  |
| Accumulated Depreciation |  | $ 28,000 |  | $ 34,000 |
| Accounts Payable |  | 5,000 |  | 5,000 |
| Interest Payable |  | –0– |  | 150 |
| Notes Payable |  | 5,000 |  | 5,000 |
| Unearned Advertising Fees |  | 7,200 |  | 5,600 |
| Salaries Payable |  | –0– |  | 1,300 |
| Common Stock |  | 25,000 |  | 25,000 |
| Retained Earnings |  | 500 |  | 500 |
| Dividends | 12,000 |  | 12,000 |  |
| Advertising Revenue |  | 58,600 |  | 62,700 |
| Salaries Expense | 10,000 |  | 11,300 |  |
| Insurance Expense |  |  | 850 |  |
| Interest Expense | 350 |  | 500 |  |
| Depreciation Expense |  |  | 6,000 |  |
| Art Supplies Expense |  |  | 3,600 |  |
| Rent Expense | 4,000 |  | 4,000 |  |
|  | $129,300 | $129,300 | $139,250 | $139,250 |

**Instructions**
(a) Journalize the annual adjusting entries that were made.
(b) Prepare an income statement and a retained earnings statement for the year ending December 31, 2008, and a balance sheet at December 31.
(c) Answer the following questions.
   (1) If the note has been outstanding 6 months, what is the annual interest rate on that note?
   (2) If the company paid $12,500 in salaries in 2008, what was the balance in Salaries Payable on December 31, 2007?

(b) Net income $36,450
Ending retained
earnings $24,950
Total assets $67,000

(c) (1) 6%
    (2) $2,500

**P3-4A**    A review of the ledger of Remington Company at December 31, 2008, produces the following data pertaining to the preparation of annual adjusting entries.

1. Salaries Payable $0. There are eight salaried employees. Salaries are paid every Friday for the current week. Five employees receive a salary of $800 each per week, and three employees earn $600 each per week. December 31 is a Tuesday. Employees do not work weekends. All employees worked the last 2 days of December.

2. Unearned Rent $324,000. The company began subleasing office space in its new building on November 1. At December 31, the company had the following rental contracts that are paid in full for the entire term of the lease.

*Preparing adjusting entries.*
(SO 5, 6)
1. Salaries expense $2,320

2. Rent revenue $74,000

| Date | Term (in months) | Monthly Rent | Number of Leases |
|------|------------------|--------------|------------------|
| Nov. 1 | 6 | $4,000 | 5 |
| Dec. 1 | 6 | 8,500 | 4 |

3. Prepaid Advertising $15,000. This balance consists of payments on two advertising contracts. The contracts provide for monthly advertising in two trade magazines. The terms of the contracts are as follows.

3. Advertising expense $4,800

| Contract | Date | Amount | Number of Magazine Issues |
|----------|------|--------|---------------------------|
| A650 | May 1 | $5,400 | 12 |
| B974 | Oct. 1 | 9,600 | 24 |

The first advertisement runs in the month in which the contract is signed.

4. Notes Payable $120,000. This balance consists of a note for one year at an annual interest rate of 9%, dated June 1.

4. Interest expense $6,300

**Instructions**
Prepare the adjusting entries at December 31, 2008. (Show all computations.)

**P3-5A**    On September 1, 2008, the account balances of Rand Equipment Repair, Inc. were as follows.

*Journalize transactions and follow through accounting cycle to preparation of financial statements.*
(SO 5, 6, 7)

| No. | Debits | | No. | Credits | |
|-----|--------|--|-----|---------|--|
| 101 | Cash | $ 4,880 | 154 | Accumulated Depreciation | $ 1,500 |
| 112 | Accounts Receivable | 3,520 | 201 | Accounts Payable | 3,400 |
| 126 | Supplies | 2,000 | 209 | Unearned Service Revenue | 1,400 |
| 153 | Store Equipment | 15,000 | 212 | Salaries Payable | 500 |
| | | | 311 | Common Stock | 15,000 |
| | | | 320 | Retained Earnings | 3,600 |
| | | $25,400 | | | $25,400 |

During September the following summary transactions were completed.

Sept.  8   Paid $1,400 for salaries due employees, of which $900 is for September.
       10   Received $1,200 cash from customers on account.
       12   Received $3,400 cash for services performed in September.
       15   Purchased store equipment on account $3,000.
       17   Purchased supplies on account $1,200.
       20   Paid creditors $4,500 on account.
       22   Paid September rent $500.
       25   Paid salaries $1,250.
       27   Performed services on account and billed customers for services provided $1,500.
       29   Received $650 from customers for future service.

Adjustment data consist of:

1.  Supplies on hand $1,200.
2.  Accrued salaries payable $400.
3.  Depreciation is $100 per month.
4.  Unearned service revenue of $1,450 is earned.

**Instructions**
(a)  Enter the September 1 balances in the ledger accounts.
(b)  Journalize the September transactions.
(c)  Post to the ledger accounts. Use J1 for the posting reference. Use the following accounts: No. 407 Service Revenue, No. 615 Depreciation Expense, No. 631 Supplies Expense, No. 726 Salaries Expense, and No. 729 Rent Expense.
(d)  Prepare a trial balance at September 30.
(e)  Journalize and post adjusting entries.
(f)  Prepare an adjusted trial balance.
(g)  Prepare an income statement and a retained earnings statement for September and a balance sheet at September 30.

*(d) Trial balance $30,150*

*(f) Adj. trial balance $30,650*

*(g) Net income $1,200*
*Ending retained earnings $4,800*
*Total assets $23,900*

*Prepare adjusting entries, adjusted trial balance, and financial statements using appendix.*

*(SO 5, 6, 7, 8)*

**\*P3-6A**  Givens Graphics Company, Inc. was organized on January 1, 2008, by Sue Givens. At the end of the first 6 months of operations, the trial balance contained the following accounts.

| **Debits** | | **Credits** | |
|---|---|---|---|
| Cash | $  9,500 | Notes Payable | $ 20,000 |
| Accounts Receivable | 14,000 | Accounts Payable | 9,000 |
| Equipment | 45,000 | Common Stock | 22,000 |
| Insurance Expense | 1,800 | Graphic Revenue | 52,100 |
| Salaries Expense | 30,000 | Consulting Revenue | 6,000 |
| Supplies Expense | 3,700 | | |
| Advertising Expense | 1,900 | | |
| Rent Expense | 1,500 | | |
| Utilities Expense | 1,700 | | |
| | $109,100 | | $109,100 |

Analysis reveals the following additional data.

1.  The $3,700 balance in Supplies Expense represents supplies purchased in January. At June 30, $1,300 of supplies was on hand.
2.  The note payable was issued on February 1. It is a 9%, 6-month note.
3.  The balance in Insurance Expense is the premium on a one-year policy, dated March 1, 2008.
4.  Consulting fees are credited to revenue when received. At June 30, consulting fees of $1,500 are unearned.

**5.** Graphic revenue earned but unrecorded at June 30 totals $2,000.
**6.** Depreciation is $2,000 per year.

**Instructions**
**(a)** Journalize the adjusting entries at June 30. (Assume adjustments are recorded every 6 months.)
**(b)** Prepare an adjusted trial balance.
**(c)** Prepare an income statement and a retained earnings statement for the 6 months ended June 30 and a balance sheet at June 30.

(b) Adj. trial balance $112,850
(c) Net income $18,750
 Ending retained
 earnings $18,750
 Total assets $72,000

## PROBLEMS: SET B

**P3-1B** Linda Ace started her own consulting firm, Modine Consulting, Inc. on May 1, 2008. The trial balance at May 31 is as follows.

*Prepare adjusting entries, post to ledger accounts, and prepare an adjusted trial balance.*
*(SO 5, 6, 7)*

### MODINE CONSULTING, INC.
Trial Balance
May 31, 2008

| Account Number | | Debit | Credit |
|---|---|---|---|
| 101 | Cash | $ 7,700 | |
| 112 | Accounts Receivable | 4,000 | |
| 126 | Supplies | 1,500 | |
| 130 | Prepaid Insurance | 4,800 | |
| 149 | Office Furniture | 9,600 | |
| 201 | Accounts Payable | | $ 3,500 |
| 209 | Unearned Service Revenue | | 3,000 |
| 311 | Common Stock | | 19,100 |
| 400 | Service Revenue | | 6,000 |
| 726 | Salaries Expense | 3,000 | |
| 729 | Rent Expense | 1,000 | |
| | | $31,600 | $31,600 |

In addition to those accounts listed on the trial balance, the chart of accounts for Modine Consulting also contains the following accounts and account numbers: No. 150 Accumulated Depreciation—Office Furniture, No. 212 Salaries Payable, No. 229 Travel Payable, No. 631 Supplies Expense, No. 717 Depreciation Expense, No. 722 Insurance Expense, and No. 736 Travel Expense.

Other data:

**1.** $500 of supplies have been used during the month.
**2.** Travel expense incurred but not paid on May 31, 2008, $200.
**3.** The insurance policy is for 2 years.
**4.** $1,000 of the balance in the unearned service revenue account remains unearned at the end of the month.
**5.** May 31 is a Wednesday, and employees are paid on Fridays. Modine Consulting has two employees, who are paid $700 each for a 5-day work week.
**6.** The office furniture has a 5-year life with no salvage value. It is being depreciated at $160 per month for 60 months.
**7.** Invoices representing $1,000 of services performed during the month have not been recorded as of May 31.

**Instructions**

**(a)** Prepare the adjusting entries for the month of May. Use J4 as the page number for your journal.

**(b)** Post the adjusting entries to the ledger accounts. Enter the totals from the trial balance as beginning account balances and place a check mark in the posting reference column.

(c) Adj. trial balance $33,800

**(c)** Prepare an adjusted trial balance at May 31, 2008.

*Prepare adjusting entries, post, and prepare adjusted trial balance, and financial statements.*

(SO 5, 6, 7)

**GLS**

**P3-2B** The Elston Motel, Inc. opened for business on May 1, 2008. Its trial balance before adjustment on May 31 is as follows.

### ELSTON MOTEL, INC.
Trial Balance
May 31, 2008

| Account Number | | Debit | Credit |
|---|---|---|---|
| 101 | Cash | $ 2,500 | |
| 126 | Supplies | 1,900 | |
| 130 | Prepaid Insurance | 2,400 | |
| 140 | Land | 15,000 | |
| 141 | Lodge | 70,000 | |
| 149 | Furniture | 16,800 | |
| 201 | Accounts Payable | | $ 5,300 |
| 208 | Unearned Rent | | 3,600 |
| 275 | Mortgage Payable | | 40,000 |
| 311 | Common Stock | | 55,000 |
| 429 | Rent Revenue | | 9,200 |
| 610 | Advertising Expense | 500 | |
| 726 | Salaries Expense | 3,000 | |
| 732 | Utilities Expense | 1,000 | |
| | | $113,100 | $113,100 |

In addition to those accounts listed on the trial balance, the chart of accounts for Elston Motel also contains the following accounts and account numbers: No. 142 Accumulated Depreciation—Lodge, No. 150 Accumulated Depreciation—Furniture, No. 212 Salaries Payable, No. 230 Interest Payable, No. 320 Retained Earnings, No. 619 Depreciation Expense—Lodge, No. 621 Depreciation Expense—Furniture, No. 631 Supplies Expense, No. 718 Interest Expense, and No. 722 Insurance Expense.

Other data:

1. Insurance expires at the rate of $200 per month.
2. A count of supplies shows $500 of unused supplies on May 31.
3. Annual depreciation is $3,600 on the lodge and $3,000 on furniture.
4. The mortgage interest rate is 12%. (The mortgage was taken out on May 1.)
5. Unearned rent of $2,500 has been earned.
6. Salaries of $800 are accrued and unpaid at May 31.

**Instructions**

**(a)** Journalize the adjusting entries on May 31.

(c) Adj. trial balance $114,850

(d) Net income $3,850
Ending retained
earnings $3,850
Total assets $106,450

**(b)** Prepare a ledger using the three-column form of account. Enter the trial balance amounts and post the adjusting entries. (Use J1 as the posting reference.)

**(c)** Prepare an adjusted trial balance on May 31.

**(d)** Prepare an income statement and a retained earnings statement for the month of May and a balance sheet at May 31.

**P3-3B** Ortega Co., Inc. was organized on July 1, 2008. Quarterly financial statements are prepared. The unadjusted and adjusted trial balances as of September 30 are shown below.

*Prepare adjusting entries and financial statements.*
(SO 5, 6, 7)

## ORTEGA CO., INC.
### Trial Balance
### September 30, 2008

|  | Unadjusted | | Adjusted | |
|---|---|---|---|---|
|  | **Dr.** | **Cr.** | **Dr.** | **Cr.** |
| Cash | $ 6,700 | | $ 6,700 | |
| Accounts Receivable | 400 | | 900 | |
| Supplies | 1,200 | | 1,000 | |
| Prepaid Rent | 1,500 | | 900 | |
| Equipment | 15,000 | | 15,000 | |
| Accumulated Depreciation—Equipment | | | | $ 350 |
| Notes Payable | | $ 5,000 | | 5,000 |
| Accounts Payable | | 1,510 | | 1,510 |
| Salaries Payable | | | | 600 |
| Interest Payable | | | | 50 |
| Unearned Rent | | 900 | | 500 |
| Common Stock | | 14,000 | | 14,000 |
| Dividends | 600 | | 600 | |
| Commission Revenue | | 14,000 | | 14,500 |
| Rent Revenue | | 400 | | 800 |
| Salaries Expense | 9,000 | | 9,600 | |
| Rent Expense | 900 | | 1,500 | |
| Depreciation Expense | | | 350 | |
| Supplies Expense | | | 200 | |
| Utilities Expense | 510 | | 510 | |
| Interest Expense | | | 50 | |
|  | $35,810 | $35,810 | $37,310 | $37,310 |

### Instructions
**(a)** Journalize the adjusting entries that were made.
**(b)** Prepare an income statement and a retained earnings statement for the 3 months ending September 30 and a balance sheet at September 30.
**(c)** If the note bears interest at 12%, how many months has it been outstanding?

(b) Net income $3,090
Ending retained
earnings $2,490
Total assets $24,150

**P3-4B** A review of the ledger of Yoda Company at December 31, 2008, produces the following data pertaining to the preparation of annual adjusting entries.

*Prepare adjusting entries*
(SO 5, 6)

1. **Prepaid Insurance $8,600.** The company has separate insurance policies on its buildings and its motor vehicles. Policy B4564 on the building was purchased on July 1, 2007, for $6,000. The policy has a term of 3 years. Policy A2958 on the vehicles was purchased on January 1, 2008, for $3,600. This policy has a term of 2 years.

1. Insurance expense $3,800

2. **Unearned Subscriptions $49,000.** The company began selling magazine subscriptions in 2008 on an annual basis. The magazine is published monthly. The selling price of a subscription is $50. A review of subscription contracts reveals the following.

2. Subscription revenue $7,000

| Subscription Date | Number of Subscriptions |
|---|---|
| October 1 | 200 |
| November 1 | 300 |
| December 1 | 480 |
|  | 980 |

3. **Notes Payable $60,000.** This balance consists of a note for 6 months at an annual interest rate of 9%, dated September 1.

3. Interest expense $1,800

4. Salaries expense $2,850

**4.** Salaries Payable $0. There are eight salaried employees. Salaries are paid every Friday for the current week. Five employees receive a salary of $500 each per week, and three employees earn $750 each per week. December 31 is a Wednesday. Employees do not work weekends. All employees worked the last 3 days of December.

**Instructions**

Prepare the adjusting entries at December 31, 2008.

*Journalize transactions and follow through accounting cycle to preparation of financial statements.*

(SO 5, 6, 7)

GLS

**P3-5B** On November 1, 2008, the account balances of Rondeli Equipment Repair were as follows.

| No. | Debits | | No. | Credits | |
|-----|--------|--|-----|---------|--|
| 101 | Cash | $ 2,790 | 154 | Accumulated Depreciation | $ 500 |
| 112 | Accounts Receivable | 2,510 | 201 | Accounts Payable | 2,100 |
| 126 | Supplies | 2,000 | 209 | Unearned Service Revenue | 1,400 |
| 153 | Store Equipment | 10,000 | 212 | Salaries Payable | 500 |
| | | | 311 | Common Stock | 10,000 |
| | | | 320 | Retained Earnings | 2,800 |
| | | $17,300 | | | $17,300 |

During November the following summary transactions were completed.

Nov. 8  Paid $1,100 for salaries due employees, of which $600 is for November.
   10  Received $1,200 cash from customers on account.
   12  Received $1,400 cash for services performed in November.
   15  Purchased store equipment on account $3,000.
   17  Purchased supplies on account $500.
   20  Paid creditors on account $2,500.
   22  Paid November rent $300.
   25  Paid salaries $1,300.
   27  Performed services on account and billed customers for services provided $400.
   29  Received $550 from customers for future service.

Adjustment data consist of:

**1.** Supplies on hand $500.
**2.** Accrued salaries payable $500.
**3.** Depreciation for the month is $100.
**4.** Unearned service revenue of $1,150 is earned.

**Instructions**

**(a)** Enter the November 1 balances in the ledger accounts.
**(b)** Journalize the November transactions.
**(c)** Post to the ledger accounts. Use J1 for the posting reference. Use the following accounts: No. 407 Service Revenue, No. 615 Depreciation Expense, No. 631 Supplies Expense, No. 726 Salaries Expense, and No. 729 Rent Expense.

(d) Trial balance $20,150

(f) Adj. trial balance $20,750

(g) Net loss $1,850; Ending retained earnings $950 Total assets $15,350

**(d)** Prepare a trial balance at November 30.
**(e)** Journalize and post adjusting entries.
**(f)** Prepare an adjusted trial balance.
**(g)** Prepare an income statement and a retained earnings statement for November and a balance sheet at November 30.

# PROBLEMS: SET C

Visit the book's website at **www.wiley.com/college/weygandt**, and choose the Student Companion site, to access Problem Set C.

# CONTINUING COOKIE CHRONICLE

(*Note*: This is a continuation of the Cookie Chronicle from Chapters 1 and 2.)

**CCC3** It is the end of November and Natalie has been in touch with her grandmother. Her grandmother asked Natalie how well things went in her first month of business. Natalie, too, would like to know if she has been profitable or not during November. Natalie realizes that in order to determine Cookie Creations' income, she must first make adjustments.

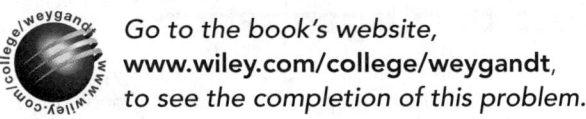

*Go to the book's website,*
**www.wiley.com/college/weygandt**,
*to see the completion of this problem.*

# BROADENING YOUR PERSPECTIVE

## FINANCIAL REPORTING AND ANALYSIS

## Financial Reporting Problem
### PepsiCo, Inc.

**BYP3-1**   The financial statements of PepsiCo are presented in Appendix A at the end of this textbook.

**Instructions**
**(a)** Using the consolidated financial statements and related information, identify items that may result in adjusting entries for prepayments.
**(b)** Using the consolidated financial statements and related information, identify items that may result in adjusting entries for accruals.
**(c)** Using the Selected Financial Data and 5-Year Summary, what has been the trend since 2001 for net income?

## Comparative Analysis Problem
### PepsiCo, Inc. vs. The Coca-Cola Company

**BYP3-2**   PepsiCo's financial statements are presented in Appendix A. Coca-Cola's financial statements are presented in Appendix B.

**Instructions**
Based on information contained in these financial statements, determine the following for each company.

**(a)** Net increase (decrease) in property, plant, and equipment (net) from 2004 to 2005.
**(b)** Increase (decrease) in selling, general, and administrative expenses from 2004 to 2005.
**(c)** Increase (decrease) in long-term debt (obligations) from 2004 to 2005.
**(d)** Increase (decrease) in net income from 2004 to 2005.
**(e)** Increase (decrease) in cash and cash equivalents from 2004 to 2005.

## Exploring the Web

**BYP3-3**   A wealth of accounting-related information is available via the Internet. For example the Rutgers Accounting Web offers access to a great variety of sources.

**Address: www.accounting.rutgers.edu/** or go to **www.wiley.com/college/weygandt**

**Steps:** Click on **Accounting Resources**. (*Note*: Once on this page, you may have to click on the **text only** box to access the available information.)

**Instructions**
**(a)** List the categories of information available through the **Accounting Resources** page.
**(b)** Select any one of these categories and briefly describe the types of information available.

# CRITICAL THINKING

## Decision Making Across the Organization

**BYP3-4**  Happy Camper Park Inc. was organized on April 1, 2007, by Amaya Berge. Amaya is a good manager but a poor accountant. From the trial balance prepared by a part-time bookkeeper, Amaya prepared the following income statement for the quarter that ended March 31, 2008.

**HAPPY CAMPER PARK INC.**
Income Statement
For the Quarter Ended March 31, 2008

| | | |
|---|---:|---:|
| Revenues | | |
| Rental revenue | | $90,000 |
| Operating expenses | | |
| Advertising | $ 5,200 | |
| Wages | 29,800 | |
| Utilities | 900 | |
| Depreciation | 800 | |
| Repairs | 4,000 | |
| Total operating expenses | | 40,700 |
| Net income | | $49,300 |

Amaya thought that something was wrong with the statement because net income had never exceeded $20,000 in any one quarter. Knowing that you are an experienced accountant, she asks you to review the income statement and other data.

You first look at the trial balance. In addition to the account balances reported above in the income statement, the ledger contains the following additional selected balances at March 31, 2008.

| | |
|---|---:|
| Supplies | $ 6,200 |
| Prepaid Insurance | 7,200 |
| Notes Payable | 12,000 |

You then make inquiries and discover the following.

1. Rental revenues include advanced rentals for summer occupancy $15,000.
2. There were $1,700 of supplies on hand at March 31.
3. Prepaid insurance resulted from the payment of a one-year policy on January 1, 2008.
4. The mail on April 1, 2008, brought the following bills: advertising for week of March 24, $110; repairs made March 10, $260; and utilities, $180.
5. There are four employees, who receive wages totaling $300 per day. At March 31, 2 days' wages have been incurred but not paid.
6. The note payable is a 3-month, 10% note dated January 1, 2008.

**Instructions**
With the class divided into groups, answer the following.

**(a)** Prepare a correct income statement for the quarter ended March 31, 2008.
**(b)** Explain to Amaya the generally accepted accounting principles that she did not recognize in preparing her income statement and their effect on her results.

## Communication Activity

**BYP3-5**  In reviewing the accounts of Keri Ann Co. at the end of the year, you discover that adjusting entries have not been made.

**Instructions**
Write a memo to Keri Ann Nickels, the owner of Keri Ann Co., that explains the following: the nature and purpose of adjusting entries, why adjusting entries are needed, and the types of adjusting entries that may be made.

# Ethics Case

**BYP3-6**  Bluestem Company is a pesticide manufacturer. Its sales declined greatly this year due to the passage of legislation outlawing the sale of several of Bluestem's chemical pesticides. In the coming year, Bluestem will have environmentally safe and competitive chemicals to replace these discontinued products. Sales in the next year are expected to greatly exceed any prior year's. The decline in sales and profits appears to be a one-year aberration. But even so, the company president fears a large dip in the current year's profits. He believes that such a dip could cause a significant drop in the market price of Bluestem's stock and make the company a takeover target.

To avoid this possibility, the company president calls in Cathi Bell, controller, to discuss this period's year-end adjusting entries. He urges her to accrue every possible revenue and to defer as many expenses as possible. He says to Cathi, "We need the revenues this year, and next year can easily absorb expenses deferred from this year. We can't let our stock price be hammered down!" Cathi didn't get around to recording the adjusting entries until January 17, but she dated the entries December 31 as if they were recorded then. Cathi also made every effort to comply with the president's request.

**Instructions**
**(a)** Who are the stakeholders in this situation?
**(b)** What are the ethical considerations of (1) the president's request and (2) Cathi's dating the adjusting entries December 31?
**(c)** Can Cathi accrue revenues and defer expenses and still be ethical?

# "All About You" Activity

**BYP3-7**  In the "All About You" feature in this chapter (p. 115), you learned how important it is that companies report or disclose information about all liabilities, including potential liabilities related to environmental clean-up. There are many situations in which you will be asked to provide personal financial information about your assets, liabilities, revenue, and expenses. Sometimes you will face difficult decisions regarding what to disclose and how to disclose it.

**Instructions**
Suppose that you are putting together a loan application to purchase a home. Based on your income and assets, you qualify for the mortgage loan, but just barely. How would you address each of the following situations in reporting your financial position for the loan application? Provide responses for each of the following questions.
**(a)** You signed a guarantee for a bank loan that a friend took out for $20,000. If your friend doesn't pay, you will have to pay. Your friend has made all of the payments so far, and it appears he will be able to pay in the future.
**(b)** You were involved in an auto accident in which you were at fault. There is the possibility that you may have to pay as much as $50,000 as part of a settlement. The issue will not be resolved before the bank processes your mortgage request.
**(c)** The company at which you work isn't doing very well, and it has recently laid off employees. You are still employed, but it is quite possible that you will lose your job in the next few months.

## Answers to Insight and Accounting Across the Organization Questions

**How Long Will "The Force" Be with Us?, p. 96**
Q: What accounting principle does this example illustrate?
A: *This situation demonstrates the difficulty of matching expenses to revenues.*
Q: How will financial results be affected if the expenses are recognized over a period that is *less than* that used for revenues?
A: *If expenses are recognized over a period that is less than that used for revenues, earnings will be understated during the early years and overstated during the later years.*
Q: What if the expenses are recognized over a period that is *longer than* that used for revenues?
A: *If the expenses are recognized over a period that is longer than that used for revenues, earnings will be overstated during the early years and understated in later years. In either case, management and stockholders could be misled.*

**Companies Change Advertising Treatment, p. 100**

Q: Why might the new accounting method cause companies sometimes to spend less on advertising?

A: *Under the old approach companies could delay to future periods the expensing of advertising costs. Under that approach, money spent this period did not necessarily immediately reduce income. Under the new approach, a dollar spent on advertising immediately reduces this year's income. If the company is concerned that it might not hit this year's earnings target, it might decide to reduce its advertising spending.*

**Turning Gift Cards into Revenue, p. 104**

Q: Suppose that Robert Jones purchases a $100 gift card at Best Buy on December 24, 2007, and gives it to his wife, Devon, on December 25, 2007. On January 3, 2008, Devon uses the card to purchase $100 worth of CDs. When do you think Best Buy should recognize revenue, and why?

A: *According to the revenue recognition principle, companies should recognize revenue when earned. In this case revenue is not earned until Best Buy provides the goods. Thus, when Best Buy receives cash in exchange for the gift card on December 24, 2007, it should recognize a liability, Unearned Revenue, for $100. On January 3, 2008, when Devon Jones exchanges the card for merchandise, Best Buy should recognize revenue and eliminate $100 from the balance in the Unearned Revenue account.*

## Authors' Comments on *All About You*: Is Your Old Computer a Liability?, p. 115

The balance sheet should provide a fair representation of what a company owns and what it owes. If significant obligations of the company are not reported on the balance sheet, the company's net worth (its equity) will be overstated. While it is true that it is not possible to estimate the *exact* amount of future environmental clean-up costs, it is becoming clear that companies will be held accountable.

Therefore, it doesn't seem reasonable to not accrue for environmental costs. Recognition of these liabilities provides a more accurate picture of the company's financial position. It also has the potential to improve the environment. As companies are forced to report these amounts on their financial statements, they will start to look for more effective and efficient means to reduce toxic waste, and therefore reduce their costs.

## Answer to PepsiCo Review It Question 4, p. 104

Per Note 4, PepsiCo's 2005 depreciation expense is $1,103 million; 2004 depreciation expense was $1,062 million.

## Answers to Self-Study Questions

**1.** c    **2.** a    **3.** d    **4.** d    **5.** d    **6.** c    **7.** a    **8.** b    **9.** b    **10.** c    ***11.** a

# Chapter 4

# Completing the Accounting Cycle

## STUDY OBJECTIVES

*After studying this chapter, you should be able to:*

1 Prepare a worksheet.
2 Explain the process of closing the books.
3 Describe the content and purpose of a post-closing trial balance.
4 State the required steps in the accounting cycle.
5 Explain the approaches to preparing correcting entries.
6 Identify the sections of a classified balance sheet.

✓ *The Navigator*

## ✓ The Navigator

| Scan **Study Objectives** | ■ |
| Read **Feature Story** | ■ |
| Read **Preview** | ■ |
| Read text and answer **Before You Go On** p. 150 ■    p. 160 ■    p. 168 ■ | |
| Work **Demonstration Problem** | ■ |
| Review **Summary of Study Objectives** | ■ |
| Answer **Self-Study Questions** | ■ |
| Complete **Assignments** | ■ |

## *Feature Story*

### EVERYONE LIKES TO WIN

When Ted Castle was a hockey coach at the University of Vermont, his players were self-motivated by their desire to win. Hockey was a game you either won or lost. But at Rhino Foods, Inc., a bakery-foods company he founded in Burlington, Vermont, he discovered that manufacturing-line workers were not so self-motivated. Ted thought, what if he turned the food-making business into a game, with rules, strategies, and trophies?

Ted knew that in a game knowing the score is all-important. He felt that only if the employees know the score—know exactly how the business is doing daily, weekly, monthly—could he turn food-making into a game. But Rhino is a closely held, family-owned business, and its financial statements

and profits were confidential. Ted wondered, should he open Rhino's books to the employees?

A consultant put Ted's concerns in perspective when he said, "Imagine you're playing touch football. You play for an hour or two, and the whole time I'm sitting there with a book, keeping score. All of a sudden I blow the whistle, and I say, 'OK, that's it. Everybody go home.' I close my book and walk away. How would you feel?" Ted opened his books and revealed the financial statements to his employees.

The next step was to teach employees the rules and strategies of how to "win" at making food. The first lesson: "Your opponent at Rhino is expenses. You must cut and control expenses." Ted and his staff distilled those lessons into daily scorecards—production reports and income statements—that keep Rhino's employees up-to-date on the game. At noon each day, Ted posts the previous day's results at the entrance to the production room. Everyone checks whether they made or lost money on what they produced the day before. And it's not just an academic exercise: There's a bonus check for each employee at the end of every four-week "game" that meets profitability guidelines.

Rhino has flourished since the first game. Employment has increased from 20 to 130 people, while both revenues and profits have grown dramatically.

 The Navigator

# Inside Chapter 4

At Rhino Foods, Inc., financial statements help employees understand what is happening in the business. In Chapter 3, we prepared financial statements directly from the adjusted trial balance. However, with so many details involved in the end-of-period accounting procedures, it is easy to make errors. One way to minimize errors in the records and to simplify the end-of-period procedures is to use a worksheet.

In this chapter we will explain the role of the worksheet in accounting. We also will study the remaining steps in the accounting cycle, especially the closing process, again using Pioneer Advertising Agency Inc. as an example. Then we will consider correcting entries and classified balance sheets. The content and organization of Chapter 4 are as follows.

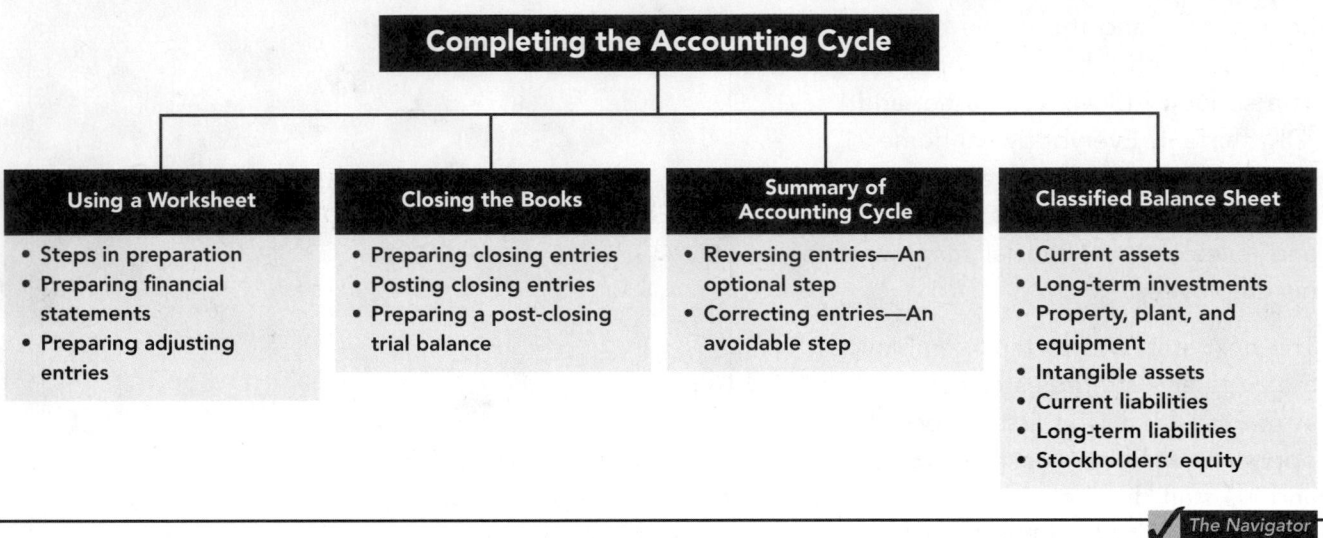

**Completing the Accounting Cycle**

| Using a Worksheet | Closing the Books | Summary of Accounting Cycle | Classified Balance Sheet |
|---|---|---|---|
| • Steps in preparation<br>• Preparing financial statements<br>• Preparing adjusting entries | • Preparing closing entries<br>• Posting closing entries<br>• Preparing a post-closing trial balance | • Reversing entries—An optional step<br>• Correcting entries—An avoidable step | • Current assets<br>• Long-term investments<br>• Property, plant, and equipment<br>• Intangible assets<br>• Current liabilities<br>• Long-term liabilities<br>• Stockholders' equity |

✔ *The Navigator*

# USING A WORKSHEET

**STUDY OBJECTIVE 1**

**Prepare a worksheet.**

A **worksheet** is a multiple-column form that companies use in the adjustment process and in preparing financial statements. As its name suggests, the worksheet is a working tool. **It is not a permanent accounting record**; it is neither a journal nor a part of the general ledger. The worksheet is merely a device used in preparing adjusting entries and the financial statements. Companies generally computerize worksheets using an electronic spreadsheet program such as Excel.

Illustration 4-1 shows the basic form of a worksheet and the five steps for preparing it. Each step is performed in sequence. **The use of a worksheet is optional.** When a company chooses to use one, it prepares financial statements from the worksheet. It enters the adjustments in the worksheet columns and then journalizes and posts the adjustments after it has prepared the financial statements. Thus, worksheets make it possible to provide the financial statements to management and other interested parties at an earlier date.

## Steps in Preparing a Worksheet

We will use the October 31 trial balance and adjustment data of Pioneer Advertising Inc., from Chapter 3, to illustrate how to prepare a worksheet. We

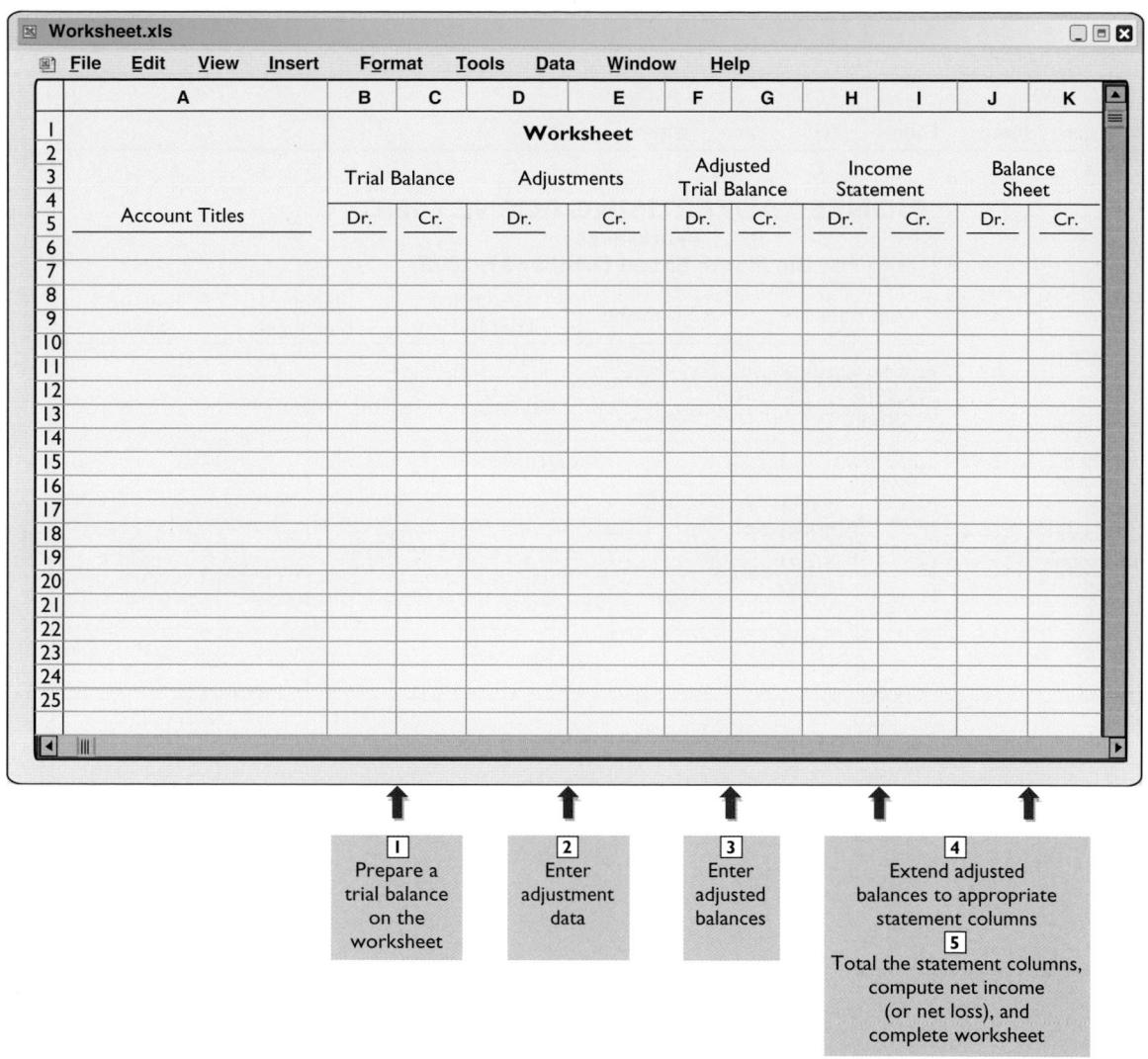

**Illustration 4-1**
Form and procedure for a worksheet

describe each step of the process and demonstrate these steps in Illustration 4-2 and transparencies 4-3A, B, C, and D.

## STEP 1. PREPARE A TRIAL BALANCE ON THE WORKSHEET

Enter all ledger accounts with balances in the account titles space. Enter debit and credit amounts from the ledger in the trial balance columns. Illustration 4-2 shows the worksheet trial balance for Pioneer Advertising Agency Inc.

## STEP 2. ENTER THE ADJUSTMENTS IN THE ADJUSTMENTS COLUMNS

**Turn over the first transparency, Illustration 4-3A.** When using a worksheet, enter all adjustments in the adjustments columns. In entering the adjustments, use applicable trial balance accounts. If additional accounts are needed, insert them on the lines immediately below the trial balance totals. A different letter identifies the debit and credit for each adjusting entry. The term used to describe this process is **keying. Companies do not journalize the adjustments until after they complete the worksheet and prepare the financial statements.**

(**Note:** Text continues on page 147, following acetate overlays.)

**Illustration 4-2**
Preparing a trial balance

```
▣ Pioneer Advertising.xls                                          ▢ ▢ ⊠
  File    Edit   View   Insert   Format   Tools   Data   Window   Help
```

| | A | B | C | D | E | F | G | H | I | J | K |
|---|---|---|---|---|---|---|---|---|---|---|---|
| 1 | | **PIONEER ADVERTISING AGENCY INC.** | | | | | | | | | |
| 2 | | **Worksheet** | | | | | | | | | |
| 3 | | **For the Month Ended October 31, 2008** | | | | | | | | | |
| 4 | | Trial Balance | | Adjustments | | Adjusted Trial Balance | | Income Statement | | Balance Sheet | |
| 5 | | | | | | | | | | | |
| 6 | | | | | | | | | | | |
| 7 | Account Titles | Dr. | Cr. | Dr. | Cr. | Dr. | Cr. | Dr. | Cr. | Dr. | Cr. |
| 8 | Cash | 15,200 | | | | | | | | | |
| 9 | Advertising Supplies | 2,500 | | | | | | | | | |
| 10 | Prepaid Insurance | 600 | | | | | | | | | |
| 11 | Office Equipment | 5,000 | | | | | | | | | |
| 12 | Notes Payable | | 5,000 | | | | | | | | |
| 13 | Accounts Payable | | 2,500 | | | | | | | | |
| 14 | Unearned Revenue | | 1,200 | | | | | | | | |
| 15 | Common Stock | | 10,000 | | | | | | | | |
| 16 | Dividends | 500 | | | | | | | | | |
| 17 | Service Revenue | | 10,000 | | | | | | | | |
| 18 | | | | | | | | | | | |
| 19 | Salaries Expense | 4,000 | | | | | | | | | |
| 20 | Rent Expense | 900 | | | | | | | | | |
| 21 | Totals | 28,700 | 28,700 | | | | | | | | |
| 22 | | | | | | | | | | | |
| 23 | | | | | | | | | | | |
| 24 | | | | | | | | | | | |
| 25 | | | | | | | | | | | |
| 26 | | | | | | | | | | | |
| 27 | | | | | | | | | | | |
| 28 | | | | | | | | | | | |
| 29 | | | | | | | | | | | |
| 30 | | | | | | | | | | | |
| 31 | | | | | | | | | | | |
| 32 | | | | | | | | | | | |
| 33 | | | | | | | | | | | |
| 34 | | | | | | | | | | | |
| 35 | | | | | | | | | | | |
| 36 | | | | | | | | | | | |

Include all accounts with balances from ledger.

Trial balance amounts come directly from ledger accounts.

The adjustments for Pioneer Advertising Agency Inc. are the same as the adjustments illustrated on page 110. They are keyed in the adjustments columns of the worksheet as follows.

**(a)** Pioneer debits an additional account, Advertising Supplies Expense, $1,500 for the cost of supplies used, and credits Advertising Supplies $1,500.

**(b)** Pioneer debits an additional account, Insurance Expense, $50 for the insurance that has expired, and credits Prepaid Insurance $50.

**(c)** The company needs two additional depreciation accounts. It debits Depreciation Expense $40 for the month's depreciation, and credits Accumulated Depreciation—Office Equipment $40.

**(d)** Pioneer debits Unearned Revenue $400 for services provided, and credits Service Revenue $400.

**(e)** Pioneer debits an additional account, Accounts Receivable, $200 for services provided but not billed, and credits Service Revenue $200.

**(f)** The company needs two additional accounts relating to interest. It debits Interest Expense $50 for accrued interest, and credits Interest Payable $50.

**(g)** Pioneer debits Salaries Expense $1,200 for accrued salaries, and credits an additional account, Salaries Payable, $1,200.

After Pioneer has entered all the adjustments, the adjustments columns are totaled to prove their equality.

## STEP 3. ENTER ADJUSTED BALANCES IN THE ADJUSTED TRIAL BALANCE COLUMNS

**Turn over the second transparency, Illustration 4-3B.** Pioneer determines the adjusted balance of an account by combining the amounts entered in the first four columns of the worksheet for each account. For example, the Prepaid Insurance account in the trial balance columns has a $600 debit balance and a $50 credit in the adjustments columns. The result is a $550 debit balance recorded in the adjusted trial balance columns. **For each account, the amount in the adjusted trial balance columns is the balance that will appear in the ledger after journalizing and posting the adjusting entries.** The balances in these columns are the same as those in the adjusted trial balance in Illustration 3-24 (page 112).

After Pioneer has entered all account balances in the adjusted trial balance columns, the columns are totaled to prove their equality. If the column totals do not agree, the financial statement columns will not balance and the financial statements will be incorrect.

## STEP 4. EXTEND ADJUSTED TRIAL BALANCE AMOUNTS TO APPROPRIATE FINANCIAL STATEMENT COLUMNS

**Turn over the third transparency, Illustration 4-3C.** The fourth step is to extend adjusted trial balance amounts to the income statement and balance sheet columns of the worksheet. Pioneer enters balance sheet accounts in the appropriate balance sheet debit and credit columns. For instance, it enters Cash in the balance sheet debit column, and Notes Payable in the credit column. Pioneer extends Accumulated Depreciation to the balance sheet credit column; the reason is that accumulated depreciation is a contra-asset account with a credit balance.

Because the worksheet does not have columns for the retained earnings statement, Pioneer extends the balances in Common Stock and Retained Earnings, if any, to the balance sheet credit column. In addition, it extends the balance in Dividends to the balance sheet debit column because it is a stockholders' equity account with a debit balance.

The company enters the expense and revenue accounts such as Salaries Expense and Service Revenue in the appropriate income statement columns. Illustration 4-3C shows all of these extensions.

**HELPFUL HINT**

Every adjusted trial balance amount must be extended to one of the four statement columns.

### STEP 5. TOTAL THE STATEMENT COLUMNS, COMPUTE THE NET INCOME (OR NET LOSS), AND COMPLETE THE WORKSHEET

**Turn over the fourth transparency, Illustration 4-3D.** The company now must total each of the financial statement columns. The net income or loss for the period is the difference between the totals of the two income statement columns. If total credits exceed total debits, the result is net income. In such a case, as shown in Illustration 4-3D, the company inserts the words "Net Income" in the account titles space. It then enters the amount in the income statement debit column and the balance sheet credit column. **The debit amount balances the income statement columns; the credit amount balances the balance sheet columns.** In addition, the credit in the balance sheet column indicates the increase in stockholders' equity resulting from net income.

What if total debits in the income statement columns exceed total credits? In that case, the company has a net loss. It enters the amount of the net loss in the income statement credit column and the balance sheet debit column.

After entering the net income or net loss, the company determines new column totals. The totals shown in the debit and credit income statement columns will match. So will the totals shown in the debit and credit balance sheet columns. If either the income statement columns or the balance sheet columns are not equal after the net income or net loss has been entered, there is an error in the worksheet. Illustration 4-3D shows the completed work sheet for Pioneer Advertising Agency Inc.

## Preparing Financial Statements from a Worksheet

After a company has completed a worksheet, it has at hand all the data required for preparation of financial statements. The income statement is prepared from the income statement columns. The balance sheet and retained earnings statement are prepared from the balance sheet columns. Illustration 4-4 shows the financial statements prepared from Pioneer's worksheet. At this point, the company has not journalized or posted adjusting entries. Therefore, ledger balances for some accounts are not the same as the financial statement amounts.

The amount shown for common stock on the worksheet does not change from the beginning to the end of the period unless the company issues additional stock during the period. Because there was no balance in Pioneer's retained earnings, the account is not listed on the worksheet. Only after dividends and net income (or loss) are posted to retained earnings does this account have a balance at the end of the first year of the business.

Using a worksheet, companies can prepare financial statements before they journalize and post adjusting entries. **However, the completed worksheet is not a substitute for formal financial statements.** The format of the data in the financial statement columns of the worksheet is not the same as the format of the financial statements. **A worksheet is essentially a working tool of the accountant;** companies do not distribute it to management and other parties.

Accounting Cycle Tutorial—
Preparing Financial
Statements and Closing the
Books

## Preparing Adjusting Entries from a Worksheet

**A worksheet is not a journal, and it cannot be used as a basis for posting to ledger accounts.** To adjust the accounts, the company must journalize the adjustments and post them to the ledger. **The adjusting entries are prepared from the adjustments columns of the worksheet.** The reference letters in the adjustments columns and the explanations of the adjustments at the bottom of the worksheet help identify

**Illustration 4-4**
Financial statements from a
worksheet

## PIONEER ADVERTISING AGENCY INC.
### Income Statement
### For the Month Ended October 31, 2008

| | | |
|---|---:|---:|
| Revenues | | |
| Service revenue | | $10,600 |
| Expenses | | |
| Salaries expense | $5,200 | |
| Advertising supplies expense | 1,500 | |
| Rent expense | 900 | |
| Insurance expense | 50 | |
| Interest expense | 50 | |
| Depreciation expense | 40 | |
| Total expenses | | 7,740 |
| Net income | | $ 2,860 |

## PIONEER ADVERTISING AGENCY INC.
### Retained Earnings Statement
### For the Month Ended October 31, 2008

| | |
|---|---:|
| Retained earnings, October 1 | $ –0– |
| Add: Net income | 2,860 |
| | 2,860 |
| Less: Dividends | 500 |
| Retained earnings, October 31 | $2,360 |

## PIONEER ADVERTISING AGENCY INC.
### Balance Sheet
### October 31, 2008

### Assets

| | | |
|---|---:|---:|
| Cash | | $15,200 |
| Accounts receivable | | 200 |
| Advertising supplies | | 1,000 |
| Prepaid insurance | | 550 |
| Office equipment | $5,000 | |
| Less: Accumulated depreciation | 40 | 4,960 |
| Total assets | | $21,910 |

### Liabilities and Stockholders' Equity

| | |
|---|---:|
| Liabilities | |
| Notes payable | $ 5,000 |
| Accounts payable | 2,500 |
| Interest payable | 50 |
| Unearned revenue | 800 |
| Salaries payable | 1,200 |
| Total liabilities | 9,550 |
| Stockholders' equity | |
| Common stock | 10,000 |
| Retained earnings | 2,360 |
| Total liabilities and stockholders' equity | $21,910 |

the adjusting entries. The journalizing and posting of adjusting entries **follows** the preparation of financial statements when a worksheet is used. The adjusting entries on October 31 for Pioneer Advertising Agency Inc. are the same as those shown in Illustration 3-22 (page 110).

## *Before You Go On...*

### REVIEW IT
1. What are the five steps in preparing a worksheet?
2. How is net income or net loss shown in a worksheet?
3. How does a worksheet relate to preparing financial statements and adjusting entries?

### DO IT
Susan Elbe is preparing a worksheet. Explain to Susan how she should extend the following adjusted trial balance accounts to the financial statement columns of the worksheet:

| | |
|---|---|
| Cash | Dividends |
| Accumulated Depreciation | Service Revenue |
| Accounts Payable | Salaries Expense |

### Action Plan
- Extend asset balances to the balance sheet debit column. Extend liability balances to the balance sheet credit column. Extend accumulated depreciation to the balance sheet credit column.
- Extend the Dividends account to the balance sheet debit column.
- Extend expenses to the income statement debit column.
- Extend revenue accounts to the income statement credit column.

### Solution
Balance sheet debit column—Cash; Dividends
Balance sheet credit column—Accumulated Depreciation; Accounts Payable
Income statement debit column—Salaries Expense
Income statement credit column—Service Revenue

Related exercise material: *BE4-1, BE4-2, BE4-3, E4-1, E4-2, E4-5, and E4-6.*

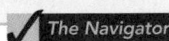 The Navigator

# CLOSING THE BOOKS

**STUDY OBJECTIVE 2**

Explain the process of closing the books.

At the end of the accounting period, the company makes the accounts ready for the next period. This is called **closing the books**. In closing the books, the company distinguishes between temporary and permanent accounts.

**Temporary accounts** relate only to a given accounting period. They include all income statement accounts and the dividends account. The company closes all temporary accounts at the end of the period.

In contrast, **permanent accounts** relate to one or more future accounting periods. They consist of all balance sheet accounts, including the stockholders' equity accounts. Permanent accounts are not closed from period to period. Instead, the

**ALTERNATIVE TERMINOLOGY**

Temporary accounts are sometimes called *nominal accounts*, and permanent accounts are sometimes called *real accounts*.

company carries forward the balances of permanent accounts into the next accounting period. Illustration 4-5 identifies the accounts in each category.

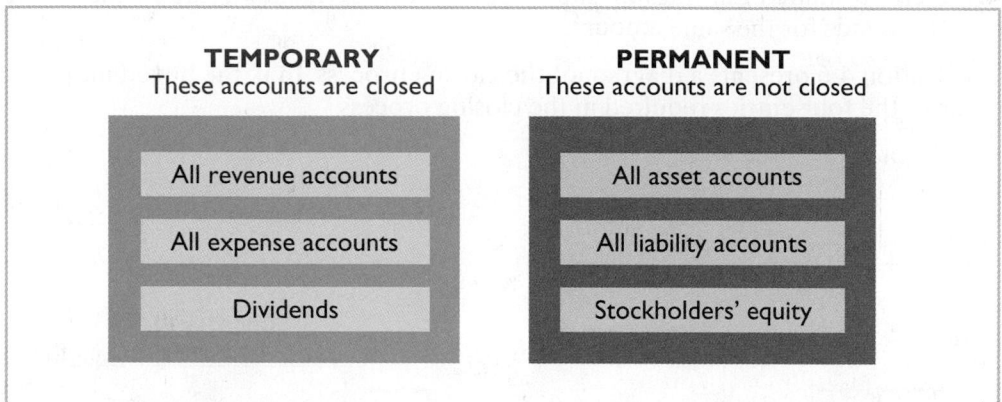

**Illustration 4-5**
Temporary versus permanent accounts

**HELPFUL HINT**

A contra-asset account, such as accumulated depreciation, is a permanent account also.

# Preparing Closing Entries

At the end of the accounting period, the company transfers temporary account balances to the permanent stockholders' equity account, Retained Earnings, by means of closing entries.

Closing entries formally recognize in the ledger the transfer of net income (or net loss) and Dividends to Retained Earnings. The retained earnings statement shows the results of these entries. **Closing entries also produce a zero balance in each temporary account.** The temporary accounts are then ready to accumulate data in the next accounting period separate from the data of prior periods. Permanent accounts are not closed.

**Journalizing and posting closing entries is a required step in the accounting cycle.** (See Illustration 4-12 on page 158.) The company performs this step after it has prepared financial statements. In contrast to the steps in the cycle that you have already studied, companies generally journalize and post closing entries **only at the end of the annual accounting period.** Thus, all temporary accounts will contain data for the entire year.

In preparing closing entries, companies could close each income statement account directly to Retained Earnings. However, to do so would result in excessive detail in the Retained Earnings account. Instead, companies close the revenue and expense accounts to another temporary account, Income Summary, and they transfer the resulting net income or net loss from this account to Retained Earnings.

Companies **record closing entries in the general journal**. A center caption, Closing Entries, inserted in the journal between the last adjusting entry and the first closing entry, identifies these entries. Then the company posts the closing entries to the ledger accounts.

Companies generally prepare closing entries directly from the adjusted balances in the ledger. They could prepare separate closing entries for each nominal account, but the following four entries accomplish the desired result more efficiently:

**1.** Debit each revenue account for its balance, and credit Income Summary for total revenues.

**HELPFUL HINT**
Dividends is closed directly to Retained Earnings and *not* to Income Summary because Dividends is not an expense.

2. Debit Income Summary for total expenses, and credit each expense account for its balance.

3. Debit Income Summary and credit Retained Earnings for the amount of net income.

4. Debit Retained Earnings for the balance in the Dividends account, and credit Dividends for the same amount.

Illustration 4-6 presents a diagram of the closing process. In it, the boxed numbers refer to the four entries required in the closing process.

**Illustration 4-6**
Diagram of closing process

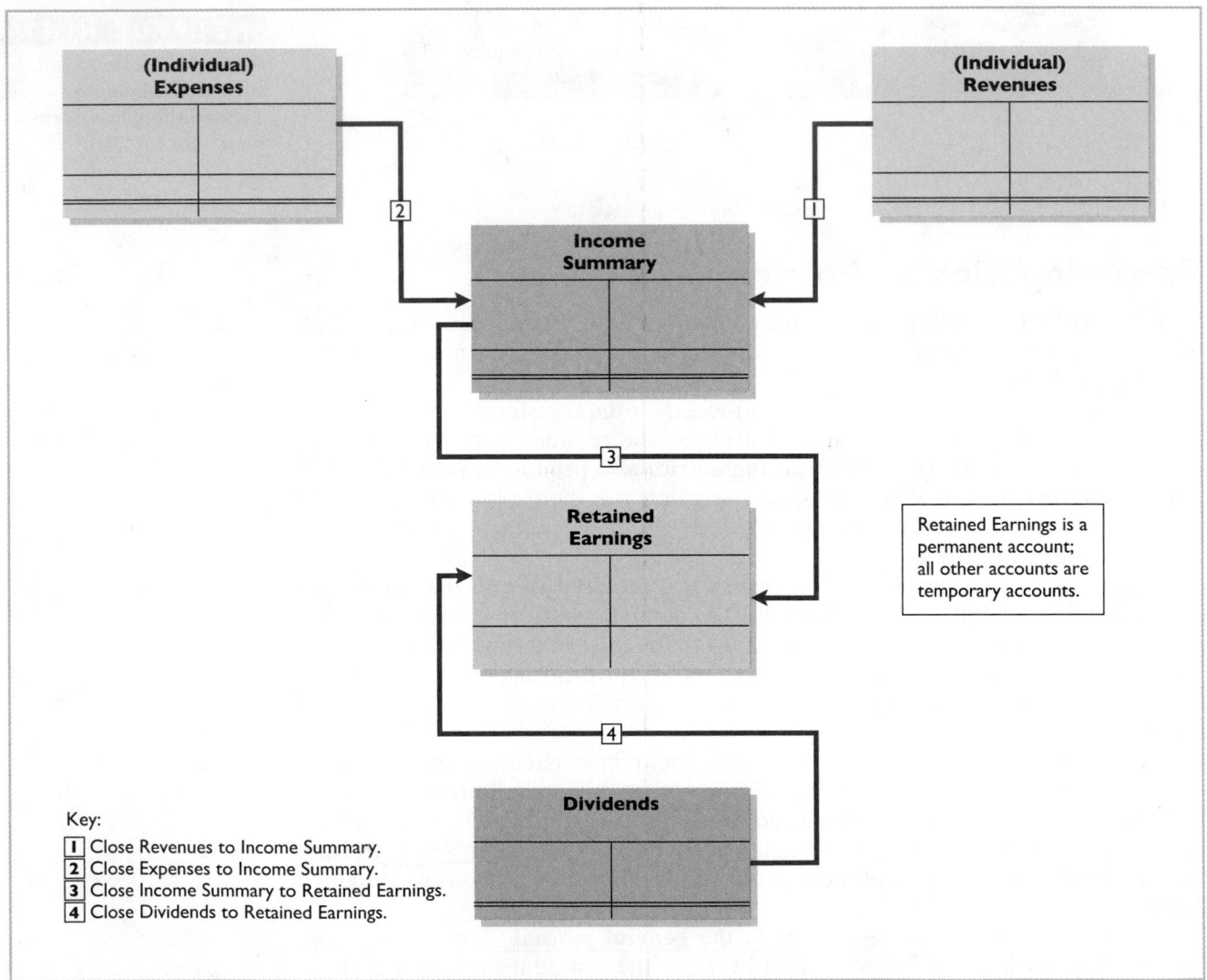

Key:
1 Close Revenues to Income Summary.
2 Close Expenses to Income Summary.
3 Close Income Summary to Retained Earnings.
4 Close Dividends to Retained Earnings.

Retained Earnings is a permanent account; all other accounts are temporary accounts.

If there were a net loss (because expenses exceeded revenues), entry 3 in Illustration 4-6 would be reversed: there would be a credit to Income Summary and a debit to Retained Earnings.

## CLOSING ENTRIES ILLUSTRATED

In practice, companies generally prepare closing entries only at the end of the annual accounting period. However, to illustrate the journalizing and posting of closing entries, we will assume that Pioneer Advertising Agency Inc. closes its books monthly. Illustration 4-7 shows the closing entries at October 31. (The numbers in parentheses before each entry correspond to the four entries diagrammed in Illustration 4-6.)

**Illustration 4-7**
Closing entries journalized

| GENERAL JOURNAL | | | | J3 |
|---|---|---|---|---|
| Date | Account Titles and Explanation | Ref. | Debit | Credit |
| | **Closing Entries** | | | |
| 2008 | (1) | | | |
| Oct. 31 | Service Revenue | 400 | 10,600 | |
| | Income Summary | 350 | | 10,600 |
| | (To close revenue account) | | | |
| | (2) | | | |
| 31 | Income Summary | 350 | 7,740 | |
| | Advertising Supplies Expense | 631 | | 1,500 |
| | Depreciation Expense | 711 | | 40 |
| | Insurance Expense | 722 | | 50 |
| | Salaries Expense | 726 | | 5,200 |
| | Rent Expense | 729 | | 900 |
| | Interest Expense | 905 | | 50 |
| | (To close expense accounts) | | | |
| | (3) | | | |
| 31 | Income Summary | 350 | 2,860 | |
| | Retained Earnings | 320 | | 2,860 |
| | (To close net income to retained earnings) | | | |
| | (4) | | | |
| 31 | Retained Earnings | 320 | 500 | |
| | Dividends | 332 | | 500 |
| | (To close dividends to capital) | | | |

Note that the amounts for Income Summary in entries (1) and (2) are the totals of the income statement credit and debit columns, respectively, in the worksheet.

A couple of cautions in preparing closing entries: (1) Avoid unintentionally doubling the revenue and expense balances rather than zeroing them. (2) Do not close Dividends through the Income Summary account. **Dividends are not an expense, and they are not a factor in determining net income.**

## Posting Closing Entries

Illustration 4-8 shows the posting of the closing entries and the ruling of the accounts. Note that all temporary accounts have zero balances after posting the closing entries. In addition, you should realize that the balance in Retained Earnings represents the accumulated undistributed earnings of the corporation at the end of the accounting period. This balance is shown on the balance sheet and is the ending amount reported on the retained earnings statement, as shown in Illustration 4-4.

**HELPFUL HINT**

The balance in Income Summary before it is closed must equal the net income or net loss for the period.

**The Income Summary account is used only in closing.** Companies do not journalize and post entries to this account during the year.

As part of the closing process, companies total, balance, and double-rule the **temporary accounts**—revenues, expenses, and Dividends—in T-account form as shown in Illustration 4-8. The **permanent accounts**—assets, liabilities, and stockholders' equity (Common Stock and Retained Earnings)—are not closed. A single rule is drawn beneath the current-period entries, and the account balance carried forward to the next period is entered below the single rule. (For example, see Retained Earnings.)

**Illustration 4-8**
Posting of closing entries

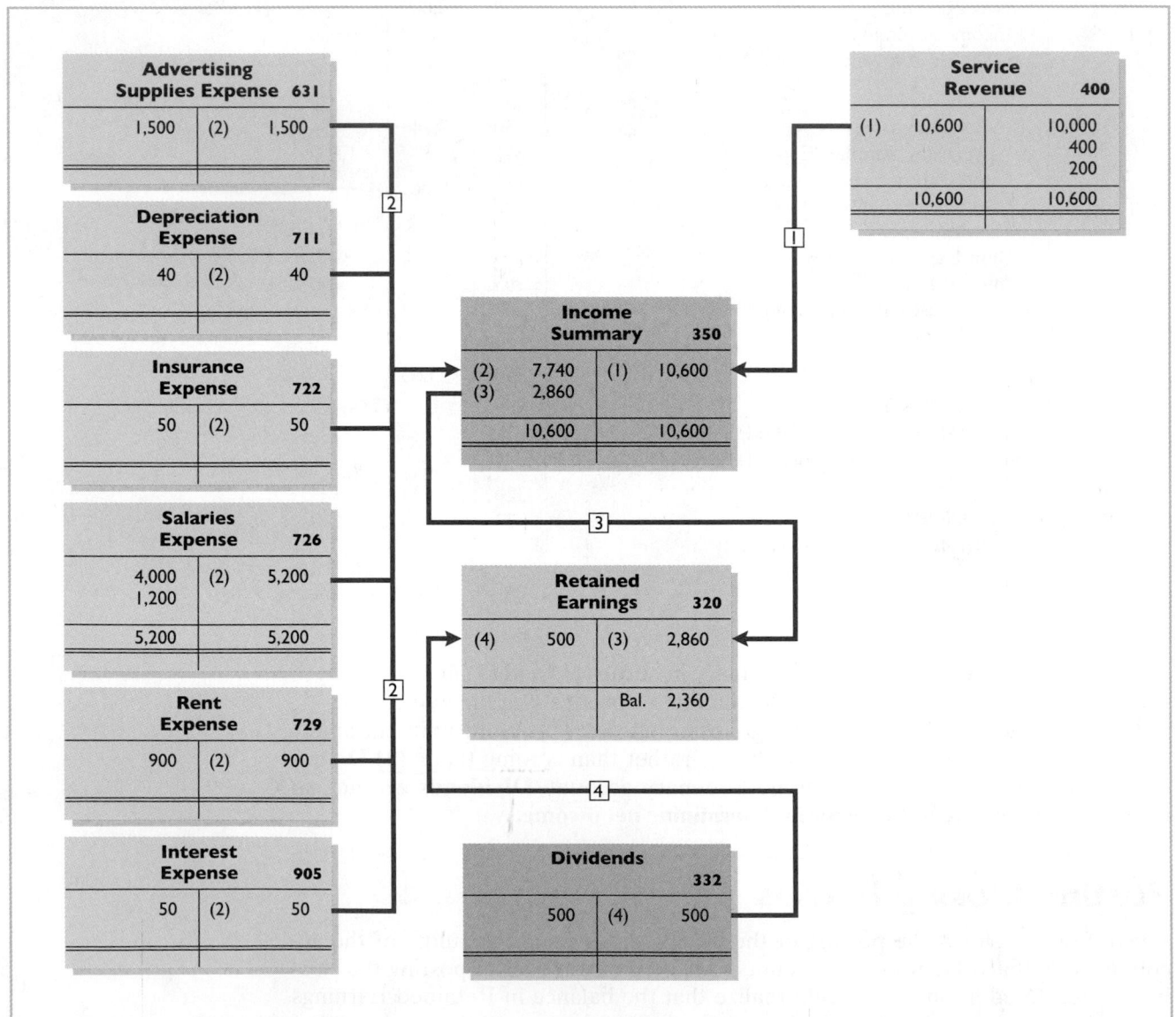

# ACCOUNTING ACROSS THE ORGANIZATION

### Cisco Performs the Virtual Close

Technology has dramatically shortened the closing process. Recent surveys have reported that the average company now takes only six to seven days to close, rather than 20 days. But a few companies do much better. Cisco Systems can perform a "virtual close"—closing within 24 hours on any day in the quarter. The same is true at Lockheed Martin Corp., which improved its closing time by 85% in just the last few years. Not very long ago it took 14 to 16 days. Managers at these companies emphasize that this increased speed has not reduced the accuracy and completeness of the data.

This is not just showing off. Knowing exactly where you are financially all of the time allows the company to respond faster than competitors. It also means that the hundreds of people who used to spend 10 to 20 days a quarter tracking transactions can now be more usefully employed on things such as mining data for business intelligence to find new business opportunities.

**Source:** "Reporting Practices: Few Do It All," *Financial Executive*, November 2003, p. 11.

**?** Who else benefits from a shorter closing process?

## Preparing a Post-Closing Trial Balance

After Pioneer has journalized and posted all closing entries, it prepares another trial balance, called a post-closing trial balance, from the ledger. The post-closing trial balance lists permanent accounts and their balances after journalizing and posting of closing entries. The purpose of the post-closing trial balance is **to prove the equality of the permanent account balances carried forward into the next accounting period.** Since all temporary accounts will have zero balances, **the post-closing trial balance will contain only permanent—balance sheet—accounts.**

Illustration 4-9 shows the post-closing trial balance for Pioneer Advertising Agency Inc.

> **STUDY OBJECTIVE 3**
>
> Describe the content and purpose of a post-closing trial balance.

**Illustration 4-9**
Post-closing trial balance

### PIONEER ADVERTISING AGENCY INC.
#### Post-Closing Trial Balance
#### October 31, 2008

|  | Debit | Credit |
|---|---|---|
| Cash | $15,200 | |
| Accounts Receivable | 200 | |
| Advertising Supplies | 1,000 | |
| Prepaid Insurance | 550 | |
| Office Equipment | 5,000 | |
| Accumulated Depreciation—Office Equipment | | $    40 |
| Notes Payable | | 5,000 |
| Accounts Payable | | 2,500 |
| Unearned Revenue | | 800 |
| Salaries Payable | | 1,200 |
| Interest Payable | | 50 |
| Common Stock | | 10,000 |
| Retained Earnings | | 2,360 |
| | $21,950 | $21,950 |

Pioneer prepares the post-closing trial balance from the permanent accounts in the ledger. Illustration 4-10 shows the permanent accounts in Pioneer's general ledger.

A post-closing trial balance provides evidence that the company has properly journalized and posted the closing entries. It also shows that the accounting equation is in balance at the end of the accounting period. However, like the trial balance, it does not prove that Pioneer has recorded all transactions or that the ledger is correct. For example, the post-closing trial balance will balance if a transaction is not journalized and posted or if a transaction is journalized and posted twice.

**Illustration 4-10**
General ledger, permanent accounts

**(Permanent Accounts Only)**

## GENERAL LEDGER

| | Cash | | | | No. 101 |
| --- | --- | --- | --- | --- | --- |
| Date | Explanation | Ref. | Debit | Credit | Balance |
| 2008 | | | | | |
| Oct. 1 | | J1 | 10,000 | | 10,000 |
| 2 | | J1 | 1,200 | | 11,200 |
| 3 | | J1 | | 900 | 10,300 |
| 4 | | J1 | | 600 | 9,700 |
| 20 | | J1 | | 500 | 9,200 |
| 26 | | J1 | | 4,000 | 5,200 |
| 31 | | J1 | 10,000 | | **15,200** |

| | Accounts Receivable | | | | No. 112 |
| --- | --- | --- | --- | --- | --- |
| Date | Explanation | Ref. | Debit | Credit | Balance |
| 2008 | | | | | |
| Oct. 31 | Adj. entry | J2 | **200** | | **200** |

| | Advertising Supplies | | | | No. 126 |
| --- | --- | --- | --- | --- | --- |
| Date | Explanation | Ref. | Debit | Credit | Balance |
| 2008 | | | | | |
| Oct. 5 | | J1 | 2,500 | | 2,500 |
| 31 | Adj. entry | J2 | | **1,500** | **1,000** |

| | Prepaid Insurance | | | | No. 130 |
| --- | --- | --- | --- | --- | --- |
| Date | Explanation | Ref. | Debit | Credit | Balance |
| 2008 | | | | | |
| Oct. 4 | | J1 | 600 | | 600 |
| 31 | Adj. entry | J2 | | **50** | **550** |

| | Office Equipment | | | | No. 157 |
| --- | --- | --- | --- | --- | --- |
| Date | Explanation | Ref. | Debit | Credit | Balance |
| 2008 | | | | | |
| Oct. 1 | | J1 | 5,000 | | **5,000** |

| | Accumulated Depreciation—Office Equipment | | | | No. 158 |
| --- | --- | --- | --- | --- | --- |
| Date | Explanation | Ref. | Debit | Credit | Balance |
| 2008 | | | | | |
| Oct. 31 | Adj. entry | J2 | | **40** | **40** |

| | Notes Payable | | | | No. 200 |
| --- | --- | --- | --- | --- | --- |
| Date | Explanation | Ref. | Debit | Credit | Balance |
| 2008 | | | | | |
| Oct. 1 | | J1 | | 5,000 | **5,000** |

| | Accounts Payable | | | | No. 201 |
| --- | --- | --- | --- | --- | --- |
| Date | Explanation | Ref. | Debit | Credit | Balance |
| 2008 | | | | | |
| Oct. 5 | | J1 | | 2,500 | **2,500** |

| | Unearned Revenue | | | | No. 209 |
| --- | --- | --- | --- | --- | --- |
| Date | Explanation | Ref. | Debit | Credit | Balance |
| 2008 | | | | | |
| Oct. 2 | | J1 | | 1,200 | 1,200 |
| 31 | Adj. entry | J2 | 400 | | **800** |

| | Salaries Payable | | | | No. 212 |
| --- | --- | --- | --- | --- | --- |
| Date | Explanation | Ref. | Debit | Credit | Balance |
| 2008 | | | | | |
| Oct. 31 | Adj. entry | J2 | | **1,200** | **1,200** |

| | Interest Payable | | | | No. 230 |
| --- | --- | --- | --- | --- | --- |
| Date | Explanation | Ref. | Debit | Credit | Balance |
| 2008 | | | | | |
| Oct. 31 | Adj. entry | J2 | | **50** | **50** |

| | Common Stock | | | | No. 311 |
| --- | --- | --- | --- | --- | --- |
| Date | Explanation | Ref. | Debit | Credit | Balance |
| 2008 | | | | | |
| Oct. 1 | | J1 | | 10,000 | 10,000 |

| | Retained Earnings | | | | No. 320 |
| --- | --- | --- | --- | --- | --- |
| Date | Explanation | Ref. | Debit | Credit | Balance |
| 2008 | | | | | |
| Oct. 1 | | | | | –0– |
| 31 | Closing entry | J3 | | 2,860 | 2,860 |
| 31 | Closing entry | J3 | 500 | | 2,360 |

*Note:* The permanent accounts for Pioneer Advertising Agency Inc. are shown here; the temporary accounts are shown in Illustration 4-11. Both permanent and temporary accounts are part of the general ledger; we segregate them here to aid in learning.

The remaining accounts in the general ledger are temporary accounts, shown in Illustration 4-11. After Pioneer correctly posts the closing entries, each temporary account has a zero balance. These accounts are double-ruled to finalize the closing process.

**Illustration 4-11**
General ledger, temporary accounts

**(Temporary Accounts Only)**

## GENERAL LEDGER

### Dividends — No. 332

| Date | Explanation | Ref. | Debit | Credit | Balance |
|---|---|---|---|---|---|
| 2008 | | | | | |
| Oct. 20 | | J1 | 500 | | 500 |
| 31 | Closing entry | J3 | | 500 | –0– |

### Income Summary — No. 350

| Date | Explanation | Ref. | Debit | Credit | Balance |
|---|---|---|---|---|---|
| 2008 | | | | | |
| Oct. 31 | Closing entry | J3 | | 10,600 | 10,600 |
| 31 | Closing entry | J3 | 7,740 | | 2,860 |
| 31 | Closing entry | J3 | 2,860 | | –0– |

### Service Revenue — No. 400

| Date | Explanation | Ref. | Debit | Credit | Balance |
|---|---|---|---|---|---|
| 2008 | | | | | |
| Oct. 31 | | J1 | | 10,000 | 10,000 |
| 31 | Adj. entry | J2 | | 400 | 10,400 |
| 31 | Adj. entry | J2 | | 200 | 10,600 |
| 31 | Closing entry | J3 | 10,600 | | –0– |

### Advertising Supplies Expense — No. 631

| Date | Explanation | Ref. | Debit | Credit | Balance |
|---|---|---|---|---|---|
| 2008 | | | | | |
| Oct. 31 | Adj. entry | J2 | 1,500 | | 1,500 |
| 31 | Closing entry | J3 | | 1,500 | –0– |

### Depreciation Expense — No. 711

| Date | Explanation | Ref. | Debit | Credit | Balance |
|---|---|---|---|---|---|
| 2008 | | | | | |
| Oct. 31 | Adj. entry | J2 | 40 | | 40 |
| 31 | Closing entry | J3 | | 40 | –0– |

### Insurance Expense — No. 722

| Date | Explanation | Ref. | Debit | Credit | Balance |
|---|---|---|---|---|---|
| 2008 | | | | | |
| Oct. 31 | Adj. entry | J2 | 50 | | 50 |
| 31 | Closing entry | J3 | | 50 | –0– |

### Salaries Expense — No. 726

| Date | Explanation | Ref. | Debit | Credit | Balance |
|---|---|---|---|---|---|
| 2008 | | | | | |
| Oct. 26 | | J1 | 4,000 | | 4,000 |
| 31 | Adj. entry | J2 | 1,200 | | 5,200 |
| 31 | Closing entry | J3 | | 5,200 | –0– |

### Rent Expense — No. 729

| Date | Explanation | Ref. | Debit | Credit | Balance |
|---|---|---|---|---|---|
| 2008 | | | | | |
| Oct. 3 | | J1 | 900 | | 900 |
| 31 | Closing entry | J3 | | 900 | –0– |

### Interest Expense — No. 905

| Date | Explanation | Ref. | Debit | Credit | Balance |
|---|---|---|---|---|---|
| 2008 | | | | | |
| Oct. 31 | Adj. entry | J2 | 50 | | 50 |
| 31 | Closing entry | J3 | | 50 | –0– |

*Note:* The temporary accounts for Pioneer Advertising Agency Inc. are shown here; Illustration 4-10 shows the permanent accounts. Both permanent and temporary accounts are part of the general ledger; we segregate them here to aid in learning.

# SUMMARY OF THE ACCOUNTING CYCLE

Illustration 4-12 (page 158) summarizes the steps in the accounting cycle. You can see that the cycle begins with the analysis of business transactions and ends with the preparation of a post-closing trial balance. Companies perform the steps in the cycle in sequence and repeat these steps in each accounting period.

**STUDY OBJECTIVE 4**
State the required steps in the accounting cycle.

Steps 1–3 may occur daily during the accounting period, as explained in Chapter 2. Companies perform Steps 4–7 on a periodic basis, such as monthly, quarterly, or annually. Steps 8 and 9—closing entries, and a post-closing trial balance—usually take place only at the end of a company's **annual** accounting period.

**Illustration 4-12**
Steps in the accounting
cycle

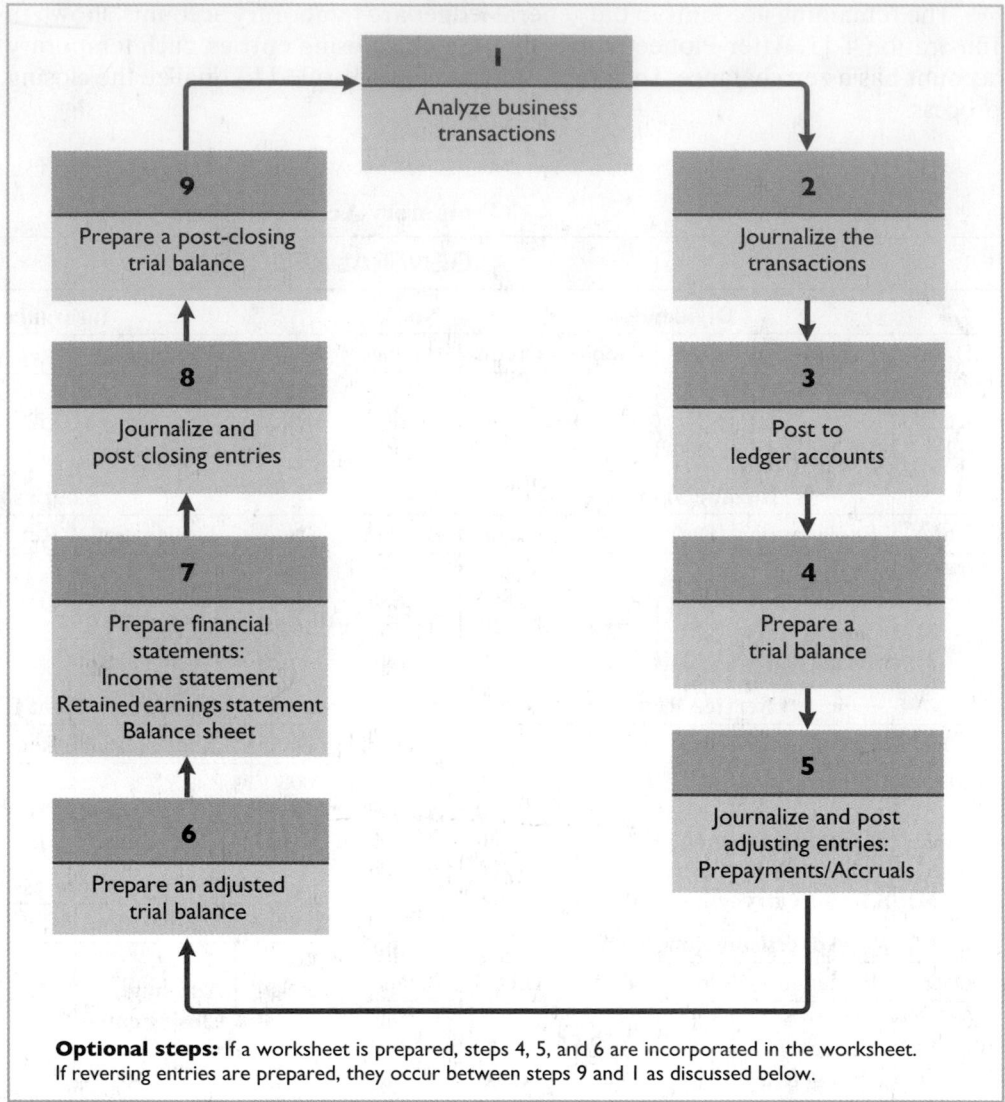

**Optional steps:** If a worksheet is prepared, steps 4, 5, and 6 are incorporated in the worksheet. If reversing entries are prepared, they occur between steps 9 and 1 as discussed below.

There are also two **optional steps** in the accounting cycle. As you have seen, companies may use a worksheet in preparing adjusting entries and financial statements. In addition, they may use reversing entries, as explained below.

## Reversing Entries—An Optional Step

Some accountants prefer to reverse certain adjusting entries by making a **reversing entry** at the beginning of the next accounting period. A reversing entry is the exact opposite of the adjusting entry made in the previous period. **Use of reversing entries is an optional bookkeeping procedure; it is not a required step in the accounting cycle.** Accordingly, we have chosen to cover this topic in an appendix at the end of the chapter.

## Correcting Entries—An Avoidable Step

STUDY OBJECTIVE 5

Explain the approaches to preparing correcting entries.

Unfortunately, errors may occur in the recording process. Companies should correct errors, **as soon as they discover them**, by journalizing and posting **correcting entries**. If the accounting records are free of errors, no correcting entries are needed.

You should recognize several differences between correcting entries and adjusting entries. First, adjusting entries are an integral part of the accounting cycle. Correcting entries, on the other hand, are unnecessary if the records are error-free. Second, companies journalize and post adjustments **only at the end of an accounting period**. In contrast, companies make correcting entries **whenever they discover an error**. Finally, adjusting entries always affect at least one balance sheet account and one income statement account. In contrast, correcting entries may involve any combination of accounts in need of correction. **Correcting entries must be posted before closing entries.**

To determine the correcting entry, it is useful to compare the incorrect entry with the correct entry. Doing so helps identify the accounts and amounts that should—and should not—be corrected. After comparison, the accountant makes an entry to correct the accounts. The following two cases for Mercato Co. illustrate this approach.

**ETHICS NOTE**

When companies find errors in previously released income statements, they restate those numbers. Perhaps because of the increased scrutiny caused by Sarbanes-Oxley, in 2005 companies filed a record 1,195 restatements.

## CASE 1

On May 10, Mercato Co. journalized and posted a $50 cash collection on account from a customer as a debit to Cash $50 and a credit to Service Revenue $50. The company discovered the error on May 20, when the customer paid the remaining balance in full.

| Incorrect Entry (May 10) | | | Correct Entry (May 10) | | |
|---|---|---|---|---|---|
| Cash | 50 | | Cash | 50 | |
| Service Revenue | | 50 | Accounts Receivable | | 50 |

**Illustration 4-13**
Comparison of entries

Comparison of the incorrect entry with the correct entry reveals that the debit to Cash $50 is correct. However, the $50 credit to Service Revenue should have been credited to Accounts Receivable. As a result, both Service Revenue and Accounts Receivable are overstated in the ledger. Mercato makes the following correcting entry.

**Illustration 4-14**
Correcting entry

| $A$ | $=$ | $L$ | $+$ | $SE$ |
|---|---|---|---|---|
| | | | | $-50$ Rev |
| $-50$ | | | | |

**Cash Flows**
no effect

| | Correcting Entry | | |
|---|---|---|---|
| May 20 | Service Revenue | 50 | |
| | Accounts Receivable | | 50 |
| | (To correct entry of May 10) | | |

## CASE 2

On May 18, Mercato purchased on account office equipment costing $450. The transaction was journalized and posted as a debit to Delivery Equipment $45 and a credit to Accounts Payable $45. The error was discovered on June 3, when Mercato received the monthly statement for May from the creditor.

**Illustration 4-15**
Comparison of entries

| Incorrect Entry (May 18) | | | Correct Entry (May 18) | | |
|---|---|---|---|---|---|
| Delivery Equipment | 45 | | Office Equipment | 450 | |
| Accounts Payable | | 45 | Accounts Payable | | 450 |

Comparison of the two entries shows that three accounts are incorrect. Delivery Equipment is overstated $45; Office Equipment is understated $450; and Accounts Payable is understated $405. Mercato makes the following correcting entry.

**Illustration 4-16**
Correcting entry

| A | = | L | + | SE |
|---|---|---|---|---|
| +450 | | | | |
| −45 | | | | |
| | | +405 | | |

**Cash Flows**
no effect

**Correcting Entry**

| | | | |
|---|---|---|---|
| June 3 | Office Equipment | 450 | |
| | Delivery Equipment | | 45 |
| | Accounts Payable | | 405 |
| | (To correct entry of May 18) | | |

Instead of preparing a correcting entry, **it is possible to reverse the incorrect entry and then prepare the correct entry**. This approach will result in more entries and postings than a correcting entry, but it will accomplish the desired result.

# ACCOUNTING ACROSS THE ORGANIZATION

### *Yale Express Loses Some Transportation Bills*

Yale Express, a short-haul trucking firm, turned over much of its cargo to local truckers to complete deliveries. Yale collected the entire delivery charge; when billed by the local trucker, Yale sent payment for the final phase to the local trucker. Yale used a cutoff period of 20 days into the next accounting period in making its adjusting entries for accrued liabilities. That is, it waited 20 days to receive the local truckers' bills to determine the amount of the unpaid but incurred delivery charges as of the balance sheet date.

On the other hand, Republic Carloading, a nationwide, long-distance freight forwarder, frequently did not receive transportation bills from truckers to whom it passed on cargo until months after the year-end. In making its year-end adjusting entries, Republic waited for months in order to include all of these outstanding transportation bills.

When Yale Express merged with Republic Carloading, Yale's vice president employed the 20-day cutoff procedure for both firms. As a result, millions of dollars of Republic's accrued transportation bills went unrecorded. When the company detected the error and made correcting entries, these and other errors changed a reported profit of $1.14 million into a loss of $1.88 million!

**?** What might Yale Express's vice president have done to produce more accurate financial statements without waiting months for Republic's outstanding transportation bills?

## *Before You Go On...*

### REVIEW IT
1. How do permanent accounts differ from temporary accounts?
2. What four different types of entries do companies make in closing the books?
3. What are the content and purpose of a post-closing trial balance?
4. What are the required and optional steps in the accounting cycle?

**DO IT**

The worksheet for Hancock Company shows the following in the financial statement columns:

Dividends $15,000

Common Stock $42,000

Net income $18,000

Prepare the closing entries at December 31 that affect owner's capital.

**Action Plan**

■ Remember to make closing entries in the correct sequence.

■ Make the first two entries to close revenues and expenses.

■ Make the third entry to close net income to retained earnings.

■ Make the final entry to close dividends to retained earnings.

**Solution**

| Dec. 31 | Income Summary | 18,000 | |
| |    Retained Earnings | | 18,000 |
| |     (To close net income to retained earnings) | | |
| 31 | Retained Earnings | 15,000 | |
| |    Dividends | | 15,000 |
| |     (To close dividends to retained earnings) | | |

Related exercise material: *BE4-4, BE4-5, BE4-6, BE4-7, BE4-8, E4-4, E4-7, E4-8, E4-10, and E4-11.*

✓ *The Navigator*

# THE CLASSIFIED BALANCE SHEET

The balance sheet presents a snapshot of a company's financial position at a point in time. To improve users' understanding of a company's financial position, companies often group similar assets and similar liabilities together. This is useful because it tells you that items within a group have similar economic characteristics. A **classified balance sheet** generally contains the standard classifications listed in Illustration 4-17.

**STUDY OBJECTIVE 6**
Identify the sections of a classified balance sheet.

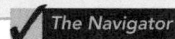

| Assets | Liabilities and Owner's Equity |
|---|---|
| Current assets | Current liabilities |
| Long-term investments | Long-term liabilities |
| Property, plant, and equipment | Stockholders' equity |
| Intangible assets | |

**Illustration 4-17**
Standard balance sheet classifications

These groupings help readers determine such things as (1) whether the company has enough assets to pay its debts as they come due, and (2) the claims of short- and long-term creditors on the company's total assets. Many of these groupings can be seen in the balance sheet of Franklin Corporation shown in Illustration 4-18 (page 162). In the sections that follow, we explain each of these groupings.

# Current Assets

Current assets are assets that a company expects to convert to cash or use up within one year. In Illustration 4-18, Franklin Corporation had current assets of $22,100. For most businesses the cutoff for classification as current assets is one year from the balance sheet date. For example, accounts receivable are current assets because the company will collect them and convert them to cash within one year. Supplies is a current asset because the company expects to use it up in operations within one year.

**Illustration 4-18**
Classified balance sheet

| FRANKLIN CORPORATION Balance Sheet October 31, 2008 | | | |
|---|---|---|---|
| **Assets** | | | |
| **Current assets** | | | |
| Cash | | $ 6,600 | |
| Short-term investments | | 2,000 | |
| Accounts receivable | | 7,000 | |
| Notes receivable | | 1,000 | |
| Inventories | | 3,000 | |
| Supplies | | 2,100 | |
| Prepaid insurance | | 400 | |
| Total current assets | | | $22,100 |
| **Long-term investments** | | | |
| Investment in stock of Walters Corp. | | 5,200 | |
| Investment in real estate | | 2,000 | 7,200 |
| **Property, plant, and equipment** | | | |
| Land | | 10,000 | |
| Office equipment | $24,000 | | |
| Less: Accumulated depreciation | 5,000 | 19,000 | 29,000 |
| **Intangible assets** | | | |
| Patents | | | 3,100 |
| Total assets | | | $61,400 |
| **Liabilities and Stockholders' Equity** | | | |
| **Current liabilities** | | | |
| Notes payable | | $11,000 | |
| Accounts payable | | 2,100 | |
| Salaries payable | | 1,600 | |
| Unearned revenue | | 900 | |
| Interest payable | | 450 | |
| Total current liabilities | | | $16,050 |
| **Long-term liabilities** | | | |
| Mortgage note payable | | 10,000 | |
| Notes payable | | 1,300 | |
| Total long-term liabilities | | | 11,300 |
| Total liabilities | | | 27,350 |
| **Stockholders' equity** | | | |
| Common stock | | 20,000 | |
| Retained earnings | | 14,050 | |
| Total stockholders' equity | | | 34,050 |
| Total liabilities and stockholders' equity | | | $61,400 |

**HELPFUL HINT**

Recall that the accounting equation is Assets = Liabilities + Stockholders' Equity.

Some companies use a period longer than one year to classify assets and liabilities as current because they have an operating cycle longer than one year. The operating cycle of a company is the average time that it takes to purchase inventory, sell it on account, and then collect cash from customers. For most businesses this cycle takes less than a year, so they use a one-year cutoff. But, for some businesses, such as vineyards or airplane manufacturers, this period may be longer than a year. **Except where noted, we will assume that companies use one year to determine whether an asset or liability is current or long-term.**

Common types of current assets are (1) cash, (2) short-term investments (such as short-term U.S. government securities), (3) receivables (notes receivable, accounts receivable, and interest receivable), (4) inventories, and (5) prepaid expenses (insurance and supplies). **On the balance sheet, companies usually list these items in the order in which they expect to convert them into cash.**

Illustration 4-19 presents the current assets of The Coca-Cola Company.

### THE COCA-COLA COMPANY
Balance Sheet (partial)
(in millions)

| Current assets | |
| --- | --- |
| Cash and cash equivalents | $ 6,707 |
| Short-term investments | 61 |
| Trade accounts receivable | 2,171 |
| Inventories | 1,420 |
| Prepaid expenses and other assets | 1,735 |
| Total current assets | $12,094 |

**Illustration 4-19**
Current assets section

As explained later in the chapter, a company's current assets are important in assessing its short-term debt-paying ability.

## Long-Term Investments

**Long-term investments** are generally investments in stocks and bonds of other companies that are normally held for many years. This category also includes investments in long-term assets such as land or buildings that a company is not currently using in its operating activities. In Illustration 4-18 Franklin Corporation reported total long-term investments of $7,200 on its balance sheet.

Yahoo! Inc. reported long-term investments in its balance sheet as shown in Illustration 4-20.

**ALTERNATIVE TERMINOLOGY**

Long-term investments are often referred to simply as *investments*.

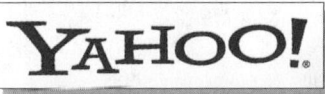

### YAHOO! INC.
Balance Sheet (partial)
(in thousands)

| Long-term investments | |
| --- | --- |
| Long-term marketable debt securities | $1,042,575 |

**Illustration 4-20**
Long-term investments section

# Property, Plant, and Equipment

**ALTERNATIVE TERMINOLOGY**

Property, plant, and equipment is sometimes called *fixed assets*.

**Property, plant, and equipment** are assets with relatively long useful lives that a company is currently using in operating the business. This category includes land, buildings, machinery and equipment, delivery equipment, and furniture. In Illustration 4-18 Franklin Corporation reported property, plant, and equipment of $29,000.

**Depreciation** is the practice of allocating the cost of assets to a number of years. Companies do this by systematically assigning a portion of an asset's cost as an expense each year (rather than expensing the full purchase price in the year of purchase). The assets that the company depreciates are reported on the balance sheet at cost less accumulated depreciation. The **accumulated depreciation** account shows the total amount of depreciation that the company has expensed thus far in the asset's life. In Illustration 4-18 Franklin Corporation reported accumulated depreciation of $5,000.

Illustration 4-21 presents the property, plant, and equipment of ski and sporting goods manufacturer K2, Inc.

**Illustration 4-21**
Property, plant, and equipment section

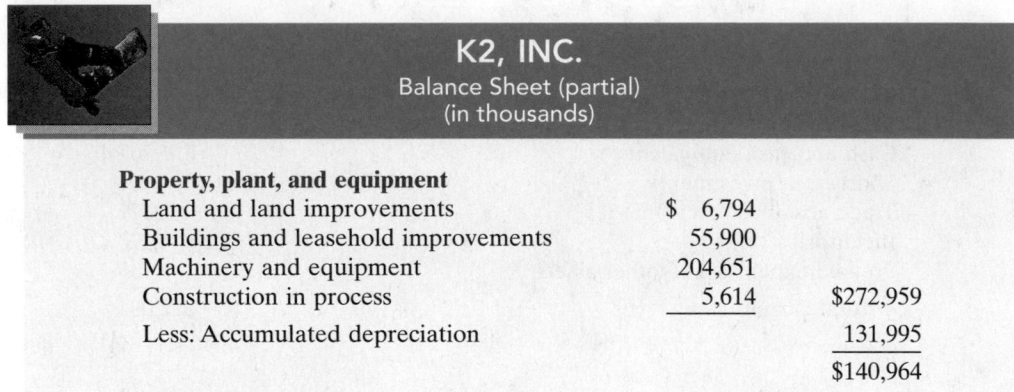

**K2, INC.**
Balance Sheet (partial)
(in thousands)

| Property, plant, and equipment | | |
|---|---:|---:|
| Land and land improvements | $ 6,794 | |
| Buildings and leasehold improvements | 55,900 | |
| Machinery and equipment | 204,651 | |
| Construction in process | 5,614 | $272,959 |
| Less: Accumulated depreciation | | 131,995 |
| | | $140,964 |

# Intangible Assets

**HELPFUL HINT**

Sometimes intangible assets are reported under a broader heading called *"Other assets."*

Many companies have assets that do not have physical substance yet often are very valuable. We call these assets **intangible assets**. One common intangible asset is goodwill. Other intangibles include patents, copyrights, and trademarks or trade names that give the company **exclusive right** of use for a specified period of time. Franklin Corporation reported intangible assets of $3,100.

Illustration 4-22 shows how media giant Time Warner, Inc. reported its intangible assets.

**Illustration 4-22**
Intangible assets section

**TIME WARNER, INC.**
Balance Sheet (partial)
(in millions)

| Intangible assets | |
|---|---:|
| Film library | $ 3,361 |
| Customer lists | 868 |
| Cable television franchises | 29,751 |
| Sports franchises | 262 |
| Brands, trademarks, and other intangible assets | 9,643 |
| | $43,885 |

# INTERNATIONAL INSIGHT

 **Big Changes Are Coming to Chinese Balance Sheets**

Beginning in 2007 many Chinese companies will be following International Financial Reporting Standards to prepare financial statements. Many people say that the largest change will occur on Chinese balance sheets. The new standards will require the companies to report a market value for many assets, including things like plant and equipment. (This, of course, is not in accordance with the cost principle, which U.S. GAAP follows.)

Chinese authorities hope that adopting international standards will give investors more confidence in the validity of Chinese financial reports.

**Source:** James T. Areddy, "Adding Up Chinese Data", *Wall Street Journal*, February 27, 2006, p. C10.

**?** What are the potential benefits and challenges presented by reporting assets like plant and equipment at their market value rather than historical cost?

## Current Liabilities

In the liabilities and stockholders' equity section of the balance sheet, the first grouping is current liabilities. **Current liabilities** are obligations that the company is to pay within the coming year. Common examples are accounts payable, wages payable, bank loans payable, interest payable, and taxes payable. Also included as current liabilities are current maturities of long-term obligations—payments to be made within the next year on long-term obligations. In Illustration 4-18 Franklin Corporation reported five different types of current liabilities, for a total of $16,050.

Within the current liabilities section, companies usually list notes payable first, followed by accounts payable. Other items then follow in the order of their magnitude. *In your homework, you should present notes payable first, followed by accounts payable, and then other liabilities in order of magnitude.*

Illustration 4-23 shows the current liabilities section adapted from the balance sheet of Marcus Corporation.

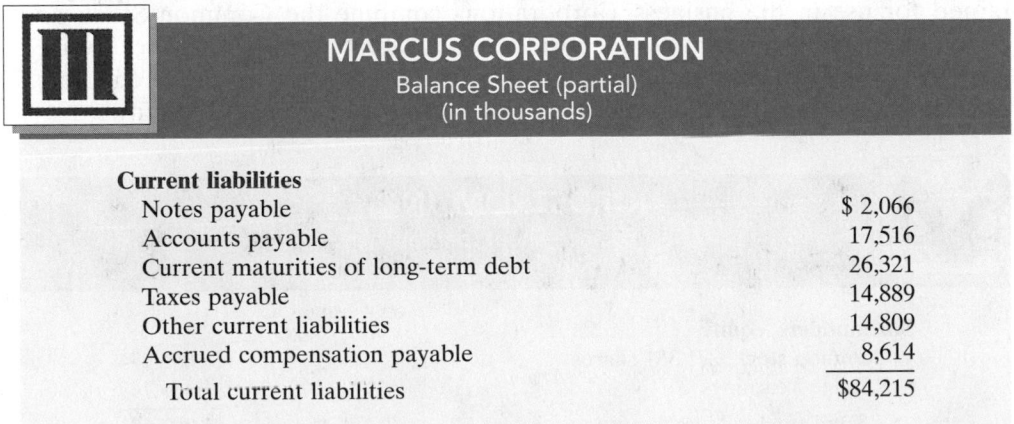

**MARCUS CORPORATION**
Balance Sheet (partial)
(in thousands)

| Current liabilities | |
| --- | --- |
| Notes payable | $ 2,066 |
| Accounts payable | 17,516 |
| Current maturities of long-term debt | 26,321 |
| Taxes payable | 14,889 |
| Other current liabilities | 14,809 |
| Accrued compensation payable | 8,614 |
| Total current liabilities | $84,215 |

**Illustration 4-23**
Current liabilities section

Users of financial statements look closely at the relationship between current assets and current liabilities. This relationship is important in evaluating a company's

**Liquidity**

**Illiquidity**

**liquidity**—its ability to pay obligations expected to be due within the next year. When current assets exceed current liabilities at the balance sheet date, the likelihood for paying the liabilities is favorable. When the reverse is true, short-term creditors may not be paid, and the company may ultimately be forced into bankruptcy.

## Long-Term Liabilities

**Long-term liabilities** are obligations that a company expects to pay **after** one year. Liabilities in this category include bonds payable, mortgages payable, long-term notes payable, lease liabilities, and pension liabilities. Many companies report long-term debt maturing after one year as a single amount in the balance sheet and show the details of the debt in notes that accompany the financial statements. Others list the various types of long-term liabilities. In Illustration 4-18 Franklin Corporation reported long-term liabilities of $11,300. *In your homework, list long-term liabilities in the order of their magnitude.*

Illustration 4-24 shows the long-term liabilities that Northwest Airlines Corporation reported in its balance sheet.

**Illustration 4-24**
Long-term liabilities section

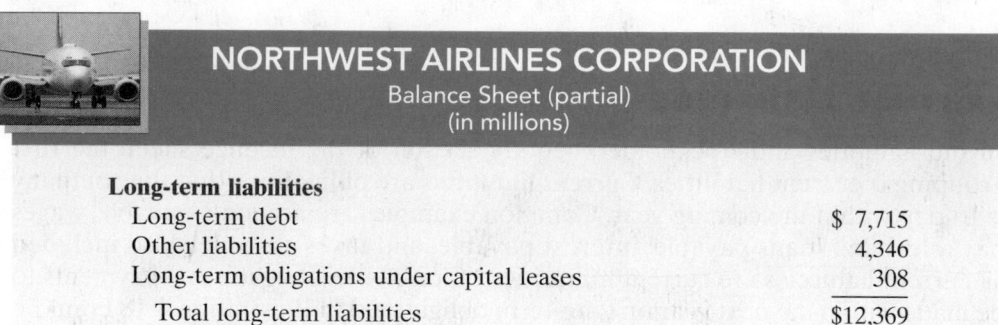

| NORTHWEST AIRLINES CORPORATION |
| Balance Sheet (partial) |
| (in millions) |

| **Long-term liabilities** | |
| Long-term debt | $ 7,715 |
| Other liabilities | 4,346 |
| Long-term obligations under capital leases | 308 |
| Total long-term liabilities | $12,369 |

## Stockholders' (Owners') Equity

The content of the owners' equity section varies with the form of business organization. In a proprietorship, there is one capital account. In a partnership, there is a capital account for each partner. Corporations divide owners' equity into two accounts—Common Stock and Retained Earnings. Corporations record stockholders' investments in the company by debiting an asset account and crediting the Common Stock account. They record in the Retained Earnings account income retained for use in the business. Corporations combine the Common Stock and Retained Earnings accounts and report them on the balance sheet as **stockholders' equity**. (We'll learn more about these corporation accounts in later chapters.) Nordstrom, Inc. recently reported its stockholders' equity section as follows.

**Illustration 4-25**
Stockholders' equity section

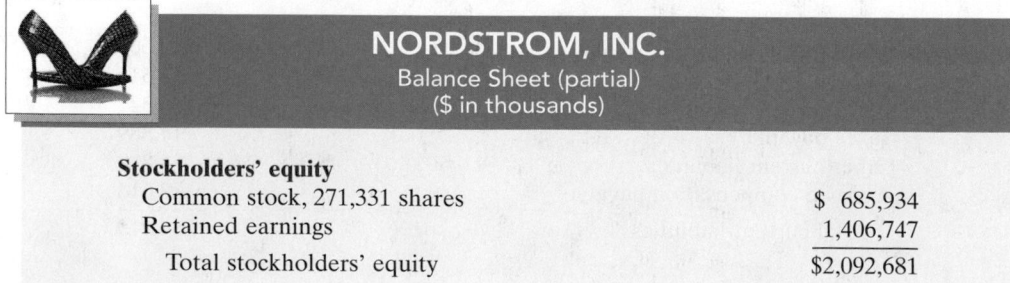

| NORDSTROM, INC. |
| Balance Sheet (partial) |
| ($ in thousands) |

| **Stockholders' equity** | |
| Common stock, 271,331 shares | $ 685,934 |
| Retained earnings | 1,406,747 |
| Total stockholders' equity | $2,092,681 |

 Be sure to read **ALL ABOUT YOU:** *Your Personal Balance Sheet* on the next page for information on how topics in this chapter apply to you.

# Your Personal Balance Sheet

By now you should be pretty comfortable with how to prepare a company's balance sheet. Maybe it is time for us to look at your personal financial position.

What are your personal assets? These are the items of value that you own. Some of your assets are *liquid*—cash or items that are easily converted to cash. Others, like cars, real estate, and some types of investments, are less liquid. Some assets, like houses and investments, tend to rise in value over time, which increases your net worth. Other assets, such as cars, tend to fall in value over time, decreasing your net worth.

What are your personal liabilities—the amounts that you owe to others? Student loans, car loans, credit card bills, and amounts owed to relatives are all personal liabilities. These liabilities are either current (to be repaid within 12 months) or long-term.

The difference between your assets and liabilities is, to use the terminology of the accounting equation, your "owner's equity." In personal finance terminology, this is your *net worth*. Having a high net worth does not guarantee happiness—but most believe that it is better than being broke. By monitoring your personal balance sheet, you can begin to take control of your financial future.

## ✺ Some Facts

* 48% of Americans think they know how much wealth they have.

* 2005 was the first year since the Depression when Americans spent more money than they made.

* The total net worth of U.S. households hit a record of $51.09 trillion during 2005.

* Economists note that a rise in house prices actually results in a fall in individual savings. It has been documented that a $1,000 rise in the value of a home results in a $50 fall in savings per year, presumably because homeowners feel more wealthy and therefore spend more (save less).

* When asked about very important wealth-building strategies for all Americans, 16% said "win the lottery."

## ✺ About the Numbers

Your ability to make good financial decisions is often influenced by your attitudes toward saving versus spending. The authors of a recent study conclude that "people commonly fall prey to psychologically driven impulses that affect their financial decisions." For example, when individuals were asked whether could they save 20% of their household income, nearly half said they couldn't. But, when asked if they could spend less, well more than half (71%) said they could live comfortably on 80% of their income. This clearly is inconsistent thinking: If you can live on 80% of your current income, you can save 20% of your current income.

**"How much could you save?"**

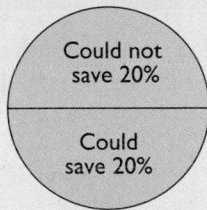

| | |
|---|---|
| Could not save 20% | Could live on 80% |
| Could save 20% | Could not live on 80% |

Nearly half could not comfortably **save 20%** of household's **annual income** at this point in life.

BUT

71% said they could comfortably **live on 80%** of household's **annual income** at this point in life.

**Source:** Northwestern Mutual Life, *www.nmfn.com/contentassets/pdfs/fin_misbehav.pdf*, p. 6.

## ✺ What Do You Think?

Should you prepare a personal balance sheet?

**YES:** In order to attain your desired financial objectives, you need to set goals early. The personal balance sheet provides a benchmark by which you can measure progress toward your financial goals. You need to do it now so that you begin to develop good financial habits. It provides a mechanism so that you don't allow your finances to get too "out-of-whack" while you are in school. That is, you don't want to dig too deep a hole.

**NO:** Your financial situation right now bears very little resemblance to what it will look like after you graduate. At that point, you will have a better job, and you won't have to pay tuition. Right now, you're just "bleeding cash."

**Sources:** Andrew Blackman, "How to Calculate Your Savings Rate; For Americans in 2005, Earnings Didn't Keep Pace with Boom in Spending," *Wall Street Journal*, January 3, 2006, p. D2; "Financial Planners Share Views on Saving," Consumer Federation of America and Financial Planning Association, January 2006.

The authors' comments on this situation appear on page 193.

## Before You Go On...

### REVIEW IT

1. What are the major sections in a classified balance sheet?
2. Using the PepsiCo annual report, determine its current liabilities at December 31, 2005, and December 25, 2004. Were current liabilities higher or lower than current assets in these two years? The answer to this question appears on page 193.

## Demonstration Problem

At the end of its first month of operations, Watson Answering Service Inc. has the following unadjusted trial balance.

**WATSON ANSWERING SERVICE INC.**
August 31, 2008
Trial Balance

| | Debit | Credit |
|---|---|---|
| Cash | $ 5,400 | |
| Accounts Receivable | 2,800 | |
| Prepaid Insurance | 2,400 | |
| Supplies | 1,300 | |
| Equipment | 60,000 | |
| Notes Payable | | $40,000 |
| Accounts Payable | | 2,400 |
| Common Stock | | 30,000 |
| Dividends | 1,000 | |
| Service Revenue | | 4,900 |
| Salaries Expense | 3,200 | |
| Utilities Expense | 800 | |
| Advertising Expense | 400 | |
| | $77,300 | $77,300 |

### action plan

✔ In completing the worksheet, be sure to (a) key the adjustments; (b) start at the top of the adjusted trial balance columns and extend adjusted balances to the correct statement columns; and (c) enter net income (or net loss) in the proper columns.

✔ In preparing a classified balance sheet, know the contents of each of the sections.

✔ In journalizing closing entries, remember that there are only four entries and that Dividends are closed to Retained Earnings.

Other data:

1. Insurance expires at the rate of $200 per month.
2. $1,000 of supplies are on hand at August 31.
3. Monthly depreciation on the equipment is $900.
4. Interest of $500 on the notes payable has accrued during August.

### Instructions

(a) Prepare a worksheet.
(b) Prepare a classified balance sheet assuming $35,000 of the notes payable are long-term.
(c) Journalize the closing entries.

**Solution**

(a)

## WATSON ANSWERING SERVICE INC.
Worksheet
For the Month Ended August 31, 2008

| Account Titles | Trial Balance Dr. | Trial Balance Cr. | Adjustments Dr. | Adjustments Cr. | Adjusted Trial Balance Dr. | Adjusted Trial Balance Cr. | Income Statement Dr. | Income Statement Cr. | Balance Sheet Dr. | Balance Sheet Cr. |
|---|---|---|---|---|---|---|---|---|---|---|
| Cash | 5,400 | | | | 5,400 | | | | 5,400 | |
| Accounts Receivable | 2,800 | | | | 2,800 | | | | 2,800 | |
| Supplies | 1,300 | | | (b) 300 | 1,000 | | | | 1,000 | |
| Prepaid Insurance | 2,400 | | | (a) 200 | 2,200 | | | | 2,200 | |
| Equipment | 60,000 | | | | 60,000 | | | | 60,000 | |
| Notes Payable | | 40,000 | | | | 40,000 | | | | 40,000 |
| Accounts Payable | | 2,400 | | | | 2,400 | | | | 2,400 |
| Common Stock | | 30,000 | | | | 30,000 | | | | 30,000 |
| Dividends | 1,000 | | | | 1,000 | | | | 1,000 | |
| Service Revenue | | 4,900 | | | | 4,900 | | 4,900 | | |
| Salaries Expense | 3,200 | | | | 3,200 | | 3,200 | | | |
| Utilities Expense | 800 | | | | 800 | | 800 | | | |
| Advertising Expense | 400 | | | | 400 | | 400 | | | |
| Totals | 77,300 | 77,300 | | | | | | | | |
| Insurance Expense | | | (a) 200 | | 200 | | 200 | | | |
| Supplies Expense | | | (b) 300 | | 300 | | 300 | | | |
| Depreciation Expense | | | (c) 900 | | 900 | | 900 | | | |
| Accumulated Depreciation— Equipment | | | | (c) 900 | | 900 | | | | 900 |
| Interest Expense | | | (d) 500 | | 500 | | 500 | | | |
| Interest Payable | | | | (d) 500 | | 500 | | | | 500 |
| Totals | | | 1,900 | 1,900 | 78,700 | 78,700 | 6,300 | 4,900 | 72,400 | 73,800 |
| Net Loss | | | | | | | | 1,400 | 1,400 | |
| Totals | | | | | | | 6,300 | 6,300 | 73,800 | 73,800 |

Explanation: (a) Insurance expired, (b) Supplies used, (c) Depreciation expensed, (d) Interest accrued.

(b)

## WATSON ANSWERING SERVICE INC.
Balance Sheet
August 31, 2008

### Assets

| | | |
|---|---|---|
| Current assets | | |
| Cash | $ 5,400 | |
| Accounts receivable | 2,800 | |
| Supplies | 1,000 | |
| Prepaid insurance | 2,200 | |
| Total current assets | | $11,400 |
| Property, plant, and equipment | | |
| Equipment | 60,000 | |
| Less: Accumulated depreciation—equipment | 900 | 59,100 |
| Total assets | | $70,500 |

### Liabilities and Stockholders' Equity

| | | |
|---|---:|---:|
| Current liabilities | | |
|   Notes payable | $ 5,000 | |
|   Accounts payable | 2,400 | |
|   Interest payable | 500 | |
|     Total current liabilities | | $7,900 |
| Long-term liabilities | | |
|   Notes payable | | 35,000 |
|     Total liabilities | | 42,900 |
| Stockholders' equity | | |
|   Common stock | 30,000 | |
|   Retained earnings | (2,400)* | |
|     Total stockholders' equity | | 27,600 |
|     Total liabilities and stockholders' equity | | $70,500 |

*Net loss of $1,400 plus dividends of $1,000.

| | | | | |
|---|---|---|---:|---:|
| **(c)** | Aug. 31 | Service Revenue | 4,900 | |
| | |   Income Summary | | 4,900 |
| | |     (To close revenue account) | | |
| | 31 | Income Summary | 6,300 | |
| | |   Salaries Expense | | 3,200 |
| | |   Depreciation Expense | | 900 |
| | |   Utilities Expense | | 800 |
| | |   Interest Expense | | 500 |
| | |   Advertising Expense | | 400 |
| | |   Supplies Expense | | 300 |
| | |   Insurance Expense | | 200 |
| | |     (To close expense accounts) | | |
| | 31 | Retained Earnings | 1,400 | |
| | |   Income Summary | | 1,400 |
| | |     (To close net loss to retained earnings) | | |
| | 31 | Retained Earnings | 1,000 | |
| | |   Dividends | | 1,000 |
| | |     (To close dividends to retained earnings) | | |

✓ The Navigator

# SUMMARY OF STUDY OBJECTIVES

**1 Prepare a worksheet.** The steps in preparing a worksheet are: (a) Prepare a trial balance on the worksheet. (b) Enter the adjustments in the adjustments columns. (c) Enter adjusted balances in the adjusted trial balance columns. (d) Extend adjusted trial balance amounts to appropriate financial statement columns. (e) Total the statement columns, compute net income (or net loss), and complete the worksheet.

**2 Explain the process of closing the books.** Closing the books occurs at the end of an accounting period. The process is to journalize and post closing entries and then rule and balance all accounts. In closing the books, companies make separate entries to close revenues and expenses to Income Summary, Income Summary to Retained Earnings, and Dividends to Retained Earnings. Only temporary accounts are closed.

**3 Describe the content and purpose of a post-closing trial balance.** A post-closing trial balance contains the balances in permanent accounts that are carried forward to the next accounting period. The purpose of this trial balance is to prove the equality of these balances.

**4 State the required steps in the accounting cycle.** The required steps in the accounting cycle are: (1) analyze business transactions, (2) journalize the transactions, (3) post to ledger accounts, (4) prepare a trial balance, (5) journalize and post adjusting entries, (6) prepare an adjusted trial balance, (7) prepare financial statements, (8) journalize and post closing entries, and (9) prepare a post-closing trial balance.

**5 Explain the approaches to preparing correcting entries.** One way to determine the correcting entry is to compare the incorrect entry with the correct entry. After comparison, the company makes a correcting entry to correct the accounts. An alternative to a correcting entry is to reverse the incorrect entry and then prepare the correct entry.

**6  Identify the sections of a classified balance sheet.** A classified balance sheet categorizes assets as current assets;

long-term investments; property, plant, and equipment; and intangibles. Liabilities are classified as either current or long-term. There is also a stockholders' (owners') equity section, which varies with the form of business organization.

# GLOSSARY

**Classified balance sheet**   A balance sheet that contains a number of standard classifications or sections. (p. 161).

**Closing entries**   Entries made at the end of an accounting period to transfer the balances of temporary accounts to a permanent stockholders' equity account, Retained Earnings. (p. 151).

**Correcting entries**   Entries to correct errors made in recording transactions. (p. 158).

**Current assets**   Assets that a company expects to convert to cash or use up within one year. (p. 162).

**Current liabilities**   Obligations that a company expects to pay from existing current assets within the coming year. (p. 165).

**Income Summary**   A temporary account used in closing revenue and expense accounts. (p. 151).

**Intangible assets**   Noncurrent assets that do not have physical substance. (p. 164).

**Liquidity**   The ability of a company to pay obligations expected to be due within the next year. (p. 166).

**Long-term investments**   Generally, investments in stocks and bonds of other companies that companies normally hold for many years. Also includes long-term assets, such as land and buildings, not currently being used in operations. (p. 163).

**Long-term liabilities**   Obligations that a company expects to pay after one year. (p. 166).

**Operating cycle**   The average time that it takes to go from cash to cash in producing revenues. (p. 163).

**Permanent (real) accounts**   Accounts that relate to one or more accounting periods. Consist of all balance sheet accounts. Balances are carried forward to next accounting period. (p. 150).

**Post-closing trial balance**   A list of permanent accounts and their balances after a company has journalized and posted closing entries. (p. 155).

**Property, plant, and equipment**   Assets with relatively long useful lives, currently being used in operations. (p. 164).

**Reversing entry**   An entry, made at the beginning of the next accounting period, that is the exact opposite of the adjusting entry made in the previous period. (p. 158).

**Stockholders' equity**   The ownership claim of shareholders on total assets. It is to a corporation what owner's equity is to a proprietorship. (p. 166).

**Temporary (nominal) accounts**   Accounts that relate only to a given accounting period. Consist of all income statement accounts and the Dividends account. All temporary accounts are closed at end of accounting period. (p. 150).

**Worksheet**   A multiple-column form that may be used in making adjusting entries and in preparing financial statements. (p. 144).

# APPENDIX **Reversing Entries**

After preparing the financial statements and closing the books, it is often helpful to reverse some of the adjusting entries before recording the regular transactions of the next period. Such entries are **reversing entries**. Companies make **a reversing entry at the beginning of the next accounting period**. Each reversing entry **is the exact opposite of the adjusting entry made in the previous period**. The recording of reversing entries is an **optional step** in the accounting cycle.

STUDY OBJECTIVE 7

Prepare reversing entries.

The purpose of reversing entries is to simplify the recording of a subsequent transaction related to an adjusting entry. For example, in Chapter 3 (page 109), the payment of salaries after an adjusting entry resulted in two debits: one to Salaries Payable and the other to Salaries Expense. With reversing entries, the company can debit the entire subsequent payment to Salaries Expense. **The use of reversing entries does not change the amounts reported in the financial statements.** What it does is simplify the recording of subsequent transactions.

# Reversing Entries Example

Companies most often use reversing entries to reverse two types of adjusting entries: accrued revenues and accrued expenses. To illustrate the optional use of reversing entries for accrued expenses, we will use the salaries expense transactions for Pioneer Advertising Agency Inc. The transaction and adjustment data are as follows.

1. October 26 (initial salary entry): Pioneer pays $4,000 of salaries earned between October 15 and October 26.

2. October 31 (adjusting entry): Salaries earned between October 29 and October 31 are $1,200. The company will pay these in the November 9 payroll.

3. November 9 (subsequent salary entry): Salaries paid are $4,000. Of this amount, $1,200 applied to accrued wages payable and $2,800 was earned between November 1 and November 9.

Illustration 4A-1 shows the entries with and without reversing entries.

**Illustration 4A-1**
Comparative entries—not reversing vs. reversing

| **Without Reversing Entries** **(per chapter)** | | | | **With Reversing Entries** **(per appendix)** | | | |
|---|---|---|---|---|---|---|---|
| *Initial Salary Entry* | | | | *Initial Salary Entry* | | | |
| Oct. 26 | Salaries Expense | 4,000 | | Oct. 26 | (Same entry) | | |
| | Cash | | 4,000 | | | | |
| *Adjusting Entry* | | | | *Adjusting Entry* | | | |
| Oct. 31 | Salaries Expense | 1,200 | | Oct. 31 | (Same entry) | | |
| | Salaries Payable | | 1,200 | | | | |
| *Closing Entry* | | | | *Closing Entry* | | | |
| Oct. 31 | Income Summary | 5,200 | | Oct. 31 | (Same entry) | | |
| | Salaries Expense | | 5,200 | | | | |
| *Reversing Entry* | | | | *Reversing Entry* | | | |
| Nov. 1 | No reversing entry is made. | | | Nov. 1 | **Salaries Payable** | **1,200** | |
| | | | | | **Salaries Expense** | | **1,200** |
| *Subsequent Salary Entry* | | | | *Subsequent Salary Entry* | | | |
| Nov. 9 | Salaries Payable | 1,200 | | Nov. 9 | **Salaries Expense** | **4,000** | |
| | Salaries Expense | 2,800 | | | **Cash** | | **4,000** |
| | Cash | | 4,000 | | | | |

The first three entries are the same whether or not Pioneer uses reversing entries. The last two entries are different. The November 1 **reversing entry** eliminates the $1,200 balance in Salaries Payable created by the October 31 adjusting entry. The reversing entry also creates a $1,200 credit balance in the Salaries Expense account. As you know, it is unusual for an expense account to have a credit balance. The balance is correct in this instance, though, because it anticipates that the entire amount of the first salary payment in the new accounting period will be debited to Salaries Expense. This debit will eliminate the credit balance. The resulting debit balance in the expense account will equal the salaries expense incurred in the new accounting period ($2,800 in this example).

If Pioneer makes reversing entries, it can debit all cash payments of expenses to the expense account. This means that on November 9 (and every payday) Pioneer can debit Salaries Expense for the amount paid, without regard to any accrued salaries payable. Being able to make the **same entry each time** simplifies the recording process: The company can record subsequent transactions as if the related adjusting entry had never been made.

Illustration 4A-2 shows the posting of the entries with reversing entries.

**Illustration 4A-2**
Postings with reversing entries

| Salaries Expense | | | | Salaries Payable | | | | |
|---|---|---|---|---|---|---|---|---|
| 10/26 Paid | 4,000 | 10/31 Closing | 5,200 | **11/1** | **Reversing** | **1,200** | 10/31 Adjusting | 1,200 |
| 31 Adjusting | 1,200 | | | | | | | |
| | 5,200 | | 5,200 | | | | | |
| 11/9 Paid | 4,000 | **11/1** | **Reversing** | **1,200** | | | | |

A company can also use reversing entries for accrued revenue adjusting entries. For Pioneer Advertising, the adjusting entry was: Accounts Receivable (Dr.) $200 and Service Revenue (Cr.) $200. Thus, the reversing entry on November 1 is:

| | | | | |
|---|---|---|---|---|
| Nov. 1 | Service Revenue | | 200 | |
| | Accounts Receivable | | | 200 |
| | (To reverse October 31 adjusting entry) | | | |

| A | = | L | + | SE |
|---|---|---|---|---|
| | | | | −200 Rev |
| −200 | | | | |

**Cash Flows**
no effect

When Pioneer collects the accrued service revenue, it debits Cash and credits Service Revenue.

**SUMMARY OF STUDY OBJECTIVE FOR APPENDIX**

**7  Prepare reversing entries.** Reversing entries are the opposite of the adjusting entries made in the preceding period. Some companies choose to make reversing entries at the beginning of a new accounting period to simplify the recording of later transactions related to the adjusting entries. In most cases, only accrued adjusting entries are reversed.

\*__Note:__ All asterisked Questions, Exercises, and Problems relate to material in the appendix to the chapter.

**SELF-STUDY QUESTIONS**

*Answers are at the end of the chapter.*

(SO 1)  **1.** Which of the following statements is *incorrect* concerning the worksheet?
 **a.** The worksheet is essentially a working tool of the accountant.
 **b.** The worksheet is distributed to management and other interested parties.
 **c.** The worksheet cannot be used as a basis for posting to ledger accounts.
 **d.** Financial statements can be prepared directly from the worksheet before journalizing and posting the adjusting entries.

**2.** In a worksheet, net income is entered in the following (SO 1) columns:
 **a.** income statement (Dr) and balance sheet (Dr).
 **b.** income statement (Cr) and balance sheet (Dr).
 **c.** income statement (Dr) and balance sheet (Cr).
 **d.** income statement (Cr) and balance sheet (Cr).

**3.** An account that will have a zero balance after closing (SO 2) entries have been journalized and posted is:
 **a.** Service Revenue.
 **b.** Advertising Supplies.
 **c.** Prepaid Insurance.
 **d.** Accumulated Depreciation.

(SO 2) **4.** When a net loss has occurred, Income Summary is:
  **a.** debited and Retained Earnings is credited.
  **b.** credited and Retained Earnings is debited.
  **c.** debited and Common Stock is credited.
  **d.** credited and Common Stock is debited.

(SO 2) **5.** The closing process involves separate entries to close (1) expenses, (2) dividends, (3) revenues, and (4) income summary. The correct sequencing of the entries is:
  **a.** (4), (3), (2), (1)
  **b.** (1), (2), (3), (4)
  **c.** (3), (1), (4), (2)
  **d.** (3), (2), (1), (4)

(SO 3) **6.** Which types of accounts will appear in the post-closing trial balance?
  **a.** Permanent (real) accounts.
  **b.** Temporary (nominal) accounts.
  **c.** Accounts shown in the income statement columns of a work sheet.
  **d.** None of the above.

(SO 4) **7.** All of the following are required steps in the accounting cycle *except*:
  **a.** journalizing and posting closing entries.
  **b.** preparing financial statements.
  **c.** journalizing the transactions.
  **d.** preparing a work sheet.

(SO 5) **8.** Cash of $100 received at the time the service was provided was journalized and posted as a debit to Cash $100 and a credit to Accounts Receivable $100. Assuming the incorrect entry is not reversed, the correcting entry is:
  **a.** debit Service Revenue $100 and credit Accounts Receivable $100.
  **b.** debit Accounts Receivable $100 and credit Service Revenue $100.
  **c.** debit Cash $100 and credit Service Revenue $100.
  **d.** debit Accounts Receivable $100 and credit Cash $100.

(SO 6) **9.** In a classified balance sheet, assets are usually classified using the following categories:
  **a.** current assets; long-term assets; property, plant, and equipment; and intangible assets.
  **b.** current assets; long-term investments; property, plant, and equipment; and other assets.
  **c.** current assets; long-term investments; tangible assets; and intangible assets.
  **d.** current assets; long-term investments; property, plant, and equipment; and intangible assets.

(SO 6) **10.** Current assets are listed:
  **a.** by liquidity.
  **b.** by importance.
  **c.** by longevity.
  **d.** alphabetically.

(SO 7) **\*11.** On December 31, Frank Voris Company correctly made an adjusting entry to recognize $2,000 of accrued salaries payable. On January 8 of the next year, total salaries of $3,400 were paid. Assuming the correct reversing entry was made on January 1, the entry on January 8 will result in a credit to Cash $3,400 and the following debit(s):
  **a.** Salaries Payable $1,400, and Salaries Expense $2,000.
  **b.** Salaries Payable $2,000 and Salaries Expense $1,400.
  **c.** Salaries Expense $3,400.
  **d.** Salaries Payable $3,400.

Go to the book's website,
**www.wiley.com/college/weygandt**,
for Additional Self-Study questions.

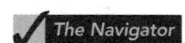 The Navigator

## QUESTIONS

**1.** "A worksheet is a permanent accounting record and its use is required in the accounting cycle." Do you agree? Explain.

**2.** Explain the purpose of the worksheet.

**3.** What is the relationship, if any, between the amount shown in the adjusted trial balance column for an account and that account's ledger balance?

**4.** If a company's revenues are $125,000 and its expenses are $113,000, in which financial statement columns of the worksheet will the net income of $12,000 appear? When expenses exceed revenues, in which columns will the difference appear?

**5.** Why is it necessary to prepare formal financial statements if all of the data are in the statement columns of the worksheet?

**6.** Identify the account(s) debited and credited in each of the four closing entries, assuming the company has net income for the year.

**7.** Describe the nature of the Income Summary account and identify the types of summary data that may be posted to this account.

**8.** What are the content and purpose of a post-closing trial balance?

**9.** Which of the following accounts would not appear in the post-closing trial balance? Interest Payable; Equipment; Depreciation Expense; Dividends; Unearned Revenue; Accumulated Depreciation—Equipment; and Service Revenue.

**10.** Distinguish between a reversing entry and an adjusting entry. Are reversing entries required?

**11.** Indicate, in the sequence in which they are made, the three required steps in the accounting cycle that involve journalizing.

**12.** Identify, in the sequence in which they are prepared, the three trial balances that are often used to report financial information about a company.

**13.** How do correcting entries differ from adjusting entries?

**14.** What standard classifications are used in preparing a classified balance sheet?

**15.** What is meant by the term "operating cycle?"

**16.** Define current assets. What basis is used for arranging individual items within the current assets section?

**17.** Distinguish between long-term investments and property, plant, and equipment.

**18.** (a) What is the term used to describe the owner's equity section of a corporation? (b) Identify the two owners' equity accounts in a corporation and indicate the purpose of each.

*19. Sanchez Company prepares reversing entries. If the adjusting entry for interest payable is reversed, what type of

an account balance, if any, will there be in Interest Payable and Interest Expense after the reversing entry is posted?

*20. At December 31, accrued salaries payable totaled $3,500. On January 10, total salaries of $8,000 are paid. (a) Assume that reversing entries are made at January 1. Give the January 10 entry, and indicate the Salaries Expense account balance after the entry is posted. (b) Repeat part (a) assuming reversing entries are not made.

# BRIEF EXERCISES

**BE4-1**    The steps in using a worksheet are presented in random order below. List the steps in the proper order by placing numbers 1–5 in the blank spaces.

*List the steps in preparing a worksheet.*

(SO 1)

**(a)** _____ Prepare a trial balance on the worksheet.
**(b)** _____ Enter adjusted balances.
**(c)** _____ Extend adjusted balances to appropriate statement columns.
**(d)** _____ Total the statement columns, compute net income (loss), and complete the worksheet.
**(e)** _____ Enter adjustment data.

**BE4-2**    The ledger of Ley Company includes the following unadjusted balances: Prepaid Insurance $3,000, Service Revenue $58,000, and Salaries Expense $25,000. Adjusting entries are required for **(a)** expired insurance $1,200; **(b)** services provided $1,100, but unbilled and uncollected; and **(c)** accrued salaries payable $800. Enter the unadjusted balances and adjustments into a worksheet and complete the worksheet for all accounts. *Note:* You will need to add the following accounts: Accounts Receivable, Salaries Payable, and Insurance Expense.

*Prepare partial worksheet.*

(SO 1)

**BE4-3**    The following selected accounts appear in the adjusted trial balance columns of the worksheet for Batan Company: Accumulated Depreciation; Depreciation Expense; Common Stock; Dividends; Service Revenue; Supplies; and Accounts Payable. Indicate the financial statement column (income statement Dr., balance sheet Cr., etc.) to which each balance should be extended.

*Identify worksheet columns for selected accounts.*

(SO 1)

**BE4-4**    The ledger of Swann Company contains the following balances: Retained Earnings $30,000; Dividends $2,000; Service Revenue $50,000; Salaries Expense $27,000; and Supplies Expense $4,000. Prepare the closing entries at December 31.

*Prepare closing entries from ledger balances.*

(SO 2)

**BE4-5**    Using the data in BE4-4, enter the balances in T accounts, post the closing entries, and rule and balance the accounts.

*Post closing entries; rule and balance T accounts.*

(SO 2)

**BE4-6**    The income statement for Crestwood Golf Club for the month ending July 31 shows Green Fee Revenue $13,600, Salaries Expense $8,200, Maintenance Expense $2,500, and Net Income $2,900. Prepare the entries to close the revenue and expense accounts. Post the entries to the revenue and expense accounts, and complete the closing process for these accounts using the three-column form of account.

*Journalize and post closing entries using the three-column form of account.*

(SO 2)

**BE4-7**    Using the data in BE4-3, identify the accounts that would be included in a post-closing trial balance.

*Identify post-closing trial balance accounts.*

(SO 3)

**BE4-8**    The steps in the accounting cycle are listed in random order below. List the steps in proper sequence, assuming no worksheet is prepared, by placing numbers 1–9 in the blank spaces.

*List the required steps in the accounting cycle in sequence.*

(SO 4)

**(a)** _____ Prepare a trial balance.
**(b)** _____ Journalize the transactions.
**(c)** _____ Journalize and post closing entries.
**(d)** _____ Prepare financial statements.
**(e)** _____ Journalize and post adjusting entries.
**(f)** _____ Post to ledger accounts.
**(g)** _____ Prepare a post-closing trial balance.
**(h)** _____ Prepare an adjusted trial balance.
**(i)** _____ Analyze business transactions.

*Prepare correcting entries.*
(SO 5)

**BE4-9**   At Batavia Company, the following errors were discovered after the transactions had been journalized and posted. Prepare the correcting entries.

1. A collection on account from a customer for $780 was recorded as a debit to Cash $780 and a credit to Service Revenue $780.
2. The purchase of store supplies on account for $1,570 was recorded as a debit to Store Supplies $1,750 and a credit to Accounts Payable $1,750.

*Prepare the current assets section of a balance sheet.*
(SO 6)

**BE4-10**   The balance sheet debit column of the worksheet for Diaz Company includes the following accounts: Accounts Receivable $12,500; Prepaid Insurance $3,600; Cash $15,400; Supplies $5,200, and Short-term Investments $6,700. Prepare the current assets section of the balance sheet, listing the accounts in proper sequence.

*Classify accounts on balance sheet.*
(SO 6)

**BE4-11**   The following are the major balance sheet classifications:

Current assets (CA)                 Current liabilities (CL)
Long-term investments (LTI)         Long-term liabilities (LTL)
Property, plant, and equipment (PPE)  Stockholders' equity (SE)
Intangible assets (IA)

Match each of the following accounts to its proper balance sheet classification.

_____ Accounts payable               _____ Income tax payable
_____ Accounts receivable            _____ Investment in long-term bonds
_____ Accumulated depreciation       _____ Land
_____ Building                       _____ Merchandise inventory
_____ Cash                           _____ Patent
_____ Copyrights                     _____ Supplies

*Prepare reversing entries.*
(SO 7)

**\*BE4-12**   At October 31, Nathan Company made an accrued expense adjusting entry of $1,400 for salaries. Prepare the reversing entry on November 1, and indicate the balances in Salaries Payable and Salaries Expense after posting the reversing entry.

# EXERCISES

*Complete the worksheet.*
(SO 1)

**E4-1**   The trial balance columns of the worksheet for Briscoe Company at June 30, 2008, are as follows.

## BRISCOE COMPANY
### Worksheet
### For the Month Ended June 30, 2008

| Account Titles | Trial Balance | |
|---|---|---|
| | Dr. | Cr. |
| Cash | $2,320 | |
| Accounts Receivable | 2,440 | |
| Supplies | 1,880 | |
| Accounts Payable | | $1,120 |
| Unearned Revenue | | 240 |
| Common Stock | | 3,600 |
| Service Revenue | | 2,400 |
| Salaries Expense | 560 | |
| Miscellaneous Expense | 160 | |
| | $7,360 | $7,360 |

Other data:

1. A physical count reveals $300 of supplies on hand.
2. $100 of the unearned revenue is still unearned at month-end.
3. Accrued salaries are $280.

**Instructions**
Enter the trial balance on a worksheet and complete the worksheet.

**E4-2**    The adjusted trial balance columns of the worksheet for Goode Company are as follows.

*Complete the worksheet.*
(SO 1)

### GOODE COMPANY
Worksheet (partial)
For the Month Ended April 30, 2008

| Account Titles | Adjusted Trial Balance Dr. | Cr. | Income Statement Dr. | Cr. | Balance Sheet Dr. | Cr. |
|---|---|---|---|---|---|---|
| Cash | 13,752 | | | | | |
| Accounts Receivable | 7,840 | | | | | |
| Prepaid Rent | 2,280 | | | | | |
| Equipment | 23,050 | | | | | |
| Accumulated Depreciation | | 4,921 | | | | |
| Notes Payable | | 5,700 | | | | |
| Accounts Payable | | 5,672 | | | | |
| Common Stock | | 25,000 | | | | |
| Retained Earnings | | 5,960 | | | | |
| Dividends | 3,650 | | | | | |
| Service Revenue | | 15,590 | | | | |
| Salaries Expense | 10,840 | | | | | |
| Rent Expense | 760 | | | | | |
| Depreciation Expense | 671 | | | | | |
| Interest Expense | 57 | | | | | |
| Interest Payable | | 57 | | | | |
| Totals | 62,900 | 62,900 | | | | |

**Instructions**
Complete the worksheet.

**E4-3**    Worksheet data for Goode Company are presented in E4-2. No common stock was issued during April.

*Prepare financial statements from worksheet.*
(SO 1, 6)

**Instructions**
Prepare an income statement, a retained earnings statement, and a classified balance sheet.

**E4-4**    Worksheet data for Goode Company are presented in E4-2.

*Journalize and post closing entries and prepare a post-closing trial balance.*
(SO 2, 3)

**Instructions**
(a) Journalize the closing entries at April 30.
(b) Post the closing entries to Income Summary and Retained Earnings. Use T accounts.
(c) Prepare a post-closing trial balance at April 30.

**E4-5**    The adjustments columns of the worksheet for Mears Company are shown below.

*Prepare adjusting entries from a worksheet, and extend balances to worksheet columns.*
(SO 1)

| Account Titles | Adjustments Debit | Credit |
|---|---|---|
| Accounts Receivable | 600 | |
| Prepaid Insurance | | 400 |
| Accumulated Depreciation | | 900 |
| Salaries Payable | | 500 |
| Service Revenue | | 600 |
| Salaries Expense | 500 | |
| Insurance Expense | 400 | |
| Depreciation Expense | 900 | |
| | 2,400 | 2,400 |

**Instructions**

**(a)** Prepare the adjusting entries.

**(b)** Assuming the adjusted trial balance amount for each account is normal, indicate the financial statement column to which each balance should be extended.

*Derive adjusting entries from worksheet data.*

*(SO 1)*

**E4-6** Selected worksheet data for Nicholson Company are presented below.

| Account Titles | Trial Balance | | Adjusted Trial Balance | |
|---|---|---|---|---|
| | Dr. | Cr. | Dr. | Cr. |
| Accounts Receivable | ? | | 34,000 | |
| Prepaid Insurance | 26,000 | | 20,000 | |
| Supplies | 7,000 | | ? | |
| Accumulated Depreciation | | 12,000 | | ? |
| Salaries Payable | | ? | | 5,000 |
| Service Revenue | | 88,000 | | 97,000 |
| Insurance Expense | | | ? | |
| Depreciation Expense | | | 10,000 | |
| Supplies Expense | | | 5,000 | |
| Salaries Expense | ? | | 49,000 | |

**Instructions**

**(a)** Fill in the missing amounts.

**(b)** Prepare the adjusting entries that were made.

*Prepare closing entries, and prepare a post-closing trial balance.*

*(SO 2, 3)*

**E4-7** Emil Skoda Company had the following adjusted trial balance.

### EMIL SKODA COMPANY
Adjusted Trial Balance
For the Month Ended June 30, 2008

| Account Titles | Adjusted Trial Balance | |
|---|---|---|
| | Debits | Credits |
| Cash | $3,712 | |
| Accounts Receivable | 3,904 | |
| Supplies | 480 | |
| Accounts Payable | | $1,792 |
| Unearned Revenue | | 160 |
| Common Stock | | 5,000 |
| Retained Earnings | | 760 |
| Dividends | 300 | |
| Service Revenue | | 4,064 |
| Salaries Expense | 1,344 | |
| Miscellaneous Expense | 256 | |
| Supplies Expense | 2,228 | |
| Salaries Payable | | 448 |
| | $12,224 | $12,224 |

**Instructions**

**(a)** Prepare closing entries at June 30, 2008.

**(b)** Prepare a post-closing trial balance.

*Journalize and post closing entries, and prepare a post-closing trial balance.*

*(SO 2, 3)*

**E4-8** Apachi Company ended its fiscal year on July 31, 2008. The company's adjusted trial balance as of the end of its fiscal year is as shown at the top of page 179.

## APACHI COMPANY
### Adjusted Trial Balance
### July 31, 2008

| No. | Account Titles | Debits | Credits |
|---|---|---|---|
| 101 | Cash | $ 14,840 | |
| 112 | Accounts Receivable | 8,780 | |
| 157 | Equipment | 15,900 | |
| 167 | Accumulated Depreciation | | $ 7,400 |
| 201 | Accounts Payable | | 4,220 |
| 208 | Unearned Rent Revenue | | 1,800 |
| 311 | Common Stock | | 20,000 |
| 320 | Retained Earnings | | 25,200 |
| 332 | Dividends | 16,000 | |
| 404 | Commission Revenue | | 65,000 |
| 429 | Rent Revenue | | 6,500 |
| 711 | Depreciation Expense | 4,000 | |
| 720 | Salaries Expense | 55,700 | |
| 732 | Utilities Expense | 14,900 | |
| | | $130,120 | $130,120 |

**Instructions**
(a) Prepare the closing entries using page J15.
(b) Post to Retained Earnings and No. 350 Income Summary accounts. (Use the three-column form.)
(c) Prepare a post-closing trial balance at July 31.

**E4-9**   The adjusted trial balance for Apachi Company is presented in E4-8.

*Prepare financial statements.*
*(SO 6)*

**Instructions**
(a) Prepare an income statement and a retained earnings statement for the year. There were no issuances of common stock during the year.
(b) Prepare a classified balance sheet at July 31.

**E4-10**   Josh Borke has prepared the following list of statements about the accounting cycle.

*Answer questions related to the accounting cycle.*
*(SO 4)*

1. "Journalize the transactions" is the first step in the accounting cycle.
2. Reversing entries are a required step in the accounting cycle.
3. Correcting entries do not have to be part of the accounting cycle.
4. If a worksheet is prepared, some steps of the accounting cycle are incorporated into the worksheet.
5. The accounting cycle begins with the analysis of business transactions and ends with the preparation of a post-closing trial balance.
6. All steps of the accounting cycle occur daily during the accounting period.
7. The step of "post to the ledger accounts" occurs before the step of "journalize the transactions."
8. Closing entries must be prepared before financial statements can be prepared.

**Instructions**
Identify each statement as true of false. If false, indicate how to correct the statement.

**E4-11**   Selected accounts for Nina's Salon are presented below. All June 30 postings are from closing entries.

*Prepare closing entries.*
*(SO 2)*

| Salaries Expense | | | |
|---|---|---|---|
| 6/10 | 3,200 | 6/30 | 8,800 |
| 6/28 | 5,600 | | |

| Service Revenue | | | |
|---|---|---|---|
| 6/30 | 15,100 | 6/15 | 6,700 |
| | | 6/24 | 8,400 |

| Retained Earnings | | | |
|---|---|---|---|
| 6/30 | 2,500 | 6/1 | 12,000 |
| | | 6/30 | 2,000 |
| | | Bal. | 11,500 |

| Supplies Expense | | | |
|---|---|---|---|
| 6/12 | 600 | 6/30 | 1,300 |
| 6/24 | 700 | | |

| Rent Expense | | | |
|---|---|---|---|
| 6/1 | 3,000 | 6/30 | 3,000 |

| Dividends | | | |
|---|---|---|---|
| 6/13 | 1,000 | 6/30 | 2,500 |
| 6/25 | 1,500 | | |

**Instructions**

(a) Prepare the closing entries that were made.

(b) Post the closing entries to Income Summary.

*Prepare correcting entries.*
(SO 5)

**E4-12**   Max Weinberg Company discovered the following errors made in January 2008.

1. A payment of Salaries Expense of $600 was debited to Equipment and credited to Cash, both for $600.
2. A collection of $1,000 from a client on account was debited to Cash $100 and credited to Service Revenue $100.
3. The purchase of equipment on account for $980 was debited to Equipment $890 and credited to Accounts Payable $890.

**Instructions**

(a) Correct the errors by reversing the incorrect entry and preparing the correct entry.

(b) Correct the errors without reversing the incorrect entry.

*Prepare correcting entries.*
(SO 5)

**E4-13**   Mason Company has an inexperienced accountant. During the first 2 weeks on the job, the accountant made the following errors in journalizing transactions. All entries were posted as made.

1. A payment on account of $630 to a creditor was debited to Accounts Payable $360 and credited to Cash $360.
2. The purchase of supplies on account for $560 was debited to Equipment $56 and credited to Accounts Payable $56.
3. A $400 cash dividend was debited to Salaries Expense $400 and credited to Cash $400.

**Instructions**

Prepare the correcting entries.

*Prepare a classified balance sheet.*
(SO 6)

**E4-14**   The adjusted trial balance for Karr Bowling Alley at December 31, 2008, contains the following accounts.

| Debits | | Credits | |
|---|---|---|---|
| Building | $128,800 | Common Stock | $100,000 |
| Accounts Receivable | 14,520 | Retained Earnings | 15,000 |
| Prepaid Insurance | 4,680 | Accumulated Depreciation—Building | 42,600 |
| Cash | 18,040 | Accounts Payable | 12,300 |
| Equipment | 62,400 | Note Payable | 97,780 |
| Land | 64,000 | Accumulated Depreciation—Equipment | 18,720 |
| Insurance Expense | 780 | Interest Payable | 2,600 |
| Depreciation Expense | 7,360 | Bowling Revenues | 14,180 |
| Interest Expense | 2,600 | | $303,180 |
| | $303,180 | | |

**Instructions**

(a) Prepare a classified balance sheet; assume that $13,900 of the note payable will be paid in 2009.

(b) ⬤━━▶ Comment on the liquidity of the company.

*Classify accounts on balance sheet.*
(SO 6)

**E4-15**   The following are the major balance sheet classifications.

Current assets (CA)   Current liabilities (CL)
Long-term investments (LTI)   Long-term liabilities (LTL)
Property, plant, and equipment (PPE)   Stockholders' equity (SE)
Intangible assets (IA)

**Instructions**

Classify each of the following accounts taken from Roberts Company's balance sheet.

_____ Accounts payable      _____ Accumulated depreciation
_____ Accounts receivable    _____ Buildings.

|  |  |
|---|---|
| _____ Cash | _____ Land |
| _____ Common Stock | _____ Long-term debt |
| _____ Patents | _____ Supplies |
| _____ Salaries payable | _____ Office equipment |
| _____ Inventories | _____ Prepaid expenses |
| _____ Investments | |

**E4-16**   The following items were taken from the financial statements of R. Stevens Company. (All dollars are in thousands.)

_Prepare a classified balance sheet._

(SO 6)

| | | | |
|---|---|---|---|
| Long-term debt | $   943 | Accumulated depreciation | $ 5,655 |
| Prepaid expenses | 880 | Accounts payable | 1,444 |
| Property, plant, and equipment | 11,500 | Notes payable after 2009 | 368 |
| Long-term investments | 264 | Common stock | 10,000 |
| Short-term investments | 3,690 | Retained earnings | 3,063 |
| Notes payable in 2009 | 481 | Accounts receivable | 1,696 |
| Cash | 2,668 | Inventories | 1,256 |

**Instructions**
Prepare a classified balance sheet in good form as of December 31, 2008.

**E4-17**   These financial statement items are for B. Snyder Company Inc. at year-end, July 31, 2008.

_Prepare financial statements._

(SO 1, 6)

| | | | |
|---|---|---|---|
| Salaries payable | $ 2,080 | Note payable (long-term) | $ 1,800 |
| Salaries expense | 51,700 | Cash | 24,200 |
| Utilities expense | 22,600 | Accounts receivable | 9,780 |
| Equipment | 18,500 | Accumulated depreciation | 6,000 |
| Accounts payable | 4,100 | Dividends | 4,000 |
| Commission revenue | 61,100 | Depreciation expense | 4,000 |
| Rent revenue | 8,500 | Retained earnings (beginning | 21,200 |
| Common stock | 30,000 | of the year) | |

**Instructions**
**(a)** Prepare an income statement and a retained earnings statement for the year.
**(b)** Prepare a classified balance sheet at July 31.

**\*E4-18**   LaBamba Company pays salaries of $10,000 every Monday for the preceding 5-day week (Monday through Friday). Assume December 31 falls on a Tuesday, so LaBamba's employes have worked 2 days without being paid.

_Use reversing entries._

(SO 7)

**Instructions**
**(a)** Assume the company does not use reversing entries. Prepare the December 31 adjusting entry and the entry on Monday, January 6, when LaBamba pays the payroll.
**(b)** Assume the company does use reversing entries. Prepare the December 31 adjusting entry, the January 1 reversing entry, and the entry on Monday, January 6, when LaBamba pays the payroll.

**\*E4-19**   On December 31, the adjusted trial balance of Oslo Employment Agency shows the following selected data.

_Prepare closing and reversing entries._

(SO 2, 4, 7)

| | | | |
|---|---|---|---|
| Accounts Receivable | $24,000 | Commission Revenue | $92,000 |
| Interest Expense | 7,800 | Interest Payable | 1,500 |

Analysis shows that adjusting entries were made to (1) accrue $4,500 of commission revenue and (2) accrue $1,500 interest expense.

**Instructions**
**(a)** Prepare the closing entries for the temporary accounts at December 31.
**(b)** Prepare the reversing entries on January 1.
**(c)** Post the entries in (a) and (b). Rule and balance the accounts. (Use T accounts.)
**(d)** Prepare the entries to record (1) the collection of the accrued commissions on January 10 and (2) the payment of all interest due ($2,500) on January 15.
**(e)** Post the entries in (d) to the temporary accounts.

Visit the book's website at **www.wiley.com/college/weygandt**, and choose the Student Companion site, to access Exercise Set B.

*Prepare worksheet, financial statements, and adjusting and closing entries.*

(SO 1, 2, 6)

**P4-1A** Thomas Magnum began operations as a private investigator on January 1, 2008. The trial balance columns of the worksheet for Thomas Magnum, P.I. at March 31 are as follows.

### THOMAS MAGNUM, P.I., INC.
Worksheet
For the Quarter Ended March 31, 2008

| | Trial Balance | |
| --- | --- | --- |
| **Account Titles** | **Dr.** | **Cr.** |
| Cash | 11,400 | |
| Accounts Receivable | 5,620 | |
| Supplies | 1,050 | |
| Prepaid Insurance | 2,400 | |
| Equipment | 30,000 | |
| Notes Payable | | 10,000 |
| Accounts Payable | | 12,350 |
| Common Stock | | 20,000 |
| Dividends | 600 | |
| Service Revenue | | 13,620 |
| Salaries Expense | 2,200 | |
| Travel Expense | 1,300 | |
| Rent Expense | 1,200 | |
| Miscellaneous Expense | 200 | |
| | 55,970 | 55,970 |

Other data:

1. Supplies on hand total $380.
2. Depreciation is $1,000 per quarter.
3. Interest accrued on 6-month note payable, issued January 1, $300.
4. Insurance expires at the rate of $200 per month.
5. Services provided but unbilled at March 31 total $530.

**Instructions**

(a) Adjusted trial balance $57,800

(b) Net income $6,680
Total assets $48,730

**(a)** Enter the trial balance on a worksheet and complete the worksheet.
**(b)** Prepare an income statement and a retained earnings statement for the quarter and a classified balance sheet at March 31. No additional common stock was issued during the quarter ended March 31, 2008.
**(c)** Journalize the adjusting entries from the adjustments columns of the worksheet.
**(d)** Journalize the closing entries from the financial statement columns of the worksheet.

*Complete worksheet; prepare financial statements, closing entries, and post-closing trial balance.*

(SO 1, 2, 3, 6)

**P4-2A** The adjusted trial balance columns of the worksheet for Porter Company are as follows.

### PORTER COMPANY
Worksheet
For the Year Ended December 31, 2008

| Account No. | Account Titles | Adjusted Trial Balance | |
| --- | --- | --- | --- |
| | | **Dr.** | **Cr.** |
| 101 | Cash | 18,800 | |
| 112 | Accounts Receivable | 16,200 | |
| 126 | Supplies | 2,300 | |

| Account No. | Account Titles | Adjusted Trial Balance Dr. | Adjusted Trial Balance Cr. |
|---|---|---|---|
| 130 | Prepaid Insurance | 4,400 | |
| 151 | Office Equipment | 44,000 | |
| 152 | Accumulated Depreciation—Office Equipment | | 20,000 |
| 200 | Notes Payable | | 20,000 |
| 201 | Accounts Payable | | 8,000 |
| 212 | Salaries Payable | | 2,600 |
| 230 | Interest Payable | | 1,000 |
| 311 | Common Stock | | 30,000 |
| 320 | Retained Earnings | | 6,000 |
| 332 | Dividends | 12,000 | |
| 400 | Service Revenue | | 77,800 |
| 610 | Advertising Expense | 12,000 | |
| 631 | Supplies Expense | 3,700 | |
| 711 | Depreciation Expense | 8,000 | |
| 722 | Insurance Expense | 4,000 | |
| 726 | Salaries Expense | 39,000 | |
| 905 | Interest Expense | 1,000 | |
| | Totals | 165,400 | 165,400 |

## Instructions

**(a)** Complete the worksheet by extending the balances to the financial statement columns.

**(b)** Prepare an income statement, a retained earnings statement, and a classified balance sheet. $10,000 of the notes payable become due in 2009. No additional issuance of common stock occurred during 2008.

**(c)** Prepare the closing entries. Use J14 for the journal page.

**(d)** Post the closing entries. Use the three-column form of account. Income Summary is account No. 350.

**(e)** Prepare a post-closing trial balance.

(a) Net income $10,100

(b) Current assets $41,700
Current liabilities $21,600

(e) Post-closing trial balance $85,700

**P4-3A**  The completed financial statement columns of the worksheet for Woods Company, Inc. are shown below.

*Prepare financial statements, closing entries, and post-closing trial balance.*

(SO 1, 2, 3, 6)

## WOODS COMPANY, INC.
Worksheet
For the Year Ended December 31, 2008

| Account No. | Account Titles | Income Statement Dr. | Income Statement Cr. | Balance Sheet Dr. | Balance Sheet Cr. |
|---|---|---|---|---|---|
| 101 | Cash | | | 8,200 | |
| 112 | Accounts Receivable | | | 7,500 | |
| 130 | Prepaid Insurance | | | 1,800 | |
| 157 | Equipment | | | 28,000 | |
| 167 | Accumulated Depreciation | | | | 8,600 |
| 201 | Accounts Payable | | | | 11,700 |
| 212 | Salaries Payable | | | | 3,000 |
| 311 | Common Stock | | | | 20,000 |
| 320 | Retained Earnings | | | | 14,000 |
| 332 | Dividends | | | 7,200 | |
| 400 | Service Revenue | | 44,000 | | |
| 622 | Repair Expense | 5,400 | | | |
| 711 | Depreciation Expense | 2,800 | | | |
| 722 | Insurance Expense | 1,200 | | | |
| 726 | Salaries Expense | 35,200 | | | |
| 732 | Utilities Expense | 4,000 | | | |
| | Totals | 48,600 | 44,000 | 52,700 | 57,300 |
| | Net Loss | | 4,600 | 4,600 | |
| | | 48,600 | 48,600 | 57,300 | 57,300 |

**Instructions**

(a) Net loss $4,600
Ending retained
earnings $2,200
Total assets $36,900

(d) Post-closing trial balance
$45,500

**(a)** Prepare an income statement, a retained earnings statement, and a classified balance sheet. No additional common stock was issued during 2008.

**(b)** Prepare the closing entries.

**(c)** Post the closing entries and rule and balance the accounts. Use T accounts. Income Summary is account No. 350.

**(d)** Prepare a post-closing trial balance.

*Complete worksheet; prepare classified balance sheet, entries, and post-closing trial balance.*

*(SO 1, 2, 3, 6)*

**P4-4A** Disney Amusement Park, Inc. has a fiscal year ending on September 30. Selected data from the September 30 worksheet are presented below.

### DISNEY AMUSEMENT PARK, INC.
Worksheet
For the Year Ended September 30, 2008

| | Trial Balance Dr. | Trial Balance Cr. | Adjusted Trial Balance Dr. | Adjusted Trial Balance Cr. |
|---|---|---|---|---|
| Cash | 41,400 | | 41,400 | |
| Supplies | 18,600 | | 1,200 | |
| Prepaid Insurance | 31,900 | | 8,900 | |
| Land | 80,000 | | 80,000 | |
| Equipment | 120,000 | | 120,000 | |
| Accumulated Depreciation | | 36,200 | | 42,200 |
| Accounts Payable | | 14,600 | | 14,600 |
| Unearned Admissions Revenue | | 3,700 | | 2,000 |
| Mortgage Note Payable | | 50,000 | | 50,000 |
| Common Stock | | 100,000 | | 100,000 |
| Retained Earnings | | 9,700 | | 9,700 |
| Dividends | 14,000 | | 14,000 | |
| Admissions Revenue | | 277,500 | | 279,200 |
| Salaries Expense | 105,000 | | 105,000 | |
| Repair Expense | 30,500 | | 30,500 | |
| Advertising Expense | 9,400 | | 9,400 | |
| Utilities Expense | 16,900 | | 16,900 | |
| Property Taxes Expense | 18,000 | | 21,000 | |
| Interest Expense | 6,000 | | 10,000 | |
| Totals | 491,700 | 491,700 | | |
| Insurance Expense | | | 23,000 | |
| Supplies Expense | | | 17,400 | |
| Interest Payable | | | | 4,000 |
| Depreciation Expense | | | 6,000 | |
| Property Taxes Payable | | | | 3,000 |
| Totals | | | 504,700 | 504,700 |

**Instructions**

(a) Net income $40,000

(b) Total current assets
$51,500

(e) Post-closing trial balance
$251,500

**(a)** Prepare a complete worksheet.

**(b)** Prepare a classified balance sheet. (*Note*: $10,000 of the mortgage note payable is due for payment in the next fiscal year.)

**(c)** Journalize the adjusting entries using the worksheet as a basis.

**(d)** Journalize the closing entries using the worksheet as a basis.

**(e)** Prepare a post-closing trial balance.

*Complete all steps in accounting cycle.*

*(SO 1, 2, 3, 4, 6)*

GLS

**P4-5A** Laura Eddy opened Eddy's Carpet Cleaners Inc. on March 1. During March, the following transactions were completed.

Mar. 1 Issued stock for $10,000 in cash.
  1 Purchased used truck for $6,000, paying $3,000 cash and the balance on account.
  3 Purchased cleaning supplies for $1,200 on account.
  5 Paid $1,200 cash on one-year insurance policy effective March 1.

14  Billed customers $4,800 for cleaning services.
18  Paid $1,500 cash on amount owed on truck and $500 on amount owed on cleaning supplies.
20  Paid $1,800 cash for employee salaries.
21  Collected $1,400 cash from customers billed on March 14.
28  Billed customers $2,500 for cleaning services.
31  Paid gas and oil for month on truck $200.
31  Declared and paid a $700 cash dividend.

The chart of accounts for Eddy's Carpet Cleaners contains the following accounts: No. 101 Cash, No. 112 Accounts Receivable, No. 128 Cleaning Supplies, No. 130 Prepaid Insurance, No. 157 Equipment, No. 158 Accumulated Depreciation—Equipment, No. 201 Accounts Payable, No. 212 Salaries Payable, No. 311 Common Stock, No. 320 Retained Earnings, No. 332 Dividends, No. 350 Income Summary, No. 400 Service Revenue, No. 633 Gas & Oil Expense, No. 634 Cleaning Supplies Expense, No. 711 Depreciation Expense, No. 722 Insurance Expense, and No. 726 Salaries Expense.

**Instructions**

(a) Journalize and post the March transactions. Use page J1 for the journal and the three-column form of account.

(b) Prepare a trial balance at March 31 on a worksheet.

(b) Trial balance $19,500

(c) Enter the following adjustments on the worksheet and complete the worksheet.

(c) Adjusted trial balance $20,950

  (1) Earned but unbilled revenue at March 31 was $700.
  (2) Depreciation on equipment for the month was $250.
  (3) One-twelfth of the insurance expired.
  (4) An inventory count shows $400 of cleaning supplies on hand at March 31.
  (5) Accrued but unpaid employee salaries were $500.

(d) Prepare the income statement and a retained earnings statement for March and a classified balance sheet at March 31.

(d) Net income $4,350
    Total assets $16,350

(e) Journalize and post adjusting entries. Use page J2 for the journal.

(f) Journalize and post closing entries and complete the closing process. Use page J3 for the journal.

(g) Prepare a post-closing trial balance at March 31.

(g) Post-closing trial balance $16,600

**P4-6A**  Joe Edmonds, CPA, was retained by Clark Cable Inc. to prepare financial statements for April 2008. Edmonds accumulated all the ledger balances per Clark's records and found the following.

*Analyze errors and prepare correcting entries and trial balance.*

(SO 5)

## CLARK CABLE INC.
### Trial Balance
### April 30, 2008

|  | Debit | Credit |
|---|---|---|
| Cash | $ 4,100 |  |
| Accounts Receivable | 3,200 |  |
| Supplies | 800 |  |
| Equipment | 10,600 |  |
| Accumulated Depreciation |  | $ 1,350 |
| Accounts Payable |  | 2,100 |
| Salaries Payable |  | 700 |
| Unearned Revenue |  | 890 |
| Common Stock |  | 10,000 |
| Retained Earnings |  | 2,900 |
| Service Revenue |  | 5,450 |
| Salaries Expense | 3,300 |  |
| Advertising Expense | 600 |  |
| Miscellaneous Expense | 290 |  |
| Depreciation Expense | 500 |  |
|  | $23,390 | $23,390 |

Joe Edmonds reviewed the records and found the following errors.

1. Cash received from a customer on account was recorded as $960 instead of $690.
2. A payment of $65 for advertising expense was entered as a debit to Miscellaneous Expense $65 and a credit to Cash $65.
3. The first salary payment this month was for $1,900, which included $700 of salaries payable on March 31. The payment was recorded as a debit to Salaries Expense $1,900 and a credit to Cash $1,900. (No reversing entries were made on April 1.)
4. The purchase on account of a printer costing $290 was recorded as a debit to Supplies and a credit to Accounts Payable for $290.
5. A cash payment of repair expense on equipment for $95 was recorded as a debit to Equipment $59 and a credit to Cash $59.

**Instructions**

**(a)** Prepare an analysis of each error showing (1) the incorrect entry, (2) the correct entry, and (3) the correcting entry. Items 4 and 5 occurred on April 30, 2008.

*Trial balance $22,690*

**(b)** Prepare a correct trial balance.

# PROBLEMS: SET B

*Prepare a worksheet, financial statements, and adjusting and closing entries.*

*(SO 1, 2, 6)*

**P4-1B** The trial balance columns of the worksheet for Everlast Roofing Inc. at March 31, 2008, are as follows.

## EVERLAST ROOFING INC.
### Worksheet
### For the Month Ended March 31, 2008

| Account Titles | Trial Balance | |
| --- | --- | --- |
| | Dr. | Cr. |
| Cash | 2,500 | |
| Accounts Receivable | 1,800 | |
| Roofing Supplies | 1,100 | |
| Equipment | 6,000 | |
| Accumulated Depreciation—Equipment | | 700 |
| Accounts Payable | | 1,400 |
| Unearned Revenue | | 300 |
| Common Stock | | 7,000 |
| Dividends | 600 | |
| Service Revenue | | 3,500 |
| Salaries Expense | 700 | |
| Miscellaneous Expense | 200 | |
| | 12,900 | 12,900 |

Other data:

1. A physical count reveals only $240 of roofing supplies on hand.
2. Depreciation for March is $200.
3. Unearned revenue amounted to $130 after adjustment on March 31.
4. Accrued salaries are $350.

**Instructions**

*(a) Adjusted trial balance $13,450*

*(b) Net income $1,360*
*Total assets $9,640*

**(a)** Enter the trial balance on a worksheet and complete the worksheet.
**(b)** Prepare an income statement and a retained earnings statement for the month of March and a classified balance sheet at March 31. Common stock of $7,000 was issued for cash at the beginning of March.
**(c)** Journalize the adjusting entries from the adjustments columns of the worksheet.
**(d)** Journalize the closing entries from the financial statement columns of the worksheet.

**P4-2B**  The adjusted trial balance columns of the worksheet for Sparks Company Inc. owned by Billy Sparks, are as follows.

*Complete worksheet; prepare financial statements, closing entries, and post-closing trial balance.*

(SO 1, 2, 3, 6)

GLS

### SPARKS COMPANY INC.
Worksheet
For the Year Ended December 31, 2008

| Account No. | Account Titles | Adjusted Trial Balance Dr. | Cr. |
|---|---|---|---|
| 101 | Cash | 11,600 | |
| 112 | Accounts Receivable | 15,400 | |
| 126 | Supplies | 2,000 | |
| 130 | Prepaid Insurance | 2,800 | |
| 151 | Office Equipment | 34,000 | |
| 152 | Accumulated Depreciation—Office Equipment | | 8,000 |
| 200 | Notes Payable | | 20,000 |
| 201 | Accounts Payable | | 9,000 |
| 212 | Salaries Payable | | 3,500 |
| 230 | Interest Payable | | 800 |
| 311 | Common Stock | | 15,000 |
| 320 | Retained Earnings | | 10,000 |
| 332 | Dividends | 10,000 | |
| 400 | Service Revenue | | 85,000 |
| 610 | Advertising Expense | 12,000 | |
| 631 | Supplies Expense | 5,700 | |
| 711 | Depreciation Expense | 8,000 | |
| 722 | Insurance Expense | 5,000 | |
| 726 | Salaries Expense | 44,000 | |
| 905 | Interest Expense | 800 | |
| | Totals | 151,300 | 151,300 |

### Instructions
**(a)** Complete the worksheet by extending the balances to the financial statement columns.
**(b)** Prepare an income statement, a retained earnings statement, and a classified balance sheet. (*Note:* $10,000 of the notes payable become due in 2009.) No additional common stock was issued during the year.
**(c)** Prepare the closing entries. Use J14 for the journal page.
**(d)** Post the closing entries. Use the three-column form of account. Income Summary is No. 350.
**(e)** Prepare a post-closing trial balance.

(a) Net income $9,500

(b) Current assets $31,800; Current liabilities $23,300

(e) Post-closing trial balance $65,800

**P4-3B**  The completed financial statement columns of the worksheet for Molinda Company are shown below and on the next page.

*Prepare financial statements, closing entries, and post-closing trial balance.*

(SO 1, 2, 3, 6)

### MOLINDA COMPANY
Worksheet
For the Year Ended December 31, 2008

| Account No. | Account Titles | Income Statement Dr. | Cr. | Balance Sheet Dr. | Cr. |
|---|---|---|---|---|---|
| 101 | Cash | | | 22,400 | |
| 112 | Accounts Receivable | | | 13,500 | |
| 130 | Prepaid Insurance | | | 3,500 | |
| 157 | Equipment | | | 26,000 | |
| 167 | Accumulated Depreciation | | | | 5,600 |
| 201 | Accounts Payable | | | | 11,300 |
| 212 | Salaries Payable | | | | 3,000 |
| 311 | Common Stock | | | | 20,000 |
| 320 | Retained Earnings | | | | 16,000 |
| 332 | Dividends | | | 14,000 | |
| 400 | Service Revenue | | 69,000 | | |
| 622 | Repair Expense | 2,000 | | | |

| Account No. | Account Titles | Income Statement Dr. | Income Statement Cr. | Balance Sheet Dr. | Balance Sheet Cr. |
|---|---|---|---|---|---|
| 711 | Depreciation Expense | 2,600 | | | |
| 722 | Insurance Expense | 2,200 | | | |
| 726 | Salaries Expense | 37,000 | | | |
| 732 | Utilities Expense | 1,700 | | | |
| | Totals | 45,500 | 69,000 | 79,400 | 55,900 |
| | Net Income | 23,500 | | | 23,500 |
| | | 69,000 | 69,000 | 79,400 | 79,400 |

### Instructions

(a) Ending retained earnings $25,500; Total current assets $39,400

(d) Post-closing trial balance $65,400

(a) Prepare an income statement, a retained earnings statement, and a classified balance sheet.

(b) Prepare the closing entries. No additional issuance of common stock occurred during the year.

(c) Post the closing entries and rule and balance the accounts. Use T accounts. Income Summary is account No. 350.

(d) Prepare a post-closing trial balance.

*Complete worksheet; prepare classified balance sheet, entries, and post-closing trial balance.*

(SO 1, 2, 3, 6)

**P4-4B** Pettengill Management Services Inc. began business on January 1, 2008, with an investment of $100,000. The company manages condominiums for owners (Service Revenue) and rents space in its own office building (Rent Revenue). The trial balance and adjusted trial balance columns of the worksheet at the end of the first year are as follows.

### PETTENGILL MANAGEMENT SERVICES INC.
Worksheet
For the Year Ended December 31, 2008

| Account Titles | Trial Balance Dr. | Trial Balance Cr. | Adjusted Trial Balance Dr. | Adjusted Trial Balance Cr. |
|---|---|---|---|---|
| Cash | 11,500 | | 11,500 | |
| Accounts Receivable | 23,600 | | 23,600 | |
| Prepaid Insurance | 3,100 | | 1,400 | |
| Land | 56,000 | | 56,000 | |
| Building | 106,000 | | 106,000 | |
| Equipment | 49,000 | | 49,000 | |
| Accounts Payable | | 10,400 | | 10,400 |
| Unearned Rent Revenue | | 5,000 | | 2,800 |
| Mortgage Note Payable | | 100,000 | | 100,000 |
| Common Stock | | 100,000 | | 100,000 |
| Retained Earnings | | 20,000 | | 20,000 |
| Dividends | 18,000 | | 18,000 | |
| Service Revenue | | 75,600 | | 75,600 |
| Rent Revenue | | 24,000 | | 26,200 |
| Salaries Expense | 35,000 | | 35,000 | |
| Advertising Expense | 17,000 | | 17,000 | |
| Utilities Expense | 15,800 | | 15,800 | |
| Totals | 335,000 | 335,000 | | |
| Insurance Expense | | | 1,700 | |
| Depreciation Expense—Building | | | 2,500 | |
| Accumulated Depreciation—Building | | | | 2,500 |
| Depreciation Expense—Equipment | | | 3,900 | |
| Accumulated Depreciation—Equipment | | | | 3,900 |
| Interest Expense | | | 9,000 | |
| Interest Payable | | | | 9,000 |
| Totals | | | 350,400 | 350,400 |

### Instructions

(a) Net income $16,900

(b) Total current assets $36,500

(a) Prepare a complete worksheet.

(b) Prepare a classified balance sheet. (*Note*: $10,000 of the mortgage note payable is due for payment next year.)

**(c)** Journalize the adjusting entries.
**(d)** Journalize the closing entries.
**(e)** Prepare a post-closing trial balance.

(e) Post-closing trial balance
$247,500

**P4-5B**    Lee Choi opened Choi's Window Washing, Inc. on July 1, 2008. During July the following transactions were completed.

*Complete all steps in accounting cycle.*

(SO 1, 2, 3, 4, 6)

July  1    Issued $12,000 of common stock for $12,000 cash.
       1    Purchased used truck for $6,000, paying $3,000 cash and the balance on account.
       3    Purchased cleaning supplies for $1,300 on account.
       5    Paid $2,400 cash on one-year insurance policy effective July 1.
      12    Billed customers $2,500 for cleaning services.
      18    Paid $1,000 cash on amount owed on truck and $800 on amount owed on cleaning supplies.
      20    Paid $1,200 cash for employee salaries.
      21    Collected $1,400 cash from customers billed on July 12.
      25    Billed customers $5,000 for cleaning services.
      31    Paid gas and oil for month on truck $200.
      31    Declared and paid $900 cash dividend.

The chart of accounts for Choi's Window Washing contains the following accounts: No. 101 Cash, No. 112 Accounts Receivable, No. 128 Cleaning Supplies, No. 130 Prepaid Insurance, No. 157 Equipment, No. 158 Accumulated Depreciation—Equipment, No. 201 Accounts Payable, No. 212 Salaries Payable, No. 311 Common Stock, No. 320 Retained Earnings, No. 332 Dividends, No. 350 Income Summary, No. 400 Service Revenue, No. 633 Gas & Oil Expense, No. 634 Cleaning Supplies Expense, No. 711 Depreciation Expense, No. 722 Insurance Expense, and No. 726 Salaries Expense.

### Instructions

**(a)** Journalize and post the July transactions. Use page J1 for the journal and the three-column form of account.
**(b)** Prepare a trial balance at July 31 on a worksheet.
**(c)** Enter the following adjustments on the worksheet and complete the worksheet.
   **(1)** Services provided but unbilled and uncollected at July 31 were $1,500.
   **(2)** Depreciation on equipment for the month was $300.
   **(3)** One-twelfth of the insurance expired.
   **(4)** An inventory count shows $400 of cleaning supplies on hand at July 31.
   **(5)** Accrued but unpaid employee salaries were $600.
**(d)** Prepare the income statement and a retained earnings statement for July and a classified balance sheet at July 31.
**(e)** Journalize and post adjusting entries. Use page J2 for the journal.
**(f)** Journalize and post closing entries and complete the closing process. Use page J3 for the journal.
**(g)** Prepare a post-closing trial balance at July 31.

(b) Trial balance $22,000

(c) Adjusted trial balance
$24,400

(d) Net income $5,600;
Total assets $19,800

(g) Post-closing trial balance
$20,100

## PROBLEMS: SET C

Visit the book's website at **www.wiley.com/college/weygandt**, and choose the Student Companion site, to access Problem Set C.

## COMPREHENSIVE PROBLEM: CHAPTERS 2 TO 4

Julie Molony opened Julie's Maids Cleaning Service Inc. on July 1, 2008. During July, the company completed the following transactions.

July  1    Issued $14,000 of common stock for $14,000 cash.
       1    Purchased a used truck for $10,000, paying $3,000 cash and the balance on account.
       3    Purchased cleaning supplies for $800 on account.
       5    Paid $1,800 on a one-year insurance policy, effective July 1.
      12    Billed customers $3,800 for cleaning services.
      18    Paid $1,000 of amount owed on truck, and $400 of amount owed on cleaning supplies.
      20    Paid $1,600 for employee salaries.
      21    Collected $1,400 from customers billed on July 12.
      25    Billed customers $1,500 for cleaning services.

31 Paid gas and oil for the month on the truck, $400.
31 Paid a $600 cash dividend.

The chart of accounts for Julie's Maids Cleaning Service contains the following accounts: No. 101 Cash, No. 112 Accounts Receivable, No. 128 Cleaning Supplies, No. 130 Prepaid Insurance, No. 157 Equipment, No. 158 Accumulated Depreciation—Equipment, No. 201 Accounts Payable, No. 212 Salaries Payable, No. 311 Common Stock, No. 320 Retained Earnings, No. 332 Dividends, No. 350 Income Summary, No. 400 Service Revenue, No. 633 Gas & Oil Expense, No. 634 Cleaning Supplies Expense, No. 711 Depreciation Expense, No. 722 Insurance Expense, and No. 726 Salaries Expense.

**Instructions**

(a) Journalize and post the July transactions. Use page J1 for the journal.

*(b) Trial balance totals $25,700*

(b) Prepare a trial balance at July 31 on a worksheet.

(c) Enter the following adjustments on the worksheet, and complete the worksheet.
  (1) Earned but unbilled fees at July 31 were $1,300.
  (2) Depreciation on equipment for the month was $200.
  (3) One-twelfth of the insurance expired.
  (4) An inventory count shows $100 of cleaning supplies on hand at July 31.
  (5) Accrued but unpaid employee salaries were $500.

*(d) Net income $3,050
Total assets $23,350*

(d) Prepare the income statement and a retained earnings statement for July, and a classified balance sheet at July 31, 2008.

(e) Journalize and post the adjusting entries. Use page J2 for the journal.

(f) Journalize and post the closing entries, and complete the closing process. Use page J3 for the journal.

*(g) Trial balance totals $23,550*

(g) Prepare a post-closing trial balance at July 31.

---

## CONTINUING COOKIE CHRONICLE

(*Note*: This is a continuation of the Cookie Chronicle from Chapters 1 through 3.)

**CCC4** Natalie had a very busy December. At the end of the month after journalizing and posting the December transactions and adjusting entries, Natalie prepared an adjusted trial balance. Using that information, she wants to prepare financial statements for the year-end, closing entries, and a post-closing trial balance.

*Go to the book's website,*
**www.wiley.com/college/weygandt,**
*to see the completion of this problem.*

---

# BROADENING YOUR PERSPECTIVE

## FINANCIAL REPORTING AND ANALYSIS

### Financial Reporting Problem
### PepsiCo, Inc.

**BYP4-1** Appendix A at the end of this textbook presents the financial statements of PepsiCo.

**Instructions**
Answer the following questions using the Consolidated Balance Sheet and the Notes to Consolidated Financial Statements section.

(a) What were PepsiCo's total current assets at December 31, 2005 and December 25, 2004?

(b) Are assets that PepsiCo included under current assets listed in proper order? Explain.

(c) How are PepsiCo's assets classified?

**(d)** What are "cash equivalents"?

**(e)** What were PepsiCo 's total current liabilities at December 31, 2005 and December 25, 2004?

## Comparative Analysis Problem
### PepsiCo, Inc. vs. The Coca-Cola Company

**BYP4-2**   Appendix A presents PepsiCo's financial statements. Appendix B presents Coca-Cola's financial statements.

**Instructions**

**(a)** Based on the information contained in these financial statements, determine each of the following for PepsiCo at December 31, 2005, and for Coca-Cola at December 31, 2005.

   **(1)** Total current assets.

   **(2)** Net amount of property, plant, and equipment (land, buildings, and equipment).

   **(3)** Total current liabilities.

   **(4)** Total stockholders' (shareholders') equity.

**(b)** What conclusions concerning the companies' respective financial positions can be drawn?

## Exploring the Web

**BYP4-3**   Numerous companies have established home pages on the Internet, e.g., Capt'n Eli Root Beer Company **(www.captneli.com/rootbeer.php)** and Kodak **(www.kodak.com)**.

**Instructions**

Examine the home pages of any two companies and answer the following questions.

**(a)** What type of information is available?

**(b)** Is any accounting-related information presented?

**(c)** Would you describe the home page as informative, promotional, or both? Why?

## CRITICAL THINKING

## Decision Making Across the Organization

**BYP4-4**   Whitegloves Janitorial Service Inc. was started 2 years ago by Nancy Kohl. Because business has been exceptionally good, Nancy decided on July 1, 2008, to expand operations by acquiring an additional truck and hiring two more assistants. To finance the expansion, Nancy obtained on July 1, 2008, a $25,000, 10% bank loan, payable $10,000 on July 1, 2009, and the balance on July 1, 2010. The terms of the loan require the borrower to have $10,000 more current assets than current liabilities at December 31, 2008. If these terms are not met, the bank loan will be refinanced at 15% interest. At December 31, 2008, the accountant for Whitegloves Janitorial Service Inc. prepared the balance sheet shown on page 192.

    Nancy presented the balance sheet to the bank's loan officer on January 2, 2009, confident that the company had met the terms of the loan. The loan officer was not impressed. She said, "We need financial statements audited by a CPA." A CPA was hired and immediately realized that the balance sheet had been prepared from a trial balance and not from an adjusted trial balance. The adjustment data at the balance sheet date consisted of the following.

**(1)** Earned but unbilled janitorial services were $3,700.

**(2)** Janitorial supplies on hand were $2,500.

**(3)** Prepaid insurance was a 3-year policy dated January 1, 2008.

**(4)** December expenses incurred but unpaid at December 31, $500.

**(5)** Interest on the bank loan was not recorded.

**(6)** The amounts for property, plant, and equipment presented in the balance sheet were reported net of accumulated depreciation (cost less accumulated depreciation). These amounts were $4,000 for cleaning equipment and $5,000 for delivery trucks as of January 1, 2008. Depreciation for 2008 was $2,000 for cleaning equipment and $5,000 for delivery trucks.

**WHITEGLOVES JANITORIAL SERVICE INC.**
Balance Sheet
December 31, 2008

| Assets | | Liabilities and Owner's Equity | |
|---|---|---|---|
| **Current assets** | | **Current liabilities** | |
| Cash | $ 6,500 | Notes payable | $10,000 |
| Accounts receivable | 9,000 | Accounts payable | 2,500 |
| Janitorial supplies | 5,200 | Total current liabilities | 12,500 |
| Prepaid insurance | 4,800 | **Long-term liability** | |
| Total current assets | 25,500 | Notes payable | 15,000 |
| **Property, plant, and equipment** | | Total liabilities | 27,500 |
| Cleaning equipment (net) | 22,000 | **Stockholders' equity** | |
| Delivery trucks (net) | 34,000 | Common stock | 40,000 |
| Total property, plant, and equipment | 56,000 | Retained earnings | 14,000 |
| Total assets | $81,500 | Total stockholders' equity | 54,000 |
| | | Total liabilities and stockholders' equity | $81,500 |

**Instructions**

With the class divided into groups, answer the following.

**(a)** Prepare a correct balance sheet.
**(b)** Were the terms of the bank loan met? Explain.

# Communication Activity

**BYP4-5**  The accounting cycle is important in understanding the accounting process.

**Instructions**

Write a memo to your instructor that lists the steps of the accounting cycle in the order they should be completed. End with a paragraph that explains the optional steps in the cycle.

# Ethics Case

**BYP4-6**  As the controller of Breathless Perfume Company, you discover a misstatement that overstated net income in the prior year's financial statements. The misleading financial statements appear in the company's annual report which was issued to banks and other creditors less than a month ago. After much thought about the consequences of telling the president, Jerry McNabb, about this misstatement, you gather your courage to inform him. Jerry says, "Hey! What they don't know won't hurt them. But, just so we set the record straight, we'll adjust this year's financial statements for last year's misstatement. We can absorb that misstatement better in this year than in last year anyway! Just don't make such a mistake again."

**Instructions**

**(a)** Who are the stakeholders in this situation?
**(b)** What are the ethical issues in this situation?
**(c)** What would you do as a controller in this situation?

 # "All About You" Activity

**BYP4-7**  Companies prepare balance sheets in order to know their financial position at a specific point in time. This enables them to make a comparison to their position at previous points in time, and gives them a basis for planning for the future. As discussed in the "All About You" feature in this chapter, in order to evaluate your financial position you need to prepare a personal balance sheet. Assume that you have compiled the following information regarding your finances. (*Hint:* Some of the items might not be used in your personal balance sheet.)

| | |
|---|---|
| Amount owed on student loan balance (long-term) | $ 5,000 |
| Balance in checking account | 1,200 |
| Certificate of deposit (6-month) | 3,000 |
| Annual earnings from part-time job | 11,300 |

| | |
|---|---|
| Automobile | 7,000 |
| Balance on automobile loan (current portion) | 1,500 |
| Balance on automobile loan (long-term portion) | 4,000 |
| Home computer | 800 |
| Amount owed to you by younger brother | 300 |
| Balance in money market account | 1,800 |
| Annual tuition | 6,400 |
| Video and stereo equipment | 1,250 |
| Balance owed on credit card (current portion) | 150 |
| Balance owed on credit card (long-term portion) | 1,650 |

**Instructions**

Prepare a personal balance sheet using the format you have learned for a classified balance sheet for a company. For the owner's equity account, use M. Y. Own, Capital.

## Answers to Insight and Accounting Across the Organization Questions

**Cisco Performs the Virtual Close, p. 155**

Q: Who else benefits from a shorter closing process?

A: *Investors and creditors benefit from a shorter closing process. The shorter the closing, the sooner the company can report its financial results. This means that the financial information is more timely, and therefore more relevant to investors and creditors.*

**Yale Express Loses Some Transportation Bills, p. 160**

Q: What might Yale Express's vice president have done to produce more accurate financial statements without waiting months for Republic's outstanding transportation bills?

A: *Yale's vice president could have engaged his accountants and auditors to prepare an adjusting entry based on an estimate of the outstanding transportation bills. (The estimate could have been made using past experience and the current volume of business.)*

**Big Changes Are Coming to Chinese Balance Sheets, p. 165**

Q: What are the potential benefits and challenges presented by reporting assets like plant and equipment at market value rather than historical cost?

A: *Reporting assets at market value will provide investors with more relevant information. Most investors are more interested in what an asset is currently worth than in what it originally cost. However, determining the market value of some assets can be very subjective. Some companies may take advantage of this in order to obtain more desirable accounting results.*

## Authors' Comments on *All About You:* Your Personal Balance Sheet, p. 167

By deciding to go to school after high school, you have taken a big step toward improving your long-term personal finances. Post-high-school education increases your job opportunities, which increases your earning potential.

Although it is true that your earnings will probably increase considerably when you graduate, you should not wait until graduation to lay the groundwork for a sound financial plan. If you do not monitor your finances closely while you are in school, you could easily dig a deep hole that would be difficult to get out of. Controlling your spending now will give you better control of your personal finances by the time you graduate. A first step toward taking control of your finances is preparing a personal balance sheet. In later chapters we discuss topics that will give you the tools that you need to improve your financial position.

Software is available to help you identify your assets and liabilities and determine your net worth. See for example the net worth calculator at *http://www.bygpub.com/finance/NetWorthCalc.htm.*

## Answers to PepsiCo Review It Question 2, p. 168

PepsiCo's current liabilities in 2005 were $9,406 million. Current liabilities in 2004 were $6,752 million. In both 2005 and 2004, current liabilities were less than current assets.

## Answers to Self-Study Questions

**1.** b  **2.** c  **3.** a  **4.** b  **5.** c  **6.** a  **7.** d  **8.** b  **9.** d  **10.** a  **11.** c

✓ *Remember to go back to the Navigator box on the chapter-opening page and check off your completed work.*

# Chapter 5

# Accounting for Merchandising Operations

## STUDY OBJECTIVES

*After studying this chapter, you should be able to:*

1 Identify the differences between service and merchandising companies.
2 Explain the recording of purchases under a perpetual inventory system.
3 Explain the recording of sales revenues under a perpetual inventory system.
4 Explain the steps in the accounting cycle for a merchandising company.
5 Distinguish between a multiple-step and a single-step income statement.
6 Explain the computation and importance of gross profit.
7 Determine cost of goods sold under a periodic inventory system. ✓ *The Navigator*

## ✓ The Navigator

| | |
|---|---|
| Scan **Study Objectives** | ■ |
| Read **Feature Story** | ■ |
| Read **Preview** | ■ |
| Read text and answer **Before You Go On** p. 203 ■  p. 205 ■  p. 208 ■  p. 214 ■ p. 216 ■ | |
| Work **Demonstration Problem** | ■ |
| Review **Summary of Study Objectives** | ■ |
| Answer **Self-Study Questions** | ■ |
| Complete **Assignments** | ■ |

## Feature Story

### WHO DOESN'T SHOP AT WAL-MART?

In his book *The End of Work,* Jeremy Rifkin notes that until the 20th century the word *consumption* evoked negative images. To be labeled a "consumer" was an insult. In fact, one of the deadliest diseases in history, tuberculosis, was often referred to as "consumption." Twentieth-century merchants realized, however, that in order to prosper, they had to convince people of the need for things not previously needed. For example, General Motors made annual changes in its cars so that people would be discontented with the cars they already owned. Thus began consumerism.

Today consumption describes the U.S. lifestyle in a nutshell. We consume twice as much today per person as we did at the end of World War II. The amount of U.S. retail space per person is vastly greater than that of any other country. It appears that we live to shop.

The first great retail giant was Sears, Roebuck and Company. It started as a catalog company enabling people in rural areas to buy things by mail. For decades it was the uncontested merchandising leader.

Today Wal-Mart (*www.walmart.com*) is the undisputed champion provider of basic (and perhaps not-so-basic) human needs. Wal-Mart opened its first store in 1962, and it now has more than 6,000 stores, serving more than 100 million customers every week. A key cause of Wal-Mart's incredible growth is its amazing system of inventory control and distribution. Wal-Mart has a management information system that employs six satellite channels, from which company computers receive 8.4 million updates every minute on what items customers buy and the relationship among items sold to each person.

Measured by sales revenues, Wal-Mart is the largest company in the world. In six years it went from selling almost no groceries to being America's largest grocery retailer.

It would appear that things have never looked better at Wal-Mart. On the other hand, a *Wall Street Journal* article entitled "How to Sell More to Those Who Think It's Cool to Be Frugal" suggests that consumerism as a way of life might be dying. Don't bet your wide-screen TV on it, though.

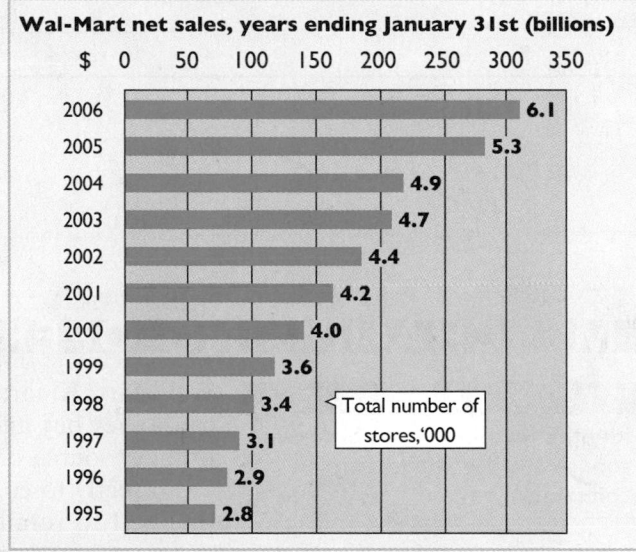

*Sources*: "How Big Can It Grow?" *The Economist*, April 17, 2004, pp. 67–69; and *www.walmart.com* (accessed May 1, 2006).

# Inside Chapter 5

**Morrow Snowboards Improves Its Stock Appeal** (p. 199)

**Should Publishers Have Liberal Return Policies?** (p. 205)

**For IBM, What Is Operating?** (p. 213)

***All About You:*** **When Is a Sale a Sale?** (p. 215)

Merchandising is one of the largest and most influential industries in the United States. It is likely that a number of you will work for a merchandiser. Therefore, understanding the financial statements of merchandising companies is important. In this chapter you will learn the basics about reporting merchandising transactions. In addition, you will learn how to prepare and analyze a commonly used form of the income statement—the multiple-step income statement. The content and organization of the chapter are as follows.

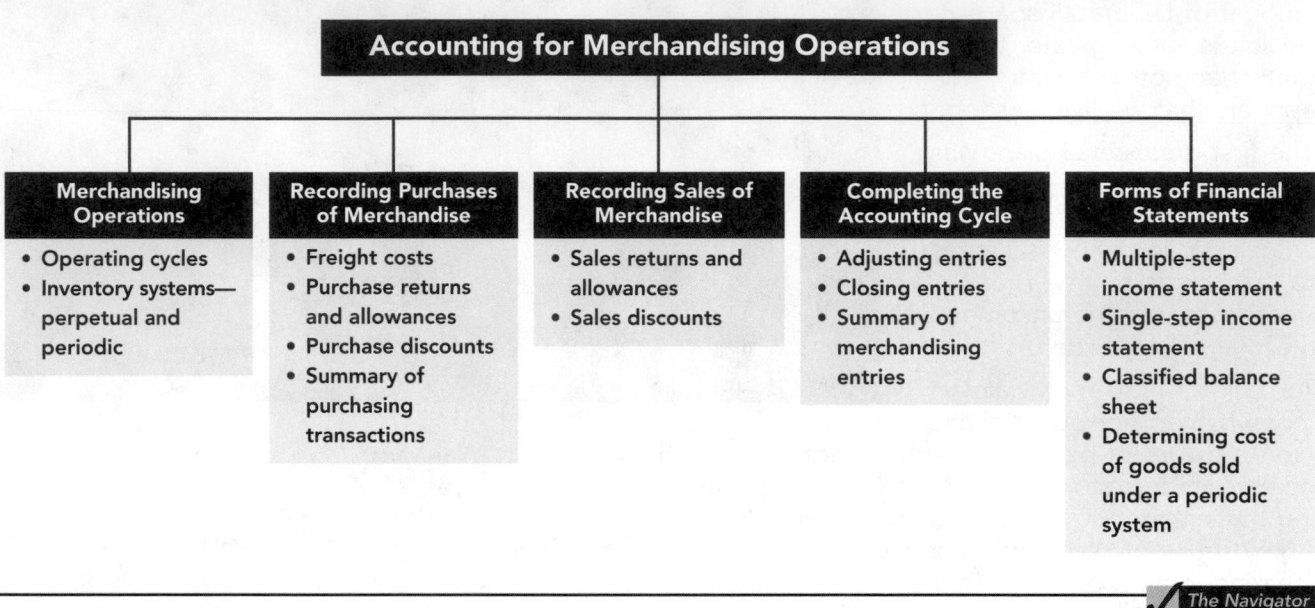

## Accounting for Merchandising Operations

| Merchandising Operations | Recording Purchases of Merchandise | Recording Sales of Merchandise | Completing the Accounting Cycle | Forms of Financial Statements |
|---|---|---|---|---|
| • Operating cycles<br>• Inventory systems—perpetual and periodic | • Freight costs<br>• Purchase returns and allowances<br>• Purchase discounts<br>• Summary of purchasing transactions | • Sales returns and allowances<br>• Sales discounts | • Adjusting entries<br>• Closing entries<br>• Summary of merchandising entries | • Multiple-step income statement<br>• Single-step income statement<br>• Classified balance sheet<br>• Determining cost of goods sold under a periodic system |

✔ *The Navigator*

# MERCHANDISING OPERATIONS

Wal-Mart, Kmart, and Target are called merchandising companies because they buy and sell merchandise rather than perform services as their primary source of revenue. Merchandising companies that purchase and sell directly to consumers are called **retailers**. Merchandising companies that sell to retailers are known as **wholesalers**. For example, retailer Walgreens might buy goods from wholesaler McKesson; retailer Office Depot might buy office supplies from wholesaler United Stationers. The primary source of revenues for merchandising companies is the sale of merchandise, often referred to simply as **sales revenue** or **sales.** A merchandising company has two categories of expenses: cost of goods sold and operating expenses.

<u>Cost of goods sold</u> is the total cost of merchandise sold during the period. This expense is directly related to the revenue recognized from the sale of goods. Illustration 5-1 (page 197) shows the income measurement process for a merchandising company. The items in the two blue boxes are unique to a merchandising company; they are not used by a service company.

## Operating Cycles

The operating cycle of a merchandising company ordinarily is longer than that of a service company. The purchase of merchandise inventory and its eventual sale

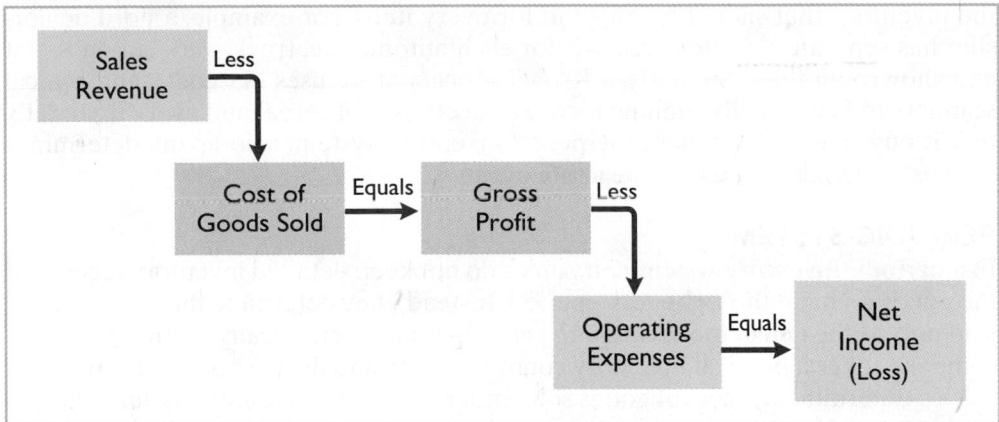

**Illustration 5-1**
Income measurement process for a merchandising company

lengthen the cycle.)Illustration 5-2 contrasts the operating cycles of service and merchandising companies. Note that the added asset account for a merchandising company is the Merchandise Inventory account. Companies report merchandise inventory as a current asset on the balance sheet.

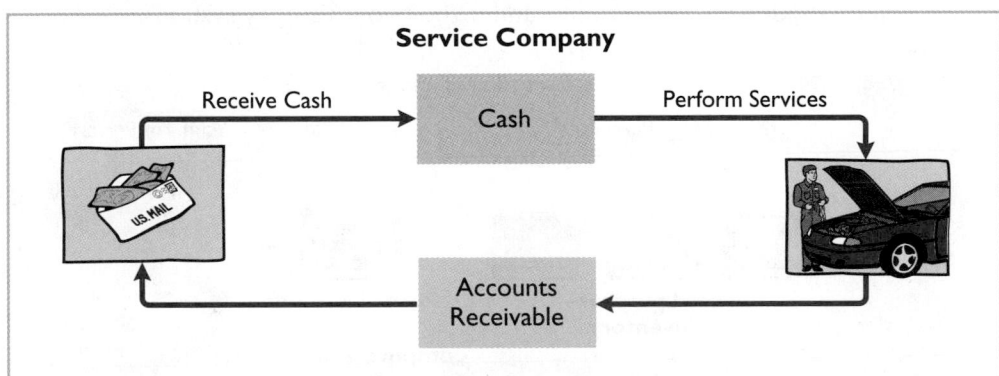

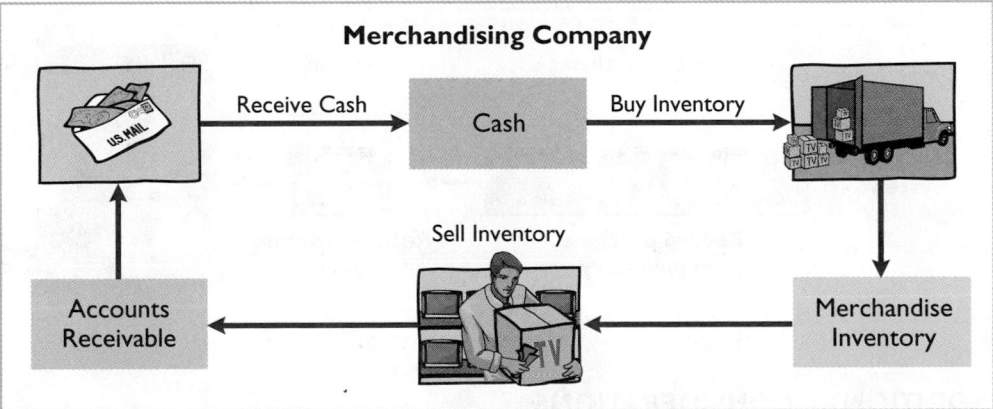

**Illustration 5-2**
Operating cycles for a service company and a merchandising company

# Inventory Systems

A merchandising company keeps track of its inventory to determine what is available for sale and what has been sold. Companies use one of two systems to account for inventory: a **perpetual inventory system** or a **periodic inventory system**.

### PERPETUAL SYSTEM

In a **perpetual inventory system**, companies keep detailed records of the cost of each inventory purchase and sale. These records continuously—perpetually—show the inventory that should be on hand for every item. For example, a Ford dealership has separate inventory records for each automobile, truck, and van on its lot and showroom floor. Similarly, a Kroger grocery store uses bar codes and optical scanners to keep a daily running record of every box of cereal and every jar of jelly that it buys and sells. Under a perpetual inventory system, a company determines the cost of goods sold **each time a sale occurs.**

### PERIODIC SYSTEM

In a **periodic inventory system,** companies do not keep detailed inventory records of the goods on hand throughout the period. Instead, they determine the cost of goods sold **only at the end of the accounting period**—that is, periodically. At that point, the company takes a physical inventory count to determine the cost of goods on hand.

To determine the cost of goods sold under a periodic inventory system, the following steps are necessary:

1. Determine the cost of goods on hand at the beginning of the accounting period.
2. Add to it the cost of goods purchased.
3. Subtract the cost of goods on hand at the end of the accounting period.

Illustration 5-3 graphically compares the sequence of activities and the timing of the cost of goods sold computation under the two inventory systems.

**Illustration 5-3**
Comparing perpetual and periodic inventory systems

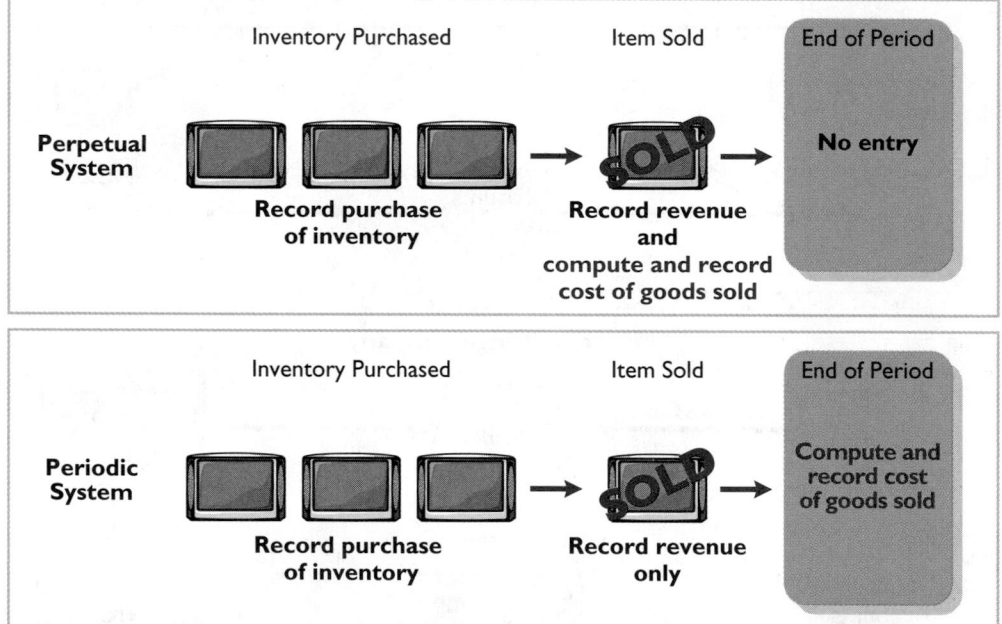

### ADDITIONAL CONSIDERATIONS

Companies that sell merchandise with high unit values, such as automobiles, furniture, and major home appliances, have traditionally used perpetual systems. The growing use of computers and electronic scanners has enabled many more companies to install perpetual inventory systems. The perpetual inventory system is so named because the accounting records continuously—perpetually—show the quantity and cost of the inventory that should be on hand at any time.

A perpetual inventory system provides better control over inventories than a periodic system. Since the inventory records show the quantities that should be on hand, the company can count the goods at any time to see whether the amount of goods actually on hand agrees with the inventory records. If shortages are uncovered, the company can investigate immediately. Although a perpetual inventory system requires additional clerical work and additional cost to maintain the subsidiary records, a computerized system can minimize this cost. As noted in the Feature Story, much of Wal-Mart's success is attributed to its sophisticated inventory system.

Some businesses find it either unnecessary or uneconomical to invest in a computerized perpetual inventory system. Many small merchandising businesses, in particular, find that a perpetual inventory system costs more than it is worth. Managers of these businesses can control their merchandise and manage day-to-day operations using a periodic inventory system.

Because the perpetual inventory system is growing in popularity and use, we illustrate it in this chapter. Appendix 5A describes the journal entries for the periodic system.

# INVESTOR INSIGHT

### Morrow Snowboards Improves Its Stock Appeal

Investors are often eager to invest in a company that has a hot new product. However, when snowboard maker Morrow Snowboards, Inc., issued shares of stock to the public for the first time, some investors expressed reluctance to invest in Morrow because of a number of accounting control problems. To reduce investor concerns, Morrow implemented a perpetual inventory system to improve its control over inventory. In addition, it stated that it would perform a physical inventory count every quarter until it felt that the perpetual inventory system was reliable.

? If a perpetual system keeps track of inventory on a daily basis, why do companies ever need to do a physical count?

# RECORDING PURCHASES OF MERCHANDISE

Companies purchase inventory using cash or credit (on account). They normally record purchases when they receive the goods from the seller. Business documents provide written evidence of the transaction. A canceled check or a cash register receipt, for example, indicate the items purchased and amounts paid for each cash purchase. Companies record cash purchases by an increase in Merchandise Inventory and a decrease in Cash.

A **purchase invoice** should support each credit purchase. This invoice indicates the total purchase price and other relevant information. The purchaser uses the copy of the sales invoice sent by the seller as a purchase invoice. In Illustration 5-4 (page 200), for example, Sauk Stereo (the buyer) uses as a purchase invoice the sales invoice prepared by PW Audio Supply Inc. (the seller).

Sauk Stereo makes the following journal entry to record its purchase from PW Audio Supply. The entry increases (debits) Merchandise Inventory and increases (credits) Accounts Payable.

> ### STUDY OBJECTIVE 2
> Explain the recording of purchases under a perpetual inventory system.

| | | | | |
|---|---|---|---|---|
| May 4 | Merchandise Inventory | | 3,800 | |
| | Accounts Payable | | | 3,800 |
| | (To record goods purchased on account from PW Audio Supply) | | | |

| A | = | L | + | SE |
|---|---|---|---|---|
| +3,800 | | | | |
| | | +3,800 | | |

**Cash Flows**
no effect

Under the perpetual inventory system, companies record in the Merchandise Inventory account the purchase of goods they intend to sell. Thus, Wal-Mart would

**Illustration 5-4**
Sales invoice used as purchase invoice by Sauk Stereo

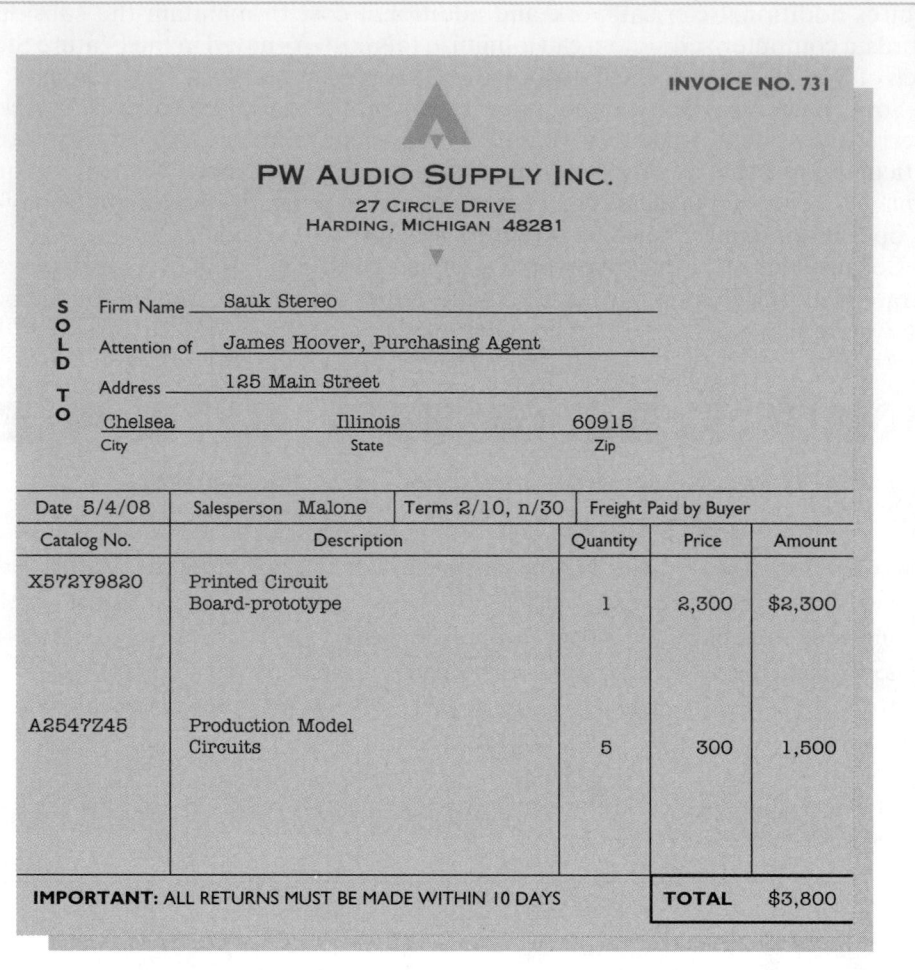

**HELPFUL HINT**
To better understand the contents of this invoice, identify these items:
1. Seller
2. Invoice date
3. Purchaser
4. Salesperson
5. Credit terms
6. Freight terms
7. Goods sold: catalog number, description, quantity, price per unit
8. Total invoice amount

increase (debit) Merchandise Inventory for clothing, sporting goods, and anything else purchased for resale to customers.

Not all purchases are debited to Merchandise Inventory, however. Companies record purchases of assets acquired for use and not for resale, such as supplies, equipment, and similar items, as increases to specific asset accounts rather than to Merchandise Inventory. For example, to record the purchase of materials used to make shelf signs or for cash register receipt paper, Wal-Mart would increase Supplies.

## Freight Costs

The sales agreement should indicate who—the seller or the buyer—is to pay for transporting the goods to the buyer's place of business. When a common carrier such as a railroad, trucking company, or airline transports the goods, the carrier prepares a freight bill in accord with the sales agreement.

Freight terms are expressed as either FOB shipping point or FOB destination. The letters FOB mean **free on board**. Thus, FOB shipping point means that the seller places the goods free on board the carrier, and the buyer pays the freight costs. Conversely, FOB destination means that the seller places the goods free on board to the buyer's place of business, and the seller pays the freight. For example, the sales invoice in Illustration 5-4 (above) indicates that the buyer (Sauk Stereo) pays the freight charges.

When the purchaser incurs the freight costs, it debits (increases) the account Merchandise Inventory for those costs. For example, if upon delivery of the goods on May 6, Sauk Stereo pays Acme Freight Company $150 for freight charges, the entry on Sauk Stereo's books is:

| | | | |
|---|---|---|---|
| May 6 | Merchandise Inventory | 150 | |
| | Cash | | 150 |
| | (To record payment of freight on goods purchased) | | |

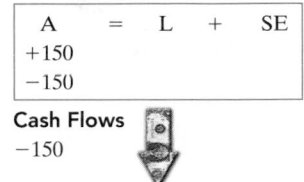

A = L + SE
+150
−150

**Cash Flows**
−150

In contrast, **freight costs incurred by the seller on outgoing merchandise are an operating expense to the seller.** These costs increase an expense account titled Freight-out or Delivery Expense. If the freight terms on the invoice in Illustration 5-4 had required PW Audio Supply to pay the freight charges, the entry by PW Audio Supply would have been:

| | | | |
|---|---|---|---|
| May 4 | Freight-out (or Delivery Expense) | 150 | |
| | Cash | | 150 |
| | (To record payment of freight on goods sold) | | |

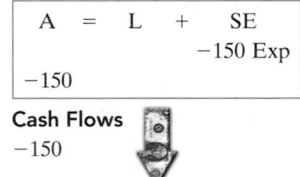

A = L + SE
                 −150 Exp
−150

**Cash Flows**
−150

When the seller pays the freight charges, it will usually establish a higher invoice price for the goods to cover the shipping expense.

## Purchase Returns and Allowances

A purchaser may be dissatisfied with the merchandise received because the goods are damaged or defective, of inferior quality, or do not meet the purchaser's specifications. In such cases, the purchaser may return the goods to the seller for credit if the sale was made on credit, or for a cash refund if the purchase was for cash. This transaction is known as a purchase return. Alternatively, the purchaser may choose to keep the merchandise if the seller is willing to grant an allowance (deduction) from the purchase price. This transaction is known as a purchase allowance.

Assume that on May 8 Sauk Stereo returned to PW Audio Supply goods costing $300. The following entry by Sauk Stereo for the returned merchandise decreases (debits) Accounts Payable and decreases (credits) Merchandise Inventory.

| | | | |
|---|---|---|---|
| May 8 | Accounts Payable | 300 | |
| | Merchandise Inventory | | 300 |
| | (To record return of goods purchased from PW Audio Supply) | | |

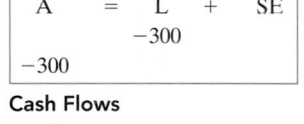

A = L + SE
        −300
−300

**Cash Flows**
no effect

Because Sauk Stereo increased Merchandise Inventory when the goods were received, Merchandise Inventory is decreased when Sauk returns the goods (or when it is granted an allowance).

## Purchase Discounts

The credit terms of a purchase on account may permit the buyer to claim a cash discount for prompt payment. The buyer calls this cash discount a purchase discount. This incentive offers advantages to both parties: The purchaser saves money, and the seller shortens the operating cycle by more quickly converting the accounts receivable into cash.

**Credit terms** specify the amount of the cash discount and time period in which it is offered. They also indicate the time period in which the purchaser is expected to pay the full invoice price. In the sales invoice in Illustration 5-4 (page 200) credit terms are 2/10, n/30, which is read "two-ten, net thirty." This means that the buyer may take a 2% cash discount on the invoice price less ("net of") any returns or allowances, if payment is made within 10 days of the invoice date (the **discount period**). If the buyer does not pay in that time, the invoice price, less any returns or allowances, is due 30 days from the invoice date.

Alternatively, the discount period may extend to a specified number of days following the month in which the sale occurs. For example, 1/10 EOM (end of month) means that a 1% discount is available if the invoice is paid within the first 10 days of the next month.

When the seller elects not to offer a cash discount for prompt payment, credit terms will specify only the maximum time period for paying the balance due. For example, the invoice may state the time period as n/30, n/60, or n/10 EOM. This means, respectively, that the buyer must pay the net amount in 30 days, 60 days, or within the first 10 days of the next month.

When the buyer pays an invoice within the discount period, the amount of the discount decreases Merchandise Inventory. Why? Because companies record inventory at cost and, by paying within the discount period, the merchandiser has reduced that cost. To illustrate, assume Sauk Stereo pays the balance due of $3,500 (gross invoice price of $3,800 less purchase returns and allowances of $300) on May 14, the last day of the discount period. The cash discount is $70 ($3,500 × 2%), and Sauk Stereo pays $3,430 ($3,500 − $70). The entry Sauk makes to record its May 14 payment decreases (debits) Accounts Payable by the amount of the gross invoice price, reduces (credits) Merchandise Inventory by the $70 discount, and reduces (credits) Cash by the net amount owed.

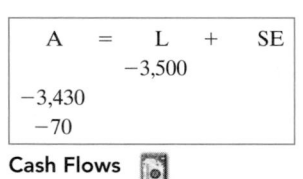

```
A   =   L   +   SE
       −3,500
−3,430
−70
```

**Cash Flows**
−3,430

| May 14 | Accounts Payable | 3,500 | |
| |    Cash | | 3,430 |
| |    Merchandise Inventory | | 70 |
| |     (To record payment within discount period) | | |

If Sauk Stereo failed to take the discount, and instead made full payment of $3,500 on June 3, it would debit Accounts Payable and credit Cash for $3,500 each.

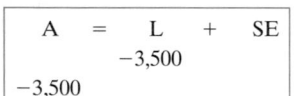

```
A   =   L   +   SE
       −3,500
−3,500
```

**Cash Flows**
−3,500

| June 3 | Accounts Payable | 3,500 | |
| |    Cash | | 3,500 |
| |     (To record payment with no discount taken) | | |

As a rule, a company usually should take all available discounts. Passing up the discount may be viewed as **paying interest** for use of the money. For example, passing up the discount offered by PW Audio would be comparable to Sauk Stereo paying an interest rate of 2% for the use of $3,500 for 20 days. This is the equivalent of an annual interest rate of approximately 36.5% (2% × 365/20). Obviously, it would be better for Sauk Stereo to borrow at prevailing bank interest rates of 6% to 10% than to lose the discount.

## Summary of Purchasing Transactions

The following T account (with transaction descriptions in blue) provides a summary of the effect of the previous transactions on Merchandise Inventory. Sauk originally purchased $3,800 worth of inventory for resale. It then returned $300 of goods. It paid $150 in freight charges, and finally, it received a $70 discount off the balance owed because it paid within the discount period. This results in a balance in Merchandise Inventory of $3,580.

**Merchandise Inventory**

| | | | | | |
|---|---|---|---|---|---|
| Purchase | May 4 | 3,800 | May 8 | 300 | Purchase return |
| Freight-in | 6 | 150 | 14 | 70 | Purchase discount |
| Balance | | 3,580 | | | |

## Before You Go On...

### REVIEW IT

1. How does a merchandising company measure net income differently from a service company?
2. In what ways is a perpetual inventory system different from a periodic system?
3. Under the perpetual inventory system, what entries do companies make to record purchases, purchase returns and allowances, purchase discounts, and freight costs?

✓ *The Navigator*

## RECORDING SALES OF MERCHANDISE

Companies record sales revenues, like service revenues, when earned, in compliance with the revenue recognition principle. Typically, companies earn sales revenues when the goods transfer from the seller to the buyer. At this point the sales transaction is complete and the sales price established.

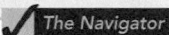

**STUDY OBJECTIVE 3**

Explain the recording of sales revenues under a perpetual inventory system.

Sales may be made on credit or for cash. A **business document** should support every sales transaction, to provide written evidence of the sale. **Cash register tapes** provide evidence of cash sales. A <u>sales invoice</u>, like the one shown in Illustration 5-4 (page 200), provides support for a credit sale. The original copy of the invoice goes to the customer, and the seller keeps a copy for use in recording the sale. The invoice shows the date of sale, customer name, total sales price, and other relevant information.

The seller makes two entries for each sale. The first entry records the sale: The seller increases (debits) Cash (or Accounts Receivable, if a credit sale), and also increases (credits) Sales for the invoice price of the goods. The second entry records the cost of the merchandise sold: The seller increases (debits) Cost of Goods Sold, and also decreases (credits) Merchandise Inventory for the cost of those goods. As a result, the Merchandise Inventory account will show at all times the amount of inventory that should be on hand.

To illustrate a credit sales transaction, PW Audio Supply records its May 4 sale of $3,800 to Sauk Stereo (see Illustration 5-4) as follows. (Here, we assume the merchandise cost PW Audio Supply $2,400.)

| | | | | |
|---|---|---|---|---|
| May 4 | Accounts Receivable | | 3,800 | |
| | Sales | | | 3,800 |
| | (To record credit sale to Sauk Stereo per invoice #731) | | | |

| A | = | L | + | SE |
|---|---|---|---|---|
| +3,800 | | | | |
| | | | | +3,800 Rev |

**Cash Flows**
no effect

| | | | | |
|---|---|---|---|---|
| 4 | Cost of Goods Sold | | 2,400 | |
| | Merchandise Inventory | | | 2,400 |
| | (To record cost of merchandise sold on invoice #731 to Sauk Stereo) | | | |

| A | = | L | + | SE |
|---|---|---|---|---|
| | | | | −2,400 Exp |
| −2,400 | | | | |

**Cash Flows**
no effect

\For internal decision-making purposes, merchandising companies may use more than one sales account\For example, PW Audio Supply may decide to keep separate sales accounts for its sales of TV sets, DVD recorders, and satellite radio receivers. Wal-Mart might use separate accounts for sporting goods, children's clothing, and hardware—or it might have even more narrowly defined accounts. By using separate sales accounts for major product lines, rather than a single combined sales account, company management can more closely monitor sales trends and respond more strategically to changes in sales patterns. For example, if HDTV sales are increasing while DVD-player sales are decreasing, PW Audio Supply might reevaluate both its advertising and pricing policies on these items to ensure they are optimal.

\ On its income statement presented to outside investors, a merchandising company normally would provide only a single sales figure—the sum of all of its individual sales accounts\This is done for two reasons. First, providing detail on all of its individual sales accounts would add considerable length to its income statement. Second, companies do not want their competitors to know the details of their operating results. However, Microsoft recently expanded its disclosure of revenue from three to five types. The reason: The additional categories will better enable financial statement users to evaluate the growth of the company's consumer and Internet businesses.

## Sales Returns and Allowances

We now look at the "flipside" of purchase returns and allowances, which the seller records as **sales returns and allowances**. PW Audio Supply's\entries to record credit for returned goods involve (1) an increase in Sales Returns and Allowances and a decrease in Accounts Receivable at the $300 selling price, and (2) an increase in Merchandise Inventory (assume a $140 cost) and a decrease in Cost of Goods Sold) as shown below. \We have assumed that the goods were not defective. If they were defective, PW Audio would make an adjustment to the inventory account to reflect their decline in value.\

```
A   =   L   +   SE
                -300 Rev
-300
```
**Cash Flows**
no effect

```
A   =   L   +   SE
+140
                +140 Exp
```
**Cash Flows**
no effect

| | | | | |
|---|---|---|---|---|
| May 8 | Sales Returns and Allowances | | 300 | |
| | Accounts Receivable | | | 300 |
| | (To record credit granted to Sauk Stereo for returned goods) | | | |
| 8 | Merchandise Inventory | | 140 | |
| | Cost of Goods Sold | | | 140 |
| | (To record cost of goods returned) | | | |

\ If Sauk returns goods because they are damaged or defective, then PW Audio Supply's entry to Merchandise Inventory and Cost of Goods Sold should be for the estimated value of the returned goods, rather than their cost\For example, if the returned goods were defective and had a scrap value of $50, PW Audio would debit Merchandise Inventory for $50, and would credit Cost of Goods Sold for $50.

\ Sales Returns and Allowances is a **contra-revenue account** to Sales.\The normal balance of Sales Returns and Allowances is a debit. Companies use a contra account, instead of debiting Sales, to disclose in the accounts and in the income statement the amount of sales returns and allowances. Disclosure of this information is important to management: Excessive returns and allowances may suggest problems—inferior merchandise, inefficiencies in filling orders, errors in billing customers, or delivery or shipment mistakes. Moreover, a decrease (debit) recorded directly to Sales would obscure the relative importance of sales returns and allowances as a percentage of sales. It also could distort comparisons between total sales in different accounting periods.

# ACCOUNTING ACROSS THE ORGANIZATION

### *Should Publishers Have Liberal Return Policies?*

In most industries sales returns are relatively minor. In the publishing industry, however, bookstores are allowed to return unsold hardcover books to the publisher. Marketing managers at the publishing companies argue that these generous return policies are necessary to encourage bookstores to buy a broader range of books, instead of focusing just on "sure things."

But with returns of hardcover books now exceeding 34% of sales, this generous return policy is taking its toll on net income. Production and inventory managers are quick to point out the many costs of excess returns. Publishers must pay to have the books shipped back to their warehouse, sorted, and then shipped to discounters. If the discounters don't sell them, the books are repackaged again, shipped back to the publisher, and destroyed. Some bookstores and publishers have proposed adopting a "no returns" policy, but no company wants to be the first to implement it.

*Source:* Jeffrey A Trachtenberg, "Quest for Best Seller Creates a Pileup of Returned Books," *Wall Street Journal* (June 3, 2005), p. A1.

**?** If a company expects significant returns, what are the implications for revenue recognition?

## Sales Discounts

As mentioned earlier, the seller may offer the customer a cash discount—called by the seller a **sales discount**—for the prompt payment of the balance due. It is based on the invoice price less returns and allowances, if any. The seller increases (debits) the Sales Discounts account for discounts that are taken. For example, PW Audio Supply makes the following entry to record the cash receipt on May 14 from Sauk Stereo within the discount period.

| May 14 | Cash | 3,430 | |
|---|---|---|---|
| | Sales Discounts | 70 | |
| |     Accounts Receivable | | 3,500 |
| |       (To record collection within 2/10, n/30 | | |
| |       discount period from Sauk Stereo) | | |

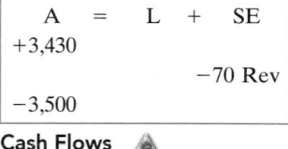

| A | = | L | + | SE |
|---|---|---|---|---|
| +3,430 | | | | |
| | | | | −70 Rev |
| −3,500 | | | | |

**Cash Flows**
+3,430

Like Sales Returns and Allowances, Sales Discounts is a **contra-revenue account** to Sales. Its normal balance is a debit. PW Audio uses this account, instead of debiting sales, to disclose the amount of cash discounts taken by customers. If Sauk Stereo does not take the discount, PW Audio Supply increases Cash for $3,500 and decreases Accounts Receivable for the same amount at the date of collection.

## Before You Go On...

### REVIEW IT

1. Under a perpetual inventory system, what are the two entries that a selling company must record at the time of each sale?
2. Why is it important to use the Sales Returns and Allowances account, rather than simply reducing the Sales account, when purchasers return goods?

## DO IT

On September 5, De La Hoya Company buys merchandise on account from Junot Diaz Company. The selling price of the goods is $1,500, and the cost to Diaz Company was $800. On September 8, De La Hoya returns defective goods with a selling price of $200 and a scrap value of $80. Record the transactions on the books of both companies.

### Action Plan

- Purchaser records goods at cost.
- Seller records both the sale and the cost of goods sold at the time of the sale.
- When goods are returned, purchaser reduces Merchandise Inventory, but seller records the return in a contra account, Sales Returns and Allowances.

### Solution

**De La Hoya Company**

| | | | | |
|---|---|---|---|---|
| Sept. | 5 | Merchandise Inventory | 1,500 | |
| | | Accounts Payable | | 1,500 |
| | | (To record goods purchased on account) | | |
| Sept. | 8 | Accounts Payable | 200 | |
| | | Merchandise Inventory | | 200 |
| | | (To record return of defective goods) | | |

**Junot Diaz Company**

| | | | | |
|---|---|---|---|---|
| Sept. | 5 | Accounts Receivable | 1,500 | |
| | | Sales | | 1,500 |
| | | (To record credit sale) | | |
| | 5 | Cost of Goods Sold | 800 | |
| | | Merchandise Inventory | | 800 |
| | | (To record cost of goods sold on account) | | |
| Sept. | 8 | Sales Returns and Allowances | 200 | |
| | | Accounts Receivable | | 200 |
| | | (To record credit granted for receipt of returned goods) | | |
| | 8 | Merchandise Inventory | 80 | |
| | | Cost of Goods Sold | | 80 |
| | | (To record scrap value of goods returned) | | |

Related exercise material: *BE5-2, BE5-3, BE5-4, E5-2, E5-3, E5-4, and E5-5.*

✓ *The Navigator*

# COMPLETING THE ACCOUNTING CYCLE

**STUDY OBJECTIVE 4**

Explain the steps in the accounting cycle for a merchandising company.

Up to this point, we have illustrated the basic entries for transactions relating to purchases and sales in a perpetual inventory system. Now we consider the remaining steps in the accounting cycle for a merchandising company. Each of the required steps described in Chapter 4 for service companies apply to merchandising companies. Appendix 5B to this chapter shows use of a worksheet by a merchandiser (an optional step).

## Adjusting Entries

A merchandising company generally has the same types of adjusting entries as a service company. However, a merchandiser using a perpetual system will require one additional adjustment to make the records agree with the actual inventory on hand. Here's why: At the end of each period, for control purposes, a merchandising company that uses a perpetual system will take a physical count of its goods on hand. The company's unadjusted balance in Merchandise Inventory usually does not agree with the actual amount of inventory on hand. The perpetual inventory records may be incorrect due to recording errors, theft, or waste. Thus, the company needs to adjust the perpetual records to make the recorded inventory amount agree with the inventory on hand. **This involves adjusting Merchandise Inventory and Cost of Goods Sold.**

For example, suppose that PW Audio Supply has an unadjusted balance of $40,500 in Merchandise Inventory. Through a physical count, PW Audio determines that its actual merchandise inventory at year-end is $40,000. The company would make an adjusting entry to debit Cost of Goods Sold for $500 and to credit Merchandise Inventory for $500.

## Closing Entries

A merchandising company, like a service company, closes to Income Summary all accounts that affect net income. In journalizing, the company credits all temporary accounts with debit balances, and debits all temporary accounts with credit balances, as shown below for PW Audio Supply. Note that PW Audio closes Cost of Goods Sold to Income Summary.

| | | | |
|---|---|---|---|
| Dec. 31 | Sales | 480,000 | |
| | Income Summary | | 480,000 |
| | (To close income statement accounts with | | |
| | credit balances) | | |
| | | | |
| 31 | Income Summary | 450,000 | |
| | Sales Returns and Allowances | | 12,000 |
| | Sales Discounts | | 8,000 |
| | Cost of Goods Sold | | 316,000 |
| | Store Salaries Expense | | 45,000 |
| | Administrative Salaries Expense | | 19,000 |
| | Freight-out | | 7,000 |
| | Advertising Expense | | 16,000 |
| | Utilities Expense | | 17,000 |
| | Depreciation Expense | | 8,000 |
| | Insurance Expense | | 2,000 |
| | (To close income statement accounts with | | |
| | debit balances) | | |
| | | | |
| 31 | Income Summary | 30,000 | |
| | Retained Earnings | | 30,000 |
| | (To close net income to retained earnings) | | |
| | | | |
| 31 | Retained Earnings | 15,000 | |
| | Dividends | | 15,000 |
| | (To close dividends to retained earnings) | | |

**HELPFUL HINT**

The easiest way to prepare the first two closing entries is to identify the temporary accounts by their balances and then prepare one entry for the credits and one for the debits.

After PW Audio has posted the closing entries, all temporary accounts have zero balances. In addition, Retained Earnings has a credit balance of $48,000: Beginning balance + Net income − Dividends ($33,000 + $30,000 − $15,000).

# Summary of Merchandising Entries

Illustration 5-5 summarizes the entries for the merchandising accounts using a perpetual inventory system.

**Illustration 5-5**
Daily recurring and adjusting and closing entries

| | Transactions | Daily Recurring Entries | Dr. | Cr. |
|---|---|---|---|---|
| **Sales Transactions** | Selling merchandise to customers. | Cash or Accounts Receivable<br>    Sales | XX | XX |
| | | Cost of Goods Sold<br>    Merchandise Inventory | XX | XX |
| | Granting sales returns or allowances to customers. | Sales Returns and Allowances<br>    Cash or Accounts Receivable | XX | XX |
| | | Merchandise Inventory<br>    Cost of Goods Sold | XX | XX |
| | Paying freight costs on sales; FOB destination. | Freight-out<br>    Cash | XX | XX |
| | Receiving payment from customers within discount period. | Cash<br>Sales Discounts<br>    Accounts Receivable | XX<br>XX | XX |
| **Purchase Transactions** | Purchasing merchandise for resale. | Merchandise Inventory<br>    Cash or Accounts Payable | XX | XX |
| | Paying freight costs on merchandise purchased; FOB shipping point. | Merchandise Inventory<br>    Cash | XX | XX |
| | Receiving purchase returns or allowances from suppliers. | Cash or Accounts Payable<br>    Merchandise Inventory | XX | XX |
| | Paying suppliers within discount period. | Accounts Payable<br>    Merchandise Inventory<br>    Cash | XX | XX<br>XX |

| Events | Adjusting and Closing Entries | Dr. | Cr. |
|---|---|---|---|
| Adjust because book amount is higher than the inventory amount determined to be on hand. | Cost of Goods Sold<br>    Merchandise Inventory | XX | XX |
| Closing temporary accounts with credit balances. | Sales<br>    Income Summary | XX | XX |
| Closing temporary accounts with debit balances. | Income Summary<br>    Sales Returns and Allowances<br>    Sales Discounts<br>    Cost of Goods Sold<br>    Freight-out<br>    Expenses | XX | XX<br>XX<br>XX<br>XX<br>XX |

## Before You Go On...

**REVIEW IT**

1. Why do merchandising companies usually need to make an adjustment to the Merchandise Inventory account?
2. What merchandising account(s) will appear in the post-closing trial balance?

**DO IT**

The trial balance of Celine's Sports Wear Shop at December 31 shows Merchandise Inventory $25,000, Sales $162,400, Sales Returns and Allowances $4,800, Sales Discounts $3,600, Cost of Goods Sold $110,000, Rental Revenue $6,000, Freight-out $1,800, Rent Expense $8,800, and Salaries and Wages Expense $22,000. Prepare the closing entries for the above accounts.

**Action Plan**

- Close all temporary accounts with credit balances to Income Summary by debiting these accounts.
- Close all temporary accounts with debit balances to Income Summary by crediting these accounts.

**Solution**  The two closing entries are:

| | | | |
|---|---|---:|---:|
| Dec. 31 | Sales | 162,400 | |
| | Rental Revenue | 6,000 | |
| |     Income Summary | | 168,400 |
| |       (To close accounts with credit balances) | | |
| | | | |
| 31 | Income Summary | 151,000 | |
| |     Cost of Goods Sold | | 110,000 |
| |     Sales Returns and Allowances | | 4,800 |
| |     Sales Discounts | | 3,600 |
| |     Freight-out | | 1,800 |
| |     Rent Expense | | 8,800 |
| |     Salaries and Wages Expense | | 22,000 |
| |       (To close accounts with debit balances) | | |

Related exercise material: *BE5-5, BE5-6, E5-6, E5-7, and E5-8.*

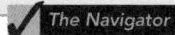 *The Navigator*

# FORMS OF FINANCIAL STATEMENTS

Merchandising companies widely use the classified balance sheet introduced in Chapter 4 and one of two forms for the income statement. This section explains the use of these financial statements by merchandisers.

**STUDY OBJECTIVE 5**

Distinguish between a multiple-step and a single-step income statement.

## Multiple-Step Income Statement

The **multiple-step income statement** is so named because it shows several steps in determining net income. Two of these steps relate to the company's principal operating activities. A multiple-step statement also distinguishes between **operating** and **non-operating activities**. Finally, the statement also highlights intermediate components of income and shows subgroupings of expenses.

### INCOME STATEMENT PRESENTATION OF SALES

The multiple-step income statement begins by presenting **sales revenue**. It then deducts contra-revenue accounts—sales returns and allowances, and sales discounts—to arrive at **net sales**. Illustration 5-6 (page 210) presents the sales revenues section for PW Audio Supply Inc., using assumed data.

**Illustration 5-6**
Computation of net sales

| PW AUDIO SUPPLY INC. | | |
| --- | --- | --- |
| Income Statement (partial) | | |
| **Sales revenues** | | |
| Sales | | $480,000 |
| Less: Sales returns and allowances | $12,000 | |
| Sales discounts | 8,000 | 20,000 |
| **Net sales** | | **$460,000** |

This presentation discloses the key data about the company's principal revenue-producing activities.

## GROSS PROFIT

**STUDY OBJECTIVE 6**

**Explain the computation and importance of gross profit.**

From Illustration 5-1, you learned that companies deduct from sales revenue the cost of goods sold in order to determine gross profit. For this computation, companies use **net sales** as the amount of sales revenue. On the basis of the sales data in Illustration 5-6 (net sales of $460,000) and cost of goods sold under the perpetual inventory system (assume $316,000), PW Audio's gross profit is $144,000, computed as follows.

*Net Sales − Costs of Goods Sold = Gross Profit*

**Illustration 5-7**
Computation of gross profit

| | |
| --- | --- |
| Net sales | $460,000 |
| Cost of goods sold | 316,000 |
| **Gross profit** | **$144,000** |

We also can express a company's gross profit as a percentage, called the gross profit rate. To do so, we divide the amount of gross profit by net sales. For PW Audio, the **gross profit rate** is 31.3%, computed as follows.

**Illustration 5-8**
Gross profit rate formula and computation

| **Gross Profit** | ÷ | **Net Sales** | = | **Gross Profit Rate** |
| --- | --- | --- | --- | --- |
| $144,000 | ÷ | $460,000 | = | 31.3% |

Analysts generally consider the gross profit **rate** to be more useful than the gross profit **amount**. The rate expresses a more meaningful (qualitative) relationship between net sales and gross profit. For example, a gross profit of $1,000,000 may sound impressive. But if it is the result of a gross profit rate of only 7%, it is not so impressive. The gross profit rate tells how many cents of each sales dollar go to gross profit.

Gross profit represents the **merchandising profit** of a company. It is not a measure of the overall profitability, because operating expenses are not yet deducted. But managers and other interested parties closely watch the amount and trend of gross profit. They compare current gross profit with amounts reported in past periods. They also compare the company's gross profit rate with rates of competitors and with industry averages. Such comparisons provide information about the effectiveness of a company's purchasing function and the soundness of its pricing policies.

## OPERATING EXPENSES AND NET INCOME

Operating expenses are the next component in measuring a merchandising company's net income. They are the expenses incurred in the process of earning sales revenue. These expenses are similar in merchandising and service enterprises. At

PW Audio, operating expenses were $114,000. The company's net income is determined by subtracting operating expenses from gross profit. Thus, net income is $30,000, as calculated below.

| | |
|---|---:|
| Gross profit | $144,000 |
| **Operating expenses** | **114,000** |
| Net income | $ 30,000 |

**Illustration 5-9**
Operating expenses in computing net income

The net income amount is the so-called "bottom line" of a company's income statement.

## SUBGROUPING OF OPERATING EXPENSES

Larger companies often subdivide operating expenses into selling expenses and administrative expenses. Selling expenses are those associated with making sales. They include expenses for sales promotion and expenses of completing the sale, such as delivery and shipping. Administrative expenses (sometimes called general expenses) relate to general operating activities such as personnel management, accounting, and store security.

When companies use these subgroupings, they may need to prorate some expenses (e.g., 70% to selling and 30% to administrative expenses). For example, if a company uses a store building for both selling and general functions, it will need to allocate to the two categories building expenses such as depreciation, utilities, and property taxes.

Any reasonable classification of expenses that serves to inform those who use the statement is satisfactory. The present tendency in statements prepared for management's internal use is to present in considerable detail expense data grouped along lines of responsibility.

## NONOPERATING ACTIVITIES

Nonoperating activities consist of various revenues and expenses and gains and losses that are unrelated to the company's main line of operations. When nonoperating items are included, the label "Income from operations" (or "Operating income") precedes them. This label clearly identifies the results of the company's normal operations, an amount determined by subtracting cost of goods sold and operating expenses from net sales. The results of nonoperating activities are shown in the categories "Other revenues and gains" and "Other expenses and losses." Illustration 5-10 lists examples of each.

**Illustration 5-10**
Other items of nonoperating activities

| **Other Revenues and Gains** |
|---|
| **Interest revenue** from notes receivable and marketable securities. |
| **Dividend revenue** from investments in capital stock. |
| **Rent revenue** from subleasing a portion of the store. |
| **Gain** from the sale of property, plant, and equipment. |
| **Other Expenses and Losses** |
| **Interest expense** on notes and loans payable. |
| **Casualty losses** from recurring causes, such as vandalism and accidents. |
| **Loss** from the sale or abandonment of property, plant, and equipment. |
| **Loss** from strikes by employees and suppliers. |

Merchandising companies report the nonoperating activities in the income statement immediately after the company's primary operating activities. Illustration 5-11 shows these sections for PW Audio Supply Inc., using assumed data.

In the nonoperating activities sections, companies generally report items at the net amount. Thus, if a company received a $2,500 insurance settlement on vandalism losses of $2,700, it reports the loss at $200. Note, too, that the company nets the results of the two nonoperating sections. (For example, PW Audio shows an amount for $1,600, which is the net of the two nonoperating activities amounts.) This difference is added to or subtracted from income from operations to determine net income. Companies often combine these two nonoperating activities sections into a single "Other revenues and expenses" section.

**ETHICS NOTE**

Companies manage earnings in various ways. ConAgra Foods recorded a non-recurring gain for $186 million from the sale of Pilgrim's Pride stock to help meet an earnings projection for the quarter.

**Illustration 5-11**
Multiple-step income statement—nonoperating sections and subgroupings of operating expenses

### PW AUDIO SUPPLY INC.
### Income Statement
### For the Year Ended December 31, 2008

Calculation of gross profit

| | | |
|---|---:|---:|
| **Sales revenues** | | |
| Sales | | $480,000 |
| Less: Sales returns and allowances | $12,000 | |
| Sales discounts | 8,000 | 20,000 |
| Net sales | | 460,000 |
| **Cost of goods sold** | | 316,000 |
| **Gross profit** | | 144,000 |

Calculation of income from operations

| | | |
|---|---:|---:|
| **Operating expenses** | | |
| **Selling expenses** | | |
| Store salaries expense | 45,000 | |
| Advertising expense | 16,000 | |
| Depreciation expense—store equipment | 8,000 | |
| Freight-out | 7,000 | |
| Total selling expenses | 76,000 | |
| **Administrative expenses** | | |
| Salaries expense | 19,000 | |
| Utilities expense | 17,000 | |
| Insurance expense | 2,000 | |
| Total administrative expenses | 38,000 | |
| Total operating expenses | | 114,000 |
| **Income from operations** | | 30,000 |

Results of nonoperating activities

| | | |
|---|---:|---:|
| **Other revenues and gains** | | |
| Interest revenue | 3,000 | |
| Gain on sale of equipment | 600 | |
| | 3,600 | |
| **Other expenses and losses** | | |
| Interest expense | 1,800 | |
| Casualty loss from vandalism | 200 | |
| | 2,000 | |
| | | 1,600 |
| **Net income** | | $ 31,600 |

The distinction between operating and nonoperating activities is crucial to many external users of financial data. These users view operating income as sustainable and many nonoperating activities as nonrecurring. Therefore, when forecasting next year's income, analysts put the most weight on this year's operating income, and less weight on this year's nonoperating activities.

## ETHICS INSIGHT

### *For IBM, What Is Operating?*

After Enron, increased investor criticism and regulator scrutiny forced many companies to improve the clarity of their financial disclosures. For example, IBM announced it would provide more detail of its "Other gains and losses." It had previously included these items in its selling, general, and administrative expenses, with little disclosure.

Disclosing other gains and losses in a separate line item on the income statement will not have any effect on bottom-line income. However, analysts complained that burying these details in the selling, general, and administrative expense line reduced their ability to fully understand how well IBM was performing. For example, previously if IBM sold one of its buildings at a gain, it would include this gain in the selling, general, and administrative expense line item, thus reducing that expense. This made it appear that the company had done a better job of controlling operating expenses than it actually had.

Other companies that also recently announced changes to increase the informativeness of their income statements include PepsiCo and General Electric.

**?** Why have investors and analysts demanded more accuracy in isolating "Other gains and losses" from operating items?

## Single-Step Income Statement

Another income statement format is the single-step income statement. The statement is so named because only one step—subtracting total expenses from total revenues—is required in determining net income.

A single-step statement classifies all data under two categories: revenues and expenses. **Revenues** include both operating revenues and other revenues and gains. **Expenses** include cost of goods sold, operating expenses, and other expenses and losses. Illustration 5-12 (page 214) shows a single-step statement for PW Audio Supply Inc.

There are two primary reasons for using the single-step format: (1) A company does not realize any type of profit or income until total revenues exceed total expenses, so it makes sense to divide the statement into these two categories. (2) The format is simpler and easier to read. *For homework problems, however, you should use the single-step format only when specifically instructed to do so.*

## Classified Balance Sheet

In the balance sheet, merchandising companies report merchandise inventory as a current asset immediately below accounts receivable. Recall from Chapter 4 that companies generally list current asset items in the order of their closeness to cash (liquidity). Merchandise inventory is less close to cash than accounts receivable, because the goods must first be sold and then collection made from the customer. Illustration 5-13 (page 214) presents the assets section of a classified balance sheet for PW Audio Supply Inc.

**Illustration 5-12**
Single-step income statement

### PW AUDIO SUPPLY INC.
Income Statement
For the Year Ended December 31, 2008

| | | |
|---|---:|---:|
| **Revenues** | | |
| Net sales | | $460,000 |
| Interest revenue | | 3,000 |
| Gain on sale of equipment | | 600 |
| Total revenues | | 463,600 |
| **Expenses** | | |
| Cost of goods sold | $316,000 | |
| Selling expenses | 76,000 | |
| Administrative expenses | 38,000 | |
| Interest expense | 1,800 | |
| Casualty loss from vandalism | 200 | |
| Total expenses | | 432,000 |
| **Net income** | | $ 31,600 |

**Illustration 5-13**
Assets section of a classified balance sheet

### PW AUDIO SUPPLY INC.
Balance Sheet (Partial)
December 31, 2008

**Assets**

| | | |
|---|---:|---:|
| Current assets | | |
| Cash | | $ 9,500 |
| Accounts receivable | | 16,100 |
| **Merchandise inventory** | | 40,000 |
| Prepaid insurance | | 1,800 |
| Total current assets | | 67,400 |
| Property, plant, and equipment | | |
| Store equipment | $80,000 | |
| Less: Accumulated depreciation—store equipment | 24,000 | 56,000 |
| Total assets | | $123,400 |

**HELPFUL HINT**

The **$40,000** is the *cost* of the inventory on hand, not its expected selling price.

## Before You Go On...

**REVIEW IT**

1. Determine PepsiCo's gross profit rate for 2005 and 2004. Indicate whether it increased or decreased from 2004 to 2005. The answer to this question appears on page 243.

2. What are nonoperating activities? How do companies report them in the income statement?

3. How does a single-step income statement differ from a multiple-step income statement?

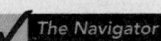

 Be sure to read **ALL ABOUT YOU:** *When Is a Sale a Sale?* on the next page for information on how topics in this chapter apply to you.

# When Is a Sale Not a Sale?

Two interesting questions about merchandising are, "When is a sale not really a sale?" and "Why does it matter?" The answer for the second question is easy. If sales increase, net income increases. Managers' bonuses and stock prices generally increase when net income increases. Therefore, managers want sales to increase, and they feel much pressure at year-end to make sure this happens.

The first question is more difficult to answer. As the chapter indicates, a sale generally occurs when the seller has earned the revenue. But what do we mean by "earning the revenue"? Sometimes, to achieve higher sales figures, managers resort to reducing sales prices at year-end. Others may go even further. One example is a practice called *channel stuffing*. This involves shipping more goods to a customer than the customer needs. This practice boosts reported sales in that quarter. In the next quarter, however, the customer frequently returns a large portion of the extra goods, or at the very least, buys fewer goods because of the inventory already on hand.

## ✲ About the Numbers

Presented below is a pie chart to illustrate that revenue recognition issues often require companies to correct—restate—their financial statements.

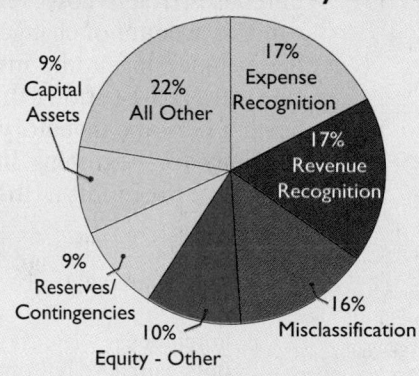

**Oops! Total 2004 Restatements by Error Category**

- 17% Expense Recognition
- 17% Revenue Recognition
- 16% Misclassification
- 10% Equity - Other
- 9% Reserves/Contingencies
- 9% Capital Assets
- 22% All Other

**Source for chart:** Terry Baldwin and Daniel Yoo, "Restatements—Traversing Shaky Ground: An Analysis for Investors," Glass Lewis & Co., June 2, 2005, p. 9, Graph 7.

## ✲ Some Facts

* In early 2005 the shareholders of Krispy Kreme Doughnuts filed a lawsuit against management, alleging that at the end of accounting quarters the company was shipping twice as many doughnuts to wholesale customers than ordered.

* The SEC investigated claims that Harley-Davidson was shipping motorcycles to dealers in excess of dealer requests, in order to give the appearance of continued strong sales.

* In a recent lawsuit settlement, pharmaceutical company Bristol-Myers Squibb paid a $150 million fine for an alleged channel stuffing scheme that began in 1991 and did not end until 2001.

* An SEC investigation concluded that The Coca-Cola Company shipped $1.2 of excessive beverage concentrate to bottlers in Japan during a three-year period. The bottlers' inventories surged 62% during this time, while their sales increased only 11%.

## ✲ What Do You Think?

Suppose that at the end of the year, your boss asks you to ship twice as many goods to your customers as they ordered. If you don't do so, you won't make your sales goal, and you won't get your bonus. You ask yourself, "Is channel stuffing an ethical business practice?"

**YES:** Motorcycles and pharmaceuticals can't be sold if they are sitting in the manufacturer's warehouse. They should be shipped to dealers and retailers so they have a chance of being sold to customers.

**NO:** If goods are intentionally shipped to customers when the customer hasn't requested them, and the seller has a high expectation that the goods will be returned, then this clearly is not a real sale. Management is providing a distorted picture of the company's sales performance, and thus misleading investors about the company's success.

**Sources:** Betsy McKay and Chad Terhune, "Coca-Cola Settles Regulatory Probe," *Wall Street Journal*, April 19, 2005, p. A3; Jay Hancock, "Check Those 4th-Quarter Earnings for Plumping," *The Baltimore Sun*, January 9, 2005, p. 1D.

# DETERMINING COST OF GOODS SOLD UNDER A PERIODIC SYSTEM

**STUDY OBJECTIVE 7**

Determine cost of goods sold under a periodic inventory system.

As shown in Illustration 5–3 (page 198), determining cost of goods sold is different under the periodic inventory system. When a company uses a perpetual inventory system, it records all transactions affecting inventory (such as purchases, freight costs, returns, and discounts) directly to the Merchandise Inventory account. In addition, at the time of each sale the perpetual system requires a reduction in Merchandise Inventory and an increase in Cost of Goods Sold.

\Under a periodic system, however, the company uses **separate accounts** to record purchases, freight costs, returns, and discounts.\Also, the company does not maintain a running account of changes in inventory. Instead, at the end of the period, it calculates the balance in ending inventory, as well as the cost of goods sold for the period. Illustration 5-14 shows the calculation of cost of goods sold for PW Audio Supply, using a periodic inventory system. Note that it includes (here, in blue type) separate amounts for beginning inventory, cost of goods purchased, and ending inventory. These are the inputs to the cost of goods sold computation under a periodic system.

**Illustration 5-14**
Cost of goods sold for a merchandising company using a periodic inventory system

**HELPFUL HINT**

Reading from right to left, the second column identifies the primary items that make up cost of goods sold of $316,000. The third column explains cost of goods purchased of $320,000. The fourth column reports contra-purchase items of $17,200.

| Cost of goods sold | | | |
|---|---|---|---|
| Inventory, January 1 | | | $36,000 |
| Purchases | | $325,000 | |
| Less: Purchase returns and | | | |
| allowances | $10,400 | | |
| Purchase discounts | 6,800 | 17,200 | |
| Net purchases | | 307,800 | |
| Add: Freight-in | | 12,200 | |
| Cost of goods purchased | | | 320,000 |
| Cost of goods available for sale | | | 356,000 |
| Inventory, December 31 | | | 40,000 |
| **Cost of goods sold** | | | **316,000** |

A company reports merchandise inventory in the current assets section whether it uses a periodic or a perpetual system.

Appendix 5A provides further detail on the use of the periodic system.

## Before You Go On...

**REVIEW IT**

1. Name two basic systems of accounting for inventory.
2. What accounts are used in determining the cost of goods purchased?
3. What is included in cost of goods available for sale?

**DO IT**

Aerosmith Company's accounting records show the following at year-end: Purchase Discounts $3,400; Freight-in $6,100; Sales $240,000; Purchases $162,500; Beginning Inventory $18,000; Ending Inventory $20,000; Sales Discounts $10,000; Purchase Returns $5,200; and Operating Expenses $57,000. Compute the following amounts for Aerosmith Company: net sales, cost of goods purchased, cost of goods sold, gross profit, and net income.

**Action Plan**

■ Understand the relationships of the cost components in measuring net income for a merchandising company.

- Compute net sales.
- Compute cost of goods purchased.
- Compute cost of goods sold.
- Compute gross profit.
- Compute net income.

**Solution**

Net sales:

Sales − Sales discounts = Net sales

$240,000 − $10,000 = $230,000

Cost of goods purchased:

Purchases − Purchase returns − Purchase discounts + Freight-in = Cost of goods purchased

$162,500 − $5,200 − $3,400 + $6,100 = $160,000

Cost of goods sold:

Beginning inventory + Cost of goods purchased − Ending inventory = Cost of goods sold

$18,000 + $160,000 − $20,000 = $158,000

Gross profit:

Net sales − Cost of goods sold = Gross profit

$230,000 − $158,000 = $72,000

Net income:

Gross profit − Operating expenses = Net income

$72,000 − $57,000 = $15,000

Related exercise material: *BE5-10, BE5-11, E5-13, E5-14, and E5-15.*

✓ The Navigator

## Demonstration Problem

The adjusted trial balance columns of Falcetto Company's worksheet for the year ended December 31, 2008, are as follows.

| Debit | | Credit | |
|---|---|---|---|
| Cash | 14,500 | Accumulated Depreciation | 18,000 |
| Accounts Receivable | 11,100 | Notes Payable | 25,000 |
| Merchandise Inventory | 29,000 | Accounts Payable | 10,600 |
| Prepaid Insurance | 2,500 | Common Stock | 50,000 |
| Store Equipment | 95,000 | Retained Earnings | 31,000 |
| Dividends | 12,000 | Sales | 536,800 |
| Sales Returns and Allowances | 6,700 | Interest Revenue | 2,500 |
| Sales Discounts | 5,000 | | 673,900 |
| Cost of Goods Sold | 363,400 | | |
| Freight-out | 7,600 | | |
| Advertising Expense | 12,000 | | |
| Store Salaries Expense | 56,000 | | |
| Utilities Expense | 18,000 | | |
| Rent Expense | 24,000 | | |
| Depreciation Expense | 9,000 | | |
| Insurance Expense | 4,500 | | |
| Interest Expense | 3,600 | | |
| | 673,900 | | |

**Instructions**

Prepare an income statement assuming Falcetto Company does not use subgroupings for operating expenses.

## action plan

✔ Remember that the key components of the income statement are net sales, cost of goods sold, gross profit, total operating expenses, and net income (loss). Report these components in the right-hand column of the income statement.

✔ Put nonoperating items after income from operations.

### Solution

**FALCETTO COMPANY**
Income Statement
For the Year Ended December 31, 2008

| | | | |
|---|---|---:|---:|
| Sales revenues | | | |
| Sales | | | $536,800 |
| Less: Sales returns and allowances | | $6,700 | |
| Sales discounts | | 5,000 | 11,700 |
| Net sales | | | 525,100 |
| Cost of goods sold | | | 363,400 |
| Gross profit | | | 161,700 |
| Operating expenses | | | |
| Store salaries expense | | 56,000 | |
| Rent expense | | 24,000 | |
| Utilities expense | | 18,000 | |
| Advertising expense | | 12,000 | |
| Depreciation expense | | 9,000 | |
| Freight-out | | 7,600 | |
| Insurance expense | | 4,500 | |
| Total operating expenses | | | 131,100 |
| Income from operations | | | 30,600 |
| Other revenues and gains | | | |
| Interest revenue | | 2,500 | |
| Other expenses and losses | | | |
| Interest expense | | 3,600 | 1,100 |
| Net income | | | $ 29,500 |

---

# SUMMARY OF STUDY OBJECTIVES

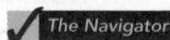

1 **Identify the differences between service and merchandising companies.** Because of inventory, a merchandising company has sales revenue, cost of goods sold, and gross profit. To account for inventory, a merchandising company must choose between a perpetual and a periodic inventory system.

2 **Explain the recording of purchases under a perpetual inventory system.** The company debits the Merchandise Inventory account for all purchases of merchandise and freight-in, and credits it for purchase discounts and purchase returns and allowances.

3 **Explain the recording of sales revenues under a perpetual inventory system.** When a merchandising company sells inventory, it debits Accounts Receivable (or Cash), and credits Sales for the **selling price** of the merchandise. At the same time, it debits Cost of Goods Sold, and credits Merchandise Inventory for the **cost** of the inventory items sold.

4 **Explain the steps in the accounting cycle for a merchandising company.** Each of the required steps in the accounting cycle for a service company applies to a merchandising company. A worksheet is again an optional step.

Under a perpetual inventory system, the company must adjust the Merchandise Inventory account to agree with the physical count.

5 **Distinguish between a multiple-step and a single-step income statement.** A multiple-step income statement shows numerous steps in determining net income, including nonoperating activities sections. A single-step income statement classifies all data under two categories, revenues or expenses, and determines net income in one step.

6 **Explain the computation and importance of gross profit.** Merchandising companies compute gross profit by subtracting cost of goods sold from net sales. Gross profit represents the merchandising profit of a company. Managers and other interested parties closely watch the amount and trend of gross profit.

7 **Determine cost of goods sold under a periodic inventory system.** (a) Determine the cost of goods on hand at the beginning of the accounting period. (b) Add to it the cost of goods purchased. (c) Subtract the cost of goods on hand at the end of the accounting period.

# GLOSSARY

**Administrative expenses** Expenses relating to general operating activities such as personnel management, accounting, and store security. (p. 211).

**Contra-revenue account** An account that is offset against a revenue account on the income statement. (p. 204).

**Cost of goods sold** The total cost of merchandise sold during the period. (p. 196).

**FOB destination** Freight terms indicating that the seller places the goods free on board to the buyer's place of business, and the seller pays the freight. (p. 200).

**FOB shipping point** Freight terms indicating that the seller places goods free on board the carrier, and the buyer pays the freight costs. (p. 200).

**Gross profit** The excess of net sales over the cost of goods sold. (p. 210).

**Gross profit rate** Gross profit expressed as a percentage, by dividing the amount of gross profit by net sales. (p. 210).

**Income from operations** Income from a company's principal operating activity; determined by subtracting cost of goods sold and operating expenses from net sales. (p. 211).

**Multiple-step income statement** An income statement that shows several steps in determining net income. (p. 209).

**Net sales** Sales less sales returns and allowances and less sales discounts. (p. 209).

**Nonoperating activities** Various revenues, expenses, gains, and losses that are unrelated to a company's main line of operations. (p. 211).

**Operating expenses** Expenses incurred in the process of earning sales revenues. (p. 210).

**Other expenses and losses** A nonoperating-activities section of the income statement that shows expenses from auxiliary operations and losses unrelated to the company's operations. (p. 211).

**Other revenues and gains** A nonoperating-activities section of the income statement that shows revenues from auxiliary operations and gains unrelated to the company's operations. (p. 211).

**Periodic inventory system** An inventory system under which the company does not keep detailed inventory records throughout the accounting period but determines the cost of goods sold only at the end of an accounting period. (p. 198).

**Perpetual inventory system** An inventory system under which the company keeps detailed records of the cost of each inventory purchase and sale and the records continuously show the inventory that should be on hand. (p. 197).

**Purchase allowance** A deduction made to the selling price of merchandise, granted by the seller so that the buyer will keep the merchandise. (p. 201).

**Purchase discount** A cash discount claimed by a buyer for prompt payment of a balance due. (p. 201).

**Purchase invoice** A document that supports each credit purchase. (p. 199).

**Purchase return** A return of goods from the buyer to the seller for a cash or credit refund. (p. 201).

**Sales discount** A reduction given by a seller for prompt payment of a credit sale. (p. 205).

**Sales invoice** A document that supports each credit sale. (p. 203).

**Sales returns and allowances** Purchase returns and allowances from the seller's perspective. See *Purchase return* and *Purchase allowance,* above. (p. 204).

**Sales revenue (Sales)** The primary source of revenue in a merchandising company. (p. 196).

**Selling expenses** Expenses associated with making sales. (p. 211).

**Single-step income statement** An income statement that shows only one step in determining net income. (p. 213).

# APPENDIX 5A   Periodic Inventory System

As described in this chapter, companies may use one of two basic systems of accounting for inventories: (1) the perpetual inventory system or (2) the periodic inventory system. In the chapter we focused on the characteristics of the perpetual inventory system. In this appendix we discuss and illustrate the **periodic inventory system**. One key difference between the two systems is the point at which the company computes cost of goods sold. For a visual reminder of this difference, you may want to refer back to Illustration 5-3 on page 198.

> **STUDY OBJECTIVE 8**
>
> Explain the recording of purchases and sales of inventory under a periodic inventory system.

## Recording Merchandise Transactions

In a **periodic inventory system**, companies record revenues from the sale of merchandise when sales are made, just as in a perpetual system. Unlike the perpetual system, however, companies **do not attempt on the date of sale to record the cost of the merchandise sold**. Instead, they take a physical inventory count at the **end of the period** to determine (1) the cost of the merchandise then on hand and (2) the cost of the goods sold during the period. And, **under a periodic system**, **companies record purchases of merchandise in the Purchases account rather than the Merchandise Inventory account**. Also, in a periodic system, purchase returns and allowances, purchase discounts, and freight costs on purchases are recorded in separate accounts.

To illustrate the recording of merchandise transactions under a periodic inventory system, we will use purchase/sale transactions between PW Audio Supply Inc. and Sauk Stereo, as illustrated for the perpetual inventory system in this chapter.

# Recording Purchases of Merchandise

On the basis of the sales invoice (Illustration 5-4, shown on page 200) and receipt of the merchandise ordered from PW Audio Supply Inc., Sauk Stereo records the $3,800 purchase as follows.

| | | | |
|---|---|---|---|
| May 4 | Purchases | 3,800 | |
| | Accounts Payable | | 3,800 |
| | (To record goods purchased on account from PW Audio Supply) | | |

Purchases is a temporary account whose normal balance is a debit.

### FREIGHT COSTS
When the purchaser directly incurs the freight costs, it debits the account Freight-in (or Transportation-in). For example, if Sauk pays Haul-It Freight Company $150 for freight charges on its purchase from PW Audio Supply on May 6, the entry on Sauk's books is:

| | | | |
|---|---|---|---|
| May 6 | Freight-in (Transportation-in) | 150 | |
| | Cash | | 150 |
| | (To record payment of freight on goods purchased) | | |

Like Purchases, Freight-in is a temporary account whose normal balance is a debit. **Freight-in is part of cost of goods purchased.** The reason is that cost of goods purchased should include any freight charges necessary to bring the goods to the purchaser. Freight costs are not subject to a purchase discount. Purchase discounts apply to the invoice cost of the merchandise.

### PURCHASE RETURNS AND ALLOWANCES
Sauk Stereo returns $300 of goods to PW Audio Supply and prepares the following entry to recognize the return.

| | | | |
|---|---|---|---|
| May 8 | Accounts Payable | 300 | |
| | Purchase Returns and Allowances | | 300 |
| | (To record return of goods purchased from PW Audio Supply) | | |

Purchase Returns and Allowances is a temporary account whose normal balance is a credit.

## PURCHASE DISCOUNTS
On May 14 Sauk Stereo pays the balance due on account to PW Audio Supply, taking the 2% cash discount allowed by PW Audio Supply for payment within 10 days. Sauk Stereo records the payment and discount as follows.

| | | | | |
|---|---|---|---|---|
| May 14 | Accounts Payable ($3,800 − $300) | | 3,500 | |
| | Purchase Discounts ($3,500 × .02) | | | 70 |
| | Cash | | | 3,430 |
| | (To record payment within the discount period) | | | |

Purchase Discounts is a temporary account whose normal balance is a credit.

# Recording Sales of Merchandise
The seller, PW Audio Supply, records the sale of $3,800 of merchandise to Sauk Stereo on May 4 (sales invoice No. 731, Illustration 5-4, page 200) as follows.

| | | | | |
|---|---|---|---|---|
| May 4 | Accounts Receivable | | 3,800 | |
| | Sales | | | 3,800 |
| | (To record credit sales per invoice #731 to Sauk Stereo) | | | |

## SALES RETURNS AND ALLOWANCES
To record the returned goods received from Sauk Stereo on May 8, PW Audio Supply records the $300 sales return as follows.

| | | | | |
|---|---|---|---|---|
| May 8 | Sales Returns and Allowances | | 300 | |
| | Accounts Receivable | | | 300 |
| | (To record credit granted to Sauk Stereo for returned goods) | | | |

## SALES DISCOUNTS
On May 14, PW Audio Supply receives payment of $3,430 on account from Sauk Stereo. PW Audio Supply honors the 2% cash discount and records the payment of Sauk's account receivable in full as follows.

| | | | | |
|---|---|---|---|---|
| May 14 | Cash | | 3,430 | |
| | Sales Discounts ($3,500 × .02) | | 70 | |
| | Accounts Receivable ($3,800 − $300) | | | 3,500 |
| | (To record collection within 2/10, n/30 discount period from Sauk Stereo) | | | |

## COMPARISON OF ENTRIES—PERPETUAL VS. PERIODIC
The following display summarizes the periodic inventory entries shown in this appendix and compares them to the perpetual-system entries from the chapter. Entries that differ in the two systems are shown in color.

## ENTRIES ON SAUK STEREO'S BOOKS

| Transaction | Perpetual Inventory System | | Periodic Inventory System | |
|---|---|---|---|---|
| May 4 Purchase of merchandise on credit. | Merchandise Inventory<br>   Accounts Payable | 3,800<br> <br>3,800 | Purchases<br>   Accounts Payable | 3,800<br> <br>3,800 |
| May 6 Freight costs on purchases. | Merchandise Inventory<br>   Cash | 150<br> <br>150 | Freight-in<br>   Cash | 150<br> <br>150 |
| May 8 Purchase returns and allowances. | Accounts Payable<br>   Merchandise Inventory | 300<br> <br>300 | Accounts Payable<br>   Purchase Returns<br>   and Allowances | 300<br> <br> <br>300 |
| May 14 Payment on account with a discount. | Accounts Payable<br>   Cash<br>   Merchandise Inventory | 3,500<br> <br>3,430<br>70 | Accounts Payable<br>   Cash<br>   Purchase Discounts | 3,500<br> <br>3,430<br>70 |

## ENTRIES ON PW AUDIO SUPPLY'S BOOKS

| Transaction | Perpetual Inventory System | | Periodic Inventory System | |
|---|---|---|---|---|
| May 4 Sale of merchandise on credit. | Accounts Receivable<br>   Sales Revenue | 3,800<br> <br>3,800 | Accounts Receivable<br>   Sales Revenue | 3,800<br> <br>3,800 |
| | Cost of Goods Sold<br>   Merchandise Inventory | 2,400<br> <br>2,400 | No entry for cost of<br>   goods sold | |
| May 8 Return of merchandise sold. | Sales Returns and<br>Allowances<br>   Accounts Receivable | <br>300<br> <br>300 | Sales Returns and<br>Allowances<br>   Accounts Receivable | <br>300<br> <br>300 |
| | Merchandise Inventory<br>   Cost of Goods Sold | 140<br> <br>140 | No entry | |
| May 14 Cash received on account with a discount. | Cash<br>Sales Discounts<br>   Accounts Receivable | 3,430<br>70<br> <br>3,500 | Cash<br>Sales Discounts<br>   Accounts Receivable | 3,430<br>70<br> <br>3,500 |

---

# SUMMARY OF STUDY OBJECTIVE FOR APPENDIX 5A

**8 Explain the recording of purchases and sales of inventory under a periodic inventory system.** In recording purchases under a periodic system, companies must make entries for (a) cash and credit purchases, (b) purchase returns and allowances, (c) purchase discounts, and (d) freight costs. In recording sales, companies must make entries for (a) cash and credit sales, (b) sales returns and allowances, and (c) sales discounts.

---

## APPENDIX 5B    Worksheet for a Merchandising Company

**STUDY OBJECTIVE 9**

Prepare a worksheet for a merchandising company.

### Using a Worksheet

As indicated in Chapter 4, a worksheet enables companies to prepare financial statements before they journalize and post adjusting entries. The steps in preparing a worksheet for a merchandising company are the same as for a service enterprise (see pages 145–148). Illustration 5B-1 shows the worksheet for PW Audio Supply (excluding nonoperating items). The unique accounts for a merchandiser using a perpetual inventory system are in boldface letters and in red.

PW Audio Supply.xls

File    Edit    View    Insert    Format    Tools    Data    Window    Help

| | A | B | C | D | E | F | G | H | I | J | K |
|---|---|---|---|---|---|---|---|---|---|---|---|
| 1 | | **PW AUDIO SUPPLY INC.** | | | | | | | | | |
| 2 | | Worksheet | | | | | | | | | |
| 3 | | For the Year Ended December 31, 2008 | | | | | | | | | |
| 4 | | Trial Balance | | Adjustments | | Adjusted Trial Balance | | Income Statement | | Balance Sheet | |
| 5 | | | | | | | | | | | |
| 6 | | | | | | | | | | | |
| 7 | Accounts | Dr. | Cr. | Dr. | Cr. | Dr. | Cr. | Dr. | Cr. | Dr. | Cr. |
| 8 | Cash | 9,500 | | | | 9,500 | | | | 9,500 | |
| 9 | Accounts Receivable | 16,100 | | | | 16,100 | | | | 16,100 | |
| 10 | **Merchandise Inventory** | **40,500** | | | (a) 500 | **40,000** | | | | **40,000** | |
| 11 | Prepaid Insurance | 3,800 | | | (b) 2,000 | 1,800 | | | | 1,800 | |
| 12 | Store Equipment | 80,000 | | | | 80,000 | | | | 80,000 | |
| 13 | Accumulated Depreciation | | 16,000 | | (c) 8,000 | | 24,000 | | | | 24,000 |
| 14 | Accounts Payable | | 20,400 | | | | 20,400 | | | | 20,400 |
| 15 | Common Stock | | 50,000 | | | | 50,000 | | | | 50,000 |
| 16 | Retained Earnings | | 33,000 | | | | 33,000 | | | | 33,000 |
| 17 | Dividends | 15,000 | | | | 15,000 | | | | 15,000 | |
| 18 | **Sales** | | **480,000** | | | | **480,000** | | **480,000** | | |
| 19 | **Sales Returns and Allowances** | **12,000** | | | | **12,000** | | **12,000** | | | |
| 20 | **Sales Discounts** | **8,000** | | | | **8,000** | | **8,000** | | | |
| 21 | **Cost of Goods Sold** | **315,500** | | (a) 500 | | **316,000** | | **316,000** | | | |
| 22 | Freight-out | 7,000 | | | | 7,000 | | 7,000 | | | |
| 23 | Advertising Expense | 16,000 | | | | 16,000 | | 16,000 | | | |
| 24 | Admin. Sal. Exp. | 19,000 | | | | 19,000 | | 19,000 | | | |
| 25 | Store Salaries Expense | 40,000 | | (d) 5,000 | | 45,000 | | 45,000 | | | |
| 26 | Utilities Expense | 17,000 | | | | 17,000 | | 17,000 | | | |
| 27 | Totals | 599,400 | 599,400 | | | | | | | | |
| 28 | Insurance Expense | | | (b) 2,000 | | 2,000 | | 2,000 | | | |
| 29 | Depreciation Expense | | | (c) 8,000 | | 8,000 | | 8,000 | | | |
| 30 | Salaries Payable | | | | (d) 5,000 | | 5,000 | | | | 5,000 |
| 31 | Totals | | | 15,500 | 15,500 | 612,400 | 612,400 | 450,000 | 480,000 | 162,400 | 132,400 |
| 32 | Net Income | | | | | | | 30,000 | | | 30,000 |
| 33 | Totals | | | | | | | 480,000 | 480,000 | 162,400 | 162,400 |
| 34 | | | | | | | | | | | |
| 35 | | | | | | | | | | | |

Key: (a) Adjustment to inventory on hand, (b) Insurance expired, (c) Depreciation expense, (d) Salaries accrued.

**Illustration 5B-1**
Worksheet for merchandising company

## TRIAL BALANCE COLUMNS
Data for the trial balance come from the ledger balances of PW Audio Supply at December 31. The amount shown for Merchandise Inventory, $40,500, is the year-end inventory amount from the perpetual inventory system.

## ADJUSTMENTS COLUMNS
A merchandising company generally has the same types of adjustments as a service company. As you see in the worksheet, adjustments (b), (c), and (d) are for insurance, depreciation, and salaries. Pioneer Advertising Agency, as illustrated in Chapters 3 and 4 also had these adjustments. Adjustment (a) was required to adjust the perpetual inventory carrying amount to the actual count.

After PW Audio enters all adjustments data on the worksheet, it establishes the equality of the adjustments column totals. It then extends the balances in all accounts to the adjusted trial balance columns.

## ADJUSTED TRIAL BALANCE
The adjusted trial balance shows the balance of all accounts after adjustment at the end of the accounting period.

### INCOME STATEMENT COLUMNS

Next, the merchandising company transfers the accounts and balances that affect the income statement from the adjusted trial balance columns to the income statement columns. PW Audio Supply shows sales of $480,000 in the credit column. It shows the contra-revenue accounts Sales Returns and Allowances $12,000 and Sales Discounts $8,000 in the debit column. The difference of $460,000 is the net sales shown on the income statement (Illustration 5-11, page 212).

Finally, the company totals all the credits in the income statement column and compares those totals to the total of the debits in the income statement column. If the credits exceed the debits, the company has net income. PW Audio Supply has net income of $30,000. If the debits exceed the credits, the company would report a net loss.

### BALANCE SHEET COLUMNS

The major difference between the balance sheets of a service company and a merchandiser is inventory. PW Audio Supply shows the ending inventory amount of $40,000 in the balance sheet debit column. The information to prepare the retained earnings statement is also found in these columns. That is, the retained earnings beginning balance is $33,000. The dividends are $15,000. Net income results when the total of the debit column exceeds the total of the credit column in the balance sheet columns. A net loss results when the total of the credits exceeds the total of the debit balances.

## SUMMARY OF STUDY OBJECTIVE

**9 Prepare a worksheet for a merchandising company.** The steps in preparing a worksheet for a merchandising company are the same as for a service company. The unique accounts for a merchandiser are Merchandise Inventory, Sales, Sales Returns and Allowances, Sales Discounts, and Cost of Goods Sold.

*Note: All **asterisked** Questions, Exercises, and Problems relate to material in the appendices to the chapter.

## SELF-STUDY QUESTIONS

*Answers are at the end of the chapter.*

(SO 1) **1.** Gross profit will result if:
  **a.** operating expenses are less than net income.
  **b.** sales revenues are greater than operating expenses.
  **c.** sales revenues are greater than cost of goods sold.
  **d.** operating expenses are greater than cost of goods sold.

(SO 2) **2.** Under a perpetual inventory system, when goods are purchased for resale by a company:
  **a.** purchases on account are debited to Merchandise Inventory.
  **b.** purchases on account are debited to Purchases.
  **c.** purchase returns are debited to Purchase Returns and Allowances.
  **d.** freight costs are debited to Freight-out.

(SO 3) **3.** The sales accounts that normally have a debit balance are:
  **a.** Sales Discounts.
  **b.** Sales Returns and Allowances.

  **c.** both (a) and (b).
  **d.** neither (a) nor (b).

(SO 3) **4.** A credit sale of $750 is made on June 13, terms 2/10, net/30. A return of $50 is granted on June 16. The amount received as payment in full on June 23 is:
  **a.** $700.
  **b.** $686.
  **c.** $685.
  **d.** $650.

(SO 2) **5.** Which of the following accounts will normally appear in the ledger of a merchandising company that uses a perpetual inventory system?
  **a.** Purchases.
  **b.** Freight-in.
  **c.** Cost of Goods Sold.
  **d.** Purchase Discounts.

(SO 5) **6.** The multiple-step income statement for a merchandising company shows each of the following features *except*:
  **a.** gross profit.
  **b.** cost of goods sold.
  **c.** a sales revenue section.
  **d.** investing activities section.

(SO 6) **7.** If sales revenues are $400,000, cost of goods sold is $310,000, and operating expenses are $60,000, the gross profit is:
  **a.** $30,000.
  **b.** $90,000.
  **c.** $340,000.
  **d.** $400,000.

(SO 5) **8.** A single-step income statement:
  **a.** reports gross profit.
  **b.** does not report cost of goods sold.
  **c.** reports sales revenues and "Other revenues and gains" in the revenues section of the income statement.
  **d.** reports operating income separately.

(SO 5) **9.** Which of the following appears on both a single-step and a multiple-step income statement?
  **a.** merchandise inventory.
  **b.** gross profit.
  **c.** income from operations.
  **d.** cost of goods sold.

(SO 7) **10.** In determining cost of goods sold:
  **a.** purchase discounts are deducted from net purchases.
  **b.** freight-out is added to net purchases.

  **c.** purchase returns and allowances are deducted from net purchases.
  **d.** freight-in is added to net purchases.

(SO 7) **11.** If beginning inventory is $60,000, cost of goods purchased is $380,000, and ending inventory is $50,000, cost of goods sold is:
  **a.** $390,000.
  **b.** $370,000.
  **c.** $330,000.
  **d.** $420,000.

(SO 8) *****12.** When goods are purchased for resale by a company using a periodic inventory system:
  **a.** purchases on account are debited to Merchandise Inventory.
  **b.** purchases on account are debited to Purchases.
  **c.** purchase returns are debited to Purchase Returns and Allowances.
  **d.** freight costs are debited to Purchases.

(SO 9) *****13.** In a worksheet, Merchandise Inventory is shown in the following columns:
  **a.** Adjusted trial balance debit and balance sheet debit.
  **b.** Income statement debit and balance sheet debit.
  **c.** Income statement credit and balance sheet debit.
  **d.** Income statement credit and adjusted trial balance debit.

Go to the book's website,
**www.wiley.com/college/weygandt**,
for Additional Self-Study questions.

 The Navigator

# QUESTIONS

**1.** (a)"The steps in the accounting cycle for a merchandising company are different from the accounting cycle for a service company." Do you agree or disagree? (b) Is the measurement of net income for a merchandising company conceptually the same as for a service company? Explain.

**2.** Why is the normal operating cycle for a merchandising company likely to be longer than for a service company?

**3.** (a) How do the components of revenues and expenses differ between merchandising and service companies? (b) Explain the income measurement process in a merchandising company.

**4.** How does income measurement differ between a merchandising and a service company?

**5.** When is cost of goods sold determined in a perpetual inventory system?

**6.** Distinguish between FOB shipping point and FOB destination. Identify the freight terms that will result in a debit to Merchandise Inventory by the purchaser and a debit to Freight-out by the seller.

**7.** Explain the meaning of the credit terms 2/10, n/30.

**8.** Goods costing $2,000 are purchased on account on July 15 with credit terms of 2/10, n/30. On July 18 the company received a $200 credit from the supplier for damaged

goods. Give the journal entry on July 24 to record payment of the balance due within the discount period using a perpetual inventory system.

**9.** Joan Roland believes revenues from credit sales may be earned before they are collected in cash. Do you agree? Explain.

**10.** (a) What is the primary source document for recording (1) cash sales, (2) credit sales. (b) Using XXs for amounts, give the journal entry for each of the transactions in part (a).

**11.** A credit sale is made on July 10 for $900, terms 2/10, n/30. On July 12, $100 of goods are returned for credit. Give the journal entry on July 19 to record the receipt of the balance due within the discount period.

**12.** Explain why the Merchandise Inventory account will usually require adjustment at year-end.

**13.** Prepare the closing entries for the Sales account, assuming a balance of $200,000 and the Cost of Goods Sold account with a $145,000 balance.

**14.** What merchandising account(s) will appear in the post-closing trial balance?

**15.** Reese Co. has sales revenue of $105,000, cost of goods sold of $70,000, and operating expenses of $20,000. What is its gross profit and its gross profit rate?

**16.** Ann Fort Company reports net sales of $800,000, gross profit of $370,000, and net income of $240,000. What are its operating expenses?

**17.** Identify the distinguishing features of an income statement for a merchandising company.

**18.** Identify the sections of a multiple-step income statement that relate to (a) operating activities, and (b) nonoperating activities.

**19.** Distinguish between the types of functional groupings of operating expenses. What problem is created by these groupings?

**20.** How does the single-step form of income statement differ from the multiple-step form?

**21.** Identify the accounts that are added to or deducted from Purchases to determine the cost of goods purchased. For each account, indicate whether it is added or deducted.

**\*22.** Goods costing $3,000 are purchased on account on July 15 with credit terms of 2/10, n/30. On July 18 a $200 credit was received from the supplier for damaged goods. Give the journal entry on July 24 to record payment of the balance due within the discount period, assuming a periodic inventory system.

**\*23.** Indicate the columns of the worksheet in which (a) merchandise inventory and (b) cost of goods sold will be shown.

---

# BRIEF EXERCISES

*Compute missing amounts in determining net income.*

*(SO 1)*

**BE5-1** Presented below are the components in Waegelain Company's income statement. Determine the missing amounts.

| | Sales | Cost of Goods Sold | Gross Profit | Operating Expenses | Net Income |
|---|---|---|---|---|---|
| **(a)** | $75,000 | ? | $30,000 | ? | $10,800 |
| **(b)** | $108,000 | $70,000 | ? | ? | $29,500 |
| **(c)** | ? | $71,900 | $79,600 | $39,500 | ? |

*Journalize perpetual inventory entries.*

*(SO 2, 3)*

**BE5-2** Hollins Company buys merchandise on account from Gordon Company. The selling price of the goods is $780, and the cost of the goods is $520. Both companies use perpetual inventory systems. Journalize the transaction on the books of both companies.

*Journalize sales transactions.*

*(SO 3)*

**BE5-3** Prepare the journal entries to record the following transactions on Monroe Company's books using a perpetual inventory system.

**(a)** On March 2, Monroe Company sold $900,000 of merchandise to Churchill Company, terms 2/10, n/30. The cost of the merchandise sold was $620,000.

**(b)** On March 6, Churchill Company returned $120,000 of the merchandise purchased on March 2 because it was defective. The cost of the returned merchandise was $90,000.

**(c)** On March 12, Monroe Company received the balance due from Churchill Company.

*Journalize purchase transactions.*

*(SO 2)*

**BE5-4** From the information in BE5-3, prepare the journal entries to record these transactions on Churchill Company's books under a perpetual inventory system.

*Prepare adjusting entry for merchandise inventory.*

*(SO 4)*

**BE5-5** At year-end the perpetual inventory records of Garbo Company showed merchandise inventory of $98,000. The company determined, however, that its actual inventory on hand was $96,500. Record the necessary adjusting entry.

*Prepare closing entries for merchandise accounts.*

*(SO 4)*

**BE5-6** Bleeker Company has the following merchandise account balances: Sales $195,000, Sales Discounts $2,000, Cost of Goods Sold $105,000, and Merchandise Inventory $40,000. Prepare the entries to record the closing of these items to Income Summary.

*Prepare sales revenues section of income statement.*

*(SO 5)*

**BE5-7** Maulder Company provides the following information for the month ended October 31, 2008: Sales on credit $280,000, cash sales $100,000, sales discounts $13,000, sales returns and allowances $11,000. Prepare the sales revenues section of the income statement based on this information.

*Contrast presentation in multiple-step and single-step income statements.*

*(SO 5)*

**BE5-8** ⬛▬ Explain where each of the following items would appear on (1) a multiple-step income statement, and on (2) a single-step income statement: **(a)** gain on sale of equipment, **(b)** casualty loss from vandalism, and **(c)** cost of goods sold.

*Compute net sales, gross profit, income from operations, and gross profit rate.*

*(SO 5, 6)*

**BE5-9** Assume Baja Company has the following account balances: Sales $510,000, Sales Returns and Allowances $15,000, Cost of Goods Sold $350,000, Selling Expenses $70,000, and Administrative Expenses $40,000. Compute the following: **(a)** net sales, **(b)** gross profit, **(c)** income from operations, and **(d)** gross profit rate. (Round to one decimal place.)

**BE5-10** Assume that Alshare Company uses a periodic inventory system and has these account balances: Purchases $450,000; Purchase Returns and Allowances $11,000; Purchase Discounts $8,000; and Freight-in $16,000. Determine net purchases and cost of goods purchased.

*Compute net purchases and cost of goods purchased.*
*(SO 7)*

**BE5-11** Assume the same information as in BE5-10 and also that Alshare Company has beginning inventory of $60,000, ending inventory of $90,000, and net sales of $630,000. Determine the amounts to be reported for cost of goods sold and gross profit.

*Compute cost of goods sold and gross profit.*
*(SO 6, 7)*

**\*BE5-12** Prepare the journal entries to record these transactions on Allied Company's books using a periodic inventory system.

*Journalize purchase transactions.*
*(SO, 8)*

**(a)** On March 2, Allied Company purchased $1,000,000 of merchandise from B. Streisand Company, terms 2/10, n/30.
**(b)** On March 6 Allied Company returned $130,000 of the merchandise purchased on March 2 because it was defective.
**(c)** On March 12 Allied Company paid the balance due to B. Streisand Company.

**\*BE5-13** Presented below is the format of the worksheet presented in Appendix 5B.

*Identify worksheet columns for selected accounts.*
*(SO 9)*

| Trial Balance | | Adjustments | | Adjusted Trial Balance | | Income Statement | | Balance Sheet | |
|---|---|---|---|---|---|---|---|---|---|
| Dr. | Cr. | Dr. | Cr. | Dr. | Cr. | Dr. | Cr. | Dr. | Cr. |

Indicate where the following items will appear on the worksheet: **(a)** Cash, **(b)** Merchandise Inventory, **(c)** Sales, **(d)** Cost of Goods Sold.

*Example:*
Cash: Trial balance debit column; Adjusted trial balance debit column; and Balance sheet debit column.

# EXERCISES

**E5-1** Mr. Wellington has prepared the following list of statements about service companies and merchandisers.

*Answer general questions on inventory.*
*(SO 1)*

1. Measuring net income for a merchandising company is conceptually the same as for a service company.
2. For a merchandising company, sales less operating expenses is called gross profit.
3. For a merchandising company, the primary source of revenues is the sale of inventory.
4. Sales salaries is an example of an operating expense.
5. The operating cycle of a merchandising company is the same as that of a service company.
6. In a perpetual inventory system, no detailed inventory records of goods on hand are maintained.
7. In a periodic inventory system, the cost of goods sold is determined only at the end of the accounting period.
8. A periodic inventory system provides better control over inventories than a perpetual system.

**Instructions**
Identify each statement as true or false. If false, indicate how to correct the statement.

**E5-2** Information related to Steffens Co. is presented below.

*Journalize purchase transactions.*
*(SO 2)*

1. On April 5, purchased merchandise from Bryant Company for $25,000 terms 2/10, net/30, FOB shipping point.
2. On April 6 paid freight costs of $900 on merchandise purchased from Bryant.
3. On April 7, purchased equipment on account for $26,000.
4. On April 8, returned damaged merchandise to Bryant Company and was granted a $4,000 credit for returned merchandise.
5. On April 15 paid the amount due to Bryant Company in full.

**Instructions**

(a) Prepare the journal entries to record these transactions on the books of Steffens Co. under a perpetual inventory system.

(b) Assume that Steffens Co. paid the balance due to Bryant Company on May 4 instead of April 15. Prepare the journal entry to record this payment.

*Journalize perpetual inventory entries.*

(SO 2, 3)

**E5-3**   On September 1, Howe Office Supply had an inventory of 30 calculators at a cost of $18 each. The company uses a perpetual inventory system. During September, the following transactions occurred.

Sept.  6   Purchased 80 calculators at $20 each from DeVito Co. for cash.
       9   Paid freight of $80 on calculators purchased from DeVito Co.
      10   Returned 2 calculators to DeVito Co. for $42 credit (including freight) because they did not meet specifications.
      12   Sold 26 calculators costing $21 (including freight) for $31 each to Mega Book Store, terms n/30.
      14   Granted credit of $31 to Mega Book Store for the return of one calculator that was not ordered.
      20   Sold 30 calculators costing $21 for $31 each to Barbara's Card Shop, terms n/30.

**Instructions**

Journalize the September transactions.

*Prepare purchase and sale entries.*

(SO 2, 3)

**E5-4**   On June 10, Meredith Company purchased $8,000 of merchandise from Leinert Company, FOB shipping point, terms 2/10, n/30. Meredith pays the freight costs of $400 on June 11. Damaged goods totaling $300 are returned to Leinert for credit on June 12. The scrap value of these goods is $150. On June 19, Meredith pays Leinert Company in full, less the purchase discount. Both companies use a perpetual inventory system.

**Instructions**

(a) Prepare separate entries for each transaction on the books of Meredith Company.

(b) Prepare separate entries for each transaction for Leinert Company. The merchandise purchased by Meredith on June 10 had cost Leinert $5,000.

*Journalize sales transactions.*

(SO 3)

**E5-5**   Presented below are transactions related to Wheeler Company.

1. On December 3, Wheeler Company sold $500,000 of merchandise to Hashmi Co., terms 2/10, n/30, FOB shipping point. The cost of the merchandise sold was $350,000.
2. On December 8, Hashmi Co. was granted an allowance of $27,000 for merchandise purchased on December 3.
3. On December 13, Wheeler Company received the balance due from Hashmi Co.

**Instructions**

(a) Prepare the journal entries to record these transactions on the books of Wheeler Company using a perpetual inventory system.

(b) Assume that Wheeler Company received the balance due from Hashmi Co. on January 2 of the following year instead of December 13. Prepare the journal entry to record the receipt of payment on January 2.

*Prepare sales revenues section and closing entries.*

(SO 4, 5)

**E5-6**   The adjusted trial balance of Zambrana Company shows the following data pertaining to sales at the end of its fiscal year October 31, 2008: Sales $800,000, Freight-out $16,000, Sales Returns and Allowances $25,000, and Sales Discounts $15,000.

**Instructions**

(a) Prepare the sales revenues section of the income statement.

(b) Prepare separate closing entries for (1) sales, and (2) the contra accounts to sales.

*Prepare adjusting and closing entries.*

(SO 4)

**E5-7**   Peter Kalle Company had the following account balances at year-end: cost of goods sold $60,000; merchandise inventory $15,000; operating expenses $29,000; sales $108,000; sales discounts $1,200; and sales returns and allowances $1,700. A physical count of inventory determines that merchandise inventory on hand is $14,100.

**Instructions**

(a) Prepare the adjusting entry necessary as a result of the physical count.

(b) Prepare closing entries.

**E5-8** Presented below is information related to Rogers Co. for the month of January 2008.

*Prepare adjusting and closing entries.*

*(SO 4)*

| | | | |
|---|---|---|---|
| Ending inventory per | | Salary expense | $ 61,000 |
| perpetual records | $ 21,600 | Sales discounts | 10,000 |
| Ending inventory actually | | Sales returns and allowances | 13,000 |
| on hand | 21,000 | Sales | 350,000 |
| Cost of goods sold | 218,000 | | |
| Freight-out | 7,000 | | |
| Insurance expense | 12,000 | | |
| Rent expense | 20,000 | | |

**Instructions**
**(a)** Prepare the necessary adjusting entry for inventory.
**(b)** Prepare the necessary closing entries.

**E5-9** In its income statement for the year ended December 31, 2008, Pele Company reported the following condensed data.

*Prepare multiple-step and single-step income statements.*

*(SO 5)*

| | | | |
|---|---|---|---|
| Administrative expenses | $ 435,000 | Selling expenses | $ 490,000 |
| Cost of goods sold | 1,289,000 | Loss on sale of equipment | 10,000 |
| Interest expense | 70,000 | Net sales | 2,312,000 |
| Interest revenue | 28,000 | | |

**Instructions**
**(a)** Prepare a multiple-step income statement.
**(b)** Prepare a single-step income statement.

**E5-10** An inexperienced accountant for Blaufuss Company made the following errors in recording merchandising transactions.

*Prepare correcting entries for sales and purchases.*

*(SO 2, 3)*

1. A $175 refund to a customer for faulty merchandise was debited to Sales $175 and credited to Cash $175.
2. A $180 credit purchase of supplies was debited to Merchandise Inventory $180 and credited to Cash $180.
3. A $110 sales discount was debited to Sales.
4. A cash payment of $20 for freight on merchandise purchases was debited to Freight-out $200 and credited to Cash $200.

**Instructions**
Prepare separate correcting entries for each error, assuming that the incorrect entry is not reversed. (Omit explanations.)

**E5-11** In 2008, Walter Payton Company had net sales of $900,000 and cost of goods sold of $540,000. Operating expenses were $230,000, and interest expense was $11,000. Payton prepares a multiple-step income statement.

*Compute various income measures.*

*(SO 5, 6)*

**Instructions**
**(a)** Compute Payton's gross profit.
**(b)** Compute the gross profit rate. Why is this rate computed by financial statement users?
**(c)** What is Payton's income from operations and net income?
**(d)** If Payton prepared a single-step income statement, what amount would it report for net income?
**(e)** In what section of its classified balance sheet should Payton report merchandise inventory?

**E5-12** Presented below is financial information for two different companies.

*Compute missing amounts and compute gross profit rate.*

*(SO 5, 6)*

| | Nam Company | Mayo Company |
|---|---|---|
| Sales | $90,000 | (d) |
| Sales returns | (a) | $ 5,000 |
| Net sales | 84,000 | 100,000 |
| Cost of goods sold | 56,000 | (e) |
| Gross profit | (b) | 41,500 |
| Operating expenses | 15,000 | (f) |
| Net income | (c) | 15,000 |

**Instructions**
(a) Determine the missing amounts on page 229.
(b) Determine the gross profit rates. (Round to one decimal place.)

*Prepare cost of goods sold section.*
*(SO 7)*

**E5-13** The trial balance of G. Durler Company at the end of its fiscal year, August 31, 2008, includes these accounts: Merchandise Inventory $17,200; Purchases $149,000; Sales $190,000; Freight-in $4,000; Sales Returns and Allowances $3,000; Freight-out $1,000; and Purchase Returns and Allowances $2,000. The ending merchandise inventory is $25,000.

**Instructions**
Prepare a cost of goods sold section for the year ending August 31 (periodic inventory).

*Compute various income statement items.*
*(SO 7)*

**E5-14** On January 1, 2008, Rachael Ray Corporation had merchandise inventory of $50,000. At December 31, 2008, Rachael Ray had the following account balances.

| | |
|---|---:|
| Freight-in | $ 4,000 |
| Purchases | 500,000 |
| Purchase discounts | 6,000 |
| Purchase returns and allowances | 2,000 |
| Sales | 800,000 |
| Sales discounts | 5,000 |
| Sales returns and allowances | 10,000 |

At December 31, 2008, Rachael Ray determines that its ending inventory is $60,000.

**Instructions**
(a) Compute Rachael Ray's 2008 gross profit.
(b) Compute Rachael Ray's 2008 operating expenses if net income is $130,000 and there are no nonoperating activities.

*Prepare cost of goods sold sections.*
*(SO 7)*

**E5-15** Below is a series of cost of goods sold sections for companies B, F, L, and R.

| | **B** | **F** | **L** | **R** |
|---|---:|---:|---:|---:|
| Beginning inventory | $ 150 | $ 70 | $1,000 | $ (j) |
| Purchases | 1,600 | 1,080 | (g) | 43,590 |
| Purchase returns and allowances | 40 | (d) | 290 | (k) |
| Net purchases | (a) | 1,030 | 6,210 | 41,090 |
| Freight-in | 110 | (e) | (h) | 2,240 |
| Cost of goods purchased | (b) | 1,280 | 7,940 | (l) |
| Cost of goods available for sale | 1,820 | 1,350 | (i) | 49,530 |
| Ending inventory | 310 | (f) | 1,450 | 6,230 |
| Cost of goods sold | (c) | 1,230 | 7,490 | 43,300 |

**Instructions**
Fill in the lettered blanks to complete the cost of goods sold sections.

*Journalize purchase transactions.*
*(SO 8)*

**\*E5-16** This information relates to Martinez Co.

1. On April 5 purchased merchandise from D. Norlan Company for $20,000, terms 2/10, net/30, FOB shipping point.
2. On April 6 paid freight costs of $900 on merchandise purchased from D. Norlan Company.
3. On April 7 purchased equipment on account for $26,000.
4. On April 8 returned some of April 5 merchandise to D. Norlan Company which cost $2,800.
5. On April 15 paid the amount due to D. Norlan Company in full.

**Instructions**
(a) Prepare the journal entries to record these transactions on the books of Martinez Co. using a periodic inventory system.
(b) Assume that Martinez Co. paid the balance due to D. Norlan Company on May 4 instead of April 15. Prepare the journal entry to record this payment.

*Journalize purchase transactions.*
*(SO 8)*

**\*E5-17** Presented below and on page 231 is information related to Chevalier Co.

1. On April 5, purchased merchandise from Paris Company for $22,000, terms 2/10, net/30, FOB shipping point.

2. On April 6, paid freight costs of $800 on merchandise purchased from Paris.
3. On April 7, purchased equipment on account from Wayne Higley Mfg. Co. for $26,000.
4. On April 8, returned damaged merchandise to Paris Company and was granted a $4,000 allowance.
5. On April 15, paid the amount due to Paris Company in full.

**Instructions**
(a) Prepare the journal entries to record these transactions on the books of Chevalier Co. using a periodic inventory system.
(b) Assume that Chevalier Co. paid the balance due to Paris Company on May 4 instead of April 15. Prepare the journal entry to record this payment.

**\*E5-18**    Presented below are selected accounts for Carpenter Company as reported in the worksheet at the end of May 2008.

*Complete worksheet.*
*(SO 9)*

| Accounts | Adjusted Trial Balance | | Income Statement | | Balance Sheet | |
|---|---|---|---|---|---|---|
| | Dr. | Cr. | Dr. | Cr. | Dr. | Cr. |
| Cash | 9,000 | | | | | |
| Merchandise Inventory | 76,000 | | | | | |
| Sales | | 450,000 | | | | |
| Sales Returns and Allowances | 10,000 | | | | | |
| Sales Discounts | 9,000 | | | | | |
| Cost of Goods Sold | 300,000 | | | | | |

**Instructions**
Complete the worksheet by extending amounts reported in the adjusted trial balance to the appropriate columns in the work sheet. Do not total individual columns.

**\*E5-19**    The trial balance columns of the worksheet for Green Company at June 30, 2008, are as follows.

*Prepare a worksheet.*
*(SO 9)*

### GREEN COMPANY
Worksheet
For the Month Ended June 30, 2008

| | Trial Balance | |
|---|---|---|
| Accounts | Debit | Credit |
| Cash | $ 2,320 | |
| Accounts Receivable | 2,440 | |
| Merchandise Inventory | 11,640 | |
| Accounts Payable | | $ 1,120 |
| Common Stock | | 3,000 |
| Retained Earnings | | 600 |
| Sales | | 42,400 |
| Cost of Goods Sold | 20,560 | |
| Operating Expenses | 10,160 | |
| | $47,120 | $47,120 |

Other data:
Operating expenses incurred on account which have not yet been recorded total $1,500.

**Instructions**
Enter the trial balance on a worksheet and complete the worksheet.

## EXERCISES: SET B

Visit the book's website at **www.wiley.com/college/weygandt**, and choose the Student Companion site, to access Exercise Set B.

*Journalize purchase and sales transactions under a perpetual inventory system.*

(SO 2, 3)

**P5-1A** Sansomite Co. distributes suitcases to retail stores and extends credit terms of 1/10, n/30 to all of its customers. At the end of June, Sansomite's inventory consisted of 40 suitcases purchased at $30 each. During the month of July the following merchandising transactions occurred.

July 1 Purchased 60 suitcases on account for $30 each from Trunk Manufacturers, FOB destination, terms 2/10, n/30. The appropriate party also made a cash payment of $100 for freight on this date.

3 Sold 40 suitcases on account to Satchel World for $50 each.

9 Paid Trunk Manufacturers in full.

12 Received payment in full from Satchel World.

17 Sold 30 suitcases on account to The Going Concern for $50 each.

18 Purchased 60 suitcases on account for $1,700 from Kingman Manufacturers, FOB shipping point, terms 1/10, n/30. The appropriate party also made a cash payment of $100 for freight on this date.

20 Received $300 credit (including freight) for 10 suitcases returned to Kingman Manufacturers.

21 Received payment in full from The Going Concern.

22 Sold 45 suitcases on account to Fly-By-Night for $50 each.

30 Paid Kingman Manufacturers in full.

31 Granted Fly-By-Night $200 credit for 4 suitcases returned costing $120.

Sansomite's chart of accounts includes the following: No. 101 Cash, No. 112 Accounts Receivable, No. 120 Merchandise Inventory, No. 201 Accounts Payable, No. 401 Sales, No. 412 Sales Returns and Allowances, No. 414 Sales Discounts, No. 505 Cost of Goods Sold.

**Instructions**

Journalize the transactions for the month of July for Sansomite using a perpetual inventory system.

*Journalize, post, and prepare a partial income statement.*

(SO 2, 3, 5, 6)

**P5-2A** Olaf Distributing Company completed the following merchandising transactions in the month of April. At the beginning of April, the ledger of Olaf showed Cash of $9,000 and Common Stock of $9,000.

Apr. 2 Purchased merchandise on account from Dakota Supply Co. $6,900, terms 1/10, n/30.

4 Sold merchandise on account $5,500, FOB destination, terms 1/10, n/30. The cost of the merchandise sold was $4,100.

5 Paid $240 freight on April 4 sale.

6 Received credit from Dakota Supply Co. for merchandise returned $500.

11 Paid Dakota Supply Co. in full, less discount.

13 Received collections in full, less discounts, from customers billed on April 4.

14 Purchased merchandise for cash $3,800.

16 Received refund from supplier for returned goods on cash purchase of April 14, $500.

18 Purchased merchandise from Skywalker Distributors $4,500, FOB shipping point, terms 2/10, n/30.

20 Paid freight on April 18 purchase $100.

23 Sold merchandise for cash $6,400. The merchandise sold had a cost of $5,120.

26 Purchased merchandise for cash $2,300.

27 Paid Skywalker Distributors in full, less discount.

29 Made refunds to cash customers for defective merchandise $90. The returned merchandise had a scrap value of $30.

30 Sold merchandise on account $3,700, terms n/30. The cost of the merchandise sold was $2,800.

Olaf Company's chart of accounts includes the following: No. 101 Cash, No. 112 Accounts Receivable, No. 120 Merchandise Inventory, No. 201 Accounts Payable, No. 311 Common Stock, No. 401 Sales, No. 412 Sales Returns and Allowances, No. 414 Sales Discounts, No. 505 Cost of Goods Sold, and No. 644 Freight-out.

**Instructions**

**(a)** Journalize the transactions using a perpetual inventory system.

**(b)** Enter the beginning cash and common stock balances, and post the transactions. (Use J1 for the journal reference.)

*(c) Gross profit $3,465*

**(c)** Prepare the income statement through gross profit for the month of April 2008.

**P5-3A**    Maine Department Store is located near the Village Shopping Mall. At the end of the company's fiscal year on December 31, 2008, the following accounts appeared in two of its trial balances.

*Prepare financial statements and adjusting and closing entries.*

*(SO 4, 5)*

| | Unadjusted | Adjusted | | Unadjusted | Adjusted |
|---|---|---|---|---|---|
| Accounts Payable | $ 79,300 | $ 79,300 | Interest Revenue | $ 4,000 | $ 4,000 |
| Accounts Receivable | 50,300 | 50,300 | Merchandise Inventory | 75,000 | 75,000 |
| Accumulated Depr.—Building | 42,100 | 52,500 | Mortgage Payable | 80,000 | 80,000 |
| Accumulated Depr.—Equipment | 29,600 | 42,900 | Office Salaries Expense | 32,000 | 32,000 |
| Building | 190,000 | 190,000 | Prepaid Insurance | 9,600 | 2,400 |
| Cash | 23,800 | 23,800 | Property Tax Expense | | 4,800 |
| Common Stock | 116,600 | 116,600 | Property Taxes Payable | | 4,800 |
| Cost of Goods Sold | 412,700 | 412,700 | Retained Earnings | 60,000 | 60,000 |
| Depr. Expense—Building | | 10,400 | Sales Salaries Expense | 76,000 | 76,000 |
| Depr. Expense—Equipment | | 13,300 | Sales | 628,000 | 628,000 |
| Dividends | 28,000 | 28,000 | Sales Commissions Expense | 10,200 | 14,500 |
| Equipment | 110,000 | 110,000 | Sales Commissions Payable | | 4,300 |
| Insurance Expense | | 7,200 | Sales Returns and Allowances | 8,000 | 8,000 |
| Interest Expense | 3,000 | 11,000 | Utilities Expense | 11,000 | 12,000 |
| Interest Payable | | 8,000 | Utilities Expense Payable | | 1,000 |

Analysis reveals the following additional data.

1. Insurance expense and utilities expense are 60% selling and 40% administrative.
2. $20,000 of the mortgage payable is due for payment next year.
3. Depreciation on the building and property tax expense are administrative expenses; depreciation on the equipment is a selling expense.

**Instructions**
**(a)** Prepare a multiple-step income statement, a retained earnings statement, and a classified balance sheet.
**(b)** Journalize the adjusting entries that were made.
**(c)** Journalize the closing entries that are necessary.

*(a)* Net income $30,100
Retained earnings $62,100
Total assets $356,100

**P5-4A**    J. Hafner, a former professional tennis star, operates Hafner's Tennis Shop at the Miller Lake Resort. At the beginning of the current season, the ledger of Hafner's Tennis Shop showed Cash $2,500, Merchandise Inventory $1,700, and Common Stock $4,200. The following transactions were completed during April.

*Journalize, post, and prepare a trial balance.*

*(SO 2, 3, 4)*

Apr.  4    Purchased racquets and balls from Wellman Co. $840, FOB shipping point, terms 2/10, n/30.
    6    Paid freight on purchase from Wellman Co. $40.
    8    Sold merchandise to members $1,150, terms n/30. The merchandise sold had a cost of $790.
    10    Received credit of $40 from Wellman Co. for a damaged racquet that was returned.
    11    Purchased tennis shoes from Venus Sports for cash, $420.
    13    Paid Wellman Co. in full.
    14    Purchased tennis shirts and shorts from Serena's Sportswear $900, FOB shipping point, terms 3/10, n/60.
    15    Received cash refund of $50 from Venus Sports for damaged merchandise that was returned.
    17    Paid freight on Serena's Sportswear purchase $30.
    18    Sold merchandise to members $810, terms n/30. The cost of the merchandise sold was $530.
    20    Received $500 in cash from members in settlement of their accounts.
    21    Paid Serena's Sportswear in full.
    27    Granted an allowance of $30 to members for tennis clothing that did not fit properly.
    30    Received cash payments on account from members, $660.

The chart of accounts for the tennis shop includes the following: No. 101 Cash, No. 112 Accounts Receivable, No. 120 Merchandise Inventory, No. 201 Accounts Payable, No. 311 Common Stock, No. 401 Sales, No. 412 Sales Returns and Allowances, No. 505 Cost of Goods Sold.

**Instructions**

(a) Journalize the April transactions using a perpetual inventory system.

(b) Enter the beginning balances in the ledger accounts and post the April transactions. (Use J1 for the journal reference.)

(c) Prepare a trial balance on April 30, 2008.

*(c) Total debits $6,160*

*Determine cost of goods sold and gross profit under periodic approach.*

*(SO 6, 7)*

**P5-5A** At the end of Gordman Department Store's fiscal year on December 31, 2008, these accounts appeared in its adjusted trial balance.

| | |
|---|---|
| Freight-in | $5,600 |
| Merchandise Inventory | 40,500 |
| Purchases | 447,000 |
| Purchase Discounts | 12,000 |
| Purchase Returns and Allowances | 6,400 |
| Sales | 718,000 |
| Sales Returns and Allowances | 8,000 |

Additional facts:

1. Merchandise inventory on December 31, 2008, is $75,000.
2. Note that Gordman Department Store uses a periodic system.

**Instructions**

*Gross profit $310,300*

Prepare an income statement through gross profit for the year ended December 31, 2008.

*Calculate missing amounts and assess profitability.*

*(SO 6, 7)*

**P5-6A** Kristen Montana operates a retail clothing operation. She purchases all merchandise inventory on credit and uses a periodic inventory system. The accounts payable account is used for recording inventory purchases only; all other current liabilities are accrued in separate accounts. You are provided with the following selected information for the fiscal years 2005, 2006, 2007, and 2008.

| | **2005** | **2006** | **2007** | **2008** |
|---|---|---|---|---|
| Inventory (ending) | $13,000 | $11,300 | $14,700 | $12,200 |
| Accounts payable (ending) | 20,000 | | | |
| Sales | | 225,700 | 227,600 | 219,500 |
| Purchases of merchandise inventory on account | | 146,000 | 145,000 | 129,000 |
| Cash payments to suppliers | | 135,000 | 161,000 | 127,000 |

**Instructions**

*(a) 2007 $141,600*

(a) Calculate cost of goods sold for each of the 2006, 2007, and 2008 fiscal years.

(b) Calculate the gross profit for each of the 2006, 2007, and 2008 fiscal years.

*(c) 2007 Ending accts payable $15,000*

(c) Calculate the ending balance of accounts payable for each of the 2006, 2007, and 2008 fiscal years.

(d) Sales declined in fiscal 2008. Does that mean that profitability, as measured by the gross profit rate, necessarily also declined? Explain, calculating the gross profit rate for each fiscal year to help support your answer. (Round to one decimal place.)

*Journalize, post, and prepare trial balance and partial income statement using periodic approach.*

*(SO 7, 8)*

**GLS**

**\*P5-7A** At the beginning of the current season, the ledger of Village Tennis Shop showed Cash $2,500; Merchandise Inventory $1,700; and Common Stock $4,200. The following transactions were completed during April.

Apr. 4 Purchased racquets and balls from Denton Co. $740, terms 3/10, n/30.
6 Paid freight on Denton Co. purchase $60.
8 Sold merchandise to members $900, terms n/30.
10 Received credit of $40 from Denton Co. for a damaged racquet that was returned.
11 Purchased tennis shoes from Newbee Sports for cash $300.
13 Paid Denton Co. in full.
14 Purchased tennis shirts and shorts from Venus's Sportswear $600, terms 2/10, n/60.
15 Received cash refund of $50 from Newbee Sports for damaged merchandise that was returned.
17 Paid freight on Venus's Sportswear purchase $30.
18 Sold merchandise to members $1,000, terms n/30.
20 Received $500 in cash from members in settlement of their accounts.
21 Paid Venus's Sportswear in full.
27 Granted an allowance of $30 to members for tennis clothing that did not fit properly.
30 Received cash payments on account from members $500.

The chart of accounts for the tennis shop includes Cash; Accounts Receivable; Merchandise Inventory; Accounts Payable; Common Stock; Sales; Sales Returns and Allowances; Purchases; Purchase Returns and Allowances; Purchase Discounts; and Freight-in.

**Instructions**

(a) Journalize the April transactions using a periodic inventory system.

(b) Using T accounts, enter the beginning balances in the ledger accounts and post the April transactions.

(c) Prepare a trial balance on April 30, 2008.

(d) Prepare an income statement through gross profit, assuming merchandise inventory on hand at April 30 is $2,296.

*(c) Tot. trial balance $6,223*

*(d) Gross profit $ 859*

**\*P5-8A**    The trial balance of Terry Manning Fashion Center contained the following accounts at November 30, the end of the company's fiscal year.

*Complete accounting cycle beginning with a worksheet.*

*(SO 4, 5, 6, 9)*

## TERRY MANNING FASHION CENTER
### Trial Balance
### November 30, 2008

|  | Debit | Credit |
|---|---|---|
| Cash | $ 28,700 | |
| Accounts Receivable | 30,700 | |
| Merchandise Inventory | 44,700 | |
| Store Supplies | 6,200 | |
| Store Equipment | 85,000 | |
| Accumulated Depreciation—Store Equipment | | $ 22,000 |
| Delivery Equipment | 48,000 | |
| Accumulated Depreciation—Delivery Equipment | | 6,000 |
| Notes Payable | | 51,000 |
| Accounts Payable | | 48,500 |
| Common Stock | | 80,000 |
| Retained Earnings | | 30,000 |
| Dividends | 12,000 | |
| Sales | | 755,200 |
| Sales Returns and Allowances | 8,800 | |
| Cost of Goods Sold | 497,400 | |
| Salaries Expense | 140,000 | |
| Advertising Expense | 24,400 | |
| Utilities Expense | 14,000 | |
| Repair Expense | 12,100 | |
| Delivery Expense | 16,700 | |
| Rent Expense | 24,000 | |
| Totals | $992,700 | $992,700 |

Adjustment data:

1. Store supplies on hand totaled $2,500.
2. Depreciation is $9,000 on the store equipment and $5,000 on the delivery equipment.
3. Interest of $4,080 is accrued on notes payable at November 30.
4. Merchandise inventory actually on hand is $44,400.

Other data:

1. Salaries expense is 70% selling and 30% administrative.
2. Rent expense and utilities expense are 80% selling and 20% administrative.
3. $30,000 of notes payable are due for payment next year.
4. Repair expense is 100% administrative.

**Instructions**

(a) Enter the trial balance on a worksheet, and complete the worksheet.

(b) Prepare a multiple-step income statement and a retained earnings statement for the year, and a classified balance sheet as of November 30, 2008.

(c) Journalize the adjusting entries.

(d) Journalize the closing entries.

(e) Prepare a post-closing trial balance.

*(a) Adj. trial balance $1,010,780*
*Net loss $4,280*

*(b) Gross profit $248,700*
*Total assets $197,300*

## PROBLEMS: SET B

*Journalize purchase and sales transactions under a perpetual inventory system.*

(SO 2, 3)

**P5-1B** Sorvino Book Warehouse distributes hardcover books to retail stores and extends credit terms of 2/10, n/30 to all of its customers. At the end of May, Sorvino's inventory consisted of 240 books purchased at $1,200. During the month of June the following merchandising transactions occurred.

June  1  Purchased 180 books on account for $5 each from Atkinson Publishers, FOB destination, terms 2/10, n/30. The appropriate party also made a cash payment of $50 for the freight on this date.
      3  Sold 120 books on account to Readers-R-Us for $10 each.
      6  Received $50 credit for 10 books returned to Atkinson Publishers.
      9  Paid Atkinson Publishers in full, less discount.
     15  Received payment in full from Readers-R-Us.
     17  Sold 150 books on account to Bargain Books for $10 each.
     20  Purchased 120 books on account for $5 each from Bookem Publishers, FOB destination, terms 2/15, n/30. The appropriate party also made a cash payment of $50 for the freight on this date.
     24  Received payment in full from Bargain Books.
     26  Paid Bookem Publishers in full, less discount.
     28  Sold 110 books on account to Read-n-Weep Bookstore for $10 each.
     30  Granted Read-n-Weep Bookstore $150 credit for 15 books returned costing $75.

Sorvino Book Warehouse's chart of accounts includes the following: No. 101 Cash, No. 112 Accounts Receivable, No. 120 Merchandise Inventory, No. 201 Accounts Payable, No. 401 Sales, No. 412 Sales Returns and Allowances, No. 414 Sales Discounts, No. 505 Cost of Goods Sold.

**Instructions**
Journalize the transactions for the month of June for Sorvino Book Warehouse using a perpetual inventory system.

*Journalize, post, and prepare a partial income statement.*

(SO 2, 3, 5, 6)

**P5-2B** Newson Hardware Store completed the following merchandising transactions in the month of May. At the beginning of May, the ledger of Newson showed Cash of $10,000 and Common Stock of $10,000.

May  1  Purchased merchandise on account from Mesa Wholesale Supply $8,000, terms 2/10, n/30.
     2  Sold merchandise on account $4,000, terms 1/10, n/30. The cost of the merchandise sold was $3,100.
     5  Received credit from Mesa Wholesale Supply for merchandise returned $600.
     9  Received collections in full, less discounts, from customers billed on sales of $4,000 on May 2.
    10  Paid Mesa Wholesale Supply in full, less discount.
    11  Purchased supplies for cash $900.
    12  Purchased merchandise for cash $2,700.
    15  Received refund for poor quality merchandise from supplier on cash purchase $230.
    17  Purchased merchandise from Sherrick Distributors $2,500, FOB shipping point, terms 2/10, n/30.
    19  Paid freight on May 17 purchase $250.
    24  Sold merchandise for cash $6,200. The merchandise sold had a cost of $4,600.
    25  Purchased merchandise from Duffy Inc. $1,000, FOB destination, terms 2/10, n/30.
    27  Paid Sherrick Distributors in full, less discount.
    29  Made refunds to cash customers for defective merchandise $100. The returned merchandise had a scrap value of $20.
    31  Sold merchandise on account $1,600, terms n/30. The cost of the merchandise sold was $1,120.

Newson Hardware's chart of accounts includes the following: No. 101 Cash, No. 112 Accounts Receivable, No. 120 Merchandise Inventory, No. 126 Supplies, No. 201 Accounts Payable, No. 311 Common Stock, No. 401 Sales, No. 412 Sales Returns and Allowances, No. 414 Sales Discounts, No. 505 Cost of Goods Sold.

**Instructions**

**(a)** Journalize the transactions using a perpetual inventory system.

**(b)** Enter the beginning cash and capital balances and post the transactions. (Use J1 for the journal reference.)

**(c)** Prepare an income statement through gross profit for the month of May 2008.

*(c) Gross profit $2,860*

**P5-3B** Huffman Department Store is located in midtown Metropolis. During the past several years, net income has been declining because of suburban shopping centers. At the end of the company's fiscal year on November 30, 2008, the following accounts appeared in two of its trial balances.

*Prepare financial statements and adjusting and closing entries.*

*(SO 4, 5)*

| | Unadjusted | Adjusted | | Unadjusted | Adjusted |
|---|---|---|---|---|---|
| Accounts Payable | $ 47,310 | $ 47,310 | Interest Revenue | $ 5,000 | $ 5,000 |
| Accounts Receivable | 11,770 | 11,770 | Merchandise Inventory | 36,200 | 36,200 |
| Accumulated Depr.—Delivery Equip. | 15,680 | 19,680 | Notes Payable | 46,000 | 46,000 |
| Accumulated Depr.—Store Equip. | 32,300 | 41,800 | Prepaid Insurance | 13,500 | 4,500 |
| Cash | 8,000 | 8,000 | Property Tax Expense | | 3,500 |
| Common Stock | 50,000 | 50,000 | Property Taxes Payable | | 3,500 |
| Cost of Goods Sold | 633,220 | 633,220 | Rent Expense | 19,000 | 19,000 |
| Delivery Expense | 8,200 | 8,200 | Retained Earnings | 34,200 | 34,200 |
| Delivery Equipment | 57,000 | 57,000 | Salaries Expense | 120,000 | 120,000 |
| Depr. Expense—Delivery Equip. | | 4,000 | Sales | 850,000 | 850,000 |
| Depr. Expense—Store Equip. | | 9,500 | Sales Commissions Expense | 8,000 | 14,000 |
| Dividends | 12,000 | 12,000 | Sales Commissions Payable | | 6,000 |
| Insurance Expense | | 9,000 | Sales Returns and Allowances | 10,000 | 10,000 |
| Interest Expense | 8,000 | 8,000 | Store Equip. | 125,000 | 125,000 |
| | | | Utilities Expense | 10,600 | 10,600 |

Analysis reveals the following additional data.

**1.** Salaries expense is 75% selling and 25% administrative.
**2.** Insurance expense is 50% selling and 50% administrative.
**3.** Rent expense, utilities expense, and property tax expense are administrative expenses.
**4.** Notes payable are due in 2011.

**Instructions**

**(a)** Prepare a multiple-step income statement, a retained earnings statement, and a classified balance sheet.

**(b)** Journalize the adjusting entries that were made.

**(c)** Journalize the closing entries that are necessary.

*(a) Net income $5,980*
*Retained earnings $28,180*
*Total assets $180,990*

**P5-4B** Mike Palmer, a former professional golf star, operates Mike's Pro Shop at Bay Golf Course. At the beginning of the current season on April 1, the ledger of Mike's Pro Shop showed Cash $2,500, Merchandise Inventory $3,500, and Common Stock $6,000. The following transactions were completed during April.

*Journalize, post, and prepare a trial balance.*

*(SO 2, 3, 4)*

Apr.  5  Purchased golf bags, clubs, and balls on account from Ramos Co. $1,500, FOB shipping point, terms 2/10, n/60.

   7  Paid freight on Ramos purchase $80.

   9  Received credit from Ramos Co. for merchandise returned $100.

  10  Sold merchandise on account to members $1,100, terms n/30. The merchandise sold had a cost of $810.

  12  Purchased golf shoes, sweaters, and other accessories on account from Penguin Sportswear $860, terms 1/10, n/30.

  14  Paid Ramos Co. in full, less discount.

  17  Received credit from Penguin Sportswear for merchandise returned $60.

  20  Made sales on account to members $700, terms n/30. The cost of the merchandise sold was $490.

  21  Paid Penguin Sportswear in full, less discount.

  27  Granted an allowance to members for clothing that did not fit properly $40.

  30  Received payments on account from members $1,000.

The chart of accounts for the pro shop includes the following: No. 101 Cash, No. 112 Accounts Receivable, No. 120 Merchandise Inventory, No. 201 Accounts Payable, No. 311 Common Stock, No. 401 Sales, No. 412 Sales Returns and Allowances, No. 505 Cost of Goods Sold.

**Instructions**
(a) Journalize the April transactions using a perpetual inventory system.
(b) Enter the beginning balances in the ledger accounts and post the April transactions. (Use J1 for the journal reference.)

*(c) Total debits $7,800*

(c) Prepare a trial balance on April 30, 2008.

*Determine cost of goods sold and gross profit under periodic approach.*

*(SO 6, 7)*

**P5-5B** At the end of Duckwall Department Store's fiscal year on November 30, 2008, these accounts appeared in its adjusted trial balance.

| | |
|---|---:|
| Freight-in | $ 5,060 |
| Merchandise Inventory | 44,360 |
| Purchases | 650,000 |
| Purchase Discounts | 7,000 |
| Purchase Returns and Allowances | 3,000 |
| Sales | 900,000 |
| Sales Returns and Allowances | 20,000 |

Additional facts:
1. Merchandise inventory on November 30, 2008, is $36,200.
2. Note that Duckwall Department Store uses a periodic system.

**Instructions**

*Gross profit $226,780*

Prepare an income statement through gross profit for the year ended November 30, 2008.

*Calculate missing amounts and assess profitability.*

*(SO 6, 7)*

**P5-6B** Howit Inc. operates a retail operation that purchases and sells snowmobiles, amongst other outdoor products. The company purchases all merchandise inventory on credit and uses a periodic inventory system. The accounts payable account is used for recording inventory purchases only; all other current liabilities are accrued in separate accounts. You are provided with the following selected information for the fiscal years 2005 through 2008, inclusive.

| | 2005 | 2006 | 2007 | 2008 |
|---|---:|---:|---:|---:|
| **Income Statement Data** | | | | |
| Sales | | $96,850 | $ (e) | $82,220 |
| Cost of goods sold | | (a) | 25,140 | 25,990 |
| Gross profit | | 69,640 | 61,540 | (i) |
| Operating expenses | | 63,500 | (f) | 52,060 |
| Net income | | $ (b) | $ 4,570 | $ (j) |
| **Balance Sheet Data** | | | | |
| Merchandise inventory | $13,000 | $ (c) | $14,700 | $ (k) |
| Accounts payable | 5,800 | 6,500 | 4,600 | (l) |
| **Additional Information** | | | | |
| Purchases of merchandise inventory on account | | $25,890 | $ (g) | $24,050 |
| Cash payments to suppliers | | (d) | (h) | 24,650 |

**Instructions**

*(c) $11,680*
*(g) $28,160*
*(i) $56,230*

(a) Calculate the missing amounts.
(b) Sales declined over the 3-year fiscal period, 2006–2008. Does that mean that profitability necessarily also declined? Explain, computing the gross profit rate and the profit margin ratio for each fiscal year to help support your answer. (Round to one decimal place.)

**\*P5-7B** At the beginning of the current season on April 1, the ledger of Four Oaks Pro Shop showed Cash $2,500; Merchandise Inventory $3,500; and Common Stock $6,000. These transactions occured during April 2008.

*Journalize, post, and prepare trial balance and partial income statement using periodic approach.*

*(SO 7, 8)*

**GLS**

Apr. 5 Purchased golf bags, clubs, and balls on account from Hardee Co. $2,200, FOB shipping point, terms 2/10, n/60.
  7 Paid freight on Hardee Co. purchases $80.
  9 Received credit from Hardee Co. for merchandise returned $200.
  10 Sold merchandise on account to members $950, terms n/30.
  12 Purchased golf shoes, sweaters, and other accessories on account from Arrow Sportswear $460, terms 1/10, n/30.
  14 Paid Hardee Co. in full.
  17 Received credit from Arrow Sportswear for merchandise returned $60.
  20 Made sales on account to members $1,000, terms n/30.
  21 Paid Arrow Sportswear in full.
  27 Granted credit to members for clothing that did not fit properly $75.
  30 Received payments on account from members $1,100.

The chart of accounts for the pro shop includes Cash; Accounts Receivable, Merchandise Inventory; Accounts Payable; Common Stock; Sales; Sales Returns and Allowances; Purchases; Purchase Returns and Allowances; Purchase Discounts, and Freight-in.

**Instructions**
**(a)** Journalize the April transactions using a periodic inventory system.
**(b)** Using T accounts, enter the beginning balances in the ledger accounts and post the April transactions.
**(c)** Prepare a trial balance on April 30, 2008.
**(d)** Prepare an income statement through gross profit, assuming merchandise inventory on hand at April 30 is $4,524.

*(c) Tot. trial balance $8,254*
*Gross profit $463*

## PROBLEMS: SET C

Visit the book's website at **www.wiley.com/college/weygandt**, and choose the Student Companion site, to access Problem Set C.

## CONTINUING COOKIE CHRONICLE

(*Note:* This is a continuation of the Cookie Chronicle from Chapters 1 through 4.)

**CCC5** Because Natalie has had such a successful first few months, she is considering other opportunities to develop her business. One opportunity is the sale of fine European mixers. The owner of Mixer Deluxe has approached Natalie to become the exclusive U.S. distributor of these fine mixers in her state. The current cost of a mixer is approximately $525 (U.S.), and Natalie would sell each one for $1,050. Natalie comes to you for advice on how to account for these mixers.

*Go to the book's website,*
**www.wiley.com/college/weygandt**,
*to see the completion of this problem.*

# BROADENING YOUR PERSPECTIVE

## FINANCIAL REPORTING AND ANALYSIS

## Financial Reporting Problem
### PepsiCo, Inc.

**BYP5-1** The financial statements of PepsiCo are presented in Appendix A at the end of this textbook.

**Instructions**
Answer the following questions using the Consolidated Statement of Income.

**(a)** What was the percentage change in (1) sales and in (2) net income from 2003 to 2004 and from 2004 to 2005?

**(b)** What was the company's gross profit rate in 2003, 2004, and 2005?

**(c)** What was the company's percentage of net income to net sales in 2003, 2004, and 2005? Comment on any trend in this percentage.

## Comparative Analysis Problem

### PepsiCo, Inc. vs. The Coca-Cola Company

**BYP5-2**    PepsiCo's financial statements are presented in Appendix A. Coca-Cola's financial statements are presented in Appendix B.

**Instructions**
**(a)** Based on the information contained in these financial statements, determine each of the following for each company.
  **(1)** Gross profit for 2005.
  **(2)** Gross profit rate for 2005.
  **(3)** Operating income for 2005.
  **(4)** Percent change in operating income from 2004 to 2005.
**(b)** What conclusions concerning the relative profitability of the two companies can you draw from these data?

## Exploring the Web

**BYP5-3**    No financial decision maker should ever rely solely on the financial information reported in the annual report to make decisions. It is important to keep abreast of financial news. This activity demonstrates how to search for financial news on the Web.

**Address: biz.yahoo.com/i**, or go to **www.wiley.com/college/weygandt**

**Steps:**
**1.** Type in either PepsiCo or Coca-Cola.
**2.** Choose **News**.
**3.** Select an article that sounds interesting to you.

**Instructions**
**(a)** What was the source of the article? (For example, Reuters, Businesswire, PR Newswire.)
**(b)** Assume that you are a personal financial planner and that one of your clients owns stock in the company. Write a brief memo to your client, summarizing the article and explaining the implications of the article for their investment.

## CRITICAL THINKING

## Decision Making Across the Organization

**BYP5-4**    Three years ago, Carrie Dungy and her brother-in-law Luke Barber opened FedCo Department Store. For the first two years, business was good, but the following condensed income statement results for 2007 were disappointing.

**FEDCO DEPARTMENT STORE**
Income Statement
For the Year Ended December 31, 2007

| | | |
|---|---:|---:|
| Net sales | | $700,000 |
| Cost of goods sold | | 553,000 |
| Gross profit | | 147,000 |
| Operating expenses | | |
| Selling expenses | $100,000 | |
| Administrative expenses | 20,000 | 120,000 |
| Net income | | $ 27,000 |

Carrie believes the problem lies in the relatively low gross profit rate (gross profit divided by net sales) of 21%. Luke believes the problem is that operating expenses are too high.

Carrie thinks the gross profit rate can be improved by making both of the following changes. She does not anticipate that these changes will have any effect on operating expenses.

1. Increase average selling prices by 17%. This increase is expected to lower sales volume so that total sales will increase only 6%.
2. Buy merchandise in larger quantities and take all purchase discounts. These changes are expected to increase the gross profit rate by 3 percentage points.

Luke thinks expenses can be cut by making both of the following changes. He feels that these changes will not have any effect on net sales.

1. Cut 2007 sales salaries of $60,000 in half and give sales personnel a commission of 2% of net sales.
2. Reduce store deliveries to one day per week rather than twice a week; this change will reduce 2007 delivery expenses of $30,000 by 40%.

Carrie and Luke come to you for help in deciding the best way to improve net income.

### Instructions

With the class divided into groups, answer the following.

**(a)** Prepare a condensed income statement for 2008 assuming (1) Carrie's changes are implemented and (2) Luke's ideas are adopted.
**(b)** What is your recommendation to Carrie and Luke?
**(c)** Prepare a condensed income statement for 2008 assuming both sets of proposed changes are made.

## Communication Activity

**BYP5-5**  The following situation is in chronological order.

1. Flutie decides to buy a surfboard.
2. He calls Surfing USA Co. to inquire about their surfboards.
3. Two days later he requests Surfing USA Co. to make him a surfboard.
4. Three days later, Surfing USA Co. sends him a purchase order to fill out.
5. He sends back the purchase order.
6. Surfing USA Co. receives the completed purchase order.
7. Surfing USA Co. completes the surfboard.
8. Flutie picks up the surfboard.
9. Surfing USA Co. bills Flutie.
10. Surfing USA Co. receives payment from Flutie.

### Instructions

In a memo to the president of Surfing USA Co., answer the following.

**(a)** When should Surfing USA Co. record the sale?
**(b)** Suppose that with his purchase order, Flutie is required to make a down payment. Would that change your answer?

## Ethics Case

**BYP5-6**  Laura McAntee was just hired as the assistant treasurer of Dorchester Stores. The company is a specialty chain store with nine retail stores concentrated in one metropolitan area. Among other things, the payment of all invoices is centralized in one of the departments Laura will manage. Her primary responsibility is to maintain the company's high credit rating by paying all bills when due and to take advantage of all cash discounts.

Danny Feeney, the former assistant treasurer who has been promoted to treasurer, is training Laura in her new duties. He instructs Laura that she is to continue the practice of preparing all checks "net of discount" and dating the checks the last day of the discount period. "But," Danny continues, "we always hold the checks at least 4 days beyond the discount period before mailing them. That way we get another 4 days of interest on our money. Most of our creditors need our business and don't complain. And, if they scream about our missing the discount period, we blame it on the mail room or the post office. We've only lost one discount out of every hundred we take that way. I think everybody does it. By the way, welcome to our team!"

**Instructions**

**(a)** What are the ethical considerations in this case?

**(b)** Who are the stakeholders that are harmed or benefitted in this situation?

**(c)** Should Laura continue the practice started by Danny? Does she have any choice?

# "All About You" Activity

**BYP5-7**  In the "All About You" feature in this chapter (page 215), you learned about channel stuffing—intentionally shipping customers more goods than they requested in order to boost reported sales. Channel stuffing is just one type of challenge to proper revenue recognition. There are many situations in business where it is difficult to determine the proper period in which to record revenue.

Suppose that after graduation with a degree in finance, you take a job as a manager at a consumer electronics store called Atlantis Electronics. The company has expanded rapidly in order to compete with Best Buy and Circuit City.

**Instructions**

Provide a response to the questions below. In each case provide reasoning to support your conclusion.

**(a)** Atlantis Electronics operates a website. It earns revenue from fees collected from advertisements placed on its site. It recently rented space on its site worth $50,000 to Lester Consumer Goods for a 2-year period. Rather than pay cash, Lester will provide space on Lester's website worth $50,000 to Atlantis for the same 2-year period. Since the amount given and received by each party is equal, no cash will change hands. How should each company record the $50,000 of advertising space? Should Atlantis record $50,000 of revenue for the advertising space given to Lester, or should it recognize no revenue at all?

**(b)** Atlantis has also begun selling gift cards for its electronic products. The cards are available in any dollar amount, and allow the holder of the card to purchase an item for up to 2 years from the time the card is purchased. If the card is not used during that 2 years, it expires. At what point should the revenue from the gift cards be recognized? Should the revenue be recognized at the time the card is sold, or should it be recorded when the card is redeemed?

**(c)** Atlantis sells extended warranties along with many of its electronics. It sells a stereo for $1,000 and a related 3-year extended warranty for $150 to cover maintenance and repair of the stereo. When should the $1,000 be recognized as revenue—at the time of sale, or at the time that the 3-year warranty is completed? At what time should the $150 for the 3-year warranty be recorded as revenue—at the time of sale, equally over the 3-year period, or at the end of the 3-year period?

# Answers to Insight and Accounting Across the Organization Questions

**Morrow Snowboards Improves Its Stock Appeal, p. 199**

Q: If a perpetual system keeps track of inventory on a daily basis, why do companies ever need to do a physical count?

A: *A perpetual system keeps track of all sales and purchases on a continuous basis. This provides a constant record of the number of units in the inventory. However, if employees make errors in recording sales or purchases, the inventory value will not be correct. As a consequence, all companies do a physical count of inventory at least once a year.*

**Should Publishers Have Liberal Return Policies?, p. 205**

Q: If a company expects significant returns, what are the implications for revenue recognition?

A: *If a company expects significant returns, it should make an adjusting entry at the end of the year reducing sales by the estimated amount of sales returns. This is necessary so as not to overstate the amount of revenue recognized in the period.*

**For IBM, What Is Operating?, p. 213**

Q: Why have investors and analysts demanded more accuracy in isolating "Other gains and losses" from operating items?

A: *Greater accuracy in the classification of operating versus nonoperating ("Other gains and losses") items permits investors and analysts to judge the real operating margin, the results of continuing operations, and management's ability to control operating expenses.*

## Authors' Comments on *All About You:* When Is a Sale a Sale?, p. 215

Channel stuffing represents a difficult area for accounting. Some instances are clearly attempts by management to overstate sales. For example, Sunbeam Corporation shipped $1.5 million of barbeque grills to a distributor; all were eventually returned. In many other instances, though, it might be argued that although such sales tactics are *aggressive*, it isn't clear that they are illegal or unethical business practices, or even that they violate good accounting practice. Even in the situation related to The Coca-Cola Company, the SEC concluded that the sales were "technically legitimate" but that Coke had not adequately disclosed the existence of these sales, nor discussed the potential negative impact they might have on future periods.

In general, if the company makes an accurate estimate of the amount of expected returns, then the shipping of excess goods is of little concern. In fact, in some industries, such as magazine and book sales, significant returns are expected and routinely estimated.

## Answer to PepsiCo Review It Question 1, p. 214

For PepsiCo, the 2005 gross profit rate is 56.5% ($18,386 ÷ $32,562). The 2004 gross profit rate was 56.7% ($16,587 ÷ $29,261). This represents a decrease.

## Answers to Self-Study Questions

**1.** c   **2.** a   **3.** c   **4.** b   **5.** c   **6.** d   **7.** b   **8.** c   **9.** d   **10.** d   **11.** a   *12. b   *13. a

# Chapter 6

# Inventories

## STUDY OBJECTIVES

*After studying this chapter, you should be able to:*

1 Describe the steps in determining inventory quantities.

2 Explain the accounting for inventories and apply the inventory cost flow methods.

3 Explain the financial effects of the inventory cost flow assumptions.

4 Explain the lower-of-cost-or-market basis of accounting for inventories.

5 Indicate the effects of inventory errors on the financial statements.

6 Compute and interpret the inventory turnover ratio.

✓ *The Navigator*

## ✓ The Navigator

| | |
|---|---|
| Scan **Study Objectives** | ■ |
| Read **Feature Story** | ■ |
| Read **Preview** | ■ |
| Read text and answer **Before You Go On** p. 249 ■     p. 258 ■     p. 262 ■ | |
| Work **Demonstration Problems** | ■ |
| Review **Summary of Study Objectives** | ■ |
| Answer **Self-Study Questions** | ■ |
| Complete **Assignments** | ■ |

## *Feature Story*

**WHERE IS THAT SPARE BULLDOZER BLADE?**

Let's talk inventory—big, bulldozer-size inventory. Caterpillar Inc. (*www.cat.com*) is the world's largest manufacturer of construction and mining equipment, diesel and natural gas engines, and industrial gas turbines. It sells its products in over 200 countries, making it one of the most successful U.S. exporters. More than 70% of its productive assets are located domestically, and nearly 50% of its sales are foreign.

During the 1980s Caterpillar's profitability suffered, but today it is very successful. A big part of this turnaround can be attributed to effective management of its inventory. Imagine what a bulldozer costs. Now imagine what it costs Caterpillar to have too many bulldozers sitting around in inventory—a situation the company definitely wants to avoid. Conversely, Caterpillar must make sure it has enough inventory to meet demand.

During a recent 7-year period, Caterpillar's sales increased by 100%, while its inventory increased by only 50%. To achieve this dramatic reduction in the amount of resources tied up in inventory, while continuing to meet customers' needs, Caterpillar used a two-pronged approach. First, it completed a factory modernization program, which dramatically increased its production efficiency. The program reduced by 60% the amount of inventory the company processed at any one time. It also reduced by an incredible 75% the time it takes to manufacture a part.

Second, Caterpillar dramatically improved its parts distribution system. It ships more than 100,000 items daily from its 23 distribution centers strategically located around the world (10 *million* square feet of warehouse space—remember, we're talking bulldozers). The company can virtually guarantee that it can get any part to anywhere in the world within 24 hours. Although this network services 550,000 part numbers, Caterpillar is able to ship 99.7% of its orders within hours. In fact, Caterpillar's distribution system is so advanced that it created a subsidiary, Caterpillar Logistics Services, Inc., that warehouses and distributes other companies' products. This subsidiary distributes products as diverse as running shoes, computer software, and auto parts all around the world.

In short, how Caterpillar manages and accounts for its inventory goes a long way in explaining how profitable it is.

✓ *The Navigator*

# *Inside Chapter 6*

In the previous chapter, we discussed the accounting for merchandise inventory using a perpetual inventory system. In this chapter, we explain the methods used to calculate the cost of inventory on hand at the balance sheet date and the cost of goods sold.

The content and organization of this chapter are as follows.

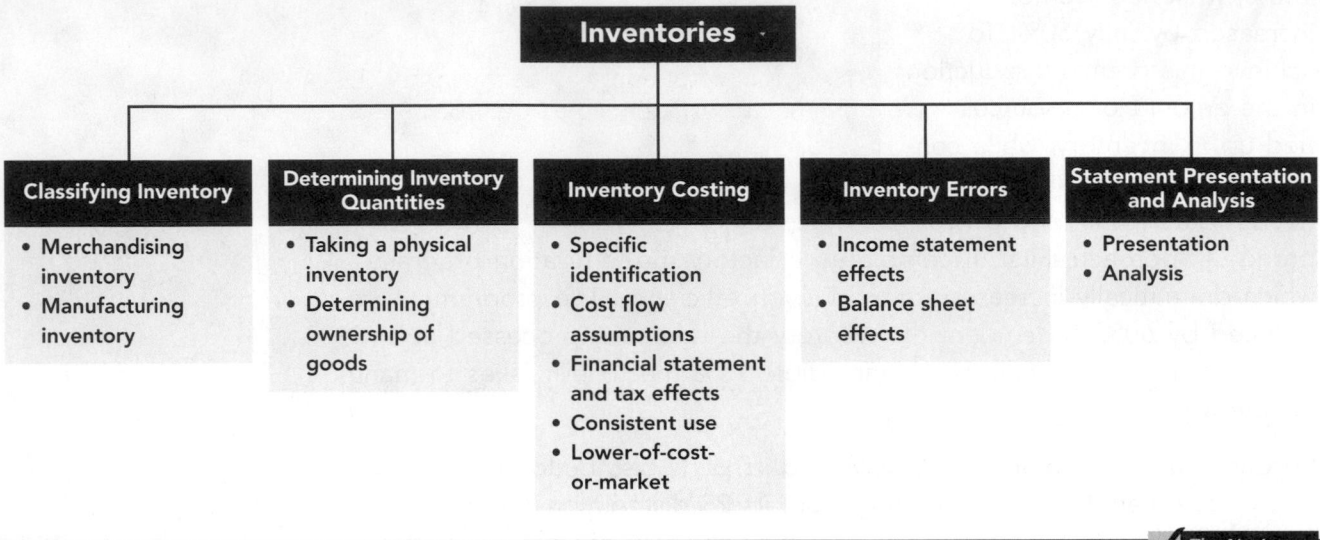

# CLASSIFYING INVENTORY

How a company classifies its inventory depends on whether the firm is a merchandiser or a manufacturer. In a **merchandising** company, such as those described in Chapter 5, inventory consists of many different items. For example, in a grocery store, canned goods, dairy products, meats, and produce are just a few of the inventory items on hand. These items have two common characteristics: (1) They are owned by the company, and (2) they are in a form ready for sale to customers in the ordinary course of business. Thus, merchandisers need only one inventory classification, **merchandise inventory**, to describe the many different items that make up the total inventory.

In a **manufacturing** company, some inventory may not yet be ready for sale. As a result, manufacturers usually classify inventory into three categories: finished goods, work in process, and raw materials. **Finished goods inventory** is manufactured items that are completed and ready for sale. **Work in process** is that portion of manufactured inventory that has been placed into the production process but is not yet complete. **Raw materials** are the basic goods that will be used in production but have not yet been placed into production.

For example, Caterpillar classifies earth-moving tractors completed and ready for sale as **finished goods**. It classifies the tractors on the assembly line in various stages of production as **work in process**. The steel, glass, tires, and other components that are on hand waiting to be used in the production of tractors are identified as **raw materials**.

**By observing the levels and changes in the levels of these three inventory types, financial statement users can gain insight into management's production plans.** For example, low levels of raw materials and high levels of finished goods suggest that management believes it has enough inventory on hand, and production will be slowing down—perhaps in anticipation of a recession. On the other hand, high levels of raw materials and low levels of finished goods probably indicate that management is planning to step up production.

**HELPFUL HINT**
Regardless of the classification, companies report all inventories under Current Assets on the balance sheet.

Many companies have significantly lowered inventory levels and costs using just-in-time (JIT) inventory methods. Under a just-in-time method, companies manufacture or purchase goods just in time for use. Dell is famous for having developed a system for making computers in response to individual customer requests. Even though it makes each computer to meet each customer's particular specifications, Dell is able to assemble the computer and put it on a truck in less than 48 hours. By integrating its information systems with those of its suppliers, Dell reduced its inventories to nearly zero. This is a huge advantage in an industry where products become obsolete nearly overnight.

The accounting concepts discussed in this chapter apply to the inventory classifications of both merchandising and manufacturing companies. Our focus here is on merchandise inventory.

# ACCOUNTING ACROSS THE ORGANIZATION

### How Wal-Mart Tracks Inventory

Wal-Mart improved its inventory control in 2004 with the introduction of electronic product codes (EPCs). Much like bar codes, which tell a retailer the number of boxes of a specific product it has, EPCs go a step farther, helping to distinguish one box of a specific product from another. EPCs use radio frequency identification (RFID) technology, the same technology behind keyless remotes used to unlock car doors.

Companies currently use EPCs to track shipments from supplier to distribution center to store. Other potential uses include help with monitoring product expiration dates and acting quickly on product recalls. Wal-Mart also anticipates faster returns and warranty processing using EPCs. This technology will further assist Wal-Mart managers in their efforts to ensure that their stores have just the right type of inventory, in just the right amount, in just the right place.

**?** Why is inventory control important to managers such as those at Wal-Mart?

# DETERMINING INVENTORY QUANTITIES

No matter whether they are using a periodic or perpetual inventory system, all companies need to determine inventory quantities at the end of the accounting period. When using a perpetual system, companies take a physical inventory for two purposes: The first purpose is to check the accuracy of their perpetual inventory records. The second is to determine the amount of inventory lost due to wasted raw materials, shoplifting, or employee theft.

**STUDY OBJECTIVE 1**

Describe the steps in determining inventory quantities.

Companies using a periodic inventory system must take a physical inventory for two *different* purposes: to determine the inventory on hand at the balance sheet date, and to determine the cost of goods sold for the period.

Determining inventory quantities involves two steps: (1) taking a physical inventory of goods on hand and (2) determining the ownership of goods.

## Taking a Physical Inventory

Taking a physical inventory involves actually counting, weighing, or measuring each kind of inventory on hand/In many companies, taking an inventory is a formidable task. Retailers such as Target, True Value Hardware, or Home Depot have thousands of different inventory items. An inventory count is generally more accurate when goods are not being sold or received during the counting. Consequently, companies often "take inventory" when the business is closed or when business is slow. Many retailers close early on a chosen day in January—after the holiday sales and returns, when inventories are at their lowest level—to count inventory. Recall from Chapter 5 that Wal-Mart had a year-end of January 31. Companies take the physical inventory at the end of the accounting period.

## ETHICS INSIGHT

### "Fill 'Em Up"—With Water, Not Oil

Over the years inventory has played a role in many fraud cases. A classic case involved salad oil. Management of a salad-oil company filled storage tanks mostly with water. Since oil rises to the top, the auditors thought the tanks were full of oil. In addition, management said they had more tanks than they really did—they repainted numbers on the tanks to confuse auditors.

More recently, managers at women's apparel maker Leslie Fay were convicted of falsifying inventory records to boost net income—and consequently to boost management bonuses.

**?** What effect does an overstatement of inventory have on a company's financial statements?

## Determining Ownership of Goods

One challenge in computing inventory quantities is determining what inventory a company owns. To determine ownership of goods, two questions must be answered: Do all of the goods included in the count belong to the company? Does the company own any goods that were not included in the count?

### GOODS IN TRANSIT

A complication in determining ownership is **goods in transit** (on board a truck, train, ship, or plane) at the end of the period. The company may have purchased goods that have not yet been received, or it may have sold goods that have not yet been delivered. To arrive at an accurate count, the company must determine ownership of these goods.

Goods in transit should be included in the inventory of the company that has legal title to the goods. Legal title is determined by the terms of the sale, as shown in Illustration 6-1 and described below.

**1.** When the terms are **FOB (free on board) shipping point**, ownership of the goods passes to the buyer when the public carrier accepts the goods from the seller.

**2.** When the terms are **FOB destination**, ownership of the goods remains with the seller until the goods reach the buyer.

If goods in transit at the statement date are ignored, inventory quantities may be seriously miscounted. Assume, for example, that Hargrove Company has 20,000 units of inventory on hand on December 31. It also has the following goods in transit: (1) sales of 1,500 units shipped December 31 FOB destination, and (2) purchases of 2,500 units shipped FOB shipping point by the seller on December 31. Hargrove has legal title to both the 1,500 units sold and the 2,500 units purchased. If the

---

[1]To estimate the cost of inventory when a physical inventory cannot be taken (e.g., the inventory is destroyed) or when it is inconvenient (e.g., during interim periods), companies can use estimation methods. We discuss these methods—gross profit method and retail inventory method—in Appendix 6B.

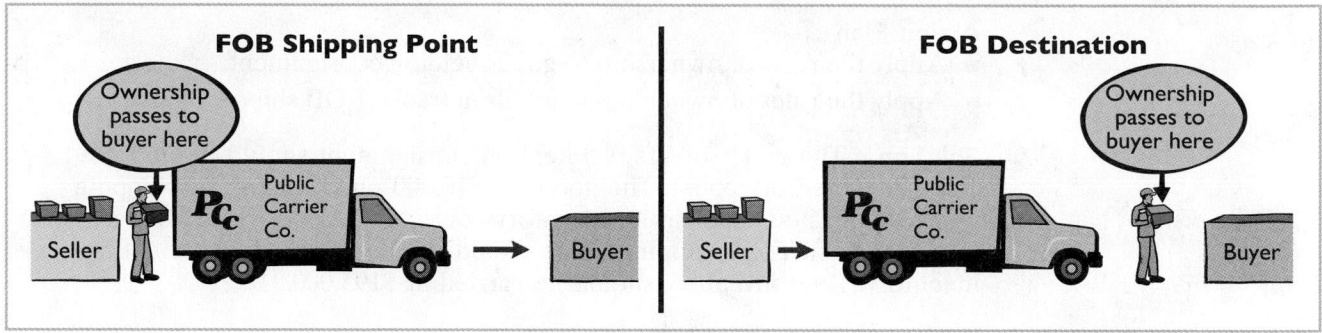

FOB Shipping Point

Ownership passes to buyer here

Seller

P<sub>CC</sub> Public Carrier Co.

Buyer

FOB Destination

Ownership passes to buyer here

Seller

P<sub>CC</sub> Public Carrier Co.

Buyer

**Illustration 6-1**
Terms of sale

company ignores the units in transit, it would understate inventory quantities by 4,000 units (1,500 + 2,500).

As we will see later in the chapter, inaccurate inventory counts affect not only the inventory amount shown on the balance sheet but also the cost of goods sold calculation on the income statement.

### CONSIGNED GOODS

In some lines of business, it is common to hold the goods of other parties and try to sell the goods for them for a fee, but without taking ownership of the goods. These are called consigned goods.

For example, you might have a used car that you would like to sell. If you take the item to a dealer, the dealer might be willing to put the car on its lot and charge you a commission if it is sold. Under this agreement the dealer would not take ownership of the car, which would still belong to you. Therefore, if an inventory count were taken, the car would not be included in the dealer's inventory.

Many car, boat, and antique dealers sell goods on consignment to keep their inventory costs down and to avoid the risk of purchasing an item that they won't be able to sell. Today even some manufacturers are making consignment agreements with their suppliers in order to keep their inventory levels low.

### Before You Go On...

**REVIEW IT**

1. What steps are involved in determining inventory quantities?
2. How is ownership determined for goods in transit at the balance sheet date?
3. Who has title to consigned goods?

**DO IT**

Hasbeen Company completed its inventory count. It arrived at a total inventory value of $200,000. As a new member of Hasbeen's accounting department, you have been given the information listed below. Discuss how this information affects the reported cost of inventory.

1. Hasbeen included in the inventory goods held on consignment for Falls Co., costing $15,000.
2. The company did not include in the count purchased goods of $10,000 which were in transit (terms: FOB shipping point).
3. The company did not include in the count sold inventory with a cost of $12,000 which was in transit (terms: FOB shipping point).

**Action Plan**

- Apply the rules of ownership to goods held on consignment.
- Apply the rules of ownership to goods in transit FOB shipping point.

**Solution**  The goods of $15,000 held on consignment should be deducted from the inventory count. The goods of $10,000 purchased FOB shipping point should be added to the inventory count. Sold goods of $12,000 which were in transit FOB shipping point should not be included in the ending inventory. Thus, inventory should be carried at $195,000.

Related exercise material: *BE6-1, E6-1, and E6-2.*

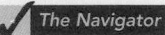 *The Navigator*

# INVENTORY COSTING

**STUDY OBJECTIVE 2**

Explain the accounting for inventories and apply the inventory cost flow methods.

After a company has determined the quantity of units of inventory, it applies unit costs to the quantities to compute the total cost of the inventory and the cost of goods sold. This process can be complicated if a company has purchased inventory items at different times and at different prices.

For example, assume that Crivitz TV Company purchases three identical 46-inch TVs on different dates at costs of $700, $750, and $800. During the year Crivitz sold two sets at $1,200 each. These facts are summarized in Illustration 6-2.

**Illustration 6-2**
Data for inventory costing example

| **Purchases** | | | |
|---|---|---|---|
| February 3 | 1 TV | at | $700 |
| March 5 | 1 TV | at | $750 |
| May 22 | 1 TV | at | $800 |
| **Sales** | | | |
| June 1 | 2 TVs | for | $2,400 ($1,200 × 2) |

Cost of goods sold will differ depending on which two TVs the company sold. For example, it might be $1,450 ($700 + $750), or $1,500 ($700 + $800), or $1,550 ($750 + $800). In this section we discuss alternative costing methods available to Crivitz.

## Specific Identification

If Crivitz sold the TVs it purchased on February 3 and May 22, then its cost of goods sold is $1,500 ($700 + $800), and its ending inventory is $750. If Crivitz can positively identify which particular units it sold and which are still in ending inventory, it can use the **specific identification method** of inventory costing (see Illustration 6-3, page 251). Using this method, companies can accurately determine ending inventory and cost of goods sold.

Specific identification requires that companies keep records of the original cost of each individual inventory item. Historically, specific identification was possible only when a company sold a limited variety of high-unit-cost items that could be identified clearly from the time of purchase through the time of sale. Examples of such products are cars, pianos, or expensive antiques.

Today, bar coding, electronic product codes, and radio frequency identification make it theoretically possible to do specific identification with nearly any type of product. The reality is, however, that this practice is still relatively

**ETHICS NOTE**

A major disadvantage of the specific identification method is that management may be able to manipulate net income. For example, it can boost net income by selling units purchased at a low cost, or reduce net income by selling units purchased at a high cost.

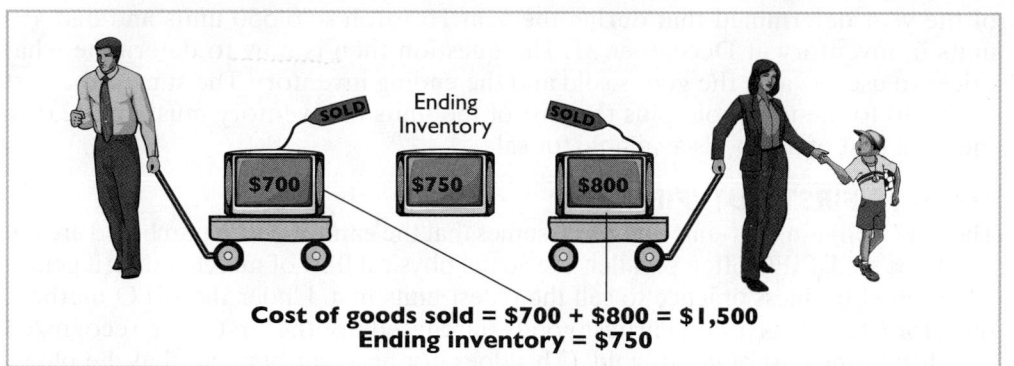

**Illustration 6-3**
Specific identification
method

rare. Instead, rather than keep track of the cost of each particular item sold, most companies make assumptions, called **cost flow assumptions**, about which units were sold.

## Cost Flow Assumptions

Because specific identification is often impractical, other cost flow methods are permitted. These differ from specific identification in that they **assume** flows of costs that may be unrelated to the physical flow of goods. There are three assumed cost flow methods:

**1.** First-in, first-out (FIFO)
**2.** Last-in, first-out (LIFO)
**3.** Average-cost

\There is no accounting requirement that the cost flow assumption be consistent with the physical movement of the goods.\Company management selects the appropriate cost flow method.

To illustrate these three inventory cost flow methods, we will assume that Houston Electronics uses a periodic inventory system and has the information shown in Illustration 6-4 for its Astro condenser.[2] (An appendix to this chapter presents the use of these methods under a perpetual system.)

**Illustration 6-4**
Cost of goods available
for sale

| | HOUSTON ELECTRONICS | | | |
|---|---|---|---|---|
| | Astro Condensers | | | |
| **Date** | **Explanation** | **Units** | **Unit Cost** | **Total Cost** |
| Jan.  1 | Beginning inventory | 100 | $10 | $ 1,000 |
| Apr. 15 | Purchase | 200 | 11 | 2,200 |
| Aug. 24 | Purchase | 300 | 12 | 3,600 |
| Nov. 27 | Purchase | 400 | 13 | 5,200 |
| | Total | 1,000 | | $12,000 |

The company had a total of 1,000 units available that it could have sold during the period. The total cost of these units was $12,000. A physical inventory at the end

---

[2]We have chosen to use the periodic approach for a number of reasons. First, many companies that use a perpetual inventory system use it to keep track of units on hand, but then determine cost of goods sold at the end of the period using one of the three cost flow approaches applied under essentially a periodic approach. In addition, because of the complexity, few companies use average cost on a perpetual basis. Also, most companies that use perpetual LIFO employ dollar-value LIFO, which is presented in more advanced texts. Furthermore, FIFO gives the same results under either perpetual or periodic. And finally, it is easier to demonstrate the cost flow assumptions under the periodic system, which makes it more pedagogically appropriate.

of the year determined that during the year Houston sold 550 units and had 450 units in inventory at December 31. The question then is how to determine what prices to use to value the goods sold and the ending inventory. The sum of the cost allocated to the units sold plus the cost of the units in inventory must be $12,000, the total cost of all goods available for sale.

### FIRST-IN, FIRST-OUT (FIFO)

The **FIFO (first-in, first-out) method** assumes that the **earliest goods** purchased are the first to be sold. FIFO often parallels the actual physical flow of merchandise; it generally is good business practice to sell the oldest units first. Under the FIFO method, therefore, the **costs** of the earliest goods purchased are the first to be recognized in determining cost of goods sold. (This does not necessarily mean that the oldest units *are* sold first, but that the costs of the oldest units are *recognized* first. In a bin of picture hangers at the hardware store, for example, no one really knows, nor would it matter, which hangers are sold first.) Illustration 6-5 shows the allocation of the cost of goods available for sale at Houston Electronics under FIFO.

**Illustration 6-5**
Allocation of costs—FIFO method

**HELPFUL HINT**

Note the sequencing of the allocation: (1) Compute ending inventory, and (2) determine cost of goods sold.

**HELPFUL HINT**

Another way of thinking about the calculation of FIFO ending inventory is the *LISH assumption—* last in still here.

### COST OF GOODS AVAILABLE FOR SALE

| Date | Explanation | Units | Unit Cost | Total Cost |
|---|---|---|---|---|
| Jan. 1 | Beginning inventory | 100 | $10 | $ 1,000 |
| Apr. 15 | Purchase | 200 | 11 | 2,200 |
| Aug. 24 | Purchase | 300 | 12 | 3,600 |
| Nov. 27 | Purchase | 400 | 13 | 5,200 |
| | Total | 1,000 | | $12,000 |

### STEP 1: ENDING INVENTORY

| Date | Units | Unit Cost | Total Cost |
|---|---|---|---|
| Nov. 27 | 400 | $13 | $5,200 |
| Aug. 24 | 50 | 12 | 600 |
| Total | 450 | | $5,800 |

### STEP 2: COST OF GOODS SOLD

| | |
|---|---|
| Cost of goods available for sale | $12,000 |
| Less: Ending inventory | 5,800 |
| Cost of goods sold | $ 6,200 |

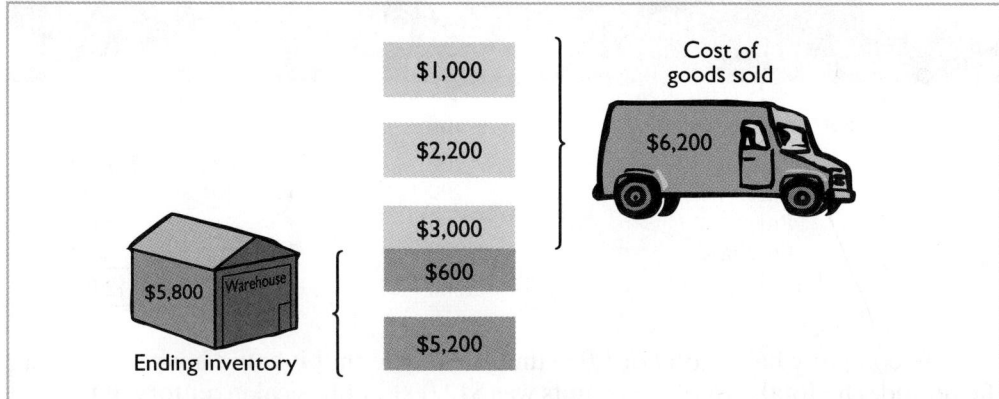

Under FIFO, since it is assumed that the first goods purchased were the first goods sold, ending inventory is based on the prices of the most recent units purchased. That is, **under FIFO, companies obtain the cost of the ending inventory by taking the unit cost of the most recent purchase and working backward until all units of inventory have been costed.** In this example, Houston Electronics prices the 450 units of ending inventory using the *most recent* prices. The last purchase was 400 units at $13 on November 27. The remaining 50 units are priced using the unit cost of the second most recent purchase, $12, on August 24. Next, Houston

Electronics calculates cost of goods sold by subtracting the cost of the units **not sold** (ending inventory) from the cost of all goods available for sale.

Illustration 6-6 demonstrates that companies also can calculate cost of goods sold by pricing the 550 units sold using the prices of the first 550 units acquired. Note that of the 300 units purchased on August 24, only 250 units are assumed sold. This agrees with our calculation of the cost of ending inventory, where 50 of these units were assumed unsold and thus included in ending inventory.

**Illustration 6-6**
Proof of cost of goods sold

| Date | Units | Unit Cost | Total Cost |
|---|---|---|---|
| Jan. 1 | 100 | $10 | $1,000 |
| Apr. 15 | 200 | 11 | 2,200 |
| Aug. 24 | 250 | 12 | 3,000 |
| Total | 550 | | $6,200 |

## LAST-IN, FIRST-OUT (LIFO)

The **LIFO (last-in, first-out) method** assumes that the **latest goods** purchased are the first to be sold. LIFO seldom coincides with the actual physical flow of inventory. (Exceptions include goods stored in piles, such as coal or hay, where goods are removed from the top of the pile as they are sold.) Under the LIFO method, the **costs** of the latest goods purchased are the first to be recognized in determining cost of goods sold. Illustration 6-7 shows the allocation of the cost of goods available for sale at Houston Electronics under LIFO.

**Illustration 6-7**
Allocation of costs—LIFO method

### COST OF GOODS AVAILABLE FOR SALE

| Date | Explanation | Units | Unit Cost | Total Cost |
|---|---|---|---|---|
| Jan. 1 | Beginning inventory | 100 | $10 | $ 1,000 |
| Apr. 15 | Purchase | 200 | 11 | 2,200 |
| Aug. 24 | Purchase | 300 | 12 | 3,600 |
| Nov. 27 | Purchase | 400 | 13 | 5,200 |
| | Total | 1,000 | | $12,000 |

### STEP 1: ENDING INVENTORY

| Date | Units | Unit Cost | Total Cost |
|---|---|---|---|
| Jan. 1 | 100 | $10 | $1,000 |
| Apr. 15 | 200 | 11 | 2,200 |
| Aug. 24 | 150 | 12 | 1,800 |
| Total | 450 | | $5,000 |

### STEP 2: COST OF GOODS SOLD

| | |
|---|---|
| Cost of goods available for sale | $12,000 |
| Less: Ending inventory | 5,000 |
| Cost of goods sold | $ 7,000 |

**HELPFUL HINT**

Another way of thinking about the calculation of LIFO ending inventory is the *FISH assumption*— first in still here.

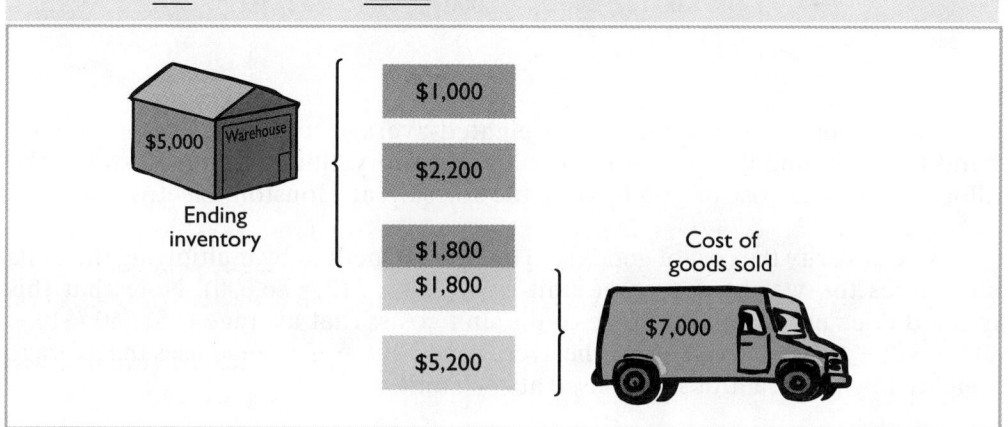

Under LIFO, since it is assumed that the first goods sold were those that were most recently purchased, ending inventory is based on the prices of the oldest units purchased. That is, **under LIFO, companies obtain the cost of the ending inventory by taking the unit cost of the earliest goods available for sale and working forward until all units of inventory have been costed.** In this example, Houston Electronics prices the 450 units of ending inventory using the *earliest* prices. The first purchase was 100 units at $10 in the January 1 beginning inventory. Then 200 units were purchased at $11. The remaining 150 units needed are priced at $12 per unit (August 24 purchase). Next, Houston Electronics calculates cost of goods sold by subtracting the cost of the units **not sold** (ending inventory) from the cost of all goods available for sale.

Illustration 6-8 demonstrates that companies also can calculate cost of goods sold by pricing the 550 units sold using the prices of the last 550 units acquired. Note that of the 300 units purchased on August 24, only 150 units are assumed sold. This agrees with our calculation of the cost of ending inventory, where 150 of these units were assumed unsold and thus included in ending inventory.

**Illustration 6-8**
Proof of cost of goods sold

| Date | Units | Unit Cost | Total Cost |
|------|-------|-----------|------------|
| Nov. 27 | 400 | $13 | $5,200 |
| Aug. 24 | 150 | 12 | 1,800 |
| Total | 550 | | $7,000 |

Under a periodic inventory system, which we are using here, **all goods purchased during the period are assumed to be available for the first sale, regardless of the date of purchase.**

### AVERAGE-COST

The **average-cost method** allocates the cost of goods available for sale on the basis of the **weighted-average unit cost** incurred. The average-cost method assumes that goods are similar in nature. Illustration 6-9 presents the formula and a sample computation of the weighted-average unit cost.

**Illustration 6-9**
Formula for weighted-average unit cost

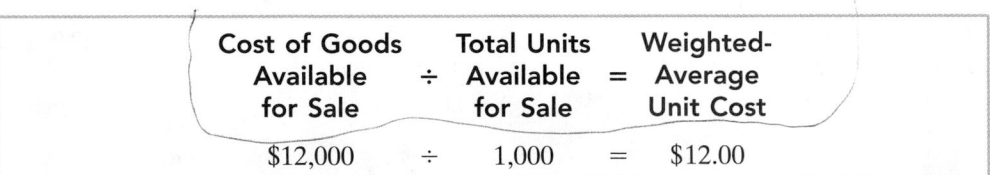

| Cost of Goods Available for Sale | ÷ | Total Units Available for Sale | = | Weighted-Average Unit Cost |
|---|---|---|---|---|
| $12,000 | ÷ | 1,000 | = | $12.00 |

The company then applies the weighted-average unit cost to the units on hand to determine the cost of the ending inventory. Illustration 6-10 shows the allocation of the cost of goods available for sale at Houston Electronics using average cost.

We can verify the cost of goods sold under this method by multiplying the units sold times the weighted-average unit cost (550 × $12 = $6,600). Note that this method does not use the average of the unit costs. That average is $11.50 ($10 + $11 + $12 + $13 = $46; $46 ÷ 4). The average cost method instead uses the average **weighted by** the quantities purchased at each unit cost.

**Illustration 6-10**
Allocation of costs—
average-cost method

## COST OF GOODS AVAILABLE FOR SALE

| Date | Explanation | Units | Unit Cost | Total Cost |
|---|---|---|---|---|
| Jan.  1 | Beginning inventory | 100 | $10 | $ 1,000 |
| Apr. 15 | Purchase | 200 | 11 | 2,200 |
| Aug. 24 | Purchase | 300 | 12 | 3,600 |
| Nov. 27 | Purchase | 400 | 13 | 5,200 |
|  | Total | 1,000 |  | $12,000 |

### STEP 1: ENDING INVENTORY

$12,000 ÷ 1,000 = $12.00

| Units | Unit Cost | Total Cost |
|---|---|---|
| 450 | $12.00 | $5,400 |

### STEP 2: COST OF GOODS SOLD

| | |
|---|---|
| Cost of goods available for sale | $12,000 |
| Less: Ending inventory | 5,400 |
| Cost of goods sold | $ 6,600 |

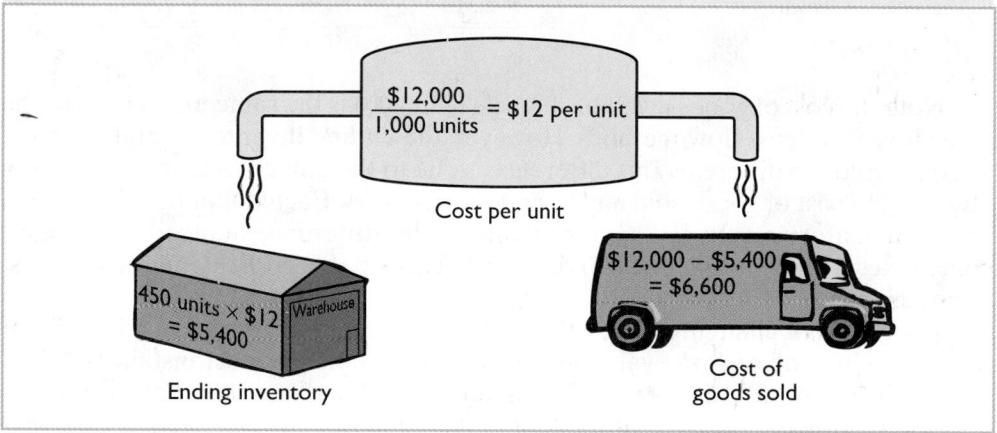

$$\frac{\$12,000}{1,000 \text{ units}} = \$12 \text{ per unit}$$

Cost per unit

450 units × $12 = $5,400    Warehouse

Ending inventory

$12,000 − $5,400 = $6,600

Cost of goods sold

# Financial Statement and Tax Effects of Cost Flow Methods

Each of the three assumed cost flow methods is acceptable for use. For example, Reebok International Ltd. and Wendy's International currently use the FIFO method of inventory costing. Campbell Soup Company, Krogers, and Walgreen Drugs use LIFO for part or all of their inventory. Bristol-Myers Squibb, Starbucks, and Motorola use the average-cost method. In fact, a company may also use more than one cost flow method at the same time. Black & Decker Manufacturing Company, for example, uses LIFO for domestic inventories and FIFO for foreign inventories. Illustration 6-11 (in the margin) shows the use of the three cost flow methods in the 600 largest U.S. companies.

The reasons companies adopt different inventory cost flow methods are varied, but they usually involve one of three factors: (1) income statement effects, (2) balance sheet effects, or (3) tax effects.

## INCOME STATEMENT EFFECTS

To understand why companies might choose a particular cost flow method, let's examine the effects of the different cost flow assumptions on the financial statements of Houston Electronics. The condensed income statements in Illustration 6-12 (page 256) assume that Houston sold its 550 units for $11,500, had operating expenses of $2,000, and is subject to an income tax rate of 30%.

**STUDY OBJECTIVE 3**

Explain the financial effects of the inventory cost flow assumptions.

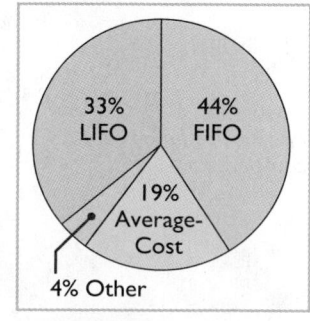

33% LIFO    44% FIFO

19% Average-Cost

4% Other

**Illustration 6-11**
Use of cost flow methods in major U.S. companies

**Illustration 6-12**
Comparative effects of cost flow methods

## HOUSTON ELECTRONICS
### Condensed Income Statements

| | FIFO | LIFO | Average-Cost |
|---|---|---|---|
| Sales | $11,500 | $11,500 | $11,500 |
| Beginning inventory | 1,000 | 1,000 | 1,000 |
| Purchases | 11,000 | 11,000 | 11,000 |
| Cost of goods available for sale | 12,000 | 12,000 | 12,000 |
| Ending inventory | **5,800** | **5,000** | **5,400** |
| Cost of goods sold | 6,200 | 7,000 | 6,600 |
| Gross profit | 5,300 | 4,500 | 4,900 |
| Operating expenses | 2,000 | 2,000 | 2,000 |
| Income before income taxes[3] | 3,300 | 2,500 | 2,900 |
| Income tax expense (30%) | 990 | 750 | 870 |
| Net income | **$ 2,310** | **$ 1,750** | **$ 2,030** |

Note the cost of goods available for sale ($12,000) is the same under each of the three inventory cost flow methods. However, the ending inventories and the costs of goods sold are different. This difference is due to the unit costs that the company allocated to cost of goods sold and to ending inventory. Each dollar of difference in ending inventory results in a corresponding dollar difference in income before income taxes. For Houston, an $800 difference exists between FIFO and LIFO cost of goods sold.

In periods of changing prices, the cost flow assumption can have a significant impact on income and on evaluations based on income. In most instances, prices are rising (inflation). In a period of inflation, FIFO produces a higher net income because the lower unit costs of the first units purchased are matched against revenues. In a period of rising prices (as is the case in the Houston example), FIFO reports the highest net income ($2,310) and LIFO the lowest ($1,750); average cost falls in the middle ($2,030). If prices are falling, the results from the use of FIFO and LIFO are reversed: FIFO will report the lowest net income and LIFO the highest.

To management, higher net income is an advantage: It causes external users to view the company more favorably. In addition, management bonuses, if based on net income, will be higher. Therefore, when prices are rising (which is usually the case), companies tend to prefer FIFO because it results in higher net income.

Some argue that the use of LIFO in a period of inflation enables the company to avoid reporting **paper** (or **phantom**) **profit** as economic gain. To illustrate, assume that Kralik Company buys 200 units of a product at $20 per unit on January 10 and 200 more on December 31 at $24 each. During the year, Kralik sells 200 units at $30 each. Illustration 6-13 shows the results under FIFO and LIFO.

**Illustration 6-13**
Income statement effects compared

| | FIFO | LIFO |
|---|---|---|
| Sales (200 × $30) | $6,000 | $6,000 |
| **Cost of goods sold** | **4,000** (200 × $20) | **4,800** (200 × $24) |
| Gross profit | $2,000 | $1,200 |

---

[3]We are assuming that Houston Electronics is a corporation, and corporations are required to pay income taxes.

Under LIFO, Kralik Company has recovered the current replacement cost ($4,800) of the units sold. Thus, the gross profit in economic terms is real. However, under FIFO, the company has recovered only the January 10 cost ($4,000). To replace the units sold, it must reinvest $800 (200 × $4) of the gross profit. Thus, $800 of the gross profit is said to be phantom or illusory. As a result, reported net income is also overstated in real terms.

## BALANCE SHEET EFFECTS

A major advantage of the FIFO method is that in a period of inflation, the costs allocated to ending inventory will approximate their current cost. For example, for Houston Electronics, 400 of the 450 units in the ending inventory are costed under FIFO at the higher November 27 unit cost of $13.

Conversely, a major shortcoming of the LIFO method is that in a period of inflation, the costs allocated to ending inventory may be significantly understated in terms of current cost. The understatement becomes greater over prolonged periods of inflation if the inventory includes goods purchased in one or more prior accounting periods. For example, Caterpillar has used LIFO for 50 years. Its balance sheet shows ending inventory of $4,675 million. But the inventory's actual current cost if FIFO had been used is $6,799 million.

## TAX EFFECTS

We have seen that both inventory on the balance sheet and net income on the income statement are higher when companies use FIFO in a period of inflation. Yet, many companies have selected LIFO. Why? The reason is that LIFO results in the lowest income taxes (because of lower net income) during times of rising prices. For example, at Houston Electronics, income taxes are $750 under LIFO, compared to $990 under FIFO. The tax savings of $240 makes more cash available for use in the business.

# Using Inventory Cost Flow Methods Consistently

Whatever cost flow method a company chooses, it should use that method consistently from one accounting period to another. This approach is often referred to as the **consistency principle**, which means that a company uses the same accounting principles and methods from year to year. Consistent application enhances the comparability of financial statements over successive time periods. In contrast, using the FIFO method one year and the LIFO method the next year would make it difficult to compare the net incomes of the two years.

Although consistent application is preferred, it does not mean that a company may *never* change its inventory costing method. When a company adopts a different method, it should disclose in the financial statements the change and its effects on net income. Illustration 6-14 shows a typical disclosure, using information from financial statements of Quaker Oats (now a unit of PepsiCo).

| QUAKER OATS |
| :---: |
| Notes to the Financial Statements |

**Note 1:** Effective July 1, the Company adopted the LIFO cost flow assumption for valuing the majority of U.S. Grocery Products inventories. The Company believes that the use of the LIFO method better matches current costs with current revenues. The effect of this change on the current year was to decrease net income by $16.0 million.

**Illustration 6-14**
Disclosure of change in cost flow method

# Lower-of-Cost-or-Market

**STUDY OBJECTIVE 4**

Explain the lower-of-cost-or-market basis of accounting for inventories.

The value of inventory for companies selling high-technology or fashion goods can drop very quickly due to changes in technology or fashions. These circumstances sometimes call for inventory valuation methods other than those presented so far. For example, purchasing managers at Ford decided to make a large purchase of palladium, a precious metal used in vehicle emission devices. They made this purchase because they feared a future shortage. The shortage did not materialize, and by the end of the year the price of palladium had plummeted. Ford's inventory was then worth $1 billion less than its original cost. Do you think Ford's inventory should have been stated at cost, in accordance with the cost principle, or at its lower replacement cost?

As you probably reasoned, this situation requires a departure from the cost basis of accounting. When the value of inventory is lower than its cost, companies can "write down" the inventory to its market value. This is done by valuing the inventory at the **lower-of-cost-or-market (LCM)** in the period in which the price decline occurs. LCM is an example of the accounting concept of **conservatism**, which means that the best choice among accounting alternatives is the method that is least likely to overstate assets and net income.

Companies apply LCM to the items in inventory after they have used one of the cost flow methods (specific identification, FIFO, LIFO, or average cost) to determine cost. Under the LCM basis, market is defined as **current replacement cost**, not selling price. For a merchandising company, market is the cost of purchasing the same goods at the present time from the usual suppliers in the usual quantities. Current replacement cost is used because a decline in the replacement cost of an item usually leads to a decline in the selling price of the item.

To illustrate the application of LCM, assume that Ken Tuckie TV has the following lines of merchandise with costs and market values as indicated. LCM produces the results shown in Illustration 6-15. Note that the amounts shown in the final column are the lower of cost or market amounts for each item.

**Illustration 6-15**
Computation of lower-of-cost-or-market

|  | Cost | Market | Lower-of-Cost-or-Market |
|---|---|---|---|
| Flatscreen TVs | $ 60,000 | $ 55,000 | $ 55,000 |
| Satellite radios | 45,000 | 52,000 | 45,000 |
| DVD recorders | 48,000 | 45,000 | 45,000 |
| DVDs | 15,000 | 14,000 | 14,000 |
| Total inventory | $168,000 | $166,000 | **$159,000** |

## Before You Go On...

**REVIEW IT**

1. What factors should management consider in selecting an inventory cost flow method?

2. What inventory cost flow method does PepsiCo use for its inventories? (*Hint:* You will need to examine the notes for PepsiCo's financial statements.) The answer to this question appears on page 291.

3. Which inventory cost flow method produces the highest net income in a period of rising prices? Which results in the lowest income taxes?

4. When should inventory be reported at a value other than cost?

**DO IT**

The accounting records of Shumway Ag Implement show the following data.

| Beginning inventory | 4,000 units at $ 3 |
|---|---|
| Purchases | 6,000 units at $ 4 |
| Sales | 7,000 units at $12 |

Determine the cost of goods sold during the period under a periodic inventory system using (a) the FIFO method, (b) the LIFO method, and (c) the average-cost method.

### Action Plan
■ Understand the periodic inventory system.
■ Allocate costs between goods sold and goods on hand (ending inventory) for each cost flow method.
■ Compute cost of goods sold for each cost flow method.

### Solution
Cost of goods available for sale = (4,000 × $3) + (6,000 × $4) = $36,000
Ending inventory = 10,000 − 7,000 = 3,000 units
(a) FIFO: $36,000 − (3,000 × $4) = $24,000
(b) LIFO: $36,000 − (3,000 × $3) = 27,000
(c) Average-cost: [(4,000 @ $3) + (6,000 @ $4)] ÷ 10,000
          = ($12,000 + $24,000) ÷ 10,000
          = $3.60 per unit; 7,000 @ $3.60 = $25,200

Related exercise material: *BE6-3, BE6-4, BE6-5, E6-3, E6-4, E6-5, E6-6, E6-7, and E6-8.*

✓ *The Navigator*

# INVENTORY ERRORS

Unfortunately, errors occasionally occur in accounting for inventory. In some cases, errors are caused by failure to count or price the inventory correctly. In other cases, errors occur because companies do not properly recognize the transfer of legal title to goods that are in transit. When errors occur, they affect both the income statement and the balance sheet.

> **STUDY OBJECTIVE 5**
> Indicate the effects of inventory errors on the financial statements.

## Income Statement Effects

As you know, both the beginning and ending inventories appear in the income statement. The ending inventory of one period automatically becomes the beginning inventory of the next period. Thus, inventory errors affect the computation of cost of goods sold and net income in two periods.

The effects on cost of goods sold can be computed by entering incorrect data in the formula in Illustration 6-16 and then substituting the correct data.

| Beginning Inventory | + | Cost of Goods Purchased | − | Ending Inventory | = | Cost of Goods Sold |
|---|---|---|---|---|---|---|

**Illustration 6-16**
Formula for cost of goods sold

If the error understates *beginning* inventory, cost of goods sold will be understated. If the error understates *ending* inventory, cost of goods sold will be overstated. Illustration 6-17 (page 260) shows the effects of inventory errors on the current year's income statement.

**Illustration 6-17**
Effects of inventory errors
on current year's income
statement

| Inventory Error | Cost of Goods Sold | Net Income |
|---|---|---|
| Understate beginning inventory | Understated | Overstated |
| Overstate beginning inventory | Overstated | Understated |
| Understate ending inventory | Overstated | Understated |
| Overstate ending inventory | Understated | Overstated |

**ETHICS NOTE**

Inventory fraud increases during recessions. Such fraud includes pricing inventory at amounts in excess of its actual value, or claiming to have inventory when no inventory exists. Inventory fraud usually overstates ending inventory, thereby understating cost of goods sold and creating higher income.

So far, the effects of inventory errors are fairly straightforward. Now, though, comes the (at first) surprising part: An error in the ending inventory of the current period will have a **reverse effect on net income of the next accounting period.** Illustration 6-18 shows this effect. As you study the illustration, you will see that the reverse effect comes from the fact that understating ending inventory in 2008 results in understating beginning inventory in 2009 and overstating net income in 2009.

Over the two years, though, total net income is correct because the errors **offset each other.** Notice that total income using incorrect data is $35,000 ($22,000 + $13,000), which is the same as the total income of $35,000 ($25,000 + $10,000) using correct data. Also note in this example that an error in the beginning inventory does not result in a corresponding error in the ending inventory for that period. The correctness of the ending inventory depends entirely on the accuracy of taking and costing the inventory at the balance sheet date under the periodic inventory system.

**Illustration 6-18**
Effects of inventory errors
on two years' income
statements

## SAMPLE COMPANY
### Condensed Income Statements

| | 2008 Incorrect | | 2008 Correct | | 2009 Incorrect | | 2009 Correct | |
|---|---|---|---|---|---|---|---|---|
| Sales | | $80,000 | | $80,000 | | $90,000 | | $90,000 |
| Beginning inventory | $20,000 | | $20,000 | | **$12,000** | | **$15,000** | |
| Cost of goods purchased | 40,000 | | 40,000 | | 68,000 | | 68,000 | |
| Cost of goods available for sale | 60,000 | | 60,000 | | 80,000 | | 83,000 | |
| Ending inventory | **12,000** | | **15,000** | | 23,000 | | 23,000 | |
| Cost of goods sold | | 48,000 | | 45,000 | | 57,000 | | 60,000 |
| Gross profit | | 32,000 | | 35,000 | | 33,000 | | 30,000 |
| Operating expenses | | 10,000 | | 10,000 | | 20,000 | | 20,000 |
| Net income | | $22,000 | | $25,000 | | $13,000 | | $10,000 |

$(3,000)
Net income
understated

$3,000
Net income
overstated

**The errors cancel. Thus the combined total
income for the 2-year period is correct.**

## Balance Sheet Effects

Companies can determine the effect of ending inventory errors on the balance sheet by using the basic accounting equation: Assets = Liabilities + Stockholders' equity. Errors in the ending inventory have the effects shown in Illustration 6-19.

| Ending Inventory Error | Assets | Liabilities | Stockholders' Equity |
|---|---|---|---|
| Overstated | Overstated | No effect | Overstated |
| Understated | Understated | No effect | Understated |

Illustration 6-19
Effects of ending inventory errors on balance sheet

# STATEMENT PRESENTATION AND ANALYSIS

## Presentation

As indicated in Chapter 5, inventory is classified as a current asset after receivables in the balance sheet. In a multiple-step income statement, cost of goods sold is subtracted from sales. There also should be disclosure of (1) the major inventory classifications, (2) the basis of accounting (cost, or lower of cost or market), and (3) the costing method (FIFO, LIFO, or average).

Wal-Mart, for example, in its January 31, 2006, balance sheet reported inventories of $32,191 million under current assets. The accompanying notes to the financial statements, as shown in Illustration 6-20, disclosed the following information.

**WAL★MART**

## WAL-MART STORES, INC.
### Notes to the Financial Statements

Illustration 6-20
Inventory disclosures by Wal-Mart

**Note 1. Summary of Significant Accounting Policies**

**Inventories**

The company values inventories at the lower-of-cost-or-market as determined primarily by the retail method of accounting, using the last-in, first-out ("LIFO") method for substantially all merchandise inventories in the United States, except SAM'S CLUB merchandise and merchandise in our distribution warehouses, which is based on cost LIFO method. Inventories of foreign operations are primarily valued by the retail method of accounting, using the first-in, first-out ("FIFO") method. At January 31, 2006 and 2005, our inventories valued at LIFO approximate those inventories as if they were valued at FIFO.

As indicated in this note, Wal-Mart values its inventories at the lower-of-cost-or-market using LIFO and FIFO.

## Analysis

The amount of inventory carried by a company has significant economic consequences. And inventory management is a double-edged sword that requires constant attention. On the one hand, management wants to have a great variety and quantity on hand so that customers have a wide selection and items are always in stock. But such a policy may incur high carrying costs (e.g., investment, storage, insurance, obsolescence, and damage). On the other hand, low inventory levels lead to stockouts and lost sales. Common ratios used to manage and evaluate inventory levels are inventory turnover and a related measure, days in inventory.

Inventory turnover measures the number of times on average the inventory is sold during the period. Its purpose is to measure the liquidity of the inventory. The inventory turnover is computed by dividing cost of goods sold by the average inventory during the period. Unless seasonal factors are significant, average inventory can be computed from the beginning and ending inventory balances. For example, Wal-Mart reported in its 2006 annual report a beginning inventory of $29,762 million, an ending inventory of $32,191 million, and cost of goods sold for the year ended January 31, 2006, of $240,391 million. The inventory turnover formula and computation for Wal-Mart are shown below.

**Illustration 6-21**
Inventory turnover formula and computation for Wal-Mart

| Cost of Goods Sold | ÷ | Average Inventory | = | Inventory Turnover |
|---|---|---|---|---|
| $240,391 | ÷ | $\dfrac{\$29{,}762 + \$32{,}191}{2}$ | = | 7.8 times |

A variant of the inventory turnover ratio is **days in inventory**. This measures the average number of days inventory is held. It is calculated as 365 divided by the inventory turnover ratio. For example, Wal-Mart's inventory turnover of 7.8 times divided into 365 is approximately 47 days. This is the approximate time that it takes a company to sell the inventory once it arrives at the store.

There are typical levels of inventory in every industry. Companies that are able to keep their inventory at lower levels and higher turnovers and still satisfy customer needs are the most successful.

# ACCOUNTING ACROSS THE ORGANIZATION

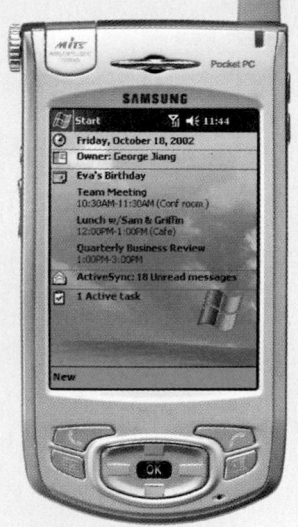

### Samsung Uses a Different Strategy

Demand for cell phones typically falls during the first quarter of each year. It is a widely held principle that a company should cut back its production and inventory levels when it anticipates that demand will decrease. Thus many industry observers were surprised when Samsung Electronics Co. chose to increase production during the first quarter of the year, for the third year in a row.

Why did Samsung do this? Its executives felt that this approach would enable it to stand out against competitors by putting "a slew of new cell phones on shelves next to graying models from its rivals." It is clear that even with just-in-time inventory techniques and highly efficient inventory systems, management still must make many critical strategic decisions regarding inventory.

**Source:** Evan Ramstad, "Samsung to Report Whether Counterintuitive Move Paid Off," *Wall Street Journal*, April 24, 2005, p. B3.

**?** If Samsung isn't successful in selling the units, what steps will it have to take, and how will this show up in its financial statements?

## Before You Go On...

**REVIEW IT**
1. How do inventory errors affect financial statements?
2. What is the purpose of the inventory turnover ratio?
3. What is the relationship between the inventory turnover ratio and average days in inventory?

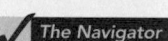 *The Navigator*

 Be sure to read **ALL ABOUT YOU:** *Employee Theft—An Inside Job* on the next page for information on how topics in this chapter apply to you.

## Employee Theft—An Inside Job

Inventory theft is a huge problem for many businesses. Few employees would be as bold as the character in a Johnny Cash song, who while working on an assembly line in Detroit, steals an entire car, one piece at a time, over the course of many years (*www.lyricsdomain.com/10/johnny_cash/one_piece_at_a_time.html*). Nonetheless, at most companies, employees are the primary culprits. While you might think that a free pizza or steak at the end of your shift isn't hurting anybody, the statistics below show that such pilferage really adds up.

Many companies use sophisticated technologies to monitor their customers and employees in order to keep their inventory from walking off. Examples include closed-circuit video cameras and radio frequency identification (RFID). Other companies use techniques that don't rely on technology, such as taking frequent (in some cases daily) inventory counts, having employees keep all personal belongings and bags in a separate changing room, and making surprise checks of employees' bags as they leave. An increasing number of companies are setting up 800 numbers that employees or customers can call to report suspicious behavior, sometimes for a reward.

### ✷ Some Facts

* The National Food Service Security Council estimates that employee theft costs U.S. restaurants $15 billion to $25 billion annually.

* The average supermarket has inventory shrinkage losses of 2.28% of sales, or $224,808 per year. Average net profit is only 1.1% of sales, so inventory shrinkage is twice the level of profits.

* Fear of getting caught and being fired ranks among one of the top reasons employees give, in surveys of reasons why they do not steal from their employer.

* Tips from customers are the No. 1 way that many stores catch thieving employees.

* The average employee caught stealing costs his or her company $1,341, while the average loss from a shoplifting incident is only $207.

### ✷ About the Numbers

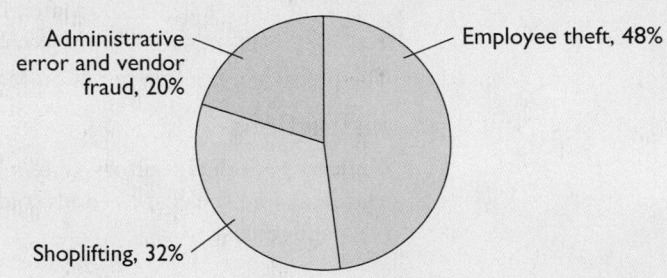

**Where Did the Inventory Go?**

- Administrative error and vendor fraud, 20%
- Employee theft, 48%
- Shoplifting, 32%

**Source:** Data from 2003 National Retail Security Survey, University of Florida.

### ✷ What Do You Think?

Suppose you own a number of wine shops selling mid-level as well as expensive bottled wine. You have been experiencing significant losses from theft at your stores. You suspect that it is a combination of both employee and customer theft. Assuming that it would be cost-effective, would you install video cameras to reduce both employee theft and customer theft?

**YES:** Most employees and customers are honest. However, some will steal if given the opportunity. Management has a responsibility to employ reasonable, cost-effective approaches to safeguard company assets.

**NO:** The use of video technology to monitor employees and customers sends a message of distrust. You run the risk of alienating your employees (who may well figure out a way around the cameras anyway). Cameras might also reduce the welcoming atmosphere for your customers, who might find the cameras offensive.

**Sources:** Bob Ingram, "Shrink Has Shrunk," *Supermarket Business*, September 15, 2000, p. 65; Lisa Bertagnoli, "Wrapping up Shrink," *Restaurants & Institutions*, May 1, 2005, pp. 89–90; Naomi R. Kooker, "Taking Aim at Crime," *Nation's Restaurant News*, May 22, 2000, pp. 114–118.

## Demonstration Problem 1

Gerald D. Englehart Company has the following inventory, purchases, and sales data for the month of March.

| | | | |
|---|---|---|---|
| Inventory: March 1 | | 200 units @ $4.00 | $ 800 |
| Purchases: | | | |
| | March 10 | 500 units @ $4.50 | 2,250 |
| | March 20 | 400 units @ $4.75 | 1,900 |
| | March 30 | 300 units @ $5.00 | 1,500 |
| Sales: | | | |
| | March 15 | 500 units | |
| | March 25 | 400 units | |

The physical inventory count on March 31 shows 500 units on hand.

### Instructions

Under a **periodic inventory system**, determine the cost of inventory on hand at March 31 and the cost of goods sold for March under (a) (FIFO), (b) (LIFO), and (c) average-cost.

## action plan

✔ Compute the cost of inventory under the periodic FIFO method by allocating to the units on hand the **latest costs**.

✔ Compute the cost of inventory under the periodic LIFO method by allocating to the units on hand the **earliest costs**.

✔ Compute the cost of inventory under the periodic average-cost method by allocating to the units on hand a **weighted-average cost**.

### Solution

The cost of goods available for sale is $6,450, as follows.

| | | |
|---|---|---|
| Inventory: | 200 units @ $4.00 | $ 800 |
| Purchases: | | |
| March 10 | 500 units @ $4.50 | 2,250 |
| March 20 | 400 units @ $4.75 | 1,900 |
| March 30 | 300 units @ $5.00 | 1,500 |
| Total cost of goods available for sale | | $6,450 |

Under a **periodic inventory system**, the cost of goods sold under each cost flow method is as follows.

### FIFO Method

Ending inventory:

| Date | Units | Unit Cost | Total Cost | |
|---|---|---|---|---|
| March 30 | 300 | $5.00 | $1,500 | |
| March 20 | 200 | 4.75 | 950 | $2,450 |

Cost of goods sold: $6,450 − $2,450 = $4,000

### LIFO Method

Ending inventory:

| Date | Units | Unit Cost | Total Cost | |
|---|---|---|---|---|
| March 1 | 200 | $4.00 | $ 800 | |
| March 10 | 300 | 4.50 | 1,350 | $2,150 |

Cost of goods sold: $6,450 − $2,150 = $4,300

### Average-Cost Method

Average unit cost: $6,450 ÷ 1,400 = $4.607
Ending inventory: 500 × $4.607 = $2,303.50

Cost of goods sold: $6,450 − $2,303.50 = $4,146.50

# SUMMARY OF STUDY OBJECTIVES

**1 Describe the steps in determining inventory quantities.** The steps are (1) take a physical inventory of goods on hand and (2) determine the ownership of goods in transit or on consignment.

**2 Explain the accounting for inventories and apply the inventory cost flow methods.** The primary basis of accounting for inventories is cost. Cost of goods available for sale includes (a) cost of beginning inventory and (b) cost of goods purchased. The inventory cost flow methods are: specific identification and three assumed cost flow methods—FIFO, LIFO, and average-cost.

**3 Explain the financial effects of the inventory cost flow assumptions.** Companies may allocate the cost of goods available for sale to cost of goods sold and ending inventory by specific identification or by a method based on an assumed cost flow. When prices are rising, the first-in, first-out (FIFO) method results in lower cost of goods sold and higher net income than the other methods. The reverse is true when prices are falling. In the balance sheet, FIFO results in an ending inventory that is closest to current value; inventory under LIFO is the farthest from current value. LIFO results in the lowest income taxes.

**4 Explain the lower-of-cost-or-market basis of accounting for inventories.** Companies may use the lower-of-cost-or-market (LCM) basis when the current replacement cost (market) is less than cost. Under LCM, companies recognize the loss in the period in which the price decline occurs.

**5 Indicate the effects of inventory errors on the financial statements.** *In the income statement of the current year:* (a) An error in beginning inventory will have a reverse effect on net income. (b) An error in ending inventory will have a similar effect on net income. If ending inventory errors are not corrected in the following period, their effect on net income for that period is reversed, and total net income for the two years will be correct.

*In the balance sheet:* Ending inventory errors will have the same effect on total assets and total stockholders' equity and no effect on liabilities.

**6 Compute and interpret the inventory turnover ratio.** The inventory turnover ratio is cost of goods sold divided by average inventory. To convert it to average days in inventory, divide 365 days by the inventory turnover ratio.  ✓ *The Navigator*

# GLOSSARY

**Average-cost method** Inventory costing method that uses the weighted average unit cost to allocate to ending inventory and cost of goods sold the cost of goods available for sale. (p. 254).

**Conservatism** Concept that dictates that when in doubt, choose the method that will be least likely to overstate assets and net income. (p. 258).

**Consigned goods** Goods held for sale by one party (the consignee) although ownership of the goods is retained by another party (the consignor). (p. 249).

**Consistency principle** Dictates that a company use the same accounting principles and methods from year to year. (p. 257).

**Current replacement cost** The current cost to replace an inventory item. (p. 258).

**Days in inventory** Measure of the average number of days inventory is held; calculated as 365 divided by inventory turnover ratio. (p. 262).

**Finished goods inventory** Manufactured items that are completed and ready for sale. (p. 246).

**First-in, first-out (FIFO) method** Inventory costing method that assumes that the costs of the earliest goods purchased are the first to be recognized as cost of goods sold. (p. 252).

**FOB (free on board) destination** Freight terms indicating that ownership of the goods remains with the seller until the goods reach the buyer. (p. 248).

**FOB (free on board) shipping point** Freight terms indicating that ownership of the goods passes to the buyer when the public carrier accepts the goods from the seller. (p. 248).

**Inventory turnover ratio** A ratio that measures the number of times on average the inventory sold during the period; computed by dividing cost of goods sold by the average inventory during the period. (p. 261).

**Just-in-time (JIT) inventory method** Inventory system in which companies manufacture or purchase goods just in time for use. (p. 247).

**Last-in, first-out (LIFO) method** Inventory costing method that assumes the costs of the latest units purchased are the first to be allocated to cost of goods sold. (p. 253).

**Lower-of-cost-or-market (LCM) basis** A basis whereby inventory is stated at the lower of either its cost or its market value as determined by current replacement cost. (p. 258).

**Raw materials** Basic goods that will be used in production but have not yet been placed into production. (p. 246).

**Specific identification method** An actual physical flow costing method in which items still in inventory are specifically costed to arrive at the total cost of the ending inventory. (p. 250).

**Weighted-average unit cost** Average cost that is weighted by the number of units purchased at each unit cost. (p. 254).

**Work in process** That portion of manufactured inventory that has been placed into the production process but is not yet complete. (p. 246).

# APPENDIX 6A Inventory Cost Flow Methods in Perpetual Inventory Systems

**Apply the inventory cost flow methods to perpetual inventory records.**

What inventory cost flow methods do companies employ if they use a perpetual inventory system? Simple—they can use any of the inventory cost flow methods described in the chapter. To illustrate the application of the three assumed cost flow methods (FIFO, LIFO, and average-cost), we will use the data shown in Illustration 6A-1 and in this chapter for Houston Electronic's Astro Condenser.

**Illustration 6A-1**
Inventoriable units and costs

### HOUSTON ELECTRONICS
#### Astro Condensers

| Date | Explanation | Units | Unit Cost | Total Cost | Balance in Units |
|------|-------------|-------|-----------|------------|------------------|
| 1/1 | Beginning inventory | 100 | $10 | $ 1,000 | 100 |
| 4/15 | Purchases | 200 | 11 | 2,200 | 300 |
| 8/24 | Purchases | 300 | 12 | 3,600 | 600 |
| 9/10 | Sale | 550 | | | 50 |
| 11/27 | Purchases | 400 | 13 | 5,200 | 450 |
| | | | | $12,000 | |

## First-In, First-Out (FIFO)

Under FIFO, the company charges to cost of goods sold the cost of the earliest goods on hand **prior to each sale**. Therefore, the cost of goods sold on September 10 consists of the units on hand January 1 and the units purchased April 15 and August 24. Illustration 6A-2 shows the inventory under a FIFO method perpetual system.

**Illustration 6A-2**
Perpetual system—FIFO

| Date | Purchases | Cost of Goods Sold | Balance (in units and cost) |
|------|-----------|--------------------|-----------------------------|
| January 1 | | | (100 @ $10)    $ 1,000 |
| April 15 | (200 @ $11)   $2,200 | | (100 @ $10) <br> (200 @ $11) } $ 3,200 |
| August 24 | (300 @ $12)   $3,600 | | (100 @ $10) <br> (200 @ $11) } $ 6,800 <br> (300 @ $12) |
| September 10 | | (100 @ $10) <br> (200 @ $11) <br> (250 @ $12) <br> $6,200 | ( 50 @ $12)    $ 600 |
| November 27 | (400 @ $13)   $5,200 | | ( 50 @ $12) <br> (400 @ $13) } $5,800 |

**Cost of goods sold**

**Ending inventory**

The ending inventory in this situation is $5,800, and the cost of goods sold is $6,200 [(100 @ $10) + (200 @ $11) + (250 @ $12)].

Compare Illustrations 6-5 (page 252) and 6A-2. You can see that the results under FIFO in a perpetual system are the **same as in a periodic system**. In both cases, the ending inventory is $5,800 and cost of goods sold is $6,200. Regardless of the system, the first costs in are the costs assigned to cost of goods sold.

## Last-In, First-Out (LIFO)

Under the LIFO method using a perpetual system, the company charges to cost of goods sold the cost of the most recent purchase prior to sale. Therefore, the cost of the goods sold on September 10 consists of all the units from the August 24 and April 15 purchases plus 50 of the units in beginning inventory. Illustration 6A-3 shows the computation of the ending inventory under the LIFO method.

**Illustration 6A-3**
Perpetual system—LIFO

| Date | Purchases | Cost of Goods Sold | Balance (in units and cost) | |
|---|---|---|---|---|
| January 1 | | | (100 @ $10) | $1,000 |
| April 15 | (200 @ $11)   $2,200 | | (100 @ $10) (200 @ $11) | $3,200 |
| August 24 | (300 @ $12)   $3,600 | | (100 @ $10) (200 @ $11) (300 @ $12) | $6,800 |
| September 10 | | (300 @ $12) (200 @ $11) ( 50 @ $10) | (50 @ $10) | $ 500 |
| | | **$6,300** | | |
| November 27 | (400 @ $13)   $5,200 | | (50 @ $10) (400 @ $13) | **$5,700** |

> Cost of goods sold
> Ending inventory

The use of LIFO in a perpetual system will usually produce cost allocations that differ from those using LIFO in a periodic system. In a perpetual system, the company allocates the latest units purchased *prior to each sale* to cost of goods sold. In contrast, in a periodic system, the latest units purchased *during the period* are allocated to cost of goods sold. Thus, when a purchase is made after the last sale, the LIFO periodic system will apply this purchase to the previous sale. Compare Illustrations 6-8 (page 254) and 6A-3. Illustration 6-8 shows that the 400 units at $13 purchased on November 27 are applied to the sale of 550 units on September 10. Under the LIFO perpetual system in Illustration 6A-3, the 400 units at $13 purchased on November 27 are all applied to the ending inventory.

The ending inventory in this LIFO perpetual illustration is $5,700, and cost of goods sold is $6,300, as compared to the LIFO periodic illustration (on page 253) where the ending inventory is $5,000 and cost of goods sold is $7,000.

## Average-Cost

The average-cost method in a perpetual inventory system is called the **moving-average method.** Under this method the company computes a new average **after each purchase**, by dividing the cost of goods available for sale by the units on hand. They then apply the average cost to: (1) the units sold, to determine the cost of goods sold, and (2) the remaining units on hand, to determine the ending inventory amount. Illustration 6A-4 shows the application of the average-cost method by Houston Electronics.

**Illustration 6A-4**
Perpetual system—average-cost method

| Date | Purchases | Cost of Goods Sold | Balance (in units and cost) | |
|---|---|---|---|---|
| January 1 | | | (100 @ $10) | $1,000 |
| April 15 | (200 @ $11)   $2,200 | | (300 @ $10.667) | $3,200 |
| August 24 | (300 @ $12)   $3,600 | | (600 @ $11.333) | $6,800 |
| September 10 | | (550 @ $11.333) | (50 @ $11.333) | $ 567 |
| | | **$6,233** | | |
| November 27 | (400 @ $13)   $5,200 | | (450 @ $12.816) | **$5,767** |

> Cost of goods sold
> Ending inventory

As indicated above, Houston Electronics computes **a new average each time it makes a purchase**. On April 15, after it buys 200 units for $2,200, a total of 300 units costing $3,200 ($1,000 + $2,200) are on hand. The average unit cost is $10.667 ($3,200 ÷ 300). On August 24, after Houston Electronics buys 300 units for $3,600, a total of 600 units costing $6,800 ($1,000 + $2,200 + $3,600) are on hand, at an average cost per unit of $11.333 ($6,800 ÷ 600). Houston Electronics uses this unit cost of $11.333 in costing sales until it makes another purchase, when the company computes a new unit cost. Accordingly, the unit cost of the 550 units sold on September 10 is $11.333, and the total cost of goods sold is $6,233. On November 27, following the purchase of 400 units for $5,200, there are 450 units on hand costing $5,767 ($567 + $5,200) with a new average cost of $12.816 ($5,767 ÷ 450).

Compare this moving-average cost under the perpetual inventory system to Illustration 6-10 (on page 255) showing the weighted-average method under a periodic inventory system.

## Demonstration Problem 2

Demonstration Problem 1 on page 264 showed cost of goods sold computations under a periodic inventory system. Now let's assume that Gerald D. Englehart Company uses a perpetual inventory system. The company has the same inventory, purchases, and sales data for the month of March as shown earlier:

| | | | |
|---|---|---|---|
| Inventory: | March 1 | 200 units @ $4.00 | $ 800 |
| Purchases: | March 10 | 500 units @ $4.50 | 2,250 |
| | March 20 | 400 units @ $4.75 | 1,900 |
| | March 30 | 300 units @ $5.00 | 1,500 |
| Sales: | March 15 | 500 units | |
| | March 25 | 400 units | |

The physical inventory count on March 31 shows 500 units on hand.

### Instructions

Under a **perpetual inventory system**, determine the cost of inventory on hand at March 31 and the cost of goods sold for March under (a) FIFO, (b) LIFO, and (c) average-cost.

### Solution

The cost of goods available for sale is $6,450, as follows.

| | | | |
|---|---|---|---|
| Inventory: | | 200 units @ $4.00 | $ 800 |
| Purchases: | March 10 | 500 units @ $4.50 | 2,250 |
| | March 20 | 400 units @ $4.75 | 1,900 |
| | March 30 | 300 units @ $5.00 | 1,500 |
| Total cost of goods available for sale | | | $6,450 |

Under a **perpetual inventory system**, the cost of goods sold under each cost flow method is as follows.

### FIFO Method

| Date | Purchases | Cost of Goods Sold | Balance |
|---|---|---|---|
| March 1 | | | (200 @ $4.00)   $ 800 |
| March 10 | (500 @ $4.50)   $2,250 | | (200 @ $4.00)⎫<br>(500 @ $4.50)⎬ $3,050 |
| March 15 | | (200 @ $4.00)<br>(300 @ $4.50)<br>―――――<br>$2,150 | (200 @ $4.50)   $ 900 |

### action plan

✔ Compute the cost of goods sold under the perpetual FIFO method by allocating to the goods sold the **earliest** cost of goods purchased.

✔ Compute the cost of goods sold under the perpetual LIFO method by allocating to the goods sold the **latest** cost of goods purchased.

✔ Compute the cost of goods sold under the perpetual average-cost method by allocating to the goods sold a **moving-average** cost.

| Date | Purchases | | Cost of Goods Sold | | Balance | |
|------|-----------|---|--------------------|---|---------|---|
| March 20 | (400 @ $4.75) | $1,900 | | | (200 @ $4.50)<br>(400 @ $4.75)} | $2,800 |
| March 25 | | | (200 @ $4.50)<br>(200 @ $4.75)<br>$1,850 | | (200 @ $4.75) | $ 950 |
| March 30 | (300 @ $5.00) | $1,500 | | | (200 @ $4.75)<br>(300 @ $5.00)} | $2,450 |
| | Ending inventory, $2,450 | | Cost of goods sold: $2,150 + $1,850 = $4,000 | | | |

### LIFO Method

| Date | Purchases | | Cost of Goods Sold | | Balance | |
|------|-----------|---|--------------------|---|---------|---|
| March 1 | | | | | (200 @ $4.00) | $ 800 |
| March 10 | (500 @ $4.50) | $2,250 | | | (200 @ $4.00)<br>(500 @ $4.50)} | $3,050 |
| March 15 | | | (500 @ $4.50) | $2,250 | (200 @ $4.00) | $ 800 |
| March 20 | (400 @ $4.75) | $1,900 | | | (200 @ $4.00)<br>(400 @ $4.75)} | $2,700 |
| March 25 | | | (400 @ $4.75) | $1,900 | (200 @ $4.00) | $ 800 |
| March 30 | (300 @ $5.00) | $1,500 | | | (200 @ $4.00)<br>(300 @ $5.00)} | $2,300 |
| | Ending inventory, $2,300 | | Cost of goods sold: $2,250 + $1,900 = $4,150 | | | |

### Moving-Average Cost Method

| Date | Purchases | | Cost of Goods Sold | | Balance | |
|------|-----------|---|--------------------|---|---------|---|
| March 1 | | | | | (200 @ $ 4.00) | $ 800 |
| March 10 | (500 @ $4.50) | $2,250 | | | (700 @ $4.357) | $3,050 |
| March 15 | | | (500 @ $4.357) | $2,179 | (200 @ $4.357) | $ 871 |
| March 20 | (400 @ $4.75) | $1,900 | | | (600 @ $4.618) | $2,771 |
| March 25 | | | (400 @ $4.618) | $1,847 | (200 @ $4.618) | $ 924 |
| March 30 | (300 @ $5.00) | $1,500 | | | (500 @ $4.848) | $2,424 |
| | Ending inventory, $2,424 | | Cost of goods sold: $2,179 + $1,847 = $4,026 | | | |

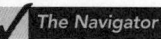
The Navigator

---

SUMMARY OF STUDY OBJECTIVE FOR APPENDIX 6A WILEY PLUS

**7 Apply the inventory cost flow methods to perpetual inventory records.** Under FIFO and a perpetual inventory system, companies charge to cost of goods sold the cost of the earliest goods on hand prior to each sale. Under LIFO and a perpetual system, companies charge to cost of goods sold the cost of the most recent purchase prior to sale. Under the moving-average (average cost) method and a perpetual system, companies compute a new average cost after each purchase.

## APPENDIX 6B Estimating Inventories

In the chapter we assumed that a company would be able to physically count its inventory. What if it cannot? What if the inventory were destroyed by fire or flood, for example? In that case, the company would use an estimate.

> **STUDY OBJECTIVE 8**
>
> Describe the two methods of estimating inventories.

Two circumstances explain why companies sometimes estimate inventories. First, a casualty such as fire, flood, or earthquake may make it impossible to take a physical inventory. Second, managers may want monthly or quarterly financial statements, but a physical inventory is taken only annually. The need for estimating inventories occurs primarily with a periodic inventory system because of the absence of perpetual inventory records.

There are two widely used methods of estimating inventories: (1) the gross profit method, and (2) the retail inventory method.

## Gross Profit Method

The **gross profit method** estimates the cost of ending inventory by applying a gross profit rate to net sales. This method is relatively simple, but effective. It will detect large errors. Accountants, auditors, and managers frequently use the gross profit method to test the reasonableness of the ending inventory amount.

To use this method, a company needs to know its net sales, cost of goods available for sale, and gross profit rate. With the gross profit rate, the company can estimate its gross profit for the period. Illustration 6B-1 shows the formulas for using the gross profit method.

**Illustration 6B-1**
Gross profit method formulas

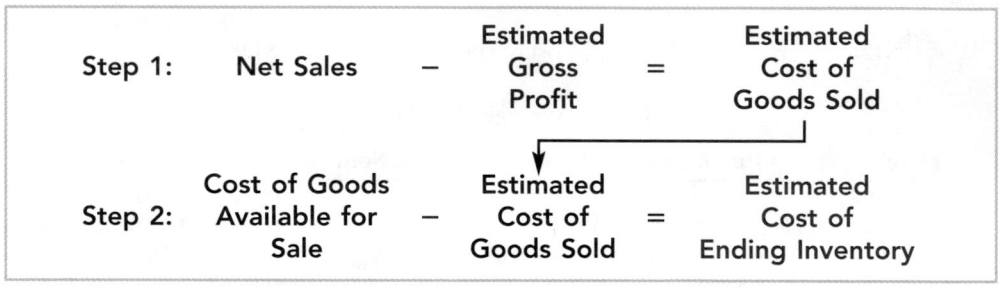

To illustrate, assume that Kishwaukee Company wishes to prepare an income statement for the month of January. Its records show net sales of $200,000, beginning inventory $40,000, and cost of goods purchased $120,000. In the preceding year, the company realized a 30% gross profit rate. It expects to earn the same rate this year. Given these facts and assumptions, Kishwaukee can compute the estimated cost of the ending inventory at January 31 under the gross profit method as follows.

**Illustration 6B-2**
Example of gross profit method

| | |
|---|---:|
| **Step 1:** | |
| Net sales | $200,000 |
| Less: Estimated gross profit (30% × $200,000) | 60,000 |
| **Estimated cost of goods sold** | **$140,000** |
| | |
| **Step 2:** | |
| Beginning inventory | $ 40,000 |
| Cost of goods purchased | 120,000 |
| Cost of goods available for sale | 160,000 |
| Less: Estimated cost of goods sold | 140,000 |
| **Estimated cost of ending inventory** | **$ 20,000** |

The gross profit method is based on the assumption that the gross profit rate will remain constant. But it may not remain constant, due to a change in merchandising policies or in market conditions. In such cases, the company should adjust the rate to reflect current operating conditions. In some cases, companies can obtain a more accurate estimate by applying this method on a department or product-line basis.

Note that companies should not use the gross profit method to prepare financial statements at the end of the year. These statements should be based on a physical inventory count.

## Retail Inventory Method

A retail store such as Home Depot, Ace Hardware, or Wal-Mart has thousands of different types of merchandise at low unit costs. In such cases it is difficult and time-consuming to apply unit costs to inventory quantities. An alternative is to use the retail inventory method to estimate the cost of inventory. Most retail companies can establish a relationship between cost and sales price. The company then applies the cost-to-retail percentage to the ending inventory at retail prices to determine inventory at cost.

Under the retail inventory method, a company's records must show both the cost and retail value of the goods available for sale. Illustration 6B-3 presents the formulas for using the retail inventory method.

| | | | | | | |
|---|---|---|---|---|---|---|
| Step 1: | Goods Available for Sale at Retail | − | Net Sales | = | Ending Inventory at Retail | |
| Step 2: | Goods Available for Sale at Cost | ÷ | Goods Available for Sale at Retail | = | Cost-to- Retail Ratio | |
| Step 3: | Ending Inventory at Retail | × | Cost-to- Retail Ratio | = | Estimated Cost of Ending Inventory | |

**Illustration 6B-3**
Retail inventory method formulas

We can demonstrate the logic of the retail method by using unit-cost data. Assume that Ortiz Inc. has marked 10 units purchased at $7 to sell for $10 per unit. Thus, the cost-to-retail ratio is 70% ($70 ÷ $100). If four units remain unsold, their retail value is $40 (4 × $10), and their cost is $28 ($40 × 70%). This amount agrees with the total cost of goods on hand on a per unit basis (4 × $7).

Illustration 6B-4 shows application of the retail method for Valley West Co. Note that it is not necessary to take a physical inventory to determine the estimated cost of goods on hand at any given time.

| | At Cost | At Retail |
|---|---|---|
| Beginning inventory | $14,000 | $ 21,500 |
| Goods purchased | 61,000 | 78,500 |
| Goods available for sale | $75,000 | 100,000 |
| Net sales | | 70,000 |
| Step (1)  Ending inventory at retail = | | $ 30,000 |
| Step (2)  Cost-to-retail ratio $75,000 ÷ $100,000 = 75% | | |
| Step (3)  Estimated cost of ending inventory = $30,000 × 75% = $22,500 | | |

**Illustration 6B-4**
Application of retail inventory method

The retail inventory method also facilitates taking a physical inventory at the end of the year. Valley West can value the goods on hand at the prices marked on the merchandise, and then apply the cost-to-retail ratio to the goods on hand at retail to determine the ending inventory at cost.

The major disadvantage of the retail method is that it is an averaging technique. Thus, it may produce an incorrect inventory valuation if the mix of the ending inventory is not representative of the mix in the goods available for sale. Assume, for example, that the cost-to-retail ratio of 75% for Valley West Co. consists of equal proportions of inventory items that have cost-to-retail ratios of 70%, 75%, and 80%. If the ending inventory contains only items with a 70% ratio, an incorrect inventory cost will result. Companies can minimize this problem by applying the retail method on a department or product-line basis.

## SUMMARY OF STUDY OBJECTIVE FOR APPENDIX 6B

**8 Describe the two methods of estimating inventories.** The two methods of estimating inventories are the gross profit method and the retail inventory method. Under the gross profit method, companies apply a gross profit rate to net sales to determine estimated cost of goods sold. They then subtract estimated cost of goods sold from cost of goods available for sale to determine the estimated cost of the ending inventory.

Under the retail inventory method, companies compute a cost-to-retail ratio by dividing the cost of goods available for sale by the retail value of the goods available for sale. They then apply this ratio to the ending inventory at retail to determine the estimated cost of the ending inventory.

## GLOSSARY FOR APPENDIX 6B

**Gross profit method** A method for estimating the cost of the ending inventory by applying a gross profit rate to net sales and subtracting the result from cost of goods available for sale. (p. 270).

**Retail inventory method** A method for estimating the cost of the ending inventory by applying a cost-to-retail ratio to the ending inventory at retail. (p. 271).

**\*Note:** All **asterisked** Questions, Exercises, and Problems relate to material in the appendices to the chapter.

## SELF-STUDY QUESTIONS

*Answers are at the end of the chapter.*

(SO 1)  **1.** Which of the following should *not* be included in the physical inventory of a company?
   **a.** Goods held on consignment from another company.
   **b.** Goods shipped on consignment to another company.
   **c.** Goods in transit from another company shipped FOB shipping point.
   **d.** None of the above.

(SO 2)  **2.** Cost of goods available for sale consist of two elements: beginning inventory and
   **a.** ending inventory.
   **b.** cost of goods purchased.
   **c.** cost of goods sold.
   **d.** all of the above.

(SO 2)  **3.** Tinker Bell Company has the following:

| | Units | Unit Cost |
|---|---|---|
| Inventory, Jan. 1 | 8,000 | $11 |
| Purchase, June 19 | 13,000 | 12 |
| Purchase, Nov. 8 | 5,000 | 13 |

If Tinker Bell has 9,000 units on hand at December 31, the cost of the ending inventory under FIFO is:
   **a.** $99,000.        **c.** $113,000.
   **b.** $108,000.       **d.** $117,000.

**4.** Using the data in (3) above, the cost of the ending inventory under LIFO is:     (SO 2)
   **a.** $113,000.       **c.** $99,000.
   **b.** $108,000.       **d.** $100,000.

**5.** In periods of rising prices, LIFO will produce:     (SO 3)
   **a.** higher net income than FIFO.
   **b.** the same net income as FIFO.
   **c.** lower net income than FIFO.
   **d.** higher net income than average costing.

**6.** Factors that affect the selection of an inventory costing     (SO 3)
   method do *not* include:
   **a.** tax effects.
   **b.** balance sheet effects.
   **c.** income statement effects.
   **d.** perpetual vs. periodic inventory system.

(SO 4)  **7.** Rickety Company purchased 1,000 widgets and has 200 widgets in its ending inventory at a cost of $91 each and a current replacement cost of $80 each. The ending inventory under lower of cost or market is:
  **a.** $91,000.
  **b.** $80,000.
  **c.** $18,200.
  **d.** $16,000.

(SO 5)  **8.** Atlantis Company's ending inventory is understated $4,000. The effects of this error on the current year's cost of goods sold and net income, respectively, are:
  **a.** understated, overstated.
  **b.** overstated, understated.
  **c.** overstated, overstated.
  **d.** understated, understated.

(SO 6)  **9.** Which of these would cause the inventory turnover ratio to increase the most?
  **a.** Increasing the amount of inventory on hand.
  **b.** Keeping the amount of inventory on hand constant but increasing sales.
  **c.** Keeping the amount of inventory on hand constant but decreasing sales.
  **d.** Decreasing the amount of inventory on hand and increasing sales.

*10. Songbird Company has sales of $150,000 and cost of goods available for sale of $135,000. If the gross profit rate is 30%, the estimated cost of the ending inventory under the gross profit method is: (SO 8)
  **a.** $15,000.
  **b.** $30,000.
  **c.** $45,000.
  **d.** $75,000.

*11. In a perpetual inventory system, (SO 7)
  **a.** LIFO cost of goods sold will be the same as in a periodic inventory system.
  **b.** average costs are based entirely on unit cost averages.
  **c.** a new average is computed under the average cost method after each sale.
  **d.** FIFO cost of goods sold will be the same as in a periodic inventory system.

Go to the book's website,
**www.wiley.com/college/weygandt**,
for Additional Self-Study questions.

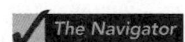

## QUESTIONS

**1.** "The key to successful business operations is effective inventory management." Do you agree? Explain.

**2.** An item must possess two characteristics to be classified as inventory by a merchandiser. What are these two characteristics?

**3.** Your friend Tom Witt has been hired to help take the physical inventory in Hawkeye Hardware Store. Explain to Tom Witt what this job will entail.

**4.** (a) Reeves Company ships merchandise to Cox Company on December 30. The merchandise reaches the buyer on January 6. Indicate the terms of sale that will result in the goods being included in (1) Reeves's December 31 inventory, and (2) Cox's December 31 inventory.
  (b) Under what circumstances should Reeves Company include consigned goods in its inventory?

**5.** Jim's Hat Shop received a shipment of hats for which it paid the wholesaler $2,970. The price of the hats was $3,000 but Jim's was given a $30 cash discount and required to pay freight charges of $50. In addition, Jim's paid $130 to cover the travel expenses of an employee who negotiated the purchase of the hats. What amount will Jim's record for inventory? Why?

**6.** Identify the distinguishing features of an income statement for a merchandiser.

**7.** David Shannon believes that the allocation of inventoriable costs should be based on the actual physical flow of the goods. Explain to David why this may be both impractical and inappropriate.

**8.** What is a major advantage and a major disadvantage of the specific identification method of inventory costing?

**9.** "The selection of an inventory cost flow method is a decision made by accountants." Do you agree? Explain.

Once a method has been selected, what accounting requirement applies?

**10.** Which assumed inventory cost flow method:
  (a) usually parallels the actual physical flow of merchandise?
  (b) assumes that goods available for sale during an accounting period are identical?
  (c) assumes that the latest units purchased are the first to be sold?

**11.** In a period of rising prices, the inventory reported in Plato Company's balance sheet is close to the current cost of the inventory. Cecil Company's inventory is considerably below its current cost. Identify the inventory cost flow method being used by each company. Which company has probably been reporting the higher gross profit?

**12.** Casey Company has been using the FIFO cost flow method during a prolonged period of rising prices. During the same time period, Casey has been paying out all of its net income as dividends. What adverse effects may result from this policy?

**13.** Peter Lunde is studying for the next accounting mid-term examination. What should Peter know about (a) departing from the cost basis of accounting for inventories and (b) the meaning of "market" in the lower-of-cost-or-market method?

**14.** Garitson Music Center has 5 CD players on hand at the balance sheet date. Each cost $400. The current replacement cost is $380 per unit. Under the lower-of-cost-or-market basis of accounting for inventories, what value should be reported for the CD players on the balance sheet? Why?

**15.** Ruthie Stores has 20 toasters on hand at the balance sheet data. Each cost $27. The current replacement cost is

$30 per unit. Under the lower-of-cost-or-market basis of accounting for inventories, what value should Ruthie report for the toasters on the balance sheet? Why?

**16.** Mintz Company discovers in 2008 that its ending inventory at December 31, 2007, was $7,000 understated. What effect will this error have on (a) 2007 net income, (b) 2008 net income, and (c) the combined net income for the 2 years?

**17.** Willingham Company's balance sheet shows Inventories $162,800. What additional disclosures should be made?

**18.** Under what circumstances might inventory turnover be too high? That is, what possible negative consequences might occur?

***19.** "When perpetual inventory records are kept, the results under the FIFO and LIFO methods are the same as they would be in a periodic inventory system." Do you agree? Explain.

***20.** How does the average-cost method of inventory costing differ between a perpetual inventory system and a periodic inventory system?

***21.** When is it necessary to estimate inventories?

***22.** Both the gross profit method and the retail inventory method are based on averages. For each method, indicate the average used, how it is determined, and how it is applied.

***23.** Maureen Company has net sales of $400,000 and cost of goods available for sale of $300,000. If the gross profit rate is 35%, what is the estimated cost of the ending inventory? Show computations.

***24.** Milo Shoe Shop had goods available for sale in 2008 with a retail price of $120,000. The cost of these goods was $84,000. If sales during the period were $80,000, what is the ending inventory at cost using the retail inventory method?

## BRIEF EXERCISES

*Identify items to be included in taking a physical inventory.*

*(SO 1)*

**BE6-1** Smart Company identifies the following items for possible inclusion in the taking of a physical inventory. Indicate whether each item should be included or excluded from the inventory taking.

**(a)** Goods shipped on consignment by Smart to another company.
**(b)** Goods in transit from a supplier shipped FOB destination.
**(c)** Goods sold but being held for customer pickup.
**(d)** Goods held on consignment from another company.

*Identify the components of goods available for sale.*

*(SO 2)*

**BE6-2** The ledger of Gomez Company includes the following items: **(a)** Freight-in, **(b)** Purchase Returns and Allowances, **(c)** Purchases, **(d)** Sales Discounts, **(e)** Purchase Discounts. Identify which items are included in goods available for sale.

*Compute ending inventory using FIFO and LIFO.*

*(SO 2)*

**BE6-3** In its first month of operations, Quirk Company made three purchases of merchandise in the following sequence: (1) 300 units at $6, (2) 400 units at $7, and (3) 200 units at $8. Assuming there are 360 units on hand, compute the cost of the ending inventory under the **(a)** FIFO method and **(b)** LIFO method. Quirk uses a periodic inventory system.

*Compute the ending inventory using average-cost.*

*(SO 2)*

**BE6-4** Data for Quirk Company are presented in BE6-3. Compute the cost of the ending inventory under the average-cost method, assuming there are 360 units on hand.

*Explain the financial statement effect of inventory cost flow assumptions.*

*(SO 3)*

**BE6-5** The management of Hoyt Corp. is considering the effects of various inventory-costing methods on its financial statements and its income tax expense. Assuming that the price the company pays for inventory is increasing, which method will:

**(a)** provide the highest net income?
**(b)** provide the highest ending inventory?
**(c)** result in the lowest income tax expense?
**(d)** result in the most stable earnings over a number of years?

*Explain the financial statement effect of inventory cost flow assumptions.*

*(SO 3)*

**BE6-6** In its first month of operation, Gulletson Company purchased 100 units of inventory for $6, then 200 units for $7, and finally 150 units for $8. At the end of the month, 180 units remained. Compute the amount of phantom profit that would result if the company used FIFO rather than LIFO. Explain why this amount is referred to as phantom profit. The company uses the periodic method.

*Determine the LCM valuation using inventory categories.*

*(SO 4)*

**BE6-7** Alou Appliance Center accumulates the following cost and market data at December 31.

| Inventory Categories | Cost Data | Market Data |
| --- | --- | --- |
| Cameras | $12,000 | $12,100 |
| Camcorders | 9,500 | 9,700 |
| VCRs | 14,000 | 12,800 |

Compute the lower-of-cost-or-market valuation for the company's total inventory.

**BE6-8**  Cody Company reports net income of $90,000 in 2008. However, ending inventory was understated $10,000. What is the correct net income for 2008? What effect, if any, will this error have on total assets as reported in the balance sheet at December 31, 2008?

*Determine correct income statement amounts.*

*(SO 5)*

**BE6-9**  At December 31, 2008, the following information was available for J. Graff Company: ending inventory $40,000, beginning inventory $60,000, cost of goods sold $270,000, and sales revenue $380,000. Calculate inventory turnover and days in inventory for J. Graff Company.

*Compute inventory turnover and days in inventory.*

*(SO 6)*

**\*BE6-10**  Jensen's Department Store uses a perpetual inventory system. Data for product E2-D2 include the following purchases.

*Apply cost flow methods to perpetual inventory records.*

*(SO 7)*

| Date | Number of Units | Unit Price |
|------|-----------------|------------|
| May 7 | 50 | $10 |
| July 28 | 30 | 13 |

On June 1 Jensen's sold 30 units, and on August 27, 40 more units. Prepare the perpetual inventory schedule for the above transactions using (1) FIFO, (2) LIFO, and (3) average-cost.

**\*BE6-11**  At May 31, Creole Company has net sales of $330,000 and cost of goods available for sale of $230,000. Compute the estimated cost of the ending inventory, assuming the gross profit rate is 35%.

*Apply the gross profit method.*

*(SO 8)*

**\*BE6-12**  On June 30, Fabre Fabrics has the following data pertaining to the retail inventory method: Goods available for sale: at cost $35,000, at retail $50,000; net sales $40,000, and ending inventory at retail $10,000. Compute the estimated cost of the ending inventory using the retail inventory method.

*Apply the retail inventory method.*

*(SO 8)*

# EXERCISES

**E6-1**  Premier Bank and Trust is considering giving Lima Company a loan. Before doing so, they decide that further discussions with Lima's accountant may be desirable. One area of particular concern is the inventory account, which has a year-end balance of $297,000. Discussions with the accountant reveal the following.

*Determine the correct inventory amount.*

*(SO 1)*

1. Lima sold goods costing $38,000 to Comerica Company, FOB shipping point, on December 28. The goods are not expected to arrive at Comerica until January 12. The goods were not included in the physical inventory because they were not in the warehouse.
2. The physical count of the inventory did not include goods costing $95,000 that were shipped to Lima FOB destination on December 27 and were still in transit at year-end.
3. Lima received goods costing $22,000 on January 2. The goods were shipped FOB shipping point on December 26 by Galant Co. The goods were not included in the physical count.
4. Lima sold goods costing $35,000 to Emerick Co., FOB destination, on December 30. The goods were received at Emerick on January 8. They were not included in Lima's physical inventory.
5. Lima received goods costing $44,000 on January 2 that were shipped FOB destination on December 29. The shipment was a rush order that was supposed to arrive December 31. This purchase was included in the ending inventory of $297,000.

**Instructions**

Determine the correct inventory amount on December 31.

**E6-2**  Kale Thompson, an auditor with Sneed CPAs, is performing a review of Strawser Company's inventory account. Strawser did not have a good year and top management is under pressure to boost reported income. According to its records, the inventory balance at year-end was $740,000. However, the following information was not considered when determining that amount.

*Determine the correct inventory amount.*

*(SO 1)*

1. Included in the company's count were goods with a cost of $250,000 that the company is holding on consignment. The goods belong to Superior Corporation.
2. The physical count did not include goods purchased by Strawser with a cost of $40,000 that were shipped FOB destination on December 28 and did not arrive at Strawser's warehouse until January 3.

3. Included in the inventory account was $17,000 of office supplies that were stored in the warehouse and were to be used by the company's supervisors and managers during the coming year.

4. The company received an order on December 29 that was boxed and was sitting on the loading dock awaiting pick-up on December 31. The shipper picked up the goods on January 1 and delivered them on January 6. The shipping terms were FOB shipping point. The goods had a selling price of $40,000 and a cost of $30,000. The goods were not included in the count because they were sitting on the dock.

5. On December 29 Strawser shipped goods with a selling price of $80,000 and a cost of $60,000 to District Sales Corporation FOB shipping point. The goods arrived on January 3. District Sales had only ordered goods with a selling price of $10,000 and a cost of $8,000. However, a sales manager at Strawser had authorized the shipment and said that if District wanted to ship the goods back next week, it could.

6. Included in the count was $40,000 of goods that were parts for a machine that the company no longer made. Given the high-tech nature of Strawser's products, it was unlikely that these obsolete parts had any other use. However, management would prefer to keep them on the books at cost, "since that is what we paid for them, after all."

**Instructions**

Prepare a schedule to determine the correct inventory amount. Provide explanations for each item above, saying why you did or did not make an adjustment for each item.

*Calculate cost of goods sold using specific identification and FIFO.*

*(SO 2, 3)*

**E6-3** On December 1, Bargain Electronics Ltd. has three DVD players left in stock. All are identical, all are priced to sell at $150. One of the three DVD players left in stock, with serial #1012, was purchased on June 1 at a cost of $100. Another, with serial #1045, was purchased on November 1 for $90. The last player, serial #1056, was purchased on November 30 for $80.

**Instructions**

(a) Calculate the cost of goods sold using the FIFO periodic inventory method assuming that two of the three players were sold by the end of December, Bargain Electronic's year-end.

(b) If Bargain Electronics used the specific identification method instead of the FIFO method, how might it alter its earnings by "selectively choosing" which particular players to sell to the two customers? What would Bargain's cost of goods sold be if the company wished to minimize earnings? Maximize earnings?

(c) Which inventory method do you recommend that Bargain use? Explain why.

*Compute inventory and cost of goods sold using FIFO and LIFO.*

*(SO 2)*

**E6-4** Boarders sells a snowboard, Xpert, that is popular with snowboard enthusiasts. Below is information relating to Boarders's purchases of Xpert snowboards during September. During the same month, 121 Xpert snowboards were sold. Boarders uses a periodic inventory system.

| Date | Explanation | Units | Unit Cost | Total Cost |
|---|---|---|---|---|
| Sept.  1 | Inventory | 26 | $ 97 | $ 2,522 |
| Sept. 12 | Purchases | 45 | 102 | 4,590 |
| Sept. 19 | Purchases | 20 | 104 | 2,080 |
| Sept. 26 | Purchases | 50 | 105 | 5,250 |
| | Totals | 141 | | $14,442 |

**Instructions**

(a) Compute the ending inventory at September 30 and cost of goods sold using the FIFO and LIFO methods. Prove the amount allocated to cost of goods sold under each method.

(b) For both FIFO and LIFO, calculate the sum of ending inventory and cost of goods sold. What do you notice about the answers you found for each method?

*Compute inventory and cost of goods sold using FIFO and LIFO.*

*(SO 2)*

**E6-5** Catlet Co. uses a periodic inventory system. Its records show the following for the month of May, in which 65 units were sold.

| | | Units | Unit Cost | Total Cost |
|---|---|---|---|---|
| May 1 | Inventory | 30 | $ 8 | $240 |
| 15 | Purchases | 25 | 11 | 275 |
| 24 | Purchases | 35 | 12 | 420 |
| | Totals | 90 | | $935 |

**Instructions**

Compute the ending inventory at May 31 and cost of goods sold using the FIFO and LIFO methods. Prove the amount allocated to cost of goods sold under each method.

**E6-6** Yount Company reports the following for the month of June.

| | | Units | Unit Cost | Total Cost |
|---|---|---|---|---|
| June 1 | Inventory | 200 | $5 | $1,000 |
| 12 | Purchase | 300 | 6 | 1,800 |
| 23 | Purchase | 500 | 7 | 3,500 |
| 30 | Inventory | 120 | | |

*Compute inventory and cost of goods sold using FIFO and LIFO.*

*(SO 2, 3)*

**Instructions**

**(a)** Compute the cost of the ending inventory and the cost of goods sold under (1) FIFO and (2) LIFO.

**(b)** Which costing method gives the higher ending inventory? Why?

**(c)** Which method results in the higher cost of goods sold? Why?

**E6-7** Jones Company had 100 units in beginning inventory at a total cost of $10,000. The company purchased 200 units at a total cost of $26,000. At the end of the year, Jones had 80 units in ending inventory.

*Compute inventory under FIFO, LIFO, and average-cost.*

*(SO 2, 3)*

**Instructions**

**(a)** Compute the cost of the ending inventory and the cost of goods sold under (1) FIFO, (2) LIFO, and (3) average-cost.

**(b)** Which cost flow method would result in the highest net income?

**(c)** Which cost flow method would result in inventories approximating current cost in the balance sheet?

**(d)** Which cost flow method would result in Jones paying the least taxes in the first year?

**E6-8** Inventory data for Yount Company are presented in E6-6.

*Compute inventory and cost of goods sold using average-cost.*

*(SO 2, 3)*

**Instructions**

**(a)** Compute the cost of the ending inventory and the cost of goods sold using the average-cost method.

**(b)** Will the results in (a) be higher or lower than the results under (1) FIFO and (2) LIFO?

**(c)** Why is the average unit cost not $6?

**E6-9** Americus Camera Shop uses the lower-of-cost-or-market basis for its inventory. The following data are available at December 31.

*Determine ending inventory under LCM.*

*(SO 4)*

| Item | Units | Unit Cost | Market |
|---|---|---|---|
| Cameras: | | | |
| Minolta | 5 | $170 | $156 |
| Canon | 6 | 150 | 152 |
| Light meters: | | | |
| Vivitar | 12 | 125 | 115 |
| Kodak | 14 | 120 | 135 |

**Instructions**

Determine the amount of the ending inventory by applying the lower-of-cost-or-market basis.

**E6-10** Conan Company applied FIFO to its inventory and got the following results for its ending inventory.

*Compute lower-of-cost-or-market.*

*(SO 4)*

| | |
|---|---|
| VCRs | 100 units at a cost per unit of $65 |
| DVD players | 150 units at a cost per unit of $75 |
| iPods | 125 units at a cost per unit of $80 |

The cost of purchasing units at year-end was VCRs $71, DVD players $69, and iPods $78.

**Instructions**

Determine the amount of ending inventory at lower-of-cost-or-market.

*Determine effects of inventory errors.*

*(SO 5)*

**E6-11**    Lebo Hardware reported cost of goods sold as follows.

| | 2008 | 2009 |
|---|---|---|
| Beginning inventory | $ 20,000 | $ 30,000 |
| Cost of goods purchased | 150,000 | 175,000 |
| Cost of goods available for sale | 170,000 | 205,000 |
| Ending inventory | 30,000 | 35,000 |
| Cost of goods sold | $140,000 | $170,000 |

Lebo made two errors: (1) 2008 ending inventory was overstated $3,000, and (2) 2009 ending inventory was understated $6,000.

**Instructions**

Compute the correct cost of goods sold for each year.

*Prepare correct income statements.*

*(SO 5)*

**E6-12**    Staley Watch Company reported the following income statement data for a 2-year period.

| | 2008 | 2009 |
|---|---|---|
| Sales | $210,000 | $250,000 |
| Cost of goods sold | | |
|   Beginning inventory | 32,000 | 44,000 |
|   Cost of goods purchased | 173,000 | 202,000 |
|   Cost of goods available for sale | 205,000 | 246,000 |
|   Ending inventory | 44,000 | 52,000 |
|     Cost of goods sold | 161,000 | 194,000 |
| Gross profit | $ 49,000 | $ 56,000 |

Staley uses a periodic inventory system. The inventories at January 1, 2008, and December 31, 2009, are correct. However, the ending inventory at December 31, 2008, was overstated $5,000.

**Instructions**

**(a)** Prepare correct income statement data for the 2 years.

**(b)** What is the cumulative effect of the inventory error on total gross profit for the 2 years?

**(c)** ▣━━━▶ Explain in a letter to the president of Staley Company what has happened—i.e., the nature of the error and its effect on the financial statements.

*Compute inventory turnover, days in inventory, and gross profit rate.*

*(SO 6)*

**E6-13**    This information is available for Santo's Photo Corporation for 2007, 2008, and 2009.

| | 2007 | 2008 | 2009 |
|---|---|---|---|
| Beginning inventory | $ 100,000 | $ 300,000 | $ 400,000 |
| Ending inventory | 300,000 | 400,000 | 480,000 |
| Cost of goods sold | 900,000 | 1,120,000 | 1,300,000 |
| Sales | 1,200,000 | 1,600,000 | 1,900,000 |

**Instructions**

Calculate inventory turnover, days in inventory, and gross profit rate (from Chapter 5) for Santo's Photo Corporation for 2007, 2008, 2009. Comment on any trends.

*Compute inventory turnover and days in inventory.*

*(SO 6)*

**E6-14**    The cost of goods sold computations for O'Brien Company and Weinberg Company are shown below.

| | O'Brien Company | Weinberg Company |
|---|---|---|
| Beginning inventory | $ 45,000 | $ 71,000 |
| Cost of goods purchased | 200,000 | 290,000 |
| Cost of goods available for sale | 245,000 | 361,000 |
| Ending inventory | 55,000 | 69,000 |
| Cost of goods sold | $190,000 | $292,000 |

**Instructions**

(a) Compute inventory turnover and days in inventory for each company.

(b) Which company moves its inventory more quickly?

**\*E6-15**    Klugman Appliance uses a perpetual inventory system. For its flat-screen television sets, the January 1 inventory was 3 sets at $600 each. On January 10, Klugman purchased 6 units at $660 each. The company sold 2 units on January 8 and 4 units on January 15.

*Apply cost flow methods to perpetual records.*

*(SO 7)*

**Instructions**

Compute the ending inventory under (1) FIFO, (2) LIFO, and (3) average-cost.

**\*E6-16**    Yount Company reports the following for the month of June.

*Calculate inventory and cost of goods sold using three cost flow methods in a perpetual inventory system.*

*(SO 7)*

| Date | Explanation | Units | Unit Cost | Total Cost |
|---|---|---|---|---|
| June  1 | Inventory | 200 | $5 | $1,000 |
| 12 | Purchase | 300 | 6 | 1,800 |
| 23 | Purchase | 500 | 7 | 3,500 |
| 30 | Inventory | 120 | | |

**Instructions**

(a) Calculate the cost of the ending inventory and the cost of goods sold for each cost flow assumption, using a perpetual inventory system. Assume a sale of 400 units occurred on June 15 for a selling price of $8 and a sale of 480 units on June 27 for $9.

(b) How do the results differ from E6-6 and E6-8?

(c) Why is the average unit cost not $6 [($5 + $6 + $7) ÷ 3 = $6]?

**\*E6-17**    Information about Boarders is presented in E6-4. Additional data regarding Boarders' sales of Xpert snowboards are provided below. Assume that Boarders uses a perpetual inventory system.

*Apply cost flow methods to perpetual records.*

*(SO 7)*

| Date | | Units | Unit Price | Total Cost |
|---|---|---|---|---|
| Sept.  5 | Sale | 12 | $199 | $ 2,388 |
| Sept. 16 | Sale | 50 | 199 | 9,950 |
| Sept. 29 | Sale | 59 | 209 | 12,331 |
| | Totals | 121 | | $24,669 |

**Instructions**

(a) Compute ending inventory at September 30 using FIFO, LIFO, and average cost.

(b) Compare ending inventory using a perpetual inventory system to ending inventory using a periodic inventory system (from E6-4).

(c) Which inventory cost flow method (FIFO, LIFO) gives the same ending inventory value under both periodic and perpetual? Which method gives different ending inventory values?

**\*E6-18**    Doc Gibbs Company reported the following information for November and December 2008.

*Use the gross profit method to estimate inventory.*

*(SO 8)*

| | November | December |
|---|---|---|
| Cost of goods purchased | $500,000 | $ 610,000 |
| Inventory, beginning-of-month | 100,000 | 120,000 |
| Inventory, end-of-month | 120,000 | ???? |
| Sales | 800,000 | 1,000,000 |

Doc Gibbs's ending inventory at December 31 was destroyed in a fire.

**Instructions**

(a) Compute the gross profit rate for November.

(b) Using the gross profit rate for November, determine the estimated cost of inventory lost in the fire.

**\*E6-19**    The inventory of Faber Company was destroyed by fire on March 1. From an examination of the accounting records, the following data for the first 2 months of the year are obtained: Sales $51,000, Sales Returns and Allowances $1,000, Purchases $31,200, Freight-in $1,200, and Purchase Returns and Allowances $1,400.

*Determine merchandise lost using the gross profit method of estimating inventory.*

*(SO 8)*

**Instructions**

Determine the merchandise lost by fire, assuming:

(a) A beginning inventory of $20,000 and a gross profit rate of 40% on net sales.

(b) A beginning inventory of $30,000 and a gross profit rate of 30% on net sales.

*Determine ending inventory at cost using retail method.*

*(SO 8)*

**\*E6-20**   Quayle Shoe Store uses the retail inventory method for its two departments, Women's Shoes and Men's Shoes. The following information for each department is obtained.

| Item | Women's Department | Men's Department |
|---|---|---|
| Beginning inventory at cost | $ 32,000 | $ 45,000 |
| Cost of goods purchased at cost | 148,000 | 136,300 |
| Net sales | 178,000 | 185,000 |
| Beginning inventory at retail | 46,000 | 60,000 |
| Cost of goods purchased at retail | 179,000 | 185,000 |

**Instructions**

Compute the estimated cost of the ending inventory for each department under the retail inventory method.

# EXERCISES: SET B

Visit the book's website at **www.wiley.com/college/weygandt**, and choose the Student Companion site, to access Exercise Set B.

# PROBLEMS: SET A

*Determine items and amounts to be recorded in inventory.*

*(SO 1)*

**P6-1A**   Heath Limited is trying to determine the value of its ending inventory at February 29, 2008, the company's year end. The accountant counted everything that was in the warehouse as of February 29, which resulted in an ending inventory valuation of $48,000. However, she didn't know how to treat the following transactions so she didn't record them.

(a) On February 26, Heath shipped to a customer goods costing $800. The goods were shipped FOB shipping point, and the receiving report indicates that the customer received the goods on March 2.

(b) On February 26, Seller Inc. shipped goods to Heath FOB destination. The invoice price was $350. The receiving report indicates that the goods were received by Heath on March 2.

(c) Heath had $500 of inventory at a customer's warehouse "on approval." The customer was going to let Heath know whether it wanted the merchandise by the end of the week, March 4.

(d) Heath also had $400 of inventory on consignment at a Jasper craft shop.

(e) On February 26, Heath ordered goods costing $750. The goods were shipped FOB shipping point on February 27. Heath received the goods on March 1.

(f) On February 29, Heath packaged goods and had them ready for shipping to a customer FOB destination. The invoice price was $350; the cost of the items was $250. The receiving report indicates that the goods were received by the customer on March 2.

(g) Heath had damaged goods set aside in the warehouse because they are no longer saleable. These goods originally cost $400 and, originally, Heath expected to sell these items for $600.

**Instructions**

For each of the above transactions, specify whether the item in question should be included in ending inventory, and if so, at what amount. For each item that is not included in ending inventory, indicate who owns it and what account, if any, it should have been recorded in.

*Determine cost of goods sold and ending inventory using FIFO, LIFO, and average-cost with analysis.*

*(SO 2, 3)*

**P6-2A**   Glanville Distribution markets CDs of the performing artist Harrilyn Clooney. At the beginning of March, Glanville had in beginning inventory 1,500 Clooney CDs with a unit cost of $7. During March Glanville made the following purchases of Clooney CDs.

| | | | |
|---|---|---|---|
| March 5 | 3,000 @ $8 | March 21 | 4,000 @ $10 |
| March 13 | 5,500 @ $9 | March 26 | 2,000 @ $11 |

During March 12,500 units were sold. Glanville uses a periodic inventory system.

**Instructions**

**(a)** Determine the cost of goods available for sale.

**(b)** Determine (1) the ending inventory and (2) the cost of goods sold under each of the assumed cost flow methods (FIFO, LIFO, and average-cost). Prove the accuracy of the cost of goods sold under the FIFO and LIFO methods. (Use three decimal places for average-cost.)

**(c)** Which cost flow method results in (1) the highest inventory amount for the balance sheet and (2) the highest cost of goods sold for the income statement?

**P6-3A** Eddings Company had a beginning inventory of 400 units of Product XNA at a cost of $8.00 per unit. During the year, purchases were:

*Determine cost of goods sold and ending inventory using FIFO, LIFO, and average-cost with analysis.*

*(SO 2, 3)*

| | | | |
|---|---|---|---|
| Feb. 20 | 600 units at $9 | Aug. 12 | 300 units at $11 |
| May 5 | 500 units at $10 | Dec. 8 | 200 units at $12 |

Eddings Company uses a periodic inventory system. Sales totaled 1,500 units.

**Instructions**

**(a)** Determine the cost of goods available for sale.

**(b)** Determine (1) the ending inventory, and (2) the cost of goods sold under each of the assumed cost flow methods (FIFO, LIFO, and average). Prove the accuracy of the cost of goods sold under the FIFO and LIFO methods.

**(c)** Which cost flow method results in (1) the lowest inventory amount for the balance sheet, and (2) the lowest cost of goods sold for the income statement?

**P6-4A** The management of Morales Co. is reevaluating the appropriateness of using its present inventory cost flow method, which is average-cost. They request your help in determining the results of operations for 2008 if either the FIFO method or the LIFO method had been used. For 2008, the accounting records show the following data.

*Compute ending inventory, prepare income statements, and answer questions using FIFO and LIFO.*

*(SO 2, 3)*

| Inventories | | Purchases and Sales | |
|---|---|---|---|
| Beginning (15,000 units) | $32,000 | Total net sales (215,000 units) | $865,000 |
| Ending (30,000 units) | | Total cost of goods purchased (230,000 units) | 595,000 |

Purchases were made quarterly as follows.

| Quarter | Units | Unit Cost | Total Cost |
|---|---|---|---|
| 1 | 60,000 | $2.40 | $144,000 |
| 2 | 50,000 | 2.50 | 125,000 |
| 3 | 50,000 | 2.60 | 130,000 |
| 4 | 70,000 | 2.80 | 196,000 |
| | 230,000 | | $595,000 |

Operating expenses were $147,000, and the company's income tax rate is 34%.

**Instructions**

**(a)** Prepare comparative condensed income statements for 2008 under FIFO and LIFO. (Show computations of ending inventory.)

**(b)** ▬▬▬▶ Answer the following questions for management.

    **(1)** Which cost flow method (FIFO or LIFO) produces the more meaningful inventory amount for the balance sheet? Why?

    **(2)** Which cost flow method (FIFO or LIFO) produces the more meaningful net income? Why?

    **(3)** Which cost flow method (FIFO or LIFO) is more likely to approximate actual physical flow of the goods? Why?

    **(4)** How much additional cash will be available for management under LIFO than under FIFO? Why?

    **(5)** Will gross profit under the average-cost method be higher or lower than (a) FIFO and (b) LIFO? (*Note:* It is not necessary to quantify your answer.)

**P6-5A** You are provided with the following information for Pavey Inc. for the month ended October 31, 2008. Pavey uses a periodic method for inventory.

| Date | Description | Units | Unit Cost or Selling Price |
|------|-------------|-------|----------------------------|
| October 1 | Beginning inventory | 60 | $25 |
| October 9 | Purchase | 120 | 26 |
| October 11 | Sale | 100 | 35 |
| October 17 | Purchase | 70 | 27 |
| October 22 | Sale | 60 | 40 |
| October 25 | Purchase | 80 | 28 |
| October 29 | Sale | 110 | 40 |

**Instructions**

(a)(iii) Gross profit:
| | |
|---|---|
| LIFO | $3,050 |
| FIFO | $3,230 |
| Average | $3,141 |

(a) Calculate (i) ending inventory, (ii) cost of goods sold, (iii) gross profit, and (iv) gross profit rate under each of the following methods.
 (1) LIFO.
 (2) FIFO.
 (3) Average-cost.
(b) Compare results for the three cost flow assumptions.

**P6-6A** You have the following information for Bernelli Diamonds. Bernelli Diamonds uses the periodic method of accounting for its inventory transactions. Bernelli only carries one brand and size of diamonds—all are identical. Each batch of diamonds purchased is carefully coded and marked with its purchase cost.

| | | |
|---|---|---|
| March 1 | Beginning inventory 150 diamonds at a cost of $300 per diamond. | |
| March 3 | Purchased 200 diamonds at a cost of $350 each. | |
| March 5 | Sold 180 diamonds for $600 each. | |
| March 10 | Purchased 350 diamonds at a cost of $375 each. | |
| March 25 | Sold 400 diamonds for $650 each. | |

**Instructions**

(a) Gross profit:
 (1) Maximum $166,750

 (2) Minimum $157,750

(a) Assume that Bernelli Diamonds uses the specific identification cost flow method.
 (1) Demonstrate how Bernelli Diamonds could maximize its gross profit for the month by specifically selecting which diamonds to sell on March 5 and March 25.
 (2) Demonstrate how Bernelli Diamonds could minimize its gross profit for the month by selecting which diamonds to sell on March 5 and March 25.
(b) Assume that Bernelli Diamonds uses the FIFO cost flow assumption. Calculate cost of goods sold. How much gross profit would Bernelli Diamonds report under this cost flow assumption?
(c) Assume that Bernelli Diamonds uses the LIFO cost flow assumption. Calculate cost of goods sold. How much gross profit would the company report under this cost flow assumption?
(d) Which cost flow method should Bernelli Diamonds select? Explain.

**P6-7A** The management of Utley Inc. asks your help in determining the comparative effects of the FIFO and LIFO inventory cost flow methods. For 2008 the accounting records show these data.

| | |
|---|---|
| Inventory, January 1 (10,000 units) | $ 35,000 |
| Cost of 120,000 units purchased | 504,500 |
| Selling price of 100,000 units sold | 665,000 |
| Operating expenses | 130,000 |

Units purchased consisted of 35,000 units at $4.00 on May 10; 60,000 units at $4.20 on August 15; and 25,000 units at $4.50 on November 20. Income taxes are 28%.

**Instructions**

Gross profit:
| | |
|---|---|
| FIFO | $259,000 |
| LIFO | $240,500 |

(a) Prepare comparative condensed income statements for 2008 under FIFO and LIFO. (Show computations of ending inventory.)
(b) ▬▬▶ Answer the following questions for management in the form of a business letter.
 (1) Which inventory cost flow method produces the most meaningful inventory amount for the balance sheet? Why?

(2) Which inventory cost flow method produces the most meaningful net income? Why?

(3) Which inventory cost flow method is most likely to approximate the actual physical flow of the goods? Why?

(4) How much more cash will be available for management under LIFO than under FIFO? Why?

(5) How much of the gross profit under FIFO is illusionary in comparison with the gross profit under LIFO?

**\*P6-8A**   Vasquez Ltd. is a retailer operating in Edmonton, Alberta. Vasquez uses the perpetual inventory method. All sales returns from customers result in the goods being returned to inventory; the inventory is not damaged. Assume that there are no credit transactions; all amounts are settled in cash. You are provided with the following information for Vasquez Ltd. for the month of January 2008.

*Calculate cost of goods sold and ending inventory for FIFO, average-cost, and LIFO under the perpetual system; compare gross profit under each assumption.*

*(SO 7)*

| Date | Description | Quantity | Unit Cost or Selling Price |
|---|---|---|---|
| December 31 | Ending inventory | 150 | $17 |
| January 2 | Purchase | 100 | 21 |
| January 6 | Sale | 150 | 40 |
| January 9 | Sale return | 10 | 40 |
| January 9 | Purchase | 75 | 24 |
| January 10 | Purchase return | 15 | 24 |
| January 10 | Sale | 50 | 45 |
| January 23 | Purchase | 100 | 28 |
| January 30 | Sale | 110 | 50 |

**Instructions**

(a) For each of the following cost flow assumptions, calculate (i) cost of goods sold, (ii) ending inventory, and (iii) gross profit. (Round average-cost to three decimal places.)

(1) LIFO.    (2) FIFO.    (3) Moving-average-cost.

(b) Compare results for the three cost flow assumptions.

Gross profit:
LIFO   $6,330
FIFO   $7,500
Average   $7,090

**\*P6-9A**   Sandoval Appliance Mart began operations on May 1. It uses a perpetual inventory system. During May the company had the following purchases and sales for its Model 25 Sureshot camera.

*Determine ending inventory under a perpetual inventory system.*

*(SO 7)*

| | Purchases | | |
|---|---|---|---|
| Date | Units | Unit Cost | Sales Units |
| May 1 | 7 | $150 | |
| 4 | | | 4 |
| 8 | 8 | $170 | |
| 12 | | | 5 |
| 15 | 6 | $185 | |
| 20 | | | 3 |
| 25 | | | 4 |

**Instructions**

(a) Determine the ending inventory under a perpetual inventory system using (1) FIFO, (2) average-cost, and (3) LIFO.

(b) Which costing method produces (1) the highest ending inventory valuation and (2) the lowest ending inventory valuation?

(a) FIFO   $925
Average   $874
LIFO   $790

**\*P6-10A**   Saffordville Company lost 70% of its inventory in a fire on March 25, 2008. The accounting records showed the following gross profit data for February and March.

*Estimate inventory loss using gross profit method.*

*(SO 8)*

| | February | March (to 3/25) |
|---|---|---|
| Net sales | $300,000 | $250,000 |
| Net purchases | 197,800 | 191,000 |
| Freight-in | 2,900 | 4,000 |
| Beginning inventory | 4,500 | 13,200 |
| Ending inventory | 13,200 | ? |

Saffordville Company is fully insured for fire losses but must prepare a report for the insurance company.

**Instructions**

(a) Gross profit $108,000

(a) Compute the gross profit rate for the month of February.

(b) Using the gross profit rate for February, determine both the estimated total inventory and inventory lost in the fire in March.

*Compute ending inventory using retail method.*

*(SO 8)*

**\*P6-11A** Neer Department Store uses the retail inventory method to estimate its monthly ending inventories. The following information is available for two of its departments at August 31, 2008.

| | Sporting Goods | | Jewelry and Cosmetics | |
|---|---|---|---|---|
| | Cost | Retail | Cost | Retail |
| Net sales | | $1,000,000 | | $1,160,000 |
| Purchases | $675,000 | 1,066,000 | $741,000 | 1,158,000 |
| Purchase returns | (26,000) | (40,000) | (12,000) | (20,000) |
| Purchase discounts | (12,360) | — | (2,440) | — |
| Freight-in | 9,000 | — | 14,000 | — |
| Beginning inventory | 47,360 | 74,000 | 39,440 | 62,000 |

At December 31, Neer Department Store takes a physical inventory at retail. The actual retail values of the inventories in each department are Sporting Goods $95,000, and Jewelry and Cosmetics $44,000.

**Instructions**

(a) Sporting Goods cost ratio 63%

(a) Determine the estimated cost of the ending inventory for each department on **August 31**, 2008, using the retail inventory method.

(b) Compute the ending inventory at cost for each department at **December 31**, assuming the cost-to-retail ratios are 60% for Sporting Goods and 64% for Jewelry and Cosmetics.

# PROBLEMS: SET B

*Determine items and amounts to be recorded in inventory.*

*(SO 1)*

**P6-1B** Slaymakker Country Limited is trying to determine the value of its ending inventory as of February 29, 2008, the company's year-end. The following transactions occurred, and the accountant asked your help in determining whether they should be recorded or not.

(a) On February 26, Slaymakker shipped goods costing $800 to a customer and charged the customer $1,000. The goods were shipped with terms FOB destination and the receiving report indicates that the customer received the goods on March 2.

(b) On February 26, Seller Inc. shipped goods to Slaymakker under terms FOB shipping point. The invoice price was $350 plus $25 for freight. The receiving report indicates that the goods were received by Slaymakker on March 2.

(c) Slaymakker had $500 of inventory isolated in the warehouse. The inventory is designated for a customer who has requested that the goods be shipped on March 10.

(d) Also included in Slaymakker's warehouse is $400 of inventory that Craft Producers shipped to Slaymakker on consignment.

(e) On February 26, Slaymakker issued a purchase order to acquire goods costing $750. The goods were shipped with terms FOB destination on February 27. Slaymakker received the goods on March 2.

(f) On February 26, Slaymakker shipped goods to a customer under terms FOB shipping point. The invoice price was $350 plus $25 for freight; the cost of the items was $300. The receiving report indicates that the goods were received by the customer on March 2.

**Instructions**

For each of the above transactions, specify whether the item in question should be included in ending inventory, and if so, at what amount.

*Determine cost of goods sold and ending inventory using FIFO, LIFO, and average-cost with analysis.*

*(SO 2, 3)*

**P6-2B** Carrington Distribution markets CDs of the performing artist Christina Spears. At the beginning of October, Carrington had in beginning inventory 1,000 Spears CDs with a unit cost of $5. During October Carrington made the following purchases of Spears CDs.

|        |              |        |             |
|--------|--------------|--------|-------------|
| Oct. 3 | 3,500 @ $6   | Oct. 19 | 2,000 @ $8 |
| Oct. 9 | 4,000 @ $7   | Oct. 25 | 2,000 @ $9 |

During October 9,500 units were sold. Carrington uses a periodic inventory system.

**Instructions**
**(a)** Determine the cost of goods available for sale.
**(b)** Determine (1) the ending inventory and (2) the cost of goods sold under each of the assumed cost flow methods (FIFO, LIFO, and average-cost). Prove the accuracy of the cost of goods sold under the FIFO and LIFO methods.
**(c)** Which cost flow method results in (1) the highest inventory amount for the balance sheet and (2) the highest cost of goods sold for the income statement?

(b)(2) Cost of goods sold:
FIFO        $62,000
LIFO        $71,000
Average   $66,880

**P6-3B**    Shellankamp Company had a beginning inventory on January 1 of 100 units of Product WD-44 at a cost of $21 per unit. During the year, the following purchases were made.

| | | | |
|--------|-------------------|---------|-------------------|
| Mar. 15 | 300 units at $24 | Sept. 4 | 300 units at $28 |
| July 20 | 200 units at $25 | Dec. 2  | 100 units at $30 |

800 units were sold. Shellankamp Company uses a periodic inventory system.

*Determine cost of goods sold and ending inventory, using FIFO, LIFO, and average-cost with analysis.*

*(SO 2, 3)*

**Instructions**
**(a)** Determine the cost of goods available for sale.
**(b)** Determine (1) the ending inventory, and (2) the cost of goods sold under each of the assumed cost flow methods (FIFO, LIFO, and average-cost). Prove the accuracy of the cost of goods sold under the FIFO and LIFO methods.
**(c)** Which cost flow method results in (1) the highest inventory amount for the balance sheet, and (2) the highest cost of goods sold for the income statement?

(b)(2) Cost of goods sold:
FIFO        $19,900
LIFO        $21,200
Average   $20,560

**P6-4B**    The management of Groneman Inc. is reevaluating the appropriateness of using its present inventory cost flow method, which is average-cost. The company requests your help in determining the results of operations for 2008 if either the FIFO or the LIFO method had been used. For 2008 the accounting records show these data:

*Compute ending inventory, prepare income statements, and answer questions using FIFO and LIFO.*

*(SO 2, 3)*

| Inventories | | Purchases and Sales | |
|-------------|---------|---------------------|---------|
| Beginning (10,000 units) | $22,800 | Total net sales (220,000 units) | $865,000 |
| Ending (20,000 units) | | Total cost of goods purchased (230,000 units) | 578,500 |

Purchases were made quarterly as follows.

| Quarter | Units | Unit Cost | Total Cost |
|---------|---------|-----------|------------|
| 1 | 60,000 | $2.30 | $138,000 |
| 2 | 50,000 | 2.50 | 125,000 |
| 3 | 50,000 | 2.60 | 130,000 |
| 4 | 70,000 | 2.65 | 185,500 |
| | 230,000 | | $578,500 |

Operating expenses were $147,000, and the company's income tax rate is 32%.

**Instructions**
**(a)** Prepare comparative condensed income statements for 2008 under FIFO and LIFO. (Show computations of ending inventory.)
**(b)** ⬛⬛⬛➤ Answer the following questions for management.
  **(1)** Which cost flow method (FIFO or LIFO) produces the more meaningful inventory amount for the balance sheet? Why?
  **(2)** Which cost flow method (FIFO or LIFO) produces the more meaningful net income? Why?
  **(3)** Which cost flow method (FIFO or LIFO) is more likely to approximate the actual physical flow of goods? Why?
  **(4)** How much more cash will be available for management under LIFO than under FIFO? Why?
  **(5)** Will gross profit under the average-cost method be higher or lower than FIFO? Than LIFO? (*Note*: It is not necessary to quantify your answer.)

(a) Gross profit:
FIFO   $316,700
LIFO   $309,500

*Calculate ending inventory, cost of goods sold, gross profit, and gross profit rate under periodic method; compare results.*

*(SO 2, 3)*

**P6-5B** You are provided with the following information for Charlote Inc. for the month ended June 30, 2008. Charlote uses the periodic method for inventory.

| Date | Description | Quantity | Unit Cost or Selling Price |
|---|---|---|---|
| June 1 | Beginning inventory | 25 | $60 |
| June 4 | Purchase | 85 | 64 |
| June 10 | Sale | 70 | 90 |
| June 11 | Sale return | 10 | 90 |
| June 18 | Purchase | 35 | 68 |
| June 18 | Purchase return | 5 | 68 |
| June 25 | Sale | 40 | 95 |
| June 28 | Purchase | 20 | 72 |

**Instructions**

*(a)(iii) Gross profit:*
| | |
|---|---|
| LIFO | $2,520 |
| FIFO | $2,900 |
| Average | $2,687.50 |

**(a)** Calculate (i) ending inventory, (ii) cost of goods sold, (iii) gross profit, and (iv) gross profit rate under each of the following methods. (Use three decimal places for average-cost.)
    **(1)** LIFO.    **(2)** FIFO.    **(3)** Average-cost.
**(b)** Compare results for the three cost flow assumptions.

*Compare specific identification, FIFO, and LIFO under periodic method; use cost flow assumption to justify price increase.*

*(SO 2, 3)*

**P6-6B** You are provided with the following information for Rondelli Inc. Rondelli Inc. uses the periodic method of accounting for its inventory transactions.

March 1   Beginning inventory 1,500 litres at a cost of 40¢ per litre.
March 3   Purchased 2,000 litres at a cost of 45¢ per litre.
March 5   Sold 1,800 litres for 60¢ per litre.
March 10  Purchased 3,500 litres at a cost of 49¢ per litre.
March 20  Purchased 2,000 litres at a cost of 55¢ per litre.
March 30  Sold 4,500 litres for 70¢ per litre.

**Instructions**

**(a)** Prepare partial income statements through gross profit, and calculate the value of ending inventory that would be reported on the balance sheet, under each of the following cost flow assumptions.

*(a)(1) Gross profit:*
Specific identification
    $1,256

  **(1)** Specific identification method assuming:
    **(i)** the March 5 sale consisted of 900 litres from the March 1 beginning inventory and 900 litres from the March 3 purchase; and
    **(ii)** the March 30 sale consisted of the following number of units sold from beginning inventory and each purchase: 400 litres from March 1; 500 litres from March 3; 2,600 litres from March 10; 1,000 litres from March 20.

*(2) FIFO   $1,358*
*(3) LIFO   $1,055*

  **(2)** FIFO.
  **(3)** LIFO.

**(b)** How can companies use a cost flow method to justify price increases? Which cost flow method would best support an argument to increase prices?

*Compute ending inventory, prepare income statements, and answer questions using FIFO and LIFO.*

*(SO 2, 3)*

**P6-7B** The management of Dains Co. asks your help in determining the comparative effects of the FIFO and LIFO inventory cost flow methods. For 2008, the accounting records show the following data.

| | |
|---|---|
| Inventory, January 1 (10,000 units) | $ 37,000 |
| Cost of 110,000 units purchased | 479,000 |
| Selling price of 90,000 units sold | 630,000 |
| Operating expenses | 120,000 |

Units purchased consisted of 40,000 units at $4.20 on May 10; 50,000 units at $4.40 on August 15; and 20,000 units at $4.55 on November 20. Income taxes are 30%.

**Instructions**

*(a) Net income*
| | |
|---|---|
| FIFO | $90,300 |
| LIFO | $80,500 |

**(a)** Prepare comparative condensed income statements for 2008 under FIFO and LIFO. (Show computations of ending inventory.)
**(b)**         Answer the following questions for management.
  **(1)** Which inventory cost flow method produces the most meaningful inventory amount for the balance sheet? Why?

(2) Which inventory cost flow method produces the most meaningful net income? Why?

(3) Which inventory cost flow method is most likely to approximate actual physical flow of the goods? Why?

(4) How much additional cash will be available for management under LIFO than under FIFO? Why?

(5) How much of the gross profit under FIFO is illusory in comparison with the gross profit under LIFO?

**\*P6-8B**    Fechter Inc. is a retailer operating in Dartmouth, Nova Scotia. Fechter uses the perpetual inventory method. All sales returns from customers result in the goods being returned to inventory; the inventory is not damaged. Assume that there are no credit transactions; all amounts are settled in cash. You are provided with the following information for Fechter Inc. for the month of January 2008.

*Calculate cost of goods sold and ending inventory under LIFO, FIFO, and average-cost under the perpetual system; compare gross profit under each assumption.*

(SO 7)

| Date | Description | Quantity | Unit Cost or Selling Price |
|---|---|---|---|
| January 1 | Beginning inventory | 50 | $12 |
| January 5 | Purchase | 100 | 14 |
| January 8 | Sale | 80 | 25 |
| January 10 | Sale return | 10 | 25 |
| January 15 | Purchase | 30 | 18 |
| January 16 | Purchase return | 5 | 18 |
| January 20 | Sale | 75 | 25 |
| January 25 | Purchase | 10 | 20 |

**Instructions**

(a) For each of the following cost flow assumptions, calculate (i) cost of goods sold, (ii) ending inventory, and (iii) gross profit. (Round moving-average-cost to three decimal places.)

(1) LIFO.        (2) FIFO.        (3) Moving-average-cost.

(b) Compare results for the three cost flow assumptions.

Gross profit:
LIFO      $1,535
FIFO      $1,695
Average   $1,608

**\*P6-9B**    Falco Co. began operations on July 1. It uses a perpetual inventory system. During July the company had the following purchases and sales.

*Determine ending inventory under a perpetual inventory system.*

(SO 7)

| Date | Purchases Units | Purchases Unit Cost | Sales Units |
|---|---|---|---|
| July 1 | 4 | $ 90 | |
| July 6 | | | 3 |
| July 11 | 5 | $ 99 | |
| July 14 | | | 2 |
| July 21 | 6 | $106 | |
| July 27 | | | 5 |

**Instructions**

(a) Determine the ending inventory under a perpetual inventory system using (1) FIFO, (2) average-cost, and (3) LIFO.

(b) Which costing method produces the highest ending inventory valuation?

(a) Ending inventory
FIFO   $530
Avg.   $513
LIFO   $493

**\*P6-10B**    Hannigan Company lost all of its inventory in a fire on December 26, 2008. The accounting records showed the following gross profit data for November and December.

*Compute gross profit rate and inventory loss using gross profit method.*

(SO 8)

| | November | December (to 12/26) |
|---|---|---|
| Net sales | $500,000 | $400,000 |
| Beginning inventory | 34,100 | 31,100 |
| Purchases | 334,975 | 246,000 |
| Purchase returns and allowances | 11,800 | 5,000 |
| Purchase discounts | 7,577 | 6,000 |
| Freight-in | 6,402 | 3,700 |
| Ending inventory | 31,100 | ? |

Hannigan is fully insured for fire losses but must prepare a report for the insurance company.

(a) Gross profit $175,000

### Instructions
(a) Compute the gross profit rate for November.
(b) Using the gross profit rate for November, determine the estimated cost of the inventory lost in the fire.

*Compute ending inventory using retail method.*

(SO 8)

**\*P6-11B** Frontenac Books uses the retail inventory method to estimate its monthly ending inventories. The following information is available for two of its departments at October 31, 2008.

| | Hardcovers | | Paperbacks | |
|---|---|---|---|---|
| | **Cost** | **Retail** | **Cost** | **Retail** |
| Beginning inventory | $ 256,000 | $ 400,000 | $ 65,000 | $ 90,000 |
| Purchases | 1,180,000 | 1,825,000 | 266,000 | 380,000 |
| Freight-in | 4,000 | | 2,000 | |
| Purchase discounts | 16,000 | | 4,000 | |
| Net sales | | 1,827,000 | | 385,000 |

At December 31, Frontenac Books takes a physical inventory at retail. The actual retail values of the inventories in each department are Hardcovers $395,000 and Paperbacks $88,000.

### Instructions

(a) Hardcovers cost ratio 64%

(a) Determine the estimated cost of the ending inventory for each department at **October 31**, 2008, using the retail inventory method.
(b) Compute the ending inventory at cost for each department at **December 31**, assuming the cost-to-retail ratios for the year are 65% for hardcovers and 70% for paperbacks.

## PROBLEMS: SET C

Visit the book's website at **www.wiley.com/college/weygandt**, and choose the Student Companion site, to access Problem Set C.

## CONTINUING COOKIE CHRONICLE

(*Note:* This is a continuation of the Cookie Chronicle from Chapters 1 through 5.)

**CCC6** Natalie is busy establishing both divisions of her business (cookie classes and mixer sales) and completing her business degree. Her goals for the next 11 months are to sell one mixer per month and to give two to three classes per week.

The cost of the fine European mixers is expected to increase. Natalie has just negotiated new terms with Kzinski that include shipping costs in the negotiated purchase price (mixers will be shipped FOB destination), but the supplier cannot guarantee the invoice price. Natalie must choose a cost flow assumption for her mixer inventory.

*Go to the book's website,*
**www.wiley.com/college/weygandt**,
*to see the completion of this problem.*

# BROADENING YOUR PERSPECTIVE

## FINANCIAL REPORTING AND ANALYSIS

## Financial Reporting Problem
### PepsiCo, Inc.

**BYP6-1** The notes that accompany a company's financial statements provide informative details that would clutter the amounts and descriptions presented in the statements. Refer to the financial statements of PepsiCo and the Notes to Consolidated Financial Statements in Appendix A.

**Instructions**

Answer the following questions. Complete the requirements in millions of dollars, as shown in PepsiCo's annual report.

**(a)** What did PepsiCo report for the amount of inventories in its consolidated balance sheet at December 31, 2005? At December 25, 2004?

**(b)** Compute the dollar amount of change and the percentage change in inventories between 2004 and 2005. Compute inventory as a percentage of current assets at December 31, 2005.

**(c)** How does PepsiCo value its inventories? Which inventory cost flow method does PepsiCo use? (See Notes to the Financial Statements.)

**(d)** What is the cost of sales (cost of goods sold) reported by PepsiCo for 2005, 2004, and 2003? Compute the percentage of cost of sales to net sales in 2005.

## Comparative Analysis Problem

### PepsiCo, Inc. vs. The Coca-Cola Company

**BYP6-2**   PepsiCo's financial statements are presented in Appendix A. Coca-Cola's financial statements are presented in Appendix B.

**Instructions**

**(a)** Based on the information contained in these financial statements, compute the following 2005 ratios for each company.
   **(1)** Inventory turnover ratio
   **(2)** Days in inventory

**(b)** What conclusions concerning the management of the inventory can you draw from these data?

## Exploring the Web

**BYP6-3**   A company's annual report usually will identify the inventory method used. Knowing that, you can analyze the effects of the inventory method on the income statement and balance sheet.

**Address: www.cisco.com**, or go to **www.wiley.com/college/weygandt**

**Instructions**

Answer the following questions based on the current year's Annual Report on Cisco's Web site.

**(a)** At Cisco's fiscal year-end, what was the inventory on the balance sheet?
**(b)** How has this changed from the previous fiscal year-end?
**(c)** How much of the inventory was finished goods?
**(d)** What inventory method does Cisco use?

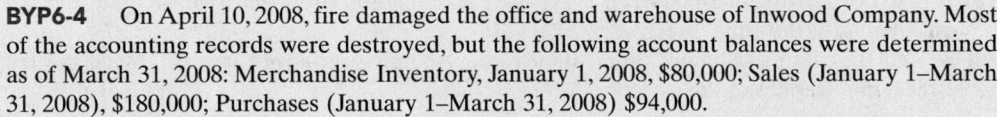

CRITICAL THINKING

## Decision Making Across the Organization

**BYP6-4**   On April 10, 2008, fire damaged the office and warehouse of Inwood Company. Most of the accounting records were destroyed, but the following account balances were determined as of March 31, 2008: Merchandise Inventory, January 1, 2008, $80,000; Sales (January 1–March 31, 2008), $180,000; Purchases (January 1–March 31, 2008) $94,000.

The company's fiscal year ends on December 31. It uses a periodic inventory system.

From an analysis of the April bank statement, you discover cancelled checks of $4,200 for cash purchases during the period April 1–10. Deposits during the same period totaled $18,500. Of that amount, 60% were collections on accounts receivable, and the balance was cash sales.

Correspondence with the company's principal suppliers revealed $12,400 of purchases on account from April 1 to April 10. Of that amount, $1,600 was for merchandise in transit on April 10 that was shipped FOB destination.

Correspondence with the company's principal customers produced acknowledgments of credit sales totaling $37,000 from April 1 to April 10. It was estimated that $5,600 of credit sales will never be acknowledged or recovered from customers.

Inwood Company reached an agreement with the insurance company that its fire-loss claim should be based on the average of the gross profit rates for the preceding 2 years. The financial statements for 2006 and 2007 showed the following data.

|  | 2007 | 2006 |
|---|---|---|
| Net sales | $600,000 | $480,000 |
| Cost of goods purchased | 404,000 | 356,000 |
| Beginning inventory | 60,000 | 40,000 |
| Ending inventory | 80,000 | 60,000 |

Inventory with a cost of $17,000 was salvaged from the fire.

**Instructions**

With the class divided into groups, answer the following.

**(a)** Determine the balances in (1) Sales and (2) Purchases at April 10.
*(b)* Determine the average profit rate for the years 2006 and 2007. (*Hint*: Find the gross profit rate for each year and divide the sum by 2.)
*(c)* Determine the inventory loss as a result of the fire, using the gross profit method.

# Communication Activity

**BYP6-5**   You are the controller of Small Toys Inc. Janice LeMay, the president, recently mentioned to you that she found an error in the 2007 financial statements which she believes has corrected itself. She determined, in discussions with the Purchasing Department, that 2007 ending inventory was overstated by $1 million. Janice says that the 2008 ending inventory is correct. Thus she assumes that 2008 income is correct. Janice says to you, "What happened has happened—there's no point in worrying about it anymore."

**Instructions**

You conclude that Janice is incorrect. Write a brief, tactful memo to Janice, clarifying the situation.

# Ethics Case

**BYP6-6**   B. J. Ortiz Wholesale Corp. uses the LIFO method of inventory costing. In the current year, profit at B. J. Ortiz is running unusually high. The corporate tax rate is also high this year, but it is scheduled to decline significantly next year. In an effort to lower the current year's net income and to take advantage of the changing income tax rate, the president of B. J. Ortiz Wholesale instructs the plant accountant to recommend to the purchasing department a large purchase of inventory for delivery 3 days before the end of the year. The price of the inventory to be purchased has doubled during the year, and the purchase will represent a major portion of the ending inventory value.

**Instructions**

**(a)** What is the effect of this transaction on this year's and next year's income statement and income tax expense? Why?
**(b)** If B. J. Ortiz Wholesale had been using the FIFO method of inventory costing, would the president give the same directive?
**(c)** Should the plant accountant order the inventory purchase to lower income? What are the ethical implications of this order?

 # "All About You" Activity

**BYP6-7**   Some of the largest business frauds ever perpetrated have involved the misstatement of inventory. Two classics were at Leslie Fay Cos., and McKesson Corporation.

**Instructions**

There is considerable information regarding inventory frauds available on the Internet. Search for information about one of the two cases mentioned above, or inventory fraud at any other company, and prepare a short explanation of the nature of the inventory fraud.

## Answers to Insight and Accounting Across the Organization Questions

**How Wal-Mart Tracks Inventory, p. 247**

Q:  Why is inventory control important to managers such as those at Wal-Mart?

A:  *In the very competitive environment of discount retailing, where Wal-Mart is the major player, small differences in price matter to the customer. Wal-Mart sells a high volume of inventory at a low gross profit rate. When operating in a high-volume, low-margin environment, small cost savings can mean the difference between being profitable or going out of business.*

**"Fill 'Em Up"—With Water, Not Oil, p. 248**

Q:  What effect does an overstatement of inventory have on a company's financial statements?

A:  *The balance sheet looks stronger because inventory and retained earnings are overstated. The income statement looks better because cost of goods sold is understated and income is overstated.*

**Samsung Uses a Different Strategy, p. 262**

Q.  If Samsung isn't successful in selling the units, what steps will it have to take, and how will this show up in its financial statements?

A.  *If Samsung increases production, but then can't sell the units, its finished goods inventory will increase. Because cell phones are constantly changing, Samsung would want to take steps to sell off the inventory before it becomes obsolete. Thus, it would need to offer big discounts. Such a strategy would get its inventory down to desirable levels, but would severely depress the company's gross profit.*

## Authors' Comments on *All About You:* Employee Theft—An Inside Job, p. 263

Opinions regarding video technology differ greatly. One chief operating officer of a pub and restaurant chain says his company considers them "Big Brother-ish and demeaning." However, others feel that they are sometimes the only effective option. When properly implemented, theft-reduction procedures don't need to offend employees or customers. Wal-Mart has long employed senior citizens as greeters at its stores. Many people don't realize that these "greeters" are actually part of Wal-Mart's anti-shoplifting efforts.

Also, the need for video cameras depends, in part, on the nature of the product. In business environments where the inventory is of lower value, and/or not easily stolen, other techniques can be effective. However, in the case of expensive inventory items that can be easily concealed (such as expensive bottles of wine), reliance on video surveillance may be necessary.

## Answer to PepsiCo Review It Question 2, p. 258

PepsiCo uses the average, FIFO, and LIFO methods to account for its inventories.

## Answers to Self-Study Questions

**1.** a    **2.** b    **3.** c    **4.** d    **5.** c    **6.** d    **7.** d    **8.** b    **9.** d    **\*10.** b    **\*11.** d

*Remember to go back to the Navigator box on the chapter-opening page and check off your completed work.*

# Chapter 7

# Accounting Principles

## STUDY OBJECTIVES

*After studying this chapter, you should be able to:*

1 Explain the meaning of GAAP and identify the key items of the conceptual framework.
2 Describe the basic objectives of financial reporting.
3 Discuss the qualitative characteristics of accounting information and elements of financial statements.
4 Identify the basic assumptions used by accountants.
5 Identify the basic principles of accounting.
6 Identify the two constraints in accounting.
7 Understand and analyze classified financial statements.
8 Explain the accounting principles used in international operations.

✓ The Navigator

## ✓ The Navigator

| | |
|---|---|
| Scan **Study Objectives** | ■ |
| Read **Feature Story** | ■ |
| Read **Preview** | ■ |
| Read text and answer **Before You Go On** p. 298 ■    p. 304 ■    p. 313 ■ | |
| Work **Demonstration Problems** | ■ |
| Review **Summary of Study Objectives** | ■ |
| Answer **Self-Study Questions** | ■ |
| Complete **Assignments** | ■ |

## *Feature Story*

**CERTAINLY WORTH INVESTIGATING!**

It is often difficult to determine in what period some revenues and expenses should be reported. There are rules that give guidance, but occasionally these rules are overlooked, misinterpreted, or even intentionally ignored. Consider the following examples.

• Policy Management Systems, which makes insurance software, said that it reported some sales before contracts were signed or products delivered.

• Sunbeam Corporation, while under the control of the (in)famous "Chainsaw" Al Dunlap, prematurely booked revenues and recorded overly large restructuring charges. Ultimately the company had to restate its net income

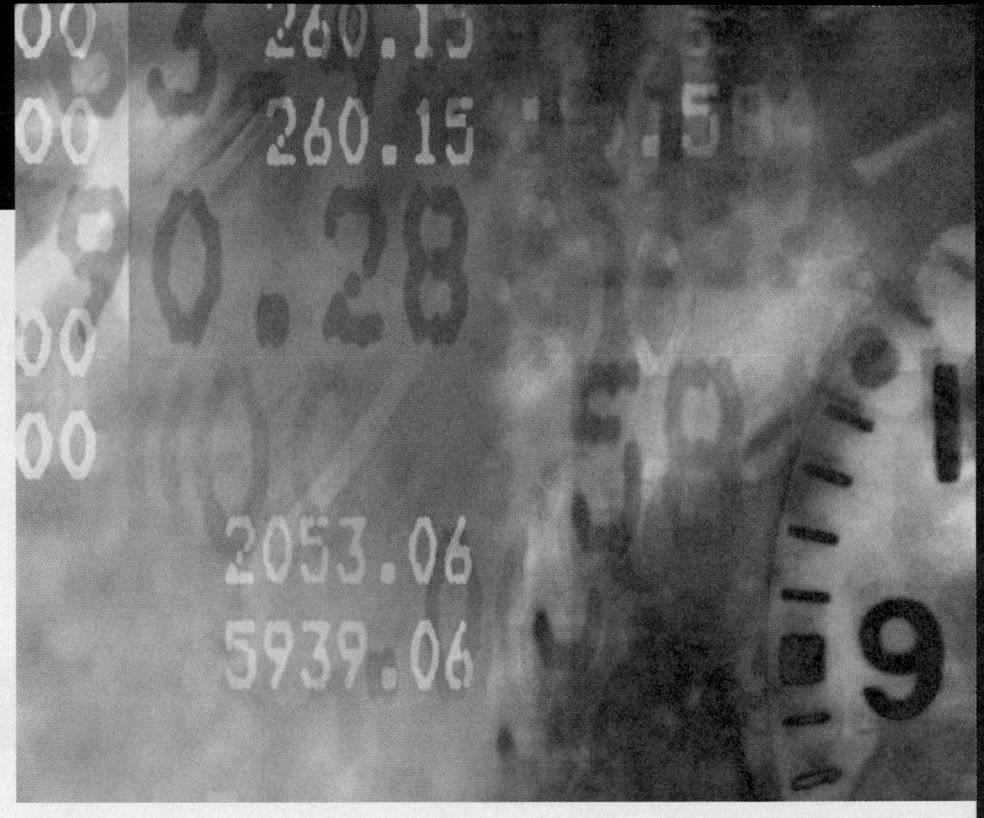

figures, and Mr. Dunlap lost his job.

- Rent-Way Inc., which owns a large chain of rent-to-own stores, saw its share price plummet from $23.44 to $5 within a week after it disclosed what the company termed "fictitious" accounting entries on its books. These entries included improper accounting for fixed-asset write-offs, and understating the amount of damaged or missing merchandise.

Often in cases such as these, the company's stockholders sue the company because of the decline in the stock price due to the disclosure of the misinformation. In light of this eventuality, why might management want to report revenues or expenses in the wrong period? Company managers are under intense pressure to report higher earnings every year. If actual performance falls short of expectations, management might be tempted to bend the rules.

One analyst suggests that investors and auditors should be suspicious of sharp increases in monthly sales at the end of each quarter or big jumps in fourth-quarter sales. Such events don't always mean management is cheating, but they are certainly worth investigating.

✓ *The Navigator*

## *Inside Chapter 7*

As indicated in the Feature Story, it is important that companies have general guidelines available to resolve accounting issues. Without these basic guidelines, each company would have to develop its own set of accounting practices. If this happened, we would have to become familiar with every company's peculiar accounting and reporting rules in order to understand its financial statements. It would be almost impossible to compare the financial statements of different companies. This chapter explores the basic accounting principles that are followed in developing specific accounting guidelines.

The content and organization of Chapter 7 are as follows.

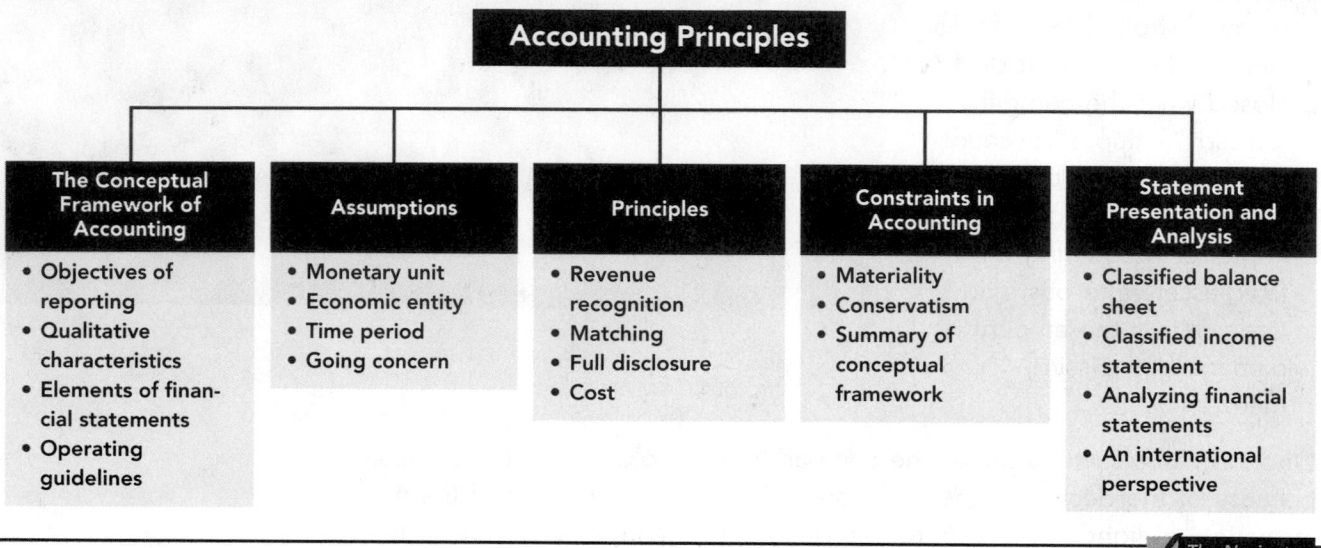

The Navigator

# THE CONCEPTUAL FRAMEWORK OF ACCOUNTING

**STUDY OBJECTIVE 1**

Explain the meaning of GAAP and identify the key items of the conceptual framework.

What you have learned up to this point in the book is a process that leads to the preparation of financial reports about a company. These are the company's financial statements. This area of accounting is called **financial accounting**. The accounting profession has established a set of standards and rules that are recognized as a general guide for financial reporting. This recognized set of standards is called **generally accepted accounting principles (GAAP)**. *Generally accepted* means that these principles have "substantial authoritative support." Such support usually comes from two standard-setting bodies: the Financial Accounting Standards Board (FASB) and the Securities and Exchange Commission (SEC).[1]

Since the early 1970s the business and governmental communities have given the FASB the responsibility for developing accounting principles in this country. This is an ongoing process; accounting principles change to reflect changes in the business environment and in the needs of users of accounting information.

---

[1]The SEC is an agency of the U.S. government that was established in 1933 to administer laws and regulations relating to the exchange of securities and the publication of financial information by U.S. businesses. The agency has the authority to mandate generally accepted accounting principles for companies under its jurisdiction. However, throughout its history, the SEC has been willing to accept the principles set forth by the FASB and similar bodies.

Prior to the establishment of the FASB, accounting principles were developed on a problem-by-problem basis. Rule-making bodies developed accounting rules and methods to solve specific problems. Critics charged that the problem-by-problem approach led over time to inconsistent rules and practices. No clearly developed conceptual framework of accounting existed to refer to in solving new problems.

In response to these criticisms, the FASB developed a conceptual framework. It serves as the basis for resolving accounting and reporting problems. The FASB spent considerable time and effort on this project. The Board views its conceptual framework as "... a constitution, a coherent system of interrelated objectives and fundamentals."[2]

The FASB's conceptual framework consists of the following four items:

1. Objectives of financial reporting.
2. Qualitative characteristics of accounting information.
3. Elements of financial statements.
4. Operating guidelines (assumptions, principles, and constraints).

We will discuss these items on the following pages.

**HELPFUL HINT**

Accounting principles are affected by economic and political conditions which change over time. As a result, accounting principles are not cut into stone like the periodic table in chemistry or a formula in math.

## Objectives of Financial Reporting

The FASB began to work on the conceptual framework by looking at the objectives of financial reporting. Determining these objectives required answers to such basic questions as: Who uses financial statements? Why? What information do they need? How knowledgeable about business and accounting are financial statement users? How should financial information be reported so that it is best understood?

In answering these questions, the FASB concluded that the objectives of financial reporting are to provide information that:

1. Is useful to those making investment and credit decisions.
2. Is helpful in assessing future cash flows.
3. Identifies the economic resources (assets), the claims to those resources (liabilities), and the changes in those resources and claims.

The FASB then undertook to describe the characteristics that make accounting information useful.

**STUDY OBJECTIVE 2**

Describe the basic objectives of financial reporting.

## Qualitative Characteristics of Accounting Information

How does a company like Microsoft decide on the amount of financial information to disclose? In what format should Walt Disney present its financial information? How should it measure assets, liabilities, revenues, and expenses? The FASB concluded that the overriding criterion for such accounting choices is **decision usefulness**. The accounting practice selected should be the one that generates the most useful financial information for making a decision. To be useful, information should possess the following qualitative characteristics: relevance, reliability, comparability, and consistency.

**STUDY OBJECTIVE 3**

Discuss the qualitative characteristics of accounting information and elements of financial statements.

[2]"Conceptual Framework for Financial Accounting and Reporting: Elements of Financial Statements and Their Measurement," *FASB Discussion Memorandum* (Stamford, Conn.: 1976), p. 1.

## RELEVANCE

Accounting information has **relevance** if it makes a difference in a decision. Relevant information has either predictive or feedback value or both. **Predictive value** helps users forecast future events. For example, when ExxonMobil issues financial statements, the information in them is considered relevant because it provides a basis for predicting future earnings. **Feedback value** confirms or corrects prior expectations. When ExxonMobil issues financial statements, it confirms or corrects prior expectations about the financial health of the company.

In addition, accounting information has relevance if it is **timely.** It must be available to decision makers before it loses its capacity to influence decisions. If ExxonMobil reports its financial information only every five years, the information is of limited use in decision-making.

## RELIABILITY

**Reliability** of information means that the information is free of error and bias. In short, it can be depended on. To be reliable, accounting information must be **verifiable**: We must be able to prove that it is free of error and bias. It also must be a **faithful representation** of what it purports to be: It must be factual. If General Motors' income statement reports sales of $225 billion when it had sales of $193.5 billion, then the statement is not a faithful representation. Finally, accounting information must be **neutral**: It cannot be selected, prepared, or presented to favor one set of interested users over another. To ensure reliability, certified public accountants audit financial statements.

## COMPARABILITY

Accounting information about an enterprise is most useful when it can be compared with accounting information about other enterprises. **Comparability** results when different companies use the same accounting principles. For example, Sears Holdings, L. L. Bean, and The Limited all use the cost principle in reporting plant assets on the balance sheet. Also, each company uses the revenue recognition and matching principles in determining its net income.

Conceptually, comparability should also extend to the methods used by companies in complying with an accounting principle. Accounting methods include the FIFO and LIFO methods of inventory costing, and various depreciation methods. At this point, comparability of methods is not required, even for companies in the same industry. Thus, Ford, General Motors, and DaimlerChrysler may use different inventory costing and depreciation methods in their financial statements. The only accounting requirement is that each company **must disclose** the accounting methods used. From the disclosures, the external user can determine whether the financial information is comparable.

## CONSISTENCY

**Consistency** means that a company uses the same accounting principles and methods from year to year. If a company selects FIFO as the inventory costing method in the first year of operations, it is expected to use FIFO in succeeding years. When a company reports financial information on a consistent basis, the financial statements permit meaningful analysis of trends within the company.

A company *can* change to a new method of accounting. To do so, management must justify that the new method results in more meaningful financial information. In the year in which the change occurs, the company must disclose the change in the notes to the financial statements. Such disclosure makes users of the financial statements aware of the lack of consistency.

Illustration 7-1 (on page 297) summarizes the characteristics that make accounting information useful.

**Relevance**
1. Provides a basis for forecasts
2. Confirms or corrects prior expectations
3. Is timely

**Reliability**
1. Is verifiable
2. Is a faithful representation
3. Is neutral

**Comparability**
Different companies use similar accounting principles

**Consistency**
Company uses same accounting methods from year to year

**Illustration 7-1**
Characteristics of useful information

# Elements of Financial Statements

An important part of the accounting conceptual framework is a set of definitions that describe the basic terms used in accounting. The FASB refers to this set of definitions as the **elements of financial statements**. They include such terms as assets, liabilities, equity, revenues, and expenses.

Because these elements are so important, it is crucial that they be precisely defined and universally applied. Finding the appropriate definition for many of these elements is not easy. For example, should the value of a company's employees be reported as an asset on a balance sheet? Should the death of the company's president be reported as a loss? A good set of definitions should provide answers to these types of questions. Because you have already encountered most of these definitions in earlier chapters, they are not repeated here.

# Operating Guidelines

The objectives of financial reporting, the qualitative characteristics of accounting information, and the elements of financial statements are very broad. Because practicing accountants must solve practical problems, they need more detailed guidelines. In its conceptual framework, the FASB recognized the need for operating guidelines. We classify these guidelines as assumptions, principles, and constraints. These guidelines are well-established and accepted in accounting.

**Assumptions** provide a foundation for the accounting process. **Principles** are specific rules that indicate how economic events should be reported in the accounting process. **Constraints** on the accounting process allow for a relaxation of the principles under certain circumstances. Illustration 7-2 provides a road-map of the operating guidelines of accounting. These guidelines (some of which you know from earlier chapters) are discussed in more detail in the following sections.

**Illustration 7-2**
The operating guidelines of accounting

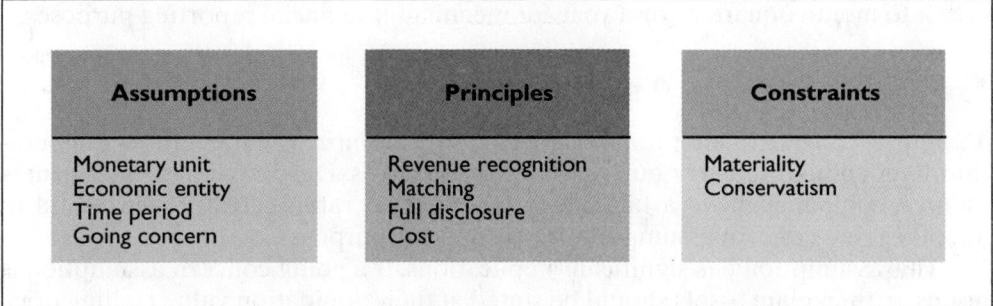

| Assumptions | Principles | Constraints |
|---|---|---|
| Monetary unit | Revenue recognition | Materiality |
| Economic entity | Matching | Conservatism |
| Time period | Full disclosure | |
| Going concern | Cost | |

*Before You Go On...*

**REVIEW IT**
1. What are generally accepted accounting principles?
2. What is stated about generally accepted accounting principles in the Independent Auditors' Report for PepsiCo? The answer to this question appears on page 336.
3. What are the basic objectives of financial information?
4. What are the qualitative characteristics that make accounting information useful? Identify two elements of the financial statements.

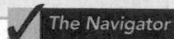 The Navigator

# ASSUMPTIONS
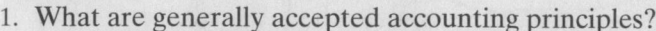

**STUDY OBJECTIVE 4**
Identify the basic assumptions used by accountants.

As noted above, assumptions provide a foundation for the accounting process. You already know three of the major assumptions—the monetary unit, economic entity, and time period assumptions. The fourth is the going concern assumption.

## Monetary Unit Assumption

The **monetary unit assumption** states that only transaction data that can be expressed in terms of money be included in the accounting records. For example, a company does not report the value of the company president in its financial records because that value cannot be expressed easily in dollars.

An important corollary to the monetary unit assumption is the assumption that the unit of measure remains relatively constant over time. We will discuss this point in more detail later in this chapter.

**ETHICS NOTE**

In an action that sent shock waves through the French business community, the CEO of Alcatel-Alsthom was taken into custody for an apparent violation of the economic entity assumption. Allegedly, the executive improperly used company funds to install an expensive security system in his home.

## Economic Entity Assumption

The **economic entity assumption** states that the activities of the entity be kept separate and distinct from the activities of the owner and of all other economic entities. For example, it is assumed that the activities of IBM can be distinguished from those of other computer companies such as Apple, Dell, and Hewlett-Packard.

## Time Period Assumption

The **time period assumption** states that the economic life of a business can be divided into artificial time periods. Thus, it is assumed that companies such as General Electric, Time Warner, and ExxonMobil, can subdivide their business activities into months, quarters, or a year for meaningful financial reporting purposes.

## Going Concern Assumption

The **going concern assumption** assumes that the company will continue in operation long enough to carry out its existing objectives. Despite numerous business failures, companies have a fairly high continuance rate. It has proved useful to adopt a going-concern assumption for accounting purposes.

This assumption has significant implications. If a going concern assumption is not used, then plant assets should be stated at their liquidation value (selling price less cost of disposal)—not at their cost. In that case, depreciation of these assets is not needed. Each period, companies would simply report these assets at their liquidation value. Also, without this assumption, the current–noncurrent classification of assets and liabilities would not matter. Labeling anything as long-term would be difficult to justify.

\Acceptance of the going-concern assumption gives credibility to the cost principle\Only when liquidation appears imminent is the going concern assumption inapplicable. In that case, assets would be better stated at liquidation value than at cost.

These basic accounting assumptions are illustrated graphically in Illustration 7-3 below.

**Illustration 7-3**
Assumptions used in accounting

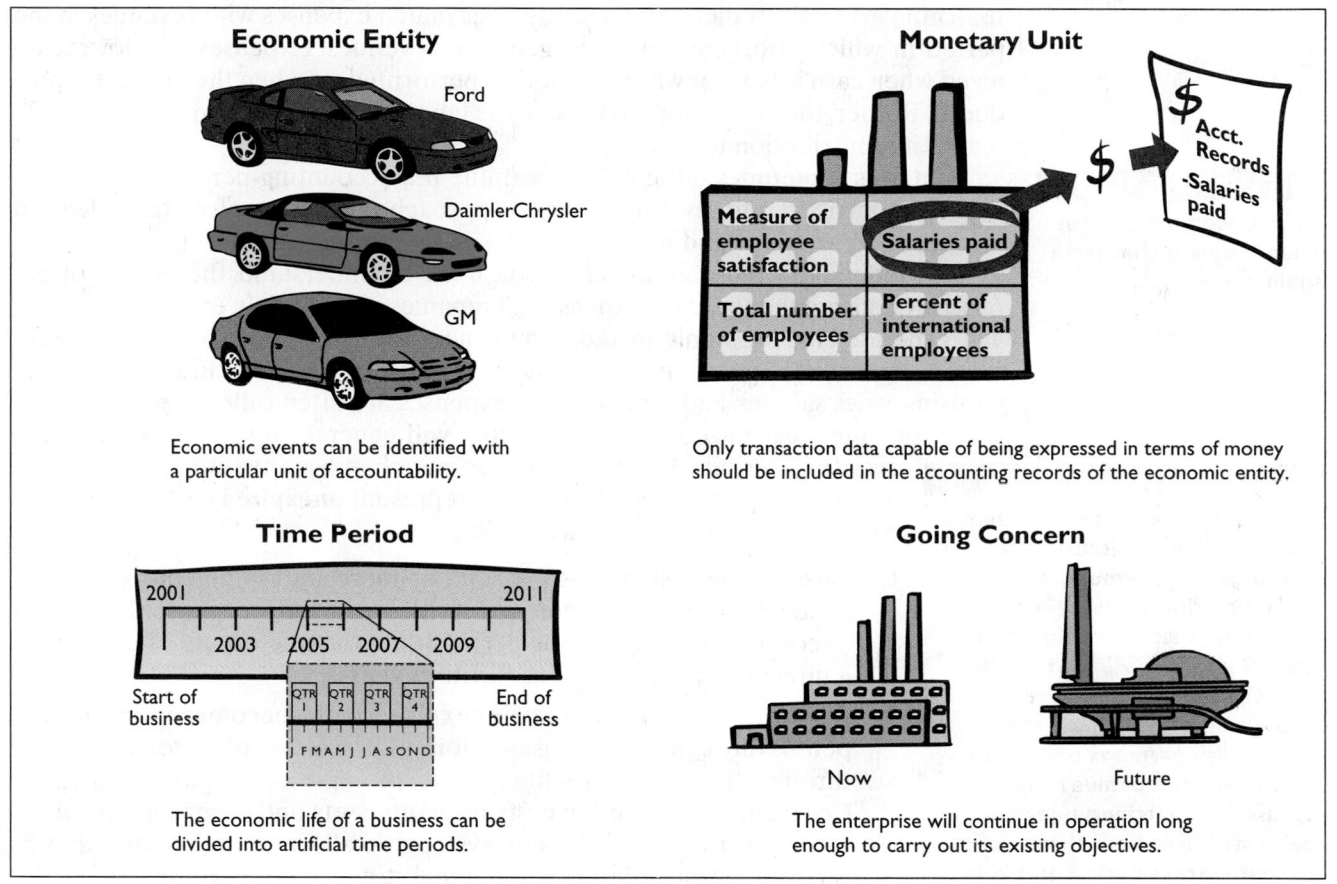

# PRINCIPLES

On the basis of the fundamental assumptions of accounting, the accounting profession has developed principles that dictate how economic events should be recorded and reported. In earlier chapters we discussed the cost principle (Chapter 1) and the revenue recognition and matching principles (Chapter 3). Here we now examine a number of reporting issues related to these principles. In addition, we introduce another principle, the full disclosure principle.

STUDY OBJECTIVE 5

Identify the basic principles of accounting.

## Revenue Recognition Principle

The **revenue recognition principle** dictates that companies should recognize revenue in the accounting period in which it is earned. But applying this general principle in practice can be difficult. For example, some companies improperly recognize revenue on goods that have not been shipped to customers. Similarly, financial institutions at one time immediately recorded a large portion of their fees for granting a loan as revenue rather than spreading those fees over the life of the loan.

When a sale is involved, companies recognize revenue at the point of sale. This **sales basis** involves an exchange transaction between the seller and buyer. The sales price is an objective measure of the amount of revenue realized. However, there are two exceptions to the sales basis for revenue recognition that have become generally accepted. These methods are left for more advanced courses.

## Matching Principle (Expense Recognition)

Expense recognition is traditionally tied to revenue recognition: "Let the expense follow the revenue." As you learned in Chapter 3, this practice is referred to as the **matching principle**. It dictates that companies match expenses with revenues in the period in which efforts are made to generate revenues. Expenses are not recognized when cash is paid, or when the work is performed, or when the product is produced. Rather, they are recognized when the labor (service) or the product actually makes its contribution to revenue.

But, it is sometimes difficult to determine the accounting period in which the expense contributed to revenues. Several approaches have therefore been devised for matching expenses and revenues on the income statement.

To understand these approaches, you need to understand the nature of expenses. Costs are the source of expenses. Companies immediately expense costs that will generate revenues only in the current accounting period. They report these costs as **operating expenses** in the income statement. Examples include costs for advertising, sales salaries, and repairs. These expenses are often called **expired costs**.

Companies recognize as assets costs that will generate revenues in future accounting periods. Examples include merchandise inventory, prepaid expenses, and plant assets. These costs represent **unexpired costs**. Unexpired costs become expenses in two ways:

1. **Cost of goods sold.** Costs carried as merchandise inventory become expenses when the inventory is sold. Companies expense these costs as cost of goods sold in the period when the sale occurs. Thus, there is a direct matching of expenses with revenues.

2. **Operating expenses.** Other unexpired costs become operating expenses through use or consumption (as in the case of store supplies) or through the passage of time (as in the case of prepaid insurance). Companies expense the costs of plant assets and other long-lived resources through rational and systematic allocation methods—that is, through periodic depreciation. Operating expenses contribute to the revenues for the period, but their association with revenues is less direct than for cost of goods sold.

Illustration 7-4 summarizes these points about expense recognition.

**Illustration 7-4**
Expense recognition pattern

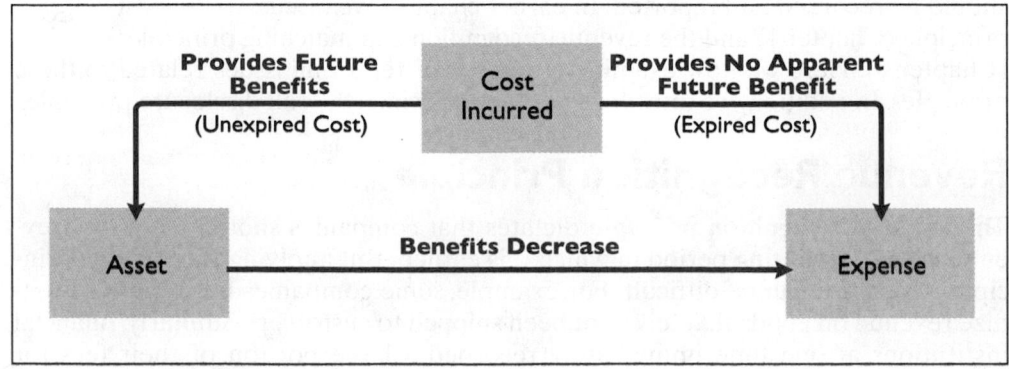

# ACCOUNTING ACROSS THE ORGANIZATION

### *When to Account for the Winning Handle Pull*

Implementing expense recognition guidelines can be difficult. Consider, for example, Harold's Club (a gambling casino) in Reno, Nevada. How should it report expenses related to the payoff of its progressive slot machines? Progressive slot machines, which generally have no ceiling on their jackpots, provide a lucky winner with all the money that many losers had previously put in. Payoffs tend to be huge, but infrequent. At Harold's, the progressive slots pay off on average every 4½ months.

The basic accounting question is: Can Harold's deduct the millions of dollars sitting in its progressive slot machines from the revenue recognized at the end of the accounting period? One might argue that no, you cannot deduct the money until the "winning handle pull." However, a winning handle pull might not occur for many months or even years. Although an estimate would have to be used, the better answer is to match these costs with the revenue recognized, assuming that an average 4½ months' payout is well documented.

**?** What accounting principles are applicable to the Harold's Club progressive slot machines? If Harold's fails to use an estimate for expenses, what effect will this have on financial statements in a period when no payouts occur?

# Full Disclosure Principle

The **full disclosure principle** requires that companies disclose circumstances and events that make a difference to financial statement users. For example, investors who lost money in Enron, WorldCom, and Global Crossing have complained that the lack of full disclosure regarding some of the companies' transactions caused the financial statements to be misleading. Investors want to be made aware of events that can affect the financial health of a company.

Compliance with the full disclosure principle occurs through the data in the financial statements and the information in the notes that accompany the statements. The first note in most cases is a **summary of significant accounting policies**. It includes, among others, the methods used for inventory costing and depreciation of plant assets.

Deciding how much disclosure is enough can be difficult. Accountants could disclose every financial event that occurs and every contingency that exists. But the benefits of providing additional information in some cases may be less than the costs of doing so. Many companies complain of an accounting standards overload. They also object to requirements that force them to disclose confidential information. Determining where to draw the line on disclosure is not easy.

One thing is certain: Financial statements were much simpler years ago. In 1930, General Electric had no notes to its financial statements. Today it has numerous pages of notes! Why this change? A major reason is that the objectives of financial statements have changed. In the past, information was generally presented on what the business had done. Today, the objectives of financial reporting are more future-oriented. The goal is to provide information that makes it possible to predict the amounts, timing, and uncertainty of future cash flows.

# ACCOUNTING ACROSS THE ORGANIZATION

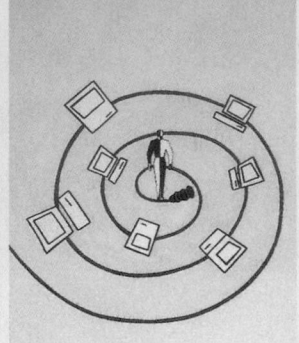

### *How About Instant Access?*

Some accountants are reconsidering the current means of financial reporting. They propose a database concept of financial reporting. In such a system, a computerized database would store all the information from transactions. Various user groups could instantly access the information. The main benefit of such a system is the ability to tailor the information requested to the needs of each user on a real-time basis.

What makes this idea controversial? Discussion currently revolves around access and aggregation issues. Questions abound: "Who should be allowed to make inquiries of the system?" "What is the lowest/smallest level of information to be provided?" "Will such a system necessarily improve on the current means of disclosure?" Such questions must be answered before database financial accounting can be implemented on a large scale.

**?** Would instant access to financial information provide more relevant information? Do you think such an approach would do away with the need for annual reports?

## Cost Principle

As you know, the cost principle dictates that companies record assets at their cost. Cost is used because it is both relevant and reliable. Cost is **relevant** because it represents the price paid, the assets sacrificed, or the commitment made at date of acquisition. Cost is **reliable** because it is objectively measurable, factual, and verifiable. It is the result of an exchange transaction. Cost is the basis used in preparing financial statements.

The cost principle, however, has come under criticism. Some criticize it as irrelevant. After acquisition, the argument goes, the cost of an asset is not equivalent to market value or current value. Also, as the purchasing power of the dollar changes, so does the meaning associated with the dollar used as the basis of measurement. Consider the classic story about the individual who went to sleep and woke up 10 years later. Hurrying to a telephone, he called his broker and asked what his formerly modest stock portfolio was worth. The broker told him that he was a multimillionaire. His General Motors stock was worth $5 million, and his Microsoft stock was up to $10 million. Elated, he was about to inquire about his other holdings, when the telephone operator cut in with "Your time is up. Please deposit $100,000 for the next three minutes."[3]

Despite the inevitability of changing prices due to inflation, the accounting profession still follows the stable monetary unit assumption in preparing the primary financial statements. While admitting that some changes in prices do occur, the profession believes the unit of measure—the dollar—has remained sufficiently constant over time to provide meaningful financial information. Sometimes, the **disclosure of price-level adjusted data is in the form of supplemental information** that accompanies the financial statements.

Illustration 7-5 (page 303) summarizes the basic principles of accounting.

> **HELPFUL HINT**
>
> Are you a winner or loser when you hold cash in a period of inflation? Answer: A loser, because the value of the cash declines as inflation climbs.

---

[3]Adapted from *Barron's*, January 28, 1980, p. 27.

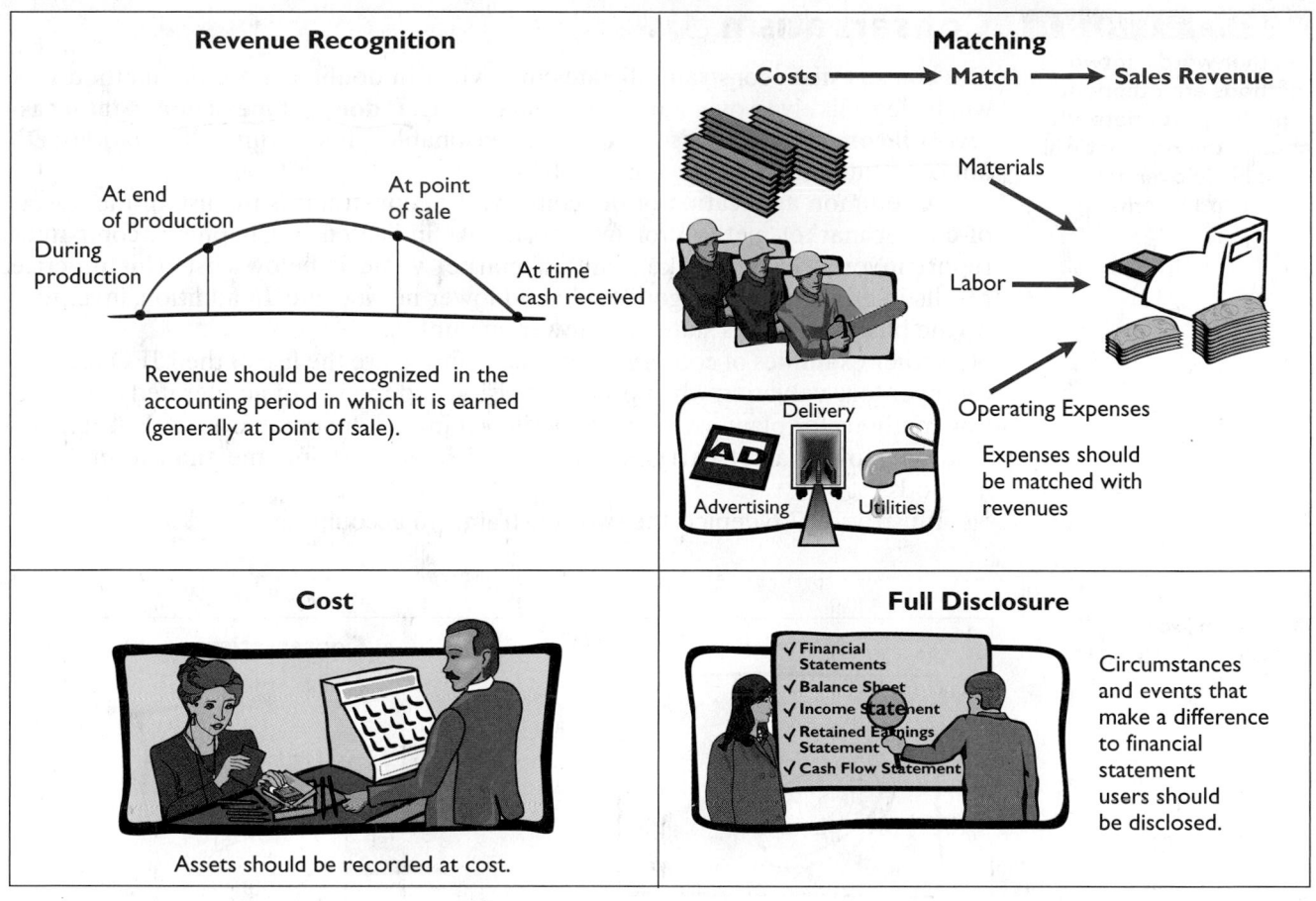

**Illustration 7-5**
Basic principles used in accounting

# CONSTRAINTS IN ACCOUNTING

**Constraints** permit a company to modify generally accepted accounting principles without reducing the usefulness of the reported information. The constraints are materiality and conservatism.

STUDY OBJECTIVE 6

Identify the two constraints in accounting.

## Materiality

Materiality relates to an item's impact on a firm's overall financial condition and operations. An item is **material** when it is likely to influence the decision of a reasonably prudent investor or creditor. It is **immaterial** if its inclusion or omission has no impact on a decision maker. In short, if the item does not make a difference in decision making, GAAP does not have to be followed. To determine the materiality of an amount, the accountant usually compares it with such items as total assets, total liabilities, and net income.

To illustrate application of the materiality constraint, assume that Rodriguez Co. purchases a number of low-cost plant assets, such as wastepaper baskets. Although the proper accounting would appear to be to depreciate these wastepaper baskets over their useful life, they usually are expensed immediately. This practice is justified because these costs are considered immaterial. Establishing depreciation schedules for these assets is costly and time-consuming and will not make a material difference on total assets and net income. Another application of the materiality constraint would be the expensing of small tools. Some companies expense any plant assets under a specified dollar amount.

## Conservatism

The **conservatism** constraint dictates that when in doubt, choose the method that will be least likely to overstate assets and income. **It does not mean understating assets or income.** Conservatism provides a reasonable guide in difficult situations: Do not overstate assets and income.

A common application of the conservatism constraint is the use of the lower-of-cost-or-market method for inventories. As indicated in Chapter 6, companies report inventories at market value if market value is below cost. This practice results in a higher cost of goods sold and lower net income. In addition, inventory on the balance sheet is stated at a lower amount.

Other examples of conservatism in accounting are the use of the LIFO method for inventory valuation when prices are rising and the use of accelerated depreciation methods for plant assets (faster write-off in earlier years). Both these methods result in lower asset carrying values and lower net income than alternative methods.

Illustration 7-6 depicts the two constraints in accounting.

**Illustration 7-6**
Constraints in accounting

**Materiality**

For small amounts, GAAP does not have to be followed.

**Conservatism**

When in doubt, choose the solution that will be least likely to overstate assets and income.

## Summary of Conceptual Framework

As we have seen, the conceptual framework for developing sound reporting practices starts with a set of objectives for financial reporting. It follows with the description of qualities that make information useful. In addition, it defines elements of financial statements and then provides more detailed operating guidelines. These guidelines take the form of assumptions and principles. The conceptual framework also recognizes that constraints exist on the reporting environment. Illustration 7-7 (page 305) shows the conceptual framework.

### Before You Go On...

**REVIEW IT**

1. What are the monetary unit assumption, the economic entity assumption, the time period assumption, and the going concern assumption?
2. What are the revenue recognition principle, the matching principle, the full disclosure principle, and the cost principle?
3. What are the materiality constraint and the conservatism constraint?

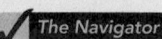

The Navigator

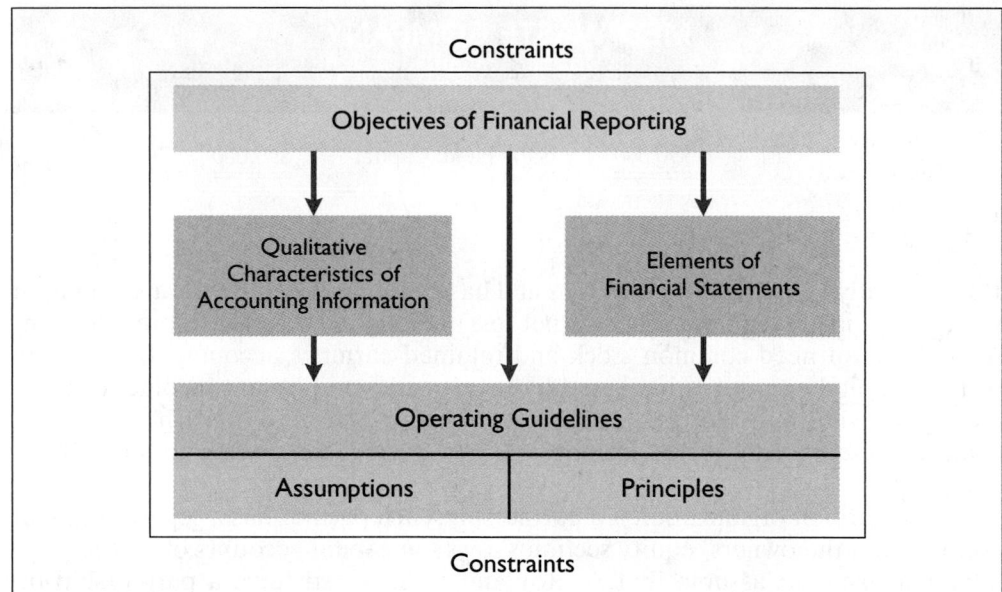

**Illustration 7-7**
Conceptual framework

# STATEMENT PRESENTATION AND ANALYSIS

Financial statements play an important role in attempting to meet the objectives of financial reporting. "Bottom line" information such as total assets and net income are useful to investors, but these single numbers lack sufficient detail for serious analysis. Investors and creditors generally find the parts of a financial statement more useful than the whole. Proper classification within the financial statements is therefore extremely important.

**STUDY OBJECTIVE 7**
Understand and analyze classified financial statements.

## Classified Balance Sheet

The balance sheet is composed of three major elements: assets, liabilities, and stockholders' equity. Additional segregation within these groups, however, is considered useful to financial statement readers. As indicated in Chapter 4, the following classification is generally found.

| Assets | Liabilities and Stockholders' Equity |
|---|---|
| Current assets | Current liabilities |
| Long-term investments | Long-term liabilities |
| Property, plant, and equipment | Stockholders' equity |
| Intangible assets | |

**Illustration 7-8**
Standard classification of balance sheet

If the form of organization is a proprietorship, the balance sheet uses the term "Owner's equity" instead of "Stockholders' equity" to describe that section. An account called Capital is reported in the owner's equity section of the balance sheet for a proprietorship. **Capital** is the owner's investment in the business.

To illustrate, assume that Sally Field invests $90,000 on July 10, 2008, to start up Med/Waste Company. The company's balance sheet immediately after the investment is shown in Illustration 7-9 on the next page.

**Illustration 7-9**
Proprietorship balance
sheet

| MED/WASTE COMPANY | | | |
|---|---|---|---|
| Balance Sheet | | | |
| July 10, 2008 | | | |
| Cash | $90,000 | Sally Field, Capital | $90,000 |

**HELPFUL HINT**

Note "Owners' equity"
instead of "Owner's
equity" is used for a
partnership to indicate
multiple owners.

Because Sally Field owns the business and has chosen not to incorporate, common stock is not issued and net income (net loss) belongs to her. Therefore, the company does not need common stock and retained earnings accounts. Instead, the owner's capital account is increased by investments and by net income. It is decreased by withdrawals of assets for personal use and by net losses. The capital account represents Sally Field's claim to the net assets (assets less liabilities) of the company.

If the form of organization is a partnership, each partner has a separate capital account, and the owners' equity section shows the capital accounts of all the partners. For example, assume that A. Roy and B. Siegfried form a partnership on December 11, 2008, at which time Roy and Siegfried each invest $60,000. The balance sheet immediately after their investments is as follows.

**Illustration 7-10**
Partnership balance sheet

| ROY AND SIEGFRIED | | | |
|---|---|---|---|
| Balance Sheet | | | |
| December 11, 2008 | | | |
| Cash | $120,000 | A. Roy, Capital | $ 60,000 |
| | | B. Siegfried, Capital | 60,000 |
| | | | $120,000 |

## Classified Income Statement

Chapter 5 presented a multiple-step income statement for PW Audio Supply, Inc. The multiple-step income statement included the following.

> **Sales revenue section**—Presents the sales, discounts, allowances, and other related information to arrive at the net amount of sales revenue.
>
> **Cost of goods sold**—Indicates the cost of goods sold to produce sales.
>
> **Operating expenses**—Provides information on both selling and administrative expenses.
>
> **Other revenues and gains**—Indicates revenues earned or gains resulting from nonoperating transactions.
>
> **Other expenses and losses**—Indicates expenses or losses incurred from nonoperating transactions.

Two additional items are income tax expense and earnings per share.

### INCOME TAX EXPENSE

Because a corporation is a legal entity separate and distinct from its owners, corporations must pay and report income taxes. Proprietorships and partnerships are not separate legal entities; owners are therefore taxed directly on their business income. Stockholders are taxed only on the dividends they receive.

Companies report corporate **income taxes (or income tax expense)** in a separate section of the income statement, before net income. The condensed income statement for Leads Inc. in Illustration 7-11 shows a typical presentation. Note that "Income before income taxes" is reported before "Income tax expense."

**LEADS INC.**
Income Statement
For the Year Ended December 31, 2008

| | |
|---|---:|
| Sales | $800,000 |
| Cost of goods sold | 600,000 |
| Gross profit | 200,000 |
| Operating expenses | 50,000 |
| Income from operations | 150,000 |
| Other revenues and gains | 10,000 |
| Other expenses and losses | 4,000 |
| **Income before income taxes** | **156,000** |
| **Income tax expense** | **46,800** |
| Net income | $109,200 |

**Illustration 7-11**
Income statement with income taxes

**HELPFUL HINT**

Corporations may also use the single-step form of income statements discussed in Chapter 5.

Income tax expense and the related liability for income taxes payable are recorded as part of the adjusting process, preceding financial statement preparation. Using the data in Illustration 7-11 for Leads Inc., the adjusting entry for income tax expense at December 31, 2008, would be as follows.

| | | |
|---|---:|---:|
| Income Tax Expense | 46,800 | |
|     Income Taxes Payable | | 46,800 |
|     (To record income taxes for 2008) | | |

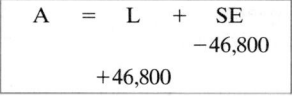

| A | = | L | + | SE |
|---|---|---|---|---|
| | | | | −46,800 |
| | | +46,800 | | |

**Cash Flows**
no effect

Other examples of income tax presentation appear in the Demonstration Problem income statement of Chapter 15 and the income statement of **PepsiCo** in Appendix A.

## EARNINGS PER SHARE

The financial press frequently reports earnings per share data and stockholders and potential investors widely use EPS data in evaluating the profitability of a company. Investors, especially, attempt to link earnings per share to the market price per share.[4] **Earnings per share (EPS)** indicates the net income earned by each share of outstanding common stock. Thus, **earnings per share is reported only for common stock**. The formula for computing earnings per share when there has been no change in outstanding shares during the year is as follows.

| Net Income | ÷ | Number of Common Shares Outstanding | = | Earnings per Share |
|---|---|---|---|---|

**Illustration 7-12**
Earnings per share formula—no change in outstanding shares

---

[4]The ratio of the market price per share to the earnings per share is referred to as the *price-earnings (P-E) ratio*. This ratio is reported in the *Wall Street Journal* and other newspapers for common stocks listed on major stock exchanges.

For example, Leads Inc. (Illustration 7-11) has net income of $109,200. Assuming that it has 54,600 shares of common stock outstanding for the year, earnings per share is $2 ($109,200 ÷ 54,600).[5]

Because of the importance of earnings per share, most companies are required to report it on the face of the income statement. Generally this amount is simply reported below net income on the statement. For Leads Inc. the presentation would be as follows.

**Illustration 7-13**
Basic earnings per share disclosure

### LEADS INC.
Income Statement (partial)
For the Year Ended December 31, 2008

| | |
|---|---|
| Net income | $109,200 |
| **Earnings per share** | **$2.00** |

## Analyzing Financial Statements

The financial statements should provide financial information that is useful for helping readers make sound investment and credit decisions. Illustrations 7-14 below and 7-15 (page 309) present the condensed balance sheet and income statement of Genlyte Inc. for 2008.

**Illustration 7-14**
Balance sheet—
Genlyte Inc.

### GENLYTE INC.
Balance Sheet
December 31, 2008

| **Assets** | | **Liabilities and Stockholders' Equity** | |
|---|---|---|---|
| Current assets | $156,000 | Current liabilities | $ 70,000 |
| Plant and equipment (net) | 74,000 | Long-term liabilities | 114,000 |
| Intangible assets | 14,000 | Stockholders' equity | 60,000 |
| Total assets | $244,000 | Total liabilities and stockholders' equity | $244,000 |

In analyzing and interpreting financial statement information, three major characteristics are generally used: **liquidity**, **profitability**, and **solvency**. A **short-term debtholder**, for example, is primarily interested in the ability of a borrower to pay obligations when they become due. The liquidity of the borrower in such a case is extremely important in assessing the safety of a loan. A **long-term debtholder**, however, looks to indicators such as profitability and solvency that point to the firm's ability to survive over a long period of time. Long-term debtholders analyze earnings per share, the relationship of income to total assets invested, and the amount of debt in relation to total assets to determine whether money should be

---

[5]Whenever the number of outstanding shares changes during the year, the calculation of EPS becomes more complicated. These computations are covered in Chapter 15.

**Illustration 7-15**
Income statement—
Genlyte Inc.

**GENLYTE INC.**
Income Statement
For the Year Ended December 31, 2008

| | |
|---|---|
| Net sales | $430,000 |
| Cost of sales | 295,000 |
| Gross profit | 135,000 |
| Selling and administrative expenses | 109,000 |
| Income from operations | 26,000 |
| Other expenses and losses | 5,000 |
| Income before income taxes | 21,000 |
| Income tax expense | 7,000 |
| Net income | $ 14,000 |
| Earnings per share | $0.35 |

lent and at what interest rate. Similarly, when assessing the likelihood of dividends and the growth potential of the common stock, **stockholders** are interested in the profitability and solvency of a company.

## LIQUIDITY

What is Genlyte's ability to pay its maturing obligations and meet unexpected needs for cash? The relationship between current assets and current liabilities is critical to helping answer this question. These relationships are expressed as a ratio, called the **current ratio**, and as a dollar amount, called **working capital**.

**Current Ratio.** The current ratio is current assets divided by current liabilities. For Genlyte Inc., the ratio is 2.23:1, computed as follows.

**Illustration 7-16**
Current ratio formula and
computation

| Current Assets | ÷ | Current Liabilities | = | Current Ratio |
|---|---|---|---|---|
| $156,000 | ÷ | $70,000 | = | 2.23:1 |

This ratio means that current assets are more than two times greater than current liabilities. Bankers, other creditors, and agencies such as Dun & Bradstreet use this ratio to determine whether the company is a good credit risk. Traditionally, a ratio of 2:1 is considered to be the standard for a good credit rating. Today, however, many sound companies have current ratios of less than 2:1. With its 2.23:1 ratio, Genlyte's short-term debt-paying ability appears to be very favorable.

From the foregoing, you might at first assume that the higher the current ratio, the better. This is not necessarily true. A very high current ratio may indicate that the company is holding more current assets than it currently needs in the business. It is possible, therefore, that the excess resources might be directed to more profitable investment opportunities.

**Working Capital.** The excess of current assets over current liabilities is called working capital. For Genlyte Inc., working capital is $86,000, as shown on page 310.

**Illustration 7-17**
Working capital formula and computation

| Current Assets | − | Current Liabilities | = | Working Capital |
|---|---|---|---|---|
| $156,000 | − | $70,000 | = | $86,000 |

The amount of working capital provides some indication of the company's ability to meet its existing current obligations. A large amount of working capital generally means a company can meet its current liabilities as they fall due and, if desired, pay dividends. Although no set standards exist for the level of working capital a company should maintain, analysts often determine the general adequacy of a company's working capital by comparing data from prior periods and from similar companies of comparable size. Genlyte's working capital appears adequate.

## PROFITABILITY

Profitability ratios measure the income or operating success of a company for a given period of time. Income, or the lack of it, affects the company's ability to obtain debt or equity financing and the company's ability to grow.

**Profit Margin Percentage.** One important profitability ratio is the **profit margin percentage** (or rate of return on sales). It measures the percentage of each dollar of sales that results in net income. It is calculated by dividing net income by net sales for the period. Genlyte Inc.'s profit margin percentage is 3.3 percent, computed as follows.

**Illustration 7-18**
Profit margin formula and computation

| Net Income | ÷ | Net Sales | = | Profit Margin Percentage |
|---|---|---|---|---|
| $14,000 | ÷ | $430,000 | = | 3.3% |

This ratio seems low. Much, however, depends on the type of industry. High-volume retailers, such as grocery stores (Safeway or Kroger) or discount stores (Wal-Mart or Kmart), generally have a low profit margin. They make a small profit on each sale but have many sales.

# INVESTOR INSIGHT

### How High Is Your Profit Margin?

The type of industry can make a difference in the profit margin percentage investors and creditors expect. Profit margins among service companies—from airlines and banks to telecommunications companies and utilities—have traditionally been lower than those among manufacturers. Verizon Communications, for example, showed a profit margin percentage of 7 percent which is high for a telecommunications company. Qwest's profit margin percentage was 4.6 percent. By contrast, the top three pharmaceutical firms—Johnson & Johnson, Pfizer, and Merck—had profit margin percentages of 20.7 percent, 39.9 percent, and 19.6 percent, respectively. Before using a ratio like the profit margin percentage to evaluate company performance, you need to know what is reasonable performance for the industry.

**?** If service companies have a profit margin much lower than manufacturers (a third as large), why would anyone invest in a service company over a manufacturer?

**Return on Assets.** In making an investment, an investor wants to know what rate of return to expect and what risks are associated with that rate of return. The greater the risk, the higher the rate of return the investor will demand on the investment.

One overall measure of profitability of a company is its rate of **return on assets**. It is calculated by dividing net income by total assets.[6] Genlyte Inc.'s rate of return is 5.7 percent, computed as follows.

| Net Income | ÷ | Total Assets | = | Return on Assets |
|---|---|---|---|---|
| $14,000 | ÷ | $244,000 | = | 5.7% |

**Illustration 7-19**
Return on assets formula and computation

The rate of return on assets is relatively low, which suggests that Genlyte may not be using its assets effectively.

**Return on Common Stockholders' Equity.** Another widely used rate that measures profitability from the common stockholders' viewpoint is **return on common stockholders' equity**. This rate shows the percentage of net income earned for each dollar of owners' investment. It is calculated by dividing net income by common stockholders' equity. In Genlyte Inc.'s case, the rate of return is 23.3 percent (or 23.3 cents per dollar), computed as follows.

| Net Income | ÷ | Common Equity | = | Return on Common Stockholders' Equity |
|---|---|---|---|---|
| $14,000 | ÷ | $60,000 | = | 23.3% |

**Illustration 7-20**
Return on common stockholders' equity formula and computation

Genlyte's return on common stockholders' equity is quite good. The reason for this high rate of return is that Genlyte's assets are earning a return higher than the borrowing costs the company incurs.

## SOLVENCY

Solvency measures the ability of an enterprise to survive over a long period of time. Long-term debtholders and stockholders are interested in a company's ability to pay periodic interest and to repay the face value of the debt at maturity.

**Debt to Total Assets.** One useful measure of solvency is the **debt to total assets ratio**. It measures the percentage of total assets that creditors, as opposed to stockholders, provide. It is calculated by dividing total debt (liabilities) by total assets, normally expressed as a percentage. Genlyte Inc.'s debt to total assets ratio is 75.4 percent, computed as follows.

| Total Debt | ÷ | Total Assets | = | Debt to Total Assets Ratio |
|---|---|---|---|---|
| $184,000 | ÷ | $244,000 | = | 75.4% |

**Illustration 7-21**
Debt to total assets formula and computation

---

[6]For simplicity, we've based the rate of return calculations on end-of-year total amounts. The more conceptually correct *average* total assets and *average* common stockholders' equity are used in later chapters.

Debt to total assets of 75.4 percent means that Genlyte's creditors have provided approximately three-quarters of its total assets. The higher the percentage of debt to total assets, the greater the risk that the company may be unable to meet its maturing obligations. The lower the percentage, the greater the "buffer" available to creditors should the company become insolvent. In Genlyte Inc.'s case, unless earnings are positive and very stable, the company may have too much debt.

Analysts and other financial statement readers often use these percentage and ratio relationships in comparison with (1) expected results, (2) prior year results, and (3) published results of other companies in the same line of business. Conclusions based on a single year's results are hazardous at best. Chapter 15 provides more detailed consideration of the analysis of financial statements.

# Financial Statement Presentation— An International Perspective

World markets are increasingly intertwined. Foreigners use American computers, eat American breakfast cereals, read American magazines, listen to American rock music, watch American movies and TV shows, and drink American soda. Americans drive Japanese cars, wear Italian shoes and Scottish woolens, drink Brazilian coffee and Indian tea, eat Swiss chocolate bars, sit on Danish furniture, and use Arabian oil. The variety and volume of exported and imported goods indicates the extensive involvement of U.S. business in international trade. Many U.S. companies consider the world their market.

Companies that conduct operations in more than one country through subsidiaries, divisions, or branches in foreign countries are referred to as **multinational corporations (MNCs)**. The accounting for such corporations is complicated because foreign currencies are involved. These international transactions must be translated into U.S. dollars.

# INTERNATIONAL INSIGHT

### *And the Correct Answer Is . . . ?*

Research and development costs are an example of different international accounting standards. Compare how four countries once accounted for research and development (R&D):

| Country | Accounting Treatment |
| --- | --- |
| United States | Expenditures are expensed. |
| United Kingdom | Certain expenditures may be capitalized. |
| Germany | Expenditures are expensed. |
| Japan | Expenditures may be capitalized and written off over 5 years. |

Thus, an R&D expenditure of $100 million is charged totally to expense in the current period in the United States and Germany. This same expense could range from zero to $100 million in the United Kingdom and from $20 million to $100 million in Japan!

What would be the advantage of similar accounting standards for all countries? How can the financial and operating performance of international companies be compared?

## DIFFERENCES IN STANDARDS

In the new global economy many investment and credit decisions require the analysis of foreign financial statements. As indicated in Chapter 1, accounting standards are not always uniform from country to country. This lack of uniformity results from differences in legal systems, in processes for developing accounting standards, in governmental requirements, and in economic environments.

## UNIFORMITY IN STANDARDS

The **International Accounting Standards Board (IASB)** is working toward the development of a single set of high-quality global accounting standards. Its purpose is to formulate international accounting standards and to promote their acceptance worldwide.

The FASB is a willing partner in trying to achieve the goal of the IASB. For example, the FASB and IASB are undertaking several joint projects. One joint project is development of a common conceptual framework for financial reporting. The goal of this project is to build a framework that both the FASB and IASB can use when developing new and revised accounting standards.

Over 7,000 listed companies in the European Union and over 100 countries around the world now use IASB standards. There may be many bumps in the road to achieve one set of worldwide standards, but progress to date is remarkable. We are optimistic that the goal of worldwide standards can be achieved, which will be of value to all.

## *Before You Go On...*

### REVIEW IT

1. What is the major difference in the equity section of the balance sheet between a corporation and proprietorship?
2. Where are income tax expense and earnings per share reported on the income statement? How is earnings per share computed?
3. How are the current ratio, working capital, profit margin percentage, return on assets, return on common stockholders' equity, and debt to total assets computed?
4. Explain how these ratios are useful in financial statement analysis.
5. What is the purpose of the International Accounting Standards Board?

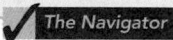 *The Navigator*

 Be sure to read **ALL ABOUT YOU:** *Corporations Have Governance Structures—Do You?* on page 314 for information on how topics in this chapter apply to you.

all about Y✻U

# Corporations Have Governance Structures—Do You?

As discussed previously in this text, the scandals and bankruptcies at Enron, WorldCom, and other companies brought many changes to the way America does business. One of the primary lessons has been that companies need to take corporate governance and management oversight more seriously. In a sense, they have to set up a conceptual framework to run their companies.

As part of this effort, many companies have developed a code of ethics. The purpose of a code of ethics is to clearly specify standards of conduct to deter wrongdoing and promote honest and ethical conduct. It also is intended to be an expression by top management of its "tone at the top" —that is, to indicate that top management takes ethics seriously. Many other organizations, including university student groups, also have formulated ethics codes.

## ✻ Some Facts

* Under Sarbanes-Oxley, a company must disclose in its annual report whether it has a code of ethics. It must also disclose any changes to or waivers of the code of ethics.
* Enron had a code of ethics. In a number of instances, Enron's board of directors knowingly waived requirements of the code so that the CFO could set up and run special purpose entities. Ultimately these waivers contributed to Enron's downfall.
* In some instances U.S. federal prosecutors have pressured companies to not pay the legal-defense bills of employees accused of wrong-doing, thus making it harder for the employees to defend themselves.
* In a recent survey of 1,436 workers, 34% said that they have seen unethical activities at their workplace, but only 47% said they are likely to report these activities. Many cited fear of retaliation by their bosses as the reason for not reporting.

## ✻ About the Numbers

Stockholders often lose money as a result of unethical behavior by management. When they do, they often file lawsuits against the company in an effort to recoup these losses. The graph below shows just how expensive these class-action lawsuits can be for companies.

**Top Class-Action Securities Settlements**

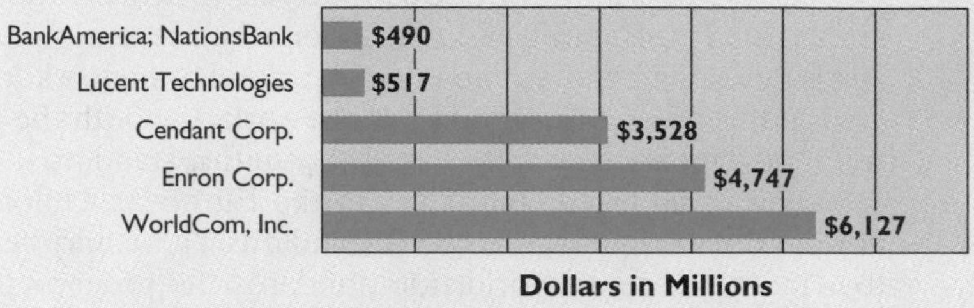
BankAmerica; NationsBank
$490
Lucent Technologies
$517
Cendant Corp.
$3,528
Enron Corp.
$4,747
WorldCom, Inc.
$6,127
Dollars in Millions

**Source:** Elaine Buckberg, Todd Foster, and Ronald I. Miller, "Recent Trends in Shareholder Class Action Litigation: Are WorldCom and Enron the New Standard?" NERA Economic Consulting, *www.nera.com* (accessed June 26, 2006).

## ✻ What Do You Think

Many universities have become concerned about student cheating. In particular, the prevalence of digital documents on the Internet has made it very easy to plagiarize. Many schools now have student ethics codes. Do you think that these ethics codes serve a useful purpose?

**YES:** Anything that will reduce unethical behavior is a good thing. An ethics code establishes what is and is not acceptable behavior, which helps universities maintain ethical standards for academic work and weed out those students who try to get ahead by non-ethical means.

**NO:** The existence of an ethics code won't affect student behavior. If students have a propensity to cheat, a document that tells them what is and is not good behavior is not going to be a deterrent. Students already know what cheating is, and that it is wrong.

**Sources:** "Whistleblowing Workers: Becoming an Endangered Species?" *HR Focus,* June 2006, p. 9; Lauren Etter, "The Enron Trial Finally Begins," *Wall Street Journal,* February 4, 2006, p. A7.


The authors' comments on this situation appear on page 335.

## Demonstration Problem 1

Presented below are a number of operational guidelines and practices that have developed over time.

### Instructions

Identify the accounting assumption, accounting principle, or reporting constraint that most appropriately justifies these procedures and practices. Use only one item per description.

**(a)** The first note, "Summary of Significant Accounting Policies," presents information on the subclassification of plant assets and discusses the company's depreciation methods.

**(b)** The local hamburger restaurant expenses all spatulas, french fry baskets, and other cooking utensils when purchased.

**(c)** Retailers recognize revenue at the point of sale.

**(d)** Green-Grow Lawn Mowers, Inc. includes an estimate of warranty expense in the year in which it sells its lawn mowers, which carry a 2-year warranty.

**(e)** Companies present sufficient financial information so that creditors and reasonably prudent investors will not be misled.

**(f)** Companies listed on U.S. stock exchanges report audited financial information annually and report unaudited information quarterly.

**(g)** Beach Resorts, Inc. does not record the 2008 value of $1.5 million for a piece of beachfront property it purchased in 1995 for $500,000.

**(h)** Office Systems, Inc. takes a $32,000 loss on a number of older microcomputers in its inventory; it paid the manufacturer $107,000 for them but can sell them for only $75,000.

**(i)** Frito Lay is a wholly owned subsidiary of PepsiCo, Inc., and Frito Lay's operating results and financial condition are included in the consolidated financial statements of PepsiCo. (Do not use full disclosure.)

**action plan**

Remember that:

✔ The four principles are cost, revenue recognition, matching, and full disclosure.

✔ The two constraints are materiality and conservatism.

✔ Full disclosure relates generally to the item; materiality to the amount.

### Solution

**(a)** Full disclosure principle

**(b)** Materiality constraint

**(c)** Revenue recognition principle

**(d)** Matching principle

**(e)** Full disclosure principle

**(f)** Time period assumption

**(g)** Cost principle

**(h)** Conservatism constraint

**(i)** Economic entity assumption

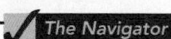

## Demonstration Problem 2

Presented below is financial information related to Notting Hill Corporation for the year 2008. All balances are ending balances unless stated otherwise.

| | |
|---|---:|
| Accounts payable | $ 868,000 |
| Accounts receivable | 700,000 |
| Accumulated depreciation—equipment | 100,000 |
| Administrative expenses | 280,000 |
| Bonds payable | 1,600,000 |
| Cash | 800,000 |
| Common stock | 500,000 |
| Cost of goods sold | 1,600,000 |
| Dividends | 60,000 |
| Equipment | 1,100,000 |

## action plan

✔ Review the format in Chapter 5, page 216, for a multiple-step income statement. Note the multiple-step income statement reports gross profit and income from operations. A single-step income statement does not report these items.

✔ Remember that income tax expense is reported immediately after "Income before income taxes" for both a multiple-step and single-step income statement.

✔ Report earnings per share on both a multiple-step and a single-step income statement.

✔ Disclose net income and dividends on a retained earnings statement.

✔ Refer to Chapter 4, page 166, for examples of a classified balance sheet.

| | |
|---|---:|
| Income tax expense | 83,000 |
| Interest expense | 60,000 |
| Interest revenue | 120,000 |
| Inventories | 500,000 |
| Loss on the sale of equipment | 35,000 |
| Marketable (trading) securities | 400,000 |
| Net sales | 2,400,000 |
| Notes payable (short-term) | 800,000 |
| Other long-term debt | 387,000 |
| Patents and other intangibles | 900,000 |
| Prepaid expenses | 200,000 |
| Retained earnings (January 1, 2008) | 80,000 |
| Selling expenses | 220,000 |
| Taxes payable | 83,000 |

Notting Hill Corporation had 88,000 shares of common stock outstanding for the entire year.

## Instructions

(a) Prepare a multiple-step income statement.
(b) Prepare a single-step income statement.
(c) Prepare a retained earnings statement.
(d) Prepare a classified balance sheet.
(e) Compute the following balance sheet relationships.
  (1) Current ratio.
  (2) The amount of working capital.
  (3) Debt to total assets ratio.
  What insights do these relationships provide to the reader of the financial statements?
(f) Compute three measures of profitability from the income statement and balance sheet information. What insights do these relationships provide to the reader of the financial statements?

### Solution

(a) Multiple-step income statement

### NOTTING HILL CORPORATION
Income Statement
For the Year Ended December 31, 2008

| | | |
|---|---:|---:|
| Net sales | | $2,400,000 |
| Cost of goods sold | | 1,600,000 |
| Gross profit | | 800,000 |
| Selling expenses | $220,000 | |
| Administrative expenses | 280,000 | 500,000 |
| Income from operations | | 300,000 |
| Other revenues and gains | | |
|   Interest revenue | | 120,000 |
| Other expenses and losses | | |
|   Loss on sale of equipment | 35,000 | |
|   Interest expense | 60,000 | 95,000 |
| Income before income taxes | | 325,000 |
| Income tax expense | | 83,000 |
| Net income | | $ 242,000 |
| Earnings per share | | $2.75 |

**(b)** Single-step income statement

## NOTTING HILL CORPORATION
Income Statement
For the Year Ended December 31, 2008

| | | |
|---|---:|---:|
| Revenues | | |
| Net sales | | $2,400,000 |
| Interest revenue | | 120,000 |
| Total revenues | | 2,520,000 |
| Expenses | | |
| Cost of goods sold | $1,600,000 | |
| Selling expenses | 220,000 | |
| Administrative expenses | 280,000 | |
| Interest expense | 60,000 | |
| Loss on the sale of equipment | 35,000 | 2,195,000 |
| Income before income taxes | | 325,000 |
| Income tax expense | | 83,000 |
| Net income | | $ 242,000 |
| Earnings per share | | $2.75 |

**(c)** Retained earnings statement

## NOTTING HILL CORPORATION
Retained Earnings Statement
For the Year Ended December 31, 2008

| | |
|---|---:|
| Retained earnings, January 1 | $ 80,000 |
| Add: Net income | 242,000 |
| | 322,000 |
| Less: Dividends | 60,000 |
| Retained earnings, December 31 | $262,000 |

**(d)** Classified balance sheet

## NOTTING HILL CORPORATION
Balance Sheet
December 31, 2008

| | | |
|---|---:|---:|
| Current assets | | |
| Cash | | $ 800,000 |
| Marketable (trading) securities | | 400,000 |
| Accounts receivable | | 700,000 |
| Inventories | | 500,000 |
| Prepaid expenses | | 200,000 |
| Total current assets | | 2,600,000 |
| Property, plant, and equipment | | |
| Equipment | $1,100,000 | |
| Less: Accumulated depreciation | 100,000 | 1,000,000 |
| Intangible assets | | |
| Patents and other intangible assets | | 900,000 |
| Total assets | | $4,500,000 |
| Current liabilities | | |
| Notes payable | | $ 800,000 |
| Accounts payable | | 868,000 |
| Taxes payable | | 83,000 |
| Total current liabilities | | 1,751,000 |

|  | Long-term liabilities | | |
|---|---|---|---|
|  | Bonds payable | $1,600,000 | |
|  | Other long-term debt | 387,000 | 1,987,000 |
|  | Total liabilities | | 3,738,000 |
|  | Stockholders' equity | | |
|  | Common stock | 500,000 | |
|  | Retained earnings | 262,000 | 762,000 |
|  | Total liabilities and stockholders' equity | | $4,500,000 |

**(e)** Balance sheet relationships

(1) $\text{Current ratio} = \dfrac{\text{Current assets}}{\text{Current liabilities}} = \dfrac{\$2,600,000}{\$1,751,000} = 1.48:1$

(2) Working capital = Current assets − Current liabilities

|  |  |
|---|---|
| Current assets | $2,600,000 |
| Current liabilities | 1,751,000 |
| Working capital | $ 849,000 |

(3) $\text{Debt to total assets} = \dfrac{\text{Debt}}{\text{Total assets}} = \dfrac{\$3,738,000}{\$4,500,000} = 83.07\%$

Notting Hill's liquidity and solvency are of mixed quality. The current ratio is satisfactory with its working capital healthy, i.e., current assets well in excess of current liabilities. However, its debt to total assets, at well over 80%, is too high. Given the company's relatively low profitability (see below), its creditors might be concerned.

**(f)** Profitability relationships

$$\text{Profit margin percentage} = \dfrac{\text{Net income}}{\text{Net sales}} = \dfrac{\$242,000}{\$2,400,000} = 10.08\%$$

$$\text{Return on assets} = \dfrac{\text{Net income}}{\text{Total assets}} = \dfrac{\$242,000}{\$4,500,000} = 5.38\%$$

$$\dfrac{\text{Return on common}}{\text{stockholders' equity}} = \dfrac{\text{Net income}}{\text{Common stockholders' equity}} = \dfrac{\$242,000}{\$762,000} = 31.76\%$$

The profit margin percentage (return on sales) for Notting Hill seems adequate. Given the company's large asset base, however, it should probably generate a higher profit. The company's overall financial picture, then, could be better.

# SUMMARY OF STUDY OBJECTIVES

**1 Explain the meaning of GAAP and identify the key items of the conceptual framework.** Generally accepted accounting principles (GAAP) are a set of rules and practices that are recognized as a general guide for financial reporting purposes. *Generally accepted* means that these principles must have "substantial authoritative support." The key items of the conceptual framework are: (1) objectives of financial reporting; (2) qualitative characteristics of accounting information; (3) elements of financial statements; and (4) operating guidelines (assumptions, principles, and constraints).

**2 Describe the basic objectives of financial reporting.** The basic objectives of financial reporting are to provide information that is (1) useful to those making investment

and credit decisions; (2) helpful in assessing future cash flows; and (3) helpful in identifying economic resources (assets), the claims to those resources (liabilities), and the changes in those resources and claims.

**3 Discuss the qualitative characteristics of accounting information and elements of financial statements.** To be judged useful, information should possess the following qualitative characteristics: relevance, reliability, comparability, and consistency. The elements of financial statements are a set of definitions that can be used to describe the basic terms used in accounting.

**4 Identify the basic assumptions used by accountants.** The major assumptions are: monetary unit, economic entity, time period, and going concern.

**5 Identify the basic principles of accounting.** The major principles are revenue recognition, matching, full disclosure, and cost.

**6 Identify the two constraints in accounting.** The major constraints are materiality and conservatism.

**7 Understand and analyze classified financial statements.** We presented classified balance sheets and classified (multiple-step) income statements in Chapters 4 and 5, respectively. Two new items added to the classified income statement in this chapter are income taxes and earnings per share. Three items used to analyze the balance sheet are the current ratio, working capital, and debt to total assets. Earnings per share, profit margin percentage (return on sales), return on assets, and return on common stockholders' equity are used to analyze profitability.

**8 Explain the accounting principles used in international operations.** There are few recognized worldwide accounting standards. The International Accounting Standards Board (IASB), of which the United States is a member, is working to obtain conformity in international accounting practices.

 The Navigator

# GLOSSARY

WILEY PLUS

**Comparability** Ability to compare accounting information of different companies because they use the same accounting principles. (p. 296).

**Conceptual framework** A coherent system of interrelated objectives and fundamentals that can lead to consistent standards. (p. 295).

**Conservatism** The approach of choosing an accounting method when in doubt that will least likely overstate assets and net income. (p. 304).

**Consistency** Use of the same accounting principles and methods from year to year within a company. (p. 296).

**Cost principle** Accounting principle that assets should be recorded at their historical cost. (p. 302).

**Current ratio** A measure that expresses the relationship of current assets to current liabilities by dividing current assets by current liabilities. (p. 309).

**Debt to total assets ratio** Solvency measure that indicates the percentage of total assets provided by creditors; calculated as total debt divided by total assets. (p. 311).

**Earnings per share (EPS)** The net income earned by each share of outstanding common stock. (p. 307).

**Economic entity assumption** Accounting assumption that economic events can be identified with a particular unit of accountability. (p. 298).

**Elements of financial statements** Definitions of basic terms used in accounting. (p. 297).

**Full disclosure principle** Accounting principle that circumstances and events that make a difference to financial statement users should be disclosed. (p. 301).

**Generally accepted accounting principles (GAAP)** A set of rules and practices, having substantial authoritative support, that are recognized as a general guide for financial reporting purposes. (p. 294).

**Going concern assumption** The assumption that the enterprise will continue in operation long enough to carry out its existing objectives and commitments. (p. 298).

**International Accounting Standards Board (IASB)** An accounting organization whose purpose is to formulate and publish international accounting standards and to promote their acceptance worldwide. (p. 313).

**Matching principle** Accounting principle that expenses should be matched with revenues in the period when efforts are expended to generate revenues. (p. 300).

**Materiality** The constraint of determining if an item is important enough to likely influence the decision of a reasonably prudent investor or creditor. (p. 303).

**Monetary unit assumption** Accounting assumption that only transaction data capable of being expressed in monetary terms should be included in accounting records. (p. 298).

**Profit margin percentage** Profitability measure that indicates the percentage of each dollar of sales that results in net income; calculated as net income divided by net sales. Also called *rate of return on sales.* (p. 310).

**Relevance** The quality of information that indicates the information makes a difference in a decision. (p. 296).

**Reliability** The quality of information that gives assurance that it is free of error and bias. (p. 296).

**Return on assets** An overall measure of a company's profitability; calculated as net income divided by total assets. (p. 311).

**Return on common stockholders' equity** Profitability measure that shows the rate of net income earned for each dollar of owners' investment; calculated as net income divided by common stockholders' equity. (p. 311).

**Revenue recognition principle** Accounting principle that revenue should be recognized in the accounting period in which it is earned (generally at the point of sale). (p. 299).

**Time period assumption** Accounting assumption that the economic life of a business can be divided into artificial time periods. (p. 298).

**Working capital** The excess of current assets over current liabilities. (p. 309).

*Answers are at the end of the chapter.*

(SO 1) **1.** Generally accepted accounting principles are:
  **a.** a set of standards and rules that are recognized as a general guide for financial reporting.
  **b.** usually established by the Internal Revenue Service.
  **c.** the guidelines used to resolve ethical dilemmas.
  **d.** fundamental truths that can be derived from the laws of nature.

(SO 2) **2.** Which of the following is *not* an objective of financial reporting?
  **a.** Provide information that is useful in investment and credit decisions.
  **b.** Provide information about economic resources, claims to those resources, and changes in them.
  **c.** Provide information that is useful in assessing future cash flows.
  **d.** Provide information on the liquidation value of a business.

(SO 3) **3.** The primary criterion by which accounting information can be judged is:
  **a.** consistency.          **c.** decision-usefulness.
  **b.** predictive value.     **d.** comparability.

(SO 3) **4.** Verifiable is an ingredient of:

|     | Reliability | Relevance |
|-----|-------------|-----------|
| **a.** | Yes | Yes |
| **b.** | No  | No  |
| **c.** | Yes | No  |
| **d.** | No  | Yes |

(SO 4, 5, 6) **5.** Valuing assets at their liquidation value rather than their cost is *inconsistent* with the:
  **a.** time period assumption.
  **b.** matching principle.
  **c.** going concern assumption.
  **d.** materiality constraint.

(SO 4, 5, 6) **6.** The accounting constraint that says that when in doubt the accountant should choose the method that will be least likely to overstate assets and income is called:
  **a.** matching principle.
  **b.** materiality.
  **c.** conservatism.
  **d.** monetary unit assumption.

(SO 7) **7.** Erika Pechacek Inc. has current assets of $90,000 and current liabilities of $30,000. Its current ratio and working capital are:
  **a.** .33:1; $60,000.       **c.** .33:1; $90,000.
  **b.** 3:1; $60,000.         **d.** 3:1; $90,000.

(SO 7) **8.** Suster Company has a retained earnings balance of $170,000 at the beginning of the period. At the end of the period, the retained earnings balance was $222,000. Assuming a dividend of $25,000 was declared and paid during the period, the net income for the period was:
  **a.** $27,000.             **c.** $77,000.
  **b.** $52,000.             **d.** $197,000.

(SO 7) **9.** The basic formula for computing earnings per share is net income divided by:
  **a.** common shares authorized.
  **b.** common shares issued.
  **c.** common shares outstanding.
  **d.** common stock purchased.

(SO 7) **10.** Phish Corp. has total liabilities of $1,200,000, total stockholders' equity of $1,800,000, current assets of $800,000, and current liabilities of $400,000. Phish's debt to total assets ratio is:
  **a.** 50%.                 **c.** 33.3%.
  **b.** 40%.                 **d.** 26.6%.

Go to the book's website,
**www.wiley.com/college/weygandt**,
for Additional Self-Study questions.

**1.** **(a)** What are generally accepted accounting principles (GAAP)? **(b)** What bodies provide authoritative support for GAAP?

**2.** What elements comprise the FASB's conceptual framework?

**3.** **(a)** What are the objectives of financial reporting? **(b)** Identify the qualitative characteristics of accounting information.

**4.** Henrik Stenson, the president of Spartan Company, is pleased. Spartan substantially increased its net income in 2008 while keeping the number of **units** in its inventory relatively the same. Brett Quiney, chief accountant, cautions Stenson, however. Quiney says that since Spartan changed its method of inventory **valuation**, there is a consistency problem and it would be difficult to determine if Spartan is better off. Is Quiney correct? Why?

**5.** What is the distinction between comparability and consistency?

**6.** Why is it necessary for accountants to assume that an economic entity will remain a going concern?

**7.** When should revenue be recognized? Why has the date of sale been chosen as the point at which to recognize the revenue resulting from the entire producing and selling process?

**8.** Distinguish between expired costs and unexpired costs.

**9.** **(a)** Where does the accountant disclose information about an entity's financial position, operations, and cash flows? **(b)** The full disclosure principle recognizes that the nature and amount of information included in financial reports reflects a series of judgmental trade-offs. What are the objectives of these trade-offs?

10. Betsy McCall is the president of Brew News. She has no accounting background. McCall cannot understand why current cost is not used as the basis for accounting measurement and reporting. Explain what basis is used and why.

11. Describe the two constraints inherent in the presentation of accounting information.

12. In February 2008, Matt Osterhaus invested an additional $5,000 in his business, Osterhaus Pharmacy, which is organized as a corporation. Osterhaus' accountant, Kate Mulgrew, recorded this receipt as an increase in cash and revenues. Is this treatment appropriate? Why or why not?

13. Identify three financial relationships that are useful in analyzing the profitability of a company. Why might we want more than one measure of profitability?

14. Natasha Company has current assets of $60,000 and current liabilities of $20,000. What is its (a) working capital and (b) current ratio?

15. If current assets are less than current liabilities, will working capital be positive or negative? Will the current ratio be greater than or less than 1:1?

16. Bozeman Inc.'s debt to total asset ratio stands at 62 percent. If you were a banker, would you be comfortable about extending additional credit to Bozeman? Why or why not?

17. Your roommate believes that international accounting standards are uniform throughout the world. Is your roommate correct? Explain.

18. What organization establishes international accounting standards?

## BRIEF EXERCISES

**BE7-1** Indicate whether each of the following statements is true or false.

(a) _____ "*Generally accepted*" means that these principles must have "substantial authoritative support."

(b) _____ Substantial authoritative support for GAAP usually comes from two standard-setting bodies: the FASB and the IRS.

(c) _____ GAAP is a set of rules and practices established by the accounting profession to serve as a general guide for financial reporting purposes.

*Identify generally accepted accounting principles.*

(SO 1)

**BE7-2** Indicate which of the following items is(are) included in the FASB's conceptual framework. (Use "Yes" or "No" to answer this question.)

(a) _____ Analysis of financial statement ratios.

(b) _____ Objectives of financial reporting.

(c) _____ Qualitative characteristics of accounting information.

*Identify items included in conceptual framework.*

(SO 1)

**BE7-3** According to the FASB's conceptual framework, which of the following are objectives of financial reporting? (Use "Yes" or "No" to answer this question.)

(a) _____ Provide information that is helpful in assessing past cash flows and stock prices.

(b) _____ Provide information that is useful to those making investment and credit decisions.

(c) _____ Provide information that identifies the economic resources (assets), the claims to those resources (liabilities), and the changes in those resources and claims.

*Identify objectives of financial reporting.*

(SO 2)

**BE7-4** Presented below is a chart of the qualitative characteristics of accounting information. Fill in the blanks from (a) to (e).

*Identify qualitative characteristics.*

(SO 3)

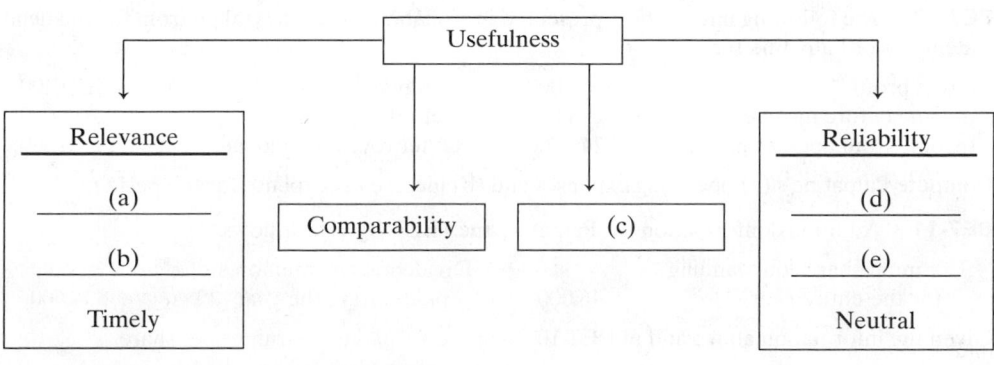

*Identify qualitative characteristics.*
(SO 3)

**BE7-5** Given the *qualitative characteristics* of accounting established by the FASB's conceptual framework, complete each of the following statements:

(a) For information to be ____, it should have predictive or feedback value, and it must be presented on a timely basis.

(b) ____ is the quality of information that gives assurance that it is free of error and bias; it can be depended on.

(c) ____ means using the same accounting principles and methods from year to year within a company.

*Identify qualitative characteristics.*
(SO 3)

**BE7-6** Presented below is a set of qualitative characteristics of accounting information.

1. Predictive value          3. Verifiable
2. Neutral                   4. Timely

Match these qualitative characteristics to the following statements, using numbers 1 through 4.

(a) ____ Accounting information should help users make predictions about the outcome of past, present, and future events.

(b) ____ Accounting information cannot be selected, prepared, or presented to favor one set of interested users over another.

(c) ____ Accounting information must be proved to be free of error and bias.

(d) ____ Accounting information must be available to decision makers before it loses its capacity to influence their decisions.

*Identify operating guidelines.*
(SO 4, 5, 6)

**BE7-7** Presented below are four concepts discussed in this chapter.

1. Time period assumption     3. Full disclosure principle
2. Cost principle             4. Conservatism

Match these concepts to the following accounting practices. Each number can be used only once.

(a) ____ Recording inventory at its purchase price.

(b) ____ Using notes and supplementary schedules in the financial statements.

(c) ____ Preparing financial statements on an annual basis.

(d) ____ Using the lower of cost or market method for inventory valuation.

*Identify the constraints that have been violated.*
(SO 6)

**BE7-8** Fast Forward Company uses the following accounting practices.

(a) Inventory is reported at cost when market value is lower.

(b) The alternative accounting methods are selected in order to avoid reporting a higher net income.

(c) Small tools are recorded as plant assets and depreciated.

(d) The income statement shows paper clips expense of $10.

Indicate the accounting constraint, if any, that has been violated by each practice.

*Perform balance sheet analysis.*
(SO 7)

**BE7-9** The following data are taken from the balance sheet of Ortiz, Inc. The data are arranged in alphabetical order (in millions).

| | | | |
|---|---|---|---|
| Accounts payable | $ 584,600 | Income taxes payable | $ 25,900 |
| Accounts receivable | 1,674,400 | Other current liabilities | 608,500 |
| Cash | 110,600 | Retained earnings | 3,043,400 |

Compute Ortiz's (a) current ratio and (b) working capital.

*Compute income statement relationships.*
(SO 7)

**BE7-10** The following information, presented in alphabetical order, is taken from the financial statements of Palpatine Inc.

| | | | |
|---|---|---|---|
| Gross profit | $907,000 | Net income | $ 179,400 |
| Income before income taxes | 276,000 | Net sales | 1,652,000 |
| Income from operations | 240,000 | Other revenues and gains | 36,000 |

Compute Palpatine's (a) operating expenses and (b) income tax expense for the period.

*Compute earnings per share.*
(SO 7)

**BE7-11** Additional information for Palpatine Inc. (BE7-10) is as follows.

| | | | |
|---|---|---|---|
| Common shares outstanding | | Dividends on common stock | |
| for the entire year | 46,000 | paid during the year | $34,500 |

Given the information above and in BE7-10, compute Palpatine's earnings per share.

# EXERCISES

**E7-1** A number of accounting reporting situations are described below.

1. Church Company recognizes revenue at the end of the production cycle, but before sale. The price of the product, as well as the amount that can be sold, is not certain.
2. In preparing its financial statements, Leask Company omitted information concerning its method of accounting for inventories.
3. Zareena Corp. charges the entire premium on a 2-year insurance policy to the first year.
4. Whitney Hospital Supply Corporation reports only current assets and current liabilities on its balance sheet. Property, plant, and equipment and bonds payable are reported as current assets and current liabilities, respectively. Liquidation of the company is unlikely.
5. Dean Inc. is carrying inventory at its current market value of $100,000. Inventory had an original cost of $110,000.
6. Hot Shot Company is in its fifth year of operation and has yet to issue financial statements. (Do not use full disclosure principle.)
7. Silas Rupe Co. has inventory on hand that cost $400,000. Rupe Co. reports inventory on its balance sheet at its current market value of $425,000.
8. Charlotte Webb, president and owner of the Always Music Company, bought a computer for her personal use. She paid for the computer by using company funds and debited the "Computers" account.

*Identify the assumption, principle, or constraint that has been violated.*

*(SO 4, 5, 6)*

**Instructions**
For each of the above, list the assumption, principle, or constraint that has been violated, if any. List only one term for each case.

**E7-2** Presented below are some business transactions that occurred during 2008 for Vicki Prowitz Company.

**(a)** Merchandise inventory with a cost of $208,000 is reported at its market value of $260,000. The following entry was made.

| | | |
|---|---|---|
| Merchandise Inventory | 52,000 | |
| Gain | | 52,000 |

**(b)** Equipment worth $62,000 was acquired at a cost of $41,000 from a company that had water damage in a flood. The following entry was made.

| | | |
|---|---|---|
| Equipment | 62,000 | |
| Cash | | 41,000 |
| Gain on Purchase of Equipment | | 21,000 |

**(c)** The president of Vicki Prowitz Company, Mark Nabke, purchased a truck for personal use and charged it to his expense account. The following entry was made.

| | | |
|---|---|---|
| Travel Expense | 18,000 | |
| Cash | | 18,000 |

**(d)** An electric pencil sharpener costing $50 is being depreciated over 5 years. The following entry was made.

| | | |
|---|---|---|
| Depreciation Expense—Pencil Sharpener | 10 | |
| Accumulated Depreciation—Pencil Sharpener | | 10 |

*Identify the assumption, principle, or constraint that has been violated and prepare correct entries.*

*(SO 4, 5, 6)*

**Instructions**
In each of the situations above, identify the assumption, principle, or constraint that has been violated, if any. Discuss the appropriateness of the journal entries, and give the correct journal entry, if necessary.

**E7-3** Presented below are the assumptions, principles, and constraints discussed in this chapter.

1. Economic entity assumption
2. Going concern assumption
3. Monetary unit assumption
4. Time period assumption
5. Cost principle
6. Matching principle
7. Full disclosure principle
8. Revenue recognition principle
9. Materiality
10. Conservatism

*Identify accounting assumptions, principles, and constraints.*

*(SO 4, 5, 6)*

**Instructions**

Identify by number the accounting assumption, principle, or constraint on page 323 that describes each situation below. Do not use a number more than once.

**(a)** Is the rationale for why plant assets are not reported at liquidation value. (Do not use historical cost principle.)

**(b)** Indicates that personal and business record-keeping should be separately maintained.

**(c)** Ensures that all relevant financial information is reported.

**(d)** Assumes that the dollar is the "measuring stick" used to report on financial performance.

**(e)** Requires that the operational guidelines be followed for all significant items.

**(f)** Separates financial information into time periods for reporting purpose.

**(g)** Requires recognition of expenses in the same period as related revenues.

**(h)** Indicates that market value changes subsequent to purchase are not recorded in the accounts.

*Determine the amount of revenue to be recognized.*

*(SO 5)*

**E7-4** Consider the following transactions of Parolini Company for 2008.

**1.** Sold a 6-month insurance policy to Orosco Corporation for $9,000 on March 1.

**2.** Leased office space to Easley Supplies for a 1-year period beginning September 1. The rent of $30,000 was paid in advance.

**3.** A sales order for merchandise costing $9,000 that had a sales price of $14,000 was received on December 28 from Guiterrez Company. The goods were shipped FOB shipping point on December 31 and Guiterrez received them on January 3, 2009.

**4.** Merchandise inventory on hand at year-end amounted to $160,000. Parolini expects to sell the inventory in 2009 for $180,000.

**Instructions**

For each item above, indicate the amount of revenue Parolini should recognize in calendar year 2008. Explain.

*Compute earnings per share.*

*(SO 7)*

**E7-5** The ledger of Jean Sartre Corporation at December 31, 2008, contains the following summary information.

| | | | |
|---|---|---|---|
| Administrative expenses | $116,000 | Other expenses and losses | $34,700 |
| Cost of goods sold | 409,200 | Other revenues and gains | 17,500 |
| Net sales | 696,000 | Selling expenses | 98,600 |

The income tax rate for all items is 30%. Sartre Corp. had 10,000 shares of common stock outstanding throughout the year, and the company paid $15,000 in dividends during 2008.

**Instructions**

Compute earnings per share for 2008.

*Prepare an income statement and calculate related information.*

*(SO 7)*

**E7-6** Presented below, in alphabetical order, is information related to Wilkinson Corporation for the year 2008.

| | |
|---|---|
| Cost of goods sold | $1,499,900 |
| Dividends on common stock | 140,000 |
| Gain on the sale of equipment | 80,000 |
| Income tax expense | 150,000 |
| Interest expense | 90,000 |
| Interest revenue | 300,000 |
| Net sales | 2,156,900 |
| Selling and administrative expenses | 340,750 |

Wilkinson had 35,500 shares outstanding for the entire year.

**Instructions**

**(a)** Prepare in good form a single-step income statement for Wilkinson Corporation for 2008.

**(b)** Assuming a multiple-step income statement was prepared instead, compute:

    **(1)** Gross profit.

    **(2)** Income from operations.

    **(3)** Net income.

**(c)** Calculate Wilkinson Corporation's profit margin percentage (rate of return on sales).

**E7-7** Net sales, net income, total assets, and total common stockholders' equity information for a recent year is available for the following three companies.

*Calculate and analyze profitability and solvency relationships.*

(SO 7)

| Company | Net Sales (in millions) | Net Income (in millions) | Total Assets (in millions) | Total Common Equity (in millions) |
|---|---|---|---|---|
| Intel Corporation | $30,141 | $5,641 | $47,143 | $37,846 |
| Johnson & Johnson | $41,862 | $7,197 | $48,263 | $26,869 |
| Motorola, Inc. | $27,058 | $ 893 | $32,098 | $12,689 |

**Instructions**
**(a)** Compute the following relationships for each company.
    **(1)** Debt to total assets ratio.
    **(2)** Profit margin percentage (rate of return on sales).
    **(3)** Return on assets.
    **(4)** Return on common stockholders' equity.
**(b)** What reasons might there be for the differing relationships among these three companies? In your answer, consider the different kinds of industries these companies represent. Do any similarities or differences in the type of business help account for the differences you see?

**E7-8** Net sales, net income, total assets, and total common stockholders' equity information for a recent year is available for the following three companies.

*Calculate and analyze profitability and solvency relationships.*

(SO 7)

| Company | Net Sales (in millions) | Net Income (in millions) | Total Assets (in millions) | Total Common Equity (in millions) |
|---|---|---|---|---|
| Southern Company | $11,251 | $1,474 | $35,045 | $ 9,648 |
| Toys "R" Us, Inc. | $11,305 | $ 229 | $10,218 | $ 4,222 |
| Intel Corp. | $30,141 | $5,641 | $47,143 | $37,846 |

**Instructions**
**(a)** Compute the following relationships for each company.
    **(1)** Debt to total assets ratio.
    **(2)** Profit margin percentage (rate of return on sales).
    **(3)** Return on assets.
    **(4)** Return on common stockholders' equity.
**(b)** What reasons might there be for the differing relationships among these three companies? In your answer, consider the different kinds of industries these companies represent. Do any similarities or differences in the type of business help account for the differences you see?

**E7-9** As of December 31, 2008, Aruba Corporation has a current ratio of 2.6:1 and working capital of $800,000. Aruba's total debt is 60% of its total assets. All of Aruba's long-term assets, which are exactly half of total assets, are properly categorized as property, plant, and equipment.

*Use balance sheet relationships to prepare a balance sheet.*

(SO 7)

**Instructions**
Prepare a summary classified balance sheet for Aruba Corporation at year-end 2008. (*Hint:* First calculate Aruba's current asset and current liability amounts.)

**E7-10** Presented on page 326 is partial balance sheet information related to Batten Ltd., a United Kingdom company at December 31. All financial information has been translated from pounds to dollars.

*Restate foreign financial statements.*

(SO 8)

### BATTEN LTD.
Balance Sheet (partial)
(in thousands)

| | | |
|---|---:|---:|
| Fixed assets | | |
| Tangible assets | | $ 900,000 |
| Current assets | | |
| Stocks (inventory) | $300,000 | |
| Debtors | 121,000 | |
| Investments | 53,000 | |
| Cash | 62,000 | |
| | 536,000 | |
| Creditors | | |
| Amount falling due within one year | 100,000 | |
| Net current assets | | 436,000 |
| Total assets less current liabilities | | 1,336,000 |
| Creditors | | |
| Amounts falling due after one year | | 240,000 |
| Total net assets | | $1,096,000 |

### Instructions

(a) Restate the asset side of the balance sheet in accordance with generally accepted accounting principles in the United States.

(b) What is the amount of total stockholders' equity?

## EXERCISES: SET B

Visit the book's website at **www.wiley.com/college/weygandt,** and choose the Student Companion site, to access Exercise Set B.

## PROBLEMS: SET A

*Analyze transactions to identify accounting principle or assumption violated, and prepare correct entries.*

(SO 4, 5)

**P7-1A**  Scott and Quick are accountants for Millenium Computers. They disagree over the following transactions that occurred during the calendar year 2008.

1. Scott suggests that equipment should be reported on the balance sheet at its liquidation value, which is $15,000 less than its cost.

2. Millenium bought a custom-made piece of equipment for $36,000. This equipment has a useful life of 6 years. Millenium depreciates equipment using the straight-line method. "Since the equipment is custom-made, it will have no resale value. Therefore, it shouldn't be depreciated but instead should be expensed immediately," argues Scott. "Besides, it provides for lower net income."

3. Depreciation for the year was $18,000. Since net income is expected to be lower this year, Scott suggests deferring depreciation to a year when there is more net income.

4. Land costing $60,000 was appraised at $90,000. Scott suggests the following journal entry.

| | | |
|---|---:|---:|
| Land | 30,000 | |
| Gain on Appreciation of Land | | 30,000 |

5. Millenium purchased equipment for $35,000 at a going-out-of-business sale. The equipment was worth $45,000. Scott believes that the following entry should be made.

| | | |
|---|---:|---:|
| Equipment | 45,000 | |
| Cash | | 35,000 |
| Gain on Purchase of Equipment | | 10,000 |

Quick disagrees with Scott on each of the above situations.

## Instructions

For each transaction, indicate why Quick disagrees. Identify the accounting principle or assumption that Scott would be violating if his suggestions were used. Prepare the correct journal entry for each transaction, if any.

**P7-2A**    Presented below are a number of business transactions that occurred during the current year for Yerkes, Inc.

*Determine the appropriateness of journal entries in terms of generally accepted accounting principles or assumptions.*
*(SO 4, 5)*

1. Because the general level of prices increased during the current year, Yerkes, Inc. determined that there was a $10,000 understatement of depreciation expense on its equipment and decided to record it in its accounts. The following entry was made.

| | | |
|---|---|---|
| Depreciation Expense | 10,000 | |
|     Accumulated Depreciation | | 10,000 |

2. Because of a "flood sale," equipment obviously worth $250,000 was acquired at a cost of $200,000. The following entry was made.

| | | |
|---|---|---|
| Equipment | 250,000 | |
|     Cash | | 200,000 |
|     Gain on Purchase of Equipment | | 50,000 |

3. The president of Yerkes, Inc. used his expense account to purchase a new Saab 9000 solely for personal use. The following entry was made.

| | | |
|---|---|---|
| Miscellaneous Expense | 34,000 | |
|     Cash | | 34,000 |

4. An order for $30,000 has been received from a customer for products on hand. This order is to be shipped on January 9 next year. The following entry was made.

| | | |
|---|---|---|
| Accounts Receivable | 30,000 | |
|     Sales | | 30,000 |

5. Materials were purchased on March 31 for $65,000. This amount was entered in the Inventory account. On December 31, the materials would have cost $80,000, so the following entry was made.

| | | |
|---|---|---|
| Inventory | 15,000 | |
|     Gain on Inventories | | 15,000 |

## Instructions

➡️ In each situation, discuss the appropriateness of the journal entries in terms of generally accepted accounting principles.

**P7-3A**    Presented below are the assumptions, principles, and constraints used in this chapter.

*Identify accounting assumptions, principles, and constraints.*
*(SO 4, 5, 6)*

1. Economic entity assumption
2. Going concern assumption
3. Monetary unit assumption
4. Time period assumption
5. Full disclosure principle
6. Revenue recognition principle
7. Matching principle
8. Cost principle
9. Materiality
10. Conservatism

Identify by number the accounting assumption, principle, or constraint that matches each description below. Do not use a number more than once.

**(a)** Assets are not stated at their liquidation value. (Do not use cost principle.)
**(b)** The death of the president is not recorded in the accounts.
**(c)** Pencil sharpeners are expensed when purchased.
**(d)** Depreciation is recorded in the accounts over the life of an asset. (Do not use the going concern assumption.)
**(e)** Each entity is kept as a unit distinct from its owner or owners.
**(f)** Reporting must be done at defined intervals.
**(g)** Revenue is recorded at the point of sale.
**(h)** When in doubt, it is better to understate rather than overstate net income.
**(i)** All important information related to inventories is presented in the footnotes or in the financial statements.

*Prepare a classified balance sheet and analyze financial position.*

(SO 7)

**P7-4A** The adjusted trial balance of Quad Cities Tours Inc. as of October 31, 2008 (its year-end) contains the following information.

| | |
|---|---:|
| Accounts payable | $170,000 |
| Accounts receivable | 15,000 |
| Accumulated depreciation—Buildings | 144,000 |
| Accumulated depreciation—Equipment | 715,000 |
| Bonds payable | 600,000 |
| Buildings—Offices and cabins | 660,000 |
| Cash | 36,000 |
| Common stock | 300,000 |
| Equipment | 840,000 |
| Income taxes payable | 56,250 |
| Interest payable | 30,000 |
| Inventories | 485,000 |
| Investment in Iowa Trading Post, Inc. (trading—short-term) | 140,000 |
| Land | 653,000 |
| Mortgage payable (on fishing cabins—long-term) | 247,750 |
| Notes payable (short-term) | 164,000 |
| Prepaid advertising | 17,000 |
| Prepaid insurance | 9,000 |
| Retained earnings (October 31, 2008) | 440,000 |
| Supplies | 12,000 |

**Instructions**

*(a) Total current liabilities $420,250*

**(a)** Prepare in good form a classified balance sheet for Quad Cities Tours Inc.

**(b)** Calculate the following balance sheet relationships: current ratio, debt to total assets ratio, and working capital.

**(c)** Assume that Quad Cities has come to you, as the senior loan officer of Big Woods Credit Union, seeking a $500,000 loan to help defray the costs of replacing much of its rental camping gear and canoes. Would you be willing to approve the loan? Is there any additional information you would like to have before making your decision?

*Prepare a multiple-step income statement and analyze profitability.*

(SO 7)

**P7-5A** The ledgers of Mid City Galleries Inc. contain the following balances as of December 31, 2008.

| | | | |
|---|---:|---|---:|
| Advertising expense | $ 123,000 | Miscellaneous administrative | |
| Commissions expense on art sales | 1,200,000 | expenses | 53,200 |
| Depreciation expense | | Miscellaneous selling expenses | 39,000 |
| (administrative) | 98,000 | Net purchases | 3,200,000 |
| Dividend revenue | 50,000 | Net sales | 9,275,000 |
| Insurance expense | 600,000 | Rent expense | 808,000 |
| Interest expense | 98,000 | Freight-in | 232,000 |
| Inventory, January 1 | 1,650,000 | Freight-out | 82,500 |
| Inventory, December 31 | 1,424,000 | Utilities expense | 117,000 |
| Loss on the sale of office | | Wages and salaries | 1,264,000 |
| equipment | 21,300 | | |

Income taxes are calculated at 30 percent of income. Mid City Galleries had 90,000 shares of common stock outstanding for the entire year. Total assets amounted to $7,509,000, and common stockholder's equity was $3,975,400.

**Instructions**

*(a) Net income $814,100*

**(a)** Prepare in good form a multiple-step income statement for Mid City Galleries.

**(b)** Calculate three measures of profitability and one ratio of solvency.

**(c)** Assume that you are considering supplying Mid City Galleries with a line of miniature replicas of fine arts sculptures for sale in its gift shops. Is this a company for which you would like to be a supplier? What additional information would you like to have before deciding to become a major supplier for Mid City Galleries?

# PROBLEMS: SET B

*Analyze transactions to identify accounting principle or assumption violated, and prepare correct entries.*

(SO 4, 5)

**P7-1B**    Mary Kate and Ashley are accountants for Olsen Printers. They disagree over the following transactions that occurred during the year.

1.  Land costing $41,000 was appraised at $49,000. Mary Kate suggests the following journal entry.

| | | |
|---|---|---|
| Land | 8,000 | |
|     Gain on Appreciation of Land | | 8,000 |

2.  Olsen bought equipment for $60,000, including installation costs. The equipment has a useful life of 5 years. Olsen depreciates equipment using the straight-line method. "Since the equipment as installed into our system cannot be removed without considerable damage, it will have no resale value. Therefore, it should not be depreciated, but instead should be expensed immediately," argues Mary Kate. "Besides, it lowers net income."

3.  Depreciation for the year was $26,000. Since net income is expected to be lower this year, Mary Kate suggests deferring depreciation to a year when there is more net income.

4.  Olsen purchased equipment at a fire sale for $18,000. The equipment was worth $26,000. Mary Kate believes that the following entry should be made.

| | | |
|---|---|---|
| Equipment | 26,000 | |
|     Cash | | 18,000 |
|     Gain on Purchase of Equipment | | 8,000 |

5.  Mary Kate suggests that Olsen should carry equipment on the balance sheet at its liquidation value, which is $20,000 less than its cost.

6.  Olsen rented office space for 1 year starting October 1, 2008. The total amount of $24,000 was paid in advance. Mary Kate believes that the following entry should be made on October 1.

| | | |
|---|---|---|
| Rent Expense | 24,000 | |
|     Cash | | 24,000 |

Ashley disagrees with Mary Kate on each of the situations above.

**Instructions**
For each transaction, indicate why Ashley disagrees. Identify the accounting principle or assumption that Mary Kate would be violating if her suggestions were used. Prepare the correct journal entry for each transaction, if any.

*Determine the appropriateness of journal entries in terms of generally accepted accounting principles or assumptions.*

(SO 4, 5)

**P7-2B**    Presented below are a number of business transactions that occurred during the current year for Renteria, Inc.

1.  Because the general level of prices increased during the current year, Renteria, Inc. determined that there was a $40,000 understatement of depreciation expense on its equipment and decided to record it in its accounts. The following entry was made.

| | | |
|---|---|---|
| Depreciation Expense | 40,000 | |
|     Accumulated Depreciation | | 40,000 |

2.  Because of a "flood sale," equipment obviously worth $300,000 was acquired at a cost of $225,000. The following entry was made.

| | | |
|---|---|---|
| Equipment | 300,000 | |
|     Cash | | 225,000 |
|     Gain on Purchase of Equipment | | 75,000 |

3.  An order for $60,000 has been received from a customer for products on hand. This order is to be shipped on January 9 next year. The following entry was made.

| | | |
|---|---|---|
| Accounts Receivable | 60,000 | |
|     Sales | | 60,000 |

4.  Land was purchased on April 30 for $200,000. This amount was entered in the Land account. On December 31, the land would have cost $240,000, so the following entry was made.

| | | |
|---|---|---|
| Land | 40,000 | |
|     Gain on Land | | 40,000 |

5. The president of Renteria, Inc. used his expense account to purchase a pre-owned Mercedes-Benz E420 solely for personal use. The following entry was made.

| | | |
|---|---|---|
| Miscellaneous Expense | 54,000 | |
|     Cash | | 54,000 |

**Instructions**

In each situation, discuss the appropriateness of the journal entries in terms of generally accepted accounting principles.

*Identify accounting assumptions, principles, and constraints.*

*(SO 4, 5, 6)*

**P7-3B** Presented below are the assumptions, principles, and constraints used in this chapter.

1. Economic entity assumption
2. Going concern assumption
3. Monetary unit assumption
4. Time period assumption
5. Full disclosure principle
6. Revenue recognition principle
7. Matching principle
8. Cost principle
9. Materiality
10. Conservatism

Identify by number the accounting assumption, principle, or constraint that matches each description below. Do not use a number more than once.

**(a)** Repair tools are expensed when purchased. (Do not use conservatism.)
**(b)** Allocates expenses to revenues in proper period.
**(c)** Assumes that the dollar is the measuring stick used to report financial information.
**(d)** Separates financial information into time periods for reporting purposes.
**(e)** Market value changes subsequent to purchase are not recorded in the accounts. (Do not use revenue recognition principle.)
**(f)** Indicates that personal and business record keeping should be separately maintained.
**(g)** Ensures that all relevant financial information is reported.
**(h)** Lower of cost or market is used to value inventories.

*Prepare a classified balance sheet and analyze financial position.*

*(SO 7)*

**P7-4B** The adjusted trial balance of Gabelli Equipment, Inc., as of June 30, 2008 (its year-end) contains the following information.

| | |
|---|---|
| Accounts payable | $ 486,000 |
| Accounts receivable | 420,000 |
| Accumulated depreciation—Buildings | 180,000 |
| Accumulated depreciation—Equipment | 577,500 |
| Bonds payable | 1,750,000 |
| Buildings—Manufacturing plant and offices | 680,000 |
| Cash | 87,000 |
| Common stock | 500,000 |
| Equipment | 1,650,000 |
| Income taxes payable | 47,000 |
| Interest payable | 70,000 |
| Interest receivable | 21,000 |
| Inventories | 845,000 |
| Investment in Spartan, Inc. bonds (held-to-maturity—long-term) | 600,000 |
| Land | 212,000 |
| Mortgage payable (on manufacturing plant—long-term) | 310,000 |
| Notes payable (short-term) | 210,000 |
| Prepaid advertising | 9,500 |
| Prepaid insurance | 21,000 |
| Retained earnings (June 30, 2008) | 447,000 |
| Supplies | 32,000 |

**Instructions**

*(a) Total current assets $1,435,500*

**(a)** Prepare in good form a classified balance sheet for Gabelli Equipment.
**(b)** Calculate the following balance sheet relationships: current ratio, debt to total assets ratio, and working capital.
**(c)** Assume that Gabelli has come to you, as vice president of Illinois National Bank, seeking a $450,000 loan to help defray the costs of upgrading some of its machinery. Would you be willing to approve the loan? Is there any additional information you would like to have before making your decision?

**P7-5B**   The ledgers of Campo Leathers Inc. contain the following balances as of January 31, 2008 (its year-end).

*Prepare a multiple-step income statement and analyze profitability.*
*(SO 7)*

| | | | |
|---|---|---|---|
| Advertising expense | $ 130,000 | Inventory, January 31, 2008 | 303,400 |
| Depreciation expense | | Managerial salaries | 129,800 |
| (administrative) | 53,000 | Miscellaneous administrative | |
| Freight-in | 27,900 | expenses | 22,200 |
| Freight-out | 6,800 | Miscellaneous selling expenses | 39,000 |
| Gain on the sale of equipment | 8,500 | Net purchases | 1,697,000 |
| Insurance expense | 57,000 | Net sales | 2,660,000 |
| Interest expense | 13,600 | Rent expense | 81,000 |
| Interest revenue | 7,000 | Sales staff wages | 155,000 |
| Inventory, February 1, 2007 | 296,400 | Utilities expense | 30,300 |

Income taxes are calculated at 30 percent of income. Campo had 84,000 shares of common stock outstanding for the entire year. Total assets amounted to $5,460,000, and common stockholders' equity was $1,966,200 at year end.

**Instructions**
**(a)** Prepare in good form a multiple-step income statement for Campo Leathers Inc.
**(b)** Calculate three measures of profitability and one ratio of solvency.
**(c)** Assume that you are considering supplying Campo Leathers with a line of wallets, key holders, and other small leather goods for sale in its two stores. Is this a company for which you would like to be a supplier? What additional information would you like to have before deciding to become a supplier for Campo Leathers?

(a) Net income $167,930

## PROBLEMS: SET C

Visit the book's website at **www.wiley.com/college/weygandt,** and choose the Student Companion site, to access Problem Set C.

## COMPREHENSIVE PROBLEM: CHAPTERS 2 TO 7

Presented below is financial information related to Nu Wood Corporation for the year 2008. Unless otherwise stated, all balances are ending balances.

| | | | |
|---|---|---|---|
| Accounts payable | $ 874,200 | Interest revenue | 99,000 |
| Accounts receivable | 1,000,800 | Inventories | 984,000 |
| Accumulated | | Marketable securities | |
| depreciation—Equipment | 1,560,000 | (short-term) | 1,175,000 |
| Administrative expenses | 420,000 | Net sales | 3,590,000 |
| Bonds payable | 3,300,000 | Notes payable (short-term) | 1,136,500 |
| Cash | 165,000 | Other long-term debt | 401,300 |
| Common stock | 2,200,000 | Patents and other intangibles | 1,150,100 |
| Cost of goods sold | 2,285,000 | Prepaid expenses | 356,100 |
| Dividends | 250,000 | Retained earnings | |
| Equipment | 5,894,000 | (January 1, 2008) | 877,200 |
| Gain on the sale of land | 87,000 | Selling expenses | 361,000 |
| Interest expense | 108,000 | Taxes payable | 234,500 |

Nu Wood Corporation had 80,000 shares of common stock outstanding for the entire year. Its effective income tax rate for state and federal income taxes combined is 35 percent.

**Instructions**
**(a)** Prepare a multiple-step income statement.
**(b)** Prepare a single-step income statement.

(a) Net income $391,300

(c) Retained earnings, Dec. 31
    $1,018,500

(c) Prepare a retained earnings statement.
(d) Prepare a classified balance sheet.
(e) Compute the following balance sheet relationships:
    (1) current ratio.
    (2) the amount of working capital.
    (3) debt to total assets ratio.
    What insights do these relationships provide to the reader of the financial statements?
(f) Compute three measures of profitability. What insights do these relationships provide to the reader of the financial statements?
(g) Compare the results for Nu Wood Corporation, calculated here, and the results for Notting Hill Corporation in Demonstration Problem 2. As an investor, which corporation seems more attractive to you? Why?

## CONTINUING COOKIE CHRONICLE

(Note: This is a continuation of the Cookie Chronicle from Chapters 1 through 6.)

**CCC7** Natalie's biggest competitor is Trial Appliances. Trial Appliances sells a fine European mixer similar to the one that customers are able to buy from Cookie Creations. Natalie estimates that Trial Appliances sells twice as many mixers as she does. Trial Appliances also sells other appliances. Natalie believes that one of the major reasons Trial Appliances sells the number of mixers that it does is because it sells all of its appliances on an extended payment plan. She would really like to generate more sales revenues and cash flow. Natalie comes to you to ask about the accounting for revenues when mixers are sold on an extended payment plan.

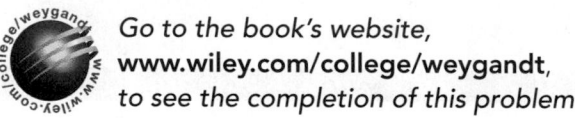 *Go to the book's website,* **www.wiley.com/college/weygandt**, *to see the completion of this problem.*

# BROADENING YOUR PERSPECTIVE

## FINANCIAL REPORTING AND ANALYSIS

## Financial Reporting Problem

**BYP7-1** Marcey Leuck successfully completed her first accounting course during the spring semester. She is now working as a management trainee for Midwest Bank, N.A. during the summer. One of her fellow management trainees, Reed LaDue, is taking the same accounting course this summer and has been having a "lot of trouble." On the second exam, for example, Reed became confused about inventory valuation methods. He completely missed all the points on a problem involving LIFO and FIFO.

Reed's instructor recently indicated that the third exam will probably have a number of essay questions dealing with accounting principles issues. Reed is quite concerned about the third exam for two reasons. First, he has never taken an accounting exam in which essay answers were required. Second, Reed feels he must do well on this exam to get an acceptable grade in the course.

Reed has asked Marcey to help him prepare for the next exam. She agrees, and suggests that Reed develop a set of possible questions on the accounting principles material that they might discuss.

### Instructions
Answer the following questions that were developed by Reed.

(a) What is a conceptual framework?
(b) Why is there a need for a conceptual framework?
(c) What are the objectives of financial reporting?
(d) If you had to explain generally accepted accounting principles to a nonaccountant, what essential characteristics would you include in your explanation?

(e) What are the qualitative characteristics of accounting? Explain each one.
(f) Identify the basic assumptions used in accounting.
(g) What are two major constraints involved in financial reporting? Explain both of them.

# Comparative Analysis Problem

## PepsiCo vs. Coca-Cola

**BYP7-2** PepsiCo's financial statements are presented in Appendix A. Coca-Cola's financial statements are presented in Appendix B.

**Instructions**
(a) Based on the information contained in these financial statements, compute the following 2005 ratios for each company.
   (1) Current ratio.                  (4) Return on assets.
   (2) Working capital.                (5) Return on common stockholders' equity.
   (3) Profit margin percentage.       (6) Debt to total assets ratio.
(b) Compare and evaluate the liquidity, profitability, and solvency of the two companies.

# Exploring the Web

**BYP7-3** The Financial Accounting Standards Board (FASB) is a private organization established to improve accounting standards and financial reporting. The FASB conducts extensive research before issuing a "Statement of Financial Accounting Standards," which represents an authoritative expression of generally accepted accounting principles.

*Address:* **www.accounting.rutgers.edu/accounting**, or go to **www.wiley.com/college/weygandt**

**Steps**

1. Choose **FASB**.
2. Choose **Facts about FASB**.

**Instructions**
Answer the following questions.

(a) What is the mission of the FASB?
(b) How are topics added to the FASB technical agenda?
(c) What characteristics make the FASB's procedures an "open" decision-making process?

# CRITICAL THINKING

# Decision Making Across the Organization

**BYP7-4** Presented below are key figures and relationships from the financial statements of a prominent company in each of three different industries for two recent fiscal years.

|  | Manufacturing | | Mining/Oil | | Merchandising | |
|---|---|---|---|---|---|---|
|  | Prior Year | Current Year | Prior Year | Current Year | Prior Year | Current Year |
| **From the balance sheets:** | | | | | | |
| Total assets (millions) | $11,079 | $11,083 | $33,884 | $35,089 | $8,524 | $9,485 |
| Current ratio | 1.72 | 1.73 | 1.14 | 1.12 | 1.51 | 1.56 |
| Working capital (millions) | $2,390 | $2,349 | $1,037 | $1,072 | $1,236 | $1,452 |
| Debt to total assets ratio | 0.45 | 0.43 | 0.59 | 0.58 | 0.72 | 0.72 |
| **Profitability:** | | | | | | |
| Total sales (millions) | $13,021 | $13,340 | $31,916 | $41,540 | $14,739 | $16,115 |
| Profit margin percentage | 10.0% | 8.7% | 0.8% | 5.2% | 2.8% | 1.9% |
| Return on assets | 11.8% | 10.4% | 0.7% | 6.1% | 4.8% | 3.2% |
| Return on common equity | 21.4% | 18.3% | 1.8% | 15.0% | 20.1% | 13.5% |
| Earnings per common share | $5.91 | $5.26 | $0.73 | $6.10 | $5.20 | $3.72 |
| **From the annual reports:** | | | | | | |
| End-of-year stock price | $67.75 | $72.63 | $85.75 | $95.25 | $56.50 | $62.00 |

**Instructions**
With the class divided into groups, answer the following.

**(a)** The benchmark for the current ratio is generally 2:1. None of these companies has a ratio that high, yet all three are well regarded firms. Why might a current ratio less than 2:1 *not* signal a problem?

**(b)** The merchandising company acquired a chain of well-known department stores two years ago. Apart from such major acquisitions, what else might contribute to differing debt to total assets ratios? Consider industry-specific as well as company-specific considerations.

**(c)** For all three companies, the ratio of debt to total assets changed little from the prior year to the current year, yet for two of the three companies return on common stockholders' equity decreased. What might cause this pattern?

**(d)** The profitability relationships and earnings per share for both the manufacturing and the merchandising companies decreased from the prior year to the current year, yet the price per share of stock for each company increased. Why might investors have been willing to pay more for these companies in the current year?

# Communication Activity

**BYP7-5** If you go on to advanced accounting courses, you'll study the differences between accounting in the business world and university accounting. You'll find that there's one major similarity: both depend heavily on the matching principle.

At Long Beach City College, a two-year community college with 30,000 students, most of the revenues come from the state of California and the federal government. As a condition of receiving these grants, "we must match expenses against revenues in the right fiscal year," says the school's accounting manager.

For example, the college receives federal funding under the Job Training Partnership Act. "We receive funding from the federal government, which allows us to offer classes to students for job preparation. The government specifies the grant periods, for instance, from July 1 to June 30. We therefore have to ensure that all transactions for that project are completed within that fiscal year." Another project is the amnesty program, the federal government's legalization of foreign nationals. Expenses to offset the grant money are mostly teaching salaries and instructional materials.

By year-end, the goal is to break even. Excess funds, if any, have to be returned. But program managers do not want a deficit, either, because these projects are accountable to the college administration and any overspending will come from the college's general fund.

**Instructions**
Write a letter to your instructor covering the following points.

**1.** Why is the matching principle important in accounting for government grants?

**2.** Give some examples of grant or special programs to which the matching principle might be applied at your college or university.

**3.** What are some examples of costs that Long Beach City College might properly charge to its grant or special programs?

# Ethics Case

**BYP7-6** When the Financial Accounting Standards Board issues new standards, the required implementation date is usually 12 months or more from the date of issuance, with early implementation encouraged. Michael Peeples, accountant at Bruno Corporation, discusses with his financial vice president the need for early implementation of a recently issued standard that would result in a much fairer presentation of the company's financial condition and earnings. When the financial vice president determines that early implementation of the standard will adversely affect reported net income for the year, he strongly discourages Michael from implementing the standard until it is required.

**Instructions**

**(a)** Who are the stakeholders in this situation?

**(b)** What, if any, are the ethical considerations in this situation?

**(c)** What does Michael have to gain by advocating early implementation? Who might be affected by the decision against early implementation?

# "All About You" Activity

**BYP7-7** In the "All About You" feature in this chapter (page 314), you learned that in response to the Sarbanes-Oxley Act, many companies have implemented formal ethics codes. Many other organizations also have ethics codes.

**Instructions**

Obtain the ethics code from an organization that you belong to (e.g., student organization, business school, employer, or a volunteer organization). Evaluate the ethics code based on how clearly it identifies proper and improper behavior. Discuss its strengths, and how it might be improved.

## Answers to Insight and Accounting Across the Organization Questions

**When to Account for the Winning Handle Pull, p. 301**

Q: What accounting principles are applicable to the Harold's Club progressive slot machines?

A: *The revenue recognition and the matching principles are applicable.*

Q: If Harold's fails to use an estimate for expenses, what effect will this have on financial statements in a period when no payouts occur?

A: *In periods without a payout, revenues will be very high, expenses will be too low, and income will be overstated. In a subsequent period, when a payout occurs, expenses will be very high and net income very low.*

**How About Instant Access?, p. 302**

Q: Would instant access to financial information provide more relevant information?

A: *Such access should be more relevant since it would be more timely.*

Q: Do you think such an approach would do away with the need for annual reports?

A: *No. To ensure compliance with GAAP and various regulatory agencies, it will still be necessary to have audited financial statements and regulatory filings. Reports based upon a consistent time period will be necessary to allow for comparison with prior years and with other companies.*

**How High Is Your Profit Margin?, p. 310**

Q: If service companies have a profit margin much lower than manufacturers (a third as large), why would anyone invest in a service company over a manufacturer?

A: *The profit margin is only a percentage, not an absolute amount. A service company may have a profit margin only a third that of a manufacturer but have a greater amount of net profit in total dollars and per-share amount.*

**And the Correct Answer Is . . .?, p. 312**

Q: What would be the advantage of similar accounting standards for all countries?

A: *Similar accounting standards would make comparable the financial statements of companies from all countries.*

Q: How can the financial and operating performance of international companies be compared?

A: *Adjustments must be made to the reported financial data to make analysis and ratios comparable.*

## Authors' Comments on *All About You*: Corporations Have Governance Structures—Do You?, p. 314

Before we address the usefulness of a student code of ethics, let's first ask whether a corporate code of ethics will ensure that employees no longer commit fraud. The answer is, "Clearly not." Does that mean a code of ethics is a waste of time? No. A code of ethics is a useful statement by the leaders of an organization about what kind of behavior is expected of the members of that organization. It provides a concrete reference point by which wrongdoing can be identified and evaluated.

Now, suppose that you were taking an exam and that you observed a number of people cheating. It would be very frustrating if you thought that your instructor, the school administrators, and other students didn't care that people were cheating. Ultimately this would encourage even more people to cheat. But if the school has defined unethical behavior, stated that it won't be tolerated, and created the necessary mechanisms for detecting and punishing unethical behavior, then it has begun the first steps in creating a more ethical environment. For an example of an ethics code for university students, see the ethics section of the Student Resources at **www.bus.wisc.edu/accounting.**

### Answer to PepsiCo Review It Question 2, p. 298

The Report of Independent Auditors indicates that PepsiCo's financial statements (balance sheet and statements of income, cash flows, and common shareholders' equity) are presented fairly, in conformity with accounting principles generally accepted in the U.S.A.

### Answers to Self-Study Questions

**1.** a   **2.** d   **3.** c   **4.** c   **5.** c   **6.** c   **7.** b   **8.** c   **9.** c   **10.** b

# Chapter 8

# Internal Control and Cash

## STUDY OBJECTIVES

*After studying this chapter, you should be able to:*

1 Define internal control.
2 Identify the principles of internal control.
3 Explain the applications of internal control principles to cash receipts.
4 Explain the applications of internal control principles to cash disbursements.
5 Describe the operation of a petty cash fund.
6 Indicate the control features of a bank account.
7 Prepare a bank reconciliation.
8 Explain the reporting of cash.

The Navigator

## ✓ The Navigator

Scan **Study Objectives** ▪

Read **Feature Story** ▪

Read **Preview** ▪

Read text and answer **Before You Go On** ▪
p. 347 ▪    p. 351 ▪    p. 355 ▪    p. 362 ▪
p. 365 ▪

Work **Demonstration Problem** ▪

Review **Summary of Study Objectives** ▪

Answer **Self-Study Questions** ▪

Complete **Assignments** ▪

## Feature Story

**MINDING THE MONEY IN MOOSE JAW**

If you're ever looking for a cappuccino in Moose Jaw, Saskatchewan, stop by Stephanie's Gourmet Coffee and More, located on Main Street. Staff there serve, on average, 650 cups of coffee a day, including both regular and specialty coffees, not to mention soups, Italian sandwiches, and a wide assortment of gourmet cheesecakes.

"We've got high school students who come here, and students from the community college," says owner/manager Stephanie Mintenko, who has run the place since opening it in 1995. "We have customers who are retired, and others who are working people and have only 30 minutes for lunch. We have to be pretty quick."

That means that the cashiers have to be efficient. Like most businesses where purchases are low-cost and high-volume, cash control has to be simple.

"We have an electronic cash register, but it's not the fancy new kind where you just punch in the item," explains Ms. Mintenko. "You have to punch in the prices." The machine does keep track of sales in several categories, however. Cashiers punch a button to indicate whether each item is a beverage, a meal, or a charge for the cafe's Internet connections. An internal tape in the machine keeps a record of all transactions; the customer receives a receipt only upon request.

There is only one cash register. "Up to three of us might operate it on any given shift, including myself," says Ms. Mintenko.

She and her staff do two "cashouts" each day—one with the shift change at 5:00 p.m. and one when the shop closes at 10:00 p.m. At each cashout, they count the cash in the register drawer. That amount, minus the cash change carried forward (the float), should match the shift total on the register tape. If there's a discrepancy, they do another count. Then, if necessary, "we go through the whole tape to find the mistake," she explains. "It usually turns out to be someone who punched in $18 instead of $1.80, or something like that."

Ms. Mintenko sends all the cash tapes and float totals to a bookkeeper, who double-checks everything and provides regular reports. "We try to keep the accounting simple, so we can concentrate on making great coffee and food."

 The Navigator

## Inside Chapter 8

## Preview of Chapter 8

As the story about recording cash sales at Stephanie's Gourmet Coffee and More indicates, control of cash is important. Companies also need controls to safeguard other types of assets. For example, Stephanie's undoubtedly has controls to prevent the theft of food and supplies, and controls to prevent the theft of tableware and dishes from its kitchen.

In this chapter, we explain the essential features of an internal control system and then describe how those controls apply to cash. The applications include some controls with which you may be already familiar. Toward the end of the chapter, we describe the use of a bank and explain how companies report cash on the balance sheet.

The content and organization of Chapter 8 are as follows.

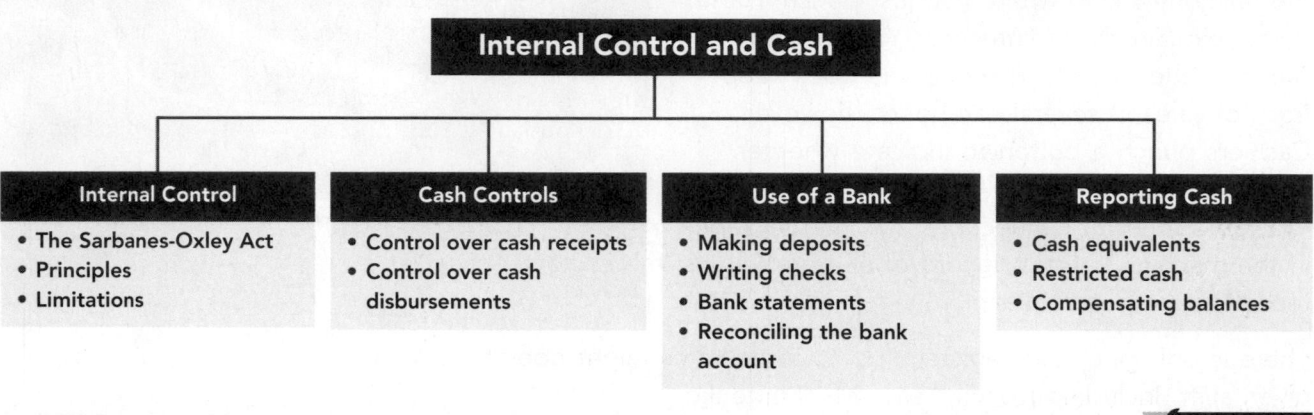

Internal Control and Cash

**Internal Control**
- The Sarbanes-Oxley Act
- Principles
- Limitations

**Cash Controls**
- Control over cash receipts
- Control over cash disbursements

**Use of a Bank**
- Making deposits
- Writing checks
- Bank statements
- Reconciling the bank account

**Reporting Cash**
- Cash equivalents
- Restricted cash
- Compensating balances

# INTERNAL CONTROL

**STUDY OBJECTIVE 1**
Define internal control.

Could there be dishonest employees where you work? Unfortunately, sometimes the answer is yes. For example, in addition to the highly publicized frauds at Enron, WorldCom, Tyco, and Global Crossing, the financial press recently reported the following.

A bookkeeper in a small company diverted $750,000 of bill payments to a personal bank account over a three-year period.

A shipping clerk with 28 years of service shipped $125,000 of merchandise to himself.

A computer operator embezzled $21 million from Wells Fargo Bank over a two-year period.

A church treasurer "borrowed" $150,000 of church funds to finance a friend's business dealings.

These situations emphasize the need for organizations to have good systems of internal control.

**Internal control** consists of all the related methods and measures adopted within an organization to:

1. **Safeguard its assets** from employee theft, robbery, and unauthorized use.
2. **Enhance the accuracy and reliability of its accounting records.** This is done by reducing the risk of **errors** (unintentional mistakes) and **irregularities** (intentional mistakes and misrepresentations) in the accounting process.

Under the Sarbanes-Oxley Act, all publicly traded U.S. corporations are **required** to maintain an adequate system of internal control. Companies that fail to comply are subject to fines, and company officers may be imprisoned.

## The Sarbanes-Oxley Act

"Better get those controls under control" was a comment often made after the numerous corporate scandals of recent years. As a result, Congress passed the Sarbanes-Oxley Act of 2002 (SOX). One of the most important laws to be passed in decades, SOX forces companies to pay more attention to internal controls.

SOX imposes more responsibilities on corporate executives and boards of directors to ensure that companies' internal controls are reliable and effective. Under one part of the law, companies must develop sound principles of control over financial reporting. They must continually verify that these controls are working. In addition, independent outside auditors must attest to the level of internal control. SOX also created the **Public Company Accounting Oversight Board (PCAOB)**, which now establishes auditing standards and regulates auditor activity.

One poll found that about 60% of investors believe that SOX will help safeguard their stock investments. Many say they would be unlikely to invest in a company that fails to follow SOX requirements. Although some corporate executives have criticized the time and expense involved in following the requirements of the law, SOX appears to be working well. For example, the chief accounting officer of Eli Lily noted that SOX triggered a comprehensive review of how the company documents its controls. This review uncovered redundancies and also pointed out controls that needed to be added. In short, it added up to time and money well spent. And the finance chief at General Electric noted, "We have seen value in SOX. It helps build investors' trust and gives them more confidence."[1]

## Principles of Internal Control

To safeguard assets and enhance the accuracy and reliability of accounting records, companies follow specific control principles. These measures vary with the size and nature of the business and with management's control philosophy. The six principles listed in Illustration 8-1 (page 342) apply to most enterprises. They are explained in the following sections.

STUDY OBJECTIVE 2

Identify the principles of internal control.

### ESTABLISHMENT OF RESPONSIBILITY

An essential principle of internal control is to assign responsibility to specific employees. **Control is most effective when only one person is responsible for a given task.**

To illustrate, assume that the cash on hand at the end of the day in a Safeway supermarket is $10 short of the cash rung up on the cash register. If only one person has operated the register, the shift manager can quickly determine responsibility for the shortage. If two or more individuals have worked the register, it may be impossible to determine who is responsible for the error unless each person is assigned a separate cash drawer and register key. In the Feature Story, the principle of establishing responsibility does not appear to be strictly applied by Stephanie's, since three people operate the cash register on any given shift. To quickly identify any shortages, employees at Stephanie's perform two cashouts each day.

Transfer of cash drawers

---

[1]"Corporate Regulation Must Be Working—There's a Backlash," *Wall Street Journal,* June 16, 2004, p. C1; and Judith Burns, "Is Sarbanes-Oxley Working?" *Wall Street Journal,* June 21, 2004, pp. R8–R9.

**Illustration 8-1**
Principles of internal control

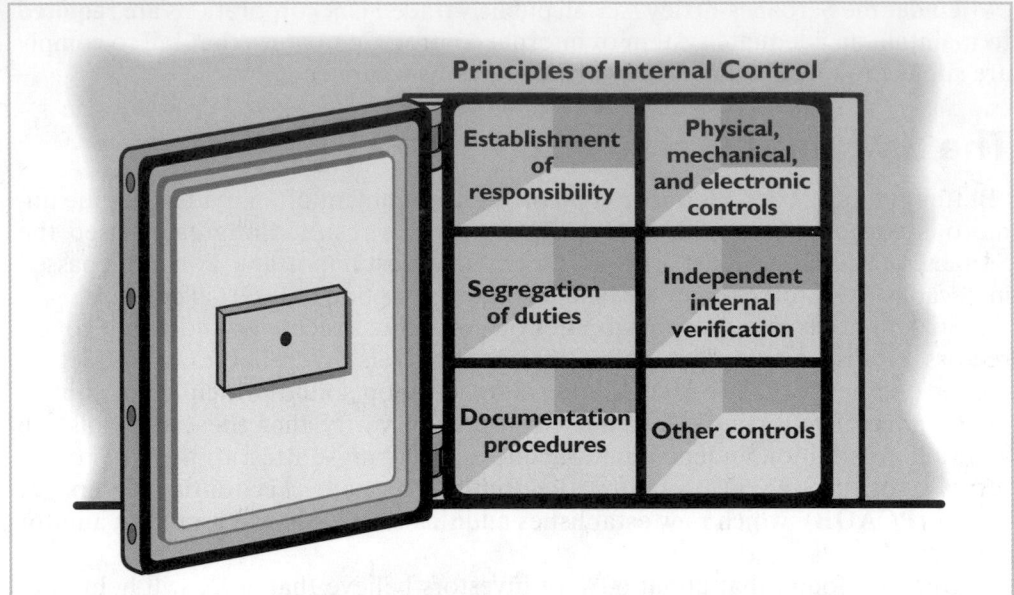

Establishing responsibility includes authorization and approval of transactions. For example, the vice president of sales should have the authority to establish policies for making credit sales. The policies ordinarily will require written credit department approval of credit sales.

## SEGREGATION OF DUTIES

Segregation of duties (also called separation of functions) is indispensable in an internal control system. There are two common applications of this principle:

1. Different individuals should be responsible for related activities.
2. The responsibility for record keeping for an asset should be separate from the physical custody of that asset.

The rationale for segregation of duties is this: **The work of one employee should, without a duplication of effort, provide a reliable basis for evaluating the work of another employee.**

**Related Activities.** In both purchasing and selling, companies should assign related activities to different individuals. **Making one individual responsible for all of the related activities increases the potential for errors and irregularities.**

Related *purchasing activities* include ordering merchandise, receiving the goods, and paying (or authorizing payment) for the merchandise. For example, a dishonest employee could place orders with friends or with suppliers who give kickbacks. An employee could do only a cursory count and inspection of delivered goods, which could lead to errors and poor-quality merchandise. An employee might authorize payment without a careful review of the invoice, or even worse, might approve fictitious invoices for payment. When a company assigns responsibility for ordering, receiving, and paying to different individuals, it minimizes the risk of such abuses.

Similarly, companies should assign related *sales activities* to different individuals. Related selling activities include making a sale, shipping (or delivering) the goods to the customer, billing the customer, and receiving payment. Various frauds are possible when one person handles related sales transactions. A salesperson could make sales at unauthorized prices to increase sales commissions. A shipping clerk could ship goods to himself. A billing clerk could understate the amount billed for sales made to friends and relatives. These abuses are less likely to occur when companies divide the sales tasks: the salespeople make the sale; the shipping department ships the goods on the basis of the sales order; and the billing department prepares the sales invoice after comparing the sales order with the report of goods shipped.

# INTERNATIONAL INSIGHT

## This Was a Penalty to Take Seriously

It's said that accountants' predecessors were the scribes of ancient Egypt, who kept the pharaohs' books. They inventoried grain, gold, and other assets. Unfortunately, some fell victim to temptation and stole from their leader, as did other employees of the king. The solution was to have two scribes independently record each transaction—perhaps the first instance of internal control. As long as the scribes' totals agreed exactly, there was no problem. But if the totals were materially different, both scribes would be put to death. That proved to be a great incentive for them to carefully check all the numbers and make sure the help wasn't stealing. In fact, fraud prevention and detection became the royal accountants' main duty.

*Source:* Joseph T. Wells, "So That's Why It's Called a Pyramid Scheme," *Journal of Accountancy* (October 2000), p. 91. Copyright © 2000 from the *Journal of Accountancy* by the *American Institute of Certified Public Accountants, Inc.* Opinions of the authors are their own and do not necessarily reflect policies of the AICPA. Reprinted with permission.

**?** Which principle of internal control was implemented in ancient Egypt? Who do you think investors today expect to detect and prevent fraud?

**Record Keeping Separate from Physical Custody.** To provide a valid basis of accountability for an asset, the accountant should have neither physical custody of the asset nor access to it. Likewise, the custodian of the asset should not maintain or have access to the accounting records. **The custodian of the asset is not likely to convert the asset to personal use when one employee maintains the record of the asset, and a different employee has physical custody of the asset.** The separation of accounting responsibility from the custody of assets is especially important for cash and inventories because these assets are very vulnerable to unauthorized use or misappropriation.

Illustration 8-2 shows the segregation of duties concept.

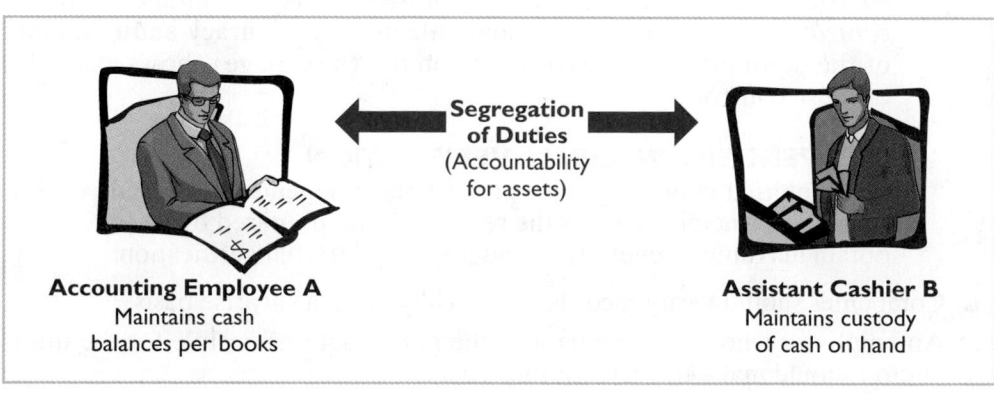

**Illustration 8-2**
The segregation of duties (accountability for assets) principle

**Prenumbered invoices**

## DOCUMENTATION PROCEDURES

Documents provide evidence that transactions and events have occurred. At Stephanie's Gourmet Coffee and More, the cash register tape is the restaurant's documentation for the sale and the amount of cash received. Similarly, a shipping document indicates that the goods have been shipped, and a sales invoice indicates that the company has billed the customer for the goods. By requiring signatures (or initials) on the documents, the company can identify the individual(s) responsible for the transaction or event. Companies should document transactions when the transaction occurs. They generally develop documentation of events, such as those leading to adjusting entries, when the adjustments are made.

Companies should establish procedures for documents. First, whenever possible, companies should use **prenumbered documents, and all documents should be accounted for**. Prenumbering helps to prevent a transaction from being recorded more than once, or conversely, from not being recorded at all. Second, the control system should require that employees **promptly forward source documents for accounting entries to the accounting department. This control measure helps to ensure timely recording of the transaction** and contributes directly to the accuracy and reliability of the accounting records.

---

# ACCOUNTING ACROSS THE ORGANIZATION

### SOX Boosts the Role of Human Resources

The human resources (HR) department has always played an important role in internal control by carefully screening potential hires. The Sarbanes-Oxley Act has increased HR's role in a number of ways. Under SOX, a company needs to keep track of employees' degrees and certifications to ensure that employees continue to meet the specified requirements of a job. Also, to ensure proper employee supervision and proper separation of duties, companies must develop and monitor an organizational chart. When one corporation went through this exercise it found that out of 17,000 employees, there were 400 people who did not report to anyone, and they had 35 people who reported to each other. In addition, if an employee complains of an unfair firing and mentions financial issues at the company, HR must refer the case to the company audit committee and possibly to its legal counsel.

 Why would unsupervised employees or employees who report to each other represent potential internal control threats?

---

**ETHICS NOTE**

Program controls built into the computer prevent intentional or unintentional errors or unauthorized access. To prevent unauthorized access, the computer system may require that users enter passwords or correctly answer random personal questions.

## PHYSICAL, MECHANICAL, AND ELECTRONIC CONTROLS

Use of physical, mechanical, and electronic controls is essential. *Physical controls* relate to the safeguarding of assets. *Mechanical* and *electronic controls* also safeguard assets and enhance the accuracy and reliability of the accounting records. Illustration 8-3 (next page) shows examples of these controls.

## INDEPENDENT INTERNAL VERIFICATION

Most internal control systems provide for **independent internal verification**. This principle involves the review of data prepared by employees. To obtain maximum benefit from independent internal verification:

**1.** Companies should verify records periodically or on a surprise basis.

**2.** An employee who is independent of the personnel responsible for the information should make the verification.

**Physical Controls**

Safes, vaults, and safety
deposit boxes for cash
and business papers

Locked warehouses
and storage cabinets for
inventories and records

Computer facilities
with pass key access
or fingerprint or
eyeball scans

**Mechanical and Electronic Controls**

Alarms to
prevent break-ins

Television monitors
and garment sensors
to deter theft

Time clocks for
recording time worked

**Illustration 8-3**
Physical, mechanical, and
electronic controls

**3.** Discrepancies and exceptions should be reported to a management level that can take appropriate corrective action.

Independent internal verification is especially useful in comparing recorded accountability with existing assets. The reconciliation of the cash register tape with the cash in the register at Stephanie's Gourmet Coffee and More is an example of this internal control principle. Another common example is the reconciliation of a company's cash balance per books with the cash balance per bank. Illustration 8-4 shows the relationship between this principle and the segregation of duties principle.

**Illustration 8-4**
Comparison of segregation
of duties principle with
independent internal
verification principle

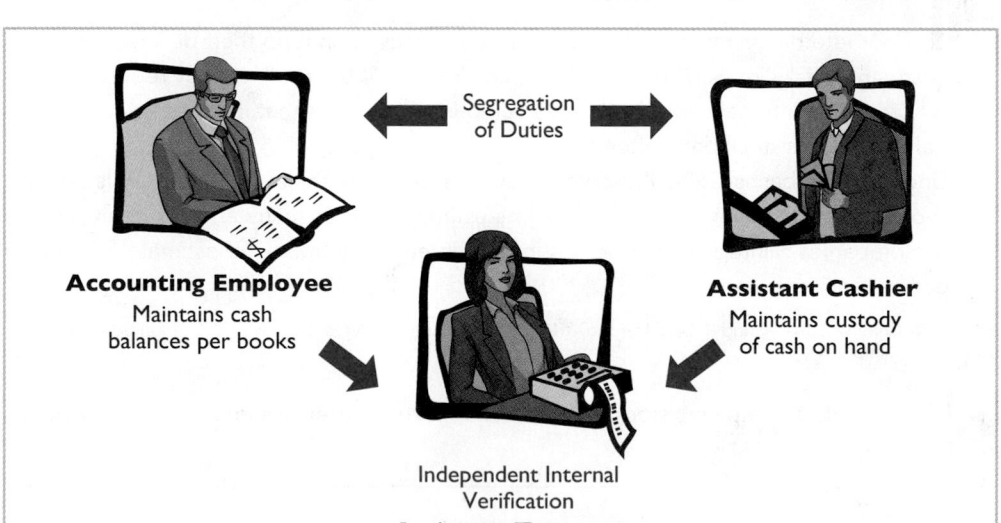

**Accounting Employee**
Maintains cash
balances per books

Segregation
of Duties

**Assistant Cashier**
Maintains custody
of cash on hand

Independent Internal
Verification
**Assistant Treasurer**
Makes monthly comparisons; reports
any unreconcilable differences to treasurer

Large companies often assign independent internal verification to internal auditors. **Internal auditors** are company employees who continuously evaluate the effectiveness of the company's internal control systems. They review the activities of departments and individuals to determine whether prescribed internal controls are being followed. They also recommend improvements when needed. In fact, most fraud is discovered by the company through internal mechanisms such as existing internal controls and internal audits. For example, the alleged fraud at WorldCom, involving billions of dollars, was uncovered by an internal auditor.

## OTHER CONTROLS
Other control measures include the following.

1. **Bond employees who handle cash.** Bonding involves obtaining insurance protection against misappropriation of assets by employees. It contributes to the safeguarding of cash in two ways: First, the insurance company carefully screens all individuals before adding them to the policy and may reject risky applicants. Second, bonded employees know that the insurance company will vigorously prosecute all offenders.

2. **Rotate employees' duties and require employees to take vacations.** These measures deter employees from attempting thefts since they will not be able to permanently conceal their improper actions. Many banks, for example, have discovered embezzlements when the perpetrator was on vacation or assigned to a new position.

3. **Conduct thorough background checks.** Many believe that the most important and inexpensive measure any business can take to reduce employee theft and fraud is for the human resources department to conduct thorough background checks. Two tips: (1) Check to see whether job applicants actually graduated from the schools they list. (2) Never use the telephone numbers for previous employers given on the reference sheet; always look them up yourself.

## INVESTOR INSIGHT

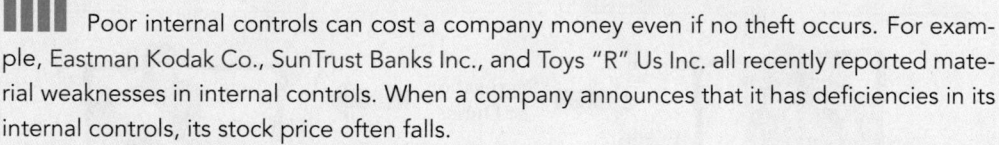

### *Poor Internal Control Can Hammer Stock Price*

Poor internal controls can cost a company money even if no theft occurs. For example, Eastman Kodak Co., SunTrust Banks Inc., and Toys "R" Us Inc. all recently reported material weaknesses in internal controls. When a company announces that it has deficiencies in its internal controls, its stock price often falls.

Under the Sarbanes-Oxley Act companies must evaluate their internal controls systems and report on any deficiencies. Some analysts estimate that as many as 10% of all publicly traded companies will report weaknesses in their internal controls. The estimate for smaller companies is even higher.

*Source:* William M. Bulkeley and Robert Tomsho, "Kodak to Get Auditors Adverse View," *Wall Street Journal Online,* January 27, 2005.

 Why would a company's stock price fall if it reports deficiencies in its internal controls?

## Limitations of Internal Control

Companies generally design their systems of internal control to provide **reasonable assurance** of proper safeguarding of assets and reliability of the accounting records. The concept of reasonable assurance rests on the premise that the costs of establishing control procedures should not exceed their expected benefit.

To illustrate, consider shoplifting losses in retail stores. Stores could eliminate such losses by having a security guard stop and search customers as they leave the store. But store managers have concluded that the negative effects of such a procedure cannot be justified. Instead, stores have attempted to control shoplifting losses by less costly procedures: They post signs saying, "We reserve the right to inspect all packages" and "All shoplifters will be prosecuted." They use hidden TV cameras and store detectives to monitor customer activity, and they install sensor equipment at exits.

The **human element** is an important factor in every system of internal control. A good system can become ineffective as a result of employee fatigue, carelessness, or indifference. For example, a receiving clerk may not bother to count goods received and may just "fudge" the counts. Occasionally, two or more individuals may work together to get around prescribed controls. Such **collusion** can significantly impair the effectiveness of a system, eliminating the protection offered by segregation of duties. No system of internal control is perfect.

The size of the business also may impose limitations on internal control. A small company, for example, may find it difficult to segregate duties or to provide for independent internal verification.

**HELPFUL HINT**

Controls may vary with the risk level of the activity. For example, management may consider cash to be high risk and maintaining inventories in the stockroom as low risk. Thus management would have stricter controls for cash.

## Before You Go On...

### REVIEW IT
1. What are the two primary objectives of internal control?
2. Identify and describe the principles of internal control.
3. What are the limitations of internal control?

### DO IT
Li Song owns a small retail store. Li wants to establish good internal control procedures but is confused about the difference between segregation of duties and independent internal verification. Explain the differences to Li.

### Action Plan
■ Understand and explain the differences between (1) segregation of duties and (2) independent internal verification.

**Solution** Segregation of duties involves assigning responsibility so that the work of one employee evaluates the work of another employee. Segregation of duties occurs daily in executing and recording transactions.

In contrast, independent internal verification involves reviewing, comparing, and reconciling data prepared by employees. Independent internal verification occurs *after the fact*, as in the case of reconciling cash register totals at the end of the day with cash on hand.

Related exercise material: *BE8-1, BE8-2, BE8-3, and E8-1.*

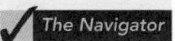 *The Navigator*

# CASH CONTROLS

Just as cash is the beginning of a company's operating cycle, so it is also usually the starting point for a company's system of internal control. Cash is the one asset that is readily convertible into any other type of asset. It also is easily concealed and transported, and is highly desired. Because of these characteristics, **cash is the asset most susceptible to improper diversion and use**. In addition, because of the large volume of cash transactions, numerous errors may occur in executing and recording them. To safeguard cash and to ensure the accuracy of the accounting records for cash, effective internal control over cash is imperative.

**Cash** consists of coins, currency (paper money), checks, money orders, and money on hand or on deposit in a bank or similar depository. The general rule is that cash is whatever the bank will accept for deposit.

In the next sections we explain the application of internal control principles to cash receipts and cash disbursements.

# Internal Control over Cash Receipts

**STUDY OBJECTIVE 3**

Explain the applications of internal control principles to cash receipts.

Cash receipts come from a variety of sources: cash sales; collections on account from customers; the receipt of interest, rent, and dividends; investments by owners; bank loans; and proceeds from the sale of noncurrent assets. Illustration 8-5 shows how the internal control principles explained earlier apply to cash receipts transactions.

**Illustration 8-5**
Application of internal control principles to cash receipts

## Internal Control over Cash Receipts

**Establishment of Responsibility**

Only designated personnel are authorized to handle cash receipts (cashiers)

**Physical, Mechanical, and Electronic Controls**

Store cash in safes and bank vaults; limit access to storage areas; use cash registers

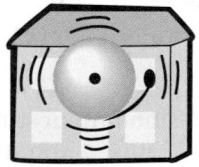

**Segregation of Duties**

Different individuals receive cash, record cash receipts, and hold the cash

**Independent Internal Verification**

Supervisors count cash receipts daily; treasurer compares total receipts to bank deposits daily

**Documentation Procedures**

Use remittance advice (mail receipts), cash register tapes, and deposit slips

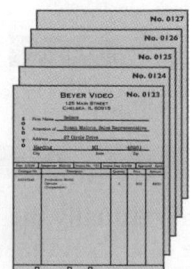

**Other Controls**

Bond personnel who handle cash; require employees to take vacations; deposit all cash in bank daily

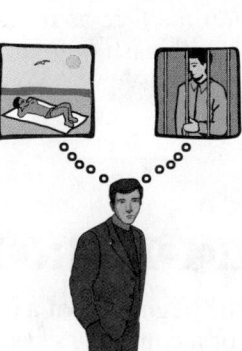

As you might expect, companies vary considerably in how they apply these principles. To illustrate internal control over cash receipts, we will examine control measures for a retail store with both over-the-counter and mail receipts.

## OVER-THE-COUNTER RECEIPTS

In retail businesses, control of over-the-counter receipts centers on cash registers that are visible to customers. Supermarkets and discount stores such as Wal-Mart, typically place cash registers in check-out lines near the exit. In stores such as Sears, Roebuck & Co. and JCPenney, each department has its own cash register. A cash sale is "rung up" on a cash register **with the amount clearly visible to the customer**. This measure prevents the cashier from ringing up a lower amount and pocketing the difference. The customer receives an itemized cash register receipt slip and is expected to count the change received.

The cash register keeps a tape locked in the register until a supervisor or manager removes it. This tape accumulates the daily transactions and totals. When the tape is removed, the supervisor compares the total with the amount of cash in the register. The tape should show all registered receipts accounted for. The supervisor reports his or her findings on a cash count sheet which both the cashier and supervisor sign. Illustration 8-6 shows a typical cash count sheet.

| | |
|---|---|
| Store No. ___8___ | Date   March 8, 2008 |
| 1. Opening cash balance | $     50.00 |
| 2. Cash sales per tape (attached) | 6,956.20 |
| 3. Total cash to be accounted for | 7,006.20 |
| 4. Cash on hand | 6,996.10 |
| 5. Cash (short) or over | $    (10.10) |
| 6. Ending cash balance | $     50.00 |
| 7. Cash for deposit (Line 4 – Line 6) | $6,946.10 |
| Cashier _J. Cruse_ | Supervisor _M. Braun_ |

**Illustration 8-6**
Cash count sheet

Next, the supervisor gives the count sheets, register tapes, and cash to the head cashier. This person prepares a daily cash summary showing the total cash received and the amount from each source, such as cash sales and collections on account. The head cashier sends one copy of the summary to the accounting department for entry. A second copy goes to the treasurer's office for later comparison with the daily bank deposit.

The head cashier prepares a deposit slip (see Illustration 8-10 on page 356) and makes the bank deposit. The total amount deposited should equal the total receipts on the daily cash summary. This will ensure that the head cashier has placed all receipts in the custody of the bank. In accepting the bank deposit, the bank stamps (authenticates) the duplicate deposit slip and sends it to the company treasurer, who compares the amount of the cash deposit with the daily cash summary.

Illustration 8-7 (page 350) graphically presents these measures for cash sales. It shows the activities of the sales department separately from those of the cashier's department to indicate the segregation of duties in handling cash.

**Illustration 8-7**
Executing over-the-counter cash sales

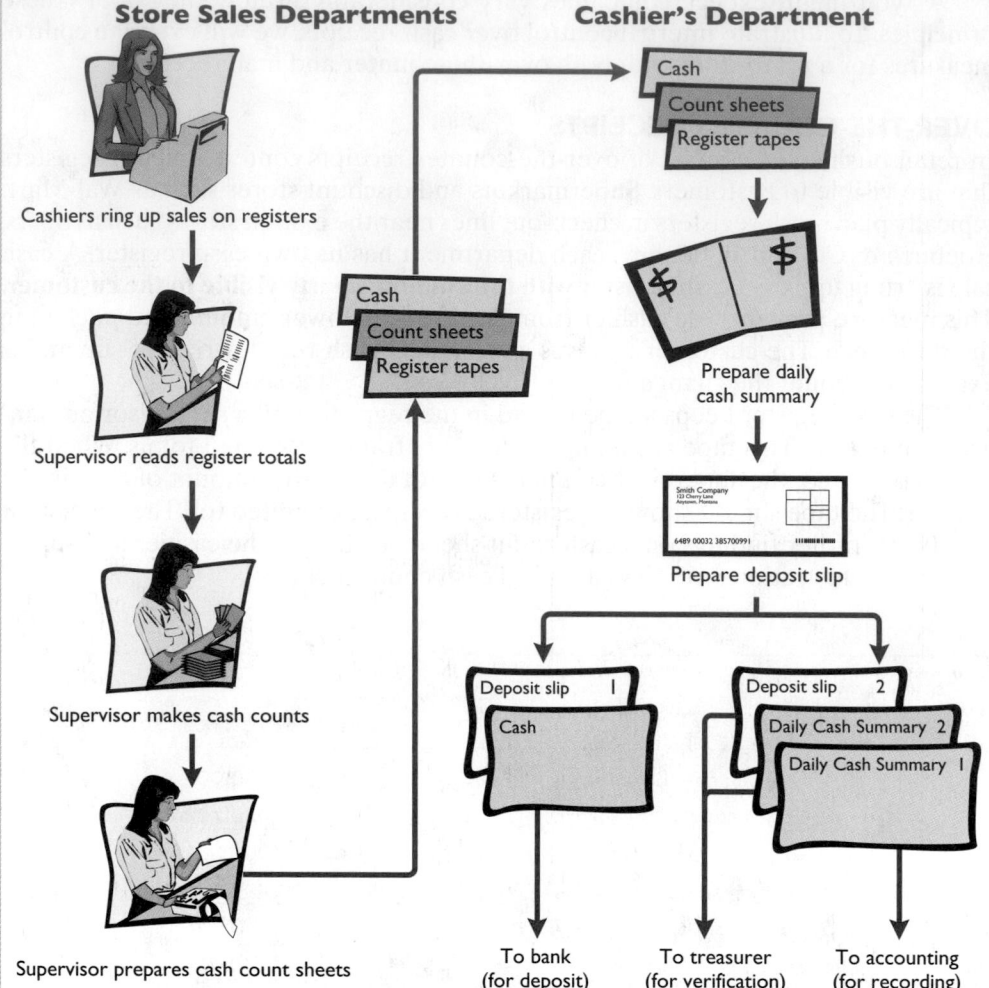

## MAIL RECEIPTS

As an individual customer, you may be more familiar with over-the-counter receipts than with mail receipts. However, mail receipts resulting from billings and credit sales are by far the most common way that companies receive cash. Think, for example, of the number of checks received through the mail daily by a national retailer such as J. Crew or American Eagle Outfitters.

All mail receipts should be opened in the presence of two mail clerks. These receipts are generally in the form of checks or money orders. A remittance advice stating the purpose of the check frequently comes with the check (sometimes attached to the check, but often a part of the bill that the customer tears off and returns). A mail clerk should endorse each check "For Deposit Only" by use of a company stamp. This **restrictive endorsement** reduces the likelihood that someone could divert the check to personal use. Banks will not give an individual cash when presented with a check that has this type of endorsement.

The mail-receipt clerks prepare, in duplicate, a list of the checks received each day. This list shows the name of the check issuer, the purpose of the payment, and the amount of the check. Each mail clerk signs the list to establish responsibility for the data. The original copy of the list, along with the checks and remittance advices, are then sent to the cashier's department. There, the cashier adds the checks to the over-the-counter receipts (if any) in preparing the daily cash summary (remember, checks are cash) and in making the daily bank deposit. Also, the mail-receipt clerks send a copy of the list to the treasurer's office for comparison with the total mail receipts shown on the daily cash summary. This copy ensures that all mail receipts have been included.

---

## Before You Go On...

### REVIEW IT

1. How do the principles of internal control apply to cash receipts?
2. What procedures do companies use for over-the-counter receipts?

### DO IT

L. R. Cortez is concerned about the control over cash receipts in his fast-food restaurant, Big Cheese. The restaurant has two cash registers. At no time do more than two employees take customer orders and ring up sales. Work shifts for employees range from 4 to 8 hours. Cortez asks your help in installing a good system of internal control over cash receipts.

### Action Plan

■ Differentiate among the internal control principles of (1) establishing responsibility, (2) using electronic controls, and (3) independent internal verification.

■ Design an effective system of internal control over cash receipts.

**Solution**    Cortez should assign a cash register to each employee at the start of each work shift, with register totals set at zero. Each employee should be instructed to use only the assigned register and to ring up all sales. At the end of each work shift, Cortez or a supervisor/manager should total the register and make a cash count to see whether all cash is accounted for.

Related exercise material: *BE8-4 and E8-2.*

---

# Internal Control over Cash Disbursements

Companies disburse cash for a variety of reasons, such as to pay expenses and liabilities or to purchase assets. **Generally, internal control over cash disbursements is more effective when companies pay by check, rather than by cash.** One exception is **for incidental amounts that are paid out of petty cash.**[2]

**STUDY OBJECTIVE 4**

Explain the applications of internal control principles to cash disbursements.

Companies generally issue checks only after following specified control procedures. Illustration 8-8 (page 352) shows how principles of internal control apply to cash disbursements.

## VOUCHER SYSTEM

Most medium and large companies use vouchers as part of their internal control over cash disbursements. A **voucher system** is a network of approvals by authorized individuals, acting independently, to ensure that all disbursements by check are proper.

The system begins with the authorization to incur a cost or expense. It ends with the issuance of a check for the liability incurred. A **voucher** is an authorization form prepared for each expenditure. Companies require vouchers for all types of cash disbursements except those from petty cash.

---

[2]We explain the operation of a petty cash fund on pages 353–355.

## Internal Control over Cash Disbursements

### Establishment of Responsibility

Only designated personnel are authorized to sign checks (treasurer)

### Physical, Mechanical, and Electronic Controls

Store blank checks in safes, with limited access; print check amounts by machine in indelible ink

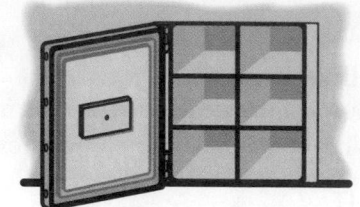

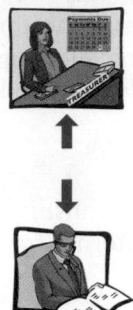

### Segregation of Duties

Different individuals approve and make payments; check signers do not record disbursements

### Independent Internal Verification

Compare checks to invoices; reconcile bank statement monthly

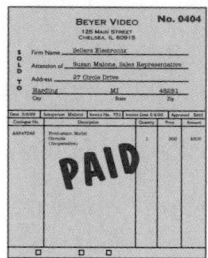

### Documentation Procedures

Use prenumbered checks and account for them in sequence; each check must have an approved invoice

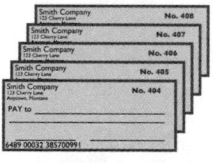

### Other Controls

Stamp invoices PAID

**Illustration 8-8**
Application of internal control principles to cash disbursements

The starting point in preparing a voucher is to fill in the appropriate information about the liability on the face of the voucher. The vendor's invoice provides most of the needed information. Then, an employee in accounts payable records the voucher (in a journal called a **voucher register**) and files it according to the date on which it is to be paid. The company issues and sends a check on that date, and stamps the voucher "paid." The paid voucher is sent to the accounting department for recording (in a journal called the **check register**). A voucher system involves two journal entries, one to issue the voucher and a second to pay the voucher.

### ELECTRONIC FUNDS TRANSFER (EFT) SYSTEM

Accounting for and controlling cash is an expensive and time-consuming process. The cost to process a check through a bank system is about $1 per check and is increasing. In contrast, it costs only 35¢ if a customer pays by credit card over the telephone, and only 1¢ if the customer pays by credit card via a computer.

It is not surprising, therefore, that companies and banks have developed approaches to transfer funds among parties without the use of paper (deposit tickets, checks, etc.). Such procedures, called **electronic funds transfers (EFT)**, are disbursement systems that use wire, telephone, or computers to transfer cash balances from one location to another. Use of EFT is quite common. For example, many employees receive no formal payroll checks from their employers. Instead, employers send electronic payroll data to the appropriate banks. Also, individuals now frequently make regular payments such as those for house, car, and utilities by EFT.

## PETTY CASH FUND

As you learned earlier in the chapter, better internal control over cash disbursements is possible when companies make payments by check. However, using checks to pay small amounts is both impractical and a nuisance. For instance, a company would not want to write checks to pay for postage due, working lunches, or taxi fares. A common way of handling such payments, while maintaining satisfactory control, is to use a petty cash fund to pay relatively small amounts. The operation of a petty cash fund, often called an **imprest system**, involves three steps: (1) establishing the fund, (2) making payments from the fund, and (3) replenishing the fund.[3]

**Establishing The Fund.** In establishing a petty cash fund, a company appoints a petty cash custodian who will be responsible for the fund. Next it determines the size of the fund. Ordinarily, a company expects the amount in the fund to cover anticipated disbursements for a three- to four-week period.

To establish the fund, a company issues a check payable to the petty cash custodian for the stipulated amount. For example, if Laird Company decides to establish a $100 fund on March 1, the journal entry is:

| Mar. 1 | Petty Cash | 100 | |
| | Cash | | 100 |
| | (To establish a petty cash fund) | | |

| A | = | L | + | SE |
|---|---|---|---|---|
| +100 | | | | |
| −100 | | | | |

**Cash Flows**
no effect

The fund custodian cashes the check and places the proceeds in a locked petty cash box or drawer. Most petty cash funds are established on a fixed-amount basis. The company will make no additional entries to the Petty Cash account unless management changes the stipulated amount of the fund. For example, if Laird Company decides on July 1 to increase the size of the fund to $250, it would debit Petty Cash $150 and credit Cash $150.

**Making Payments from the Fund.** The petty cash fund custodian has the authority to make payments from the fund that conform to prescribed management policies. Usually, management limits the size of expenditures that come from petty cash. Likewise, it may not permit use of the fund for certain types of transactions (such as making short-term loans to employees).

Each payment from the fund must be documented on a prenumbered petty cash receipt (or petty cash voucher) as shown in Illustration 8-9 (page 354). Note that the signatures of both the fund custodian and the person receiving payment are required on the receipt. If other supporting documents such as a freight bill or invoice are available, they should be attached to the petty cash receipt.

The fund custodian keeps the receipts in the petty cash box until the fund is replenished. The sum of the petty cash receipts and the money in the fund should equal the established total at all times. Management can (and should) make surprise counts at any time to determine whether the fund is being maintained correctly.

The company does not make an accounting entry to record a payment when it is made from petty cash. Instead, the company recognizes the accounting effects of each payment when it replenishes the fund.

---

[3]The term "imprest" means an advance of money for a designated purpose.

**Illustration 8-9**
Petty cash receipt

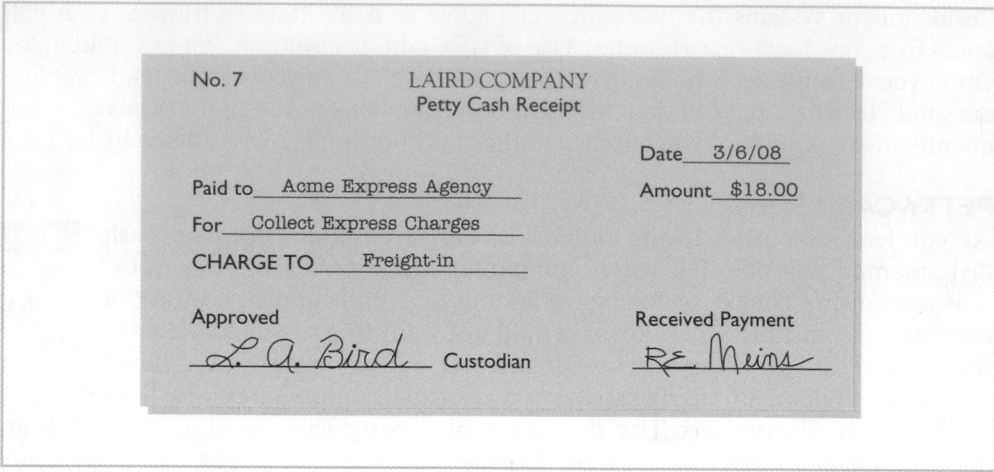

**Replenishing the Fund.** When the money in the petty cash fund reaches a minimum level, the company replenishes the fund. The petty cash custodian initiates a request for reimbursement. He or she prepares a schedule (or summary) of the payments that have been made and sends the schedule, supported by petty cash receipts and other documentation, to the treasurer's office. Someone in the treasurer's office examines the receipts and supporting documents to verify that they were proper payments from the fund. The treasurer then approves the request and issues a check to restore the fund to its established amount. At the same time, all supporting documentation is stamped "paid" so that it cannot be submitted again for payment.

To illustrate, assume that on March 15 Laird's petty cash custodian requests a check for $87. The fund contains $13 cash and petty cash receipts for postage $44, freight-out $38, and miscellaneous expenses $5. The general journal entry to record the check is:

```
A   =   L   +   SE
                -44 Exp
                -38 Exp
                 -5 Exp
-87
```
**Cash Flows**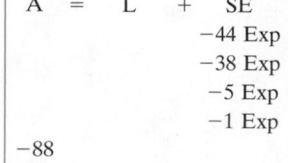
-87

| Mar. 15 | Postage Expense | 44 | |
| | Freight-out | 38 | |
| | Miscellaneous Expense | 5 | |
| |    Cash | | 87 |
| |     (To replenish petty cash fund) | | |

Note that the reimbursement entry does not affect the Petty Cash account. Replenishment changes the composition of the fund by replacing the petty cash receipts with cash. It does not change the balance in the fund.

Occasionally, in replenishing a petty cash fund, the company may need to recognize a cash shortage or overage. This results when the total of the cash plus receipts in the petty cash box does not equal the established amount of the petty cash fund. To illustrate, assume that Laird's petty cash custodian has only $12 in cash in the fund plus the receipts as listed above. The request for reimbursement would, therefore, be for $88, and Laird would make the following entry:

<table>
<tr><td colspan="2">HELPFUL HINT</td></tr>
</table>

Cash over and short situations result from mathematical errors or from failure to keep accurate records.

```
A   =   L   +   SE
                -44 Exp
                -38 Exp
                 -5 Exp
                 -1 Exp
-88
```
**Cash Flows**
-88

| Mar. 15 | Postage Expense | 44 | |
| | Freight-out | 38 | |
| | Miscellaneous Expense | 5 | |
| | Cash Over and Short | 1 | |
| |    Cash | | 88 |
| |     (To replenish petty cash fund) | | |

Conversely, if the custodian has $14 in cash, the reimbursement request would be for $86, and the company would credit Cash Over and Short for $1 (overage). A company reports a debit balance in Cash Over and Short in the income statement as miscellaneous expense. It reports a credit balance in the account as miscellaneous revenue. The company closes Cash Over and Short to Income Summary at the end of the year.

Companies should replenish a petty cash fund at the end of the accounting period, regardless of the cash in the fund. Replenishment at this time is necessary in order to recognize the effects of the petty cash payments on the financial statements.

**ETHICS NOTE**

Internal control over a petty cash fund is strengthened by: (1) having a supervisor make surprise counts of the fund to confirm whether the paid vouchers and fund cash equal the imprest amount, and (2) canceling or mutilating the paid vouchers so they cannot be resubmitted for reimbursement.

## Before You Go On...

**REVIEW IT**

1. How do the principles of internal control apply to cash disbursements?
2. What are the entries required in a petty cash system?

✓ *The Navigator*

# USE OF A BANK

**The use of a bank contributes significantly to good internal control over cash.** A company can safeguard its cash by using a bank as a depository and as a clearing house for checks received and written. Use of a bank minimizes the amount of currency that a company must keep on hand. Also, use of a bank facilitates the control of cash because it creates a double record of all bank transactions—one by the company and the other by the bank. The asset account Cash maintained by the company should have the same balance as the bank's liability account for that company. A 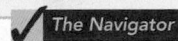 bank reconciliation compares the bank's balance with the company's balance and explains any differences to make them agree.

Many companies have more than one bank account. For efficiency of operations and better control, national retailers like Wal-Mart and Target may have regional bank accounts. Large companies, with tens of thousands of employees, may have a payroll bank account, as well as one or more general bank accounts. Also, a company may maintain several bank accounts in order to have more than one source for short-term loans when needed.

**STUDY OBJECTIVE 6**

Indicate the control features of a bank account.

## Making Bank Deposits

An authorized employee, such as the head cashier, should make a company's bank deposits. Each deposit must be documented by a deposit slip (ticket), as shown in Illustration 8-10 (page 356).

Deposit slips are prepared in duplicate. The bank retains the original; the depositor keeps the duplicate, machine-stamped by the bank to establish its authenticity.

## Writing Checks

Most of us write checks, without thinking very much about them. A **check** is a written order signed by the depositor directing the bank to pay a specified sum of money to a designated recipient. There are three parties to a check: (1) the **maker** (or drawer) who issues the check, (2) the **bank** (or payer) on which the check is

**Illustration 8-10**
Deposit slip

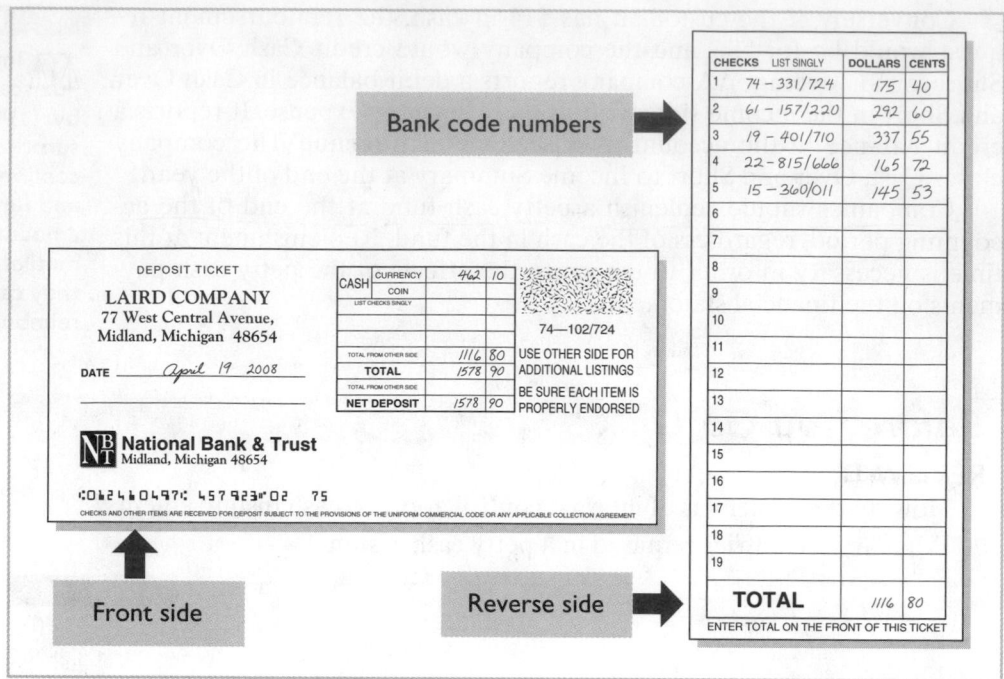

drawn, and (3) the **payee** to whom the check is payable. A check is a **negotiable instrument** that one party can transfer to another party by endorsement. Each check should be accompanied by an explanation of its purpose. In many companies, a remittance advice attached to the check, as shown in Illustration 8-11 explains the check's purpose.

**Illustration 8-11**
Check with remittance advice

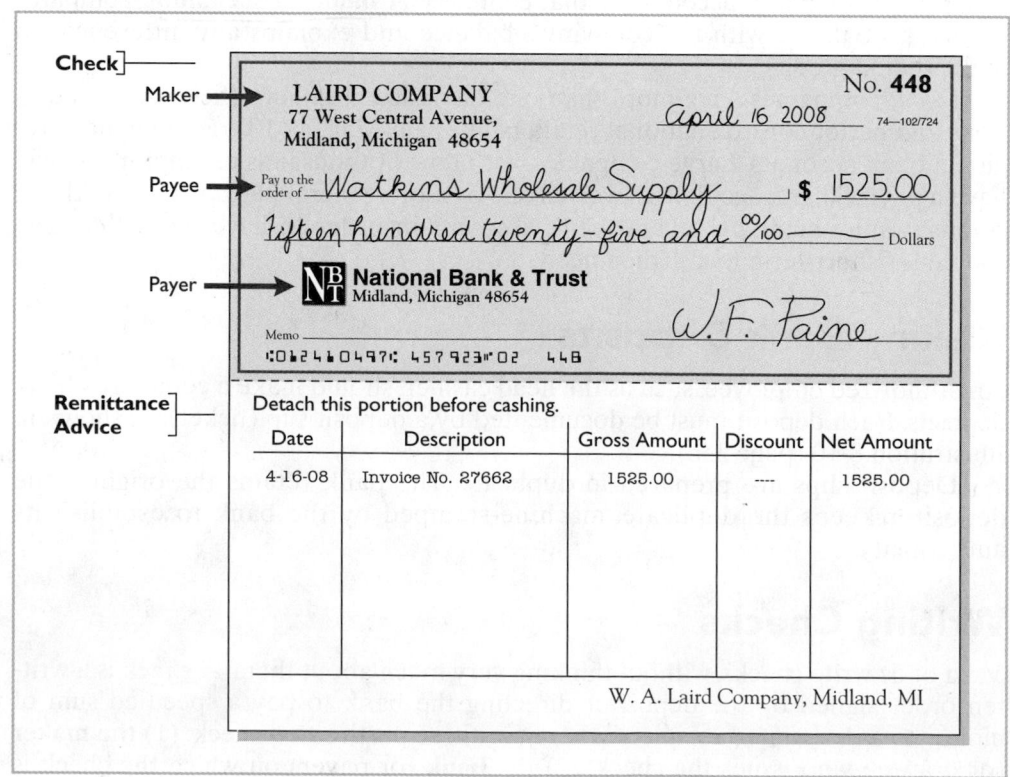

It is important to know the balance in the checking account at all times. To keep the balance current, the depositor should enter each deposit and check on running-balance memo forms provided by the bank or on the check stubs in the checkbook.

## ACCOUNTING ACROSS THE ORGANIZATION

### Cash? What Cash?

Cash is virtually obsolete. Today, many people use debit cards and credit cards to pay for most of their purchases. But debit cards are usable only at specified locations, and credit cards are cumbersome for small transactions. They are no good for transferring cash between individuals or to small companies that do not want to pay credit card fees. Digital cash may be the next online wave.

There are many digital-cash companies. One of the most flexible appears to be PayPal (*www.paypal.com*). PayPal became popular with users of the auction site eBay, because it allows them to transfer funds to each other as easily as sending e-mail. (PayPal is now owned by eBay, though it is operated as an independent site.)

*Source:* Mathew Ingram, "Will Digital Cash Work This Time?" *The Globe and Mail*, March 18, 2000, p. N4.

**?** Will "cash" be obsolete in terms of financial statement reporting?

## Bank Statements

If you have a personal checking account, you are probably familiar with bank statements. A **bank statement** shows the depositor's bank transactions and balances.[4] Each month, a depositor receives a statement from the bank. Illustration 8-12 (page 358) presents a typical bank statement. It shows: (1) checks paid and other debits that reduce the balance in the depositor's account, (2) deposits and other credits that increase the balance in the account, and (3) the account balance after each day's transactions.

> **HELPFUL HINT**
> Essentially, the bank statement is a copy of the bank's records sent to the customer for periodic review.

The bank statement lists in numerical sequence all "paid" checks, along with the date the check was paid and its amount. Upon paying a check, the bank stamps the check "paid." (A paid check is sometimes referred to as a **canceled** check.) On the statement the bank also includes memoranda explaining other debits and credits it made to the depositor's account.

### DEBIT MEMORANDUM
Some banks charge a monthly fee for their services. Often they charge this fee only when the average monthly balance in a checking account falls below a specified amount. They identify the fee, called a **bank service charge**, on the bank statement by a symbol such as **SC**. The bank also sends with the statement a debit memorandum explaining the charge noted on the statement. Other debit memoranda may also be issued for other bank services such as the cost of printing checks, issuing traveler's checks, and wiring funds to other locations. The symbol **DM** is often used for such charges.

---

[4]Our presentation assumes that the depositor makes all adjustments at the end of the month. In practice, a company may also make journal entries during the month as it receives information from the bank regarding its account.

**Illustration 8-12**
Bank statement

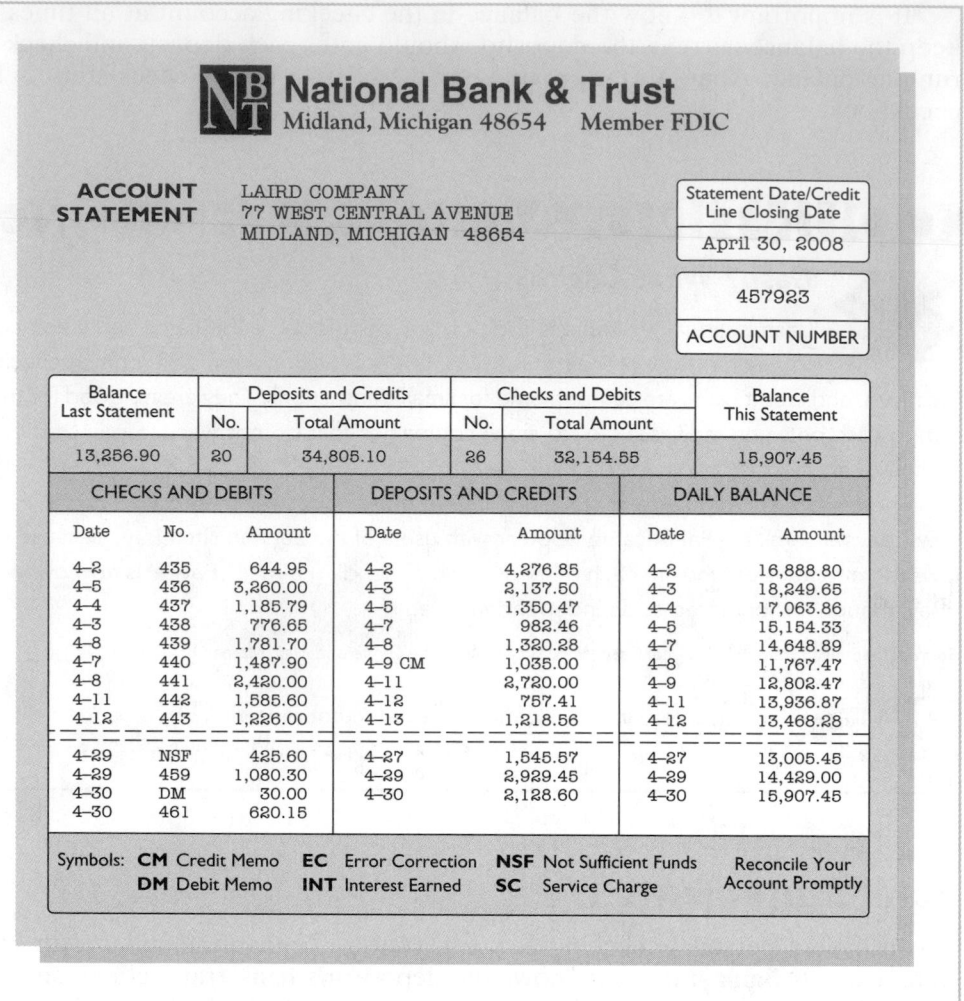

Banks also use a debit memorandum when a deposited check from a customer "bounces" because of insufficient funds. For example, assume that Scott Company, a customer of Laird Company, sends a check for $800 to Laird Company for services provided. Unfortunately, Scott does not have sufficient funds at its bank to pay for these services. In such a case, Scott's bank marks the check <u>NSF</u> (not sufficient funds) and returns it to Laird's (the depositor's) bank. Laird's bank then debits Laird's account, as shown by the symbol NSF on the bank statement in Illustration 8-12 (above). The bank sends the NSF check and debit memorandum to Laird as notification of the charge. Laird then records an Account Receivable from Scott Company (the writer of the bad check) and reduces cash for the NSF check.

### CREDIT MEMORANDUM

Sometimes a depositor asks the bank to collect its notes receivable. In such a case, the bank will credit the depositor's account for the cash proceeds of the note. This is illustrated by the symbol **CM** on the Laird Company bank statement. The bank issues and sends with the statement a credit memorandum to explain the entry. Many banks also offer interest on checking accounts. The interest earned may be indicated on the bank statement by the symbol **CM** or **INT**.

# Reconciling the Bank Account

The bank and the depositor maintain independent records of the depositor's checking account. People tend to assume that the respective balances will always agree. In fact, the two balances are seldom the same at any given time. Therefore it is necessary to make the balance per books agree with the balance per bank—a process called **reconciling the bank account**. The lack of agreement between the two balances has two causes:

**STUDY OBJECTIVE 7**

Prepare a bank reconciliation.

1. **Time lags** that prevent one of the parties from recording the transaction in the same period as the other party.

2. **Errors** by either party in recording transactions.

Time lags occur frequently. For example, several days may elapse between the time a company mails a check to a payee and the date the bank pays the check. Similarly, when the depositor uses the bank's night depository to make its deposits, there will be a difference of at least one day between the time the depositor records the deposit and the time the bank does so. A time lag also occurs whenever the bank mails a debit or credit memorandum to the depositor.

The incidence of errors depends on the effectiveness of the internal controls of the depositor and the bank. Bank errors are infrequent. However, either party could accidentally record a $450 check as $45 or $540. In addition, the bank might mistakenly charge a check to a wrong account by keying in an incorrect account name or number.

## RECONCILIATION PROCEDURE

**The bank reconciliation should be prepared by an employee who has no other responsibilities pertaining to cash.** If a company fails to follow this internal control principle of independent internal verification, cash embezzlements may go unnoticed. For example, a cashier who prepares the reconciliation can embezzle cash and conceal the embezzlement by misstating the reconciliation. Thus, the bank accounts would reconcile, and the embezzlement would not be detected.

In reconciling the bank account, it is customary to reconcile the balance per books and balance per bank to their adjusted (correct or true) cash balances. The starting point in preparing the reconciliation is to enter the balance per bank statement and balance per books on the reconciliation schedule. The company then makes various adjustments, as shown in Illustration 8-13 (page 360).

The following steps should reveal all the reconciling items that cause the difference between the two balances.

**Step 1. Deposits in transit.** Compare the individual deposits listed on the bank statement with deposits in transit from the preceding bank reconciliation and with the deposits per company records or duplicate deposit slips. Deposits recorded by the depositor that have not been recorded by the bank are the **deposits in transit**. Add these deposits to the balance per bank.

**Step 2. Outstanding checks.** Compare the paid checks shown on the bank statement with (a) checks outstanding from the previous bank reconciliation, and (b) checks issued by the company as recorded in the cash payments journal (or in the check register in your personal checkbook). Issued checks recorded by the company but that have not yet been paid by the bank are **outstanding checks**. Deduct outstanding checks from the balance per the bank.

**Step 3. Errors.** Note any errors discovered in the foregoing steps and list them in the appropriate section of the reconciliation schedule. For example, if the company mistakenly recorded as $169 a paid check correctly written

**HELPFUL HINT**

Deposits in transit and outstanding checks are reconciling items because of time lags.

Illustration 8-13
Bank reconciliation
procedures

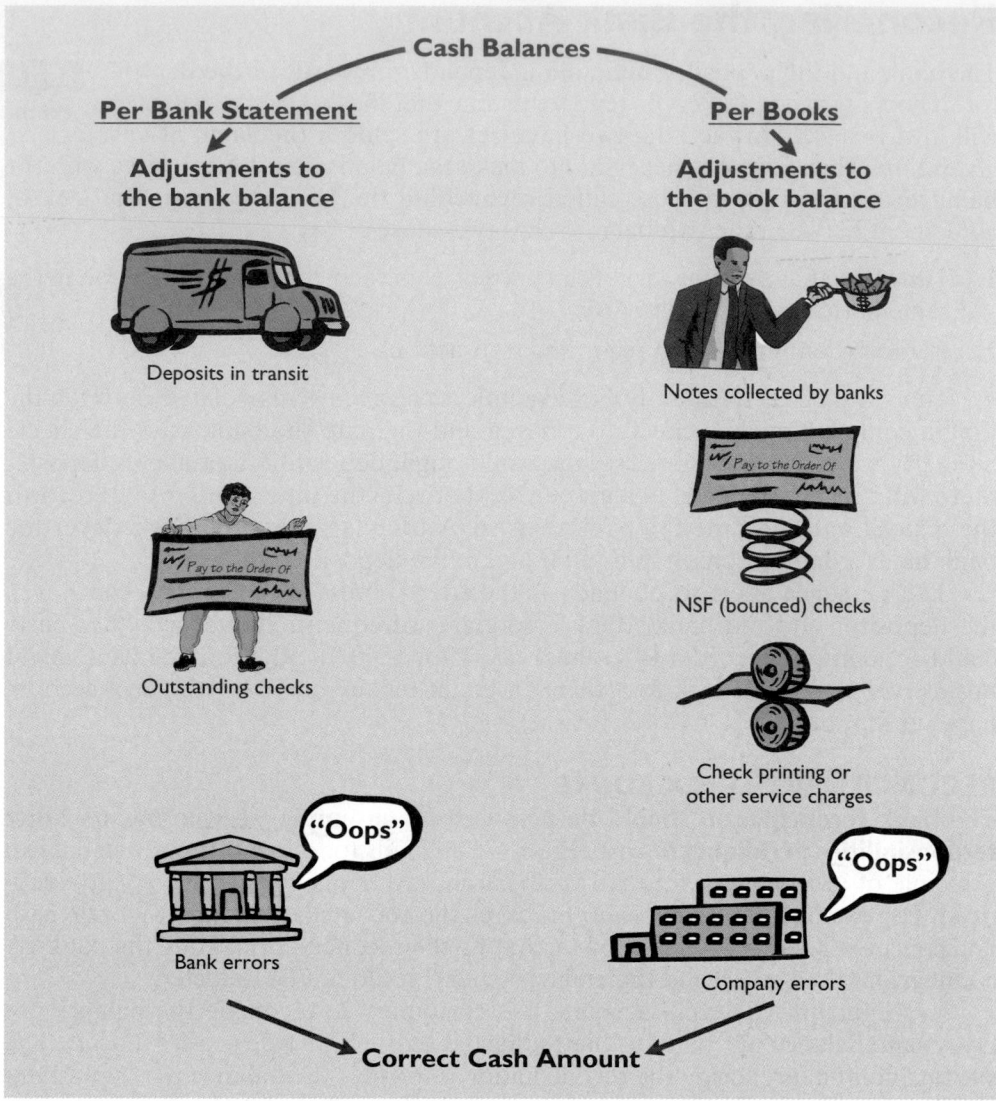

Note in the bank state-
ment on page 358 that
checks no. 459 and 461
have been paid but check
no. 460 is not listed. Thus,
this check is outstanding.
If a complete bank state-
ment were provided,
checks no. 453 and 457
would also not be listed.
The amounts for these
three checks are obtained
from the company's cash
payments records.

for $196, it would deduct the error of $27 from the balance per books. All
errors made by the depositor are reconciling items in determining the
adjusted cash balance per books. In contrast, all errors made by the bank
are reconciling items in determining the adjusted cash balance per the
bank.

**Step 4. Bank memoranda.** Trace bank memoranda to the depositor's records. List
in the appropriate section of the reconciliation schedule any unrecorded
memoranda. For example, the company would deduct from the balance per
books a $5 debit memorandum for bank service charges. Similarly, it would
add to the balance per books $32 of interest earned.

## BANK RECONCILIATION ILLUSTRATED

The bank statement for Laird Company, in Illustration 8-12, shows a balance per
bank of $15,907.45 on April 30, 2008. On this date the balance of cash per books is
$11,589.45. Using the four reconciliation steps, Laird determines the following rec-
onciling items.

**Step 1. Deposits in transit:** April 30 deposit (received by
bank on May 1).                                                      $2,201.40

**Step 2. Outstanding checks:** No. 453, $3,000.00; no. 457,
$1,401.30; no. 460, $1,502.70.                                         5,904.00

**Step 3. Errors:** Laird wrote check no. 443 for $1,226.00 and the
bank correctly paid that amount. However, Laird recorded
the check as $1,262.00.                                                  36.00

**Step 4. Bank memoranda:**
    **a.** Debit—NSF check from J. R. Baron for $425.60         425.60
    **b.** Debit—Charge for printing company checks $30.00         30.00
    **c.** Credit—Collection of note receivable for $1,000
        plus interest earned $50, less bank collection fee $15.00   1,035.00

Illustration 8-14 shows Laird's bank reconciliation.

**Illustration 8-14**
Bank reconciliation

| LAIRD COMPANY | | |
|---|---|---|
| Bank Reconciliation | | |
| April 30, 2008 | | |

| | | |
|---|---|---|
| Cash balance per bank statement | | $15,907.45 |
| Add: Deposits in transit | | 2,201.40 |
| | | 18,108.85 |
| Less: Outstanding checks | | |
| No. 453 | $3,000.00 | |
| No. 457 | 1,401.30 | |
| No. 460 | 1,502.70 | 5,904.00 |
| **Adjusted cash balance per bank** | | **$12,204.85** ← |
| | | |
| Cash balance per books | | $11,589.45 |
| Add: Collection of note receivable $1,000, plus interest | | |
|     earned $50, less collection fee $15 | $1,035.00 | |
|     Error in recording check no. 443 | 36.00 | 1,071.00 |
| | | 12,660.45 |
| Less: NSF check | 425.60 | |
|     Bank service charge | 30.00 | 455.60 |
| **Adjusted cash balance per books** | | **$12,204.85** ← |

**ALTERNATIVE TERMINOLOGY**

The terms *adjusted balance, true cash balance,* and *correct cash balance* are used interchangeably.

## ENTRIES FROM BANK RECONCILIATION

The company records each reconciling item used to determine the **adjusted cash balance per books. If the company does not journalize and post these items, the Cash account will not show the correct balance.** Laird Company would make the following entries on April 30.

**Collection of Note Receivable.** This entry involves four accounts. Assuming that the interest of $50 has not been accrued and the collection fee is charged to Miscellaneous Expense, the entry is:

| Apr. 30 | Cash | 1,035.00 | |
|---|---|---|---|
| | Miscellaneous Expense | 15.00 | |
| |     Notes Receivable | | 1,000.00 |
| |     Interest Revenue | | 50.00 |
| |         (To record collection of note | | |
| |         receivable by bank) | | |

**HELPFUL HINT**

The entries that follow are adjusting entries. In prior chapters, Cash was an account that did not require adjustment. That was a simplifying assumption for learning purposes, because we had not yet explained a bank reconciliation.

| A | = | L | + | SE |
|---|---|---|---|---|
| +1,035 | | | | |
| | | | | −15 Exp |
| −1,000 | | | | |
| | | | | +50 Rev |

**Cash Flows**
+1,035

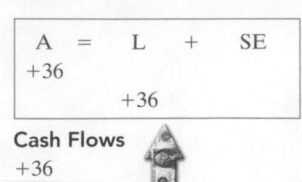

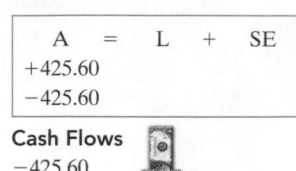

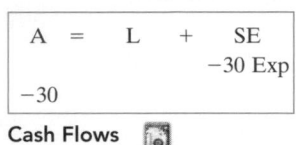

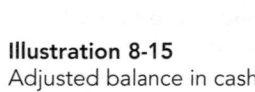

**Illustration 8-15**
Adjusted balance in cash account

**Book Error.** The cash disbursements journal shows that check no. 443 was a payment on account to Andrea Company, a supplier. The correcting entry is:

| Apr. 30 | Cash | 36.00 | |
| | Accounts Payable—Andrea Company | | 36.00 |
| | (To correct error in recording check no. 443) | | |

**NSF Check.** As indicated earlier, an NSF check becomes an account receivable to the depositor. The entry is:

| Apr. 30 | Accounts Receivable—J. R. Baron | 425.60 | |
| | Cash | | 425.60 |
| | (To record NSF check) | | |

**Bank Service Charges.** Depositors debit check printing charges (DM) and other bank service charges (SC) to Miscellaneous Expense, because they are usually nominal in amount. The entry is:

| Apr. 30 | Miscellaneous Expense | 30.00 | |
| | Cash | | 30.00 |
| | (To record charge for printing company checks) | | |

Instead of making four separate entries, Laird could combine them into one compound entry.

After Laird has posted the entries, the Cash account will show the following.

| Cash | | | | | |
| --- | --- | --- | --- | --- | --- |
| Apr. 30 Bal. | 11,589.45 | Apr. 30 | | | 425.60 |
| 30 | 1,035.00 | 30 | | | 30.00 |
| 30 | 36.00 | | | | |
| Apr. 30 Bal. | **12,204.85** | | | | |

The adjusted cash balance in the ledger should agree with the adjusted cash balance per books in the bank reconciliation in Illustration 8-14.

What entries does the bank make? If the company discovers any bank errors in preparing the reconciliation, it should notify the bank. The bank then can make the necessary corrections in its records. The bank does not make any entries for deposits in transit or outstanding checks. Only when these items reach the bank will the bank record these items.

## Before You Go On...

### REVIEW IT
1. Why is it necessary to reconcile a bank account?
2. What steps are involved in the reconciliation procedure?
3. What information does a bank reconciliation include?

### DO IT
Sally Kist owns Linen Kist Fabrics. Sally asks you to explain how she should treat the following reconciling items when reconciling the company's bank account: (1) a debit memorandum for an NSF check, (2) a credit memorandum for a note collected by the bank, (3) outstanding checks, and (4) a deposit in transit.

**Action Plan**

- Understand the purpose of a bank reconciliation.
- Identify time lags and explain how they cause reconciling items.

**Solution**    Sally should treat the reconciling items as follows.

(1)  NSF check: Deduct from balance per books.

(2)  Collection of note: Add to balance per books.

(3)  Outstanding checks: Deduct from balance per bank.

(4)  Deposit in transit: Add to balance per bank.

Related exercise material: *BE8-8, BE8-9, BE8-10, BE8-11, E8-9, E8-10, E8-11, E8-12, and E8-13.*

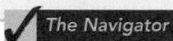 *The Navigator*

# REPORTING CASH

On the balance sheet, companies often combine cash on hand, cash in banks, and petty cash and report the total simply as **Cash**. Because it is the most liquid asset owned by a company, cash is listed first in the current assets section of the balance sheet. Some companies use the term "Cash and cash equivalents" in reporting cash, as shown in Illustration 8-16.

**STUDY OBJECTIVE 8**
Explain the reporting of cash.

### EASTMAN KODAK COMPANY
Balance Sheets (partial)

|  | **2005** | **2004** |
|---|---|---|
| Current assets (in millions) | | |
| Cash and cash equivalents | $1,255 | $1,665 |

**Illustration 8-16**
Presentation of cash and cash equivalents

**Cash equivalents** are short-term, highly liquid investments that can be converted into a specific amount of cash. At the time of purchase, they typically have maturities of three months or less. They include money market funds, bank certificates of deposit, and U.S. Treasury bills and notes.

A company may have cash that is restricted for a special purpose. An example is a payroll bank account for paying salaries and wages. Another would be a plant expansion cash fund for financing new construction. Companies should report **restricted cash** separately on the balance sheet. If a company expects to use the restricted cash **within the next year**, the amount should be reported as a current asset. Otherwise, it should be reported as a noncurrent asset. Since a payroll bank account will be used as early as the next payday, it is reported as a current asset. In contrast, unless the new construction will begin within the next year, cash for plant expansion would be classified as a noncurrent asset (long-term investment).

When making loans to depositors, banks commonly require borrowers to maintain minimum cash balances. These minimum balances, called **compensating balances**, provide the bank with support for the loans. They are a restriction on the use of cash that may affect a company's liquidity. Thus, companies should disclose compensating balances in the notes to the financial statements.

 Be sure to read **ALL ABOUT YOU:** *Protecting Yourself from Identity Theft* on page 364 for information on how topics in this chapter apply to you.

## Protecting Yourself from Identity Theft

As a result of the Sarbanes-Oxley Act, companies have done a lot to improve their internal controls to help protect themselves from both internal and external thieves. What have you done lately to shore up your own personal internal controls? You've heard the stories about hackers cleaning out people's online investment accounts or running up credit card bills that would take you most of your life to pay off. (If you don't have a credit card, they'll open an account for you.) The identity thieves aren't going away. So what can you do to protect yourself? Many of the same common-sense controls discussed in this chapter can be implemented in your personal life.

### ✸ Some Facts

* Identity thieves determine your identity by going through your mail or trash, stealing your credit cards, redirecting mail through change of address forms, or acquiring personal information you share on unsecured sites. In a recent year, more than 7 million people were victims of identity theft.

* During a single computer-virus outbreak, called the "Hearse," thieves stole 90,000 pieces of personal data.

* The average identity-theft victim spends 600 hours clearing up his or her finances and financial and other records to recover from the crime.

* Victims incur an average of $1,400 in out-of-pocket expenses.

* Consumers have $1.7 trillion worth of assets with online brokerage firms. Many of the largest identity theft losses have been the result of thieves completely cleaning out online brokerage accounts.

* The Federal Trade Commission reports identify theft is the No. 1 fraud complaint among consumers. Phoenix and Las Vegas top the list for identity theft per capita.

### ✸ About the Numbers

The following chart shows the most common survey responses from victims of identity theft when asked how their information was used by the thieves. (Note that respondents chose more than one type of use.)

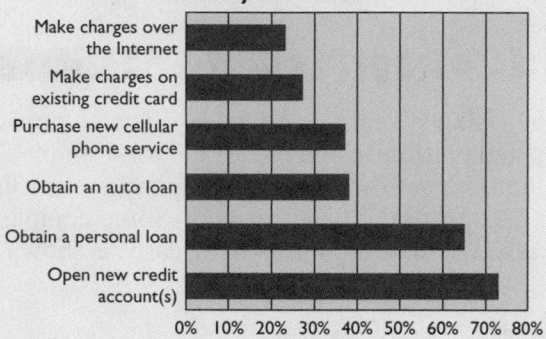

**Common Ways That Thieves Use Stolen Identity Information**

**Source:** The Identity Theft Resource Center, *Identity Theft: The Aftermath 2003*, *www.idtheftcenter.org/idaftermath.pdf* (accessed May 2006).

### ✸ What Do You Think

Do you feel it is safe to store personal financial data (such as Social Security numbers and bank and credit account numbers) on your computer?

**YES:** I have anti-virus software that will detect and stop any intruder.

**NO:** Even the best anti-virus software does not detect every kind of intruder.

---

**Sources:** Amy Borrus, "Invasion of the Stock Hackers," *Business Week*, November 14, 2005, pp. 38-40; Brian Grow, "Nasty, Brutish, and Sneaky," *Business Week*, April 10, 2006, p. 37; Federal Trade Commission, *www.consumer.gov/idtheft/*.

## Before You Go On...

### REVIEW IT

1. What do companies generally report as cash on the balance sheet?
2. What are cash equivalents? What are compensating balances? What is restricted cash?
3. At what amount does PepsiCo report cash and cash equivalents in its 2005 consolidated balance sheet? The answer to this question appears on page 383.

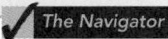 The Navigator

---

### Demonstration Problem

Poorten Company's bank statement for May 2008 shows the following data.

| Balance 5/1 | $12,650 | Balance 5/31 | $14,280 |
| Debit memorandum: | | Credit memorandum: | |
| NSF check | $175 | Collection of note receivable | $505 |

The cash balance per books at May 31 is $13,319. Your review of the data reveals the following.

1. The NSF check was from Copple Co., a customer.
2. The note collected by the bank was a $500, 3-month, 12% note. The bank charged a $10 collection fee. No interest has accrued.
3. Outstanding checks at May 31 total $2,410.
4. Deposits in transit at May 31 total $1,752.
5. A Poorten Company check for $352, dated May 10, cleared the bank on May 25. The company recorded this check, which was a payment on account, for $325.

### Instructions

**(a)** Prepare a bank reconciliation at May 31.
**(b)** Journalize the entries required by the reconciliation.

### Solution

**(a)**
### POORTEN COMPANY
Bank Reconciliation
May 31, 2008

| | | |
|---|---:|---:|
| Cash balance per bank statement | | $14,280 |
| Add: Deposits in transit | | 1,752 |
| | | 16,032 |
| Less: Outstanding checks | | 2,410 |
| Adjusted cash balance per bank | | $13,622 |
| | | |
| Cash balance per books | | $13,319 |
| Add: Collection of note receivable $500, plus $15* | | |
| interest, less collection fee $10 | | 505 |
| | | 13,824 |
| Less: NSF check | $175 | |
| Error in recording check | 27 | 202 |
| Adjusted cash balance per books | | $13,622 |

*500 × .12 × 3/12

### action plan

✔ Follow the four steps in the reconciliation procedure. (pp. 359–360).

✔ Work carefully to minimize mathematical errors in the reconciliation.

✔ Prepare adjusting entries from reconciling items per books.

✔ Make sure the cash ledger balance after posting the reconciling entries agrees with the adjusted cash balance per books.

**(b)**

| | | | | |
|---|---|---|---|---|
| May 31 | Cash | | 505 | |
| | Miscellaneous Expense | | 10 | |
| |     Notes Receivable | | | 500 |
| |     Interest Revenue | | | 15 |
| |       (To record collection of note by bank) | | | |
| 31 | Accounts Receivable—Copple Co. | | 175 | |
| |     Cash | | | 175 |
| |       (To record NSF check from Copple Co.) | | | |
| 31 | Accounts Payable | | 27 | |
| |     Cash | | | 27 |
| |       (To correct error in recording check) | | | |

# SUMMARY OF STUDY OBJECTIVES

**1 Define internal control.** Internal control is the related methods and procedures adopted within an organization to safeguard its assets and to enhance the accuracy and reliability of its accounting records.

**2 Identify the principles of internal control.** The principles of internal control are: establishment of responsibility; segregation of duties; documentation procedures; physical, mechanical, and electronic controls; independent internal verification; and other controls such as bonding and requiring employees to take vacations.

**3 Explain the applications of internal control principles to cash receipts.** Internal controls over cash receipts include: (a) designating specific personnel to handle cash; (b) assigning different individuals to receive cash, record cash, and maintain custody of cash; (c) using remittance advices for mail receipts, cash register tapes for over-the-counter receipts, and deposit slips for bank deposits; (d) using company safes and bank vaults to store cash with access limited to authorized personnel, and using cash registers in executing over-the-counter receipts; (e) making independent daily counts of register receipts and daily comparison of total receipts with total deposits; and (f) bonding personnel that handle cash and requiring them to take vacations.

**4 Explain the applications of internal control principles to cash disbursements.** Internal controls over cash disbursements include: (a) having specific individuals such as the treasurer authorized to sign checks; (b) assigning different individuals to approve items for payment, pay the items, and record the payment; (c) using prenumbered checks and accounting for all checks, with each check supported by an approved invoice; (d) storing blank checks in a safe or vault with access restricted to authorized personnel, and using a checkwriting machine to imprint amounts on checks; (e) comparing each check with the approved invoice before issuing the check, and making monthly reconciliations of bank and book balances; and (f) after payment, stamping each approved invoice "paid."

**5 Describe the operation of a petty cash fund.** Companies operate a petty cash fund to pay relatively small amounts of cash. They must establish the fund, make payments from the fund, and replenish the fund when the cash in the fund reaches a minimum level.

**6 Indicate the control features of a bank account.** A bank account contributes to good internal control by providing physical controls for the storage of cash. It minimizes the amount of currency that a company must keep on hand, and it creates a double record of a depositor's bank transactions.

**7 Prepare a bank reconciliation.** It is customary to reconcile the balance per books and balance per bank to their adjusted balances. The steps in the reconciling process are to determine deposits in transit, outstanding checks, errors by the depositor or the bank, and unrecorded bank memoranda.

**8 Explain the reporting of cash.** Companies list cash first in the current assets section of the balance sheet. In some cases, they report cash together with cash equivalents. Cash restricted for a special purpose is reported separately as a current asset or as a noncurrent asset, depending on when the cash is expected to be used.

# GLOSSARY

**Bank reconciliation** The process of comparing the bank's balance of an account with the company's balance and explaining any differences to make them agree. (p. 355).

**Bank service charge** A fee charged by a bank for the use of its services. (p. 357).

**Bank statement** A monthly statement from the bank that shows the depositor's bank transactions and balances. (p. 357).

**Bonding** Obtaining insurance protection against misappropriation of assets by employees. (p. 346).

**Cash**  Resources that consist of coins, currency, checks, money orders, and money on hand or on deposit in a bank or similar depository. (p. 348).

**Cash equivalents**  Short-term, highly liquid investments that can be converted to a specific amount of cash. (p. 363).

**Check**  A written order signed by a bank depositor, directing the bank to pay a specified sum of money to a designated recipient. (p. 355).

**Compensating balances**  Minimum cash balances required by a bank in support of bank loans. (p. 363).

**Deposits in transit**  Deposits recorded by the depositor but not yet been recorded by the bank. (p. 359).

**Electronic funds transfer (EFT)**  A disbursement system that uses wire, telephone, or computers to transfer funds from one location to another. (p. 352).

**Internal auditors**  Company employees who continuously evaluate the effectiveness of the company's internal control system. (p. 345).

**Internal control**  All of the related methods and measures adopted within an organization to safeguard its assets and enhance the accuracy and reliability of its accounting records. (p. 340).

**NSF check**  A check that is not paid by a bank because of insufficient funds in a customer's bank account. (p. 358).

**Outstanding checks**  Checks issued and recorded by a company but not yet paid by the bank. (p. 359).

**Petty cash fund**  A cash fund used to pay relatively small amounts. (p. 353).

**Restricted cash**  Cash that must be used for a special purpose. (p. 363).

**Sarbanes-Oxley Act**  Regulations passed by Congress in 2002 to try to reduce unethical corporate behavior. (p. 341).

**Voucher**  An authorization form prepared for each payment in a voucher system. (p. 351).

**Voucher system**  A network of approvals by authorized individuals acting independently to ensure that all disbursements by check are proper. (p. 351).

## SELF-STUDY QUESTIONS

*Answers are at the end of the chapter.*

(SO 1)  **1.** An organization uses internal control to enhance the accuracy and reliability of its accounting records and to:
   **a.** safeguard its assets.
   **b.** prevent fraud.
   **c.** produce correct financial statements.
   **d.** deter employee dishonesty.

(SO 2)  **2.** The principles of internal control do *not* include:
   **a.** establishment of responsibility.
   **b.** documentation procedures.
   **c.** management responsibility.
   **d.** independent internal verification.

(SO 2)  **3.** Physical controls do *not* include:
   **a.** safes and vaults to store cash.
   **b.** independent bank reconciliations.
   **c.** locked warehouses for inventories.
   **d.** bank safety deposit boxes for important papers.

(SO 3)  **4.** Which of the following items in a cash drawer at November 30 is *not* cash?
   **a.** Money orders.
   **b.** Coins and currency.
   **c.** A customer check dated December 1.
   **d.** A customer check dated November 28.

(SO 3)  **5.** Permitting only designated personnel to handle cash receipts is an application of the principle of:
   **a.** segregation of duties.
   **b.** establishment of responsibility.
   **c.** independent check.
   **d.** other controls.

(SO 4)  **6.** The use of prenumbered checks in disbursing cash is an application of the principle of:
   **a.** establishment of responsibility.
   **b.** segregation of duties.
   **c.** physical, mechanical, and electronic controls.
   **d.** documentation procedures.

**7.** A company writes a check to replenish a $100 petty cash (SO 5) fund when the fund contains receipts of $94 and $3 in cash. In recording the check, the company should:
   **a.** debit Cash Over and Short for $3.
   **b.** debit Petty Cash for $94.
   **c.** credit Cash for $94.
   **d.** credit Petty Cash for $3.

**8.** The control features of a bank account do *not* include:  (SO 6)
   **a.** having bank auditors verify the correctness of the bank balance per books.
   **b.** minimizing the amount of cash that must be kept on hand.
   **c.** providing a double record of all bank transactions.
   **d.** safeguarding cash by using a bank as a depository.

**9.** In a bank reconciliation, deposits in transit are:  (SO 7)
   **a.** deducted from the book balance.
   **b.** added to the book balance.
   **c.** added to the bank balance.
   **d.** deducted from the bank balance.

**10.** The reconciling item in a bank reconciliation that will result in an adjusting entry by the depositor is:  (SO 7)
   **a.** outstanding checks.
   **b.** deposit in transit.
   **c.** a bank error.
   **d.** bank service charges.

**11.** Which of the following statements correctly describes the (SO 8) reporting of cash?
   **a.** Cash cannot be combined with cash equivalents.
   **b.** Restricted cash funds may be combined with Cash.
   **c.** Cash is listed first in the current assets section.
   **d.** Restricted cash funds cannot be reported as a current asset.

Go to the book's website,
**www.wiley.com/college/weygandt**,
for Additional Self-Study questions.

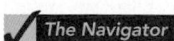

# QUESTIONS

1. "Internal control is concerned only with enhancing the accuracy of the accounting records." Do you agree? Explain.

2. What principles of internal control apply to most organizations?

3. At the corner grocery store, all sales clerks make change out of one cash register drawer. Is this a violation of internal control? Why?

4. Meg Lucas is reviewing the principle of segregation of duties. What are the two common applications of this principle?

5. How do documentation procedures contribute to good internal control?

6. What internal control objectives are met by physical, mechanical, and electronic controls?

7. (a) Explain the control principle of independent internal verification. (b) What practices are important in applying this principle?

8. The management of Sewell Company asks you, as the company accountant, to explain (a) the concept of reasonable assurance in internal control and (b) the importance of the human factor in internal control.

9. McCartney Fertilizer Co. owns the following assets at the balance sheet date.

| | |
|---|---|
| Cash in bank savings account | $ 8,000 |
| Cash on hand | 850 |
| Cash refund due from the IRS | 1,000 |
| Checking account balance | 12,000 |
| Postdated checks | 500 |

What amount should McCartney report as cash in the balance sheet?

10. What principle(s) of internal control is (are) involved in making daily cash counts of over-the-counter receipts?

11. Jacobs Department Stores has just installed new electronic cash registers in its stores. How do cash registers improve internal control over cash receipts?

12. At Hummel Wholesale Company, two mail clerks open all mail receipts. How does this strengthen internal control?

13. "To have maximum effective internal control over cash disbursements, all payments should be made by check." Is this true? Explain.

14. Joe Griswold Company's internal controls over cash disbursements provide for the treasurer to sign checks imprinted by a checkwriting machine in indelible ink after comparing the check with the approved invoice. Identify the internal control principles that are present in these controls.

15. How do the principles of (a) physical, mechanical, and electronic controls and (b) other controls apply to cash disbursements?

16. (a) What is a voucher system? (b) What principles of internal control apply to a voucher system?

17. What is the essential feature of an electronic funds transfer (EFT) procedure?

18. (a) Identify the three activities that pertain to a petty cash fund, and indicate an internal control principle that is applicable to each activity. (b) When are journal entries required in the operation of a petty cash fund?

19. "The use of a bank contributes significantly to good internal control over cash." Is this true? Why or why not?

20. Lori Figgs is confused about the lack of agreement between the cash balance per books and the balance per the bank. Explain the causes for the lack of agreement to Lori, and give an example of each cause.

21. What are the four steps involved in finding differences between the balance per books and balance per bank?

22. Kristen Hope asks your help concerning an NSF check. Explain to Kristen (a) what an NSF check is, (b) how it is treated in a bank reconciliation, and (c) whether it will require an adjusting entry.

23. (a) "Cash equivalents are the same as cash." Do you agree? Explain. (b) How should restricted cash funds be reported on the balance sheet?

# BRIEF EXERCISES

*Indicate internal control concepts.*

*(SO 1)*

**BE8-1**  Jim Gaffigan has prepared the following list of statements about internal control.

1. One of the objectives of internal control is to safeguard assets from employee theft, robbery, and unauthorized use.
2. One of the objectives of internal control is to enhance the accuracy and reliability of the accounting records.
3. No laws require U.S. corporations to maintain an adequate system of internal control.

**Instructions**
Identify each statement as true or false. If false, indicate how to correct the statement.

*Explain the importance of internal control.*

*(SO 1)*

**BE8-2**  Heather Bailiff is the new owner of Ready Parking. She has heard about internal control but is not clear about its importance for her business. Explain to Heather the two purposes of internal control and give her one application of each purpose for Ready Parking.

*Identify internal control principles.*

*(SO 2)*

**BE8-3**  The internal control procedures in Weiser Company provide that:

(a) Employees who have physical custody of assets do not have access to the accounting records.

**(b)** Each month the assets on hand are compared to the accounting records by an internal auditor.
**(c)** A prenumbered shipping document is prepared for each shipment of goods to customers.

Identify the principles of internal control that are being followed.

**BE8-4** Knobloch Company has the following internal control procedures over cash receipts. *Identify the internal control principles applicable to cash receipts.*
Identify the internal control principle that is applicable to each procedure.

*(SO 3)*

1. All over-the-counter receipts are registered on cash registers.
2. All cashiers are bonded.
3. Daily cash counts are made by cashier department supervisors.
4. The duties of receiving cash, recording cash, and custody of cash are assigned to different individuals.
5. Only cashiers may operate cash registers.

**BE8-5** Mingenback Company has the following internal control procedures over cash dis- *Identify the internal control principles applicable to cash disbursements.*
bursements. Identify the internal control principle that is applicable to each procedure.

*(SO 4)*

1. Company checks are prenumbered.
2. The bank statement is reconciled monthly by an internal auditor.
3. Blank checks are stored in a safe in the treasurer's office.
4. Only the treasurer or assistant treasurer may sign checks.
5. Check signers are not allowed to record cash disbursement transactions.

**BE8-6** On March 20, Terrell's petty cash fund of $100 is replenished when the fund contains $7 *Prepare entry to replenish a petty cash fund.*
in cash and receipts for postage $52, freight-out $26, and travel expense $10. Prepare the journal
entry to record the replenishment of the petty cash fund.

*(SO 5)*

**BE8-7** Gary Cunningham is uncertain about the control features of a bank account. Explain *Identify the control features of a bank account.*
the control benefits of **(a)** a check and **(b)** a bank statement.

*(SO 6)*

**BE8-8** The following reconciling items are applicable to the bank reconciliation for Stormont *Indicate location of reconciling items in a bank reconciliation.*
Company: (1) outstanding checks, (2) bank debit memorandum for service charge, (3) bank
credit memorandum for collecting a note for the depositor, (4) deposits in transit. Indicate how
each item should be shown on a bank reconciliation.

*(SO 7)*

**BE8-9** Using the data in BE8-8, indicate **(a)** the items that will result in an adjustment to the *Identify reconciling items that require adjusting entries.*
depositor's records and **(b)** why the other items do not require adjustment.

*(SO 7)*

**BE8-10** At July 31, Kuhlmann Company has the following bank information: cash balance per *Prepare partial bank reconciliation.*
bank $7,420, outstanding checks $762, deposits in transit $1,120, and a bank service charge $20.
Determine the adjusted cash balance per bank at July 31.

*(SO 7)*

**BE8-11** At August 31, Felipe Company has a cash balance per books of $8,500 and the follow- *Prepare partial bank reconciliation.*
ing additional data from the bank statement: charge for printing Felipe Company checks $35,
interest earned on checking account balance $40, and outstanding checks $800. Determine the
adjusted cash balance per books at August 31.

*(SO 7)*

**BE8-12** Quirk Company has the following cash balances: Cash in Bank $15,742, Payroll Bank *Explain the statement presentation of cash balances.*
Account $6,000, and Plant Expansion Fund Cash $25,000. Explain how each balance should be
reported on the balance sheet.

*(SO 8)*

# EXERCISES

**E8-1** Sue Merando is the owner of Merando's Pizza. Merando's is operated strictly on a carry- *Identify the principles of internal control.*
out basis. Customers pick up their orders at a counter where a clerk exchanges the pizza for cash.
While at the counter, the customer can see other employees making the pizzas and the large *(SO 2)*
ovens in which the pizzas are baked.

**Instructions**
Identify the six principles of internal control and give an example of each principle that you might
observe when picking up your pizza. (*Note*: It may not be possible to observe all the principles.)

**E8-2** The following control procedures are used at Gonzales Company for over-the-counter *Identify internal control weaknesses over cash receipts and suggest improvements.*
cash receipts.

1. To minimize the risk of robbery, cash in excess of $100 is stored in an unlocked attaché case in *(SO 2, 3)*
the stock room until it is deposited in the bank.

2. All over-the-counter receipts are registered by three clerks who use a cash register with a single cash drawer.
3. The company accountant makes the bank deposit and then records the day's receipts.
4. At the end of each day, the total receipts are counted by the cashier on duty and reconciled to the cash register total.
5. Cashiers are experienced; they are not bonded.

**Instructions**

(a) For each procedure, explain the weakness in internal control, and identify the control principle that is violated.
(b) For each weakness, suggest a change in procedure that will result in good internal control.

*Identify internal control weaknesses over cash disbursements and suggest improvements.*

*(SO 2, 4)*

**E8-3** The following control procedures are used in Benton's Boutique Shoppe for cash disbursements.

1. The company accountant prepares the bank reconciliation and reports any discrepancies to the owner.
2. The store manager personally approves all payments before signing and issuing checks.
3. Each week, Benton leaves 100 company checks in an unmarked envelope on a shelf behind the cash register.
4. After payment, bills are filed in a paid invoice folder.
5. The company checks are unnumbered.

**Instructions**

(a) For each procedure, explain the weakness in internal control, and identify the internal control principle that is violated.
(b) For each weakness, suggest a change in the procedure that will result in good internal control.

*Identify internal control weaknesses for cash disbursements and suggest improvements.*

*(SO 4)*

**E8-4** At Hutchingson Company, checks are not prenumbered because both the puchasing agent and the treasurer are authorized to issue checks. Each signer has access to unissued checks kept in an unlocked file cabinet. The purchasing agent pays all bills pertaining to goods purchased for resale. Prior to payment, the purchasing agent determines that the goods have been received and verifies the mathematical accuracy of the vendor's invoice. After payment, the invoice is filed by vendor, and the purchasing agent records the payment in the cash disbursements journal. The treasurer pays all other bills following approval by authorized employees. After payment, the treasurer stamps all bills PAID, files them by payment date, and records the checks in the cash disbursements journal. Hutchingson Company maintains one checking account that is reconciled by the treasurer.

**Instructions**

(a) List the weaknesses in internal control over cash disbursements.
(b) ➤ Write a memo to the company treasurer indicating your recommendations for improvement.

*Indicate whether procedure is good or weak internal control.*

*(SO 2, 3, 4)*

**E8-5** Listed below are five procedures followed by The Beat Company.

1. Several individuals operate the cash register using the same register drawer.
2. A monthly bank reconciliation is prepared by someone who has no other cash responsibilities.
3. Ellen May writes checks and also records cash payment journal entries.
4. One individual orders inventory, while a different individual authorizes payments.
5. Unnumbered sales invoices from credit sales are forwarded to the accounting department every four weeks for recording.

**Instructions**

Indicate whether each procedure is an example of good internal control or of weak internal control. If it is an example of good internal control, indicate which internal control principle is being followed. If it is an example of weak internal control, indicate which internal control principle is violated. Use the table below.

| Procedure | IC Good or Weak? | Related Internal Control Principle |
|---|---|---|
| 1. | | |
| 2. | | |
| 3. | | |
| 4. | | |
| 5. | | |

**E8-6** Listed below are five procedures followed by Collins Company.

*Indicate whether procedure is good or weak internal control.*

*(SO 2, 3, 4)*

1. Employees are required to take vacations.
2. Any member of the sales department can approve credit sales.
3. Jethro Bodine ships goods to customers, bills customers, and receives payment from customers.
4. Total cash receipts are compared to bank deposits daily by someone who has no other cash responsibilities.
5. Time clocks are used for recording time worked by employees.

**Instructions**

Indicate whether each procedure is an example of good internal control or of weak internal control. If it is an example of good internal control, indicate which internal control principle is being followed. If it is an example of weak internal control, indicate which internal control principle is violated. Use the table below.

| Procedure | IC Good or Weak? | Related Internal Control Principle |
|---|---|---|
| 1. | | |
| 2. | | |
| 3. | | |
| 4. | | |
| 5. | | |

**E8-7** James Hughes Company established a petty cash fund on May 1, cashing a check for $100. The company reimbursed the fund on June 1 and July 1 with the following results.

*Prepare journal entries for a petty cash fund.*

*(SO 5)*

> June 1: Cash in fund $2.75. Receipts: delivery expense $31.25; postage expense $39.00; and miscellaneous expense $25.00.
>
> July 1: Cash in fund $3.25. Receipts: delivery expense $21.00; entertainment expense $51.00; and miscellaneous expense $24.75.

On July 10, James Hughes increased the fund from $100 to $150.

**Instructions**

Prepare journal entries for James Hughes Company for May 1, June 1, July 1, and July 10.

**E8-8** Lincolnville Company uses an imprest petty cash system. The fund was established on March 1 with a balance of $100. During March the following petty cash receipts were found in the petty cash box.

*Prepare journal entries for a petty cash fund.*

*(SO 5)*

| Date | Receipt No. | For | Amount |
|---|---|---|---|
| 3/5 | 1 | Postage Expense | $39 |
| 7 | 2 | Freight-out | 21 |
| 9 | 3 | Miscellaneous Expense | 6 |
| 11 | 4 | Travel Expense | 24 |
| 14 | 5 | Miscellaneous Expense | 5 |

The fund was replenished on March 15 when the fund contained $3 in cash. On March 20, the amount in the fund was increased to $150.

**Instructions**

Journalize the entries in March that pertain to the operation of the petty cash fund.

**E8-9** Anna Pelo is unable to reconcile the bank balance at January 31. Anna's reconciliation is as follows.

*Prepare bank reconciliation and adjusting entries.*

*(SO 7)*

| | |
|---|---|
| Cash balance per bank | $3,560.20 |
| Add: NSF check | 690.00 |
| Less: Bank service charge | 25.00 |
| Adjusted balance per bank | $4,225.20 |
| | |
| Cash balance per books | $3,875.20 |
| Less: Deposits in transit | 530.00 |
| Add: Outstanding checks | 930.00 |
| Adjusted balance per books | $4,275.20 |

**Instructions**

**(a)** Prepare a correct bank reconciliation.

**(b)** Journalize the entries required by the reconciliation.

*Determine outstanding checks.*

*(SO 7)*

**E8-10**    On April 30, the bank reconciliation of Galena Company shows three outstanding checks: no. 254, $650, no. 255, $820, and no. 257, $410. The May bank statement and the May cash payments journal show the following.

| Bank Statement | | | Cash Payments Journal | | |
|---|---|---|---|---|---|
| Checks Paid | | | Checks Issued | | |
| Date | Check No. | Amount | Date | Check No. | Amount |
| 5/4 | 254 | 650 | 5/2 | 258 | 159 |
| 5/2 | 257 | 410 | 5/5 | 259 | 275 |
| 5/17 | 258 | 159 | 5/10 | 260 | 890 |
| 5/12 | 259 | 275 | 5/15 | 261 | 500 |
| 5/20 | 261 | 500 | 5/22 | 262 | 750 |
| 5/29 | 263 | 480 | 5/24 | 263 | 480 |
| 5/30 | 262 | 750 | 5/29 | 264 | 560 |

**Instructions**

Using step 2 in the reconciliation procedure, list the outstanding checks at May 31.

*Prepare bank reconciliation and adjusting entries.*

*(SO 7)*

**E8-11**    The following information pertains to Family Video Company.

**1.** Cash balance per bank, July 31, $7,263.

**2.** July bank service charge not recorded by the depositor $28.

**3.** Cash balance per books, July 31, $7,284.

**4.** Deposits in transit, July 31, $1,500.

**5.** Bank collected $900 note for Family in July, plus interest $36, less fee $20. The collection has not been recorded by Family, and no interest has been accrued.

**6.** Outstanding checks, July 31, $591.

**Instructions**

**(a)** Prepare a bank reconciliation at July 31.

**(b)** Journalize the adjusting entries at July 31 on the books of Family Video Company.

*Prepare bank reconciliation and adjusting entries.*

*(SO 7)*

**E8-12**    The information below relates to the Cash account in the ledger of Robertson Company.

Balance September 1—$17,150; Cash deposited—$64,000.

Balance September 30—$17,404; Checks written—$63,746.

The September bank statement shows a balance of $16,422 on September 30 and the following memoranda.

| Credits | | Debits | |
|---|---|---|---|
| Collection of $1,500 note plus interest $30 | $1,530 | NSF check: J. E. Hoover | $425 |
| Interest earned on checking account | $45 | Safety deposit box rent | $65 |

At September 30, deposits in transit were $4,450, and outstanding checks totaled $2,383.

**Instructions**

**(a)** Prepare the bank reconciliation at September 30.

**(b)** Prepare the adjusting entries at September 30, assuming (1) the NSF check was from a customer on account, and (2) no interest had been accrued on the note.

*Compute deposits in transit and outstanding checks for two bank reconciliations.*

*(SO 7)*

**E8-13**    The cash records of Givens Company show the following four situations.

**1.** The June 30 bank reconciliation indicated that deposits in transit total $720. During July the general ledger account Cash shows deposits of $15,750, but the bank statement indicates that only $15,600 in deposits were received during the month.

**2.** The June 30 bank reconciliation also reported outstanding checks of $680. During the month of July, Givens Company books show that $17,200 of checks were issued. The bank statement showed that $16,400 of checks cleared the bank in July.

3. In September, deposits per the bank statement totaled $26,700, deposits per books were $25,400, and deposits in transit at September 30 were $2,100.
4. In September, cash disbursements per books were $23,700, checks clearing the bank were $25,000, and outstanding checks at September 30 were $2,100.

There were no bank debit or credit memoranda. No errors were made by either the bank or Givens Company.

**Instructions**
Answer the following questions.

**(a)** In situation (1), what were the deposits in transit at July 31?
**(b)** In situation (2), what were the outstanding checks at July 31?
**(c)** In situation (3), what were the deposits in transit at August 31?
**(d)** In situation (4), what were the outstanding checks at August 31?

**E8-14** Lipkus Company has recorded the following items in its financial records.

| | |
|---|---|
| Cash in bank | $ 47,000 |
| Cash in plant expansion fund | 100,000 |
| Cash on hand | 12,000 |
| Highly liquid investments | 34,000 |
| Petty cash | 500 |
| Receivables from customers | 89,000 |
| Stock investments | 61,000 |

*Show presentation of cash in financial statements.*

*(SO 8)*

The cash in bank is subject to a compensating balance of $5,000. The highly liquid investments had maturities of 3 months or less when they were purchased. The stock investments will be sold in the next 6 to 12 months. The plant expansion project will begin in 3 years.

**Instructions**
**(a)** What amount should Lipkus report as "Cash and cash equivalents" on its balance sheet?
**(b)** Where should the items not included in part (a) be reported on the balance sheet?
**(c)** What disclosures should Lipkus make in its financial statements concerning "cash and cash equivalents"?

# EXERCISES: SET B

Visit the book's website at **www.wiley.com/college/weygandt**, and choose the Student Companion site, to access Exercise Set B.

# PROBLEMS: SET A

**P8-1A** Luby Office Supply Company recently changed its system of internal control over cash disbursements. The system includes the following features.

Instead of being unnumbered and manually prepared, all checks must now be prenumbered and written by using the new checkwriting machine purchased by the company. Before a check can be issued, each invoice must have the approval of Sally Morgan, the purchasing agent, and John Countryman, the receiving department supervisor. Checks must be signed by either Ann Lynn, the treasurer, or Bob Skabo, the assistant treasurer. Before signing a check, the signer is expected to compare the amount of the check with the amount on the invoice.

After signing a check, the signer stamps the invoice PAID and inserts within the stamp, the date, check number, and amount of the check. The "paid" invoice is then sent to the accounting department for recording.

Blank checks are stored in a safe in the treasurer's office. The combination to the safe is known only by the treasurer and assistant treasurer. Each month, the bank statement is reconciled with the bank balance per books by the assistant chief accountant.

*Identify internal control principles over cash disbursements.*

*(SO 2, 4)*

**Instructions**
Identify the internal control principles and their application to cash disbursements of Luby Office Supply Company.

*Journalize and post petty cash fund transactions.*

(SO 5)

GLS

**P8-2A** Winningham Company maintains a petty cash fund for small expenditures. The following transactions occurred over a 2-month period.

July  1   Established petty cash fund by writing a check on Cubs Bank for $200.
     15   Replenished the petty cash fund by writing a check for $196.00. On this date the fund consisted of $4.00 in cash and the following petty cash receipts: freight-out $94.00, postage expense $42.40, entertainment expense $46.60, and miscellaneous expense $11.20.
     31   Replenished the petty cash fund by writing a check for $192.00. At this date, the fund consisted of $8.00 in cash and the following petty cash receipts: freight-out $82.10, charitable contributions expense $45.00, postage expense $25.50, and miscellaneous expense $39.40.
Aug. 15   Replenished the petty cash fund by writing a check for $187.00. On this date, the fund consisted of $13.00 in cash and the following petty cash receipts: freight-out $75.60, entertainment expense $43.00, postage expense $33.00, and miscellaneous expense $37.00.
     16   Increased the amount of the petty cash fund to $300 by writing a check for $100.
     31   Replenished petty cash fund by writing a check for $284.00. On this date, the fund consisted of $16 in cash and the following petty cash receipts: postage expense $140.00, travel expense $95.60, and freight-out $47.10.

**Instructions**

(a) July 15, Cash short $1.80

(b) Aug. 31 balance $300

**(a)** Journalize the petty cash transactions.
**(b)** Post to the Petty Cash account.
**(c)** What internal control features exist in a petty cash fund?

*Prepare a bank reconciliation and adjusting entries.*

(SO 7)

**P8-3A** On May 31, 2008, James Logan Company had a cash balance per books of $6,781.50. The bank statement from Farmers State Bank on that date showed a balance of $6,404.60. A comparison of the statement with the cash account revealed the following facts.

1. The statement included a debit memo of $40 for the printing of additional company checks.
2. Cash sales of $836.15 on May 12 were deposited in the bank. The cash receipts journal entry and the deposit slip were incorrectly made for $886.15. The bank credited Logan Company for the correct amount.
3. Outstanding checks at May 31 totaled $576.25. Deposits in transit were $1,916.15.
4. On May 18, the company issued check No. 1181 for $685 to Barry Trest, on account. The check, which cleared the bank in May, was incorrectly journalized and posted by Logan Company for $658.
5. A $2,500 note receivable was collected by the bank for Logan Company on May 31 plus $80 interest. The bank charged a collection fee of $20. No interest has been accrued on the note.
6. Included with the cancelled checks was a check issued by Bridgetown Company to Tom Lujak for $800 that was incorrectly charged to Logan Company by the bank.
7. On May 31, the bank statement showed an NSF charge of $680 for a check issued by Sandy Grifton, a customer, to Logan Company on account.

**Instructions**

(a) Adjusted cash balance per bank $8,544.50

**(a)** Prepare the bank reconciliation at May 31, 2008.
**(b)** Prepare the necessary adjusting entries for Logan Company at May 31, 2008.

*Prepare a bank reconciliation and adjusting entries from detailed data.*

(SO 7)

**P8-4A** The bank portion of the bank reconciliation for Backhaus Company at November 30, 2008, was as follows.

### BACKHAUS COMPANY
Bank Reconciliation
November 30, 2008

| | | |
|---|---|---|
| Cash balance per bank | | $14,367.90 |
| Add: Deposits in transit | | 2,530.20 |
| | | 16,898.10 |
| Less: Outstanding checks | | |

| Check Number | Check Amount | |
|---|---|---|
| 3451 | $2,260.40 | |
| 3470 | 720.10 | |
| 3471 | 844.50 | |
| 3472 | 1,426.80 | |
| 3474 | 1,050.00 | 6,301.80 |
| Adjusted cash balance per bank | | $10,596.30 |

The adjusted cash balance per bank agreed with the cash balance per books at November 30. The December bank statement showed the following checks and deposits.

**Bank Statement**

| | Checks | | | Deposits | |
|---|---|---|---|---|---|
| Date | Number | Amount | Date | | Amount |
| 12-1 | 3451 | $ 2,260.40 | 12-1 | | $ 2,530.20 |
| 12-2 | 3471 | 844.50 | 12-4 | | 1,211.60 |
| 12-7 | 3472 | 1,426.80 | 12-8 | | 2,365.10 |
| 12-4 | 3475 | 1,640.70 | 12-16 | | 2,672.70 |
| 12-8 | 3476 | 1,300.00 | 12-21 | | 2,945.00 |
| 12-10 | 3477 | 2,130.00 | 12-26 | | 2,567.30 |
| 12-15 | 3479 | 3,080.00 | 12-29 | | 2,836.00 |
| 12-27 | 3480 | 600.00 | 12-30 | | 1,025.00 |
| 12-30 | 3482 | 475.50 | Total | | $18,152.90 |
| 12-29 | 3483 | 1,140.00 | | | |
| 12-31 | 3485 | 540.80 | | | |
| | Total | $15,438.70 | | | |

The cash records per books for December showed the following.

**Cash Payments Journal**

| Date | Number | Amount | Date | Number | Amount |
|---|---|---|---|---|---|
| 12-1 | 3475 | $1,640.70 | 12-20 | 3482 | $ 475.50 |
| 12-2 | 3476 | 1,300.00 | 12-22 | 3483 | 1,140.00 |
| 12-2 | 3477 | 2,130.00 | 12-23 | 3484 | 798.00 |
| 12-4 | 3478 | 621.30 | 12-24 | 3485 | 450.80 |
| 12-8 | 3479 | 3,080.00 | 12-30 | 3486 | 1,889.50 |
| 12-10 | 3480 | 600.00 | Total | | $14,933.20 |
| 12-17 | 3481 | 807.40 | | | |

**Cash Receipts Journal**

| Date | Amount |
|---|---|
| 12-3 | $ 1,211.60 |
| 12-7 | 2,365.10 |
| 12-15 | 2,672.70 |
| 12-20 | 2,954.00 |
| 12-25 | 2,567.30 |
| 12-28 | 2,836.00 |
| 12-30 | 1,025.00 |
| 12-31 | 1,690.40 |
| Total | $17,322.10 |

The bank statement contained two memoranda:

1. A credit of $4,145 for the collection of a $4,000 note for Backhaus Company plus interest of $160 and less a collection fee of $15. Backhaus Company has not accrued any interest on the note.
2. A debit of $572.80 for an NSF check written by D. Chagnon, a customer. At December 31, the check had not been redeposited in the bank.

At December 31 the cash balance per books was $12,985.20, and the cash balance per the bank statement was $20,654.30. The bank did not make any errors, but two errors were made by Backhaus Company.

**Instructions**
(a) Using the four steps in the reconciliation procedure, prepare a bank reconciliation at December 31.
(b) Prepare the adjusting entries based on the reconciliation. (*Hint*: The correction of any errors pertaining to recording checks should be made to Accounts Payable. The correction of any errors relating to recording cash receipts should be made to Accounts Receivable.)

**P8-5A**  Haverman Company maintains a checking account at the Commerce Bank. At July 31, selected data from the ledger balance and the bank statement are shown on page 376.

(a) Adjusted balance per books $15,958.40

*Prepare a bank reconciliation and adjusting entries.*

(SO 7)

| | Cash in Bank | |
|---|---|---|
| | **Per Books** | **Per Bank** |
| Balance, July 1 | $17,600 | $16,800 |
| July receipts | 81,400 | |
| July credits | | 82,470 |
| July disbursements | 77,150 | |
| July debits | | 74,756 |
| Balance, July 31 | $21,850 | $24,514 |

Analysis of the bank data reveals that the credits consist of $79,000 of July deposits and a credit memorandum of $3,470 for the collection of a $3,400 note plus interest revenue of $70. The July debits per bank consist of checks cleared $74,700 and a debit memorandum of $56 for printing additional company checks.

You also discover the following errors involving July checks: (1) A check for $230 to a creditor on account that cleared the bank in July was journalized and posted as $320. (2) A salary check to an employee for $255 was recorded by the bank for $155.

The June 30 bank reconciliation contained only two reconciling items: deposits in transit $7,000 and outstanding checks of $6,200.

**Instructions**

(a) Adjusted balance per books $25,354

**(a)** Prepare a bank reconciliation at July 31.

**(b)** Journalize the adjusting entries to be made by Haverman Company at July 31, 2008. Assume that interest on the note has not been accrued.

*Identify internal control weaknesses in cash receipts and cash disbursements.*

*(SO 2, 3, 4)*

**P8-6A** Emporia Middle School wants to raise money for a new sound system for its auditorium. The primary fund-raising event is a dance at which the famous disc jockey Obnoxious Ed will play classic and not-so-classic dance tunes. Tom Wickman, the music and theater instructor, has been given the responsibility for coordinating the fund-raising efforts. This is Tom's first experience with fund-raising. He decides to put the eighth-grade choir in charge of the event; he will be a relatively passive observer.

Tom had 500 unnumbered tickets printed for the dance. He left the tickets in a box on his desk and told the choir students to take as many tickets as they thought they could sell for $5 each. In order to ensure that no extra tickets would be floating around, he told them to dispose of any unsold tickets. When the students received payment for the tickets, they were to bring the cash back to Tom, and he would put it in a locked box in his desk drawer.

Some of the students were responsible for decorating the gymnasium for the dance. Tom gave each of them a key to the money box and told them that if they took money out to purchase materials, they should put a note in the box saying how much they took and what it was used for. After 2 weeks the money box appeared to be getting full, so Tom asked Luke Gilmor to count the money, prepare a deposit slip, and deposit the money in a bank account Tom had opened.

The day of the dance, Tom wrote a check from the account to pay the DJ. Obnoxious Ed, however, said that he accepted only cash and did not give receipts. So Tom took $200 out of the cash box and gave it to Ed. At the dance Tom had Mel Harris working at the entrance to the gymnasium, collecting tickets from students and selling tickets to those who had not prepurchased them. Tom estimated that 400 students attended the dance.

The following day Tom closed out the bank account, which had $250 in it, and gave that amount plus the $180 in the cash box to Principal Foran. Principal Foran seemed surprised that, after generating roughly $2,000 in sales, the dance netted only $430 in cash. Tom did not know how to respond.

**Instructions**

Identify as many internal control weaknesses as you can in this scenario, and suggest how each could be addressed.

# PROBLEMS: SET B

*Identify internal control weaknesses over cash receipts.*

*(SO 2, 3)*

**P8-1B** Starr Theater is located in the Zurbrugg Mall. A cashier's booth is located near the entrance to the theater. Two cashiers are employed. One works from 1–5 P.M., the other from 5–9 P.M. Each cashier is bonded. The cashiers receive cash from customers and operate a machine that ejects serially numbered tickets. The rolls of tickets are inserted and locked into the machine by the theater manager at the beginning of each cashier's shift.

After purchasing a ticket, the customer takes the ticket to an usher stationed at the entrance of the theater lobby some 60 feet from the cashier's booth. The usher tears the ticket in half, admits the customer, and returns the ticket stub to the customer. The other half of the ticket is dropped into a locked box by the usher.

At the end of each cashier's shift, the theater manager removes the ticket rolls from the machine and makes a cash count. The cash count sheet is initialed by the cashier. At the end of the day, the manager deposits the receipts in total in a bank night deposit vault located in the mall. The manager also sends copies of the deposit slip and the initialed cash count sheets to the theater company treasurer for verification and to the company's accounting department. Receipts from the first shift are stored in a safe located in the manager's office.

**Instructions**

**(a)** Identify the internal control principles and their application to the cash receipts transactions of the Starr Theater.

**(b)** If the usher and cashier decide to collaborate to misappropriate cash, what actions might they take?

**P8-2B** Cushenberry Company maintains a petty cash fund for small expenditures. The following transactions occurred over a 2-month period.

*Journalize and post petty cash fund transactions.*

*(SO 5)*

| July | 1 | Established petty cash fund by writing a check on Landmark Bank for $200. |
| | 15 | Replenished the petty cash fund by writing a check for $194.30. On this date the fund consisted of $5.70 in cash and the following petty cash receipts: freight-out $94.00, postage expense $42.40, entertainment expense $45.90, and miscellaneous expense $10.70. |
| | 31 | Replenished the petty cash fund by writing a check for $192.00. At this date, the fund consisted of $8.00 in cash and the following petty cash receipts: freight-out $82.10, charitable contributions expense $30.00, postage expense $47.80, and miscellaneous expense $32.10. |
| Aug. | 15 | Replenished the petty cash fund by writing a check for $188.00. On this date, the fund consisted of $12.00 in cash and the following petty cash receipts: freight-out $74.40, entertainment expense $41.50, postage expense $33.00, and miscellaneous expense $36.00. |
| | 16 | Increased the amount of the petty cash fund to $300 by writing a check for $100. |
| | 31 | Replenished petty cash fund by writing a check for $283.00. On this date, the fund consisted of $17 in cash and the following petty cash receipts: postage expense $145.00, entertainment expense $90.60, and freight-out $46.00. |

**Instructions**

**(a)** Journalize the petty cash transactions.

**(b)** Post to the Petty Cash account.

**(c)** What internal control features exist in a petty cash fund?

*(a) July 15 Cash short $1.30*
*(b) Aug. 31 balance $300*

**P8-3B** Flint Hills Genetics Company of Lawrence, Kansas, spreads herbicides and applies liquid fertilizer for local farmers. On May 31, 2008, the company's cash account per its general ledger showed the following balance.

*Prepare a bank reconciliation and adjusting entries.*

*(SO 7)*

### CASH                                             NO. 101

| Date | Explanation | Ref. | Debit | Credit | Balance |
|------|-------------|------|-------|--------|---------|
| May 31 | Balance | | | | 6,781.50 |

The bank statement from Lawrence State Bank on that date showed the following balance.

### LAWRENCE STATE BANK

| Checks and Debits | Deposits and Credits | Daily Balance |
|-------------------|----------------------|---------------|
| XXX | XXX | 5/31   6,804.60 |

A comparison of the details on the bank statement with the details in the cash account revealed the following facts.

**1.** The statement included a debit memo of $40 for the printing of additional company checks.

**2.** Cash sales of $836.15 on May 12 were deposited in the bank. The cash receipts journal entry and the deposit slip were incorrectly made for $846.15. The bank credited Flint Hills Genetics Company for the correct amount.

3. Outstanding checks at May 31 totaled $515.25, and deposits in transit were $936.15.
4. On May 18, the company issued check no. 1181 for $685 to M. Datz, on account. The check, which cleared the bank in May, was incorrectly journalized and posted by Flint Hills Genetics Company for $658.
5. A $2,000 note receivable was collected by the bank for Flint Hills Genetics Company on May 31 plus $80 interest. The bank charged a collection fee of $25. No interest has been accrued on the note.
6. Included with the cancelled checks was a check issued by Bohr Company to Fred Mertz for $600 that was incorrectly charged to Flint Hills Genetics Company by the bank.
7. On May 31, the bank statement showed an NSF charge of $934 for a check issued by Tyler Gricius, a customer, to Flint Hills Genetics Company on account.

**Instructions**

(a) Adj. cash bal. $7,825.50

(a) Prepare the bank reconciliation at May 31, 2008.
(b) Prepare the necessary adjusting entries for Flint Hills Genetics Company at May 31, 2008.

*Prepare a bank reconciliation and adjusting entries from detailed data.*

(SO 7)

**P8-4B** The bank portion of the bank reconciliation for Conlin Company at October 31, 2008 was as follows.

## CONLIN COMPANY
Bank Reconciliation
October 31, 2008

| | | |
|---|---|---|
| Cash balance per bank | | $11,444.70 |
| Add: Deposits in transit | | 1,530.20 |
| | | 12,974.90 |
| Less: Outstanding checks | | |

| Check Number | Check Amount | |
|---|---|---|
| 2451 | $1,260.40 | |
| 2470 | 720.10 | |
| 2471 | 844.50 | |
| 2472 | 503.60 | |
| 2474 | 1,050.00 | 4,378.60 |
| Adjusted cash balance per bank | | $ 8,596.30 |

The adjusted cash balance per bank agreed with the cash balance per books at October 31. The November bank statement showed the following checks and deposits:

| Bank Statement | | | | | |
|---|---|---|---|---|---|
| Checks | | | Deposits | | |
| Date | Number | Amount | Date | Amount | |
| 11-1 | 2470 | $ 720.10 | 11-1 | $ 1,530.20 | |
| 11-2 | 2471 | 844.50 | 11-4 | 1,211.60 | |
| 11-5 | 2474 | 1,050.00 | 11-8 | 990.10 | |
| 11-4 | 2475 | 1,640.70 | 11-13 | 2,575.00 | |
| 11-8 | 2476 | 2,830.00 | 11-18 | 1,472.70 | |
| 11-10 | 2477 | 600.00 | 11-21 | 2,945.00 | |
| 11-15 | 2479 | 1,750.00 | 11-25 | 2,567.30 | |
| 11-18 | 2480 | 1,330.00 | 11-28 | 1,650.00 | |
| 11-27 | 2481 | 695.40 | 11-30 | 1,186.00 | |
| 11-30 | 2483 | 575.50 | Total | $16,127.90 | |
| 11-29 | 2486 | 900.00 | | | |
| | Total | $12,936.20 | | | |

The cash records per books for November showed the following.

| Cash Payments Journal | | | | | | Cash Receipts Journal | |
|---|---|---|---|---|---|---|---|
| Date | Number | Amount | Date | Number | Amount | Date | Amount |
| 11-1 | 2475 | $1,640.70 | 11-20 | 2483 | $ 575.50 | 11-3 | $ 1,211.60 |
| 11-2 | 2476 | 2,830.00 | 11-22 | 2484 | 829.50 | 11-7 | 990.10 |
| 11-2 | 2477 | 600.00 | 11-23 | 2485 | 974.80 | 11-12 | 2,575.00 |
| 11-4 | 2478 | 538.20 | 11-24 | 2486 | 900.00 | 11-17 | 1,472.70 |
| 11-8 | 2479 | 1,570.00 | 11-29 | 2487 | 398.00 | 11-20 | 2,954.00 |
| 11-10 | 2480 | 1,330.00 | 11-30 | 2488 | 1,200.00 | 11-24 | 2,567.30 |
| 11-15 | 2481 | 695.40 | Total | | $14,694.10 | 11-27 | 1,650.00 |
| 11-18 | 2482 | 612.00 | | | | 11-29 | 1,186.00 |
| | | | | | | 11-30 | 2,338.00 |
| | | | | | | Total | $16,944.70 |

The bank statement contained two bank memoranda:

1. A credit of $2,505.00 for the collection of a $2,400 note for Conlin Company plus interest of $120 and less a collection fee of $15. Conlin Company has not accrued any interest on the note.
2. A debit for the printing of additional company checks $72.

At November 30, the cash balance per books was $10,846.90, and the cash balance per the bank statement was $17,069.40. The bank did not make any errors, but two errors were made by Conlin Company.

**Instructions**

(a) Using the four steps in the reconciliation procedure described on page 357, prepare a bank reconciliation at November 30.

(b) Prepare the adjusting entries based on the reconciliation. (*Hint*: The correction of any errors pertaining to recording checks should be made to Accounts Payable. The correction of any errors relating to recording cash receipts should be made to Accounts Receivable).

*(a) Adjusted cash balance per bank $13,090.90*

**P8-5B** Baumgardner Company's bank statement from Last National Bank at August 31, 2008, shows the following information.

*Prepare a bank reconciliation and adjusting entries.*

*(SO 7)*

| | | | | |
|---|---|---|---|---|
| Balance, August 1 | $17,400 | Bank credit memoranda: | | |
| August deposits | 73,110 | Collection of note | | |
| Checks cleared in August | 71,500 | receivable plus $130 | | |
| Balance, August 31 | 25,932 | interest | $6,930 | |
| | | Interest earned | 32 | |
| | | Bank debit memorandum: | | |
| | | Safety deposit box rent | 40 | |

A summary of the Cash account in the ledger for August shows: Balance, August 1, $16,900; receipts $77,000; disbursements $73,570; and balance, August 31, $20,330. Analysis reveals that the only reconciling items on the July 31 bank reconciliation were a deposit in transit for $4,000 and outstanding checks of $4,500. The deposit in transit was the first deposit recorded by the bank in August. In addition, you determine that there were two errors involving company checks drawn in August: (1) A check for $240 to a creditor on account that cleared the bank in August was journalized and posted for $420. (2) A salary check to an employee for $275 was recorded by the bank for $278.

**Instructions**

(a) Prepare a bank reconciliation at August 31.

(b) Journalize the adjusting entries to be made by Baumgardner Company at August 31. Assume that interest on the note has not been accrued by the company.

*(a) Adjusted balance per books $27,432*

**P8-6B** Richardson Company is a very profitable small business. It has not, however, given much consideration to internal control. For example, in an attempt to keep clerical and office expenses to a minimum, the company has combined the jobs of cashier and bookkeeper. As a result, Jake Stickyfingers handles all cash receipts, keeps the accounting records, and prepares the monthly bank reconciliations.

The balance per the bank statement on October 31, 2008, was $18,180. Outstanding checks were: no. 62 for $126.75, no. 183 for $150, no. 284 for $253.25, no. 862 for $190.71, no. 863 for

*Prepare comprehensive bank reconciliation with theft and internal control deficiencies.*

*(SO 2, 3, 4, 7)*

$226.80, and no. 864 for $165.28. Included with the statement was a credit memorandum of $400 indicating the collection of a note receivable for Richardson Company by the bank on October 25. This memorandum has not been recorded by Richardson Company.

The company's ledger showed one cash account with a balance of $21,892.72. The balance included undeposited cash on hand. Because of the lack of internal controls, Stickyfingers took for personal use all of the undeposited receipts in excess of $3,795.51. He then prepared the following bank reconciliation in an effort to conceal his theft of cash.

## BANK RECONCILIATION

| | | |
|---|---:|---:|
| Cash balance per books, October 31 | | $21,892.72 |
| Add: Outstanding checks | | |
| No. 862 | $190.71 | |
| No. 863 | 226.80 | |
| No. 864 | 165.28 | 482.79 |
| | | 22,375.51 |
| Less: Undeposited receipts | | 3,795.51 |
| Unadjusted balance per bank, October 31 | | 18,580.00 |
| Less: Bank credit memorandum | | 400.00 |
| Cash balance per bank statement, October 31 | | $18,180.00 |

### Instructions

(a) Adjusted balance per books $20,862.72

**(a)** Prepare a correct bank reconciliation. (*Hint:* Deduct the amount of the theft from the adjusted balance per books.)

**(b)** Indicate the three ways that Stickyfingers attempted to conceal the theft and the dollar amount pertaining to each method.

**(c)** What principles of internal control were violated in this case?

## PROBLEMS: SET C

Visit the book's website at **www.wiley.com/college/weygandt**, and choose the Student Companion site, to access Problem Set C.

## CONTINUING COOKIE CHRONICLE

(Note: This is a continuation of the Cookie Chronicle from Chapters 1 through 7.)

**CCC8   Part 1**   Natalie is struggling to keep up with the recording of her accounting transactions. She is spending a lot of time marketing and selling mixers and giving her cookie classes. Her friend John is an accounting student who runs his own accounting service. He has asked Natalie if she would like to have him do her accounting. John and Natalie meet and discuss her business.

**Part 2**   Natalie decides that she cannot afford to hire John to do her accounting. One way that she can ensure that her cash account does not have any errors and is accurate and up-to-date is to prepare a bank reconciliation at the end of each month. Natalie would like you to help her.

*Go to the book's website,*
**www.wiley.com/college/weygandt,**
*to see the completion of this problem.*

# BROADENING YOUR PERSPECTIVE

## FINANCIAL REPORTING AND ANALYSIS

### Financial Reporting Problem
#### PepsiCo, Inc.

**BYP8-1**   The financial statements of PepsiCo, Inc., are presented in Appendix A at the end of this textbook.

**Instructions**

(a) What comments, if any, are made about cash in the report of the independent auditors?

(b) What data about cash and cash equivalents are shown in the consolidated balance sheet?

(c) In its notes to Consolidated Financial Statements, how does PepsiCo define cash equivalents?

(d) In management's letter that assumes "Responsibility for Financial Reporting," what does PepsiCo's management say about internal control? (See page A3 in Appendix A of the back of the book.)

# Comparative Analysis Problem
## PepsiCo, Inc. vs. The Coca-Cola Company

**BYP8-2** PepsiCo's financial statements are presented in Appendix A. Coca-Cola's financial statements are presented in Appendix B.

**Instructions**

(a) Based on the information contained in these financial statements, determine each of the following for each company:

    **(1)** Cash and cash equivalents balance at December 31, 2005, for PepsiCo and at December 31, 2005, for Coca-Cola.

    **(2)** Increase (decrease) in cash and cash equivalents from 2004 to 2005.

    **(3)** Cash provided by operating activities during the year ended December 2005 (from statement of cash flows).

(b) What conclusions concerning the management of cash can be drawn from these data?

# Exploring the Web

**BYP8-3** All organizations should have systems of internal control. Universities are no exception. This site discusses the basics of internal control in a university setting.

**Address: www.bc.edu/offices/audit/controls**, or go to **www.wiley.com/college/weygandt**

**Steps:** Go to the site shown above.

**Instructions**

The front page of this site provides links to pages that answer six critical questions. Use these links to answer the following questions.

(a) In a university setting who has responsibility for evaluating the adequacy of the system of internal control?

(b) What do reconciliations ensure in the university setting? Who should review the reconciliation?

(c) What are some examples of physical controls?

(d) What are two ways to accomplish inventory counts?

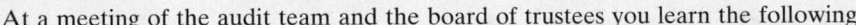

# CRITICAL THINKING

# Decision Making Across the Organization

**BYP8-4** The board of trustees of a local church is concerned about the internal accounting controls for the offering collections made at weekly services. The trustees ask you to serve on a three-person audit team with the internal auditor of a local college and a CPA who has just joined the church.

At a meeting of the audit team and the board of trustees you learn the following.

1. The church's board of trustees has delegated responsibility for the financial management and audit of the financial records to the finance committee. This group prepares the annual budget and approves major disbursements. It is not involved in collections or record keeping. No audit has been made in recent years because the same trusted employee has kept church records and served as financial secretary for 15 years. The church does not carry any fidelity insurance.

2. The collection at the weekly service is taken by a team of ushers who volunteer to serve one month. The ushers take the collection plates to a basement office at the rear of the church. They hand their plates to the head usher and return to the church service. After all plates have been turned in, the head usher counts the cash received. The head usher then places

the cash in the church safe along with a notation of the amount counted. The head usher volunteers to serve for 3 months.

3. The next morning the financial secretary opens the safe and recounts the collection. The secretary withholds $150–$200 in cash, depending on the cash expenditures expected for the week, and deposits the remainder of the collections in the bank. To facilitate the deposit, church members who contribute by check are asked to make their checks payable to "Cash."

4. Each month, the financial secretary reconciles the bank statement and submits a copy of the reconciliation to the board of trustees. The reconciliations have rarely contained any bank errors and have never shown any errors per books.

**Instructions**

With the class divided into groups, answer the following.

**(a)** Indicate the weaknesses in internal accounting control over the handling of collections.

**(b)** List the improvements in internal control procedures that you plan to make at the next meeting of the audit team for (1) the ushers, (2) the head usher, (3) the financial secretary, and (4) the finance committee.

**(c)** What church policies should be changed to improve internal control?

# Communication Activity

**BYP8-5**    As a new auditor for the CPA firm of Croix, Marais, and Kale, you have been assigned to review the internal controls over mail cash receipts of Manhattan Company. Your review reveals the following: Checks are promptly endorsed "For Deposit Only," but no list of the checks is prepared by the person opening the mail. The mail is opened either by the cashier or by the employee who maintains the accounts receivable records. Mail receipts are deposited in the bank weekly by the cashier.

**Instructions**

Write a letter to Jerry Mays, owner of the Manhattan Company, explaining the weaknesses in internal control and your recommendations for improving the system.

# Ethics Case

**BYP8-6**    You are the assistant controller in charge of general ledger accounting at Riverside Bottling Company. Your company has a large loan from an insurance company. The loan agreement requires that the company's cash account balance be maintained at $200,000 or more, as reported monthly.

At June 30 the cash balance is $80,000, which you report to Gena Schmitt, the financial vice president. Gena excitedly instructs you to keep the cash receipts book open for one additional day for purposes of the June 30 report to the insurance company. Gena says, "If we don't get that cash balance over $200,000, we'll default on our loan agreement. They could close us down, put us all out of our jobs!" Gena continues, "I talked to Oconto Distributors (one of Riverside's largest customers) this morning. They said they sent us a check for $150,000 yesterday. We should receive it tomorrow. If we include just that one check in our cash balance, we'll be in the clear. It's in the mail!"

**Instructions**

**(a)** Who will suffer negative effects if you do not comply with Gena Schmitt's instructions? Who will suffer if you do comply?

**(b)** What are the ethical considerations in this case?

**(c)** What alternatives do you have?

 # "All About You" Activity

**BYP8-7**    The "All About You" feature in this chapter (page 364) indicates potential security risks that may arise from your personal computer. It is important to keep in mind, however, that there are also many other ways that your identity can be stolen other than from your computer. The federal government provides many resources to help protect you from identity thieves.

**Instructions**

Go to **http://onguardonline.gov/idtheft.html**, and click on ID Theft Faceoff. Complete the quiz provided there.

## Answers to Insight and Accounting Across the Organization Questions

**This Was a Penalty to Take Seriously, p. 343**

Q: Which principle of internal control was implemented in ancient Egypt?

A: *The system in ancient Egypt used the principle of independent internal verification.*

Q: Who do you think investors today expect to detect and prevent fraud?

A: *Today, investors probably expect independent auditors to detect and prevent fraud. In reality, management is assigned this important responsibility. Auditors attest to compliance with GAAP and specifically state that financial statements and the system of internal control are management's responsibility.*

**SOX Boosts the Role of Human Resources, p. 344**

Q: Why would unsupervised employees or employees who report to each other represent potential internal control threats?

A. *An unsupervised employee may have a fraudulent job (or may even be a fictitious person— e.g., a person drawing a paycheck without working). Or, if two employees supervise each other, there is no real separation of duties, and they can conspire to defraud the company.*

**Poor Internal Control Can Hammer Stock Price, p. 346**

Q. Why would a company's stock price fall if it reports deficiencies in its internal controls?

A. *Internal controls protect against employee theft, but they also provide protection against manipulation of accounting numbers. If a company has poor internal controls, investors will have less confidence that its financial statements are accurate. As a consequence, its stock price might suffer.*

**Cash? What Cash?, p. 357**

Q: Will "cash" be obsolete in terms of financial statement reporting?

A: *Cash, as the most liquid asset, will continue to be reported on balance sheets, and cash flows will still be reported on the statement of cash flows. Coins and currency may be less popular, but cash in the form of virtual cash (balances or deposits in accounts) will exist in a big way and will continue to appear in financial statements.*

## Authors' Comments on *All About You*: Protecting Yourself from Identity Theft, p. 364

Most experts discourage storing sensitive financial information on your computer. In recent years there have been countless examples of hackers penetrating sophisticated corporate systems to steal personal data. If hackers can beat sophisticated systems, it is unlikely that you can do better.

The Federal Trade Commission recommends that you frequently update your anti-virus software. Use a firewall program and a secure browser that encrypts all online transactions. If you do store financial information on your computer, make sure that it is password-protected with a password that is an unrecognizable combination of upper- and lower-case letters, numbers, and symbols. Change the password periodically. When you dispose of your old computer, make sure that you use a wiping utility to destroy all information on the hard drive.

Be careful, too, not to focus all of your internal control efforts on your computer. Most identity theft still derives from very non-technical sources—such as your trash can. You should take the following steps to minimize non-computer-related risks: Use passwords on your credit card, bank, and phone accounts. Make sure that all personal information in your home is in a secure place, especially if you have roommates or employ outside help. Don't give out personal information unless you initiated the contact or you are sure you know whom you are dealing with. Deposit outgoing mail in post-office collection boxes (not in your mailbox with the red flag up), and promptly remove all mail from your mailbox. Use a cross-cut shredder to shred all charge receipts, insurance forms, bank statements, etc. that might reveal personal information.

## Answer to PepsiCo Review It Question 3, p. 365

PepsiCo reports cash and cash equivalents on its balance sheet for 2005 of $1,716 million.

## Answers to Self-Study Questions

**1.** a  **2.** c  **3.** b  **4.** c  **5.** b  **6.** d  **7.** a  **8.** a  **9.** c  **10.** d  **11.** c

# Chapter 9

# Accounting for Receivables

## STUDY OBJECTIVES

*After studying this chapter, you should be able to:*

1 Identify the different types of receivables.
2 Explain how companies recognize accounts receivable.
3 Distinguish between the methods and bases companies use to value accounts receivable.
4 Describe the entries to record the disposition of accounts receivable.
5 Compute the maturity date of and interest on notes receivable.
6 Explain how companies recognize notes receivable.
7 Describe how companies value notes receivable.
8 Describe the entries to record the disposition of notes receivable.
9 Explain the statement presentation and analysis of receivables. ✔ The Navigator

## ✔ The Navigator

| Scan **Study Objectives** | ■ |
| Read **Feature Story** | ■ |
| Read **Preview** | ■ |
| Read text and answer **Before You Go On** p. 394 ■  p. 397 ■  p. 402 ■  p. 404 ■ | |
| Work **Demonstration Problem** | ■ |
| Review **Summary of Study Objectives** | ■ |
| Answer **Self-Study Questions** | ■ |
| Complete **Assignments** | ■ |

## Feature Story

**A DOSE OF CAREFUL MANAGEMENT KEEPS RECEIVABLES HEALTHY**

"Sometimes you have to know when to be very tough, and sometimes you can give them a bit of a break," says Vivi Su. She's not talking about her children, but about the customers of a subsidiary of pharmaceutical company Whitehall-Robins (*www.whitehall-robins.com*), where she works as supervisor of credit and collections.

For example, while the company's regular terms are 1/15, n/30 (1% discount if paid within 15 days), a customer might ask for and receive a few days of grace and still get the discount. Or a customer might place orders above its credit limit, in which case, depending on its payment history and the circumstances, Ms. Su might authorize shipment of the goods anyway.

Nearly all of the company's sales come through the credit accounts Ms. Su manages. The process starts with the decision to grant a customer an account in the first place, Ms. Su explains. The sales rep gives the customer a credit application. "My department reviews this application very carefully; a customer needs to supply three good references, and we also run a check with a credit firm like Equifax. If we accept them, then based on their size and history, we assign a credit limit."

Once accounts are established, the company supervises them very carefully. "I get an aging report every single day," says Ms. Su.

"The rule of thumb is that we should always have at least 85% of receivables current—meaning they were billed less than 30 days ago," she continues. "But we try to do even better than that—I like to see 90%." Similarly, her guideline is never to have more than 5% of receivables at over 90 days. But long before that figure is reached, "we jump on it," she says firmly.

At 15 days overdue, Whitehall-Robins phones the client. Often there's a reasonable explanation for the delay—an invoice may have gone astray, or the payables clerk is away. "But if a customer keeps on delaying, and tells us several times that it'll only be a few more days, we know there's a problem," says Ms. Su. After 45 days, "I send a letter. Then a second notice is sent in writing. After the third and final notice, the client has 10 days to pay, and then I hand it over to a collection agency, and it's out of my hands."

Ms. Su knows that management of receivables is crucial to the profitability of Whitehall-Robins. "Receivables are generally the second-largest asset of any company (after its capital assets)," she points out. "So it's no wonder we keep a very close eye on them."

✓ *The Navigator*

# Inside Chapter 9

- **Be Sure to Read the Fine Print** (p. 388)

- **When Investors Ignore Warning Signs** (p. 394)

- **How Does a Credit Card Work?** (p. 397)

- **Who Gets Credit?** (p. 402)

- *All About You:* **Should You Be Carrying Plastic?** (p. 405)

As indicated in the Feature Story, receivables are a significant asset for many pharmaceutical companies. Because a significant portion of sales in the United States are done on credit, receivables are significant to companies in other industries as well. As a consequence, companies must pay close attention to their receivables and manage them carefully. In this chapter you will learn what journal entries companies make when they sell products, when they collect cash from those sales, and when they write off accounts they cannot collect.

The content and organization of the chapter are as follows.

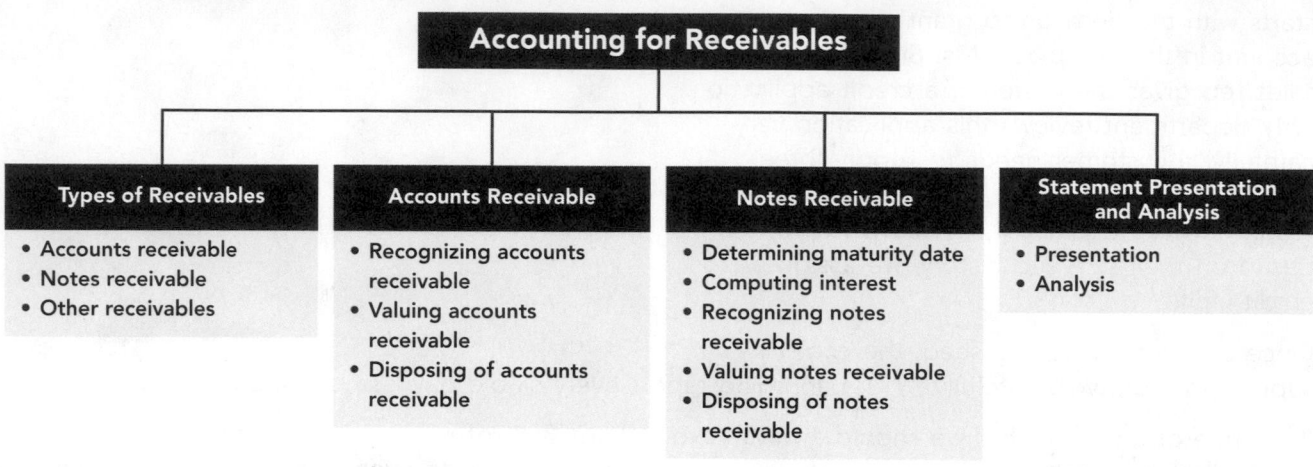

✓ *The Navigator*

# TYPES OF RECEIVABLES

**STUDY OBJECTIVE 1**

Identify the different types of receivables.

The term **receivables** refers to amounts due from individuals and other companies. Receivables are claims that are expected to be collected in cash. They are frequently classified as (1) accounts receivable, (2) notes receivable, and (3) other receivables.

**Accounts receivable** are amounts owed by customers on account. They result from the sale of goods and services. Companies generally expect to collect these receivables within 30 to 60 days. Accounts receivable are the most significant type of claim held by a company.

**Notes receivable** are claims for which formal instruments of credit are issued as proof of the debt. A note receivable normally extends for time periods of 60–90 days or longer and requires the debtor to pay interest. Notes and accounts receivable that result from sales transactions are often called **trade receivables**.

**ETHICS NOTE**

⚖ Companies report receivables from employees separately in the financial statements. The reason: Sometimes those assets are not the result of an "arm's-length" transaction.

**Other receivables** include nontrade receivables. Examples are interest receivable, loans to company officers, advances to employees, and income taxes refundable. These do not generally result from the operations of the business. Therefore companies generally classify and report them as separate items in the balance sheet.

# ACCOUNTS RECEIVABLE

Three accounting issues associated with accounts receivable are:

1. **Recognizing** accounts receivable.
2. **Valuing** accounts receivable.
3. **Disposing of** accounts receivable.

# Recognizing Accounts Receivable

Recognizing accounts receivable is relatively straightforward. In Chapter 5 we saw how the sale of merchandise affects accounts receivable. To review, assume that Jordache Co. on July 1, 2008, sells merchandise on account to Polo Company for $1,000 terms 2/10, n/30. On July 5, Polo returns merchandise worth $100 to Jordache Co. On July 11, Jordache receives payment from Polo Company for the balance due. The journal entries to record these transactions on the books of Jordache Co. are as follows.

| July 1 | Accounts Receivable—Polo Company | 1,000 | |
| | Sales | | 1,000 |
| | (To record sales on account) | | |
| July 5 | Sales Returns and Allowances | 100 | |
| | Accounts Receivable—Polo Company | | 100 |
| | (To record merchandise returned) | | |
| July 11 | Cash ($900−$18) | 882 | |
| | Sales Discounts ($900 × .02) | 18 | |
| | Accounts Receivable—Polo Company | | 900 |
| | (To record collection of accounts receivable) | | |

**HELPFUL HINT**

These entries are the same as those described in Chapter 5. For simplicity, we have omitted inventory and cost of goods sold from this set of journal entries and from end-of-chapter material.

The opportunity to receive a cash discount usually occurs when a manufacturer sells to a wholesaler or a wholesaler sells to a retailer. The selling company gives a discount in these situations either to encourage prompt payment or for competitive reasons.

Retailers rarely grant cash discounts to customers. In fact, when you use a retailer's credit card (Sears, for example), instead of giving a discount, the retailer charges interest on the balance due if not paid within a specified period (usually 25–30 days).

To illustrate, assume that you use your J.C. Penney Company credit card to purchase clothing with a sales price of $300. J.C. Penney will make the following entry at the date of sale.

| Accounts Receivable | 300 | |
| Sales | | 300 |
| (To record sale of merchandise) | | |

| A | = | L | + | SE |
|---|---|---|---|---|
| +300 | | | | |
| | | | | +300 Rev |

**Cash Flows**
no effect

J.C. Penney will send you a monthly statement of this transaction and any others that have occurred during the month. If you do not pay in full within 30 days, J.C. Penney adds an interest (financing) charge to the balance due. Although interest rates vary by region and over time, a common rate for retailers is 18% per year (1.5% per month).

The seller recognizes interest revenue when it adds financing charges. Assuming that you owe $300 at the end of the month, and J.C. Penney charges 1.5% per month on the balance due, the adjusting entry to record interest revenue of $4.50 ($300 × 1.5%) is as follows.

| Accounts Receivable | 4.50 | |
| Interest Revenue | | 4.50 |
| (To record interest on amount due) | | |

| A | = | L | + | SE |
|---|---|---|---|---|
| +4.50 | | | | |
| | | | | +4.50 Rev |

**Cash Flows**
no effect

Interest revenue is often substantial for many retailers.

# ACCOUNTING ACROSS THE ORGANIZATION

### Be Sure to Read the Fine Print

Interest rates on most credit cards are quite high, sometimes 18% or higher. As a result, consumers often look for companies that charge lower rates. Be careful—some companies offer lower interest rates but have eliminated the standard 25-day grace period before finance charges kick in. Other companies encourage consumers to increase their debt by advertising that only a $1 minimum payment is due on a $1,000 account balance. The less you pay off, the more interest they earn! Several banks market a credit card that allows cardholders to skip a payment twice a year. However, the outstanding balance continues to incur interest. Other credit card companies calculate finance charges on two-month, rather than one-month, averages, a practice that often translates into higher interest charges. In short, read the fine print in your credit agreement.

**?** Why are credit card companies willing to offer relaxed payment options?

## Valuing Accounts Receivable

**STUDY OBJECTIVE 3**

Distinquish between the methods and bases companies use to value accounts receivable.

Once companies record receivables in the accounts, the next question is: How should they report receivables in the financial statements? Companies report accounts receivable on the balance sheet as an asset. But determining the **amount** to report is sometimes difficult because some receivables will become uncollectible.

Each customer must satisfy the credit requirements of the seller before the credit sale is approved. Inevitably, though, some accounts receivable become uncollectible. For example, a customer may not be able to pay because of a decline in its sales revenue due to a downturn in the economy. Similarly, individuals may be laid off from their jobs or faced with unexpected hospital bills. Companies record credit losses as debits to <u>Bad Debts Expense</u> (or Uncollectible Accounts Expense). Such losses are a normal and necessary risk of doing business on a credit basis.

Two methods are used in accounting for uncollectible accounts: (1) the direct write-off method and (2) the allowance method. The following sections explain these methods.

### DIRECT WRITE-OFF METHOD FOR UNCOLLECTIBLE ACCOUNTS

Under the **direct write-off method**, when a company determines a particular account to be uncollectible, it charges the loss to Bad Debts Expense. Assume, for example, that on December 12 Warden Co. writes off as uncollectible M. E. Doran's $200 balance. The entry is:

| | | | |
|---|---|---|---|
| A = L + SE | | | |
| | | −200 Exp | |
| −200 | | | |

**Cash Flows**
no effect

| Dec. 12 | Bad Debts Expense | 200 | |
|---------|-------------------|-----|-----|
| | Accounts Receivable—M. E. Doran | | 200 |
| | (To record write-off of M. E. Doran account) | | |

Under this method, Bad Debts Expense will show only **actual losses** from uncollectibles. The company will report accounts receivable at its gross amount.

Although this method is simple, its use can reduce the usefulness of both the income statement and balance sheet. Consider the following example. Assume that in 2008, Quick Buck Computer Company decided it could increase its revenues by offering computers to college students without requiring any money down and with no credit-approval process. On campuses across the country it distributed one million computers with a selling price of $800 each. This increased Quick Buck's revenues and receivables by $800 million. The promotion was a huge success! The 2008 balance sheet and income statement looked great. Unfortunately, during 2009, nearly 40% of the customers defaulted on their loans. This made the 2009 income statement and balance sheet look terrible. Illustration 9-1 shows the effect of these events on the financial statements if the direct write-off method is used.

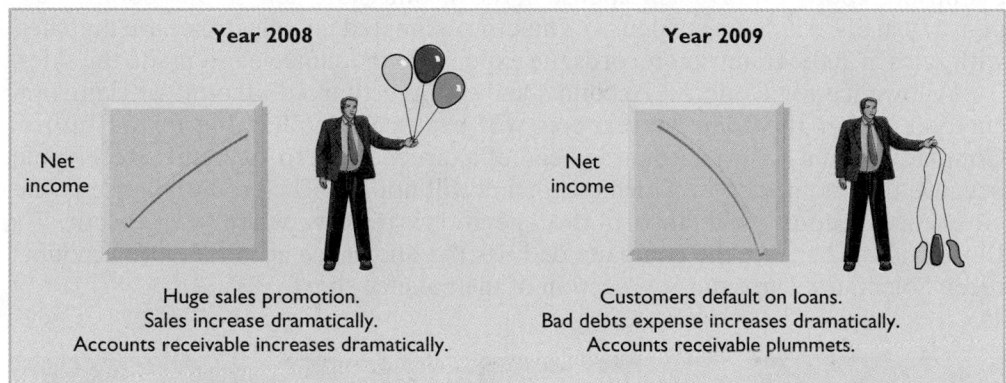

**Year 2008**

Net income

Huge sales promotion.
Sales increase dramatically.
Accounts receivable increases dramatically.

**Year 2009**

Net income

Customers default on loans.
Bad debts expense increases dramatically.
Accounts receivable plummets.

**Illustration 9-1**
Effects of direct write-off method

Under the direct write-off method, companies often record bad debts expense in a period different from the period in which they record the revenue. The method does not attempt to match bad debts expense to sales revenues in the income statement. Nor does the direct write-off method show accounts receivable in the balance sheet at the amount the company actually expects to receive. **Consequently, unless bad debts losses are insignificant, the direct write-off method is not acceptable for financial reporting purposes.**

## ALLOWANCE METHOD FOR UNCOLLECTIBLE ACCOUNTS

The **allowance method** of accounting for bad debts involves estimating uncollectible accounts at the end of each period. This provides better matching on the income statement. It also ensures that companies state receivables on the balance sheet at their cash (net) realizable value. **Cash (net) realizable value** is the net amount the company expects to receive in cash. It excludes amounts that the company estimates it will not collect. Thus, this method reduces receivables in the balance sheet by the amount of estimated uncollectible receivables.

GAAP requires the allowance method for financial reporting purposes when bad debts are material in amount. This method has three essential features:

1. Companies **estimate** uncollectible accounts receivable. They match this estimated expense **against revenues** in the same accounting period in which they record the revenues.

2. Companies debit estimated uncollectibles to Bad Debts Expense and credit them to Allowance for Doubtful Accounts (a contra-asset account) through an adjusting entry at the end of each period.

3. When companies write off a specific account, they debit actual uncollectibles to Allowance for Doubtful Accounts and credit that amount to Accounts Receivable.

> **HELPFUL HINT**
> In this context, *material* means significant or important to financial statement users.

**Recording Estimated Uncollectibles.** To illustrate the allowance method, assume that Hampson Furniture has credit sales of $1,200,000 in 2008. Of this amount, $200,000 remains uncollected at December 31. The credit manager estimates that $12,000 of these sales will be uncollectible. The adjusting entry to record the estimated uncollectibles is:

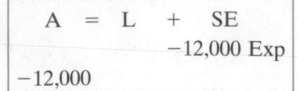

| A | = | L | + | SE |
|---|---|---|---|---|
| | | | | −12,000 Exp |
| −12,000 | | | | |

**Cash Flows**

no effect

| Dec. 31 | Bad Debts Expense | 12,000 | |
| | Allowance for Doubtful Accounts | | 12,000 |
| | (To record estimate of uncollectible accounts) | | |

Hampson reports Bad Debts Expense in the income statement as an operating expense (usually as a selling expense). Thus, the estimated uncollectibles are matched with sales in 2008. Hampson records the expense in the same year it made the sales.

Allowance for Doubtful Accounts shows the estimated amount of claims on customers that the company expects will become uncollectible in the future. Companies use a contra account instead of a direct credit to Accounts Receivable because they do not know which customers will not pay. The credit balance in the allowance account will absorb the specific write-offs when they occur. As Illustration 9-2 shows, the company deducts the allowance account from accounts receivable in the current assets section of the balance sheet.

**Illustration 9-2**
Presentation of allowance for doubtful accounts

| HAMPSON FURNITURE | | |
|---|---|---|
| Balance Sheet (partial) | | |
| Current assets | | |
| Cash | | $ 14,800 |
| **Accounts receivable** | $200,000 | |
| **Less: Allowance for doubtful accounts** | 12,000 | 188,000 |
| Merchandise inventory | | 310,000 |
| Prepaid expense | | 25,000 |
| Total current assets | | $537,800 |

**HELPFUL HINT**

Cash realizable value is sometimes referred to as *accounts receivable (net)*.

The amount of $188,000 in Illustration 9-2 represents the expected **cash realizable value** of the accounts receivable at the statement date. **Companies do not close Allowance for Doubtful Accounts at the end of the fiscal year.**

**Recording the Write-Off of an Uncollectible Account.** As described in the Feature Story, companies use various methods of collecting past-due accounts, such as letters, calls, and legal action. When they have exhausted all means of collecting a past-due account and collection appears impossible, the company should write off the account. In the credit card industry, for example, it is standard practice to write off accounts that are 210 days past due. To prevent premature or unauthorized write-offs, management should formally approve, in writing, each write-off. To maintain good internal control, companies should not give authorization to write off accounts to someone who also has daily responsibilities related to cash or receivables.

To illustrate a receivables write-off, assume that the financial vice-president of Hampson Furniture authorizes a write-off of the $500 balance owed by R. A. Ware on March 1, 2009. The entry to record the write-off is:

| A | = | L | + | SE |
|---|---|---|---|---|
| +500 | | | | |
| −500 | | | | |

**Cash Flows**

no effect

| Mar. 1 | Allowance for Doubtful Accounts | 500 | |
| | Accounts Receivable—R. A. Ware | | 500 |
| | (Write-off of R. A. Ware account) | | |

Bad Debts Expense does not increase when the write-off occurs. **Under the allowance method, companies debit every bad debt write-off to the allowance account rather than to Bad Debts Expense.** A debit to Bad Debts Expense would be incorrect because the company has already recognized the expense when it made the adjusting entry for estimated bad debts. Instead, the entry to record the write-off of an uncollectible account reduces both Accounts Receivable and the Allowance for Doubtful Accounts. After posting, the general ledger accounts will appear as in Illustration 9-3.

| Accounts Receivable | | | Allowance for Doubtful Accounts | | |
|---|---|---|---|---|---|
| Jan. 1 Bal. 200,000 | Mar. 1 | 500 | Mar. 1 | 500 | Jan. 1 Bal. 12,000 |
| Mar. 1 Bal. 199,500 | | | | | Mar. 1 Bal. 11,500 |

**Illustration 9-3**
General ledger balances after write-off

A write-off affects **only balance sheet accounts**—not income statement accounts. The write-off of the account reduces both Accounts Receivable and Allowance for Doubtful Accounts. Cash realizable value in the balance sheet, therefore, remains the same, as Illustration 9-4 shows.

| | Before Write-off | After Write-off |
|---|---|---|
| Accounts receivable | $200,000 | $199,500 |
| Allowance for doubtful accounts | 12,000 | 11,500 |
| **Cash realizable value** | **$188,000** | **$188,000** |

**Illustration 9-4**
Cash realizable value comparison

**Recovery of an Uncollectible Account.** Occasionally, a company collects from a customer after it has written off the account as uncollectible. The company makes two entries to record the recovery of a bad debt: (1) It reverses the entry made in writing off the account. This reinstates the customer's account. (2) It journalizes the collection in the usual manner.

To illustrate, assume that on July 1, R. A. Ware pays the $500 amount that Hampson had written off on March 1. These are the entries:

| | (1) | | |
|---|---|---|---|
| July 1 | Accounts Receivable—R. A. Ware | 500 | |
| | Allowance for Doubtful Accounts | | 500 |
| | (To reverse write-off of R. A. Ware account) | | |

| A | = | L | + | SE |
|---|---|---|---|---|
| +500 | | | | |
| −500 | | | | |

**Cash Flows**
no effect

| | (2) | | |
|---|---|---|---|
| July 1 | Cash | 500 | |
| | Accounts Receivable—R. A. Ware | | 500 |
| | (To record collection from R. A. Ware) | | |

| A | = | L | + | SE |
|---|---|---|---|---|
| +500 | | | | |
| −500 | | | | |

**Cash Flows**
+500

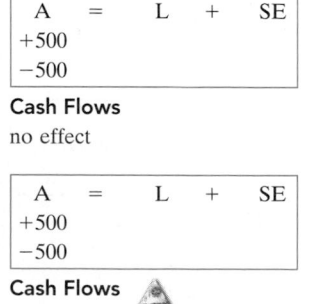

Note that the recovery of a bad debt, like the write-off of a bad debt, affects **only balance sheet accounts.** The net effect of the two entries above is a debit to Cash and a credit to Allowance for Doubtful Accounts for $500. Accounts Receivable and the Allowance for Doubtful Accounts both increase in entry (1) for two reasons: First, the company made an error in judgment when it wrote off the account receivable. Second, after R. A. Ware did pay, Accounts Receivable in the general ledger and Ware's account in the subsidiary ledger should show the collection for possible future credit purposes.

**Bases Used For Allowance Method.** To simplify the preceding explanation, we assumed we knew the amount of the expected uncollectibles. In "real life," companies must estimate that amount when they use the allowance method. Two bases are used to determine this amount: **(1) percentage of sales**, and **(2) percentage of receivables**. Both bases are generally accepted. The choice is a management decision. It depends on the relative emphasis that management wishes to give to expenses and revenues on the one hand or to cash realizable value of the accounts receivable on the other. The choice is whether to emphasize income statement or balance sheet relationships. Illustration 9-5 compares the two bases.

**Illustration 9-5**
Comparison of bases for estimating uncollectibles

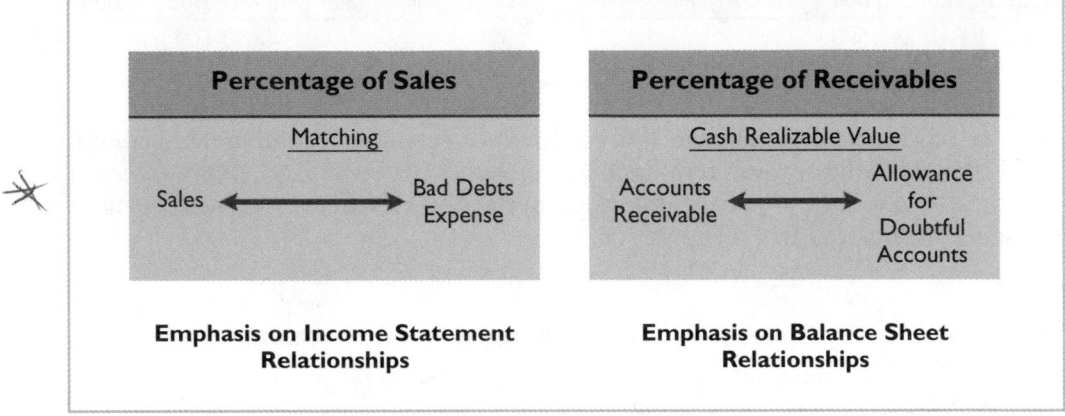

The percentage-of-sales basis results in a better matching of expenses with revenues—an income statement viewpoint. The percentage-of-receivables basis produces the better estimate of cash realizable value—a balance sheet viewpoint. Under both bases, the company must determine its past experience with bad debt losses.

*Percentage-of-Sales.* In the **percentage-of-sales basis**, management estimates what percentage of credit sales will be uncollectible. This percentage is based on past experience and anticipated credit policy.

The company applies this percentage to either total credit sales or net credit sales of the current year. To illustrate, assume that Gonzalez Company elects to use the percentage-of-sales basis. It concludes that 1% of net credit sales will become uncollectible. If net credit sales for 2008 are $800,000, the estimated bad debts expense is $8,000 (1% × $800,000). The adjusting entry is:

| A | = | L | + | SE |
|---|---|---|---|---|
| | | | | −8,000 Exp |
| −8,000 | | | | |

**Cash Flows**
no effect

| Dec. 31 | Bad Debts Expense | 8,000 | |
| | Allowance for Doubtful Accounts | | 8,000 |
| | (To record estimated bad debts for year) | | |

After the adjusting entry is posted, assuming the allowance account already has a credit balance of $1,723, the accounts of Gonzalez Company will show the following:

**Illustration 9-6**
Bad debts accounts after posting

| Bad Debts Expense | | Allowance for Doubtful Accounts | |
|---|---|---|---|
| Dec. 31 Adj. **8,000** | | Jan. 1 Bal. 1,723 | |
| | | Dec. 31 Adj. **8,000** | |
| | | Dec. 31 Bal. 9,723 | |

   **This basis of estimating uncollectibles emphasizes the matching of expenses with revenues.** As a result, Bad Debts Expense will show a direct percentage relationship to the sales base on which it is computed. **When the company makes the adjusting entry, it disregards the existing balance in Allowance for Doubtful Accounts.** The adjusted balance in this account should be a reasonable approximation of the realizable value of the receivables. If actual write-offs differ significantly from the amount estimated, the company should modify the percentage for future years.

   *Percentage-of-Receivables.*   Under the percentage-of-receivables basis, management estimates what percentage of receivables will result in losses from uncollectible accounts. The company prepares an **aging schedule**, in which it classifies customer balances by the length of time they have been unpaid. Because of its emphasis on time, the analysis is often called aging the accounts receivable. In the opening story, Whitehall-Robins prepared an aging report daily.

   After the company arranges the accounts by age, it determines the expected bad debt losses. It applies percentages based on past experience to the totals in each category. The longer a receivable is past due, the less likely it is to be collected. Thus, the estimated percentage of uncollectible debts increases as the number of days past due increases. Illustration 9-7 shows an aging schedule for Dart Company. Note that the estimated percentage uncollectible increases from 2 to 40% as the number of days past due increases.

**Illustration 9-7**
Aging schedule

### Worksheet.xls

File    Edit    View    Insert    Format    Tools    Data    Window    Help

| | A | B | C | D | E | F | G |
|---|---|---|---|---|---|---|---|
| 1 | | | | | **Number of Days Past Due** | | |
| 2 | | | **Not** | | | | |
| 3 | **Customer** | **Total** | **Yet Due** | **1–30** | **31–60** | **61–90** | **Over 90** |
| 4 | T. E. Adert | $  600 | | $  300 | | $  200 | $  100 |
| 5 | R. C. Bortz | 300 | $  300 | | | | |
| 6 | B. A. Carl | 450 | | 200 | $  250 | | |
| 7 | O. L. Diker | 700 | 500 | | | 200 | |
| 8 | T. O. Ebbet | 600 | | | 300 | | 300 |
| 9 | Others | 36,950 | 26,200 | 5,200 | 2,450 | 1,600 | 1,500 |
| 10 | | $39,600 | $27,000 | $5,700 | $3,000 | $2,000 | $1,900 |
| 11 | Estimated Percentage Uncollectible | | 2% | 4% | 10% | 20% | 40% |
| 12 | Total Estimated Bad Debts | $ 2,228 | $  540 | $  228 | $  300 | $  400 | $  760 |
| 13 | | | | | | | |

**HELPFUL HINT**
The older categories have higher percentages because the longer an account is past due, the less likely it is to be collected.

   Total estimated bad debts for Dart Company ($2,228) represent the amount of existing customer claims the company expects will become uncollectible in the future. This amount represents the **required balance** in Allowance for Doubtful Accounts at the balance sheet date. **The amount of the bad debt adjusting entry is the difference between the required balance and the existing balance in the allowance account.** If the trial balance shows Allowance for Doubtful Accounts with a credit balance of $528, the company will make an adjusting entry for $1,700 ($2,228 − $528), as shown here.

| | | | | |
|---|---|---|---|---|
| Dec. 31 | Bad Debts Expense | | 1,700 | |
| | Allowance for Doubtful Accounts | | | 1,700 |
| | (To adjust allowance account to total estimated uncollectibles) | | | |

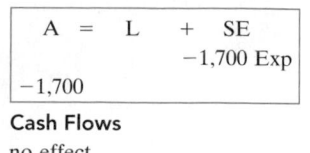

$$A = L + SE$$
−1,700         −1,700 Exp

**Cash Flows**
no effect

After the adjusting entry is posted, the accounts of the Dart Company will show:

**Illustration 9-8**
Bad debts accounts after posting

| Bad Debts Expense | | Allowance for Doubtful Accounts | |
|---|---|---|---|
| Dec. 31 Adj. **1,700** | | Bal. | 528 |
| | | Dec. 31 Adj. **1,700** | |
| | | Bal. | 2,228 |

Occasionally the allowance account will have a **debit balance** prior to adjustment. This occurs when write-offs during the year have exceeded previous provisions for bad debts. In such a case the company **adds the debit balance to the required balance** when it makes the adjusting entry. Thus, if there had been a $500 debit balance in the allowance account before adjustment, the adjusting entry would have been for $2,728 ($2,228 + $500) to arrive at a credit balance of $2,228. The percentage-of-receivables basis will normally result in the better approximation of cash realizable value.

# INVESTOR INSIGHT

### When Investors Ignore Warning Signs

Recently Nortel Networks announced that half of its previous year's earnings were "fake." Should investors have seen this coming? Well, there were issues in its annual report that should at least have caused investors to ask questions. The company had cut its allowance for doubtful accounts on all receivables from $1,253 million to $544 million, even though its total balance of receivables remained relatively unchanged.

This reduction in bad debts expense was responsible for a very large part of the company's earnings that year. At the time it was unclear whether Nortel might have set the reserves too high originally and needed to reduce them, or whether it slashed the allowance to artificially boost earnings. But one thing is certain—when a company makes an accounting change of this magnitude, investors need to ask questions.

*Source:* Jonathan Weil, "Outside Audit: At Nortel, Warning Signs Existed Months Ago," *Wall Street Journal*, May, 18, 2004, p. C3.

When would it be appropriate for a company to lower its allowance for doubtful accounts as a percentage of its receivables?

## Before You Go On...

### REVIEW IT
1. What is the primary criticism of the direct write-off method?
2. Explain the difference between the percentage-of-sales and the percentage-of-receivables methods.
3. What percentage does PepsiCo's allowance for doubtful accounts represent as a percent of its gross receivables? (*Hint:* See PepsiCo's Note 14.) The answer to this question appears on page 423.

### DO IT
Brule Co. has been in business 5 years. The ledger at the end of the current year shows: Accounts Receivable $30,000, Sales $180,000, and Allowance for

Doubtful Accounts with a debit balance of $2,000. Bad debts are estimated to be 10% of receivables. Prepare the entry to adjust the Allowance for Doubtful Accounts.

### Action Plan
- Report receivables at their cash (net) realizable value.
- Estimate the amount the company does not expect to collect.
- Consider the existing balance in the allowance account when using the percentage-of-receivables basis.

**Solution**   The following entry should be made to bring the balance in the Allowance for Doubtful Accounts up to a balance of $3,000 (0.1 × $30,000):

| | | |
|---|---|---|
| Bad Debts Expense | 5,000 | |
|    Allowance for Doubtful Accounts | | 5,000 |
|      (To record estimate of uncollectible accounts) | | |

Related exercise material: *BE9-3, BE9-4, BE9-5, BE9-6, BE9-7, E9-3, E9-4, E9-5, and E9-6.*

*The Navigator*

# Disposing of Accounts Receivable

In the normal course of events, companies collect accounts receivable in cash and remove the receivables from the books. However, as credit sales and receivables have grown in significance, the "normal course of events" has changed. Companies now frequently sell their receivables to another company for cash, thereby shortening the cash-to-cash operating cycle.

> **STUDY OBJECTIVE 4**
> Describe the entries to record the disposition of accounts receivable.

Companies sell receivables for two major reasons. First, **they may be the only reasonable source of cash.** When money is tight, companies may not be able to borrow money in the usual credit markets. Or, if money is available, the cost of borrowing may be prohibitive.

A second reason for selling receivables is that **billing and collection are often time-consuming and costly.** It is often easier for a retailer to sell the receivables to another party with expertise in billing and collection matters. Credit card companies such as MasterCard, Visa, and Discover specialize in billing and collecting accounts receivable.

## SALE OF RECEIVABLES

A common sale of receivables is a sale to a factor. A **factor** is a finance company or bank that buys receivables from businesses and then collects the payments directly from the customers. Factoring is a multibillion dollar business.

Factoring arrangements vary widely. Typically the factor charges a commission to the company that is selling the receivables. This fee ranges from 1–3% of the amount of receivables purchased. To illustrate, assume that Hendredon Furniture factors $600,000 of receivables to Federal Factors. Federal Factors assesses a service charge of 2% of the amount of receivables sold. The journal entry to record the sale by Hendredon Furniture is as follows.

| | | |
|---|---|---|
| Cash | 588,000 | |
| Service Charge Expense (2% × $600,000) | 12,000 | |
|    Accounts Receivable | | 600,000 |
|      (To record the sale of accounts receivable) | | |

| A | = | L | + | SE |
|---|---|---|---|---|
| +588,000 | | | | |
| | | | | −12,000 Exp |
| −600,000 | | | | |

**Cash Flows**
+588,000

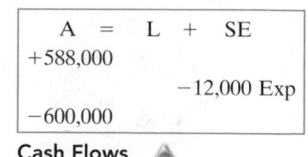

If the company often sells its receivables, it records the service charge expense (such as that incurred by Hendredon) as selling expense. If the company infrequently sells receivables, it may report this amount in the "Other expenses and losses" section of the income statement.

### CREDIT CARD SALES

Over one billion credit cards are in use in the United States—more than three credit cards for every man, woman, and child in this country. Visa, MasterCard, and American Express are the national credit cards that most individuals use. Three parties are involved when national credit cards are used in retail sales: (1) the credit card issuer, who is independent of the retailer, (2) the retailer, and (3) the customer. A retailer's acceptance of a national credit card is another form of selling (factoring) the receivable.

Illustration 9-9 shows the major advantages of national credit cards to the retailer. In exchange for these advantages, the retailer pays the credit card issuer a fee of 2–6% of the invoice price for its services.

**Illustration 9-9**
Advantages of credit cards to the retailer

### Accounting for Credit Card Sales.

The retailer generally considers sales from the use of national credit card sales as *cash sales.* The retailer must pay to the bank that issues the card a fee of 2 to 4% for processing the transactions. The retailer records the credit card slips in a similar manner as checks deposited from a cash sale.

To illustrate, Anita Ferreri purchases $1,000 of compact discs for her restaurant from Karen Kerr Music Co., using her Visa First Bank Card. First Bank charges a service fee of 3%. The entry to record this transaction by Karen Kerr Music is as follows.

| | | |
|---|---|---|
| Cash | 970 | |
| Service Charge Expense | 30 | |
|     Sales | | 1,000 |
|       (To record Visa credit card sales) | | |

| A | = | L | + | SE |
|---|---|---|---|---|
| +970 | | | | |
| | | | | −30 Exp |
| | | | | +1,000 Rcv |

**Cash Flows**
+970

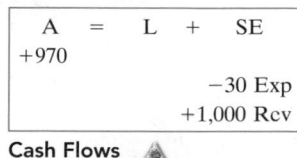

# ACCOUNTING ACROSS THE ORGANIZATION

## How Does a Credit Card Work?

Most of you know how to *use* a credit card, but do you know what happens in the transaction and how the transaction is processed? Suppose that you use a Visa card to purchase some new ties at Nordstrom. The salesperson swipes your card, and the swiping machine reads the information on the magnetic strip on the back of the card. The salesperson then types in the amount of the purchase. The machine contacts the Visa computer, which routes the call back to the bank that issued your Visa card. The issuing bank verifies that the account exists, that the card is not stolen, and that you have not exceeded your credit limit. At this point, the slip is printed, which you sign.

Visa acts as the clearing agent for the transaction. It transfers funds from the issuing bank to Nordstrom's bank account. Generally this transfer of funds, from sale to the receipt of funds in the merchant's account, takes two to three days.

In the meantime, Visa puts a pending charge on your account for the amount of the tie purchase; that amount counts immediately against your available credit limit. At the end of the billing period, Visa sends you an invoice (your credit card bill) which shows the various charges you made, and the amounts that Visa expended on your behalf, for the month. You then must "pay the piper" for your stylish new ties.

**?** Assume that Nordstrom prepares a bank reconciliation at the end of each month. If some credit card sales have not been processed by the bank, how should Nordstrom treat these transactions on its bank reconciliation?

## Before You Go On...

### REVIEW IT

1. Why do companies sell their receivables?
2. What is the journal entry when a company sells its receivables to a factor?
3. How do companies report sales using Visa or MasterCard?

### DO IT

Mehl Wholesalers Co. has been expanding faster than it can raise capital. According to its local banker, the company has reached its debt ceiling. Mehl's customers are slow in paying (60–90 days), but its suppliers (creditors) are demanding 30-day payment. Mehl has a cash flow problem.

Mehl needs $120,000 in cash to safely cover next Friday's employee payroll. Its balance of outstanding receivables totals $750,000. What might Mehl do to alleviate this cash crunch? Record the entry that Mehl would make when it raises the needed cash.

**Action Plan**

- To speed up the collection of cash, sell receivables to a factor.
- Calculate service charge expense as a percentage of the factored receivables.

**Solution**   Assuming that Mehl Wholesalers factors $125,000 of its accounts receivable at a 1% service charge, it would make the following entry.

| | | |
|---|---:|---:|
| Cash | 123,750 | |
| Service Charge Expense | 1,250 | |
|     Accounts Receivable | | 125,000 |
|       (To record sale of receivables to factor) | | |

Related exercise material: *BE9-8, E9-7, E9-8, and E9-9.*

✓ The Navigator

# NOTES RECEIVABLE

Companies may also grant credit in exchange for a promissory note. A **promissory note** is a written promise to pay a specified amount of money on demand or at a definite time. Notes receivable give the payee a stronger legal claim to assets than accounts receivable. Promissory notes may be used: (1) when individuals and companies lend or borrow money, (2) when the amount of the transaction and the credit period exceed normal limits, or (3) in settlement of accounts receivable.

In a promissory note, the party making the promise to pay is called the **maker**. The party to whom payment is to be made is called the **payee**. The note may specifically identify the payee by name or may designate the payee simply as the bearer of the note. In the note shown in Illustration 9-10, Calhoun Company is the maker, Wilma Company is the payee. To Wilma Company, the promissory note is a note receivable; to Calhoun Company, it is a note payable.

**Illustration 9-10**
Promissory note

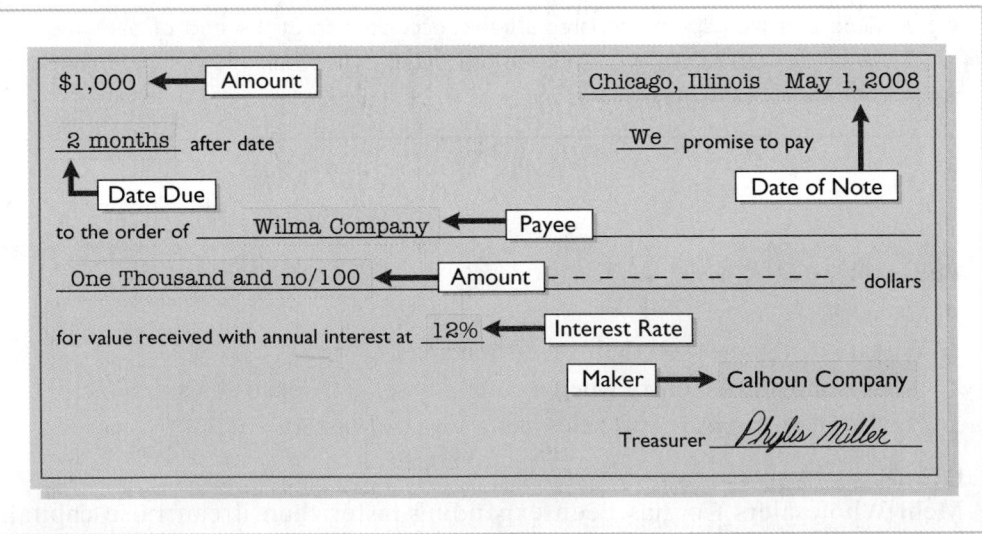

Like accounts receivable, notes receivable can be readily sold to another party. Promissory notes are negotiable instruments (as are checks), which means that they can be transferred to another party by endorsement.

Companies frequently accept notes receivable from customers who need to extend the payment of an account receivable. They often require such notes from high-risk customers. In some industries (such as the pleasure boat industry), all credit sales are supported by notes. The majority of notes originate from loans.

The basic issues in accounting for notes receivable are the same as those for accounts receivable:

1. **Recognizing** notes receivable.
2. **Valuing** notes receivable.
3. **Disposing of** notes receivable.

On the following pages, we will look at these issues. Before we do, we need to consider two issues that did not apply to accounts receivable: maturity date and computing interest.

## Determining the Maturity Date

When the life of a note is expressed in terms of months, you find the date when it matures by counting the months from the date of issue. For example, the maturity date of a three-month note dated May 1 is August 1. A note drawn on the last day of a month matures on the last day of a subsequent month. That is, a July 31 note due in two months matures on September 30.

When the due date is stated in terms of days, you need to count the exact number of days to determine the maturity date. In counting, **omit the date the note is issued but include the due date**. For example, the maturity date of a 60-day note dated July 17 is September 15, computed as follows.

| Term of note | | 60 days |
|---|---|---|
| July (31−17) | 14 | |
| August | 31 | 45 |
| **Maturity date: September** | | **15** |

**Illustration 9-11**
Computation of maturity date

Illustration 9-12 shows three ways of stating the maturity date of a promissory note.

On demand

On a stated date

At the end of a stated period of time

**Illustration 9-12**
Maturity date of different notes

## Computing Interest

As indicated in Chapter 3, the basic formula for computing interest on an interest-bearing note is:

$$\text{Face Value of Note} \times \text{Annual Interest Rate} \times \text{Time in Terms of One Year} = \text{Interest}$$

The interest rate specified in a note is an **annual** rate of interest. There are many different ways to calculate interest. The time factor in the formula in Illustration 9-13 expresses the fraction of a year that the note is outstanding. When the maturity date is stated in days, the time factor is often the number of days divided by 360. When the due date is stated in months, the time factor is the number of months divided by 12. Illustration 9-14 shows computation of interest for various time periods.

| Terms of Note | Interest Computation |
| --- | --- |
| | **Face × Rate × Time = Interest** |
| $ 730, 18%, 120 days | $ 730 × 18% × 120/360 = $ 43.80 |
| $1,000, 15%, 6 months | $1,000 × 15% × 6/12 = $ 75.00 |
| $2,000, 12%, 1 year | $2,000 × 12% × 1/1 = $240.00 |

The computation above assumed 360 days for the length of the year. Financial instruments actually use 365 days. In order to simplify calculations in our illustrations, we have assumed 360 days. *For homework problems, assume 360 days.*

## Recognizing Notes Receivable

To illustrate the basic entry for notes receivable, we will use the $1,000, two-month, 12% promissory note on page 398. Assuming that Calhoun Company wrote the note to settle an open account, Wilma Company makes the following entry for the receipt of the note.

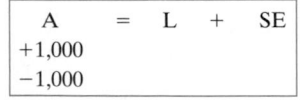

| A | = | L | + | SE |
| --- | --- | --- | --- | --- |
| +1,000 | | | | |
| −1,000 | | | | |

**Cash Flows**
no effect

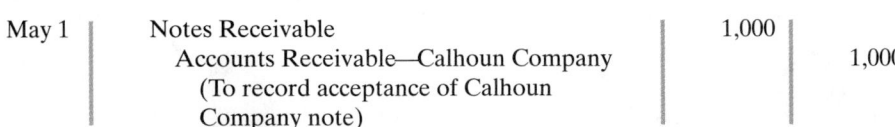

| May 1 | Notes Receivable | 1,000 | |
| --- | --- | --- | --- |
| | Accounts Receivable—Calhoun Company | | 1,000 |
| | (To record acceptance of Calhoun Company note) | | |

The company records the note receivable at its **face value,** the amount shown on the face of the note. No interest revenue is reported when the note is accepted, because the revenue recognition principle does not recognize revenue until earned. Interest is earned (accrued) as time passes.

If a company lends money using a note, the entry is a debit to Notes Receivable and a credit to Cash in the amount of the loan.

## Valuing Notes Receivable

Valuing short-term notes receivable is the same as valuing accounts receivable. Like accounts receivable, companies report short-term notes receivable at their **cash (net) realizable value.** The notes receivable allowance account is Allowance for Doubtful Accounts. The estimations involved in determining cash realizable value and in recording bad debts expense and the related allowance are done similarly to accounts receivable.

## Disposing of Notes Receivable

Notes may be held to their maturity date, at which time the maker must pay the face value plus accrued interest. Sometimes the maker of the note defaults and the payee must make an adjustment to the accounts. At other times the holder of the note speeds up the conversion to cash by selling the note receivable.

### HONOR OF NOTES RECEIVABLE

A note is **honored** when its maker pays it in full at its maturity date. For an interest-bearing note, the amount due at maturity is the face value of the note plus interest for the length of time specified on the note.

To illustrate, assume that Betty Co. lends Wayne Higley Inc. $10,000 on June 1, accepting a five-month, 9% interest-bearing note. Interest will be $375 ($10,000 $\times$ 9% $\times$ 5/12). The maturity value will be $10,375. To obtain payment, Betty Co. (the payee) must present the note either to Wayne Higley Inc. (the maker) or to the maker's designated agent, such as a bank. Assuming that Betty Co. presents the note to Wayne Higley Inc. on the maturity date, Betty Co.'s entry to record the collection is:

| Nov. 1 | Cash | 10,375 | |
| | Notes Receivable | | 10,000 |
| | Interest Revenue | | 375 |
| | (To record collection of Higley Inc. note) | | |

| A | = | L | + | SE |
|---|---|---|---|---|
| +10,375 | | | | |
| −10,000 | | | | |
| | | | | +375 Rev |

**Cash Flows**
+10,375

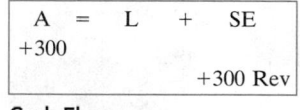

If Betty Co. prepares financial statements as of September 30, it must accrue interest. In this case, Betty Co. would make the adjusting entry shown below to record 4 months' interest ($300).

| Sept. 30 | Interest Receivable ($10,000 $\times$ 9% $\times$ 4/12) | 300 | |
| | Interest Revenue | | 300 |
| | (To accrue 4 months' interest) | | |

| A | = | L | + | SE |
|---|---|---|---|---|
| +300 | | | | |
| | | | | +300 Rev |

**Cash Flows**
no effect

When interest has been accrued, the company must credit Interest Receivable at maturity. In addition, since an additional month has passed, it must record one month of interest revenue. The entry by Betty Co. to record the honoring of the Wayne Higley Inc. note on November 1 is:

| Nov. 1 | Cash | 10,375 | |
| | Notes Receivable | | 10,000 |
| | Interest Receivable | | 300 |
| | Interest Revenue ($10,000 $\times$ 9% $\times$ 1/12) | | 75 |
| | (To record collection of note at maturity) | | |

| A | = | L | + | SE |
|---|---|---|---|---|
| +10,375 | | | | |
| −10,000 | | | | |
| −300 | | | | |
| | | | | +75 Rev |

**Cash Flows**
+10,375

In this case, Betty Co. credits Interest Receivable because the receivable was established in the adjusting entry of September 30.

### DISHONOR OF NOTES RECEIVABLE

A **dishonored note** is a note that is not paid in full at maturity. A dishonored note receivable is no longer negotiable. However, the payee still has a claim against the maker of the note. Therefore the note holder usually transfers the Notes Receivable account to an Account Receivable.

To illustrate, assume that Wayne Higley Inc. on November 1 indicates that it cannot pay at the present time. The entry to record the dishonor of the note depends on whether Betty Co. expects eventual collection. If it does expect eventual collection, Betty Co. debits the amount due (face value and interest) on the note to Accounts Receivable. It would make the following entry at the time the note is dishonored (assuming no previous accrual of interest).

| A | = | L | + | SE |
|---|---|---|---|---|
| +10,375 | | | | |
| −10,000 | | | | |
| | | | | +375 Rev |

**Cash Flows**
no effect

| Nov. 1 | Accounts Receivable—Wayne Higley Inc. | 10,375 | |
| | Notes Receivable | | 10,000 |
| | Interest Revenue | | 375 |
| | (To record the dishonor of Higley Inc. note) | | |

If instead, on November 1, there is no hope of collection, the note holder would write off the face value of the note by debiting the Allowance for Doubtful Accounts. No interest revenue would be recorded because collection will not occur.

# ACCOUNTING ACROSS THE ORGANIZATION

### Who Gets Credit?

Management must decide to whom it will grant credit. This is one of the hardest, and most critical, decisions that it makes. Consider the case of Mitsubishi Motors. It had been floundering, reporting large losses for a number of years in a row. Then management came up with what appeared to be a great plan. It began a marketing campaign aimed at giving Mitsubishi a hip image (think flashy ads with loud music), thus making its vehicles attractive to single people in their early twenties. The company combined this campaign with easy credit-terms—so called "zero-zero-zero" deals. This meant no down-payment, no payments for the first six months, and 0% financing.

The plan worked great—sort of. Sales took off. But then the twenty-somethings started defaulting on their loans. Soon Mitsubishi's losses were even bigger than before. It has since refocused its ads and credit terms. It now focuses on people who are "young at heart" (as opposed to just young)—and "economically safer."

**Source:** Todd Zaun, "Bad Loans Bump Mitsubishi Motors Off Road to Recovery," *Wall Street Journal*, November 12, 2003.

 How would reported net income likely differ during the first year of this promotion if Mitsubishi used the direct write-off method versus the allowance method?

## SALE OF NOTES RECEIVABLE

The accounting for the sale of notes receivable is recorded similarly to the sale of accounts receivable. The accounting entries for the sale of notes receivable are left for a more advanced course.

### Before You Go On...

**REVIEW IT**
1. What is the basic formula for computing interest?
2. At what value do companies report notes receivable on the balance sheet?
3. Explain the difference between honoring and dishonoring a note receivable.

**DO IT**

Gambit Stores accepts from Leonard Co. a $3,400, 90-day, 12% note dated May 10 in settlement of Leonard's overdue account. What is the maturity date of the note? What is the entry made by Gambit at the maturity date, assuming Leonard pays the note and interest in full at that time?

**Action Plan**

- Count the exact number of days to determine the maturity date. Omit the date the note is issued, but include the due date.
- Determine whether interest was accrued. The entry here assumes that no interest has been previously accrued on this note.

**Solution**   The maturity date is August 8, computed as follows.

| | | |
|---|---|---|
| Term of note: | | 90 days |
| May (31 – 10) | 21 | |
| June | 30 | |
| July | 31 | 82 |
| Maturity date: August | | 8 |

The interest payable at maturity date is $102, computed as follows.

$$\text{Face} \ \times \ \text{Rate} \times \text{Time} \ = \text{Interest}$$
$$\$3,400 \ \times \ 12\% \ \times 90/360 = \ \$102$$

The entry recorded by Gambit Stores at the maturity date is:

| | | |
|---|---|---|
| Cash | 3,502 | |
|     Notes Receivable | | 3,400 |
|     Interest Revenue | | 102 |
|     (To record collection of Leonard note) | | |

Related exercise material: *BE9-9, BE9-10, BE9-11, E9-10, E9-11, E9-12, and E9-13.*

✔ *The Navigator*

# STATEMENT PRESENTATION AND ANALYSIS

## ✱Presentation

Companies should identify in the balance sheet or in the notes to the financial statements each of the major types of receivables. Short-term receivables appear in the current assets section of the balance sheet, below short-term investments. Short-term investments appear before receivables, because short-term investments are more liquid (nearer to cash). Companies report both the gross amount of receivables and the allowance for doubtful accounts.

In a multiple-step income statement, companies report bad debts expense and service charge expense as selling expenses in the operating expenses section. Interest revenue appears under "Other revenues and gains" in the nonoperating activities section of the income statement.

**STUDY OBJECTIVE 9**

Explain the statement presentation and analysis of receivables.

## Analysis

Investors and corporate managers compute financial ratios to evaluate the liquidity of a company's accounts receivable. They use the **accounts receivable turnover ratio** to assess the liquidity of the receivables. This ratio measures the number of times, on average, the company collects accounts receivable during the period. It is computed by dividing net credit sales (net sales less cash sales) by the average net accounts receivable during the year. Unless seasonal factors are significant, average net accounts receivable outstanding can be computed from the beginning and ending balances of net accounts receivable.

For example, in a recent year Cisco Systems had net sales of $24,801 million for the year. It had a beginning accounts receivable (net) balance of $1,825 million and an ending accounts receivable (net) balance of $2,216 million. Assuming that Cisco's sales were all on credit, its accounts receivable turnover ratio is computed as follows.

**Illustration 9-15**
Accounts receivable turnover ratio and computation

| Net Credit Sales | ÷ | Average Net Accounts Receivable | = | Accounts Receivable Turnover |
|---|---|---|---|---|
| $24,801 | ÷ | $\dfrac{\$1,825 + \$2,216}{2}$ | = | 12.3 times |

The result indicates an accounts receivable turnover ratio of 12.3 times per year. The higher the turnover ratio the more liquid the company's receivables.

A variant of the accounts receivable turnover ratio that makes the liquidity even more evident is its conversion into an **average collection period** in terms of days. This is done by dividing the turnover ratio into 365 days. For example, Cisco's turnover of 12.3 times is divided into 365 days, as shown in Illustration 9-16, to obtain approximately 29.7 days. This means that it takes Cisco about 30 days to collect its accounts receivable.

**Illustration 9-16**
Average collection period for receivables formula and computation

| Days in Year | ÷ | Accounts Receivable Turnover | = | Average Collection Period in Days |
|---|---|---|---|---|
| 365 days | ÷ | 12.3 times | = | 29.7 days |

Companies frequently use the average collection period to assess the effectiveness of a company's credit and collection policies. The general rule is that the collection period should not greatly exceed the credit term period (that is, the time allowed for payment).

## Before You Go On...

### REVIEW IT
1. Explain where companies report accounts and notes receivable on the balance sheet.
2. Where do companies report bad debts expense, service charge expense, and interest revenue on the multiple-step income statement?

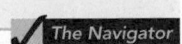

 Be sure to read **ALL ABOUT YOU:** *Should You Be Carrying Plastic?* on the next page for information on how topics in this chapter apply to you.

## Should You Be Carrying Plastic?

Smart business people carefully consider their use of credit. They evaluate who they lend to, and how they finance their own operations. They know that getting overextended on credit can destroy their business.

Individuals need to evaluate their personal credit positions using the same thought processes used by business people. Some of you might consider the idea of not having a credit card a ridiculous proposition. But the reality is that the misuse of credit cards brings financial hardship to millions of Americans each year. Credit card companies aggressively market their cards with images of glamour and happiness. But there isn't much glamour in paying an 18% to 21% interest rate, and there is very little happiness to be found in filing for personal bankruptcy.

### ❂ Some Facts

* About 70% of undergraduates at 4-year colleges carry at least one credit card in their own name. Approximately 22% of college students got their first credit cards in high school.

* The average monthly debt on a college student's charge account, according to one study, is close to $2,000.

* In a recent year, Americans charged more than $1 trillion in purchases with their credit cards. That was more than they spent in cash.

* During one quarter in 2006, the percentage of delinquent credit card payments rose to 5% from 4.3%. Card write-offs increased from 5.6% to 6.4%. Until this year, both numbers were declining.

* Significant increases in consumer bankruptcy filings occurred in every region of the country. There were 2,043,535 new filings in 2005, up 31.6% from 1,552,967 in 2004—that is, one in every 53 households filed a bankruptcy petition.

### ❂ About the Numbers

Presented below is a chart that shows the major causes of personal financial problems. Note the excessive use of credit, which is cited as the number-one cause. This often translates into addiction to credit cards.

**Causes of Personal Financial Problems**

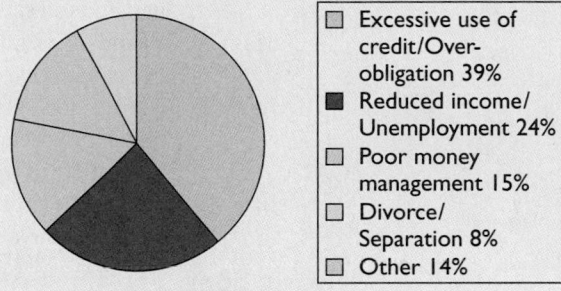

- ☐ Excessive use of credit/Over-obligation 39%
- ■ Reduced income/Unemployment 24%
- ☐ Poor money management 15%
- ☐ Divorce/Separation 8%
- ☐ Other 14%

**Source:** Debt Solutions of America, *www.becomedebtfree.com* (accessed May 2006).

### ❂ What Do You Think?

Should you cut up your credit card(s)?

**YES:** Americans are carrying huge personal debt burdens. Credit cards encourage unnecessary, spontaneous expenditures. The interest rates on credit cards are extremely high, which causes debt problems to escalate exponentially.

**NO:** Credit cards are a necessity for transactions in today's economy. In fact, many transactions are difficult or impossible to carry out without a credit card. People should learn to use credit cards responsibly.

**Sources:** Debtsmart, *www.debtsmart.com/pages/debt_stats.html*; Robin Marantz Henig, "Teen Credit Cards Actually Teach Responsibility," *USAToday.com*, July 30, 2001.

### Demonstration Problem

The following selected transactions relate to Falcetto Company.

Mar. 1 Sold $20,000 of merchandise to Potter Company, terms 2/10, n/30.
11 Received payment in full from Potter Company for balance due.
12 Accepted Juno Company's $20,000, 6-month, 12% note for balance due.
13 Made Falcetto Company credit card sales for $13,200.
15 Made Visa credit card sales totaling $6,700. A 3% service fee is charged by Visa.

Apr. 11 Sold accounts receivable of $8,000 to Harcot Factor. Harcot Factor assesses a service charge of 2% of the amount of receivables sold.
13 Received collections of $8,200 on Falcetto Company credit card sales and added finance charges of 1.5% to the remaining balances.

May 10 Wrote off as uncollectible $16,000 of accounts receivable. Falcetto uses the percentage-of-sales basis to estimate bad debts.

June 30 Credit sales recorded during the first 6 months total $2,000,000. The bad debt percentage is 1% of credit sales. At June 30, the balance in the allowance account is $3,500.

July 16 One of the accounts receivable written off in May was from J. Simon, who pays the amount due, $4,000, in full.

### Instructions

Prepare the journal entries for the transactions.

### Solution

| | | | |
|---|---|---|---|
| Mar. 1 | Accounts Receivable–Potter | 20,000 | |
| | Sales | | 20,000 |
| | (To record sales on account) | | |
| | | | |
| Mar. 11 | Cash | 19,600 | |
| | Sales Discounts (2% × $20,000) | 400 | |
| | Accounts Receivable—Potter | | 20,000 |
| | (To record collection of accounts receivable) | | |
| | | | |
| Mar. 12 | Notes Receivable | 20,000 | |
| | Accounts Receivable—Juno | | 20,000 |
| | (To record acceptance of Juno Company note) | | |
| | | | |
| Mar. 13 | Accounts Receivable | 13,200 | |
| | Sales | | 13,200 |
| | (To record company credit card sales) | | |
| | | | |
| Mar. 15 | Cash | 6,499 | |
| | Service Charge Expense (3% × $6,700) | 201 | |
| | Sales | | 6,700 |
| | (To record credit card sales) | | |
| | | | |
| Apr. 11 | Cash | 7,840 | |
| | Service Charge Expense (2% × $8,000) | 160 | |
| | Accounts Receivable | | 8,000 |
| | (To record sale of receivables to factor) | | |
| | | | |
| Apr. 13 | Cash | 8,200 | |
| | Accounts Receivable | | 8,200 |
| | (To record collection of accounts receivable) | | |

### action plan

✔ Generally, record accounts receivable at invoice price.

✔ Recognize that sales returns and allowances and cash discounts reduce the amount received on accounts receivable.

✔ Record a service charge expense on the seller's books when accounts receivable are sold.

✔ Prepare an adjusting entry for bad debts expense.

✔ Ignore any balance in the allowance account under the percentage-of-sales basis. Recognize the balance in the allowance account under the percentage-of-receivables basis.

✔ Record write-offs of accounts receivable only in balance sheet accounts.

| | | | | |
|---|---|---|---|---|
| | Accounts Receivable [($13,200 − $8,200) × 1.5%] | | 75 | |
| |    Interest Revenue | | | 75 |
| |    (To record interest on amount due) | | | |
| May 10 | Allowance for Doubtful Accounts | | 16,000 | |
| |    Accounts Receivable | | | 16,000 |
| |    (To record write-off of accounts receivable) | | | |
| June 30 | Bad Debts Expense ($2,000,000 × 1%) | | 20,000 | |
| |    Allowance for Doubtful Accounts | | | 20,000 |
| |    (To record estimate of uncollectible accounts) | | | |
| July 16 | Accounts Receivable—J. Simon | | 4,000 | |
| |    Allowance for Doubtful Accounts | | | 4,000 |
| |    (To reverse write-off of accounts receivable) | | | |
| | Cash | | 4,000 | |
| |    Accounts Receivable—J. Simon | | | 4,000 |
| |    (To record collection of accounts receivable) | | | |

✔ *The Navigator*

# SUMMARY OF STUDY OBJECTIVES

1 **Identify the different types of receivables.** Receivables are frequently classified as (1) accounts, (2) notes, and (3) other. Accounts receivable are amounts customers owe on account. Notes receivable are claims for which lenders issue formal instruments of credit as proof of the debt. Other receivables include nontrade receivables such as interest receivable, loans to company officers, advances to employees, and income taxes refundable.

2 **Explain how companies recognize accounts receivable.** Companies record accounts receivable at invoice price. They are reduced by sales returns and allowances. Cash discounts reduce the amount received on accounts receivable. When interest is charged on a past due receivable, the company adds this interest to the accounts receivable balance and recognizes it as interest revenue.

3 **Distinguish between the methods and bases companies use to value accounts receivable.** There are two methods of accounting for uncollectible accounts: the allowance method and the direct write-off method. Companies may use either the percentage-of-sales or the percentage-of-receivables basis to estimate uncollectible accounts using the allowance method. The percentage-of-sales basis emphasizes the matching principle. The percentage-of-receivables basis emphasizes the cash realizable value of the accounts receivable. An aging schedule is often used with this basis.

4 **Describe the entries to record the disposition of accounts receivable.** When a company collects an account receivable, it credits Accounts Receivable. When a company sells (factors) an account receivable, a service charge expense reduces the amount received.

5 **Compute the maturity date of and interest on notes receivable.** For a note stated in months, the maturity date is found by counting the months from the date of issue. For a note stated in days, the number of days is counted, omitting the issue date and counting the due date. The formula for computing interest is: Face value × Interest rate × Time.

6 **Explain how companies recognize notes receivable.** Companies record notes receivable at face value. In some cases, it is necessary to accrue interest prior to maturity. In this case, companies debit Interest Receivable and credit Interest Revenue.

7 **Describe how companies value notes receivable.** As with accounts receivable, companies report notes receivable at their cash (net) realizable value. The notes receivable allowance account is the Allowance for Doubtful Accounts. The computation and estimations involved in valuing notes receivable at cash realizable value, and in recording the proper amount of bad debts expense and related allowance are similar to those for accounts receivable.

8 **Describe the entries to record the disposition of notes receivable.** Notes can be held to maturity. At that time the face value plus accrued interest is due, and the note is removed from the accounts. In many cases, the holder of the note speeds up the conversion by selling the receivable to another party (a factor). In some situations, the maker of the note dishonors the note (defaults), in which case the company transfers the note and accrued interest to an account receivable or writes off the note.

9 **Explain the statement presentation and analysis of receivables.** Companies should identify in the balance sheet

or in the notes to the financial statements each major type of receivable. Short-term receivables are considered current assets. Companies report the gross amount of receivables and the allowance for doubtful accounts. They report bad debts and service charge expenses in the multiple-step income statement as operating (selling) expenses; interest revenue appears under other revenues and gains in the nonoperating activities section of the statement. Managers and investors evaluate accounts receivable for liquidity by computing a turnover ratio and an average collection period.

# GLOSSARY

**Accounts receivable** Amounts owed by customers on account. (p. 386).

**Accounts receivable turnover ratio** A measure of the liquidity of accounts receivable; computed by dividing net credit sales by average net accounts receivable. (p. 403).

**Aging the accounts receivable** The analysis of customer balances by the length of time they have been unpaid. (p. 393).

**Allowance method** A method of accounting for bad debts that involves estimating uncollectible accounts at the end of each period. (p. 389).

**Average collection period** The average amount of time that a receivable is outstanding; calculated by dividing 365 days by the accounts receivables turnover ratio. (p. 404).

**Bad Debts Expense** An expense account to record uncollectible receivables. (p. 388).

**Cash (net) realizable value** The net amount a company expects to receive in cash. (p. 389).

**Direct write-off method** A method of accounting for bad debts that involves expensing accounts at the time they are determined to be uncollectible. (p. 388).

**Dishonored note** A note that is not paid in full at maturity. (p. 401).

**Factor** A finance company or bank that buys receivables from businesses and then collects the payments directly from the customers. (p. 395).

**Maker** The party in a promissory note who is making the promise to pay. (p. 398).

**Notes receivable** Claims for which formal instruments of credit are issued as proof of the debt. (p. 386).

**Other receivables** Various forms of nontrade receivables, such as interest receivable and income taxes refundable. (p. 386).

**Payee** The party to whom payment of a promissory note is to be made. (p. 398).

**Percentage-of-receivables basis** Management estimates what percentage of receivables will result in losses from uncollectible accounts. (p. 393).

**Percentage-of-sales basis** Management estimates what percentage of credit sales will be uncollectible. (p. 392).

**Promissory note** A written promise to pay a specified amount of money on demand or at a definite time. (p. 398).

**Receivables** Amounts due from individuals and other companies. (p. 386).

**Trade receivables** Notes and accounts receivable that result from sales transactions. (p. 386).

# SELF-STUDY QUESTIONS

*Answers are at the end of the chapter.*

(SO 2) **1.** Buehler Company on June 15 sells merchandise on account to Chaz Co. for $1,000, terms 2/10, n/30. On June 20, Chaz Co. returns merchandise worth $300 to Buehler Company. On June 24, payment is received from Chaz Co. for the balance due. What is the amount of cash received?
 **a.** $700.
 **b.** $680.
 **c.** $686.
 **d.** None of the above.

(SO 3) **2.** Which of the following approaches for bad debts is best described as a balance sheet method?
 **a.** Percentage-of-receivables basis.
 **b.** Direct write-off method.
 **c.** Percentage-of-sales basis.
 **d.** Both a and b.

(SO 3) **3.** Net sales for the month are $800,000, and bad debts are expected to be 1.5% of net sales. The company uses the percentage-of-sales basis. If the Allowance for Doubtful Accounts has a credit balance of $15,000 before adjustment, what is the balance after adjustment?
 **a.** $15,000.
 **b.** $27,000.
 **c.** $23,000.
 **d.** $31,000.

**4.** In 2008, Roso Carlson Company had net credit sales of (SO 3) $750,000. On January 1, 2008, Allowance for Doubtful Accounts had a credit balance of $18,000. During 2008, $30,000 of uncollectible accounts receivable were written off. Past experience indicates that 3% of net credit sales become uncollectible. What should be the adjusted balance of Allowance for Doubtful Accounts at December 31, 2008?
 **a.** $10,050.
 **b.** $10,500.
 **c.** $22,500.
 **d.** $40,500.

(SO 3)  **5.** An analysis and aging of the accounts receivable of Prince Company at December 31 reveals the following data.

Accounts receivable                          $800,000
Allowance for doubtful
  accounts per books before
  adjustment                                        50,000
Amounts expected to become
  uncollectible                                       65,000

The cash realizable value of the accounts receivable at December 31, after adjustment, is:
  **a.** $685,000.
  **b.** $750,000.
  **c.** $800,000.
  **d.** $735,000.

(SO 6)  **6.** One of the following statements about promissory notes is incorrect. The *incorrect* statement is:
  **a.** The party making the promise to pay is called the maker.
  **b.** The party to whom payment is to be made is called the payee.
  **c.** A promissory note is not a negotiable instrument.
  **d.** A promissory note is often required from high-risk customers.

(SO 4)  **7.** Which of the following statements about Visa credit card sales is *incorrect*?
  **a.** The credit card issuer makes the credit investigation of the customer.
  **b.** The retailer is not involved in the collection process.
  **c.** Two parties are involved.
  **d.** The retailer receives cash more quickly than it would from individual customers on account.

(SO 4)  **8.** Blinka Retailers accepted $50,000 of Citibank Visa credit card charges for merchandise sold on July 1. Citibank charges 4% for its credit card use. The entry to record this transaction by Blinka Retailers will include a credit to Sales of $50,000 and a debit(s) to:

  **a.** Cash                                               $48,000
      and Service Charge Expense                2,000
  **b.** Accounts Receivable                      $48,000
      and Service Charge Expense              $2,000
  **c.** Cash                                               $50,000
  **d.** Accounts Receivable                      $50,000

**9.** Foti Co. accepts a $1,000, 3-month, 12% promissory note (SO 6) in settlement of an account with Bartelt Co. The entry to record this transaction is as follows.

  **a.** Notes Receivable              | 1,030 |
            Accounts Receivable      |       | 1,030
  **b.** Notes Receivable              | 1,000 |
            Accounts Receivable      |       | 1,000
  **c.** Notes Receivable              | 1,000 |
            Sales                            |       | 1,000
  **d.** Notes Receivable              | 1,020 |
            Accounts Receivable      |       | 1,020

**10.** Ginter Co. holds Kolar Inc.'s $10,000, 120-day, 9% note. (SO 8) The entry made by Ginter Co. when the note is collected, assuming no interest has been previously accrued, is:

  **a.** Cash                               | 10,300 |
            Notes Receivable          |         | 10,300
  **b.** Cash                               | 10,000 |
            Notes Receivable          |         | 10,000
  **c.** Accounts Receivable         | 10,300 |
            Notes Receivable          |         | 10,000
            Interest Revenue           |         | 300
  **d.** Cash                               | 10,300 |
            Notes Receivable          |         | 10,000
            Interest Revenue           |         | 300

Go to the book's website,
**www.wiley.com/college/weygandt**,
for Additional Self-Study questions.

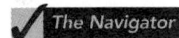 The Navigator

## QUESTIONS

**1.** What is the difference between an account receivable and a note receivable?

**2.** What are some common types of receivables other than accounts receivable and notes receivable?

**3.** Texaco Oil Company issues its own credit cards. Assume that Texaco charges you $40 on an unpaid balance. Prepare the journal entry that Texaco makes to record this revenue.

**4.** What are the essential features of the allowance method of accounting for bad debts?

**5.** Jerry Gatewood cannot understand why cash realizable value does not decrease when an uncollectible account is written off under the allowance method. Clarify this point for Jerry Gatewood.

**6.** Distinguish between the two bases that may be used in estimating uncollectible accounts.

**7.** Eaton Company has a credit balance of $3,500 in Allowance for Doubtful Accounts. The estimated bad debts expense under the percentage-of-sales basis is $4,100. The total estimated uncollectibles under the percentage-of-

receivables basis is $5,800. Prepare the adjusting entry under each basis.

**8.** How are bad debts accounted for under the direct write-off method? What are the disadvantages of this method?

**9.** DeVito Company accepts both its own credit cards and national credit cards. What are the advantages of accepting both types of cards?

**10.** An article recently appeared in the *Wall Street Journal* indicating that companies are selling their receivables at a record rate. Why are companies selling their receivables?

**11.** Pinkston Textiles decides to sell $600,000 of its accounts receivable to First Factors Inc. First Factors assesses a service charge of 3% of the amount of receivables sold. Prepare the journal entry that Pinkston Textiles makes to record this sale.

**12.** Your roommate is uncertain about the advantages of a promissory note. Compare the advantages of a note receivable with those of an account receivable.

**13.** How may the maturity date of a promissory note be stated?

**14.** Indicate the maturity date of each of the following promissory notes:

| Date of Note | Terms |
| --- | --- |
| (a) March 13 | one year after date of note |
| (b) May 4 | 3 months after date |
| (c) June 20 | 30 days after date |
| (d) July 1 | 60 days after date |

**15.** Compute the missing amounts for each of the following notes.

| | Principal | Annual Interest Rate | Time | Total Interest |
| --- | --- | --- | --- | --- |
| (a) | ? | 9% | 120 days | $ 600 |
| (b) | $30,000 | 10% | 3 years | ? |
| (c) | $60,000 | ? | 5 months | $2,000 |
| (d) | $45,000 | 8% | ? | $1,200 |

**16.** In determining interest revenue, some financial institutions use 365 days per year and others use 360 days. Why might a financial institution use 360 days?

**17.** Cain Company dishonors a note at maturity. What actions by Cain may occur with the dishonoring of the note?

**18.** General Motors Corporation has accounts receivable and notes receivable. How should the receivables be reported on the balance sheet?

**19.** The accounts receivable turnover ratio is 8.14, and average net receivables during the period are $400,000. What is the amount of net credit sales for the period?

---

# BRIEF EXERCISES

*Identify different types of receivables.*

*(SO 1)*

**BE9-1** Presented below are three receivables transactions. Indicate whether these receivables are reported as accounts receivable, notes receivable, or other receivables on a balance sheet.

**(a)** Sold merchandise on account for $64,000 to a customer.
**(b)** Received a promissory note of $57,000 for services performed.
**(c)** Advanced $10,000 to an employee.

*Record basic accounts receivable transactions.*

*(SO 2)*

**BE9-2** Record the following transactions on the books of Keyser Co.

**(a)** On July 1, Keyser Co. sold merchandise on account to Maxfield Inc. for $15,200, terms 2/10, n/30.
**(b)** On July 8, Maxfield Inc. returned merchandise worth $3,800 to Keyser Co.
**(c)** On July 11, Maxfield Inc. paid for the merchandise.

*Prepare entry for allowance method and partial balance sheet.*

*(SO 3, 9)*

**BE9-3** During its first year of operations, Henley Company had credit sales of $3,000,000; $600,000 remained uncollected at year-end. The credit manager estimates that $35,000 of these receivables will become uncollectible.

**(a)** Prepare the journal entry to record the estimated uncollectibles.
**(b)** Prepare the current assets section of the balance sheet for Henley Company. Assume that in addition to the receivables it has cash of $90,000, merchandise inventory of $130,000, and prepaid expenses of $7,500.

*Prepare entry for write-off; determine cash realizable value.*

*(SO 3)*

**BE9-4** At the end of 2008, Delong Co. has accounts receivable of $700,000 and an allowance for doubtful accounts of $54,000. On January 24, 2009, the company learns that its receivable from Ristau Inc. is not collectible, and management authorizes a write-off of $5,400.

**(a)** Prepare the journal entry to record the write-off.
**(b)** What is the cash realizable value of the accounts receivable (1) before the write-off and (2) after the write-off?

*Prepare entries for collection of bad debts write-off.*

*(SO 3)*

**BE9-5** Assume the same information as BE9-4. On March 4, 2009, Delong Co. receives payment of $5,400 in full from Ristau Inc. Prepare the journal entries to record this transaction.

*Prepare entry using percentage-of-sales method.*

*(SO 3)*

**BE9-6** Nieto Co. elects to use the percentage-of-sales basis in 2008 to record bad debts expense. It estimates that 2% of net credit sales will become uncollectible. Sales are $800,000 for 2008, sales returns and allowances are $45,000, and the allowance for doubtful accounts has a credit balance of $9,000. Prepare the adjusting entry to record bad debts expense in 2008.

*Prepare entry using percentage-of-receivables method.*

*(SO 3)*

**BE9-7** Linhart Co. uses the percentage-of-receivables basis to record bad debts expense. It estimates that 1% of accounts receivable will become uncollectible. Accounts receivable are $450,000 at the end of the year, and the allowance for doubtful accounts has a credit balance of $1,500.

**(a)** Prepare the adjusting journal entry to record bad debts expense for the year.

**(b)** If the allowance for doubtful accounts had a debit balance of $800 instead of a credit balance of $1,500, determine the amount to be reported for bad debts expense.

**BE9-8** Presented below are two independent transactions.

*Prepare entries to dispose of accounts receivable.*

*(SO 4)*

**(a)** St. Pierre Restaurant accepted a Visa card in payment of a $150 lunch bill. The bank charges a 4% fee. What entry should St. Pierre make?

**(b)** Jamar Company sold its accounts receivable of $60,000. What entry should Jamar make, given a service charge of 3% on the amount of receivables sold?

**BE9-9** Compute interest and find the maturity date for the following notes.

*Compute interest and determine maturity dates on notes.*

*(SO 5)*

| | Date of Note | Principal | Interest Rate (%) | Terms |
|---|---|---|---|---|
| **(a)** | June 10 | $80,000 | 6% | 60 days |
| **(b)** | July 14 | $50,000 | 7% | 90 days |
| **(c)** | April 27 | $12,000 | 8% | 75 days |

**BE9-10** Presented below are data on three promissory notes. Determine the missing amounts.

*Determine maturity dates and compute interest and rates on notes.*

*(SO 5)*

| Date of Note | Terms | Maturity Date | Principal | Annual Interest Rate | Total Interest |
|---|---|---|---|---|---|
| **(a)** April 1 | 60 days | ? | $600,000 | 9% | ? |
| **(b)** July 2 | 30 days | ? | 90,000 | ? | $600 |
| **(c)** March 7 | 6 months | ? | 120,000 | 10% | ? |

**BE9-11** On January 10, 2008, Edmunds Co. sold merchandise on account to Jeff Gallup for $13,600, n/30. On February 9, Jeff Gallup gave Edmunds Co. a 10% promissory note in settlement of this account. Prepare the journal entry to record the sale and the settlement of the account receivable.

*Prepare entry for notes receivable exchanged for account receivable.*

*(SO 6)*

**BE9-12** The financial statements of Minnesota Mining and Manufacturing Company (3M) report net sales of $20.0 billion. Accounts receivable (net) are $2.7 billion at the beginning of the year and $2.8 billion at the end of the year. Compute 3M's accounts receivable turnover ratio. Compute 3M's average collection period for accounts receivable in days.

*Compute ratios to analyze receivables.*

*(SO 9)*

# EXERCISES

**E9-1** Presented below are selected transactions of Pale Force Company. Pale Force sells in large quantities to other companies and also sells its product in a small retail outlet.

*Journalize entries related to accounts receivable.*

*(SO 2)*

| March | 1 | Sold merchandise on account to CC Company for $3,000, terms 2/10, n/30. |
|---|---|---|
| | 3 | CC Company returned merchandise worth $500 to Pale Force. |
| | 9 | Pale Force collected the amount due from CC Company from the March 1 sale. |
| | 15 | Pale Force sold merchandise for $400 in its retail outlet. The customer used his Pale Force credit card. |
| | 31 | Pale Force added 1.5% monthly interest to the customer's credit card balance. |

**Instructions**

Prepare journal entries for the transactions above.

**E9-2** Presented below are two independent situations.

*Journalize entries for recognizing accounts receivable.*

*(SO 2)*

**(a)** On January 6, Arneson Co. sells merchandise on account to Cortez Inc. for $9,000, terms 2/10, n/30. On January 16, Cortez Inc. pays the amount due. Prepare the entries on Arneson's books to record the sale and related collection.

**(b)** On January 10, Mary Dawes uses her Pierson Co. credit card to purchase merchandise from Pierson Co. for $9,000. On February 10, Dawes is billed for the amount due of $9,000. On February 12, Dawes pays $5,000 on the balance due. On March 10, Dawes is billed for the amount due, including interest at 2% per month on the unpaid balance as of February 12. Prepare the entries on Pierson Co.'s books related to the transactions that occurred on January 10, February 12, and March 10.

*Journalize entries to record allowance for doubtful accounts using two different bases.*

**E9-3** The ledger of Hixson Company at the end of the current year shows Accounts Receivable $120,000, Sales $840,000, and Sales Returns and Allowances $30,000.

*(SO 3)*

**Instructions**

**(a)** If Hixson uses the direct write-off method to account for uncollectible accounts, journalize the adjusting entry at December 31, assuming Hixson determines that Fell's $1,400 balance is uncollectible.

**(b)** If Allowance for Doubtful Accounts has a credit balance of $2,100 in the trial balance, journalize the adjusting entry at December 31, assuming bad debts are expected to be (1) 1% of net sales, and (2) 10% of accounts receivable.

**(c)** If Allowance for Doubtful Accounts has a debit balance of $200 in the trial balance, journalize the adjusting entry at December 31, assuming bad debts are expected to be (1) 0.75% of net sales and (2) 6% of accounts receivable.

*Determine bad debts expense; prepare the adjusting entry for bad debts expense.*

*(SO 3)*

**E9-4**   Ingles Company has accounts receivable of $93,100 at March 31. An analysis of the accounts shows the following.

| Month of Sale | Balance, March 31 |
|---|---|
| March | $60,000 |
| February | 17,600 |
| January | 8,500 |
| Prior to January | 7,000 |
| | $93,100 |

Credit terms are 2/10, n/30. At March 31, Allowance for Doubtful Accounts has a credit balance of $1,200 prior to adjustment. The company uses the percentage-of-receivables basis for estimating uncollectible accounts. The company's estimate of bad debts is as follows.

| Age of Accounts | Estimated Percentage Uncollectible |
|---|---|
| 1–30 days | 2.0% |
| 31–60 days | 5.0% |
| 61–90 days | 30.0% |
| Over 90 days | 50.0% |

**Instructions**

**(a)** Determine the total estimated uncollectibles.

**(b)** Prepare the adjusting entry at March 31 to record bad debts expense.

*Journalize write-off and recovery.*

*(SO 3)*

**E9-5**   At December 31, 2007, Braddock Company had a balance of $15,000 in the Allowance for Doubtful Accounts. During 2008, Braddock wrote off accounts totaling $13,000. One of those accounts ($1,800) was later collected. At December 31, 2008, an aging schedule indicated that the balance in the Allowance for Doubtful Accounts should be $19,000.

**Instructions**

Prepare journal entries to record the 2008 transactions of Braddock Company.

*Journalize percentage of sales basis, write-off, recovery.*

*(SO 3)*

**E9-6**   On December 31, 2008, Jarnigan Co. estimated that 2% of its net sales of $400,000 will become uncollectible. The company recorded this amount as an addition to Allowance for Doubtful Accounts. On May 11, 2009, Jarnigan Co. determined that Terry Frye's account was uncollectible and wrote off $1,100. On June 12, 2009, Frye paid the amount previously written off.

**Instructions**

Prepare the journal entries on December 31, 2008, May 11, 2009, and June 12, 2009.

*Journalize entries for the sale of accounts receivable.*

*(SO 4)*

**E9-7**   Presented below are two independent situations.

**(a)** On March 3, Cornwell Appliances sells $680,000 of its receivables to Marsh Factors Inc. Marsh Factors assesses a finance charge of 3% of the amount of receivables sold. Prepare the entry on Cornwell Appliances' books to record the sale of the receivables.

**(b)** On May 10, Dale Company sold merchandise for $3,500 and accepted the customer's America Bank MasterCard. America Bank charges a 4% service charge for credit card sales. Prepare the entry on Dale Company's books to record the sale of merchandise.

*Journalize entries for credit card sales.*

*(SO 4)*

**E9-8**   Presented below and on page 413 are two independent situations.

**(a)** On April 2, Nancy Hansel uses her J. C. Penney Company credit card to purchase merchandise from a J. C. Penney store for $1,500. On May 1, Hansel is billed for the $1,500 amount due. Hansel pays $700 on the balance due on May 3. On June 1, Hansel receives a bill for the amount due, including interest at 1% per month on the unpaid balance as of May 3. Prepare the entries on J. C. Penney Co.'s books related to the transactions that occurred on April 2, May 3, and June 1.

**(b)** On July 4, Kimble's Restaurant accepts a Visa card for a $200 dinner bill. Visa charges a 3% service fee. Prepare the entry on Kimble's books related to this transaction.

**E9-9**   Topeka Stores accepts both its own and national credit cards. During the year the following selected summary transactions occurred.

Jan. 15   Made Topeka credit card sales totaling $18,000. (There were no balances prior to January 15.)

20   Made Visa credit card sales (service charge fee 2%) totaling $4,300.

Feb. 10   Collected $10,000 on Topeka credit card sales.

15   Added finance charges of 1% to Topeka credit card balance.

*Journalize credit card sales, and indicate the statement presentation of financing charges and service charge expense.*

*(SO 4)*

**Instructions**

**(a)** Journalize the transactions for Topeka Stores.

**(b)** Indicate the statement presentation of the financing charges and the credit card service charge expense for Topeka Stores.

**E9-10**   Orosco Supply Co. has the following transactions related to notes receivable during the last 2 months of 2008.

Nov. 1   Loaned $15,000 cash to Sally Givens on a 1-year, 10% note.

Dec. 11   Sold goods to John Countryman, Inc., receiving a $6,750, 90-day, 8% note.

16   Received a $4,000, 6-month, 9% note in exchange for Bob Reber's outstanding accounts receivable.

31   Accrued interest revenue on all notes receivable.

*Journalize entries for notes receivable transactions.*

*(SO 5, 6)*

**Instructions**

**(a)** Journalize the transactions for Orosco Supply Co.

**(b)** Record the collection of the Givens note at its maturity in 2009.

**E9-11**   Record the following transactions for Sandwich Co. in the general journal.

**2008**

May 1   Received a $7,500, 1-year, 10% note in exchange for Julia Gonzalez's outstanding accounts receivable.

Dec. 31   Accrued interest on the Gonzalez note.

Dec. 31   Closed the interest revenue account.

**2009**

May 1   Received principal plus interest on the Gonzalez note. (No interest has been accrued in 2009.)

*Journalize entries for notes receivable.*

*(SO 5, 6)*

**E9-12**   Singletary Company had the following select transactions.

Apr. 1, 2008   Accepted Wilson Company's 1-year, 12% note in settlement of a $20,000 account receivable.

July 1, 2008   Loaned $25,000 cash to Richard Dent on a 9-month, 10% note.

Dec. 31, 2008   Accrued interest on all notes receivable.

Apr. 1, 2009   Received principal plus interest on the Wilson note.

Apr. 1, 2009   Richard Dent dishonored its note; Singletary expects it will eventually collect.

*Prepare entries for note receivable transactions.*

*(SO 5, 6, 8)*

**Instructions**

Prepare journal entries to record the transactions. Singletary prepares adjusting entries once a year on December 31.

**E9-13**   On May 2, Kleinsorge Company lends $7,600 to Everhart, Inc., issuing a 6-month, 9% note. At the maturity date, November 2, Everhart indicates that it cannot pay.

*Journalize entries for dishonor of notes receivable.*

*(SO 5, 8)*

**Instructions**

**(a)** Prepare the entry to record the issuance of the note.

**(b)** Prepare the entry to record the dishonor of the note, assuming that Kleinsorge Company expects collection will occur.

**(c)** Prepare the entry to record the dishonor of the note, assuming that Kleinsorge Company does not expect collection in the future.

*Determine missing amounts related to sales and accounts receivable.*

*(SO 2, 4, 9)*

**E9-14**  The following information pertains to Napa Merchandising Company.

| | |
|---|---:|
| Merchandise inventory at end of year | $33,000 |
| Accounts receivable at beginning of year | 24,000 |
| Cash sales made during the year | 18,000 |
| Gross profit on sales | 20,000 |
| Accounts receivable written off during the year | 1,000 |
| Purchases made during the year | 60,000 |
| Accounts receivable collected during the year | 78,000 |
| Merchandise inventory at beginning of year | 36,000 |

**Instructions**

(a) Calculate the amount of credit sales made during the year. (*Hint:* You will need to use income statement relationships—introduced in Chapter 5—in order to determine this.)

(b) Calculate the balance of accounts receivable at the end of the year.

*Compute accounts receivable turnover and average collection period.*

*(SO 9)*

**E9-15**  Bledel Company had accounts receivable of $100,000 on January 1, 2008. The only transactions that affected accounts receivable during 2008 were net credit sales of $1,000,000, cash collections of $900,000, and accounts written off of $30,000.

**Instructions**

(a) Compute the ending balance of accounts receivable.

(b) Compute the accounts receivable turnover ratio for 2008.

(c) Compute the average collection period in days.

# EXERCISES: SET B

Visit the book's website at **www.wiley.com/college/weygandt**, and choose the Student Companion site, to access Exercise Set B.

# PROBLEMS: SET A

*Prepare journal entries related to bad debts expense.*

*(SO 2, 3, 9)*

**P9-1A**  At December 31, 2007, Leis Co. reported the following information on its balance sheet.

| | |
|---|---:|
| Accounts receivable | $960,000 |
| Less: Allowance for doubtful accounts | 80,000 |

During 2008, the company had the following transactions related to receivables.

| | |
|---|---:|
| 1. Sales on account | $3,200,000 |
| 2. Sales returns and allowances | 50,000 |
| 3. Collections of accounts receivable | 2,810,000 |
| 4. Write-offs of accounts receivable deemed uncollectible | 90,000 |
| 5. Recovery of bad debts previously written off as uncollectible | 24,000 |

**Instructions**

(a) Prepare the journal entries to record each of these five transactions. Assume that no cash discounts were taken on the collections of accounts receivable.

*(b) Accounts receivable $1,210,000 ADA $14,000*

*(c) Bad debts expense $101,000*

(b) Enter the January 1, 2008, balances in Accounts Receivable and Allowance for Doubtful Accounts, post the entries to the two accounts (use T accounts), and determine the balances.

(c) Prepare the journal entry to record bad debts expense for 2008, assuming that an aging of accounts receivable indicates that expected bad debts are $115,000.

(d) Compute the accounts receivable turnover ratio for 2008.

*Compute bad debts amounts.*

*(SO 3)*

**P9-2A**  Information related to Hermesch Company for 2008 is summarized below.

| | |
|---|---:|
| Total credit sales | $2,200,000 |
| Accounts receivable at December 31 | 825,000 |
| Bad debts written off | 33,000 |

**Instructions**

(a) What amount of bad debts expense will Hermesch Company report if it uses the direct write-off method of accounting for bad debts?

(b) Assume that Hermesch Company estimates its bad debts expense to be 2% of credit sales. What amount of bad debts expense will Hermesch record if it has an Allowance for Doubtful Accounts credit balance of $4,000?

**(c)** Assume that Hermesch Company estimates its bad debts expense based on 6% of accounts receivable. What amount of bad debts expense will Hermesch record if it has an Allowance for Doubtful Accounts credit balance of $3,000?

**(d)** Assume the same facts as in (c), except that there is a $3,000 debit balance in Allowance for Doubtful Accounts. What amount of bad debts expense will Hermesch record?

**(e)** What is the weakness of the direct write-off method of reporting bad debts expense?

**P9-3A**    Presented below is an aging schedule for Zillmann Company.

*Journalize entries to record transactions related to bad debts.*

*(SO 2, 3)*

**Worksheet.xls**

File    Edit    View    Insert    Format    Tools    Data    Window    Help

| | A | B | C | D | E | F | G |
|---|---|---|---|---|---|---|---|
| 1 | | | Not Yet Due | Number of Days Past Due | | | |
| 2 | | | | | | | |
| 3 | Customer | Total | | 1–30 | 31–60 | 61–90 | Over 90 |
| 4 | Arndt | $ 22,000 | | $10,000 | $12,000 | | |
| 5 | Blair | 40,000 | $ 40,000 | | | | |
| 6 | Chase | 57,000 | 16,000 | 6,000 | | $35,000 | |
| 7 | Drea | 34,000 | | | | | $34,000 |
| 8 | Others | 132,000 | 96,000 | 16,000 | 14,000 | | 6,000 |
| 9 | | $285,000 | $152,000 | $32,000 | $26,000 | $35,000 | $40,000 |
| 10 | Estimated Percentage Uncollectible | | 3% | 6% | 13% | 25% | 60% |
| 11 | Total Estimated Bad Debts | $ 42,610 | $ 4,560 | $ 1,920 | $ 3,380 | $ 8,750 | $24,000 |
| 12 | | | | | | | |

At December 31, 2008, the unadjusted balance in Allowance for Doubtful Accounts is a credit of $12,000.

**Instructions**

**(a)** Journalize and post the adjusting entry for bad debts at December 31, 2008.

*(a) Bad debts expense $30,610*

**(b)** Journalize and post to the allowance account the following events and transactions in the year 2009.

**(1)** On March 31, a $1,000 customer balance originating in 2008 is judged uncollectible.

**(2)** On May 31, a check for $1,000 is received from the customer whose account was written off as uncollectible on March 31.

**(c)** Journalize the adjusting entry for bad debts on December 31, 2009, assuming that the unadjusted balance in Allowance for Doubtful Accounts is a debit of $800 and the aging schedule indicates that total estimated bad debts will be $28,600.

*(c) Bad debts expense $29,400*

**P9-4A**    Wall Inc. uses the allowance method to estimate uncollectible accounts receivable. The company produced the following aging of the accounts receivable at year end.

*Journalize transactions related to bad debts.*

*(SO 2, 3)*

**Worksheet.xls**

File    Edit    View    Insert    Format    Tools    Data    Window    Help

| | A | B | C | D | E | F | G |
|---|---|---|---|---|---|---|---|
| 1 | | | Number of Days Outstanding | | | | |
| 2 | | | | | | | |
| 3 | | Total | 0–30 | 31–60 | 61–90 | 91–120 | Over 120 |
| 4 | Accounts receivable | $375,000 | $220,000 | $90,000 | $40,000 | $10,000 | $15,000 |
| 5 | % uncollectible | | 1% | 4% | 5% | 8% | 10% |
| 6 | Estimated bad debts | | | | | | |
| 7 | | | | | | | |

**Instructions**

**(a)** Calculate the total estimated bad debts based on the above information.

*(a) Tot. est. bad debts $10,100*

**(b)** Prepare the year-end adjusting journal entry to record the bad debts using the aged uncollectible accounts receivable determined in (a). Assume the current balance in Allowance for Doubtful Accounts is an $8,000 debit.

**(c)** Of the above accounts, $5,000 is determined to be specifically uncollectible. Prepare the journal entry to write off the uncollectible account.

**(d)** The company collects $5,000 subsequently on a specific account that had previously been determined to be uncollectible in (c). Prepare the journal entry(ies) necessary to restore the account and record the cash collection.

**(e)**  Comment on how your answers to (a)–(d) would change if Wall Inc. used 3% of *total* accounts receivable, rather than aging the accounts receivable. What are the advantages to the company of aging the accounts receivable rather than applying a percentage to total accounts receivable?

*Journalize entries to record transactions related to bad debts.*

*(SO 3)*

**P9-5A** At December 31, 2008, the trial balance of Worcester Company contained the following amounts before adjustment.

|  | Debits | Credits |
|---|---|---|
| Accounts Receivable | $385,000 | |
| Allowance for Doubtful Accounts | | $ 2,000 |
| Sales | | 950,000 |

**Instructions**

**(a)** Based on the information given, which method of accounting for bad debts is Worcester Company using—the direct write-off method or the allowance method? How can you tell?

*(b) (2) $9,500*

**(b)** Prepare the adjusting entry at December 31, 2008, for bad debts expense under each of the following independent assumptions.

**(1)** An aging schedule indicates that $11,750 of accounts receivable will be uncollectible.

**(2)** The company estimates that 1% of sales will be uncollectible.

**(c)** Repeat part (b) assuming that instead of a credit balance there is an $2,000 debit balance in Allowance for Doubtful Accounts.

**(d)** During the next month, January 2009, a $3,000 account receivable is written off as uncollectible. Prepare the journal entry to record the write-off.

**(e)** Repeat part (d) assuming that Worcester uses the direct write-off method instead of the allowance method in accounting for uncollectible accounts receivable.

**(f)**  What type of account is Allowance for Doubtful Accounts? How does it affect how accounts receivable is reported on the balance sheet at the end of the accounting period?

*Prepare entries for various notes receivable transactions.*

*(SO 2, 4, 5, 8, 9)*

GLS

**P9-6A** Mendosa Company closes its books monthly. On September 30, selected ledger account balances are:

| Notes Receivable | $33,000 |
|---|---|
| Interest Receivable | $ 170 |

Notes Receivable include the following.

| Date | Maker | Face | Term | Interest |
|---|---|---|---|---|
| Aug. 16 | Chang Inc. | $ 8,000 | 60 days | 8% |
| Aug. 25 | Hughey Co. | 9,000 | 60 days | 10% |
| Sept. 30 | Skinner Corp. | 16,000 | 6 months | 9% |

Interest is computed using a 360-day year. During October, the following transactions were completed.

Oct. 7 Made sales of $6,900 on Mendosa credit cards.
 12 Made sales of $900 on MasterCard credit cards. The credit card service charge is 3%.
 15 Added $460 to Mendosa customer balances for finance charges on unpaid balances.
 15 Received payment in full from Chang Inc. on the amount due.
 24 Received notice that the Hughey note has been dishonored. (Assume that Hughey is expected to pay in the future.)

**Instructions**

**(a)** Journalize the October transactions and the October 31 adjusting entry for accrued interest receivable.

*(b) Accounts receivable $16,510*

**(b)** Enter the balances at October 1 in the receivable accounts. Post the entries to all of the receivable accounts.

*(c) Total receivables $32,630*

**(c)** Show the balance sheet presentation of the receivable accounts at October 31.

*Prepare entries for various receivable transactions.*

*(SO 2, 4, 5, 6, 7, 8)*

**P9-7A** On January 1, 2008, Kloppenberg Company had Accounts Receivable $139,000, Notes Receivable $25,000, and Allowance for Doubtful Accounts $13,200. The note receivable is from

Sara Rogers Company. It is a 4-month, 12% note dated December 31, 2007. Kloppenberg Company prepares financial statements annually. During the year the following selected transactions occurred.

Jan.   5  Sold $20,000 of merchandise to Dedonder Company, terms n/15.
       20  Accepted Dedonder Company's $20,000, 3-month, 9% note for balance due.
Feb.  18  Sold $8,000 of merchandise to Ludwig Company and accepted Ludwig's $8,000, 6-month, 9% note for the amount due.
Apr.  20  Collected Dedonder Company note in full.
       30  Received payment in full from Sara Rogers Company on the amount due.
May   25  Accepted Jenks Inc.'s $4,000, 3-month, 7% note in settlement of a past-due balance on account.
Aug.  18  Received payment in full from Ludwig Company on note due.
       25  The Jenks Inc. note was dishonored. Jenks Inc. is not bankrupt; future payment is anticipated.
Sept.  1  Sold $12,000 of merchandise to Lena Torme Company and accepted a $12,000, 6-month, 10% note for the amount due.

**Instructions**
Journalize the transactions.

# PROBLEMS: SET B

**P9-1B**   At December 31, 2007, Pickeril Imports reported the following information on its balance sheet.

*Prepare journal entries related to bad debts expense.*

(SO 2, 3, 9)

|  |  |
|---|---|
| Accounts receivable | $1,000,000 |
| Less: Allowance for doubtful accounts | 60,000 |

During 2008, the company had the following transactions related to receivables.

| | |
|---|---|
| 1. Sales on account | $2,570,000 |
| 2. Sales returns and allowances | 40,000 |
| 3. Collections of accounts receivable | 2,300,000 |
| 4. Write-offs of accounts receivable deemed uncollectible | 65,000 |
| 5. Recovery of bad debts previously written off as uncollectible | 25,000 |

**Instructions**
(a) Prepare the journal entries to record each of these five transactions. Assume that no cash discounts were taken on the collections of accounts receivable.
(b) Enter the January 1, 2008, balances in Accounts Receivable and Allowance for Doubtful Accounts. Post the entries to the two accounts (use T accounts), and determine the balances.
(c) Prepare the journal entry to record bad debts expense for 2008, assuming that an aging of accounts receivable indicates that estimated bad debts are $90,000.
(d) Compute the accounts receivable turnover ratio for the year 2008.

(b) Accounts receivable
$1,165,000
ADA $20,000

(c) Bad debts expense
$70,000

**P9-2B**   Information related to Hively Company for 2008 is summarized below.

| | |
|---|---|
| Total credit sales | $1,540,000 |
| Accounts receivable at December 31 | 520,000 |
| Bad debts written off | 26,000 |

*Compute bad debts amounts.*

(SO 3)

**Instructions**
(a) What amount of bad debts expense will Hively Company report if it uses the direct write-off method of accounting for bad debts?
(b) Assume that Hively Company decides to estimate its bad debts expense to be 2% of credit sales. What amount of bad debts expense will Hively record if Allowance for Doubtful Accounts has a credit balance of $3,000?
(c) Assume that Hively Company decides to estimate its bad debts expense based on 5% of accounts receivable. What amount of bad debts expense will Hively Company record if Allowance for Doubtful Accounts has a credit balance of $4,000?
(d) Assume the same facts as in (c), except that there is a $2,000 debit balance in Allowance for Doubtful Accounts. What amount of bad debts expense will Hively record?
(e) ◀■■■■■■■▶   What is the weakness of the direct write-off method of reporting bad debts expense?

*Journalize entries to record transactions related to bad debts.*

(SO 2, 3)

**P9-3B**   Presented below is an aging schedule for Lawrenz Company.

| | Worksheet.xls | | | | | | |
|---|---|---|---|---|---|---|---|
| | File   Edit   View   Insert   Format   Tools   Data   Window   Help | | | | | | |
| | A | B | C | D | E | F | G |
| | | | Not | | Number of Days Past Due | | |
| 3 | Customer | Total | Yet Due | 1–30 | 31–60 | 61–90 | Over 90 |
| 4 | Akers | $ 20,000 | | $ 9,000 | $11,000 | | |
| 5 | Baietto | 30,000 | $ 30,000 | | | | |
| 6 | Comer | 50,000 | 15,000 | 5,000 | | $30,000 | |
| 7 | DeJong | 38,000 | | | | | $38,000 |
| 8 | Others | 126,000 | 92,000 | 15,000 | 13,000 | | 6,000 |
| 9 | | $264,000 | $137,000 | $29,000 | $24,000 | $30,000 | $44,000 |
| 10 | Estimated Percentage Uncollectible | | 2% | 5% | 10% | 24% | 50% |
| 11 | Total Estimated Bad Debts | $ 35,790 | $ 2,740 | $ 1,450 | $ 2,400 | $ 7,200 | $22,000 |

At December 31, 2008, the unadjusted balance in Allowance for Doubtful Accounts is a credit of $10,000.

**Instructions**

(a) Bad debts expense $25,790

**(a)** Journalize and post the adjusting entry for bad debts at December 31, 2008.

**(b)** Journalize and post to the allowance account the following events and transactions in the year 2009.

    **(1)** March 1, an $1,100 customer balance originating in 2008 is judged uncollectible.

    **(2)** May 1, a check for $1,100 is received from the customer whose account was written off as uncollectible on March 1.

(c) Bad debts expense $29,500

**(c)** Journalize the adjusting entry for bad debts on December 31, 2009. Assume that the unadjusted balance in Allowance for Doubtful Accounts is a debit of $1,200, and the aging schedule indicates that total estimated bad debts will be $28,300.

*Journalize transactions related to bad debts.*

(SO 2, 3)

**P9-4B**   The following represents selected information taken from a company's aging schedule to estimate uncollectible accounts receivable at year end.

| | Worksheet.xls | | | | | | |
|---|---|---|---|---|---|---|---|
| | File   Edit   View   Insert   Format   Tools   Data   Window   Help | | | | | | |
| | A | B | C | D | E | F | G |
| | | | Number of Days Outstanding | | | | |
| 3 | | Total | 0–30 | 31–60 | 61–90 | 91–120 | Over 120 |
| 4 | Accounts receivable | $260,000 | $100,000 | $60,000 | $50,000 | $30,000 | $20,000 |
| 5 | % uncollectible | | 1% | 5% | 7.5% | 10% | 15% |
| 6 | Estimated bad debts | | | | | | |

**Instructions**

(a) Tot. est. bad debts $13,750

**(a)** Calculate the total estimated bad debts based on the above information.

**(b)** Prepare the year-end adjusting journal entry to record the bad debts using the allowance method and the aged uncollectible accounts receivable determined in (a). Assume the current balance in the Allowance for Doubtful Accounts account is a $10,000 credit.

**(c)** Of the above accounts, $2,000 is determined to be specifically uncollectible. Prepare the journal entry to write off the uncollectible accounts.

**(d)** The company subsequently collects $1,000 on a specific account that had previously been determined to be uncollectible in (c). Prepare the journal entry(ies) necessary to restore the account and record the cash collection.

**(e)** Explain how establishing an allowance account satisfies the matching principle.

**P9-5B**   At December 31, 2008, the trial balance of Schnakenberg Company contained the following amounts before adjustment.

*Journalize entries to record transactions related to bad debts.*

*(SO 3)*

|  | **Debits** | **Credits** |
|---|---|---|
| Accounts Receivable | $350,000 |  |
| Allowance for Doubtful Accounts |  | $  1,500 |
| Sales |  | 850,000 |

**Instructions**
**(a)** Prepare the adjusting entry at December 31, 2008, to record bad debts expense under each of the following independent assumptions.

*(a) (2) $17,000*

   **(1)** An aging schedule indicates that $17,550 of accounts receivable will be uncollectible.
   **(2)** The company estimates that 2% of sales will be uncollectible.
**(b)** Repeat part (a) assuming that instead of a credit balance, there is a $1,500 debit balance in Allowance for Doubtful Accounts.
**(c)** During the next month, January 2009, a $4,500 account receivable is written off as uncollectible. Prepare the journal entry to record the write-off.
**(d)** Repeat part (c) assuming that Schnakenberg Company uses the direct write-off method instead of the allowance method in accounting for uncollectible accounts receivable.
**(e)** ◄▬▬▬▬► What are the advantages of using the allowance method in accounting for uncollectible accounts as compared to the direct write-off method?

**P9-6B**   Schottenheimer Co. closes its books monthly. On June 30, selected ledger account balances are:

*Prepare entries for various notes receivable transactions.*

*(SO 2, 4, 5, 8, 9)*

GLS

| Notes Receivable | $46,000 |
|---|---|
| Interest Receivable | $    300 |

Notes Receivable include the following.

| **Date** | **Maker** | **Face** | **Term** | **Interest** |
|---|---|---|---|---|
| May 16 | Baylor Inc. | $ 6,000 | 60 days | 10% |
| May 25 | Felter Co. | 25,000 | 60 days | 9% |
| June 30 | ERV Corp. | 15,000 | 6 months | 8% |

During July, the following transactions were completed.

July  5  Made sales of $6,200 on Schottenheimer Co. credit cards.
   14  Made sales of $700 on Visa credit cards. The credit card service charge is 3%.
   14  Added $440 to Schottenheimer Co. credit card customer balances for finance charges on unpaid balances.
   15  Received payment in full from Baylor Inc. on the amount due.
   25  Received notice that the Felter Co. note has been dishonored. (Assume that Felter Co. is expected to pay in the future.)

**Instructions**
**(a)** Journalize the July transactions and the July 31 adjusting entry for accrued interest receivable. (Interest is computed using 360 days.)
**(b)** Enter the balances at July 1 in the receivable accounts. Post the entries to all of the receivable accounts.
**(c)** Show the balance sheet presentation of the receivable accounts at July 31.

*(b) Accounts receivable $32,015*

*(c) Total receivables $47,115*

**P9-7B**   On January 1, 2008, Frybendall Company had Accounts Receivable $56,900 and Allowance for Doubtful Accounts $4,700. Frybendall Company prepares financial statements annually. During the year the following selected transactions occurred.

*Prepare entries for various receivable transactions.*

*(SO 2, 4, 5, 6, 7, 8)*

Jan.  5  Sold $6,300 of merchandise to Klosterman Company, terms n/30.
Feb.  2  Accepted a $6,300, 4-month, 10% promissory note from Klosterman Company for the balance due.
   12  Sold $7,800 of merchandise to Menard Company and accepted Menard's $7,800, 2-month, 10% note for the balance due.
   26  Sold $4,000 of merchandise to Louk Co., terms n/10.
Apr.  5  Accepted a $4,000, 3-month, 8% note from Louk Co. for the balance due.
   12  Collected Menard Company note in full.
June  2  Collected Klosterman Company note in full.

July 5 Louk Co. dishonors its note of April 5. It is expected that Louk will eventually pay the amount owed.

15 Sold $7,000 of merchandise to Peck Co. and accepted Peck's $7,000, 3-month, 12% note for the amount due.

Oct. 15 Peck Co.'s note was dishonored. Peck Co. is bankrupt, and there is no hope of future settlement.

**Instructions**
Journalize the transactions.

## PROBLEMS: SET C

Visit the book's website at **www.wiley.com/college/weygandt**, and choose the Student Companion site, to access Problem Set C.

## CONTINUING COOKIE CHRONICLE

(*Note:* This is a continuation of the Cookie Chronicle from Chapters 1 through 8.)

**CCC9** One of Natalie's friends, Curtis Lesperance, runs a coffee shop where he sells specialty coffees and prepares and sells muffins and cookies. He is eager to buy one of Natalie's fine European mixers, which would enable him to make larger batches of muffins and cookies. However, Curtis cannot afford to pay for the mixer for at least 30 days. He asks Natalie if she would be willing to sell him the mixer on credit. Natalie comes to you for advice.

*Go to the book's website,*
**www.wiley.com/college/weygandt**,
*to see the completion of this problem.*

# BROADENING YOUR PERSPECTIVE

## FINANCIAL REPORTING AND ANALYSIS

### Financial Reporting Problem
### SEK Company

**BYP9-1** SEK Company sells office equipment and supplies to many organizations in the city and surrounding area on contract terms of 2/10, n/30. In the past, over 75% of the credit customers have taken advantage of the discount by paying within 10 days of the invoice date.

The number of customers taking the full 30 days to pay has increased within the last year. Current indications are that less than 60% of the customers are now taking the discount. Bad debts as a percentage of gross credit sales have risen from the 2.5% provided in past years to about 4.5% in the current year.

The company's Finance Committee has requested more information on the collections of accounts receivable. The controller responded to this request with the report reproduced below.

**SEK COMPANY**
Accounts Receivable Collections
May 31, 2008

The fact that some credit accounts will prove uncollectible is normal. Annual bad debts write-offs have been 2.5% of gross credit sales over the past 5 years. During the last fiscal year, this percentage increased to slightly less than 4.5%. The current Accounts Receivable balance is $1,400,000. The condition of this balance in terms of age and probability of collection is as follows.

| Proportion of Total | Age Categories | Probability of Collection |
|---|---|---|
| 62% | not yet due | 98% |
| 20% | less than 30 days past due | 96% |
| 9% | 30 to 60 days past due | 94% |
| 5% | 61 to 120 days past due | 91% |
| 2½% | 121 to 180 days past due | 75% |
| 1½% | over 180 days past due | 30% |

The Allowance for Doubtful Accounts had a credit balance of $29,500 on June 1, 2007. SEK has provided for a monthly bad debts expense accrual during the current fiscal year based on the assumption that 4.5% of gross credit sales will be uncollectible. Total gross credit sales for the 2007–08 fiscal year amounted to $2,900,000. Write-offs of bad accounts during the year totaled $102,000.

**Instructions**

(a) Prepare an accounts receivable aging schedule for SEK Company using the age categories identified in the controller's report to the Finance Committee showing the following.
  (1) The amount of accounts receivable outstanding for each age category and in total.
  (2) The estimated amount that is uncollectible for each category and in total.
(b) Compute the amount of the year-end adjustment necessary to bring Allowance for Doubtful Accounts to the balance indicated by the age analysis. Then prepare the necessary journal entry to adjust the accounting records.
(c) In a recessionary environment with tight credit and high interest rates:
  (1) Identify steps SEK Company might consider to improve the accounts receivable situation.
  (2) Then evaluate each step identified in terms of the risks and costs involved.

## Comparative Analysis Problem
### PepsiCo, Inc. vs. The Coca-Cola Company

**BYP9-2**  PepsiCo's financial statements are presented in Appendix A. Coca-Cola's financial statements are presented in Appendix B.

**Instructions**

(a) Based on the information in these financial statements, compute the following 2005 ratios for each company. (Assume all sales are credit sales. Also, see PepsiCo's Note 14.)
  (1) Accounts receivable turnover ratio.
  (2) Average collection period for receivables.
(b) What conclusions about managing accounts receivable can you draw from these data?

## Exploring the Web

**BYP9-3**  **Purpose:** To learn more about factoring services.

*Address:* **www.invoicefinancial.com**, or go to **www.wiley.com/college/weygandt**

**Steps:** Go to the website and answer the following questions.

(a) What are some of the benefits of factoring?
(b) What is the range of the percentages of the typical discount rate?
(c) If a company factors its receivables, what percentage of the value of the receivables can it expect to receive from the factor in the form of cash, and how quickly will it receive the cash?

## CRITICAL THINKING

## Decision Making Across the Organization

**BYP9-4**  Molly and Joe Mayne own Campus Fashions. From its inception Campus Fashions has sold merchandise on either a cash or credit basis, but no credit cards have been accepted. During the past several months, the Maynes have begun to question their sales policies. First, they have lost some sales because of refusing to accept credit cards. Second, representatives of two metropolitan banks have been persuasive in almost convincing them to accept their national credit cards. One bank, City National Bank, has stated that its credit card fee is 4%.

The Maynes decide that they should determine the cost of carrying their own credit sales. From the accounting records of the past 3 years they accumulate the following data.

| | 2008 | 2007 | 2006 |
|---|---|---|---|
| Net credit sales | $500,000 | $600,000 | $400,000 |
| Collection agency fees for slow-paying customers | 2,450 | 2,500 | 2,400 |
| Salary of part-time accounts receivable clerk | 4,100 | 4,100 | 4,100 |

Credit and collection expenses as a percentage of net credit sales are: uncollectible accounts 1.6%, billing and mailing costs 0.5%, and credit investigation fee on new customers 0.15%.

Molly and Joe also determine that the average accounts receivable balance outstanding during the year is 5% of net credit sales. The Maynes estimate that they could earn an average of 8% annually on cash invested in other business opportunities.

**Instructions**

With the class divided into groups, answer the following.

**(a)** Prepare a table showing, for each year, total credit and collection expenses in dollars and as a percentage of net credit sales.

**(b)** Determine the net credit and collection expense in dollars and as a percentage of sales after considering the revenue not earned from other investment opportunities.

**(c)** Discuss both the financial and nonfinancial factors that are relevant to the decision.

# Communication Activity

**BYP9-5**   Rene Mai, a friend of yours, overheard a discussion at work about changes her employer wants to make in accounting for uncollectible accounts. Rene knows little about accounting, and she asks you to help make sense of what she heard. Specifically, she asks you to explain the differences between the percentage-of-sales, percentage-of-receivables, and the direct write-off methods for uncollectible accounts.

**Instructions**

In a letter of one page (or less), explain to Rene the three methods of accounting for uncollectibles. Be sure to discuss differences among these methods.

# Ethics Case

**BYP9-6**   The controller of Ruiz Co. believes that the yearly allowance for doubtful accounts for Ruiz Co. should be 2% of net credit sales. The president of Ruiz Co., nervous that the stockholders might expect the company to sustain its 10% growth rate, suggests that the controller increase the allowance for doubtful accounts to 4%. The president thinks that the lower net income, which reflects a 6% growth rate, will be a more sustainable rate for Ruiz Co.

**Instructions**

**(a)** Who are the stakeholders in this case?

**(b)** Does the president's request pose an ethical dilemma for the controller?

**(c)** Should the controller be concerned with Ruiz Co.'s growth rate? Explain your answer.

 # "All About You" Activity

**BYP9-7**   As the "All About You" feature in this chapter (page 405) indicates, credit card usage in the United States is substantial. Many startup companies use credit cards as a way to help meet short-term financial needs. The most common forms of debt for startups are use of credit cards and loans from relatives.

Suppose that you start up Brothers Sandwich Shop. You invested your savings of $20,000 and borrowed $70,000 from your relatives. Although sales in the first few months are good, you see that you may not have sufficient cash to pay expenses and maintain your inventory at acceptable levels, at least in the short term. You decide you may need to use one or more credit cards to fund the possible cash shortfall.

**Instructions**

**(a)** Go to the Web and find two sources that provide insight into how to compare credit card terms.

**(b)** Develop a list, in descending order of importance, as to what features are most important to you in selecting a credit card for your business.

**(c)** Examine the features of your present credit card. (If you do not have a credit card, select a likely one online for this exercise.) Given your analysis above, what are the three major disadvantages of your present credit card?

## Answers to Insight and Accounting Across the Organization Questions

**Be Sure to Read the Fine Print, p. 388**

Q: Why are credit card companies willing to offer relaxed repayment options?

A: *Credit card companies generate their income primarily from interest charges on cardholders' balances. The larger the outstanding balances, the greater the interest income.*

**When Investors Ignore Warning Signs, p. 394**

Q: When would it be appropriate for a company to lower its allowance for doubtful accounts as a percentage of its receivables?

A: *It could do so if the company's collection experience had improved, or was expected to improve, and therefore the company expected lower defaults as a percentage of receivables.*

**How Does a Credit Card Work?, p. 397**

Q: Assume that Nordstrom prepares a bank reconciliation at the end of each month. If some credit card sales have not been processed by the bank, how should Nordstrom treat these transactions on its bank reconciliation?

A: *Nordstrom would treat the credit card receipts as deposits in transit. It has already recorded the receipts as cash. Its bank will increase Nordstrom's cash account when it receives the receipts.*

**Who Gets Credit?, p. 402**

Q: How would reported net income likely differ during the first year of this promotion if Mitsubishi used the direct write-off method versus the allowance method?

A: *Under the direct write-off method, Mitsubishi would not record bad debt expense until a customer defaulted on a loan. Under the allowance method, it would estimate how many of its loans would default rather than waiting until they default. The direct write-off method would have resulted in higher net income during the first year of the promotion.*

## Authors' Comments on *All About You:* Should You Be Carrying Plastic?, p. 405

We aren't going to tell you to cut up your credit card(s). Well, we aren't going to tell *all* of you to do so. Credit cards, when used properly, can serve a very useful purpose. They provide great convenience, are widely accepted, and can be a source of security in an emergency. But too many Americans use credit cards inappropriately. When businesses purchase short-term items such as inventory and supplies, they use short-term credit, which they expect to pay back very quickly. The same should be true of your credit card. When you make purchases of everyday items, you should completely pay off those items within a month or two. If you don't, you are living beyond your means, and you will soon dig yourself a deep financial pit.

Longer-term items should not be purchased with credit cards, since the interest rate is too high. If you currently have a large balance on your credit card(s), we encourage you to cut up your card(s) until you have paid off your balance(s).

## Answer to PepsiCo Review It Question 3, p. 394

According to Note 14, PepsiCo's gross receivables were $3,336 million. Its allowance for doubtful accounts was $75 million. Therefore, the allowance is 2.2% of the gross receivables balance.

## Answers to Self-Study Questions

**1.** c   **2.** a   **3.** b   **4.** b   **5.** d   **6.** c   **7.** c   **8.** a   **9.** b   **10.** d

 *Remember to go back to the Navigator box on the chapter-opening page and check off your completed work.*

# Chapter 10

# Plant Assets, Natural Resources, and Intangible Assets

## STUDY OBJECTIVES

*After studying this chapter, you should be able to:*

1 Describe how the cost principle applies to plant assets.
2 Explain the concept of depreciation.
3 Compute periodic depreciation using different methods.
4 Describe the procedure for revising periodic depreciation.
5 Distinguish between revenue and capital expenditures, and explain the entries for each.
6 Explain how to account for the disposal of a plant asset.
7 Compute periodic depletion of natural resources.
8 Explain the basic issues related to accounting for intangible assets.
9 Indicate how plant assets, natural resources, and intangible assets are reported.

*The Navigator*

## ✓ The Navigator

| | |
|---|---|
| Scan **Study Objectives** | ■ |
| Read **Feature Story** | ■ |
| Read **Preview** | ■ |
| Read text and answer **Before You Go On** p. 430 ■   p. 437 ■   p. 441 ■   p. 449 ■ | |
| Work **Demonstration Problems** | ■ |
| Review **Summary of Study Objectives** | ■ |
| Answer **Self-Study Questions** | ■ |
| Complete **Assignments** | ■ |

## Feature Story

### HOW MUCH FOR A RIDE TO THE BEACH?

It's spring break. Your plane has landed, you've finally found your bags, and you're dying to hit the beach—but first you need a "vehicular unit" to get

you there. As you turn away from baggage claim you see a long row of rental agency booths. Many are names you are familiar with—Hertz, Avis, and Budget. But a booth at the far end catches your eye—Rent-A-Wreck (*www.rent-a-wreck.com*). Now there's a company making a clear statement!

Any company that relies on equipment to generate revenues must make decisions about what kind of equipment to buy, how long to keep it, and how vigorously to maintain it. Rent-A-Wreck has decided to rent used rather than new cars and trucks. It rents these vehicles across the United States, Europe, and Asia. While the big-name agencies push vehicles with that "new car smell," Rent-A-Wreck competes on price. The message is simple: Rent a used car and save some cash. It's not a message that appeals to everyone. If you're a marketing executive wanting to impress a big client, you probably don't want to pull up in a Rent-A-Wreck car. But if you want to get from point A to point B for the minimum cash per mile, then they are playing your tune. The company's message seems to be getting across to the right clientele. Revenues have increased significantly.

When you rent a car from Rent-A-Wreck, you are renting from an independent business person who has paid a "franchise fee" for the right to use the Rent-A-Wreck name. In order to gain a franchise, he or she must meet financial and other criteria, and must agree to run the rental agency according to rules prescribed by Rent-A-Wreck. Some of these rules require that each franchise maintain its cars in a reasonable fashion. This ensures that, though you won't be cruising down Daytona Beach's Atlantic Avenue in a Mercedes convertible, you can be reasonably assured that you won't be calling a towtruck.

✓ *The Navigator*

## *Inside Chapter 10*

The accounting for long-term assets has important implications for a company's reported results. In this chapter, we explain the application of the cost principle of accounting to property, plant, and equipment, such as Rent-A-Wreck vehicles, as well as to natural resources and intangible assets such as the "Rent-A-Wreck" trademark. We also describe the methods that companies may use to allocate an asset's cost over its useful life. In addition, we discuss the accounting for expenditures incurred during the useful life of assets, such as the cost of replacing tires and brake pads on rental cars.

The content and organization of Chapter 10 are as follows.

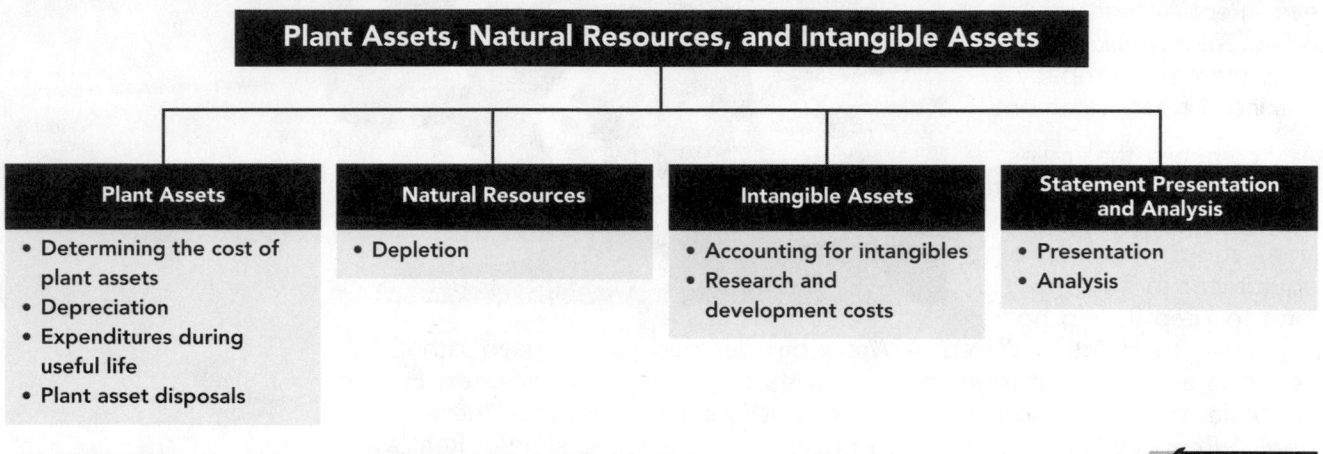

✓ *The Navigator*

# SECTION 1 **Plant Assets**

Plant assets are resources that have three characteristics: they have a physical substance (a definite size and shape), are used in the operations of a business, and are not intended for sale to customers. They are also called **property**, **plant**, **and equipment**; **plant and equipment**; and **fixed assets**. These assets are expected to provide services to the company for a number of years. Except for land, plant assets decline in service potential over their useful lives.

Because plant assets play a key role in ongoing operations, companies keep plant assets in good operating condition. They also replace worn-out or outdated plant assets, and expand productive resources as needed. Many companies have substantial investments in plant assets. Illustration 10-1 shows the

**Illustration 10-1**
Percentages of plant assets in relation to total assets

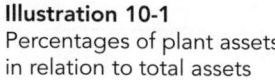

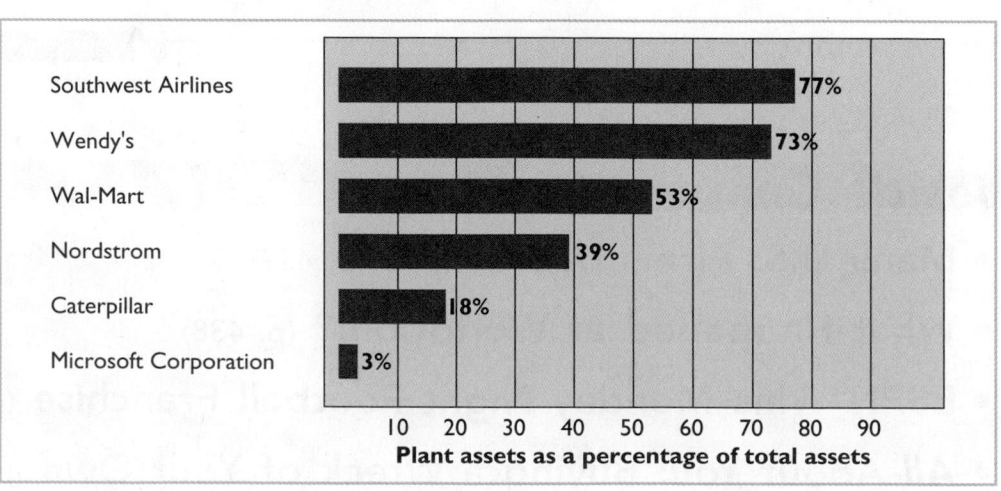

percentages of plant assets in relation to total assets of companies in a number of industries.

# DETERMINING THE COST OF PLANT ASSETS

The cost principle requires that companies record plant assets at cost. Thus Rent-A-Wreck records its vehicles at cost( **Cost consists of all expenditures necessary to acquire the asset and make it ready for its intended use.**) For example, the cost of factory machinery includes the purchase price, freight costs paid by the purchaser, and installation costs. Once cost is established, the company uses that amount as the basis of accounting for the plant asset over its useful life.

**STUDY OBJECTIVE 1**

Describe how the cost principle applies to plant assets.

In the following sections, we explain the application of the cost principle to each of the major classes of plant assets.

## Land

Companies acquire **land** for use as a site upon which to build a manufacturing plant, store, warehouse, or office.\The cost of land includes (1) the cash purchase price, (2) closing costs such as title and attorney's fees, (3) real estate brokers' commissions, and (4) accrued property taxes and other liens assumed by the purchaser.\ For example, if the cash price is $50,000 and the purchaser agrees to pay accrued taxes of $5,000, the cost of the land is $55,000.

\Companies record as debits (increases) to the Land account all necessary costs incurred to make land **ready for its intended use.**\When a company acquires vacant land, these costs include expenditures for clearing, draining, filling, and grading. Sometimes the land has a building on it that must be removed before construction of a new building. In this case, the company debits to the Land account all demolition and removal costs, less any proceeds from salvaged materials.

**HELPFUL HINT**

Management's intended use is important in applying the cost principle.

To illustrate, assume that Hayes Manufacturing Company acquires real estate at a cash cost of $100,000. The property contains an old warehouse that is razed at a net cost of $6,000 ($7,500 in costs less $1,500 proceeds from salvaged materials). Additional expenditures are the attorney's fee, $1,000, and the real estate broker's commission, $8,000. The cost of the land is $115,000, computed as follows.

**Illustration 10-2**
Computation of cost of land

| Land | |
|---|---|
| Cash price of property | $100,000 |
| Net removal cost of warehouse | 6,000 |
| Attorney's fee | 1,000 |
| Real estate broker's commission | 8,000 |
| **Cost of land** | **$115,000** |

When Hayes records the acquisition, it debits Land for $115,000 and credits Cash for $115,000.

## Land Improvements

**Land improvements** are structural additions made to land. Examples are driveways, parking lots, fences, landscaping, and underground sprinklers. The cost of land improvements includes all expenditures necessary to make the improvements ready for their intended use. For example, the cost of a new parking lot for Home Depot includes the amount paid for paving, fencing, and lighting. Thus Home Depot debits to Land Improvements the total of all of these costs.

Land improvements have limited useful lives, and their maintenance and replacement are the responsibility of the company. Because of their limited useful life, companies expense (depreciate) the cost of land improvements over their useful lives.

## Buildings

**Buildings** are facilities used in operations, such as stores, offices, factories, warehouses, and airplane hangars. Companies debit to the Buildings account all necessary expenditures related to the purchase or construction of a building. When a building is **purchased**, such costs include the purchase price, closing costs (attorney's fees, title insurance, etc.) and real estate broker's commission. Costs to make the building ready for its intended use include expenditures for remodeling and replacing or repairing the roof, floors, electrical wiring, and plumbing. When a new building is **constructed**, cost consists of the contract price plus payments for architects' fees, building permits, and excavation costs.

In addition, companies charge certain interest costs to the Buildings account. Interest costs incurred to finance the project are included in the cost of the building when a significant period of time is required to get the building ready for use. In these circumstances, interest costs are considered as necessary as materials and labor. However, the inclusion of interest costs in the cost of a constructed building is **limited to the construction period**. When construction has been completed, the company records subsequent interest payments on funds borrowed to finance the construction as debits (increases) to Interest Expense.

## Equipment

**Equipment** includes assets used in operations, such as store check-out counters, office furniture, factory machinery, delivery trucks, and airplanes. The cost of equipment, such as Rent-A-Wreck vehicles, consists of the **cash purchase price**, **sales taxes**, **freight charges**, **and insurance during transit paid by the purchaser.** It also includes expenditures required in assembling, installing, and testing the unit. However, Rent-A-Wreck does not include motor vehicle licenses and accident insurance on company vehicles in the cost of equipment. These costs represent annual recurring expenditures and do not benefit future periods. Thus, they are treated as expenses as they are incurred.

To illustrate, assume Merten Company purchases factory machinery at a cash price of $50,000. Related expenditures are for sales taxes $3,000, insurance during shipping $500, and installation and testing $1,000. The cost of the factory machinery is $54,500, computed as follows.

**Illustration 10-3**
Computation of cost of factory machinery

| Factory Machinery | |
| --- | ---: |
| Cash price | $50,000 |
| Sales taxes | 3,000 |
| Insurance during shipping | 500 |
| Installation and testing | 1,000 |
| **Cost of factory machinery** | **$54,500** |

Merten makes the following summary entry to record the purchase and related expenditures:

| | | |
|---|---|---|
| Factory Machinery | 54,500 | |
| Cash | | 54,500 |
| (To record purchase of factory machine) | | |

| A | = | L | + | SE |
|---|---|---|---|---|
| +54,500 | | | | |
| −54,500 | | | | |

**Cash Flows**
−54,500

For another example, assume that Lenard Company purchases a delivery truck at a cash price of $22,000. Related expenditures consist of sales taxes $1,320, painting and lettering $500, motor vehicle license $80, and a three-year accident insurance policy $1,600. The cost of the delivery truck is $23,820, computed as follows.

**Illustration 10-4**
Computation of cost of delivery truck

| **Delivery Truck** | |
|---|---|
| Cash price | $22,000 |
| Sales taxes | 1,320 |
| Painting and lettering | 500 |
| **Cost of delivery truck** | **$23,820** |

Lenard treats the cost of the motor vehicle license as an expense, and the cost of the insurance policy as a prepaid asset. Thus, Lenard makes the following entry to record the purchase of the truck and related expenditures:

| | | |
|---|---|---|
| Delivery Truck | 23,820 | |
| License Expense | 80 | |
| Prepaid Insurance | 1,600 | |
| Cash | | 25,500 |
| (To record purchase of delivery truck and related expenditures) | | |

| A | = | L | + | SE |
|---|---|---|---|---|
| +23,820 | | | | |
| | | | | −80 Exp |
| +1,600 | | | | |
| −25,500 | | | | |

**Cash Flows**
−25,500

# ACCOUNTING ACROSS THE ORGANIZATION

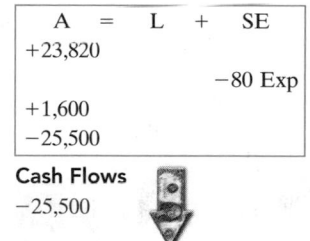

### *Many U.S. Firms Use Leases*

Leasing is big business for U.S. companies. For example, business investment in equipment in 2004 totaled $709 billion. Leasing accounted for about 31% of all business investment ($218 billion).

Who does the most leasing? Interestingly major banks, such as Continental Bank, J.P. Morgan Leasing, and US Bancorp Equipment Finance, are the major lessors. Also, many companies have established separate leasing companies, such as Boeing Capital Corporation, Dell Financial Services, and John Deere Capital Corporation. And, as an excellent example of the magnitude of leasing, leased planes account for nearly 40% of the U.S. fleet of commercial airlines. In addition, leasing is becoming increasingly common in the hotel industry. Marriott, Hilton, and InterContinental are increasingly choosing to lease hotels that are owned by someone else.

 Why might airline managers choose to lease rather than purchase their planes?

## *Before You Go On...*

### REVIEW IT

1. What are plant assets? What are the major classes of plant assets? How do companies apply the cost principle to accounting for plant assets?
2. What classifications and amounts are shown in PepsiCo's Note 4 to explain its total property, plant, and equipment (net) of $8,681,000,000? The answer to this question appears on p. 471.

### DO IT

Assume that Drummond Heating and Cooling Co. purchases a delivery truck for $15,000 cash, plus sales taxes of $900 and delivery costs to the dealer of $500. The buyer also pays $200 for painting and lettering, $600 for an annual insurance policy, and $80 for a motor vehicle license. Explain how each of these costs would be accounted for.

### Action Plan

■ Identify expenditures made in order to get delivery equipment ready for its intended use.
■ Treat operating costs as expenses.

**Solution**   The first four payments ($15,000, $900, $500, and $200) are expenditures necessary to make the truck ready for its intended use. Thus, the cost of the truck is $16,600. The payments for insurance and the license are operating costs and therefore are expensed.

*Related exercise material: BE10-1, BE10-2, E10-1, E10-2, and E10-3.*

✓ *The Navigator*

# DEPRECIATION

**STUDY OBJECTIVE 2**

Explain the concept of depreciation.

As explained in Chapter 3, **depreciation is the process of allocating to expense the cost of a plant asset over its useful (service) life in a rational and systematic manner.** Cost allocation enables companies to properly match expenses with revenues in accordance with the matching principle (see Illustration 10-5).

**Illustration 10-5**
Depreciation as an allocation concept

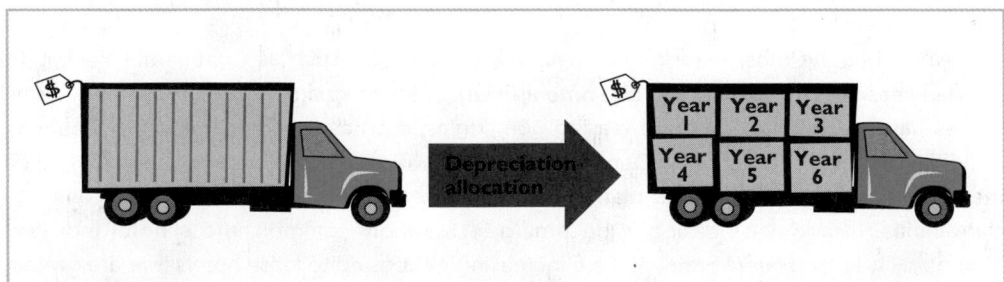

It is important to understand that **depreciation is a process of cost allocation, not a process of asset valuation.** No attempt is made to measure the change in an asset's market value during ownership. So, the **book value** (cost less accumulated depreciation) of a plant asset may be quite different from its market value.

Depreciation applies to three classes of plant assets: land improvements, buildings, and equipment. Each asset in these classes is considered to be a **depreciable asset**. Why? Because the usefulness to the company and revenue-producing ability of each asset will decline over the asset's useful life. Depreciation **does not apply to land** because its usefulness and revenue-producing ability generally remain intact over time. In fact, in many cases, the usefulness of land is greater over time because of the scarcity of good land sites. Thus, **land is not a depreciable asset**.

During a depreciable asset's useful life its revenue-producing ability declines because of **wear and tear**. A delivery truck that has been driven 100,000 miles will be less useful to a company than one driven only 800 miles.

Revenue-producing ability may also decline because of obsolescence. **Obsolescence** is the process of becoming out of date before the asset physically wears out. For example, major airlines moved from Chicago's Midway Airport to Chicago-O'Hare International Airport because Midway's runways were too short for jumbo jets. Similarly, many companies replace their computers long before they originally planned to do so because improvements in new computing technology make the old computers obsolete.

**Recognizing depreciation on an asset does not result in an accumulation of cash for replacement of the asset**. The balance in Accumulated Depreciation represents the total amount of the asset's cost that the company has charged to expense. It is not a cash fund.

Note that the concept of depreciation is consistent with the going-concern assumption. The **going-concern assumption** states that the company will continue in operation for the foreseeable future. If a company does not use a going-concern assumption, then plant assets should be stated at their market value. In that case, depreciation of these assets is not needed.

> **ETHICS NOTE**
>
> When a business is acquired, proper allocation of the purchase price to various asset classes is important, since different depreciation treatment can materially affect income. For example, buildings are depreciated, but land is not.

## Factors in Computing Depreciation

Three factors affect the computation of depreciation:

1. **Cost.** Earlier, we explained the issues affecting the cost of a depreciable asset. Recall that companies record plant assets at cost, in accordance with the cost principle.

2. **Useful life.** Useful life is an estimate of the expected *productive life*, also called *service life*, of the asset. Useful life may be expressed in terms of time, units of activity (such as machine hours), or units of output. Useful life is an estimate. In making the estimate, management considers such factors as the intended use of the asset, its expected repair and maintenance, and its vulnerability to obsolescence. Past experience with similar assets is often helpful in deciding on expected useful life. We might reasonably expect Rent-A-Wreck and Avis to use different estimated useful lives for their vehicles.

3. **Salvage value.** Salvage value is an estimate of the asset's value at the end of its useful life. This value may be based on the asset's worth as scrap or on its expected trade-in value. Like useful life, salvage value is an estimate. In making the estimate, management considers how it plans to dispose of the asset and its experience with similar assets.

> **ALTERNATIVE TERMINOLOGY**
>
> Another term sometimes used for salvage value is *residual value*.

Illustration 10-6 (on page 432) summarizes the three factors used in computing depreciation.

**Illustration 10-6**
Three factors in computing depreciation

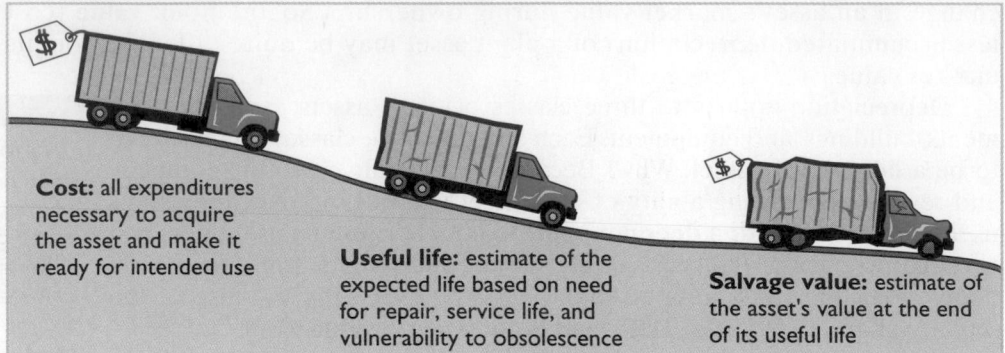

**Cost:** all expenditures necessary to acquire the asset and make it ready for intended use

**Useful life:** estimate of the expected life based on need for repair, service life, and vulnerability to obsolescence

**Salvage value:** estimate of the asset's value at the end of its useful life

# Depreciation Methods

**STUDY OBJECTIVE 3**

Compute periodic depreciation using different methods.

Depreciation is generally computed using one of the following methods:

1. Straight-line
2. Units-of-activity
3. Declining-balance

Each method is acceptable under generally accepted accounting principles. Management selects the method(s) it believes to be appropriate. The objective is to select the method that best measures an asset's contribution to revenue over its useful life. Once a company chooses a method, it should apply it consistently over the useful life of the asset. Consistency enhances the comparability of financial statements. Depreciation affects the balance sheet through accumulated depreciation and the income statement through depreciation expense.

We will compare the three depreciation methods using the following data for a small delivery truck purchased by Barb's Florists on January 1, 2008.

**Illustration 10-7**
Delivery truck data

| | |
|---|---|
| Cost | $13,000 |
| Expected salvage value | $ 1,000 |
| Estimated useful life in years | 5 |
| Estimated useful life in miles | 100,000 |

Illustration 10-8 (in the margin) shows the use of the primary depreciation methods in 600 of the largest companies in the United States.

**STRAIGHT-LINE**

Under the straight-line method, companies expense the same amount of depreciation for each year of the asset's useful life. It is measured solely by the passage of time.

In order to compute depreciation expense under the straight-line method, companies need to determine depreciable cost. Depreciable cost is the cost of the asset less its salvage value. It represents the total amount subject to depreciation. Under the straight-line method, to determine annual depreciation expense, we divide depreciable cost by the asset's useful life. Illustration 10-9 (next page) shows the computation of the first year's depreciation expense for Barb's Florists.

Alternatively, we also can compute an annual **rate** of depreciation. In this case, the rate is 20% (100% ÷ 5 years). When a company uses an annual straight-line rate, it applies the percentage rate to the depreciable cost of the asset. Illustration 10-10 shows a **depreciation schedule** using an annual rate.

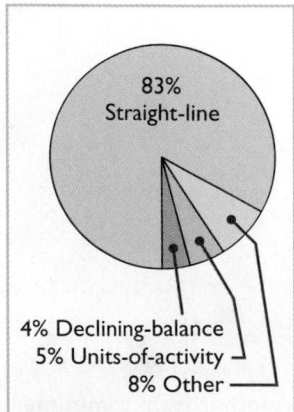

83% Straight-line

4% Declining-balance
5% Units-of-activity
8% Other

**Illustration 10-8**
Use of depreciation methods in 600 large U.S. companies

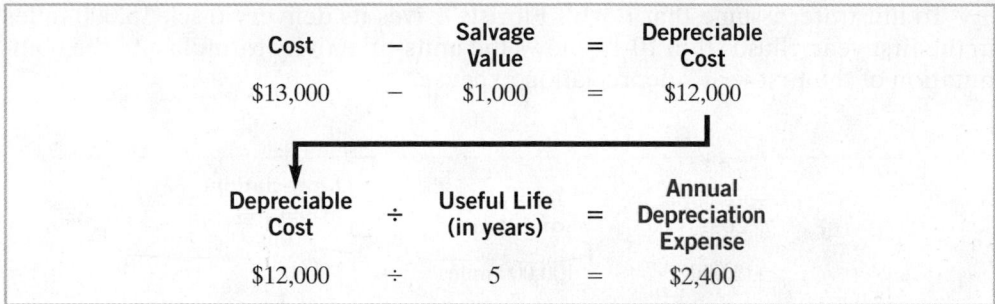

**Illustration 10-9**
Formula for straight-line method

| | | **BARB'S FLORISTS** | | | | |
|---|---|---|---|---|---|---|
| | **Computation** | | | **Annual** | **End of Year** | |
| **Year** | **Depreciable Cost** | × | **Depreciation Rate** = | **Depreciation Expense** | **Accumulated Depreciation** | **Book Value** |
| 2008 | $12,000 | | 20% | **$2,400** | $ 2,400 | $10,600* |
| 2009 | 12,000 | | 20 | **2,400** | 4,800 | 8,200 |
| 2010 | 12,000 | | 20 | **2,400** | 7,200 | 5,800 |
| 2011 | 12,000 | | 20 | **2,400** | 9,600 | 3,400 |
| 2012 | 12,000 | | 20 | **2,400** | 12,000 | **1,000** |

*Book Value = Cost − Accumulated depreciation = ($13,000 − $2,400).

**Illustration 10-10**
Straight-line depreciation schedule

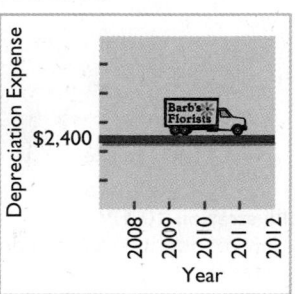

Note that the depreciation expense of $2,400 is the same each year. The book value (computed as cost minus accumulated depreciation) at the end of the useful life is equal to the expected $1,000 salvage value.

What happens to these computations for an asset purchased **during** the year, rather than on January 1? In that case, it is necessary to **prorate the annual depreciation** on a time basis. If Barb's Florists had purchased the delivery truck on April 1, 2008, the company would own the truck for nine months of the first year (April–December). Thus, depreciation for 2008 would be $1,800 ($12,000 × 20% × 9/12 of a year).

The straight-line method predominates in practice. Such large companies as Campbell Soup, Marriott, and General Mills use the straight-line method. It is simple to apply, and it matches expenses with revenues when the benefit received from the asset is reasonably uniform throughout the service life. For simplicity, Rent-A-Wreck is probably using the straight-line method of depreciation for its vehicles.

## UNITS-OF-ACTIVITY

Under the units-of-activity method, useful life is expressed in terms of the total units of production or use expected from the asset, rather than as a time period. The units-of-activity method is ideally suited to factory machinery. Manufacturing companies can measure production in units of output or in machine hours. This method can also be used for such assets as delivery equipment (miles driven) and airplanes (hours in use). The units-of-activity method is generally not suitable for buildings or furniture, because depreciation for these assets is more a function of time than of use.

To use this method, companies estimate the total units of activity for the entire useful life, and then divide these units into depreciable cost. The resulting number represents the depreciation cost per unit. The depreciation cost per unit is then applied to the units of activity during the year to determine the annual depreciation expense.

**ALTERNATIVE TERMINOLOGY**

Another term often used is the *units-of-production method.*

**HELPFUL HINT**

Under any method, depreciation stops when the asset's book value equals expected salvage value.

To illustrate, assume that Barb's Florists drives its delivery truck 15,000 miles in the first year. Illustration 10-11 shows the units-of-activity formula and the computation of the first year's depreciation expense.

**Illustration 10-11**
Formula for units-of-activity method

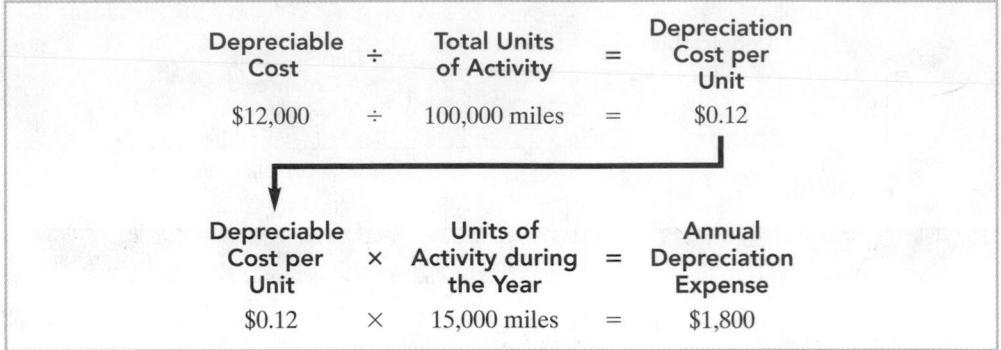

The units-of-activity depreciation schedule, using assumed mileage, is as follows.

**Illustration 10-12**
Units-of-activity depreciation schedule

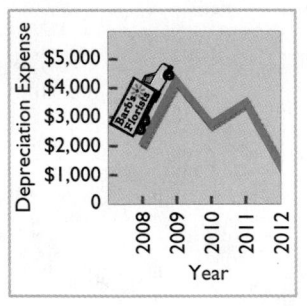

| | Computation | | | Annual | End of Year | |
|---|---|---|---|---|---|---|
| Year | Units of Activity | × | Depreciation Cost/Unit | = Annual Depreciation Expense | Accumulated Depreciation | Book Value |
| 2008 | 15,000 | | $0.12 | **$1,800** | $ 1,800 | $11,200* |
| 2009 | 30,000 | | 0.12 | **3,600** | 5,400 | 7,600 |
| 2010 | 20,000 | | 0.12 | **2,400** | 7,800 | 5,200 |
| 2011 | 25,000 | | 0.12 | **3,000** | 10,800 | 2,200 |
| 2012 | 10,000 | | 0.12 | **1,200** | 12,000 | **1,000** |

*($13,000 − $1,800).

**BARB'S FLORISTS**

This method is easy to apply for assets purchased mid-year. In such a case, the company computes the depreciation using the productivity of the asset for the partial year.

The units-of-activity method is not nearly as popular as the straight-line method (see Illustration 10-8, page 432), primarily because it is often difficult for companies to reasonably estimate total activity. However, some very large companies, such as Chevron and Boise Cascade (a forestry company), do use this method. When the productivity of an asset varies significantly from one period to another, the units-of-activity method results in the best matching of expenses with revenues.

## DECLINING-BALANCE

The **declining-balance method** produces a decreasing annual depreciation expense over the asset's useful life. The method is so named because the periodic depreciation is based on a **declining book value** (cost less accumulated depreciation) of the asset. With this method, companies compute annual depreciation expense by multiplying the book value at the beginning of the year by the declining-balance depreciation rate. **The depreciation rate remains constant from year to year, but the book value to which the rate is applied declines each year.**

( At the beginning of the first year, book value is the cost of the asset.)This is so because the balance in accumulated depreciation at the beginning of the asset's useful life is zero. In subsequent years, book value is the difference between cost and accumulated depreciation to date. Unlike the other depreciation methods, the declining-balance method does not use depreciable cost. That is, **it ignores salvage value in determining the amount to which the declining-balance rate is applied.** Salvage value, however, does limit the total depreciation that can be taken. Depreciation stops when the asset's book value equals expected salvage value.

A common declining-balance rate is double the straight-line rate. The method is often called the **double-declining-balance method.** If Barb's Florists uses the double-declining-balance method, it uses a depreciation rate of 40% (2 × the straight-line rate of 20%). Illustration 10-13 shows the declining-balance formula and the computation of the first year's depreciation on the delivery truck.

| Book Value at Beginning of Year | × | Declining-Balance Rate | = | Annual Depreciation Expense |
|---|---|---|---|---|
| $13,000 | × | 40% | = | $5,200 |

**Illustration 10-13**
Formula for declining-balance method

The depreciation schedule under this method is as follows.

**Illustration 10-14**
Double-declining-balance depreciation schedule

### BARB'S FLORISTS

| | Computation | | | Annual | End of Year | |
| Year | Book Value Beginning of Year | × Depreciation Rate = | | Depreciation Expense | Accumulated Depreciation | Book Value |
|---|---|---|---|---|---|---|
| 2008 | $13,000 | 40% | | **$5,200** | $ 5,200 | $7,800 |
| 2009 | 7,800 | 40 | | **3,120** | 8,320 | 4,680 |
| 2010 | 4,680 | 40 | | **1,872** | 10,192 | 2,808 |
| 2011 | 2,808 | 40 | | **1,123** | 11,315 | 1,685 |
| 2012 | 1,685 | 40 | | **685*** | 12,000 | **1,000** |

*Computation of $674 ($1,685 × 40%) is adjusted to $685 in order for book value to equal salvage value.

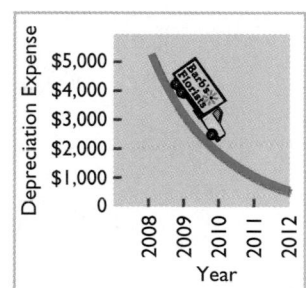

The delivery equipment is 69% depreciated ($8,320 ÷ $12,000) at the end of the second year. Under the straight-line method, the truck would be depreciated 40% ($4,800 ÷ $12,000) at that time. Because the declining-balance method produces higher depreciation expense in the early years than in the later years, it is considered an accelerated-depreciation method. The declining-balance method is compatible with the matching principle. It matches the higher depreciation expense in early years with the higher benefits received in these years. It also recognizes lower depreciation expense in later years, when the asset's contribution to revenue is less. Some assets lose usefulness rapidly because of obsolescence. In these cases, the declining-balance method provides the most appropriate depreciation amount.

When a company purchases an asset during the year, it must pro-rate the first year's declining-balance depreciation on a time basis. For example, if Barb's Florists had purchased the truck on April 1, 2008, depreciation for 2008 would become $3,900 ($13,000 × 40% × 9/12). The book value at the beginning of 2009 is then $9,100 ($13,000 − $3,900), and the 2009 depreciation is $3,640 ($9,100 × 40%). Subsequent computations would follow from those amounts.

**HELPFUL HINT**

The method recommended for an asset that is expected to be significantly more productive in the first half of its useful life is the declining-balance method.

## COMPARISON OF METHODS

Illustration 10-15 compares annual and total depreciation expense under each of the three methods for Barb's Florists.

**Illustration 10-15**
Comparison of depreciation methods

| Year | Straight-Line | Units-of-Activity | Declining-Balance |
|------|---------------|-------------------|-------------------|
| 2008 | $ 2,400 | $ 1,800 | $ 5,200 |
| 2009 | 2,400 | 3,600 | 3,120 |
| 2010 | 2,400 | 2,400 | 1,872 |
| 2011 | 2,400 | 3,000 | 1,123 |
| 2012 | 2,400 | 1,200 | 685 |
| | **$12,000** | **$12,000** | **$12,000** |

Annual depreciation varies considerably among the methods, but **total depreciation is the same for the five-year period** under all three methods. Each method is acceptable in accounting, because each recognizes in a rational and systematic manner the decline in service potential of the asset. Illustration 10-16 graphs the depreciation expense pattern under each method.

**Illustration 10-16**
Patterns of depreciation

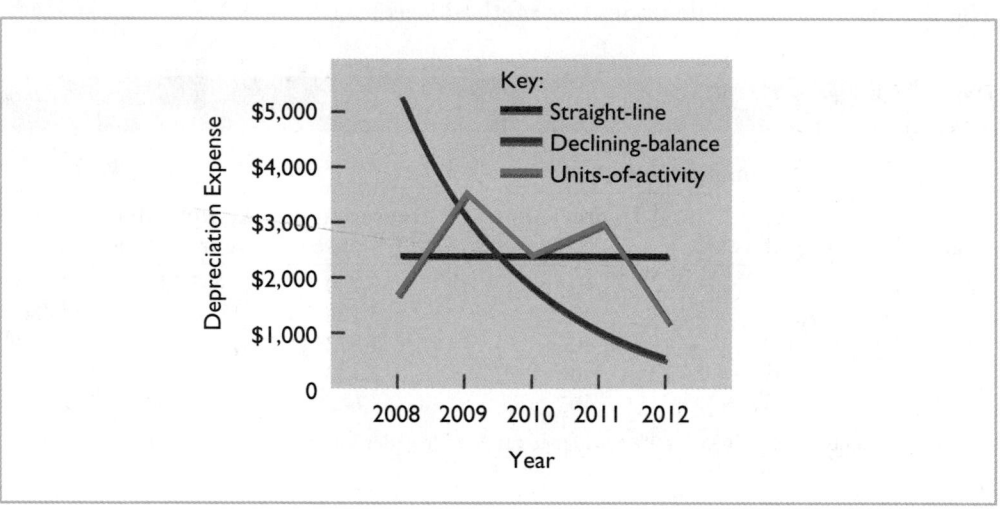

## Depreciation and Income Taxes

The Internal Revenue Service (IRS) allows corporate taxpayers to deduct depreciation expense when they compute taxable income. However, the IRS does not require the taxpayer to use the same depreciation method on the tax return that is used in preparing financial statements.

Many corporations use straight-line in their financial statements to maximize net income. At the same time, they use a special accelerated-depreciation method on their tax returns to minimize their income taxes. Taxpayers must use on their tax returns either the straight-line method or a special accelerated-depreciation method called the **Modified Accelerated Cost Recovery System** (MACRS).

## Revising Periodic Depreciation

Depreciation is one example of the use of estimation in the accounting process. Management should periodically review annual depreciation expense. If wear and tear or obsolescence indicate that annual depreciation estimates are inadequate or excessive, the company should change the amount of depreciation expense.⟩

⟨When a change in an estimate is required, the company makes the change in **current and future years. It does not change depreciation in prior periods.**⟩The rationale is that continual restatement of prior periods would adversely affect confidence in financial statements.

To determine the new annual depreciation expense, the company first computes the asset's depreciable cost at the time of the revision. It then allocates the revised depreciable cost to the remaining useful life.

To illustrate, assume that Barb's Florists decides on January 1, 2011, to extend the useful life of the truck one year because of its excellent condition. The company has used the straight-line method to depreciate the asset to date, and book value is $5,800 ($13,000 − $7,200). The new annual depreciation is $1,600, computed as follows.

| | | |
|---|---:|---|
| Book value, 1/1/11 | $5,800 | |
| Less: Salvage value | 1,000 | |
| Depreciable cost | $4,800 | |
| Remaining useful life | 3 years | (2011–2013) |
| **Revised annual depreciation ($4,800 ÷ 3)** | **$1,600** | |

**Illustration 10-17**
Revised depreciation computation

Barb's Florists makes no entry for the change in estimate. On December 31, 2011, during the preparation of adjusting entries, it records depreciation expense of $1,600. Companies must describe in the financial statements significant changes in estimates.

**HELPFUL HINT**
Use a step-by-step approach: (1) determine new depreciable cost; (2) divide by remaining useful life.

## *Before You Go On...*

### REVIEW IT

1. What is the relationship, if any, of depreciation to (a) cost allocation, (b) asset valuation, and (c) cash accumulation?

2. Explain the factors that affect the computation of depreciation.

3. What are the formulas for computing annual depreciation under each of the depreciation methods?

4. How do the methods differ in terms of their effects on annual depreciation over the useful life of the asset?

5. Do companies make revisions of periodic depreciation to prior periods? Explain.

### DO IT

On January 1, 2008, Iron Mountain Ski Corporation purchased a new snow-grooming machine for $50,000. The machine is estimated to have a 10-year life with a $2,000 salvage value. What journal entry would Iron Mountain Ski Corporation make at December 31, 2008, if it uses the straight-line method of depreciation?

### Action Plan

■ Calculate depreciable cost (Cost − Salvage value).
■ Divide the depreciable cost by the estimated useful life.

### Solution

$$\text{Depreciation expense} = \frac{\text{Cost} - \text{Salvage value}}{\text{Useful life}} = \frac{\$50,000 - \$2,000}{10} = \$4,800$$

The entry to record the first year's depreciation would be:

| Dec. 31 | Depreciation Expense | 4,800 | |
| | Accumulated Depreciation | | 4,800 |
| | (To record annual depreciation on snow-grooming machine) | | |

Related exercise material: *BE10-3, BE10-4, BE10-5, BE10-6, BE10-7, E10-5, E10-6, E10-7, and E10-8.*

✓ *The Navigator*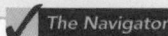

# EXPENDITURES DURING USEFUL LIFE

**STUDY OBJECTIVE 5**

Distinguish between revenue and capital expenditures, and explain the entries for each.

During the useful life of a plant asset, a company may incur costs for ordinary repairs, additions, or improvements. **Ordinary repairs** are expenditures to **maintain** the operating efficiency and productive life of the unit. They usually are fairly small amounts that occur frequently. Examples are motor tune-ups and oil changes, the painting of buildings, and the replacing of worn-out gears on machinery. Companies record such repairs as debits to Repair (or Maintenance) Expense as they are incurred. Because they are immediately charged as an expense against revenues, these costs are often referred to as **revenue expenditures**.

**Additions and improvements** are costs incurred to **increase** the operating efficiency, productive capacity, or useful life of a plant asset. They are usually material in amount and occur infrequently. Additions and improvements increase the company's investment in productive facilities. Companies generally debit these amounts to the plant asset affected. They are often referred to as **capital expenditures**. Most major U.S. corporations disclose annual capital expenditures.

Companies must use good judgment in deciding between a revenue expenditure and capital expenditure. For example, assume that Rodriguez Co. purchases a number of wastepaper baskets. Although the proper accounting would appear to be to capitalize and then depreciate these wastepaper baskets over their useful life, it would be more usual for Rodriguez to expense them immediately. This practice is justified on the basis of **materiality**. Materiality refers to the impact of an item's size on a company's financial operations. The **materiality principle** states that if an item would not make a difference in decision making, the company does not have to follow GAAP in reporting that item.

# ETHICS INSIGHT

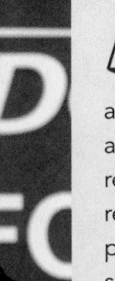

### *What Happened at WorldCom?*

In what could become one of the largest accounting frauds in history, WorldCom announced the discovery of $7 billion in expenses improperly booked as capital expenditures, a gimmick that boosted profit over a recent five-quarter period. If these expenses had been recorded properly, WorldCom, one of the biggest stock market stars of the 1990s, would have reported a net loss for 2001, as well as for the first quarter of 2002. Instead, WorldCom reported a profit of $1.4 billion for 2001 and $130 million for the first quarter of 2002. As a result of these problems, WorldCom declared bankruptcy, to the dismay of its investors and creditors.

**?** What erroneous accounting entries (accounts debited and credited) did WorldCom make? What is the correcting entry that should be recorded, and what is its effect on WorldCom's financial statements?

# PLANT ASSET DISPOSALS

Companies dispose of plant assets in three ways—retirement, sale, or exchange—as Illustration 10-18 shows. Whatever the method, at the time of disposal the company must determine the book value of the plant asset. As noted earlier, book value is the difference between the cost of a plant asset and the accumulated depreciation to date.

**STUDY OBJECTIVE 6**

Explain how to account for the disposal of a plant asset.

**Retirement**
Equipment is scrapped or discarded.

**Sale**
Equipment is sold to another party.

**Exchange**
Existing equipment is traded for new equipment.

**Illustration 10-18**
Methods of plant asset disposal

At the time of disposal, the company records depreciation for the fraction of the year to the date of disposal. The book value is then eliminated by two entries: (1) debiting (decreasing) Accumulated Depreciation for the total depreciation to date, and (2) crediting (decreasing) the asset account for the cost of the asset. In this chapter we examine the accounting for the retirement and sale of plant assets. In the appendix to the chapter we discuss and illustrate the accounting for exchanges of plant assets.

## Retirement of Plant Assets

To illustrate the retirement of plant assets, assume that Hobart Enterprises retires its computer printers, which cost $32,000. The accumulated depreciation on these printers is $32,000. The equipment, therefore, is fully depreciated (zero book value). The entry to record this retirement is as follows.

| | | |
|---|---|---|
| Accumulated Depreciation—Printing Equipment | 32,000 | |
|     Printing Equipment | | 32,000 |
|       (To record retirement of fully depreciated equipment) | | |

| A | = | L | + | SE |
|---|---|---|---|---|
| +32,000 | | | | |
| −32,000 | | | | |

**Cash Flows**
no effect

What happens if a fully depreciated plant asset is still useful to the company? In this case, the asset and its accumulated depreciation continue to be reported on the balance sheet, without further depreciation adjustment, until the company retires the asset. Reporting the asset and related accumulated depreciation on the balance sheet informs the financial statement reader that the asset is still in use. Once fully depreciated, no additional depreciation should be taken, even if an asset is still being used. In no situation can the accumulated depreciation on a plant asset exceed its cost.

If a company retires a plant asset before it is fully depreciated, and no cash is received for scrap or salvage value, a loss on disposal occurs. For example, assume that Sunset Company discards delivery equipment that cost $18,000 and has accumulated depreciation of $14,000. The entry is as follows.

**HELPFUL HINT**

When a company disposes of a plant asset, the company must remove from the accounts all amounts related to the asset. This includes the original cost in the asset account and the total depreciation to date in the accumulated depreciation account.

| | | |
|---|---|---|
| Accumulated Depreciation—Delivery Equipment | 14,000 | |
| Loss on Disposal | 4,000 | |
|     Delivery Equipment | | 18,000 |
|       (To record retirement of delivery equipment at a loss) | | |

| A | = | L | + | SE |
|---|---|---|---|---|
| +14,000 | | | | |
| | | | | −4,000 Exp |
| −18,000 | | | | |

**Cash Flows**
no effect

Companies report a loss on disposal in the "Other expenses and losses" section of the income statement.

## Sale of Plant Assets

In a disposal by sale, the company compares the book value of the asset with the proceeds received from the sale. If the proceeds of the sale **exceed** the book value of the plant asset, **a gain on disposal occurs**. If the proceeds of the sale **are less than** the book value of the plant asset sold, **a loss on disposal occurs**.

Only by coincidence will the book value and the fair market value of the asset be the same when the asset is sold. Gains and losses on sales of plant assets are therefore quite common. For example, Delta Airlines reported a $94,343,000 gain on the sale of five Boeing B727-200 aircraft and five Lockheed L-1011-1 aircraft.

### GAIN ON DISPOSAL

To illustrate a gain, assume that on July 1, 2008, Wright Company sells office furniture for $16,000 cash. The office furniture originally cost $60,000. As of January 1, 2008, it had accumulated depreciation of $41,000. Depreciation for the first six months of 2008 is $8,000. Wright records depreciation expense and updates accumulated depreciation to July 1 with the following entry.

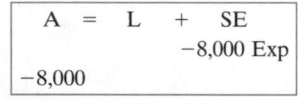

**Cash Flows**
no effect

| | | | |
|---|---|---|---|
| July 1 | Depreciation Expense | 8,000 | |
| |     Accumulated Depreciation—Office Furniture | | 8,000 |
| |       (To record depreciation expense for the first | | |
| |       6 months of 2008) | | |

After the accumulated depreciation balance is updated, the company computes the gain or loss. Illustration 10-19 shows this computation for Wright Company, which has a gain on disposal of $5,000.

**Illustration 10-19**
Computation of gain on disposal

| | |
|---|---|
| Cost of office furniture | $60,000 |
| Less: Accumulated depreciation ($41,000 + $8,000) | 49,000 |
| Book value at date of disposal | 11,000 |
| Proceeds from sale | 16,000 |
| **Gain on disposal** | **$ 5,000** |

Wright records the sale and the gain on disposal as follows.

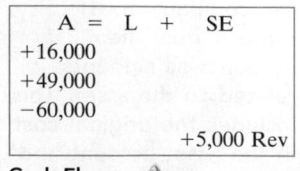

**Cash Flows**
+16,000

| | | | |
|---|---|---|---|
| July 1 | Cash | 16,000 | |
| | Accumulated Depreciation—Office Furniture | 49,000 | |
| |     Office Furniture | | 60,000 |
| |     Gain on Disposal | | 5,000 |
| |       (To record sale of office furniture at a gain) | | |

Companies report a gain on disposal in the "Other revenues and gains" section of the income statement.

### LOSS ON DISPOSAL

Assume that instead of selling the office furniture for $16,000, Wright sells it for $9,000. In this case, Wright computes a loss of $2,000 as follows:

| | | |
|---|---|---|
| Cost of office furniture | $60,000 | |
| Less: Accumulated depreciation | 49,000 | |
| Book value at date of disposal | 11,000 | |
| Proceeds from sale | 9,000 | |
| **Loss on disposal** | **$ 2,000** | |

**Illustration 10-20**
Computation of loss on disposal

Wright records the sale and the loss on disposal as follows.

| July 1 | Cash | 9,000 | |
|---|---|---|---|
| | Accumulated Depreciation—Office Furniture | 49,000 | |
| | Loss on Disposal | 2,000 | |
| |     Office Furniture | | 60,000 |
| |       (To record sale of office furniture at a loss) | | |

| A | = | L | + | SE |
|---|---|---|---|---|
| +9,000 | | | | |
| +49,000 | | | | |
| | | | | −2,000 Exp |
| −60,000 | | | | |

**Cash Flows**
+9,000

Companies report a loss on disposal in the "Other expenses and losses" section of the income statement.

## Before You Go On...

### REVIEW IT
1. How does a capital expenditure differ from a revenue expenditure?
2. What is the proper accounting for the retirement and sale of plant assets?

### DO IT
Overland Trucking has an old truck that cost $30,000. The truck has accumulated depreciation of $16,000 and a fair value of $17,000. Overland has decided to sell the truck. (a) What is the entry that Overland Trucking would make to record the sale of the truck for $17,000 cash? (b) What is the entry that Overland trucking would make to record the sale of the truck for $10,000 cash?

### Action Plan
- At the time of disposal, determine the book value of the asset.
- Compare the asset's book value with the proceeds received to determine whether a gain or loss has occurred.

### Solution
(a) Sale of truck for cash at a gain:

| Cash | 17,000 | |
|---|---|---|
| Accumulated Depreciation—Truck | 16,000 | |
|     Truck | | 30,000 |
|     Gain on Disposal [$17,000 − ($30,000 − $16,000)] | | 3,000 |
|       (To record sale of truck at a gain) | | |

(b) Sale of truck for cash at a loss:

| Cash | 10,000 | |
|---|---|---|
| Loss on Disposal [$10,000 − ($30,000 − $16,000)] | 4,000 | |
| Accumulated Depreciation—Truck | 16,000 | |
|     Truck | | 30,000 |
|       (To record sale of truck at a loss) | | |

Related exercise material: *BE10-9, BE10-10, E10-9, and E10-10.*

✓ The Navigator

# SECTION 2 Natural Resources

<u>Natural resources</u> consist of standing timber and underground deposits of oil, gas, and minerals. These long-lived productive assets have two distinguishing characteristics: (1) They are physically extracted in operations (such as mining, cutting, or pumping). (2) They are replaceable only by an act of nature.

The acquisition cost of a natural resource is the price needed to acquire the resource **and** prepare it for its intended use. For an already-discovered resource, such as an existing coal mine, cost is the price paid for the property.

The allocation of the cost of natural resources to expense in a rational and systematic manner over the resource's useful life is called <u>depletion</u>. (That is, *depletion* is to natural resources as *depreciation* is to plant assets.) **Companies generally use the units-of-activity method** (learned earlier in the chapter) **to compute depletion.** The reason is that **depletion generally is a function of the units extracted during the year.**

**STUDY OBJECTIVE 7**

Compute periodic depletion of natural resources.

Under the units-of-activity method, companies divide the total cost of the natural resource minus salvage value by the number of units estimated to be in the resource. The result is a **depletion cost per unit of product.** They then multiply the depletion cost per unit by the number of units extracted and sold. The result is the **annual depletion expense.** Illustration 10-21 shows the formula to compute depletion expense.

**Illustration 10-21**
Formula to compute depletion expense

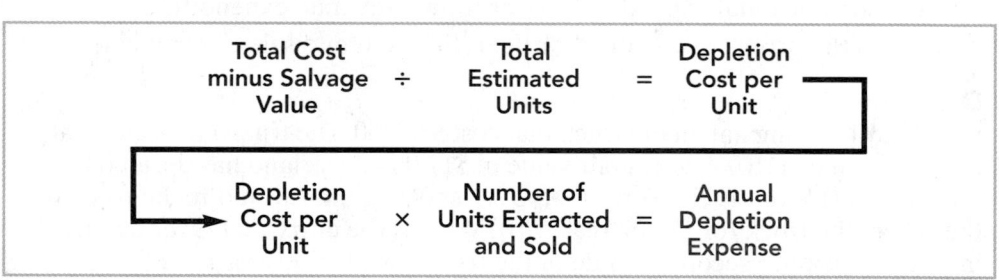

To illustrate, assume that Lane Coal Company invests $5 million in a mine estimated to have 10 million tons of coal and no salvage value. In the first year, Lane extracts and sells 800,000 tons of coal. Using the formulas above, Lane computes the depletion expense as follows:

$$\$5,000,000 \div 10,000,000 = \$0.50 \text{ depletion cost per ton}$$

$$\$0.50 \times 800,000 = \$400,000 \text{ annual depletion expense}$$

Lane records depletion expense for the first year of operation as follows.

| A = L + SE | |
|---|---|
| | −400,000 Exp |
| −400,000 | |

**Cash Flows**
no effect

| Dec. 31 | Depletion Expense | 400,000 | |
| | Accumulated Depletion | | 400,000 |
| | (To record depletion expense on coal deposits) | | |

The company reports the account Depletion Expense as a part of the cost of producing the product. Accumulated Depletion is a contra-asset account, similar to accumulated depreciation. It is deducted from the cost of the natural resource in the balance sheet, as Illustration 10-22 shows.

| LANE COAL COMPANY | | |
| --- | --- | --- |
| Balance Sheet (partial) | | |
| Coal mine | $5,000,000 | |
| Less: Accumulated depletion | 400,000 | $4,600,000 |

Illustration 10-22
Statement presentation of
accumulated depletion

Many companies do not use an Accumulated Depletion account. In such cases, the company credits the amount of depletion directly to the natural resources account.

Sometimes, a company will extract natural resources in one accounting period but not sell them until a later period. In this case, the company does not expense the depletion until it sells the resource. It reports the amount not sold as inventory in the current assets section.

# SECTION 3 Intangible Assets

Intangible assets are rights, privileges, and competitive advantages that result from the ownership of long-lived assets that do not possess physical substance. Evidence of intangibles may exist in the form of contracts or licenses. Intangibles may arise from the following sources:

1. Government grants, such as patents, copyrights, and trademarks.
2. Acquisition of another business, in which the purchase price includes a payment for the company's favorable attributes (called *goodwill*).
3. Private monopolistic arrangements arising from contractual agreements, such as franchises and leases.

Some widely known intangibles are Microsoft's patents, McDonald's franchises, Apple's trade name iPod, J.K. Rowlings' copyrights on the Harry Potter books, and the trademark Rent-A-Wreck in the Feature Story.

# ACCOUNTING FOR INTANGIBLE ASSETS

Companies record intangible assets at cost. Intangibles are categorized as having either a limited life or an indefinite life. If an intangible has a **limited life**, the company allocates its cost over the asset's useful life using a process similar to depreciation. The process of allocating the cost of intangibles is referred to as amortization. The cost of intangible assets with **indefinite lives should not be amortized.**

To record amortization of an intangible asset, a company increases (debits) Amortization Expense, and decreases (credits) the specific intangible asset. (Unlike depreciation, no contra account, such as Accumulated Amortization, is usually used.)

Intangible assets are typically amortized on a straight-line basis. For example, the legal life of a patent is 20 years. Companies **amortize the cost of a patent over its 20-year life or its useful life, whichever is shorter**. To illustrate the computation of patent amortization, assume that National Labs purchases a patent at a cost of $60,000. If National estimates the useful life of the patent to be eight years, the

**STUDY OBJECTIVE 8**
Explain the basic issues related to accounting for intangible assets.

**HELPFUL HINT**
*Amortization* is to intangibles what *depreciation* is to plant assets and *depletion* is to natural resources.

annual amortization expense is $7,500 ($60,000 ÷ 8). National records the annual amortization as follows.

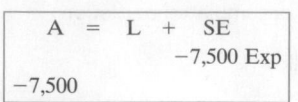

| A = L + SE | |
|---|---|
| | −7,500 Exp |
| −7,500 | |

**Cash Flows**
no effect

| Dec. 31 | Amortization Expense—Patent | 7,500 | |
|---|---|---|---|
| | Patent | | 7,500 |
| | (To record patent amortization) | | |

Companies classify Amortization Expense—Patents as an operating expense in the income statement. There is a difference between intangible assets and plant assets in determining cost. For plant assets, cost includes both the purchase price of the asset and the costs incurred in designing and constructing the asset. In contrast, cost for an intangible asset includes **only the purchase price.** Companies expense any costs incurred in developing an intangible asset.

## Patents

A **patent** is an exclusive right issued by the U.S. Patent Office that enables the recipient to manufacture, sell, or otherwise control an invention for a period of 20 years from the date of the grant. A patent is nonrenewable. But companies can extend the legal life of a patent by obtaining new patents for improvements or other changes in the basic design. **The initial cost of a patent is the cash or cash equivalent price paid to acquire the patent.**

The saying, "A patent is only as good as the money you're prepared to spend defending it" is very true. Many patents are subject to litigation. Any legal costs an owner incurs in successfully defending a patent in an infringement suit are considered necessary to establish the patent's validity. **The owner adds those costs to the Patent account and amortizes them over the remaining life of the patent.**

**The patent holder amortizes the cost of a patent over its 20-year legal life or its useful life, whichever is shorter.** Companies consider obsolescence and inadequacy in determining useful life. These factors may cause a patent to become economically ineffective before the end of its legal life.

## Copyrights

The federal government grants **copyrights** which give the owner the exclusive right to reproduce and sell an artistic or published work. Copyrights extend for the life of the creator plus 70 years. The cost of a copyright is the **cost of acquiring and defending it.** The cost may be only the $10 fee paid to the U.S. Copyright Office. Or it may amount to much more if an infringement suit is involved.

The useful life of a copyright generally is significantly shorter than its legal life. Therefore, copyrights usually are amortized over a relatively short period of time.

## Trademarks and Trade Names

A **trademark** or **trade name** is a word, phrase, jingle, or symbol that identifies a particular enterprise or product. Trade names like Wheaties, Game Boy, Frappuccino, Kleenex, Windows, Coca-Cola, and Jeep create immediate product identification. They also generally enhance the sale of the product. The creator or original user may obtain exclusive legal right to the trademark or trade name by registering it with the U.S. Patent Office. Such registration provides 20 years of protection. The registration may be renewed indefinitely as long as the trademark or trade name is in use.

If a company purchases the trademark or trade name, its cost is the purchase price. If a company develops and maintains the trademark or trade name, any costs related to these activities are expensed as incurred. Because trademarks and trade names have indefinite lives, they are not amortized.

## Franchises and Licenses

When you fill up your tank at the corner Shell station, eat lunch at Taco Bell, or rent a car from Rent-A-Wreck, you are dealing with franchises. A franchise is a contractual arrangement between a franchisor and a franchisee. The franchisor grants the franchisee the right to sell certain products, provide specific services, or use certain trademarks or trade names, usually within a designated geographical area.

Another type of franchise is that entered into between a governmental body (commonly municipalities) and a company. This franchise permits the company to use public property in performing its services. Examples are the use of city streets for a bus line or taxi service, use of public land for telephone and electric lines, and the use of airwaves for radio or TV broadcasting. Such operating rights are referred to as licenses. **When a company can identify costs with the purchase of a franchise or license, it should recognize an intangible asset.** Companies should amortize the cost of a limited-life franchise (or license) over its useful life. If the life is indefinite, the cost is not amortized. Annual payments made under a franchise agreement are recorded as **operating expenses** in the period in which they are incurred.

## ACCOUNTING ACROSS THE ORGANIZATION

### *ESPN Wins Monday Night Football Franchise*

What is a well-known franchise worth? Recently ESPN outbid its rivals for the right to broadcast Monday Night Football. At a price of $1.1 billion per year— nearly twice what rival ABC paid in previous years—it isn't clear who won and who lost.

When bidding for a unique franchise like Monday Night Football, management must consider many factors to determine a price. As part of the deal, ESPN also got wireless rights and Spanish-language telecasts. By its estimation, ESPN will generate a profit of $200 million per year from Monday Night Football. ABC was losing $150 million per year.

Another factor in the decision was ESPN management's concern that if ESPN didn't win the bid, a buyer would emerge that would use Monday Night Football as a launching pad for a new sports network. ESPN doesn't want any more competitors than it already has. It is hard to put a price tag on the value of keeping the competition to a minimum.

*Source:* Ronald Grover and Tom Lowry, "A Ball ESPN Couldn't Afford to Drop," *BusinessWeek*, May 2, 2005, p. 42.

 How should ESPN account for the $1.1 billion per year franchise fee?

## Goodwill

Usually, the largest intangible asset that appears on a company's balance sheet is goodwill. Goodwill represents the value of all favorable attributes that relate to a company. These include exceptional management, desirable location, good customer relations, skilled employees, high-quality products, and harmonious relations with labor unions. Goodwill is unique: Unlike assets such as investments and plant assets, which can be sold *individually* in the marketplace, goodwill can be identified only with the business as a whole.

If goodwill can be identified only with the business as a whole, how can its amount be determined? One could try to put a dollar value on the factors listed above (exceptional management, desirable location, and so on). But the results would be very subjective, and such subjective valuations would not contribute to the reliability of financial statements. **Therefore, companies record goodwill only when an entire business is purchased. In that case, goodwill is the excess of cost over the fair market value of the net assets (assets less liabilities) acquired.**

In recording the purchase of a business, the company debits (increases) the net assets at their fair market values, credits (decreases) cash for the purchase price, and debits goodwill for the difference) **Goodwill is not amortized** (because it is considered to have an indefinite life). Companies report goodwill in the balance sheet under intangible assets.

# RESEARCH AND DEVELOPMENT COSTS

**HELPFUL HINT**
Research and development (R&D) costs are not intangible assets. But because they may lead to patents and copyrights, we discuss them in this section.

**Research and development costs** are expenditures that may lead to patents, copyrights, new processes, and new products. Many companies spend considerable sums of money on research and development (R&D). For example, in a recent year IBM spent over $5.1 billion on R&D.

Research and development costs present accounting problems. For one thing, it is sometimes difficult to assign the costs to specific projects. Also, there are uncertainties in identifying the extent and timing of future benefits. As a result, companies usually record R&D costs **as an expense when incurred**, whether the research and development is successful or not.

To illustrate, assume that Laser Scanner Company spent $3 million on R&D. This expenditure resulted in two highly successful patents, obtained with $20,000 in lawyers' fees. The company would add the lawyers' fees to the patent account. The R&D costs, however, cannot be included in the cost of the patent. Instead, the company would record the R&D costs as an expense when incurred.

Many disagree with this accounting approach. They argue that expensing R&D costs leads to understated assets and net income. Others, however, argue that capitalizing these costs will lead to highly speculative assets on the balance sheet. It is difficult to determine who is right. The controversy illustrates how difficult it can be to establish proper guidelines for financial reporting.

# STATEMENT PRESENTATION AND ANALYSIS

## Presentation

**STUDY OBJECTIVE 9**
Indicate how plant assets, natural resources, and intangible assets are reported.

Usually companies combine plant assets and natural resources under "Property, plant, and equipment" in the balance sheet. They show intangibles separately. Companies disclose either in the balance sheet or the notes the balances of the major classes of assets, such as land, buildings, and equipment, and accumulated depreciation by major classes or in total. In addition, they should describe the depreciation and amortization methods that were used, as well as disclose the amount of depreciation and amortization expense for the period.

Illustration 10-23 (next page) shows the financial statement presentation of property, plant, and equipment and intangibles by The Procter & Gamble Company (P&G) in its 2005 balance sheet. The notes to P&G's financial statements present greater details about the accounting for its long-term tangible and intangible assets.

Illustration 10-24 (next page) shows another comprehensive presentation of property, plant, and equipment, from the balance sheet of Owens-Illinois. The notes to the financial statements of Owens-Illinois identify the major classes of property, plant, and equipment. They also indicate that depreciation and amortization are by the straight-line method, and depletion is by the units-of-activity method.

## Analysis

Using ratios, we can analyze how efficiently a company uses its assets to generate sales. The **asset turnover ratio** analyzes the productivity of a company's assets. It tells us how many dollars of sales a company generates for each dollar invested in assets. This ratio is computed by dividing net sales by average total assets for

## P&G — THE PROCTER & GAMBLE COMPANY
Balance Sheet (partial)
(in millions)

|  | June 30 | |
|  | 2005 | 2004 |
| --- | --- | --- |
| Property, plant, and equipment | | |
| Buildings | $ 5,292 | $ 5,206 |
| Machinery and equipment | 20,397 | 19,456 |
| Land | 636 | 642 |
|  | 26,325 | 25,304 |
| Accumulated depreciation | (11,993) | (11,196) |
| Net property, plant, and equipment | 14,332 | 14,108 |
| Goodwill and other intangible assets | | |
| Goodwill | 19,816 | 19,610 |
| Trademarks and other intangible assets, net | 4,347 | 4,290 |
| Net goodwill and other intangible assets | $24,163 | $23,900 |

## OWENS-ILLINOIS, INC.
Balance Sheet (partial)
(in millions)

| Property, plant, and equipment | | | |
| --- | --- | --- | --- |
| Timberlands, at cost, less accumulated depletion | | $ 95.4 | |
| Buildings and equipment, at cost | $2,207.1 | | |
| Less: Accumulated depreciation | 1,229.0 | 978.1 | |
| Total property, plant, and equipment | | $1,073.5 | |
| Intangibles | | | |
| Patents | | 410.0 | |
| Total | | $1,483.5 | |

the period. The formula in Illustration 10-25 shows the computation of the asset turnover ratio for The Procter & Gamble Company. P&G's net sales for 2005 were $56,741 million. Its total ending assets were $61,527 million, and beginning assets were $57,048 million.

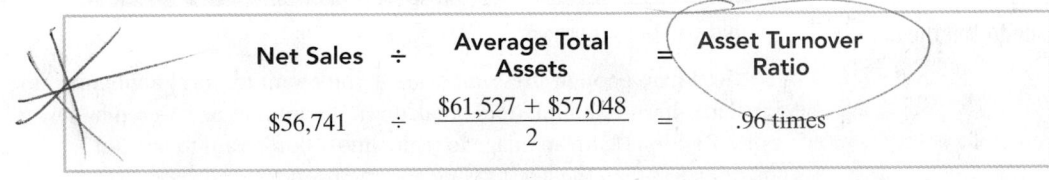

$$\text{Net Sales} \div \text{Average Total Assets} = \text{Asset Turnover Ratio}$$

$$\$56,741 \div \frac{\$61,527 + \$57,048}{2} = .96 \text{ times}$$

**Illustration 10-25**
Asset turnover formula and computation

Thus, each dollar invested in assets produced $0.96 in sales for P&G. If a company is using its assets efficiently, each dollar of assets will create a high amount of sales. This ratio varies greatly among different industries—from those that are asset intensive (utilities) to those that are not (services).

 Be sure to read **ALL ABOUT YOU:** *Buying a Wreck of Your Own* on page 448 for information on how topics in this chapter apply to you.

# Buying a Wreck of Your Own

The opening story to this chapter discusses car rental company Rent-A-Wreck. Recall that Rent-A-Wreck determined it can maximize its profitability by buying and renting used, rather than new, cars. What about *you*? Could you maximize your economic well-being by buying a used car rather than a new one?

## ✹ Some Facts

* In a recent year, nearly 17 million new cars were sold in the U.S., compared to sales of 44 million used cars.

* The cost of an average new car has risen in recent years, to about $22,000. The price of the average used car has actually been falling, and is now about $8,100.

* Financial institutions typically require a down payment of at least 10% of the value of a vehicle on a vehicle loan. Thus, the average new car will require a much higher down payment. However, interest rates on used-car loans are higher than on new-car loans.

* A new car typically loses at least 30% of its value during the first two years, and about 40 to 50% after three years. Some brands maintain their value better than others.

* The price of new cars has increased faster than average annual incomes in recent years.

* To keep monthly car payments down, car companies will now provide financing for up to six years. (It used to be two or three years.) With such a long loan, you might end up "upside down on the loan"—that is, you might actually owe more money than the car is worth if you decide to sell the car before the end of the loan.

## ✹ About the Numbers

There are many costs to consider in deciding whether to buy a new or used car. These costs include the down payment, monthly loan payments, insurance, maintenance and repair costs, and state (department of motor vehicle) fees. The graph below compares the total costs over five years for the typical new versus used car.

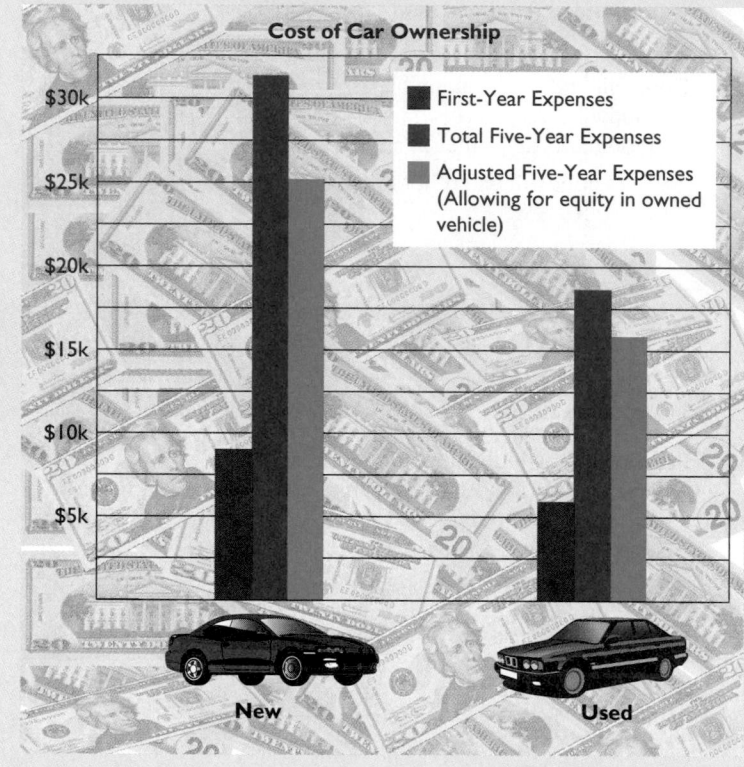

**Source for graph:** Phillip Reed, "Compare the Costs: Buying vs. Leasing vs. Buying a Used Car," *www.edmunds.com/advice/buying/articles/47079/article.html* (accessed May 2006).

## ✹ What Do You Think?

Should you buy a new car?

**YES:** I have enough stress in my life. I don't want to worry about my car breaking down—and if it does break down, I want it to be covered by a warranty. Besides, I have an image to maintain—I don't want to be seen in anything less than the latest styling and the latest technology.

**NO:** I'm a college student, and I need to keep my costs down. Also, used cars are a lot more dependable than they used to be. In addition, my self-image is strong enough that I don't need a fancy new car to feel good about myself (despite what the car advertisements say).

**Source:** Michelle Krebs, "Should You Buy New or Used?" *www.cars.com/go/advice,* May 3, 2005.

## Before You Go On...

### REVIEW IT

1. How is depletion expense computed?
2. What are the main differences between accounting for intangible assets and for plant assets?
3. Identify the major types of intangibles and the proper accounting for them.
4. Explain the accounting for research and development costs.
5. What ratio may be computed to analyze property, plant, and equipment?

✔ The Navigator

## Demonstration Problem 1

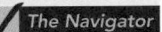

DuPage Company purchases a factory machine at a cost of $18,000 on January 1, 2008. DuPage expects the machine to have a salvage value of $2,000 at the end of its 4-year useful life.

During its useful life, the machine is expected to be used 160,000 hours. Actual annual hourly use was: 2008, 40,000; 2009, 60,000; 2010, 35,000; and 2011, 25,000.

### Instructions

Prepare depreciation schedules for the following methods: (a) straight-line, (b) units-of-activity, and (c) declining-balance using double the straight-line rate.

### Solution

**(a)**

**Straight-Line Method**

| | Computation | | | Annual | End of Year | |
|---|---|---|---|---|---|---|
| Year | Depreciable Cost* | × | Depreciation Rate | = Depreciation Expense | Accumulated Depreciation | Book Value |
| 2008 | $16,000 | | 25% | $4,000 | $ 4,000 | $14,000** |
| 2009 | 16,000 | | 25% | 4,000 | 8,000 | 10,000 |
| 2010 | 16,000 | | 25% | 4,000 | 12,000 | 6,000 |
| 2011 | 16,000 | | 25% | 4,000 | 16,000 | 2,000 |

*$18,000 − $2,000.
**$18,000 − $4,000.

**(b)**

**Units-of-Activity Method**

| | Computation | | | Annual | End of Year | |
|---|---|---|---|---|---|---|
| Year | Units of Activity | × | Depreciation Cost/Unit | = Depreciation Expense | Accumulated Depreciation | Book Value |
| 2008 | 40,000 | | $0.10* | $4,000 | $ 4,000 | $14,000 |
| 2009 | 60,000 | | 0.10 | 6,000 | 10,000 | 8,000 |
| 2010 | 35,000 | | 0.10 | 3,500 | 13,500 | 4,500 |
| 2011 | 25,000 | | 0.10 | 2,500 | 16,000 | 2,000 |

*($18,000 − $2,000) ÷ 160,000.

### action plan

✔ Under the straight-line method, apply the depreciation rate to depreciable cost.

✔ Under the units-of-activity method, compute the depreciation cost per unit by dividing depreciable cost by total units of activity.

✔ Under the declining-balance method, apply the depreciation rate to **book value** at the beginning of the year.

**(c)**

## Declining-Balance Method

| | Computation | | | | End of Year | |
|---|---|---|---|---|---|---|
| Year | Book Value Beginning of Year | × Depreciation Rate* | = | Annual Depreciation Expense | Accumulated Depreciation | Book Value |
| 2008 | $18,000 | 50% | | $9,000 | $ 9,000 | $9,000 |
| 2009 | 9,000 | 50% | | 4,500 | 13,500 | 4,500 |
| 2010 | 4,500 | 50% | | 2,250 | 15,750 | 2,250 |
| 2011 | 2,250 | 50% | | 250** | 16,000 | 2,000 |

*¼ × 2.
**Adjusted to $250 because ending book value should not be less than expected salvage value.

---

## Demonstration Problem 2

On January 1, 2006, Skyline Limousine Co. purchased a limo at an acquisition cost of $28,000. The vehicle has been depreciated by the straight-line method using a 4-year service life and a $4,000 salvage value. The company's fiscal year ends on December 31.

### Instructions

Prepare the journal entry or entries to record the disposal of the limousine assuming that it was:

**(a)** Retired and scrapped with no salvage value on January 1, 2010.
**(b)** Sold for $5,000 on July 1, 2009.

### Solution

**action plan**

✔ At the time of disposal, determine the book value of the asset.

✔ Recognize any gain or loss from disposal of the asset.

✔ Remove the book value of the asset from the records by debiting Accumulated Depreciation for the total depreciation to date of disposal and crediting the asset account for the cost of the asset.

| | | | | |
|---|---|---|---|---|
| **(a)** | 1/1/10 | Accumulated Depreciation—Limousine | 24,000 | |
| | | Loss on Disposal | 4,000 | |
| | |     Limousine | | 28,000 |
| | |     (To record retirement of limousine) | | |
| **(b)** | 7/1/09 | Depreciation Expense | 3,000 | |
| | |     Accumulated Depreciation—Limousine | | 3,000 |
| | |     (To record depreciation to date of disposal) | | |
| | 7/1/09 | Cash | 5,000 | |
| | | Accumulated Depreciation—Limousine | 21,000 | |
| | | Loss on Disposal | 2,000 | |
| | |     Limousine | | 28,000 |
| | |     (To record sale of limousine) | | |

---

# SUMMARY OF STUDY OBJECTIVES

**1 Describe how the cost principle applies to plant assets.** The cost of plant assets includes all expenditures necessary to acquire the asset and make it ready for its intended use. Cost is measured by the cash or cash equivalent price paid.

**2 Explain the concept of depreciation.** Depreciation is the allocation of the cost of a plant asset to expense over its useful (service) life in a rational and systematic manner. Depreciation is not a process of valuation, nor is it a process that results in an accumulation of cash.

**3 Compute periodic depreciation using different methods.** Three depreciation methods are:

| Method | Effect on Annual Depreciation | Formula |
|---|---|---|
| Straight-line | Constant amount | Depreciable cost ÷ Useful life (in years) |
| Units-of-activity | Varying amount | Depreciation cost per unit × Units of activity during the year |
| Declining-balance | Decreasing amount | Book value at beginning of year × Declining-balance rate |

**4 Describe the procedure for revising periodic depreciation.** Companies make revisions of periodic depreciation in present and future periods, not retroactively. They determine the new annual depreciation by dividing the depreciable cost at the time of the revision by the remaining useful life.

**5 Distinguish between revenue and capital expenditures, and explain the entries for each.** Companies incur revenue expenditures to maintain the operating efficiency and productive life of an asset. They debit these expenditures to Repair Expense as incurred. Capital expenditures increase the operating efficiency, productive capacity, or expected useful life of the asset. Companies generally debit these expenditures to the plant asset affected.

**6 Explain how to account for the disposal of a plant asset.** The accounting for disposal of a plant asset through retirement or sale is as follows:

**(a)** Eliminate the book value of the plant asset at the date of disposal.

**(b)** Record cash proceeds, if any.

**(c)** Account for the difference between the book value and the cash proceeds as a gain or loss on disposal.

**7 Compute periodic depletion of natural resources.** Companies compute depletion cost per unit by dividing the total cost of the natural resource minus salvage value by the number of units estimated to be in the resource. They then multiply the depletion cost per unit by the number of units extracted and sold.

**8 Explain the basic issues related to accounting for intangible assets.** The process of allocating the cost of an intangible asset is referred to as amortization. The cost of intangible assets with indefinite lives are not amortized. Companies normally use the straight-line method for amortizing intangible assets.

**9 Indicate how plant assets, natural resources, and intangible assets are reported.** Companies usually combine plant assets and natural resources under property, plant, and equipment; they show intangibles separately under intangible assets. Either within the balance sheet or in the notes, companies should disclose the balances of the major classes of assets, such as land, buildings, and equipment, and accumulated depreciation by major classes or in total. They also should describe the depreciation and amortization methods used, and should disclose the amount of depreciation and amortization expense for the period. The asset turnover ratio measures the productivity of a company's assets in generating sales.

# GLOSSARY

**Accelerated-depreciation method** Depreciation method that produces higher depreciation expense in the early years than in the later years. (p. 435).

**Additions and improvements** Costs incurred to increase the operating efficiency, productive capacity, or useful life of a plant asset. (p. 438).

**Amortization** The allocation of the cost of an intangible asset to expense over its useful life in a systematic and rational manner. (p. 443).

**Asset turnover ratio** A measure of how efficiently a company uses its assets to generate sales; calculated as net sales divided by average total assets. (p. 446).

**Capital expenditures** Expenditures that increase the company's investment in productive facilities. (p. 438).

**Copyright** Exclusive grant from the federal government that allows the owner to reproduce and sell an artistic or published work. (p. 444).

**Declining-balance method** Depreciation method that applies a constant rate to the declining book value of the asset and produces a decreasing annual depreciation expense over the useful life of the asset. (p. 434).

**Depletion** The allocation of the cost of a natural resource to expense in a rational and systematic manner over the resource's useful life. (p. 442).

**Depreciation** The process of allocating to expense the cost of a plant asset over its useful (service) life in a rational and systematic manner. (p. 430).

**Depreciable cost** The cost of a plant asset less its salvage value. (p. 432).

**Franchise (license)** A contractual arrangement under which the franchisor grants the franchisee the right to sell certain products, provide specific services, or use certain trademarks or trade names, usually within a designated geographical area. (p. 445).

**Going-concern assumption** States that the company will continue in operation for the foreseeable future. (p. 431).

**Goodwill** The value of all favorable attributes that relate to a business enterprise. (p. 445).

**Intangible assets** Rights, privileges, and competitive advantages that result from the ownership of long-lived assets that do not possess physical substance. (p. 443).

**Licenses** Operating rights to use public property, granted to a business enterprise by a governmental agency. (p. 445).

**Materiality principle** If an item would not make a difference in decision making, a company does not have to follow GAAP in reporting it. (p. 438).

**Natural resources** Assets that consist of standing timber and underground deposits of oil, gas, or minerals. (p. 442).

**Ordinary repairs** Expenditures to maintain the operating efficiency and productive life of the unit. (p. 438).

**Patent** An exclusive right issued by the U.S. Patent Office that enables the recipient to manufacture, sell, or otherwise control an invention for a period of 20 years from the date of the grant. (p. 444).

**Plant assets** Tangible resources that are used in the operations of the business and are not intended for sale to customers. (p. 426).

**Research and development (R&D) costs** Expenditures that may lead to patents, copyrights, new processes, or new products. (p. 446).

**Revenue expenditures** Expenditures that are immediately charged against revenues as an expense. (p. 438).

**Salvage value** An estimate of an asset's value at the end of its useful life. (p. 431).

**Straight-line method** Depreciation method in which periodic depreciation is the same for each year of the asset's useful life. (p. 432).

**Trademark (trade name)** A word, phrase, jingle, or symbol that identifies a particular enterprise or product. (p. 444).

**Units-of-activity method** Depreciation method in which useful life is expressed in terms of the total units of production or use expected from an asset. (p. 433).

**Useful life** An estimate of the expected productive life, also called service life, of an asset. (p. 431).

# APPENDIX **Exchange of Plant Assets**

**STUDY OBJECTIVE 10**

**Explain how to account for the exchange of plant assets.**

Ordinarily, companies record a gain or loss on the exchange of plant assets. The rationale for recognizing a gain or loss is that most exchanges have **commercial substance**. An exchange has commercial substance if the future cash flows change as a result of the exchange.

To illustrate, Ramos Co. exchanges some of its equipment for land held by Brodhead Inc. It is likely that the timing and amount of the cash flows arising from the land will differ significantly from the cash flows arising from the equipment. As a result, both Ramos and Brodhead are in different economic positions. Therefore **the exchange has commercial substance**, and the companies recognize a gain or loss in the exchange. Because most exchanges have commercial substance (even when similar assets are exchanged), we illustrate only this type of situation, for both a loss and a gain.

## Loss Treatment

To illustrate an exchange that results in a loss, assume that Roland Company exchanged a set of used trucks plus cash for a new semi-truck. The used trucks have a combined book value of $42,000 (cost $64,000 less $22,000 accumulated depreciation). Roland's purchasing agent, experienced in the second-hand market, indicates that the used trucks have a fair market value of $26,000. In addition to the trucks, Roland must pay $17,000 for the semi-truck. Roland computes the cost of the semi-truck as follows

**Illustration 10A-1**
Cost of semi-truck

| | |
|---|---:|
| Fair value of used trucks | $26,000 |
| Cash paid | 17,000 |
| Cost of semi-truck | $43,000 |

Roland incurs a loss on disposal of $16,000 on this exchange. The reason is that the book value of the used trucks is greater than the fair market value of these trucks. The computation is as follows.

| Book value of used trucks ($64,000 − $22,000) | $42,000 |
| Fair market value of used trucks | 26,000 |
| **Loss on disposal** | **$16,000** |

**Illustration 10A-2**
Computation of loss on disposal

In recording an exchange at a loss, three steps are required: (1) Eliminate the book value of the asset given up, (2) record the cost of the asset acquired, and (3) recognize the loss on disposal. Roland Company thus records the exchange on the loss as follows.

| | | | |
|---|---|---|---|
| Semi-truck | 43,000 | | |
| Accumulated Depreciation—Used Trucks | 22,000 | | |
| Loss on Disposal | 16,000 | | |
|    Used Trucks | | 64,000 | |
|    Cash | | 17,000 | |
|      (To record exchange of used trucks for semi-truck.) | | | |

A = L + SE
+43,000
+22,000
         −16,000 Exp
−64,000
−17,000

**Cash Flows**
−17,000

## Gain Treatment

To illustrate a gain situation, assume that Mark Express Delivery decides to exchange its old delivery equipment plus cash of $3,000 for new delivery equipment. The book value of the old delivery equipment is $12,000 (cost $40,000 less accumulated depreciation $28,000). The fair market value of the old delivery equipment is $19,000.

The cost of the new asset is the fair market value of the old asset exchanged plus any cash paid (or other consideration given up). The cost of the new delivery equipment is $22,000 computed as follows.

| Fair market value of old delivery equipment | $19,000 |
| Cash paid | 3,000 |
| **Cost of new delivery equipment** | **$22,000** |

**Illustration 10A-3**
Cost of new delivery equipment

A gain results when the fair market value of the old delivery equipment is greater than its book value. For Mark Express there is a gain of $7,000 on disposal, computed as follows.

| Fair market value of old delivery equipment | $19,000 |
| Book value of old delivery equipment ($40,000 − $28,000) | 12,000 |
| **Gain on disposal** | **$ 7,000** |

**Illustration 10A-4**
Computation of gain on disposal

Mark Express Delivery records the exchange as follows.

| | | | |
|---|---|---|---|
| Delivery Equipment (new) | 22,000 | | |
| Accumulated Depreciation—Delivery Equipment (old) | 28,000 | | |
|    Delivery Equipment (old) | | 40,000 | |
|    Gain on Disposal | | 7,000 | |
|    Cash | | 3,000 | |
|      (To record exchange of old delivery equipment for new delivery equipment) | | | |

A = L + SE
+22,000
+28,000
−40,000
         +7,000 Rev
−3,000

**Cash Flows**
−3,000

In recording an exchange at a gain, the following three steps are involved: (1) Eliminate the book value of the asset given up, (2) record the cost of the asset acquired, and (3) recognize the gain on disposal. Accounting for exchanges of plant assets becomes more complex if the transaction does not have commercial substance. This issue is discussed in more advanced accounting classes.

**10 Explain how to account for the exchange of plant assets.** Ordinarily companies record a gain or loss on the exchange of plant assets. The rationale for recognizing a gain or loss is that most exchanges have commercial substance. An exchange has commercial substance if the future cash flows change as a result of the exchange.

*Note: All **asterisked** Questions, Exercises, and Problems relate to material in the appendix to the chapter.

**SELF-STUDY QUESTIONS**

*Answers are at the end of the chapter.*

(SO 1) **1.** Erin Danielle Company purchased equipment and incurred the following costs.

| | |
|---|---|
| Cash price | $24,000 |
| Sales taxes | 1,200 |
| Insurance during transit | 200 |
| Installation and testing | 400 |
| Total costs | $25,800 |

What amount should be recorded as the cost of the equipment?
  **a.** $24,000.
  **b.** $25,200.
  **c.** $25,400.
  **d.** $25,800.

(SO 2) **2.** Depreciation is a process of:
  **a.** valuation.
  **b.** cost allocation.
  **c.** cash accumulation.
  **d.** appraisal.

(SO 3) **3.** Micah Bartlett Company purchased equipment on January 1, 2007, at a total invoice cost of $400,000. The equipment has an estimated salvage value of $10,000 and an estimated useful life of 5 years. The amount of accumulated depreciation at December 31, 2008, if the straight-line method of depreciation is used, is:
  **a.** $80,000.
  **b.** $160,000.
  **c.** $78,000.
  **d.** $156,000.

(SO 3) **4.** Ann Torbert purchased a truck for $11,000 on January 1, 2007. The truck will have an estimated salvage value of $1,000 at the end of 5 years. Using the units-of-activity method, the balance in accumulated depreciation at December 31, 2008, can be computed by the following formula:
  **a.** ($11,000 ÷ Total estimated activity) × Units of activity for 2008.
  **b.** ($10,000 ÷ Total estimated activity) × Units of activity for 2008.
  **c.** ($11,000 ÷ Total estimated activity) × Units of activity for 2007 and 2008.
  **d.** ($10,000 ÷ Total estimated activity) × Units of activity for 2007 and 2008.

(SO 4) **5.** When there is a change in estimated depreciation:
  **a.** previous depreciation should be corrected.
  **b.** current and future years' depreciation should be revised.
  **c.** only future years' depreciation should be revised.
  **d.** None of the above.

(SO 5) **6.** Additions to plant assets are:
  **a.** revenue expenditures.
  **b.** debited to a Repair Expense account.
  **c.** debited to a Purchases account.
  **d.** capital expenditures.

(SO 7) **7.** Maggie Sharrer Company expects to extract 20 million tons of coal from a mine that cost $12 million. If no salvage value is expected, and 2 million tons are mined and sold in the first year, the entry to record depletion will include a:
  **a.** debit to Accumulated Depletion of $2,000,000.
  **b.** credit to Depletion Expense of $1,200,000.
  **c.** debit to Depletion Expense of $1,200,000.
  **d.** credit to Accumulated Depletion of $2,000,000.

(SO 8) **8.** Martha Beyerlein Company incurred $150,000 of research and development costs in its laboratory to develop a patent granted on January 2, 2008. On July 31, 2008, Beyerlein paid $35,000 for legal fees in a successful defense of the patent. The total amount debited to Patents through July 31, 2008, should be:
  **a.** $150,000.
  **b.** $35,000.
  **c.** $185,000.
  **d.** $170,000.

(SO 9) **9.** Indicate which of the following statements is *true*.
  **a.** Since intangible assets lack physical substance, they need be disclosed only in the notes to the financial statements.
  **b.** Goodwill should be reported as a contra-account in the owner's equity section.
  **c.** Totals of major classes of assets can be shown in the balance sheet, with asset details disclosed in the notes to the financial statements.
  **d.** Intangible assets are typically combined with plant assets and natural resources and shown in the property, plant, and equipment section.

**(SO 10)** *10. Schopenhauer Company exchanged an old machine, with a book value of $39,000 and a fair market value of $35,000, and paid $10,000 cash for a similar new machine. The transaction has commercial substance. At what amount should the machine acquired in the exchange be recorded on Schopenhauer's books?

    **a.** $45,000.
    **b.** $46,000.
    **c.** $49,000.
    **d.** $50,000.

*11. In exchanges of assets in which the exchange has commercial substance: **(SO 10)**

    **a.** neither gains nor losses are recognized immediately.
    **b.** gains, but not losses, are recognized immediately.
    **c.** losses, but not gains, are recognized immediately.
    **d.** both gains and losses are recognized immediately.

Go to the book's website, **www.wiley.com/college/ weygandt**, for Additional Self-Study questions.

 The Navigator

# QUESTIONS

1. Tim Hoover is uncertain about the applicability of the cost principle to plant assets. Explain the principle to Tim.

2. What are some examples of land improvements?

3. Dain Company acquires the land and building owned by Corrs Company. What types of costs may be incurred to make the asset ready for its intended use if Dain Company wants to use (a) only the land, and (b) both the land and the building?

4. In a recent newspaper release, the president of Keene Company asserted that something has to be done about depreciation. The president said, "Depreciation does not come close to accumulating the cash needed to replace the asset at the end of its useful life." What is your response to the president?

5. Robert is studying for the next accounting examination. He asks your help on two questions: (a) What is salvage value? (b) Is salvage value used in determining periodic depreciation under each depreciation method? Answer Robert's questions.

6. Contrast the straight-line method and the units-of-activity method as to (a) useful life, and (b) the pattern of periodic depreciation over useful life.

7. Contrast the effects of the three depreciation methods on annual depreciation expense.

8. In the fourth year of an asset's 5-year useful life, the company decides that the asset will have a 6-year service life. How should the revision of depreciation be recorded? Why?

9. Distinguish between revenue expenditures and capital expenditures during useful life.

10. How is a gain or loss on the sale of a plant asset computed?

11. Mendez Corporation owns a machine that is fully depreciated but is still being used. How should Mendez account for this asset and report it in the financial statements?

12. What are natural resources, and what are their distinguishing characteristics?

13. Explain what depletion is and how it is computed.

14. What are the similarities and differences between the terms depreciation, depletion, and amortization?

15. Pendergrass Company hires an accounting intern who says that intangible assets should always be amortized over their legal lives. Is the intern correct? Explain.

16. Goodwill has been defined as the value of all favorable attributes that relate to a business enterprise. What types of attributes could result in goodwill?

17. Kenny Sain, a business major, is working on a case problem for one of his classes. In the case problem, the company needs to raise cash to market a new product it developed. Joe Morris, an engineering major, takes one look at the company's balance sheet and says, "This company has an awful lot of goodwill. Why don't you recommend that they sell some of it to raise cash?" How should Kenny respond to Joe?

18. Under what conditions is goodwill recorded?

19. Often research and development costs provide companies with benefits that last a number of years. (For example, these costs can lead to the development of a patent that will increase the company's income for many years.) However, generally accepted accounting principles require that such costs be recorded as an expense when incurred. Why?

20. McDonald's Corporation reports total average assets of $28.9 billion and net sales of $20.5 billion. What is the company's asset turnover ratio?

21. Resco Corporation and Yapan Corporation operate in the same industry. Resco uses the straight-line method to account for depreciation; Yapan uses an accelerated method. Explain what complications might arise in trying to compare the results of these two companies.

22. Lopez Corporation uses straight-line depreciation for financial reporting purposes but an accelerated method for tax purposes. Is it acceptable to use different methods for the two purposes? What is Lopez's motivation for doing this?

23. You are comparing two companies in the same industry. You have determined that May Corp. depreciates its plant assets over a 40-year life, whereas Won Corp. depreciates its plant assets over a 20-year life. Discuss the implications this has for comparing the results of the two companies.

24. Wade Company is doing significant work to revitalize its warehouses. It is not sure whether it should capitalize these costs or expense them. What are the implications for current-year net income and future net income of expensing versus capitalizing these costs?

*25. When assets are exchanged in a transaction involving commercial substance, how is the gain or loss on disposal computed?

*26. Tatum Refrigeration Company trades in an old machine on a new model when the fair market value of the old

machine is greater than its book value. The transaction has commercial substance. Should Tatum recognize a gain on disposal? If the fair market value of the old machine is less than its book value, should Tatum recognize a loss on disposal?

# BRIEF EXERCISES

*Determine the cost of land.*

*(SO 1)*

**BE10-1** The following expenditures were incurred by Obermeyer Company in purchasing land: cash price $70,000, accrued taxes $3,000, attorneys' fees $2,500, real estate broker's commission $2,000, and clearing and grading $3,500. What is the cost of the land?

*Determine the cost of a truck.*

*(SO 1)*

**BE10-2** Neeley Company incurs the following expenditures in purchasing a truck: cash price $30,000, accident insurance $2,000, sales taxes $1,500, motor vehicle license $100, and painting and lettering $400. What is the cost of the truck?

*Compute straight-line depreciation.*

*(SO 3)*

**BE10-3** Conlin Company acquires a delivery truck at a cost of $42,000. The truck is expected to have a salvage value of $6,000 at the end of its 4-year useful life. Compute annual depreciation for the first and second years using the straight-line method.

*Compute depreciation and evaluate treatment.*

*(SO 3)*

**BE10-4** Ecklund Company purchased land and a building on January 1, 2008. Management's best estimate of the value of the land was $100,000 and of the building $200,000. But management told the accounting department to record the land at $220,000 and the building at $80,000. The building is being depreciated on a straight-line basis over 20 years with no salvage value. Why do you suppose management requested this accounting treatment? Is it ethical?

*Compute declining-balance depreciation.*

*(SO 3)*

**BE10-5** Depreciation information for Conlin Company is given in BE10-3. Assuming the declining-balance depreciation rate is double the straight-line rate, compute annual depreciation for the first and second years under the declining-balance method.

*Compute depreciation using the units-of-activity method.*

*(SO 3)*

**BE10-6** Speedy Taxi Service uses the units-of-activity method in computing depreciation on its taxicabs. Each cab is expected to be driven 150,000 miles. Taxi no. 10 cost $33,500 and is expected to have a salvage value of $500. Taxi no. 10 is driven 30,000 miles in year 1 and 20,000 miles in year 2. Compute the depreciation for each year.

*Compute revised depreciation.*

*(SO 4)*

**BE10-7** On January 1, 2008, the Ramirez Company ledger shows Equipment $29,000 and Accumulated Depreciation $9,000. The depreciation resulted from using the straight-line method with a useful life of 10 years and salvage value of $2,000. On this date, the company concludes that the equipment has a remaining useful life of only 4 years with the same salvage value. Compute the revised annual depreciation.

*Prepare entries for delivery truck costs.*

*(SO 5)*

**BE10-8** Firefly Company had the following two transactions related to its delivery truck.

1. Paid $45 for an oil change.
2. Paid $400 to install special shelving units, which increase the operating efficiency of the truck.

Prepare Firefly's journal entries to record these two transactions.

*Prepare entries for disposal by retirement.*

*(SO 6)*

**BE10-9** Prepare journal entries to record the following.

(a) Gomez Company retires its delivery equipment, which cost $41,000. Accumulated depreciation is also $41,000 on this delivery equipment. No salvage value is received.

(b) Assume the same information as (a), except that accumulated depreciation for Gomez Company is $39,000, instead of $41,000.

*Prepare entries for disposal by sale.*

*(SO 6)*

**BE10-10** Chan Company sells office equipment on September 30, 2008, for $20,000 cash. The office equipment originally cost $72,000 and as of January 1, 2008, had accumulated depreciation of $42,000. Depreciation for the first 9 months of 2008 is $5,250. Prepare the journal entries to (a) update depreciation to September 30, 2008, and (b) record the sale of the equipment.

*Prepare depletion expense entry and balance sheet presentation for natural resources.*

*(SO 7)*

**BE10-11** Olpe Mining Co. purchased for $7 million a mine that is estimated to have 35 million tons of ore and no salvage value. In the first year, 6 million tons of ore are extracted and sold.

(a) Prepare the journal entry to record depletion expense for the first year.

(b) Show how this mine is reported on the balance sheet at the end of the first year.

**BE10-12**   Galena Company purchases a patent for $120,000 on January 2, 2008. Its estimated useful life is 10 years.

**(a)** Prepare the journal entry to record patent amortization expense for the first year.
**(b)** Show how this patent is reported on the balance sheet at the end of the first year.

*Prepare patent expense entry and balance sheet presentation for intangibles.*
*(SO 8)*

**BE10-13**   Information related to plant assets, natural resources, and intangibles at the end of 2008 for Spain Company is as follows: buildings $1,100,000; accumulated depreciation—buildings $650,000; goodwill $410,000; coal mine $500,000; accumulated depletion—coal mine $108,000. Prepare a partial balance sheet of Spain Company for these items.

*Classify long-lived assets on balance sheet.*
*(SO 9)*

**BE10-14**   In its 2005 annual report Target reported beginning total assets of $32.2 billion; ending total assets of $35.0 billion; property and equipment (net) of $19.4 billion; and net sales of $51.2 billion. Compute Target's asset turnover ratio.

*Analyze long-lived assets.*
*(SO 9)*

**\*BE10-15**   Rivera Company exchanges old delivery equipment for new delivery equipment. The book value of the old delivery equipment is $31,000 (cost $61,000 less accumulated depreciation $30,000). Its fair market value is $19,000, and cash of $5,000 is paid. Prepare the entry to record the exchange, assuming the transaction has commercial substance.

*Prepare entry for disposal by exchange.*
*(SO 10)*

**\*BE10-16**   Assume the same information as BE10-15, except that the fair market value of the old delivery equipment is $38,000. Prepare the entry to record the exchange.

*Prepare entry for disposal by exchange.*
*(SO 10)*

# EXERCISES

**E10-1**   The following expenditures relating to plant assets were made by Spaulding Company during the first 2 months of 2008.

*Determine cost of plant acquisitions.*
*(SO 1)*

1. Paid $5,000 of accrued taxes at time plant site was acquired.
2. Paid $200 insurance to cover possible accident loss on new factory machinery while the machinery was in transit.
3. Paid $850 sales taxes on new delivery truck.
4. Paid $17,500 for parking lots and driveways on new plant site.
5. Paid $250 to have company name and advertising slogan painted on new delivery truck.
6. Paid $8,000 for installation of new factory machinery.
7. Paid $900 for one-year accident insurance policy on new delivery truck.
8. Paid $75 motor vehicle license fee on the new truck.

**Instructions**
**(a)**  ✏️  Explain the application of the cost principle in determining the acquisition cost of plant assets.
**(b)** List the numbers of the foregoing transactions, and opposite each indicate the account title to which each expenditure should be debited.

**E10-2**   Trudy Company incurred the following costs.

*Determine property, plant, and equipment costs.*
*(SO 1)*

| | |
|---|---|
| 1. Sales tax on factory machinery purchased | $5,000 |
| 2. Painting of and lettering on truck immediately upon purchase | 700 |
| 3. Installation and testing of factory machinery | 2,000 |
| 4. Real estate broker's commission on land purchased | 3,500 |
| 5. Insurance premium paid for first year's insurance on new truck | 880 |
| 6. Cost of landscaping on property purchased | 7,200 |
| 7. Cost of paving parking lot for new building constructed | 17,900 |
| 8. Cost of clearing, draining, and filling land | 13,300 |
| 9. Architect's fees on self-constructed building | 10,000 |

**Instructions**
Indicate to which account Trudy would debit each of the costs.

**E10-3**   On March 1, 2008, Penner Company acquired real estate on which it planned to construct a small office building. The company paid $80,000 in cash. An old warehouse on the property was razed at a cost of $8,600; the salvaged materials were sold for $1,700. Additional expenditures before construction began included $1,100 attorney's fee for work concerning the land purchase, $5,000 real estate broker's fee, $7,800 architect's fee, and $14,000 to put in driveways and a parking lot.

*Determine acquisition costs of land.*
*(SO 1)*

### Instructions
**(a)** Determine the amount to be reported as the cost of the land.
**(b)** For each cost not used in part (a), indicate the account to be debited.

*Understand depreciation concepts.*

*(SO 2)*

**E10-4**   Chris Rock has prepared the following list of statements about depreciation.

1. Depreciation is a process of asset valuation, not cost allocation.
2. Depreciation provides for the proper matching of expenses with revenues.
3. The book value of a plant asset should approximate its market value.
4. Depreciation applies to three classes of plant assets: land, buildings, and equipment.
5. Depreciation does not apply to a building because its usefulness and revenue-producing ability generally remain intact over time.
6. The revenue-producing ability of a depreciable asset will decline due to wear and tear and to obsolescence.
7. Recognizing depreciation on an asset results in an accumulation of cash for replacement of the asset.
8. The balance in accumulated depreciation represents the total cost that has been charged to expense.
9. Depreciation expense and accumulated depreciation are reported on the income statement.
10. Four factors affect the computation of depreciation: cost, useful life, salvage value, and residual value.

### Instructions
Identify each statement as true or false. If false, indicate how to correct the statement.

*Compute depreciation under units-of-activity method.*

*(SO 3)*

**E10-5**   Younger Bus Lines uses the units-of-activity method in depreciating its buses. One bus was purchased on January 1, 2008, at a cost of $168,000. Over its 4-year useful life, the bus is expected to be driven 100,000 miles. Salvage value is expected to be $8,000.

### Instructions
**(a)** Compute the depreciation cost per mile.
**(b)** Prepare a depreciation schedule assuming actual mileage was: 2008, 26,000; 2009, 32,000; 2010, 25,000; and 2011, 17,000.

*Determine depreciation for partial periods.*

*(SO 3)*

**E10-6**   Kelm Company purchased a new machine on October 1, 2008, at a cost of $120,000. The company estimated that the machine will have a salvage value of $12,000. The machine is expected to be used for 10,000 working hours during its 5-year life.

### Instructions
Compute the depreciation expense under the following methods for the year indicated.

**(a)** Straight-line for 2008.
**(b)** Units-of-activity for 2008, assuming machine usage was 1,700 hours.
**(c)** Declining-balance using double the straight-line rate for 2008 and 2009.

*Compute depreciation using different methods.*

*(SO 3)*

**E10-7**   Brainiac Company purchased a delivery truck for $30,000 on January 1, 2008. The truck has an expected salvage value of $2,000, and is expected to be driven 100,000 miles over its estimated useful life of 8 years. Actual miles driven were 15,000 in 2008 and 12,000 in 2009.

### Instructions
**(a)** Compute depreciation expense for 2008 and 2009 using (1) the straight-line method, (2) the units-of-activity method, and (3) the double-declining balance method.
**(b)** Assume that Brainiac uses the straight-line method.
  (1) Prepare the journal entry to record 2008 depreciation.
  (2) Show how the truck would be reported in the December 31, 2008, balance sheet.

*Compute revised annual depreciation.*

*(SO 4)*

**E10-8**   Jerry Grant, the new controller of Blackburn Company, has reviewed the expected useful lives and salvage values of selected depreciable assets at the beginning of 2008. His findings are as follows.

| Type of Asset | Date Acquired | Cost | Accumulated Depreciation 1/1/08 | Useful Life in Years | | Salvage Value | |
|---|---|---|---|---|---|---|---|
| | | | | Old | Proposed | Old | Proposed |
| Building | 1/1/02 | $800,000 | $114,000 | 40 | 50 | $40,000 | $37,000 |
| Warehouse | 1/1/03 | 100,000 | 19,000 | 25 | 20 | 5,000 | 3,600 |

All assets are depreciated by the straight-line method. Blackburn Company uses a calendar year in preparing annual financial statements. After discussion, management has agreed to accept Jerry's proposed changes.

**Instructions**

**(a)** Compute the revised annual depreciation on each asset in 2008. (Show computations.)

**(b)** Prepare the entry (or entries) to record depreciation on the building in 2008.

**E10-9** Presented below are selected transactions at Ingles Company for 2008.

Jan. 1 Retired a piece of machinery that was purchased on January 1, 1998. The machine cost $62,000 on that date. It had a useful life of 10 years with no salvage value.

June 30 Sold a computer that was purchased on January 1, 2005. The computer cost $40,000. It had a useful life of 5 years with no salvage value. The computer was sold for $14,000.

Dec. 31 Discarded a delivery truck that was purchased on January 1, 2004. The truck cost $39,000. It was depreciated based on a 6-year useful life with a $3,000 salvage value.

*Journalize entries for disposal of plant assets.*
*(SO 6)*

**Instructions**

Journalize all entries required on the above dates, including entries to update depreciation, where applicable, on assets disposed of. Ingles Company uses straight-line depreciation. (Assume depreciation is up to date as of December 31, 2007.)

**E10-10** Beka Company owns equipment that cost $50,000 when purchased on January 1, 2005. It has been depreciated using the straight-line method based on estimated salvage value of $5,000 and an estimated useful life of 5 years.

*Journalize entries for disposal of equipment.*
*(SO 6)*

**Instructions**

Prepare Beka Company's journal entries to record the sale of the equipment in these four independent situations. Update depreciation on assets disposed of at time of sale.

**(a)** Sold for $28,000 on January 1, 2008.

**(b)** Sold for $28,000 on May 1, 2008.

**(c)** Sold for $11,000 on January 1, 2008.

**(d)** Sold for $11,000 on October 1, 2008.

**E10-11** On July 1, 2008, Hurtig Inc. invested $720,000 in a mine estimated to have 800,000 tons of ore of uniform grade. During the last 6 months of 2008, 100,000 tons of ore were mined and sold.

*Journalize entries for natural resources depletion.*
*(SO 7)*

**Instructions**

**(a)** Prepare the journal entry to record depletion expense.

**(b)** Assume that the 100,000 tons of ore were mined, but only 80,000 units were sold. How are the costs applicable to the 20,000 unsold units reported?

**E10-12** The following are selected 2008 transactions of Franco Corporation.

Jan. 1 Purchased a small company and recorded goodwill of $150,000. Its useful life is indefinite.

May 1 Purchased for $90,000 a patent with an estimated useful life of 5 years and a legal life of 20 years.

*Prepare adjusting entries for amortization.*
*(SO 8)*

**Instructions**

Prepare necessary adjusting entries at December 31 to record amortization required by the events above.

**E10-13** Herzogg Company, organized in 2008, has the following transactions related to intangible assets.

| | | |
|---|---|---|
| 1/2/08 | Purchased patent (7-year life) | $560,000 |
| 4/1/08 | Goodwill purchased (indefinite life) | 360,000 |
| 7/1/08 | 10-year franchise; expiration date 7/1/2018 | 440,000 |
| 9/1/08 | Research and development costs | 185,000 |

*Prepare entries to set up appropriate accounts for different intangibles; amortize intangible assets.*
*(SO 8)*

**Instructions**

Prepare the necessary entries to record these intangibles. All costs incurred were for cash. Make the adjusting entries as of December 31, 2008, recording any necessary amortization and reporting all intangible asset balances accurately as of that date.

**E10-14** During 2008 Nasra Corporation reported net sales of $4,900,000 and net income of $1,500,000. Its balance sheet reported average total assets of $1,400,000.

*Calculate asset turnover ratio.*
*(SO 9)*

**Instructions**
Calculate the asset turnover ratio.

*Journalize entries for exchanges.*
*(SO 10)*

**\*E10-15**   Presented below are two independent transactions. Both transactions have commercial substance.

1. Sidney Co. exchanged old trucks (cost $64,000 less $22,000 accumulated depreciation) plus cash of $17,000 for new trucks. The old trucks had a fair market value of $36,000.
2. Lupa Inc. trades its used machine (cost $12,000 less $4,000 accumulated depreciation) for a new machine. In addition to exchanging the old machine (which had a fair market value of $9,000), Lupa also paid cash of $3,000.

**Instructions**
(a) Prepare the entry to record the exchange of assets by Sidney Co.
(b) Prepare the entry to record the exchange of assets by Lupa Inc.

*Journalize entries for the exchange of plant assets.*
*(SO 10)*

**\*E10-16**   Coran's Delivery Company and Enright's Express Delivery exchanged delivery trucks on January 1, 2008. Coran's truck cost $22,000. It has accumulated depreciation of $15,000 and a fair market value of $4,000. Enright's truck cost $10,000. It has accumulated depreciation of $8,000 and a fair market value of $4,000. The transaction has commercial substance.

**Instructions**
(a) Journalize the exchange for Coran's Delivery Company.
(b) Journalize the exchange for Enright's Express Delivery.

# EXERCISES: SET B

Visit the book's website at **www.wiley.com/college/weygandt**, and choose the Student Companion site, to access Exercise Set B.

# PROBLEMS: SET A

*Determine acquisition costs of land and building.*
*(SO 1)*

**P10-1A**   Diaz Company was organized on January 1. During the first year of operations, the following plant asset expenditures and receipts were recorded in random order.

Debits

| | |
|---|---:|
| **1.** Cost of filling and grading the land | $ 4,000 |
| **2.** Full payment to building contractor | 700,000 |
| **3.** Real estate taxes on land paid for the current year | 5,000 |
| **4.** Cost of real estate purchased as a plant site (land $100,000 and building $45,000) | 145,000 |
| **5.** Excavation costs for new building | 35,000 |
| **6.** Architect's fees on building plans | 10,000 |
| **7.** Accrued real estate taxes paid at time of purchase of real estate | 2,000 |
| **8.** Cost of parking lots and driveways | 14,000 |
| **9.** Cost of demolishing building to make land suitable for construction of new building | 15,000 |
| | $930,000 |

Credits

| | |
|---|---:|
| **10.** Proceeds from salvage of demolished building | $ 3,500 |

**Instructions**

*Totals*
Land $162,500
Building $745,000

Analyze the foregoing transactions using the following column headings. Insert the number of each transaction in the Item space, and insert the amounts in the appropriate columns. For amounts entered in the Other Accounts column, also indicate the account titles.

| Item | Land | Building | Other Accounts |
|------|------|----------|----------------|

*Compute depreciation under different methods.*
*(SO 3)*

**P10-2A**   In recent years, Juresic Transportation purchased three used buses. Because of frequent turnover in the accounting department, a different accountant selected the depreciation method for each bus, and various methods were selected. Information concerning the buses is summarized on the next page.

| Bus | Acquired | Cost | Salvage Value | Useful Life in Years | Depreciation Method |
|-----|----------|------|---------------|----------------------|---------------------|
| 1 | 1/1/06 | $ 96,000 | $ 6,000 | 5 | Straight-line |
| 2 | 1/1/06 | 120,000 | 10,000 | 4 | Declining-balance |
| 3 | 1/1/07 | 80,000 | 8,000 | 5 | Units-of-activity |

For the declining-balance method, the company uses the double-declining rate. For the units-of-activity method, total miles are expected to be 120,000. Actual miles of use in the first 3 years were: 2007, 24,000; 2008, 34,000; and 2009, 30,000.

**Instructions**
**(a)** Compute the amount of accumulated depreciation on each bus at December 31, 2008.
**(b)** If bus no. 2 was purchased on April 1 instead of January 1, what is the depreciation expense for this bus in (1) 2006 and (2) 2007?

*(a) Bus 2, 2007, $90,000*

**P10-3A**   On January 1, 2008, Pele Company purchased the following two machines for use in its production process.

*Compute depreciation under different methods.*

*(SO 3)*

Machine A:  The cash price of this machine was $38,000. Related expenditures included: sales tax $1,700, shipping costs $150, insurance during shipping $80, installation and testing costs $70, and $100 of oil and lubricants to be used with the machinery during its first year of operations. Pele estimates that the useful life of the machine is 5 years with a $5,000 salvage value remaining at the end of that time period. Assume that the straight-line method of depreciation is used.

Machine B:  The recorded cost of this machine was $160,000. Pele estimates that the useful life of the machine is 4 years with a $10,000 salvage value remaining at the end of that time period.

**Instructions**
**(a)** Prepare the following for Machine A.
   **(1)** The journal entry to record its purchase on January 1, 2008.
   **(2)** The journal entry to record annual depreciation at December 31, 2008.
**(b)** Calculate the amount of depreciation expense that Pele should record for machine B each year of its useful life under the following assumptions.
   **(1)** Pele uses the straight-line method of depreciation.
   **(2)** Pele uses the declining-balance method. The rate used is twice the straight-line rate.
   **(3)** Pele uses the units-of-activity method and estimates that the useful life of the machine is 125,000 units. Actual usage is as follows: 2008, 45,000 units; 2009, 35,000 units; 2010, 25,000 units; 2011, 20,000 units.
**(c)** Which method used to calculate depreciation on machine B reports the highest amount of depreciation expense in year 1 (2008)? The highest amount in year 4 (2011)? The highest total amount over the 4-year period?

*(b) (2) 2008 DDB depreciation $80,000*

**P10-4A**   At the beginning of 2006, Lehman Company acquired equipment costing $90,000. It was estimated that this equipment would have a useful life of 6 years and a residual value of $9,000 at that time. The straight-line method of depreciation was considered the most appropriate to use with this type of equipment. Depreciation is to be recorded at the end of each year.

*Calculate revisions to depreciation expense.*

*(SO 3, 4)*

   During 2008 (the third year of the equipment's life), the company's engineers reconsidered their expectations, and estimated that the equipment's useful life would probably be 7 years (in total) instead of 6 years. The estimated residual value was not changed at that time. However, during 2011 the estimated residual value was reduced to $5,000.

**Instructions**
Indicate how much depreciation expense should be recorded each year for this equipment, by completing the following table.

| Year | Depreciation Expense | Accumulated Depreciation |
|------|----------------------|--------------------------|
| 2006 | | |
| 2007 | | |
| 2008 | | |
| 2009 | | |
| 2010 | | |
| 2011 | | |
| 2012 | | |

*2012 depreciation expense, $12,800*

*Journalize a series of equipment transactions related to purchase, sale, retirement, and depreciation.*

*(SO 1, 3, 6, 9)*

**P10-5A**   At December 31, 2008, Jimenez Company reported the following as plant assets.

| | | |
|---|---:|---:|
| Land | | $ 4,000,000 |
| Buildings | $28,500,000 | |
| Less: Accumulated depreciation—buildings | 12,100,000 | 16,400,000 |
| Equipment | 48,000,000 | |
| Less: Accumulated depreciation—equipment | 5,000,000 | 43,000,000 |
| Total plant assets | | $63,400,000 |

During 2009, the following selected cash transactions occurred.

April 1   Purchased land for $2,130,000.
May   1   Sold equipment that cost $780,000 when purchased on January 1, 2005. The equipment was sold for $450,000.
June  1   Sold land purchased on June 1, 1999, for $1,500,000. The land cost $400,000.
July   1   Purchased equipment for $2,000,000.
Dec. 31  Retired equipment that cost $500,000 when purchased on December 31, 1999. No salvage value was received.

**Instructions**

**(a)** Journalize the above transactions. The company uses straight-line depreciation for buildings and equipment. The buildings are estimated to have a 50-year life and no salvage value. The equipment is estimated to have a 10-year useful life and no salvage value. Update depreciation on assets disposed of at the time of sale or retirement.

(b) Depreciation Expense—
building $570,000;
equipment $4,772,000
(c) Total plant assets
$61,270,000

**(b)** Record adjusting entries for depreciation for 2009.
**(c)** Prepare the plant assets section of Jimenez's balance sheet at December 31, 2009.

*Record disposals.*

*(SO 6)*

**P10-6A**   Puckett Co. has office furniture that cost $75,000 and that has been depreciated $50,000. Record the disposal under the following assumptions.

**(a)** It was scrapped as having no value.
**(b)** It was sold for $21,000.
**(c)** It was sold for $31,000.

*Prepare entries to record transactions related to acquisition and amortization of intangibles; prepare the intangible assets section.*

*(SO 8, 9)*

**P10-7A**   The intangible assets section of Redeker Company at December 31, 2008, is presented below.

| | |
|---|---:|
| Patent ($70,000 cost less $7,000 amortization) | $63,000 |
| Franchise ($48,000 cost less $19,200 amortization) | 28,800 |
| Total | $91,800 |

The patent was acquired in January 2008 and has a useful life of 10 years. The franchise was acquired in January 2005 and also has a useful life of 10 years. The following cash transactions may have affected intangible assets during 2009.

Jan. 2   Paid $45,000 legal costs to successfully defend the patent against infringement by another company.
Jan.–June   Developed a new product, incurring $140,000 in research and development costs. A patent was granted for the product on July 1. Its useful life is equal to its legal life.
Sept. 1   Paid $50,000 to an extremely large defensive lineman to appear in commercials advertising the company's products. The commercials will air in September and October.
Oct. 1   Acquired a franchise for $100,000. The franchise has a useful life of 50 years.

(b) Amortization Expense—
Patents $12,000
Amortization Expense—
Franchise $5,300
(c) Total intangible assets
$219,500

**Instructions**

**(a)** Prepare journal entries to record the transactions above.
**(b)** Prepare journal entries to record the 2009 amortization expense.
**(c)** Prepare the intangible assets section of the balance sheet at December 31, 2009.

*Prepare entries to correct errors made in recording and amortizing intangible assets.*

*(SO 8)*

**P10-8A**   Due to rapid turnover in the accounting department, a number of transactions involving intangible assets were improperly recorded by Thorne Company in 2008.

**1.** Thorne developed a new manufacturing process, incurring research and development costs of $136,000. The company also purchased a patent for $60,000. In early January, Thorne capitalized $196,000 as the cost of the patents. Patent amortization expense of $9,800 was recorded based on a 20-year useful life.

2. On July 1, 2008, Thorne purchased a small company and as a result acquired goodwill of $92,000. Thorne recorded a half-year's amortization in 2008, based on a 50-year life ($920 amortization). The goodwill has an indefinite life.

**Instructions**

Prepare all journal entries necessary to correct any errors made during 2008. Assume the books have not yet been closed for 2008.

*1. R&D Exp. $136,000*

**P10-9A**   Lebo Company and Ritter Corporation, two corporations of roughly the same size, are both involved in the manufacture of in-line skates. Each company depreciates its plant assets using the straight-line approach. An investigation of their financial statements reveals the following information.

*Calculate and comment on asset turnover ratio.*

*(SO 9)*

|  | **Lebo Co.** | **Ritter Corp.** |
|---|---|---|
| Net income | $ 800,000 | $1,000,000 |
| Sales | 1,200,000 | 1,080,000 |
| Average total assets | 2,500,000 | 2,000,000 |
| Average plant assets | 1,800,000 | 1,000,000 |

**Instructions**

(a) For each company, calculate the asset turnover ratio.

(b) ━━━▶ Based on your calculations in part (a), comment on the relative effectiveness of the two companies in using their assets to generate sales and produce net income.

# PROBLEMS: SET B

**P10-1B**   Selmon Company was organized on January 1. During the first year of operations, the following plant asset expenditures and receipts were recorded in random order.

*Determine acquisition costs of land and building.*

*(SO 1)*

### Debits

| | |
|---|---|
| 1. Accrued real estate taxes paid at time of purchase of real estate | $  2,000 |
| 2. Real estate taxes on land paid for the current year | 3,000 |
| 3. Full payment to building contractor | 600,000 |
| 4. Excavation costs for new building | 22,000 |
| 5. Cost of real estate purchased as a plant site (land $100,000 and building $25,000) | 125,000 |
| 6. Cost of parking lots and driveways | 15,000 |
| 7. Architect's fees on building plans | 10,000 |
| 8. Installation cost of fences around property | 4,000 |
| 9. Cost of demolishing building to make land suitable for construction of new building | 24,000 |
| | $805,000 |

### Credit

| | |
|---|---|
| 10. Proceeds from salvage of demolished building | $  2,500 |

**Instructions**

Analyze the foregoing tranactions using the following column headings. Insert the number of each transaction in the Item space, and insert the amounts in the appropriate columns. For amounts entered in the Other Accounts column, also indicate the account title.

| Item | Land | Building | Other Accounts |
|---|---|---|---|

*Totals*

*Land $148,500*
*Building $632,000*

**P10-2B**   In recent years, Escobar Company purchased three machines. Because of heavy turnover in the accounting department, a different accountant was in charge of selecting the depreciation method for each machine, and various methods were selected. Information concerning the machines is summarized on the next page.

*Compute depreciation under different methods.*

*(SO 3)*

| Machine | Acquired | Cost | Salvage Value | Useful Life in Years | Depreciation Method |
|---------|----------|------|---------------|----------------------|---------------------|
| 1 | 1/1/05 | $86,000 | $ 6,000 | 10 | Straight-line |
| 2 | 1/1/06 | 100,000 | 10,000 | 8 | Declining-balance |
| 3 | 11/1/08 | 78,000 | 6,000 | 6 | Units-of-activity |

For the declining-balance method, the company uses the double-declining rate. For the units-of-activity method, total machine hours are expected to be 24,000. Actual hours of use in the first 3 years were: 2008, 1,000; 2009, 4,500; and 2010, 5,000.

**Instructions**

(a) Machine 2, 2007, $18,750

**(a)** Compute the amount of accumulated depreciation on each machine at December 31, 2008.

**(b)** If machine 2 had been purchased on April 1 instead of January 1, what would be the depreciation expense for this machine in (1) 2006 and (2) 2007?

*Compute depreciation under different methods.*

*(SO 3)*

**P10-3B**   On January 1, 2008, Guthrie Company purchased the following two machines for use in its production process.

> Machine A: The cash price of this machine was $46,500. Related expenditures included: sales tax $2,200, shipping costs $175, insurance during shipping $75, installation and testing costs $50, and $90 of oil and lubricants to be used with the machinery during its first year of operation. Guthrie estimates that the useful life of the machine is 4 years with a $5,000 salvage value remaining at the end of that time period.

> Machine B: The recorded cost of this machine was $120,000. Guthrie estimates that the useful life of the machine is 4 years with a $8,000 salvage value remaining at the end of that time period.

**Instructions**

(a) (2) $11,000

**(a)** Prepare the following for Machine A.

   **(1)** The journal entry to record its purchase on January 1, 2008.

   **(2)** The journal entry to record annual depreciation at December 31, 2008, assuming the straight-line method of depreciation is used.

**(b)** Calculate the amount of depreciation expense that Guthrie should record for machine B each year of its useful life under the following assumption.

   **(1)** Guthrie uses the straight-line method of depreciation.

   **(2)** Guthrie uses the declining-balance method. The rate used is twice the straight-line rate.

   **(3)** Guthrie uses the units-of-activity method and estimates the useful life of the machine is 25,000 units. Actual usage is as follows: 2008, 6,500 units; 2009, 7,500 units; 2010, 6,000 units; 2011, 5,000 units.

**(c)** Which method used to calculate depreciation on machine B reports the lowest amount of depreciation expense in year 1 (2008)? The lowest amount in year 4 (2011)? The lowest total amount over the 4-year period?

*Calculate revisions to depreciation expense.*

*(SO 3, 4)*

**P10-4B**   At the beginning of 2006, Hadaway Company acquired equipment costing $80,000. It was estimated that this equipment would have a useful life of 6 years and a residual value of $8,000 at that time. The straight-line method of depreciation was considered the most appropriate to use with this type of equipment. Depreciation is to be recorded at the end of each year.

During 2008 (the third year of the equipment's life), the company's engineers reconsidered their expectations, and estimated that the equipment's useful life would probably be 7 years (in total) instead of 6 years. The estimated residual value was not changed at that time. However, during 2011 the estimated residual value was reduced to $4,000.

**Instructions**

Indicate how much depreciation expense should be recorded for this equipment each year by completing the following table.

| Year | Depreciation Expense | Accumulated Depreciation |
|------|----------------------|--------------------------|
| 2006 | | |
| 2007 | | |
| 2008 | | |
| 2009 | | |
| 2010 | | |
| 2011 | | |
| 2012 | | |

2012 depreciation expense, $11,600

**P10-5B**   At December 31, 2008, Yockey Company reported the following as plant assets.

| | | |
|---|---:|---:|
| Land | | $ 3,000,000 |
| Buildings | $26,500,000 | |
| Less: Accumulated depreciation—buildings | 12,100,000 | 14,400,000 |
| Equipment | 40,000,000 | |
| Less: Accumulated depreciation—equipment | 5,000,000 | 35,000,000 |
| Total plant assets | | $52,400,000 |

*Journalize a series of equipment transactions related to purchase, sale, retirement, and depreciation.*

*(SO 1, 3, 6, 9)*

During 2009, the following selected cash transactions occurred.

April 1   Purchased land for $2,200,000.
May  1   Sold equipment that cost $600,000 when purchased on January 1, 2005. The equipment was sold for $360,000.
June 1   Sold land purchased on June 1, 1999, for $1,800,000. The land cost $600,000.
July 1   Purchased equipment for $1,800,000.
Dec. 31   Retired equipment that cost $500,000 when purchased on December 31, 1999. No salvage value was received.

**Instructions**
**(a)** Journalize the above transactions. Yockey uses straight-line depreciation for buildings and equipment. The buildings are estimated to have a 50-year useful life and no salvage value. The equipment is estimated to have a 10-year useful life and no salvage value. Update depreciation on assets disposed of at the time of sale or retirement.
**(b)** Record adjusting entries for depreciation for 2009.
**(c)** Prepare the plant assets section of Yockey's balance sheet at December 31, 2009.

*(b) Depreciation expense— Building $530,000; Equipment $3,980,000*
*(c) Total plant assets $50,880,000*

**P10-6B**   Riggs Co. has delivery equipment that cost $50,000 and that has been depreciated $24,000. Record the disposal under the following assumptions.

**(a)** It was scrapped as having no value.
**(b)** It was sold for $31,000.
**(c)** It was sold for $18,000.

*Record disposals.*

*(SO 6)*

**P10-7B**   The intangible assets section of Justen Company at December 31, 2008, is presented below.

| | |
|---|---:|
| Patent ($60,000 cost less $6,000 amortization) | $54,000 |
| Copyright ($36,000 cost less $14,400 amortization) | 21,600 |
| Total | $75,600 |

*Prepare entries to record transactions related to acquisition and amortization of intangibles; prepare the intangible assets section.*

*(SO 8, 9)*

The patent was acquired in January 2008 and has a useful life of 10 years. The copyright was acquired in January 2005 and also has a useful life of 10 years. The following cash transactions may have affected intangible assets during 2009.

Jan. 2   Paid $27,000 legal costs to successfully defend the patent against infringement by another company.
Jan.–June   Developed a new product, incurring $140,000 in research and development costs. A patent was granted for the product on July 1. Its useful life is equal to its legal life.
Sept. 1   Paid $75,000 to a quarterback to appear in commercials advertising the company's products. The commercials will air in September and October.
Oct. 1   Acquired a copyright for $120,000. The copyright has a useful life of 50 years.

**Instructions**
**(a)** Prepare journal entries to record the transactions above.
**(b)** Prepare journal entries to record the 2009 amortization expense for intangible assets.
**(c)** Prepare the intangible assets section of the balance sheet at December 31, 2009.
**(d)** ✏ Prepare the note to the financials on Justen's intangibles as of December 31, 2009.

*(b) Amortization Expense— Patents $9,000; Amortization Expense— Copyrights $4,200*
*(c) Total intangible assets, $209,400*

**P10-8B**   Due to rapid turnover in the accounting department, a number of transactions involving intangible assets were improperly recorded by Duby Company in 2008.

**1.** Duby developed a new manufacturing process, incurring research and development costs of $95,000. The company also purchased a patent for $40,000. In early January, Duby capitalized $135,000 as the cost of the patents. Patent amortization expense of $6,750 was recorded based on a 20-year useful life.

*Prepare entries to correct errors made in recording and amortizing intangible assets.*

*(SO 8)*

2. On July 1, 2008, Duby purchased a small company and as a result acquired goodwill of $80,000. Duby recorded a half-year's amortization in 2008, based on a 50-year life ($800 amortization). The goodwill has an indefinite life.

**Instructions**

*R&D Exp. $95,000*

Prepare all journal entries necessary to correct any errors made during 2008. Assume the books have not yet been closed for 2008.

*Calculate and comment on asset turnover ratio.*

*(SO 9)*

**P10-9B**  Gavin Corporation and Keady Corporation, two corporations of roughly the same size, are both involved in the manufacture of canoes and sea kayaks. Each company depreciates its plant assets using the straight-line approach. An investigation of their financial statements reveals the following information.

|  | Gavin Corp. | Keady Corp. |
|---|---|---|
| Net income | $ 400,000 | $ 420,000 |
| Sales | 1,300,000 | 1,140,000 |
| Average total assets | 2,000,000 | 1,500,000 |
| Average plant assets | 1,500,000 | 800,000 |

**Instructions**

**(a)** For each company, calculate the asset turnover ratio.

**(b)** Based on your calculations in part (a), comment on the relative effectiveness of the two companies in using their assets to generate sales and produce net income.

## PROBLEMS: SET C

Visit the book's website at **www.wiley.com/college/weygandt**, and choose the Student Companion site, to access Problem Set C.

## COMPREHENSIVE PROBLEM: CHAPTERS 3 TO 10

Winterschid Company's trial balance at December 31, 2008, is presented below. All 2008 transactions have been recorded except for the items described on page 467.

|  | Debit | Credit |
|---|---|---|
| Cash | $ 28,000 | |
| Accounts Receivable | 36,800 | |
| Notes Receivable | 10,000 | |
| Interest Receivable | –0– | |
| Merchandise Inventory | 36,200 | |
| Prepaid Insurance | 3,600 | |
| Land | 20,000 | |
| Building | 150,000 | |
| Equipment | 60,000 | |
| Patent | 9,000 | |
| Allowance for Doubtful Accounts | | $ 500 |
| Accumulated Depreciation—Building | | 50,000 |
| Accumulated Depreciation—Equipment | | 24,000 |
| Accounts Payable | | 27,300 |
| Salaries Payable | | –0– |
| Unearned Rent | | 6,000 |
| Notes Payable (short-term) | | 11,000 |
| Interest Payable | | –0– |
| Notes Payable (long-term) | | 35,000 |
| Common Stock | | 75,000 |
| Retained Earnings | | 38,600 |
| Dividends | 12,000 | |
| Sales | | 900,000 |

| | | |
|---|---|---|
| Interest Revenue | | –0– |
| Rent Revenue | | –0– |
| Gain on Disposal | | –0– |
| Bad Debts Expense | –0– | |
| Cost of Goods Sold | 630,000 | |
| Depreciation Expense—Buildings | –0– | |
| Depreciation Expense—Equipment | –0– | |
| Insurance Expense | –0– | |
| Interest Expense | –0– | |
| Other Operating Expenses | 61,800 | |
| Amortization Expense—Patents | –0– | |
| Salaries Expense | 110,000 | |
| Total | $1,167,400 | $1,167,400 |

Unrecorded transactions

1. On May 1, 2008, Winterschid purchased equipment for $13,200 plus sales taxes of $600 (all paid in cash).
2. On July 1, 2008, Winterschid sold for $3,500 equipment which originally cost $5,000. Accumulated depreciation on this equipment at January 1, 2008, was $1,800; 2008 depreciation prior to the sale of equipment was $450.
3. On December 31, 2008, Winterschid sold for $9,000 on account inventory that cost $6,300.
4. Winterschid estimates that uncollectible accounts receivable at year-end is $4,000.
5. The note receivable is a one-year, 8% note dated April 1, 2008. No interest has been recorded.
6. The balance in prepaid insurance represents payment of a $3,600 6-month premium on September 1, 2008.
7. The building is being depreciated using the straight-line method over 30 years. The salvage value is $30,000.
8. The equipment owned prior to this year is being depreciated using the straight-line method over 5 years. The salvage value is 10% of cost.
9. The equipment purchased on May 1, 2008, is being depreciated using the straight-line method over 5 years, with a salvage value of $1,800.
10. The patent was acquired on January 1, 2008, and has a useful life of 10 years from that date.
11. Unpaid salaries at December 31, 2008, total $2,200.
12. The unearned rent of $6,000 was received on December 1, 2008, for 3 months rent.
13. Both the short-term and long-term notes payable are dated January 1, 2008, and carry a 9% interest rate. All interest is payable in the next 12 months.

**Instructions**
(a) Prepare journal entries for the transactions listed above.
(b) Prepare an updated December 31, 2008, trial balance.
(c) Prepare a 2008 income statement and a retained earnings statement.
(d) Prepare a December 31, 2008, classified balance sheet.

## CONTINUING COOKIE CHRONICLE

(*Note:* This is a continuation of the Cookie Chronicle from Chapters 1 through 9.)
**CCC10**

**Part 1**    Now that she is selling mixers and her customers can use credit cards to pay for them, Natalie is thinking of upgrading her website to include the online sale of mixers and payment by credit card. This would enable her to sell these mixers to a wider range of customers using the Internet.

**Part 2**    Natalie is also thinking of buying a van that will be used only for business. Natalie is concerned about the impact of the van's cost on her income statement and balance sheet. She has come to you for advice on calculating the van's depreciation.

*Go to the book's website,*
**www.wiley.com/college/weygandt**,
*to see the completion of this problem.*

# BROADENING YOUR PERSPECTIVE

## FINANCIAL REPORTING AND ANALYSIS

## Financial Reporting Problem

### PepsiCo, Inc.

**BYP10-1** The financial statements and the Notes to Consolidated Financial Statements of PepsiCo are presented in Appendix A.

**Instructions**

Refer to PepsiCo's financial statements and answer the following questions.

**(a)** What was the total cost and book value of property, plant, and equipment at December 31, 2005?
**(b)** What method or methods of depreciation are used by the company for financial reporting purposes?
**(c)** What was the amount of depreciation and amortization expense for each of the three years 2003–2005?
**(d)** Using the statement of cash flows, what is the amount of capital spending in 2005 and 2004?
**(e)** Where does the company disclose its intangible assets, and what types of intangibles did it have at December 31, 2005?

## Comparative Analysis Problem

### PepsiCo, Inc. vs. The Coca-Cola Company

**BYP10-2** PepsiCo's financial statements are presented in Appendix A. Coca-Cola's financial statements are presented in Appendix B.

**Instructions**

**(a)** Compute the asset turnover ratio for each company for 2005.
**(b)** What conclusions concerning the efficiency of assets can be drawn from these data?

## Exploring the Web

**BYP10-3** A company's annual report identifies the amount of its plant assets and the depreciation method used.

**Address: www.reportgallery.com**, or go to **www.wiley.com/college/weygandt**

**Steps**

1. From Report Gallery Homepage, choose **Search by Alphabet**, and pick a letter.
2. Select a particular company.
3. Choose the most recent **Annual Report**.
4. Follow instructions below.

**Instructions**

**(a)** What is the name of the company?
**(b)** At fiscal year-end, what is the net amount of its plant assets?
**(c)** What is the accumulated depreciation?
**(d)** Which method of depreciation does the company use?

## CRITICAL THINKING

## Decision Making Across the Organization

**BYP10-4** Reimer Company and Lingo Company are two proprietorships that are similar in many respects. One difference is that Reimer Company uses the straight-line method and Lingo

Company uses the declining-balance method at double the straight-line rate. On January 2, 2006, both companies acquired the following depreciable assets.

| Asset | Cost | Salvage Value | Useful Life |
|---|---|---|---|
| Building | $320,000 | $20,000 | 40 years |
| Equipment | 110,000 | 10,000 | 10 years |

Including the appropriate depreciation charges, annual net income for the companies in the years 2006, 2007, and 2008 and total income for the 3 years were as follows.

| | 2006 | 2007 | 2008 | Total |
|---|---|---|---|---|
| Reimer Company | $84,000 | $88,400 | $90,000 | $262,400 |
| Lingo Company | 68,000 | 76,000 | 85,000 | 229,000 |

At December 31, 2008, the balance sheets of the two companies are similar except that Lingo Company has more cash than Reimer Company.

Sally Vogts is interested in buying one of the companies. She comes to you for advice.

**Instructions**

With the class divided into groups, answer the following.

**(a)** Determine the annual and total depreciation recorded by each company during the 3 years.

**(b)** Assuming that Lingo Company also uses the straight-line method of depreciation instead of the declining-balance method as in (a), prepare comparative income data for the 3 years.

**(c)** Which company should Sally Vogts buy? Why?

# Communication Activity

**BYP10-5** The following was published with the financial statements to American Exploration Company.

## AMERICAN EXPLORATION COMPANY
### Notes to the Financial Statements

**Property, Plant, and Equipment**—The Company accounts for its oil and gas exploration and production activities using the successful efforts method of accounting. Under this method, acquisition costs for proved and unproved properties are capitalized when incurred.... The costs of drilling exploratory wells are capitalized pending determination of whether each well has discovered proved reserves. If proved reserves are not discovered, such drilling costs are charged to expense.... Depletion of the cost of producing oil and gas properties is computed on the units-of-activity method.

**Instructions**

Write a brief memo to your instructor discussing American Exploration Company's note regarding property, plant, and equipment. Your memo should address what is meant by the "successful efforts method" and "units-of-activity method."

# Ethics Case

**BYP10-6** Buster Container Company is suffering declining sales of its principal product, non-biodegradeable plastic cartons. The president, Dennis Harwood, instructs his controller, Shelly McGlone, to lengthen asset lives to reduce depreciation expense. A processing line of automated plastic extruding equipment, purchased for $3.1 million in January 2008, was originally estimated to have a useful life of 8 years and a salvage value of $300,000. Depreciation has been recorded for 2 years on that basis. Dennis wants the estimated life changed to 12 years total, and the straight-line method continued. Shelly is hesitant to make the change, believing it is unethical to increase net income in this manner. Dennis says, "Hey, the life is only an estimate, and I've heard that our competition uses a 12-year life on their production equipment."

**Instructions**

**(a)** Who are the stakeholders in this situation?

**(b)** Is the change in asset life unethical, or is it simply a good business practice by an astute president?

**(c)** What is the effect of Dennis Harwood's proposed change on income before taxes in the year of change?

 # "All About You" Activity

**BYP10-7** Both the "All About You" story and the Feature Story at the beginning of the chapter discussed the company Rent-A-Wreck. Note that the tradename Rent-A-Wreck is a very important asset to the company, as it creates immediate product identification. As indicated in the chapter, companies invest substantial sums to ensure that their product is well-known to the consumer. Test your knowledge of who owns some famous brands and their impact on the financial statements.

**Instructions**

**(a)** Provide an answer to the five multiple-choice questions below.

(1) Which company owns both Taco Bell and Pizza Hut?
- **(a)** McDonald's.
- **(c)** Yum Brands.
- **(b)** CKE.
- **(d)** Wendy's.

(2) Dairy Queen belongs to:
- **(a)** Breyer.
- **(c)** GE.
- **(b)** Berkshire Hathaway.
- **(d)** The Coca-Cola Company.

(3) Phillip Morris, the cigarette maker, is owned by:
- **(a)** Altria.
- **(c)** Boeing.
- **(b)** GE.
- **(d)** ExxonMobil.

(4) AOL, a major Internet provider, belongs to:
- **(a)** Microsoft.
- **(c)** NBC.
- **(b)** Cisco.
- **(d)** Time Warner.

(5) ESPN, the sports broadcasting network, is owned by:
- **(a)** Procter & Gamble.
- **(c)** Walt Disney.
- **(b)** Altria.
- **(d)** The Coca-Cola Company.

**(b)** How do you think the value of these brands is reported on the parent company's balance sheet?

 ## Answers to Insight and Accounting Across the Organization Questions

**Many U.S. Firms Use Leases, p. 429**

Q: Why might airline managers choose to lease rather than purchase their planes?

A: *The reasons for leasing include favorable tax treatment, better financing options, increased flexibility, reduced risk of obsolescence, and low airline income.*

**What Happened at WorldCom?, p. 438**

Q: What erroneous accounting entries (accounts debited and credited) were made by WorldCom?

A: *WorldCom erroneously debited Assets and credited Cash/Accounts Payable.*

Q: What is the correcting entry that should be recorded, and what is its effect on WorldCom's financial statements?

A: *The correcting entry would be a debit to Expenses and a credit to Assets. This correction would decrease reported income, assets, and retained earnings as well as increase expenses.*

**ESPN Wins Monday Night Football Franchise, p. 445**

Q: How should ESPN account for the $1.1 billion per year franchise fee?

A: *Since this is an annual franchise fee, ESPN should expense it each year, rather than capitalizing and amortizing it.*

 ## Authors' Comments on *All About You: Buying a Wreck of Your Own*, p. 448

As the data in the box suggest, this decision can have significant implications for your personal budget. For many college students, vehicle costs are among their biggest expenses—and vehicle expenses often offer the greatest opportunities for savings. But for many people their vehicle choice is not just about how to get around. Some view their car as an expression of their personality. That said, many people simply don't realize just how much this particular expression of their personality is actually costing them.

You should approach this decision using the skills you have acquired in your business studies. Evaluate your transportation needs, collect information about all of your alternatives, and understand exactly what the real costs are of each. For example, everyone knows that the original purchase price of a new car is higher than a used car, but few people stop to consider the fact that insurance costs and annual motor vehicle costs on a new vehicle are also much higher.

We cannot tell you whether a new or used car is right for you, but we do hope that we have convinced you to carefully consider all aspects of the financial implications of your decision the next time you shop for new wheels. In later chapters we will provide you with additional tools to help you evaluate this decision.

## Answer to PepsiCo Review It Question 2, p. 430

PepsiCo reports the following categories and amounts under the heading "Property, plant, and equipment (net)": Land and improvements \$685,000,000; Buildings and improvements \$3,736,000,000; Machinery and equipment, including fleet and software \$11,658,000,000; and Construction in progress \$1,066,000,000. In addition, accumulated depreciation of \$8,464,000,000 was deducted.

## Answers to Self-Study Questions

**1.** d   **2.** b   **3.** d   **4.** d   **5.** b   **6.** d   **7.** c   **8.** b   **9.** c   **10.** a   **11.** d

# Chapter 11

# Liabilities

### STUDY OBJECTIVES

*After studying this chapter, you should be able to:*

1 Explain a current liability, and identify the major types of current liabilities.

2 Describe the accounting for notes payable.

3 Explain the accounting for other current liabilities.

4 Explain why bonds are issued, and identify the types of bonds.

5 Prepare the entries for the issuance of bonds and interest expense.

6 Describe the entries when bonds are redeemed or converted.

7 Describe the accounting for long-term notes payable.

8 Identify the methods for the presentation and analysis of long-term liabilities.

 The Navigator

### ✓ The Navigator

| | |
|---|---|
| Scan **Study Objectives** | ■ |
| Read **Feature Story** | ■ |
| Read **Preview** | ■ |
| Read text and answer **Before You Go On** p. 481 ■  p. 487 ■  p. 490 ■  p. 492 ■ p. 495 ■ | |
| Work **Demonstration Problem** | ■ |
| Review **Summary of Study Objectives** | ■ |
| Answer **Self-Study Questions** | ■ |
| Complete **Assignments** | ■ |

## *Feature Story*

**FINANCING HIS DREAMS**

What would you do if you had a great idea for a new product, but couldn't come up with the cash to get the business off the ground? Small businesses often cannot attract investors. Nor can they obtain traditional debt financing through bank loans or bond issuances. Instead, they often resort to unusual, and costly, forms of nontraditional financing.

Such was the case for Wilbert Murdock. Murdock grew up in a New York housing project, and always had great ambitions. This ambitious spirit led him into some business ventures that failed: a medical diagnostic tool, a device to eliminate carpal-tunnel syndrome, custom-designed sneakers, and a device to

keep people from falling asleep while driving.

Another idea was computerized golf clubs that analyze a golfer's swing and provide immediate feedback. Murdock saw great potential in the idea: Many golfers are willing to shell out considerable sums of money for devices that might improve their game. But Murdock had no cash to develop his product, and banks and other lenders had shied away. Rather than give up, Murdock resorted to credit cards—in a big way. He quickly owed $25,000 to credit card companies.

While funding a business with credit cards might sound unusual, it isn't. A recent study found that one-third of businesses with fewer than 20 employees financed at least part of their operations with credit cards. As Murdock explained, credit cards are an appealing way to finance a start-up because "credit-card companies don't care how the money is spent." However, they do care how they are paid. And so Murdock faced high interest charges and a barrage of credit card collection letters.

Murdock's debt forced him to sacrifice nearly everything in order to keep his business afloat. His car stopped running, he barely had enough money to buy food, and he lived and worked out of a dimly lit apartment in his mother's basement. Through it all he tried to maintain a positive spirit, joking that, if he becomes successful, he might some day get to appear in an American Express commercial.

**Source:** Rodney Ho, "Banking on Plastic: To Finance a Dream, Many Entrepreneurs Binge on Credit Cards," *Wall Street Journal*, March 9, 1998, p. A1.

✓ The Navigator

# Inside Chapter 11

Inventor-entrepreneur Wilbert Murdock, as you can tell from the Feature Story, had to use multiple credit cards to finance his business ventures. Murdock's credit card debts would be classified as *current liabilities* because they are due every month. Yet by making minimal payments and paying high interest each month, Murdock used this credit source long-term. Some credit card balances remain outstanding for years as they accumulate interest.

In Chapter 4, we defined liabilities as creditors' claims on total assets and as existing debts and obligations. These claims, debts, and obligations must be settled or paid at some time **in the future** by the transfer of assets or services. The future date on which they are due or payable (maturity date) is a significant feature of liabilities. This "future date" feature gives rise to two basic classifications of liabilities: (1) current liabilities and (2) long-term liabilities. Our discussion in this chapter is divided into these two classifications.

The content and organization of Chapter 11 are as follows.

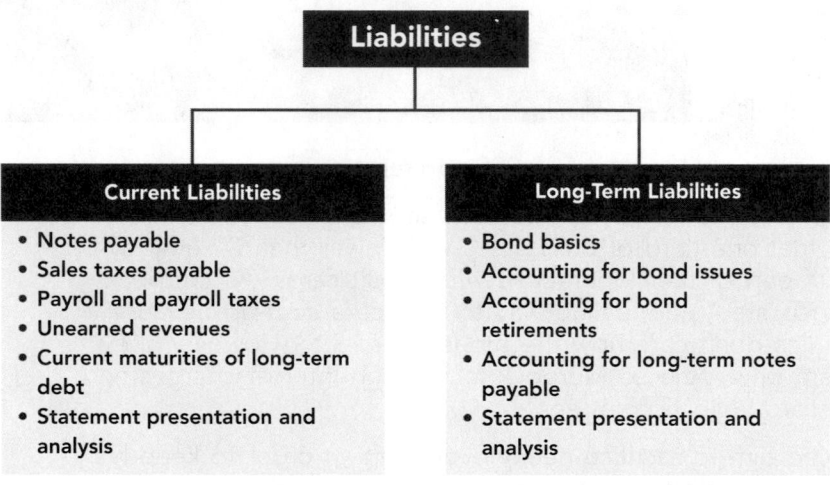

The Navigator

# SECTION 1 **Current Liabilities**

## WHAT IS A CURRENT LIABILITY?

**STUDY OBJECTIVE 1**

Explain a current liability, and identify the major types of current liabilities.

As explained in Chapter 4, a **current liability** is a debt with two key features: (1) The company reasonably expects to pay the debt from existing current assets or through the creation of other current liabilities. (2) The company will pay the debt within one year or the operating cycle, whichever is longer. Debts that do not meet **both criteria** are classified as long-term liabilities. Most companies pay current liabilities within one year out of current assets, rather than by creating other liabilities.

Companies must carefully monitor the relationship of current liabilities to current assets. This relationship is critical in evaluating a company's short-term debt-paying ability. A company that has more current liabilities than current assets may not be able to meet its current obligations when they become due.

Current liabilities include notes payable, accounts payable, and unearned revenues. They also include accrued liabilities such as taxes, salaries and wages, and interest payable. In previous chapters we explained the entries for accounts payable and adjusting entries for some current liabilities. In the following sections, we discuss other types of current liabilities.

# Notes Payable

Companies record obligations in the form of written promissory notes, called **notes payable**. Notes payable are often used instead of accounts payable because they give the lender formal proof of the obligation in case legal remedies are needed to collect the debt. Notes payable usually require the borrower to pay interest. Companies frequently issue them to meet short-term financing needs.

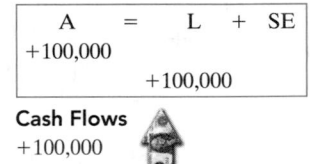

**STUDY OBJECTIVE 2**

Describe the accounting for notes payable.

Notes are issued for varying periods. **Those due for payment within one year of the balance sheet date are usually classified as current liabilities.**

To illustrate the accounting for notes payable, assume that First National Bank agrees to lend $100,000 on March 1, 2008, if Cole Williams Co. signs a $100,000, 12%, four-month note. With an interest-bearing promissory note, the amount of assets received upon issuance of the note generally equals the note's face value. Cole Williams Co. therefore will receive $100,000 cash and will make the following journal entry.

| | | | |
|---|---|---|---|
| Mar. 1 | Cash | 100,000 | |
| |     Notes Payable | | 100,000 |
| |     (To record issuance of 12%, 4-month note | | |
| |     to First National Bank) | | |

```
A     =    L    +   SE
+100,000
               +100,000
Cash Flows
+100,000
```

Interest accrues over the life of the note, and the company must periodically record that accrual. If Cole Williams Co. prepares financial statements on June 30, it makes an adjusting entry at June 30 to recognize interest expense and interest payable of $4,000 ($100,000 × 12% × 4/12). Illustration 11-1 shows the formula for computing interest, and its application to Cole Williams Co.'s note.

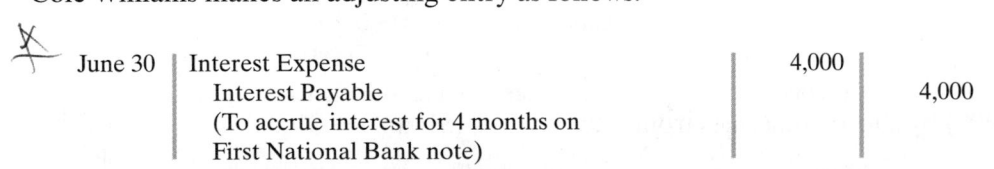

**Illustration 11-1**
Formula for computing interest

| Face Value of Note | × | Annual Interest Rate | × | Time in Terms of One Year | = | Interest |
|---|---|---|---|---|---|---|
| $100,000 | × | 12% | × | 4/12 | = | $4,000 |

Cole Williams makes an adjusting entry as follows:

| | | | |
|---|---|---|---|
| June 30 | Interest Expense | 4,000 | |
| |     Interest Payable | | 4,000 |
| |     (To accrue interest for 4 months on | | |
| |     First National Bank note) | | |

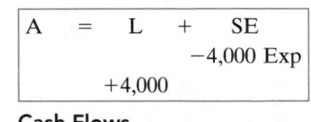

```
A    =    L    +    SE
                -4,000 Exp
          +4,000
Cash Flows
no effect
```

In the June 30 financial statements, the current liabilities section of the balance sheet will show notes payable $100,000 and interest payable $4,000. In addition, the company will report interest expense of $4,000 under "Other expenses and losses" in the income statement. If Cole Williams Co. prepared financial statements monthly, the adjusting entry at the end of each month would have been $1,000 ($100,000 × 12% × 1/12).

At maturity (July 1, 2008), Cole Williams Co. must pay the face value of the note ($100,000) plus $4,000 interest ($100,000 × 12% × 4/12). It records payment of the note and accrued interest as shown on the next page.

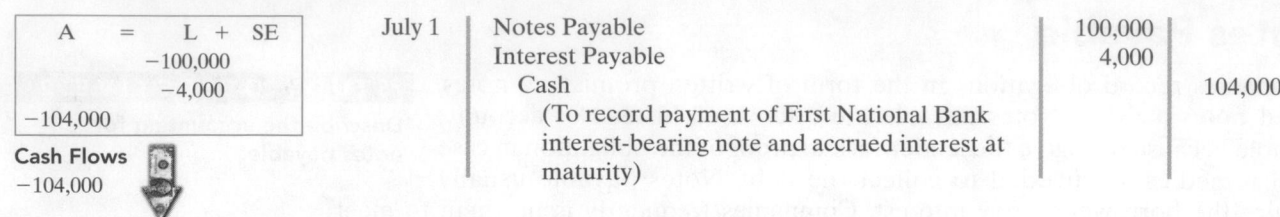

| A | = | L | + | SE |
|---|---|---|---|---|
| | | −100,000 | | |
| | | −4,000 | | |
| −104,000 | | | | |

**Cash Flows**
−104,000

| July 1 | Notes Payable | 100,000 | |
|--------|---------------|---------|--------|
| | Interest Payable | 4,000 | |
| |     Cash | | 104,000 |
| |     (To record payment of First National Bank | | |
| |     interest-bearing note and accrued interest at | | |
| |     maturity) | | |

## Sales Taxes Payable

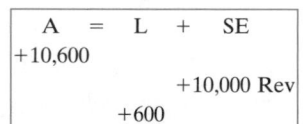

**STUDY OBJECTIVE 3**

Explain the accounting for other current liabilities.

As a consumer, you know that many of the products you purchase at retail stores are subject to sales taxes. Many states also are now collecting sales taxes on purchases made on the Internet. Sales taxes are expressed as a stated percentage of the sales price. The retailer collects the tax from the customer when the sale occurs. Periodically (usually monthly), the retailer remits the collections to the state's department of revenue.

Under most state sales tax laws, the selling company must ring up separately on the cash register the amount of the sale and the amount of the sales tax collected. (Gasoline sales are a major exception.) The company then uses the cash register readings to credit Sales and Sales Taxes Payable. For example, if the March 25 cash register reading for Cooley Grocery shows sales of $10,000 and sales taxes of $600 (sales tax rate of 6%), the journal entry is:

| A | = | L | + | SE |
|---|---|---|---|---|
| +10,600 | | | | |
| | | | | +10,000 Rev |
| | | +600 | | |

**Cash Flows**
+10,600

| Mar. 25 | Cash | 10,600 | |
|---------|------|--------|--------|
| |     Sales | | 10,000 |
| |     Sales Taxes Payable | | 600 |
| |     (To record daily sales and sales taxes) | | |

When the company remits the taxes to the taxing agency, it debits Sales Taxes Payable and credits Cash. The company does not report sales taxes as an expense. It simply forwards to the government the amount paid by the customers. Thus, Cooley Grocery serves only as a **collection agent** for the taxing authority.

Sometimes companies do not ring up sales taxes separately on the cash register. To determine the amount of sales in such cases, divide total receipts by 100% plus the sales tax percentage. To illustrate, assume that in the above example Cooley Grocery rings up total receipts of $10,600. The receipts from the sales are equal to the sales price (100%) plus the tax percentage (6% of sales), or 1.06 times the sales total. We can compute the sales amount as follows.

**HELPFUL HINT**

Alternatively, Cooley could find the tax by multiplying sales by the sales tax rate ($10,000 × .06).

$$\$10,600 \div 1.06 = \$10,000$$

Thus, Cooley Grocery could find the sales tax amount it must remit to the state ($600) by subtracting sales from total receipts ($10,600 − $10,000).

## Payroll and Payroll Taxes Payable

Every employer incurs liabilities relating to employees' salaries and wages. One is the amount of wages and salaries owed to employees—**wages and salaries payable**. Another is the amount required by law to be withheld from employees' gross pay. Until a company remits these **withholding taxes** (federal and state income taxes, and Social Security taxes) to the governmental taxing authorities, they are credited to appropriate liability accounts. For example, if a corporation withholds taxes from its employees' wages and salaries, it would record accrual and payment of a $100,000 payroll as shown on the next page.

| March 7 | Salaries and Wages Expense | 100,000 | | | A = L + SE |
|---|---|---|---|---|---|
| | FICA Taxes Payable[1] | | 7,650 | | −100,000 |
| | Federal Income Taxes Payable | | 21,864 | | +7,650 |
| | State Income Taxes Payable | | 2,922 | | +21,864 |
| | Salaries and Wages Payable | | 67,564 | | +2,922 |
| | (To record payroll and withholding taxes for the week ending March 7) | | | | +67,564 |

**Cash Flows**
no effect

| March 11 | Salaries and Wages Payable | 67,564 | | | A = L + SE |
|---|---|---|---|---|---|
| | Cash | | 67,564 | | −67,564 |
| | (To record payment of the March 7 payroll) | | | | −67,564 |

**Cash Flows**
−67,564

Illustration 11-2 summarizes the types of payroll deductions.

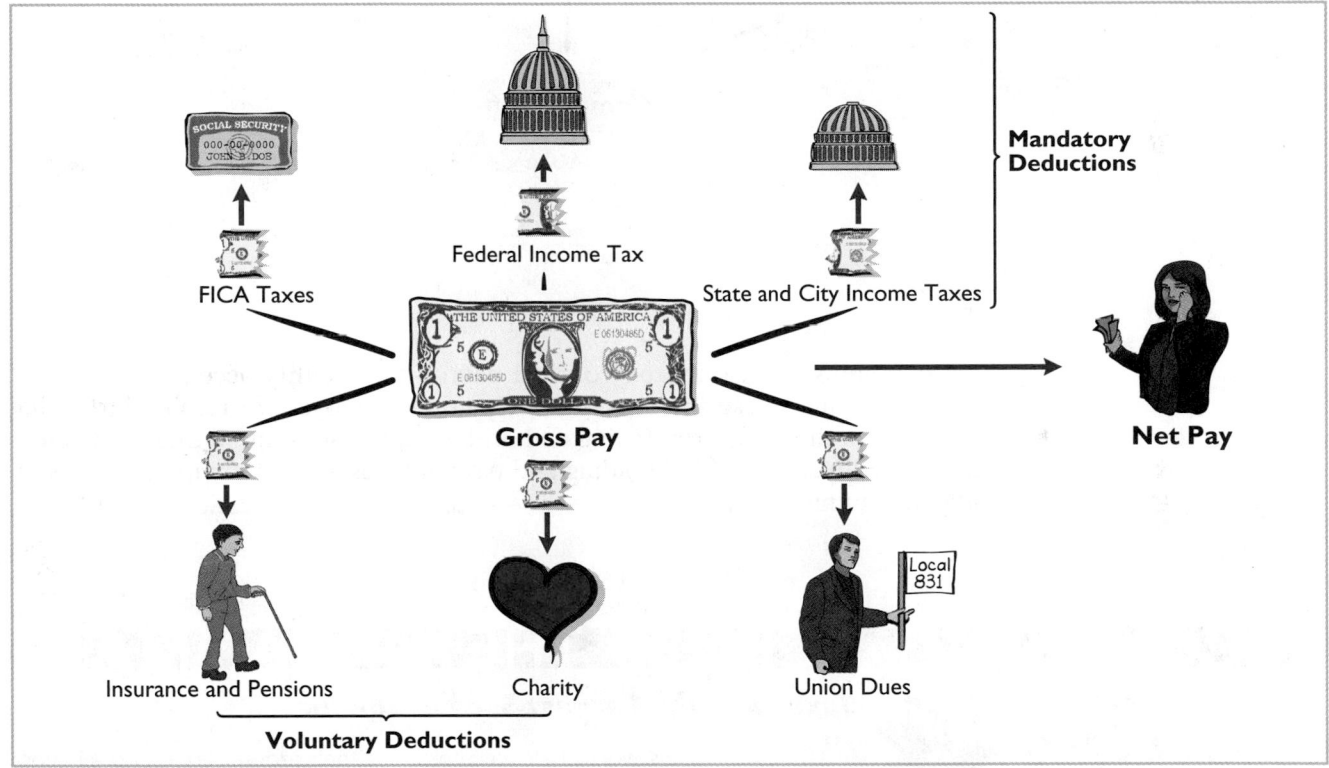

**Illustration 11-2**
Payroll deductions

Also, with every payroll, the employer incurs liabilities to pay various **payroll taxes** levied upon the employer. These payroll taxes include the employer's share of Social Security taxes and the state and federal unemployment taxes. Based on the $100,000 payroll in the previous example, the company would make the following entry to record the employer's expense and liability for these payroll taxes.

| March 7 | Payroll Tax Expense | 13,850 | | | A = L + SE |
|---|---|---|---|---|---|
| | FICA Taxes Payable | | 7,650 | | −13,850 |
| | Federal Unemployment Taxes Payable | | 800 | | +7,650 |
| | State Unemployment Taxes Payable | | 5,400 | | +800 |
| | (To record employer's payroll taxes on March 7 payroll) | | | | +5,400 |

**Cash Flows**
no effect

---

[1] In 2007 FICA includes 6.2% of the first $97,500 for Old-Age, Survivors, and Disability Insurance (OASDI) and 1.45% of all wages for Hospital Insurance (HI).

Illustration 11-3 shows the types of taxes levied on employers.

**Illustration 11-3**
Employer payroll taxes

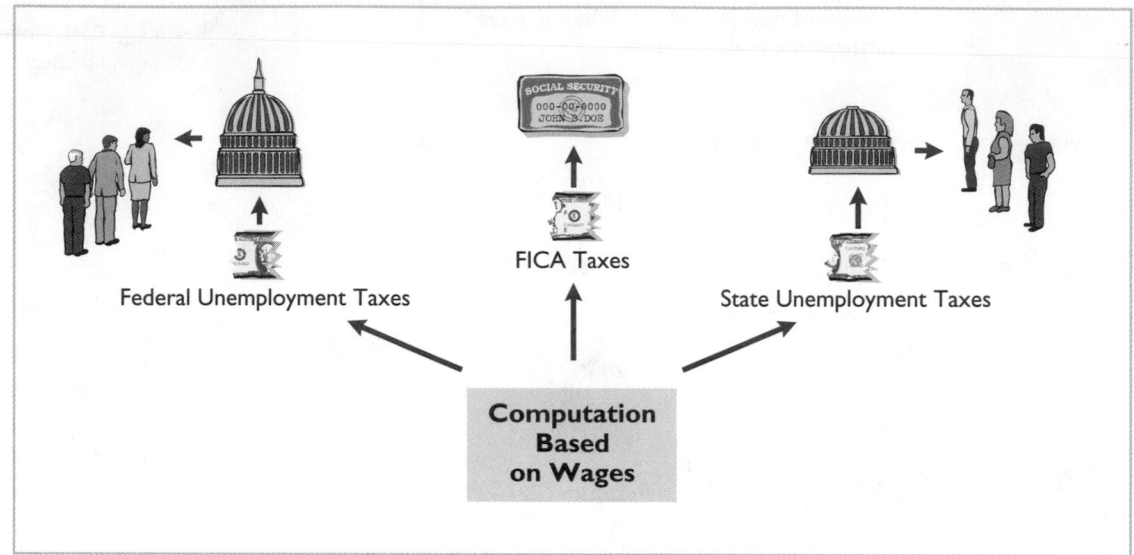

Companies classify the payroll and payroll tax liability accounts as current liabilities because these amounts must be paid to employees or remitted to taxing authorities in the near term. Taxing authorities impose substantial fines and penalties on employers if the withholding and payroll taxes are not computed correctly and paid on time.

# ACCOUNTING ACROSS THE ORGANIZATION

### Taxes Are the Largest Slice of the Pie

In 2007, Americans worked 79 days to afford their federal taxes and 41 more days to afford state and local taxes, according to the Tax Foundation. Each year this foundation calculates the mathematical average of tax collections in the United States, using a formula that divides the year's total tax collections (federal, state, and local taxes) by all income earned (the "national income"). The resulting national "tax burden" varies each year, and the tax burden also varies by state.

National taxation in 2007 was a bigger burden than average expenditures on housing and household operation (62 days), health and medical care (52 days), food (30 days), transportation (30 days), recreation (22 days), or clothing and accessories (13 days).

*Source: www.taxfoundation.org/taxfreedomday* (accessed June 2007). For a map of tax burden by states, see Figure 5 at that site.

**?** If the information on 2007 taxation depicted your spending patterns, on what date (starting on January 1) will you have earned enough to pay all of your taxes? This date is often referred to as Tax Freedom Day.

## Unearned Revenues

A magazine publisher, such as Sports Illustrated, receives customers' checks when they order magazines. An airline company, such as American Airlines, receives cash when it sells tickets for future flights. Through these transactions, both companies have incurred **unearned revenues**—revenues that are received before the company delivers goods or provides services. How do companies account for unearned revenues?

1. When a company receives the advance payment, it debits Cash, and credits a current liability account identifying the source of the unearned revenue.
2. When the company earns the revenue, it debits the Unearned Revenue account, and credits an earned revenue account.

To illustrate, assume that Superior University sells 10,000 season football tickets at $50 each for its five-game home schedule. The university makes the following entry for the sale of season tickets:

| | | | |
|---|---|---|---|
| Aug. 6 | Cash | 500,000 | |
| | Unearned Football Ticket Revenue | | 500,000 |
| | (To record sale of 10,000 season tickets) | | |

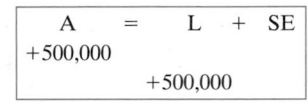

As the school completes each of the five home games, it earns one-fifth of the revenue. The following entry records the revenue earned.

| | | | |
|---|---|---|---|
| Sept. 7 | Unearned Football Ticket Revenue | 100,000 | |
| | Football Ticket Revenue | | 100,000 |
| | (To record football ticket revenue earned) | | |

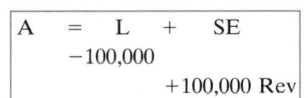

Organizations report any balance in an unearned revenue account (in Unearned Football Ticket Revenue, for example) as a current liability in the balance sheet. As they earn the revenue, a transfer from unearned revenue to earned revenue occurs. Unearned revenue is material for some companies. In the airline industry, for example, tickets sold for future flights represent almost 30% of total current liabilities. At United Air Lines, unearned ticket revenue is the largest current liability, recently amounting to over $1.5 billion.

Illustration 11-4 shows specific unearned and earned revenue accounts used in selected types of businesses.

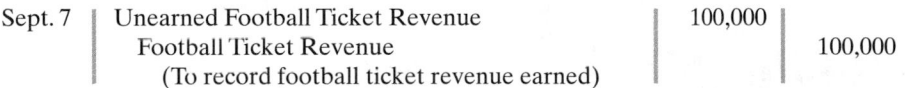

| Type of Business | Account Title | |
|---|---|---|
| | **Unearned Revenue** | **Earned Revenue** |
| Airline | Unearned Passenger Ticket Revenue | Passenger Revenue |
| Magazine publisher | Unearned Subscription Revenue | Subscription Revenue |
| Hotel | Unearned Rental Revenue | Rental Revenue |
| Insurance company | Unearned Premium Revenue | Premium Revenue |

**Illustration 11-4**
Unearned and earned revenue accounts

## Current Maturities of Long-Term Debt

Companies often have a portion of long-term debt that comes due in the current year. That amount is considered a current liability. For example, assume that Wendy Construction issues a five-year interest-bearing $25,000 note on January 1, 2008. Each January 1, starting January 1, 2009, $5,000 of the note is due to be paid. When Wendy Construction prepares financial statements on December 31, 2008, it should report $5,000 as a current liability. It would report the remaining $20,000 on the note as a long-term liability. Current maturities of long-term debt are often termed **long-term debt due within one year**.

It is not necessary to prepare an adjusting entry to recognize the current maturity of long-term debt. The company will recognize the proper statement classification of each balance sheet account when it prepares the balance sheet.

# STATEMENT PRESENTATION AND ANALYSIS

## Presentation

As indicated in Chapter 4, current liabilities are the first category under liabilities on the balance sheet. Each of the principal types of current liabilities is listed separately. In addition, companies disclose the terms of notes payable and other key information about the individual items in the notes to the financial statements.

Companies seldom list current liabilities in the order of liquidity. The reason is that varying maturity dates may exist for specific obligations such as notes payable. A more common method of presenting current liabilities is to list them by **order of magnitude**, with the largest ones first. Or, as a matter of custom, many companies show notes payable first, and then accounts payable, regardless of amount. Then the remaining current liabilities are listed by magnitude. (*Use this approach in your homework.*) The following adapted excerpt from the balance sheet of Caterpillar Inc. illustrates its order of presentation.

**Illustration 11-5**
Balance sheet presentation of current liabilities

**CATERPILLAR®**

### CATERPILLAR INC.
Balance Sheet
(partial)
(in millions)

#### Assets

| | |
|---|---:|
| Current assets | $20,856 |
| Property, plant and equipment (net) | 7,682 |
| Other long-term assets | 14,553 |
| Total assets | $43,091 |

#### Liabilities and Stockholders' Equity

| | |
|---|---:|
| **Current liabilities** | |
| Short-term borrowings (notes payable) | $ 4,157 |
| Accounts payable | 3,990 |
| Accrued expenses | 1,847 |
| Accrued wages, salaries, and employee benefits | 1,730 |
| Customer advances | 555 |
| Dividends payable | 141 |
| Deferred and current income taxes payable | 259 |
| Long-term debt due within one year | 3,531 |
| Total current liabilities | 16,210 |
| Noncurrent liabilities | 19,414 |
| Total liabilities | 35,624 |
| Stockholders' equity | 7,467 |
| Total liabilities and stockholders' equity | $43,091 |

**HELPFUL HINT**

For other examples of current liabilities sections, refer to the PepsiCo and Coca-Cola balance sheets in Appendixes A and B.

# Analysis

Use of current and noncurrent classifications makes it possible to analyze a company's liquidity. **Liquidity** refers to the ability to pay maturing obligations and meet unexpected needs for cash. The relationship of current assets to current liabilities is critical in analyzing liquidity. We can express this relationship as a dollar amount (working capital) and as a ratio (the current ratio).

The excess of current assets over current liabilities is **working capital**. Illustration 11-6 shows the formula for the computation of Caterpillar's working capital (dollar amounts in millions).

| Current Assets | − | Current Liabilities | = | Working Capital |
|:---:|:---:|:---:|:---:|:---:|
| $20,856 | − | $16,210 | = | $4,646 |

**Illustration 11-6**
Working capital formula and computation

As an absolute dollar amount, working capital offers limited informational value. For example, $1 million of working capital may be far more than needed for a small company but be inadequate for a large corporation. Also, $1 million of working capital may be adequate for a company at one time but inadequate at another time.

The **current ratio** permits us to compare the liquidity of different-sized companies and of a single company at different times. The current ratio is calculated as current assets divided by current liabilities. The formula for this ratio is illustrated below, along with its computation using Caterpillar's current asset and current liability data (dollar amounts in millions).

| Current Assets | ÷ | Current Liabilities | = | Current Ratio |
|:---:|:---:|:---:|:---:|:---:|
| $20,856 | ÷ | $16,210 | = | 1.29:1 |

**Illustration 11-7**
Current ratio formula and computation

Historically, companies and analysts considered a current ratio of 2:1 to be the standard for a good credit rating. In recent years, however, many healthy companies have maintained ratios well below 2:1 by improving management of their current assets and liabilities. Caterpillar's ratio of 1.29:1 is adequate but certainly below the standard of 2:1.

## Before You Go On...

### REVIEW IT
1. What are the two criteria for classifying a debt as a current liability?
2. Identify the liabilities classified as current by PepsiCo. The answer to this question appears on page 531.
3. What entries does a company make for an interest-bearing note payable?
4. How do retailers record sales taxes? Identify three unearned revenues.
5. What are the three taxes generally withheld from employees' wages or salaries?
6. How may the liquidity of a company be analyzed?

## DO IT

You and several classmates are studying for the next accounting examination. They ask you to answer the following questions: (1) How is the sales tax amount determined when the cash register total includes sales taxes? (2) What is payroll tax expense related to Social Security taxes if salaries and wages for the week are $10,000?

### Action Plan

■ Remove the sales tax from the total sales.
■ Multiply the FICA tax rate times the salary and wages expense amount.

### Solution

(1) First, divide the total proceeds by 100% plus the sales tax percentage to find the sales amount. Second, subtract the sales amount from the total proceeds to determine the sales taxes.
(2) Social Security taxes (FICA) = $10,000 \times 7.65\% = \$765$.

*Related exercise material: BE11-1, BE11-2, BE11-3, BE11-4, BE11-5, BE11-6, E11-1, E11-2, E11-3, E11-4, E11-5, E11-6, and E11-7.*

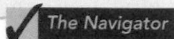

# SECTION 2 **Long-Term Liabilities**

**Long-term liabilities** are obligations that are expected to be paid after one year. In this section we will explain the accounting for the principal types of obligations reported in the long-term liability section of the balance sheet. These obligations often are in the form of bonds or long-term notes.

# BOND BASICS

**STUDY OBJECTIVE 4**
Explain why bonds are issued, and identify the types of bonds.

**Bonds** are a form of interest-bearing notes payable. To obtain **large amounts of long-term capital**, corporate management usually must decide whether to issue common stock (equity financing) or bonds. Bonds offer three advantages over common stock, as shown in Illustration 11-8.

**Illustration 11-8**
Advantages of bond financing over common stock

| **Bond Financing** | **Advantages** |
| --- | --- |
| | 1. **Stockholder control is not affected.**<br>Bondholders do not have voting rights, so current owners (stockholders) retain full control of the company. |
| | 2. **Tax savings result.**<br>Bond interest is deductible for tax purposes; dividends on stock are not. |
| | 3. **Earnings per share may be higher.**<br>Although bond interest expense reduces net income, earnings per share on common stock often is higher under bond financing because no additional shares of common stock are issued. |

As the illustration shows, one reason to issue bonds is that they do not affect stockholder control. Because bondholders do not have voting rights, owners can raise capital with bonds and still maintain corporate control. In addition, bonds are attractive to corporations because the cost of bond interest is tax-deductible. As a result of this tax treatment, which stock dividends do not offer, bonds may result in lower cost of capital than equity financing.

To illustrate the third advantage, on earnings per share, assume that Microsystems, Inc. is considering two plans for financing the construction of a new $5 million plant. Plan A involves issuance of 200,000 shares of common stock at the current market price of $25 per share. Plan B involves issuance of $5 million, 8% bonds at face value. Income before interest and taxes on the new plant will be $1.5 million. Income taxes are expected to be 30%. Microsystems currently has 100,000 shares of common stock outstanding. Illustration 11-9 shows the alternative effects on earnings per share.

|  | Plan A<br>Issue Stock | Plan B<br>Issue Bonds |
|---|---|---|
| Income before interest and taxes | $1,500,000 | $1,500,000 |
| Interest (8% × $5,000,000) | — | 400,000 |
| Income before income taxes | 1,500,000 | 1,100,000 |
| Income tax expense (30%) | 450,000 | 330,000 |
| Net income | $1,050,000 | $ 770,000 |
| Outstanding shares | 300,000 | 100,000 |
| **Earnings per share** | **$3.50** | **$7.70** |

**Illustration 11-9**
Effects on earnings per share—stocks vs. bonds

Note that net income is $280,000 less ($1,050,000 − $770,000) with long-term debt financing (bonds). However, earnings per share is higher because there are 200,000 fewer shares of common stock outstanding.

One disadvantage in using bonds is that the company must **pay interest** on a periodic basis. In addition, the company must also **repay the principal** at the due date. A company with fluctuating earnings and a relatively weak cash position may have great difficulty making interest payments when earnings are low.

A corporation may also obtain long-term financing from notes payable and leasing. However, notes payable and leasing are seldom sufficient to furnish the amount of funds needed for plant expansion and major projects like new buildings.

Bonds are sold in relatively small denominations (usually $1,000 multiples). As a result of their size, and the variety of their features, bonds attract many investors.

## Types of Bonds

Bonds may have many different features. In the following sections, we describe the types of bonds commonly issued.

### SECURED AND UNSECURED BONDS

Secured bonds have specific assets of the issuer pledged as collateral for the bonds. A bond secured by real estate, for example, is called a mortgage bond. A bond secured by specific assets set aside to retire the bonds is called a sinking fund bond.

**HELPFUL HINT**

Besides corporations, governmental agencies and universities also issue bonds to raise capital.

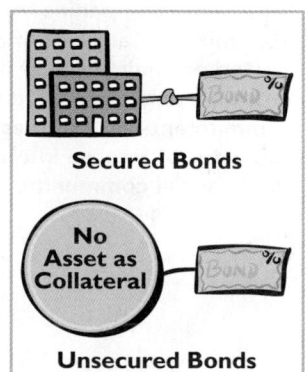

**Secured Bonds**

**Unsecured Bonds**

**Unsecured bonds**, also called **debenture bonds**, are issued against the general credit of the borrower. Companies with good credit ratings use these bonds extensively. For example, in a recent annual report, DuPont reported over $2 billion of debenture bonds outstanding.

### TERM AND SERIAL BONDS

Bonds that mature—are due for payment—at a single specified future date are **term bonds**. In contrast, bonds that mature in installments are **serial bonds**.

### REGISTERED AND BEARER BONDS

Bonds issued in the name of the owner are **registered bonds**. Interest payments on registered bonds are made by check to bondholders of record. Bonds not registered are **bearer** (or **coupon**) **bonds**. Holders of bearer bonds must send in coupons to receive interest payments. Most bonds issued today are registered bonds.

### CONVERTIBLE AND CALLABLE BONDS

Bonds that can be converted into common stock at the bondholder's option are **convertible bonds**. The conversion feature generally is attractive to bond buyers. Bonds that the issuing company can retire at a stated dollar amount prior to maturity are **callable bonds**. A call feature is included in nearly all corporate bond issues.

Convertible Bonds

"Hey Harv, Call in those bonds"

Callable Bonds

## Issuing Procedures

State laws grant corporations the power to issue bonds. Both the board of directors and stockholders usually must approve bond issues. **In authorizing the bond issue, the board of directors must stipulate the number of bonds to be authorized, total face value, and contractual interest rate.** The total bond authorization often exceeds the number of bonds the company originally issues. This gives the corporation the flexibility to issue more bonds, if needed, to meet future cash requirements.

The **face value** is the amount of principal the issuing company must pay at the maturity date. The **contractual interest rate**, often referred to as the **stated rate**, is the rate used to determine the amount of cash interest the borrower pays and the investor receives. Usually the contractual rate is stated as an annual rate. Interest is generally paid semiannually.

The terms of the bond issue are set forth in a legal document called a **bond indenture**. The indenture shows the terms and summarizes the rights of the bondholders and their trustees, and the obligations of the issuing company. The **trustee** (usually a financial institution) keeps records of each bondholder, maintains custody of unissued bonds, and holds conditional title to pledged property.

In addition, the issuing company arranges for the printing of **bond certificates**. The indenture and the certificate are separate documents. As shown in Illustration 11-10 (page 485), a bond certificate provides the following information: name of the issuer, face value, contractual interest rate, and maturity date. An investment company that specializes in selling securities generally sells the bonds for the issuing company.

## Bond Trading

Bondholders have the opportunity to convert their holdings into cash at any time by selling the bonds at the current market price on national securities exchanges. **Bond prices are quoted as a percentage of the face value of the bond, which is usually $1,000.** A $1,000 bond with a quoted price of 97 means that the selling price of

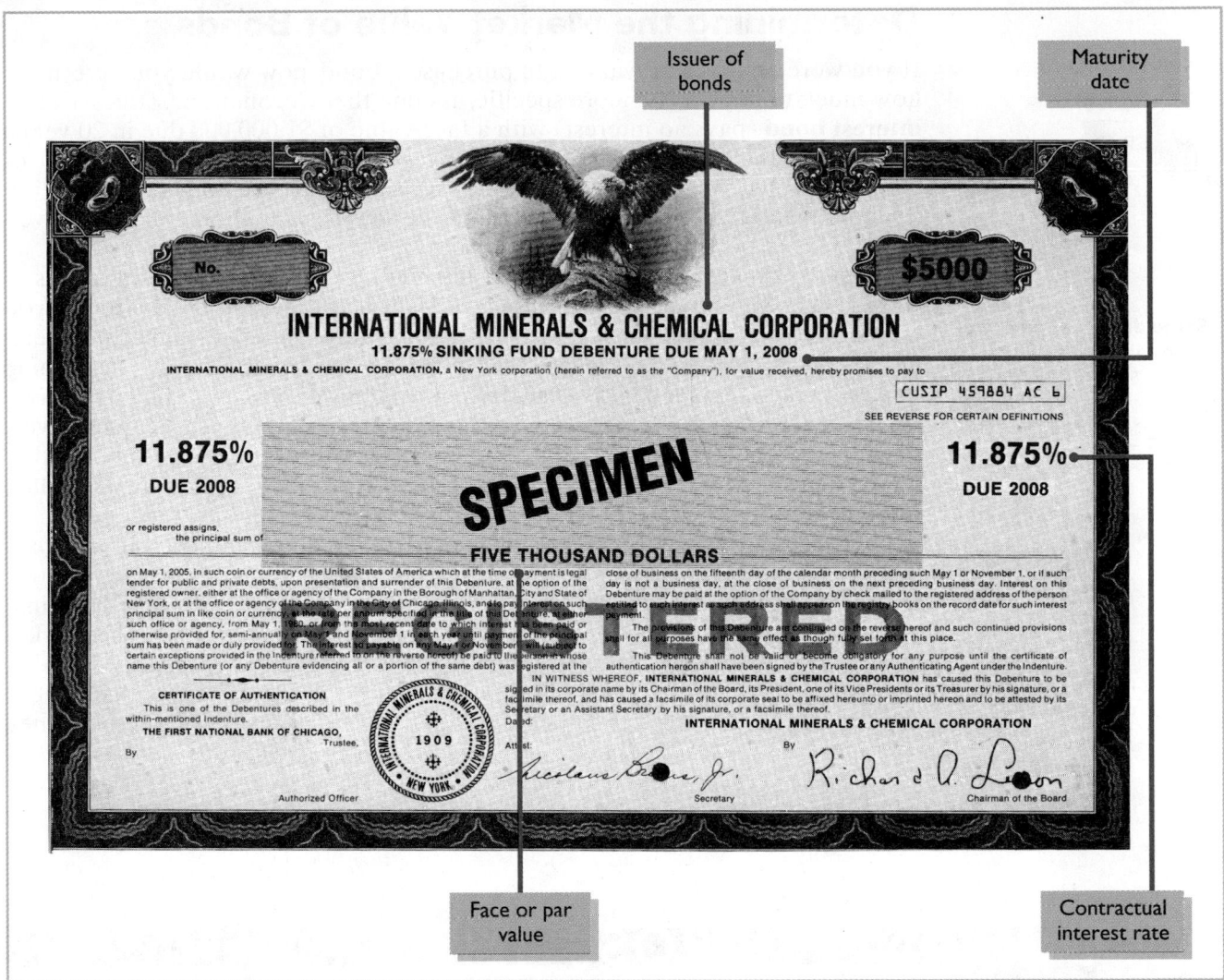

**Illustration 11-10**
Bond certificate

the bond is 97% of face value, or $970. Newspapers and the financial press publish bond prices and trading activity daily as illustrated by the following.

| Bonds | Maturity | Close | Yield | Est. Volume (000) |
|---|---|---|---|---|
| Boeing Co. 5.125 | Feb. 15, 2011 | 96.595 | 5.747 | 33,965 |

**Illustration 11-11**
Market information for bonds

This bond listing indicates that Boeing Co. has outstanding 5.125%, $1,000 bonds that mature in 2011. They currently yield a 5.747% return. On this day, $33,965,000 of these bonds were traded. At the close of trading, the price was 96.595% of face value, or $965.95.

A corporation makes journal entries **only when it issues or buys back bonds**, or when bondholders convert bonds into common stock. For example, DuPont **does not journalize** transactions between its bondholders and other investors. If Tom Smith sells his DuPont bonds to Faith Jones, DuPont does not journalize the transaction. (DuPont or its trustee does, however, keep records of the names of bondholders in the case of registered bonds.)

**HELPFUL HINT**

(1) What is the price of a $1,000 bond trading at 95¼?

(2) What is the price of a $1,000 bond trading at 101⅞?

Answers: (1) $952.50.
(2) $1,018.75.

# Determining the Market Value of Bonds

**Same dollars at different times are not equal.**

If you were an investor wanting to purchase a bond, how would you determine how much to pay? To be more specific, assume that Coronet, Inc. issues a **zero-interest bond** (pays no interest) with a face value of $1,000,000 due in 20 years. For this bond, the only cash you receive is a million dollars at the end of 20 years. Would you pay a million dollars for this bond? We hope not! A million dollars received 20 years from now is not the same as a million dollars received today.

The reason you should not pay a million dollars for Coronet's bond relates to what is called the **time value of money**. If you had a million dollars today, you would invest it. From that investment, you would earn interest such that at the end of 20 years, you would have much more than a million dollars. If someone is going to pay you a million dollars 20 years from now, you would want to find its equivalent today. In other words, you would want to determine how much you must invest today at current interest rates to have a million dollars in 20 years. The amount that must be invested today at a given rate of interest over a specified time is called **present value**.

The present value of a bond is the value at which it should sell in the marketplace. Market value therefore is a function of the three factors that determine present value: (1) the dollar amounts to be received, (2) the length of time until the amounts are received, and (3) the market rate of interest. The **market interest rate** is the rate investors demand for loaning funds. Appendix 11A discusses the process of finding the present value for bonds. Appendix C near the end of the book also provides additional material for time value of money computations.

# ACCOUNTING ACROSS THE ORGANIZATION

### When to Go Long-Term

A decision that all companies must make is to what extent to rely on short-term versus long-term financing. The critical nature of this decision was highlighted in the fall of 2001, after the World Trade Center disaster. Prior to September 11, short-term interest rates had been extremely low relative to long-term rates. In order to minimize interest costs, many companies were relying very heavily on short-term financing to purchase things they normally would have used long-term debt for. The problem with short-term financing is that it requires companies to continually find new financing as each loan comes due. This makes them vulnerable to sudden changes in the economy.

After September 11, lenders and short-term investors became very reluctant to loan money. This put the squeeze on many companies: as short-term loans came due, they were unable to refinance. Some were able to get other financing, but at extremely high rates (for example, 12% as compared to 3%). Others were unable to get loans and instead had to sell assets to generate cash for their immediate needs.

*Source:* Henny Sender, "Firms Feel Consequences of Short-Term Borrowing," *Wall Street Journal Online* (October 12, 2001).

 Based on this story, what is a good general rule to use in choosing between short-term and long-term financing?

# ACCOUNTING FOR BOND ISSUES

Bonds may be issued at face value, below face value (at a discount), or above face value (at a premium).

> **STUDY OBJECTIVE 5**
>
> Prepare the entries for the issuance of bonds and interest expense.

## Issuing Bonds at Face Value

To illustrate the accounting for bonds, assume that on January 1, 2008, Candlestick Corporation issues $100,000, five-year, 10% bonds at 100 (100% of face value). The entry to record the sale is:

| Jan. 1 | Cash | 100,000 | |
| | Bonds Payable | | 100,000 |
| | (To record sale of bonds at face value) | | |

| A | = | L | + | SE |
|---|---|---|---|---|
| +100,000 | | | | +100,000 |

**Cash Flows**
+100,000

Candlestick reports bonds payable in the long-term liabilities section of the balance sheet because the maturity date is more than one year away.

Over the term (life) of the bonds, companies make entries to record bond interest. Interest on bonds payable is computed in the same manner as interest on notes payable, as explained on page 475. Assume that interest is payable semiannually on January 1 and July 1 on the bonds described above. In that case, Candlestick must pay interest of $5,000 ($100,000 × 10% × 6/12) on July 1, 2008. The entry for the payment, assuming no previous accrual of interest, is:

| July 1 | Bond Interest Expense | 5,000 | |
| | Cash | | 5,000 |
| | (To record payment of bond interest) | | |

| A | = | L | + | SE |
|---|---|---|---|---|
| | | | | −5,000 Exp |
| −5,000 | | | | |

**Cash Flows**
−5,000

At December 31, Candlestick recognizes the $5,000 of interest expense incurred since July 1 with the following adjusting entry:

| Dec. 31 | Bond Interest Expense | 5,000 | |
| | Bond Interest Payable | | 5,000 |
| | (To accrue bond interest) | | |

| A | = | L | + | SE |
|---|---|---|---|---|
| | | | | −5,000 Exp |
| | | +5,000 | | |

**Cash Flows**
no effect

**Companies classify bond interest payable as a current liability**, because it is scheduled for payment within the next year. When Candlestick pays the interest on January 1, 2009, it debits (decreases) Bond Interest Payable and credits (decreases) Cash for $5,000.

## Discount or Premium on Bonds

In the Candlestick illustrations above, we assumed that the contractual (stated) interest rate paid on the bonds and the market (effective) interest rate were the same.

Recall that the **contractual interest rate** is the rate applied to the face (par) value to arrive at the interest paid in a year. The **market interest rate** is the rate investors demand for loaning funds to the corporation. When the contractual interest rate and the market interest rate are the same, bonds sell **at face value.**

However, market interest rates change daily. The type of bond issued, the state of the economy, current industry conditions, and the company's performance all affect market interest rates. Contractual and market interest rates often differ. As a result, bonds often sell below or above face value.

To illustrate, suppose that a company issues 10% bonds at a time when other bonds of similar risk are paying 12%. Investors will not be interested in buying the 10% bonds, so their value will fall below their face value. In this case, we say the 10% bonds are **selling at a discount.** As a result of the decline in the bonds' selling price, the actual interest rate incurred by the company increases to the level of the current market interest rate.

Conversely, if the market rate of interest is **lower than** the contractual interest rate, investors will have to pay more than face value for the bonds. That is, if the market rate of interest is 8% but the contractual interest rate on the bonds is 10%, the issuer will require more funds from the investor. In these cases, **bonds sell at a premium.** Illustration 11-12 shows these relationships graphically.

**Illustration 11-12**
Interest rates and bond prices

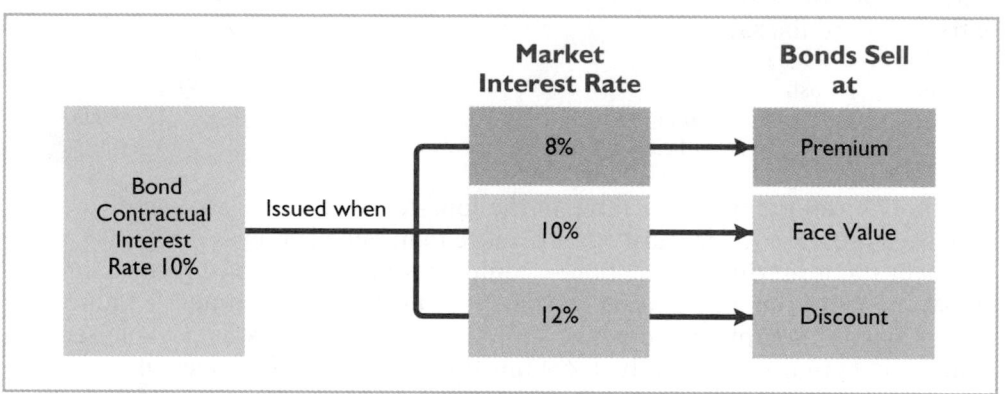

Issuing bonds at an amount different from face value is quite common. By the time a company prints the bond certificates and markets the bonds, it will be a coincidence if the market rate and the contractual rate are the same. Thus, the sale of bonds at a discount does not mean that the issuer's financial strength is suspect. Nor does the sale of bonds at a premium indicate exceptional financial strength.

## Issuing Bonds at a Discount

To illustrate issuance of bonds at a discount, assume that on January 1, 2008, Candlestick, Inc. sells $100,000, five-year, 10% bonds for $92,639 (92.639% of face value). Interest is payable on July 1 and January 1. The entry to record the issuance is:

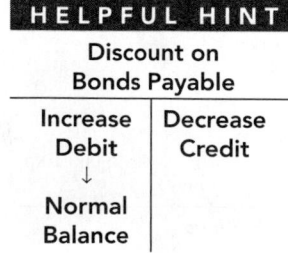
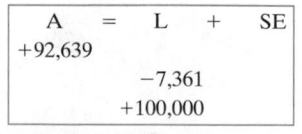

**HELPFUL HINT**

Discount on
Bonds Payable

| Increase<br>Debit<br>↓ | Decrease<br>Credit |
|---|---|
| Normal<br>Balance | |

| A | = | L | + | SE |
|---|---|---|---|---|
| +92,639 | | | | |
| | | −7,361 | | |
| | | +100,000 | | |

Cash Flows
+92,639

| Jan. 1 | Cash | 92,639 | |
|---|---|---|---|
| | Discount on Bonds Payable | 7,361 | |
| |   Bonds Payable | | 100,000 |
| |    (To record sale of bonds at a discount) | | |

Although Discount on Bonds Payable has a debit balance, **it is not an asset.** Rather, it is a **contra account.** This account is **deducted from bonds payable** on the balance sheet, as shown in Illustration 11-13.

Illustration 11-13
Statement presentation of
discount on bonds payable

| CANDLESTICK, INC. | | |
|---|---|---|
| Balance Sheet (partial) | | |
| Long-term liabilities | | |
| Bonds payable | $100,000 | |
| **Less: Discount on bonds payable** | 7,361 | $92,639 |

The $92,639 represents the **carrying (or book) value** of the bonds. On the date of issue this amount equals the market price of the bonds.

The issuance of bonds below face value—at a discount—causes the total cost of borrowing to differ from the bond interest paid. That is, the issuing corporation must pay not only the contractual interest rate over the term of the bonds, but also the face value (rather than the issuance price) at maturity. Therefore, the difference between the issuance price and face value of the bonds—the discount—is an **additional cost of borrowing**. The company records this additional cost as **bond interest expense** over the life of the bonds. Appendices 11B and 11C show the procedures for recording this additional cost.

The total cost of borrowing $92,639 for Candlestick, Inc. is $57,361, computed as follows.

**HELPFUL HINT**

Carrying value (book value) of bonds issued at a discount is determined by subtracting the balance of the discount account from the balance of the Bonds Payable account.

Illustration 11-14
Total cost of borrowing—
bonds issued at a discount

| Bonds Issued at a Discount | |
|---|---|
| Semiannual interest payments | |
| ($100,000 × 10% × ½ = $5,000; $5,000 × 10) | $50,000 |
| Add: Bond discount ($100,000 − $92,639) | 7,361 |
| **Total cost of borrowing** ⊂ Interest Payments + Discount | **$57,361** |

Alternatively, we can compute the total cost of borrowing as follows.

Illustration 11-15
Alternative computation of
total cost of borrowing—
bonds issued at a discount

| Bonds Issued at a Discount | |
|---|---|
| Principal at maturity | $100,000 |
| Semiannual interest payments ($5,000 × 10) | 50,000 |
| Cash to be paid to bondholders | 150,000 |
| Cash received from bondholders | 92,639 |
| **Total cost of borrowing** | **$ 57,361** |

## Issuing Bonds at a Premium

To illustrate the issuance of bonds at a premium, we now assume the Candlestick, Inc. bonds described above sell for $108,111 (108.111% of face value) rather than for $92,639. The entry to record the sale is:

| Jan. 1 | Cash | 108,111 | |
|---|---|---|---|
| | Bonds Payable | | 100,000 |
| | Premium on Bonds Payable | | 8,111 |
| | (To record sale of bonds at a premium) | | |

| A | = | L | + | SE |
|---|---|---|---|---|
| +108,111 | | | | |
| | | +100,000 | | |
| | | +8,111 | | |

**Cash Flows**
+108,111

Candlestick adds the premium on bonds payable **to the bonds payable amount** on the balance sheet, as shown in Illustration 11-16 on the next page.

**Illustration 11-16**
Statement presentation of bond premium

| CANDLESTICK, INC. | | |
| :-- | --: | --: |
| Balance Sheet (partial) | | |
| Long-term liabilities | | |
| Bonds payable | $100,000 | |
| **Add: Premium on bonds payable** | **8,111** | $108,111 |

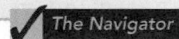

**HELPFUL HINT**

**Premium on Bonds Payable**

| Decrease | Increase |
| :-- | :-- |
| Debit | Credit |
| | ↓ |
| | Normal |
| | Balance |

The sale of bonds above face value causes the total cost of borrowing to be **less than the bond interest paid.** The bond premium is considered to be **a reduction in the cost of borrowing.** The company credits the bond premium to Bond Interest Expense over the life of the bonds. Appendices 11B and 11C show the procedures for recording this reduction in the cost of borrowing. The total cost of borrowing $108,111 for Candlestick, Inc. is computed as follows.

**Illustration 11-17**
Total cost of borrowing—bonds issued at a premium

| Bonds Issued at a Premium | |
| :-- | --: |
| Semiannual interest payments | |
| ($100,000 × 10% × ½ = $5,000; $5,000 × 10) | $50,000 |
| Less: Bond premium ($108,111 − $100,000) | 8,111 |
| **Total cost of borrowing** = Interest Payment - Bond premium | **$41,889** |

Alternatively, we can compute the cost of borrowing as follows.

**Illustration 11-18**
Alternative computation of total cost of borrowing—bonds issued at a premium

| Bonds Issued at a Premium | |
| :-- | --: |
| Principal at maturity | $100,000 |
| Semiannual interest payments ($5,000 × 10) | 50,000 |
| Cash to be paid to bondholders | 150,000 |
| Cash received from bondholders | 108,111 |
| **Total cost of borrowing** | **$ 41,889** |

## Before You Go On...

**REVIEW IT**

1. What entry would a company make to record the issuance of bonds payable of $1 million at 100? At 96? At 102?
2. Why do bonds sell at a discount? At a premium? At face value?

Related exercise material: *BE11-7, BE11-8, BE11-9, BE11-10, E11-8, E11-9, E11-10, E11-11, and E11-12.*

✓ *The Navigator*

# ACCOUNTING FOR BOND RETIREMENTS

**STUDY OBJECTIVE 6**

Describe the entries when bonds are redeemed or converted.

An issuing corporation retires bonds either when it redeems the bonds or when bondholders convert them into common stock. We explain the entries for these transactions in the following sections.

## Redeeming Bonds at Maturity

Regardless of the issue price of bonds, the book value of the bonds at maturity will equal their face value. Assuming that the company pays and records separately the interest for the last interest period, Candlestick records the redemption of its bonds at maturity as follows:

| | | |
|---|---|---|
| Bonds Payable | 100,000 | |
|    Cash | | 100,000 |
|       (To record redemption of bonds at maturity) | | |

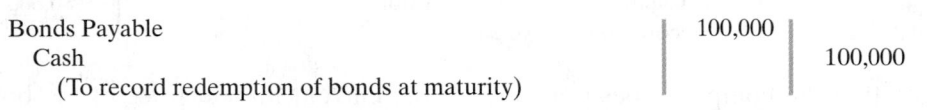

A = L + SE
−100,000
−100,000

**Cash Flows**
−100,000

## Redeeming Bonds before Maturity

Bonds also may be redeemed before maturity. A company may decide to retire bonds before maturity to reduce interest cost and to remove debt from its balance sheet. A company should retire debt early only if it has sufficient cash resources.

When a company retires bonds before maturity, it is necessary to: (1) eliminate the carrying value of the bonds at the redemption date; (2) record the cash paid; and (3) recognize the gain or loss on redemption. The carrying value of the bonds is the face value of the bonds less unamortized bond discount or plus unamortized bond premium at the redemption date.

To illustrate, assume that Candlestick, Inc. has sold its bonds at a premium. At the end of the eighth period, Candlestick retires these bonds at 103 after paying the semiannual interest. Assume also that the carrying value of the bonds at the redemption date is $101,623. Candlestick makes the following entry to record the redemption at the end of the eighth interest period (January 1, 2012):

| | | | |
|---|---|---|---|
| Jan. 1 | Bonds Payable | 100,000 | |
| | Premium on Bonds Payable | 1,623 | |
| | Loss on Bond Redemption | 1,377 | |
| |    Cash | | 103,000 |
| |       (To record redemption of bonds at 103) | | |

A = L + SE
−100,000
−1,623
−1,377 Exp
−103,000

**Cash Flows**
−103,000

Note that the loss of $1,377 is the difference between the cash paid of $103,000 and the carrying value of the bonds of $101,623.

**HELPFUL HINT**

Question: A bond is redeemed prior to its maturity date. Its carrying value exceeds its redemption price. Will the retirement result in a gain or a loss on redemption? Answer: Gain.

## Converting Bonds into Common Stock

**Convertible bonds** have features that are attractive both to bondholders and to the issuer. The conversion often gives bondholders an opportunity to benefit if the market price of the common stock increases substantially. Until conversion, though, the bondholder receives interest on the bond. For the issuer of convertible bonds, the bonds sell at a higher price and pay a lower rate of interest than comparable debt securities without the conversion option. Many corporations, such as USAir, USX Corp., and DaimlerChrysler Corporation, have convertible bonds outstanding.

When the issuing company records a conversion, the company ignores the current market prices of the bonds and stock. Instead, the company transfers the **carrying value** of the bonds to paid-in capital accounts. **No gain or loss is recognized.**

To illustrate, assume that on July 1 Saunders Associates converts $100,000 bonds sold at face value into 2,000 shares of $10 par value common stock. Both the bonds and the common stock have a market value of $130,000. Saunders makes the following entry to record the conversion:

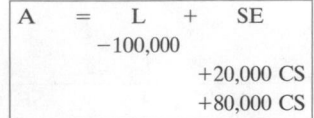

| A | = | L | + | SE |
|---|---|---|---|---|
| −100,000 | | | | |
| | | | | +20,000 CS |
| | | | | +80,000 CS |

**Cash Flows**
no effect

| July 1 | Bonds Payable | 100,000 | |
|---|---|---|---|
| | Common Stock | | 20,000 |
| | Paid-in Capital in Excess of Par Value | | 80,000 |
| | (To record bond conversion) | | |

Note that the company does not consider the current market price of the bonds and stock ($130,000) in making the entry. This method of recording the bond conversion is often referred to as the **carrying (or book) value method.**

## Before You Go On...

### REVIEW IT

1. Explain the accounting for redemption of bonds at maturity, before maturity by payment in cash, and by conversion into common stock.

2. Did PepsiCo redeem any of its debt during the fiscal year ended December 31, 2005? (*Hint:* Examine PepsiCo's statement of cash flows. The answer to this question appears on page 531.)

### DO IT

R & B Inc. issued $500,000, 10-year bonds at a premium. Prior to maturity, when the carrying value of the bonds is $508,000, the company retires the bonds at 102. Prepare the entry to record the redemption of the bonds.

### Action Plan

■ Determine and eliminate the carrying value of the bonds.

■ Record the cash paid.

■ Compute and record the gain (loss) (the difference between the first two items).

**Solution**   There is a loss on redemption: The cash paid, $510,000 ($500,000 × 102%), is greater than the carrying value of $508,000. The entry is:

| Bonds Payable | 500,000 | |
|---|---|---|
| Premium on Bonds Payable | 8,000 | |
| Loss on Bond Redemption | 2,000 | |
| Cash | | 510,000 |
| (To record redemption of bonds at 102) | | |

Related exercise material: *BE11-11, E11-13, and E11-14.*

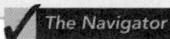
The Navigator

# ACCOUNTING FOR LONG-TERM NOTES PAYABLE

**STUDY OBJECTIVE 7**

Describe the accounting for long-term notes payable.

The use of notes payable in long-term debt financing is quite common. **Long-term notes payable** are similar to short-term interest-bearing notes payable except that the term of the notes exceeds one year.

A long-term note may be secured by a **mortgage** that pledges title to specific assets as security for a loan. Individuals widely use mortgage notes payable to purchase homes, and many small and some large companies use them to acquire plant assets. At one time, approximately 18% of McDonald's long-term debt related to mortgage notes on land, buildings, and improvements.

Mortgage loan terms may stipulate either a **fixed** or an **adjustable** interest rate. The interest rate on a fixed-rate mortgage remains the same over the life of the mortgage. The interest rate on an adjustable-rate mortgage is adjusted periodically to reflect changes in the market rate of interest. Typically, the terms require the borrower to make installment payments over the term of the loan. Each payment consists of (1) interest on the unpaid balance of the loan and (2) a reduction of loan principal. The interest decreases each period, while the portion applied to the loan principal increases.

Companies initially record mortgage notes payable at face value. They subsequently make entries for each installment payment. To illustrate, assume that Porter Technology Inc. issues a $500,000, 12%, 20-year mortgage note on December 31, 2008, to obtain needed financing for a new research laboratory. The terms provide for semiannual installment payments of $33,231 (not including real estate taxes and insurance). The installment payment schedule for the first two years is as follows.

| Semiannual Interest Period | (A) Cash Payment | (B) Interest Expense (D) × 6% | (C) Reduction of Principal (A) − (B) | (D) Principal Balance (D) − (C) |
|---|---|---|---|---|
| 12/31/08 | | | | $500,000 |
| 06/30/09 | $33,231 | $30,000 | $3,231 | 496,769 |
| 12/31/09 | 33,231 | 29,806 | 3,425 | 493,344 |
| 06/30/10 | 33,231 | 29,601 | 3,630 | 489,714 |
| 12/31/10 | 33,231 | 29,383 | 3,848 | 485,866 |

**Illustration 11-19**
Mortgage installment payment schedule

Porter records the mortgage loan and first installment payment as follows.

| Dec. 31 | Cash | 500,000 | |
| | Mortgage Notes Payable | | 500,000 |
| | (To record mortgage loan) | | |

| A | = | L | + | SE |
|---|---|---|---|---|
| +500,000 | | | | |
| | | | | +500,000 |

**Cash Flows**
+500,000

| June 30 | Interest Expense | 30,000 | |
| | Mortgage Notes Payable | 3,231 | |
| | Cash | | 33,231 |
| | (To record semiannual payment on mortgage) | | |

| A | = | L | + | SE |
|---|---|---|---|---|
| | | | | −30,000 Exp |
| | | −3,231 | | |
| −33,231 | | | | |

**Cash Flows**
−33,231

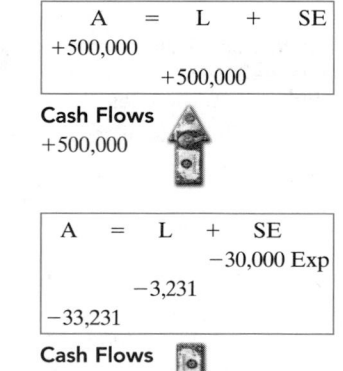

**In the balance sheet, the company reports the reduction in principal for the next year as a current liability, and it classifies the remaining unpaid principal balance as a long-term liability.** At December 31, 2009, the total liability is $493,344. Of that amount, $7,478 ($3,630 + $3,848) is current, and $485,866 ($493,344 − $7,478) is long-term.

# ACCOUNTING ACROSS THE ORGANIZATION

### Search for Your Best Rate

Companies spend a great deal of time shopping for the best loan terms. You should do the same. Suppose that you have a used car that you are planning to trade in on the purchase of a new car. Experts suggest that you view this deal as three separate transactions: (1) the purchase of a new car, (2) the trade in or sale of an old car, and (3) shopping for an interest rate.

Studies suggest that too many people neglect transaction number 3. One survey found that 63% of people planned on shopping for the best car-loan interest rate online the next time they bought a car. But a separate study found that only 15% of people who bought a car actually shopped around for the best online rate. Too many people simply take the interest rate offered at the car dealership. Many lenders will pre-approve you for a loan up to a specific dollar amount, and many will then give you a blank check (negotiable for up to that amount) that you can take to the car dealer.

*Source:* Ron Lieber, "How to Haggle the Best Car Loan," *Wall Street Journal*, March 25, 2006, p. B1.

**?** What should you do if the dealer "trash-talks" your lender, or refuses to sell you the car for the agreed-upon price unless you get your car loan through the dealer?

# STATEMENT PRESENTATION AND ANALYSIS

## Presentation

**STUDY OBJECTIVE 8**

Identify the methods for the presentation and analysis of long-term liabilities.

Companies report long-term liabilities in a separate section of the balance sheet immediately following current liabilities, as shown in Illustration 11-20. Alternatively, companies may present summary data in the balance sheet, with detailed data (interest rates, maturity dates, conversion privileges, and assets pledged as collateral) shown in a supporting schedule. Companies report the current maturities of long-term debt under current liabilities if they are to be paid from current assets.

**Illustration 11-20**
Balance sheet presentation of long-term liabilities

| LAX CORPORATION | | |
|---|---|---|
| Balance Sheet (partial) | | |
| Long-term liabilities | | |
| Bonds payable 10% due in 2015 | $1,000,000 | |
| Less: Discount on bonds payable | 80,000 | $ 920,000 |
| Mortgage notes payable, 11%, due in 2021 and secured by plant assets | | 500,000 |
| Lease liability | | 440,000 |
| Total long-term liabilities | | $1,860,000 |

## Analysis

Long-term creditors and stockholders are interested in a company's long-run solvency. Of particular interest is the company's ability to pay interest as it comes due and to repay the face value of the debt at maturity. Debt to total assets and times interest earned are two ratios that provide information about debt-paying ability and long-run solvency.

The **debt to total assets ratio** measures the percentage of the total assets provided by creditors. As shown in the formula in Illustration 11-21, it is computed by dividing total debt (both current and long-term liabilities) by total assets. The higher the percentage of debt to total assets, the greater the risk that the company may be unable to meet its maturing obligations.

The **times interest earned ratio** indicates the company's ability to meet interest payments as they come due. It is computed by dividing income before income taxes and interest expense by interest expense.

To illustrate these ratios, we will use data from Kellogg Company's 2005 annual report. The company had total liabilities of $8,290.8 million, total assets of $10,574.5 million, interest expense of $300.3 million, income taxes of $444.7 million, and net income of $980.4 million. Kellogg's debt to total assets ratio and times interest earned ratio are shown below.

| **Total Debt** | ÷ | **Total Assets** | = | **Debt to Total Assets** |
|---|---|---|---|---|
| $8,290.8 | ÷ | $10,574.5 | = | 78.4% |
| **Income before Income Taxes and Interest Expense** | ÷ | **Interest Expense** | = | **Times Interest Earned** |
| $980.4 + $444.7 + $300.3 | ÷ | $300.3 | = | 5.75 times |

**Illustration 11-21**
Debt to total assets and times interest earned ratios, with computations

Kellogg has a relatively high debt to total assets percentage of 78.4%. Its interest coverage of 5.75 times is considered safe.

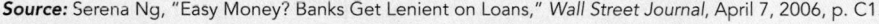

# INVESTOR INSIGHT

### They Thought It Was Easy Money

Lending markets change over time. Sometimes it is easy to borrow money, while at other times the credit market dries up. During the spring of 2006 many observers noted that money was flowing very freely. This was a concern to some analysts, who noted that many lenders had cut back on the number and restrictiveness of loan covenants that they required of borrowers. *Covenants* are performance hurdles that companies agree to in order to obtain a loan. For example, many loan covenants specify required values for debt to total assets or times interest earned measures that must be maintained while the debt is outstanding. In the words of one observer, "Credit quality is still strong, but this trend of shrinking covenants is laying the groundwork for the next round of credit problems."

*Source:* Serena Ng, "Easy Money? Banks Get Lenient on Loans," *Wall Street Journal*, April 7, 2006, p. C1.

**?** What do you think happens when a company violates its debt covenants?

## Before You Go On...

### REVIEW IT
1. Explain the accounting for long-term mortgage notes payable.
2. Where in the financial statements do companies report current maturities of long-term debt?
3. What ratios may be computed to analyze a company's long-run solvency?

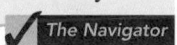

 Be sure to read **ALL ABOUT YOU:** *Your Boss Wants to Know If You Ran Today* on page 496 for information on how topics in this chapter apply to you.

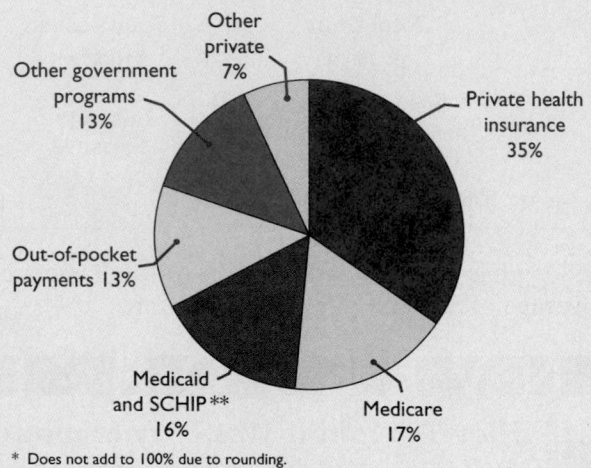

# Your Boss Wants to Know If You Ran Today

A you saw in this chapter, compensation packages often include fringe benefits in addition to basic salary. Health insurance is one benefit that many employers offer. In recent years, as the cost of health insurance has sky-rocketed, many employers either have shifted some of the cost of health insurance onto employees, or have discontinued health insurance coverage altogether.

## ✱ Some Facts

* Health-care spending in the U.S. was $1.9 trillion in 2004, and is projected to be $2.9 trillion by 2009. It is four times the amount spent on national defense and represents 16% of U.S. gross domestic product.

* About 45 million Americans are without any form of health insurance. Many of these people are employed, but their jobs don't provide a health-care benefit.

* For employers, the average cost of health-care benefits per employee is about $6,700 per year.

* The rate of increase of employer health-care costs has slowed somewhat as employers raised the employee share of premiums and raised deductibles (the amount of a bill that the employee pays before insurance coverage begins).

* More than 30% of small employers have a deductible of $1,000 for employee health insurance.

## ✱ About the Numbers

As the graph below shows, private health insurance, such as that provided by employers, pays for less than half of health-care costs in the U.S. If employers continue to cut their health-care benefits, more of the burden will shift to the government or to individuals as out-of-pocket costs.

**The Nation's Health-Care Dollar: Where it Comes From\***

- Other private 7%
- Other government programs 13%
- Private health insurance 35%
- Out-of-pocket payments 13%
- Medicaid and SCHIP\*\* 16%
- Medicare 17%

\* Does not add to 100% due to rounding.
\*\* State Children's Health Insurance Program.

**Source:** Data for 2004, from Centers for Medicare and Medicaid Services, Office of the Actuary, National Health Statistics Group.

## ✱ What Do You Think?

Suppose you own a business. About a quarter of your employees smoke, and an even higher percentage are overweight. You decide to implement a mandatory health program that requires employees to quit smoking and to exercise regularly, with regular monitoring. If employees do not participate in the program, they will have to pay their own insurance premiums. Is this fair?

**YES:** It is the responsibility of management to try to maximize a company's profit. Employees with unhealthy habits drive up the cost of health insurance because they require more frequent and more costly medical attention.

**NO:** What people do on their own time is their own business. This represents an invasion of privacy, and is a form of discrimination.

**Source:** Dee Gill, "Get Healthy . . . Or Else," *Inc.* Magazine, April 2006; "Health Insurance Cost," The National Coalition on Health Care, *www.nchc.org/facts/cost.shtml* (accessed May 2006).

The authors' comments on this situation appear on page 531.

Snyder Software Inc. has successfully developed a new spreadsheet program. To produce and market the program, the company needed $2 million of additional financing. On January 1, 2009, Snyder borrowed money as follows.

1. Snyder issued $500,000, 11%, 10-year convertible bonds. The bonds sold at face value and pay semiannual interest on January 1 and July 1. Each $1,000 bond is convertible into 30 shares of Snyder's $20 par value common stock.
2. Snyder issued $1 million, 10%, 10-year bonds at face value. Interest is payable semiannually on January 1 and July 1.
3. Snyder also issued a $500,000, 12%, 15-year mortgage note payable. The terms provide for semiannual installment payments of $36,324 on June 30 and December 31.

## Instructions

1. For the convertible bonds, prepare journal entries for:

   (a) The issuance of the bonds on January 1, 2009.
   (b) Interest expense on July 1 and December 31, 2009.
   (c) The payment of interest on January 1, 2010.
   (d) The conversion of all bonds into common stock on January 1, 2010, when the market value of the common stock was $67 per share.

2. For the 10-year, 10% bonds:

   (a) Journalize the issuance of the bonds on January 1, 2009.
   (b) Prepare the journal entries for interest expense in 2009. Assume no accrual of interest on July 1.
   (c) Prepare the entry for the redemption of the bonds at 101 on January 1, 2012, after paying the interest due on this date.

3. For the mortgage note payable:

   (a) Prepare the entry for the issuance of the note on January 1, 2009.
   (b) Prepare a payment schedule for the first four installment payments.
   (c) Indicate the current and noncurrent amounts for the mortgage note payable at December 31, 2009.

## Solution

**1. (a) 2009**

| | | | |
|---|---|---|---|
| Jan. 1 | Cash | 500,000 | |
| | Bonds Payable | | 500,000 |
| | (To record issue of 11%, 10-year convertible bonds at face value) | | |

**(b) 2009**

| | | | |
|---|---|---|---|
| July 1 | Bond Interest Expense | 27,500 | |
| | Cash ($500,000 × 0.055) | | 27,500 |
| | (To record payment of semiannual interest) | | |
| Dec. 31 | Bond Interest Expense | 27,500 | |
| | Bond Interest Payable | | 27,500 |
| | (To record accrual of semiannual bond interest) | | |

### action plan

✔ Compute interest semiannually (six months).

✔ Record the accrual and payment of interest on appropriate dates.

✔ Record the conversion of the bonds into common stock by removing the book (carrying) value of the bonds from the liability account.

**(c)** 2010

| | | | |
|---|---|---|---|
| Jan. 1 | Bond Interest Payable | 27,500 | |
| |     Cash | | 27,500 |
| |     (To record payment of accrued | | |
| |     interest) | | |

**(d)** Jan. 1

| | | | |
|---|---|---|---|
| | Bonds Payable | 500,000 | |
| |     Common Stock | | 300,000* |
| |     Paid-in Capital in Excess of Par Value | | 200,000 |
| |     (To record conversion of bonds into | | |
| |     common stock) | | |
| |     *($500,000 ÷ $1,000 = 500 bonds; | | |
| |     500 × 30 = 15,000 shares; | | |
| |     15,000 × $20 = $300,000) | | |

## action plan

✔ Record the issuance of the bonds.

✔ Compute interest expense for each period.

✔ Compute the loss on bond redemption as the excess of the cash paid over the carrying value of the redeemed bonds.

**2. (a)** 2009

| | | | |
|---|---|---|---|
| Jan. 1 | Cash | 1,000,000 | |
| |     Bonds Payable | | 1,000,000 |
| |     (To record issuance of bonds) | | |

**(b)** 2009

| | | | |
|---|---|---|---|
| July 1 | Bond Interest Expense | 50,000 | |
| |     Cash | | 50,000 |
| |     (To record payment of semiannual | | |
| |     interest) | | |
| Dec. 31 | Bond Interest Expense | 50,000 | |
| |     Bond Interest Payable | | 50,000 |
| |     (To record accrual of semiannual | | |
| |     interest) | | |

**(c)** 2012

| | | | |
|---|---|---|---|
| Jan. 1 | Bonds Payable | 1,000,000 | |
| | Loss on Bond Redemption | 10,000* | |
| |     Cash | | 1,010,000 |
| |     (To record redemption of bonds at | | |
| |     101) | | |
| |     *($1,010,000 − $1,000,000) | | |

## action plan

✔ Compute periodic interest expense on a mortgage note, recognizing that as the principal amount decreases, so does the interest expense.

✔ Record mortgage payments, recognizing that each payment consists of (1) interest on the unpaid loan balance and (2) a reduction of the loan principal.

**3. (a)** 2009

| | | | |
|---|---|---|---|
| Jan. 1 | Cash | 500,000 | |
| |     Mortgage Notes Payable | | 500,000 |
| |     (To record issuance of mortgage note | | |
| |     payable) | | |

**(b)**

| Semiannual Interest Period | Cash Payment | Interest Expense | Reduction of Principal | Principal Balance |
|---|---|---|---|---|
| Issue date | | | | $500,000 |
| 1 | $36,324 | $30,000 | $6,324 | 493,676 |
| 2 | 36,324 | 29,621 | 6,703 | 486,973 |
| 3 | 36,324 | 29,218 | 7,106 | 479,867 |
| 4 | 36,324 | 28,792 | 7,532 | 472,335 |

**(c)**   Current liability      $14,638 ($7,106 + $7,532)
      Long-term liability    $472,335

✔ The Navigator

**1 Explain a current liability, and identify the major types of current liabilities.** A current liability is a debt that can reasonably be expected to be paid (1) from existing current assets or through the creation of other current liabilities, and (2) within one year or the operating cycle, whichever is longer. The major types of current liabilities are notes payable, accounts payable, sales taxes payable, unearned revenues, and accrued liabilities such as taxes, salaries and wages, and interest payable.

**2 Describe the accounting for notes payable.** When a promissory note is interest-bearing, the amount of assets received upon the issuance of the note is generally equal to the face value of the note. Interest expense is accrued over the life of the note. At maturity, the amount paid is equal to the face value of the note plus accrued interest.

**3 Explain the accounting for other current liabilities.** Sales taxes payable are recorded at the time the related sales occur. The company serves as a collection agent for the taxing authority. Sales taxes are not an expense to the company. Until employee withholding taxes are remitted to governmental taxing authorities, they are credited to appropriate liability accounts. Unearned revenues are initially recorded in an unearned revenue account. As the revenue is earned, a transfer from unearned revenue to earned revenue occurs. The current maturities of long-term debt should be reported as a current liability in the balance sheet.

**4 Explain why bonds are issued, and identify the types of bonds.** Bonds may be sold to many investors, and they offer the following advantages over common stock: (a) stockholder control is not affected, (b) tax savings result, and (c) earnings per share of common stock may be higher. The following different types of bonds may be issued:

secured and unsecured bonds, term and serial bonds, registered and bearer bonds, convertible and callable bonds.

**5 Prepare the entries for the issuance of bonds and interest expense.** When bonds are issued, Cash is debited for the cash proceeds, and Bonds Payable is credited for the face value of the bonds. The account Premium on Bonds Payable is used to show a bond premium; Discount on Bonds Payable is used to show a bond discount.

**6 Describe the entries when bonds are redeemed or converted.** When bonds are redeemed at maturity, Cash is credited and Bonds Payable is debited for the face value of the bonds. When bonds are redeemed before maturity, it is necessary to (a) eliminate the carrying value of the bonds at the redemption date, (b) record the cash paid, and (c) recognize the gain or loss on redemption. When bonds are converted to common stock, the carrying (or book) value of the bonds is transferred to appropriate paid-in capital accounts; no gain or loss is recognized.

**7 Describe the accounting for long-term notes payable.** Each payment consists of (1) interest on the unpaid balance of the loan and (2) a reduction of loan principal. The interest decreases each period, while the portion applied to the loan principal increases.

**8 Identify the methods for the presentation and analysis of long-term liabilities.** The nature and amount of each long-term debt should be reported in the balance sheet or in the notes accompanying the financial statements. Stockholders and long-term creditors are interested in a company's long-run solvency. Debt to total assets and times interest earned are two ratios that provide information about debt-paying ability and long-run solvency.

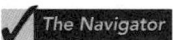

*The Navigator*

**GLOSSARY**

**Bearer (coupon) bonds** Bonds not registered. (p. 484).

**Bond certificate** A legal document that indicates the name of the issuer, the face value of the bonds, and such other data as the contractual interest rate and maturity date of the bonds. (p. 484).

**Bond discount** The amount by which a bond sells at less than its face value. (p. 488).

**Bond indenture** A legal document that sets forth the terms of the bond issue. (p. 484).

**Bond premium** The amount by which a bond sells above its face value. (p. 488).

**Bonds** A form of interest-bearing notes payable issued by corporations, universities, and governmental entities. (p. 482).

**Callable bonds** Bonds that are subject to retirement at a stated dollar amount prior to maturity at the option of the issuer. (p. 484).

**Contractual interest rate** Rate used to determine the amount of interest the borrower pays and the investor receives. (p. 484).

**Convertible bonds** Bonds that permit bondholders to convert them into common stock at their option. (p. 484).

**Current liabilities** Debts that a company reasonably expects to pay from existing current assets within the next year or operating cycle. (p. 474).

**Current ratio** A measure of a company's liquidity; computed as current assets divided by current liabilities. (p. 481).

**Debenture bonds** Bonds issued against the general credit of the borrower. Also called unsecured bonds. (p. 484).

**Debt to total assets ratio** A solvency measure that indicates the percentage of total assets provided by creditors; computed as total debt divided by total assets. (p. 495).

**Face value** Amount of principal the issuer must pay at the maturity date of the bond. (p. 484).

**Long-term liabilities** Obligations expected to be paid after one year. (p. 482).

**Market interest rate** The rate investors demand for loaning funds to the corporation. (p. 486).

**Mortgage bond** A bond secured by real estate. (p. 483).

**Mortgage note payable** A long-term note secured by a mortgage that pledges title to specific assets as security for a loan. (p. 493).

**Notes payable** Obligations in the form of written promissory notes. (p. 475).

**Registered bonds** Bonds issued in the name of the owner. (p. 484).

**Secured bonds** Bonds that have specific assets of the issuer pledged as collateral. (p. 483).

**Serial bonds** Bonds that mature in installments. (p. 484).

**Sinking fund bonds** Bonds secured by specific assets set aside to retire them. (p. 483).

**Term bonds** Bonds that mature at a single specified future date. (p. 484).

**Times interest earned ratio** A solvency measure that indicates a company's ability to meet interest payments; computed by dividing income before income taxes and interest expense by interest expense. (p. 495).

**Unsecured bonds** Bonds issued against the general credit of the borrower. Also called debenture bonds. (p. 484).

**Working capital** A measure of a company's liquidity; computed as current assets minus current liabilities. (p. 481).

# APPENDIX 11A **Present Value Concepts Related to Bond Pricing**

Congratulations! You have a winning lottery ticket and the state has provided you with three possible options for payment. They are:

1. Receive $10,000,000 in three years.
2. Receive $7,000,000 immediately.
3. Receive $3,500,000 at the end of each year for three years.

Which of these options would you select? The answer is not easy to determine at a glance. To make a dollar-maximizing choice, you must perform present value computations. A present value computation is based on the concept of time value of money. Time value of money concepts are useful for the lottery situation and for pricing other amounts to be received in the future. This appendix discusses how to use present value concepts to price bonds. It also will tell you how to determine what option you should take as a lottery winner.

## Present Value of Face Value

**STUDY OBJECTIVE 9**

**Compute the market price of a bond.**

To illustrate present value concepts, assume that you are willing to invest a sum of money that will yield $1,000 at the end of one year. In other words, what amount would you need to invest today to have $1,000 one year from now? If you want to earn 10%, the investment (or present value) is $909.09 ($1,000 ÷ 1.10). Illustration 11A-1 shows the computation.

**Illustration 11A-1**
Present value computation—$1,000 discounted at 10% for one year

| Present Value | × | (1 + Interest Rate) | = | Future Amount |
|---|---|---|---|---|
| Present value | × | (1 + 10%) | = | $1,000 |
| Present value | | | = | $1,000 ÷ 1.10 |
| Present value | | | = | $909.09 |

The future amount ($1,000), the interest rate (10%), and the number of periods (1) are known. We can depict the variables in this situation as shown in the time diagram in Illustration 11A-2.

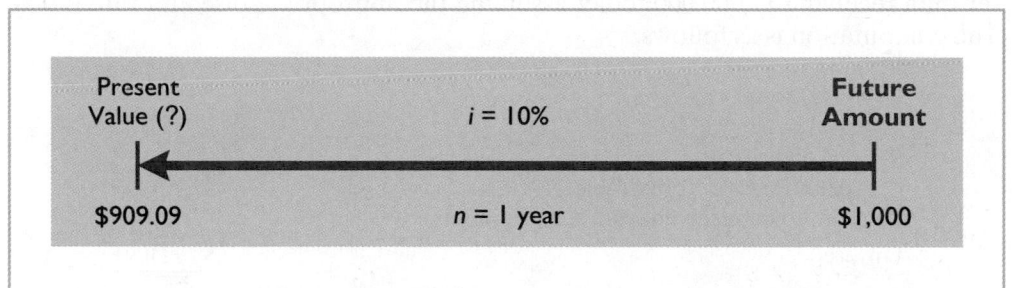

**Illustration 11A-2**
Finding present value if discounted for one period

If you are to receive the single future amount of $1,000 **in two years**, discounted at 10%, its present value is $826.45 [($1,000 ÷ 1.10) ÷ 1.10], depicted as follows.

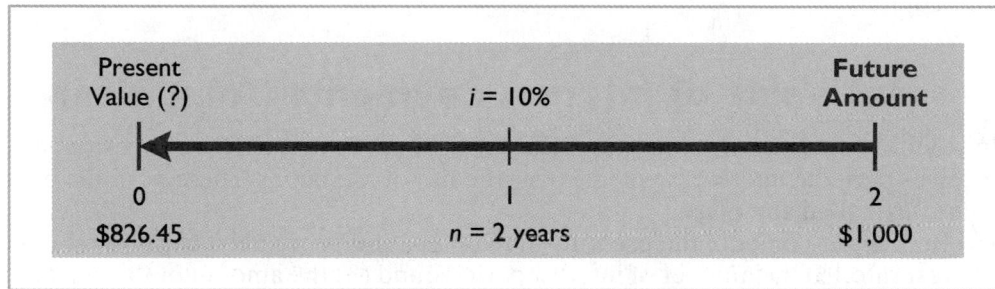

**Illustration 11A-3**
Finding present value if discounted for two periods

We also can determine the present value of 1 through tables that show the present value of 1 for $n$ periods. In Table 11A-1 below, $n$ is the number of discounting periods involved. The percentages are the periodic interest rates, and the five-digit decimal numbers in the respective columns are the factors for the present value of 1.

When using Table 11A-1, we multiply the future amount by the present value factor specified at the intersection of the number of periods and the interest rate. For example, the present value factor for 1 period at an interest rate of 10% is .90909, which equals the $909.09 ($1,000 × .90909) computed in Illustration 11A-1.

## TABLE 11A-1
### Present Value of 1

| (n) Periods | 4% | 5% | 6% | 8% | 9% | 10% | 11% | 12% | 15% |
|---|---|---|---|---|---|---|---|---|---|
| 1 | .96154 | .95238 | .94340 | .92593 | .91743 | .90909 | .90090 | .89286 | .86957 |
| 2 | .92456 | .90703 | .89000 | .85734 | .84168 | .82645 | .81162 | .79719 | .75614 |
| 3 | .88900 | .86384 | .83962 | .79383 | .77218 | .75132 | .73119 | .71178 | .65752 |
| 4 | .85480 | .82270 | .79209 | .73503 | .70843 | .68301 | .65873 | .63552 | .57175 |
| 5 | .82193 | .78353 | .74726 | .68058 | .64993 | .62092 | .59345 | .56743 | .49718 |
| 6 | .79031 | .74622 | .70496 | .63017 | .59627 | .56447 | .53464 | .50663 | .43233 |
| 7 | .75992 | .71068 | .66506 | .58349 | .54703 | .51316 | .48166 | .45235 | .37594 |
| 8 | .73069 | .67684 | .62741 | .54027 | .50187 | .46651 | .43393 | .40388 | .32690 |
| 9 | .70259 | .64461 | .59190 | .50025 | .46043 | .42410 | .39092 | .36061 | .28426 |
| 10 | .67556 | .61391 | .55839 | .46319 | .42241 | .38554 | .35218 | .32197 | .24719 |

For two periods at an interest rate of 10%, the present value factor is .82645, which equals the $826.45 ($1,000 × .82645) computed previously.

Let's now go back to our lottery example. Given the present value concepts just learned, we can determine whether receiving $10,000,000 in three years is better than receiving $7,000,000 today, assuming the appropriate discount rate is 9%. The computation is as follows.

**Illustration 11A-4**
Present value of $10,000,000 to be received in three years

| | |
|---|---:|
| $10,000,000 × PV of 1 due in 3 years at 9% = | |
| $10,000,000 × .77218 (Table 11A-1) | $7,721,800 |
| Amount to be received from state immediately | 7,000,000 |
| Difference | $ 721,800 |

What this computation shows you is that you would be $721,800 better off receiving the $10,000,000 at the end of three years rather than taking $7,000,000 immediately.

## Present Value of Interest Payments (Annuities)

In addition to receiving the face value of a bond at maturity, an investor also receives periodic interest payments over the life of the bonds. These periodic payments are called **annuities**.

In order to compute the present value of an annuity, we need to know: (1) the interest rate, (2) the number of interest periods, and (3) the amount of the periodic receipts or payments. To illustrate the computation of the present value of an annuity, assume that you will receive $1,000 cash annually for three years and the interest rate is 10%. The time diagram in Illustration 11A-5 depicts this situation.

**Illustration 11A-5**
Time diagram for a three-year annuity

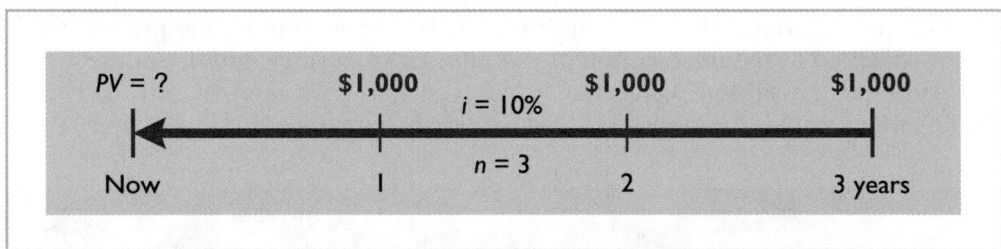

The present value in this situation may be computed as follows.

**Illustration 11A-6**
Present value of a series of future amounts computation

| Future Amount | × | Present Value of 1 Factor at 10% | = | Present Value |
|---|---|:---:|---|---:|
| $1,000 (1 year away) | | .90909 | | $ 909.09 |
| 1,000 (2 years away) | | .82645 | | 826.45 |
| 1,000 (3 years away) | | .75132 | | 751.32 |
| | | 2.48686 | | **$2,486.86** |

We also can use annuity tables to value annuities. As illustrated in Table 11A-2 below, these tables show the present value of 1 to be received periodically for a given number of periods.

| **TABLE 11A-2**<br>Present Value of an Annuity of 1 | | | | | | | | |
|---|---|---|---|---|---|---|---|---|
| **(n)**<br>**Periods** | **4%** | **5%** | **6%** | **8%** | **9%** | **10%** | **11%** | **12%** | **15%** |
| 1 | .96154 | .95238 | .94340 | .92593 | .91743 | .90909 | .90090 | .89286 | .86957 |
| 2 | 1.88609 | 1.85941 | 1.83339 | 1.78326 | 1.75911 | 1.73554 | 1.71252 | 1.69005 | 1.62571 |
| 3 | 2.77509 | 2.72325 | 2.67301 | 2.57710 | 2.53130 | 2.48685 | 2.44371 | 2.40183 | 2.28323 |
| 4 | 3.62990 | 3.54595 | 3.46511 | 3.31213 | 3.23972 | 3.16986 | 3.10245 | 3.03735 | 2.85498 |
| 5 | 4.45182 | 4.32948 | 4.21236 | 3.99271 | 3.88965 | 3.79079 | 3.69590 | 3.60478 | 3.35216 |
| 6 | 5.24214 | 5.07569 | 4.91732 | 4.62288 | 4.48592 | 4.35526 | 4.23054 | 4.11141 | 3.78448 |
| 7 | 6.00205 | 5.78637 | 5.58238 | 5.20637 | 5.03295 | 4.86842 | 4.71220 | 4.56376 | 4.16042 |
| 8 | 6.73274 | 6.46321 | 6.20979 | 5.74664 | 5.53482 | 5.33493 | 5.14612 | 4.96764 | 4.48732 |
| 9 | 7.43533 | 7.10782 | 6.80169 | 6.24689 | 5.99525 | 5.75902 | 5.53705 | 5.32825 | 4.77158 |
| 10 | 8.11090 | 7.72173 | 7.36009 | 6.71008 | 6.41766 | 6.14457 | 5.88923 | 5.65022 | 5.01877 |

From Table 11A-2 you can see that the present value factor of an annuity of 1 for three periods at 10% is 2.48685.[1] This present value factor is the total of the three individual present value factors as shown in Illustration 11A-6. Applying this amount to the annual cash flow of $1,000 produces a present value of $2,486.85.

Let's now go back to our lottery example. We determined that you would get more money if you wait and take the $10,000,000 in three years rather than take $7,000,000 immediately. But there is still another option—to receive $3,500,000 at the end of **each year** for three years (an annuity). The computation to evaluate this option (again assuming a 9% discount rate) is as follows.

| | |
|---|---|
| $3,500,000 × PV of 1 due yearly for 3 years at 9% =<br>  $3,500,000 × 2.53130 (Table 11A-2) | $8,859,550 |
| Present value of $10,000,000 to be received in 3 years | 7,721,800 |
| Difference | $1,137,750 |

**Illustration 11A-7**
Present value of lottery payments to be received over three years

If you take the annuity of $3,500,000 for each of three years, you will be $1,137,750 richer as a result.

## Time Periods and Discounting

We have used an **annual** interest rate to determine present value. Present value computations may also be done over shorter periods of time, such as monthly, quarterly,

---

[1]The difference of .00001 between 2.48686 and 2.48685 is due to rounding.

or semiannually. When the time frame is less than one year, it is necessary to convert the annual interest rate to the shorter time frame.

Assume, for example, that the investor in Illustration 11A-6 received $500 **semiannually** for three years instead of $1,000 annually. In this case, the number of periods becomes six (3 × 2), the interest rate is 5% (10% ÷ 2), the present value factor from Table 11A-2 is 5.07569, and the present value of the future cash flows is $2,537.85 (5.07569 × $500). This amount is slightly higher than the $2,486.86 computed in Illustration 11A-6 because interest is computed twice during the same year. That is, interest is earned on the first half year's interest.

## Computing the Present Value of a Bond

The present value (or market price) of a bond is a function of three variables: (1) the payment amounts, (2) the length of time until the amounts are paid, and (3) the interest (discount) rate.

The first variable (dollars to be paid) is made up of two elements: (1) a series of interest payments (an annuity), and (2) the principal amount (a single sum). To compute the present value of the bond, we must discount both the interest payments and the principal amount.

When the investor's interest (discount) rate is equal to the bond's contractual interest rate, the present value of the bonds will equal the face value of the bonds. To illustrate, assume a bond issue of 10%, five-year bonds with a face value of $100,000 with interest payable **semiannually** on January 1 and July 1. If the discount rate is the same as the contractual rate, the bonds will sell **at face value**. In this case, the investor will receive: (1) $100,000 at maturity and (2) a series of ten $5,000 interest payments [$100,000 × (10% ÷ 2)] over the term of the bonds. The length of time is expressed in terms of interest periods (in this case, 10) and the discount rate per interest period (5%). The time diagram in Illustration 11A-8 below depicts the variables involved in this discounting situation.

**Illustration 11A-8**
Time diagram for the present value of a 10%, five-year bond paying interest semiannually

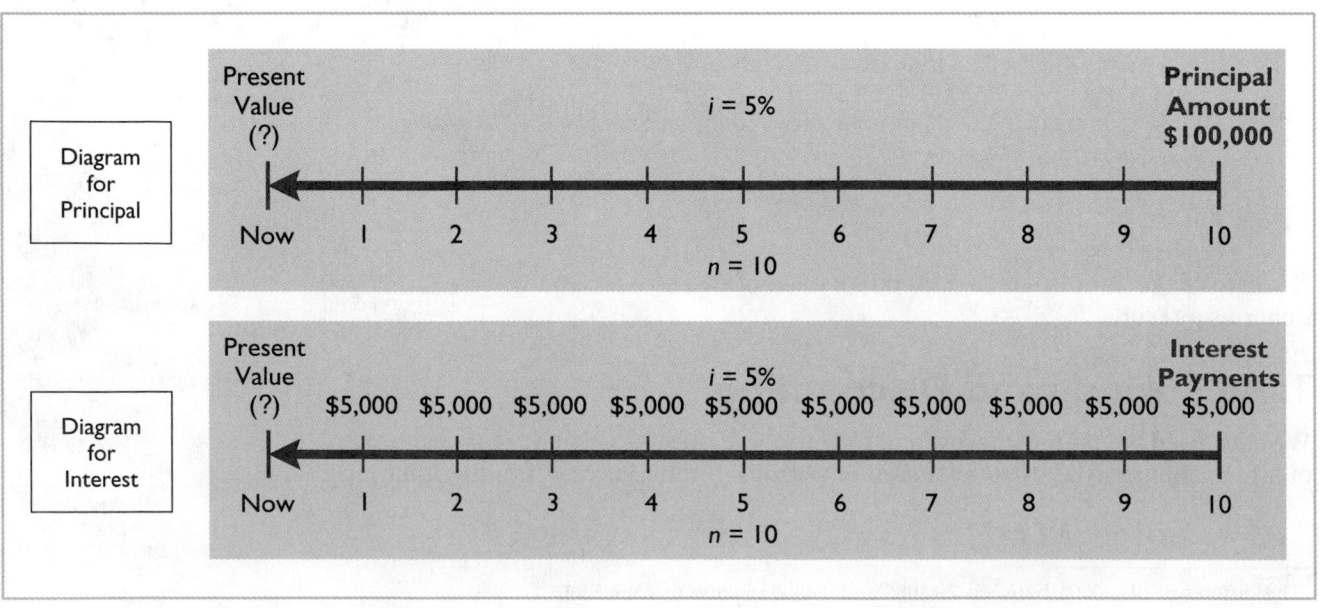

The computation of the present value of Candlestick's bonds, assuming they were issued at face value (page 487), is shown below.

| 10% Contractual Rate—10% Discount Rate | |
|---|---:|
| **Present value of principal to be received at maturity** | |
| $100,000 × PV of 1 due in 10 periods at 5% | |
| $100,000 × .61391 (Table 11A-1) | $ 61,391 |
| **Present value of interest to be received periodically** | |
| **over the term of the bonds** | |
| $5,000 × PV of 1 due periodically for 10 periods at 5% | |
| $5,000 × 7.72173 (Table 11A-2) | 38,609* |
| **Present value of bonds** | **$100,000** |

*Rounded.

**Illustration 11A-9**
Present value of principal and interest (face value)

Now assume that the investor's required rate of return is 12%, not 10%. The future amounts are again $100,000 and $5,000, respectively. But now we must use a discount rate of 6% (12% ÷ 2). The present value of Candlestick's bonds issued at a discount (page 488) is $92,639 as computed below.

| 10% Contractual Rate—12% Discount Rate | |
|---|---:|
| **Present value of principal to be received at maturity** | |
| $100,000 × .55839 (Table 11A-1) | $55,839 |
| **Present value of interest to be received periodically** | |
| **over the term of the bonds** | |
| $5,000 × 7.36009 (Table 11A-2) | 36,800 |
| **Present value of bonds** | **$92,639** |

**Illustration 11A-10**
Present value of principal and interest (discount)

If the discount rate is 8% and the contractual rate is 10%, the present value of Candlestick's bonds issued at a premium (page 489) is $108,111 as computed below.

| 10% Contractual Rate—8% Discount Rate | |
|---|---:|
| **Present value of principal to be received at maturity** | |
| $100,000 × .67556 (Table 11A-1) | $67,556 |
| **Present value of interest to be received periodically** | |
| **over the term of the bonds** | |
| $5,000 × 8.11090 (Table 11A-2) | 40,555 |
| **Present value of bonds** | **$108,111** |

**Illustration 11A-11**
Present value of principal and interest (premium)

**9 Compute the market price of a bond.** Time value of money concepts are useful for pricing bonds. The present value (or market price) of a bond is a function of three variables: (1) the payment amounts, (2) the length of time until the amounts are paid, and (3) the interest rate.

# APPENDIX 11B Effective-Interest Method of Bond Amortization

**STUDY OBJECTIVE 10**

Apply the effective-interest method of amortizing bond discount and bond premium.

Under the **effective-interest method**, the amortization of bond discount or bond premium results in periodic interest expense equal to a **constant percentage** of the carrying value of the bonds. The effective-interest method results in varying amounts of amortization and interest expense per period but **a constant percentage rate**.

The following steps are required under the effective-interest method.

1. Compute the **bond interest expense**. To do so, multiply the carrying value of the bonds at the beginning of the interest period by the effective-interest rate.

2. Compute the **bond interest paid** (or accrued). To do so, multiply the face value of the bonds by the contractual interest rate.

3. Compute the **amortization amount**. To do so, determine the difference between the amounts computed in steps (1) and (2).

Illustration 11B-1 depicts these steps.

**Illustration 11B-1**
Computation of amortization—effective-interest method

| (1) Bond Interest Expense | | (2) Bond Interest Paid | | (3) |
|---|---|---|---|---|
| $\left(\begin{array}{c}\text{Carrying Value of Bonds at Beginning of Period}\end{array} \times \begin{array}{c}\text{Effective Interest Rate}\end{array}\right)$ | $-$ | $\left(\begin{array}{c}\text{Face Amount of Bonds}\end{array} \times \begin{array}{c}\text{Contractual Interest Rate}\end{array}\right)$ | $=$ | Amortization Amount |

When the difference between the straight-line method of amortization (Appendix 11C) and the effective-interest method is material, GAAP requires the use of the effective-interest method.

## Amortizing Bond Discount

To illustrate the effective-interest method of bond discount amortization, assume that Candlestick, Inc. issues $100,000 of 10%, five-year bonds on January 1, 2008, with interest payable each July 1 and January 1 (pages 488–489). The bonds sell for $92,639 (92.639% of face value). This sales price results in bond discount of $7,361 ($100,000 − $92,639) and an effective-interest rate of 12%. A bond discount amortization schedule, as shown in Illustration 11B-2 (page 507), facilitates the recording of interest expense and the discount amortization. Note that interest expense as a percentage of carrying value remains constant at 6%.

We have highlighted columns (A), (B), and (C) in the amortization schedule to emphasize their importance. These three columns provide the numbers for each period's journal entries. They are the primary reason for preparing the schedule.

**Candlestick Inc.xls**

File    Edit    View    Insert    Format    Tools    Data    Window    Help

### CANDLESTICK, INC.
#### Bond Discount Amortization
#### Effective-Interest Method—Semiannual Interest Payments
#### 10% Bonds Issued at 12%

| Semiannual Interest Periods | (A) Interest to Be Paid (5% × $100,000) | (B) Interest Expense to Be Recorded (6% × Preceding Bond Carrying Value) | | (C) Discount Amortization (B) − (A) | (D) Unamortized Discount (D) − (C) | (E) Bond Carrying Value ($100,000 − D) |
|---|---|---|---|---|---|---|
| Issue date | | | | | $7,361 | $92,639 |
| 1 | $ 5,000 | $ 5,558 | (6% × $92,639) | $ 558 | 6,803 | 93,197 |
| 2 | 5,000 | 5,592 | (6% × $93,197) | 592 | 6,211 | 93,789 |
| 3 | 5,000 | 5,627 | (6% × $93,789) | 627 | 5,584 | 94,416 |
| 4 | 5,000 | 5,665 | (6% × $94,416) | 665 | 4,919 | 95,081 |
| 5 | 5,000 | 5,705 | (6% × $95,081) | 705 | 4,214 | 95,786 |
| 6 | 5,000 | 5,747 | (6% × $95,786) | 747 | 3,467 | 96,533 |
| 7 | 5,000 | 5,792 | (6% × $96,533) | 792 | 2,675 | 97,325 |
| 8 | 5,000 | 5,840 | (6% × $97,325) | 840 | 1,835 | 98,165 |
| 9 | 5,000 | 5,890 | (6% × $98,165) | 890 | 945 | 99,055 |
| 10 | 5,000 | 5,945* | (6% × $99,055) | 945 | –0– | 100,000 |
| | $50,000 | $57,361 | | $7,361 | | |

Column (A) remains constant because the face value of the bonds ($100,000) is multiplied by the semiannual contractual interest rate (5%) each period.

Column (B) is computed as the preceding bond carrying value times the semiannual effective-interest rate (6%).

Column (C) indicates the discount amortization each period.

Column (D) decreases each period until it reaches zero at maturity.

Column (E) increases each period until it equals face value at maturity.

*$2 difference due to rounding.

**Illustration 11B-2**
Bond discount amortization schedule

For the first interest period, the computations of bond interest expense and the bond discount amortization are:

| | |
|---|---|
| Bond interest expense ($92,639 × 6%) | $5,558 |
| Contractual interest ($100,000 × 5%) | 5,000 |
| **Bond discount amortization** | $  558 |

**Illustration 11B-3**
Computation of bond discount amortization

Candlestick records the payment of interest and amortization of bond discount on July 1, 2008, as follows.

| July 1 | Bond Interest Expense | 5,558 | |
|---|---|---|---|
| | Discount on Bonds Payable | | 558 |
| | Cash | | 5,000 |
| | (To record payment of bond interest and amortization of bond discount) | | |

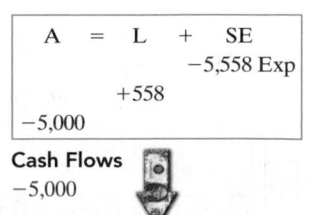

A  =  L  +  SE
−5,558 Exp
+558
−5,000

**Cash Flows**
−5,000

For the second interest period, bond interest expense will be $5,592 ($93,197 × 6%), and the discount amortization will be $592. At December 31, Candlestick makes the following adjusting entry.

| A | = | L | + | SE |
|---|---|---|---|---|
| | | | | −5,592 Exp |
| | +592 | | | |
| | +5,000 | | | |

| Dec. 31 | Bond Interest Expense | 5,592 | |
|---|---|---|---|
| | Discount on Bonds Payable | | 592 |
| | Bond Interest Payable | | 5,000 |
| | (To record accrued interest and amortization of bond discount) | | |

**Cash Flows**

no effect

**HELPFUL HINT**

When a bond sells for $108,111, it is quoted as 108.111% of face value. Note that $108,111 can be proven as shown in Appendix 11A.

Total bond interest expense for 2008 is $11,150 ($5,558 + $5,592). On January 1, Candlestick records payment of the interest by a debit to Bond Interest Payable and a credit to Cash.

## Amortizing Bond Premium

The amortization of bond premium by the effective-interest method is similar to the procedures described for bond discount. For example, assume that Candlestick, Inc. issues $100,000, 10%, five-year bonds on January 1, 2008, with interest payable on July 1 and January 1 (pages 489–490). In this case, the bonds sell for $108,111. This sales price results in bond premium of $8,111 and an effective-interest rate of 8%. Illustration 11B-4 shows the bond premium amortization schedule.

**Illustration 11B-4**
Bond premium amortization schedule

**Candlestick Inc.xls**

File   Edit   View   Insert   Format   Tools   Data   Window   Help

**CANDLESTICK, INC.**
**Bond Premium Amortization**
**Effective-Interest Method—Semiannual Interest Payments**
**10% Bonds Issued at 8%**

| Semiannual Interest Periods | (A) Interest to Be Paid (5% × $100,000) | (B) Interest Expense to Be Recorded (4% × Preceding Bond Carrying Value) | | (C) Premium Amortization (A) − (B) | (D) Unamortized Premium (D) − (C) | (E) Bond Carrying Value ($100,000 + D) |
|---|---|---|---|---|---|---|
| Issue date | | | | | $8,111 | $108,111 |
| 1 | $ 5,000 | $ 4,324 | (4% × $108,111) | $ 676 | 7,435 | 107,435 |
| 2 | 5,000 | 4,297 | (4% × $107,435) | 703 | 6,732 | 106,732 |
| 3 | 5,000 | 4,269 | (4% × $106,732) | 731 | 6,001 | 106,001 |
| 4 | 5,000 | 4,240 | (4% × $106,001) | 760 | 5,241 | 105,241 |
| 5 | 5,000 | 4,210 | (4% × $105,241) | 790 | 4,451 | 104,451 |
| 6 | 5,000 | 4,178 | (4% × $104,451) | 822 | 3,629 | 103,629 |
| 7 | 5,000 | 4,145 | (4% × $103,629) | 855 | 2,774 | 102,774 |
| 8 | 5,000 | 4,111 | (4% × $102,774) | 889 | 1,885 | 101,885 |
| 9 | 5,000 | 4,075 | (4% × $101,885) | 925 | 960 | 100,960 |
| 10 | 5,000 | 4,040* | (4% × $100,960) | 960 | –0– | 100,000 |
| | $50,000 | $41,889 | | $8,111 | | |

Column **(A)** remains constant because the face value of the bonds ($100,000) is multiplied by the semiannual contractual interest rate (5%) each period.

Column **(B)** is computed as the carrying value of the bonds times the semiannual effective-interest rate (4%).

Column **(C)** indicates the premium amortization each period.

Column **(D)** decreases each period until it reaches zero at maturity.

Column **(E)** decreases each period until it equals face value at maturity.

*$2 difference due to rounding.

For the first interest period, the computations of bond interest expense and the bond premium amortization are:

| | | |
|---|---|---|
| Bond interest expense ($108,111 × 4%) | $4,324 | |
| Contractual interest ($100,000 × 5%) | 5,000 | |
| **Bond premium amortization** | **$ 676** | |

**Illustration 11B-5**
Computation of bond premium amortization

Candlestick records payments on the first interest date as follows.

| July 1 | Bond Interest Expense | 4,324 | |
|---|---|---|---|
| | Premium on Bonds Payable | 676 | |
| |     Cash | | 5,000 |
| |         (To record payment of bond interest and | | |
| |         amortization of bond premium) | | |

| A | = | L | + | SE |
|---|---|---|---|---|
| | | | | −4,324 Exp |
| | | −676 | | |
| −5,000 | | | | |

**Cash Flows**
−5,000

For the second interest period, interest expense will be $4,297, and the premium amortization will be $703. Total bond interest expense for 2008 is $8,621 ($4,324 + $4,297).

---

## Demonstration Problem for Appendix 11B

Gardner Corporation issues $1,750,000, 10-year, 12% bonds on January 1, 2008, at $1,820,000, to yield 10%. The bonds pay semiannual interest July 1 and January 1. Gardner uses the effective-interest method of amortization.

### Instructions

**(a)** Prepare the journal entry to record the issuance of the bonds.
**(b)** Prepare the journal entry to record the payment of interest on July 1, 2008.

### Solution

**(a)** 2008

| Jan. 1 | Cash | 1,820,000 | |
|---|---|---|---|
| |     Bonds Payable | | 1,750,000 |
| |     Premium on Bonds Payable | | 70,000 |
| |         (To record issuance of bonds at a premium) | | |

**(b)** 2008

| July 1 | Bond Interest Expense | 91,000* | |
|---|---|---|---|
| | Premium on Bonds Payable | 14,000** | |
| |     Cash | | 105,000 |
| |         (To record payment of semiannual interest | | |
| |         and amortization of bond premium) | | |
| |         *($1,820,000 × 5%) | | |
| |         **($105,000 − $91,000) | | |

✔ *The Navigator*

### action plan

✔ Compute interest expense by multiplying bond carrying value at the beginning of the period by the effective-interest rate.

✔ Compute credit to cash (or bond interest payable) by multiplying the face value of the bonds by the contractual interest rate.

✔ Compute bond premium or discount amortization, which is the difference between interest expense and cash paid.

✔ Interest expense decreases when the effective-interest method is used for bonds issued at a premium. The reason is that a constant percentage is applied to a decreasing book value to compute interest expense.

---

## SUMMARY OF STUDY OBJECTIVE FOR APPENDIX 11B

**10 Apply the effective-interest method of amortizing bond discount and bond premium.** The effective-interest method results in varying amounts of amortization and interest expense per period but a *constant percentage rate* of interest. When the difference between the straight-line and effective-interest method is material, GAAP requires the use of the effective-interest method.

**Effective-interest method of amortization** A method of amortizing bond discount or bond premium that results in periodic interest expense equal to a constant percentage of the carrying value of the bonds. (p. 506).

# APPENDIX 11C Straight-Line Amortization

## Amortizing Bond Discount

To follow the matching principle, companies should allocate bond discount systematically to each period in which the bonds are outstanding. The straight-line method of amortization allocates the **same amount to interest expense** in each interest period. The amount is determined using the formula in Illustration 11C-1.

**Illustration 11C-1**
Formula for straight-line method of bond discount amortization

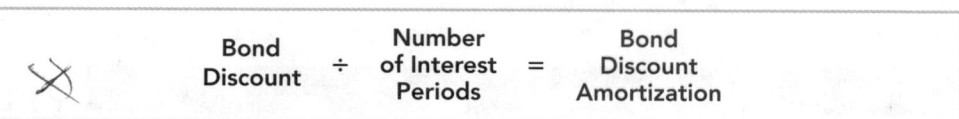

In the Candlestick, Inc. example (page 488), the company sold $100,000, five-year, 10% bonds on January 1, 2008, for $92,639. This price resulted in a $7,361 bond discount ($100,000 − $92,639). Interest is payable on July 1 and January 1. The bond discount amortization for each interest period is $736 ($7,361 ÷ 10). Candlestick records the payment of bond interest and the amortization of bond discount on the first interest date (July 1, 2008) as follows.

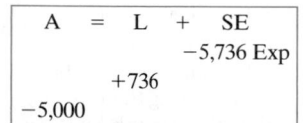

**Cash Flows**
−5,000

| July 1 | Bond Interest Expense | 5,736 | |
| | Discount on Bonds Payable | | 736 |
| | Cash | | 5,000 |
| | (To record payment of bond interest and amortization of bond discount) | | |

At December 31, Candlestick makes the following adjusting entry.

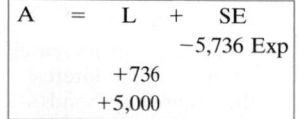

**Cash Flows**
no effect

| Dec. 31 | Bond Interest Expense | 5,736 | |
| | Discount on Bonds Payable | | 736 |
| | Bond Interest Payable | | 5,000 |
| | (To record accrued bond interest and amortization of bond discount) | | |

Over the term of the bonds, the balance in Discount on Bonds Payable will decrease annually by the **same amount** until it has a zero balance at the maturity date of the bonds. Thus, the carrying value of the bonds at maturity will be equal to the face value.

It is useful to prepare a bond discount amortization schedule as shown in Illustration 11C-2 (page 511). The schedule shows interest expense, discount amortization, and the carrying value of the bond for each interest period. As indicated, the interest expense recorded **each period** for the Candlestick bond is $5,736. Also note that the carrying value of the bond increases $736 each period until it reaches its face value $100,000 at the end of period 10.

**Illustration 11C-2**
Bond discount amortization schedule

```
Candlestick Inc.xls                                              _ ☐ ☒
 File    Edit    View    Insert    Format    Tools    Data    Window    Help
```

|  | A | B | C | D | E | F |
|---|---|---|---|---|---|---|
| 1 | | | **CANDLESTICK, INC.** | | | |
| 2 | | | **Bond Discount Amortization** | | | |
| 3 | | | | | | |
| 4 | | | **Straight-Line Method—Semiannual Interest Payments** | | | |
| 5 | | **(A)** | **(B)** | **(C)** | **(D)** | **(E)** |
| 6 | **Semiannual** | **Interest to** | **Interest Expense** | **Discount** | **Unamortized** | **Bond** |
| 7 | **Interest** | **Be Paid** | **to Be Recorded** | **Amortization** | **Discount** | **Carrying Value** |
| 8 | **Periods** | **(5% × $100,000)** | **(A) + (C)** | **($7,361 ÷ 10)** | **(D) − (C)** | **($100,000 − D)** |
| 9 | Issue date | | | | $7,361 | $92,639 |
| 10 | 1 | $ 5,000 | $ 5,736 | $ 736 | 6,625 | 93,375 |
| 11 | 2 | 5,000 | 5,736 | 736 | 5,889 | 94,111 |
| 12 | 3 | 5,000 | 5,736 | 736 | 5,153 | 94,847 |
| 13 | 4 | 5,000 | 5,736 | 736 | 4,417 | 95,583 |
| 14 | 5 | 5,000 | 5,736 | 736 | 3,681 | 96,319 |
| 15 | 6 | 5,000 | 5,736 | 736 | 2,945 | 97,055 |
| 16 | 7 | 5,000 | 5,736 | 736 | 2,209 | 97,791 |
| 17 | 8 | 5,000 | 5,736 | 736 | 1,473 | 98,527 |
| 18 | 9 | 5,000 | 5,736 | 736 | 737 | 99,263 |
| 19 | 10 | 5,000 | 5,737* | 737* | –0– | 100,000 |
| 20 | | $50,000 | $57,361 | $7,361 | | |
| 21 | | | | | | |
| 22 | Column **(A)** remains constant because the face value of the bonds ($100,000) is multiplied by the | | | | | |
| 23 | semiannual contractual interest rate (5%) each period. | | | | | |
| 24 | Column **(B)** is computed as the interest paid (Column A) plus the discount amortization (Column C). | | | | | |
| 25 | Column **(C)** indicates the discount amortization each period. | | | | | |
| 26 | Column **(D)** decreases each period by the same amount until it reaches zero at maturity. | | | | | |
| 27 | Column **(E)** increases each period by the same amount of discount amortization until it equals the | | | | | |
| 28 | face value at maturity. | | | | | |
| 29 | *One dollar difference due to rounding. | | | | | |

We have highlighted columns (A), (B), and (C) in the amortization schedule to emphasize their importance. These three columns provide the numbers for each period's journal entries. They are the primary reason for preparing the schedule.

## Amortizing Bond Premium

The amortization of bond premium parallels that of bond discount. Illustration 11C-3 presents the formula for determining bond premium amortization under the straight-line method.

$$\text{Bond Premium} \div \text{Number of Interest Periods} = \text{Bond Premium Amortization}$$

**Illustration 11C-3**
Formula for straight-line method of bond premium amortization

Continuing our example, assume that Candlestick sells the bonds for $108,111, rather than $92,639 (page 489). This sale price results in a bond premium of $8,111 ($108,111 − $100,000). The bond premium amortization for each interest period is $811 ($8,111 ÷ 10). Candlestick records the first payment of interest on July 1 as follows.

| July 1 | Bond Interest Expense | 4,189 | |
|---|---|---|---|
| | Premium on Bonds Payable | 811 | |
| | Cash | | 5,000 |
| | (To record payment of bond interest and amortization of bond premium) | | |

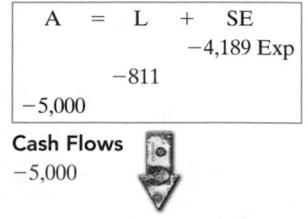

| A | = | L | + | SE |
|---|---|---|---|---|
| | | | | −4,189 Exp |
| | | −811 | | |
| −5,000 | | | | |

**Cash Flows**
−5,000

At December 31, the company makes the following adjusting entry.

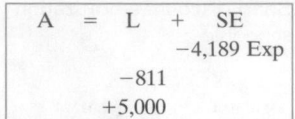

A = L + SE
   −4,189 Exp
 −811
 +5,000

**Cash Flows**
no effect

| Dec. 31 | Bond Interest Expense | 4,189 | |
| | Premium on Bonds Payable | 811 | |
| |  Bond Interest Payable | | 5,000 |
| |  (To record accrued bond interest and | | |
| |  amortization of bond premium) | | |

Over the term of the bonds, the balance in Premium on Bonds Payable will decrease annually **by the same amount** until it has a zero balance at maturity.

It is useful to prepare a bond premium amortization schedule as shown in Illustration 11C-4. It shows interest expense, premium amortization, and the carrying value of the bond. The interest expense recorded each period for the Candlestick bond is $4,189. Also note that the carrying value of the bond decreases $811 each period until it reaches its face value $100,000 at the end of period 10.

**Illustration 11C-4**
Bond premium amortization schedule

☒ **Candlestick Inc.xls**

File Edit View Insert Format Tools Data Window Help

### CANDLESTICK, INC.
### Bond Premium Amortization
### Straight-Line Method—Semiannual Interest Payments

| | (A) | (B) | (C) | (D) | (E) |
|---|---|---|---|---|---|
| **Semiannual Interest Periods** | **Interest to Be Paid (5% × $100,000)** | **Interest Expense to Be Recorded (A) − (C)** | **Premium Amortization ($8,111 ÷ 10)** | **Unamortized Premium (D) − (C)** | **Bond Carrying Value ($100,000 + D)** |
| Issue date | | | | $8,111 | $108,111 |
| 1 | $ 5,000 | $ 4,189 | $ 811 | 7,300 | 107,300 |
| 2 | 5,000 | 4,189 | 811 | 6,489 | 106,489 |
| 3 | 5,000 | 4,189 | 811 | 5,678 | 105,678 |
| 4 | 5,000 | 4,189 | 811 | 4,867 | 104,867 |
| 5 | 5,000 | 4,189 | 811 | 4,056 | 104,056 |
| 6 | 5,000 | 4,189 | 811 | 3,245 | 103,245 |
| 7 | 5,000 | 4,189 | 811 | 2,434 | 102,434 |
| 8 | 5,000 | 4,189 | 811 | 1,623 | 101,623 |
| 9 | 5,000 | 4,189 | 811 | 812 | 100,812 |
| 10 | 5,000 | 4,188* | 812* | −0− | 100,000 |
| | $50,000 | $41,889 | $8,111 | | |

Column **(A)** remains constant because the face value of the bonds ($100,000) is multiplied by the semiannual contractual interest rate (5%) each period.
Column **(B)** is computed as the interest paid (Column A) less the premium amortization (Column C).
Column **(C)** indicates the premium amortization each period.
Column **(D)** decreases each period by the same amount until it reaches zero at maturity.
Column **(E)** decreases each period by the amount of premium amortization until it equals the face value at maturity.
*One dollar difference due to rounding.

## Demonstration Problem for Appendix 11C

Glenda Corporation issues $1,750,000, 10-year, 12% bonds on January 1, 2008, for $1,820,000 to yield 10%. The bonds pay semiannual interest July 1 and January 1. Glenda uses the straight-line method of amortization.

### Instructions

**(a)** Prepare the journal entry to record the issuance of the bonds.
**(b)** Prepare the journal entry to record the payment of interest on July 1, 2008.

### Solution

**(a)** 2008

| Jan. 1 | Cash | 1,820,000 | |
| | Bonds Payable | | 1,750,000 |
| | Premium on Bonds Payable | | 70,000 |

**(b)** 2008

| July 1 | Bond Interest Expense | 101,500** | |
| | Premium on Bonds Payable | 3,500* | |
| | Cash | | 105,000 |

*$70,000 ÷ 20
**$105,000 − $3,500

✔ *The Navigator*

## SUMMARY OF STUDY OBJECTIVE FOR APPENDIX 11C

**11 Apply the straight-line method of amortizing bond discount and bond premium.** The straight-line method of amortization results in a *constant amount* of amortization and interest expense per period.

## GLOSSARY FOR APPENDIX 11C

**Straight-line method of amortization.** A method of amortizing bond discount or bond premium that results in allocating the same amount to interest expense in each interest period. (p. 510)

*****Note**: All asterisked Questions, Exercises, and Problems relate to material in the appendices to the chapter.

## SELF-STUDY QUESTIONS

*Answers are at the end of the chapter.*

(SO 1) **1.** The time period for classifying a liability as current is one year or the operating cycle, whichever is:
   **a.** longer.
   **b.** shorter.
   **c.** probable.
   **d.** possible.

(SO 1) **2.** To be classified as a current liability, a debt must be expected to be paid:
   **a.** out of existing current assets.
   **b.** by creating other current liabilities.
   **c.** within 2 years.
   **d.** both (a) and (b).

(SO 2) **3.** Maggie Sharrer Company borrows $88,500 on September 1, 2008, from Sandwich State Bank by signing an $88,500, 12%, one-year note. What is the accrued interest at December 31, 2008?
   **a.** $2,655.
   **b.** $3,540.
   **c.** $4,425.
   **d.** $10,620.

(SO 3) **4.** Becky Sherrick Company has total proceeds from sales of $4,515. If the proceeds include sales taxes of 5%, the amount to be credited to Sales is:

   **a.** $4,000.
   **b.** $4,300.
   **c.** $4,289.25.
   **d.** No correct answer given.

(SO 4) **5.** The term used for bonds that are unsecured is:
   **a.** callable bonds.
   **b.** indenture bonds.
   **c.** debenture bonds.
   **d.** bearer bonds.

(SO 5) **6.** Karson Inc. issues 10-year bonds with a maturity value of $200,000. If the bonds are issued at a premium, this indicates that:
   **a.** the contractual interest rate exceeds the market interest rate.
   **b.** the market interest rate exceeds the contractual interest rate.
   **c.** the contractual interest rate and the market interest rate are the same.
   **d.** no relationship exists between the two rates.

(SO 6) **7.** Gester Corporation retires its $100,000 face value bonds at 105 on January 1, following the payment of semiannual interest. The carrying value of the bonds at the redemption date is $103,745. The entry to record the redemption will include a:

a. credit of $3,745 to Loss on Bond Redemption.
b. debit of $3,745 to Premium on Bonds Payable.
c. credit of $1,255 to Gain on Bond Redemption.
d. debit of $5,000 to Premium on Bonds Payable.

(SO 6) **8.** Colson Inc. converts $600,000 of bonds sold at face value into 10,000 shares of common stock, par value $1. Both the bonds and the stock have a market value of $760,000. What amount should be credited to Paid-in Capital in Excess of Par as a result of the conversion?
a. $10,000.
b. $160,000.
c. $600,000.
d. $590,000.

(SO 7) **9.** Andrews Inc. issues a $497,000, 10% 3-year mortgage note on January 1. The note will be paid in three annual installments of $200,000, each payable at the end of the year. What is the amount of interest expense that should be recognized by Andrews Inc. in the second year?
a. $16,567.
b. $49,700.
c. $34,670.
d. $346,700.

(SO 10) **\*10.** On January 1, Besalius Inc. issued $1,000,000, 9% bonds for $939,000. The market rate of interest for these bonds is 10%. Interest is payable annually on December 31. Besalius uses the effective-interest method of amortizing bond discount. At the end of the first year, Besalius should report unamortized bond discount of:

a. $54,900.        c. $51,610.
b. $57,100.        d. $51,000.

**\*11.** On January 1, Dias Corporation issued $1,000,000, 14%, (SO 10) 5-year bonds with interest payable on July 1 and January 1. The bonds sold for $1,098,540. The market rate of interest for these bonds was 12%. On the first interest date, using the effective-interest method, the debit entry to Bond Interest Expense is for:
a. $60,000.        c. $65,912.
b. $76,898.        d. $131,825.

**\*12.** On January 1, Hurley Corporation issues $500,000, 5-year, (SO 11) 12% bonds at 96 with interest payable on July 1 and January 1. The entry on July 1 to record payment of bond interest and the amortization of bond discount using the straight-line method will include a:
a. debit to Interest Expense $30,000.
b. debit to Interest Expense $60,000.
c. credit to Discount on Bonds Payable $4,000.
d. credit to Discount on Bonds Payable $2,000.

**\*13.** For the bonds issued in question 9, above, what is the carry- (SO 11) ing value of the bonds at the end of the third interest period?
a. $486,000.        c. $472,000.
b. $488,000.        d. $464,000.

Go to the book's website,
**www.wiley.com/college/weygandt,**
for Additional Self-Study questions.

The Navigator

# QUESTIONS

**1.** Jill Loomis believes a current liability is a debt that can be expected to be paid in one year. Is Jill correct? Explain.

**2.** Frederickson Company obtains $40,000 in cash by signing a 9%, 6-month, $40,000 note payable to First Bank on July 1. Frederickson's fiscal year ends on September 30. What information should be reported for the note payable in the annual financial statements?

**3.** (a) Your roommate says, "Sales taxes are reported as an expense in the income statement." Do you agree? Explain.
(b) Planet Hollywood has cash proceeds from sales of $7,400. This amount includes $400 of sales taxes. Give the entry to record the proceeds.

**4.** Baylor University sold 10,000 season football tickets at $80 each for its five-game home schedule. What entries should be made (a) when the tickets were sold, and (b) after each game?

**5.** What is liquidity? What are two measures of liquidity?

**6.** Identify three taxes commonly withheld by the employer from an employee's gross pay.

**7.** (a) What are long-term liabilities? Give three examples.
(b) What is a bond?

**8.** (a) As a source of long-term financing, what are the major advantages of bonds over common stock? (b) What are the major disadvantages in using bonds for long-term financing?

**9.** Contrast the following types of bonds: (a) secured and unsecured, (b) term and serial, (c) registered and bearer, and (d) convertible and callable.

**10.** The following terms are important in issuing bonds: (a) face value, (b) contractual interest rate, (c) bond indenture, and (d) bond certificate. Explain each of these terms.

**11.** Describe the two major obligations incurred by a company when bonds are issued.

**12.** Assume that Koslowski Inc. sold bonds with a par value of $100,000 for $104,000. Was the market interest rate equal to, less than, or greater than the bonds' contractual interest rate? Explain.

**13.** If a 7%, 10-year, $800,000 bond is issued at par and interest is paid semiannually, what is the amount of the interest payment at the end of the first semiannual period?

**14.** If the Bonds Payable account has a balance of $900,000 and the Discount on Bonds Payable account has a balance of $40,000, what is the carrying value of the bonds?

**15.** Which accounts are debited and which are credited if a bond issue originally sold at a premium is redeemed before maturity at 97 immediately following the payment of interest?

**16.** Henricks Corporation is considering issuing a convertible bond. What is a convertible bond? Discuss the advantages of a convertible bond from the standpoint of (a) the bond-holders and (b) the issuing corporation.

**17.** Tim Brown, a friend of yours, has recently purchased a home for $125,000, paying $25,000 down and the remainder financed by a 10.5%, 20-year mortgage, payable at $998.38 per month. At the end of the first month, Tim receives a statement from the bank indicating that only $123.38 of principal was paid during the month. At this rate, he calculates that it will take over 67 years to pay off the mortgage. Is he right? Discuss.

**18.** In general, what are the requirements for the financial statement presentation of long-term liabilities?

***19.** Laura Hiatt is discussing the advantages of the effective-interest method of bond amortization with her accounting staff. What do you think Laura is saying?

***20.** Markham Corporation issues $500,000 of 9%, 5-year bonds on January 1, 2008, at 104. If Markham uses the effective-interest method in amortizing the premium, will the annual interest expense increase or decrease over the life of the bonds? Explain.

***21.** Tina Cruz and Dale Commons are discussing how the market price of a bond is determined. Tina believes that the market price of a bond is solely a function of the amount of the principal payment at the end of the term of a bond. Is she right? Discuss.

***22.** Explain the straight-line method of amortizing discount and premium on bonds payable.

***23.** DeWeese Corporation issues $400,000 of 8%, 5-year bonds on January 1, 2008, at 105. Assuming that the straight-line method is used to amortize the premium, what is the total amount of interest expense for 2008?

# BRIEF EXERCISES

**BE11-1**    Buffaloe Company has the following obligations at December 31: **(a)** a note payable for $100,000 due in 2 years, **(b)** a 10-year mortgage payable of $300,000 payable in ten $30,000 annual payments, **(c)** interest payable of $15,000 on the mortgage, and **(d)** accounts payable of $60,000. For each obligation, indicate whether it should be classified as a current liability. (Assume an operating cycle of less than one year.)

*Identify whether obligations are current liabilities.*

*(SO 1)*

**BE11-2**    Hanna Company borrows $80,000 on July 1 from the bank by signing a $80,000, 10%, one-year note payable.

**(a)** Prepare the journal entry to record the proceeds of the note.
**(b)** Prepare the journal entry to record accrued interest at December 31, assuming adjusting entries are made only at the end of the year.

*Prepare entries for an interest-bearing note payable.*

*(SO 2)*

**BE11-3**    Leister Auto Supply does not segregate sales and sales taxes at the time of sale. The register total for March 16 is $15,540. All sales are subject to a 5% sales tax. Compute sales taxes payable, and make the entry to record sales taxes payable and sales.

*Compute and record sales taxes payable.*

*(SO 3)*

**BE11-4**    Emporia State University sells 4,000 season basketball tickets at $180 each for its 12-game home schedule. Give the entry to record **(a)** the sale of the season tickets and **(b)** the revenue earned by playing the first home game.

*Prepare entries for unearned revenues.*

*(SO 3)*

**BE11-5**    Cindy Neuer's regular hourly wage rate is $16, and she receives an hourly rate of $24 for work in excess of 40 hours. During a January pay period, Cindy works 47 hours. Cindy's federal income tax withholding is $95, and she has no voluntary deductions. Compute Cindy Neuer's gross earnings and net pay for the pay period. Assume that the FICA tax rate is 8%.

*Compute gross earnings and net pay.*

*(SO 3)*

**BE11-6**    Data for Cindy Neuer are presented in BE11-5. Prepare the journal entries to record **(a)** Cindy's pay for the period and **(b)** the payment of Cindy's wages. Use January 15 for the end of the pay period and the payment date.

*Record a payroll and the payment of wages.*

*(SO 3)*

**BE11-7**    Mareska Inc. is considering two alternatives to finance its construction of a new $2 million plant.

**(a)** Issuance of 200,000 shares of common stock at the market price of $10 per share.
**(b)** Issuance of $2 million, 8% bonds at par.

*Compare bond versus stock financing.*

*(SO 4)*

Complete the following table, and indicate which alternative is preferable.

| | Issue Stock | Issue Bond |
|---|---|---|
| Income before interest and taxes | $700,000 | $700,000 |
| Interest expense from bonds | _____ | _____ |
| Income before income taxes | $ | $ |
| Income tax expense (30%) | _____ | _____ |
| Net income | $ | $ |
| Outstanding shares | _____ | 500,000 |
| Earnings per share | _____ | _____ |

*Prepare entries for bonds issued at face value.*

*(SO 5)*

**BE11-8**  Pruitt Corporation issued 3,000, 8%, 5-year, $1,000 bonds dated January 1, 2008, at 100.

**(a)** Prepare the journal entry to record the sale of these bonds on January 1, 2008.

**(b)** Prepare the journal entry to record the first interest payment on July 1, 2008 (interest payable semiannually), assuming no previous accrual of interest.

**(c)** Prepare the adjusting journal entry on December 31, 2008, to record interest expense.

*Prepare entries for bonds sold at a discount and a premium.*

*(SO 5)*

**BE11-9**  Ratzlaff Company issues $2 million, 10-year, 8% bonds at 97, with interest payable on July 1 and January 1.

**(a)** Prepare the journal entry to record the sale of these bonds on January 1, 2008.

**(b)** Assuming instead that the above bonds sold for 104, prepare the journal entry to record the sale of these bonds on January 1, 2008.

*Prepare entries for bonds issued.*

*(SO 5)*

**BE11-10**  Halloway Company has issued three different bonds during 2008. Interest is payable semiannually on each of these bonds.

**1.** On January 1, 2008, 1,000, 8%, 5-year, $1,000 bonds dated January 1, 2008, were issued at face value.

**2.** On July 1, $800,000, 9%, 5-year bonds dated July 1, 2008, were issued at 102.

**3.** On September 1, $200,000, 7%, 5-year bonds dated September 1, 2008, were issued at 98.

Prepare the journal entry to record each bond transaction at the date of issuance.

*Prepare entry for redemption of bonds.*

*(SO 6)*

**BE11-11**  The balance sheet for Lemay Company reports the following information on July 1, 2008.

| Long-term liabilities | | |
|---|---|---|
| Bonds payable | $1,000,000 | |
| Less: Discount on bonds payable | 60,000 | $940,000 |

Lemay decides to redeem these bonds at 101 after paying semiannual interest. Prepare the journal entry to record the redemption on July 1, 2008.

*Prepare entries for long-term notes payable.*

*(SO 7)*

**BE11-12**  Pickeril Inc. issues a $600,000, 10%, 10-year mortgage note on December 31, 2008, to obtain financing for a new building. The terms provide for semiannual installment payments of $48,145. Prepare the entry to record the mortgage loan on December 31, 2008, and the first installment payment.

*Prepare statement presentation of long-term liabilities.*

*(SO 8)*

**BE11-13**  Presented below are long-term liability items for Molini Company at December 31, 2008. Prepare the long-term liabilities section of the balance sheet for Molini Company.

| | |
|---|---|
| Bonds payable, due 2010 | $500,000 |
| Lease liability | 70,000 |
| Notes payable, due 2013 | 80,000 |
| Discount on bonds payable | 45,000 |

*Determine present value.*

*(SO 9)*

**\*BE11-14**  **(a)** What is the present value of $10,000 due 8 periods from now, discounted at 10%?

**(b)** What is the present value of $20,000 to be received at the end of each of 6 periods, discounted at 8%?

*Use effective-interest method of bond amortization.*

*(SO 10)*

**\*BE11-15**  Presented on the next page is the partial bond discount amortization schedule for Morales Corp. Morales uses the effective-interest method of amortization.

| Semiannual Interest Periods | Interest to Be Paid | Interest Expense to Be Recorded | Discount Amortization | Unamortized Discount | Bond Carrying Value |
|---|---|---|---|---|---|
| Issue date | | | | $62,311 | $937,689 |
| 1 | $45,000 | $46,884 | $1,884 | 60,427 | 939,573 |
| 2 | 45,000 | 46,979 | 1,979 | 58,448 | 941,552 |

**Instructions**

**(a)** Prepare the journal entry to record the payment of interest and the discount amortization at the end of period 1.

**(b)**  Explain why interest expense is greater than interest paid.

**(c)** Explain why interest expense will increase each period.

**\*BE11-16**   Deane Company issues $5 million, 10-year, 9% bonds at 96, with interest payable on July 1 and January 1. The straight-line method is used to amortize bond discount.

*Prepare entries for bonds issued at a discount.*

(SO 11)

**(a)** Prepare the journal entry to record the sale of these bonds on January 1, 2008.

**(b)** Prepare the journal entry to record interest expense and bond discount amortization on July 1, 2008, assuming no previous accrual of interest.

**\*BE11-17**   Coates Inc. issues $3 million, 5-year, 10% bonds at 102, with interest payable on July 1 and January 1. The straight-line method is used to amortize bond premium.

*Prepare entries for bonds issued at a premium.*

(SO 11)

**(a)** Prepare the journal entry to record the sale of these bonds on January 1, 2008.

**(b)** Prepare the journal entry to record interest expense and bond premium amortization on July 1, 2008, assuming no previous accrual of interest.

## EXERCISES

**E11-1**   Rob Judson Company had the following transactions involving notes payable.

*Prepare entries for interest-bearing notes.*

(SO 2)

| | |
|---|---|
| July 1, 2008 | Borrows $50,000 from Third National Bank by signing a 9-month, 12% note. |
| Nov. 1, 2008 | Borrows $60,000 from DeKalb State Bank by signing a 3-month, 10% note. |
| Dec. 31, 2008 | Prepares adjusting entries. |
| Feb. 1, 2009 | Pays principal and interest to DeKalb State Bank. |
| Apr. 1, 2009 | Pays principal and interest to Third National Bank. |

**Instructions**

Prepare journal entries for each of the transactions shown above.

**E11-2**   On June 1, Melendez Company borrows $90,000 from First Bank on a 6-month, $90,000, 12% note.

*Prepare entries for interest-bearing notes.*

(SO 2)

**Instructions**

**(a)** Prepare the entry on June 1.

**(b)** Prepare the adjusting entry on June 30.

**(c)** Prepare the entry at maturity (December 1), assuming monthly adjusting entries have been made through November 30.

**(d)** What was the total financing cost (interest expense)?

**E11-3**   In providing accounting services to small businesses, you encounter the following situations pertaining to cash sales.

*Journalize sales and related taxes.*

(SO 3)

**1.** Warkentinne Company rings up sales and sales taxes separately on its cash register. On April 10, the register totals are sales $30,000 and sales taxes $1,500.

**2.** Rivera Company does not segregate sales and sales taxes. Its register total for April 15 is $23,540, which includes a 7% sales tax.

**Instructions**

Prepare the entry to record the sales transactions and related taxes for each client.

**E11-4**   Guyer Company publishes a monthly sports magazine, *Fishing Preview*. Subscriptions to the magazine cost $20 per year. During November 2008, Guyer sells 12,000 subscriptions beginning with the December issue. Guyer prepares financial statements quarterly and recognizes

*Journalize unearned subscription revenue.*

(SO 3)

subscription revenue earned at the end of the quarter. The company uses the accounts Unearned Subscriptions and Subscription Revenue.

**Instructions**

**(a)** Prepare the entry in November for the receipt of the subscriptions.

**(b)** Prepare the adjusting entry at December 31, 2008, to record subscription revenue earned in December 2008.

**(c)** Prepare the adjusting entry at March 31, 2009, to record subscription revenue earned in the first quarter of 2009.

*Calculate and record net pay.*

*(SO 3)*

**E11-5** Don Walls's gross earnings for the week were $1,780, his federal income tax withholding was $301.63, and his FICA total was $135.73.

**Instructions**

**(a)** What was Walls's net pay for the week?

**(b)** Journalize the entry for the recording of his pay in the general journal. (*Note:* Use Salaries Payable; not Cash.)

**(c)** Record the issuing of the check for Walls's pay in the general journal.

*Record accrual of payroll taxes.*

*(SO 3)*

**E11-6** According to the accountant of Ulner Inc., its payroll taxes for the week were as follows: $198.40 for FICA taxes, $19.84 for federal unemployment taxes, and $133.92 for state unemployment taxes.

**Instruction**

Journalize the entry to record the accrual of the payroll taxes.

*Calculate and analyze current ratio and working capital.*

*(SO 3)*

**E11-7** The following financial data were reported by 3M Company for 2005 and 2006 (dollars in millions).

### 3M COMPANY
Balance Sheets (partial)

|  | 2006 | 2005 |
|---|---|---|
| Current assets |  |  |
| Cash and cash equivalents | $1,918 | $1,072 |
| Accounts receivable, net | 3,769 | 2,838 |
| Inventories | 2,601 | 2,162 |
| Other current assets | 658 | 1,043 |
| Total current assets | $8,946 | $7,115 |
| Current liabilities | $7,323 | $5,238 |

**Instructions**

**(a)** Calculate the current ratio and working capital for 3M for 2005 and 2006.

**(b)** Suppose at the end of 2006, 3M management used $300 million cash to pay off $300 million of accounts payable. How would the current ratio and working capital have changed?

*Evaluate statements about bonds.*

*(SO 4)*

**E11-8** Jim Thome has prepared the following list of statements about bonds.

1. Bonds are a form of interest-bearing notes payable.
2. When seeking long-term financing, an advantage of issuing bonds over issuing common stock is that stockholder control is not affected.
3. When seeking long-term financing, an advantage of issuing common stock over issuing bonds is that tax savings result.
4. Secured bonds have specific assets of the issuer pledged as collateral for the bonds.
5. Secured bonds are also known as debenture bonds.
6. Bonds that mature in installments are called term bonds.
7. A conversion feature may be added to bonds to make them more attractive to bond buyers.
8. The rate used to determine the amount of cash interest the borrower pays is called the stated rate.
9. Bond prices are usually quoted as a percentage of the face value of the bond.
10. The present value of a bond is the value at which it should sell in the marketplace.

**Instructions**

Identify each statement above as true or false. If false, indicate how to correct the statement.

**E11-9** Northeast Airlines is considering two alternatives for the financing of a purchase of a fleet of airplanes. These two alternatives are:

1. Issue 60,000 shares of common stock at $45 per share. (Cash dividends have not been paid nor is the payment of any contemplated).
2. Issue 10%, 10-year bonds at par for $2,700,000.

It is estimated that the company will earn $800,000 before interest and taxes as a result of this purchase. The company has an estimated tax rate of 30% and has 90,000 shares of common stock outstanding prior to the new financing.

**Instructions**
Determine the effect on net income and earnings per share for these two methods of financing.

*Compare two alternatives of financing—issuance of common stock vs. issuance of bonds.*
*(SO 4)*

**E11-10** On January 1, Neuer Company issued $500,000, 10%, 10-year bonds at par. Interest is payable semiannually on July 1 and January 1.

**Instructions**
Present journal entries to record the following.

(a) The issuance of the bonds.
(b) The payment of interest on July 1, assuming that interest was not accrued on June 30.
(c) The accrual of interest on December 31.

*Prepare entries for issuance of bonds, and payment and accrual of bond interest.*
*(SO 5)*

**E11-11** On January 1, Flory Company issued $300,000, 8%, 5-year bonds at face value. Interest is payable semiannually on July 1 and January 1.

**Instructions**
Prepare journal entries to record the following events.

(a) The issuance of the bonds.
(b) The payment of interest on July 1, assuming no previous accrual of interest.
(c) The accrual of interest on December 31.

*Prepare entries for bonds issued at face value.*
*(SO 5)*

**E11-12** Deng Company issued $500,000 of 5-year, 8% bonds at 97 on January 1, 2008. The bonds pay interest twice a year.

**Instructions**
(a) (1) Prepare the journal entry to record the issuance of the bonds.
(2) Compute the total cost of borrowing for these bonds.
(b) Repeat the requirements from part (a), assuming the bonds were issued at 105.

*Prepare entries to record issuance of bonds at discount and premium.*
*(SO 5)*

**E11-13** The following section is taken from Budke Corp.'s balance sheet at December 31, 2007.

| | |
|---|---|
| Current liabilities | |
| Bond interest payable | $ 72,000 |
| Long-term liabilities | |
| Bonds payable, 9%, due January 1, 2012 | 1,600,000 |

Interest is payable semiannually on January 1 and July 1. The bonds are callable on any interest date.

**Instructions**
(a) Journalize the payment of the bond interest on January 1, 2008.
(b) Assume that on January 1, 2008, after paying interest, Budke calls bonds having a face value of $600,000. The call price is 104. Record the redemption of the bonds.
(c) Prepare the entry to record the payment of interest on July 1, 2008, assuming no previous accrual of interest on the remaining bonds.

*Prepare entries for bond interest and redemption.*
*(SO 5, 6)*

**E11-14** Presented below and on the next page are three independent situations.

1. Sigel Corporation retired $130,000 face value, 12% bonds on June 30, 2008, at 102. The carrying value of the bonds at the redemption date was $117,500. The bonds pay semiannual interest, and the interest payment due on June 30, 2008, has been made and recorded.
2. Diaz Inc. retired $150,000 face value, 12.5% bonds on June 30, 2008, at 98. The carrying value of the bonds at the redemption date was $151,000. The bonds pay semiannual interest, and the interest payment due on June 30, 2008, has been made and recorded.

*Prepare entries for redemption of bonds and conversion of bonds into common stock.*
*(SO 6)*

**3.** Haas Company has $80,000, 8%, 12-year convertible bonds outstanding. These bonds were sold at face value and pay semiannual interest on June 30 and December 31 of each year. The bonds are convertible into 30 shares of Haas $5 par value common stock for each $1,000 worth of bonds. On December 31, 2008, after the bond interest has been paid, $20,000 face value bonds were converted. The market value of Haas common stock was $44 per share on December 31, 2008.

**Instructions**

For each independent situation above, prepare the appropriate journal entry for the redemption or conversion of the bonds.

*Prepare entries to record mortgage note and installment payments.*

*(SO 7)*

**E11-15**   Leoni Co. receives $240,000 when it issues a $240,000, 10%, mortgage note payable to finance the construction of a building at December 31, 2008. The terms provide for semiannual installment payments of $20,000 on June 30 and December 31.

**Instructions**

Prepare the journal entries to record the mortgage loan and the first two installment payments.

*Prepare long-term liabilities section.*

*(SO 8)*

**E11-16**   The adjusted trial balance for Gilligan Corporation at the end of the current year contained the following accounts.

| | |
|---|---:|
| Bond Interest Payable | $ 9,000 |
| Lease Liability | 89,500 |
| Bonds Payable, due 2013 | 180,000 |
| Premium on Bonds Payable | 32,000 |

**Instructions**

Prepare the long-term liabilities section of the balance sheet.

*Compute market price of bonds.*

*(SO 9)*

**\*E11-17**   Banzai Corporation is issuing $200,000 of 8%, 5-year bonds when potential bond investors want a return of 10%. Interest is payable semiannually.

**Instructions**

Compute the market price (present value) of the bonds.

*Prepare entries for issuance of bonds, payment of interest, and amortization of discount using effective-interest method*

*(SO 10)*

**\*E11-18**   Hrabik Corporation issued $600,000, 9%, 10-year bonds on January 1, 2008, for $562,613. This price resulted in an effective-interest rate of 10% on the bonds. Interest is payable semiannually on July 1 and January 1. Hrabik uses the effective-interest method to amortize bond premium or discount.

**Instructions**

Prepare the journal entries to record the following. (Round to the nearest dollar.)

**(a)** The issuance of the bonds.

**(b)** The payment of interest and the discount amortization on July 1, 2008, assuming that interest was not accrued on June 30.

**(c)** The accrual of interest and the discount amortization on December 31, 2008.

*Prepare entries for issuance of bonds, payment of interest, and amortization of premium using effective-interest method.*

*(SO 10)*

**\*E11-19**   Siburo Company issued $300,000, 11%, 10-year bonds on January 1, 2008, for $318,694. This price resulted in an effective-interest rate of 10% on the bonds. Interest is payable semiannually on July 1 and January 1. Siburo uses the effective-interest method to amortize bond premium or discount.

**Instructions**

Prepare the journal entries to record the following. (Round to the nearest dollar).

**(a)** The issuance of the bonds.

**(b)** The payment of interest and the premium amortization on July 1, 2008, assuming that interest was not accrued on June 30.

**(c)** The accrual of interest and the premium amortization on December 31, 2008.

*Prepare entries to record issuance of bonds, payment of interest, amortization of premium, and redemption at maturity.*

*(SO 5, 11)*

**\*E11-20**   Patino Company issued $400,000, 9%, 20-year bonds on January 1, 2008, at 103. Interest is payable semiannually on July 1 and January 1. Patino uses straight-line amortization for bond premium or discount.

**Instructions**

Prepare the journal entries to record the following.

**(a)** The issuance of the bonds.

**(b)** The payment of interest and the premium amortization on July 1, 2008, assuming that interest was not accrued on June 30.

**(c)** The accrual of interest and the premium amortization on December 31, 2008.

**(d)** The redemption of the bonds at maturity, assuming interest for the last interest period has been paid and recorded.

**\*E11-21** Joseph Company issued $800,000, 11%, 10-year bonds on December 31, 2007, for $730,000. Interest is payable semiannually on June 30 and December 31. Joseph Company uses the straight-line method to amortize bond premium or discount.

*Prepare entries to record issuance of bonds, payment of interest, amortization of discount, and redemption at maturity.*

*(SO 5, 11)*

**Instructions**

Prepare the journal entries to record the following.

**(a)** The issuance of the bonds.

**(b)** The payment of interest and the discount amortization on June 30, 2008.

**(c)** The payment of interest and the discount amortization on December 31, 2008.

**(d)** The redemption of the bonds at maturity, assuming interest for the last interest period has been paid and recorded.

# EXERCISES: SET B

Visit the book's website at **www.wiley.com/college/weygandt**, and choose the Student Companion site, to access Exercise Set B.

# PROBLEMS: SET A

**P11-1A** On January 1, 2008, the ledger of Mane Company contains the following liability accounts.

| | |
|---|---|
| Accounts Payable | $52,000 |
| Sales Taxes Payable | 7,700 |
| Unearned Service Revenue | 16,000 |

*Prepare current liability entries, adjusting entries, and current liabilities section.*

*(SO 1, 2, 3)*

GLS

During January the following selected transactions occurred.

Jan. 5 Sold merchandise for cash totaling $22,680, which includes 8% sales taxes.
   12 Provided services for customers who had made advance payments of $10,000. (Credit Service Revenue.)
   14 Paid state revenue department for sales taxes collected in December 2007 ($7,700).
   20 Sold 800 units of a new product on credit at $50 per unit, plus 8% sales tax.
   21 Borrowed $18,000 from UCLA Bank on a 3-month, 8%, $18,000 note.
   25 Sold merchandise for cash totaling $12,420, which includes 8% sales taxes.

**Instructions**

**(a)** Journalize the January transactions.

**(b)** Journalize the adjusting entries at January 31 for the outstanding notes payable. (*Hint:* Use one-third of a month for the UCLA Bank note.)

**(c)** Prepare the current liabilities section of the balance sheet at January 31, 2008. Assume no change in accounts payable.

*(c) Current liability total $81,840*

**P11-2A** The following are selected transactions of Winsky Company. Winsky prepares financial statements quarterly.

*Journalize and post note transactions; show balance sheet presentation.*

*(SO 2)*

Jan. 2 Purchased merchandise on account from Yokum Company, $30,000, terms 2/10, n/30.

Feb. 1 Issued a 9%, 2-month, $30,000 note to Yokum in payment of account.

Mar. 31 Accrued interest for 2 months on Yokum note.

Apr. 1 Paid face value and interest on Yokum note.

July 1 Purchased equipment from Korsak Equipment paying $11,000 in cash and signing a 10%, 3-month, $40,000 note.

Sept. 30 Accrued interest for 3 months on Korsak note.

Oct. 1 Paid face value and interest on Korsak note.

Dec. 1 Borrowed $15,000 from the Otago Bank by issuing a 3-month, 8% interest-bearing note with a face value of $15,000.

Dec. 31 Recognized interest expense for 1 month on Otago Bank note.

**Instructions**

**(a)** Prepare journal entries for the above transactions and events.

**(b)** Post to the accounts Notes Payable, Interest Payable, and Interest Expense.

**(c)** Show the balance sheet presentation of notes and interest payable at December 31.

*(d) $1,550*

**(d)** What is total interest expense for the year?

*Prepare entries to record issuance of bonds, interest accrual, and bond redemption.*

*(SO 5, 6, 8)*

**P11-3A** On May 1, 2008, Newby Corp. issued $600,000, 9%, 5-year bonds at face value. The bonds were dated May 1, 2008, and pay interest semiannually on May 1 and November 1. Financial statements are prepared annually on December 31.

**Instructions**

**(a)** Prepare the journal entry to record the issuance of the bonds.

**(b)** Prepare the adjusting entry to record the accrual of interest on December 31, 2008.

**(c)** Show the balance sheet presentation on December 31, 2008.

*(d) Int. exp. $18,000*

**(d)** Prepare the journal entry to record payment of interest on May 1, 2009, assuming no accrual of interest from January 1, 2009, to May 1, 2009.

**(e)** Prepare the journal entry to record payment of interest on November 1, 2009.

*(f) Loss $12,000*

**(f)** Assume that on November 1, 2009, Newby calls the bonds at 102. Record the redemption of the bonds.

*Prepare entries to record issuance of bonds, interest accrual, and bond redemption.*

*(SO 5, 6, 8)*

**P11-4A** Kusmaul Electric sold $500,000, 10%, 10-year bonds on January 1, 2008. The bonds were dated January 1 and paid interest on January 1 and July 1. The bonds were sold at 104.

**Instructions**

**(a)** Prepare the journal entry to record the issuance of the bonds on January 1, 2008.

**(b)** At December 31, 2008, the balance in the Premium on Bonds Payable account is $18,000. Show the balance sheet presentation of accrued interest and the bond liability at December 31, 2008.

*(c) Loss $9,000*

**(c)** On January 1, 2010, when the carrying value of the bonds was $516,000, the company redeemed the bonds at 105. Record the redemption of the bonds assuming that interest for the period has already been paid.

*Prepare installment payments schedule and journal entries for a mortgage note payable.*

*(SO 7)*

**P11-5A** Fordyce Electronics issues a $400,000, 8%, 10-year mortgage note on December 31, 2007. The proceeds from the note are to be used in financing a new research laboratory. The terms of the note provide for semiannual installment payments, exclusive of real estate taxes and insurance, of $29,433. Payments are due June 30 and December 31.

**Instructions**

*(b) June 30 Mortgage Notes Payable $13,433*

**(a)** Prepare an installment payments schedule for the first 2 years.

**(b)** Prepare the entries for (1) the loan and (2) the first two installment payments.

*(c) Current liability—2008: $29,639*

**(c)** Show how the total mortgage liability should be reported on the balance sheet at December 31, 2008.

*Prepare entries to record issuance of bonds, payment of interest, and amortization of bond premium using effective-interest method.*

*(SO 5, 10)*

**\*P11-6A** On July 1, 2008, Atwater Corporation issued $2,000,000 face value, 10%, 10-year bonds at $2,271,813. This price resulted in an effective-interest rate of 8% on the bonds. Atwater uses the effective-interest method to amortize bond premium or discount. The bonds pay semiannual interest July 1 and January 1.

**Instructions**

(Round all computations to the nearest dollar.)

**(a)** Prepare the journal entry to record the issuance of the bonds on July 1, 2008.

**(b)** Prepare an amortization table through December 31, 2009 (3 interest periods) for this bond issue.

*(c) Amortization $9,127*

**(c)** Prepare the journal entry to record the accrual of interest and the amortization of the premium on December 31, 2008.

**(d)** Prepare the journal entry to record the payment of interest and the amortization of the premium on July 1, 2009, assuming no accrual of interest on June 30.

**(e)** Prepare the journal entry to record the accrual of interest and the amortization of the premium on December 31, 2009.

*(d) Amortization $9,493*

*(e) Amortization $9,872*

**\*P11-7A**    On July 1, 2008, Rossillon Company issued $4,000,000 face value, 8%, 10-year bonds at $3,501,514. This price resulted in an effective-interest rate of 10% on the bonds. Rossillon uses the effective-interest method to amortize bond premium or discount. The bonds pay semiannual interest July 1 and January 1.

*Prepare entries to record issuance of bonds, payment of interest, and amortization of discount using effective-interest method. In addition, answer questions.*

**Instructions**

(Round all computations to the nearest dollar.)

*(SO 5, 10)*

**(a)** Prepare the journal entries to record the following transactions.
   **(1)** The issuance of the bonds on July 1, 2008.
   **(2)** The accrual of interest and the amortization of the discount on December 31, 2008.
   **(3)** The payment of interest and the amortization of the discount on July 1, 2009, assuming no accrual of interest on June 30.
   **(4)** The accrual of interest and the amortization of the discount on December 31, 2009.
**(b)** Show the proper balance sheet presentation for the liability for bonds payable on the December 31, 2009, balance sheet.
**(c)** ━━━━━━▶ Provide the answers to the following questions in letter form.
   **(1)** What amount of interest expense is reported for 2009?
   **(2)** Would the bond interest expense reported in 2009 be the same as, greater than, or less than the amount that would be reported if the straight-line method of amortization were used?
   **(3)** Determine the total cost of borrowing over the life of the bond.
   **(4)** Would the total bond interest expense be greater than, the same as, or less than the total interest expense that would be reported if the straight-line method of amortization were used?

*(a) (3) Amortization $15,830*

*(a) (4) Amortization $16,621*

*(b) Bond carrying value $3,549,041*

**\*P11-8A**    Soprano Electric sold $3,000,000, 10%, 10-year bonds on January 1, 2008. The bonds were dated January 1 and pay interest July 1 and January 1. Soprano Electric uses the straight-line method to amortize bond premium or discount. The bonds were sold at 104. Assume no interest is accrued on June 30.

*Prepare entries to record issuance of bonds, interest accrual, and straight-line amortization for 2 years.*

*(SO 5, 11)*

**Instructions**

**(a)** Prepare the journal entry to record the issuance of the bonds on January 1, 2008.
**(b)** Prepare a bond premium amortization schedule for the first 4 interest periods.
**(c)** Prepare the journal entries for interest and the amortization of the premium in 2008 and 2009.
**(d)** Show the balance sheet presentation of the bond liability at December 31, 2009.

*(b) Amortization $6,000*

*(d) Premium on bonds payable $96,000*

**\*P11-9A**    Elkins Company sold $2,500,000, 8%, 10-year bonds on July 1, 2008. The bonds were dated July 1, 2008, and pay interest July 1 and January 1. Elkins Company uses the straight-line method to amortize bond premium or discount. Assume no interest is accrued on June 30.

*Prepare entries to record issuance of bonds, interest, and straight-line amortization of bond premium and discount.*

*(SO 5, 11)*

**Instructions**

**(a)** Prepare all the necessary journal entries to record the issuance of the bonds and bond interest expense for 2008, assuming that the bonds sold at 104.
**(b)** Prepare journal entries as in part (a) assuming that the bonds sold at 98.
**(c)** Show balance sheet presentation for each bond issue at December 31, 2008.

*(a) Amortization $5,000*
*(b) Amortization $2,500*
*(c) Premium on bonds payable $95,000*
*Discount on bonds payable $47,500*

**\*P11-10A**    The following is taken from the Pinkston Company balance sheet.

*Prepare entries to record interest payments, straight-line premium amortization, and redemption of bonds.*

*(SO 6, 11)*

**PINKSTON COMPANY**
Balance Sheet (partial)
December 31, 2008

| | | |
|---|---:|---:|
| Current liabilities | | |
| Bond interest payable (for 6 months from July 1 to December 31) | | $  105,000 |
| Long-term liabilities | | |
| Bonds payable, 7% due January 1, 2019 | $3,000,000 | |
| Add: Premium on bonds payable | 200,000 | $3,200,000 |

Interest is payable semiannually on January 1 and July 1. The bonds are callable on any semi-annual interest date. Pinkston uses straight-line amortization for any bond premium or discount. From December 31, 2008, the bonds will be outstanding for an additional 10 years (120 months).

**Instructions**

(b) Amortization $10,000

(c) Gain $64,000

(d) Amortization $6,000

(a) Journalize the payment of bond interest on January 1, 2009.
(b) Prepare the entry to amortize bond premium and to pay the interest due on July 1, 2009, assuming no accrual of interest on June 30.
(c) Assume that on July 1, 2009, after paying interest, Pinkston Company calls bonds having a face value of $1,200,000. The call price is 101. Record the redemption of the bonds.
(d) Prepare the adjusting entry at December 31, 2009, to amortize bond premium and to accrue interest on the remaining bonds.

# PROBLEMS: SET B

*Prepare current liability entries, adjusting entries, and current liabilities section.*

(SO 1, 2, 3)

**P11-1B** On January 1, 2008, the ledger of Payless Software Company contains the following liability accounts.

| | |
|---|---|
| Accounts Payable | $42,500 |
| Sales Taxes Payable | 5,800 |
| Unearned Service Revenue | 15,000 |

During January the following selected transactions occurred.

Jan. 1 Borrowed $30,000 in cash from Amsterdam Bank on a 4-month, 8%, $30,000 note.
5 Sold merchandise for cash totaling $10,400, which includes 4% sales taxes.
12 Provided services for customers who had made advance payments of $9,000. (Credit Service Revenue.)
14 Paid state treasurer's department for sales taxes collected in December 2007, $5,800.
20 Sold 900 units of a new product on credit at $52 per unit, plus 4% sales tax.
25 Sold merchandise for cash totaling $18,720, which includes 4% sales taxes.

**Instructions**

(c) Current liability total $81,692

(a) Journalize the January transactions.
(b) Journalize the adjusting entries at January 31 for the outstanding notes payable.
(c) Prepare the current liabilities section of the balance sheet at January 31, 2008. Assume no change in accounts payable.

*Prepare entries to record issuance of bonds, interest accrual, and bond redemption.*

(SO 5, 6, 8)

**P11-2B** On June 1, 2008, Logsdon Corp. issued $1,500,000, 8%, 5-year bonds at face value. The bonds were dated June 1, 2008, and pay interest semiannually on June 1 and December 1. Financial statements are prepared annually on December 31.

**Instructions**

(d) Int. exp. $50,000

(f) Loss $30,000

(a) Prepare the journal entry to record the issuance of the bonds.
(b) Prepare the adjusting entry to record the accrual of interest on December 31, 2008.
(c) Show the balance sheet presentation on December 31, 2008.
(d) Prepare the journal entry to record payment of interest on June 1, 2009, assuming no accrual of interest from January 1, 2009, to June 1, 2009.
(e) Prepare the journal entry to record payment of interest on December 1, 2009.
(f) Assume that on December 1, 2009, Logsdon calls the bonds at 102. Record the redemption of the bonds.

*Prepare entries to record issuance of bonds, interest accrual, and bond redemption.*

(SO 5, 6, 8)

**P11-3B** Merendo Co. sold $600,000, 9%, 10-year bonds on January 1, 2008. The bonds were dated January 1, and interest is paid on January 1 and July 1. The bonds were sold at 105.

**Instructions**

(a) Prepare the journal entry to record the issuance of the bonds on January 1, 2008.
(b) At December 31, 2008, the balance in the Premium on Bonds Payable account is $27,000. Show the balance sheet presentation of accrued interest and the bond liability at December 31, 2008.

**(c)** On January 1, 2010, when the carrying value of the bonds was $624,000, the company redeemed the bonds at 105. Record the redemption of the bonds assuming that interest for the period has already been paid.

**P11-4B**    Egan Electronics issues an $500,000, 8%, 10-year mortgage note on December 31, 2008, to help finance a plant expansion program. The terms provide for semiannual installment payments, not including real estate taxes and insurance, of $36,791. Payments are due June 30 and December 31.

**Instructions**
**(a)** Prepare an installment payments schedule for the first 2 years.
**(b)** Prepare the entries for (1) the mortgage loan and (2) the first two installment payments.
**(c)** Show how the total mortgage liability should be reported on the balance sheet at December 31, 2009.

**\*P11-5B**    On July 1, 2008, Matlock Satellites issued $2,700,000 face value, 9%, 10-year bonds at $2,531,760. This price resulted in an effective-interest rate of 10% on the bonds. Matlock uses the effective-interest method to amortize bond premium or discount. The bonds pay semiannual interest July 1 and January 1.

**Instructions**
(Round all computations to the nearest dollar.)
**(a)** Prepare the journal entry to record the issuance of the bonds on July 1, 2008.
**(b)** Prepare an amortization table through December 31, 2009 (3 interest periods) for this bond issue.
**(c)** Prepare the journal entry to record the accrual of interest and the amortization of the discount on December 31, 2008.
**(d)** Prepare the journal entry to record the payment of interest and the amortization of the discount on July 1, 2009, assuming that interest was not accrued on June 30.
**(e)** Prepare the journal entry to record the accrual of interest and the amortization of the discount on December 31, 2009.

**\*P11-6B**    On July 1, 2008, S. Posadas Chemical Company issued $3,000,000 face value, 10%, 10-year bonds at $3,407,720. This price resulted in an 8% effective-interest rate on the bonds. Posadas uses the effective-interest method to amortize bond premium or discount. The bonds pay semiannual interest on each July 1 and January 1.

**Instructions**
(Round all computations to the nearest dollar.)
**(a)** Prepare the journal entries to record the following transactions.
   **(1)** The issuance of the bonds on July 1, 2008.
   **(2)** The accrual of interest and the amortization of the premium on December 31, 2008.
   **(3)** The payment of interest and the amortization of the premium on July 1, 2009, assuming no accrual of interest on June 30.
   **(4)** The accrual of interest and the amortization of the premium on December 31, 2009.
**(b)** Show the proper balance sheet presentation for the liability for bonds payable on the December 31, 2009, balance sheet.
**(c)** ▬▬▬▶ Provide the answers to the following questions in letter form.
   **(1)** What amount of interest expense is reported for 2009?
   **(2)** Would the bond interest expense reported in 2009 be the same as, greater than, or less than the amount that would be reported if the straight-line method of amortization were used?
   **(3)** Determine the total cost of borrowing over the life of the bond.
   **(4)** Would the total bond interest expense be greater than, the same as, or less than the total interest expense if the straight-line method of amortization were used?

**\*P11-7B**    Roeder Company sold $4,000,000, 9%, 20-year bonds on January 1, 2008. The bonds were dated January 1, 2008, and pay interest on January 1 and July 1. Roeder Company uses the straight-line method to amortize bond premium or discount. The bonds were sold at 96. Assume no interest is accrued on June 30.

**Instructions**
**(a)** Prepare the journal entry to record the issuance of the bonds on January 1, 2008.
**(b)** Prepare a bond discount amortization schedule for the first 4 interest periods.

**(c)** Prepare the journal entries for interest and the amortization of the discount in 2008 and 2009.

**(d)** Show the balance sheet presentation of the bond liability at December 31, 2009.

(d) Discount on bonds
    payable $144,000

*Prepare entries to record
issuance of bonds, interest, and
straight-line amortization of
bond premium and discount.*

(SO 5, 11)

(a) Amortization $7,500
(b) Amortization $10,000
(c) Premium on bonds
    payable $135,000
    Discount on bonds
    payable $180,000

*Prepare entries to record
interest payments, straight-line
discount amortization, and
redemption of bonds.*

(SO 6, 11)

**\*P11-8B**  Karjala Corporation sold $5,000,000, 8%, 10-year bonds on January 1, 2008. The bonds were dated January 1, 2008, and pay interest on July 1 and January 1. Karjala Corporation uses the straight-line method to amortize bond premium or discount. Assume no interest is accrued on June 30.

**Instructions**

**(a)** Prepare all the necessary journal entries to record the issuance of the bonds and bond interest expense for 2008, assuming that the bonds sold at 103.

**(b)** Prepare journal entries as in part (a) assuming that the bonds sold at 96.

**(c)** Show balance sheet presentation for each bond issue at December 31, 2008.

**\*P11-9B**  The following is taken from the Magana Corp. balance sheet.

**MAGANA CORPORATION**
Balance Sheet (partial)
December 31, 2008

Current liabilities
  Bond interest payable (for 6 months
    from July 1 to December 31)       $ 84,000
Long-term liabilities
  Bonds payable, 7%, due
    January 1, 2019     $2,400,000
    Less: Discount on bonds payable   90,000   $2,310,000

Interest is payable semiannually on January 1 and July 1. The bonds are callable on any semiannual interest date. Magana uses straight-line amortization for any bond premium or discount. From December 31, 2008, the bonds will be outstanding for an additional 10 years (120 months).

**Instructions**
(Round all computations to the nearest dollar).

**(a)** Journalize the payment of bond interest on January 1, 2009.

(b) Amortization $4,500

**(b)** Prepare the entry to amortize bond discount and to pay the interest due on July 1, 2009, assuming that interest was not accrued on June 30.

(c) Loss $36,500

**(c)** Assume that on July 1, 2009, after paying interest, Magana Corp. calls bonds having a face value of $800,000. The call price is 101. Record the redemption of the bonds.

(d) Amortization $3,000

**(d)** Prepare the adjusting entry at December 31, 2009, to amortize bond discount and to accrue interest on the remaining bonds.

## PROBLEMS: SET C

Visit the book's website at **www.wiley.com/college/weygandt**, and choose the Student Companion site, to access Problem Set C.

## COMPREHENSIVE PROBLEM: CHAPTERS 6–11

Paris Company and Troyer Company are competing businesses. Both began operations 6 years ago and are quite similar in most respects. The current balance sheet data for the two companies are shown on the next page.

| | Paris Company | Troyer Company |
|---|---|---|
| Cash | $ 70,300 | $ 48,400 |
| Accounts receivable | 309,700 | 312,500 |
| Allowance for doubtful accounts | (13,600) | –0– |
| Merchandise inventory | 463,900 | 520,200 |
| Plant and equipment | 255,300 | 257,300 |
| Accumulated depreciation, plant and equipment | (112,650) | (189,850) |
| Total assets | 972,950 | $948,550 |
| Current liabilities | $440,200 | $436,500 |
| Long-term liabilities | 78,000 | 80,000 |
| Total liabilities | 518,200 | 516,500 |
| Stockholders' equity | 454,750 | 432,050 |
| Total liabilities and stockholders' equity | $972,950 | $948,550 |

You have been engaged as a consultant to conduct a review of the two companies. Your goal is to determine which of them is in the stronger financial position.

Your review of their financial statements quickly reveals that the two companies have not followed the same accounting practices. The differences and your conclusions regarding them are summarized below.

1. Paris Company has used the allowance method of accounting for bad debts. A review shows that the amount of its write-offs each year has been quite close to the allowances that have been provided. It therefore seems reasonable to have confidence in its current estimate of bad debts.

   Troyer Company has used the direct write-off method for bad debts, and it has been somewhat slow to write off its uncollectible accounts. Based upon an aging analysis and review of its accounts receivable, it is estimated that $20,000 of its existing accounts will probably prove to be uncollectible.

2. Paris Company has determined the cost of its merchandise inventory on a LIFO basis. The result is that its inventory appears on the balance sheet at an amount that is below its current replacement cost. Based upon a detailed physical examination of its merchandise on hand, the current replacement cost of its inventory is estimated at $517,000.

   Troyer Company has used the FIFO method of valuing its merchandise inventory. Its ending inventory appears on the balance sheet at an amount that quite closely approximates its current replacement cost.

3. Paris Company estimated a useful life of 12 years and a salvage value of $30,000 for its plant and equipment. It has been depreciating them on a straight-line basis.

   Troyer Company has the same type of plant and equipment. However, it estimated a useful life of 10 years and a salvage value of $10,000. It has been depreciating its plant and equipment using the double-declining-balance method.

   Based upon engineering studies of these types of plant and equipment, you conclude that Troyer's estimates and method for calculating depreciation are the more appropriate.

4. Among its current liabilities, Paris has included the portions of long-term liabilities that become due within the next year. Troyer has not done so.

   You find that $16,000 of Troyer's $80,000 of long-term liabilities are due to be repaid in the current year.

**Instructions**
(a) Revise the balance sheets presented above so that the data are comparable and reflect the current financial position for each of the two companies.
(b) ➤ Prepare a brief report to your client stating your conclusions.

(a) Total assets:
Paris $950,325
Troyer $928,550

## CONTINUING COOKIE CHRONICLE

(*Note*: This is a continuation of the Cookie Chronicle from Chapters 1 through 10.)

**CCC11** Natalie is thinking of repaying all amounts outstanding to her grandmother. Recall that Cookie Creations borrowed $2,000 on November 16, 2007, from Natalie's grandmother. Interest on the note is 6% per year, and the note plus interest was to be repaid in 24 months. Recall that a monthly adjusting journal entry was prepared for the months of November 2007 (1/2 month), December 2007, and January 2008.

Natalie needs to know the interest expense and interest payable, and she needs to record the loan repayment.

*Go to the book's website,*
**www.wiley.com/college/weygandt,**
*to see the completion of this problem.*

# BROADENING YOUR PERSPECTIVE

## FINANCIAL REPORTING AND ANALYSIS

## Financial Reporting Problem
### PepsiCo

**BYP11-1** The financial statements of PepsiCo and the Notes to Consolidated Financial Statements appear in Appendix A.

**Instructions**
Refer to PepsiCo's financial statements and answer the following questions about current and long-term liabilities.

**(a)** What were PepsiCo's total current liabilities at December 31, 2005? What was the increase/decrease in PepsiCo's total current liabilities from the prior year?

**(b)** In PepsiCo's Note 2 ("Our Significant Accounting Policies"), the company explains the nature of its contingencies. Under what conditions does PepsiCo recognize (record and report) liabilities for contingencies?

**(c)** What were the components of total current liabilities on December 31, 2005?

**(d)** What was PepsiCo's total long-term debt (excluding deferred income taxes) at December 31, 2005? What was the increase/decrease in total long-term debt (excluding deferred income taxes) from the prior year? What does Note 9 to the financial statements indicate about the composition of PepsiCo's long-term debt obligation?

**(e)** What are the total long-term contractual commitments that PepsiCo reports as of December 31, 2005? (See Note 9.)

## Comparative Analysis Problem
### PepsiCo vs. Coca-Cola

**BYP11-2** PepsiCo's financial statements are presented in Appendix A. Coca-Cola's financial statements are presented in Appendix B.

**Instructions**
**(a)** At December 31, 2005, what was PepsiCo's largest current liability account? What were its total current liabilities? At December 31, 2005, what was Coca-Cola's largest current liability account? What were its total current liabilities?

**(b)** Based on information contained in those financial statements, compute the following 2005 values for each company.
**(1)** Working capital.
**(2)** Current ratio.

**(c)** What conclusions concerning the relative liquidity of these companies can be drawn from these data?

**(d)** Based on the information contained in these financial statements, compute the following 2005 ratios for each company.

  **(1)** Debt (excluding "deferred income taxes") to total assets.

  **(2)** Times interest earned.

**(e)** What conclusions concerning the companies' long-run solvency can be drawn from these ratios?

# Exploring the Web

**BYP11-3**    Bond or debt securities pay a stated rate of interest. This rate of interest is dependent on the risk associated with the investment. Moody's Investment Service provides ratings for companies that issue debt securities.

**Address: www.moodys.com**, or go to **www.wiley.com/college/weygandt**

**Steps:** From Moody's homepage, choose **About Moody's**.

**Instructions**

**(a)** What year did Moody's introduce the first bond rating? (See Moody's History.)

**(b)** What is the total amount of debt securities that Moody's analysts "track"? (See **An Introduction**.)

**(c)** What characteristics must debt ratings have in order to be useful to the capital markets? (See **Understand Risk: The Truth About Credit Ratings**.)

# CRITICAL THINKING

# Decision Making Across the Organization

**BYP11-4**    On January 1, 2006, Bailey Corporation issued $6,000,000 of 5-year, 8% bonds at 96. The bonds pay interest semiannually on July 1 and January 1. By January 1, 2008, the market rate of interest for bonds of similar risk had risen. As a result, the market value of the Bailey Corporation bonds was $5,000,000 on January 1, 2008—below their carrying value.

Debbie Bailey, president of the company, suggests repurchasing all of these bonds in the open market at the $5,000,000 price. To do so, the company would have to issue $5,000,000 (face value) of new 10-year, 11% bonds at par. The president asks you, as controller, "What is the feasibility of my proposed repurchase plan?"

**Instructions**

With the class divided into groups, answer the following.

*__(a)__ What is the carrying value of the outstanding Bailey Corporation 5-year bonds on January 1, 2008? (Assume straight-line amortization.)

**(b)** Prepare the journal entry to retire the 5-year bonds on January 1, 2008. Prepare the journal entry to issue the new 10-year bonds.

**(c)** Prepare a list of talking points for your use in meeting with the president in response to her request for advice. List the economic factors that you believe should be considered for her repurchase proposal.

# Communication Activity

**BYP11-5**    Ken Robson, president of the Robson Corporation, is considering the issuance of bonds to finance an expansion of his business. He has asked you to (a) discuss the advantages of bonds over common stock financing, (b) indicate the types of bonds he might issue, and (c) explain the issuing procedures used in bond transactions.

**Instructions**

Write a memo to the president, answering his request.

## Ethics Case

**BYP11-6**   Sam Farr is the president, founder, and majority owner of Galena Medical Corporation, an emerging medical technology products company. Galena is in dire need of additional capital to keep operating and to bring several promising products to final development, testing, and production. Sam, as owner of 51% of the outstanding stock, manages the company's operations. He places heavy emphasis on research and development and on long-term growth. The other principal stockholder is Jill Hutton who, as a nonemployee investor, owns 40% of the stock. Jill would like to deemphasize the R&D functions and emphasize the marketing function, to maximize short-run sales and profits from existing products. She believes this strategy would raise the market price of Galena's stock.

All of Sam's personal capital and borrowing power is tied up in his 51% stock ownership. He knows that any offering of additional shares of stock will dilute his controlling interest because he won't be able to participate in such an issuance. But, Jill has money and would likely buy enough shares to gain control of Galena. She then would dictate the company's future direction, even if it meant replacing Sam as president and CEO.

The company already has considerable debt. Raising additional debt will be costly, will adversely affect Galena's credit rating, and will increase the company's reported losses due to the growth in interest expense. Jill and the other minority stockholders express opposition to the assumption of additional debt, fearing the company will be pushed to the brink of bankruptcy. Wanting to maintain his control and to preserve the direction of "his" company, Sam is doing everything to avoid a stock issuance. He is contemplating a large issuance of bonds, even if it means the bonds are issued with a high effective-interest rate.

**Instructions**
**(a)** Who are the stakeholders in this situation?
**(b)** What are the ethical issues in this case?
**(c)** What would you do if you were Sam?

##  "All About You" Activity

**BYP11-7**   As indicated in the "All About You" feature in this chapter (page 496), medical costs are substantial and rising. But will medical costs be your most substantial expense over your lifetime? Not likely. Will it be housing or food? Again, not likely. The answer is in the *Accounting Across the Organization* box on page 478: taxes. On average, Americans work 79 days to afford their federal taxes. Companies, too, have large tax burdens. They look very hard at tax issues in deciding where to build their plants and where to locate their administrative headquarters.

**Instructions**
**(a)** Determine what your state income taxes are if your taxable income is $60,000 and you file as a single taxpayer in the state in which you live.
**(b)** Assume that you own a home worth $200,000 in your community and the tax rate is 2.1%. Compute the property taxes you would pay.
**(c)** Assume that the total gasoline bill for your automobile is $1,200 a year (400 gallons at $3 per gallon). What are the amounts of state and federal taxes that you pay on the $1,200?
**(d)** Assume that your purchases for the year total $9,000. Of this amount, $5,000 was for food and prescription drugs. What is the amount of sales tax you would pay on these purchases? (Note that many states do not have a sales tax for food or prescription drug purchases. Does yours?).
**(e)** Determine what your Social Security taxes are if your income is $60,000.
**(f)** Determine what your federal income taxes are if your taxable income is $60,000 and you file as a single taxpayer.
**(g)** Determine your *total* taxes paid based on the above calculations, and determine the percentage of income that you would pay in taxes based on the following formula: Total taxes paid ÷ Total income.

## Answers to Insight and Accounting Across the Organization Questions

### Taxes Are the Largest Slice of the Pie, p. 478

Q: If the information on 2006 taxation depicted your spending patterns, on what date (starting on January 1) will you have earned enough to pay all of your taxes?

A: *As indicated in the story, it takes 116 (77 + 39) days to pay your taxes. Thus, April 26 is Tax Freedom Day. Tax Freedom Day for the past 26 years has occurred in April, except for the year 2000 when it occurred in May.*

### When to Go Long-Term, p. 486

Q: Based on this story, what is a good general rule to use in choosing between short-term and long-term financing?

A: *In general, it is best to finance short-term assets with short-term liabilities and long-term assets with long-term liabilities, in order to reduce the likelihood of a liquidity crunch such as this.*

### Search for Your Best Rate, p. 494

Q: What should you do if the dealer "trash-talks" your lender, or refuses to sell you the car for the agreed-upon price unless you get your car loan through the dealer?

A: *Experts suggest that if the dealer "trash-talks" your lender or refuses to sell you the car at the agreed-upon price unless you get your financing through the dealer, get up and leave, and buy your car somewhere else.*

### They Thought It Was Easy Money, p. 495

Q: What do you think happens when a company violates its debt covenants?

A: *If a company violates its debt covenants the lender can "call the loan." This means that the company is required to repay the loan immediately, even though the maturity date of the loan has not been reached. In practice, many lenders will renegotiate the terms of the loan rather than force the company to repay immediately.*

## Authors' Comments on *All About You:* Your Boss Wants to Know If You Ran Today, p. 496

On the one hand, a company's insurance premiums would be substantially lower if its employees did not smoke and if they were in better shape. Some argue that employees with unhealthy habits place a burden on healthy employees because they increase the share of insurance premiums that all employees have to pay, and because unhealthy employees miss more days of work. On the other hand, some argue that this approach discriminates in favor of "healthy" people. Also, it is not illegal to smoke or to be overweight. Should an employer really be able to dictate against non-illegal behavior that employees do on their own time? The cost of health care is a huge problem in the U.S., with no easy answers.

## Answers to PepsiCo Review It Questions

### Question 2, p. 481

Under the heading of current liabilities, PepsiCo has listed short-term obligations, accounts payable and other current liabilities, and income taxes payable.

### Question 2, p. 492

An examination of PepsiCo's statement of cash flows indicates the following reductions of debt: payments of long-term debt, $177 million, and payments of short-term borrowings of more than 3 months, $85 million.

## Answers to Self-Study Questions

**1.** a    **2.** d    **3.** b    **4.** b    **5.** c    **6.** a    **7.** b    **8.** d    **9.** c    *10. b    *11. c    *12. d    *13. a

# Corporations: Organization, Stock Transactions, Dividends, and Retained Earnings

## STUDY OBJECTIVES

*After studying this chapter, you should be able to:*

1 Identify the major characteristics of a corporation.
2 Record the issuance of common stock.
3 Explain the accounting for treasury stock.
4 Differentiate preferred stock from common stock.
5 Prepare the entries for cash dividends and stock dividends.
6 Identify the items that are reported in a retained earnings statement.
7 Prepare and analyze a comprehensive stockholders' equity section.

*The Navigator*

## ✓ The Navigator

| | |
|---|---|
| Understand **Concepts for Review** | ■ |
| Read **Feature Story** | ■ |
| Scan **Study Objectives** | ■ |
| Read **Preview** | ■ |
| Read text and answer **Before You Go On** | |
| p. 540 ■  p. 543 ■  p. 546 ■  p. 550 ■ | |
| p. 552 ■  p. 559 ■  p. 563 ■  p. 566 ■ | |
| Work **Demonstration Problem** | ■ |
| Review **Summary of Study Objectives** | ■ |
| Answer **Self-Study Questions** | ■ |
| Complete **Assignments** | ■ |

## Feature Story

### "HAVE YOU DRIVEN A FORD LATELY?"

A company that has produced such renowned successes as the Model T and the Mustang, and such a dismal failure as the Edsel, would have some interesting tales to tell. Henry Ford was a defiant visionary from the day

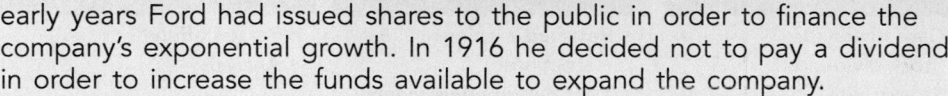

Ford Motor Company (*www.ford.com*) was formed in 1903. His goal from day one was to design a car he could mass-produce and sell at a price that was affordable to the masses. In short order he accomplished this goal. By 1920, 60% of all vehicles on U.S. roads were Fords.

Henry Ford was intolerant of anything that stood between him and success. In the early years Ford had issued shares to the public in order to finance the company's exponential growth. In 1916 he decided not to pay a dividend in order to increase the funds available to expand the company.

The shareholders sued. Henry Ford's reaction was swift and direct: If the shareholders didn't see things his way, he would get rid of them. In 1919 the Ford family purchased 100 percent of the outstanding shares of Ford, eliminating any outside "interference." It was over 35 years before shares were again issued to the public.

Ford Motor Company has continued to evolve and grow over the years into one of the largest international corporations. Today there are nearly a billion shares of publicly traded Ford stock outstanding. But some aspects of the company have changed very little. The Ford family still retains a significant stake in Ford Motor Company. In a move Henry Ford might have supported, top management recently decided to centralize decision making—that is, to have more key decisions made by top management, rather than by division managers. And, reminiscent of Henry Ford's most famous car, the company is attempting to make a "global car"—a mass-produced car that can be sold around the world with only minor changes.

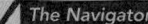 The Navigator

# Inside Chapter 12

Corporations like Ford Motor Company have substantial resources. In fact, the corporation is the dominant form of business organization in the United States in terms of dollar volume of sales and earnings, and number of employees. All of the 500 largest companies in the United States are corporations. In this chapter we will explain the essential features of a corporation and the accounting for a corporation's capital stock transactions, dividends, and retained earnings.

The content and organization of Chapter 12 are as follows.

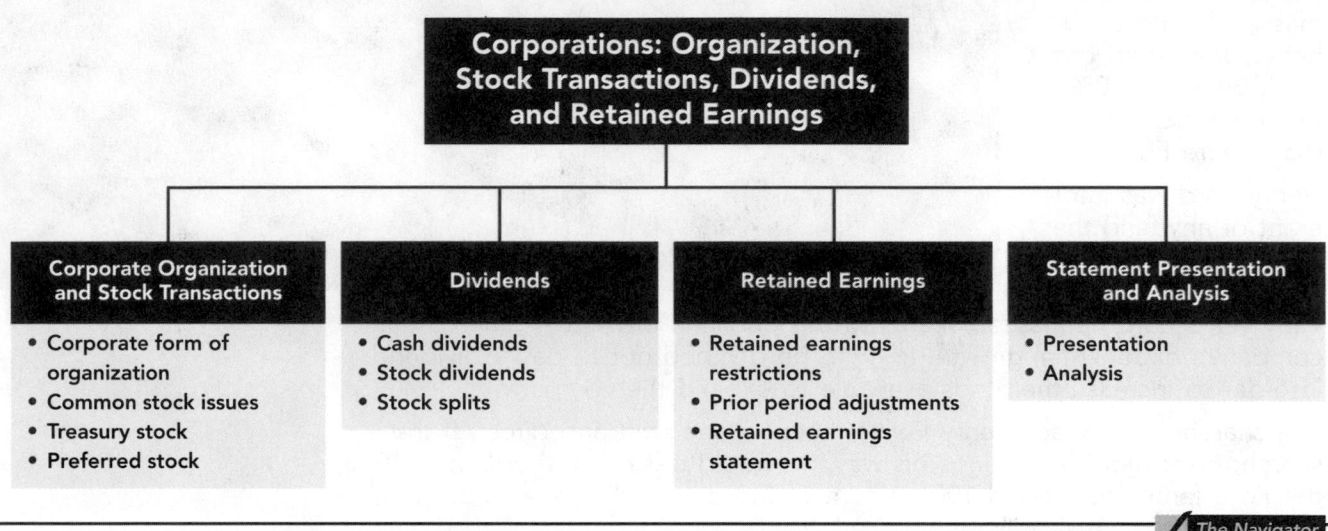

| Corporations: Organization, Stock Transactions, Dividends, and Retained Earnings | | | |
|---|---|---|---|
| **Corporate Organization and Stock Transactions** | **Dividends** | **Retained Earnings** | **Statement Presentation and Analysis** |
| • Corporate form of organization<br>• Common stock issues<br>• Treasury stock<br>• Preferred stock | • Cash dividends<br>• Stock dividends<br>• Stock splits | • Retained earnings restrictions<br>• Prior period adjustments<br>• Retained earnings statement | • Presentation<br>• Analysis |

✔ *The Navigator*

# SECTION 1 The Corporate Organization and Stock Transactions

## THE CORPORATE FORM OF ORGANIZATION

In 1819, Chief Justice John Marshall defined a corporation as "an artificial being, invisible, intangible, and existing only in contemplation of law." This definition is the foundation for the prevailing legal interpretation that a **corporation** is an **entity separate and distinct from its owners**.

A corporation is created by law, and its continued existence depends upon the statutes of the state in which it is incorporated. As a legal entity, a corporation has most of the rights and privileges of a person. The major exceptions relate to privileges that only a living person can exercise, such as the right to vote or to hold public office. A corporation is subject to the same duties and responsibilities as a person. For example, it must abide by the laws, and it must pay taxes.

Two common ways to classify corporations are by purpose and by ownership. A corporation may be organized for the purpose of making a **profit**, or it may be **not-for-profit**. For-profit corporations include such well-known companies as McDonald's, Ford Motor Company, PepsiCo, and Google. Not-for-profit corporations are organized for charitable, medical, or educational purposes. Examples are the Salvation Army, the American Cancer Society, and the Bill & Melinda Gates Foundation.

Classification by **ownership** distinguishes between publicly held and privately held corporations. A **publicly held corporation** may have thousands of stockholders. Its stock is regularly traded on a national securities exchange such as the

**ALTERNATIVE TERMINOLOGY**

Privately held corporations are also referred to as *closely held corporations*.

New York Stock Exchange. Most of the largest U.S. corporations are publicly held. Examples of publicly held corporations are Intel, IBM, Caterpillar Inc., and General Electric.

In contrast, a **privately held corporation** usually has only a few stockholders, and does not offer its stock for sale to the general public. Privately held companies are generally much smaller than publicly held companies, although some notable exceptions exist. Cargill Inc., a private corporation that trades in grain and other commodities, is one of the largest companies in the United States.

# Characteristics of a Corporation

A number of characteristics distinguish corporations from proprietorships and partnerships. We explain the most important of these characteristics below.

STUDY OBJECTIVE 1

Identify the major characteristics of a corporation.

### SEPARATE LEGAL EXISTENCE

As an entity separate and distinct from its owners, the corporation acts under its own name rather than in the name of its stockholders. Ford Motor Company may buy, own, and sell property. It may borrow money, and may enter into legally binding contracts in its own name. It may also sue or be sued, and it pays its own taxes.

Remember that in a partnership the acts of the owners (partners) bind the partnership. In contrast, the acts of its owners (stockholders) do not bind the corporation unless such owners are **agents** of the corporation. For example, if you owned shares of Ford Motor Company stock, you would not have the right to purchase automobile parts for the company unless you were appointed as an agent of the company, such as a purchasing manager.

### LIMITED LIABILITY OF STOCKHOLDERS

Since a corporation is a separate legal entity, creditors have recourse only to corporate assets to satisfy their claims. The liability of stockholders is normally limited to their investment in the corporation. Creditors have no legal claim on the personal assets of the owners unless fraud has occurred. Even in the event of bankruptcy, stockholders' losses are generally limited to their capital investment in the corporation.

### TRANSFERABLE OWNERSHIP RIGHTS

Shares of capital stock give ownership in a corporation. These shares are transferable units. Stockholders may dispose of part or all of their interest in a corporation simply by selling their stock. Remember that the transfer of an ownership interest in a partnership requires the consent of each owner. In contrast, the transfer of stock is entirely at the discretion of the stockholder. It does not require the approval of either the corporation or other stockholders.

The transfer of ownership rights between stockholders normally has no effect on the daily operating activities of the corporation. Nor does it affect the corporation's assets, liabilities, and total ownership equity. The transfer of these ownership rights is a transaction between individual owners. After it first issues the capital stock, the company does not participate in such transfers.

### ABILITY TO ACQUIRE CAPITAL

It is relatively easy for a corporation to obtain capital through the issuance of stock. Investors buy stock in a corporation to earn money over time as the share price grows, and because a stockholder has limited liability and shares of stock are readily transferable. Also, individuals can become stockholders by investing relatively small amounts of money. In sum, the ability of a successful corporation to obtain capital is virtually unlimited.

Stockholders

**Legal existence separate from owners**

Stockholders

**Limited liability of stockholders**

**Transferable ownership rights**

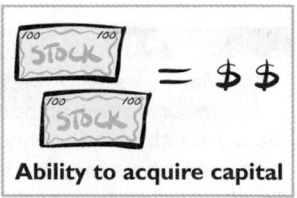

**Ability to acquire capital**

**Continuous life**

## CONTINUOUS LIFE

The life of a corporation is stated in its charter. The life may be perpetual, or it may be limited to a specific number of years. If it is limited, the company can extend the life through renewal of the charter. Since a corporation is a separate legal entity, its continuance as a going concern is not affected by the withdrawal, death, or incapacity of a stockholder, employee, or officer. As a result, a successful enterprise can have a continuous and perpetual life.

## CORPORATION MANAGEMENT

As in **Ford Motor Company**, stockholders legally own the corporation. But they manage the corporation indirectly through a board of directors they elect. The board, in turn, formulates the operating policies for the company. The board also selects officers, such as a president and one or more vice presidents, to execute policy and to perform daily management functions.

Illustration 12-1 presents a typical organization chart showing the delegation of responsibility. The chief executive officer (CEO) has overall responsibility for managing the business. As the organization chart shows, the CEO delegates responsibility to other officers.

**Illustration 12-1**
Corporation organization chart

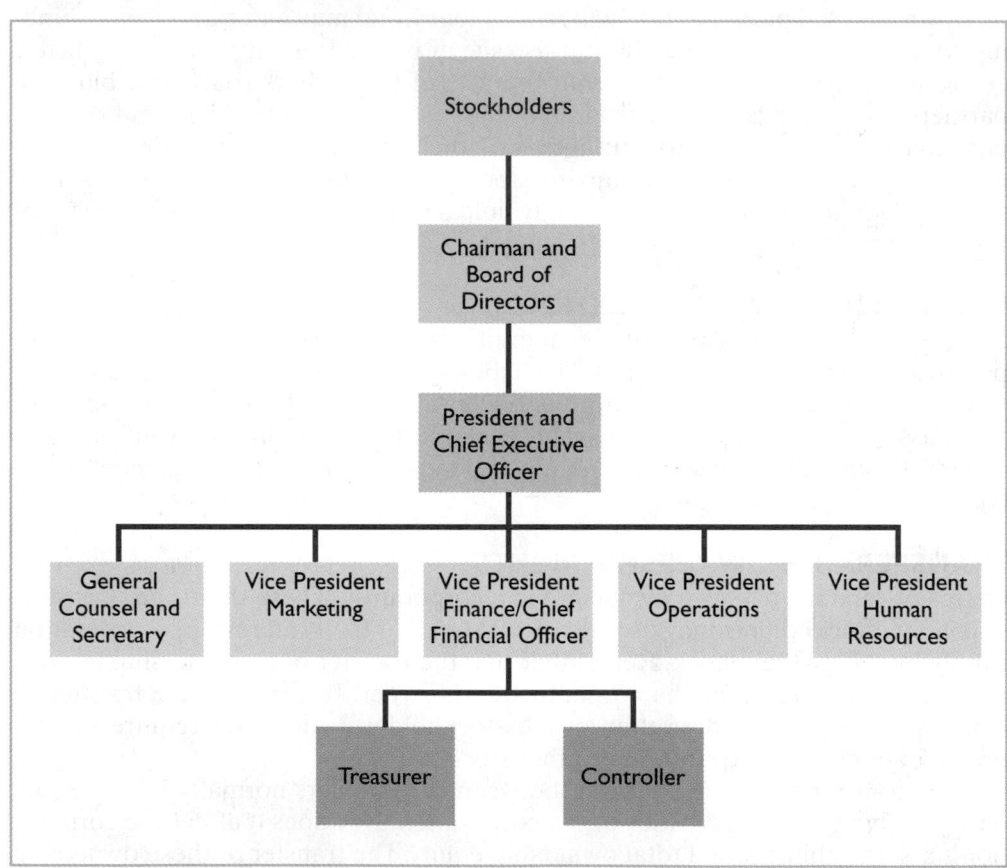

The chief accounting officer is the **controller**. The controller's responsibilities include (1) maintaining the accounting records, (2) maintaining an adequate system of internal control, and (3) preparing financial statements, tax returns, and internal reports. The **treasurer** has custody of the corporation's funds and is responsible for maintaining the company's cash position.

The organizational structure of a corporation enables a company to hire professional managers to run the business. On the other hand, the separation of ownership and management prevents owners from having an active role in managing the company, which some owners like to have.

**ETHICS NOTE**

Managers who are not owners are often compensated based on the performance of the firm. They thus may be tempted to exaggerate firm performance by inflating income figures.

# ETHICS INSIGHT

### Directors Take on More Accountability

In the wake of Enron's collapse, the members of Enron's board of directors were questioned and scrutinized to determine what they knew, and when they knew it. A *Wall Street Journal* story reported that Enron's board contends it was "kept in the dark" by management and by Arthur Andersen—Enron's longtime auditors—and didn't learn about the company's troublesome accounting until October 2001. But, the *Wall Street Journal* reported that according to outside attorneys, "directors on at least two occasions waived Enron's ethical code of conduct to approve partnerships between Enron and its chief financial officer. Those partnerships kept significant debt off of Enron's books and masked actual company finances."

Since Enron's demise, passage of the Sarbanes-Oxley Act and proposals by the SEC and the stock exchanges have created a new corporate-governance climate: Stronger boards, with more independent directors, are now in favor.

**Source:** Carol Hymowitz, "Serving on a Board Now Means Less Talk, More Accountability," *Wall Street Journal*, January 29, 2002.

**?** Was Enron's board of directors fulfilling its role in a corporate organization when it waived Enron's ethical code on two occasions?

## GOVERNMENT REGULATIONS

A corporation is subject to numerous state and federal regulations. State laws usually prescribe the requirements for issuing stock, the distributions of earnings permitted to stockholders, and the effects of retiring stock. Federal securities laws govern the sale of capital stock to the general public. Also, most publicly held corporations are required to make extensive disclosure of their financial affairs to the Securities and Exchange Commission (SEC) through quarterly and annual reports. In addition, when a corporation lists its stock on organized securities exchanges, it must comply with the reporting requirements of these exchanges. Government regulations are designed to protect the owners of the corporation.

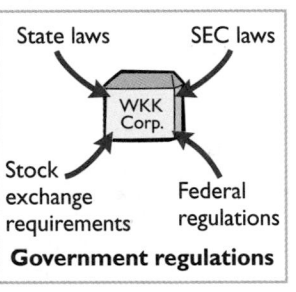

**Government regulations**

## ADDITIONAL TAXES

Neither proprietorships nor partnerships pay income taxes separate from the owner's share of earnings. Sole proprietors and partners report earnings on their personal income tax returns and pay taxes on this amount. Corporations, on the other hand, must pay federal and state income taxes **as a separate legal entity**. These taxes are substantial.

In addition, stockholders must pay taxes on cash dividends (pro rata distributions of net income). Thus, many argue that the government taxes corporate income **twice (double taxation)**—once at the corporate level, and again at the individual level.

In summary, we can identify the following advantages and disadvantages of a corporation compared to a proprietorship and a partnership.

**Additional taxes**

| Advantages | Disadvantages |
|---|---|
| Separate legal existence | Corporation management—separation of ownership and management |
| Limited liability of stockholders | Government regulations |
| Transferable ownership rights | Additional taxes |
| Ability to acquire capital | |
| Continuous life | |
| Corporation management—professional managers | |

**Illustration 12-2**
Advantages and disadvantages of a corporation

# Forming a Corporation

The initial step in forming a corporation is to file an application with the Secretary of State in the state in which incorporation is desired. The application contains such information as: (1) the name and purpose of the proposed corporation; (2) amounts, kinds, and number of shares of capital stock to be authorized; (3) the names of the incorporators; and (4) the shares of stock to which each has subscribed.

After the state approves the application, it grants a **charter**. The charter may be an approved copy of the application form, or it may be a separate document containing the same basic data. The issuance of the charter creates the corporation. Upon receipt of the charter, the corporation develops its by-laws. The **by-laws** establish the internal rules and procedures for conducting the affairs of the corporation. They also indicate the powers of the stockholders, directors, and officers of the enterprise.[1]

Regardless of the number of states in which a corporation has operating divisions, it is incorporated in only one state. It is to the company's advantage to incorporate in a state whose laws are favorable to the corporate form of business organization. General Motors, for example, is incorporated in Delaware, whereas Qualcomm is a New Jersey corporation. Many corporations choose to incorporate in states with rules favorable to existing management. For example, Gulf Oil at one time changed its state of incorporation to Delaware to thwart possible unfriendly takeovers. There, state law allows boards of directors to approve certain defensive tactics against takeovers without a vote by shareholders.

Corporations engaged in interstate commerce must also obtain a license from each state in which they do business. The license subjects the corporation's operating activities to the corporation laws of the state.

Costs incurred in the formation of a corporation are called **organization costs**. These costs include legal and state fees, and promotional expenditures involved in the organization of the business. **Corporations expense organization costs as incurred.** To determine the amount and timing of future benefits is so difficult that it is standard procedure to take a conservative approach of expensing these costs immediately.

**ALTERNATIVE TERMINOLOGY**

The charter is often referred to as the *articles of incorporation*.

# Ownership Rights of Stockholders

When chartered, the corporation may begin selling ownership rights in the form of shares of stock. When a corporation has only one class of stock, it is **common stock**. Each share of common stock gives the stockholder the ownership rights pictured in Illustration 12-3 (next page). A corporation's articles of incorporation or its by-laws state the ownership rights of a share of stock.

Proof of stock ownership is evidenced by a form known as a **stock certificate**. As Illustration 12-4 (next page) shows, the face of the certificate shows the name of the corporation, the stockholder's name, the class and special features of the stock, the number of shares owned, and the signatures of authorized corporate officials. Prenumbered certificates facilitate accountability. They may be issued for any quantity of shares.

---

[1] Following approval by two-thirds of the stockholders, the by-laws become binding upon all stockholders, directors, and officers. Legally, a corporation is regulated first by the laws of the state, second by its charter, and third by its by-laws. Corporations must take care to ensure that the provisions of the by-laws are not in conflict with either state laws or the charter.

**Stockholders have the right to:**

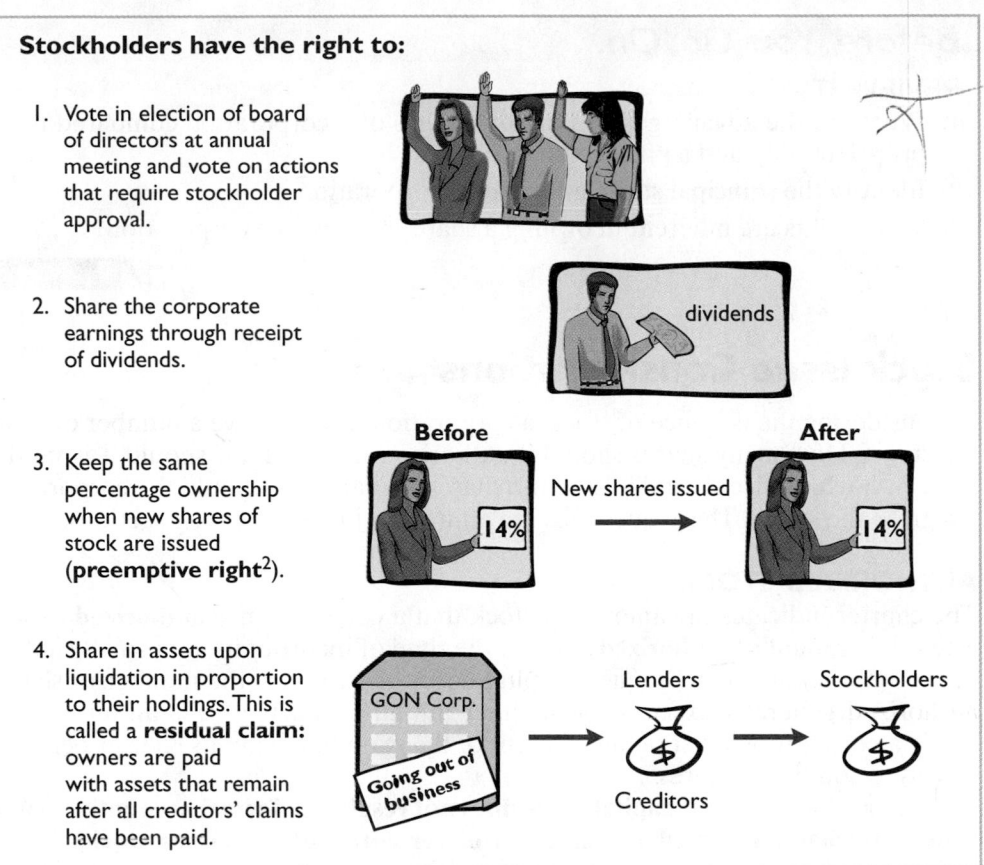

1. Vote in election of board of directors at annual meeting and vote on actions that require stockholder approval.

2. Share the corporate earnings through receipt of dividends.

3. Keep the same percentage ownership when new shares of stock are issued (**preemptive right**[2]).

4. Share in assets upon liquidation in proportion to their holdings. This is called a **residual claim**: owners are paid with assets that remain after all creditors' claims have been paid.

**Illustration 12-3**
Ownership rights of stockholders

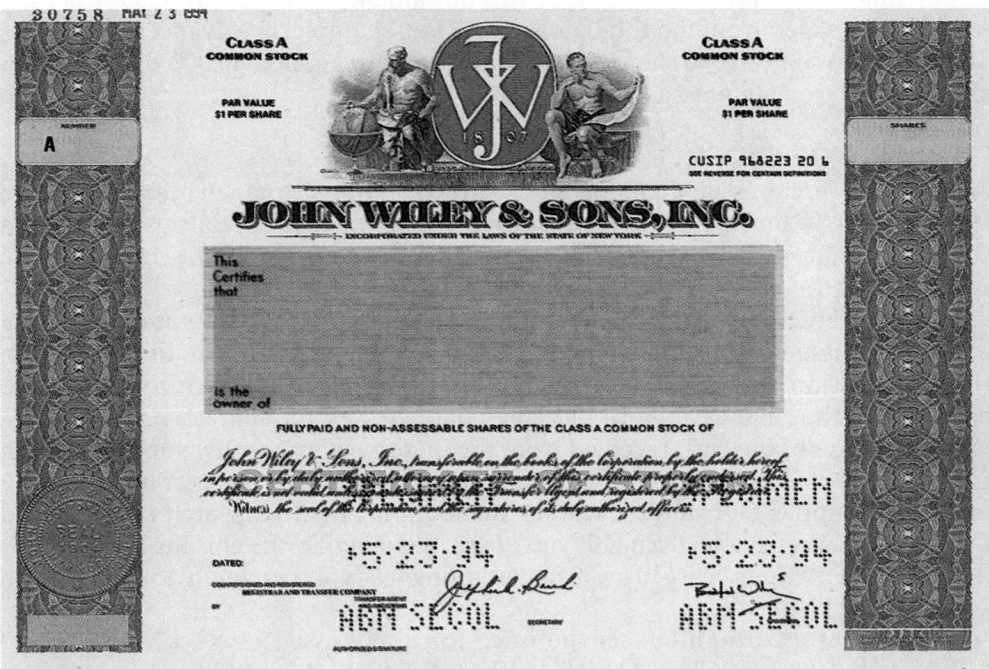

**Illustration 12-4**
A stock certificate

---

[2]A number of companies have eliminated the preemptive right, because they believe it makes an unnecessary and cumbersome demand on management. For example, by stockholder approval, IBM has dropped its preemptive right for stockholders.

## *Before You Go On...*

**REVIEW IT**

1. What are the advantages and disadvantages of a corporation compared to a proprietorship and a partnership?
2. Identify the principal steps in forming a corporation.
3. What rights are inherent in owning a share of stock in a corporation?

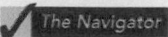 *The Navigator*

# Stock Issue Considerations

In considering the issuance of stock, a corporation must resolve a number of basic questions: How many shares should it authorize for sale? How should it issue the stock? At what price should it issue the shares? What value should the corporation assign to the stock? These questions are addressed in the following sections.

### AUTHORIZED STOCK

The charter indicates the amount of stock that a corporation is **authorized** to sell. The total amount of authorized stock at the time of incorporation normally anticipates both initial and subsequent capital needs. As a result, the number of shares authorized generally exceeds the number initially sold. If it sells all authorized stock, a corporation must obtain consent of the state to amend its charter before it can issue additional shares.

**The authorization of capital stock does not result in a formal accounting entry. This event has no immediate effect on either corporate assets or stockholders' equity.** However, the number of authorized shares is often reported in the stockholders' equity section. It is then simple to determine the number of unissued shares that the corporation can issue without amending the charter: subtract the total shares issued from the total authorized. For example, if Advanced Micro was authorized to sell 100,000 shares of common stock and issued 80,000 shares, 20,000 shares would remain unissued.

### ISSUANCE OF STOCK

**Indirect Issuance**

A corporation can issue common stock **directly** to investors. Or it can issue the stock **indirectly** through an investment banking firm that specializes in bringing securities to market. Direct issue is typical in closely held companies. Indirect issue is customary for a publicly held corporation.

In an indirect issue, the investment banking firm may agree to **underwrite** the entire stock issue. In this arrangement, the investment banker buys the stock from the corporation at a stipulated price and resells the shares to investors. The corporation thus avoids any risk of being unable to sell the shares. Also, it obtains immediate use of the cash received from the underwriter. The investment banking firm, in turn, assumes the risk of reselling the shares, in return for an underwriting fee.[3] For example, Google (the world's number-one Internet search engine) used underwriters when it issued a highly successful initial public offering, raising $1.67 billion. The underwriters charged a 3% underwriting fee (approximately $50 million) on Google's stock offering.

How does a corporation set the price for a new issue of stock? Among the factors to be considered are: (1) the company's anticipated future earnings, (2) its

---

[3]Alternatively, the investment banking firm may agree only to enter into a **best-efforts** contract with the corporation. In such cases, the banker agrees to sell as many shares as possible at a specified price. The corporation bears the risk of unsold stock. Under a best-efforts arrangement, the banking firm is paid a fee or commission for its services.

expected dividend rate per share, (3) its current financial position, (4) the current state of the economy, and (5) the current state of the securities market. The calculation can be complex and is properly the subject of a finance course.

## MARKET VALUE OF STOCK

The stock of publicly held companies is traded on organized exchanges. The interaction between buyers and sellers determines the prices per share. In general, the prices set by the marketplace tend to follow the trend of a company's earnings and dividends. But, factors beyond a company's control, such as an oil embargo, changes in interest rates, and the outcome of a presidential election, may cause day-to-day fluctuations in market prices.

## INVESTOR INSIGHT

 ### How to Read Stock Quotes

The volume of trading on national and international exchanges is heavy. Shares in excess of a billion are often traded daily on the New York Stock Exchange (NYSE) alone. For each listed stock, the *Wall Street Journal* and other financial media report the total volume of stock traded for a given day, the high and low price for the day, the closing market price, and the net change for the day. A recent stock quote for PepsiCo, listed on the NYSE under the ticker symbol PEP, is shown below.

| Stock | Volume | High | Low | Close | Net Change |
|-------|--------|------|-----|-------|------------|
| PepsiCo | 4,305,600 | 60.30 | 59.32 | 60.02 | +0.41 |

These numbers indicate that PepsiCo's trading volume was 4,305,600 shares. The high, low, and closing prices for that date were $60.30, $59.32, and $60.02, respectively. The net change for the day was an increase of $0.41 per share.

**?** For stocks traded on organized stock exchanges, how are the dollar prices per share established? What factors might influence the price of shares in the marketplace?

The trading of capital stock on securities exchanges involves the transfer of **already issued shares** from an existing stockholder to another investor. These transactions have **no impact** on a corporation's stockholders' equity.

## PAR AND NO-PAR-VALUE STOCKS

**Par-value stock** is capital stock to which the charter has assigned a value per share. Years ago, par value determined the **legal capital** per share that a company must retain in the business for the protection of corporate creditors; that amount was not available for withdrawal by stockholders. Thus, in the past, most states required the corporation to sell its shares at par or above.

However, par value was often immaterial relative to the value of the company's stock—even at the time of issue. Thus, its usefulness as a protective device to creditors was questionable. For example, Reebok's par value is $0.01 per share, yet a new issue in 2006 would have sold at a **market value** in the $33 per share range. Thus, par has no relationship with market value; in the vast majority of cases, it is an immaterial amount. As a consequence, today many states do not require a par value. Instead, they use other means to determine legal capital to protect creditors.

No-par-value stock is capital stock to which the charter has not assigned a value. No-par-value stock is quite common today. For example, Nike, Procter & Gamble, and North American Van Lines all have no-par stock. In many states the board of directors assigns a stated value to no-par shares.

## Corporate Capital

Owners' equity is identified by various names: **stockholders' equity**, **shareholders' equity**, or **corporate capital**. The stockholders' equity section of a corporation's balance sheet consists of two parts: (1) paid-in (contributed) capital and (2) retained earnings (earned capital).

The distinction between **paid-in capital** and **retained earnings** is important from both a legal and a financial point of view. Legally, corporations can make distributions of earnings (declare dividends) out of retained earnings in all states. However, in many states they cannot declare dividends out of paid-in capital. Management, stockholders, and others often look to retained earnings for the continued existence and growth of the corporation.

### PAID-IN CAPITAL

Paid-in capital is the total amount of cash and other assets paid in to the corporation by stockholders in exchange for capital stock. As noted earlier, when a corporation has only one class of stock, it is **common stock**.

### RETAINED EARNINGS

Retained earnings is net income that a corporation retains for future use. Net income is recorded in Retained Earnings by a closing entry that debits Income Summary and credits Retained Earnings. For example, assuming that net income for Delta Robotics in its first year of operations is $130,000, the closing entry is:

| A | = | L | + | SE |
|---|---|---|---|---|
| | | | | −130,000 Inc |
| | | | | +130,000 RE |

**Cash Flows**
no effect

| | | |
|---|---|---|
| Income Summary | 130,000 | |
|    Retained Earnings | | 130,000 |
|     (To close Income Summary and transfer net income | | |
|     to retained earnings) | | |

If Delta Robotics has a balance of $800,000 in common stock at the end of its first year, its stockholders' equity section is as follows.

**Illustration 12-5**
Stockholders' equity section

| DELTA ROBOTICS | | |
|---|---|---|
| Balance Sheet (partial) | | |
| Stockholders' equity | | |
|   **Paid-in capital** | | |
|     Common stock | $800,000 | |
|   **Retained earnings** | 130,000 | |
|     Total stockholders' equity | | **$930,000** |

Illustration 12-6 compares the owners' equity (stockholders' equity) accounts reported on a balance sheet for a proprietorship and a corporation.

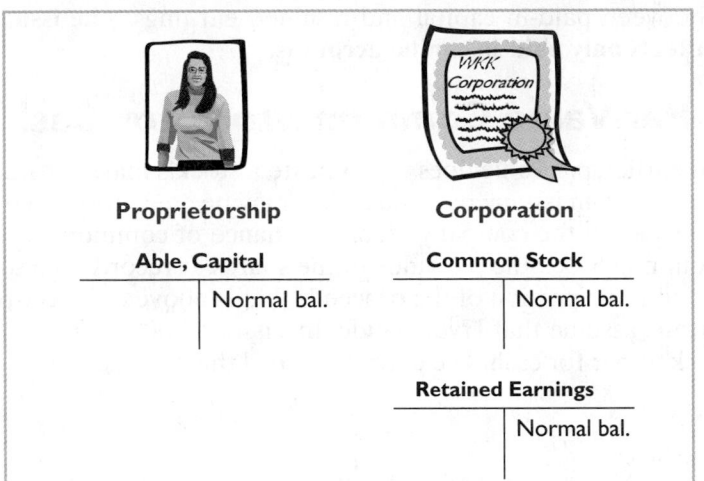

Illustration 12-6
Comparison of owners'
equity accounts

## Before You Go On...

### REVIEW IT

1. Of what significance to a corporation is the amount of authorized stock?
2. What alternative approaches may a corporation use in issuing stock?
3. Distinguish between par value and market value.
4. What are the two types of corporate capital shown on a balance sheet?

### DO IT

At the end of its first year of operation, Doral Corporation has $750,000 of common stock and net income of $122,000. Prepare (a) the closing entry for net income and (b) the stockholders' equity section at year-end.

### Action Plan

- Record net income in Retained Earnings by a closing entry in which Income Summary is debited and Retained Earnings is credited.
- In the stockholders' equity section, show (1) paid-in capital and (2) retained earnings.

### Solution

**(a)**
| | | |
|---|---:|---:|
| Income Summary | 122,000 | |
|     Retained Earnings | | 122,000 |
|     (To close Income Summary and transfer net income to retained earnings) | | |

**(b)** Stockholders' equity

| | | |
|---|---:|---:|
| Paid-in capital | | |
|     Common stock | $750,000 | |
|     Retained earnings | 122,000 | |
|         Total stockholders' equity | | $872,000 |

Related exercise material: *BE12-1, E12-1, and E12-2.*

✓ *The Navigator*

# ACCOUNTING FOR COMMON STOCK ISSUES

Let's now look at how to account for issues of common stock. The primary objectives in accounting for the issuance of common stock are: (1) to identify the specific sources of paid-in capital, and (2) to maintain the

**STUDY OBJECTIVE 2**

Record the issuance of common stock.

distinction between paid-in capital and retained earnings. **The issuance of common stock affects only paid-in capital accounts.**

## Issuing Par-Value Common Stock for Cash

As discussed earlier, par value does not indicate a stock's market value. Therefore, the cash proceeds from issuing par-value stock may be equal to, greater than, or less than par value. When the company records issuance of common stock for cash, it credits to Common Stock the par value of the shares. It records in a separate paid-in capital account the portion of the proceeds that is above or below par value.

To illustrate, assume that Hydro-Slide, Inc. issues 1,000 shares of $1 par-value common stock at par for cash. The entry to record this transaction is:

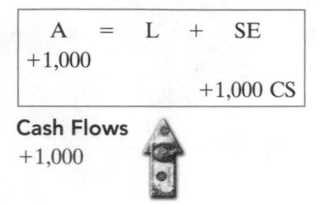

| A | = | L | + | SE |
|---|---|---|---|---|
| +1,000 | | | | |
| | | | | +1,000 CS |

**Cash Flows**
+1,000

| | | |
|---|---|---|
| Cash | 1,000 | |
|     Common Stock | | 1,000 |
|         (To record issuance of 1,000 shares of $1 par common stock at par) | | |

If Hydro-Slide issues an additional 1,000 shares of the $1 par-value common stock for cash at $5 per share, the entry is:

| A | = | L | + | SE |
|---|---|---|---|---|
| +5,000 | | | | |
| | | | | +1,000 CS |
| | | | | +4,000 CS |

**Cash Flows**
+5,000

| | | |
|---|---|---|
| Cash | 5,000 | |
|     Common Stock | | 1,000 |
|     Paid-in Capital in Excess of Par Value | | 4,000 |
|         (To record issuance of 1,000 shares of $1 par common stock) | | |

The total paid-in capital from these two transactions is $6,000, and the legal capital is $2,000. Assuming Hydro-Slide, Inc. has retained earnings of $27,000, Illustration 12-7 shows the company's stockholders' equity section.

**Illustration 12-7**
Stockholders' equity—paid-in capital in excess of par value

| HYDRO-SLIDE, INC. |
|---|
| Balance Sheet (partial) |

| Stockholders' equity | |
|---|---|
|   Paid-in capital | |
|     Common stock | $ 2,000 |
|     **Paid-in capital in excess of par value** | **4,000** |
|       Total paid-in capital | 6,000 |
|   Retained earnings | 27,000 |
|       Total stockholders' equity | $33,000 |

**ALTERNATIVE TERMINOLOGY**

Paid-in Capital in Excess of Par is also called *Premium on Stock.*

When a corporation issues stock for less than par value, it debits the account Paid-in Capital in Excess of Par Value, if a credit balance exists in this account. If a credit balance does not exist, then the corporation debits to Retained Earnings the amount less than par. This situation occurs only rarely: Most states do not permit the sale of common stock below par value, because stockholders may be held personally liable for the difference between the price paid upon original sale and par value.

## Issuing No-Par Common Stock for Cash

When no-par common stock has a stated value, the entries are similar to those illustrated for par-value stock. The corporation credits the stated value to Common Stock. Also, when the selling price of no-par stock exceeds stated value, the corporation credits the excess to Paid-in Capital in Excess of Stated Value.

For example, assume that instead of $1 par-value stock, Hydro-Slide, Inc. has $5 stated value no-par stock and the company issues 5,000 shares at $8 per share for cash. The entry is:

| | | |
|---|---|---|
| Cash | 40,000 | |
|    Common Stock | | 25,000 |
|    Paid-in Capital in Excess of Stated Value | | 15,000 |
|       (To record issue of 5,000 shares of $5 stated value no-par stock) | | |

| A | = | L | + | SE |
|---|---|---|---|---|
| +40,000 | | | | |
| | | | | +25,000 CS |
| | | | | +15,000 CS |

Cash Flows
+40,000

Hydro-Slide, Inc. reports Paid-in Capital in Excess of Stated Value as part of paid-in capital in the stockholders' equity section.

What happens when no-par stock does not have a stated value? In that case, the corporation credits the entire proceeds to Common Stock. Thus, if Hydro-Slide does not assign a stated value to its no-par stock, it would record the issuance of the 5,000 shares at $8 per share for cash as follows.

| | | |
|---|---|---|
| Cash | 40,000 | |
|    Common Stock | | 40,000 |
|       (To record issue of 5,000 shares of no-par stock) | | |

| A | = | L | + | SE |
|---|---|---|---|---|
| +40,000 | | | | |
| | | | | +40,000 CS |

Cash Flows
+40,000

# Issuing Common Stock for Services or Noncash Assets

Corporations also may issue stock for services (compensation to attorneys or consultants) or for noncash assets (land, buildings, and equipment). In such cases, what cost should be recognized in the exchange transaction? To comply with the **cost principle**, in a noncash transaction **cost is the cash equivalent price**. Thus, **cost is either the fair market value of the consideration given up, or the fair market value of the consideration received**, whichever is more clearly determinable.

To illustrate, assume that attorneys have helped Jordan Company incorporate. They have billed the company $5,000 for their services. They agree to accept 4,000 shares of $1 par value common stock in payment of their bill. At the time of the exchange, there is no established market price for the stock. In this case, the market value of the consideration received, $5,000, is more clearly evident. Accordingly, Jordan Company makes the following entry:

| | | |
|---|---|---|
| Organization Expense | 5,000 | |
|    Common Stock | | 4,000 |
|    Paid-in Capital in Excess of Par Value | | 1,000 |
|       (To record issuance of 4,000 shares of $1 par value stock to attorneys) | | |

| A | = | L | + | SE |
|---|---|---|---|---|
| | | | | −5,000 Exp |
| | | | | +4,000 CS |
| | | | | +1,000 CS |

Cash Flows
no effect

As explained on page 538, organization costs are expensed as incurred.

In contrast, assume that Athletic Research Inc. is an existing publicly held corporation. Its $5 par value stock is actively traded at $8 per share. The company issues 10,000 shares of stock to acquire land recently advertised for sale at $90,000. The most clearly evident value in this noncash transaction is the market price of the consideration given, $80,000. The company records the transaction as follows.

| | | |
|---|---|---|
| Land | 80,000 | |
|    Common Stock | | 50,000 |
|    Paid-in Capital in Excess of Par Value | | 30,000 |
|       (To record issuance of 10,000 shares of $5 par value stock for land) | | |

| A | = | L | + | SE |
|---|---|---|---|---|
| +80,000 | | | | |
| | | | | +50,000 CS |
| | | | | +30,000 CS |

Cash Flows
no effect

As illustrated in these examples, **the par value of the stock is never a factor in determining the cost of the assets received**. This is also true of the stated value of no-par stock.

---

## Before You Go On...

PEPSI.

### REVIEW IT

1. Explain the accounting for par and no-par common stock issued for cash.
2. Explain the accounting for the issuance of stock for services or noncash assets.
3. What is the par or stated value per share of PepsiCo's common stock? How many shares has PepsiCo issued at December 31, 2005? The answers to these questions appear on page 592.

### DO IT

Cayman Corporation begins operations on March 1 by issuing 100,000 shares of $10 par value common stock for cash at $12 per share. On March 15 it issues 5,000 shares of common stock to attorneys in settlement of their bill of $50,000 for organization costs. Journalize the issuance of the shares, assuming the stock is not publicly traded.

#### Action Plan

- In issuing shares for cash, credit Common Stock for par value per share.
- Credit any additional proceeds in excess of par value to a separate paid-in capital account.
- When stock is issued for services, use the cash equivalent price.
- For the cash equivalent price use either the fair market value of what is given up or the fair market value of what is received, whichever is more clearly determinable.

#### Solution

| Mar. 1 | Cash | 1,200,000 | |
|---|---|---|---|
| | Common Stock | | 1,000,000 |
| | Paid-in Capital in Excess of Par Value | | 200,000 |
| | (To record issuance of 100,000 shares at $12 per share) | | |
| | | | |
| Mar. 15 | Organization Expense | 50,000 | |
| | Common Stock | | 50,000 |
| | (To record issuance of 5,000 shares for attorneys' fees) | | |

Related exercise material: *BE12-2, BE12-3, BE12-4, E12-3, E12-4, and E12-8.*

✓ The Navigator

---

# ACCOUNTING FOR TREASURY STOCK

STUDY OBJECTIVE 3

Explain the accounting for treasury stock.

**Treasury stock** is a corporation's own stock that it has issued and subsequently reacquired from shareholders, but not retired. A corporation may acquire treasury stock for various reasons:

1. To reissue the shares to officers and employees under bonus and stock compensation plans.
2. To signal to the stock market that management believes the stock is underpriced, in the hope of enhancing its market value.

3. To have additional shares available for use in the acquisition of other companies.
4. To reduce the number of shares outstanding and thereby increase earnings per share.
5. To rid the company of disgruntled investors, perhaps to avoid a takeover, as illustrated in the Ford Motor Company Feature Story.

Many corporations have treasury stock. One survey of 600 U.S. companies found that approximately two-thirds have treasury stock.[4] Buybacks are becoming more popular. For example, ExxonMobil Corp., Microsoft Corp., and Time Warner Inc. purchased a combined $14.37 billion of their shares in the first quarter of 2005.

## Purchase of Treasury Stock

Companies generally account for treasury stock by **the cost method**. This method uses the cost of the shares purchased to value the treasury stock. Under the cost method, the company debits **Treasury Stock** for the **price paid to reacquire the shares**.

When the company disposes of the shares, it credits to Treasury Stock **the same amount** it paid to reacquire the shares. To illustrate, assume that on January 1, 2008, the stockholders' equity section of Mead, Inc. has 100,000 shares of $5 par value common stock outstanding (all issued at par value) and Retained Earnings of $200,000. The stockholders' equity section before purchase of treasury stock is as follows.

**Illustration 12-8**
Stockholders' equity with no treasury stock

| MEAD, INC. | |
|---|---|
| Balance Sheet (partial) | |
| Stockholders' equity | |
| Paid-in capital | |
| Common stock, $5 par value, 100,000 shares | |
|     issued and outstanding | $500,000 |
| Retained earnings | 200,000 |
|     Total stockholders' equity | $700,000 |

On February 1, 2008, Mead acquires 4,000 shares of its stock at $8 per share. The entry is:

| Feb. 1 | Treasury Stock | 32,000 | |
|---|---|---|---|
| |     Cash | | 32,000 |
| |     (To record purchase of 4,000 shares | | |
| |     of treasury stock at $8 per share) | | |

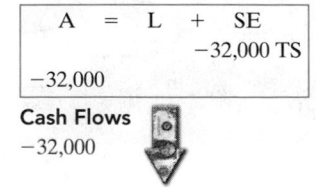

A = L + SE
−32,000 TS
−32,000

**Cash Flows**
−32,000

Note that Mead debits Treasury Stock for the cost of the shares purchased. Is the original paid-in capital account, Common Stock, affected? No, because the number of issued shares does not change. In the stockholders' equity section of the balance sheet, Mead deducts treasury stock from total paid-in capital and retained earnings. Treasury Stock is a **contra stockholders' equity account**. Thus, the acquisition of treasury stock reduces stockholders' equity.

---

[4]*Accounting Trends & Techniques 2005* (New York: American Institute of Certified Public Accountants).

The stockholders' equity section of Mead, Inc. after purchase of treasury stock is as follows.

**Illustration 12-9**
Stockholders' equity with treasury stock

| MEAD, INC. | |
| --- | --- |
| Balance Sheet (partial) | |
| Stockholders' equity | |
| Paid-in capital | |
| Common stock, $5 par value, 100,000 shares issued and 96,000 shares outstanding | $500,000 |
| Retained earnings | 200,000 |
| Total paid-in capital and retained earnings | 700,000 |
| **Less: Treasury stock (4,000 shares)** | **32,000** |
| Total stockholders' equity | $668,000 |

### ETHICS NOTE

The purchase of treasury stock reduces the cushion for creditors and preferred stockholders. A restriction for the cost of treasury stock purchased is often required. The restriction is usually applied to retained earnings.

In the balance sheet, Mead discloses both the number of shares issued (100,000) and the number in the treasury (4,000). The difference between these two amounts is the number of shares of stock outstanding (96,000). The term **outstanding stock** means the number of shares of issued stock that are being held by stockholders.

Some maintain that companies should report treasury stock as an asset because it can be sold for cash. Under this reasoning, companies should also show unissued stock as an asset, clearly an erroneous conclusion. Rather than being an asset, treasury stock reduces stockholder claims on corporate assets. This effect is correctly shown by reporting treasury stock as a deduction from total paid-in capital and retained earnings.

# ACCOUNTING ACROSS THE ORGANIZATION

### Why Did Reebok Buy Its Own Stock?

In a bold (and some would say risky) move, Reebok at one time bought back nearly a *third* of its shares. This repurchase of shares dramatically reduced Reebok's available cash. In fact, the company borrowed significant funds to accomplish the repurchase. In a press release, management stated that it was repurchasing the shares because it believed its stock was severely underpriced. The repurchase of so many shares was meant to signal management's belief in good future earnings.

Skeptics, however, suggested that Reebok's management was repurchasing shares to make it less likely that another company would acquire Reebok (in which case Reebok's top managers would likely lose their jobs). By depleting its cash, Reebok became a less likely acquisition target. Acquiring companies like to purchase companies with large cash balances so they can pay off debt used in the acquisition.

**?** What signal might a large stock repurchase send to investors regarding management's belief about the company's growth opportunities?

## Disposal of Treasury Stock

Treasury stock is usually sold or retired. The accounting for its sale differs when treasury stock is sold above cost than when it is sold below cost.

## SALE OF TREASURY STOCK ABOVE COST

If the selling price of the treasury shares is equal to their cost, the company records the sale of the shares by a debit to Cash and a credit to Treasury Stock. When the selling price of the shares is greater than their cost, the company credits the difference to Paid-in Capital from Treasury Stock.

To illustrate, assume that on July 1, Mead sells for $10 per share the 1,000 shares of its treasury stock, previously acquired at $8 per share. The entry is as follows.

| July 1 | Cash | 10,000 | |
| |     Treasury Stock | | 8,000 |
| |     Paid-in Capital from Treasury Stock | | 2,000 |
| |       (To record sale of 1,000 shares of treasury | | |
| |       stock above cost) | | |

```
A   =  L  +   SE
+10,000
                +8,000 TS
                +2,000 TS
Cash Flows
+10,000
```

Mead does not record a $2,000 gain on sale of treasury stock for two reasons: (1) Gains on sales occur when **assets** are sold, and treasury stock is not an asset. (2) A corporation does not realize a gain or suffer a loss from stock transactions with its own stockholders. Thus, companies should not include in net income any paid-in capital arising from the sale of treasury stock. Instead, they report Paid-in Capital from Treasury Stock separately on the balance sheet, as a part of paid-in capital.

## SALE OF TREASURY STOCK BELOW COST

When a company sells treasury stock below its cost, it usually debits to Paid-in Capital from Treasury Stock the excess of cost over selling price. Thus, if Mead, Inc. sells an additional 800 shares of treasury stock on October 1 at $7 per share, it makes the following entry.

| Oct. 1 | Cash | 5,600 | |
| | Paid-in Capital from Treasury Stock | 800 | |
| |     Treasury Stock | | 6,400 |
| |       (To record sale of 800 shares of treasury | | |
| |       stock below cost) | | |

```
A   =  L  +   SE
+5,600
                -800 TS
                +6,400 TS
Cash Flows
+5,600
```

Observe the following from the two sales entries: (1) Mead credits Treasury Stock at cost in each entry. (2) Mead uses Paid-in Capital from Treasury Stock for the difference between cost and the resale price of the shares. (3) The original paid-in capital account, Common Stock, is not affected. **The sale of treasury stock increases both total assets and total stockholders' equity.**

After posting the foregoing entries, the treasury stock accounts will show the following balances on October 1.

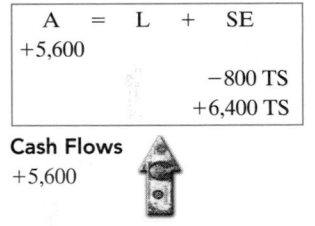
**Illustration 12-10**
Treasury stock accounts

| Treasury Stock | | | | Paid-in Capital from Treasury Stock | | | |
|---|---|---|---|---|---|---|---|
| Feb. 1 | 32,000 | July 1 | 8,000 | Oct. 1 | 800 | July 1 | 2,000 |
| | | Oct. 1 | 6,400 | | | | |
| | | | | | | Oct. 1 Bal. | 1,200 |
| Oct. 1 Bal. | 17,600 | | | | | | |

When a company fully depletes the credit balance in Paid-in Capital from Treasury Stock, it debits to Retained Earnings any additional excess of cost over selling price. To illustrate, assume that Mead, Inc. sells its remaining 2,200 shares at $7 per share on December 1. The excess of cost over selling price is $2,200 [2,200 × ($8 − $7)]. In this case, Mead debits $1,200 of the excess to Paid-in

Capital from Treasury Stock. It debits the remainder to Retained Earnings. The entry is:

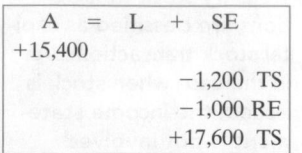

| A = L + SE | | |
|---|---|---|
| +15,400 | | |
| | −1,200 TS | |
| | −1,000 RE | |
| | +17,600 TS | |

**Cash Flows**
+15,400

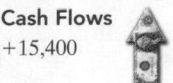

| Dec. 1 | Cash | 15,400 | |
|---|---|---|---|
| | Paid-in Capital from Treasury Stock | 1,200 | |
| | Retained Earnings | 1,000 | |
| |     Treasury Stock | | 17,600 |
| |     (To record sale of 2,200 shares of treasury | | |
| |     stock at $7 per share) | | |

## *Before You Go On...*

### REVIEW IT

1. What is treasury stock, and why do companies acquire it?
2. How do companies record treasury stock?
3. Where do companies report treasury stock in the financial statements? Does a company record gains and losses on treasury stock transactions? Explain.
4. How many shares of treasury stock did PepsiCo have at December 31, 2005, and at December 25, 2004? The answer to this question appears on page 592.

### DO IT

Santa Anita Inc. purchases 3,000 shares of its $50 par value common stock for $180,000 cash on July 1. It will hold the shares in the treasury until resold. On November 1, the corporation sells 1,000 shares of treasury stock for cash at $70 per share. Journalize the treasury stock transactions.

### Action Plan

- Record the purchase of treasury stock at cost.
- When treasury stock is sold above its cost, credit the excess of the selling price over cost to Paid-in Capital from Treasury Stock.
- When treasury stock is sold below its cost, debit the excess of cost over selling price to Paid-in Capital from Treasury Stock.

### Solution

| July 1 | Treasury Stock | 180,000 | |
|---|---|---|---|
| |     Cash | | 180,000 |
| |     (To record the purchase of 3,000 shares at | | |
| |     $60 per share) | | |
| | | | |
| Nov. 1 | Cash | 70,000 | |
| |     Treasury Stock | | 60,000 |
| |     Paid-in Capital from Treasury Stock | | 10,000 |
| |     (To record the sale of 1,000 shares at $70 | | |
| |     per share) | | |

Related exercise material: *BE12-5, E12-5, and E12-9.*

*The Navigator*

# PREFERRED STOCK

**STUDY OBJECTIVE 4**

**Differentiate preferred stock from common stock.**

To appeal to more investors, a corporation may issue an additional class of stock, called preferred stock. **Preferred stock** has provisions that give it some preference or priority over common stock. Typically, preferred stockholders have a priority as to (1) distributions of earnings (dividends) and (2) assets in the event of liquidation. However, they generally do not have voting rights.

Like common stock, corporations may issue preferred stock for cash or for noncash assets. The entries for these transactions are similar to the entries for common stock. When a corporation has more than one class of stock, each paid-in capital account title should identify the stock to which it relates. A company might have the following accounts: Preferred Stock, Common Stock, Paid-in Capital in Excess of Par Value—Preferred Stock, and Paid-in Capital in Excess of Par Value—Common Stock. For example, if Stine Corporation issues 10,000 shares of $10 par value preferred stock for $12 cash per share, the entry to record the issuance is:

| | | |
|---|---|---|
| Cash | 120,000 | |
|     Preferred Stock | | 100,000 |
|     Paid-in Capital in Excess of Par Value–Preferred Stock | | 20,000 |
|     (To record the issuance of 10,000 shares of $10 par | | |
|     value preferred stock) | | |

| A | = | L | + | SE |
|---|---|---|---|---|
| +120,000 | | | | |
| | | | | +100,000 PS |
| | | | | +20,000 PS |

**Cash Flows**
+120,000

Preferred stock may have either a par value or no-par value. In the stockholders' equity section of the balance sheet, companies list preferred stock first because of its dividend and liquidation preferences over common stock.

We discuss various features associated with the issuance of preferred stock on the following pages.

## Dividend Preferences

As noted earlier, **preferred stockholders have the right to receive dividends before common stockholders.** For example, if the dividend rate on preferred stock is $5 per share, common shareholders will not receive any dividends in the current year until preferred stockholders have received $5 per share. The first claim to dividends does not, however, guarantee the payment of dividends. Dividends depend on many factors, such as adequate retained earnings and availability of cash. If a company does not pay dividends to preferred stockholders, it cannot of course pay dividends to common stockholders.

The per share dividend amount is stated as a percentage of the preferred stock's par value or as a specified amount. For example, at one time Crane Company specified a 3¾% dividend on its $100 par value preferred ($100 × 3¾% = $3.75 per share). PepsiCo has a $5.46 series of no-par preferred stock.

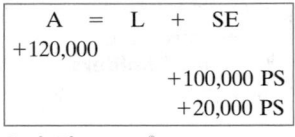

I hope there is some money left when it's my turn.

Preferred    Common
stockholders  stockholders

**Dividend Preference**

### CUMULATIVE DIVIDEND

Preferred stock often contains a cumulative dividend feature. This means that preferred stockholders must be paid both current-year dividends and any unpaid prior-year dividends before common stockholders receive dividends. When preferred stock is cumulative, preferred dividends not declared in a given period are called **dividends in arrears.**

To illustrate, assume that Scientific Leasing has 5,000 shares of 7%, $100 par value, cumulative preferred stock outstanding. The annual dividend is $35,000 (5,000 × $7 per share), but dividends are two years in arrears. In this case, preferred stockholders are entitled to receive the following dividends in the current year.

| | |
|---|---|
| Dividends in arrears ($35,000 × 2) | $ 70,000 |
| Current-year dividends | 35,000 |
| **Total preferred dividends** | **$105,000** |

**Illustration 12-11**
Computation of total dividends to preferred stock

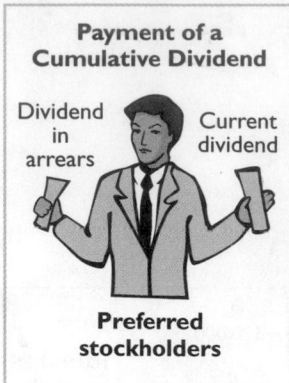

**Payment of a Cumulative Dividend**

Dividend in arrears

Current dividend

**Preferred stockholders**

The company cannot pay dividends to common stockholders until it pays the entire preferred dividend. In other words, companies cannot pay dividends to common stockholders while any preferred stock is in arrears.

Are dividends in arrears considered a liability? **No—no payment obligation exists until the board of directors declares a dividend**. However, companies should disclose in the notes to the financial statements the amount of dividends in arrears. Doing so enables investors to assess the potential impact of this commitment on the corporation's financial position.

Companies that are unable to meet their dividend obligations are not looked upon favorably by the investment community. As a financial officer noted in discussing one company's failure to pay its cumulative preferred dividend for a period of time, "Not meeting your obligations on something like that is a major black mark on your record." The accounting entries for preferred stock dividends are explained later in the chapter.

## Liquidation Preference

Most preferred stocks also have a preference on corporate assets if the corporation fails. This feature provides security for the preferred stockholder. The preference to assets may be for the par value of the shares or for a specified liquidating value. For example, EarthLink's preferred stock entitles its holders to receive $20.83 per share, plus accrued and unpaid dividends, in the event of involuntary liquidation. The liquidation preference establishes the respective claims of creditors and preferred stockholders.

### Before You Go On...

**REVIEW IT**

1. Preferred stock has what preferences over common stock?
2. Why are dividends in arrears on preferred stock not considered a liability?
3. Of what value is the preference in liquidation to preferred stockholders?

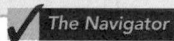
*The Navigator*

## SECTION 2 Dividends

A **dividend** is a corporation's distribution of cash or stock to its stockholders on a pro rata (proportional) basis. Investors are very interested in a company's dividend policies and practices. Dividends can take four forms: cash, property, scrip (a promissory note to pay cash), or stock. Cash dividends predominate in practice. Also, companies declare stock dividends with some frequency. These two forms of dividends will be the focus of discussion in this chapter.

Dividends may be expressed in two ways: (1) as a percentage of the par or stated value of the stock, or (2) as a dollar amount per share. The financial press generally reports **dividends as a dollar amount per share**. For example, Boeing Company's dividend rate is $1.05 a share, Hershey Foods Corp.'s is $0.93, and Nike's is $0.95.

## CASH DIVIDENDS

A **cash dividend** is a pro rata distribution of cash to stockholders. For a corporation to pay a cash dividend, it must have:

1. **Retained earnings.** The legality of a cash dividend depends on the laws of the state in which the company is incorporated. Payment of cash dividends from

retained earnings is legal in all states. In general, cash dividend distributions from only the balance in common stock (legal capital) are illegal.

A dividend declared out of paid-in capital is termed a **liquidating dividend**. Such a dividend reduces or "liquidates" the amount originally paid in by stockholders. Statutes vary considerably with respect to cash dividends based on paid-in capital in excess of par or stated value. Many states permit such dividends.

2. **Adequate cash.** The legality of a dividend and the ability to pay a dividend are two different things. For example, Nike, with retained earnings of over $3 billion, could legally declare a dividend of at least $3 billion. But Nike's cash balance is only $198 million.

   Before declaring a cash dividend, a company's board of directors must carefully consider both current and future demands on the company's cash resources. In some cases, current liabilities may make a cash dividend inappropriate. In other cases, a major plant expansion program may warrant only a relatively small dividend.

3. **A declaration of dividends.** A company does not pay dividends unless its board of directors decides to do so, at which point the board "declares" the dividend. The board of directors has full authority to determine the amount of income to distribute in the form of a dividend and the amount to retain in the business. Dividends do not accrue like interest on a note payable, and they are not a liability until declared.

The amount and timing of a dividend are important issues. The payment of a large cash dividend could lead to liquidity problems for the company. On the other hand, a small dividend or a missed dividend may cause unhappiness among stockholders. Many stockholders expect to receive a reasonable cash payment from the company on a periodic basis. Many companies declare and pay cash dividends quarterly.

## Entries for Cash Dividends

Three dates are important in connection with dividends: (1) the declaration date, (2) the record date, and (3) the payment date. Normally, there are two to four weeks between each date. Companies make accounting entries on two of the dates—the declaration date and the payment date.

On the **declaration date**, the board of directors formally declares (authorizes) the cash dividend and announces it to stockholders. Declaration of a cash dividend **commits the corporation to a legal obligation**. The obligation is binding and cannot be rescinded. The company makes an entry to recognize the decrease in retained earnings and the increase in the liability Dividends Payable.

To illustrate, assume that on December 1, 2008, the directors of Media General declare a 50¢ per share cash dividend on 100,000 shares of $10 par value common stock. The dividend is $50,000 (100,000 × 50¢) The entry to record the declaration is:

**Declaration Date**

| | | | |
|---|---|---|---|
| Dec. 1 | Retained Earnings | 50,000 | |
| | Dividends Payable | | 50,000 |
| | (To record declaration of cash dividend) | | |

| A | = | L | + | SE |
|---|---|---|---|---|
| | | | | −50,000 Div |
| | | +50,000 | | |

**Cash Flows**
no effect

Dividends Payable is a current liability: it will normally be paid within the next several months.

Instead of debiting Retained Earnings, the company may debit the account Dividends. This account provides additional information in the ledger. Also, a company may have separate dividend accounts for each class of stock. When using a dividend account, the company transfers the balance of that account to Retained Earnings at the end of the year by a closing entry. Whichever account is used for the dividend declaration, the effect is the same: Retained earnings decreases, and a current liability increases. *For homework problems, you should use the Retained Earnings account for recording dividend declarations.*

At the <u>record date</u>, the company determines ownership of the outstanding shares for dividend purposes. The records maintained by the corporation supply this information. In the interval between the declaration date and the record date, the corporation updates its stock ownership records. For Media General, the record date is December 22. No entry is required on this date because the corporation's liability recognized on the declaration date is unchanged.

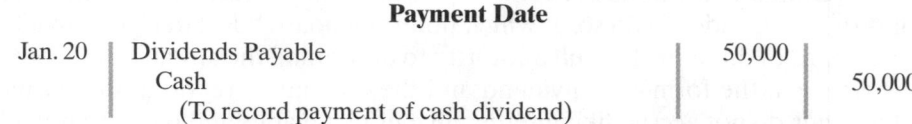

**Record Date**

Dec. 22 | No entry necessary

On the **payment date**, the company mails dividend checks to the stockholders and records the payment of the dividend. Assuming that the payment date is January 20 for Media General, the entry on that date is:

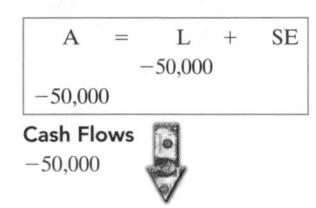

A = L + SE
           −50,000
−50,000

**Cash Flows**
−50,000

**Payment Date**

| Jan. 20 | Dividends Payable | 50,000 | |
| | Cash | | 50,000 |
| | (To record payment of cash dividend) | | |

Note that payment of the dividend reduces both current assets and current liabilities. It has no effect on stockholders' equity. The **cumulative effect** of the **declaration and payment** of a cash dividend is to **decrease both stockholders' equity and total assets**. Illustration 12-12 summarizes the three important dates associated with dividends for Media General.

**Illustration 12-12**
Key dividend dates

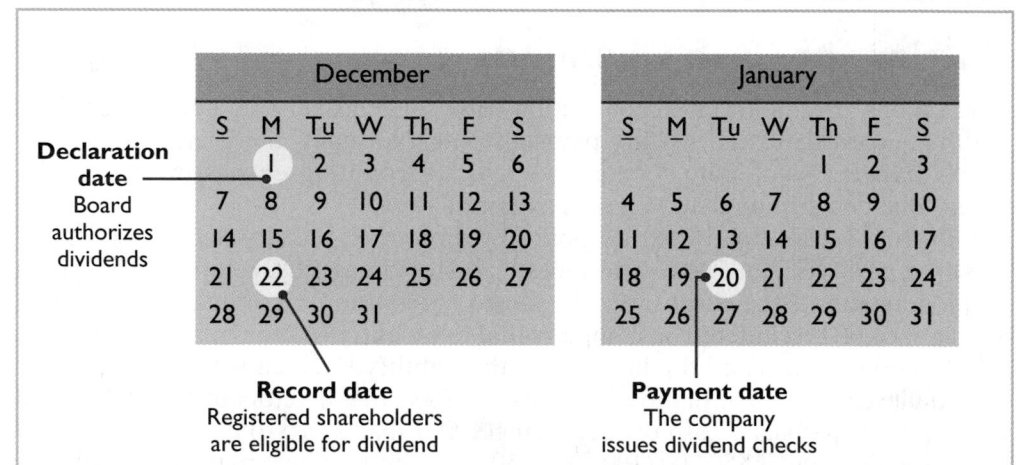

## Allocating Cash Dividends between Preferred and Common Stock

As explained earlier in the chapter, preferred stock has priority over common stock in regard to dividends. Holders of cumulative preferred stock must be paid any unpaid prior-year dividends before common stockholders receive dividends.

To illustrate, assume that at December 31, 2008, IBR Inc. has 1,000 shares of 8%, $100 par value cumulative preferred stock. It also has 50,000 shares of $10 par value common stock outstanding. The dividend per share for preferred stock is $8 ($100 par value × 8%). The required annual dividend for preferred stock is therefore $8,000 (1,000 × $8). At December 31, 2008, the directors declare a $6,000 cash dividend. In this case, the entire dividend amount goes to preferred stockholders because of their dividend preference. The entry to record the declaration of the dividend is:

| | | | |
|---|---|---|---|
| Dec. 31 | Retained Earnings | 6,000 | |
| | Dividends Payable | | 6,000 |
| | (To record $6 per share cash dividend to preferred stockholders) | | |

```
A  =  L  +  SE
              -6,000 Div
     +6,000
```
**Cash Flows**
no effect

Because of the cumulative feature, dividends of $2 per share are in arrears on preferred stock for 2008. The company must pay these dividends to preferred stockholders before it can pay any future dividends to common stockholders. IBR should disclose dividends in arrears in the financial statements.

At December 31, 2009, IBR declares a $50,000 cash dividend. The allocation of the dividend to the two classes of stock is as follows.

| | | |
|---|---|---|
| Total dividend | | $50,000 |
| Allocated to preferred stock | | |
| **Dividends in arrears, 2008 (1,000 × $2)** | **$2,000** | |
| **2009 dividend (1,000 × $8)** | **8,000** | 10,000 |
| Remainder allocated to common stock | | $40,000 |

**Illustration 12-13**
Allocating dividends to preferred and common stock

The entry to record the declaration of the dividend is:

| | | | |
|---|---|---|---|
| Dec. 31 | Retained Earnings | 50,000 | |
| | Dividends Payable | | 50,000 |
| | (To record declaration of cash dividends of $10,000 to preferred stock and $40,000 to common stock) | | |

```
A  =  L  +  SE
              -50,000 Div
     +50,000
```
**Cash Flows**
no effect

What if IBR's preferred stock were not cumulative? In that case preferred stockholders would have received only $8,000 in dividends in 2009. Common stockholders would have received $42,000.

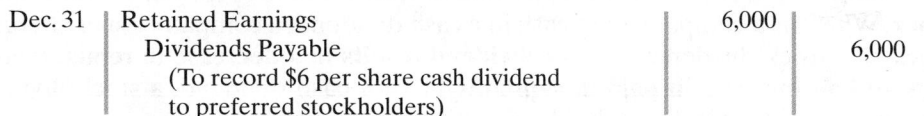

# ACCOUNTING ACROSS THE ORGANIZATION

## *Why Are Companies Increasing Their Dividends?*

The decision whether to pay a cash dividend, and how much to pay, is a very important management decision. During 2004 cash dividend payments were a record $181 billion—not including a one-time $32.6 billion dividend by Microsoft. The $181 billion does include a 44% dividend increase by Wal-Mart and a doubling of the dividend payment by Intel.

One explanation for the increase is that Congress lowered, from 39% to 15%, the tax rate paid by investors on dividends received, making dividends more attractive to investors. Another driving force for the dividend increases was that companies were sitting on record amounts of cash. Because they did not see a lot of good expansion opportunities, companies decided to return the cash to shareholders.

Bigger dividends are still possible in the future. Large companies paid out 34% of their earnings as dividends in 2004—well below the historical average payout of 54% of earnings.

*Source:* Alan Levinsohn, "Divine Dividends," *Strategic Finance,* May 2005, pp. 59–60.

 What factors must management consider in deciding how large a dividend to pay?

# STOCK DIVIDENDS

A **stock dividend** is a pro rata distribution to stockholders of the corporation's own stock. Whereas a company pays cash in a cash dividend, a company issues shares of stock in a stock dividend. **A stock dividend results in a decrease in retained earnings and an increase in paid-in capital.** Unlike a cash dividend, a stock dividend does not decrease total stockholders' equity or total assets.

To illustrate, assume that you have a 2% ownership interest in Cetus Inc.; you own 20 of its 1,000 shares of common stock. If Cetus declares a 10% stock dividend, it would issue 100 shares (1,000 × 10%) of stock. You would receive two shares (2% × 100). Would your ownership interest change? No, it would remain at 2% (22 ÷ 1,100). **You now own more shares of stock, but your ownership interest has not changed.** Illustration 12-14 shows the effect of a stock dividend for stockholders.

**Illustration 12-14**
Effect of stock dividend for stockholders

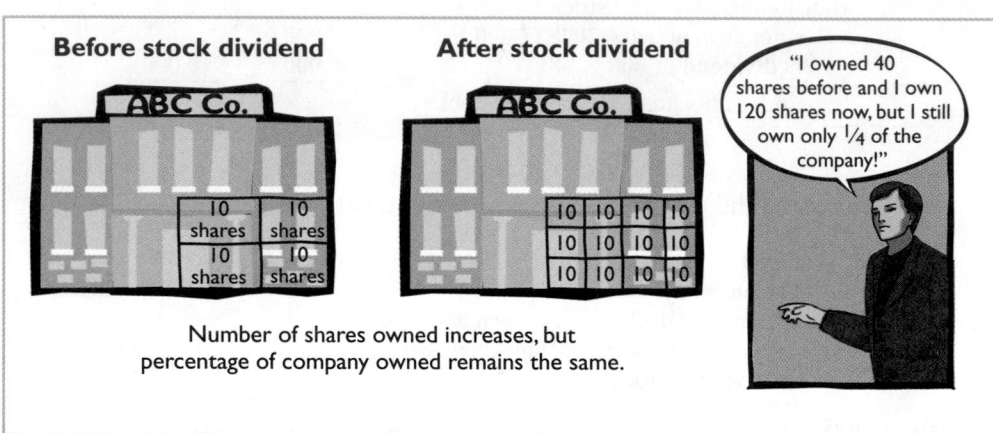

Number of shares owned increases, but percentage of company owned remains the same.

The company has disbursed no cash, and has assumed no liabilities. What are the purposes and benefits of a stock dividend? Corporations issue stock dividends generally for one or more of the following reasons.

1. To satisfy stockholders' dividend expectations without spending cash.
2. To increase the marketability of the corporation's stock. When the number of shares outstanding increases, the market price per share decreases. Decreasing the market price of the stock makes it easier for smaller investors to purchase the shares.
3. To emphasize that a portion of stockholders' equity has been permanently reinvested in the business (and is unavailable for cash dividends).

When the dividend is declared, the board of directors determines the size of the stock dividend and the value assigned to each dividend. Generally, if the company issues a **small stock dividend** (less than 20–25% of the corporation's issued stock), the value assigned to the dividend is the fair market value per share. This treatment is based on the assumption that a small stock dividend will have little effect on the market price of the outstanding shares. Many stockholders consider small stock dividends to be distributions of earnings equal to the fair market value of the shares distributed. If a company issues a **large stock dividend** (greater than 20–25%), the value assigned to the dividend is the par or stated value. Small stock dividends predominate in practice. Thus, we will illustrate only entries for small stock dividends.

# Entries for Stock Dividends

To illustrate the accounting for small stock dividends, assume that Medland Corporation has a balance of $300,000 in retained earnings. It declares a 10% stock dividend on its 50,000 shares of $10 par value common stock. The current fair market value of its stock is $15 per share. The number of shares to be issued is 5,000 (10% × 50,000). Therefore the total amount to be debited to Retained Earnings is $75,000 (5,000 × $15). The entry to record the declaration of the stock dividend is as follows.

| | | |
|---|---|---|
| Retained Earnings | 75,000 | |
|    Common Stock Dividends Distributable | | 50,000 |
|    Paid-in Capital in Excess of Par Value | | 25,000 |
|      (To record declaration of 10% stock dividend) | | |

A = L + SE
−75,000 Div
+50,000 CS
+25,000 CS

**Cash Flows**
no effect

Medland debits Retained Earnings for the fair market value of the stock issued ($15 × 5,000). It credits to Common Stock Dividends Distributable the par value of the dividend shares ($10 × 5,000), and credits to Paid-in Capital in Excess of Par Value the excess over par ($5 × 5,000).

Common Stock Dividends Distributable is a **stockholders' equity account**. It is not a liability because assets will not be used to pay the dividend. If the company prepares a balance sheet before it issues the dividend shares, it reports the distributable account under Paid-in capital as shown in Illustration 12-15.

| | | |
|---|---|---|
| Paid-in capital | | |
|    Common stock | $500,000 | |
|    **Common stock dividends distributable** | **50,000** | $550,000 |

**Illustration 12-15**
Statement presentation of common stock dividends distributable

When Medland issues the dividend shares, it debits Common Stock Dividends Distributable, and credits Common Stock, as follows.

| | | |
|---|---|---|
| Common Stock Dividends Distributable | 50,000 | |
|    Common Stock | | 50,000 |
|      (To record issuance of 5,000 shares in a stock dividend) | | |

A = L + SE
−50,000 CS
+50,000 CS

**Cash Flows**
no effect

# Effects of Stock Dividends

How do stock dividends affect stockholders' equity? They **change the composition of stockholders' equity**, because they transfer to paid-in capital a portion of retained earnings. However, **total stockholders' equity remains the same**. Stock dividends also have no effect on the par or stated value per share. But the number of shares outstanding increases, and the book value per share decreases. Illustration 12-16 shows these effects for Medland Corporation.

| | Before Dividend | After Dividend |
|---|---|---|
| Stockholders' equity | | |
|   Paid-in capital | | |
|     Common stock, $10 par | $500,000 | $550,000 |
|     Paid-in capital in excess of par value | — | 25,000 |
|      Total paid-in capital | 500,000 | 575,000 |
|   Retained earnings | 300,000 | 225,000 |
|     **Total stockholders' equity** | **$800,000** | **$800,000** |
| **Outstanding shares** | **50,000** | **55,000** |
| **Book value per share** | **$16.00** | **$14.55** |

**Illustration 12-16**
Stock dividend effects

In this example, total paid-in capital increases by $75,000, and retained earnings decreases by the same amount. Note also that total stockholders' equity remains unchanged at $800,000.

# STOCK SPLITS

A **stock split**, like a stock dividend, involves issuance of additional shares to stockholders according to their percentage ownership. **A stock split results in a reduction in the par or stated value per share.** The purpose of a stock split is to increase the marketability of the stock by lowering its market value per share.

The effect of a split on market value is generally *inversely proportional* to the size of the split. For example, after a recent 2-for-1 stock split, the market value of Nike's stock fell from $111 to approximately $55. The lower market value stimulated market activity, and within one year the stock was trading above $100 again.

In a stock split, the number of shares increases in the same proportion that par or stated value per share decreases. For example, in a 2-for-1 split, one share of $10 par value stock is exchanged for two shares of $5 par value stock. **A stock split does not have any effect on total paid-in capital, retained earnings, or total stockholders' equity.** But the number of shares outstanding increases, and book value per share decreases. Illustration 12-17 shows these effects for Medland Corporation, assuming that it splits its 50,000 shares of common stock on a 2-for-1 basis.

**Illustration 12-17**
Stock split effects

|  | Before Stock Split | After Stock Split |
|---|---|---|
| Stockholders' equity |  |  |
| Paid-in capital |  |  |
| Common stock | $500,000 | $500,000 |
| Paid-in capital in excess of par value | –0– | –0– |
| Total paid-in capital | 500,000 | 500,000 |
| Retained earnings | 300,000 | 300,000 |
| **Total stockholders' equity** | **$800,000** | **$800,000** |
| **Outstanding shares** | **50,000** | **100,000** |
| **Book value per share** | **$16.00** | **$8.00** |

A stock split does not affect the balances in any stockholders' equity accounts. Therefore **it is not necessary to journalize a stock split**.

Illustration 12-18 summarizes the significant differences between stock splits and stock dividends.

**Illustration 12-18**
Differences between the effects of stock splits and stock dividends

| Item | Stock Split | Stock Dividend |
|---|---|---|
| Total paid-in capital | No change | Increase |
| Total retained earnings | No change | Decrease |
| Total par value (common stock) | No change | Increase |
| Par value per share | Decrease | No change |

## Before You Go On...

### REVIEW IT

1. What entries do companies make for cash dividends on (a) the declaration date, (b) the record date, and (c) the payment date?

2. Distinguish between a small and large stock dividend, and indicate the basis for valuing each kind of dividend.

3. Contrast the effects of a small stock dividend and a 2-for-1 stock split on (a) stockholders' equity, (b) outstanding shares, and (c) book value per share.

4. What were the amounts of the dividends PepsiCo declared per share of common stock during the years 2001 to 2005? Is the trend in dividends consistent with the company's net income trend during that period? The answers to these questions appear on page 592.

### DO IT

Sing CD Company has had five years of record earnings. Due to this success, the market price of its 500,000 shares of $2 par value common stock has tripled from $15 per share to $45. During this period, paid-in capital remained the same at $2,000,000. Retained earnings increased from $1,500,000 to $10,000,000. CEO Joan Elbert is considering either (1) a 10% stock dividend or (2) a 2-for-1 stock split. She asks you to show the before-and-after effects of each option on (a) retained earnings and (b) book value per share.

### Action Plan

- Calculate the stock dividend's effect on retained earnings by multiplying the number of new shares times the market price of the stock (or par value for a large stock dividend).

- Recall that a stock dividend increases the number of shares without affecting total equity, thus decreasing the book value per share.

- Recall that a stock split only increases the number of shares outstanding and decreases the par value per share.

### Solution

**(a)** (1) The stock dividend amount is $2,250,000 [(500,000 × 10%) × $45]. The new balance in retained earnings is $7,750,000 ($10,000,000 − $2,250,000).

(2) The retained earnings balance after the stock split would be the same as it was before the split: $10,000,000.

**(b)** The book value effects are as follows:

|  | Original Balances | After Dividend | After Split |
|---|---|---|---|
| Paid-in capital | $ 2,000,000 | $ 4,250,000 | $ 2,000,000 |
| Retained earnings | 10,000,000 | 7,750,000 | 10,000,000 |
| Total stockholders' equity | $12,000,000 | $12,000,000 | $12,000,000 |
| Shares outstanding | 500,000 | 550,000 | 1,000,000 |
| Book value per share | $24 | $21.82 | $12 |

Related exercise material: *BE12-8, BE12-9, E12-14, and E12-15.*

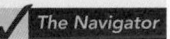

## SECTION 3 **Retained Earnings**

As you learned earlier in the chapter, retained earnings is net income that a company retains for use in the business. The balance in retained earnings is part of the stockholders' claim on the total assets of the corporation. It does not, though, represent a claim on any specific asset. Nor can the amount of retained earnings be associated with the balance of any asset account. For example, a $100,000 balance in retained earnings does not mean that there should be $100,000 in cash. The reason is that the company may have used the cash resulting from the excess of revenues over expenses to purchase buildings, equipment, and other assets.

To demonstrate that retained earnings and cash may be quite different, Illustration 12-19 shows recent amounts of retained earnings and cash in selected companies.

**Illustration 12-19**
Retained earnings and cash balances

| | | (in millions) | |
|---|---|---|---|
| **Company** | | **Retained Earnings** | **Cash** |
| Disney Co. | | $17,775 | $1,723 |
| Intel Corp. | | 29,810 | 7,324 |
| Kellogg Co. | | 3,266.1 | 219.1 |
| Amazon.com | | (2,027) | 1,013 |

Remember that when a company has net income, it closes net income to retained earnings. The closing entry is a debit to Income Summary and a credit to Retained Earnings.

When a company has a **net loss** (expenses exceed revenues), it also closes this amount to retained earnings. The closing entry in this case is a debit to Retained Earnings and a credit to Income Summary. This is done even if it results in a debit balance in Retained Earnings. **Companies do not debit net losses to paid-in capital accounts.** To do so would destroy the distinction between paid-in and earned capital. A debit balance in Retained Earnings is identified as a deficit. It is reported as a deduction in the stockholders' equity section, as shown below.

**Illustration 12-20**
Stockholders' equity with deficit

| **Balance Sheet (partial)** | |
|---|---|
| Stockholders' equity | |
| Paid-in capital | |
| Common stock | $800,000 |
| **Retained earnings (deficit)** | **(50,000)** |
| Total stockholders' equity | $750,000 |

# RETAINED EARNINGS RESTRICTIONS

The balance in retained earnings is generally available for dividend declarations. Some companies state this fact. For example, Lockheed Martin Corporation states the following in the notes to its financial statements.

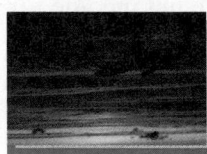

## LOCKHEED MARTIN CORPORATION
### Notes to the Financial Statements

At December 31, retained earnings were unrestricted and available for dividend payments.

**Illustration 12-21**
Disclosure of unrestricted retained earnings

In some cases, there may be **retained earnings restrictions**. These make a portion of the retained earnings balance currently unavailable for dividends. Restrictions result from one or more of the following causes.

1. **Legal restrictions.** Many states require a corporation to restrict retained earnings for the cost of treasury stock purchased. The restriction keeps intact the corporation's legal capital that is being temporarily held as treasury stock. When the company sells the treasury stock, the restriction is lifted.

2. **Contractual restrictions.** Long-term debt contracts may restrict retained earnings as a condition for the loan. The restriction limits the use of corporate assets for payment of dividends. Thus, it increases the likelihood that the corporation will be able to meet required loan payments.

3. **Voluntary restrictions.** The board of directors may voluntarily create retained earnings restrictions for specific purposes. For example, the board may authorize a restriction for future plant expansion. By reducing the amount of retained earnings available for dividends, the company makes more cash available for the planned expansion.

Companies generally disclose **retained earnings restrictions** in the notes to the financial statements. For example, Tektronix Inc., a manufacturer of electronic measurement devices, had total retained earnings of $774 million, but the unrestricted portion was only $223.8 million.

## TEKTRONIX INC.
### Notes to the Financial Statements

Certain of the Company's debt agreements require compliance with debt covenants. Management believes that the Company is in compliance with such requirements. The Company had unrestricted retained earnings of $223.8 million after meeting those requirements.

**Illustration 12-22**
Disclosure of restriction

# PRIOR PERIOD ADJUSTMENTS

Suppose that a corporation has closed its books and issued financial statements. The corporation then discovers that it made a material error in reporting net income of a prior year. How should the company record this situation in the accounts and report it in the financial statements?

The correction of an error in previously issued financial statements is known as a **prior period adjustment**. The company makes the correction directly to Retained Earnings, because the effect of the error is now in this account. The net income for the prior period has been recorded in retained earnings through the journalizing and posting of closing entries.

To illustrate, assume that General Microwave discovers in 2008 that it understated depreciation expense in 2007 by $300,000 due to computational errors. These errors overstated both net income for 2007 and the current balance in retained earnings. The entry for the prior period adjustment, ignoring all tax effects, is as follows.

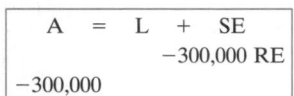

**Cash Flows**
no effect

| | | |
|---|---|---|
| Retained Earnings | 300,000 | |
|    Accumulated Depreciation | | 300,000 |
|      (To adjust for understatement of depreciation in a prior period) | | |

A debit to an income statement account in 2008 is incorrect because the error pertains to a prior year.

Companies report prior period adjustments in the retained earnings statement. They add (or deduct, as the case may be) these adjustments from the beginning retained earnings balance. This results in an adjusted beginning balance. For example, assuming a beginning balance of $800,000 in retained earnings, General Microwave reports the prior period adjustment as follows.

**Illustration 12-23**
Statement presentation of prior period adjustments

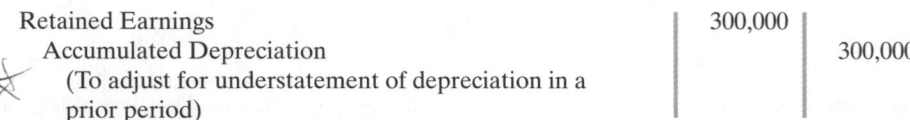

| GENERAL MICROWAVE | |
|---|---|
| Retained Earnings Statement (partial) | |
| Balance, January 1, as reported | $ 800,000 |
| **Correction for overstatement of net income in prior period (depreciation error)** | **(300,000)** |
| Balance, January 1, as adjusted | $ 500,000 |

Again, reporting the correction in the current year's income statement would be incorrect because it applies to a prior year's income statement.

# RETAINED EARNINGS STATEMENT

The **retained earnings statement** shows the changes in retained earnings during the year. The company prepares the statement from the Retained Earnings account. Illustration 12-24 shows (in account form) transactions that affect retained earnings.

| Retained Earnings | |
|---|---|
| 1. Net loss | 1. Net income |
| 2. Prior period adjustments for overstatement of net income | 2. Prior period adjustments for understatement of net income |
| 3. Cash dividends and stock dividends | |
| 4. Some disposals of treasury stock | |

**Illustration 12-24**
Debits and credits to retained earnings

As indicated, net income increases retained earnings, and a net loss decreases retained earnings. Prior period adjustments may either increase or decrease retained earnings. Both cash dividends and stock dividends decrease retained earnings. The circumstances under which treasury stock transactions decrease retained earnings are explained on page 549.

A complete retained earnings statement for Graber Inc., based on assumed data, is as follows.

**Illustration 12-25**
Retained earnings statement

| GRABER INC. Retained Earnings Statement For the Year Ended December 31, 2008 | | |
|---|---|---|
| Balance, January 1, as reported | | $1,050,000 |
| Correction for understatement of net income in prior period (inventory error) | | 50,000 |
| Balance, January 1, as adjusted | | 1,100,000 |
| Add: Net income | | 360,000 |
| | | 1,460,000 |
| Less: Cash dividends | $100,000 | |
| Stock dividends | 200,000 | 300,000 |
| Balance, December 31 | | $1,160,000 |

## Before You Go On...

### REVIEW IT
1. How are retained earnings restrictions generally reported?
2. What is a prior period adjustment, and how is it reported?
3. What are the principal sources of debits and credits to Retained Earnings?

### DO IT
Vega Corporation has retained earnings of $5,130,000 on January 1, 2008. During the year, Vega earns $2,000,000 of net income. It declares and pays a $250,000 cash dividend. In 2008, Vega records an adjustment of $180,000 due to the understatement of 2007 depreciation expense from a mathematical error. Prepare a retained earnings statement for 2008.

### Action Plan
- Recall that a retained earnings statement begins with retained earnings, as reported at the end of the previous year.

- Add or subtract any prior period adjustments to arrive at the adjusted beginning figure.
- Add net income and subtract dividends declared to arrive at the ending balance in retained earnings.

**Solution**

### VEGA CORPORATION
Retained Earnings Statement
For the Year Ended December 31, 2008

| | |
|---|---:|
| Balance, January 1, as reported | $5,130,000 |
| Correction for overstatement of net income in prior period (depreciation error) | (180,000) |
| Balance, January 1, as adjusted | 4,950,000 |
| Add: Net income | 2,000,000 |
| | 6,950,000 |
| Less: Cash dividends | 250,000 |
| Balance, December 31 | $6,700,000 |

Related exercise material: *BE12-10, BE12-11, and E12-17.*

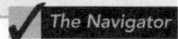 The Navigator

# STATEMENT PRESENTATION AND ANALYSIS

**STUDY OBJECTIVE 7**

Prepare and analyze a comprehensive stockholders' equity section.

In the stockholders' equity section of the balance sheet, paid-in capital and retained earnings are reported. The specific sources of paid-in capital are identified. Within paid-in capital, two classifications are recognized:

1. **Capital stock.** This category consists of preferred and common stock. Preferred stock is shown before common stock because of its preferential rights. Par value, shares authorized, shares issued, and shares outstanding are reported for each class of stock.

2. **Additional paid-in capital.** This includes the excess of amounts paid over par or stated value and paid-in capital from treasury stock.

## Presentation

The stockholders' equity section of Graber Inc.'s balance sheet is presented in Illustration 12-26 (next page). Note the following: (1) "Common stock dividends distributable" is shown under "Capital stock," in "Paid-in capital." (2) A retained earnings restriction is disclosed in the notes.

The stockholders' equity section of Graber Inc. in Illustration 12-26 (next page) includes most of the accounts discussed in this chapter. The disclosures pertaining to Graber's common stock indicate that: 400,000 shares are issued; 100,000 shares are unissued (500,000 authorized less 400,000 issued); and 390,000 shares are outstanding (400,000 issued less 10,000 shares in treasury).

In published annual reports, the individual sources of additional paid-in capital are often combined and reported as a single amount, as shown in Illustration 12-27 (next page). In addition, authorized shares are sometimes not reported.

Illustration 12-26
Comprehensive stock-
holders' equity section

### GRABER INC.
Balance Sheet (partial)

Stockholders' equity
  Paid-in capital
    Capital stock

| | | |
|---|---:|---:|
| 9% Preferred stock, $100 par value, cumulative, callable at $120, 10,000 shares authorized, 6,000 shares issued and outstanding | | $ 600,000 |
| Common stock, no par, $5 stated value, 500,000 shares authorized, 400,000 shares issued and 390,000 outstanding | $2,000,000 | |
| **Common stock dividends distributable** | **50,000** | 2,050,000 |
| Total capital stock | | 2,650,000 |
| Additional paid-in capital | | |
| In excess of par value—preferred stock | 30,000 | |
| In excess of stated value—common stock | 1,050,000 | |
| Total additional paid-in capital | | 1,080,000 |
| Total paid-in capital | | 3,730,000 |
| Retained earnings **(see Note R)** | | 1,160,000 |
| Total paid-in capital and retained earnings | | 4,890,000 |
| Less: Treasury stock—common (10,000 shares) | | 80,000 |
| Total stockholders' equity | | $4,810,000 |

**Note R:** Retained earnings is restricted for the cost of treasury stock, $80,000.

Illustration 12-27
Published stockholders'
equity section

### KELLOGG COMPANY
Balance Sheet (partial)
($ in millions)

Stockholders' equity
Common stock, $0.25 par value, 1,000,000,000 shares authorized

| | |
|---|---:|
| Issued: 418,515,339 shares | $ 104.6 |
| Capital in excess of par value | 292.3 |
| Retained earnings | 3,630.4 |
| Treasury stock, at cost 20,817,930 shares | (912.1) |
| Accumulated other comprehensive income | (1,046.2) |
| Total stockholders' equity | $2,069.0 |

In practice, the term "capital surplus" is sometimes used in place of additional paid-in capital and "earned surplus" in place of retained earnings. The use of the term "surplus" suggests that an excess amount of funds is available. Such is not necessarily the case. Therefore, **the term "surplus" should not be employed in accounting**. Unfortunately, a number of financial statements still do use it.

Instead of presenting a detailed stockholders' equity section in the balance sheet and a retained earnings statement, many companies prepare a **stockholders' equity statement**. This statement shows the changes in each stockholders' equity account and in total that have occurred during the year. An example of a stockholders' equity statement is illustrated in PepsiCo's financial statements in Appendix A and in an appendix to this chapter (Illustration 12-A1).

## Analysis

Profitability from the viewpoint of the common stockholder can be measured by the **return on common stockholders' equity**. This ratio shows how many dollars of net income were earned for each dollar invested by the stockholders. It is computed by dividing net income available to common stockholders (which is net income minus preferred stock dividends) by average common stockholders' equity.

To illustrate, Kellogg Company's beginning-of-the-year and end-of-the-year common stockholders' equity were $2,283.7 and $2,069.0 million respectively. Its net income was $1,004.1 million, and no preferred stock was outstanding. The return on common stockholders' equity ratio is computed as follows.

**Illustration 12-28**
Return on common stockholders' equity ratio and computation

| Net Income minus Preferred Dividends | ÷ | Average Common Stockholders' Equity | = | Return on Common Stockholders' Equity |
|---|---|---|---|---|
| ($1,004.1 − $0) | ÷ | $\dfrac{(\$2{,}283.7 + \$2{,}069.0)}{2}$ | = | 46.1% |

As shown in Illustration 12-28, if a company has preferred stock, the amount of **preferred dividends** is deducted from net income to compute income available to common stockholders. Also, the par value of preferred stock is deducted from total average stockholders' equity to arrive at the amount of common stockholders' equity.

## *Before You Go On...*

### REVIEW IT

1. Identify the classifications within the paid-in capital section and the totals that are stated in the stockholders' equity section of a balance sheet.
2. Explain the return on common stockholders' equity ratio.

 *The Navigator*

 Be sure to read **ALL ABOUT YOU:** *Home-Equity Loans* on the next page for information on how topics in this chapter apply to you.

## Home-Equity Loans

In this chapter you learned that companies sometimes reduce their stockholders' equity by buying treasury stock or paying dividends. They do this for a variety of reasons—some good, and some not so good. Individuals who own homes sometimes engage in equity reducing transactions by using home-equity loans. Home-equity loans use the equity existing in the home as collateral for borrowing additional monies.

Many banks encourage people to take out home-equity loans. As a result of the dramatic increase in home values in the United States in recent years, many people have significant equity in their homes. Thus, many people have chosen to use home-equity loans to finance vacations, new cars, improvements to the home, educational pursuits, and so on, or to consolidate debt. However, by taking out a home-equity loan, a homeowner is reducing the equity in that home.

### ✱ Some Facts

* PNC Financial Services Group Inc. offered gifts—in some cases, two airline tickets—to borrowers who took out a new home-equity loan.

* Many banks are extending the length of home-equity loans. Regions Financial Corp. introduced a fixed-rate home-equity loan with a term of up to 15 years. It had previously been five years.

* While home-equity loans tend to have fixed rates, home-equity lines of credit, which allow the homeowner to borrow up to a certain amount whenever they want to, have variable rates. Rates on home-equity lines of credit averaged 8.33% in April 2006, versus about 14% for credit card debt.

* Home-equity loan interest is tax deductible (like home mortgage interest). Interest on car loans, most student loans, and credit cards is not.

### ✱ About the Numbers

Home-equity loans can be very tempting. Suppose that you wanted to borrow $5,000 to take a vacation. You could spread your payments over 15 years and you would have to pay only about $50 per month. But look what your total payments would be over the life of the 15-year loan. Some vacation!

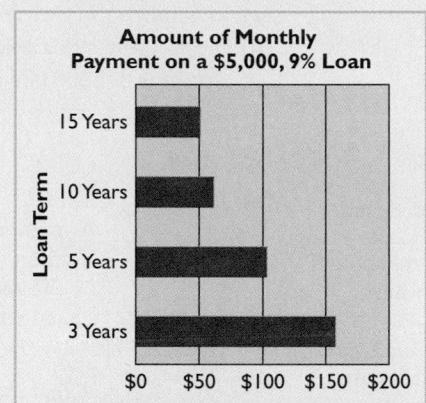

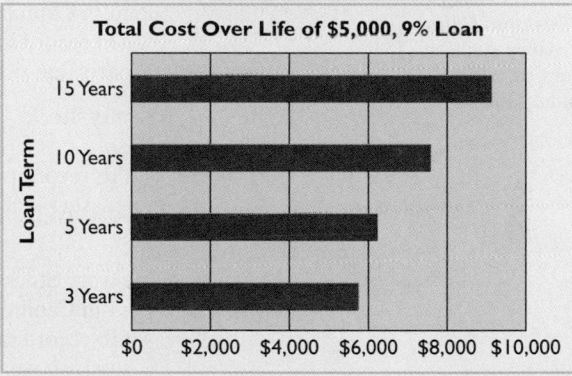

**Source:** Data from Marc Eisenson and Nancy Castleman, "When Mining Your Home for Money, Beware of Fool's Gold," Good Advice Press, *www.goodadvicepress.com/omhomeequity.htm* (accessed June 20, 2006).

### ✱ What Do You Think?

Your home has increased in value by $50,000 during the last five years. You have very little savings outside of the equity in your home. You desperately need a vacation, and you are considering taking out a $5,000 home-equity loan to finance a two-week dream vacation in Europe. Is this is a bad idea?

**YES:** This represents a significant portion of your savings. Home-equity loans should be used to finance investments of a lasting nature, not items of a fleeting nature like vacations.

**NO:** You need a vacation. If you use a little of the equity in your home now, you can make it up when your house increases in value in the future.

**Source:** Ruth Simon, "Lenders Push Home-Equity Deals," *Wall Street Journal*, April 27, 2006, page D1; Marc Eisenson and Nancy Castleman, "When Mining Your Home for Money, Beware of Fool's Gold," Good Advice Press, *www.goodadvicepress.com/omhomeequity.htm* (accessed June 20, 2006).

The Rolman Corporation is authorized to issue 1,000,000 shares of $5 par value common stock. In its first year, the company has the following stock transactions.

Jan. 10   Issued 400,000 shares of stock at $8 per share.
July 1    Issued 100,000 shares of stock for land. The land had an asking price of $900,000. The stock is currently selling on a national exchange at $8.25 per share.
Sept. 1   Purchased 10,000 shares of common stock for thc treasury at $9 per share.
Dec. 1    Sold 4,000 shares of the treasury stock at $10 per share.

**Instructions**

**(a)** Journalize the transactions.
**(b)** Prepare the stockholders' equity section assuming the company had retained earnings of $200,000 at December 31.

## action plan

✔ When common stock has a par value, credit Common Stock for par value.

✔ Use fair market value in a noncash transaction.

✔ Debit and credit the Treasury Stock account at cost.

✔ Record differences between the cost and selling price of treasury stock in stockholders' equity accounts, not as gains or losses.

## Solution

**(a)**

| | | | | |
|---|---|---|---|---|
| Jan. 10 | Cash | | 3,200,000 | |
| | Common Stock | | | 2,000,000 |
| | Paid-in Capital in Excess of Par Value | | | 1,200,000 |
| | (To record issuance of 400,000 shares of $5 par value stock) | | | |
| July 1 | Land | | 825,000 | |
| | Common Stock | | | 500,000 |
| | Paid-in Capital in Excess of Par Value | | | 325,000 |
| | (To record issuance of 100,000 shares of $5 par value stock for land) | | | |
| Sept. 1 | Treasury Stock | | 90,000 | |
| | Cash | | | 90,000 |
| | (To record purchase of 10,000 shares of treasury stock at cost) | | | |
| Dec. 1 | Cash | | 40,000 | |
| | Treasury Stock | | | 36,000 |
| | Paid-in Capital from Treasury Stock | | | 4,000 |
| | (To record sale of 4,000 shares of treasury stock above cost) | | | |

**(b)**

### ROLMAN CORPORATION
#### Balance Sheet (partial)

| | | |
|---|---|---|
| Stockholders' equity | | |
| Paid-in capital | | |
| Capital stock | | |
| Common stock, $5 par value, 1,000,000 shares authorized, 500,000 shares issued, 494,000 shares outstanding | | $2,500,000 |
| Additional paid-in capital | | |
| In excess of par value | $1,525,000 | |
| From treasury stock | 4,000 | |
| Total additional paid-in capital | | 1,529,000 |
| Total paid-in capital | | 4,029,000 |
| Retained earnings | | 200,000 |
| Total paid-in capital and retained earnings | | 4,229,000 |
| Less: Treasury stock (6,000 shares) | | (54,000) |
| Total stockholders' equity | | $4,175,000 |

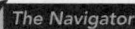

# SUMMARY OF STUDY OBJECTIVES

1 **Identify the major characteristics of a corporation.** The major characteristics of a corporation are separate legal existence, limited liability of stockholders, transferable ownership rights, ability to acquire capital, continuous life, corporation management, government regulations, and additional taxes.

2 **Record the issuance of common stock.** When the issuance of common stock for cash is recorded, the par value of the shares is credited to Common Stock. The portion of the proceeds that is above or below par value is recorded in a separate paid-in capital account. When no-par common stock has a stated value, the entries are similar to those for par value stock. When no-par stock does not have a stated value, the entire proceeds are credited to Common Stock.

3 **Explain the accounting for treasury stock.** The cost method is generally used in accounting for treasury stock. Under this approach, Treasury Stock is debited at the price paid to reacquire the shares. The same amount is credited to Treasury Stock when the shares are sold. The difference between the sales price and cost is recorded in stockholders' equity accounts, not in income statement accounts.

4 **Differentiate preferred stock from common stock.** Preferred stock has contractual provisions that give it priority over common stock in certain areas. Typically, preferred stockholders have a preference to (1) dividends and (2) assets in liquidation. They usually do not have voting rights.

5 **Prepare the entries for cash dividends and stock dividends.** Entries for both cash and stock dividends are required on the declaration date and the payment date. At the declaration date the entries are: cash dividend—debit Retained Earnings, and credit Dividends Payable; small stock dividend—debit Retained Earnings, credit Paid-in Capital in Excess of Par (or Stated) Value, and credit Common Stock Dividends Distributable. On the payment date, the entries for cash and stock dividends are: cash dividend—debit Dividends Payable and credit Cash; small stock dividend—debit Common Stock Dividends Distributable and credit Common Stock.

6 **Identify the items that are reported in a retained earnings statement.** Each of the individual debits and credits to retained earnings should be reported in the retained earnings statement. Additions consist of net income and prior period adjustments to correct understatements of prior years' net income. Deductions consist of net loss, adjustments to correct overstatements of prior years' net income, cash and stock dividends, and some disposals of treasury stock.

7 **Prepare and analyze a comprehensive stockholders' equity section.** In the stockholders' equity section, paid-in capital and retained earnings are reported and specific sources of paid-in capital are identified. Within paid-in capital, two classifications are shown: capital stock and additional paid-in capital. If a corporation has treasury stock, the cost of treasury stock is deducted from total paid-in capital and retained earnings to obtain total stockholders' equity. One measure of profitability is the return on common stockholders' equity. It is calculated by dividing net income minus preferred stock dividends by average common stockholders' equity.

✓ The Navigator

# GLOSSARY

**Authorized stock** The amount of stock that a corporation is authorized to sell as indicated in its charter. (p. 540).

**By-laws** The internal rules and procedures for conducting the affairs of a corporation. (p. 538).

**Cash dividend** A pro rata distribution of cash to stockholders. (p. 552).

**Charter** A document that creates a corporation. (p. 538).

**Corporation** A business organized as a legal entity separate and distinct from its owners under state corporation law. (p. 534).

**Cumulative dividend** A feature of preferred stock entitling the stockholder to receive current and unpaid prior-year dividends before common stockholders receive any dividends. (p. 557).

**Declaration date** The date the board of directors formally declares the dividend and announces it to stockholders. (p. 553).

**Deficit** A debit balance in retained earnings. (p. 560).

**Dividend** A distribution by a corporation to its stockholders on a pro rata (proportional) basis. (p. 552).

**Liquidating dividend** A dividend declared out of paid-in capital. (p. 553).

**No-par-value stock** Capital stock that has not been assigned a value in the corporate charter. (p. 542).

**Organization costs** Costs incurred in the formation of a corporation. (p. 538).

**Outstanding stock** Capital stock that has been issued and is being held by stockholders. (p. 548).

**Paid-in capital** Total amount of cash and other assets paid in to the corporation by stockholders in exchange for capital stock. (p. 542).

**Par-value stock** Capital stock that has been assigned a value per share in the corporate charter. (p. 541).

**Payment date** The date dividend checks are mailed to stockholders. (p. 554).

**Preferred stock** Capital stock that has some contractual preferences over common stock. (p. 550).

**Prior period adjustment** The correction of an error in previously issued financial statements. (p. 562).

**Privately held corporation** A corporation that has only a few stockholders and whose stock is not available for sale to the general public. (p. 535).

**Publicly held corporation** A corporation that may have thousands of stockholders and whose stock is regularly traded on a national securities exchange. (p. 534).

**Record date** The date when ownership of outstanding shares is determined for dividend purposes. (p. 554).

**Retained earnings** Net income that a corporation retains for future use. (p. 542, 560).

**Retained earnings restrictions** Circumstances that make a portion of retained earnings currently unavailable for dividends. (p. 561).

**Retained earnings statement** A financial statement that shows the changes in retained earnings during the year. (p. 562).

**Return on common stockholders' equity ratio** A ratio that measures profitability from the stockholders' point of view. It is computed by dividing net income available to common stockholders by average common stockholders' equity. (p. 566).

**Stated value** The amount per share assigned by the board of directors to no-par stock that becomes legal capital per share. (p. 542).

**Stock dividend** A pro rata distribution of the corporation's own stock to stockholders. (p. 556).

**Stock split** The issuance of additional shares of stock to stockholders accompanied by a reduction in the par or stated value per share. (p. 558).

**Stockholders' equity statement** A statement that shows the changes in each stockholders' equity account and in total stockholders' equity during the year. (p. 565).

**Treasury stock** A corporation's own stock that the corporation has issued, fully paid for, and reacquired but not retired. (p. 546).

# APPENDIX 12A **Stockholders' Equity Statement**

**STUDY OBJECTIVE 8**

**Describe the use and content of the stockholders' equity statement.**

When balance sheets and income statements are presented by a corporation, changes in the separate accounts comprising stockholders' equity should also be disclosed. Disclosure of such changes is necessary to make the financial statements sufficiently informative for users. The disclosures may be made in an additional statement or in the notes to the financial statements.

Many corporations make the disclosures in a **stockholders' equity statement**. The statement shows the changes in **each** stockholders' equity account and in **total** stockholders' equity during the year. As shown in Illustration 12A-1 the stockholders' equity statement is prepared in columnar form. It contains columns for each account and for total stockholders' equity. The transactions are then identified and their effects are shown in the appropriate columns.

**Illustration 12A-1**
Stockholders' equity statement

| HAMPTON CORPORATION | | | | |
|---|---|---|---|---|
| Stockholders' Equity Statement | | | | |
| For the Year Ended December 31, 2008 | | | | |
| | Common Stock ($5 Par) | Paid-in Capital in Excess of Par | Retained Earnings | Treasury Stock | Total |
|---|---|---|---|---|---|
| Balance January 1 | $300,000 | $200,000 | $650,000 | $(34,000) | $1,116,000 |
| Issued 5,000 shares of common stock at $15 | 25,000 | 50,000 | | | 75,000 |
| Declared a $40,000 cash dividend | | | (40,000) | | (40,000) |
| Purchased 2,000 shares for treasury at $16 | | | | (32,000) | (32,000) |
| Net income for year | | | 240,000 | | 240,000 |
| Balance December 31 | $325,000 | $250,000 | $850,000 | $(66,000) | $1,359,000 |

In practice, additional columns are usually provided to show the number of shares of issued stock and treasury stock. The stockholders' equity statement for PepsiCo, for a three-year period, is shown in Appendix A. **When a stockholders' equity statement is presented, a retained earnings statement is not necessary** because the retained earnings column explains the changes in this account.

## SUMMARY OF STUDY OBJECTIVE FOR APPENDIX 12A

**8   Describe the use and content of the stockholders' equity statement.** Corporations must disclose changes in stockholders' equity accounts and may choose to do so by issuing a separate stockholders' equity statement. This statement, prepared in columnar form, shows changes in each stockholders' equity account and in total stockholders' equity during the accounting period. When this statement is presented, a retained earnings statement is not necessary.

## APPENDIX 12B   Book Value—Another Per-Share Amount

### Book Value Per Share

You have learned about a number of per share amounts in this chapter. Another per-share amount of some importance is book value per share. It represents **the equity a common stockholder has in the net assets of the corporation** from owning one share of stock. Remember that the net assets (total assets minus total liabilities) of a corporation must be equal to total stockholders' equity. Therefore, the formula for computing book value per share when a company has only one class of stock outstanding is:

> **STUDY OBJECTIVE 9**
> Compute book value per share.

| Total Stockholders' Equity | ÷ | Number of Common Shares Outstanding | = | Book Value per Share |
|---|---|---|---|---|

**Illustration 12B-1**
Book value per share formula

Thus, if Marlo Corporation has total stockholders' equity of $1,500,000 (common stock $1,000,000 and retained earnings $500,000) and 50,000 shares of common stock outstanding, book value per share is $30 ($1,500,000 ÷ 50,000).

When a company has both preferred and common stock, the computation of book value is more complex. Since preferred stockholders have a prior claim on net assets over common stockholders, their equity must be deducted from total stockholders' equity. Then we can determine the stockholders' equity that applies to the common stock. The computation of book value per share involves the following steps.

1.  **Compute the preferred stock equity.** This equity is equal to the sum of the call price of preferred stock plus any cumulative dividends in arrears. If the preferred stock does not have a call price, the par value of the stock is used.

2.  **Determine the common stock equity.** Subtract the preferred stock equity from total stockholders' equity.

3.  **Determine book value per share.** Divide common stock equity by shares of common stock outstanding.

**EXAMPLE**

We will use the stockholders' equity section of Graber Inc. shown in Illustration 12-26. Graber's preferred stock is callable at $120 per share and is cumulative. Assume that dividends on Graber's preferred stock were in arrears for one year, $54,000 (6,000 × $9). The computation of preferred stock equity (Step 1 in the preceding list) is:

**Illustration 12B-2**
Computation of preferred stock equity—Step 1

| | |
|---|---|
| Call price (6,000 shares × $120) | $720,000 |
| Dividends in arrears (6,000 shares × $9) | 54,000 |
| **Preferred stock equity** | **$774,000** |

The computation of book value (Steps 2 and 3) is as follows.

**Illustration 12B-3**
Computation of book value per share with preferred stock—Steps 2 and 3

| | |
|---|---|
| Total stockholders' equity | $4,810,000 |
| Less: **Preferred stock equity** | 774,000 |
| **Common stock equity** | **$4,036,000** |
| **Shares of common stock outstanding** | 390,000 |
| **Book value per share** ($4,036,000 ÷ 390,000) | **$10.35** |

Note that we used the call price of $120 instead of the par value of $100. Note also that the paid-in capital in excess of par value of preferred stock, $30,000, **is not assigned to the preferred stock equity**. Preferred stockholders ordinarily do not have a right to amounts paid-in in excess of par value. Therefore, such amounts are assigned to the common stock equity in computing book value.

## Book Value versus Market Value

Be sure you understand that **book value per share may not equal market value per share**. Book value generally is based on recorded costs. Market value reflects the subjective judgments of thousands of stockholders and prospective investors about a company's potential for future earnings and dividends. Market value per share may exceed book value per share, but that fact does not necessarily mean that the stock is overpriced. The correlation between book value and the annual range of a company's market value per share is often remote, as indicated by the following recent data.

**Illustration 12B-4**
Book and market values compared

| Company | Book Value (year-end) | Market Range (for year 2005) |
|---|---|---|
| The Limited, Inc. | $13.38 | $31.03–$22.89 |
| H. J. Heinz Company | $ 7.48 | $40.61–$34.53 |
| Cisco Systems | $ 3.66 | $21.24–$17.01 |
| Wal-Mart Stores | $12.79 | $50.87–$42.31 |

Book value per share **is useful** in determining the trend of a stockholder's per share equity in a corporation. It is also significant in many contracts and in court cases where the rights of individual parties are based on cost information.

**9 Compute book value per share.** Book value per share represents the equity a common stockholder has in the net assets of a corporation from owning one share of stock. When there is only common stock outstanding, the formula for computing book value is: Total stockholders' equity ÷ Number of common shares outstanding = Book value per share.

## GLOSSARY FOR APPENDIX 12B

**Book value per share** The equity a common stockholder has in the net assets of the corporation from owning one share of stock. (p. 571).

*****Note:** All asterisked Questions, Exercises, and Problems relate to material in the appendices to the chapter.

## SELF-STUDY QUESTIONS

*Answers are at the end of the chapter.*

(SO 1) **1.** Which of the following is *not* a major advantage of a corporation?
  **a.** Separate legal existence.
  **b.** Continuous life.
  **c.** Government regulations.
  **d.** Transferable ownership rights.

(SO 1) **2.** A major disadvantage of a corporation is:
  **a.** limited liability of stockholders.
  **b.** additional taxes.
  **c.** transferable ownership rights.
  **d.** none of the above.

(SO 2) **3.** Which of the following statements is *false*?
  **a.** Ownership of common stock gives the owner a voting right.
  **b.** The stockholders' equity section begins with paid-in capital.
  **c.** The authorization of capital stock does not result in a formal accounting entry.
  **d.** The par value of a share of stock is equal to its market value.

(SO 2) **4.** ABC Corporation issues 1,000 shares of $10 par value common stock at $12 per share. In recording the transaction, credits are made to:
  **a.** Common Stock $10,000 and Paid-in Capital in Excess of Stated Value $2,000.
  **b.** Common Stock $12,000.
  **c.** Common Stock $10,000 and Paid-in Capital in Excess of Par Value $2,000.
  **d.** Common Stock $10,000 and Retained Earnings $2,000.

(SO 3) **5.** XYZ, Inc. sells 100 shares of $5 par value treasury stock at $13 per share. If the cost of acquiring the shares was $10 per share, the entry for the sale should include credits to:
  **a.** Treasury Stock $1,000 and Paid-in Capital from Treasury Stock $300.
  **b.** Treasury Stock $500 and Paid-in Capital from Treasury Stock $800.

  **c.** Treasury Stock $1,000 and Retained Earnings $300.
  **d.** Treasury Stock $500 and Paid-in Capital in Excess of Par Value $800.

**6.** In the stockholders' equity section, the cost of treasury (SO 3) stock is deducted from:
  **a.** total paid-in capital and retained earnings.
  **b.** retained earnings.
  **c.** total stockholders' equity.
  **d.** common stock in paid-in capital.

**7.** Preferred stock may have priority over common stock (SO 4) *except* in:
  **a.** dividends.
  **b.** assets in the event of liquidation.
  **c.** cumulative dividend features.
  **d.** voting.

**8.** Entries for cash dividends are required on the: (SO 5)
  **a.** declaration date and the payment date.
  **b.** record date and the payment date.
  **c.** declaration date, record date, and payment date.
  **d.** declaration date and the record date.

**9.** Which of the following statements about small stock divi- (SO 5) dends is true?
  **a.** A debit to Retained Earnings for the par value of the shares issued should be made.
  **b.** A small stock dividend decreases total stockholders' equity.
  **c.** Market value per share should be assigned to the dividend shares.
  **d.** A small stock dividend ordinarily will have no effect on book value per share of stock.

**10.** All *but one* of the following is reported in a retained earn- (SO 6) ings statement. The exception is:
  **a.** cash and stock dividends.
  **b.** net income and net loss.
  **c.** some disposals of treasury stock below cost.
  **d.** sales of treasury stock above cost.

(SO 6) **11.** A prior period adjustment is:
a. reported in the income statement as a nontypical item.
b. a correction of an error that is made directly to retained earnings.
c. reported directly in the stockholders' equity section.
d. reported in the retained earnings statement as an adjustment of the ending balance of retained earnings.

(SO 8) *12. When a stockholders' equity statement is presented, it is not necessary to prepare a(an):
a. retained earnings statement.
b. balance sheet.
c. income statement.
d. None of the above.

(SO 9) *13. The ledger of JFK, Inc. shows common stock, common treasury stock, and no preferred stock. For this company, the formula for computing book value per share is:

a. Total paid-in capital and retained earnings divided by the number of shares of common stock issued.
b. Common stock divided by the number of shares of common stock issued.
c. Total stockholders' equity divided by the number of shares of common stock outstanding.
d. Total stockholders' equity divided by the number of shares of common stock issued.

Go to the book's website,
**www.wiley.com/college/weygandt**,
for Additional Self-Study questions.

 *The Navigator*

# QUESTIONS

**1.** Mike Horn, a student, asks your help in understanding the following characteristics of a corporation: (a) separate legal existence, (b) limited liability of stockholders, and (c) transferable ownership rights. Explain these characteristics to Mike.

**2.** (a) Your friend Veena Gall cannot understand how the characteristic of corporation management is both an advantage and a disadvantage. Clarify this problem for Veena.
(b) Identify and explain two other disadvantages of a corporation.

**3.** Kari Jonas believes a corporation must be incorporated in the state in which its headquarters office is located. Is Kari correct? Explain.

**4.** What are the basic ownership rights of common stockholders in the absence of restrictive provisions?

**5.** A corporation has been defined as an entity separate and distinct from its owners. In what ways is a corporation a separate legal entity?

**6.** (a) What are the two principal components of stockholders' equity?
(b) What is paid-in capital? Give three examples.

**7.** The corporate charter of Sokol Corporation allows the issuance of a maximum of 100,000 shares of common stock. During its first two years of operations, Sokol sold 80,000 shares to stockholders and reacquired 7,000 of these shares. After these transactions, how many shares are authorized, issued, and outstanding?

**8.** Which is the better investment—common stock with a par value of $5 per share, or common stock with a par value of $20 per share? Why?

**9.** What factors help determine the market value of stock?

**10.** Why is common stock usually not issued at a price that is less than par value?

**11.** Land appraised at $80,000 is purchased by issuing 1,000 shares of $20 par value common stock. The market price of the shares at the time of the exchange, based on active trading in the securities market, is $90 per share. Should the land be recorded at $20,000, $80,000, or $90,000? Explain.

**12.** For what reasons might a company like IBM repurchase some of its stock (treasury stock)?

**13.** Chen, Inc. purchases 1,000 shares of its own previously issued $5 par common stock for $12,000. Assuming the shares are held in the treasury, what effect does this transaction have on (a) net income, (b) total assets, (c) total paid-in capital, and (d) total stockholders' equity?

**14.** The treasury stock purchased in question 13 is resold by Chen, Inc. for $15,000. What effect does this transaction have on (a) net income, (b) total assets, (c) total paid-in capital, and (d) total stockholders' equity?

**15.** (a) What are the principal differences between common stock and preferred stock?
(b) Preferred stock may be cumulative. Discuss this feature.
(c) How are dividends in arrears presented in the financial statements?

**16.** Identify the events that result in credits and debits to retained earnings.

**17.** Indicate how each of the following accounts should be classified in the stockholders' equity section.
(a) Common Stock.
(b) Paid-in Capital in Excess of Par Value.
(c) Retained Earnings.
(d) Treasury Stock.
(e) Paid-in Capital from Treasury Stock.
(f) Paid-in Capital in Excess of Stated Value.
(g) Preferred Stock.

**18.** What three conditions must exist before a cash dividend is paid?

**19.** Three dates associated with Naperville Company's cash dividend are May 1, May 15, and May 31. Discuss the significance of each date and give the entry at each date.

20. Contrast the effects of a cash dividend and a stock dividend on a corporation's balance sheet.

21. Mark Federia asks, "Since stock dividends don't change anything, why declare them?" What is your answer to Mark?

22. Fields Corporation has 20,000 shares of $10 par value common stock outstanding when it announces a 2-for-1 stock split. Before the split, the stock had a market price of $120 per share. After the split, how many shares of stock will be outstanding? What will be the approximate market price per share?

23. The board of directors is considering either a stock split or a stock dividend. They understand that total stockholders'

equity will remain the same under either action. However, they are not sure of the different effects of the two types of actions on other aspects of stockholders' equity. Explain the differences to the directors.

24. What is a prior period adjustment, and how is it reported in the financial statements?

25. What is the purpose of a retained earnings restriction? Identify the possible causes of retained earnings restrictions.

*26. What is the formula for computing book value per share when a corporation has only common stock?

*27. Alou Inc.'s common stock has a par value of $1, a book value of $29, and a current market value of $15. Explain why these amounts are all different.

## BRIEF EXERCISES

**BE12-1**   Ron Child is studying for his accounting midterm examination. Identify for Ron the advantages and disadvantages of the corporate form of business organization.

*List the advantages and disadvantages of a corporation.*
(SO 1)

**BE12-2**   On May 10, Romano Corporation issues 1,000 shares of $10 par value common stock for cash at $18 per share. Journalize the issuance of the stock.

*Prepare entry for issuance of par value common stock.*
(SO 2)

**BE12-3**   On June 1, Herrera Inc. issues 3,000 shares of no-par common stock at a cash price of $7 per share. Journalize the issuance of the shares assuming the stock has a stated value of $1 per share.

*Prepare entry for issuance of no-par value common stock.*
(SO 2)

**BE12-4**   Tara Inc.'s $10 par value common stock is actively traded at a market value of $16 per share. Tara issues 5,000 shares to purchase land advertised for sale at $85,000. Journalize the issuance of the stock in acquiring the land.

*Prepare entry for issuance of stock in a noncash transaction.*
(SO 2)

**BE12-5**   On July 1, Fritz Corporation purchases 500 shares of its $5 par value common stock for the treasury at a cash price of $9 per share. On September 1, it sells 300 shares of the treasury stock for cash at $11 per share. Journalize the two treasury stock transactions.

*Prepare entries for treasury stock transactions.*
(SO 3)

**BE12-6**   Ervay Inc. issues 5,000 shares of $100 par value preferred stock for cash at $120 per share. Journalize the issuance of the preferred stock.

*Prepare entry for issuance of preferred stock.*
(SO 4)

**BE12-7**   Chavez Corporation has 50,000 shares of common stock outstanding. It declares a $1 per share cash dividend on November 1 to stockholders of record on December 1. The dividend is paid on December 31. Prepare the entries on the appropriate dates to record the declaration and payment of the cash dividend.

*Prepare entries for a cash dividend.*
(SO 5)

**BE12-8**   Walters Corporation has 60,000 shares of $10 par value common stock outstanding. It declares a 10% stock dividend on December 1 when the market value per share is $16. The dividend shares are issued on December 31. Prepare the entries for the declaration and distribution of the stock dividend.

*Prepare entries for a stock dividend.*
(SO 5)

**BE12-9**   The stockholders' equity section of Martin Corporation consists of common stock ($10 par) $2,000,000 and retained earnings $300,000. A 10% stock dividend (20,000 shares) is declared when the market value per share is $14. Show the before and after effects of the dividend on the following.

*Show before and after effects of a stock dividend.*
(SO 5)

(a) The components of stockholders' equity.
(b) Shares outstanding.

**BE12-10**   For the year ending December 31, 2008, Mount Inc. reports net income $120,000 and dividends $85,000. Prepare the retained earnings statement for the year assuming the balance in retained earnings on January 1, 2008, was $220,000.

*Prepare a retained earnings statement.*
(SO 6)

*Prepare a retained earnings statement.*
(SO 6)

**BE12-11**   The balance in retained earnings on January 1, 2008, for Ola Smith Inc, was $800,000. During the year, the corporation paid cash dividends of $90,000 and distributed a stock dividend of $8,000. In addition, the company determined that it had understated its depreciation expense in prior years by $50,000. Net income for 2008 was $150,000. Prepare the retained earnings statement for 2008.

*Prepare stockholders' equity section.*
(SO 7)

**BE12-12**   Ingram Corporation has the following accounts at December 31: Common Stock, $10 par, 5,000 shares issued, $50,000; Paid-in Capital in Excess of Par Value $10,000; Retained Earnings $45,000; and Treasury Stock—Common, 500 shares, $11,000. Prepare the stockholders' equity section of the balance sheet.

*Compute book value per share.*
(SO 9)

**\*BE12-13**   The balance sheet for Jimenez Inc. shows the following: total paid-in capital and retained earnings $870,000, total stockholders' equity $810,000, common stock issued 44,000 shares, and common stock outstanding 40,000 shares. Compute the book value per share.

# EXERCISES

*Identify characteristics of a corporation.*
(SO 1)

**E12-1**   Jeff Lynne has prepared the following list of statements about corporations.

1. A corporation is an entity separate and distinct from its owners.
2. As a legal entity, a corporation has most of the rights and privileges of a person.
3. Most of the largest U.S. corporations are privately held corporations.
4. Corporations may buy, own, and sell property; borrow money; enter into legally binding contracts; and sue and be sued.
5. The net income of a corporation is not taxed as a separate entity.
6. Creditors have a legal claim on the personal assets of the owners of a corporation if the corporation does not pay its debts.
7. The transfer of stock from one owner to another requires the approval of either the corporation or other stockholders.
8. The board of directors of a corporation legally owns the corporation.
9. The chief accounting officer of a corporation is the controller.
10. Corporations are subject to less state and federal regulations than partnerships or proprietorships.

**Instructions**
Identify each statement as true or false. If false, indicate how to correct the statement.

*Identify characteristics of a corporation.*
(SO 1, 2)

**E12-2**   Jeff Lynne (see E12-1) has studied the information you gave him in that exercise and has come to you with more statements about corporation.

1. Corporation management is both an advantage and a disadvantage of a corporation compared to a proprietorship or a partnership.
2. Limited liability of stockholders, government regulations, and additional taxes are the major disadvantages of a corporation.
3. When a corporation is formed, organization costs are recorded as an asset.
4. Each share of common stock gives the stockholder the ownership rights to vote at stockholder meetings, share in corporate earnings, keep the same percentage ownership when new shares of stock are issued, and share in assets upon liquidation.
5. The number of issued shares is always greater than or equal to the number of authorized shares.
6. A journal entry is required for the authorization of capital stock.
7. Publicly held corporations usually issue stock directly to investors.
8. The trading of capital stock on a securities exchange involves the transfer of already issued shares from an existing stockholder to another investor.
9. The market value of common stock is usually the same as its par value.
10. Retained earnings is the total amount of cash and other assets paid in to the corporation by stockholders in exchange for capital stock.

**Instructions**
Identify each statement as true or false. If false, indicate how to correct the statement.

**E12-3**  During its first year of operations, Klumpe Corporation had the following transactions pertaining to its common stock.

*Journalize issuance of common stock.*

*(SO 2)*

Jan. 10   Issued 70,000 shares for cash at $5 per share.
July  1   Issued 40,000 shares for cash at $8 per share.

**Instructions**
**(a)** Journalize the transactions, assuming that the common stock has a par value of $5 per share.
**(b)** Journalize the transactions, assuming that the common stock is no-par with a stated value of $1 per share.

**E12-4**  Grossman Corporation issued 1,000 shares of stock.

*Journalize issuance of common stock.*

*(SO 2)*

**Instructions**
Prepare the entry for the issuance under the following assumptions.

**(a)** The stock had a par value of $5 per share and was issued for a total of $52,000.
**(b)** The stock had a stated value of $5 per share and was issued for a total of $52,000.
**(c)** The stock had no par or stated value and was issued for a total of $52,000.
**(d)** The stock had a par value of $5 per share and was issued to attorneys for services during incorporation valued at $52,000.
**(e)** The stock had a par value of $5 per share and was issued for land worth $52,000.

**E12-5**  Mad City Corporation purchased from its stockholders 5,000 shares of its own previously issued stock for $250,000. It later resold 2,000 shares for $54 per share, then 2,000 more shares for $49 per share, and finally 1,000 shares for $40 per share.

*Journalize treasury stock transactions.*

*(SO 3)*

**Instructions**
Prepare journal entries for the purchase of the treasury stock and the three sales of treasury stock.

**E12-6**  AI Corporation issued 100,000 shares of $20 par value, cumulative, 8% preferred stock on January 1, 2007, for $2,100,000. In December 2009, AI declared its first dividend of $500,000.

*Differentiate between preferred and common stock.*

*(SO 4)*

**Instructions**
**(a)** Prepare AI's journal entry to record the issuance of the preferred stock.
**(b)** If the preferred stock is *not* cumulative, how much of the $500,000 would be paid to **common** stockholders?
**(c)** If the preferred stock is cumulative, how much of the $500,000 would be paid to **common** stockholders?

**E12-7**  Garza Co. had the following transactions during the current period.

*Journalize issuance of common and preferred stock and purchase of treasury stock.*

*(SO 2, 3, 4)*

Mar.  2   Issued 5,000 shares of $1 par value common stock to attorneys in payment of a bill for $30,000 for services provided in helping the company to incorporate.
June 12   Issued 60,000 shares of $1 par value common stock for cash of $375,000.
July 11   Issued 1,000 shares of $100 par value preferred stock for cash at $110 per share.
Nov. 28   Purchased 2,000 shares of treasury stock for $80,000.

**Instructions**
Journalize the transactions.

**E12-8**  As an auditor for the CPA firm of Agler and Carl, you encounter the following situations in auditing different clients.

*Journalize noncash common stock transactions.*

*(SO 2)*

**1.** Desi Corporation is a closely held corporation whose stock is not publicly traded. On December 5, the corporation acquired land by issuing 5,000 shares of its $20 par value common stock. The owners' asking price for the land was $120,000, and the fair market value of the land was $110,000.
**2.** Lucille Corporation is a publicly held corporation whose common stock is traded on the securities markets. On June 1, it acquired land by issuing 20,000 shares of its $10 par value stock. At the time of the exchange, the land was advertised for sale at $250,000. The stock was selling at $11 per share.

**Instructions**
Prepare the journal entries for each of the situations above.

*Journalize treasury stock transactions.*

*(SO 3)*

**E12-9** On January 1, 2008, the stockholders' equity section of Rowen Corporation shows: Common stock ($5 par value) $1,500,000; paid-in capital in excess of par value $1,000,000; and retained earnings $1,200,000. During the year, the following treasury stock transactions occurred.

Mar. 1 Purchased 50,000 shares for cash at $16 per share.
July 1 Sold 10,000 treasury shares for cash at $17 per share.
Sept. 1 Sold 8,000 treasury shares for cash at $15 per share.

**Instructions**
**(a)** Journalize the treasury stock transactions.
**(b)** Restate the entry for September 1, assuming the treasury shares were sold at $13 per share.

*Journalize preferred stock transactions and indicate statement presentation.*

*(SO 4, 7)*

**E12-10** Tinker Corporation is authorized to issue both preferred and common stock. The par value of the preferred is $50. During the first year of operations, the company had the following events and transactions pertaining to its preferred stock.

Feb. 1 Issued 20,000 shares for cash at $51 per share.
July 1 Issued 10,000 shares for cash at $57 per share.

**Instructions**
**(a)** Journalize the transactions.
**(b)** Post to the stockholders' equity accounts.
**(c)** Indicate the financial statement presentation of the related accounts.

*Answer questions about stockholders' equity section.*

*(SO 2, 3, 4, 7)*

**E12-11** The stockholders' equity section of Lumley Corporation at December 31 is as follows.

### LUMLEY CORPORATION
Balance Sheet (partial)

| | |
|---|---:|
| Paid-in capital | |
| Preferred stock, cumulative, 10,000 shares authorized, 6,000 shares issued and outstanding | $ 600,000 |
| Common stock, no par, 750,000 shares authorized, 600,000 shares issued | 1,200,000 |
| Total paid-in capital | 1,800,000 |
| Retained earnings | 1,858,000 |
| Total paid-in capital and retained earnings | 3,658,000 |
| Less: Treasury stock (12,000 common shares) | (64,000) |
| Total stockholders' equity | $3,594,000 |

**Instructions**
From a review of the stockholders' equity section, as chief accountant, write a memo to the president of the company answering the following questions.
**(a)** How many shares of common stock are outstanding?
**(b)** Assuming there is a stated value, what is the stated value of the common stock?
**(c)** What is the par value of the preferred stock?
**(d)** If the annual dividend on preferred stock is $30,000, what is the dividend rate on preferred stock?
**(e)** If dividends of $60,000 were in arrears on preferred stock, what would be the balance in Retained Earnings?

*Prepare correct entries for capital stock transactions.*

*(SO 2, 3, 4)*

**E12-12** Flores Corporation recently hired a new accountant with extensive experience in accounting for partnerships. Because of the pressure of the new job, the accountant was unable to review his textbooks on the topic of corporation accounting. During the first month, the accountant made the following entries for the corporation's capital stock.

| | | | | |
|---|---|---|---:|---:|
| May 2 | Cash | | 120,000 | |
| | Capital Stock | | | 120,000 |
| | (Issued 10,000 shares of $10 par value common stock at $12 per share) | | | |
| 10 | Cash | | 600,000 | |
| | Capital Stock | | | 600,000 |
| | (Issued 10,000 shares of $50 par value preferred stock at $60 per share) | | | |

| 15 | Capital Stock | 14,000 | |
| | Cash | | 14,000 |
| | (Purchased 1,000 shares of common stock for the treasury at $14 per share) | | |
| 31 | Cash | 8,000 | |
| | Capital Stock | | 5,000 |
| | Gain on Sale of Stock | | 3,000 |
| | (Sold 500 shares of treasury stock at $16 per share) | | |

**Instructions**

On the basis of the explanation for each entry, prepare the entry that should have been made for the capital stock transactions.

**E12-13**    On January 1, Armada Corporation had 95,000 shares of no-par common stock issued and outstanding. The stock has a stated value of $5 per share. During the year, the following occurred.

*Journalize cash dividends; indicate statement presentation.*

*(SO 5)*

Apr.  1    Issued 15,000 additional shares of common stock for $17 per share.
June 15    Declared a cash dividend of $1 per share to stockholders of record on June 30.
July 10    Paid the $1 cash dividend.
Dec.  1    Issued 2,000 additional shares of common stock for $19 per share.
     15    Declared a cash dividend on outstanding shares of $1.20 per share to stockholders of record on December 31.

**Instructions**

**(a)** Prepare the entries, if any, on each of the three dividend dates.
**(b)** How are dividends and dividends payable reported in the financial statements prepared at December 31?

**E12-14**    On January 1, 2008, Abdella Corporation had $1,000,000 of common stock outstanding that was issued at par. It also had retained earnings of $750,000. The company issued 60,000 shares of common stock at par on July 1 and earned net income of $400,000 for the year.

*Journalize stock dividends.*

*(SO 5)*

**Instructions**

Journalize the declaration of a 15% stock dividend on December 10, 2008, for the following independent assumptions.
**1.** Par value is $10, and market value is $18.
**2.** Par value is $5, and market value is $20.

**E12-15**    On October 31, the stockholders' equity section of Omar Company consists of common stock $600,000 and retained earnings $900,000. Omar is considering the following two courses of action: (1) declaring a 5% stock dividend on the 60,000, $10 par value shares outstanding, or (2) effecting a 2-for-1 stock split that will reduce par value to $5 per share. The current market price is $14 per share.

*Compare effects of a stock dividend and a stock split.*

*(SO 5)*

**Instructions**

Prepare a tabular summary of the effects of the alternative actions on the components of stockholders' equity, outstanding shares, and book value per share. Use the following column headings: Before Action, After Stock Dividend, and After Stock Split.

**E12-16**    Before preparing financial statements for the current year, the chief accountant for Springer Company discovered the following errors in the accounts.

*Prepare correcting entries for dividends and a stock split.*

*(SO 5)*

**1.** The declaration and payment of $50,000 cash dividend was recorded as a debit to Interest Expense $50,000 and a credit to Cash $50,000.
**2.** A 10% stock dividend (1,000 shares) was declared on the $10 par value stock when the market value per share was $16. The only entry made was: Retained Earnings (Dr.) $10,000 and Dividends Payable (Cr.) $10,000. The shares have not been issued.
**3.** A 4-for-1 stock split involving the issue of 400,000 shares of $5 par value common stock for 100,000 shares of $20 par value common stock was recorded as a debit to Retained Earnings $2,000,000 and a credit to Common Stock $2,000,000.

**Instructions**

Prepare the correcting entries at December 31.

*Prepare a retained earnings statement.*

*(SO 6)*

**E12-17**  On January 1, 2008, Castle Corporation had retained earnings of $550,000. During the year, Castle had the following selected transactions.

1. Declared cash dividends of $120,000.
2. Corrected overstatement of 2007 net income because of depreciation error $30,000.
3. Earned net income of $350,000.
4. Declared stock dividends of $80,000.

**Instructions**
Prepare a retained earnings statement for the year.

*Prepare a retained earnings statement.*

*(SO 6)*

**E12-18**  Sasha Company reported retained earnings at December 31, 2007, of $310,000. Sasha had 200,000 shares of common stock outstanding throughout 2008.
The following transactions occurred during 2008.

1. An error was discovered: in 2006, depreciation expense was recorded at $70,000, but the correct amount was $50,000.
2. A cash dividend of $0.50 per share was declared and paid.
3. A 5% stock dividend was declared and distributed when the market price per share was $15 per share.
4. Net income was $285,000.

**Instructions**
Prepare a retained earnings statement for 2008.

*Classify stockholders' equity accounts.*

*(SO 7)*

**E12-19**  The ledger of O'Dell Corporation contains the following accounts: Common Stock, Preferred Stock, Treasury Stock—Common, Paid-in Capital in Excess of Par Value—Preferred Stock, Paid-in Capital in Excess of Stated Value—Common Stock, Paid-in Capital from Treasury Stock, and Retained Earnings.

**Instructions**
Classify each account using the following table headings.

| | **Paid-in Capital** | | | |
| **Account** | **Capital Stock** | **Additional** | **Retained Earnings** | **Other** |
|---|---|---|---|---|

*Prepare a stockholders' equity section.*

*(SO 7)*

**E12-20**  The following accounts appear in the ledger of Tiger Inc. after the books are closed at December 31.

| | |
|---|---:|
| Common Stock, no par, $1 stated value, 400,000 shares authorized; 300,000 shares issued | $ 300,000 |
| Common Stock Dividends Distributable | 60,000 |
| Paid-in Capital in Excess of Stated Value—Common Stock | 1,200,000 |
| Preferred Stock, $5 par value, 8%, 40,000 shares authorized; 30,000 shares issued | 150,000 |
| Retained Earnings | 700,000 |
| Treasury Stock (10,000 common shares) | 74,000 |
| Paid-in Capital in Excess of Par Value—Preferred Stock | 344,000 |

**Instructions**
Prepare the stockholders' equity section at December 31, assuming retained earnings is restricted for plant expansion in the amount of $100,000.

*Prepare stockholders' equity section.*

*(SO 7)*

**E12-21**  Kelly Groucutt Company reported the following balances at December 31, 2007: common stock $400,000; paid-in capital in excess of par value $100,000; retained earnings $250,000. During 2008, the following transactions affected stockholder's equity.

1. Issued preferred stock with a par value of $125,000 for $200,000.
2. Purchased treasury stock (common) for $40,000.
3. Earned net income of $140,000.
4. Declared and paid cash dividends of $56,000.

**Instructions**

Prepare the stockholders' equity section of Kelly Groucutt Company's December 31, 2008, balance sheet.

**E12-22** In 2008, Mike Singletary Corporation had net sales of $600,000 and cost of goods sold of $360,000. Operating expenses were $153,000, and interest expense was $7,500. The corporation's tax rate is 30%. The corporation declared preferred dividends of $15,000 in 2008, and its average common stockholders' equity during the year was $200,000.

*Prepare an income statement and compute return on equity.*

*(SO 7)*

**Instructions**

**(a)** Prepare an income statement for Mike Singletary Corporation.

**(b)** Compute Mike Singletary Corporation's return on common stockholders' equity for 2008.

**E12-23** McCoy Corporation has outstanding at December 31, 2008, 50,000 shares of $20 par value, cumulative, 8% preferred stock and 200,000 shares of $5 par value common stock. All shares were outstanding the entire year. During 2008, McCoy earned total revenues of $2,000,000 and incurred total expenses (except income taxes) of $1,200,000. McCoy's income tax rate is 30%.

*Compute EPS.*

*(SO 7)*

**Instructions**

Compute McCoy's 2008 earnings per share.

**\*E12-24** In a recent year, the stockholders' equity section of **Aluminum Company of America (Alcoa)** showed the following (in alphabetical order): additional paid-in capital $6,101, common stock $925, preferred stock $56, retained earnings $7,428, and treasury stock $2,828. All dollar data are in millions.

The preferred stock has 557,740 shares authorized, with a par value of $100 and an annual $3.75 per share cumulative dividend preference. At December 31, 557,649 shares of preferred are issued and 546,024 shares are outstanding. There are 1.8 billion shares of $1 par value common stock authorized, of which 924.6 million are issued and 844.8 million are outstanding at December 31.

*Prepare a stockholders' equity section.*

*(SO 7, 9)*

**Instructions**

**(a)** Prepare the stockholders' equity section, including disclosure of all relevant data.

**(b)** Compute the book value per share of common stock, assuming there are no preferred dividends in arrears. (Round to two decimals.)

**\*E12-25** At December 31, Missouri Corporation has total stockholders' equity of $3,000,000. Included in this total are preferred stock $500,000 and paid-in capital in excess of par value—preferred stock $50,000. There are 10,000 shares of $50 par value 10% cumulative preferred stock outstanding. At year-end, 200,000 shares of common stock are outstanding.

*Compute book value per share with preferred stock.*

*(SO 4, 9)*

**Instructions**

Compute the book value per share of common stock, under each of the following assumptions.

**(a)** There are no preferred dividends in arrears, and the preferred stock does not have a call price.

**(b)** Preferred dividends are one year in arrears, and the preferred stock has a call price of $60 per share.

**\*E12-26** On October 1, Chile Corporation's stockholders' equity is as follows.

*Compute book value per share; indicate account balances after a stock dividend.*

*(SO 5, 7, 9)*

| | |
|---|---|
| Common stock, $5 par value | $200,000 |
| Paid-in capital in excess of par value | 25,000 |
| Retained earnings | 75,000 |
| Total stockholders' equity | $300,000 |

On October 1, Chile declares and distributes a 10% stock dividend when the market value of the stock is $15 per share.

**Instructions**

**(a)** Compute the book value per share (1) before the stock dividend and (2) after the stock dividend. (Round to two decimals.)

**(b)** Indicate the balances in the three stockholders' equity accounts after the stock dividend shares have been distributed.

# EXERCISES: SET B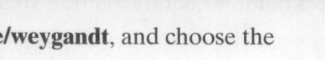

Visit the book's website at **www.wiley.com/college/weygandt**, and choose the Student Companion site, to access Exercise Set B.

# PROBLEMS: SET A

*Journalize stock transactions, post, and prepare paid-in capital section.*

(SO 2, 4, 7)

**P12-1A** Hayslett Corporation was organized on January 1, 2008. It is authorized to issue 20,000 shares of 6%, $50 par value preferred stock, and 500,000 shares of no-par common stock with a stated value of $2 per share. The following stock transactions were completed during the first year.

Jan. 10 Issued 100,000 shares of common stock for cash at $3 per share.
Mar. 1 Issued 10,000 shares of preferred stock for cash at $55 per share.
Apr. 1 Issued 25,000 shares of common stock for land. The asking price of the land was $90,000. The company's estimate of the fair market value of the land was $85,000.
May 1 Issued 75,000 shares of common stock for cash at $4 per share.
Aug. 1 Issued 10,000 shares of common stock to attorneys in payment of their bill for $50,000 for services provided in helping the company organize.
Sept. 1 Issued 5,000 shares of common stock for cash at $6 per share.
Nov. 1 Issued 2,000 shares of preferred stock for cash at $58 per share.

**Instructions**
(a) Journalize the transactions.

*(c) Total paid-in capital $1,431,000*

(b) Post to the stockholders' equity accounts. (Use J1 as the posting reference.)
(c) Prepare the paid-in capital section of stockholders' equity at December 31, 2008.

*Journalize and post treasury stock transactions, and prepare stockholders' equity section.*

(SO 3, 7)

**P12-2A** Greeve Corporation had the following stockholders' equity accounts on January 1, 2008: Common Stock ($1 par) $400,000, Paid-in Capital in Excess of Par Value $500,000, and Retained Earnings $100,000. In 2008, the company had the following treasury stock transactions.

Mar. 1 Purchased 5,000 shares at $7 per share.
June 1 Sold 1,000 shares at $10 per share.
Sept. 1 Sold 2,000 shares at $9 per share.
Dec. 1 Sold 1,000 shares at $5 per share.

Greeve Corporation uses the cost method of accounting for treasury stock. In 2008, the company reported net income of $60,000.

**Instructions**
(a) Journalize the treasury stock transactions, and prepare the closing entry at December 31, 2008, for net income.

*(b) Treasury Stock $7,000*

*(c) Total stockholders' equity $1,058,000*

(b) Open accounts for (1) Paid-in Capital from Treasury Stock, (2) Treasury Stock, and (3) Retained Earnings. Post to these accounts using J12 as the posting reference.
(c) Prepare the stockholders' equity section for Greeve Corporation at December 31, 2008.

*Journalize and post transactions, prepare stockholders' equity section.*

(SO 2, 3, 4, 7, 9)

**P12-3A** The stockholders' equity accounts of Jajoo Corporation on January 1, 2008, were as follows.

| | |
|---|---:|
| Preferred Stock (10%, $100 par noncumulative, 5,000 shares authorized) | $ 300,000 |
| Common Stock ($5 stated value, 300,000 shares authorized) | 1,000,000 |
| Paid-in Capital in Excess of Par Value—Preferred Stock | 20,000 |
| Paid-in Capital in Excess of Stated Value—Common Stock | 425,000 |
| Retained Earnings | 488,000 |
| Treasury Stock—Common (5,000 shares) | 40,000 |

During 2008, the corporation had the following transactions and events pertaining to its stockholders' equity.

Feb. 1 Issued 3,000 shares of common stock for $25,000.
Mar. 20 Purchased 1,500 additional shares of common treasury stock at $8 per share.
June 14 Sold 4,000 shares of treasury stock—common for $36,000.
Sept. 3 Issued 2,000 shares of common stock for a patent valued at $17,000.
Dec. 31 Determined that net income for the year was $340,000.

**Instructions**
(a) Journalize the transactions and the closing entry for net income.
(b) Enter the beginning balances in the accounts and post the journal entries to the stockholders' equity accounts. (Use J1 as the posting reference.)
(c) Prepare a stockholders' equity section at December 31, 2008.
*(d) Compute the book value per share of common stock at December 31, 2008. (Round to two decimals.)

*(c) Total stockholders' equity
$2,599,000*

**P12-4A** On January 1, 2008, Galactica Corporation had the following stockholders' equity accounts.

*Prepare dividend entries and stockholders' equity section.*

*(SO 5, 7)*

| Common Stock ($20 par value, 60,000 shares issued and outstanding) | $1,200,000 |
| Paid-in Capital in Excess of Par Value | 200,000 |
| Retained Earnings | 500,000 |

During the year, the following transactions occurred.

Feb. 1 Declared a $1 cash dividend per share to stockholders of record on February 15, payable March 1.
Mar. 1 Paid the dividend declared in February.
Apr. 1 Announced a 5-for-1 stock split. Prior to the split, the market price per share was $35.
July 1 Declared a 5% stock dividend to stockholders of record on July 15, distributable July 31. On July 1, the market price of the stock was $7 per share.
July 31 Issued the shares for the stock dividend.
Dec. 1 Declared a $0.50 per share dividend to stockholders of record on December 15, payable January 5, 2009.
31 Determined that net income for the year was $380,000.

**Instructions**
(a) Journalize the transactions and closing entries.
(b) Enter the beginning balances and post the entries to the stockholders' equity accounts. (*Note:* Open additional stockholders' equity accounts as needed.)
(c) Prepare a stockholders' equity section at December 31.

*(c) Total stockholders' equity
$2,062,500*

**P12-5A** The ledger of Nakona Corporation at December 31, 2008, after the books have been closed, contains the following stockholders' equity accounts.

*Prepare retained earnings statement and stockholders' equity section, and compute earnings per share.*

*(SO 5, 6, 7)*

| Preferred Stock (10,000 shares issued) | $1,000,000 |
| Common Stock (400,000 shares issued) | 2,000,000 |
| Paid-in Capital in Excess of Par Value—Preferred | 200,000 |
| Paid-in Capital in Excess of Stated Value—Common | 1,100,000 |
| Common Stock Dividends Distributable | 200,000 |
| Retained Earnings | 2,365,000 |

A review of the accounting records reveals the following.

1. No errors have been made in recording 2008 transactions or in preparing the closing entry for net income.
2. Preferred stock is 8%, $100 par value, noncumulative, and callable at $125. Since January 1, 2007, 10,000 shares have been outstanding; 20,000 shares are authorized.
3. Common stock is no-par with a stated value of $5 per share; 600,000 shares are authorized.
4. The January 1 balance in Retained Earnings was $2,450,000.
5. On October 1, 100,000 shares of common stock were sold for cash at $8 per share.
6. A cash dividend of $600,000 was declared and properly allocated to preferred and common stock on November 1. No dividends were paid to preferred stockholders in 2007.
7. On December 31, a 10% common stock dividend was declared out of retained earnings on common stock when the market price per share was $7.
8. Net income for the year was $795,000.
9. On December 31, 2008, the directors authorized disclosure of a $100,000 restriction of retained earnings for plant expansion. (Use Note A.)

**Instructions**
(a) Reproduce the Retained Earnings account (T-account) for the year.
(b) Prepare a retained earnings statement for the year.

*(b) Retained earnings
$2,365,000*

(c) Total stockholders' equity
$6,865,000

**(c)** Prepare a stockholders' equity section at December 31.

**(d)** Compute the earnings per share of common stock using 325,000 as the weighted average shares outstanding for the year.

**(e)** Compute the allocation of the cash dividend to preferred and common stock.

*Prepare entries for stock transactions and stockholders' equity section.*

*(SO 2, 3, 4, 7)*

**P12-6A**    Arnold Corporation has been authorized to issue 40,000 shares of $100 par value, 8%, noncumulative preferred stock and 2,000,000 shares of no-par common stock. The corporation assigned a $5 stated value to the common stock. At December 31, 2008, the ledger contained the following balances pertaining to stockholders' equity.

| | |
|---|---:|
| Preferred Stock | $ 240,000 |
| Paid-in Capital in Excess of Par Value—Preferred | 56,000 |
| Common Stock | 2,000,000 |
| Paid-in Capital in Excess of Stated Value—Common | 5,700,000 |
| Treasury Stock—Common (1,000 shares) | 22,000 |
| Paid-in Capital from Treasury Stock | 3,000 |
| Retained Earnings | 560,000 |

The preferred stock was issued for land having a fair market value of $296,000. All common stock issued was for cash. In November, 1,500 shares of common stock were purchased for the treasury at a per share cost of $22. In December, 500 shares of treasury stock were sold for $28 per share. No dividends were declared in 2008.

**Instructions**

**(a)** Prepare the journal entries for the:

   **(1)** Issuance of preferred stock for land.

   **(2)** Issuance of common stock for cash.

   **(3)** Purchase of common treasury stock for cash.

   **(4)** Sale of treasury stock for cash.

(b) Total stockholders' equity
$8,537,000

**(b)** Prepare the stockholders' equity section at December 31, 2008.

*Prepare dividend entries and stockholders' equity section.*

*(SO 5, 7)*

**P12-7A**    On January 1, 2008, Snider Corporation had the following stockholders' equity accounts.

| | |
|---|---:|
| Common Stock ($10 par value, 90,000 shares issued and outstanding) | $900,000 |
| Paid-in Capital in Excess of Par Value | 200,000 |
| Retained Earnings | 540,000 |

During the year, the following transactions occurred.

Jan.  15  Declared a $1 cash dividend per share to stockholders of record on January 31, payable February 15.

Feb.  15  Paid the dividend declared in January.

Apr. 15  Declared a 10% stock dividend to stockholders of record on April 30, distributable May 15. On April 15, the market price of the stock was $15 per share.

May 15  Issued the shares for the stock dividend.

July   1  Announced a 2-for-1 stock split. The market price per share prior to the announcement was $17. (The new par value is $5.)

Dec.   1  Declared a $0.50 per share cash dividend to stockholders of record on December 15, payable January 10, 2009.

     31  Determined that net income for the year was $250,000.

**Instructions**

**(a)** Journalize the transactions and the closing entry for net income.

**(b)** Enter the beginning balances, and post the entries to the stockholders' equity accounts. (*Note*: Open additional stockholders' equity accounts as needed.)

(c) Total stockholders' equity
$1,701,000

**(c)** Prepare a stockholders' equity section at December 31.

*Prepare stockholders' equity section; compute book value per share.*

*(SO 7, 9)*

**\*P12-8A**    The following stockholders' equity accounts arranged alphabetically are in the ledger of McGrath Corporation at December 31, 2008.

| | |
|---|---:|
| Common Stock ($10 stated value) | $1,500,000 |
| Paid-in Capital from Treasury Stock | 6,000 |
| Paid-in Capital in Excess of Stated Value—Common Stock | 690,000 |

| Paid-in Capital in Excess of Par Value—Preferred Stock | 288,400 |
| Preferred Stock (8%, $100 par, noncumulative) | 400,000 |
| Retained Earnings | 776,000 |
| Treasury Stock—Common (8,000 shares) | 88,000 |

**Instructions**

(a) Prepare a stockholders' equity section at December 31, 2008.

(b) Compute the book value per share of the common stock, assuming the preferred stock has a call price of $110 per share.

*Total stockholders' equity $3,572,400*

**\*P12-9A**  On January 1, 2008, Hamblin Inc. had the following stockholders' equity balances.

*Prepare stockholders' equity statement.*

*(SO 8)*

| Common Stock (500,000 shares issued) | $1,000,000 |
| Paid-in Capital in Excess of Par Value | 500,000 |
| Common Stock Dividends Distributable | 100,000 |
| Retained Earnings | 600,000 |

During 2008, the following transactions and events occurred.

1. Issued 50,000 shares of $2 par value common stock as a result of 10% stock dividend declared on December 15, 2007.
2. Issued 30,000 shares of common stock for cash at $5 per share.
3. Purchased 25,000 shares of common stock for the treasury at $6 per share.
4. Declared and paid a cash dividend of $111,000.
5. Sold 8,000 shares of treasury stock for cash at $6 per share.
6. Earned net income of $360,000.

**Instructions**

Prepare a stockholders' equity statement for the year.

*Total stockholders' equity $2,497,000*

# PROBLEMS: SET B

**P12-1B**  Keeler Corporation was organized on January 1, 2008. It is authorized to issue 10,000 shares of 8%, $100 par value preferred stock, and 500,000 shares of no-par common stock with a stated value of $3 per share. The following stock transactions were completed during the first year.

*Journalize stock transactions, post, and prepare paid-in capital section.*

*(SO 2, 4, 7)*

GLS

| Jan. | 10 | Issued 80,000 shares of common stock for cash at $4 per share. |
| Mar. | 1 | Issued 5,000 shares of preferred stock for cash at $105 per share. |
| Apr. | 1 | Issued 24,000 shares of common stock for land. The asking price of the land was $90,000. The fair market value of the land was $85,000. |
| May | 1 | Issued 80,000 shares of common stock for cash at $4.50 per share. |
| Aug. | 1 | Issued 10,000 shares of common stock to attorneys in payment of their bill of $40,000 for services provided in helping the company organize. |
| Sept. | 1 | Issued 10,000 shares of common stock for cash at $5 per share. |
| Nov. | 1 | Issued 1,000 shares of preferred stock for cash at $109 per share. |

**Instructions**

(a) Journalize the transactions.

(b) Post to the stockholders' equity accounts. (Use J5 as the posting reference.)

(c) Prepare the paid-in capital section of stockholders' equity at December 31, 2008.

*(c) Total paid-in capital $1,489,000*

**P12-2B**  Goldberg Corporation had the following stockholders' equity accounts on January 1, 2008: Common Stock ($5 par) $500,000, Paid-in Capital in Excess of Par Value $200,000, and Retained Earnings $100,000. In 2008, the company had the following treasury stock transactions.

*Journalize and post treasury stock transactions, and prepare stockholders' equity section.*

*(SO 3, 7)*

| Mar. | 1 | Purchased 5,000 shares at $8 per share. |
| June | 1 | Sold 1,000 shares at $12 per share. |
| Sept. | 1 | Sold 2,000 shares at $10 per share. |
| Dec. | 1 | Sold 1,000 shares at $6 per share. |

Goldberg Corporation uses the cost method of accounting for treasury stock. In 2008, the company reported net income of $40,000.

**Instructions**

(a) Journalize the treasury stock transactions, and prepare the closing entry at December 31, 2008, for net income.

(b) Treasury Stock $8,000

(c) Total stockholders' equity $838,000

(b) Open accounts for (1) Paid-in Capital from Treasury Stock, (2) Treasury Stock, and (3) Retained Earnings. Post to these accounts using J10 as the posting reference.

(c) Prepare the stockholders' equity section for Goldberg Corporation at December 31, 2008.

*Journalize and post transactions, prepare stockholders' equity section.*

(SO 2, 3, 4, 7, 9)

GLS

**P12-3B** The stockholders' equity accounts of Port Corporation on January 1, 2008, were as follows.

| | |
|---|---|
| Preferred Stock (8%, $50 par cumulative, 10,000 shares authorized) | $ 400,000 |
| Common Stock ($1 stated value, 2,000,000 shares authorized) | 1,000,000 |
| Paid-in Capital in Excess of Par Value—Preferred Stock | 100,000 |
| Paid-in Capital in Excess of Stated Value—Common Stock | 1,450,000 |
| Retained Earnings | 1,816,000 |
| Treasury Stock—Common (10,000 shares) | 40,000 |

During 2008, the corporation had the following transactions and events pertaining to its stockholders' equity.

Feb. 1 Issued 25,000 shares of common stock for $100,000.
Apr. 14 Sold 6,000 shares of treasury stock—common for $33,000.
Sept. 3 Issued 5,000 shares of common stock for a patent valued at $30,000.
Nov. 10 Purchased 1,000 shares of common stock for the treasury at a cost of $6,000.
Dec. 31 Determined that net income for the year was $452,000.

No dividends were declared during the year.

**Instructions**

(a) Journalize the transactions and the closing entry for net income.

(b) Enter the beginning balances in the accounts, and post the journal entries to the stockholders' equity accounts. (Use J5 for the posting reference.)

(c) Total stockholders' equity $5,335,000

(c) Prepare a stockholders' equity section at December 31, 2008, including the disclosure of the preferred dividends in arrears.

*(d) Compute the book value per share of common stock at December 31, 2008, assuming the preferred stock does not have a call price.

*Prepare dividend entries and stockholders' equity section.*

(SO 5, 7)

GLS

**P12-4B** On January 1, 2008, Argentina Corporation had the following stockholders' equity accounts.

| | |
|---|---|
| Common Stock ($20 par value, 75,000 shares issued and outstanding) | $1,500,000 |
| Paid-in Capital in Excess of Par Value | 200,000 |
| Retained Earnings | 600,000 |

During the year, the following transactions occurred.

Feb. 1 Declared a $1 cash dividend per share to stockholders of record on February 15, payable March 1.
Mar. 1 Paid the dividend declared in February.
Apr. 1 Announced a 2-for-1 stock split. Prior to the split, the market price per share was $36.
July 1 Declared a 10% stock dividend to stockholders of record on July 15, distributable July 31. On July 1, the market price of the stock was $13 per share.
31 Issued the shares for the stock dividend.
Dec. 1 Declared a $0.50 per share dividend to stockholders of record on December 15, payable January 5, 2009.
31 Determined that net income for the year was $350,000.

**Instructions**

(a) Journalize the transactions and the closing entry for net income.

(b) Enter the beginning balances, and post the entries to the stockholders' equity accounts. (*Note*: Open additional stockholders' equity accounts as needed.)

(c) Total stockholders' equity $2,492,500

(c) Prepare a stockholders' equity section at December 31.

**P12-5B**    On December 31, 2007, Bradstrom Company had 1,500,000 shares of $10 par common stock issued and outstanding. The stockholders' equity accounts at December 31, 2007, had the following balances.

*Prepare retained earnings statement and stockholders' equity section.*

*(SO 6, 7)*

| | |
|---|---:|
| Common Stock | $15,000,000 |
| Additional Paid-in Capital | 1,500,000 |
| Retained Earnings | 900,000 |

Transactions during 2008 and other information related to stockholders' equity accounts were as follows.

1. On January 10, 2008, Bradstrom issued at $105 per share 100,000 shares of $100 par value, 7% cumulative preferred stock.
2. On February 8, 2008, Bradstrom reacquired 15,000 shares of its common stock for $16 per share.
3. On June 8, 2008, Bradstrom declared a cash dividend of $1 per share on the common stock outstanding, payable on July 10, 2008, to stockholders of record on July 1, 2008.
4. On December 15, 2008, Bradstrom declared the yearly cash dividend on preferred stock, payable January 10, 2009, to stockholders of record on December 15, 2008.
5. Net income for the year is $3,600,000.
6. It was discovered that depreciation expense had been overstated in 2007 by $80,000.

**Instructions**
(a) Prepare a retained earnings statement for the year ended December 31, 2008.
(b) Prepare the stockholders' equity section of Bradstrom's balance sheet at December 31, 2008.

(b) Total stockholders' equity
$29,155,000

**P12-6B**    The post-closing trial balance of Chen Corporation at December 31, 2008, contains the following stockholders' equity accounts.

*Prepare retained earnings statement and stockholders' equity section, and compute earnings per share.*

*(SO 5, 6, 7)*

| | |
|---|---:|
| Preferred Stock (15,000 shares issued) | $ 750,000 |
| Common Stock (250,000 shares issued) | 2,500,000 |
| Paid-in Capital in Excess of Par Value—Preferred | 250,000 |
| Paid-in Capital in Excess of Par Value—Common | 400,000 |
| Common Stock Dividends Distributable | 250,000 |
| Retained Earnings | 902,000 |

A review of the accounting records reveals the following.

1. No errors have been made in recording 2008 transactions or in preparing the closing entry for net income.
2. Preferred stock is $50 par, 8%, and cumulative; 15,000 shares have been outstanding since January 1, 2007.
3. Authorized stock is 20,000 shares of preferred, 500,000 shares of common with a $10 par value.
4. The January 1 balance in Retained Earnings was $1,170,000.
5. On July 1, 20,000 shares of common stock were sold for cash at $16 per share.
6. On September 1, the company discovered an understatement error of $90,000 in computing depreciation in 2007. The net of tax effect of $63,000 was properly debited directly to Retained Earnings.
7. A cash dividend of $250,000 was declared and properly allocated to preferred and common stock on October 1. No dividends were paid to preferred stockholders in 2007.
8. On December 31, a 10% common stock dividend was declared out of retained earnings on common stock when the market price per share was $18.
9. Net income for the year was $495,000.
10. On December 31, 2008, the directors authorized disclosure of a $200,000 restriction of retained earnings for plant expansion. (Use Note X.)

**Instructions**
(a) Reproduce the Retained Earnings account for the year.
(b) Prepare a retained earnings statement for the year.
(c) Prepare a stockholders' equity section at December 31.
(d) Compute the earnings per share of common stock using 240,000 as the weighted average shares outstanding for the year.
(e) Compute the allocation of the cash dividend to preferred and common stock.

(b) Retained earnings
$902,000

(c) Total stockholders' equity
$5,052,000

*Prepare stockholders' equity section; compute book value per share.*

(SO 7, 9)

**\*P12-7B**    The following stockholders' equity accounts arranged alphabetically are in the ledger of Rizzo Corporation at December 31, 2008.

| | |
|---|---|
| Common Stock ($5 stated value) | $2,500,000 |
| Paid-in Capital from Treasury Stock | 10,000 |
| Paid-in Capital in Excess of Stated Value—Common Stock | 1,600,000 |
| Paid-in Capital in Excess of Par Value—Preferred Stock | 679,000 |
| Preferred Stock (8%, $50 par, noncumulative) | 800,000 |
| Retained Earnings | 1,448,000 |
| Treasury Stock—Common (10,000 shares) | 130,000 |

**Instructions**

*Total stockholders' equity $6,907,000*

**(a)** Prepare a stockholders' equity section at December 31, 2008.

**(b)** Compute the book value per share of the common stock, assuming the preferred stock has a call price of $60 per share.

# PROBLEMS: SET C

Visit the book's website at **www.wiley.com/college/weygandt**, and choose the Student Companion site, to access Problem Set C.

# CONTINUING COOKIE CHRONICLE

(*Note*: This is a continuation of the Cookie Chronicle from Chapters 1 through 11.)

**CCC12**    Natalie and her friend Curtis Lesperance decide that they can benefit from joining Cookie Creations and Curtis's coffee shop. In the first part of this problem, they come to you with questions about setting up a corporation for their new business. In the second part of the problem, they want your help in preparing financial information following the first year of operations of their new business, Cookie & Coffee Creations.

*Go to the book's website,*
**www.wiley.com/college/weygandt**,
*to see the completion of this problem.*

# BROADENING YOUR PERSPECTIVE

# FINANCIAL REPORTING AND ANALYSIS

## Financial Reporting Problem
### PepsiCo, Inc.

**BYP12-1**    The stockholders' equity section for PepsiCo, Inc. is shown in Appendix A. You will also find data relative to this problem on other pages of the appendix.

**Instructions**

**(a)** What is the par or stated value per share of PepsiCo's common stock?

**(b)** What percentage of PepsiCo's authorized common stock was issued at December 31, 2005?

**(c)** How many shares of common stock were outstanding at December 31, 2005, and at December 25, 2004?

\*(d) What was the book value per share at December 31, 2005, and at December 25, 2004?

(e) What were the high and low market price per share in the fourth quarter of fiscal 2005, as reported under Selected Financial Data?

## Comparative Analysis Problem
### PepsiCo, Inc. vs. The Coca-Cola Company

**BYP12-2** PepsiCo's financial statements are presented in Appendix A. Coca-Cola's financial statements are presented in Appendix B.

### Instructions

(a) Based on the information contained in these financial statements, compute the 2005 book value per share for each company. (*Hint:* Use the value reported for "common shareholders' equity" as the numerator for PepsiCo.)

(b) Compare the market value per share for each company to the book value per share at year-end 2005. Assume that the market value of Coca-Cola's stock was $50.90 at year-end 2005.

(c) Why are book value and market value per share different?

(d) Compute earnings per share and return on common stockholders' equity for both companies for the year ending in January 2005. Assume PepsiCo's weighted average shares were 1,718 million and Coca-Cola's weighted average shares were 2,462 million. Can these measures be used to compare the profitability of the two companies? Why or why not?

(e) What was the total amount of dividends paid by each company in 2005?

## Exploring the Web

**BYP12-3** Use the stockholders' equity section of an annual report and identify the major components.

**Address: www.reportgallery.com**, or go to **www.wiley.com/college/weygandt**

### Steps

1. From Report Gallery Homepage, choose **Search by Alphabet**, and choose a letter.
2. Select a particular company.
3. Choose Annual Report.
4. Follow instructions below.

### Instructions

Answer the following questions.

(a) What is the company's name?
(b) What classes of capital stock has the company issued?
(c) For each class of stock:
  (1) How many shares are authorized, issued, and/or outstanding?
  (2) What is the par value?
(d) What are the company's retained earnings?
(e) Has the company acquired treasury stock? How many shares?

## CRITICAL THINKING

## Decision Making Across the Organization

**BYP12-4** The stockholders' meeting for Harris Corporation has been in progress for some time. The chief financial officer for Harris is presently reviewing the company's financial statements and is explaining the items that comprise the stockholders' equity section of the balance sheet for the current year. The stockholders' equity section of Harris Corporation at December 31, 2008, is shown on page 590.

HARRIS CORPORATION
Balance Sheet (partial)
December 31, 2008

| | | |
|---|---|---|
| Paid in capital | | |
| Capital stock | | |
| Preferred stock, authorized 1,000,000 shares | | |
| cumulative, $100 par value, $8 per share, 6,000 | | |
| shares issued and outstanding | | $ 600,000 |
| Common stock, authorized 5,000,000 shares, $1 par | | |
| value, 3,000,000 shares issued, and 2,700,000 | | |
| outstanding | | 3,000,000 |
| Total capital stock | | 3,600,000 |
| Additional paid-in capital | | |
| In excess of par value—preferred stock | $ 50,000 | |
| In excess of par value—common stock | 25,000,000 | |
| Total additional paid-in capital | | 25,050,000 |
| Total paid-in capital | | 28,650,000 |
| Retained earnings | | 900,000 |
| Total paid-in capital and retained earnings | | 29,550,000 |
| Less: Common treasury stock (300,000 shares) | | 9,300,000 |
| Total stockholders' equity | | $20,250,000 |

At the meeting, stockholders have raised a number of questions regarding the stockholders' equity section.

**Instructions**
With the class divided into groups, answer the following questions as if you were the chief financial officer for Harris Corporation.

**(a)** "What does the cumulative provision related to the preferred stock mean?"
**(b)** "I thought the common stock was presently selling at $29.75, but the company has the stock stated at $1 per share. How can that be?"
**(c)** "Why is the company buying back its common stock? Furthermore, the treasury stock has a debit balance because it is subtracted from stockholders' equity. Why is treasury stock not reported as an asset if it has a debit balance?"
**(d)** "Why is it necessary to show additional paid-in capital? Why not just show common stock at the total amount paid in?"

# Communication Activity

**BYP12-5** Sal Greco, your uncle, is an inventor who has decided to incorporate. Uncle Sal knows that you are an accounting major at U.N.O. In a recent letter to you, he ends with the question, "I'm filling out a state incorporation application. Can you tell me the difference in the following terms: (1) authorized stock, (2) issued stock, (3) outstanding stock, (4) preferred stock?"

**Instructions**
In a brief note, differentiate for Uncle Sal among the four different stock terms. Write the letter to be friendly, yet professional.

# Ethics Case

**BYP12-6** The R&D division of Healy Chemical Corp. has just developed a chemical for sterilizing the vicious Brazilian "killer bees" which are invading Mexico and the southern states of the United States. The president of Healy is anxious to get the chemical on the market to boost Healy's profits. He believes his job is in jeopardy because of decreasing sales and profits. Healy has an opportunity to sell this chemical in Central American countries, where the laws are much more relaxed than in the United States.

The director of Healy's R&D division strongly recommends further testing in the laboratory for side-effects of this chemical on other insects, birds, animals, plants, and even humans. He cautions the president, "We could be sued from all sides if the chemical has tragic side-effects that we didn't even test for in the labs." The president answers, "We can't wait an additional year for your lab tests. We can avoid losses from such lawsuits by establishing a separate wholly owned corporation to shield Healy Corp. from such lawsuits. We can't lose any more than our investment in the new corporation, and we'll invest just the patent covering this chemical. We'll reap the benefits if the chemical works and is safe, and avoid the losses from lawsuits if it's a disaster." The following week Healy creates a new wholly owned corporation called Dryden Inc., sells the chemical patent to it for $10, and watches the spraying begin.

### Instructions
**(a)** Who are the stakeholders in this situation?
**(b)** Are the president's motives and actions ethical?
**(c)** Can Healy shield itself against losses of Dryden Inc.?

# "All About You" Activity

**BYP12-7**    A high percentage of Americans own stock in corporations. As a shareholder in a corporation, you will receive an annual report. One of the goals of this course is for you to learn how to navigate your way around an annual report.

### Instructions
Use the annual report provided in Appendix A to answer the following questions.

**(a)** What CPA firm performed the audit of PepsiCo's financial statements?
**(b)** What was the amount of PepsiCo's earnings per share in 2005?
**(c)** What are the company's net sales to foreign countries?
**(d)** What were net sales in 2001?
**(e)** How many shares of treasury stock did the company have at the end of 2005?
**(f)** How much cash did PepsiCo spend on capital expenditures in 2005?
**(g)** Over what life does the company depreciate its buildings?
**(h)** What was the total amount of dividends paid in 2005?

## Answers to Insight and Accounting Across the Organization Questions

**Directors Take on More Accountability, p. 537**
Q: Was Enron's board of directors fulfilling its role in a corporate organization when it waived Enron's ethical code on two occasions?
A: *The board of directors is elected by the owners (stockholders) of the corporation to manage the corporation. One of its roles is to formulate the ethical and operating policies for the company and to assume an oversight responsibility on behalf of the stockholders and other third parties. It was the responsibility of the board of directors to enforce the corporation's ethical code, not to waive it.*

**How to Read Stock Quotes, p. 541**
Q: For stocks traded on organized stock exchanges, how are the dollar prices per share established?
A: *The dollar prices per share are established by the interaction between buyers and sellers of the shares.*
Q: What factors might influence the price of shares in the marketplace?
A: *The price of shares is influenced by a company's earnings and dividends as well as by factors beyond a company's control, such as changes in interest rates, labor strikes, scarcity of supplies or resources, and politics. The number of willing buyers and sellers (demand and supply) also plays a part in the price of shares.*

**Why Did Reebok Buy Its Own Stock?, p. 548**
Q: What signal might a large stock repurchase send to investors regarding management's belief about the company's growth opportunities?
A: *When a company has many growth opportunities it will normally conserve its cash in order to be better able to fund expansion. A large use of cash to buy back stock (and essentially shrink the company) would suggest that management was not optimistic about its growth opportunities.*

**Why Are Companies Increasing Their Dividends?, p. 555**

Q: What factors must management consider in deciding how large a dividend to pay?

A: *Management must consider the size of its retained earnings balance, the amount of available cash, its expected near-term cash needs, its growth opportunities, and what level of dividend it will be able to sustain based upon its expected future earnings.*

## Authors' Comments on *All About You:* Home Equity Loans, p. 567

The reasons why people reduce the equity in their homes with home-equity loans are as varied as the reasons why companies reduce their stockholders' equity by buying treasury stock or paying dividends. There are good and bad reasons to buy treasury stock and pay dividends, and there are good and bad reasons to use a home-equity loan.

Suppose you are considering putting an addition on your house which would increase its value. That may be a good use of a home-equity loan, since it increases the value of your investment. Or suppose that you need to buy a new car. Financing the purchase with a home-equity loan can make good financial sense, since the interest on a home-equity loan is tax-deductible, while the interest on a car loan is not. But you should be sure you repay the home-equity loan over the same time period that you would have repaid the car loan. As the graphs in the box show, if you spread the loan over a long period you could end up owing more money than the car is worth when it comes time to sell it.

Borrowing against the equity in your home to go on a vacation is not a financially prudent thing to do. If you want to go on a vacation, you should set up a separate travel fund as part of your personal budget, and go on the vacation only when you can actually afford it.

The bottom line is this: Reducing equity, either corporate or personal, increases reliance on debt and therefore increases risk. It is a decision that should be carefully considered.

## Answers to PepsiCo Review It Questions
### Question 3, p. 546

**3.** The par value of PepsiCo's common stock is $0.0166 per share. On December 31, 2005, PepsiCo had issued 1,782 million shares.

### Question 4, p. 550

**4.** Treasury shares held by PepsiCo on December 31, 2005, were 126 million, and on December 25, 2004, were 103 million.

### Question 4, p. 559

Dividends per share of common stock declared by PepsiCo were $0.575 in 2001; $0.595 in 2002; $0.630 in 2003; $0.850 in 2004; and $1.01 in 2005. During this same period net income increased in a similar fashion, except from 2004 and 2005 when net income declined.

## Answers to Self-Study Questions
**1.** c   **2.** b   **3.** d   **4.** c   **5.** a   **6.** a   **7.** d   **8.** a   **9.** c   **10.** d   **11.** b   **\*12.** a   **\*13.** c

# Chapter 13

# Investments

## STUDY OBJECTIVES

*After studying this chapter, you should be able to:*

1 Discuss why corporations invest in debt and stock securities.
2 Explain the accounting for debt investments.
3 Explain the accounting for stock investments.
4 Describe the use of consolidated financial statements.
5 Indicate how debt and stock investments are reported in financial statements.
6 Distinguish between short-term and long-term investments.

✓ *The Navigator*

## ✓ The Navigator

| | |
|---|---|
| Scan **Study Objectives** | ■ |
| Read **Feature Story** | ■ |
| Read **Preview** | ■ |
| Read text and answer **Before You Go On** p. 599 ■    p. 604 ■    p. 610 ■ | |
| Work **Demonstration Problem** | ■ |
| Review **Summary of Study Objectives** | ■ |
| Answer **Self-Study Questions** | ■ |
| Complete **Assignments** | ■ |

## Feature Story

**"IS THERE ANYTHING ELSE WE CAN BUY?"**

In a rapidly changing world you must change rapidly or suffer the consequences. In business, change requires investment.

A case in point is found in the entertainment industry. Technology is bringing about innovations so quickly that it is nearly impossible to guess which technologies will last and which will soon fade away. For example, will both satellite TV and cable TV survive, or will just one succeed, or will both be replaced by something else? Or consider the publishing industry. Will paper newspapers and magazines be replaced by online news via the World Wide Web? If you are a publisher, you have to make your best guess about what the future holds and invest accordingly.

Time Warner, Inc. (*www.timewarner.com*) lives at the center of this arena. It is not an environment for the timid, and Time Warner's philosophy is anything

but timid. It might be characterized as, "If we can't beat you, we will buy you." Its mantra is "invest, invest, invest." A list of Time Warner's holdings gives an idea of its reach. Magazines: *People, Time, Life, Sports Illustrated, Fortune.* Book publishers: Time-Life Books, Book-of-the-Month Club, Little, Brown & Co, Sunset Books. Television and movies: Warner Bros. ("ER," "Without a Trace," the WB Network), HBO, and movies like *Harry Potter and the Goblet of Fire, and Batman Begins.* Broadcasting: TNT, CNN news, and Turner's library of thousands of classic movies. Internet: America Online, and AOL Anywhere. Time Warner owns more information and entertainment copyrights and brands than any other company in the world.

So what has Time Warner's aggressive acquisition spree meant for the bottom line? It has left the company with an accumulated deficit of approximately $93 billion. Some of the acquisitions have not come cheap, resulting in large amounts of reported goodwill and related intangible assets. The merger of America Online (AOL) with Time Warner was billed as a merger of equals. But, it was AOL's phenomenal growth and astronomical stock price that made this merger possible. Unfortunately, investors involved in this merger have faired poorly. From a high of $95.80, Time Warner's stock price recently sold at $17.08 per share.

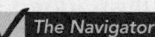 The Navigator

# Inside Chapter 13

Time Warner's management believes in aggressive growth through investing in the stock of existing companies. Besides purchasing stock, companies also purchase other securities such as bonds issued by corporations or by governments. Companies can make investments for a short or long period of time, as a passive investment, or with the intent to control another company. As you will see in this chapter, the way in which a company accounts for its investments is determined by a number of factors.

The content and organization of Chapter 13 are as follows.

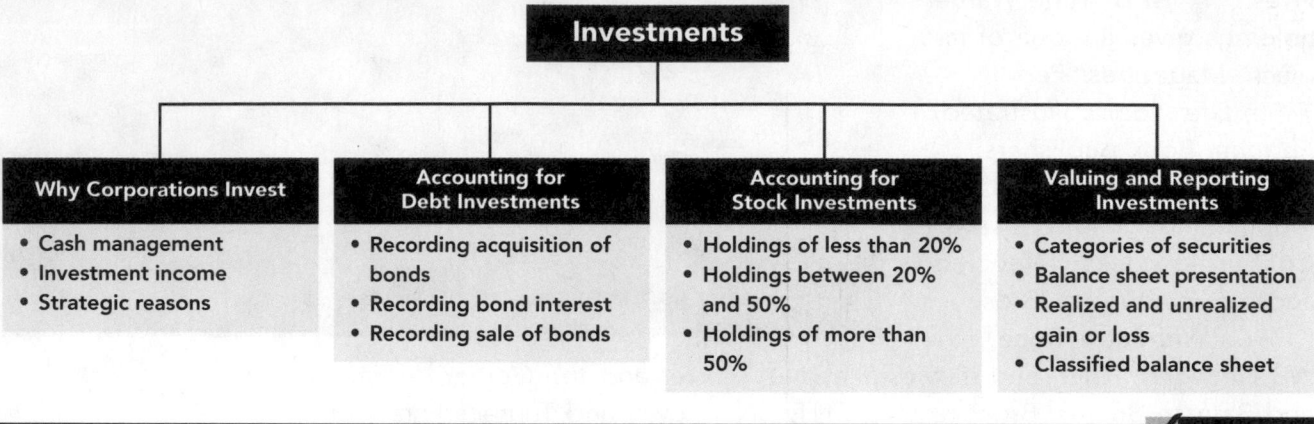

**Investments**

| Why Corporations Invest | Accounting for Debt Investments | Accounting for Stock Investments | Valuing and Reporting Investments |
|---|---|---|---|
| • Cash management<br>• Investment income<br>• Strategic reasons | • Recording acquisition of bonds<br>• Recording bond interest<br>• Recording sale of bonds | • Holdings of less than 20%<br>• Holdings between 20% and 50%<br>• Holdings of more than 50% | • Categories of securities<br>• Balance sheet presentation<br>• Realized and unrealized gain or loss<br>• Classified balance sheet |

✓ *The Navigator*

# WHY CORPORATIONS INVEST

**STUDY OBJECTIVE 1**

**Discuss why corporations invest in debt and stock securities.**

Corporations purchase investments in debt or stock securities generally for one of three reasons. First, a corporation may **have excess cash** that it does not need for the immediate purchase of operating assets. For example, many companies experience seasonal fluctuations in sales. A Cape Cod marina has more sales in the spring and summer than in the fall and winter. At the end of an operating cycle, the marina may have cash on hand that is temporarily idle until the start of another operating cycle. It may invest the excess funds to earn a greater return than it would get by just holding the funds in the bank. Illustration 13-1 depicts the role that such temporary investments play in the operating cycle.

**Illustration 13-1**
Temporary investments and the operating cycle

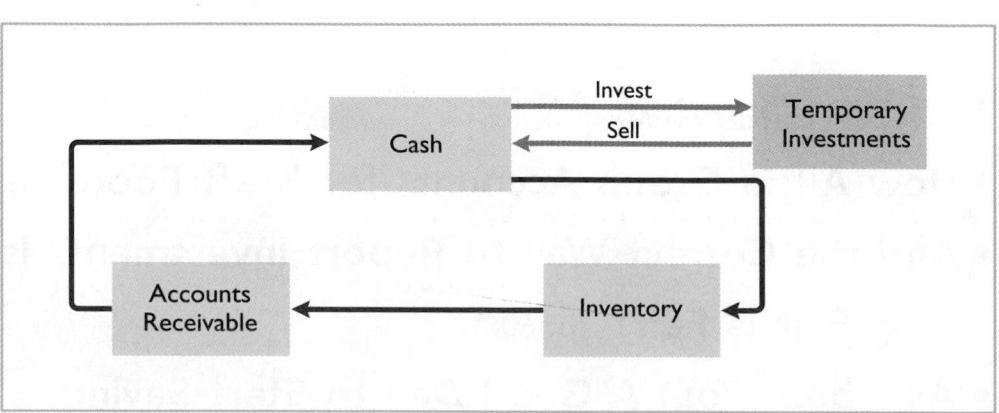

Excess cash may also result from economic cycles. For example, when the economy is booming, General Electric generates considerable excess cash. It uses some of this cash to purchase new plant and equipment and pays out some of the cash in dividends. But it may also invest excess cash in liquid assets in anticipation of a future downturn in the economy. It can then liquidate these investments during a recession, when sales slow and cash is scarce.

When investing excess cash for short periods of time, corporations invest in low-risk, highly liquid securities—most often short-term government securities. It is generally not wise to invest short-term excess cash in shares of common stock because stock investments can experience rapid price changes. If you did invest your short-term excess cash in stock and the price of the stock declined significantly just before you needed cash again, you would be forced to sell your stock investment at a loss.

A second reason some companies purchase investments is to generate **earnings from investment income**. For example, banks make most of their earnings by lending money, but they also generate earnings by investing in debt. Conversely, mutual stock funds invest primarily in equity securities in order to benefit from stock-price appreciation and dividend revenue.

Third, companies also invest for **strategic reasons**. A company can exercise some influence over a customer or supplier by purchasing a significant, but not controlling, interest in that company. Or, a company may purchase a noncontrolling interest in another company in a related industry in which it wishes to establish a presence. For example, Time Warner initially purchased an interest of less than 20% in Turner Broadcasting to have a stake in Turner's expanding business opportunities. At a later date Time Warner acquired the remaining 80%. Subsequently, Time Warner merged with AOL and became AOL Time Warner, Inc. Now, it is again just Time Warner, Inc., having dropped the "AOL" from its name in late 2003.

A corporation may also choose to purchase a controlling interest in another company. For example, in the *Accounting Across the Organization* box on page 603, Philip Morris purchased Kraft Foods. Such purchases might be done to enter a new industry without incurring the tremendous costs and risks associated with starting from scratch. Or a company might purchase another company in its same industry.

In summary, businesses invest in other companies for the reasons shown in Illustration 13-2.

| Reason | Typical Investment |
|---|---|
| To house excess cash until needed | Low-risk, high-liquidity, short-term securities such as government-issued securities |
| To generate earnings | Debt securities (banks and other financial institutions); and stock securities (mutual funds and pension funds) |
| To meet strategic goals | Stocks of companies in a related industry or in an unrelated industry that the company wishes to enter |

**Illustration 13-2**
Why corporations invest

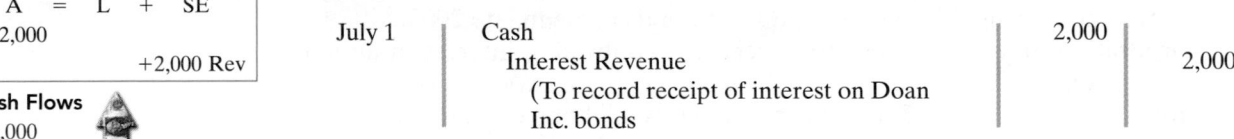

## ACCOUNTING FOR DEBT INVESTMENTS

**Debt investments** are investments in government and corporation bonds. In accounting for debt investments, companies make entries to record (1) the acquisition, (2) the interest revenue, and (3) the sale.

### Recording Acquisition of Bonds

**At acquisition, the cost principle applies.** Cost includes all expenditures necessary to acquire these investments, such as the price paid plus brokerage fees (commissions), if any.

Assume, for example, that Kuhl Corporation acquires 50 Doan Inc. 8%, 10-year, $1,000 bonds on January 1, 2008, for $54,000, including brokerage fees of $1,000. The entry to record the investment is:

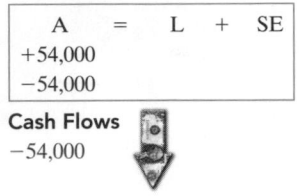

| Jan. 1 | Debt Investments | 54,000 | |
| |     Cash | | 54,000 |
| |     (To record purchase of 50 Doan Inc. bonds) | | |

### Recording Bond Interest

The Doan, Inc. bonds pay interest of $2,000 semiannually on July 1 and January 1 ($50,000 × 8% × ½). The entry for the receipt of interest on July 1 is:

| July 1 | Cash | 2,000 | |
| |     Interest Revenue | | 2,000 |
| |     (To record receipt of interest on Doan Inc. bonds | | |

If Kuhl Corporation's fiscal year ends on December 31, it accrues the interest of $2,000 earned since July 1. The adjusting entry is:

| Dec. 31 | Interest Receivable | 2,000 | |
| |     Interest Revenue | | 2,000 |
| |     (To accrue interest on Doan Inc. bonds) | | |

Kuhl reports Interest Receivable as a current asset in the balance sheet. It reports Interest Revenue under "Other revenues and gains" in the income statement.

Kuhl reports receipt of the interest on January 1 as follows.

| Jan. 1 | Cash | 2,000 | |
| |     Interest Receivable | | 2,000 |
| |     (To record receipt of accrued interest) | | |

A credit to Interest Revenue at this time is incorrect because the company earned and accrued interest revenue in the *preceding* accounting period.

### Recording Sale of Bonds

When Kuhl sells the bonds, it credits the investment account for the cost of the bonds. Kuhl records as a gain or loss any difference between the net proceeds from the sale (sales price less brokerage fees) and the cost of the bonds.

Assume, for example, that Kuhl Corporation receives net proceeds of $58,000 on the sale of the Doan Inc. bonds on January 1, 2009, after receiving the interest due. Since the securities cost $54,000, the company realizes a gain of $4,000. It records the sale as:

| Jan. 1 | Cash | 58,000 | |
| | Debt Investments | | 54,000 |
| | Gain on Sale of Debt Investments | | 4,000 |
| | (To record sale of Doan Inc. bonds) | | |

| A | = | L | + | SE |
|---|---|---|---|---|
| +58,000 | | | | |
| −54,000 | | | | |
| | | | | +4,000 Rev |

**Cash Flows**
+58,000

Kuhl reports the gain on sale of debt investments under "Other revenues and gains" in the income statement and reports losses under "Other expenses and losses."

## Before You Go On...

### REVIEW IT
1. Why might a company make investments in debt or stock securities?
2. What entries are required in accounting for debt investments?
3. How do companies report gains and losses from the sale of bonds in the income statement?

### DO IT
Waldo Corporation had the following transactions pertaining to debt investments.

Jan. 1   Purchased 30, $1,000 Hillary Co. 10% bonds for $30,000, plus brokerage fees of $900. Interest is payable semiannually on July 1 and January 1.
July 1   Received semiannual interest on Hillary Co. bonds.
July 1   Sold 15 Hillary Co. bonds for $15,000, less $400 brokerage fees.

**(a)** Journalize the transactions, and **(b)** prepare the adjusting entry for the accrual of interest on December 31.

### Action Plan
- Record bond investments at cost.
- Record interest when received and/or accrued.
- When bonds are sold, credit the investment account for the cost of the bonds.
- Record any difference between the cost and the net proceeds as a gain or loss.

### Solution

| (a) Jan. 1 | Debt Investments | 30,900 | |
| | Cash | | 30,900 |
| | (To record purchase of 30 Hillary Co. bonds) | | |

| July 1 | Cash | 1,500 | |
| | Interest Revenue ($30,000 × .10 × 6/12) | | 1,500 |
| | (To record receipt of interest on Hillary Co. bonds) | | |

| July 1 | Cash | 14,600 | |
| | Loss on Sale of Debt Investments | 850 | |
| | Debt Investments ($30,900 × 15/30) | | 15,450 |
| | (To record sale of 15 Hillary Co. bonds) | | |

| (b) Dec. 31 | Interest Receivable | 750 | |
| | Interest Revenue ($15,000 × .10 × 6/12) | | 750 |
| | (To accrue interest on Hillary Co. bonds) | | |

Related exercise material: *BE13-1, E13-2, and E13-3.*

The Navigator

# ACCOUNTING FOR STOCK INVESTMENTS

**STUDY OBJECTIVE 3**

Explain the accounting for stock investments.

**Stock investments** are investments in the capital stock of other corporations. When a company holds stock (and/or debt) of several different corporations, the group of securities is identified as an **investment portfolio**.

The accounting for investments in common stock depends on the extent of the investor's influence over the operating and financial affairs of the issuing corporation (the **investee**). Illustration 13-3 shows the general guidelines.

**Illustration 13-3**
Accounting guidelines for stock investments

| Investor's Ownership Interest in Investee's Common Stock | Presumed Influence on Investee | Accounting Guidelines |
|---|---|---|
| Less than 20% | Insignificant | Cost method |
| Between 20% and 50% | Significant | Equity method |
| More than 50% | Controlling | Consolidated financial statements |

Companies are required to use judgment instead of blindly following the guidelines.[1] On the following pages we will explain the application of each guideline.

## Holdings of Less than 20%

**HELPFUL HINT**

The entries for investments in common stock also apply to investments in preferred stock.

In accounting for stock investments of less than 20%, companies use the cost method. Under the <u>cost method</u>, companies record the investment at cost, and recognize revenue only when cash dividends are received.

### RECORDING ACQUISITION OF STOCK INVESTMENTS

At acquisition, the cost principle applies. Cost includes all expenditures necessary to acquire these investments, such as the price paid plus any brokerage fees (commissions).

Assume, for example, that on July 1, 2008, Sanchez Corporation acquires 1,000 shares (10% ownership) of Beal Corporation common stock. Sanchez pays $40 per share plus brokerage fees of $500. The entry for the purchase is:

| A | = | L | + | SE |
|---|---|---|---|---|
| +40,500 | | | | |
| −40,500 | | | | |

**Cash Flows**
−40,500

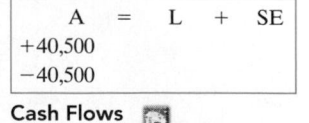

| July 1 | Stock Investments | 40,500 | |
| | Cash | | 40,500 |
| | (To record purchase of 1,000 shares of Beal Corporation common stock) | | |

---

[1]Among the questions that are considered in determining an investor's influence are these: (1) Does the investor have representation on the investee's board? (2) Does the investor participate in the investee's policy-making process? (3) Are there material transactions between the investor and investee? (4) Is the common stock held by other stockholders concentrated or dispersed?

### RECORDING DIVIDENDS

During the time Sanchez owns the stock, it makes entries for any cash dividends received. If Sanchez receives a $2 per share dividend on December 31, the entry is:

| Dec. 31 | Cash (1,000 × $2) | 2,000 | |
| | Dividend Revenue | | 2,000 |
| | (To record receipt of a cash dividend) | | |

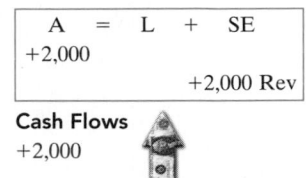

| A | = | L | + | SE |
|---|---|---|---|---|
| +2,000 | | | | |
| | | | | +2,000 Rev |

**Cash Flows**
+2,000

Sanchez reports Dividend Revenue under "Other revenues and gains" in the income statement. Unlike interest on notes and bonds, dividends do not accrue. Therefore, companies do not make adjusting entries to accrue dividends.

### RECORDING SALE OF STOCK

When a company sells a stock investment, it recognizes as a gain or a loss the difference between the net proceeds from the sale (sales price less brokerage fees) and the cost of the stock.

Assume that Sanchez Corporation receives net proceeds of $39,500 on the sale of its Beal stock on February 10, 2009. Because the stock cost $40,500, Sanchez incurred a loss of $1,000. The entry to record the sale is:

| Feb. 10 | Cash | 39,500 | |
| | Loss on Sale of Stock Investments | 1,000 | |
| | Stock Investments | | 40,500 |
| | (To record sale of Beal common stock) | | |

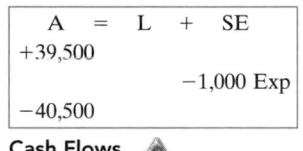

| A | = | L | + | SE |
|---|---|---|---|---|
| +39,500 | | | | |
| | | | | −1,000 Exp |
| −40,500 | | | | |

**Cash Flows**
+39,500

Sanchez reports the loss under "Other expenses and losses" in the income statement. It would show a gain on sale under "Other revenues and gains."

## Holdings Between 20% and 50%

When an investor company owns only a small portion of the shares of stock of another company, the investor cannot exercise control over the investee. But, when an investor owns between 20% and 50% of the common stock of a corporation, it is presumed that the investor has significant influence over the financial and operating activities of the investee. The investor probably has a representative on the investee's board of directors, and through that representative, may exercise some control over the investee. The investee company in some sense becomes part of the investor company.

For example, even prior to purchasing all of Turner Broadcasting, Time Warner owned 20% of Turner. Because it exercised significant control over major decisions made by Turner, Time Warner used an approach called the equity method. Under the equity method, **the investor records its share of the net income of the investee in the year when it is earned**. An alternative might be to delay recognizing the investor's share of net income until the investee declares a cash dividend. But that approach would ignore the fact that the investor and investee are, in some sense, one company, making the investor better off by the investee's earned income.

Under the equity method, the investor company initially records the investment in common stock at cost. After that, it **annually adjusts** the investment account to show the investor's equity in the investee. Each year, the investor does the following: (1) It increases (debits) the investment account and increases (credits) revenue for its share of the investee's net income.[2] (2) The investor also decreases

> **HELPFUL HINT**
> Under the equity method, the investor recognizes revenue on the accrual basis—i.e., when it is earned by the investee.

---

[2] Or, the investor increases (debits) a loss account and decreases (credits) the investment account for its share of the investee's net loss.

(credits) the investment account for the amount of dividends received. The investment account is reduced for dividends received, because payment of a dividend decreases the net assets of the investee.

## RECORDING ACQUISITION OF STOCK INVESTMENTS

Assume that Milar Corporation acquires 30% of the common stock of Beck Company for $120,000 on January 1, 2008. Milar records this transaction as:

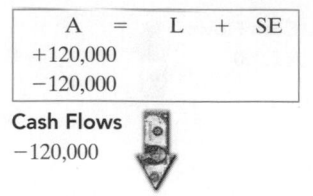

| | | | |
|---|---|---|---|
| Jan. 1 | Stock Investments | 120,000 | |
| |    Cash | | 120,000 |
| |    (To record purchase of Beck common stock) | | |

## RECORDING REVENUE AND DIVIDENDS

For 2008, Beck reports net income of $100,000. It declares and pays a $40,000 cash dividend. Milar records (1) its share of Beck's income, $30,000 (30% × $100,000) and (2) the reduction in the investment account for the dividends received, $12,000 ($40,000 × 30%). The entries are:

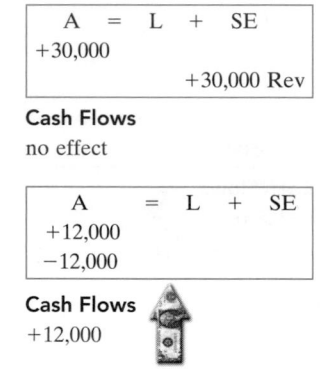

(1)

| | | | |
|---|---|---|---|
| Dec. 31 | Stock Investments | 30,000 | |
| |    Revenue from Investment in Beck Company | | 30,000 |
| |    (To record 30% equity in Beck's 2008 net income) | | |

(2)

| | | | |
|---|---|---|---|
| Dec. 31 | Cash | 12,000 | |
| |    Stock Investments | | 12,000 |
| |    (To record dividends received) | | |

After Milar posts the transactions for the year, its investment and revenue accounts will show the following.

**Illustration 13-4**
Investment and revenue accounts after posting

| Stock Investments | | | | Revenue from Investment in Beck Company | |
|---|---|---|---|---|---|
| Jan. 1 | 120,000 | Dec. 31 | 12,000 | | |
| Dec. 31 | 30,000 | | | | Dec. 31     30,000 |
| Dec. 31 Bal. | 138,000 | | | | |

During the year, the net increase in the investment account was $18,000. As indicated above, the investment account increased by $30,000 due to Milar's share of Beck's income, and it decreased by $12,000 due to dividends received from Beck. In addition, Milar reports $30,000 of revenue from its investment, which is 30% of Beck's net income of $100,000.

Note that the difference between reported revenue under the cost method and reported revenue under the equity method can be significant. For example, Milar would report only $12,000 of dividend revenue (30% × $40,000) if it used the cost method.

## Holdings of More than 50%

STUDY OBJECTIVE 4
Describe the use of consolidated financial statements.

A company that owns more than 50% of the common stock of another entity is known as the **parent company**. The entity whose stock the parent company owns is called the **subsidiary (affiliated) company**. Because of its stock ownership, the parent company has a <u>controlling interest</u> in the subsidiary.

When a company owns more than 50% of the common stock of another company, it usually prepares <u>consolidated financial statements</u>. These statements present the total assets and liabilities controlled by the parent company. They also present the total revenues and expenses of the subsidiary companies. Companies prepare consolidated statements **in addition to** the financial statements for the parent and individual subsidiary companies.

As noted earlier, when Time Warner had a 20% investment in Turner, it reported this investment in a single line item—Other Investments. After the merger, Time Warner instead consolidated Turner's results with its own. Under this approach, Time Warner included Turner's individual assets and liabilities with its own: its plant and equipment were added to Time Warner's plant and equipment, its receivables were added to Time Warner's receivables, and so on.

# ACCOUNTING ACROSS THE ORGANIZATION

### How Altria Group Accounts for Kraft Foods

Altria Group Inc. (formerly Philip Morris) owns 98.3% of the common stock of Kraft Foods, Inc. The common stockholders of Altria elect the board of directors of the company, who, in turn, select the officers and managers of the company. Altria's board of directors controls the property owned by the corporation, which includes the common stock of Kraft. Thus, they are in a position to elect the board of directors of Kraft and, in effect, control its operations. These relationships are graphically illustrated here.

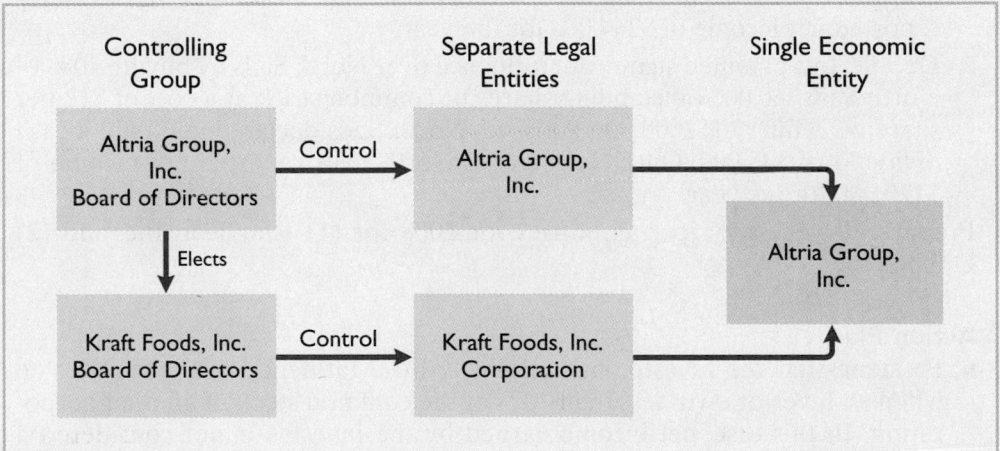

**?** Where on Altria Group's balance sheet will you find its investment in Kraft Foods, Inc.?

**Consolidated statements are useful to the stockholders, board of directors, and managers of the parent company. These statements indicate the magnitude and scope of operations of the companies under common control.** For example, regulators and the courts undoubtedly used the consolidated statements of AT&T to determine whether a breakup of AT&T was in the public interest. Listed at the top of page 604 are three companies that prepare consolidated statements and some of the companies they have owned. One, Disney, is Time Warner's arch rival.

**Illustration 13-5**
Examples of consolidated companies and their subsidiaries

| Toys "R" Us, Inc. | Cendant | The Disney Company |
|---|---|---|
| Kids "R" Us | Howard Johnson | Capital Cities/ABC, Inc. |
| Babies "R" Us | Ramada Inn | Disneyland, Disney World |
| Imaginarium | Century 21 | Mighty Ducks |
| Toysrus.com | Coldwell Banker | Anaheim Angels |
| | Avis | ESPN |

## Before You Go On...

### REVIEW IT

1. What are the accounting entries for stock investments of less than 20%?
2. What entries are made under the equity method when (a) the investor receives a cash dividend from the investee and (b) the investee reports net income for the year?
3. What is the purpose of consolidated financial statements?
4. What does PepsiCo state regarding its accounting policy involving consolidated financial statements? The answer to this question appears on page 635.

### DO IT

Presented below are two independent situations.

1. Rho Jean Inc. acquired 5% of the 400,000 shares of common stock of Stillwater Corp. at a total cost of $6 per share on May 18, 2008. On August 30, Stillwater declared and paid a $75,000 dividend. On December 31, Stillwater reported net income of $244,000 for the year.
2. Debbie, Inc. obtained significant influence over North Sails by buying 40% of North Sails' 60,000 outstanding shares of common stock at a cost of $12 per share on January 1, 2008. On April 15, North Sails declared and paid a cash dividend of $45,000. On December 31, North Sails reported net income of $120,000 for the year.

Prepare all necessary journal entries for 2008 for (1) Rho Jean Inc. and (2) Debbie, Inc.

### Action Plan

- Presume that the investor has relatively little influence over the investee when an investor owns less than 20% of the common stock of another corporation. In this case, net income earned by the investee is not considered a proper basis for recognizing income from the investment by the investor.
- Presume significant influence for investments of 20%–50%. Therefore, record the investor's share of the net income of the investee.

### Solution

| | | | | |
|---|---|---|---|---|
| **(1)** May 18 | Stock Investments (400,000 × 5% × $6) | | 120,000 | |
| | Cash | | | 120,000 |
| | (To record purchase of 20,000 shares of Stillwater Co. stock) | | | |
| Aug. 30 | Cash | | 3,750 | |
| | Dividend Revenue ($75,000 × 5%) | | | 3,750 |
| | (To record receipt of cash dividend) | | | |

| (2) Jan. 1 | Stock Investments (60,000 × 40% × $12) | 288,000 | |
| | Cash | | 288,000 |
| | (To record purchase of 24,000 shares of North Sails' stock) | | |
| Apr. 15 | Cash | 18,000 | |
| | Stock Investments ($45,000 × 40%) | | 18,000 |
| | (To record receipt of cash dividend) | | |
| Dec. 31 | Stock Investments ($120,000 × 40%) | 48,000 | |
| | Revenue from Investment in North Sails | | 48,000 |
| | (To record 40% equity in North Sails' net income) | | |

Related exercise material: *BE13-2, BE13-3, E13-4, E13-5, E13-6, E13-7, and E13-8.*

✔ *The Navigator*

# VALUING AND REPORTING INVESTMENTS

The value of debt and stock investments may fluctuate greatly during the time they are held. For example, in one 12-month period, the stock price of Dell Computer Corp. hit a high of $41.99 and a low of $23.60. In light of such price fluctuations, how should companies value investments at the balance sheet date? Valuation could be at cost, at fair value (market value), or at the lower-of-cost-or-market value.

STUDY OBJECTIVE 5

Indicate how debt and stock investments are reported in financial statements.

Many people argue that fair value offers the best approach because it represents the expected cash realizable value of securities. **Fair value** is the amount for which a security could be sold in a normal market. Others counter that, unless a security is going to be sold soon, the fair value is not relevant because the price of the security will likely change again.

## Categories of Securities

For purposes of valuation and reporting at a financial statement date, companies classify debt and stock investments into three categories:

1. **Trading securities** are bought and held primarily for sale in the near term to generate income on short-term price differences.

2. **Available-for-sale securities** are held with the intent of selling them sometime in the future.

3. **Held-to-maturity securities** are debt securities that the investor has the intent and ability to hold to maturity.[3]

Illustration 13-6 (on page 606) shows the valuation guidelines for these securities. **These guidelines apply to all debt securities and all stock investments in which the holdings are less than 20%.**

### TRADING SECURITIES

Companies hold trading securities with the intention of selling them in a short period (generally less than a month). *Trading* means frequent buying and selling. Companies report trading securities at fair value, and report changes from cost as part of net income. The changes are reported as **unrealized gains or losses** because

---

[3]This category is provided for completeness. The accounting and valuation issues related to held-to-maturity securities are discussed in more advanced accounting courses.

**Illustration 13-6**
Valuation guidelines

the securities have not been sold. The unrealized gain or loss is the difference between the **total cost** of trading securities and their **total fair value.** Companies classify trading securities as current assets.

Illustration 13-7 shows the cost and fair values for investments Pace classified as trading securities on December 31, 2008. Pace has an unrealized gain of $7,000 because total fair value of $147,000 is $7,000 greater than total cost of $140,000.

**Illustration 13-7**
Valuation of trading
securities

| Trading Securities, December 31, 2008 | | | |
|---|---|---|---|
| **Investments** | **Cost** | **Fair Value** | **Unrealized Gain (Loss)** |
| Yorkville Company bonds | $ 50,000 | $ 48,000 | $ (2,000) |
| Kodak Company stock | 90,000 | 99,000 | 9,000 |
| Total | $140,000 | $147,000 | $ 7,000 |

**HELPFUL HINT**

The fact that trading securities are short-term investments increases the likelihood that they will be sold at fair value (the company may not be able to time their sale) and that there will be realized gains or losses.

| A | = | L | + | SE |
|---|---|---|---|---|
| +7,000 | | | | |
| | | | | +7,000 Rev |

**Cash Flows**
no effect

Pace records fair value and unrealized gain or loss through an adjusting entry at the time it prepares financial statements. In this entry, the company uses a valuation allowance account, Market Adjustment—Trading, to record the difference between the total cost and the total fair value of the securities. The adjusting entry for Pace Corporation is:

| Dec. 31 | Market Adjustment—Trading | 7,000 | |
| | Unrealized Gain—Income | | 7,000 |
| | (To record unrealized gain on trading | | |
| | securities) | | |

Use of a Market Adjustment—Trading account enables Pace to maintain a record of the investment cost. It needs actual cost to determine the gain or loss realized when it sells the securities. Pace adds the Market Adjustment—Trading balance to the cost of the investments to arrive at a fair value for the trading securities. **The fair value of the securities is the amount Pace reports on its balance sheet.** It reports the unrealized gain in the income statement in the "Other revenues and gains" section. The term "Income" in the account title indicates that the gain affects net income.

If the total cost of the trading securities is greater than total fair value, an unrealized loss has occurred. In such a case, the adjusting entry is a debit to Unrealized Loss—Income and a credit to Market Adjustment—Trading. Companies report the unrealized loss under "Other expenses and losses" in the income statement.

The market adjustment account is carried forward into future accounting periods. The company does not make any entry to the account until the end of each reporting period. At that time, the company adjusts the balance in the account to the difference between cost and fair value. For trading securities, it closes the Unrealized Gain (Loss)—Income account at the end of the reporting period.

# ACCOUNTING ACROSS THE ORGANIZATION

### And the Correct Way to Report Investments Is...?

The accompanying graph presents an estimate of the percentage of companies on the major exchanges that have investments in the equity of other entities.

As the graph indicates, many companies have equity investments of some type. These investments can be substantial. For example, the total amount of equity-method investments appearing on company balance sheets is approximately $403 billion, and the amount shown in the income statements in any one year for all companies is approximately $38 billion.

**Source:** "Report and Recommendations Pursuant to Section 401(c) of the Sarbanes-Oxley Act of 2002 on Arrangements with Off-Balance Sheet Implications, Special Purpose Entities, and Transparency of Filings by Issuers," United States Securities and Exchange Commission—Office of Chief Accountant, Office of Economic Analyses, Division of Corporation Finance (June 2005), pp. 36–39.

**?** Why might the use of the equity method not lead to full disclosure in the financial statements?

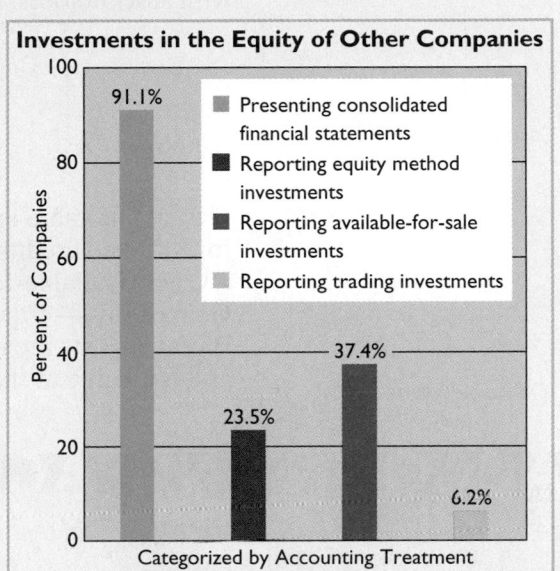

## AVAILABLE-FOR-SALE SECURITIES

As indicated earlier, companies hold available-for-sale securities with the intent of selling these investments sometime in the future. If the intent is to sell the securities within the next year or operating cycle, the investor classifies the securities as current assets in the balance sheet. Otherwise, it classifies them as long-term assets in the investments section of the balance sheet.

Companies report available-for-sale securities at fair value. The procedure for determining fair value and the unrealized gain or loss for these securities is the same as for trading securities. To illustrate, assume that Ingrao Corporation has two securities that it classifies as available-for-sale. Illustration 13-8 provides information on their valuation. There is an unrealized loss of $9,537 because total cost of $293,537 is $9,537 more than total fair value of $284,000.

> **ETHICS NOTE**
>
> Some managers seem to hold their available-for-sale securities that have experienced losses, while selling those that have gains, thus increasing income. Do you think this is ethical?

| Available-for-Sale Securities, December 31, 2008 | | | |
|---|---|---|---|
| Investments | Cost | Fair Value | Unrealized Gain (Loss) |
| Campbell Soup Corporation 8% bonds | $ 93,537 | $103,600 | $10,063 |
| Hershey Corporation stock | 200,000 | 180,400 | (19,600) |
| Total | $293,537 | $284,000 | $(9,537) |

**Illustration 13-8**
Valuation of available-for-sale securities

Both the adjusting entry and the reporting of the unrealized gain or loss for Ingrao's available-for-sale securities differ from those illustrated for trading securities. The differences result because Ingrao does not expect to sell these securities in the near term. Thus, prior to actual sale it is more likely that changes in fair value may change either unrealized gains or losses. Therefore, Ingrao does not report an unrealized gain or loss in the income statement. Instead, it reports it as a **separate component of stockholders' equity**.

In the adjusting entry, Ingrao identifies the market adjustment account with available-for-sale securities, and it identifies the unrealized gain or loss account with stockholders' equity. Ingrao records the unrealized loss of $9,537 as follows:

**Cash Flows**
no effect

| Dec. 31 | Unrealized Gain or Loss—Equity | 9,537 | |
| | Market Adjustment—Available-for-Sale | | 9,537 |
| | (To record unrealized loss on available-for-sale securities) | | |

If total fair value exceeds total cost, Ingrao debits Market Adjustment—Available for Sale and credits Unrealized Gain or Loss—Equity.

For available-for-sale securities, the company carries forward the Unrealized Gain or Loss—Equity account to future periods. At each future balance sheet date, Ingrao adjusts the market adjustment account to show the difference between cost and fair value at that time.

# ACCOUNTING ACROSS THE ORGANIZATION

### How Fair Is Fair?

In the fall of 2000, Wall Street brokerage firm Morgan Stanley told investors that rumors of big losses in its bond portfolio were "greatly exaggerated." As it turns out, Morgan Stanley also was exaggerating.

Recently, the SEC accused Morgan Stanley of violating securities laws by overstating the value of certain bonds by $75 million. The overvaluations stemmed more from wishful thinking than reality, the SEC said. "In effect, Morgan Stanley valued its positions at the price at which it thought a willing buyer and seller should enter into an exchange, rather than at a price at which a willing buyer and a willing seller would enter into a current exchange," the SEC wrote.

The SEC also noted that Morgan Stanley in some instances used its own more optimistic assumptions as a substitute for external pricing sources. "What that is saying is: 'Fair value is what you want the value to be. Pick a number...' That's especially troublesome."

 What do you believe is a major concern in valuing securities at fair value in the financial statements?

## Balance Sheet Presentation

In the balance sheet, companies classify investments as either short-term or long-term.

### SHORT-TERM INVESTMENTS

**Short-term investments** (also called **marketable securities**) are securities held by a company that are (1) **readily marketable** and (2) **intended to be converted into cash** within the next year or operating cycle, whichever is longer. Investments that do not meet **both criteria** are classified as **long-term investments**.

**Readily Marketable.** **An investment is readily marketable when it can be sold easily whenever the need for cash arises.** Short-term paper[4] meets this criterion. It can be readily sold to other investors. Stocks and bonds traded on organized securities exchanges, such as the New York Stock Exchange, are readily marketable. They can be bought and sold daily. In contrast, there may be only a limited market for the securities issued by small corporations, and no market for the securities of a privately held company.

**Intent to Convert.** **Intent to convert means that management intends to sell the investment within the next year or operating cycle, whichever is longer.** Generally, this criterion is satisfied when the investment is considered a resource that the investor will use whenever the need for cash arises. For example, a ski resort may invest idle cash during the summer months with the intent to sell the securities to buy supplies and equipment shortly before the winter season. This investment is considered short-term even if lack of snow cancels the next ski season and eliminates the need to convert the securities into cash as intended.

Because of their high liquidity, short-term investments appear immediately below Cash in the "Current assets" section of the balance sheet. They are reported at fair value. For example, Pace Corporation would report its trading securities as shown in Illustration 13-9.

| PACE CORPORATION | |
|---|---|
| Balance Sheet (partial) | |
| Current assets | |
| Cash | $ 21,000 |
| Short-term investments, at fair value | 147,000 |

**Illustration 13-9**
Presentation of short-term investments

### LONG-TERM INVESTMENTS

Companies generally report long-term investments in a separate section of the balance sheet immediately below "Current assets," as shown later in Illustration 13-12 (page 611). Long-term investments in available-for-sale securities are reported at fair value. Investments in common stock accounted for under the equity method are reported at their equity value.

## Presentation of Realized and Unrealized Gain or Loss

Companies must present in the financial statements gains and losses on investments, whether realized or unrealized. In the income statement, companies report gains and losses in the nonoperating activities section under the categories listed in Illustration 13-10. Interest and dividend revenue are also reported in that section.

| **Other Revenue and Gains** | **Other Expenses and Losses** |
|---|---|
| Interest Revenue | Loss on Sale of Investments |
| Dividend Revenue | Unrealized Loss—Income |
| Gain on Sale of Investments | |
| Unrealized Gain—Income | |

**Illustration 13-10**
Nonoperating items related to investments

---

[4]**Short-term paper** includes (1) certificates of deposit (CDs) issued by banks, (2) money market certificates issued by banks and savings and loan associations, (3) Treasury bills issued by the U.S. government, and (4) commercial paper (notes) issued by corporations with good credit ratings.

As indicated earlier, companies report an unrealized gain or loss on available-for-sale securities as a separate component of stockholders' equity. To illustrate, assume that Dawson Inc. has common stock of $3,000,000, retained earnings of $1,500,000, and an unrealized loss on available-for-sale securities of $100,000. Illustration 13-11 shows the balance sheet presentation of the unrealized loss.

**Illustration 13-11**
Unrealized loss in stockholders' equity section

| DAWSON INC. Balance Sheet (partial) | |
|---|---:|
| Stockholders' equity | |
| Common stock | $3,000,000 |
| Retained earnings | 1,500,000 |
| Total paid-in capital and retained earnings | 4,500,000 |
| **Less: Unrealized loss on available-for-sale securities** | **(100,000)** |
| Total stockholders' equity | $4,400,000 |

Note that the loss decreases stockholders' equity. An unrealized gain is added to stockholders' equity. Reporting the unrealized gain or loss in the stockholders' equity section serves two purposes: (1) It reduces the volatility of net income due to fluctuations in fair value. (2) It informs the financial statement user of the gain or loss that would occur if the securities were sold at fair value.

Companies must report items such as this, which affect stockholders' equity but are not included in the calculation of net income, as part of a more inclusive measure called *comprehensive income*. We discuss comprehensive income briefly in Chapter 15.

## Classified Balance Sheet

We have presented many sections of classified balance sheets in this and preceding chapters. The classified balance sheet in Illustration 13-12 (page 611) includes, in one place, key topics from previous chapters: the issuance of par value common stock, restrictions of retained earnings, and issuance of long-term bonds. From this chapter, the statement includes (highlighted in red) short-term and long-term investments. The investments in short-term securities are considered trading securities. The long-term investments in stock of less than 20% owned companies are considered available-for-sale securities. Illustration 13-12 also includes a long-term investment reported at equity and descriptive notations within the statement, such as the basis for valuing merchandise and one note to the statement.

---

### *Before You Go On...*

**REVIEW IT**

1. What is the proper valuation and reporting of trading and available-for-sale securities on a balance sheet?
2. Explain how companies report the unrealized gain or loss for both trading and available-for-sale securities.
3. Explain where to report short- and long-term investments on a balance sheet.

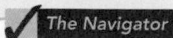 The Navigator

---

 Be sure to read **ALL ABOUT YOU: *A Good Day to Start Saving*** on page 612 for information on how topics in this chapter apply to you.

Illustration 13-12
Classified balance sheet

## PACE CORPORATION
Balance Sheet
December 31, 2008

### Assets

| | | |
|---|---:|---:|
| Current assets | | |
| Cash | | $ 21,000 |
| **Short-term investments, at fair value** | | **147,000** |
| Accounts receivable | $ 84,000 | |
| Less: Allowance for doubtful accounts | 4,000 | 80,000 |
| Merchandise inventory, at FIFO cost | | 43,000 |
| Prepaid insurance | | 23,000 |
| Total current assets | | 314,000 |
| Investments | | |
| **Investments in stock of less than 20%** | | |
| **owned companies, at fair value** | **50,000** | |
| **Investment in stock of 20–50% owned** | | |
| **company, at equity** | **150,000** | |
| Total investments | | 200,000 |
| Property, plant, and equipment | | |
| Land | | 200,000 |
| Buildings | $800,000 | |
| Less: Accumulated depreciation | 200,000 | 600,000 |
| Equipment | 180,000 | |
| Less: Accumulated depreciation | 54,000 | 126,000 |
| Total property, plant, and equipment | | 926,000 |
| Intangible assets | | |
| Goodwill | | 270,000 |
| Total assets | | $1,710,000 |

### Liabilities and Stockholders' Equity

| | | |
|---|---:|---:|
| Current liabilities | | |
| Accounts payable | | $185,000 |
| Federal income taxes payable | | 60,000 |
| Bond interest payable | | 10,000 |
| Total current liabilities | | 255,000 |
| Long-term liabilities | | |
| Bonds payable, 10%, due 2019 | $ 300,000 | |
| Less: Discount on bonds | 10,000 | |
| Total long-term liabilities | | 290,000 |
| Total liabilities | | 545,000 |
| Stockholders' equity | | |
| Paid-in capital | | |
| Common stock, $10 par value, 200,000 shares | | |
| authorized, 80,000 shares issued and outstanding | 800,000 | |
| Paid-in capital in excess of par value | 100,000 | |
| Total paid-in capital | 900,000 | |
| Retained earnings (Note 1) | 255,000 | |
| Total paid-in capital and retained earnings | 1,155,000 | |
| **Add: Unrealized gain on available-for-sale** | | |
| **securities** | **10,000** | |
| Total stockholders' equity | | 1,165,000 |
| Total liabilities and stockholders' equity | | $1,710,000 |

**Note 1.** Retained earnings of $100,000 is restricted for plant expansion.

# A Good Day to Start Saving

Compared to citizens in many other nations, Americans are very poor savers. It isn't that we don't know that we should save. It is just that we would rather spend. When *is* a good time to get serious about saving? Maybe you should start saving when you've graduated and have a good job, but then there will be those student loans to pay off, and your car loans as well. Maybe you should start after you've purchased your first home—and furnished it. Oh, and you might have kids, so you might wait until after they've gone off to college. You get the picture: there's always a reason not to start saving. Given that, *today* is as good a day as any to start saving.

## ✳ Some Facts

* Only about 48% of people in their twenties whose employers have a 401(k) plan participate in that plan. [401(k) plans allow you to put part of your pre-tax salary into investments. The investment and its earnings are not taxed until you withdraw them in retirement.] Many employers automatically enroll employees in 401(k) plans when they hire them.

* Only 40% of working couples currently are covered by pension plans, but 61% of workers expect to get income from a company pension plan.

* More than half of workers age 55 and older have less than $50,000 in retirement savings.

* 80% of individuals between the ages of 18 to 26 said that, if given $10,000, they would deposit the money into a traditional bank savings account rather than invest in the stock market. Many stated that they are intimidated by the stock market, and choose to give up the added returns the stock market offers over the long run, rather than face the market.

## ✳ About the Numbers

The message to start saving early has been presented in many different ways. The chart below presents the facts in very blunt terms. When you are 25 years old, if you start putting $300 per month into an investment earning 8%, by the age of 65 you will have accumulated more than $1 million. But if you wait until age 55, you will accumulate only about $55,000. Notice the sharp drop-off between ages 25 and 35.

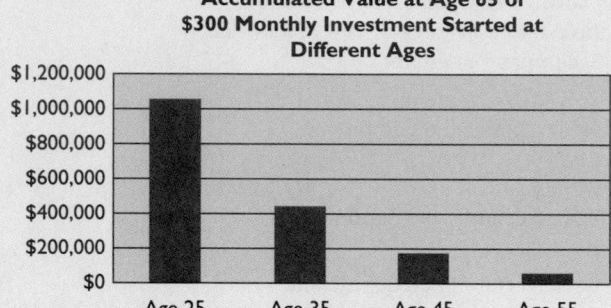

**Accumulated Value at Age 65 of $300 Monthly Investment Started at Different Ages**

## ✳ What Do You Think?

You've got $3,000 in credit card bills at an 18% interest rate. Your employer has a 401(k) plan in which it will match your contributions, up to 10% of your annual salary. Should you pay off your credit card bills before you start putting money into the 401(k)?

**YES:** Paying off an 18% debt, and thus avoiding 18% interest payments, is essentially equivalent to earning 18% on investments. Reducing your debts reduces your financial vulnerability.

**NO:** You need to get in the savings habit as soon as possible. You should take part of the money you would have used to pay off your debt each month and instead put it into the 401(k).

---

**Sources:** Kelly Greene, "Workers' Views On Retirement May Be Too Rosy," *Wall Street Journal*, April 4, 2006, p. D2; Ron Lieber, "Getting Younger Folk to Save," *Wall Street Journal*, June 17, 2006, p. B1; Eric A. Henon, "Why and How Generation Y Saves and Spends," *Benefits & Compensation Digest*, February 2006, pp. 30–32.

## Demonstration Problem

In its first year of operations, DeMarco Company had the following selected transactions in stock investments that are considered trading securities.

June 1 Purchased for cash 600 shares of Sanburg common stock at $24 per share, plus $300 brokerage fees.

July 1 Purchased for cash 800 shares of Cey common stock at $33 per share, plus $600 brokerage fees.

Sept. 1 Received a $1 per share cash dividend from Cey Corporation.

Nov. 1 Sold 200 shares of Sanburg common stock for cash at $27 per share, less $150 brokerage fees.

Dec. 15 Received a $0.50 per share cash dividend on Sanburg common stock.

At December 31, the fair values per share were: Sanburg $25 and Cey $30.

### Instructions

**(a)** Journalize the transactions.
**(b)** Prepare the adjusting entry at December 31 to report the securities at fair value.

## Solution

| | | | |
|---|---|---:|---:|
| **(a)** June 1 | Stock Investments | 14,700 | |
| |     Cash (600 × $24) + $300 | | 14,700 |
| |     (To record purchase of 600 shares of | | |
| |     Sanburg common stock) | | |
| | | | |
| July 1 | Stock Investments | 27,000 | |
| |     Cash (800 × $33) + $600 | | 27,000 |
| |     (To record purchase of 800 shares of Cey | | |
| |     common stock) | | |
| | | | |
| Sept. 1 | Cash (800 × $1.00) | 800 | |
| |     Dividend Revenue | | 800 |
| |     (To record receipt of $1 per share cash | | |
| |     dividend from Cey Corporation) | | |
| | | | |
| Nov. 1 | Cash (200 × $27) − $150 | 5,250 | |
| |     Stock Investments ($14,700 × 200/600) | | 4,900 |
| |     Gain on Sale of Stock Investments | | 350 |
| |     (To record sale of 200 shares of Sanburg | | |
| |     common stock) | | |
| | | | |
| Dec. 15 | Cash (600 − 200) × $0.50 | 200 | |
| |     Dividend Revenue | | 200 |
| |     (To record receipt of $0.50 per share | | |
| |     dividend from Sanburg Corporation) | | |
| | | | |
| **(b)** Dec. 31 | Unrealized Loss—Income | 2,800 | |
| |     Market Adjustment—Trading | | 2,800 |
| |     (To record unrealized loss on trading | | |
| |     securities) | | |

| Investment | Cost | Fair Value | Unrealized Gain (Loss) |
|---|---:|---:|---:|
| Sanburg common stock | $ 9,800 | $10,000 | $ 200 |
| Cey common stock | 27,000 | 24,000 | (3,000) |
| Totals | $36,800 | $34,000 | $(2,800) |

## action plan

✔ Include the price paid plus brokerage fees in the cost of the investment.

✔ Compute the gain or loss on sales as the difference between net selling price and the cost of the securities.

✔ Base the adjustment to fair value on the total difference between the cost and the fair value of the securities.

The Navigator

# SUMMARY OF STUDY OBJECTIVES

**1 Discuss why corporations invest in debt and stock securities.** Corporations invest for three primary reasons: (a) They have excess cash. (b) They view investments as a significant revenue source. (c) They have strategic goals such as gaining control of a competitor or moving into a new line of business.

**2 Explain the accounting for debt investments.** Companies record investments in debt securities when they purchase bonds, receive or accrue interest, and sell the bonds. They report gains or losses on the sale of bonds in the "Other revenues and gains" or "Other expenses and losses" sections of the income statement.

**3 Explain the accounting for stock investments.** Companies record investments in common stock when they purchase the stock, receive dividends, and sell the stock. When ownership is less than 20%, the cost method is used. When ownership is between 20% and 50%, the equity method should be used. When ownership is more than 50%, companies prepare consolidated financial statements.

**4 Describe the use of consolidated financial statements.** When a company owns more than 50% of the common

stock of another company, it usually prepares consolidated financial statements. These statements indicate the magnitude and scope of operations of the companies under common control.

**5 Indicate how debt and stock investments are reported in financial statements.** Investments in debt and stock securities are classified as trading, available-for-sale, or held-to-maturity securities for valuation and reporting purposes. Trading securities are reported as current assets at fair value, with changes from cost reported in net income. Available-for-sale securities are also reported at fair value, with the changes from cost reported in stockholders' equity. Available-for-sale securities are classified as short-term or long-term depending on their expected future sale date.

**6 Distinguish between short-term and long-term investments.** Short-term investments are securities that are (a) readily marketable and (b) intended to be converted to cash within the next year or operating cycle, whichever is longer. Investments that do not meet both criteria are classified as long-term investments.

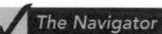

# GLOSSARY

**Available-for-sale securities** Securities that are held with the intent of selling them sometime in the future. (p. 605).

**Consolidated financial statements** Financial statements that present the assets and liabilities controlled by the parent company and the total revenues and expenses of the subsidiary companies. (p. 603).

**Controlling interest** Ownership of more than 50% of the common stock of another entity. (p. 603).

**Cost method** An accounting method in which the investment in common stock is recorded at cost, and revenue is recognized only when cash dividends are received. (p. 600).

**Debt investments** Investments in government and corporation bonds. (p. 598).

**Equity method** An accounting method in which the investment in common stock is initially recorded at cost, and the investment account is then adjusted annually to show the investor's equity in the investee. (p. 601).

**Fair value** Amount for which a security could be sold in a normal market. (p. 605).

**Held-to-maturity securities** Debt securities that the investor has the intent and ability to hold to their maturity date. (p. 605).

**Investment portfolio** A group of stocks and/or debt securities in different corporations held for investment purposes. (p. 600).

**Long-term investments** Investments that are not readily marketable or that management does not intend to convert into cash within the next year or operating cycle, whichever is longer. (p. 608).

**Parent company** A company that owns more than 50% of the common stock of another entity. (p. 602).

**Short-term investments** Investments that are readily marketable and intended to be converted into cash within the next year or operating cycle, whichever is longer. (p. 608).

**Stock investments** Investments in the capital stock of other corporations. (p. 600).

**Subsidiary (affiliated) company** A company in which more than 50% of its stock is owned by another company. (p. 602).

**Trading securities** Securities bought and held primarily for sale in the near term to generate income on short-term price differences. (p. 605).

# APPENDIX **Preparing Consolidated Financial Statements**

Most of the large U.S. corporations are holding companies that own other corporations. They therefore prepare **consolidated** financial statements that combine the separate companies.

## Consolidated Balance Sheet

Companies prepare consolidated balance sheets from the individual balance sheets of their affiliated companies. They do not prepare consolidated statements from ledger accounts kept by the consolidated entity because only the separate legal entities maintain accounting records.

All items in the individual balance sheets are included in the consolidated balance sheet except amounts that pertain to transactions between the affiliated companies. Transactions between the affiliated companies are identified as **intercompany transactions**. The process of excluding these transactions in preparing consolidated statements is referred to as **intercompany eliminations**. These eliminations are necessary to avoid overstating assets, liabilities, and stockholders' equity in the consolidated balance sheet. For example, amounts owed by a subsidiary to a parent company and the related receivable reported by the parent company would be eliminated. The objective in a consolidated balance sheet is to show only obligations to and receivables from parties who are not part of the affiliated group of companies.

To illustrate, assume that on January 1, 2008, Powers Construction Company pays $150,000 in cash for 100% of Serto Brick Company's common stock. Powers Company records the investment at cost, as required by the cost principle. Illustration 13A-1 presents the separate balance sheets of the two companies immediately after the purchase, together with combined and consolidated data.[1] Powers obtains the balances in the "combined" column are obtained by adding the items in the separate balance sheets of the affiliated companies. The combined totals do not represent a consolidated balance sheet, because there has been a double counting of assets and owners' equity in the amount of $150,000.

> **HELPFUL HINT**
> Eliminations are aptly named because they eliminate duplicate data. They are not adjustments.

> **Illustration 13A-1**
> Combined and consolidated data

### POWERS COMPANY AND SERTO COMPANY
#### Balance Sheet
#### January 1, 2008

| Assets | Powers Company | Serto Company | Combined Data | Consolidated Data |
|---|---|---|---|---|
| Current assets | $ 50,000 | $ 80,000 | $130,000 | **$130,000** |
| Investment in Serto Company common stock | 150,000 | | 150,000 | **–0–** |
| Plant and equipment (net) | 325,000 | 145,000 | 470,000 | **470,000** |
| Total assets | $525,000 | $225,000 | $750,000 | **$600,000** |
| | | | | |
| **Liabilities and Stockholders' Equity** | | | | |
| Current liabilities | $ 50,000 | $ 75,000 | $125,000 | **$125,000** |
| Common stock | 300,000 | 100,000 | 400,000 | **300,000** |
| Retained earnings | 175,000 | 50,000 | 225,000 | **175,000** |
| Total liabilities and stockholders' equity | $525,000 | $225,000 | $750,000 | **$600,000** |

---

[1] We use condensed data throughout this material to keep details at a minimum.

The Investment in Serto Company common stock that appears on the balance sheet of Powers Company represents an interest in the net assets of Serto. As a result, there has been a double counting of assets. Similarly, there has been a double counting in stockholders' equity, because the common stock of Serto Company is completely owned by the stockholders of Powers Company.

The balances in the consolidated data column are the amounts that should appear in the consolidated balance sheet. The double counting has been eliminated by showing Investment in Serto Company at zero and by reporting only the common stock and retained earnings of Powers Company as stockholders' equity.

## USE OF A WORKSHEET—COST EQUAL TO BOOK VALUE

**STUDY OBJECTIVE 7**

Describe the content of a worksheet for a consolidated balance sheet.

**The preparation of consolidated balance sheets is usually facilitated by the use of a worksheet.** As shown in Illustration 13A-2, the worksheet for a consolidated balance sheet contains columns for (1) the balance sheet data for the separate legal entities, (2) intercompany eliminations, and (3) consolidated data. All data in the worksheet relate to the preceding example in which Powers Company acquires 100% ownership of Serto Company for $150,000. In this case, the cost of the investment, $150,000, is equal to the book value $150,000 ($225,000 − $75,000) of the subsidiary's net assets. The intercompany elimination results in a credit to the Investment account maintained by Powers Company for its balance, $150,000, and debits to the Common Stock and Retained Earnings accounts of Serto Company for their respective balances, $100,000 and $50,000.

**Illustration 13A-2**
Worksheet—Cost equal to book value

| | Powers Company | Serto Company | Eliminations Dr. | Eliminations Cr. | Consolidated Data |
|---|---|---|---|---|---|
| **Assets** | | | | | |
| Current assets | 50,000 | 80,000 | | | 130,000 |
| Investment in Serto Company common stock | 150,000 | | | 150,000 | –0– |
| Plant and equipment (net) | 325,000 | 145,000 | | | 470,000 |
| Totals | 525,000 | 225,000 | | | 600,000 |
| | | | | | |
| **Liabilities and Stockholders' Equity** | | | | | |
| Current liabilities | 50,000 | 75,000 | | | 125,000 |
| Common stock—Powers Company | 300,000 | | | | 300,000 |
| Common stock—Serto Company | | 100,000 | 100,000 | | –0– |
| Retained earnings—Powers Company | 175,000 | | | | 175,000 |
| Retained earnings—Serto Company | | 50,000 | 50,000 | | –0– |
| Totals | 525,000 | 225,000 | 150,000 | 150,000 | 600,000 |

POWERS COMPANY AND SUBSIDIARY
Worksheet—Consolidated Balance Sheet
January 1, 2008 (Acquisition Date)

**HELPFUL HINT**

As in the case of the worksheets explained earlier in this textbook, consolidated worksheets are also optional.

**It is important to recognize that companies make intercompany eliminations are made solely on the worksheet to present correct consolidated data. Neither of the affiliated companies journalizes or posts the eliminations. Therefore, eliminations do not affect the ledger accounts.** Powers Company's investment account and Serto Company's common stock and retained earnings accounts are reported by the separate entities in preparing their own financial statements.

## USE OF A WORKSHEET—COST ABOVE BOOK VALUE

The cost of acquiring the common stock of another company may be above or below its book value. The management of the parent company may pay more than book value for the stock. Why? Because it believes the fair market values of identifiable assets such as land, buildings, and equipment are higher than their recorded book values. Or it may believe the subsidiary's future earnings prospects warrant a payment for goodwill.

To illustrate, assume the same data used above, except that Powers Company pays $165,000 in cash for 100% of Serto's common stock. The excess of cost over book value is $15,000 ($165,000 − $150,000). Powers recognizes this amount separately in eliminating the parent company's investment account, as shown in Illustration 13A-3. Total assets and total liabilities and stockholders' equity are the same as in the preceding example ($600,000). However, in this case, total assets include $15,000 of Excess of Cost Over Book Value of Subsidiary. The disposition of the excess is explained in the next section.

**Illustration 13A-3**
Worksheet—Cost above book value

Powers Company.xls

**POWERS COMPANY AND SUBSIDIARY**
Worksheet—Consolidated Balance Sheet
January 1, 2008 (Acquisition Date)

| Assets | Powers Company | Serto Company | Eliminations Dr. | Eliminations Cr. | Consolidated Data |
|---|---|---|---|---|---|
| Current assets | 35,000 | 80,000 | | | 115,000 |
| Investment in Serto Company common stock | 165,000 | | | 165,000 | –0– |
| Plant and equipment (net) | 325,000 | 145,000 | | | 470,000 |
| **Excess of cost over book value of subsidiary** | | | 15,000 | | 15,000 |
| Totals | 525,000 | 225,000 | | | 600,000 |
| | | | | | |
| **Liabilities and Stockholders' Equity** | | | | | |
| Current liabilities | 50,000 | 75,000 | | | 125,000 |
| Common stock—Powers Company | 300,000 | | | | 300,000 |
| Common stock—Serto Company | | 100,000 | 100,000 | | –0– |
| Retained earnings—Powers Company | 175,000 | | | | 175,000 |
| Retained earnings—Serto Company | | 50,000 | 50,000 | | –0– |
| Totals | 525,000 | 225,000 | 165,000 | 165,000 | 600,000 |

Note that a separate line is added to the worksheet for the excess of cost over book value of subsidiary.

## CONTENT OF A CONSOLIDATED BALANCE SHEET

To illustrate a consolidated balance sheet, we will use the worksheet shown in Illustration 13A-3. This worksheet shows an excess of cost over book value of $15,000. In the consolidated balance sheet, Powers first allocates this amount to specific assets, such as inventory and plant equipment, if their fair market values on the acquisition date exceed their book values. Any remainder is considered to be goodwill. For Serto Company, assume that the fair market value of property and equipment is $155,000. Thus, Powers allocates $10,000 of the excess of cost over book value to property and equipment, and the remainder, $5,000, to goodwill. Illustration 13A-4 (next page) shows the condensed consolidated balance sheet of Powers Company.

### POWERS COMPANY
#### Consolidated Balance Sheet
#### January 1, 2008

**Assets**

| | | |
|---|---|---|
| Current assets | | $115,000 |
| Plant and equipment (net) | | 480,000 |
| Goodwill | | 5,000 |
| Total assets | | $600,000 |

**Liabilities and Stockholders' Equity**

| | | |
|---|---|---|
| Current liabilities | | $125,000 |
| Stockholders' equity | | |
| Common stock | $300,000 | |
| Retained earnings | 175,000 | 475,000 |
| Total liabilities and stockholders' equity | | $600,000 |

Through innovative financial restructuring, The Coca-Cola Company at one time eliminated a substantial amount of non-intercompany debt. It sold to the public 51% of two bottling companies. The "49% solution," as insiders call the strategy, enabled Coca-Cola to keep effective control over the businesses, and it swept $3 billion of debt from its consolidated balance sheet. (It no longer consolidated the two bottling companies.) At the same time the new companies obtained independent access to equity markets to satisfy their own voracious appetites for capital.

## Consolidated Income Statement

Affiliated companies also prepare a consolidated income statement. This statement shows the results of operations of affiliated companies as though they are one economic unit. This means that the statement shows only revenue and expense transactions between the consolidated entity and companies and individuals who are outside the affiliated group.

Consequently, all intercompany revenue and expense transactions must be eliminated. Intercompany transactions such as sales between affiliates and interest on loans charged by one affiliate to another must be eliminated. A worksheet facilitates the preparation of consolidated income statements in the same manner as it does for the balance sheet.

## SUMMARY OF STUDY OBJECTIVE FOR APPENDIX

**7 Describe the content of a worksheet for a consolidated balance sheet.** The worksheet for a consolidated balance sheet contains columns for (a) the balance sheet data for the separate entities, (b) intercompany eliminations, and (c) consolidated data.

**8 Explain the form and content of consolidated financial statements.** Consolidated financial statements are similar in form and content to the financial statements of an individual corporation. A consolidated balance sheet shows the assets and liabilities controlled by the parent company. A consolidated income statement shows the results of operations of affiliated companies as though they are one economic unit.

## GLOSSARY FOR APPENDIX

**Intercompany eliminations** Eliminations made to exclude the effects of intercompany transactions in preparing consolidated statements. (p. 615).

**Intercompany transactions** Transactions between affiliated companies. (p. 615).

***Note:** All asterisked Questions, Exercises, and Problems relate to material in the appendix to the chapter.

Answers are at the end of the chapter.

(SO 2) **1.** Debt investments are initially recorded at:
   **a.** cost.
   **b.** cost plus accrued interest.
   **c.** fair value.
   **d.** None of the above.

(SO 2) **2.** Hanes Company sells debt investments costing $26,000 for $28,000, plus accrued interest that has been recorded. In journalizing the sale, credits are to:
   **a.** Debt Investments and Loss on Sale of Debt Investments.
   **b.** Debt Investments, Gain on Sale of Debt Investments, and Bond Interest Receivable.
   **c.** Stock Investments and Bond Interest Receivable.
   **d.** No correct answer given.

(SO 3) **3.** Pryor Company receives net proceeds of $42,000 on the sale of stock investments that cost $39,500. This transaction will result in reporting in the income statement a:
   **a.** loss of $2,500 under "Other expenses and losses."
   **b.** loss of $2,500 under "Operating expenses."
   **c.** gain of $2,500 under "Other revenues and gains."
   **d.** gain of $2,500 under "Operating revenues."

(SO 3) **4.** The equity method of accounting for long-term investments in stock should be used when the investor has significant influence over an investee and owns:
   **a.** between 20% and 50% of the investee's common stock.
   **b.** 20% or more of the investee's common stock.
   **c.** more than 50% of the investee's common stock.
   **d.** less than 20% of the investee's common stock.

(SO 4) **5.** Which of the following statements is *not true*? Consolidated financial statements are useful to:
   **a.** determine the profitability of specific subsidiaries.
   **b.** determine the total profitability of enterprises under common control.
   **c.** determine the breadth of a parent company's operations.
   **d.** determine the full extent of total obligations of enterprises under common control.

(SO 5) **6.** At the end of the first year of operations, the total cost of the trading securities portfolio is $120,000. Total fair value is $115,000. The financial statements should show:
   **a.** a reduction of an asset of $5,000 and a realized loss of $5,000.
   **b.** a reduction of an asset of $5,000 and an unrealized loss of $5,000 in the stockholders' equity section.
   **c.** a reduction of an asset of $5,000 in the current assets section and an unrealized loss of $5,000 in "Other expenses and losses."
   **d.** a reduction of an asset of $5,000 in the current assets section and a realized loss of $5,000 in "Other expenses and losses."

**7.** In the balance sheet, a debit balance in Unrealized Gain (SO 5) or Loss—Equity is reported as a:
   **a.** contra asset account.
   **b.** contra stockholders' equity account.
   **c.** loss in the income statement.
   **d.** loss in the retained earnings statement.

**8.** Short-term debt investments must be readily marketable (SO 6) and be expected to be sold within:
   **a.** 3 months from the date of purchase.
   **b.** the next year or operating cycle, whichever is shorter.
   **c.** the next year or operating cycle, whichever is longer.
   **d.** the operating cycle.

*9. Pate Company pays $175,000 for 100% of Sinko's com- (SO 7) mon stock when Sinko's stockholders' equity consists of Common Stock $100,000 and Retained Earnings $60,000. In the worksheet for the consolidated balance sheet, the eliminations will include a:
   **a.** credit to Investment in Sinko Common Stock $160,000.
   **b.** credit to Excess of Book Value over Cost of Subsidiary $15,000.
   **c.** debit to Retained Earnings $75,000.
   **d.** debit to Excess of Cost over Book Value of Subsidiary $15,000.

*10. Which of the following statements about intercompany (SO 7) eliminations is *true*?
   **a.** They are not journalized or posted by any of the subsidiaries.
   **b.** They do not affect the ledger accounts of any of the subsidiaries.
   **c.** Intercompany eliminations are made solely on the worksheet to arrive at correct consolidated data.
   **d.** All of these statements are true.

*11. Which one of the following statements about consolidated (SO 8) income statements is *false*?
   **a.** A worksheet facilitates the preparation of the statement.
   **b.** The consolidated income statement shows the results of operations of affiliated companies as a single economic unit.
   **c.** All revenue and expense transactions between parent and subsidiary companies are eliminated.
   **d.** When a subsidiary is wholly owned, the form and content of the statement will differ from the income statement of an individual corporation.

Go to the book's website,
**www.wiley.com/college/ weygandt**,
for Additional Self-Study questions.

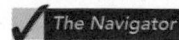

# QUESTIONS

1. What are the reasons that corporations invest in securities?

2. (a) What is the cost of an investment in bonds?
   (b) When is interest on bonds recorded?

3. Tino Martinez is confused about losses and gains on the sale of debt investments. Explain to Tino (a) how the gain or loss is computed, and (b) the statement presentation of the gains and losses.

4. Olindo Company sells Gish's bonds costing $40,000 for $45,000, including $500 of accrued interest. In recording the sale, Olindo books a $5,000 gain. Is this correct? Explain.

5. What is the cost of an investment in stock?

6. To acquire Kinston Corporation stock, R. Neal pays $62,000 in cash, plus $1,200 broker's fees. What entry should be made for this investment, assuming the stock is readily marketable?

7. (a) When should a long-term investment in common stock be accounted for by the equity method? (b) When is revenue recognized under this method?

8. Rijo Corporation uses the equity method to account for its ownership of 30% of the common stock of Pippen Packing. During 2008 Pippen reported a net income of $80,000 and declares and pays cash dividends of $10,000. What recognition should Rijo Corporation give to these events?

9. What constitutes "significant influence" when an investor's financial interest is below the 50% level?

10. Distinguish between the cost and equity methods of accounting for investments in stocks.

11. What are consolidated financial statements?

12. What are the valuation guidelines for investments at a balance sheet date?

13. Tina Eddings is the controller of Mendez Inc. At December 31, the company's investments in trading securities cost $74,000. They have a fair value of $70,000. Indicate how Tina would report these data in the financial statements prepared on December 31.

14. Using the data in question 13, how would Tina report the data if the investment were long-term and the securities were classified as available-for-sale?

15. Hashmi Company's investments in available-for-sale securities at December 31 show total cost of $195,000 and total fair value of $205,000. Prepare the adjusting entry.

16. Using the data in question 15, prepare the adjusting entry assuming the securities are classified as trading securities.

17. What is the proper statement presentation of the account Unrealized Loss—Equity?

18. What purposes are served by reporting Unrealized Gains (Losses)—Equity in the stockholders' equity section?

19. Altoona Wholesale Supply owns stock in Key Corporation. Altoona intends to hold the stock indefinitely because of some negative tax consequences if sold. Should the investment in Key be classified as a short-term investment? Why or why not?

*20. (a) What asset and stockholders' equity balances are eliminated in preparing a consolidated balance sheet for a parent and a wholly owned subsidiary? (b) Why are they eliminated?

*21. Bohanon Company pays $318,000 to purchase all the outstanding common stock of Erin Corporation. At the date of purchase the net assets of Erin have a book value of $290,000. Bohanon's management allocates $20,000 of the excess cost to undervalued land on the books of Erin. What should be done with the rest of the excess?

# BRIEF EXERCISES

*Journalize entries for debt investments.*

*(SO 2)*

**BE13-1** Coffey Corporation purchased debt investments for $52,000 on January 1, 2008. On July 1, 2008, Coffey received cash interest of $2,340. Journalize the purchase and the receipt of interest. Assume that no interest has been accrued.

*Journalize entries for stock investments.*

*(SO 3)*

**BE13-2** On August 1, Wade Company buys 1,000 shares of Morgan common stock for $35,000 cash, plus brokerage fees of $700. On December 1, Wade sells the stock investments for $40,000 in cash. Journalize the purchase and sale of the common stock.

*Record transactions under the equity method of accounting.*

*(SO 3)*

**BE13-3** Kayser Company owns 25% of Fort Company. For the current year Fort reports net income of $180,000 and declares and pays a $50,000 cash dividend. Record Kayser's equity in Fort's net income and the receipt of dividends from Fort.

*Prepare adjusting entry using fair value.*

*(SO 5)*

**BE13-4** The cost of the trading securities of Cepeda Company at December 31, 2008, is $62,000. At December 31, 2008, the fair value of the securities is $59,000. Prepare the adjusting entry to record the securities at fair value.

*Indicate statement presentation using fair value.*

*(SO 5, 6)*

**BE13-5** For the data presented in BE13-4, show the financial statement presentation of the trading securities and related accounts.

*Prepare adjusting entry using fair value.*

*(SO 5)*

**BE13-6** Garrett Corporation holds as a long-term investment available-for-sale stock securities costing $72,000. At December 31, 2008, the fair value of the securities is $66,000. Prepare the adjusting entry to record the securities at fair value.

**BE13-7** For the data presented in BE13-6, show the financial statement presentation of the available-for-sale securities and related accounts. Assume the available-for-sale securities are noncurrent.

*Indicate statements presentation using fair value.*
*(SO 5, 6)*

**BE13-8** Gowdy Corporation has the following long-term investments: (1) Common stock of Dixen Co. (10% ownership) held as available-for-sale securities, cost $108,000, fair value $115,000. (2) Common stock of Ely Inc. (30% ownership), cost $210,000, equity $270,000. Prepare the investments section of the balance sheet.

*Prepare investments section of balance sheet.*
*(SO 5, 6)*

**\*BE13-9** Paula Company acquires 100% of the common stock of Shannon Company for $190,000 cash. On the acquisition date, Shannon's ledger shows Common Stock $120,000 and Retained Earnings $70,000. Complete the worksheet for the following accounts: Paula—Investment in Shannon Common Stock, Shannon—Common Stock, and Shannon—Retained Earnings.

*Prepare partial consolidated worksheet when cost equals book value.*
*(SO 7)*

**\*BE13-10** Data for the Paula and Shannon companies are given in BE13-9. Instead of paying $190,000, assume that Paula pays $200,000 to acquire the 100% interest in Shannon Company. Complete the worksheet for the accounts identified in BE13-9 and for the excess of cost over book value.

*Prepare partial consolidated worksheet when cost exceeds book value.*
*(SO 7)*

# EXERCISES

**E13-1** Max Weinberg is studying for an accounting test and has developed the following questions about investments.

*Understand debt and stock investments.*
*(SO 1)*

1. What are three reasons why companies purchase investments in debt or stock securities?
2. Why would a corporation have excess cash that it does not need for operations?
3. What is the typical investment when investing cash for short periods of time?
4. What is the typical investment when investing cash to generate earnings?
5. Why would a company invest in securities that provide no current cash flows?
6. What is the typical investment when investing cash for strategic reasons?

**Instructions**
Provide answers for Max.

**E13-2** Foren Corporation had the following transactions pertaining to debt investments.

*Journalize debt investment transactions and accrue interest.*
*(SO 2)*

Jan. 1 Purchased 50 8%, $1,000 Choate Co. bonds for $50,000 cash plus brokerage fees of $900. Interest is payable semiannually on July 1 and January 1.
July 1 Received semiannual interest on Choate Co. bonds.
July 1 Sold 30 Choate Co. bonds for $34,000 less $500 brokerage fees.

**Instructions**
(a) Journalize the transactions.
(b) Prepare the adjusting entry for the accrual of interest at December 31.

**E13-3** EmmyLou Company purchased 70 Harris Company 12%, 10-year, $1,000 bonds on January 1, 2008, for $73,000. EmmyLou Company also had to pay $500 of broker's fees. The bonds pay interest semiannually. On January 1, 2009, after receipt of interest, EmmyLou Company sold 40 of the bonds for $40,100.

*Journalize debt investment transactions, accrue interest, and record sale.*
*(SO 2)*

**Instructions**
Prepare the journal entries to record the transactions described above.

**E13-4** Dossett Company had the following transactions pertaining to stock investments.

*Journalize stock investment transactions.*
*(SO 3)*

Feb. 1 Purchased 600 shares of Goetz common stock (2%) for $6,000 cash, plus brokerage fees of $200.
July 1 Received cash dividends of $1 per share on Goetz common stock.
Sept. 1 Sold 300 shares of Goetz common stock for $4,400, less brokerage fees of $100.
Dec. 1 Received cash dividends of $1 per share on Goetz common stock.

**Instructions**
(a) Journalize the transactions.
(b) Explain how dividend revenue and the gain (loss) on sale should be reported in the income statement.

*Journalize transactions for
investments in stocks.*

*(SO 3)*

**E13-5**  Wyrick Inc. had the following transactions pertaining to investments in common stock.

Jan.   1  Purchased 2,500 shares of Murphy Corporation common stock (5%) for $140,000 cash plus $2,100 broker's commission.
July   1  Received a cash dividend of $3 per share.
Dec.   1  Sold 500 shares of Murphy Corporation common stock for $32,000 cash, less $800 broker's commission.
Dec. 31  Received a cash dividend of $3 per share.

**Instructions**
Journalize the transactions.

*Journalize transactions for
investments in stocks.*

*(SO 3)*

**E13-6**  On February 1, Neil Company purchased 500 shares (2% ownership) of Young Company common stock for $30 per share plus brokerage fees of $400. On March 20, Neil Company sold 100 shares of Young stock for $2,900, less a $50 brokerage fee. Neil received a dividend of $1.00 per share on April 25. On June 15, Neil sold 200 shares of Young stock for $7,400, less a $90 brokerage fee. On July 28, Neil received a dividend of $1.25 per share.

**Instructions**
Prepare the journal entries to record the transactions described above.

*Journalize and post
transactions, and contrast cost
and equity method results.*

*(SO 3)*

**E13-7**  On January 1 Kwun Corporation purchased a 25% equity in Connors Corporation for $180,000. At December 31 Connors declared and paid a $60,000 cash dividend and reported net income of $200,000.

**Instructions**
**(a)** Journalize the transactions.
**(b)** Determine the amount to be reported as an investment in Connors stock at December 31.

*Journalize entries under cost
and equity methods.*

*(SO 3)*

**E13-8**  Presented below are two independent situations.

1. Heath Cosmetics acquired 15% of the 200,000 shares of common stock of Van Fashion at a total cost of $13 per share on March 18, 2008. On June 30, Van declared and paid a $60,000 dividend. On December 31, Van reported net income of $122,000 for the year. At December 31, the market price of Van Fashion was $15 per share. The stock is classified as available-for-sale.
2. Yoder, Inc., obtained significant influence over Parks Corporation by buying 30% of Parks 30,000 outstanding shares of common stock at a total cost of $9 per share on January 1, 2008. On June 15, Parks declared and paid a cash dividend of $30,000. On December 31, Parks reported a net income of $80,000 for the year.

**Instructions**
Prepare all the necessary journal entries for 2008 for (a) Heath Cosmetics and (b) Yoder, Inc.

*Understand the usefulness of
consolidated statements.*

*(SO 4)*

**E13-9**  Ryan Company purchased 70% of the outstanding common stock of Wayne Corporation.

**Instructions**
**(a)** Explain the relationship between Ryan Company and Wayne Corporation.
**(b)** How should Ryan account for its investment in Wayne?
**(c)** Why is the accounting treatment described in **(b)** useful?

*Prepare adjusting entry to
record fair value, and indicate
statement presentation.*

*(SO 5, 6)*

**E13-10**  At December 31, 2008, the trading securities for Natoli, Inc. are as follows.

| Security | Cost | Fair Value |
|----------|------|------------|
| A | $17,500 | $16,000 |
| B | 12,500 | 14,000 |
| C | 23,000 | 19,000 |
| | $53,000 | $49,000 |

**Instructions**
**(a)** Prepare the adjusting entry at December 31, 2008, to report the securities at fair value.
**(b)** Show the balance sheet and income statement presentation at December 31, 2008, after adjustment to fair value.

*Prepare adjusting entry to
record fair value, and indicate
statement presentation.*

*(SO 5, 6)*

**E13-11**  Data for investments in stock classified as trading securities are presented in E13-10. Assume instead that the investments are classified as available-for-sale securities. They have the same cost and fair value. The securities are considered to be a long-term investment.

## Instructions
**(a)** Prepare the adjusting entry at December 31, 2008, to report the securities at fair value.
**(b)** Show the statement presentation at December 31, 2008, after adjustment to fair value.
**(c)**  M. Linquist, a member of the board of directors, does not understand the reporting of the unrealized gains or losses. Write a letter to Mr. Linquist explaining the reporting and the purposes that it serves.

**E13-12**   McGee Company has the following data at December 31, 2008.

| Securities | Cost | Fair Value |
|---|---|---|
| Trading | $120,000 | $124,000 |
| Available-for-sale | 100,000 | 94,000 |

The available-for-sale securities are held as a long-term investment.

*Prepare adjusting entries for fair value, and indicate statement presentation for two classes of securities.*
*(SO 5, 6)*

## Instructions
**(a)** Prepare the adjusting entries to report each class of securities at fair value.
**(b)** Indicate the statement presentation of each class of securities and the related unrealized gain (loss) accounts.

**\*E13-13**   On January 1, 2008, Lennon Corporation acquires 100% of Ono Inc. for $220,000 in cash. The condensed balance sheets of the two corporations immediately following the acquisition are as follows.

*Prepare consolidated worksheet when cost equals book value.*
*(SO 7, 8)*

| | Lennon Corporation | Ono Inc. |
|---|---|---|
| Current assets | $ 60,000 | $ 50,000 |
| Investment in Ono Inc. common stock | 220,000 | |
| Plant and equipment (net) | 300,000 | 220,000 |
| | $580,000 | $270,000 |
| Current liabilities | $180,000 | $ 50,000 |
| Common stock | 230,000 | 80,000 |
| Retained earnings | 170,000 | 140,000 |
| | $580,000 | $270,000 |

## Instructions
Prepare a worksheet for a consolidated balance sheet.

**\*E13-14**   Data for the Lennon and Ono corporations are presented in E13-13. Assume that instead of paying $220,000 in cash for Ono Inc., Lennon Corporation pays $225,000 in cash. Thus, at the acquisition date, the assets of Lennon Corporation are: Current assets $55,000, Investment in Ono Inc. common stock $225,000, and Plant and equipment (net) $300,000.

*Prepare consolidated worksheet when cost exceeds book value.*
*(SO 7, 8)*

## Instructions
Prepare a worksheet for a consolidated balance sheet.

## EXERCISES: SET B

Visit the book's website at **www.wiley.com/college/weygandt**, and choose the Student Companion site, to access Exercise Set B.

## PROBLEMS: SET A

**P13-1A**   Davison Carecenters Inc. provides financing and capital to the health-care industry, with a particular focus on nursing homes for the elderly. The following selected transactions relate to bonds acquired as an investment by Davison, whose fiscal year ends on December 31.

*Journalize debt investment transactions and show financial statement presentation.*
*(SO 2, 5, 6)*

**2008**

Jan.  1  Purchased at par $2,000,000 of Hannon Nursing Centers, Inc., 10-year, 8% bonds dated January 1, 2008, directly from Hannon.
July  1  Received the semiannual interest on the Hannon bonds.
Dec. 31  Accrual of interest at year-end on the Hannon bonds.

(Assume that all intervening transactions and adjustments have been properly recorded and that the number of bonds owned has not changed from December 31, 2008, to December 31, 2010.)

**2011**

Jan.  1  Received the semiannual interest on the Hannon bonds.

Jan.  1  Sold $1,000,000 Hannon bonds at 106. The broker deducted $6,000 for commissions and fees on the sale.

July  1  Received the semiannual interest on the Hannon bonds.

Dec. 31  Accrual of interest at year-end on the Hannon bonds.

**Instructions**

(a) Gain on sale of debt investment $54,000

(a) Journalize the listed transactions for the years 2008 and 2011.

(b) Assume that the fair value of the bonds at December 31, 2008, was $2,200,000. These bonds are classified as available-for-sale securities. Prepare the adjusting entry to record these bonds at fair value.

(c) Based on your analysis in part (b), show the balance sheet presentation of the bonds and interest receivable at December 31, 2008. Assume the investments are considered long-term. Indicate where any unrealized gain or loss is reported in the financial statements.

*Journalize investment transactions, prepare adjusting entry, and show statement presentation.*

*(SO 2, 3, 5, 6)*

**P13-2A**  In January 2008, the management of Noble Company concludes that it has sufficient cash to permit some short-term investments in debt and stock securities. During the year, the following transactions occurred.

Feb.  1  Purchased 600 shares of Hiens common stock for $31,800, plus brokerage fees of $600.

Mar.  1  Purchased 800 shares of Pryce common stock for $20,000, plus brokerage fees of $400.

Apr.  1  Purchased 50 $1,000, 7% Roy bonds for $50,000, plus $1,000 brokerage fees. Interest is payable semiannually on April 1 and October 1.

July  1  Received a cash dividend of $0.60 per share on the Hiens common stock.

Aug.  1  Sold 200 shares of Hiens common stock at $58 per share less brokerage fees of $200.

Sept. 1  Received a $1 per share cash dividend on the Pryce common stock.

Oct.  1  Received the semiannual interest on the Roy bonds.

Oct.  1  Sold the Roy bonds for $50,000 less $1,000 brokerage fees.

At December 31, the fair value of the Hiens common stock was $55 per share. The fair value of the Pryce common stock was $24 per share.

**Instructions**

(a) Gain on stock sale $600

(a) Journalize the transactions and post to the accounts Debt Investments and Stock Investments. (Use the T-account form.)

(b) Prepare the adjusting entry at December 31, 2008, to report the investment securities at fair value. All securities are considered to be trading securities.

(c) Show the balance sheet presentation of investment securities at December 31, 2008.

(d) Identify the income statement accounts and give the statement classification of each account.

*Journalize transactions and adjusting entry for stock investments.*

*(SO 3, 5, 6)*

**P13-3A**  On December 31, 2008, Ramey Associates owned the following securities, held as a long-term investment. The securities are not held for influence or control of the investee.

| **Common Stock** | **Shares** | **Cost** |
|---|---|---|
| Hurst Co. | 2,000 | $60,000 |
| Pine Co. | 5,000 | 45,000 |
| Scott Co. | 1,500 | 30,000 |

On December 31, 2008, the total fair value of the securities was equal to its cost. In 2009, the following transactions occurred.

July  1  Received $1 per share semiannual cash dividend on Pine Co. common stock.

Aug.  1  Received $0.50 per share cash dividend on Hurst Co. common stock.

Sept. 1  Sold 1,500 shares of Pine Co. common stock for cash at $8 per share, less brokerage fees of $300.

Oct.  1  Sold 800 shares of Hurst Co. common stock for cash at $33 per share, less brokerage fees of $500.

Nov.  1  Received $1 per share cash dividend on Scott Co. common stock.

Dec. 15  Received $0.50 per share cash dividend on Hurst Co. common stock.

     31  Received $1 per share semiannual cash dividend on Pine Co. common stock.

At December 31, the fair values per share of the common stocks were: Hurst Co. $32, Pine Co. $8, and Scott Co. $18.

**Instructions**

(a) Journalize the 2009 transactions and post to the account Stock Investments. (Use the T-account form.)

(b) Prepare the adjusting entry at December 31, 2009, to show the securities at fair value. The stock should be classified as available-for-sale securities.

(b) Unrealized loss $4,100

(c) Show the balance sheet presentation of the investments at December 31, 2009. At this date, Ramey Associates has common stock $1,500,000 and retained earnings $1,000,000.

**P13-4A** Glaser Services acquired 30% of the outstanding common stock of Nickels Company on January 1, 2008, by paying $800,000 for the 45,000 shares. Nickels declared and paid $0.30 per share cash dividends on March 15, June 15, September 15, and December 15, 2008. Nickels reported net income of $320,000 for the year. At December 31, 2008, the market price of Nickels common stock was $24 per share.

*Prepare entries under the cost and equity methods, and tabulate differences.*

*(SO 3)*

**Instructions**

(a) Prepare the journal entries for Glaser Services for 2008 assuming Glaser cannot exercise significant influence over Nickels. (Use the cost method and assume that Nickels common stock should be classified as a trading security.)

*(a) Total dividend revenue $54,000*

(b) Prepare the journal entries for Glaser Services for 2008, assuming Glaser can exercise significant influence over Nickels. Use the equity method.

*(b) Revenue from investments $96,000*

(c) In tabular form, indicate the investment and income statement account balances at December 31, 2008, under each method of accounting.

**P13-5A** The following securities are in Pascual Company's portfolio of long-term available-for-sale securities at December 31, 2008.

*Journalize stock investment transactions and show statement presentation.*

*(SO 3, 5, 6)*

|  | **Cost** |
|---|---|
| 1,000 shares of Abel Corporation common stock | $52,000 |
| 1,400 shares of Frey Corporation common stock | 84,000 |
| 1,200 shares of Weiss Corporation preferred stock | 33,600 |

On December 31, 2008, the total cost of the portfolio equaled total fair value. Pascual had the following transactions related to the securities during 2009.

Jan. 20 Sold 1,000 shares of Abel Corporation common stock at $55 per share less brokerage fees of $600.

28 Purchased 400 shares of $70 par value common stock of Rosen Corporation at $78 per share, plus brokerage fees of $480.

30 Received a cash dividend of $1.15 per share on Frey Corp. common stock.

Feb. 8 Received cash dividends of $0.40 per share on Weiss Corp. preferred stock.

18 Sold all 1,200 shares of Weiss Corp. preferred stock at $27 per share less brokerage fees of $360.

July 30 Received a cash dividend of $1.00 per share on Frey Corp. common stock.

Sept. 6 Purchased an additional 900 shares of $70 par value common stock of Rosen Corporation at $82 per share, plus brokerage fees of $1,200.

Dec. 1 Received a cash dividend of $1.50 per share on Rosen Corporation common stock.

At December 31, 2009, the fair values of the securities were:

| | |
|---|---|
| Frey Corporation common stock | $64 per share |
| Rosen Corporation common stock | $72 per share |

Pascual Company uses separate account titles for each investment, such as "Investment in Frey Corporation Common Stock."

**Instructions**

(a) Prepare journal entries to record the transactions.

(b) Post to the investment accounts. (Use T accounts.)

(c) Prepare the adjusting entry at December 31, 2009 to report the portfolio at fair value.

(d) Show the balance sheet presentation at December 31, 2009.

*(a) Loss on sale of preferred stock $1,560*

*(c) Unrealized loss $7,480*

**P13-6A** The data on page 626, presented in alphabetical order, are taken from the records of Urbina Corporation.

*Prepare a balance sheet.*

*(SO 5, 6)*

| | |
|---|---:|
| Accounts payable | $ 240,000 |
| Accounts receivable | 140,000 |
| Accumulated depreciation—building | 180,000 |
| Accumulated depreciation—equipment | 52,000 |
| Allowance for doubtful accounts | 6,000 |
| Bonds payable (10%, due 2016) | 500,000 |
| Buildings | 950,000 |
| Cash | 42,000 |
| Common stock ($10 par value; 500,000 shares authorized, | |
|    150,000 shares issued) | 1,500,000 |
| Dividends payable | 80,000 |
| Equipment | 275,000 |
| Goodwill | 200,000 |
| Income taxes payable | 120,000 |
| Investment in Flott common stock (10% ownership), at cost | 278,000 |
| Investment in Portico common stock (30% ownership), at equity | 380,000 |
| Land | 390,000 |
| Market adjustment—available-for-sale securities (Dr) | 8,000 |
| Merchandise inventory | 170,000 |
| Notes payable (due 2009) | 70,000 |
| Paid-in capital in excess of par value | 130,000 |
| Premium on bonds payable | 40,000 |
| Prepaid insurance | 16,000 |
| Retained earnings | 103,000 |
| Short-term stock investment, at fair value (and cost) | 180,000 |
| Unrealized gain—available-for-sale securities | 8,000 |

The investment in Flott common stock is considered to be a long-term available-for-sale security.

**Instructions**

Total assets $2,791,000

Prepare a balance sheet at December 31, 2008.

*Prepare consolidated worksheet and balance sheet when cost exceeds book value.*

(SO 7, 8)

**\*P13-7A**  Robinson Corporation purchased all the outstanding common stock of Hoffman Plastics, Inc. on December 31, 2008. Just before the purchase, the condensed balance sheets of the two companies appeared as follows.

| | Robinson Corporation | Hoffman Plastics, Inc. |
|---|---:|---:|
| Current assets | $1,480,000 | $ 435,500 |
| Plant and equipment (net) | 2,100,000 | 676,000 |
| | $3,580,000 | $1,111,500 |
| | | |
| Current liabilities | $ 578,000 | $ 92,500 |
| Common stock | 1,950,000 | 525,000 |
| Retained earnings | 1,052,000 | 494,000 |
| | $3,580,000 | $1,111,500 |

Robinson used current assets of $1,225,000 to acquire the stock of Hoffman Plastics. The excess of this purchase price over the book value of Hoffman Plastics' net assets is determined to be attributable $86,000 to Hoffman Plastics' plant and equipment and the remainder to goodwill.

**Instructions**

Excess cost over book value $120,000

**(a)** Prepare the entry for Robinson's acquisition of Hoffman Plastics, Inc. stock.
**(b)** Prepare a consolidated worksheet at December 31, 2008.
**(c)** Prepare a consolidated balance sheet at December 31, 2008.

# PROBLEMS: SET B

*Journalize debt investment transactions and show financial statement presentation.*

(SO 2, 5, 6)

**P13-1B**  Marshall Farms is a grower of hybrid seed corn for DeKalb Genetics Corporation. It has had two exceptionally good years and has elected to invest its excess funds in bonds. The selected transactions on page 627 relate to bonds acquired as an investment by Marshall Farms, whose fiscal year ends on December 31.

### 2008

Jan.  1   Purchased at par $600,000 of Kenner Corporation 10-year, 9% bonds dated January 1, 2008, directly from the issuing corporation.

July  1   Received the semiannual interest on the Kenner bonds.

Dec. 31   Accrual of interest at year-end on the Kenner bonds.

(Assume that all intervening transactions and adjustments have been properly recorded and the number of bonds owned has not changed from December 31, 2008, to December 31, 2010.)

### 2011

Jan.  1   Received the semiannual interest on the Kenner bonds.

Jan.  1   Sold $300,000 Kenner bonds at 114. The broker deducted $7,000 for commissions and fees on the sale.

July  1   Received the semiannual interest on the Kenner bonds.

Dec. 31   Accrual of interest at year-end on the Kenner bonds.

**Instructions**

**(a)** Journalize the listed transactions for the years 2008 and 2011.

**(b)** Assume that the fair value of the bonds at December 31, 2008, was $580,000. These bonds are classified as available-for-sale securities. Prepare the adjusting entry to record these bonds at fair value.

**(c)** Based on your analysis in part (b) show the balance sheet presentation of the bonds and interest receivable at December 31, 2008. Assume the investments are considered long-term. Indicate where any unrealized gain or loss is reported in the financial statements.

*(a) Gain on sale of debt investments $35,000*

**P13-2B**   In January 2008, the management of Pandya Company concludes that it has sufficient cash to purchase some short-term investments in debt and stock securities. During the year, the following transactions occurred.

*Journalize investment transactions, prepare adjusting entry, and show statement presentation.*

*(SO 2, 3, 5, 6)*

**GLS**

Feb.  1   Purchased 600 shares of EMP common stock for $40,000, plus brokerage fees of $800.

Mar.  1   Purchased 500 shares of SEK common stock for $15,000, plus brokerage fees of $300.

Apr.  1   Purchased 60 $1,000, 9% CRE bonds for $60,000, plus $1,200 brokerage fees. Interest is payable semiannually on April 1 and October 1.

July  1   Received a cash dividend of $0.60 per share on the EMP common stock.

Aug.  1   Sold 300 shares of EMP common stock at $72 per share, less brokerage fees of $350.

Sept. 1   Received a $1 per share cash dividend on the SEK common stock.

Oct.  1   Received the semiannual interest on the CRE bonds.

Oct.  1   Sold the CRE bonds for $64,000, less $1,000 brokerage fees.

At December 31, the fair value of the EMP common stock was $66 per share. The fair value of the SEK common stock was $29 per share.

**Instructions**

**(a)** Journalize the transactions and post to the accounts Debt Investments and Stock Investments. (Use the T-account form.)

**(b)** Prepare the adjusting entry at December 31, 2008, to report the investments at fair value. All securities are considered to be trading securities.

*(b) Unrealized loss $1,400*

**(c)** Show the balance sheet presentation of investment securities at December 31, 2008.

**(d)** Identify the income statement accounts and give the statement classification of each account.

**P13-3B**   On December 31, 2008, Hastco Associates owned the following securities, held as long-term investments.

*Journalize transactions and adjusting entry for stock investments.*

*(SO 3, 5, 6)*

**GLS**

| Common Stock | Shares | Cost |
|---|---|---|
| Agee Co. | 3,000 | $60,000 |
| Burns Co. | 6,000 | 36,000 |
| Corea Co. | 1,200 | 24,000 |

On this date, the total fair value of the securities was equal to its cost. The securities are not held for influence or control over the investees. In 2009, the following transactions occurred.

July  1   Received $1 per share semiannual cash dividend on Burns Co. common stock.

Aug.  1   Received $0.50 per share cash dividend on Agee Co. common stock.

Sept. 1   Sold 2,000 shares of Burns Co. common stock for cash at $8 per share, less brokerage fees of $300.

Oct.  1   Sold 600 shares of Agee Co. common stock for cash at $28 per share, less brokerage fees of $600.

Nov.  1   Received $1 per share cash dividend on Corea Co. common stock.

Dec. 15   Received $0.50 per share cash dividend on Agee Co. common stock.

    31   Received $1 per share semiannual cash dividend on Burns Co. common stock.

At December 31, the fair values per share of the common stocks were: Agee Co. $18, Burns Co. $6, and Corea Co. $19.

**Instructions**

*(a) Gain on sale, $3,700 and $4,200*

**(a)** Journalize the 2009 transactions and post to the account Stock Investments. (Use the T-account form.)

**(b)** Prepare the adjusting entry at December 31, 2009, to show the securities at fair value. The stock should be classified as available-for-sale securities.

**(c)** Show the balance sheet presentation of the investments at December 31, 2009. At this date, Hastco Associates has common stock $2,000,000 and retained earnings $1,200,000.

*Prepare entries under the cost and equity methods, and tabulate differences.*

*(SO 3)*

**P13-4B**   Keady's Concrete acquired 30% of the outstanding common stock of Washburn, Inc. on January 1, 2008, by paying $1,600,000 for 60,000 shares. Washburn declared and paid a $0.50 per share cash dividend on June 30 and again on December 31, 2008. Washburn reported net income of $600,000 for the year. At December 31, 2008, the market price of Washburn's common stock was $30 per share.

**Instructions**

*(a) Total dividend revenue $60,000*

**(a)** Prepare the journal entries for Keady's Concrete for 2008 assuming Keady's cannot exercise significant influence over Washburn. (Use the cost method and assume Washburn common stock should be classified as available-for-sale.)

*(b) Revenue from investments $180,000*

**(b)** Prepare the journal entries for Keady's Concrete for 2008, assuming Keady's can exercise significant influence over Washburn. (Use the equity method.)

**(c)** In tabular form, indicate the investment and income account balances at December 31, 2008, under each method of accounting.

*Journalize stock investment transactions and show statement presentation.*

*(SO 3, 5, 6)*

**P13-5B**   The following are in Madisen Company's portfolio of long-term available-for-sale securities at December 31, 2008.

|  | Cost |
|---|---|
| 500 shares of Bonds Corporation common stock | $26,000 |
| 700 shares of Mays Corporation common stock | 42,000 |
| 600 shares of Dukakis Corporation preferred stock | 16,800 |

On December 31, the total cost of the portfolio equaled total fair value. Madisen Company had the following transactions related to the securities during 2009.

Jan.  7   Sold 500 shares of Bonds Corporation common stock at $56 per share, less brokerage fees of $700.

   10   Purchased 200 shares, $70 par value common stock of Petengill Corporation at $78 per share, plus brokerage fees of $240.

   26   Received a cash dividend of $1.15 per share on Mays Corporation common stock.

Feb.  2   Received cash dividends of $0.40 per share on Dukakis Corporation preferred stock.

   10   Sold all 600 shares of Dukakis Corporation preferred stock at $26 per share less brokerage fees of $180.

July  1   Received a cash dividend of $1.00 per share on Mays Corporation common stock.

Sept. 1   Purchased an additional 600 shares of the $70 par value common stock of Petengill Corporation at $75 per share, plus brokerage fees of $900.

Dec. 15   Received a cash dividend of $1.50 per share on Petengill Corporation common stock.

At December 31, 2009, the fair values of the securities were:

| Mays Corporation common stock | $63 per share |
|---|---|
| Petengill Corporation common stock | $72 per share |

Madisen uses separate account titles for each investment, such as Investment in Mays Corporation Common Stock.

**Instructions**

(a) Prepare journal entries to record the transactions.

(b) Post to the investment accounts. (Use T accounts.)

(c) Prepare the adjusting entry at December 31, 2009, to report the portfolio at fair value.

(d) Show the balance sheet presentation at December 31, 2009.

(a) Loss on sale $1,380

(c) Unrealized loss $2,040

**P13-6B** The following data, presented in alphabetical order, are taken from the records of Manning Corporation.

*Prepare a balance sheet.*
*(SO 5, 6)*

| | |
|---|---:|
| Accounts payable | $ 250,000 |
| Accounts receivable | 90,000 |
| Accumulated depreciation—building | 180,000 |
| Accumulated depreciation—equipment | 52,000 |
| Allowance for doubtful accounts | 6,000 |
| Bonds payable (10%, due 2018) | 400,000 |
| Buildings | 900,000 |
| Cash | 142,000 |
| Common stock ($5 par value; 500,000 shares authorized, | |
| 300,000 shares issued) | 1,500,000 |
| Discount on bonds payable | 20,000 |
| Dividends payable | 50,000 |
| Equipment | 275,000 |
| Goodwill | 200,000 |
| Income taxes payable | 120,000 |
| Investment in Tabares Inc. stock (30% ownership), at equity | 600,000 |
| Land | 520,000 |
| Merchandise inventory | 170,000 |
| Notes payable (due 2009) | 70,000 |
| Paid-in capital in excess of par value | 200,000 |
| Prepaid insurance | 16,000 |
| Retained earnings | 290,000 |
| Short-term stock investment, at fair value (and cost) | 185,000 |

**Instructions**

Prepare a balance sheet at December 31, 2008.

Total assets $2,860,000

**\*P13-7B** Patel Company purchased all the outstanding common stock of Singh Company on December 31, 2008. Just before the purchase, the condensed balance sheets of the two companies were as follows.

*Prepare consolidated worksheet and balance sheet when cost exceeds book value.*
*(SO 7, 8)*

| | **Patel Company** | **Singh Company** |
|---|---:|---:|
| Current assets | $1,478,000 | $379,000 |
| Plant and equipment (net) | 1,882,000 | 351,000 |
| | $3,360,000 | $730,000 |
| | | |
| Current liabilities | $ 870,000 | $ 90,000 |
| Common stock | 1,947,000 | 360,000 |
| Retained earnings | 543,000 | 280,000 |
| | $3,360,000 | $730,000 |

Patel used current assets of $710,000 to acquire the stock of Singh. The excess of this purchase price over the book value of Patel's net assets is determined to be attributable $20,000 to Singh's plant and equipment and the remainder to goodwill.

**Instructions**

(a) Prepare the entry for Patel Company's acquisition of Singh Company stock.

(b) Prepare a consolidated worksheet at December 31, 2008.

(c) Prepare a consolidated balance sheet at December 31, 2008.

Excess of cost over book value $50,000

Visit the book's website at **www.wiley.com/college/weygandt**, and choose the Student Companion site, to access Problem Set C.

## COMPREHENSIVE PROBLEM: CHAPTERS 11 TO 13

### Part I

Mindy Feldkamp and her two colleagues, Oscar Lopez and Lori Melton, are personal trainers at an upscale health spa/resort in Tampa, Florida. They want to start a health club that specializes in health plans for people in the 50+ age range. The growing population in this age range and strong consumer interest in the health benefits of physical activity have convinced them they can profitably operate their own club. In addition to many other decisions, they need to determine what type of business organization they want. Oscar believes there are more advantages to the corporate form than a partnership, but he hasn't yet convinced Mindy and Lori. They have come to you, a small business consulting specialist, seeking information and advice regarding the choice of starting a partnership versus a corporation.

**Instructions**

**(a)** ━━━▶ Prepare a memo (dated May 26, 2007) that describes the advantages and disadvantages of both partnerships and corporations. Advise Mindy, Oscar, and Lori regarding which organizational form you believe would better serve their purposes. Make sure to include reasons supporting your advice.

### Part II

After deciding to incorporate, each of the three investors receives 20,000 shares of $2 par common stock on June 12, 2007, in exchange for their co-owned building ($200,000 market value) and $100,000 total cash they contributed to the business. The next decision that Mindy, Oscar, and Lori need to make is how to obtain financing for renovation and equipment. They understand the difference between equity securities and debt securities, but do not understand the tax, net income, and earnings per share consequences of equity versus debt financing on the future of their business.

**Instructions**

**(b)** Prepare notes for a discussion with the three entrepreneurs in which you will compare the consequences of using equity versus debt financing. As part of your notes, show the differences in interest and tax expense assuming $1,400,000 is financed with common stock, and then alternatively with debt. Assume that when common stock is used, 140,000 shares will be issued. When debt is used, assume the interest rate on debt is 9%, the tax rate is 32%, and income before interest and taxes is $300,000. (You may want to use an electronic spreadsheet.)

### Part III

During the discussion about financing, Lori mentions that one of her clients, Roberto Marino, has approached her about buying a significant interest in the new club. Having an interested investor sways the three to issue equity securities to provide the financing they need. On July 21, 2007, Mr. Marino buys 90,000 shares at a price of $10 per share.

The club, LifePath Fitness, opens on January 12, 2008, and after a slow start, begins to produce the revenue desired by the owners. The owners decide to pay themselves a stock dividend, since cash has been less than abundant since they opened their doors. The 10% stock dividend is declared by the owners on July 27, 2008. The market value of the stock is $3 on the declaration date. The date of record is July 31, 2008 (there have been no changes in stock ownership since the initial issuance), and the issue date is August 15, 2008. By the middle of the fourth quarter of 2008, the cash flow of LifePath Fitness has improved to the point that the owners feel ready to pay themselves a cash dividend. They declare a $0.05 cash dividend on December 4, 2008. The record date is December 14, 2008, and the payment date is December 24, 2008.

**Instructions**

**(c) (1)** Record all of the transactions related to the common stock of LifePath Fitness during the years 2007 and 2008. **(2)** Indicate how many shares are issued and outstanding after the stock dividend is issued.

**Part IV**

Since the club opened, a major concern has been the pool facilities. Although the existing pool is adequate, Mindy, Oscar, and Lori all desire to make LifePath a cutting-edge facility. Until the end of 2008, financing concerns prevented this improvement. However, because there has been steady growth in clientele, revenue, and income since the fourth quarter of 2008, the owners have explored possible financing options. They are hesitant to issue stock and change the ownership mix because they have been able to work together as a team with great effectiveness. They have formulated a plan to issue secured term bonds to raise the needed $600,000 for the pool facilities. By the end of April 2009 everything was in place for the bond issue to go ahead. On June 1, 2009, the bonds were issued for $548,000. The bonds pay semiannual interest of 3% (6% annual) on December 1 and June 1 of each year. The bonds mature in 10 years, and amortization is computed using the straight-line method.

**Instructions**

**(d)** Record **(1)** the issuance of the secured bonds, **(2)** the interest payment made on December 1, 2009, **(3)** the adjusting entry required at December 31, 2009, and **(4)** the interest payment made on June 1, 2010.

**Part V**

Mr. Marino's purchase of LifePath Fitness was done through his business. The investment has always been accounted for using the cost method on his firm's books. However, early in 2010 he decided to take his company public. He is preparing an IPO (initial public offering), and he needs to have the firm's financial statements audited. One of the issues to be resolved is to restate the investment in LifePath Fitness using the equity method, since Mr. Marino's ownership percentage is greater than 20%.

**Instructions**

**(e) (1)** Give the entries that would have been made on Marino's books if the equity method of accounting for investments had been used since the initial investment. Assume the following data for LifePath.

|                     | 2007    | 2008    | 2009     |
|---------------------|---------|---------|----------|
| Net income          | $30,000 | $70,000 | $105,000 |
| Total cash dividends | $ 2,100 | $20,000 | $ 50,000 |

**(2)** Compute the balance in the LifePath Investment account at the end of 2009.

---

## CONTINUING COOKIE CHRONICLE

(*Note:* This is a continuation of the Cookie Chronicle from Chapters 1 through 12.)

**CCC13**    Natalie has been approached by Ken Thornton, a shareholder of The Beanery Coffee Inc. Ken wants to retire and would like to sell his 1,000 shares in The Beanery Coffee, which represents 20% of all shares issued. The Beanery is currently operated by Ken's twin daughters, who each own 40% of the common shares. The Beanery not only operates a coffee shop but also roasts and sells beans to retailers, under the name "Rocky Mountain Beanery."

Ken has met with Curtis and Natalie to discuss the business operation. All have concluded that there would be many advantages for Cookie & Coffee Creations Inc. to acquire an interest in The Beanery Coffee. Despite the apparent advantages, Natalie and Curtis are still not convinced that they should participate in this business venture.

*Go to the book's website,*
**www.wiley.com/college/weygandt,**
*to see the completion of this problem.*

# BROADENING YOUR PERSPECTIVE

## FINANCIAL REPORTING AND ANALYSIS

### Financial Reporting Problem

#### PepsiCo, Inc.

**BYP13-1**   The annual report of PepsiCo is presented in Appendix A.

**Instructions**

**(a)** See Note 1 to the financial statements and indicate what the consolidated financial statements include.

**(b)** Using PepsiCo's consolidated statement of cash flows, determine how much was spent for capital acquisitions during the current year.

### Comparative Analysis Problem

#### PepsiCo, Inc. vs. The Coca-Cola Company

**BYP13-2**   PepsiCo's financial statements are presented in Appendix A. Coca-Cola's financial statements are presented in Appendix B.

**Instructions**

**(a)** Based on the information contained in these financial statements, determine each of the following for each company.
  **(1)** Net cash used for investing (investment) activities for the current year (from the statement of cash flows).
  **(2)** Cash used for capital expenditures during the current year.

**(b)** Each of PepsiCo's financial statements is labeled "consolidated." What has been consolidated? That is, from the contents of PepsiCo's annual report, identify by name the corporations that have been consolidated (parent and subsidiaries).

### Exploring the Web

**BYP13-3**   Most publicly traded companies are analyzed by numerous analysts. These analysts often don't agree about a company's future prospects. In this exercise you will find analysts' ratings about companies and make comparisons over time and across companies in the same industry. You will also see to what extent the analysts experienced "earnings surprises." Earnings surprises can cause changes in stock prices.

**Address: biz.yahoo.com/i**, or go to **www.wiley.com/college/weygandt**

**Steps**
**1.** Choose a company.
**2.** Use the index to find the company's name.
**3.** Choose **Research**.

**Instructions**

**(a)** How many analysts rated the company?
**(b)** What percentage rated it a strong buy?
**(c)** What was the average rating for the week?
**(d)** Did the average rating improve or decline relative to the previous week?
**(e)** How do the analysts rank this company among all the companies in its industry?
**(f)** What was the amount of the earnings surprise percentage during the last quarter?

## CRITICAL THINKING

## Decision Making Across the Organization

**BYP13-4** At the beginning of the question and answer portion of the annual stockholders' meeting of Kemper Corporation, stockholder Mike Kerwin asks, "Why did management sell the holdings in UMW Company at a loss when this company has been very profitable during the period its stock was held by Kemper?"

Since president Tony Chavez has just concluded his speech on the recent success and bright future of Kemper, he is taken aback by this question and responds, "I remember we paid $1,300,000 for that stock some years ago, and I am sure we sold that stock at a much higher price. You must be mistaken."

Kerwin retorts, "Well, right here in footnote number 7 to the annual report it shows that 240,000 shares, a 30% interest in UMW, were sold on the last day of the year. Also, it states that UMW earned $520,000 this year and paid out $160,000 in cash dividends. Further, a summary statement indicates that in past years, while Kemper held UMW stock, UMW earned $1,240,000 and paid out $440,000 in dividends. Finally, the income statement for this year shows a loss on the sale of UMW stock of $180,000. So, I doubt that I am mistaken."

Red-faced, president Chavez turns to you.

### Instructions

With the class divided into groups, answer the following.

**(a)** What dollar amount did Kemper receive upon the sale of the UMW stock?
**(b)** Explain why both stockholder Kerwin and president Chavez are correct.

## Communication Activity

**BYP13-5** Bunge Corporation has purchased two securities for its portfolio. The first is a stock investment in Longley Corporation, one of its suppliers. Bunge purchased 10% of Longley with the intention of holding it for a number of years, but has no intention of purchasing more shares. The second investment was a purchase of debt securities. Bunge purchased the debt securities because its analysts believe that changes in market interest rates will cause these securities to increase in value in a short period of time. Bunge intends to sell the securities as soon as they have increased in value.

### Instructions

Write a memo to Max Scholes, the chief financial officer, explaining how to account for each of these investments. Explain what the implications for reported income are from this accounting treatment.

## Ethics Case

**BYP13-6** Bartlet Financial Services Company holds a large portfolio of debt and stock securities as an investment. The total fair value of the portfolio at December 31, 2008, is greater than total cost. Some securities have increased in value and others have decreased. Deb Faust, the financial vice president, and Jan McCabe, the controller, are in the process of classifying for the first time the securities in the portfolio.

Faust suggests classifying the securities that have increased in value as trading securities in order to increase net income for the year. She wants to classify the securities that have decreased in value as long-term available-for-sale securities, so that the decreases in value will not affect 2008 net income.

McCabe disagrees. She recommends classifying the securities that have decreased in value as trading securities and those that have increased in value as long-term available-for-sale securities. McCabe argues that the company is having a good earnings year and that recognizing the losses now will help to smooth income for this year. Moreover, for future years, when the company may not be as profitable, the company will have built-in gains.

**Instructions**

**(a)** Will classifying the securities as Faust and McCabe suggest actually affect earnings as each says it will?

**(b)** Is there anything unethical in what Faust and McCabe propose? Who are the stakeholders affected by their proposals?

**(c)** Assume that Faust and McCabe properly classify the portfolio. Assume, at year-end, that Faust proposes to sell the securities that will increase 2008 net income, and that McCabe proposes to sell the securities that will decrease 2008 net income. Is this unethical?

 # "All About You" Activity

**BYP13-7** The Securities and Exchange Commission (SEC) is the primary regulatory agency of U.S. financial markets. Its job is to ensure that the markets remain fair for all investors. The following SEC sites provide useful information for investors.

Address: **www.sec.gov/answers.shtml** and **http://www.sec.gov/investor/tools/quiz.htm**, or go to **www.wiley.com/college/weygandt**.

**Instructions**

**(a)** Go to the first SEC site and find the definition of the following terms.
    (i)   Ask price.
    (ii)  Margin account.
    (iii) Prospectus.
    (iv) Index fund.

**(b)** Go to the second SEC site and take the short quiz.

 ## Answers to Insight and Accounting Across the Organization Questions

**How Altria Group Accounts for Kraft Foods, p. 603**

Q:  Where on Altria Group's balance sheet will you find its investment in Kraft Foods, Inc.?

A:  *Because Altria owns 98.3% of Kraft, Altria Group does not report Kraft in the investment section of its balance sheet. Instead, Kraft's assets and liabilities are included and commingled with the assets and liabilities of Altria Group.*

**And the Correct Way to Report Investments Is . . . ?, p. 607**

Q:  Why might the use of the equity method not lead to full disclosure in the financial statements?

A:  *Under the equity method, the investment in common stock of another company is initially recorded at cost. After that, the investment account is adjusted at each reporting date to show the investor's equity in the investee. However, on the investor's balance sheet, only the investment account is shown. The pro-rata share of the investee's assets and liabilities are not reported. Because the pro-rata share of the investee's assets and liabilities are not shown, some argue that the full disclosure principle is violated.*

**How Fair Is Fair?, p. 608**

Q:  What do you believe is a major concern in valuing securities at fair value in the financial statements?

A:  *Some question the relevance of fair value measures for investments in securities, arguing in favor of reporting based on cost. They believe that cost provides relevant information: it focuses on the decision to acquire the asset, the earning effects of that decision that will be realized over time, and the ultimate recoverable value of the asset. They argue that fair value ignores those concepts. Instead, fair value focuses on the effects of transactions and events that do not involve the company, reflecting opportunity gains and losses whose recognition in the financial statements is, in their view, not appropriate until realized.*

 ## Authors' Comments on *All About You*: A Good Day to Start Saving, p. 612

We believe that the correct answer to this situation is both *yes* and *no*. Here is what we propose: You need to cut up your credit cards, and then pay down your credit card debt. You should prepare a budget and figure out an affordable monthly payment that will pay off your debt as fast as possible. After you have paid off the credit card, you should continue to make this same payment into some form of savings account. If your employer has a 401(k) plan, then you should put the payment into that, since it has significant tax advantages. Otherwise set up an Individual Retirement Account (IRA). Most local banks or brokerage houses would be happy to help you set up an account.

A final note: All of us want to have financial security when we retire. We don't want to be a burden to anyone. That means that we should, whenever possible, participate in any tax-advantaged savings programs available to us, such as the 401(k) and IRAs. This is especially true given the concerns that many people have about the long-term viability of Social Security.

## Answer to PepsiCo Review It Question 4, page 604

In Note 1, the following statement is made regarding PepsiCo's consolidation policy:

> Our financial statements include the consolidated accounts of PepsiCo, Inc. and the affiliates that we control. In addition, we include our share of the results of certain other affiliates based on our economic ownership interest. We do not control these other affiliates, as our ownership in these other affiliates is generally less than fifty percent. Our share of the net income of noncontrolled bottling affiliates is reported in our income statement as bottling equity income. Bottling equity income also includes any changes in our ownership interests of these affiliates. In 2005, bottling equity income includes $126 million of pre-tax gains on our sales of PBG stock. See Note 8 for additional information on our noncontrolled bottling affiliates. Our share of other noncontrolled affiliates is included in division operating profit. Intercompany balances and transactions are eliminated.

## Answers to Self-Study Questions

**1.** a   **2.** b   **3.** c   **4.** a   **5.** a   **6.** c   **7.** b   **8.** c   *__9.__ d   *__10.__ d   *__11.__ d

# Statement of Cash Flows

## STUDY OBJECTIVES

*After studying this chapter, you should be able to:*

1 Indicate the usefulness of the statement of cash flows.

2 Distinguish among operating, investing, and financing activities.

3 Prepare a statement of cash flows using the indirect method.

4 Analyze the statement of cash flows.

✔ *The Navigator*

### ✔ The Navigator

| | |
|---|---|
| Scan **Study Objectives** | ▣ |
| Read **Feature Story** | ▣ |
| Read **Preview** | ▣ |
| Read text and answer **Before You Go On** p. 642 ▣  p. 644 ▣  p. 652 ▣  p. 657 ▣ | |
| Work **Demonstration Problem 1** | ▣ |
| Review **Summary of Study Objectives** | ▣ |
| Work **Demonstration Problem 2** | ▣ |
| Answer **Self-Study Questions** | ▣ |
| Complete **Assignments** | ▣ |

## *Feature Story*

### GOT CASH?

In today's environment, companies must be ready to respond to changes quickly in order to survive and thrive. They need to produce new products and expand into new markets continually. To do this takes cash—lots and lots of cash. Keeping lots of cash available is a real challenge for a young company. It requires careful cash management and attention to cash flow.

One company that managed cash successfully in its early years was Microsoft (*www.microsoft.com*). During those years the company paid much of its payroll with stock options (rights to purchase company stock in the future at a given price) instead of cash. This strategy conserved cash, and turned more than a thousand of its employees into millionaires during the company's first 20 years of business.

In recent years Microsoft has had a different kind of cash problem. Now that it has reached a more "mature" stage in life, it generates so much cash—roughly $1 billion per month—that it cannot always figure out what to do with it. By 2004 Microsoft had accumulated $60 billion.

The company said it was accumulating cash to invest in new opportunities, buy other companies, and pay off pending lawsuits. But for years, the federal government has blocked attempts by Microsoft to buy anything other than small firms because it feared that purchase of a large firm would only increase Microsoft's monopolistic position. In addition, even the largest estimates of Microsoft's legal obligations related to pending lawsuits would use up only about $6 billion in cash.

Microsoft's stockholders have complained for years that holding all this cash was putting a drag on the company's profitability. Why? Because Microsoft had the cash invested in very low-yielding government securities. Stockholders felt that the company either should find new investment projects that would bring higher returns, or return some of the cash to stockholders.

Finally, in July 2004 Microsoft announced a plan to return cash to stockholders, by paying a special one-time $32 billion dividend in December 2004. This special dividend was so large that, according to the U.S. Commerce Department, it caused total personal income in the United States to rise by 3.7% in one month—the largest monthly increase ever recorded by the agency. (It also made the holiday season brighter, especially for retailers in the Seattle area.) Microsoft also doubled its regular annual dividend to $3.50 per share. Further, it announced that it would spend another $30 billion over the next four years buying treasury stock. These actions will help to deplete some of its massive cash horde, but as you will see in this chapter, for a cash-generating machine like Microsoft, the company will be anything but cash-starved.

*Source:* "Business: An End to Growth? Microsoft's Cash Bonanza," *The Economist*, July 23, 2005, p. 61.

✓ The Navigator

# Inside Chapter 14

- **Net *What?*** (p. 641)

- **Cash Flow Isn't Always What It Seems** (p. 644)

- **GM Must Sell More Cars** (p. 650)

- ***All About You:* Where Does the Money Go?** (p. 656)

The balance sheet, income statement, and retained earnings statement do not always show the whole picture of the financial condition of a company or institution. In fact, looking at the financial statements of some well-known companies, a thoughtful investor might ask questions like these: How did Eastman Kodak finance cash dividends of $649 million in a year in which it earned only $17 million? How could United Airlines purchase new planes that cost $1.9 billion in a year in which it reported a net loss of over $2 billion? How did the companies that spent a combined fantastic $3.4 trillion on mergers and acquisitions in a recent year finance those deals? Answers to these and similar questions can be found in this chapter, which presents the statement of cash flows.

The content and organization of this chapter are as follows.

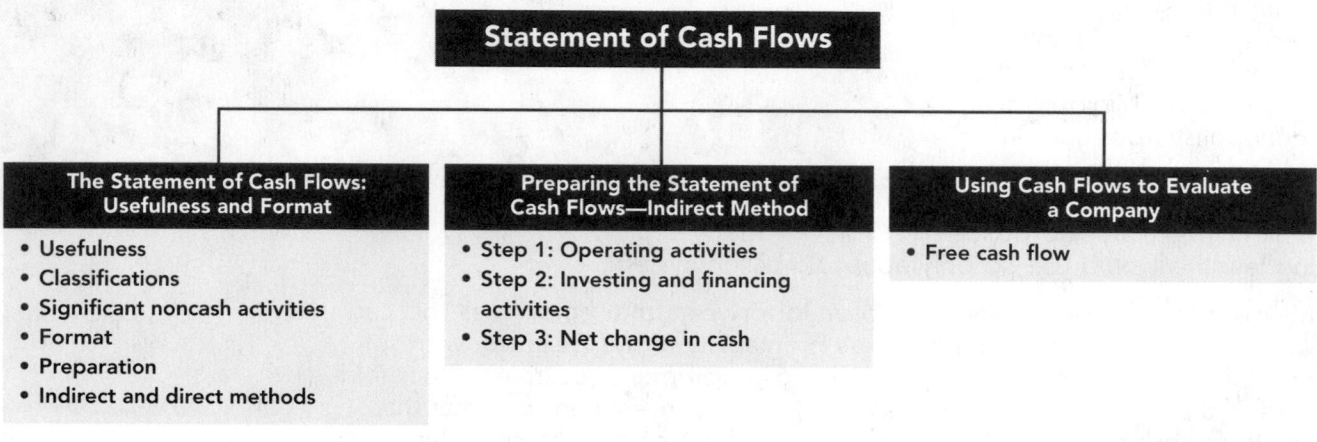

The Navigator

# THE STATEMENT OF CASH FLOWS: USEFULNESS AND FORMAT

The balance sheet, income statement, and retained earnings statement provide only limited information about a company's cash flows (cash receipts and cash payments). For example, comparative balance sheets show the increase in property, plant, and equipment during the year. But they do not show how the additions were financed or paid for. The income statement shows net income. But it does not indicate the amount of cash generated by operating activities. The retained earnings statement shows cash dividends declared but not the cash dividends paid during the year. None of these statements presents a detailed summary of where cash came from and how it was used.

## Usefulness of the Statement of Cash Flows

**STUDY OBJECTIVE 1**
Indicate the usefulness of the statement of cash flows.

The **statement of cash flows** reports the cash receipts, cash payments, and net change in cash resulting from operating, investing, and financing activities during a period. The information in a statement of cash flows should help investors, creditors, and others assess:

1. **The entity's ability to generate future cash flows.** By examining relationships between items in the statement of cash flows, investors can make predictions of the amounts, timing, and uncertainty of future cash flows better than they can from accrual basis data.

2. **The entity's ability to pay dividends and meet obligations.** If a company does not have adequate cash, it cannot pay employees, settle debts, or pay dividends. Employees, creditors, and stockholders should be particularly interested in this statement, because it alone shows the flows of cash in a business.

3. **The reasons for the difference between net income and net cash provided (used) by operating activities.** Net income provides information on the success or failure of a business enterprise. However, some financial statement users are critical of accrual-basis net income because it requires many estimates. As a result, users often challenge the reliability of the number. Such is not the case with cash. Many readers of the statement of cash flows want to know the reasons for the difference between net income and net cash provided by operating activities. Then they can assess for themselves the reliability of the income number.

4. **The cash investing and financing transactions during the period.** By examining a company's investing and financing transactions, a financial statement reader can better understand why assets and liabilities changed during the period.

> ### ETHICS NOTE
> Though we would discourage reliance on cash flows to the exclusion of accrual accounting, comparing cash from operations to net income can reveal important information about the "quality" of reported net income. Such a comparison can reveal the extent to which net income provides a good measure of actual performance.

## Classification of Cash Flows

The statement of cash flows classifies cash receipts and cash payments as operating, investing, and financing activities. Transactions and other events characteristic of each kind of activity are as follows.

> ### STUDY OBJECTIVE 2
> Distinguish among operating, investing, and financing activities.

1. **Operating activities** include the cash effects of transactions that create revenues and expenses. They thus enter into the determination of net income.

2. **Investing activities** include (a) acquiring and disposing of investments and property, plant, and equipment, and (b) lending money and collecting the loans.

3. **Financing activities** include (a) obtaining cash from issuing debt and repaying the amounts borrowed, and (b) obtaining cash from stockholders, repurchasing shares, and paying dividends.

The operating activities category is the most important. It shows the cash provided by company operations. This source of cash is generally considered to be the best measure of a company's ability to generate sufficient cash to continue as a going concern.

Illustration 14-1 (page 640) lists typical cash receipts and cash payments within each of the three classifications. **Study the list carefully.** It will prove very useful in solving homework exercises and problems.

Note the following general guidelines:

1. Operating activities involve income statement items.

2. Investing activities involve cash flows resulting from changes in investments and long-term asset items.

3. Financing activities involve cash flows resulting from changes in long-term liability and stockholders' equity items.

Companies classify as operating activities some cash flows related to investing or financing activities. For example, receipts of investment revenue (interest and dividends) are classified as operating activities. So are payments of interest to lenders. Why are these considered operating activities? **Because companies report these items in the income statement, where results of operations are shown.**

Illustration 14-1
Typical receipt and payment classifications

**Operating activities**

**Investing activities**

**Financing activities**

## TYPES OF CASH INFLOWS AND OUTFLOWS

**Operating activities—Income statement items**
Cash inflows:
From sale of goods or services.
From interest received and dividends received.
Cash outflows:
To suppliers for inventory.
To employees for services.
To government for taxes.
To lenders for interest.
To others for expenses.

**Investing activities—Changes in investments and long-term assets**
Cash inflows:
From sale of property, plant, and equipment.
From sale of investments in debt or equity securities of other entities.
From collection of principal on loans to other entities.
Cash outflows:
To purchase property, plant, and equipment.
To purchase investments in debt or equity securities of other entities.
To make loans to other entities.

**Financing activities—Changes in long-term liabilities and stockholders' equity**
Cash inflows:
From sale of common stock.
From issuance of long-term debt (bonds and notes).
Cash outflows:
To stockholders as dividends.
To redeem long-term debt or reacquire capital stock (treasury stock).

## Significant Noncash Activities

Not all of a company's significant activities involve cash. Examples of significant noncash activities are:

**1.** Direct issuance of common stock to purchase assets.

**2.** Conversion of bonds into common stock.

**3.** Direct issuance of debt to purchase assets.

**4.** Exchanges of plant assets.

**Companies do not report in the body of the statement of cash flows significant financing and investing activities that do not affect cash.** Instead, they report these activities in either a **separate schedule** at the bottom of the statement of cash flows or in a **separate note or supplementary schedule** to the financial statements. The reporting of these noncash activities in a separate schedule satisfies the **full disclosure principle**.

*In solving homework assignments you should present significant noncash investing and financing activities in a separate schedule at the bottom of the statement of cash flows. (See the last entry in Illustration 14-2, at the bottom of page 641, for an example.)*

# ACCOUNTING ACROSS THE ORGANIZATION

### Net *What?*

Net income is not the same as net cash provided by operating activities. Below are some results from recent annual reports (dollars in millions). Note the wide disparity among these companies, all of which engaged in retail merchandising.

| Company | Net Income | Net Cash Provided by Operating Activities |
|---|---|---|
| Kohl's Corporation | $ 730 | $ 948 |
| Wal-Mart Stores, Inc. | 10,267 | 15,044 |
| J. C. Penney Company, Inc. | 524 | 61 |
| Costco Wholesale Corp. | 882 | 2,099 |
| Target Corporation | 3,198 | 3,195 |

 In general, why do differences exist between net income and net cash provided by operating activities?

## Format of the Statement of Cash Flows

The general format of the statement of cash flows presents the results of the three activities discussed previously—operating, investing, and financing—plus the significant noncash investing and financing activities. Illustration 14–2 shows a widely used form of the statement of cash flows.

**Illustration 14-2**
Format of statement of cash flows

| COMPANY NAME Statement of Cash Flows Period Covered | | |
|---|---|---|
| **Cash flows from operating activities** | | |
| (List of individual items) | XX | |
| Net cash provided (used) by operating activities | | XXX |
| **Cash flows from investing activities** | | |
| (List of individual inflows and outflows) | XX | |
| Net cash provided (used) by investing activities | | XXX |
| **Cash flows from financing activities** | | |
| (List of individual inflows and outflows) | XX | |
| Net cash provided (used) by financing activities | | XXX |
| **Net increase (decrease) in cash** | | XXX |
| **Cash at beginning of period** | | XXX |
| **Cash at end of period** | | XXX |
| **Noncash investing and financing activities** | | |
| (List of individual noncash transactions) | | XXX |

The cash flows from operating activities section always appears first, followed by the investing activities section and then the financing activities section.

## Before You Go On...

### REVIEW IT

1. Why is the statement of cash flows useful?
2. What are the major classifications of cash flows on the statement of cash flows?
3. What are some examples of significant noncash activities?
4. What is the general format of the statement of cash flows? In what sequence are the three types of business activities presented?
5. In its 2005 statement of cash flows, what amounts did PepsiCo report for net cash (a) provided by operating activities, (b) used for investing activities, and (c) used for financing activities? The answer to this question appears on page 695.

### DO IT

During its first week, Duffy & Stevenson Company had these transactions.

1. Issued 100,000 shares of $5 par value common stock for $800,000 cash.
2. Borrowed $200,000 from Castle Bank, signing a 5-year note bearing 8% interest.
3. Purchased two semi-trailer trucks for $170,000 cash.
4. Paid employees $12,000 for salaries and wages.
5. Collected $20,000 cash for services provided.

Classify each of these transactions by type of cash flow activity.

### Action Plan

- Identify the three types of activities used to report all cash inflows and outflows.
- Report as operating activities the cash effects of transactions that create revenues and expenses and enter into the determination of net income.
- Report as investing activities transactions that (a) acquire and dispose of investments and productive long-lived assets and (b) lend money and collect loans.
- Report as financing activities transactions that (a) obtain cash from issuing debt and repay the amounts borrowed and (b) obtain cash from stockholders and pay them dividends.

### Solution

1. Financing activity
2. Financing activity
3. Investing activity
4. Operating activity
5. Operating activity

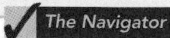

## Preparing the Statement of Cash Flows

Companies prepare the statement of cash flows differently from the three other basic financial statements. First, it is not prepared from an adjusted trial balance. It requires detailed information concerning the changes in account balances that occurred between two points in time. An adjusted trial balance will not provide the necessary data. Second, the statement of cash flows deals with cash receipts and payments. As a result, the company **must adjust** the effects of the use of accrual accounting **to determine cash flows**.

The information to prepare this statement usually comes from three sources:

- **Comparative balance sheets.** Information in the comparative balance sheets indicates the amount of the changes in assets, liabilities, and stockholders' equities from the beginning to the end of the period.
- **Current income statement.** Information in this statement helps determine the amount of cash provided or used by operations during the period.
- **Additional information.** Such information includes transaction data that are needed to determine how cash was provided or used during the period.

Preparing the statement of cash flows from these data sources involves three major steps, explained in Illustration 14-3 below.

**Step 1: Determine net cash provided/used by operating activities by converting net income from an accrual basis to a cash basis.**

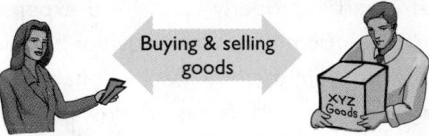

This step involves analyzing not only the current year's income statement but also comparative balance sheets and selected additional data.

**Step 2: Analyze changes in noncurrent asset and liability accounts and record as investing and financing activities, or disclose as noncash transactions.**

This step involves analyzing comparative balance sheet data and selected additional information for their effects on cash.

**Step 3: Compare the net change in cash on the statement of cash flows with the change in the cash account reported on the balance sheet to make sure the amounts agree.**

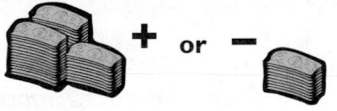

The difference between the beginning and ending cash balances can be easily computed from comparative balance sheets.

**Illustration 14-3**
Three major steps in preparing the statement of cash flows

## Indirect and Direct Methods

In order to perform step 1, a company **must convert net income from an accrual basis to a cash basis**. This conversion may be done by either of two methods: (1) the indirect method or (2) the direct method. **Both methods arrive at the same total amount** for "Net cash provided by operating activities." They differ in **how** they arrive at the amount.

The **indirect method** adjusts net income for items that do not affect cash. A great majority of companies (98.8%) use this method, as shown in the nearby chart.[1] Companies favor the indirect method for two reasons: (1) It is easier and

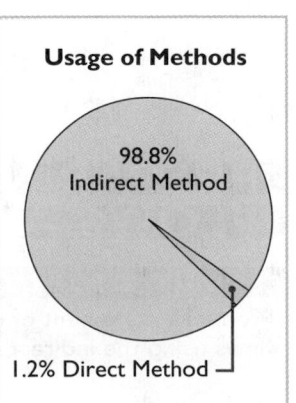

**Usage of Methods**

98.8% Indirect Method

1.2% Direct Method

---

[1] *Accounting Trends and Techniques—2005* (New York: American Institute of Certified Public Accountants, 2005).

less costly to prepare, and (2) it focuses on the differences between net income and net cash flow from operating activities.

The **direct method** shows operating cash receipts and payments, making it more consistent with the objective of a statement of cash flows. The FASB has expressed a preference for the direct method, but allows the use of either method.

The next section illustrates the more popular indirect method. Appendix 14B illustrates the direct method.

## INVESTOR INSIGHT

 ### Cash Flow Isn't Always What It Seems

Some managers have taken actions that artificially increase cash flow from operating activities. They do this by moving negative amounts out of the operating section and into the investing or financing section.

For example, WorldCom, Inc. disclosed that it had improperly capitalized expenses: It had moved $3.8 billion of cash outflows from the "Cash from operating activities" section of the cash flow statement to the "Investing activities" section, thereby greatly enhancing cash provided by operating activities. Similarly, Dynegy, Inc. restated its cash flow statement because it had improperly included in operating activities, instead of in financing activities, $300 million from natural gas trading. The restatement resulted in a drop of 37% in cash flow from operating activities.

*Source:* Henny Sender, "Sadly, These Days Even Cash Flow Isn't Always What It Seems To Be," *Wall Street Journal*, May 8, 2002.

**?** For what reasons might managers at WorldCom and at Dynegy take the actions noted above?

## Before You Go On...

**REVIEW IT**
1. What are the three major steps in preparing a statement of cash flows?
2. What is the primary difference between the indirect and direct approaches to the statement of cash flows?
3. Which method of preparing the statement of cash flows is more commonly used in practice?

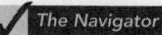 *The Navigator*

# PREPARING THE STATEMENT OF CASH FLOWS—INDIRECT METHOD

**STUDY OBJECTIVE 3**

Prepare a statement of cash flows using the indirect method.

To explain how to prepare a statement of cash flows using the indirect method, we use financial information from Computer Services Company. Illustration 14-4 presents Computer Services' current and previous-year balance sheets, its current-year income statement, and related financial information for the current year.

## COMPUTER SERVICES COMPANY
### Comparative Balance Sheets
### December 31

**Illustration 14-4**
Comparative balance sheets, income statement, and additional information for Computer Services Company

| Assets | 2008 | 2007 | Change in Account Balance Increase/Decrease |
|---|---|---|---|
| Current assets | | | |
| Cash | $ 55,000 | $ 33,000 | $ 22,000 Increase |
| Accounts receivable | 20,000 | 30,000 | 10,000 Decrease |
| Merchandise inventory | 15,000 | 10,000 | 5,000 Increase |
| Prepaid expenses | 5,000 | 1,000 | 4,000 Increase |
| Property, plant, and equipment | | | |
| Land | 130,000 | 20,000 | 110,000 Increase |
| Building | 160,000 | 40,000 | 120,000 Increase |
| Accumulated depreciation—building | (11,000) | (5,000) | 6,000 Increase |
| Equipment | 27,000 | 10,000 | 17,000 Increase |
| Accumulated depreciation—equipment | (3,000) | (1,000) | 2,000 Increase |
| Total assets | $398,000 | $138,000 | |

| Liabilities and Stockholders' Equity | | | |
|---|---|---|---|
| Current liabilities | | | |
| Accounts payable | $ 28,000 | $ 12,000 | $ 16,000 Increase |
| Income tax payable | 6,000 | 8,000 | 2,000 Decrease |
| Long-term liabilities | | | |
| Bonds payable | 130,000 | 20,000 | 110,000 Increase |
| Stockholders' equity | | | |
| Common stock | 70,000 | 50,000 | 20,000 Increase |
| Retained earnings | 164,000 | 48,000 | 116,000 Increase |
| Total liabilities and stockholders' equity | $398,000 | $138,000 | |

## COMPUTER SERVICES COMPANY
### Income Statement
### For the Year Ended December 31, 2008

| | | |
|---|---|---|
| Revenues | | $507,000 |
| Cost of goods sold | $150,000 | |
| Operating expenses (excluding depreciation) | 111,000 | |
| Depreciation expense | 9,000 | |
| Loss on sale of equipment | 3,000 | |
| Interest expense | 42,000 | 315,000 |
| Income before income tax | | 192,000 |
| Income tax expense | | 47,000 |
| Net income | | $145,000 |

**Additional information for 2008:**
1. The company declared and paid a $29,000 cash dividend.
2. Issued $110,000 of long-term bonds in direct exchange for land.
3. A building costing $120,000 was purchased for cash. Equipment costing $25,000 was also purchased for cash.
4. The company sold equipment with a book value of $7,000 (cost $8,000, less accumulated depreciation $1,000) for $4,000 cash.
5. Issued common stock for $20,000 cash.
6. Depreciation expense was comprised of $6,000 for building and $3,000 for equipment.

We will now apply the three steps to the information provided for Computer Services Company.

# Step 1: Operating Activities

**DETERMINE NET CASH PROVIDED/USED BY OPERATING ACTIVITIES BY CONVERTING NET INCOME FROM AN ACCRUAL BASIS TO A CASH BASIS**

To determine net cash provided by operating activities under the indirect method, companies **adjust net income in numerous ways**. A useful starting point is to understand **why** net income must be converted to net cash provided by operating activities.

Under generally accepted accounting principles, most companies use the accrual basis of accounting. As you have learned, this basis requires that companies record revenue when earned and record expenses when incurred. Earned revenues may include credit sales for which the company has not yet collected cash. Expenses incurred may include some items that it has not yet paid in cash. Thus, under the accrual basis of accounting, net income is not the same as net cash provided by operating activities.

Therefore, under the **indirect method**, companies must adjust net income to convert certain items to the cash basis. The indirect method (or reconciliation method) starts with net income and converts it to net cash provided by operating activities. Illustration 14-5 lists the three types of adjustments.

**Illustration 14-5**
Three types of adjustments to convert net income to net cash provided by operating activities

| Net Income | +/− | Adjustments | = | Net Cash Provided/ Used by Operating Activities |
|---|---|---|---|---|
| | | • **Add back noncash expenses**, such as depreciation expense, amortization, or depletion.<br>• **Deduct gains and add losses** that resulted from investing and financing activities.<br>• **Analyze changes** to noncash current asset and current liability accounts. | | |

We explain the three types of adjustments in the next three sections.

### DEPRECIATION EXPENSE

Computer Services' income statement reports depreciation expense of $9,000. Although depreciation expense reduces net income, it does not reduce cash. In other words, depreciation expense is a noncash charge. The company must add it back to net income to arrive at net cash provided by operating activities. Computer Services reports depreciation expense as follows in the statement of cash flows.

**Depreciation is similar to any other expense in that it reduces net income. It differs in that it does not involve a current cash outflow; that is why it must be *added back* to net income to arrive at cash provided by operating activities.**

**Illustration 14-6**
Adjustment for depreciation

| Cash flows from operating activities | |
|---|---|
| Net income | $145,000 |
| Adjustments to reconcile net income to net cash provided by operating activities: | |
| **Depreciation expense** | **9,000** |
| Net cash provided by operating activities | $154,000 |

As the first adjustment to net income in the statement of cash flows, companies frequently list depreciation and similar noncash charges such as amortization of intangible assets, depletion expense, and bad debt expense.

## LOSS ON SALE OF EQUIPMENT

Illustration 14-1 states that the investing activities section should report cash received from the sale of plant assets. Sales of plant assets are therefore not considered operating activities. Because of this, **companies must eliminate from net income all gains and losses related to the disposal of plant assets, to arrive at cash provided by operating activities.**

In our example, Computer Services' income statement reports a $3,000 loss on the sale of equipment (book value $7,000, less $4,000 cash received from sale of equipment). Illustration 14-7 shows that the $3,000 loss is eliminated by adding $3,000 back to net income to arrive at net cash provided by operating activities.

| | | | Illustration 14-7 |
|---|---|---|---|
| Cash flows from operating activities | | | Adjustment for loss on sale of equipment |
| Net income | | $145,000 | |
| Adjustments to reconcile net income to net cash | | | |
| provided by operating activities: | | | |
| Depreciation expense | $9,000 | | |
| **Loss on sale of equipment** | **3,000** | 12,000 | |
| Net cash provided by operating activities | | $157,000 | |

If a gain on sale occurs, the company deducts the gain from its net income in order to determine net cash provided by operating activities. **In the case of either a gain or a loss, companies report as a source of cash in the investing activities section of the statement of cash flows the actual amount of cash received from the sale.**

## CHANGES TO NONCASH CURRENT ASSET AND CURRENT LIABILITY ACCOUNTS

A final adjustment in reconciling net income to net cash provided by operating activities involves examining all changes in noncash current asset and current liability accounts. The accrual accounting process records revenues in the period earned and expenses in the period incurred. For example, companies use Accounts Receivable to record amounts owed to the company for sales that have been made but for which cash collections have not yet been received. They use the Prepaid Insurance account to reflect insurance that has been paid for, but which has not yet expired, and therefore has not been expensed. Similarly, the Salaries Payable account reflects salaries expense that has been incurred by the company but has not been paid.

As a result, we need to adjust net income for these accruals and prepayments to determine net cash provided by operating activities. Thus we must analyze the change in each noncash current asset and current liability account to determine its impact on net income and cash.

CHANGES IN NONCASH CURRENT ASSETS. The adjustments required for changes in noncash current asset accounts are as follows: **Deduct from net income increases in current asset accounts, and add to net income decreases in current asset accounts, to arrive at net cash provided by operating activities.** We can observe these relationships by analyzing the accounts of Computer Services Company.

**Decrease in Accounts Receivable.** Computer Services Company's accounts receivable decreased by $10,000 (from $30,000 to $20,000) during the period. For Computer Services this means that cash receipts were $10,000 higher than revenues. The Accounts Receivable account in Illustration 14-8 shows that Computer Services Company had $507,000 in revenues (as reported on the income statement), but it collected $517,000 in cash. As shown in Illustration 14-9 (below), to adjust net income to net cash provided by operating activities, the company adds to net income the decrease of $10,000 in accounts receivable.

**Illustration 14-8**
Analysis of accounts receivable

| Accounts Receivable | | | | |
|---|---|---|---|---|
| 1/1/08 | Balance | 30,000 | **Receipts from customers** | **517,000** |
| | **Revenues** | **507,000** | | |
| 12/31/08 | Balance | 20,000 | | |

When the Accounts Receivable balance increases, cash receipts are lower than revenue earned under the accrual basis. Therefore, the company deducts from net income the amount of the increase in accounts receivable, to arrive at net cash provided by operating activities.

**Increase in Merchandise Inventory.** Computer Services Company's Merchandise Inventory balance increased $5,000 (from $10,000 to $15,000) during the period. The change in the Merchandise Inventory account reflects the difference between the amount of inventory purchased and the amount sold. For Computer Services this means that the cost of merchandise purchased exceeded the cost of goods sold by $5,000. As a result, cost of goods sold does not reflect $5,000 of cash payments made for merchandise. The company deducts from net income this inventory increase of $5,000 during the period, to arrive at net cash provided by operating activities (see Illustration 14-9). If inventory decreases, the company adds to net income the amount of the change, to arrive at net cash provided by operating activities.

**Increase in Prepaid Expenses.** Computer Services' prepaid expenses increased during the period by $4,000. This means that cash paid for expenses is higher than expenses reported on an accrual basis. In other words, the company has made cash payments in the current period, but will not charge expenses to income until future periods (as charges to the income statement). To adjust net income to net cash provided by operating activities, the company deducts from net income the $4,000 increase in prepaid expenses (see Illustration 14-9).

**Illustration 14-9**
Adjustments for changes in current asset accounts

| | | |
|---|---|---|
| Cash flows from operating activities | | |
| Net income | | $145,000 |
| Adjustments to reconcile net income to net cash provided by operating activities: | | |
| Depreciation expense | $ 9,000 | |
| Loss on sale of equipment | 3,000 | |
| **Decrease in accounts receivable** | **10,000** | |
| **Increase in merchandise inventory** | **(5,000)** | |
| **Increase in prepaid expenses** | **(4,000)** | 13,000 |
| Net cash provided by operating activities | | $158,000 |

If prepaid expenses decrease, reported expenses are higher than the expenses paid. Therefore, the company adds to net income the decrease in prepaid expenses, to arrive at net cash provided by operating activities.

CHANGES IN CURRENT LIABILITIES. The adjustments required for changes in current liability accounts are as follows: **Add to net income increases in current liability accounts, and deduct from net income decreases in current liability accounts, to arrive at net cash provided by operating activities.**

**Increase in Accounts Payable.** For Computer Services Company, Accounts Payable increased by $16,000 (from $12,000 to $28,000) during the period. That means the company received $16,000 more in goods than it actually paid for. As shown in Illustration 14-10 (below), to adjust net income to determine net cash provided by operating activities, the company adds to net income the $16,000 increase in Accounts Payable.

**Decrease in Income Taxes Payable.** When a company incurs income tax expense but has not yet paid its taxes, it records income tax payable. A change in the Income Tax Payable account reflects the difference between income tax expense incurred and income tax actually paid. Computer Services' Income Tax Payable account decreased by $2,000. That means the $47,000 of income tax expense reported on the income statement was $2,000 less than the amount of taxes paid during the period of $49,000. As shown in Illustration 14-10, to adjust net income to a cash basis, the company must reduce net income by $2,000.

| | | |
|---|---:|---:|
| Cash flows from operating activities | | |
| Net income | | $145,000 |
| Adjustments to reconcile net income to net cash provided by operating activities: | | |
| Depreciation expense | $ 9,000 | |
| Loss on sale of equipment | 3,000 | |
| Decrease in accounts receivable | 10,000 | |
| Increase in merchandise inventory | (5,000) | |
| Increase in prepaid expenses | (4,000) | |
| **Increase in accounts payable** | **16,000** | |
| **Decrease in income tax payable** | **(2,000)** | 27,000 |
| Net cash provided by operating activities | | $172,000 |

**Illustration 14-10**
Adjustments for changes in current liability accounts

Illustration 14-10 shows that, after starting with net income of $145,000, the sum of all of the adjustments to net income was $27,000. This resulted in net cash provided by operating activities of $172,000.

## SUMMARY OF CONVERSION TO NET CASH PROVIDED BY OPERATING ACTIVITIES—INDIRECT METHOD

As shown in the previous illustrations, the statement of cash flows prepared by the indirect method starts with net income. It then adds or deducts items to arrive at net cash provided by operating activities. The required adjustments are of three types:

1. Noncash charges such as depreciation, amortization, and depletion.
2. Gains and losses on the sale of plant assets.
3. Changes in noncash current asset and current liability accounts.

Illustration 14-11 (page 650) provides a summary of these changes.

**Illustration 14-11**
Adjustments required to convert net income to net cash provided by operating activities

|  |  |  | Adjustment Required to Convert Net Income to Net Cash Provided by Operating Activities |
|---|---|---|---|
| Noncash Charges | { | Depreciation expense | Add |
|  |  | Patent amortization expense | Add |
|  |  | Depletion expense | Add |
| Gains and Losses | { | Loss on sale of plant asset | Add |
|  |  | Gain on sale of plant asset | Deduct |
| Changes in Current Assets and Current Liabilities | { | Increase in current asset account | Deduct |
|  |  | Decrease in current asset account | Add |
|  |  | Increase in current liability account | Add |
|  |  | Decrease in current liability account | Deduct |

# ACCOUNTING ACROSS THE ORGANIZATION

### GM Must Sell More Cars

Market share matters—and it shows up in the accounting numbers. Just ask General Motors. In recent years GM has seen its market share erode until, at 25.6% of the market, the company reached the point where it actually consumed more cash than it generated. It isn't time to panic yet—GM has about $20 billion in cash on hand—but it is time to come up with a plan.

To address immediate cash needs, GM management may have to quit paying its $1.1 billion annual dividend, and it may have to sell off some assets and businesses. But in the long term, GM must either increase its market share, or shrink its operations to fit its sales figures. The following table shows net income and cash provided by operating activities at various market-share levels.

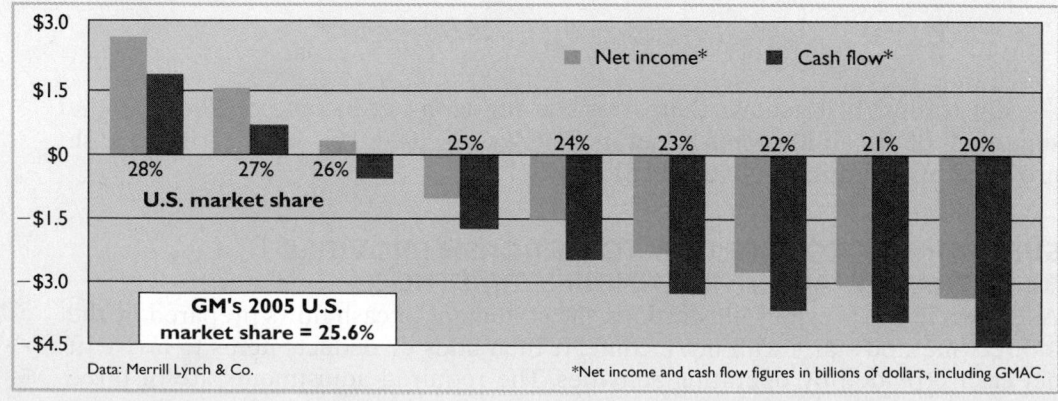

Data: Merrill Lynch & Co.

*Net income and cash flow figures in billions of dollars, including GMAC.

**Source:** David Welch and Dan Beucke, "Why GM's Plan Won't Work," *Business Week*, May 9, 2005, pp. 85–93.

**?** Why does GM's cash provided by operating activities drop so precipitously when the company's sales figures decline?

# Step 2: Investing and Financing Activities

## ANALYZE CHANGES IN NONCURRENT ASSET AND LIABILITY ACCOUNTS AND RECORD AS INVESTING AND FINANCING ACTIVITIES, OR DISCLOSE AS NONCASH TRANSACTIONS

**Increase in Land.** As indicated from the change in the Land account and the additional information, the company purchased land of $110,000 through the issuance of long-term bonds. The issuance of bonds payable for land has no effect on cash. But it is a significant noncash investing and financing activity that merits disclosure in a separate schedule. (See Illustration 14-13 on page 652.)

**Increase in Building.** As the additional data indicate, Computer Services Company acquired an office building for $120,000 cash. This is a cash outflow reported in the investing section. (See Illustration 14-13 on page 652.)

**Increase in Equipment.** The Equipment account increased $17,000. The additional information explains that this was a net increase that resulted from two transactions: (1) a purchase of equipment of $25,000, and (2) the sale for $4,000 of equipment costing $8,000. These transactions are investing activities. The company should report each transaction separately. Thus it reports the purchase of equipment as an outflow of cash for $25,000. It reports the sale as an inflow of cash for $4,000. The T account below shows the reasons for the change in this account during the year.

> **HELPFUL HINT**
> The investing and financing activities are measured and reported in the same way under both the direct and indirect methods.

| Equipment | | | | |
|---|---|---|---|---|
| 1/1/08 Balance | 10,000 | Cost of equipment sold | | 8,000 |
| **Purchase of equipment** | **25,000** | | | |
| 12/31/08 Balance | 27,000 | | | |

**Illustration 14-12**
Analysis of equipment

The following entry shows the details of the equipment sale transaction.

| | | |
|---|---|---|
| Cash | 4,000 | |
| Accumulated Depreciation | 1,000 | |
| Loss on Sale of Equipment | 3,000 | |
| Equipment | | 8,000 |

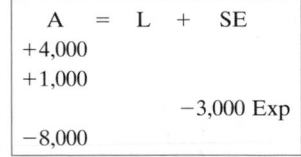

$$A = L + SE$$
$$+4,000$$
$$+1,000$$
$$-3,000 \text{ Exp}$$
$$-8,000$$

Cash Flows
+4,000

**Increase in Bonds Payable.** The Bonds Payable account increased $110,000. As indicated in the additional information, the company acquired land from the issuance of these bonds. It reports this noncash transaction in a separate schedule at the bottom of the statement.

**Increase in Common Stock.** The balance sheet reports an increase in Common Stock of $20,000. The additional information section notes that this increase resulted from the issuance of new shares of stock. This is a cash inflow reported in the financing section.

**Increase in Retained Earnings.** Retained earnings increased $116,000 during the year. This increase can be explained by two factors: (1) Net income of $145,000 increased retained earnings. (2) Dividends of $29,000 decreased retained earnings. The company adjusts net income to net cash provided by operating activities in the operating activities section. Payment of the dividends (not the declaration) is a **cash outflow that the company reports as a financing activity.**

> **HELPFUL HINT**
> When companies issue stocks or bonds for cash, the actual proceeds will appear in the statement of cash flows as a financing inflow (rather than the par value of the stocks or face value of bonds).

### STATEMENT OF CASH FLOWS—2008

Using the previous information, we can now prepare a statement of cash flows for 2008 for Computer Services Company as shown in Illustration 14-13.

**Illustration 14-13**
Statement of cash flows, 2008—indirect method

| COMPUTER SERVICES COMPANY Statement of Cash Flows—Indirect Method For the Year Ended December 31, 2008 | | |
|---|---:|---:|
| Cash flows from operating activities | | |
| Net income | | $145,000 |
| Adjustments to reconcile net income to net cash provided by operating activities: | | |
| Depreciation expense | $ 9,000 | |
| Loss on sale of equipment | 3,000 | |
| Decrease in accounts receivable | 10,000 | |
| Increase in merchandise inventory | (5,000) | |
| Increase in prepaid expenses | (4,000) | |
| Increase in accounts payable | 16,000 | |
| Decrease in income tax payable | (2,000) | 27,000 |
| Net cash provided by operating activities | | 172,000 |
| Cash flows from investing activities | | |
| Purchase of building | (120,000) | |
| Purchase of equipment | (25,000) | |
| Sale of equipment | 4,000 | |
| Net cash used by investing activities | | (141,000) |
| Cash flows from financing activities | | |
| Issuance of common stock | 20,000 | |
| Payment of cash dividends | (29,000) | |
| Net cash used by financing activities | | (9,000) |
| Net increase in cash | | 22,000 |
| Cash at beginning of period | | 33,000 |
| Cash at end of period | | $ 55,000 |
| | | |
| **Noncash investing and financing activities** | | |
| Issuance of bonds payable to purchase land | | $110,000 |

> **HELPFUL HINT**
>
> Note that in the investing and financing activities sections, positive numbers indicate cash inflows (receipts), and negative numbers indicate cash outflows (payments).

## Step 3: Net Change in Cash

### COMPARE THE NET CHANGE IN CASH ON THE STATEMENT OF CASH FLOWS WITH THE CHANGE IN THE CASH ACCOUNT REPORTED ON THE BALANCE SHEET TO MAKE SURE THE AMOUNTS AGREE

Illustration 14-13 indicates that the net change in cash during the period was an increase of $22,000. This agrees with the change in Cash account reported on the balance sheet in Illustration 14-4 (page 645).

### *Before You Go On...*

**REVIEW IT**

1. What is the format of the operating activities section?
2. Where is depreciation expense shown on a statement of cash flows?
3. Where are significant noncash investing and financing activities shown?

**DO IT**

Use the information on page 653 to prepare a statement of cash flows using the indirect method.

## REYNOLDS COMPANY
### Comparative Balance Sheets
### December 31

| Assets | 2008 | 2007 | Change Increase/Decrease |
|---|---|---|---|
| Cash | $ 54,000 | $ 37,000 | $ 17,000 Increase |
| Accounts receivable | 68,000 | 26,000 | 42,000 Increase |
| Inventories | 54,000 | –0– | 54,000 Increase |
| Prepaid expenses | 4,000 | 6,000 | 2,000 Decrease |
| Land | 45,000 | 70,000 | 25,000 Decrease |
| Buildings | 200,000 | 200,000 | –0– |
| Accumulated depreciation—buildings | (21,000) | (11,000) | 10,000 Increase |
| Equipment | 193,000 | 68,000 | 125,000 Increase |
| Accumulated depreciation—equipment | (28,000) | (10,000) | 18,000 Increase |
| Totals | $569,000 | $386,000 | |

| Liabilities and Stockholders' Equity | | | |
|---|---|---|---|
| Accounts payable | $ 23,000 | $ 40,000 | $ 17,000 Decrease |
| Accrued expenses payable | 10,000 | –0– | 10,000 Increase |
| Bonds payable | 110,000 | 150,000 | 40,000 Decrease |
| Common stock ($1 par) | 220,000 | 60,000 | 160,000 Increase |
| Retained earnings | 206,000 | 136,000 | 70,000 Increase |
| Totals | $569,000 | $386,000 | |

## REYNOLDS COMPANY
### Income Statement
### For the Year Ended December 31, 2008

| | | |
|---|---|---|
| Revenues | | $890,000 |
| Cost of goods sold | $465,000 | |
| Operating expenses | 221,000 | |
| Interest expense | 12,000 | |
| Loss on sale of equipment | 2,000 | 700,000 |
| Income before income taxes | | 190,000 |
| Income tax expense | | 65,000 |
| Net income | | $125,000 |

**Additional information:**
1. Operating expenses include depreciation expense of $33,000 and charges from prepaid expenses of $2,000.
2. Land was sold at its book value for cash.
3. Cash dividends of $55,000 were declared and paid in 2008.
4. Interest expense of $12,000 was paid in cash.
5. Equipment with a cost of $166,000 was purchased for cash. Equipment with a cost of $41,000 and a book value of $36,000 was sold for $34,000 cash.
6. Bonds of $10,000 were redeemed at their book value for cash. Bonds of $30,000 were converted into common stock.
7. Common stock ($1 par) of $130,000 was issued for cash.
8. Accounts payable pertain to merchandise suppliers.

### Action Plan
▪ Determine net cash provided/used by operating activities by adjusting net income for items that did not affect cash.

■ Determine net cash provided/used by investing activities and financing activities.
■ Determine the net increase/decrease in cash.

**Solution**

1. Determine net cash provided/used by operating activities, recognizing that operating activities generally relate to changes in current assets and current liabilities.

2. Determine net cash provided/used by investing activities, recognizing that investing activities generally relate to changes in noncurrent assets.

3. Determine net cash provided/used by financing activities, recognizing that financing activities generally relate to changes in long-term liabilities and stockholders' equity accounts.

## REYNOLDS COMPANY
### Statement of Cash Flows—Indirect Method
### For the Year Ended December 31, 2008

| | | |
|---|---:|---:|
| Cash flows from operating activities | | |
| Net income | | $125,000 |
| Adjustments to reconcile net income to net cash | | |
| provided by operating activities: | | |
| Depreciation expense | $ 33,000 | |
| Loss on sale of equipment | 2,000 | |
| Increase in accounts receivable | (42,000) | |
| Increase in inventories | (54,000) | |
| Decrease in prepaid expenses | 2,000 | |
| Decrease in accounts payable | (17,000) | |
| Increase in accrued expenses payable | 10,000 | (66,000) |
| Net cash provided by operating activities | | 59,000 |
| Cash flows from investing activities | | |
| Sale of land | 25,000 | |
| Sale of equipment | 34,000 | |
| Purchase of equipment | (166,000) | |
| Net cash used by investing activities | | (107,000) |
| Cash flows from financing activities | | |
| Redemption of bonds | (10,000) | |
| Sale of common stock | 130,000 | |
| Payment of dividends | (55,000) | |
| Net cash provided by financing activities | | 65,000 |
| Net increase in cash | | 17,000 |
| Cash at beginning of period | | 37,000 |
| Cash at end of period | | $ 54,000 |
| | | |
| **Noncash investing and financing activities** | | |
| Conversion of bonds into common stock | | $ 30,000 |

Related exercise material: *BE14-4, BE14-5, BE14-6, BE14-7, E14-4, E14-5, and E14-6.*

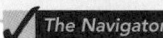
✓ *The Navigator*

# USING CASH FLOWS TO EVALUATE A COMPANY

Traditionally, investors and creditors have most commonly used ratios based on accrual accounting. These days, cash-based ratios are gaining increased acceptance among analysts.

## Free Cash Flow

In the statement of cash flows, cash provided by operating activities is intended to indicate the cash-generating capability of the company. Analysts have noted, however, that **cash provided by operating activities fails to take into account that a company must invest in new fixed assets** just to maintain its current level of operations. Companies also must at least **maintain dividends at current levels** to satisfy investors. The measurement of free cash flow provides additional insight regarding a company's cash-generating ability. **Free cash flow** describes the cash remaining from operations after adjustment for capital expenditures and dividends.

Consider the following example: Suppose that MPC produced and sold 10,000 personal computers this year. It reported $100,000 cash provided by operating activities. In order to maintain production at 10,000 computers, MPC invested $15,000 in equipment. It chose to pay $5,000 in dividends. Its free cash flow was $80,000 ($100,000 − $15,000 − $5,000). The company could use this $80,000 either to purchase new assets to expand the business or to pay an $80,000 dividend and continue to produce 10,000 computers. In practice, free cash flow is often calculated with the formula in Illustration 14-14. Alternative definitions also exist.

| Free Cash Flow | = | Cash Provided by Operating Activities | − | Capital Expenditures | − | Cash Dividends |
|---|---|---|---|---|---|---|

**Illustration 14-14**
Free cash flow

Illustration 14-15 provides basic information excerpted from the 2004 statement of cash flows of Microsoft Corporation.

**Illustration 14-15**
Microsoft cash flow information ($ in millions)

### MICROSOFT CORPORATION
Statement of Cash Flows (partial)
2004

| | | |
|---|---|---|
| Cash provided by operating activities | | $14,626 |
| Cash flows from investing activities | | |
| Additions to property and equipment | $ (1,109) | |
| Purchases of investments | (92,495) | |
| Sales of investments | 85,302 | |
| Acquisitions of companies | (4) | |
| Maturities of investments | 5,561 | |
| Cash used by investing activities | | (2,745) |
| Cash paid for dividends | | (1,729) |

Microsoft's free cash flow is calculated as shown in Illustration 14-16.

**Illustration 14-16**
Calculation of Microsoft's free cash flow ($ in millions)

| | |
|---|---|
| Cash provided by operating activities | $14,626 |
| Less: Expenditures on property, plant, and equipment | 1,109 |
| Dividends paid | 1,729 |
| Free cash flow | $11,788 |

This is a tremendous amount of cash generated in a single year. It is available for the acquisition of new assets, the retirement of stock or debt, or the payment of dividends. Also note that this amount far exceeds Microsoft's 2004 net income of $8,168 million. This lends additional credibility to Microsoft's income number as an indicator of potential future performance. If anything, Microsoft's net income might understate its actual performance.

Oracle Corporation is one of the world's largest sellers of database software and information management services. Like Microsoft, its success depends on continuing to improve its existing products while developing new products to keep pace with rapid changes in technology. Oracle's free cash flow for 2004 was $2,988 million. This is impressive, but significantly less than Microsoft's amazing ability to generate cash.

 Be sure to read **ALL ABOUT YOU:** *Where Does the Money Go?* on page 656 for information on how topics in this chapter apply to you.

# Where Does the Money Go?

**W**hen a company's cash flow from operating activities does not cover its cash needs, it must borrow money. In the short term this is OK, but in the long-term it can spell disaster. Sooner or later the company needs to increase its cash from operations or cut back on its expenditures, or it will go broke. Guess what? The same is true for you and me.

Where do you spend your cash? Most of us know how much we spend each month on rent and car payments. But how much do you spend each month on soda, coffee, pizza, video rentals, music downloads, and your cell phone service? Don't think it matters? Suppose you spend an average of only $4 per day on unneeded "incidentals." That's $120 a month, or almost $1,500 per year.

## ✹ Some Facts

* College students spend about $200 billion per year on consumer products. Of that amount, $41 billion is "discretionary" in nature.

* More than 70% of college students own a cell phone, and 71% own a car.

* College students spend more than $8 billion per year purchasing DVDs, CDs, music downloads, and video games.

* Annual spending on travel by college students is about $4.6 billion.

* 78% of college students work, earning an average of $821 per month.

## ✹ About the Numbers

College students spend an average of $287 per month on discretionary items (defined as anything other than tuition, room/board, rent, books, and school fees). A large chunk of that—more than $11 billion—is spent on beverages and snack foods. Maybe this would be a good place to start cutting your expenditures.

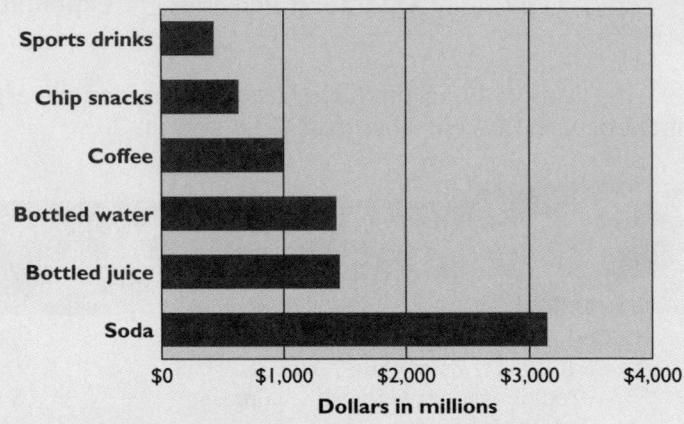

**Annual Spending by College Students on Beverages and Snacks**

**Source:** "College Students Spend $200 Billion per Year," HarrisInteractive, *www.harrisinteractive.com/news/allnewsbydate.asp?NewsID=480* (accessed May 2006).

## ✹ What Do You Think?

Let's say that you live on campus and own a car. You use the car for pleasure and to drive to a job that is three miles away. Suppose your annual cash flow statement includes the following items.

| | |
|---|---|
| Cash inflows: | |
| Wages | $ 9,000 |
| Student loans | 5,000 |
| Credit card debt | 4,000 |
| Cash outflows: | |
| Tuition, books, room, and board | 13,000 |
| Vehicle costs | 2,000 |
| Vacation | 2,000 |
| Cell phone service | 500 |
| Snacks and beverages | 500 |

Should you get rid of your car and cell phone, quit eating snacks, and give up the idea of a vacation?

**YES:** At this rate you will accumulate nearly $40,000 in debts by the time you graduate. It is not fun to spend most of the paycheck of your post-graduation job paying off the debts you accumulated while in school.

**NO:** Give me a break. A person has to have some fun. Life wouldn't be worth living if I couldn't be drinking a Starbucks while cruising down the road talking on my cell phone.

**Sources:** Becky Ebenkamp, "College Communications 101," *Brandweek*, August 22-29, 2005, p. 16.

**The authors' comments on this situation appear on page 695.**

## Before You Go On...

**REVIEW IT**

1. What is the difference between cash from operations and free cash flow?
2. What does it mean if a company has negative free cash flow?

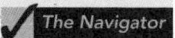 The Navigator

**Demonstration Problem 1**

The income statement for the year ended December 31, 2008, for John Kosinski
Manufacturing Company contains the following condensed information.

### JOHN KOSINSKI MANUFACTURING COMPANY
#### Income Statement

| | | |
|---|---:|---:|
| Revenues | | $6,583,000 |
| Operating expenses (excluding depreciation) | $4,920,000 | |
| Depreciation expense | 880,000 | 5,800,000 |
| Income before income taxes | | 783,000 |
| Income tax expense | | 353,000 |
| Net income | | $ 430,000 |

Included in operating expenses is a $24,000 loss resulting from the sale of machinery
for $270,000 cash. Machinery was purchased at a cost of $750,000.

The following balances are reported on Kosinski's comparative balance sheets at
December 31.

### JOHN KOSINSKI MANUFACTURING COMPANY
#### Comparative, Balance Sheets (partial)

| | **2008** | **2007** |
|---|---:|---:|
| Cash | $672,000 | $130,000 |
| Accounts receivable | 775,000 | 610,000 |
| Inventories | 834,000 | 867,000 |
| Accounts payable | 521,000 | 501,000 |

Income tax expense of $353,000 represents the amount paid in 2008. Dividends
declared and paid in 2008 totaled $200,000.

### Instructions

Prepare the statement of cash flows using the indirect method.

### Solution

### JOHN KOSINSKI MANUFACTURING COMPANY
#### Statement of Cash Flows—Indirect Method
#### For the Year Ended December 31, 2008

| | | |
|---|---:|---:|
| Cash flows from operating activities | | |
| Net income | | $ 430,000 |
| Adjustments to reconcile net income to net cash | | |
| provided by operating activities: | | |
| Depreciation expense | $ 880,000 | |
| Loss on sale of machinery | 24,000 | |
| Increase in accounts receivable | (165,000) | |
| Decrease in inventories | 33,000 | |
| Increase in accounts payable | 20,000 | 792,000 |
| Net cash provided by operating activities | | 1,222,000 |

**action plan**

✔ Determine net cash from
operating activities.
Operating activities generally relate to changes in current assets and current liabilities.

✔ Determine net cash
from investing activities.
Investing activities
generally relate to changes
in noncurrent assets.

✔ Determine net cash from
financing activities. Financing
activities generally relate to
changes in long-term liabilities and stockholders'
equity accounts.

| Cash flows from investing activities | | | |
|---|---|---|---|
| Sale of machinery | 270,000 | | |
| Purchase of machinery | (750,000) | | |
| Net cash used by investing activities | | (480,000) | |
| Cash flows from financing activities | | | |
| Payment of cash dividends | | (200,000) | |
| Net increase in cash | | 542,000 | |
| Cash at beginning of period | | 130,000 | |
| Cash at end of period | | $ 672,000 | |

## SUMMARY OF STUDY OBJECTIVES

**1 Indicate the usefulness of the statement of cash flows.** The statement of cash flows provides information about the cash receipts, cash payments, and net change in cash resulting from the operating, investing, and financing activities of a company during the period.

**2 Distinguish among operating, investing, and financing activities.** Operating activities include the cash effects of transactions that enter into the determination of net income. Investing activities involve cash flows resulting from changes in investments and long-term asset items. Financing activities involve cash flows resulting from changes in long-term liability and stockholders' equity items.

**3 Prepare a statement of cash flows using the indirect method.** The preparation of a statement of cash flows involves three major steps: (1) Determine net cash provided/used by operating activities by converting net income from an accrual basis to a cash basis. (2) Analyze changes in noncurrent asset and liability accounts and record as investing and financing activities, or disclose as noncash transactions. (3) Compare the net change in cash on the statement of cash flows with the change in the cash account reported on the balance sheet to make sure the amounts agree.

**4 Analyze the statement of cash flows.** Free cash flow indicates the amount of cash a company generated during the current year that is available for the payment of additional dividends or for expansion.

## GLOSSARY

**Direct method** A method of determining net cash provided by operating activities by adjusting each item in the income statement from the accrual basis to the cash basis. (p. 644)

**Financing activities** Cash flow activities that include (a) obtaining cash from issuing debt and repaying the amounts borrowed and (b) obtaining cash from stockholders, repurchasing shares, and paying dividends. (p. 639).

**Free cash flow** Cash provided by operating activities adjusted for capital expenditures and dividends paid. (p. 655).

**Indirect method** A method of preparing a statement of cash flows in which net income is adjusted for items that do not affect cash, to determine net cash provided by operating activities. (pp. 643, 646).

**Investing activities** Cash flow activities that include (a) purchasing and disposing of investments and property, plant, and equipment using cash and (b) lending money and collecting the loans. (p. 639).

**Operating activities** Cash flow activities that include the cash effects of transactions that create revenues and expenses and thus enter into the determination of net income. (p. 639).

**Statement of cash flows** A basic financial statement that provides information about the cash receipts, cash payments, and net change in cash during a period, resulting from operating, investing, and financing activities. (p. 638).

# APPENDIX 14A  Using a Worksheet to Prepare the Statement of Cash Flows—Indirect Method

When preparing a statement of cash flows, companies may need to make numerous adjustments of net income. In such cases, they often use **a worksheet to assemble and classify the data that will appear on the statement**. The worksheet is merely an aid in preparing the statement. Its use is optional. Illustration 14A-1 shows the skeleton format of the worksheet for preparation of the statement of cash flows.

**Illustration 14A-1**
Format of worksheet

| XYZ Company.xls | | | | |
|---|---|---|---|---|
| File   Edit   View   Insert   Format   Tools   Data   Window   Help | | | | |
| **A** | **B** | **C** | **D** | **E** |
| | **XYZ COMPANY** Worksheet Statement of Cash Flows For the Year Ended . . . | | | |
| | **End of Last Year Balances** | **Reconciling Items** | | **End of Current Year Balances** |
| **Balance Sheet Accounts** | | **Debit** | **Credit** | |
| Debit balance accounts | XX | XX | XX | XX |
| | XX | XX | XX | XX |
| Totals | XXX | | | XXX |
| Credit balance accounts | XX | XX | XX | XX |
| | XX | XX | XX | XX |
| Totals | XXX | | | XXX |
| **Statement of Cash** | | | | |
| **Flows Effects** | | | | |
| Operating activities | | | | |
| Net income | | XX | | |
| Adjustments to net income | | XX | XX | |
| Investing activities | | | | |
| Receipts and payments | | XX | XX | |
| Financing activities | | | | |
| Receipts and payments | | XX | XX | |
| Totals | | XXX | XXX | |
| Increase (decrease) in cash | | (XX) | XX | |
| Totals | | XXX | XXX | |

The following guidelines are important in preparing a worksheet.

1. In the balance sheet accounts section, **list accounts with debit balances separately from those with credit balances**. This means, for example, that Accumulated Depreciation appears under credit balances and not as a contra account under debit balances. Enter the beginning and ending balances of each account in the appropriate columns. Enter as reconciling items in the two middle columns the transactions that caused the change in the account balance during the year.

   After all reconciling items have been entered, each line pertaining to a balance sheet account should "foot across." That is, the beginning balance plus or minus the reconciling item(s) must equal the ending balance. When this agreement exists for all balance sheet accounts, all changes in account balances have been reconciled.

2. The bottom portion of the worksheet consists of the operating, investing, and financing activities sections. It provides the information necessary to prepare the formal statement of cash flows. **Enter inflows of cash as debits in the reconciling columns. Enter outflows of cash as credits in the reconciling columns.** Thus, in this section, the sale of equipment for cash at book value appears as a debit under investing activities. Similarly, the purchase of land for cash appears as a credit under investing activities.

3. **The reconciling items shown in the worksheet are not entered in any journal or posted to any account.** They do not represent either adjustments or corrections of the balance sheet accounts. They are used only to facilitate the preparation of the statement of cash flows.

## Preparing the Worksheet

As in the case of worksheets illustrated in earlier chapters, preparing a worksheet involves a series of prescribed steps. The steps in this case are:

1. Enter in the balance sheet accounts section the balance sheet accounts and their beginning and ending balances.

2. Enter in the reconciling columns of the worksheet the data that explain the changes in the balance sheet accounts other than cash and their effects on the statement of cash flows.

3. Enter on the cash line and at the bottom of the worksheet the increase or decrease in cash. This entry should enable the totals of the reconciling columns to be in agreement.

To illustrate the preparation of a worksheet, we will use the 2008 data for Computer Services Company. Your familiarity with these data (from the chapter) should help you understand the use of a worksheet. For ease of reference, the comparative balance sheets, income statement, and selected data for 2008 are presented in Illustration 14A-2.

### DETERMINING THE RECONCILING ITEMS

Companies can use one of several approaches to determine the reconciling items. For example, they can first complete the changes affecting net cash provided by operating activities, and then can determine the effects of financing and investing transactions. Or, they can analyze the balance sheet accounts in the order in which they are listed on the worksheet. We will follow this latter approach for Computer Services, except for cash. As indicated in step 3, **cash is handled last**.

**Accounts Receivable**   The decrease of $10,000 in accounts receivable means that cash collections from revenues are higher than the revenues reported in the income statement. To convert net income to net cash provided by operating activities, we add the decrease of $10,000 to net income. The entry in the reconciling columns of the worksheet is:

| (a) | Operating—Decrease in Accounts Receivable | 10,000 | |
| | Accounts Receivable | | 10,000 |

**Merchandise Inventory**   Computer Services Company's Merchandise Inventory balance increases $5,000 during the period. The Merchandise Inventory account reflects the difference between the amount of inventory that the company purchased and the amount that it sold. For Computer Services this means that the cost of merchandise purchased exceeds the cost of goods sold by $5,000. As a

**Computer Services Company.xls**

File   Edit   View   Insert   Format   Tools   Data   Window   Help

| | A | B | C | D |
|---|---|---|---|---|
| 1 | **COMPUTER SERVICES COMPANY** | | | |
| 2 | Comparative Balance Sheets | | | |
| 3 | December 31 | | | |
| 4 | | | | **Change in** |
| 5 | | | | **Account Balance** |
| 6 | **Assets** | **2008** | **2007** | **Increase/Decrease** |
| 7 | Current assets | | | |
| 8 | Cash | $ 55,000 | $ 33,000 | $ 22,000 Increase |
| 9 | Accounts receivable | 20,000 | 30,000 | 10,000 Decrease |
| 10 | Merchandise inventory | 15,000 | 10,000 | 5,000 Increase |
| 11 | Prepaid expenses | 5,000 | 1,000 | 4,000 Increase |
| 12 | Property, plant, and equipment | | | |
| 13 | Land | 130,000 | 20,000 | 110,000 Increase |
| 14 | Building | 160,000 | 40,000 | 120,000 Increase |
| 15 | Accumulated depreciation—building | (11,000) | (5,000) | 6,000 Increase |
| 16 | Equipment | 27,000 | 10,000 | 17,000 Increase |
| 17 | Accumulated depreciation—equipment | (3,000) | (1,000) | 2,000 Increase |
| 18 | Total | $398,000 | $138,000 | |
| 19 | | | | |
| 20 | **Liabilities and Stockholders' Equity** | | | |
| 21 | Current liabilities | | | |
| 22 | Accounts payable | $ 28,000 | $ 12,000 | $ 16,000 Increase |
| 23 | Income tax payable | 6,000 | 8,000 | 2,000 Decrease |
| 24 | Long-term liabilities | | | |
| 25 | Bonds payable | 130,000 | 20,000 | 110,000 Increase |
| 26 | Stockholders' equity | | | |
| 27 | Common stock | 70,000 | 50,000 | 20,000 Increase |
| 28 | Retained earnings | 164,000 | 48,000 | 116,000 Increase |
| 29 | Total liabilities and stockholders' equity | $398,000 | $138,000 | |

Sheet 1 / Sheet 2

**Computer Services Company.xls**

File   Edit   View   Insert   Format   Tools   Data   Window   Help

| | A | B | C | D |
|---|---|---|---|---|
| 1 | **COMPUTER SERVICES COMPANY** | | | |
| 2 | Income Statement | | | |
| 3 | For the Year Ended December 31, 2008 | | | |
| 4 | | | | |
| 5 | Revenues | | | $507,000 |
| 6 | Cost of goods sold | | $150,000 | |
| 7 | Operating expenses (excluding depreciation) | | 111,000 | |
| 8 | Depreciation expense | | 9,000 | |
| 9 | Loss on sale of equipment | | 3,000 | |
| 10 | Interest expense | | 42,000 | 315,000 |
| 11 | Income before income tax | | | 192,000 |
| 12 | Income tax expense | | | 47,000 |
| 13 | Net income | | | $145,000 |
| 14 | | | | |

Sheet 1 / Sheet 2

**Additional information for 2008:**
1. The company declared and paid a $29,000 cash dividend.
2. Issued $110,000 of long-term bonds in direct exchange for land.
3. A building costing $120,000 was purchased for cash. Equipment costing $25,000 was also purchased for cash.
4. The company sold equipment with a book value of $7,000 (cost $8,000, less accumulated depreciation $1,000) for $4,000 cash.
5. Issued common stock for $20,000 cash.
6. Depreciation expense was comprised of $6,000 for building and $3,000 for equipment.

result, cost of goods sold does not reflect $5,000 of cash payments made for merchandise. We deduct this inventory increase of $5,000 during the period from net income to arrive at net cash provided by operating activities. The worksheet entry is:

| (b) | Merchandise Inventory | 5,000 | |
| | Operating—Increase in Merchandise | | |
| | Inventory | | 5,000 |

**Prepaid Expenses**   An increase of $4,000 in prepaid expenses means that expenses deducted in determining net income are less than expenses that were paid in cash. We deduct the increase of $4,000 from net income in determining net cash provided by operating activities. The worksheet entry is:

| (c) | Prepaid Expenses | 4,000 | |
| | Operating—Increase in Prepaid Expenses | | 4,000 |

**HELPFUL HINT**

These amounts are asterisked in the worksheet to indicate that they result from a significant noncash transaction.

**Land**   The increase in land of $110,000 resulted from a purchase through the issuance of long-term bonds. The company should report this transaction as a significant noncash investing and financing activity. The worksheet entry is:

| (d) | Land | 110,000 | |
| | Bonds Payable | | 110,000 |

**Building**   The cash purchase of a building for $120,000 is an investing activity cash outflow. The entry in the reconciling columns of the worksheet is:

| (e) | Building | 120,000 | |
| | Investing—Purchase of Building | | 120,000 |

**Equipment**   The increase in equipment of $17,000 resulted from a cash purchase of $25,000 and the sale of equipment costing $8,000. The book value of the equipment was $7,000, the cash proceeds were $4,000, and a loss of $3,000 was recorded. The worksheet entries are:

| (f) | Equipment | 25,000 | |
| | Investing—Purchase of Equipment | | 25,000 |

| (g) | Investing—Sale of Equipment | 4,000 | |
| | Operating—Loss on Sale of Equipment | 3,000 | |
| | Accumulated Depreciation—Equipment | 1,000 | |
| | Equipment | | 8,000 |

**Accounts Payable**   We must add the increase of $16,000 in accounts payable to net income to determine net cash provided by operating activities. The worksheet entry is:

| (h) | Operating—Increase in Accounts Payable | 16,000 | |
| | Accounts Payable | | 16,000 |

**Income Taxes Payable**   When a company incurs income tax expense but has not yet paid its taxes, it records income tax payable. A change in the Income Tax Payable account reflects the difference between income tax expense incurred and income tax actually paid. Computer Services' Income Tax Payable account decreases by $2,000. That means the $47,000 of income tax expense reported on the income statement was $2,000 less than the amount of taxes paid during the period of $49,000. To adjust net income to a cash basis, we must reduce net income by $2,000. The worksheet entry is:

| (i) | Income Taxes Payable | 2,000 | |
| | Operating—Decrease in Income Taxes | | |
| | Payable | | 2,000 |

**Bonds Payable**    The increase of $110,000 in this account resulted from the issuance of bonds for land. This is a significant noncash investing and financing activity. Worksheet entry (d) above is the only entry necessary.

**Common Stock**    The balance sheet reports an increase in Common Stock of $20,000. The additional information section notes that this increase resulted from the issuance of new shares of stock. This is a cash inflow reported in the financing section. The worksheet entry is:

| (j) | Financing—Issuance of Common Stock | 20,000 | |
| | Common Stock | | 20,000 |

**Accumulated Depreciation—Building, and Accumulated Depreciation—Equipment**    Increases in these accounts of $6,000 and $3,000, respectively, resulted from depreciation expense. Depreciation expense is a **noncash charge that we must add to net income** to determine net cash provided by operating activities. The worksheet entries are:

| (k) | Operating—Depreciation Expense—Building | 6,000 | |
| | Accumulated Depreciation—Building | | 6,000 |

| (l) | Operating—Depreciation Expense—Equipment | 3,000 | |
| | Accumulated Depreciation—Equipment | | 3,000 |

**Retained Earnings**    The $116,000 increase in retained earnings resulted from net income of $145,000 and the declaration and payment of a $29,000 cash dividend. Net income is included in net cash provided by operating activities, and the dividends are a financing activity cash outflow. The entries in the reconciling columns of the worksheet are:

| (m) | Operating—Net Income | 145,000 | |
| | Retained Earnings | | 145,000 |

| (n) | Retained Earnings | 29,000 | |
| | Financing—Payment of Dividends | | 29,000 |

**Disposition of Change in Cash**    The firm's cash increased $22,000 in 2008. The final entry on the worksheet, therefore, is:

| (o) | Cash | 22,000 | |
| | Increase in Cash | | 22,000 |

As shown in the worksheet, we enter the increase in cash in the reconciling credit column as a **balancing** amount. This entry should complete the reconciliation of the changes in the balance sheet accounts. Also, it should permit the totals of the reconciling columns to be in agreement. When all changes have been explained and the reconciling columns are in agreement, the reconciling columns are ruled to complete the worksheet. The completed worksheet for Computer Services Company is shown in Illustration 14A-3 (page 664).

Illustration 14A-3
Completed worksheet—
indirect method

| | Computer Services Company.xls | | | | |
|---|---|---|---|---|---|
| | File Edit View Insert Format Tools Data Window Help | | | | |

**COMPUTER SERVICES COMPANY**
**Worksheet**
**Statement of Cash Flows For the Year Ended December 31, 2008**

| | A | B | C | D | E |
|---|---|---|---|---|---|
| | | Balance | Reconciling Items | | Balance |
| 6 | Balance Sheet Accounts | 12/31/07 | Debit | Credit | 12/31/08 |
| 7 | Debits | | | | |
| 8 | Cash | 33,000 | (o) 22,000 | | 55,000 |
| 9 | Accounts Receivable | 30,000 | | (a) 10,000 | 20,000 |
| 10 | Merchandise Inventory | 10,000 | (b) 5,000 | | 15,000 |
| 11 | Prepaid Expenses | 1,000 | (c) 4,000 | | 5,000 |
| 12 | Land | 20,000 | (d) 110,000* | | 130,000 |
| 13 | Building | 40,000 | (e) 120,000 | | 160,000 |
| 14 | Equipment | 10,000 | (f) 25,000 | (g) 8,000 | 27,000 |
| 15 | Total | 144,000 | | | 412,000 |
| 16 | Credits | | | | |
| 17 | Accounts Payable | 12,000 | | (h) 16,000 | 28,000 |
| 18 | Income Taxes Payable | 8,000 | (i) 2,000 | | 6,000 |
| 19 | Bonds Payable | 20,000 | | (d) 110,000* | 130,000 |
| 20 | Accumulated Depreciation—Building | 5,000 | | (k) 6,000 | 11,000 |
| 21 | Accumulated Depreciation—Equipment | 1,000 | (g) 1,000 | (l) 3,000 | 3,000 |
| 22 | Common Stock | 50,000 | | (j) 20,000 | 70,000 |
| 23 | Retained Earnings | 48,000 | (n) 29,000 | (m) 145,000 | 164,000 |
| 24 | Total | 144,000 | | | 412,000 |
| 25 | **Statement of Cash Flows Effects** | | | | |
| 26 | Operating activities | | | | |
| 27 | Net income | | (m) 145,000 | | |
| 28 | Decrease in accounts receivable | | (a) 10,000 | | |
| 29 | Increase in merchandise inventory | | | (b) 5,000 | |
| 30 | Increase in prepaid expenses | | | (c) 4,000 | |
| 31 | Increase in accounts payable | | (h) 16,000 | | |
| 32 | Decrease in income taxes payable | | | (i) 2,000 | |
| 33 | Depreciation expense—building | | (k) 6,000 | | |
| 34 | Depreciation expense—equipment | | (l) 3,000 | | |
| 35 | Loss on sale of equipment | | (g) 3,000 | | |
| 36 | Investing activities | | | | |
| 37 | Purchase of building | | | (e) 120,000 | |
| 38 | Purchase of equipment | | | (f) 25,000 | |
| 39 | Sale of equipment | | (g) 4,000 | | |
| 40 | Financing activities | | | | |
| 41 | Issuance of common stock | | (j) 20,000 | | |
| 42 | Payment of dividends | | | (n) 29,000 | |
| 43 | Totals | | 525,000 | 503,000 | |
| 44 | Increase in cash | | | (o) 22,000 | |
| 45 | Totals | | 525,000 | 525,000 | |
| 46 | | | | | |

\* Significant noncash investing and financing activity.

## SUMMARY OF STUDY OBJECTIVE FOR APPENDIX 14A

**5 Explain how to use a worksheet to prepare the statement of cash flows using the indirect method.** When there are numerous adjustments, a worksheet can be a helpful tool in preparing the statement of cash flows. Key guidelines for using a worksheet are: (1) List accounts with debit balances separately from those with credit balances. (2) In the reconciling columns in the bottom portion of the worksheet, show cash inflows as debits and cash outflows as credits. (3) Do not enter reconciling items in any journal or account, but use them only to help prepare the statement of cash flows.

The steps in preparing the worksheet are: (1) Enter beginning and ending balances of balance sheet accounts. (2) Enter debits and credits in reconciling columns. (3) Enter the increase or decrease in cash in two places as a balancing amount.

# APPENDIX 14B Statement of Cash Flows— Direct Method

To explain and illustrate the direct method, we will use the transactions of Juarez Company for 2008, to prepare a statement of cash flows. Illustration 14B-1 presents information related to 2008 for Juarez Company.

**STUDY OBJECTIVE 6**

Prepare a statement of cash flows using the direct method.

**Illustration 14B-1**
Comparative balance sheets, income statement, and additional information for Juarez Company

### JUAREZ COMPANY
Comparative Balance Sheets
December 31

| Assets | 2008 | 2007 | Change Increase/Decrease |
|---|---|---|---|
| Cash | $191,000 | $159,000 | $ 32,000 Increase |
| Accounts receivable | 12,000 | 15,000 | 3,000 Decrease |
| Inventory | 170,000 | 160,000 | 10,000 Increase |
| Prepaid expenses | 6,000 | 8,000 | 2,000 Decrease |
| Land | 140,000 | 80,000 | 60,000 Increase |
| Equipment | 160,000 | –0– | 160,000 Increase |
| Accumulated depreciation—equipment | (16,000) | –0– | 16,000 Increase |
| Total | $663,000 | $422,000 | |

| Liabilities and Stockholders' Equity | | | |
|---|---|---|---|
| Accounts payable | $ 52,000 | $ 60,000 | $  8,000 Decrease |
| Accrued expenses payable | 15,000 | 20,000 | 5,000 Decrease |
| Income taxes payable | 12,000 | –0– | 12,000 Increase |
| Bonds payable | 130,000 | –0– | 130,000 Increase |
| Common stock | 360,000 | 300,000 | 60,000 Increase |
| Retained earnings | 94,000 | 42,000 | 52,000 Increase |
| Total | $663,000 | $422,000 | |

### JUAREZ COMPANY
Income Statement
For the Year Ended December 31, 2008

| | | |
|---|---|---|
| Revenues | | $975,000 |
| Cost of goods sold | $660,000 | |
| Operating expenses (excluding depreciation) | 176,000 | |
| Depreciation expense | 18,000 | |
| Loss on sale of store equipment | 1,000 | 855,000 |
| Income before income taxes | | 120,000 |
| Income tax expense | | 36,000 |
| Net income | | $ 84,000 |

**Additional information:**
1. In 2008, the company declared and paid a $32,000 cash dividend.
2. Bonds were issued at face value for $130,000 in cash.
3. Equipment costing $180,000 was purchased for cash.
4. Equipment costing $20,000 was sold for $17,000 cash when the book value of the equipment was $18,000.
5. Common stock of $60,000 was issued to acquire land.

To prepare a statement of cash flows under the direct approach, we will apply the three steps outlined in Illustration 14-3 (page 643).

## Step 1: Operating Activities

### DETERMINE NET CASH PROVIDED/USED BY OPERATING ACTIVITIES BY CONVERTING NET INCOME FROM AN ACCRUAL BASIS TO A CASH BASIS

Under the **direct method**, companies compute net cash provided by operating activities by **adjusting each item in the income statement** from the accrual basis to the cash basis. To simplify and condense the operating activities section, companies **report only major classes of operating cash receipts and cash payments**. For these major classes, the difference between cash receipts and cash payments is the net cash provided by operating activities. These relationships are as shown in Illustration 14B-2.

**Illustration 14B-2**
Major classes of cash receipts and payments

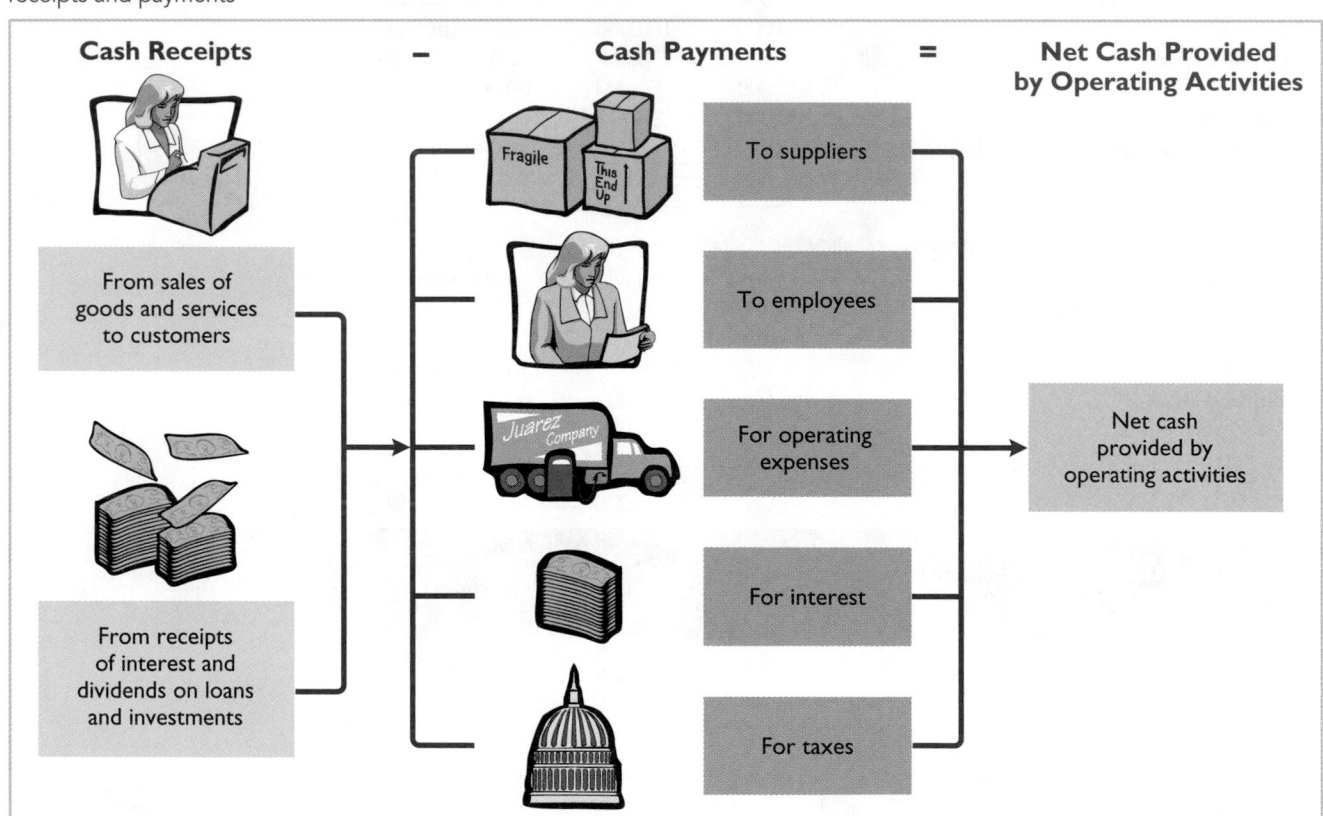

An efficient way to apply the direct method is to analyze the items reported in the income statement in the order in which they are listed. We then determine cash receipts and cash payments related to these revenues and expenses. The following pages present the adjustments required to prepare a statement of cash flows for Juarez Company using the direct approach.

### CASH RECEIPTS FROM CUSTOMERS

The income statement for Juarez Company reported revenues from customers of $975,000. How much of that was cash receipts? To answer that, companies need to consider the change in accounts receivable during the year. When accounts receivable increase during the year, revenues on an accrual basis are higher than cash receipts from customers. Operations led to revenues, but not all of these revenues resulted in cash receipts.

To determine the amount of cash receipts, the company deducts from sales revenues the increase in accounts receivable. On the other hand, there may be a decrease in accounts receivable. That would occur if cash receipts from customers exceeded sales revenues. In that case, the company adds to sales revenues the decrease in accounts receivable.

For Juarez Company, accounts receivable decreased $3,000. Thus, cash receipts from customers were $978,000, computed as shown in Illustration 14B-3.

| | |
|---|---|
| Revenues from sales | $ 975,000 |
| Add: Decrease in accounts receivable | 3,000 |
| **Cash receipts from customers** | **$ 978,000** |

**Illustration 14B-3**
Computation of cash receipts from customers

Juarez can also determine cash receipts from customers from an analysis of the Accounts Receivable account, as shown in Illustration 14B-4.

| **Accounts Receivable** | | | |
|---|---|---|---|
| 1/1/08  Balance | 15,000 | **Receipts from customers** | **978,000** |
| Revenues from sales | 975,000 | | |
| 12/31/08  Balance | 12,000 | | |

**Illustration 14B-4**
Analysis of accounts receivable

**HELPFUL HINT**
The T account shows that revenue plus decrease in receivables equals cash receipts.

Illustration 14B-5 shows the relationships among cash receipts from customers, revenues from sales, and changes in accounts receivable.

| Cash Receipts from Customers | = | Revenues from Sales | $\Big\{$ | + Decrease in Accounts Receivable<br>or<br>− Increase in Accounts Receivable |
|---|---|---|---|---|

**Illustration 14B-5**
Formula to compute cash receipts from customers—direct method

## CASH PAYMENTS TO SUPPLIERS

Juarez Company reported cost of goods sold of $660,000 on its income statement. How much of that was cash payments to suppliers? To answer that, it is first necessary to find purchases for the year. To find purchases, companies adjust cost of goods sold for the change in inventory. When inventory increases during the year, purchases for the year have exceeded cost of goods sold. As a result, to determine the amount of purchases, the company adds to cost of goods sold the increase in inventory.

In 2008, Juarez Company's inventory increased $10,000. It computes purchases as follows.

| | |
|---|---|
| Cost of goods sold | $660,000 |
| Add: Increase in inventory | 10,000 |
| **Purchases** | **$670,000** |

**Illustration 14B-6**
Computation of purchases

After computing purchases, a company can determine cash payments to suppliers. This is done by adjusting purchases for the change in accounts payable.

When accounts payable increase during the year, purchases on an accrual basis are higher than they are on a cash basis. As a result, to determine cash payments to suppliers, a company deducts from purchases the increase in accounts payable. On the other hand, if cash payments to suppliers exceed purchases, there will be a decrease in accounts payable. In that case, a company adds to purchases the decrease in accounts payable.

For Juarez Company, cash payments to suppliers were $678,000, computed as follows.

**Illustration 14B-7**
Computation of cash payments to suppliers

| | |
|---|---|
| Purchases | $670,000 |
| Add: Decrease in accounts payable | 8,000 |
| **Cash payments to suppliers** | **$678,000** |

Juarez also can determine cash payments to suppliers from an analysis of the Accounts Payable account, as shown in Illustration 14B-8.

**Illustration 14B-8**
Analysis of accounts payable

| Accounts Payable | | | | |
|---|---|---|---|---|
| **Payments to suppliers** | **678,000** | 1/1/08 Balance | | 60,000 |
| | | Purchases | | 670,000 |
| | | 12/31/08 Balance | | 52,000 |

**HELPFUL HINT**

The T account shows that purchases plus decrease in accounts payable equals payments to suppliers.

Illustration 14B-9 shows the relationships among cash payments to suppliers, cost of goods sold, changes in inventory, and changes in accounts payable.

**Illustration 14B-9**
Formula to compute cash payments to suppliers— direct method

$$\text{Cash Payments to Suppliers} = \text{Cost of Goods Sold} \begin{cases} + \text{ Increase in Inventory} \\ \text{or} \\ - \text{ Decrease in Inventory} \end{cases} \begin{cases} + \text{ Decrease in Accounts Payable} \\ \text{or} \\ - \text{ Increase in Accounts Payable} \end{cases}$$

## CASH PAYMENTS FOR OPERATING EXPENSES

Juarez reported on its income statement operating expenses of $176,000. How much of that amount was cash paid for operating expenses? To answer that, we need to adjust this amount for any changes in prepaid expenses and accrued expenses payable. For example, if prepaid expenses increased during the year, cash paid for operating expenses is higher than operating expenses reported on the income statement. To convert operating expenses to cash payments for operating expenses, a company adds the increase to operating expenses. On the other hand, if prepaid expenses decrease during the year, it deducts the decrease from operating expenses.

Companies must also adjust operating expenses for changes in accrued expenses payable. When accrued expenses payable increase during the year, operating expenses on an accrual basis are higher than they are in a cash basis. As a result, to determine cash payments for operating expenses, a company deducts from operating expenses an increase in accrued expenses payable. On the other hand, a company adds to operating expenses a decrease in accrued expenses payable because cash payments exceed operating expenses.

Juarez Company's cash payments for operating expenses were $179,000, computed as follows.

| | |
|---|---|
| Operating expenses | $176,000 |
| Deduct: Decrease in prepaid expenses | (2,000) |
| Add: Decrease in accrued expenses payable | 5,000 |
| **Cash payments for operating expenses** | **$179,000** |

**Illustration 14B-10**
Computation of cash payments for operating expenses

Illustration 14B-11 shows the relationships among cash payments for operating expenses, changes in prepaid expenses, and changes in accrued expenses payable.

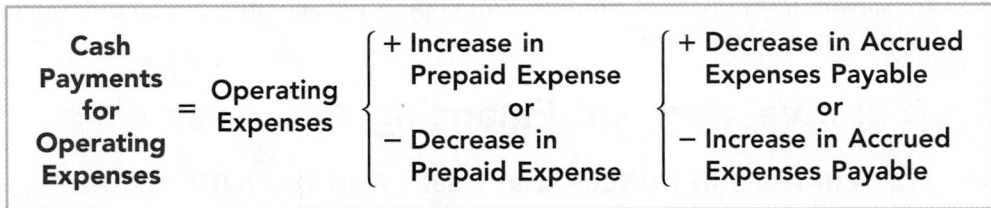

**Illustration 14B-11**
Formula to compute cash payments for operating expenses—direct method

## DEPRECIATION EXPENSE AND LOSS ON SALE OF EQUIPMENT

Companies show operating expenses exclusive of depreciation. Juarez's depreciation expense in 2008 was $18,000. Depreciation expense is not shown on a statement of cash flows because it is a noncash charge. If the amount for operating expenses includes depreciation expense, the company must reduce operating expenses by the amount of depreciation to determine cash payments for operating expenses.

The loss on sale of equipment of $1,000 is also a noncash charge. The loss on sale of equipment reduces net income, but it does not reduce cash. Thus, companies do not report on a statement of cash flows the loss on sale of equipment.

Other charges to expense that do not require the use of cash, such as the amortization of intangible assets, depletion expense, and bad debt expense, are treated in the same manner as depreciation.

## CASH PAYMENTS FOR INCOME TAXES

Juarez reported income tax expense of $36,000 on the income statement. Income taxes payable, however, increased $12,000. This increase means that the company has not yet paid $12,000 of the income taxes. As a result, income taxes paid were less than income taxes reported in the income statement. Cash payments for income taxes were, therefore, $24,000 as shown below.

| | |
|---|---|
| Income tax expense | $36,000 |
| Deduct: Increase in income taxes payable | 12,000 |
| **Cash payments for income taxes** | **$24,000** |

**Illustration 14B-12**
Computation of cash payments for income taxes

Illustration 14B-13 shows the relationships among cash payments for income taxes, income tax expense, and changes in income taxes payable.

| Cash Payments for Income Taxes | = | Income Tax Expense | { + Decrease in Income Taxes Payable  or  − Increase in Income Taxes Payable |
|---|---|---|---|

**Illustration 14B-13**
Formula to compute cash payments for income taxes—direct method

The operating activities section of the statement of cash flows of Juarez Company is shown in Illustration 14B-14.

**Illustration 14B-14**
Operating activities section of the statement of cash flows

| Cash flows from operating activities | | |
|---|---:|---:|
| Cash receipts from customers | | $978,000 |
| Less: Cash payments: | | |
| To suppliers | $678,000 | |
| For operating expenses | 179,000 | |
| For income taxes | 24,000 | 881,000 |
| Net cash provided by operating activities | | $ 97,000 |

When a company uses the direct method, it must also provide in a **separate schedule** (not shown here) the net cash flows from operating activities as computed under the indirect method.

# Step 2: Investing and Financing Activities

### ANALYZE CHANGES IN NONCURRENT ASSET AND LIABILITY ACCOUNTS AND RECORD AS INVESTING AND FINANCING ACTIVITIES, OR DISCLOSE AS NONCASH TRANSACTIONS

**Increase in Land.** Juarez's land increased $60,000. The additional information section indicates that the company issued common stock to purchase the land. The issuance of common stock for land has no effect on cash. But it is a **significant noncash investing and financing transaction**. This transaction requires disclosure in a separate schedule at the bottom of the statement of cash flows.

**Increase in Equipment.** The comparative balance sheets show that equipment increased $160,000 in 2008. The additional information in Illustration 14B-1 indicated that the increase resulted from two investing transactions: (1) Juarez purchased for cash equipment costing $180,000. And (2) it sold for $17,000 cash equipment costing $20,000, whose book value was $18,000. The relevant data for the statement of cash flows is the cash paid for the purchase and the cash proceeds from the sale. For Juarez Company, the investing activities section will show the following: The $180,000 purchase of equipment as an outflow of cash, and the $17,000 sale of equipment as an inflow of cash. The company **should not net** the two amounts. **Both individual outflows and inflows of cash should be shown.**

The analysis of the changes in equipment should include the related Accumulated Depreciation account. These two accounts for Juarez Company are shown in Illustration 14B-15.

**Illustration 14B-15**
Analysis of equipment and related accumulated depreciation

| Equipment | | | | |
|---|---|---:|---|---:|
| 1/1/08 | Balance | –0– | Cost of equipment sold | 20,000 |
| | **Cash purchase** | **180,000** | | |
| 12/31/08 | Balance | 160,000 | | |

| Accumulated Depreciation—Equipment | | | | | |
|---|---:|---|---|---|---:|
| Sale of equipment | 2,000 | 1/1/08 | Balance | | –0– |
| | | | Depreciation expense | | 18,000 |
| | | 12/31/08 | Balance | | 16,000 |

**Increase in Bonds Payable.**   Bonds Payable increased $130,000. The additional information in Illustration 14B-1 indicated that Juarez issued, for $130,000 cash, bonds with a face value of $130,000. The issuance of bonds is a financing activity. For Juarez Company, there is an inflow of cash of $130,000 from the issuance of bonds.

**Increase in Common Stock.**   The Common Stock account increased $60,000. The additional information indicated that Juarez acquired land from the issuance of common stock. This transaction is a **significant noncash investing and financing transaction** which the company should report separately at the bottom of the statement.

**Increase in Retained Earnings.**   The $52,000 net increase in Retained Earnings resulted from net income of $84,000 and the declaration and payment of a cash dividend of $32,000. Companies **do not report net income in the statement of cash flows under the direct method**. Cash dividends paid of $32,000 are reported in the financing activities section as an outflow of cash.

### STATEMENT OF CASH FLOWS—2008

Illustration 14B-16 shows the statement of cash flows for Juarez.

**Illustration 14B-16**
Statement of cash flows, 2008—direct method

| JUAREZ COMPANY<br>Statement of Cash Flows—Direct Method<br>For the Year Ended December 31, 2008 | | |
|---|---:|---:|
| Cash flows from operating activities | | |
| Cash receipts from customers | | $ 978,000 |
| Less: Cash payments: | | |
| To suppliers | $ 678,000 | |
| For operating expenses | 179,000 | |
| For income taxes | 24,000 | 881,000 |
| Net cash provided by operating activities | | 97,000 |
| Cash flows from investing activities | | |
| Purchase of equipment | (180,000) | |
| Sale of equipment | 17,000 | |
| Net cash used by investing activities | | (163,000) |
| Cash flows from financing activities | | |
| Issuance of bonds payable | 130,000 | |
| Payment of cash dividends | (32,000) | |
| Net cash provided by financing activities | | 98,000 |
| Net increase in cash | | 32,000 |
| Cash at beginning of period | | 159,000 |
| Cash at end of period | | $ 191,000 |
| | | |
| **Noncash investing and financing activities** | | |
| Issuance of common stock to purchase land | | $  60,000 |

# Step 3: Net Change in Cash

### COMPARE THE NET CHANGE IN CASH ON THE STATEMENT OF CASH FLOWS WITH THE CHANGE IN THE CASH ACCOUNT REPORTED ON THE BALANCE SHEET TO MAKE SURE THE AMOUNTS AGREE

Illustration 14B-16 indicates that the net change in cash during the period was an increase of $32,000. This agrees with the change in balances in the cash account reported on the balance sheets in Illustration 14B-1 (page 665).

**6 Prepare a statement of cash flows using the direct method.** The preparation of the statement of cash flows involves three major steps: (1) Determine net cash provided/used by operating activities by converting net income from an accrual basis to a cash basis. (2) Analyze changes in noncurrent asset and liability accounts and record as investing and financing activities, or disclose as noncash transactions. (3) Compare the net change in cash on the statement of cash flows with the change in the cash account reported on the balance sheet to make sure the amounts agree. The direct method reports cash receipts less cash payments to arrive at net cash provided by operating activities.

**Direct method** A method of determining net cash provided by operating activities by adjusting each item in the income statement from the accrual basis to the cash basis. (p. 666)

---

**Demonstration Problem 2**

The income statement for Kosinski Manufacturing Company contains the following condensed information.

### KOSINSKI MANUFACTURING COMPANY
**Income Statement**
**For the Year Ended December 31, 2008**

| | | |
|---|---|---|
| Revenues | | $6,583,000 |
| Operating expenses, excluding depreciation | $4,920,000 | |
| Depreciation expense | 880,000 | 5,800,000 |
| Income before income taxes | | 783,000 |
| Income tax expense | | 353,000 |
| Net income | | $ 430,000 |

Included in operating expenses is a $24,000 loss resulting from the sale of machinery for $270,000 cash. Machinery was purchased at a cost of $750,000. The following balances are reported on Kosinski's comparative balance sheet at December 31.

| | 2008 | 2007 |
|---|---|---|
| Cash | $672,000 | $130,000 |
| Accounts receivable | 775,000 | 610,000 |
| Inventories | 834,000 | 867,000 |
| Accounts payable | 521,000 | 501,000 |

Income tax expense of $353,000 represents the amount paid in 2008. Dividends declared and paid in 2008 totaled $200,000.

### Instructions

Prepare the statement of cash flows using the direct method.

**Solution**

### KOSINSKI MANUFACTURING COMPANY
#### Statement of Cash Flows—Direct Method
#### For the Year Ended December 31, 2008

| | | |
|---|---:|---:|
| Cash flows from operating activities | | |
| Cash collections from customers | | $6,418,000* |
| Cash payments: | | |
| For operating expenses | $4,843,000** | |
| For income taxes | 353,000 | 5,196,000 |
| Net cash provided by operating activities | | 1,222,000 |
| Cash flows from investing activities | | |
| Sale of machinery | 270,000 | |
| Purchase of machinery | (750,000) | |
| Net cash used by investing activities | | (480,000) |
| Cash flows from financing activities | | |
| Payment of cash dividends | | (200,000) |
| Net increase in cash | | 542,000 |
| Cash at beginning of period | | 130,000 |
| Cash at end of period | | $ 672,000 |

*Direct-Method Computations:*

| | |
|---|---:|
| *Computation of cash collections from customers: | |
| Revenues per the income statement | $6,583,000 |
| Deduct: Increase in accounts receivable | (165,000) |
| Cash collections from customers | $6,418,000 |
| **Computation of cash payments for operating expenses: | |
| Operating expenses per the income statement | $4,920,000 |
| Deduct: Loss from sale of machinery | (24,000) |
| Deduct: Decrease in inventories | (33,000) |
| Deduct: Increase in accounts payable | (20,000) |
| Cash payments for operating expenses | $4,843,000 |

✓ Determine net cash from operating activities. Each item in the income statement must be adjusted to the cash basis.

✓ Determine net cash from investing activities. Investing activities generally relate to changes in noncurrent assets.

✓ Determine net cash from financing activities. Financing activities generally relate to changes in long-term liabilities and stockholders' equity accounts.

✓ *The Navigator*

**Note:** All Questions, Exercises, and Problems marked with an asterisk relate to material in the appendices to the chapter.

## SELF-STUDY QUESTIONS

*WILEY PLUS*

*Answers are at the end of the chapter.*

(SO 1)  **1.** Which of the following is *incorrect* about the statement of cash flows?
  **a.** It is a fourth basic financial statement.
  **b.** It provides information about cash receipts and cash payments of an entity during a period.
  **c.** It reconciles the ending cash account balance to the balance per the bank statement.
  **d.** It provides information about the operating, investing, and financing activities of the business.

(SO 2)  **2.** The statement of cash flows classifies cash receipts and cash payments by these activities:
  **a.** operating and nonoperating.
  **b.** investing, financing, and operating.

  **c.** financing, operating, and nonoperating.
  **d.** investing, financing, and nonoperating.

**3.** Which is an example of a cash flow from an operating (SO 2) activity?
  **a.** Payment of cash to lenders for interest.
  **b.** Receipt of cash from the sale of capital stock.
  **c.** Payment of cash dividends to the company's stockholders.
  **d.** None of the above.

**4.** Which is an example of a cash flow from an investing (SO 2) activity?
  **a.** Receipt of cash from the issuance of bonds payable.
  **b.** Payment of cash to repurchase outstanding capital stock.

**c.** Receipt of cash from the sale of equipment.

**d.** Payment of cash to suppliers for inventory.

(SO 2) **5.** Cash dividends paid to stockholders are classified on the statement of cash flows as:

**a.** operating activities.

**b.** investing activities.

**c.** a combination of (a) and (b).

**d.** financing activities.

(SO 2) **6.** Which is an example of a cash flow from a financing activity?

**a.** Receipt of cash from sale of land.

**b.** Issuance of debt for cash.

**c.** Purchase of equipment for cash.

**d.** None of the above

(SO 2) **7.** Which of the following is *incorrect* about the statement of cash flows?

**a.** The direct method may be used to report cash provided by operations.

**b.** The statement shows the cash provided (used) for three categories of activity.

**c.** The operating section is the last section of the statement.

**d.** The indirect method may be used to report cash provided by operations.

**Questions 8 and 9 apply only to the indirect method.**

(SO 3) **8.** Net income is $132,000, accounts payable increased $10,000 during the year, inventory decreased $6,000 during the year, and accounts receivable increased $12,000 during the year. Under the indirect method, what is net cash provided by operating activities?

**a.** $102,000.          **c.** $124,000.

**b.** $112,000.          **d.** $136,000.

(SO 3) **9.** Items that are added back to net income in determining cash provided by operating activities under the indirect method do *not* include:

**a.** depreciation expense.

**b.** an increase in inventory.

**c.** amortization expense.

**d.** loss on sale of equipment.

(SO 4) **10.** The statement of cash flows should *not* be used to evaluate an entity's ability to:

**a.** earn net income.

**b.** generate future cash flows.

**c.** pay dividends.

**d.** meet obligations.

(SO 4) **11.** Free cash flow provides an indication of a company's ability to:

**a.** generate net income.

**b.** generate cash to pay dividends.

**c.** generate cash to invest in new capital expenditures.

**d.** both (b) and (c).

(SO 5) *12. In a worksheet for the statement of cash flows, a decrease in accounts receivable is entered in the reconciling columns as a credit to Accounts Receivable and a debit in the:

**a.** investing activities section.

**b.** operating activities section.

**c.** financing activities section.

**d.** None of the above.

**Questions 13 and 14 apply only to the direct method.**

(SO 6) *13. The beginning balance in accounts receivable is $44,000, the ending balance is $42,000, and sales during the period are $129,000. What are cash receipts from customers?

**a.** $127,000.          **c.** $131,000.

**b.** $129,000.          **d.** $141,000.

(SO 6) *14. Which of the following items is reported on a cash flow statement prepared by the direct method?

**a.** Loss on sale of building.

**b.** Increase in accounts receivable.

**c.** Depreciation expense.

**d.** Cash payments to suppliers.

Go to the book's website,
**www.wiley.com/college/weygandt**,
for Additional Self-Study questions.

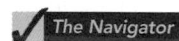

The Navigator

---

# QUESTIONS

**1. (a)** What is a statement of cash flows?

**(b)** John Norris maintains that the statement of cash flows is an optional financial statement. Do you agree? Explain.

**2.** What questions about cash are answered by the statement of cash flows?

**3.** Distinguish among the three types of activities reported in the statement of cash flows.

**4. (a)** What are the major sources (inflows) of cash in a statement of cash flows?

**(b)** What are the major uses (outflows) of cash?

**5.** Why is it important to disclose certain noncash transactions? How should they be disclosed?

**6.** Wilma Flintstone and Barny Rublestone were discussing the format of the statement of cash flows of Hart Candy Co. At the bottom of Hart Candy's statement of cash flows

was a separate section entitled "Noncash investing and financing activities." Give three examples of significant noncash transactions that would be reported in this section.

**7.** Why is it necessary to use comparative balance sheets, a current income statement, and certain transaction data in preparing a statement of cash flows?

**8.** Contrast the advantages and disadvantages of the direct and indirect methods of preparing the statement of cash flows. Are both methods acceptable? Which method is preferred by the FASB? Which method is more popular?

**9.** When the total cash inflows exceed the total cash outflows in the statement of cash flows, how and where is this excess identified?

**10.** Describe the indirect method for determining net cash provided (used) by operating activities.

**11.** Why is it necessary to convert accrual-based net income to cash-basis income when preparing a statement of cash flows?

**12.** The president of Ferneti Company is puzzled. During the last year, the company experienced a net loss of $800,000, yet its cash increased $300,000 during the same period of time. Explain to the president how this could occur.

**13.** Identify five items that are adjustments to convert net income to net cash provided by operating activities under the indirect method.

**14.** Why and how is depreciation expense reported in a statement prepared using the indirect method?

**15.** Why is the statement of cash flows useful?

**16.** During 2008 Doubleday Company converted $1,700,000 of its total $2,000,000 of bonds payable into common stock. Indicate how the transaction would be reported on a statement of cash flows, if at all.

**\*17.** Why is it advantageous to use a worksheet when preparing a statement of cash flows? Is a worksheet required to prepare a statement of cash flows?

**\*18.** Describe the direct method for determining net cash provided by operating activities.

**\*19.** Give the formulas under the direct method for computing (a) cash receipts from customers and (b) cash payments to suppliers.

**\*20.** Garcia Inc. reported sales of $2 million for 2008. Accounts receivable decreased $200,000 and accounts payable increased $300,000. Compute cash receipts from customers, assuming that the receivable and payable transactions related to operations.

**\*21.** In the direct method, why is depreciation expense not reported in the cash flows from operating activities section?

# BRIEF EXERCISES

**BE14-1**   Each of these items must be considered in preparing a statement of cash flows for Kiner Co. for the year ended December 31, 2008. For each item, state how it should be shown in the statement of cash flows for 2008.

(a) Issued bonds for $200,000 cash.
(b) Purchased equipment for $150,000 cash.
(c) Sold land costing $20,000 for $20,000 cash.
(d) Declared and paid a $50,000 cash dividend.

*Indicate statement presentation of selected transactions.*
*(SO 2)*

**BE14-2**   Classify each item as an operating, investing, or financing activity. Assume all items involve cash unless there is information to the contrary.

(a) Purchase of equipment.          (d) Depreciation.
(b) Sale of building.               (e) Payment of dividends.
(c) Redemption of bonds.           (f) Issuance of capital stock.

*Classify items by activities.*
*(SO 2)*

**BE14-3**   The following T account is a summary of the cash account of Edmonds Company.

*Identify financing activity transactions.*
*(SO 2)*

### Cash (Summary Form)

| Balance, Jan. 1 | 8,000 | | |
|---|---|---|---|
| Receipts from customers | 364,000 | Payments for goods | 200,000 |
| Dividends on stock investments | 6,000 | Payments for operating expenses | 140,000 |
| Proceeds from sale of equipment | 36,000 | Interest paid | 10,000 |
| Proceeds from issuance of | | Taxes paid | 8,000 |
| bonds payable | 300,000 | Dividends paid | 50,000 |
| Balance, Dec. 31 | 306,000 | | |

What amount of net cash provided (used) by financing activities should be reported in the statement of cash flows?

**BE14-4**   Martinez, Inc. reported net income of $2.5 million in 2008. Depreciation for the year was $160,000, accounts receivable decreased $350,000, and accounts payable decreased $280,000. Compute net cash provided by operating activities using the indirect method.

*Compute cash provided by operating activities—indirect method.*
*(SO 3)*

**BE14-5**   The net income for Adcock Co. for 2008 was $280,000. For 2008 depreciation on plant assets was $70,000, and the company incurred a loss on sale of plant assets of $12,000. Compute net cash provided by operating activities under the indirect method.

*Compute cash provided by operating activities—indirect method.*
*(SO 3)*

**BE14-6**   The comparative balance sheets for Goltra Company show these changes in noncash current asset accounts: accounts receivable decrease $80,000, prepaid expenses increase $28,000, and inventories increase $30,000. Compute net cash provided by operating activities using the indirect method assuming that net income is $200,000.

*Compute net cash provided by operating activities—indirect method.*
*(SO 3)*

*Determine cash received from sale of equipment.*
*(SO 3)*

**BE14-7** The T accounts for Equipment and the related Accumulated Depreciation for Pettengill Company at the end of 2008 are shown here.

| Equipment | | | | Accumulated Depreciation | | | |
|---|---|---|---|---|---|---|---|
| Beg. bal. | 80,000 | Disposals | 22,000 | Disposals | 5,500 | Beg. bal. | 44,500 |
| Acquisitions | 41,600 | | | | | Depr. exp. | 12,000 |
| End. bal. | 99,600 | | | | | End. bal. | 51,000 |

In addition, Pettengill Company's income statement reported a loss on the sale of equipment of $5,500. What amount was reported on the statement of cash flows as "cash flow from sale of equipment"?

*Calculate free cash flow.*
*(SO 4)*

**BE14-8** In a recent year, Cypress Semiconductor Corporation reported cash provided by operating activities of $155,793,000, cash used in investing of $207,826,000, and cash used in financing of $33,372,000. In addition, cash spent for fixed assets during the period was $132,280,000. No dividends were paid. Calculate free cash flow.

*Calculate free cash flow.*
*(SO 4)*

**BE14-9** Lott Corporation reported cash provided by operating activities of $360,000, cash used by investing activities of $250,000, and cash provided by financing activities of $70,000. In addition, cash spent for capital assets during the period was $200,000. No dividends were paid. Calculate free cash flow.

*Calculate free cash flow.*
*(SO 4)*

**BE14-10** Alliance Atlantis Communications Inc. reported a $35.8 million increase in operating cash flow for its first quarter of 2005. Alliance reported cash provided by operating activities of $45,600,000 and revenues of $264,800,000. Cash spent on plant asset additions during the quarter was $1,600,000. Calculate free cash flow.

*Calculate and analyze free cash flow.*
*(SO 4)*

**BE14-11** The management of Radar Inc. is trying to decide whether it can increase its dividend. During the current year it reported net income of $875,000. It had cash provided by operating activities of $734,000, paid cash dividends of $70,000, and had capital expenditures of $280,000. Compute the company's free cash flow, and discuss whether an increase in the dividend appears warranted. What other factors should be considered?

*Indicate entries in worksheet.*
*(SO 5)*

**\*BE14-12** During the year, prepaid expenses decreased $6,600, and accrued expenses increased $2,400. Indicate how the changes in prepaid expenses and accrued expenses payable should be entered in the reconciling columns of a worksheet. Assume that beginning balances were: Prepaid expenses $18,600 and Accrued expenses payable $8,200.

*Compute receipts from customers—direct method.*
*(SO 6)*

**\*BE14-13** Columbia Sportswear Company had accounts receivable of $206,024,000 at the beginning of a recent year, and $267,653,000 at year-end. Sales revenues were $1,095,307,000 for the year. What is the amount of cash receipts from customers?

*Compute cash payments for income taxes—direct method.*
*(SO 6)*

**\*BE14-14** Young Corporation reported income taxes of $340,000,000 on its 2008 income statement and income taxes payable of $277,000,000 at December 31, 2007, and $522,000,000 at December 31, 2008. What amount of cash payments were made for income taxes during 2008?

*Compute cash payments for operating expenses—direct method.*
*(SO 6)*

**\*BE14-15** Flynn Corporation reports operating expenses of $80,000 excluding depreciation expense of $15,000 for 2008. During the year prepaid expenses decreased $6,600 and accrued expenses payable increased $4,400. Compute the cash payments for operating expenses in 2008.

# EXERCISES

*Classify transactions by type of activity.*
*(SO 2)*

**E14-1** Pioneer Corporation had these transactions during 2008.

(a) Issued $50,000 par value common stock for cash.
(b) Purchased a machine for $30,000, giving a long-term note in exchange.
(c) Issued $200,000 par value common stock upon conversion of bonds having a face value of $200,000.
(d) Declared and paid a cash dividend of $18,000.
(e) Sold a long-term investment with a cost of $15,000 for $15,000 cash.
(f) Collected $16,000 of accounts receivable.
(g) Paid $18,000 on accounts payable.

**Instructions**

Analyze the transactions and indicate whether each transaction resulted in a cash flow from operating activities, investing activities, financing activities, or noncash investing and financing activities.

**E14-2** An analysis of comparative balance sheets, the current year's income statement, and the general ledger accounts of Gagliano Corp. uncovered the following items. Assume all items involve cash unless there is information to the contrary.

*Classify transactions by type of activity.*
*(SO 2)*

**(a)** Payment of interest on notes payable.
**(b)** Exchange of land for patent.
**(c)** Sale of building at book value.
**(d)** Payment of dividends.
**(e)** Depreciation.
**(f)** Receipt of dividends on investment in stock.
**(g)** Receipt of interest on notes receivable.

**(h)** Issuance of capital stock.
**(i)** Amortization of patent.
**(j)** Issuance of bonds for land.
**(k)** Purchase of land.
**(l)** Conversion of bonds into common stock.
**(m)** Loss on sale of land.
**(n)** Retirement of bonds.

**Instructions**

Indicate how each item should be classified in the statement of cash flows using these four major classifications: operating activity (indirect method), investing activity, financing activity, and significant noncash investing and financing activity.

**E14-3** Rachael Ray Corporation had the following transactions.

*Prepare journal entry and determine effect on cash flows.*
*(SO 2)*

1. Sold land (cost $12,000) for $15,000.
2. Issued common stock for $20,000.
3. Recorded depreciation of $17,000.
4. Paid salaries of $9,000.
5. Issued 1,000 shares of $1 par value common stock for equipment worth $8,000.
6. Sold equipment (cost $10,000, accumulated depreciation $7,000) for $1,200.

**Instructions**

For each transaction above, **(a)** prepare the journal entry, and **(b)** indicate how it would affect the statement of cash flows.

**E14-4** Villa Company reported net income of $195,000 for 2008. Villa also reported depreciation expense of $45,000 and a loss of $5,000 on the sale of equipment. The comparative balance sheet shows a decrease in accounts receivable of $15,000 for the year, a $17,000 increase in accounts payable, and a $4,000 decrease in prepaid expenses.

*Prepare the operating activities section—indirect method.*
*(SO 3)*

**Instructions**

Prepare the operating activities section of the statement of cash flows for 2008. Use the indirect method.

**E14-5** The current sections of Bellinham Inc.'s balance sheets at December 31, 2007 and 2008, are presented here.

*Prepare the operating activities section—indirect method.*
*(SO 3)*

Bellinham's net income for 2008 was $153,000. Depreciation expense was $24,000.

|  | 2008 | 2007 |
|---|---|---|
| Current assets | | |
| Cash | $105,000 | $ 99,000 |
| Accounts receivable | 110,000 | 89,000 |
| Inventory | 158,000 | 172,000 |
| Prepaid expenses | 27,000 | 22,000 |
| Total current assets | $400,000 | $382,000 |
| Current liabilities | | |
| Accrued expenses payable | $ 15,000 | $ 5,000 |
| Accounts payable | 85,000 | 92,000 |
| Total current liabilities | $100,000 | $ 97,000 |

**Instructions**

Prepare the net cash provided by operating activities section of the company's statement of cash flows for the year ended December 31, 2008, using the indirect method.

*Prepare partial statement of cash flows—indirect method.*

(SO 3)

**E14-6** The three accounts shown below appear in the general ledger of Cesar Corp. during 2008.

**Equipment**

| Date | | Debit | Credit | Balance |
|------|------|------|------|------|
| Jan. 1 | Balance | | | 160,000 |
| July 31 | Purchase of equipment | 70,000 | | 230,000 |
| Sept. 2 | Cost of equipment constructed | 53,000 | | 283,000 |
| Nov. 10 | Cost of equipment sold | | 49,000 | 234,000 |

**Accumulated Depreciation—Equipment**

| Date | | Debit | Credit | Balance |
|------|------|------|------|------|
| Jan. 1 | Balance | | | 71,000 |
| Nov. 10 | Accumulated depreciation on equipment sold | 30,000 | | 41,000 |
| Dec. 31 | Depreciation for year | | 28,000 | 69,000 |

**Retained Earnings**

| Date | | Debit | Credit | Balance |
|------|------|------|------|------|
| Jan. 1 | Balance | | | 105,000 |
| Aug. 23 | Dividends (cash) | 14,000 | | 91,000 |
| Dec. 31 | Net income | | 67,000 | 158,000 |

**Instructions**

From the postings in the accounts, indicate how the information is reported on a statement of cash flows using the indirect method. The loss on sale of equipment was $5,000. (*Hint:* Cost of equipment constructed is reported in the investing activities section as a decrease in cash of $53,000.)

*Prepare statement of cash flows and compute free cash flow.*

(SO 3, 4)

**E14-7** Scully Corporation's comparative balance sheets are presented below.

### SCULLY CORPORATION
Comparative Balance Sheets
December 31

| | 2008 | 2007 |
|------|------|------|
| Cash | $ 14,300 | $ 10,700 |
| Accounts receivable | 21,200 | 23,400 |
| Land | 20,000 | 26,000 |
| Building | 70,000 | 70,000 |
| Accumulated depreciation | (15,000) | (10,000) |
| Total | $110,500 | $120,100 |
| | | |
| Accounts payable | $12,370 | $31,100 |
| Common stock | 75,000 | 69,000 |
| Retained earnings | 23,130 | 20,000 |
| Total | $110,500 | $120,100 |

Additional information:

1. Net income was $22,630. Dividends declared and paid were $19,500.
2. All other changes in noncurrent account balances had a direct effect on cash flows, except the change in accumulated depreciation. The land was sold for $4,900.

**Instructions**
(a) Prepare a statement of cash flows for 2008 using the indirect method.
(b) Compute free cash flow.

**E14-8**    Here are comparative balance sheets for Taguchi Company.

*Prepare a statement of cash flows—indirect method.*
(SO 3)

### TAGUCHI COMPANY
Comparative Balance Sheets
December 31

| Assets | 2008 | 2007 |
|---|---|---|
| Cash | $ 73,000 | $ 22,000 |
| Accounts receivable | 85,000 | 76,000 |
| Inventories | 170,000 | 189,000 |
| Land | 75,000 | 100,000 |
| Equipment | 260,000 | 200,000 |
| Accumulated depreciation | (66,000) | (32,000) |
| Total | $597,000 | $555,000 |
| | | |
| **Liabilities and Stockholders' Equity** | | |
| Accounts payable | $ 39,000 | $ 47,000 |
| Bonds payable | 150,000 | 200,000 |
| Common stock ($1 par) | 216,000 | 174,000 |
| Retained earnings | 192,000 | 134,000 |
| Total | $597,000 | $555,000 |

Additional information:

1. Net income for 2008 was $103,000.
2. Cash dividends of $45,000 were declared and paid.
3. Bonds payable amounting to $50,000 were redeemed for cash $50,000.
4. Common stock was issued for $42,000 cash.
5. No equipment was sold during 2008; land was sold at cost.

**Instructions**
Prepare a statement of cash flows for 2008 using the indirect method.

**E14-9**    Muldur Corporation's comparative balance sheets are presented below.

*Prepare statement of cash flows and compute free cash flow.*
(SO 3, 4)

### MULDUR CORPORATION
Comparative Balance Sheets
December 31

| | 2008 | 2007 |
|---|---|---|
| Cash | $ 15,200 | $ 17,700 |
| Accounts receivable | 25,200 | 22,300 |
| Investments | 20,000 | 16,000 |
| Equipment | 60,000 | 70,000 |
| Accumulated depreciation | (14,000) | (10,000) |
| Total | $106,400 | $116,000 |
| | | |
| Accounts payable | $ 14,600 | $ 11,100 |
| Bonds payable | 10,000 | 30,000 |
| Common stock | 50,000 | 45,000 |
| Retained earnings | 31,800 | 29,900 |
| Total | $106,400 | $116,000 |

Additional information:

**1.** Net income was $18,300. Dividends declared and paid were $16,400.
**2.** Equipment which cost $10,000 and had accumulated depreciation of $1,200 was sold for $3,300.
**3.** All other changes in noncurrent account balances had a direct effect on cash flows, except the change in accumulated depreciation.

**Instructions**
**(a)** Prepare a statement of cash flows for 2008 using the indirect method.
**(b)** Compute free cash flow.

*Prepare a worksheet.*
*(SO 5)*

**\*E14-10**  Comparative balance sheets for Eddie Murphy Company are presented below.

### EDDIE MURPHY COMPANY
Comparative Balance Sheets
December 31

| Assets | 2008 | 2007 |
| --- | --- | --- |
| Cash | $ 63,000 | $ 22,000 |
| Accounts receivable | 85,000 | 76,000 |
| Inventories | 180,000 | 189,000 |
| Land | 75,000 | 100,000 |
| Equipment | 260,000 | 200,000 |
| Accumulated depreciation | (66,000) | (42,000) |
| Total | $597,000 | $545,000 |

| Liabilities and Stockholders' Equity | 2008 | 2007 |
| --- | --- | --- |
| Accounts payable | $ 34,000 | $ 47,000 |
| Bonds payable | 150,000 | 200,000 |
| Common stock ($1 par) | 214,000 | 164,000 |
| Retained earnings | 199,000 | 134,000 |
| Total | $597,000 | $545,000 |

Additional information:

**1.** Net income for 2008 was $125,000.
**2.** Cash dividends of $60,000 were declared and paid.
**3.** Bonds payable amounting to $50,000 were redeemed for cash $50,000.
**4.** Common stock was issued for $50,000 cash.
**5.** Depreciation expense was $24,000.
**6.** Sales for the year were $978,000.

**Instructions**
Prepare a worksheet for a statement of cash flows for 2008 using the indirect method. Enter the reconciling items directly on the worksheet, using letters to cross-reference each entry.

*Compute cash provided by operating activities—direct method.*
*(SO 6)*

**\*E14-11**  Hairston Company completed its first year of operations on December 31, 2008. Its initial income statement showed that Hairston had revenues of $192,000 and operating expenses of $78,000. Accounts receivable and accounts payable at year-end were $60,000 and $23,000, respectively. Assume that accounts payable related to operating expenses. Ignore income taxes.

**Instructions**
Compute net cash provided by operating activities using the direct method.

*Compute cash payments—direct method.*
*(SO 6)*

**\*E14-12**  The 2004 income statement for McDonald's Corporation shows cost of goods sold $4,852.7 million and operating expenses (including depreciation expense of $1,201 million) $10,671.5 million. The comparative balance sheet for the year shows that inventory increased $18.1 million, prepaid expenses increased $56.3 million, accounts payable (merchandise suppliers) increased $136.9 million, and accrued expenses payable increased $160.9 million.

**Instructions**
Using the direct method, compute (a) cash payments to suppliers and (b) cash payments for operating expenses.

**\*E14-13**   The 2008 accounting records of Verlander Transport reveal these transactions and events.

*Compute cash flow from operating activities—direct method.*
(SO 6)

| | | | |
|---|---|---|---|
| Payment of interest | $ 10,000 | Collection of accounts receivable | $182,000 |
| Cash sales | 48,000 | Payment of salaries and wages | 53,000 |
| Receipt of dividend revenue | 18,000 | Depreciation expense | 16,000 |
| Payment of income taxes | 12,000 | Proceeds from sale of vehicles | 12,000 |
| Net income | 38,000 | Purchase of equipment for cash | 22,000 |
| Payment of accounts payable | | Loss on sale of vehicles | 3,000 |
| for merchandise | 115,000 | Payment of dividends | 14,000 |
| Payment for land | 74,000 | Payment of operating expenses | 28,000 |

**Instructions**
Prepare the cash flows from operating activities section using the direct method. (Not all of the items will be used.)

**\*E14-14**   The following information is taken from the 2008 general ledger of Pierzynski Company.

*Calculate cash flows—direct method.*
(SO 6)

| | | |
|---|---|---|
| Rent | Rent expense | $ 40,000 |
| | Prepaid rent, January 1 | 5,900 |
| | Prepaid rent, December 31 | 9,000 |
| Salaries | Salaries expense | $ 54,000 |
| | Salaries payable, January 1 | 10,000 |
| | Salaries payable, December 31 | 8,000 |
| Sales | Revenue from sales | $170,000 |
| | Accounts receivable, January 1 | 16,000 |
| | Accounts receivable, December 31 | 7,000 |

**Instructions**
In each case, compute the amount that should be reported in the operating activities section of the statement of cash flows under the direct method.

# EXERCISES: SET B

Visit the book's website at **www.wiley.com/college/weygandt**, and choose the Student Companion site, to access Exercise Set B.

# PROBLEMS: SET A

**P14-1A**   You are provided with the following transactions that took place during a recent fiscal year.

*Distinguish among operating, investing, and financing activities.*
(SO 2)

| Transaction | Where Reported on Statement | Cash Inflow, Outflow, or No Effect? |
|---|---|---|
| (a)  Recorded depreciation expense on the plant assets. | | |
| (b)  Recorded and paid interest expense. | | |
| (c)  Recorded cash proceeds from a sale of plant assets. | | |
| (d)  Acquired land by issuing common stock. | | |
| (e)  Paid a cash dividend to preferred stockholders. | | |
| (f)  Distributed a stock dividend to common stockholders. | | |
| (g)  Recorded cash sales. | | |
| (h)  Recorded sales on account. | | |
| (i)  Purchased inventory for cash. | | |
| (j)  Purchased inventory on account. | | |

**Instructions**

Complete the table indicating whether each item (1) should be reported as an operating (O) activity, investing (I) activity, financing (F) activity, or as a noncash (NC) transaction reported in a separate schedule, and (2) represents a cash inflow or cash outflow or has no cash flow effect. Assume use of the indirect approach.

*Determine cash flow effects of changes in equity accounts.*

*(SO 3)*

**P14-2A** The following account balances relate to the stockholders' equity accounts of Gore Corp. at year-end.

|  | 2008 | 2007 |
|---|---|---|
| Common stock, 10,500 and 10,000 shares, respectively, for 2008 and 2007 | $160,000 | $140,000 |
| Preferred stock, 5,000 shares | 125,000 | 125,000 |
| Retained earnings | 300,000 | 260,000 |

A small stock dividend was declared and issued in 2008. The market value of the shares was $10,500. Cash dividends were $15,000 in both 2008 and 2007. The common stock has no par or stated value.

**Instructions**

*(a) Net income  $65,500*

**(a)** What was the amount of net income reported by Gore Corp. in 2008?

**(b)** Determine the amounts of any cash inflows or outflows related to the common stock and dividend accounts in 2008.

**(c)** Indicate where each of the cash inflows or outflows identified in (b) would be classified on the statement of cash flows.

*Prepare the operating activities section—indirect method.*

*(SO 3)*

**P14-3A** The income statement of Elbert Company is presented here.

### ELBERT COMPANY
Income Statement
For the Year Ended November 30, 2008

| | | |
|---|---|---|
| Sales | | $7,700,000 |
| Cost of goods sold | | |
| Beginning inventory | $1,900,000 | |
| Purchases | 4,400,000 | |
| Goods available for sale | 6,300,000 | |
| Ending inventory | 1,400,000 | |
| Total cost of goods sold | | 4,900,000 |
| Gross profit | | 2,800,000 |
| Operating expenses | | |
| Selling expenses | 450,000 | |
| Administrative expenses | 700,000 | 1,150,000 |
| Net income | | $1,650,000 |

Additional information:

1. Accounts receivable increased $250,000 during the year, and inventory decreased $500,000.
2. Prepaid expenses increased $150,000 during the year.
3. Accounts payable to suppliers of merchandise decreased $340,000 during the year.
4. Accrued expenses payable decreased $100,000 during the year.
5. Administrative expenses include depreciation expense of $90,000.

*Cash from operations $1,400,000*

**Instructions**

Prepare the operating activities section of the statement of cash flows for the year ended November 30, 2008, for Elbert Company, using the indirect method.

*Prepare the operating activities section—direct method.*

*(SO 6)*

**\*P14-4A** Data for Elbert Company are presented in P14-3A.

**Instructions**
Prepare the operating activities section of the statement of cash flows using the direct method.

Cash from operations
$1,400,000

**P14-5A**    Grania Company's income statement contained the condensed information below.

*Prepare the operating activities section—indirect method.*

(SO 3)

### GRANIA COMPANY
Income Statement
For the Year Ended December 31, 2008

| | | |
|---|---:|---:|
| Revenues | | $970,000 |
| Operating expenses, excluding depreciation | $624,000 | |
| Depreciation expense | 60,000 | |
| Loss on sale of equipment | 16,000 | 700,000 |
| Income before income taxes | | 270,000 |
| Income tax expense | | 40,000 |
| Net income | | $230,000 |

Grania's balance sheet contained the comparative data at December 31, shown below.

| | 2008 | 2007 |
|---|---:|---:|
| Accounts receivable | $75,000 | $60,000 |
| Accounts payable | 41,000 | 28,000 |
| Income taxes payable | 11,000 | 7,000 |

Accounts payable pertain to operating expenses.

**Instructions**
Prepare the operating activities section of the statement of cash flows using the indirect method.

Cash from operations
$308,000

**\*P14-6A**    Data for Grania Company are presented in P14-5A.

*Prepare the operating activities section—direct method.*

(SO 6)    Cash from
operations
$308,000

**Instructions**
Prepare the operating activities section of the statement of cash flows using the direct method.

**P14-7A**    Presented below are the financial statements of Weller Company.

*Prepare a statement of cash flows—indirect method, and compute free cash flow.*

(SO 3, 4)

### WELLER COMPANY
Comparative Balance Sheets
December 31

| Assets | 2008 | 2007 |
|---|---:|---:|
| Cash | $ 35,000 | $ 20,000 |
| Accounts receivable | 33,000 | 14,000 |
| Merchandise inventory | 27,000 | 20,000 |
| Property, plant, and equipment | 60,000 | 78,000 |
| Accumulated depreciation | (29,000) | (24,000) |
| Total | $126,000 | $108,000 |

| Liabilities and Stockholders' Equity | 2008 | 2007 |
|---|---:|---:|
| Accounts payable | $ 29,000 | $ 15,000 |
| Income taxes payable | 7,000 | 8,000 |
| Bonds payable | 27,000 | 33,000 |
| Common stock | 18,000 | 14,000 |
| Retained earnings | 45,000 | 38,000 |
| Total | $126,000 | $108,000 |

## WELLER COMPANY
### Income Statement
### For the Year Ended December 31, 2008

| | | |
|---|---:|---:|
| Sales | | $242,000 |
| Cost of goods sold | | 175,000 |
| Gross profit | | 67,000 |
| Selling expenses | $18,000 | |
| Administrative expenses | 6,000 | 24,000 |
| Income from operations | | 43,000 |
| Interest expense | | 3,000 |
| Income before income taxes | | 40,000 |
| Income tax expense | | 8,000 |
| Net income | | $ 32,000 |

Additional data:

1. Dividends declared and paid were $25,000.
2. During the year equipment was sold for $8,500 cash. This equipment cost $18,000 originally and had a book value of $8,500 at the time of sale.
3. All depreciation expense, $14,500, is in the selling expense category.
4. All sales and purchases are on account.

**Instructions**

(a) Prepare a statement of cash flows using the indirect method.
(b) Compute free cash flow.

*(a) Cash from operations $33,500*

*Prepare a statement of cash flows—direct method, and compute free cash flow.*

*(SO 4, 6)*

*(a) Cash from operations $33,500*

*Prepare a statement of cash flows—indirect method.*

*(SO 3)*

**\*P14-8A**  Data for Weller Company are presented in P14-7A. Further analysis reveals the following.

1. Accounts payable pertain to merchandise suppliers.
2. All operating expenses except for depreciation were paid in cash.

**Instructions**

(a) Prepare a statement of cash flows for Weller Company using the direct method.
(b) Compute free cash flow.

**P14-9A**  Condensed financial data of Arma Inc. follow.

## ARMA INC.
### Comparative Balance Sheets
### December 31

| Assets | 2008 | 2007 |
|---|---:|---:|
| Cash | $ 90,800 | $ 48,400 |
| Accounts receivable | 92,800 | 33,000 |
| Inventories | 112,500 | 102,850 |
| Prepaid expenses | 28,400 | 26,000 |
| Investments | 138,000 | 114,000 |
| Plant assets | 270,000 | 242,500 |
| Accumulated depreciation | (50,000) | (52,000) |
| Total | $682,500 | $514,750 |

| Liabilities and Stockholders' Equity | 2008 | 2007 |
|---|---:|---:|
| Accounts payable | $112,000 | $ 67,300 |
| Accrued expenses payable | 16,500 | 17,000 |
| Bonds payable | 110,000 | 150,000 |
| Common stock | 220,000 | 175,000 |
| Retained earnings | 224,000 | 105,450 |
| Total | $682,500 | $514,750 |

## ARMA INC.
Income Statement
For the Year Ended December 31, 2008

| | | |
|---|---:|---:|
| Sales | | $392,780 |
| Less: | | |
| Cost of goods sold | $135,460 | |
| Operating expenses, excluding depreciation | 12,410 | |
| Depreciation expense | 46,500 | |
| Income taxes | 27,280 | |
| Interest expense | 4,730 | |
| Loss on sale of plant assets | 7,500 | 233,880 |
| Net income | | $158,900 |

Additional information:

1. New plant assets costing $85,000 were purchased for cash during the year.
2. Old plant assets having an original cost of $57,500 were sold for $1,500 cash.
3. Bonds matured and were paid off at face value for cash.
4. A cash dividend of $40,350 was declared and paid during the year.

**Instructions**
Prepare a statement of cash flows using the indirect method.

*Cash from operations*
*$185,250*

**\*P14-10A**    Data for Arma Inc. are presented in P14-9A. Further analysis reveals that accounts payable pertain to merchandise creditors.

*Prepare a statement of cash flows—direct method.*

**Instructions**
Prepare a statement of cash flows for Arma Inc. using the direct method.

*(SO 6)*
*Cash from operations*
*$185,250*

**P14-11A**    The comparative balance sheets for Ramirez Company as of December 31 are presented below.

*Prepare a statement of cash flows—indirect method.*

*(SO 3)*

## RAMIREZ COMPANY
Comparative Balance Sheets
December 31

| Assets | 2008 | 2007 |
|---|---:|---:|
| Cash | $ 71,000 | $ 45,000 |
| Accounts receivable | 44,000 | 62,000 |
| Inventory | 151,450 | 142,000 |
| Prepaid expenses | 15,280 | 21,000 |
| Land | 105,000 | 130,000 |
| Equipment | 228,000 | 155,000 |
| Accumulated depreciation—equipment | (45,000) | (35,000) |
| Building | 200,000 | 200,000 |
| Accumulated depreciation—building | (60,000) | (40,000) |
| Total | $709,730 | $680,000 |
| | | |
| **Liabilities and Stockholders' Equity** | | |
| Accounts payable | $ 47,730 | $ 40,000 |
| Bonds payable | 260,000 | 300,000 |
| Common stock, $1 par | 200,000 | 160,000 |
| Retained earnings | 202,000 | 180,000 |
| Total | $709,730 | $680,000 |

Additional information:

1. Operating expenses include depreciation expense of $42,000 and charges from prepaid expenses of $5,720.
2. Land was sold for cash at book value.

3. Cash dividends of $15,000 were paid.
4. Net income for 2008 was $37,000.
5. Equipment was purchased for $95,000 cash. In addition, equipment costing $22,000 with a book value of $10,000 was sold for $6,000 cash.
6. Bonds were converted at face value by issuing 40,000 shares of $1 par value common stock.

*Cash from operations*
*$105,000*

**Instructions**
Prepare a statement of cash flows for the year ended December 31, 2008, using the indirect method.

*Prepare a worksheet—indirect method.*

*(SO 5)*

**\*P14-12A**  Condensed financial data of Oprah Company appear below.

### OPRAH COMPANY
Comparative Balance Sheets
December 31

| Assets | 2008 | 2007 |
|---|---|---|
| Cash | $ 92,700 | $ 47,250 |
| Accounts receivable | 90,800 | 57,000 |
| Inventories | 121,900 | 102,650 |
| Investments | 84,500 | 87,000 |
| Plant assets | 250,000 | 205,000 |
| Accumulated depreciation | (49,500) | (40,000) |
| | $590,400 | $458,900 |

| Liabilities and Stockholders' Equity | | |
|---|---|---|
| Accounts payable | $ 57,700 | $ 48,280 |
| Accrued expenses payable | 12,100 | 18,830 |
| Bonds payable | 100,000 | 70,000 |
| Common stock | 250,000 | 200,000 |
| Retained earnings | 170,600 | 121,790 |
| | $590,400 | $458,900 |

### OPRAH COMPANY
Income Statement
For the Year Ended December 31, 2008

| | | |
|---|---|---|
| Sales | | $297,500 |
| Gain on sale of plant assets | | 8,750 |
| | | 306,250 |
| Less: | | |
| Cost of goods sold | $99,460 | |
| Operating expenses (excluding depreciation expense) | 14,670 | |
| Depreciation expense | 49,700 | |
| Income taxes | 7,270 | |
| Interest expense | 2,940 | 174,040 |
| Net income | | $132,210 |

Additional information:

1. New plant assets costing $92,000 were purchased for cash during the year.
2. Investments were sold at cost.
3. Plant assets costing $47,000 were sold for $15,550, resulting in gain of $8,750.
4. A cash dividend of $83,400 was declared and paid during the year.

**Instructions**

*Reconciling items*
*total $610,210*

Prepare a worksheet for the statement of cash flows using the indirect method. Enter the reconciling items directly in the worksheet columns, using letters to cross-reference each entry.

# PROBLEMS: SET B

**P14-1B**    You are provided with the following transactions that took place during a recent fiscal year.

*Distinguish among operating, investing, and financing activities.*

*(SO 2)*

| Transaction | Where Reported on Statement | Cash Inflow, Outflow, or No Effect? |
|---|---|---|
| (a) Recorded depreciation expense on the plant assets. | | |
| (b) Incurred a loss on disposal of plant assets. | | |
| (c) Acquired a building by paying cash. | | |
| (d) Made principal repayments on a mortgage. | | |
| (e) Issued common stock. | | |
| (f) Purchased shares of another company to be held as a long-term equity investment. | | |
| (g) Paid dividends to common stockholders. | | |
| (h) Sold inventory on credit. The company uses a perpetual inventory system. | | |
| (i) Purchased inventory on credit. | | |
| (j) Paid wages to employees. | | |

**Instructions**
Complete the table indicating whether each item (1) should be reported as an operating (O) activity, investing (I) activity, financing (F) activity, or as a noncash (NC) transaction reported in a separate schedule, and (2) represents a cash inflow or cash outflow or has no cash flow effect. Assume use of the indirect approach.

**P14-2B**    The following selected account balances relate to the plant asset accounts of Zambia Inc. at year-end.

*Determine cash flow effects of changes in plant asset accounts.*

*(SO 3)*

|  | 2008 | 2007 |
|---|---|---|
| Accumulated depreciation—buildings | $337,500 | $300,000 |
| Accumulated depreciation—equipment | 144,000 | 96,000 |
| Buildings | 750,000 | 750,000 |
| Depreciation expense | 101,500 | 85,500 |
| Equipment | 300,000 | 240,000 |
| Land | 100,000 | 70,000 |
| Loss on sale of equipment | 3,000 | 0 |

**Additional information:**

1. Zambia purchased $85,000 of equipment and $30,000 of land for cash in 2008.
2. Zambia also sold equipment in 2008.
3. Depreciation expense in 2008 was $37,500 on building and $64,000 on equipment.

**Instructions**
**(a)** Determine the amounts of any cash inflows or outflows related to the plant asset accounts in 2008.
**(b)** Indicate where each of the cash inflows or outflows identified in (a) would be classified on the statement of cash flows.

*(a) Cash proceeds    $6,000*

**P14-3B**    The income statement of Marquette Company is presented on page 688.

Additional information:

1. Accounts receivable decreased $520,000 during the year, and inventory increased $140,000.
2. Prepaid expenses increased $175,000 during the year.
3. Accounts payable to merchandise suppliers increased $50,000 during the year.
4. Accrued expenses payable increased $165,000 during the year.

*Prepare the operating activities section—indirect method.*

*(SO 3)*

## MARQUETTE COMPANY
### Income Statement
For the Year Ended December 31, 2008

| | | |
|---|---:|---:|
| Sales | | $5,400,000 |
| Cost of goods sold | | |
| Beginning inventory | $1,780,000 | |
| Purchases | 3,430,000 | |
| Goods available for sale | 5,210,000 | |
| Ending inventory | 1,920,000 | |
| Total cost of goods sold | | 3,290,000 |
| Gross profit | | 2,110,000 |
| Operating expenses | | |
| Selling expenses | 420,000 | |
| Administrative expense | 525,000 | |
| Depreciation expense | 105,000 | |
| Amortization expense | 20,000 | 1,070,000 |
| Net income | | $1,040,000 |

*Cash from operations*
*$1,585,000*

**Instructions**

Prepare the operating activities section of the statement of cash flows for the year ended December 31, 2008, for Marquette Company, using the indirect method.

*Prepare the operating activities section—direct method.*

*(SO 6)*

*Cash from operations*
*$1,585,000*

**\*P14-4B**  Data for Marquette Company are presented in P14-3B.

**Instructions**

Prepare the operating activities section of the statement of cash flows using the direct method.

*Prepare the operating activities section—indirect method.*

*(SO 3)*

**P14-5B**  The income statement of Shapiro Inc. reported the following condensed information.

## SHAPIRO INC.
### Income Statement
For the Year Ended December 31, 2008

| | |
|---|---:|
| Revenues | $545,000 |
| Operating expenses | 400,000 |
| Income from operations | 145,000 |
| Income tax expense | 47,000 |
| Net income | $ 98,000 |

Shapiro's balance sheet contained these comparative data at December 31.

| | 2008 | 2007 |
|---|---:|---:|
| Accounts receivable | $50,000 | $75,000 |
| Accounts payable | 30,000 | 51,000 |
| Income taxes payable | 10,000 | 4,000 |

Shapiro has no depreciable assets. Accounts payable pertain to operating expenses.

*Cash from operations*
*$108,000*

**Instructions**

Prepare the operating activities section of the statement of cash flows using the indirect method.

*Prepare the operating activities section—direct method.*

*(SO 6)*

*Cash from operations*
*$108,000*

**\*P14-6B**  Data for Shapiro Inc. are presented in P14-5B.

**Instructions**

Prepare the operating activities section of the statement of cash flows using the direct method.

**P14-7B**    Presented below are the financial statements of Molina Company.

*Prepare a statement of cash flows—indirect method, and compute free cash flow.*
(SO 3, 4)

## MOLINA COMPANY
### Comparative Balance Sheets
#### December 31

| Assets | | 2008 | | 2007 |
|---|---|---|---|---|
| Cash | | $ 28,000 | | $ 33,000 |
| Accounts receivable | | 23,000 | | 14,000 |
| Merchandise inventory | | 41,000 | | 25,000 |
| Property, plant, and equipment | $ 70,000 | | $ 78,000 | |
| Less: Accumulated depreciation | (27,000) | 43,000 | (24,000) | 54,000 |
| Total | | $135,000 | | $126,000 |

| Liabilities and Stockholders' Equity | 2008 | 2007 |
|---|---|---|
| Accounts payable | $ 31,000 | $ 43,000 |
| Income taxes payable | 26,000 | 20,000 |
| Bonds payable | 20,000 | 10,000 |
| Common stock | 25,000 | 25,000 |
| Retained earnings | 33,000 | 28,000 |
| Total | $135,000 | $126,000 |

## MOLINA COMPANY
### Income Statement
#### For the Year Ended December 31, 2008

| | | |
|---|---|---|
| Sales | | $286,000 |
| Cost of goods sold | | 194,000 |
| Gross profit | | 92,000 |
| Selling expenses | $28,000 | |
| Administrative expenses | 9,000 | 37,000 |
| Income from operations | | 55,000 |
| Interest expense | | 7,000 |
| Income before income taxes | | 48,000 |
| Income tax expense | | 10,000 |
| Net income | | $ 38,000 |

Additional data:

1. Dividends of $33,000 were declared and paid.
2. During the year equipment was sold for $10,000 cash. This equipment cost $13,000 originally and had a book value of $10,000 at the time of sale.
3. All depreciation expense, $6,000, is in the selling expense category.
4. All sales and purchases are on account.
5. Additional equipment was purchased for $5,000 cash.

**Instructions**
(a) Prepare a statement of cash flows using the indirect method.
(b) Compute free cash flow.

(a) Cash from operations
$13,000

**\*P14-8B**    Data for Molina Company are presented in P14-7B. Further analysis reveals the following.

*Prepare a statement of cash flows—direct method, and compute free cash flow.*
(SO 4, 6)

1. Accounts payable pertains to merchandise creditors.
2. All operating expenses except for depreciation are paid in cash.

**Instructions**
(a) Prepare a statement of cash flows using the direct method.
(b) Compute free cash flow.

(a) Cash from operations
$13,000

*Prepare a statement of cash flows—indirect method.*
(SO 3)

**P14-9B** Condensed financial data of Yaeger Company are shown below.

### YAEGER COMPANY
Comparative Balance Sheets
December 31

| Assets | 2008 | 2007 |
|---|---|---|
| Cash | $ 97,700 | $ 33,400 |
| Accounts receivable | 70,800 | 37,000 |
| Inventories | 121,900 | 102,650 |
| Investments | 89,500 | 107,000 |
| Plant assets | 310,000 | 205,000 |
| Accumulated depreciation | (49,500) | (40,000) |
| Total | $640,400 | $445,050 |

| Liabilities and Stockholders' Equity | | |
|---|---|---|
| Accounts payable | $ 62,700 | $ 48,280 |
| Accrued expenses payable | 15,100 | 18,830 |
| Bonds payable | 140,000 | 70,000 |
| Common stock | 250,000 | 200,000 |
| Retained earnings | 172,600 | 107,940 |
| Total | $640,400 | $445,050 |

### YAEGER COMPANY
Income Statement
For the Year Ended December 31, 2008

| | | |
|---|---|---|
| Sales | | $297,500 |
| Gain on sale of plant assets | | 5,000 |
| | | 302,500 |
| Less: | | |
| Cost of goods sold | $99,460 | |
| Operating expenses, excluding depreciation expense | 14,670 | |
| Depreciation expense | 35,500 | |
| Income taxes | 27,270 | |
| Interest expense | 2,940 | 179,840 |
| Net income | | $122,660 |

Additional information:

1. New plant assets costing $141,000 were purchased for cash during the year.
2. Investments were sold at cost.
3. Plant assets costing $36,000 were sold for $15,000, resulting in a gain of $5,000.
4. A cash dividend of $58,000 was declared and paid during the year.

*Cash from operations $110,800*

**Instructions**
Prepare a statement of cash flows using the indirect method.

*Prepare a statement of cash flows—direct method.*
(SO 6)

**\*P14-10B** Data for Yaeger Company are presented in P14-9B. Further analysis reveals that accounts payable pertain to merchandise creditors.

*Cash from operations $110,800*

**Instructions**
Prepare a statement of cash flows for Yaeger Company using the direct method.

**P14-11B**    Presented below are the comparative balance sheets for Lewis Company at December 31.

*Prepare a statement of cash flows—indirect method.*

(SO 3)

### LEWIS COMPANY
Comparative Balance Sheets
December 31

| Assets | 2008 | 2007 |
|---|---|---|
| Cash | $ 31,000 | $ 57,000 |
| Accounts receivable | 77,000 | 64,000 |
| Inventory | 192,000 | 140,000 |
| Prepaid expenses | 12,140 | 16,540 |
| Land | 100,000 | 150,000 |
| Equipment | 215,000 | 175,000 |
| Accumulated depreciation—equipment | (70,000) | (42,000) |
| Building | 250,000 | 250,000 |
| Accumulated depreciation—building | (70,000) | (50,000) |
| Total | $737,140 | $760,540 |

| Liabilities and Stockholders' Equity | | |
|---|---|---|
| Accounts payable | $ 58,000 | $ 45,000 |
| Bonds payable | 235,000 | 265,000 |
| Common stock, $1 par | 280,000 | 250,000 |
| Retained earnings | 164,140 | 200,540 |
| Total | $737,140 | $760,540 |

Additional information:

1. Operating expenses include depreciation expense $65,000 and charges from prepaid expenses of $4,400.
2. Land was sold for cash at cost.
3. Cash dividends of $69,290 were paid.
4. Net income for 2008 was $32,890.
5. Equipment was purchased for $80,000 cash. In addition, equipment costing $40,000 with a book value of $23,000 was sold for $25,000 cash.
6. Bonds were converted at face value by issuing 30,000 shares of $1 par value common stock.

**Instructions**

Prepare a statement of cash flows for 2008 using the indirect method.

*Cash from operations*
*$48,290*

## PROBLEMS: SET C

Visit the book's website at **www.wiley.com/college/weygandt** and choose the Student Companion site to access Problem Set C.

## CONTINUING COOKIE CHRONICLE

(*Note:* This is a continuation of the Cookie Chronicle from Chapters 1 through 13.)

**CCC14**    Natalie has prepared the balance sheet and income statement of Cookie & Coffee Creations Inc. and would like you to prepare the cash flow statement.

*Go to the book's website,*
**www.wiley.com/college/weygandt**,
*to see the completion of this problem.*

# BROADENING YOUR PERSPECTIVE

## FINANCIAL REPORTING AND ANALYSIS

## Financial Reporting Problem

### PepsiCo, Inc.

**BYP14-1** Refer to the financial statements of PepsiCo, presented in Appendix A, and answer the following questions.

**(a)** What was the amount of net cash provided by operating activities for the year ended December 31, 2005? For the year ended December 25, 2004?

**(b)** What was the amount of increase or decrease in cash and cash equivalents for the year ended December 31, 2005?

**(c)** Which method of computing net cash provided by operating activities does PepsiCo use?

**(d)** From your analysis of the 2005 statement of cash flows, did the change in accounts and notes receivable require or provide cash? Did the change in inventories require or provide cash? Did the change in accounts payable and other current liabilities require or provide cash?

**(e)** What was the net outflow or inflow of cash from investing activities for the year ended December 31, 2005?

**(f)** What was the amount of interest paid in the year ended December 31, 2005? What was the amount of income taxes paid in the year ended December 31, 2005? (See Note 14.)

## Comparative Analysis Problem

### PepsiCo, Inc. vs. The Coca-Cola Company

**BYP14-2** PepsiCo's financial statements are presented in Appendix A. Coca-Cola's financial statements are presented in Appendix B.

**Instructions**

**(a)** Based on the information contained in these financial statements, compute free cash flow for each company.

**(b)** What conclusions concerning the management of cash can be drawn from these data?

## Exploring the Web

**BYP14-3** Purpose: Learn about the SEC.

**Address: www.sec.gov/index.html**, or go to **www.wiley.com/college/weygandt**

From the SEC homepage, choose **About the SEC**.

**Instructions**

Answer the following questions.

**(a)** How many enforcement actions does the SEC take each year against securities law violators? What are typical infractions?

**(b)** After the Depression, Congress passed the Securities Acts of 1933 and 1934 to improve investor confidence in the markets. What two "common sense" notions are these laws based on?

**(c)** Who was the President of the United States at the time of the creation of the SEC? Who was the first SEC Chairperson?

**BYP14-4** Purpose: Use the Internet to view SEC filings.

**Address: biz.yahoo.com/i**, or go to **www.wiley.com/college/weygandt**

**Steps**

1. Type in a company name.
2. Choose **Profile**.
3. Choose **SEC**. (This will take you to Yahoo-Edgar Online.)

**Instructions**

Answer the following questions.

**(a)** What company did you select?

**(b)** Which filing is the most recent? What is the date?

**(c)** What other recent SEC filings are available for your viewing?

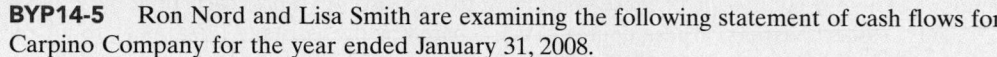

## Decision Making Across the Organization

**BYP14-5** Ron Nord and Lisa Smith are examining the following statement of cash flows for Carpino Company for the year ended January 31, 2008.

### CARPINO COMPANY
Statement of Cash Flows
For the Year Ended January 31, 2008

| | |
|---|---:|
| Sources of cash | |
| From sales of merchandise | $380,000 |
| From sale of capital stock | 420,000 |
| From sale of investment (purchased below) | 80,000 |
| From depreciation | 55,000 |
| From issuance of note for truck | 20,000 |
| From interest on investments | 6,000 |
| Total sources of cash | 961,000 |
| Uses of cash | |
| For purchase of fixtures and equipment | 330,000 |
| For merchandise purchased for resale | 258,000 |
| For operating expenses (including depreciation) | 160,000 |
| For purchase of investment | 75,000 |
| For purchase of truck by issuance of note | 20,000 |
| For purchase of treasury stock | 10,000 |
| For interest on note payable | 3,000 |
| Total uses of cash | 856,000 |
| Net increase in cash | $ 105,000 |

Ron claims that Carpino's statement of cash flows is an excellent portrayal of a superb first year with cash increasing $105,000. Lisa replies that it was not a superb first year. Rather, she says, the year was an operating failure, that the statement is presented incorrectly, and that $105,000 is not the actual increase in cash. The cash balance at the beginning of the year was $140,000.

**Instructions**

With the class divided into groups, answer the following.

**(a)** Using the data provided, prepare a statement of cash flows in proper form using the indirect method. The only noncash items in the income statement are depreciation and the gain from the sale of the investment.

**(b)** With whom do you agree, Ron or Lisa? Explain your position.

## Communication Activity

**BYP14-6** Kyle Benson, the owner-president of Computer Services Company, is unfamiliar with the statement of cash flows that you, as his accountant, prepared. He asks for further explanation.

**Instructions**

Write him a brief memo explaining the form and content of the statement of cash flows as shown in Illustration 14-13 (page 652).

## Ethics Case

**BYP14-7**  Tappit Corp. is a medium-sized wholesaler of automotive parts. It has 10 stockholders who have been paid a total of $1 million in cash dividends for 8 consecutive years. The board's policy requires that, for this dividend to be declared, net cash provided by operating activities as reported in Tappit's current year's statement of cash flows must exceed $1 million. President and CEO Willie Morton's job is secure so long as he produces annual operating cash flows to support the usual dividend.

At the end of the current year, controller Robert Jennings presents president Willie Morton with some disappointing news: The net cash provided by operating activities is calculated by the indirect method to be only $970,000. The president says to Robert, "We must get that amount above $1 million. Isn't there some way to increase operating cash flow by another $30,000?" Robert answers, "These figures were prepared by my assistant. I'll go back to my office and see what I can do." The president replies, "I know you won't let me down, Robert."

Upon close scrutiny of the statement of cash flows, Robert concludes that he can get the operating cash flows above $1 million by reclassifying a $60,000, 2-year note payable listed in the financing activities section as "Proceeds from bank loan—$60,000." He will report the note instead as "Increase in payables—$60,000" and treat it as an adjustment of net income in the operating activities section. He returns to the president, saying, "You can tell the board to declare their usual dividend. Our net cash flow provided by operating activities is $1,030,000." "Good man, Robert! I knew I could count on you," exults the president.

### Instructions

**(a)** Who are the stakeholders in this situation?

**(b)** Was there anything unethical about the president's actions? Was there anything unethical about the controller's actions?

**(c)** Are the board members or anyone else likely to discover the misclassification?

## "All About You" Activity

**BYP14-8**   In this chapter you learned that companies prepare a statement of cash flows in order to keep track of their sources and uses of cash and to help them plan for their future cash needs. Planning for your own short- and long-term cash needs is every bit as important as it is for a company.

### Instructions

Read the article provided at **www.fool.com/savings/shortterm/02.htm**, and answer the following questions.

**(a)** Describe the three factors that determine how much money you should set aside for short-term needs.

**(b)** How many months of living expenses does the article suggest to set aside?

**(c)** Estimate how much you should set aside based upon your current situation. Are you closer to Cliff's scenario or to Prudence's?

## Answers to Insight and Accounting Across the Organization Questions

**Net *What?*, p. 641**

Q:  In general, why do differences exist between net income and net cash provided by operating activities?

A:  *The differences are explained by differences in the timing of the reporting of revenues and expenses under accrual accounting versus cash. Under accrual accounting, companies report revenues when earned, even if cash hasn't been received, and they report expenses when incurred, even if cash hasn't been paid.*

**Cash Flow Isn't Always What It Seems, p. 644**

Q:  For what reasons might managers at WorldCom and at Dynegy take the actions noted above?

A:  *Analysts increasingly use cash-flow-based measures of income, such as cash flow provided by operations, in addition to net income. More investors now focus on cash flow from operations, and some compensation contracts now have bonuses tied to cash-flow numbers. Thus, some managers have taken actions that artificially increase cash flow from operations.*

**GM Must Sell More Cars, p. 650**

Q: Why does GM's cash provided by operating activities drop so precipitously when the company's sales figures decline?

A: *GM's cash inflow is directly related to how many cars it sells. But many of its cash outflows are not tied to sales—they are "fixed." For example, many of its employee payroll costs are very rigid due to labor contracts. Therefore, even though sales (and therefore cash inflows) fall, these cash outflows don't decline.*

## Authors' Comments on *All About You*: Where Does the Money Go?, p. 656

There are really two issues to consider here. The first centers on the problems associated with accumulating debt to support discretionary expenditures. If you think that you will simply pay off your debts when you graduate, consider the fact that it is not unusual for people to spend 10 years to pay off the debts they accumulated during college.

A second issue relates to the impact that working so many hours can have on your academic performance. Research shows that college students today spend more hours working at jobs and fewer hours studying than at any time in the past. This same research shows that academic performance declines when students work too many hours at their jobs. If you could cut back on your discretionary expenditures, you could quit working so many hours, which would mean that you would do better in school, which would mean that you would have a better shot at a good job after college.

The bottom line: While we think that borrowing to invest in yourself through your education makes good sense, we think that borrowing to support a Starbucks habit is a bad idea. For more ideas on how to get your cash flow under control, see *http://financialplan.about.com/cs/college/a/MoneyCollege.htm.*

## Answer to PepsiCo Review It Question 5, p. 642

In its 2005 statement of cash flows, PepsiCo reported:

**(1)** net cash provided by operating activities of $5.852 billion;
**(2)** net cash used for investing activities of $3.517 million; and
**(3)** net cash used for financing activities of $1.878 billion.

## Answers to Self-Study Questions

1. c   2. b   3. a   4. c   5. d   6. b   7. c   8. d   9. b   10. a   11. d   *12. b   *13. c   *14. d

# Chapter 15

# Financial Statement Analysis

The Navigator

# Feature Story

**"FOLLOW THAT STOCK!"**

If you thought cab drivers with cell phones were scary, how about a cab driver with a trading desk in the front seat?

When a stoplight turns red or traffic backs up, New York City cabby Carlos Rubino morphs into a day trader, scanning real-time quotes of his favorite stocks as they spew across a PalmPilot mounted next to the steering wheel. "It's kind of stressful," he says, "but I like it."

Itching to know how a particular stock is doing? Mr. Rubino is happy to look up quotes for passengers. Yahoo! and Amazon.com are two of the most requested ones. He even lets customers use his laptop computer to send urgent e-mails from the back seat. Aware of a local law prohibiting cabbies from using cell phones while they're driving, Mr. Rubino extends that rule to his trading. "I stop the cab at the side of the road if I have to make a trade," he says. "Safety first."

Originally from São Paulo, Brazil, Mr. Rubino has been driving his cab since 1987, and started trading stocks a few years ago. His curiosity grew as he began to educate himself by reading business publications. The Wall Street brokers he picks up are usually impressed with his knowledge, he says. But the feeling generally isn't mutual. Some of them "don't know much," he says. "They buy what people tell them to buy—they're like a toll collector."

Mr. Rubino is an enigma to his fellow cab drivers. A lot of his colleagues say they want to trade too. "But cab drivers are a little cheap," he says. "The [real-time] quotes cost $100 a month. The wireless Internet access is $54 a month."

Will he give up his brokerage firm on wheels for a stationary job? Not likely. Though he claims a 70% return on his investments in some months, he says he makes $1,300 and up a week driving his cab—more than he does trading. Besides, he adds, "Why go somewhere and have a boss?"

*Source:* Excerpted from Barbara Boydston, "With This Cab, People Jump in and Shout, 'Follow that Stock!'," *Wall Street Journal*, August 18, 1999, p. C1. Reprinted by permission of the Wall Street Journal © 1999 Dow Jones & Company, Inc. All Rights Reserved Worldwide.

✔ The Navigator

## Inside Chapter 15

We can learn an important lesson from the Feature Story: Experience is the best teacher. By now you have learned a significant amount about financial reporting by U.S. companies. Using some of the basic decision tools presented in this book, you can perform a rudimentary analysis on any U.S. company and draw basic conclusions about its financial health. Although it would not be wise for you to bet your life savings on a company's stock relying solely on your current level of knowledge, we strongly encourage you to practice your new skills wherever possible. Only with practice will you improve your ability to interpret financial numbers.

Before unleashing you on the world of high finance, we will present a few more important concepts and techniques, as well as provide you with one more comprehensive review of corporate financial statements. We use all of the decision tools presented in this text to analyze a single company—J.C. Penney Company, one of the country's oldest and largest retail store chains.

The content and organization of Chapter 15 are as follows.

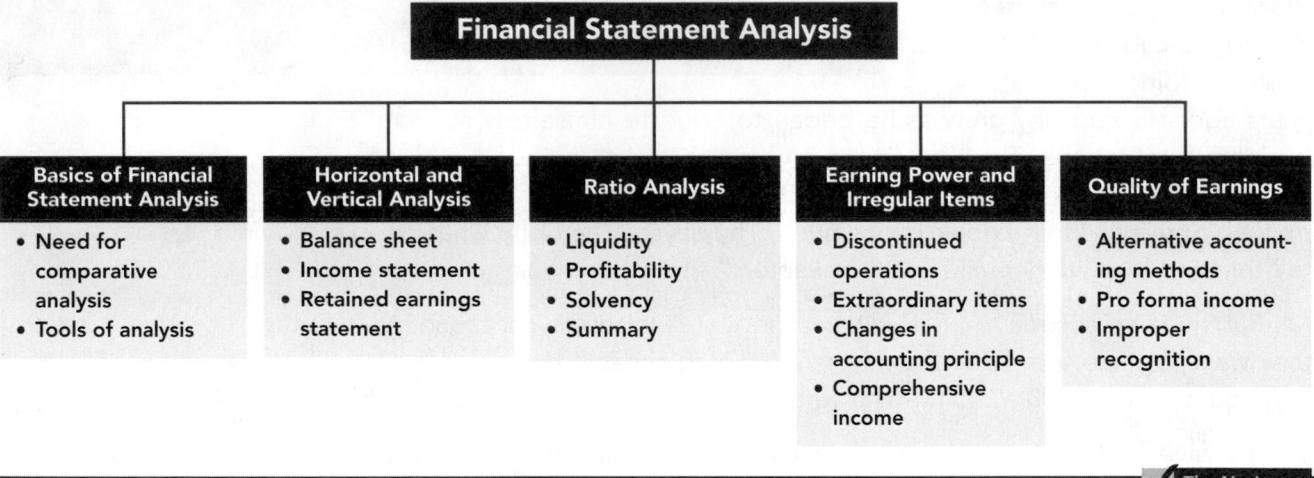

**Financial Statement Analysis**

| Basics of Financial Statement Analysis | Horizontal and Vertical Analysis | Ratio Analysis | Earning Power and Irregular Items | Quality of Earnings |
|---|---|---|---|---|
| • Need for comparative analysis <br> • Tools of analysis | • Balance sheet <br> • Income statement <br> • Retained earnings statement | • Liquidity <br> • Profitability <br> • Solvency <br> • Summary | • Discontinued operations <br> • Extraordinary items <br> • Changes in accounting principle <br> • Comprehensive income | • Alternative accounting methods <br> • Pro forma income <br> • Improper recognition |

✓ *The Navigator*

# BASICS OF FINANCIAL STATEMENT ANALYSIS

Analyzing financial statements involves evaluating three characteristics: a company's liquidity, profitability, and solvency. A **short-term creditor**, such as a bank, is primarily interested in liquidity—the ability of the borrower to pay obligations when they come due. The liquidity of the borrower is extremely important in evaluating the safety of a loan. A **long-term creditor**, such as a bondholder, looks to profitability and solvency measures that indicate the company's ability to survive over a long period of time. Long-term creditors consider such measures as the amount of debt in the company's capital structure and its ability to meet interest payments. Similarly, **stockholders** look at the profitability and solvency of the company. They want to assess the likelihood of dividends and the growth potential of the stock.

## Need for Comparative Analysis

**STUDY OBJECTIVE 1**

Discuss the need for comparative analysis.

Every item reported in a financial statement has significance. When J.C. Penney Company, Inc. reports cash of $3,016 million on its balance sheet, we know the company had that amount of cash on the balance sheet date. But, we do not know whether the amount represents an increase over prior years, or whether it is adequate in relation to the company's need for cash. To obtain such information, we need to compare the amount of cash with other financial statement data.

Comparisons can be made on a number of different bases. Three are illustrated in this chapter:

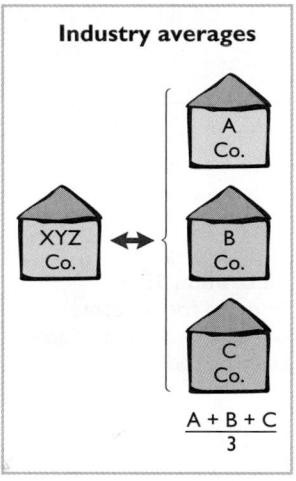

1. **Intracompany basis.** This basis compares an item or financial relationship **within a company** in the current year with the same item or relationship in one or more prior years. For example, J.C. Penney can compare its cash balance at the end of the current year with last year's balance to find the amount of the increase or decrease. Likewise, J.C. Penney can compare the percentage of cash to current assets at the end of the current year with the percentage in one or more prior years. Intracompany comparisons are useful in detecting changes in financial relationships and significant trends.

2. **Industry averages.** This basis compares an item or financial relationship of a company with **industry averages** (or **norms**) published by financial ratings organizations such as Dun & Bradstreet, Moody's, and Standard & Poor's. For example, J.C. Penney's net income can be compared with the average net income of all companies in the retail chain-store industry. Comparisons with industry averages provide information as to a company's relative performance within the industry.

3. **Intercompany basis.** This basis compares an item or financial relationship of one company with the same item or relationship in **one or more competing companies**. Analysts make these comparisons on the basis of the published financial statements of the individual companies. For example, we can compare J.C. Penney's total sales for the year with the total sales of a major competitor such as Kmart. Intercompany comparisons are useful in determining a company's competitive position.

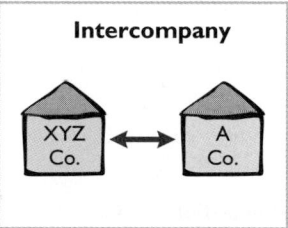

## Tools of Analysis

We use various tools to evaluate the significance of financial statement data. Three commonly used tools are these:

- **Horizontal analysis** evaluates a series of financial statement data over a period of time.
- **Vertical analysis** evaluates financial statement data by expressing each item in a financial statement as a percent of a base amount.
- **Ratio analysis** expresses the relationship among selected items of financial statement data.

*Horizontal analysis* is used primarily in intracompany comparisons. Two features in published financial statements facilitate this type of comparison: First, each of the basic financial statements presents comparative financial data for a minimum of two years. Second, a summary of selected financial data is presented for a series of five to ten years or more. *Vertical analysis* is used in both intra- and intercompany comparisons. *Ratio analysis* is used in all three types of comparisons. In the following sections, we explain and illustrate each of the three types of analysis.

# HORIZONTAL ANALYSIS

**Horizontal analysis**, also called **trend analysis**, is a technique for evaluating a series of financial statement data over a period of time. Its purpose is to determine the increase or decrease that has taken place. This change may be expressed as either an amount or a percentage. For example, the recent net sales figures of J.C. Penney Company are as follows.

**Illustration 15-1**
J.C. Penney Company's net sales

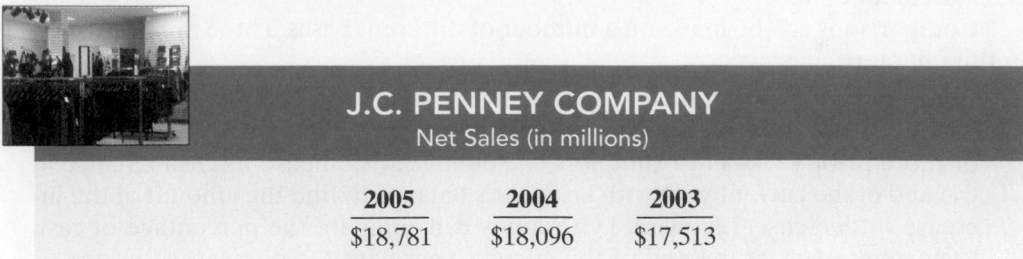

## J.C. PENNEY COMPANY
### Net Sales (in millions)

| 2005 | 2004 | 2003 |
|------|------|------|
| $18,781 | $18,096 | $17,513 |

If we assume that 2003 is the base year, we can measure all percentage increases or decreases from this base period amount as follows.

**Illustration 15-2**
Formula for horizontal analysis of changes since base period

$$\text{Change Since Base Period} = \frac{\text{Current Year Amount} - \text{Base Year Amount}}{\text{Base Year Amount}}$$

For example, we can determine that net sales for J.C. Penney increased from 2003 to 2004 approximately 3.3% [($18,096 − $17,513) ÷ $17,513]. Similarly, we can determine that net sales increased from 2003 to 2005 approximately 7.2% [($18,781 − $17,513) ÷ $17,513].

Alternatively, we can express current year sales as a percentage of the base period. We do this by dividing the current year amount by the base year amount, as shown below.

**Illustration 15-3**
Formula for horizontal analysis of current year in relation to base year

$$\text{Current Results in Relation to Base Period} = \frac{\text{Current Year Amount}}{\text{Base Year Amount}}$$

Illustration 15-4 presents this analysis for J.C. Penney for a three-year period using 2003 as the base period.

**Illustration 15-4**
Horizontal analysis of J.C. Penney Company's net sales in relation to base period

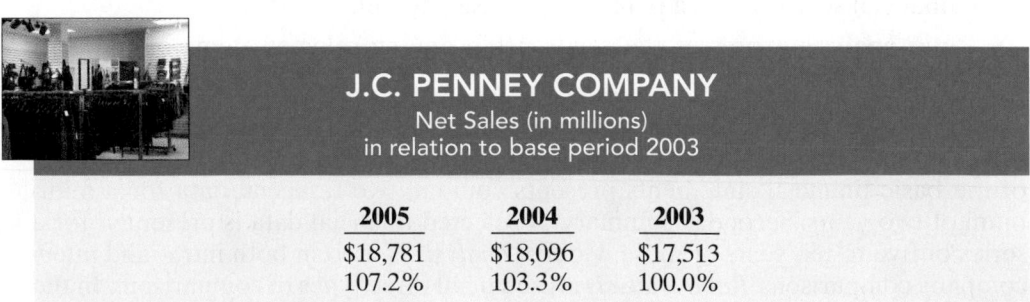

## J.C. PENNEY COMPANY
### Net Sales (in millions)
### in relation to base period 2003

| 2005 | 2004 | 2003 |
|------|------|------|
| $18,781 | $18,096 | $17,513 |
| 107.2% | 103.3% | 100.0% |

## Balance Sheet

To further illustrate horizontal analysis, we will use the financial statements of Quality Department Store Inc., a fictional retailer. Illustration 15-5 presents a horizontal analysis of its two-year condensed balance sheets, showing dollar and percentage changes.

**Illustration 15-5**
Horizontal analysis of
balance sheets

## QUALITY DEPARTMENT STORE INC.
### Condensed Balance Sheets
### December 31

| | 2005 | 2004 | Increase or (Decrease) during 2005 Amount | Increase or (Decrease) during 2005 Percent |
|---|---|---|---|---|
| **Assets** | | | | |
| Current assets | $1,020,000 | $ 945,000 | $ 75,000 | 7.9% |
| Plant assets (net) | 800,000 | 632,500 | 167,500 | 26.5% |
| Intangible assets | 15,000 | 17,500 | (2,500) | (14.3%) |
| Total assets | $1,835,000 | $1,595,000 | $240,000 | 15.0% |
| **Liabilities** | | | | |
| Current liabilities | $ 344,500 | $ 303,000 | $ 41,500 | 13.7% |
| Long-term liabilities | 487,500 | 497,000 | (9,500) | (1.9%) |
| Total liabilities | 832,000 | 800,000 | 32,000 | 4.0% |
| **Stockholders' Equity** | | | | |
| Common stock, $1 par | 275,400 | 270,000 | 5,400 | 2.0% |
| Retained earnings | 727,600 | 525,000 | 202,600 | 38.6% |
| Total stockholders' equity | 1,003,000 | 795,000 | 208,000 | 26.2% |
| Total liabilities and stockholders' equity | $1,835,000 | $1,595,000 | $240,000 | 15.0% |

The comparative balance sheets in Illustration 15-5 show that a number of significant changes have occurred in Quality Department Store's financial structure from 2004 to 2005:

- In the assets section, plant assets (net) increased $167,500, or 26.5%.
- In the liabilities section, current liabilities increased $41,500, or 13.7%.
- In the stockholders' equity section, retained earnings increased $202,600, or 38.6%.

These changes suggest that the company expanded its asset base during 2005 and **financed this expansion primarily by retaining income** rather than assuming additional long-term debt.

## Income Statement

Illustration 15-6 (page 702) presents a horizontal analysis of the two-year condensed income statements of Quality Department Store Inc. for the years 2005 and 2004. Horizontal analysis of the income statements shows the following changes:

- Net sales increased $260,000, or 14.2% ($260,000 ÷ $1,837,000).
- Cost of goods sold increased $141,000, or 12.4% ($141,000 ÷ $1,140,000).
- Total operating expenses increased $37,000, or 11.6% ($37,000 ÷ $320,000).

Overall, gross profit and net income were up substantially. Gross profit increased 17.1%, and net income, 26.5%. Quality's profit trend appears favorable.

**Illustration 15-6**
Horizontal analysis of
income statements

## QUALITY DEPARTMENT STORE INC.
### Condensed Income Statements
### For the Years Ended December 31

| | | | Increase or (Decrease) during 2005 | |
|---|---|---|---|---|
| | **2005** | **2004** | **Amount** | **Percent** |
| Sales | $2,195,000 | $1,960,000 | $235,000 | 12.0% |
| Sales returns and allowances | 98,000 | 123,000 | (25,000) | (20.3%) |
| Net sales | 2,097,000 | 1,837,000 | 260,000 | 14.2% |
| Cost of goods sold | 1,281,000 | 1,140,000 | 141,000 | 12.4% |
| Gross profit | 816,000 | 697,000 | 119,000 | 17.1% |
| Selling expenses | 253,000 | 211,500 | 41,500 | 19.6% |
| Administrative expenses | 104,000 | 108,500 | (4,500) | (4.1%) |
| Total operating expenses | 357,000 | 320,000 | 37,000 | 11.6% |
| Income from operations | 459,000 | 377,000 | 82,000 | 21.8% |
| Other revenues and gains | | | | |
| Interest and dividends | 9,000 | 11,000 | (2,000) | (18.2%) |
| Other expenses and losses | | | | |
| Interest expense | 36,000 | 40,500 | (4,500) | (11.1%) |
| Income before income taxes | 432,000 | 347,500 | 84,500 | 24.3% |
| Income tax expense | 168,200 | 139,000 | 29,200 | 21.0% |
| Net income | $ 263,800 | $ 208,500 | $ 55,300 | 26.5% |

**HELPFUL HINT**

Note that though the amount column is additive (the total is $55,300), the percentage column is not additive (26.5% is not the total). A separate percentage has been calculated for each item.

## Retained Earnings Statement

Illustration 15-7 presents a horizontal analysis of Quality Department Store's comparative retained earnings statements. Analyzed horizontally, net income increased $55,300, or 26.5%, whereas dividends on the common stock increased only $1,200, or 2%. We saw in the horizontal analysis of the balance sheet that ending retained earnings increased 38.6%. As indicated earlier, the company retained a significant portion of net income to finance additional plant facilities.

**Illustration 15-7**
Horizontal analysis of
retained earnings statements

## QUALITY DEPARTMENT STORE INC.
### Retained Earnings Statements
### For the Years Ended December 31

| | | | Increase or (Decrease) during 2005 | |
|---|---|---|---|---|
| | **2005** | **2004** | **Amount** | **Percent** |
| Retained earnings, Jan. 1 | $525,000 | $376,500 | $148,500 | 39.4% |
| Add: Net income | 263,800 | 208,500 | 55,300 | 26.5% |
| | 788,800 | 585,000 | 203,800 | |
| Deduct: Dividends | 61,200 | 60,000 | 1,200 | 2.0% |
| Retained earnings, Dec. 31 | $727,600 | $525,000 | $202,600 | 38.6% |

Horizontal analysis of changes from period to period is relatively straightforward and is quite useful. But complications can occur in making the computations. If an item has no value in a base year or preceding year but does have a value in the next year, we cannot compute a percentage change. Similarly, if a negative amount appears in the base or preceding period and a positive amount exists the following year (or vice versa), no percentage change can be computed.

# VERTICAL ANALYSIS

**Vertical analysis**, also called **common-size analysis**, is a technique that expresses each financial statement item as a percent of a base amount. On a balance sheet we might say that current assets are 22% of total assets—*total assets* being the base amount. Or on an income statement, we might say that selling expenses are 16% of net sales—*net sales* being the base amount.

## Balance Sheet

Illustration 15-8 presents the vertical analysis of Quality Department Store Inc.'s comparative balance sheets. The base for the asset items is **total assets**. The base for the liability and stockholders' equity items is **total liabilities and stockholders' equity**.

**Illustration 15-8**
Vertical analysis of balance sheets

### QUALITY DEPARTMENT STORE INC.
Condensed Balance Sheets
December 31

|  | 2005 Amount | 2005 Percent | 2004 Amount | 2004 Percent |
|---|---|---|---|---|
| **Assets** | | | | |
| Current assets | $1,020,000 | 55.6% | $ 945,000 | 59.2% |
| Plant assets (net) | 800,000 | 43.6% | 632,500 | 39.7% |
| Intangible assets | 15,000 | 0.8% | 17,500 | 1.1% |
| Total assets | $1,835,000 | 100.0% | $1,595,000 | 100.0% |
| **Liabilities** | | | | |
| Current liabilities | $ 344,500 | 18.8% | $ 303,000 | 19.0% |
| Long-term liabilities | 487,500 | 26.5% | 497,000 | 31.2% |
| Total liabilities | 832,000 | 45.3% | 800,000 | 50.2% |
| **Stockholders' Equity** | | | | |
| Common stock, $1 par | 275,400 | 15.0% | 270,000 | 16.9% |
| Retained earnings | 727,600 | 39.7% | 525,000 | 32.9% |
| Total stockholders' equity | 1,003,000 | 54.7% | 795,000 | 49.8% |
| Total liabilities and stockholders' equity | $1,835,000 | 100.0% | $1,595,000 | 100.0% |

**HELPFUL HINT**

The formula for calculating these balance sheet percentages is:

$$\frac{\text{Each item on B/S}}{\text{Total assets}} = \%$$

Vertical analysis shows the relative size of each category in the balance sheet. It also can show the **percentage change** in the individual asset, liability, and stockholders' equity items. For example, we can see that current assets decreased from 59.2% of total assets in 2004 to 55.6% in 2005 (even though the absolute dollar amount increased $75,000 in that time). Plant assets (net) have increased from 39.7% to 43.6% of total assets. Retained earnings have increased from 32.9% to 39.7% of total liabilities and stockholders' equity. These results reinforce the earlier observations that **Quality is choosing to finance its growth through retention of earnings rather than through issuing additional debt**.

## Income Statement

Illustration 15-9 (page 704) shows vertical analysis of Quality's income statements. Cost of goods sold as a percentage of net sales declined 1% (62.1% vs. 61.1%), and total operating expenses declined 0.4% (17.4% vs. 17.0%). As a result, it is not surprising to see net income as a percent of net sales increase from 11.4% to 12.6%. Quality appears to be a profitable enterprise that is becoming even more successful.

**Illustration 15-9**
Vertical analysis of income statements

### QUALITY DEPARTMENT STORE INC.
#### Condensed Income Statements
#### For the Years Ended December 31

| | 2005 Amount | 2005 Percent | 2004 Amount | 2004 Percent |
|---|---|---|---|---|
| Sales | $2,195,000 | 104.7% | $1,960,000 | 106.7% |
| Sales returns and allowances | 98,000 | 4.7% | 123,000 | 6.7% |
| Net sales | 2,097,000 | 100.0% | 1,837,000 | 100.0% |
| Cost of goods sold | 1,281,000 | 61.1% | 1,140,000 | 62.1% |
| Gross profit | 816,000 | 38.9% | 697,000 | 37.9% |
| Selling expenses | 253,000 | 12.0% | 211,500 | 11.5% |
| Administrative expenses | 104,000 | 5.0% | 108,500 | 5.9% |
| Total operating expenses | 357,000 | 17.0% | 320,000 | 17.4% |
| Income from operations | 459,000 | 21.9% | 377,000 | 20.5% |
| Other revenues and gains | | | | |
| Interest and dividends | 9,000 | 0.4% | 11,000 | 0.6% |
| Other expenses and losses | | | | |
| Interest expense | 36,000 | 1.7% | 40,500 | 2.2% |
| Income before income taxes | 432,000 | 20.6% | 347,500 | 18.9% |
| Income tax expense | 168,200 | 8.0% | 139,000 | 7.5% |
| Net income | $ 263,800 | 12.6% | $ 208,500 | 11.4% |

**HELPFUL HINT**
The formula for calculating these income statement percentages is:

$$\frac{\text{Each item on I/S}}{\text{Net sales}} = \%$$

An associated benefit of vertical analysis is that it enables you to compare companies of different sizes. For example, Quality's main competitor is a JC Penney store in a nearby town. Using vertical analysis, we can compare the condensed income statements of Quality Department Store Inc. (a small retail company) with J.C. Penney Company, Inc. (a giant international retailer), as shown in Illustration 15-10.

**Illustration 15-10**
Intercompany income statement comparison

### CONDENSED INCOME STATEMENTS
#### (in thousands)

| | Quality Department Store Inc. Dollars | Quality Department Store Inc. Percent | J. C. Penney Company[1] Dollars | J. C. Penney Company[1] Percent |
|---|---|---|---|---|
| Net sales | $2,097 | 100.0% | $18,781,000 | 100.0% |
| Cost of goods sold | 1,281 | 61.1% | 11,405,000 | 60.7% |
| Gross profit | 816 | 38.9% | 7,376,000 | 39.3% |
| Selling and administrative expenses | 357 | 17.0% | 5,799,000 | 30.9% |
| Income from operations | 459 | 21.9% | 1,577,000 | 8.4% |
| Other expenses and revenues | | | | |
| (including income taxes) | 195 | 9.3% | 489,000 | 2.6% |
| Net income | $ 264 | 12.6% | $ 1,088,000 | 5.8% |

[1]*2005 Annual Report* J.C. Penney Company, Inc. (Dallas, Texas).

J.C. Penney's net sales are 8,956 times greater than the net sales of relatively tiny Quality Department Store. But vertical analysis eliminates this difference in size. The percentages show that Quality's and J.C. Penney's gross profit rates were comparable at 38.9% and 39.3%. However, the percentages related to income from operations were significantly different at 21.9% and 8.4%. This disparity can be attributed to Quality's selling and administrative expense percentage (17%) which is much lower than J.C. Penney's (30.9%). Although J.C. Penney earned net income more than 4,121 times larger than Quality's, J.C. Penney's net income as a **percent of each sales dollar** (5.8%) is only 46% of Quality's (12.6%).

## *Before You Go On...*

### REVIEW IT

1. What are the different tools that might be used to compare financial information?
2. What is horizontal analysis?
3. What is vertical analysis?
4. Identify the specific sections in PepsiCo's 2005 annual report where horizontal and vertical analysis of financial data is presented. The answer to this question is provided on page 747.

### DO IT

Summary financial information for Rosepatch Company is as follows.

|  | December 31, 2008 | December 31, 2007 |
|---|---|---|
| Current assets | $234,000 | $180,000 |
| Plant assets (net) | 756,000 | 420,000 |
| Total assets | $990,000 | $600,000 |

Compute the amount and percentage changes in 2008 using horizontal analysis, assuming 2007 is the base year.

### Action Plan

■ Find the percentage change by dividing the amount of the increase by the 2007 amount (base year).

### Solution

| | Increase in 2008 | |
|---|---|---|
| | **Amount** | **Percent** |
| Current assets | $ 54,000 | 30% [($234,000 − $180,000) ÷ $180,000] |
| Plant assets (net) | 336,000 | 80% [($756,000 − $420,000) ÷ $420,000] |
| Total assets | $390,000 | 65% [($990,000 − $600,000) ÷ $600,000] |

Related exercise material: *BE15-2, BE15-3, BE15-5, BE15-6, BE15-7, E15-1, E15-3, and E15-4.*

 *The Navigator*

# ▍RATIO ANALYSIS

**Ratio analysis** expresses the relationship among selected items of financial statement data. A **ratio** expresses the mathematical relationship between one quantity and another. The relationship is expressed in terms of either a percentage, a rate, or a simple proportion. To illustrate, in 2005 Nike, Inc., had current assets of $6,351.1

million and current liabilities of $1,999.2 million. We can find the relationship between these two measures by dividing current assets by current liabilities. The alternative means of expression are:

| | |
|---|---|
| **Percentage:** | Current assets are 318% of current liabilities. |
| **Rate:** | Current assets are 3.18 times current liabilities. |
| **Proportion:** | The relationship of current assets to liabilities is 3.18:1. |

To analyze the primary financial statements, we can use ratios to evaluate liquidity, profitability, and solvency. Illustration 15-11 describes these classifications.

**Illustration 15-11**
Financial ratio classifications

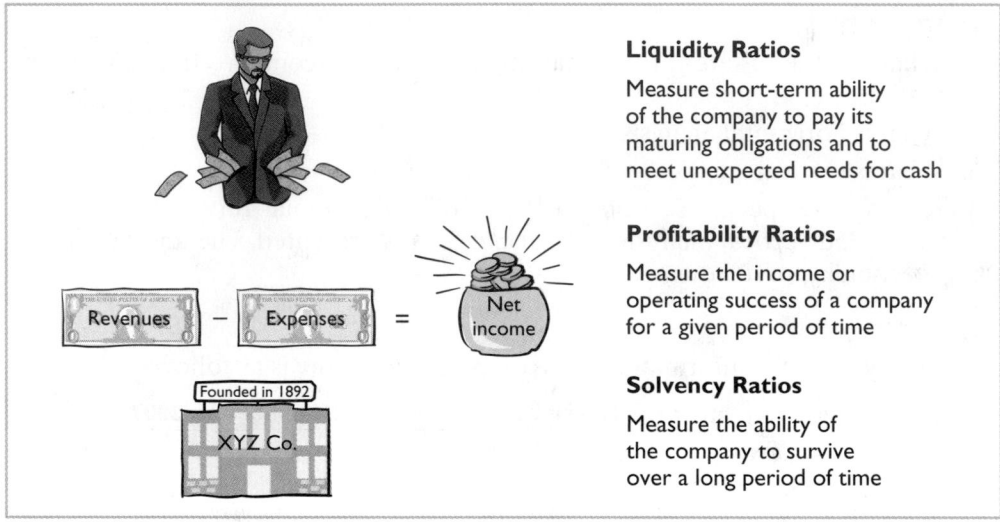

**Liquidity Ratios**

Measure short-term ability of the company to pay its maturing obligations and to meet unexpected needs for cash

**Profitability Ratios**

Measure the income or operating success of a company for a given period of time

**Solvency Ratios**

Measure the ability of the company to survive over a long period of time

Ratios can provide clues to underlying conditions that may not be apparent from individual financial statement components. However, a single ratio by itself is not very meaningful. Thus, in the discussion of ratios we will use the following types of comparisons.

1. **Intracompany comparisons** for two years for Quality Department Store.
2. **Industry average comparisons** based on median ratios for department stores.
3. **Intercompany comparisons** based on J.C. Penney Company as Quality Department Store's principal competitor.

## Liquidity Ratios

**Liquidity ratios** measure the short-term ability of the company to pay its maturing obligations and to meet unexpected needs for cash. Short-term creditors such as bankers and suppliers are particularly interested in assessing liquidity. The ratios we can use to determine the enterprise's short-term debt-paying ability are the current ratio, the acid-test ratio, receivables turnover, and inventory turnover.

### 1. CURRENT RATIO

The **current ratio** is a widely used measure for evaluating a company's liquidity and short-term debt-paying ability. The ratio is computed by dividing current assets by current liabilities. Illustration 15-12 shows the 2005 and 2004 current ratios for Quality Department Store and comparative data.

Illustration 15-12
Current ratio

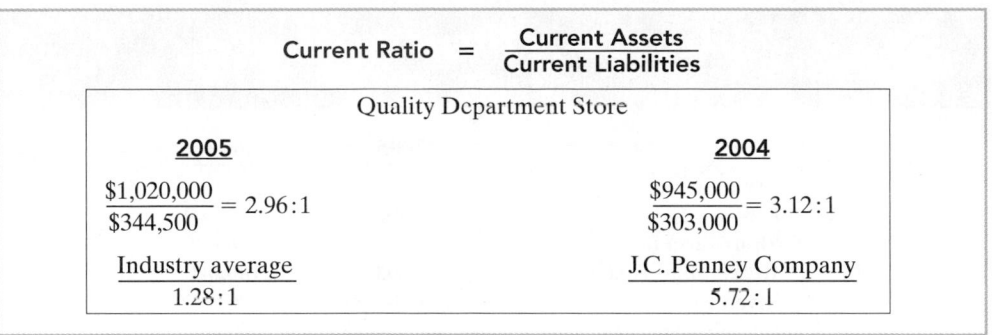

$$\text{Current Ratio} = \frac{\text{Current Assets}}{\text{Current Liabilities}}$$

Quality Department Store

| 2005 | 2004 |
|------|------|
| $\dfrac{\$1,020,000}{\$344,500} = 2.96:1$ | $\dfrac{\$945,000}{\$303,000} = 3.12:1$ |
| Industry average | J.C. Penney Company |
| 1.28:1 | 5.72:1 |

**HELPFUL HINT**

Can any company operate successfully without working capital? Yes, if it has very predictable cash flows and solid earnings. A number of companies (e.g., Whirlpool, American Standard, and Campbell's Soup) are pursuing this goal. The rationale: Less money tied up in working capital means more money to invest in the business.

What does the ratio actually mean? The 2005 ratio of 2.96:1 means that for every dollar of current liabilities, Quality has $2.96 of current assets. Quality's current ratio has decreased in the current year. But, compared to the industry average of 1.28:1, Quality appears to be reasonably liquid. J.C. Penney has a very high current ratio of 5.72 which indicates it has considerable current assets relative to its current liabilities.

The current ratio is sometimes referred to as the **working capital ratio**; **working capital** is current assets minus current liabilities. The current ratio is a more dependable indicator of liquidity than working capital. Two companies with the same amount of working capital may have significantly different current ratios.

The current ratio is only one measure of liquidity. It does not take into account the **composition** of the current assets. For example, a satisfactory current ratio does not disclose the fact that a portion of the current assets may be tied up in slow-moving inventory. A dollar of cash would be more readily available to pay the bills than a dollar of slow-moving inventory.

# ACCOUNTING ACROSS THE ORGANIZATION

### How to Manage the Current Ratio

The apparent simplicity of the current ratio can have real-world limitations. An addition of equal amounts to both the numerator and the denominator causes the ratio to change.

Assume, for example, that a company has $2,000,000 of current assets and $1,000,000 of current liabilities. Its current ratio is 2:1. If it purchases $1,000,000 of inventory on account, it will have $3,000,000 of current assets and $2,000,000 of current liabilities. Its current ratio will decrease to 1.5:1. If, instead, the company pays off $500,000 of its current liabilities, it will have $1,500,000 of current assets and $500,000 of current liabilities, and its current ratio will increase to 3:1. Thus, any trend analysis should be done with care, because the ratio is susceptible to quick changes and is easily influenced by management.

 How might management influence the company's current ratio?

## 2. ACID-TEST RATIO

The **acid-test (quick) ratio** is a measure of a company's immediate short-term liquidity. We compute this ratio by dividing the sum of cash, short-term investments, and net receivables by current liabilities. Thus, it is an important complement to the current ratio. For example, assume that the current assets of Quality Department Store for 2005 and 2004 consist of the items shown in Illustration 15-13 (page 708).

**ALTERNATIVE TERMINOLOGY**

The acid-test ratio is also called the *quick ratio*.

Illustration 15-13
Current assets of Quality
Department Store

| QUALITY DEPARTMENT STORE INC. | | |
| --- | --- | --- |
| Balance Sheet (partial) | | |
| | 2005 | 2004 |
| Current assets | | |
| **Cash** | $ 100,000 | $155,000 |
| **Short-term investments** | 20,000 | 70,000 |
| **Receivables (net*)** | 230,000 | 180,000 |
| Inventory | 620,000 | 500,000 |
| Prepaid expenses | 50,000 | 40,000 |
| Total current assets | $1,020,000 | $945,000 |

*Allowance for doubtful accounts is $10,000 at the end of each year.

Cash, short-term investments, and receivables (net) are highly liquid compared to inventory and prepaid expenses. The inventory may not be readily saleable, and the prepaid expenses may not be transferable to others. Thus, the acid-test ratio measures **immediate** liquidity. The 2005 and 2004 acid-test ratios for Quality Department Store and comparative data are as follows.

Illustration 15-14
Acid-test ratio

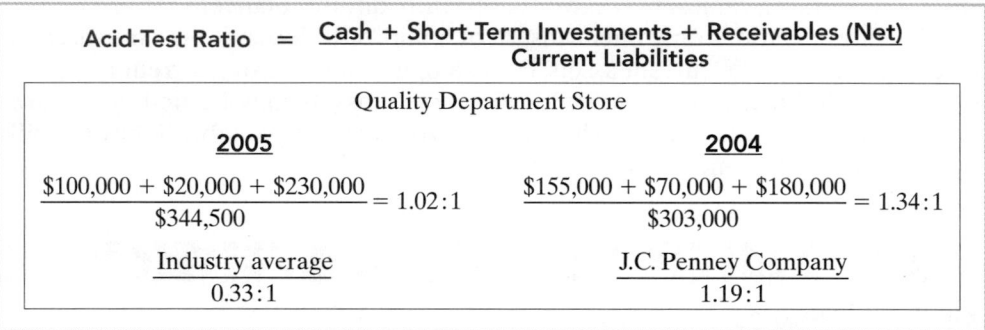

$$\text{Acid-Test Ratio} = \frac{\text{Cash + Short-Term Investments + Receivables (Net)}}{\text{Current Liabilities}}$$

Quality Department Store

**2005**

$$\frac{\$100,000 + \$20,000 + \$230,000}{\$344,500} = 1.02:1$$

Industry average
0.33:1

**2004**

$$\frac{\$155,000 + \$70,000 + \$180,000}{\$303,000} = 1.34:1$$

J.C. Penney Company
1.19:1

The ratio has declined in 2005. Is an acid-test ratio of 1.02:1 adequate? This depends on the industry and the economy. When compared with the industry average of 0.33:1 and Penney's of 1.19:1, Quality's acid-test ratio seems adequate.

### 3. RECEIVABLES TURNOVER

We can measure liquidity by how quickly a company can convert certain assets to cash. How liquid, for example, are the receivables? The ratio used to assess the liquidity of the receivables is **receivables turnover**. It measures the number of times, on average, the company collects receivables during the period. We compute receivables turnover by dividing net credit sales (net sales less cash sales) by the average net receivables. Unless seasonal factors are significant, average net receivables can be computed from the beginning and ending balances of the net receivables.[2]

Assume that all sales are credit sales. The balance of net receivables at the beginning of 2004 is $200,000. Illustration 15-15 shows the receivables turnover for Quality Department Store and comparative data. Quality's receivables turnover improved in 2005. The turnover of 10.2 times is substantially lower than J.C. Penney's 69 times, but is similar to the department store industry's average of 10.8 times.

---

[2]If seasonal factors are significant, the average receivables balance might be determined by using monthly amounts.

Illustration 15-15
Receivables turnover

$$\text{Receivables Turnover} = \frac{\text{Net Credit Sales}}{\text{Average Net Receivables}}$$

Quality Department Store

| **2005** | | **2004** | |
|---|---|---|---|
| $\dfrac{\$2,097,000}{\left[\dfrac{\$180,000 + \$230,000}{2}\right]} = 10.2$ times | | $\dfrac{\$1,837,000}{\left[\dfrac{\$200,000 + \$180,000}{2}\right]} = 9.7$ times | |
| Industry average | | J.C. Penney Company | |
| 10.8 times | | 69 times | |

**Average Collection Period.** A popular variant of the receivables turnover ratio is to convert it to an **average collection period** in terms of days. To do so, we divide the receivables turnover ratio into 365 days. For example, the receivables turnover of 10.2 times divided into 365 days gives an average collection period of approximately 36 days. This means that receivables are collected on average every 36 days, or about every 5 weeks. Analysts frequently use the average collection period to assess the effectiveness of a company's credit and collection policies. The general rule is that the collection period should not greatly exceed the credit term period (the time allowed for payment).

## 4. INVENTORY TURNOVER

**Inventory turnover** measures the number of times, on average, the inventory is sold during the period. Its purpose is to measure the liquidity of the inventory. We compute the inventory turnover by dividing cost of goods sold by the average inventory. Unless seasonal factors are significant, we can use the beginning and ending inventory balances to compute average inventory.

Assuming that the inventory balance for Quality Department Store at the beginning of 2004 was $450,000, its inventory turnover and comparative data are as shown in Illustration 15-16. Quality's inventory turnover declined slightly in 2005. The turnover of 2.3 times is relatively low compared with the industry average of 6.7 and J.C. Penney's 3.6. Generally, the faster the inventory turnover, the less cash a company has tied up in inventory and the less the chance of inventory obsolescence.

Illustration 15-16
Inventory turnover

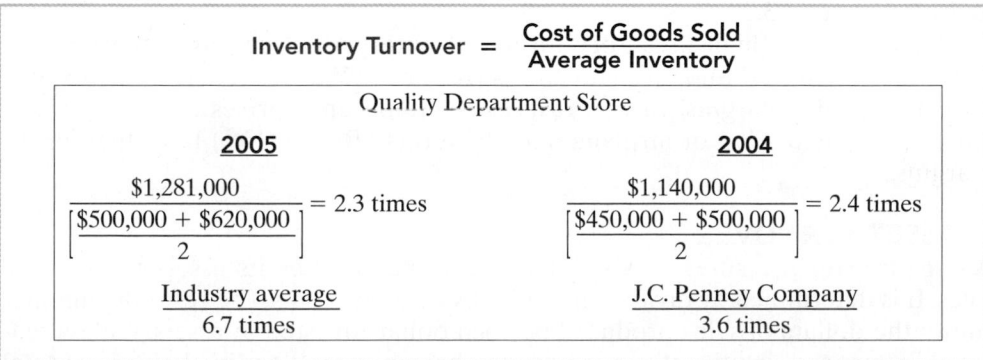

$$\text{Inventory Turnover} = \frac{\text{Cost of Goods Sold}}{\text{Average Inventory}}$$

Quality Department Store

| **2005** | | **2004** | |
|---|---|---|---|
| $\dfrac{\$1,281,000}{\left[\dfrac{\$500,000 + \$620,000}{2}\right]} = 2.3$ times | | $\dfrac{\$1,140,000}{\left[\dfrac{\$450,000 + \$500,000}{2}\right]} = 2.4$ times | |
| Industry average | | J.C. Penney Company | |
| 6.7 times | | 3.6 times | |

**Days in Inventory.** A variant of inventory turnover is the **days in inventory**. We calculate it by dividing the inventory turnover into 365. For example, Quality's 2005 inventory turnover of 2.3 times divided into 365 is approximately 159 days. An average selling time of 159 days is also relatively high compared with the industry average of 54.5 days (365 ÷ 6.7) and J.C. Penney's 101.4 days (365 ÷ 3.6).

Inventory turnover ratios vary considerably among industries. For example, grocery store chains have a turnover of 10 times and an average selling period of 37 days. In contrast, jewelry stores have an average turnover of 1.3 times and an average selling period of 281 days.

## Profitability Ratios

**Profitability ratios** measure the income or operating success of a company for a given period of time. Income, or the lack of it, affects the company's ability to obtain debt and equity financing. It also affects the company's liquidity position and the company's ability to grow. As a consequence, both creditors and investors are interested in evaluating earning power—profitability. Analysts frequently use profitability as the ultimate test of management's operating effectiveness.

**ALTERNATIVE TERMINOLOGY**

Profit margin is also called the *rate of return on sales.*

### 5. PROFIT MARGIN

**Profit margin** is a measure of the percentage of each dollar of sales that results in net income. We can compute it by dividing net income by net sales. Illustration 15-17 shows Quality Department Store's profit margin and comparative data.

**Illustration 15-17**
Profit margin

$$\text{Profit Margin} = \frac{\text{Net Income}}{\text{Net Sales}}$$

Quality Department Store

| **2005** | **2004** |
|---|---|
| $\dfrac{\$263,800}{\$2,097,000} = 12.6\%$ | $\dfrac{\$208,500}{\$1,837,000} = 11.4\%$ |
| Industry average 3.6% | J.C. Penney Company 3.7% |

Quality experienced an increase in its profit margin from 2004 to 2005. Its profit margin is unusually high in comparison with the industry average of 3.6% and J.C. Penney's 3.7%.

High-volume (high inventory turnover) enterprises such as grocery stores (Safeway or Kroger) and discount stores (Kmart or Wal-Mart) generally experience low profit margins. In contrast, low-volume enterprises such as jewelry stores (Tiffany & Co.) or airplane manufacturers (Boeing Co.) have high profit margins.

### 6. ASSET TURNOVER

**Asset turnover** measures how efficiently a company uses its assets to generate sales. It is determined by dividing net sales by average assets. The resulting number shows the dollars of sales produced by each dollar invested in assets. Unless seasonal factors are significant, we can use the beginning and ending balance of total assets to determine average total assets. Assuming that total assets at the beginning of 2004 were $1,446,000, the 2005 and 2004 asset turnover for Quality Department Store and comparative data are shown in Illustration 15-18.

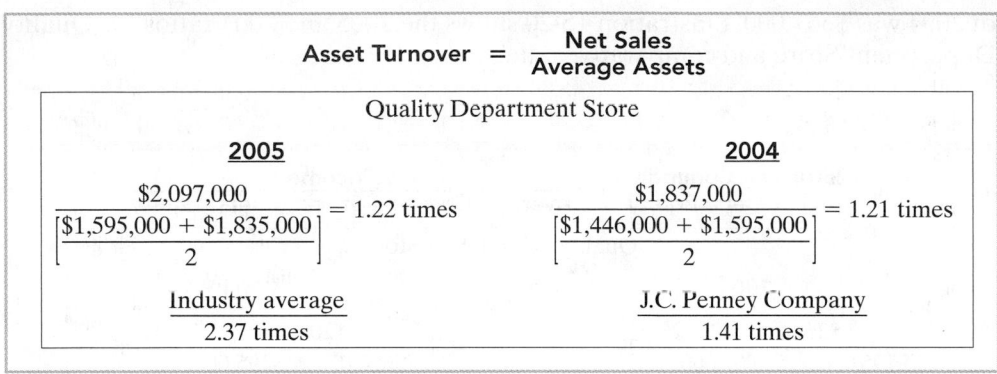

**Illustration 15-18**
Asset turnover

Asset turnover shows that in 2005 Quality generated sales of $1.22 for each dollar it had invested in assets. The ratio changed little from 2004 to 2005. Quality's asset turnover is below the industry average of 2.37 times and J.C. Penney's ratio of 1.41 times.

Asset turnover ratios vary considerably among industries. For example, a large utility company like Consolidated Edison (New York) has a ratio of 0.49 times, and the large grocery chain Kroger Stores has a ratio of 4.34 times.

## 7. RETURN ON ASSETS

An overall measure of profitability is **return on assets**. We compute this ratio by dividing net income by average assets. The 2005 and 2004 return on assets for Quality Department Store and comparative data are shown below.

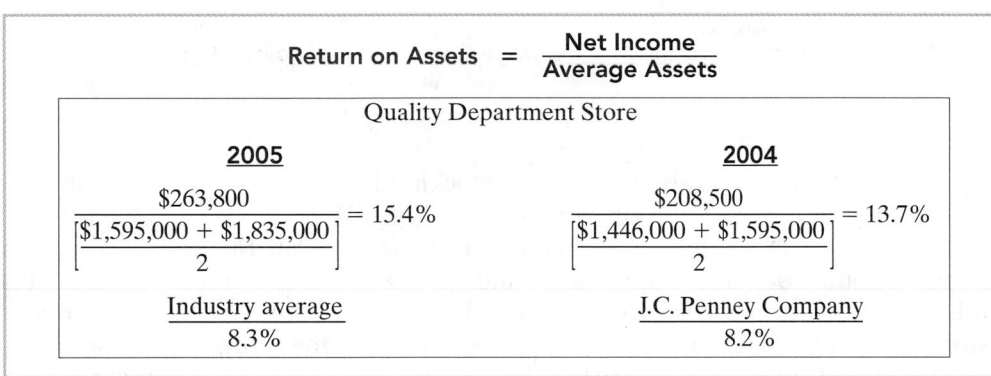

**Illustration 15-19**
Return on assets

Quality's return on assets improved from 2004 to 2005. Its return of 15.4% is very high compared with the department store industry average of 8.3% and J.C. Penney's 8.2%.

## 8. RETURN ON COMMON STOCKHOLDERS' EQUITY

Another widely used profitability ratio is **return on common stockholders' equity**. It measures profitability from the common stockholders' viewpoint. This ratio shows how many dollars of net income the company earned for each dollar invested by the owners. We compute it by dividing net income by average common stockholders' equity. Assuming that common stockholders' equity at the beginning of 2004 was $667,000, Illustration 15-20 shows the 2005 and 2004 ratios for Quality Department Store and comparative data.

Illustration 15-20
Return on common
stockholders' equity

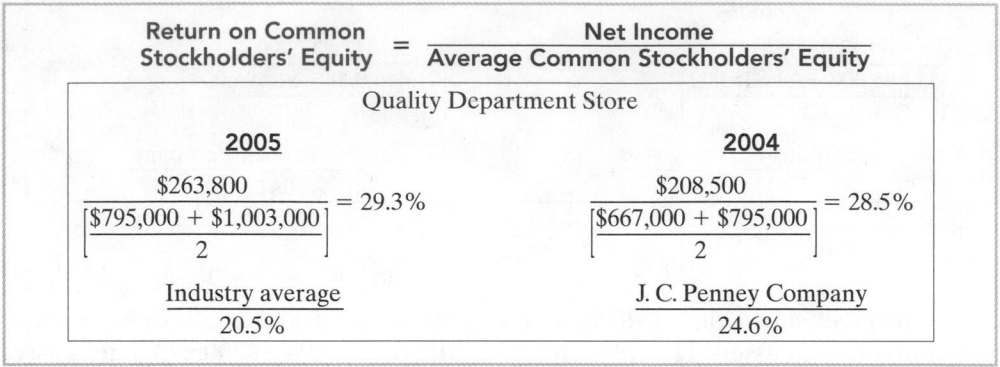

$$\text{Return on Common Stockholders' Equity} = \frac{\text{Net Income}}{\text{Average Common Stockholders' Equity}}$$

Quality Department Store

| 2005 | 2004 |
|------|------|
| $\dfrac{\$263,800}{\left[\dfrac{\$795,000 + \$1,003,000}{2}\right]} = 29.3\%$ | $\dfrac{\$208,500}{\left[\dfrac{\$667,000 + \$795,000}{2}\right]} = 28.5\%$ |
| Industry average | J. C. Penney Company |
| 20.5% | 24.6% |

Quality's rate of return on common stockholders' equity is high at 29.3%, considering an industry average of 20.5% and a rate of 24.6% for J.C. Penney.

**With Preferred Stock.** When a company has preferred stock, we must deduct **preferred dividend** requirements from net income to compute income available to common stockholders. Similarly, we deduct the par value of preferred stock (or call price, if applicable) from total stockholders' equity to determine the amount of common stockholders' equity used in this ratio. The ratio then appears as follows.

Illustration 15-21
Return on common
stockholders' equity with
preferred stock

$$\text{Return on Common Stockholders' Equity} = \frac{\text{Net Income} - \text{Preferred Dividends}}{\text{Average Common Stockholders' Equity}}$$

Note that Quality's rate of return on stockholders' equity (29.3%) is substantially higher than its rate of return on assets (15.4%). The reason is that Quality has made effective use of **leverage**. **Leveraging** or **trading on the equity** at a gain means that the company has borrowed money at a lower rate of interest than it is able to earn by using the borrowed money. Leverage enables Quality Department Store to use money supplied by nonowners to increase the return to the owners. A comparison of the rate of return on total assets with the rate of interest paid for borrowed money indicates the profitability of trading on the equity. Quality Department Store earns more on its borrowed funds than it has to pay in the form of interest. Thus the return to stockholders exceeds the return on the assets, due to benefits from the positive leveraging.

### 9. EARNINGS PER SHARE (EPS)

**Earnings per share (EPS)** is a measure of the net income earned on each share of common stock. It is computed by dividing net income by the number of weighted average common shares outstanding during the year. A measure of net income earned on a per share basis provides a useful perspective for determining profitability. Assuming that there is no change in the number of outstanding shares during 2004 and that the 2005 increase occurred midyear, Illustration 15-22 shows the net income per share for Quality Department Store for 2005 and 2004.

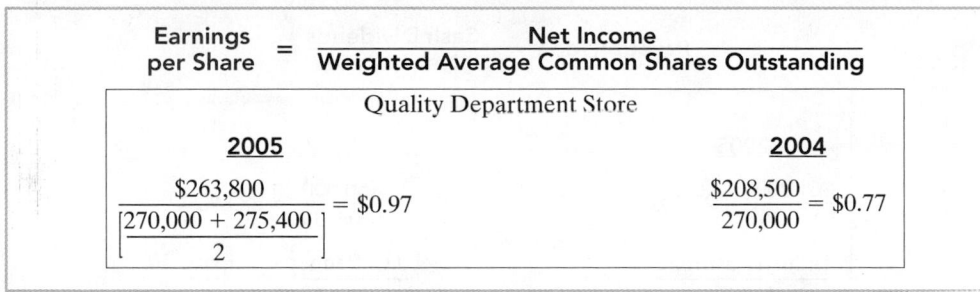

**Illustration 15-22**
Earnings per share

Note that no industry or J.C. Penney data are presented. Such comparisons are not meaningful because of the wide variations in the number of shares of outstanding stock among companies. The only meaningful EPS comparison is an intracompany trend comparison: Quality's earnings per share increased 20 cents per share in 2005. This represents a 26% increase over the 2004 earnings per share of 77 cents.

The terms "earnings per share" and "net income per share" refer to the amount of net income applicable to each share of **common stock**. Therefore, in computing EPS, if there are preferred dividends declared for the period, we must deduct them from net income to determine income available to the common stockholders.

## 10. PRICE-EARNINGS RATIO

The **price-earnings (P-E) ratio** is an oft-quoted measure of the ratio of the market price of each share of common stock to the earnings per share. The price-earnings (P-E) ratio reflects investors' assessments of a company's future earnings. We compute it by dividing the market price per share of the stock by earnings per share. Assuming that the market price of Quality Department Store Inc. stock is $8 in 2004 and $12 in 2005, the price-earnings ratio computation is as follows.

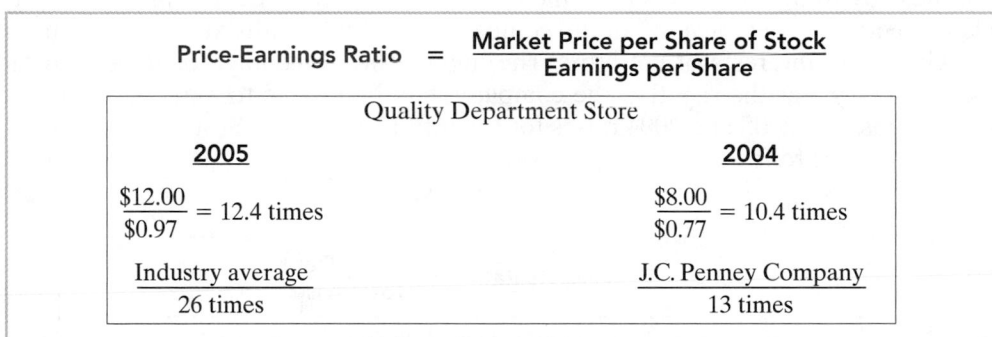

**Illustration 15-23**
Price-earnings ratio

In 2005 each share of Quality's stock sold for 12.4 times the amount that the company earned on each share. Quality's price-earnings ratio is lower than the industry average of 26 times, but almost the same as the ratio of 13 times for J.C. Penney. The average price-earnings ratio for the stocks that constitute the Standard and Poor's 500 Index (500 largest U.S. firms) in early 2006 was a little less than 20 times.

## 11. PAYOUT RATIO

The **payout ratio** measures the percentage of earnings distributed in the form of cash dividends. We compute it by dividing cash dividends by net income. Companies that have high growth rates generally have low payout ratios because they reinvest most of their net income into the business. The 2005 and 2004 payout ratios for Quality Department Store are computed as shown in Illustration 15-24 (page 714).

**Illustration 15-24**
Payout ratio

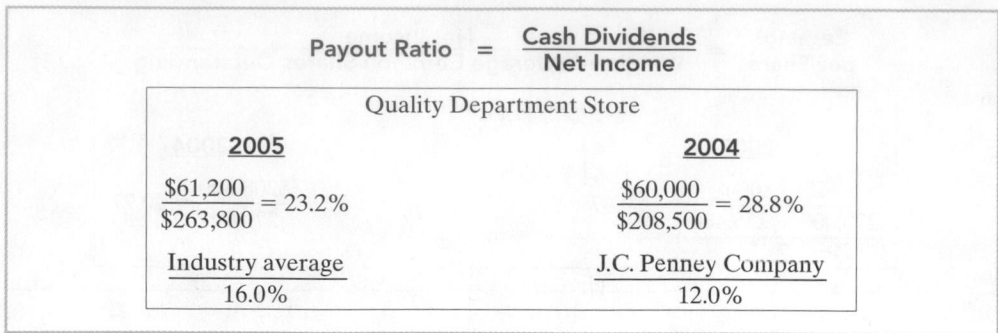

Quality's payout ratio is higher than J.C. Penney's payout ratio of 12.0%. As indicated earlier (page 703), Quality funded its purchase of plant assets through retention of earnings but still is able to pay dividends.

## Solvency Ratios

**Solvency ratios** measure the ability of a company to survive over a long period of time. Long-term creditors and stockholders are particularly interested in a company's ability to pay interest as it comes due and to repay the face value of debt at maturity. Debt to total assets and times interest earned are two ratios that provide information about debt-paying ability.

### 12. DEBT TO TOTAL ASSETS RATIO

The **debt to total assets ratio** measures the percentage of the total assets that creditors provide. We compute it by dividing total debt (both current and long-term liabilities) by total assets. This ratio indicates the company's degree of leverage. It also provides some indication of the company's ability to withstand losses without impairing the interests of creditors. The higher the percentage of debt to total assets, the greater the risk that the company may be unable to meet its maturing obligations. The 2005 and 2004 ratios for Quality Department Store and comparative data are as follows.

**Illustration 15-25**
Debt to total assets ratio

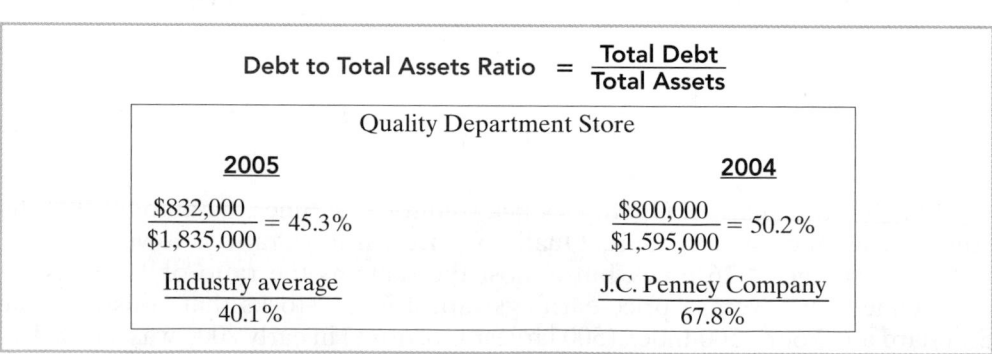

A ratio of 45.3% means that creditors have provided 45.3% of Quality Department Store's total assets. Quality's 45.3% is above the industry average of 40.1%. It is considerably below the high 67.8% ratio of J.C. Penney. The lower the ratio, the more equity "buffer" there is available to the creditors. Thus, from the creditors' point of view, a low ratio of debt to total assets is usually desirable.

The adequacy of this ratio is often judged in the light of the company's earnings. Generally, companies with relatively stable earnings (such as public utilities) have higher debt to total assets ratios than cyclical companies with widely fluctuating earnings (such as many high-tech companies).

## 13. TIMES INTEREST EARNED

**Times interest earned** provides an indication of the company's ability to meet interest payments as they come due. We compute it by dividing income before interest expense and income taxes by interest expense. Illustration 15-26 shows the 2005 and 2004 ratios for Quality Department Store and comparative data. Note that times interest earned uses income before income taxes and interest expense. This represents the amount available to cover interest. For Quality Department Store the 2005 amount of $468,000 is computed by taking the income before income taxes of $432,000 and adding back the $36,000 of interest expense.

**ALTERNATIVE TERMINOLOGY**

Times interest earned is also called *interest coverage*.

$$\text{Times Interest Earned} = \frac{\text{Income before Income Taxes and Interest Expense}}{\text{Interest Expense}}$$

| Quality Department Store | |
|---|---|
| **2005** | **2004** |
| $\dfrac{\$468,000}{\$36,000} = 13$ times | $\dfrac{\$388,000}{\$40,500} = 9.6$ times |
| Industry average | J.C. Penney Company |
| 12 times | 10.2 times |

**Illustration 15-26**
Times interest earned

Quality's interest expense is well covered at 13 times, compared with the industry average of 12 times and J.C. Penney's 10.2 times.

# INVESTOR INSIGHT

 *Keeping Up to Date as an Investor*

Today, investors have access to information provided by corporate managers that used to be available only to professional analysts. Corporate managers have always made themselves available to security analysts for questions at the end of every quarter. Now, because of a combination of new corporate disclosure requirements by the Securities and Exchange Commission and technologies that make communication to large numbers of people possible at a very low price, the average investor can listen in on these discussions. For example, one individual investor, Matthew Johnson, a Nortel Networks local area network engineer in Belfast, Northern Ireland, "stayed up past midnight to listen to Apple Computer's recent Internet conference call. Hearing the company's news 'from the dog's mouth,' he says 'gave me better information' than hunting through chat-rooms."

*Source:* Jeff D. Opdyke, "Individuals Pick Up on Conference Calls," *Wall Street Journal*, November 20, 2000.

**?** If you want to keep current with the financial and operating developments of a company in which you own shares, what are some ways you can do so?

# Summary of Ratios

**Illustration 15-27**
Summary of liquidity, profitability, and solvency ratios

Illustration 15-27 summarizes the ratios discussed in this chapter. The summary includes the formula and purpose or use of each ratio.

| Ratio | Formula | Purpose or Use |
|---|---|---|
| **Liquidity Ratios** | | |
| 1. Current ratio | $\dfrac{\text{Current assets}}{\text{Current liabilities}}$ | Measures short-term debt-paying ability. |
| 2. Acid-test (quick) ratio | $\dfrac{\text{Cash + Short-term investments + Receivables (net)}}{\text{Current liabilities}}$ | Measures immediate short-term liquidity. |
| 3. Receivables turnover | $\dfrac{\text{Net credit sales}}{\text{Average net receivables}}$ | Measures liquidity of receivables. |
| 4. Inventory turnover | $\dfrac{\text{Cost of goods sold}}{\text{Average inventory}}$ | Measures liquidity of inventory. |
| **Profitability Ratios** | | |
| 5. Profit margin | $\dfrac{\text{Net income}}{\text{Net sales}}$ | Measures net income generated by each dollar of sales. |
| 6. Asset turnover | $\dfrac{\text{Net sales}}{\text{Average assets}}$ | Measures how efficiently assets are used to generate sales. |
| 7. Return on assets | $\dfrac{\text{Net income}}{\text{Average assets}}$ | Measures overall profitability of assets. |
| 8. Return on common stockholders' equity | $\dfrac{\text{Net income}}{\text{Average common stockholders' equity}}$ | Measures profitability of owners' investment. |
| 9. Earnings per share (EPS) | $\dfrac{\text{Net income}}{\text{Weighted average common shares outstanding}}$ | Measures net income earned on each share of common stock. |
| 10. Price-earnings (P-E) ratio | $\dfrac{\text{Market price per share of stock}}{\text{Earnings per share}}$ | Measures the ratio of the market price per share to earnings per share. |
| 11. Payout ratio | $\dfrac{\text{Cash dividends}}{\text{Net income}}$ | Measures percentage of earnings distributed in the form of cash dividends. |
| **Solvency Ratios** | | |
| 12. Debt to total assets ratio | $\dfrac{\text{Total debt}}{\text{Total assets}}$ | Measures the percentage of total assets provided by creditors. |
| 13. Times interest earned | $\dfrac{\text{Income before income taxes and interest expense}}{\text{Interest expense}}$ | Measures ability to meet interest payments as they come due. |

## Before You Go On...

### REVIEW IT

1. What are liquidity ratios? Explain the current ratio, acid-test ratio, receivables turnover, and inventory turnover.
2. What are profitability ratios? Explain the profit margin, asset turnover ratio, return on assets, return on common stockholders' equity, earnings per share, price-earnings ratio, and payout ratio.
3. What are solvency ratios? Explain the debt to total assets ratio and times interest earned.

**DO IT**

Selected financial data for Drummond Company at December 31, 2008, are as follows: cash $60,000; receivables (net) $80,000; inventory $70,000; current liabilities $140,000. Compute the current and acid-test ratios.

**Action Plan**

■ Use the formula for the current ratio: Current assets ÷ Current liabilities.

■ Use the formula for the acid-test ratio: Cash + Short-term investments + Receivables (net) ÷ Current liabilities.

**Solution** The current ratio is 1.5:1 ($210,000 ÷ $140,000). The acid-test ratio is 1:1 ($140,000 ÷ $140,000).

Related exercise material: *BE15-9, BE15-10, BE15-11, BE15-12, BE15-13, E15-5, E15-6, E15-7, E15-8, E15-9, E15-10, and E15-11.*

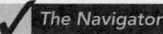 The Navigator

# EARNING POWER AND IRREGULAR ITEMS

Users of financial statements are interested in the concept of earning power. **Earning power** means the normal level of income to be obtained in the future. Earning power differs from actual net income by the amount of irregular revenues, expenses, gains, and losses. Users are interested in earning power because it helps them derive an estimate of future earnings without the "noise" of irregular items.

STUDY OBJECTIVE 6

Understand the concept of earning power, and how irregular items are presented.

For users of financial statements to determine earning power or regular income, the "irregular" items are separately identified on the income statement. Companies report two types of "irregular" items.

**1.** Discontinued operations.

**2.** Extraordinary items.

These "irregular" items are reported net of income taxes. That is, the income statement first reports income tax on the income before "irregular" items. Then the amount of tax for each of the listed "irregular" items is computed. The general concept is "let the tax follow income or loss."

## Discontinued Operations

**Discontinued operations** refers to the disposal of a **significant component** of a business. Examples involve stopping an entire activity or eliminating a major class of customers. For example, Kmart reported as discontinued operations its decision to terminate its interest in four business activities, including PACE Membership Warehouse and PayLess Drug Stores Northwest.

Following the disposal of a significant component, the company should report on its income statement both income from continuing operations and income (or loss) from discontinued operations. **The income (loss) from discontinued operations consists of two parts: the income (loss) from operations** and **the gain (loss) on disposal of the segment**.

To illustrate, assume that during 2008 Acro Energy Inc. has income before income taxes of $800,000. During 2008 Acro discontinued and sold its unprofitable chemical division. The loss in 2008 from chemical operations (net of $60,000 taxes) was $140,000. The loss on disposal of the chemical division (net of $30,000 taxes) was $70,000. Assuming a 30% tax rate on income, Illustration 15-28 shows Acro's income statement presentation.

Illustration 15-28
Statement presentation of
discontinued operations

**HELPFUL HINT**

Observe the dual disclosures: (1) The results of operations of the discontinued division must be eliminated from the results of continuing operations. (2) The company must also report the disposal of the operation.

| ACRO ENERGY INC. Income Statement (partial) For the Year Ended December 31, 2008 | | |
|---|---|---|
| Income before income taxes | | $800,000 |
| Income tax expense | | 240,000 |
| Income from continuing operations | | 560,000 |
| **Discontinued operations** | | |
| Loss from operations of chemical division, net of $60,000 income tax saving | $140,000 | |
| Loss from disposal of chemical division, net of $30,000 income tax saving | 70,000 | 210,000 |
| Net income | | $350,000 |

Note that the statement uses the caption "Income from continuing operations," and adds a new section "Discontinued operations". **The new section reports both the operating loss and the loss on disposal net of applicable income taxes.** This presentation clearly indicates the separate effects of continuing operations and discontinued operations on net income.

## Extraordinary Items

Extraordinary items are events and transactions that meet two conditions: They are (1) **unusual in nature,** and (2) **infrequent in occurrence**. To be *unusual*, the item should be abnormal and only incidentally related to the company's customary activities. To be *infrequent*, the item should not be reasonably expected to recur in the foreseeable future.

A company must evaluate both criteria in terms of its operating environment. Thus, Weyerhaeuser Co. reported the $36 million in damages to its timberland caused by the volcanic eruption of Mount St. Helens as an extraordinary item. The eruption was both unusual and infrequent. In contrast, Florida Citrus Company does not report frost damage to its citrus crop as an extraordinary item, because frost damage is not infrequent. Illustration 15-29 (next page) shows the classification of extraordinary and ordinary items.

**Companies report extraordinary items net of taxes in a separate section of the income statement, immediately below discontinued operations.** To illustrate, assume that in 2008 a foreign government expropriated property held as an investment by Acro Energy Inc. If the loss is $70,000 before applicable income taxes of $21,000, the income statement will report a deduction of $49,000, as shown in Illustration 15-30 (next page). When there is an extraordinary item to report, the company adds the caption "Income before extraordinary item" immediately before the section for the extraordinary item. This presentation clearly indicates the effect of the extraordinary item on net income.

What if a transaction or event meets one (but not both) of the criteria for an extraordinary item? In that case the company reports it under either "Other revenues and gains" or "Other expenses and losses" at its gross amount (not net of

## Extraordinary items

1. Effects of major natural casualties, if rare in the area.

2. Expropriation (takeover) of property by a foreign government.

3. Effects of a newly enacted law or regulation, such as a property condemnation action.

## Ordinary items

1. Effects of major natural casualties, not uncommon in the area.

2. Write-down of inventories or write-off of receivables.

3. Losses attributable to labor strikes.

4. Gains or losses from sales of property, plant, or equipment.

**Illustration 15-29**
Examples of extraordinary and ordinary items

tax). This is true, for example, of gains (losses) resulting from the sale of property, plant, and equipment, as explained in Chapter 10. It is quite common for companies to use the label "Nonrecurring charges" for losses that do not meet the extraordinary item criteria.

**Illustration 15-30**
Statement presentation of extraordinary items

### ACRO ENERGY INC.
Income Statement (partial)
For the Year Ended December 31, 2008

| | | |
|---|---|---|
| Income before income taxes | | $800,000 |
| Income tax expense | | 240,000 |
| Income from continuing operations | | 560,000 |
| Discontinued operations | | |
| Loss from operations of chemical division, net of $60,000 income tax saving | $140,000 | |
| Loss from disposal of chemical division, net of $30,000 income tax saving | 70,000 | 210,000 |
| Income before extraordinary item | | 350,000 |
| **Extraordinary item** | | |
| **Expropriation of investment, net of $21,000 income tax saving** | | 49,000 |
| Net income | | $301,000 |

**HELPFUL HINT**

If there are no discontinued operations, the third line of the income statement would be labeled "Income before extraordinary item."

### What Is Extraordinary?

Many companies these days are incurring restructuring charges as a result of attempting to reduce costs. Are these costs ordinary or extraordinary? Some companies report "one-time" restructuring charges over and over. Case in point: Toothpaste and diapers giant Procter & Gamble Co. reported a restructuring charge in 12 consecutive quarters, and Motorola had "special" charges 14 quarters in a row. On the other hand, some companies take a restructuring charge only once in five years. The one-size-fits-all classification therefore will not work. There appears to be no substitute for a careful analysis of the numbers that comprise net income.

**?** If a company takes a large restructuring charge, what is the effect on the company's current income statement versus future ones?

## Changes in Accounting Principle

> **ETHICS NOTE**
>
> Changes in accounting principle should result in financial statements that are more informative for statement users. They should *not* be used to artificially improve the reported performance or financial position of the corporation.

For ease of comparison, users of financial statements expect companies to prepare such statements on a basis **consistent** with the preceding period. A change in accounting principle occurs when the principle used in the current year is different from the one used in the preceding year. Accounting rules permit a change when management can show that the new principle is preferable to the old principle. An example is a change in inventory costing methods (such as FIFO to average cost).

Companies report most changes in accounting principle retroactively. That is, they report both the current period and previous periods using the new principle. As a result the same principle applies in all periods. This treatment improves the ability to compare results across years.

## Comprehensive Income

The income statement reports most revenues, expenses, gains, and losses recognized during the period. However, over time, specific exceptions to this general practice have developed. Certain items now bypass income and are reported directly in stockholders' equity.

For example, in Chapter 13 you learned that companies do not include in income any unrealized gains and losses on available-for-sale securities. Instead, they report such gains and losses in the balance sheet as adjustments to stockholders' equity. Why are these gains and losses on available-for-sale securities excluded from net income? Because disclosing them separately (1) reduces the volatility of net income due to fluctuations in fair value, yet (2) informs the financial statement user of the gain or loss that would be incurred if the securities were sold at fair value.

Many analysts have expressed concern over the significant increase in the number of items that bypass the income statement. They feel that such reporting has reduced the usefulness of the income statement. To address this concern, in addition to reporting net income, a company must also report comprehensive income. Comprehensive income includes all changes in stockholders' equity during a period except those resulting from investments by stockholders and distributions to stockholders. A number of alternative formats for reporting comprehensive income are allowed. These formats are discussed in advanced accounting courses.

## Before You Go On...

**REVIEW IT**

1. What are the similarities and differences in reporting material items not typical of regular operations?
2. What is included in comprehensive income?

**DO IT**

In its proposed 2008 income statement, AIR Corporation reports income before income taxes $400,000, extraordinary loss $100,000, income taxes (30%) $120,000, and net income $210,000. Prepare a correct income statement, beginning with income before income taxes.

**Action Plan**

- Recall that the loss is extraordinary because it meets the criteria of being both unusual and infrequent.
- Disclose the income tax effect of each component of income, beginning with income before any irregular items.
- Report irregular items net of any income tax effect.

**Solution**

### AIR CORPORATION
Income Statement (partial)

| | |
|---|---:|
| Income before income taxes | $400,000 |
| Income tax expense (30%) | 120,000 |
| Income before extraordinary item | 280,000 |
| Extraordinary loss net of $30,000 income tax saving | 70,000 |
| Net income | $210,000 |

Related exercise material: *BE15-14, BE15-15, E15-12, and E15-13.*

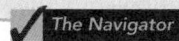 The Navigator

# QUALITY OF EARNINGS

In evaluating the financial performance of a company, the quality of a company's earnings is of extreme importance to analysts. A company that has a high **quality of earnings** provides full and transparent information that will not confuse or mislead users of the financial statements.

**STUDY OBJECTIVE 7**
Understand the concept of quality of earnings.

The issue of quality of earnings has taken on increasing importance because recent accounting scandals suggest that some companies are spending too much time managing their income and not enough time managing their business. Here are some of the factors affecting quality of earnings.

## Alternative Accounting Methods

Variations among companies in the application of generally accepted accounting principles may hamper comparability and reduce quality of earnings. For example, one company may use the FIFO method of inventory costing, while another company in the same industry may use LIFO. If inventory is a significant asset to both companies, it is unlikely that their current ratios are comparable. For example, if General Motors Corporation had used FIFO instead of LIFO for inventory valuation, its inventories in a recent year would have been 26% higher, which significantly affects the current ratio (and other ratios as well).

In addition to differences in inventory costing methods, differences also exist in reporting such items as depreciation, depletion, and amortization. Although these differences in accounting methods might be detectable from reading the notes to the financial statements, adjusting the financial data to compensate for the different methods is often difficult, if not impossible.

## Pro Forma Income

Companies whose stock is publicly traded are required to present their income statement following generally accepted accounting principles (GAAP). In recent years, many companies have also reported a second measure of income, called pro forma income. **Pro forma income** usually excludes items that the company thinks are unusual or nonrecurring. For example, in a recent year, Cisco Systems (a high-tech company) reported a quarterly net loss under GAAP of $2.7 billion. Cisco reported pro forma income for the same quarter as a profit of $230 million. This large difference in profits between GAAP income numbers and pro forma income is not unusual these days. For example, during one recent 9-month period the 100 largest firms on the Nasdaq stock exchange reported a total pro forma income of $19.1 billion, but a total loss as measured by GAAP of $82.3 billion—a difference of about $100 billion!

To compute pro forma income, companies generally can exclude any items they deem inappropriate for measuring their performance. Many analysts and investors are critical of the practice of using pro forma income because these numbers often make companies look better than they really are. As the financial press noted, pro forma numbers might be called EBS, which stands for "earnings before bad stuff." Companies, on the other hand, argue that pro forma numbers more clearly indicate sustainable income because they exclude unusual and nonrecurring expenses. "Cisco's technique gives readers of financial statements a clear picture of Cisco's normal business activities," the company said in a statement issued in response to questions about its pro forma income accounting.

Recently, the SEC provided some guidance on how companies should present pro forma information. Stay tuned: Everyone seems to agree that pro forma numbers can be useful if they provide insights into determining a company's sustainable income. However, many companies have abused the flexibility that pro forma numbers allow and have used the measure as a way to put their companies in a good light.

## Improper Recognition

Because some managers have felt pressure from Wall Street to continually increase earnings, they have manipulated the earnings numbers to meet these expectations. The most common abuse is the improper recognition of revenue. One practice that companies are using is *channel stuffing*: Offering deep discounts on their products to customers, companies encourage their customers to buy early (stuff the channel) rather than later. This lets the company report good earnings in the current period, but it often leads to a disaster in subsequent periods because customers have no need for additional goods. To illustrate, Bristol-Myers Squibb recently indicated that it used sales incentives to encourage wholesalers to buy more drugs than needed to meet patients' demands. As a result, the company had to issue revised financial statements showing corrected revenues and income.

Another practice is the improper capitalization of operating expenses. The classic case is WorldCom. It capitalized over $7 billion dollars of operating expenses so that it would report positive net income. In other situations, companies fail to report all their liabilities. Enron had promised to make payments on certain contracts if financial difficulty developed, but these guarantees were not reported as liabilities. In addition, disclosure was so lacking in transparency that it was impossible to understand what was happening at the company.

 Be sure to read **ALL ABOUT YOU:** *Should I Play the Market Yet?* on the next page for information on how topics in this chapter apply to you.

# Should I Play the Market Yet?

In this chapter you learned how to use many tools for performing a financial analysis of a company. Sometimes companies fail even though they have a good product and good sales growth. All too often the cause of failure is something that should have caused only momentary discomfort. But if a company lacks sufficient liquidity, a momentary hiccup can be fatal. This is true for individuals as well.

For example, the decision to invest in common stock can be risky. As a company's net income changes, its stock price can be volatile. You must take this into consideration when deciding whether to buy stock. You don't want to be in a situation where you have to sell a stock whose price has fallen in order to raise cash to pay your bills.

## ✱ Some Facts

* 83.4 million Americans own stock investments, either through mutual funds or individual stocks; 89% of stock investors own stock mutual funds.

* 44% of the people who own stock bought their first stock before 1990.

* The typical equity investor is in his or her late 40s, is married, is employed, and has a household income in the low $60,000s.

* 58% of people who own stock said that they rely on professional financial advisors when making decisions regarding the purchase and sale of stock.

* 46% of people who own stock used the Internet to check stock prices, and 38% use it to read online financial publications.

## ✱ About the Numbers

The percentage of Americans who buy stock, either through mutual funds or individual shares, has increased significantly in recent years. A big part of this increase is due to the increasing prevalence of employer-sponsored retirement plans, such as 401(k) plans.

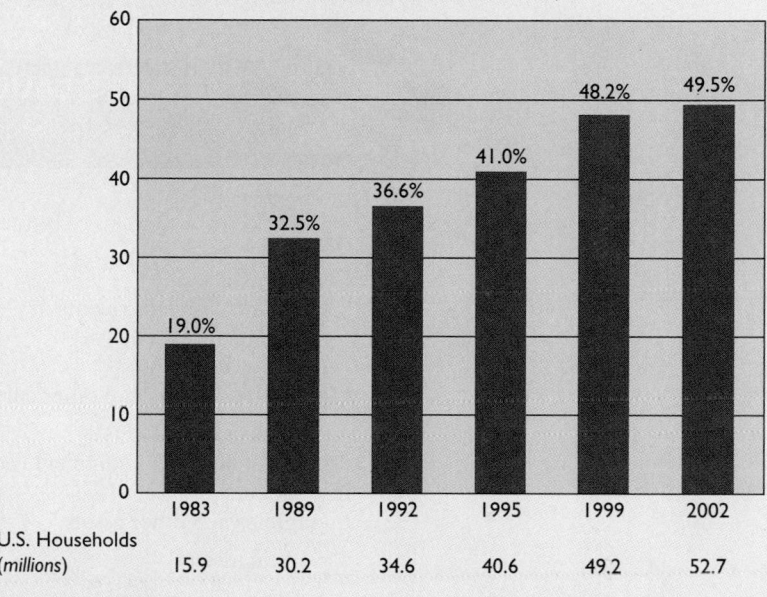

**Equity Ownership in the U.S., 1983–2002, Selected Years**
*(number and percent of U.S. households)*

| Year | Percent | U.S. Households (millions) |
|------|---------|----------------------------|
| 1983 | 19.0% | 15.9 |
| 1989 | 32.5% | 30.2 |
| 1992 | 36.6% | 34.6 |
| 1995 | 41.0% | 40.6 |
| 1999 | 48.2% | 49.2 |
| 2002 | 49.5% | 52.7 |

**Source:** "Equity Ownership in America," Investment Company Institute and the Securities Industry Association, 2002, p. 1.

## ✱ What Do You Think?

Rachael West has been working at her new job for six months. She has a good salary, with lots of opportunities for growth. She has already accumulated $8,000 in savings, which right now is sitting in a bank savings account earning very little interest. She has decided to take $7,000 out of this savings account and buy common stock of her employer, a young company that has been in business for two years. Rachael's liquid assets, including her savings account, total $10,000. Her monthly expenses are approximately $3,000. Should Rachael make this investment?

**YES:** She has a good income, and this is a great opportunity for her to get in on the ground floor of her employer's fast-growing company.

**NO:** She shouldn't invest all of her money in one company, particularly the company at which she works.

**Source:** "Equity Ownership in America," Investment Company Institute and the Securities Industry Association, 2002.

The authors' comments on this situation appear on p. 746.

## Before You Go On...

**REVIEW IT**

1. What is meant by *quality of earnings?*
2. Give examples of alternative accounting methods that hamper comparability.
3. What is pro forma income and why are analysts often critical of this number?

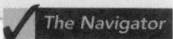 The Navigator

**Demonstration Problem 1**  WILEY PLUS

The condensed financial statements ot The Estée Lauder Companies, Inc., for the years ended June 30, 2005 and 2004, are presented below.

## THE ESTÉE LAUDER COMPANIES, INC.
### Balance Sheets
### June 30

| Assets | (in millions) 2005 | 2004 |
|---|---|---|
| Current assets | | |
| Cash and cash equivalents | $ 553.3 | $ 611.6 |
| Accounts receivable (net) | 776.6 | 664.9 |
| Inventories | 768.3 | 653.5 |
| Prepaid expenses and other current assets | 204.4 | 269.2 |
| Total current assets | 2,302.6 | 2,199.2 |
| Property, plant, and equipment (net) | 694.2 | 647.0 |
| Investments | 12.3 | 12.6 |
| Intangibles and other assets | 876.7 | 849.3 |
| Total assets | $3,885.8 | $3,708.1 |
| **Liabilities and Stockholders' Equity** | | |
| Current liabilities | $1,497.7 | $1,322.0 |
| Long-term liabilities | 679.5 | 637.1 |
| Stockholders' equity—common | 1,708.6 | 1,749.0 |
| Total liabilities and stockholders' equity | $3,885.8 | $3,708.1 |

## THE ESTÉE LAUDER COMPANIES, INC.
### Income Statements
### For the Year Ended June 30

| | (in millions) 2005 | 2004 |
|---|---|---|
| Revenues | $6,336.3 | $5,790.4 |
| Costs and expenses | | |
| Cost of goods sold | 1,617.4 | 1,476.3 |
| Selling and administrative expenses | 4,007.6 | 3,679.0 |
| Interest expense | 13.9 | 27.1 |
| Total costs and expenses | 5,638.9 | 5,182.4 |
| Income before income taxes | 697.4 | 608.0 |
| Income tax expense | 291.3 | 232.6 |
| Net income | $ 406.1 | $ 375.4 |

## Solution

| | 2005 | 2004 |
|---|---|---|
| **(a)** Current ratio: | | |
| $2,302.6 ÷ $1,497.7 = | 1.5:1 | |
| $2,199.2 ÷ $1,322.0 = | | 1.7:1 |
| **(b)** Inventory turnover: | | |
| $1,617.4 ÷ [($768.3 + $653.5) ÷ 2] = | 2.3 times | |
| $1,476.3 ÷ [($653.5 + $599.0) ÷ 2] = | | 2.4 times |
| **(c)** Profit margin: | | |
| $406.1 ÷ $6,336.3 | 6.4% | |
| $375.4 ÷ $5,790.4 | | 6.5% |
| **(d)** Return on assets: | | |
| $406.1 ÷ [($3,885.8 + $3,708.1) ÷ 2] = | 10.7% | |
| $375.4 ÷ [($3,708.1 + $3,349.9) ÷ 2] = | | 10.6% |
| **(e)** Return on common stockholders' equity: | | |
| $406.1 ÷ [($1,708.6 + $1,749.0) ÷ 2] = | 23.5% | |
| $375.4 ÷ [($1,749.0 + $1,795.9) ÷ 2] = | | 21.2% |
| **(f)** Debt to total assets ratio: | | |
| ($1,497.7 + $679.5) ÷ $3,885.8 = | 56.0% | |
| ($1,322.0 + $637.1) ÷ $3,708.1 = | | 52.8% |
| **(g)** Times interest earned: | | |
| ($406.1 + $291.3 + $13.9) ÷ $13.9 = | 51.2 times | |
| ($375.4 + $232.6 + $27.1) ÷ $27.1 = | | 23.4 times |

✓ The Navigator

**action plan**

✔ Remember that the current ratio includes all current assets. The acid-test ratio uses only cash, short-term investments, and net receivables.

✔ Use average balances for turnover ratios like inventory, receivables, and assets.

---

## Demonstration Problem 2

The events and transactions of Dever Corporation for the year ending December 31, 2008, resulted in the following data.

| | |
|---|---|
| Cost of goods sold | $2,600,000 |
| Net sales | 4,400,000 |
| Other expenses and losses | 9,600 |
| Other revenues and gains | 5,600 |
| Selling and administrative expenses | 1,100,000 |
| Income from operations of plastics division | 70,000 |
| Gain from disposal of plastics division | 500,000 |
| Loss from tornado disaster (extraordinary loss) | 600,000 |

Analysis reveals that:

**1.** All items are before the applicable income tax rate of 30%.
**2.** The plastics division was sold on July 1.
**3.** All operating data for the plastics division have been segregated.

**Instructions**

Prepare an income statement for the year.

## action plan

✔ Report material items not typical of operations in separate sections, net of taxes.

✔ Associate income taxes with the item that affects the taxes.

✔ Apply the corporate tax rate to income before income taxes to determine tax expense.

✔ Recall that all data presented in determining income before income taxes are the same as for unincorporated companies.

### Solution

**DEVER CORPORATION**
Income Statement
For the Year Ended December 31, 2008

| | | | |
|---|---|---|---|
| Net sales | | | $4,400,000 |
| Cost of goods sold | | | 2,600,000 |
| Gross profit | | | 1,800,000 |
| Selling and administrative expenses | | | 1,100,000 |
| Income from operations | | | 700,000 |
| Other revenues and gains | | $5,600 | |
| Other expenses and losses | | 9,600 | 4,000 |
| Income before income taxes | | | 696,000 |
| Income tax expense ($696,000 × 30%) | | | 208,800 |
| Income from continuing operations | | | 487,200 |
| Discontinued operations | | | |
| Income from operations of plastics division, net of $21,000 income taxes ($70,000 × 30%) | | 49,000 | |
| Gain from disposal of plastics division, net of $150,000 income taxes ($500,000 × 30%) | | 350,000 | 399,000 |
| Income before extraordinary item | | | 886,200 |
| Extraordinary item | | | |
| Tornado loss, net of $180,000 income tax saving ($600,000 × 30%) | | | 420,000 |
| Net income | | | $ 466,200 |

---

# SUMMARY OF STUDY OBJECTIVES

**1 Discuss the need for comparative analysis.** There are three bases of comparison: (1) Intracompany, which compares an item or financial relationship with other data within a company. (2) Industry, which compares company data with industry averages. (3) Intercompany, which compares an item or financial relationship of a company with data of one or more competing companies.

**2 Identify the tools of financial statement analysis.** Financial statements can be analyzed horizontally, vertically, and with ratios.

**3 Explain and apply horizontal analysis.** Horizontal analysis is a technique for evaluating a series of data over a period of time to determine the increase or decrease that has taken place, expressed as either an amount or a percentage.

**4 Describe and apply vertical analysis.** Vertical analysis is a technique that expresses each item within a financial statement in terms of a percentage of a relevant total or a base amount.

**5 Identify and compute ratios used in analyzing a firm's liquidity, profitability, and solvency.** The formula and purpose of each ratio was presented in Illustration 15-27 (page 716).

**6 Understand the concept of earning power, and how irregular items are presented.** Earning power refers to a company's ability to sustain its profits from operations. "Irregular items"—discontinued operations and extraordinary items—are presented net of tax below income from continuing operations to highlight their unusual nature.

**7 Understand the concept of quality of earnings.** A high quality of earnings provides full and transparent information that will not confuse or mislead users of the financial statements. Issues related to quality of earnings are (1) alternative accounting methods, (2) pro forma income, and (3) improper recognition.

---

# GLOSSARY

**Acid-test (quick) ratio** A measure of a company's immediate short-term liquidity; computed by dividing the sum of cash, short-term investments, and net receivables by current liabilities. (p. 707).

**Asset turnover** A measure of how efficiently a company uses its assets to generate sales; computed by dividing net sales by average assets. (p. 710).

**Change in accounting principle** The use of a principle in the current year that is different from the one used in the preceding year. (p. 720).

**Comprehensive income** Includes all changes in stockholders' equity during a period except those resulting from investments by stockholders and distributions to stockholders. (p. 720).

**Current ratio** A measure used to evaluate a company's liquidity and short-term debt-paying ability; computed by dividing current assets by current liabilities. (p. 706).

**Debt to total assets ratio** Measures the percentage of total assets provided by creditors; computed by dividing total debt by total assets. (p. 714).

**Discontinued operations** The disposal of a significant segment of a business. (p. 717).

**Earnings per share (EPS)** The net income earned on each share of common stock; computed by dividing net income by the number of weighted average common shares outstanding. (p. 712).

**Extraordinary items** Events and transactions that are unusual in nature and infrequent in occurrence. (p. 718).

**Horizontal analysis** A technique for evaluating a series of financial statement data over a period of time, to determine the increase (decrease) that has taken place, expressed as either an amount or a percentage. (p. 699).

**Inventory turnover** A measure of the liquidity of inventory; computed by dividing cost of goods sold by average inventory. (p. 709).

**Leveraging** See Trading on the equity.

**Liquidity ratios** Measures of the short-term ability of the enterprise to pay its maturing obligations and to meet unexpected needs for cash. (p. 706).

**Payout ratio** Measures the percentage of earnings distributed in the form of cash dividends; computed by dividing cash dividends by net income. (p. 713).

**Price-earnings (P-E) ratio** Measures the ratio of the market price of each share of common stock to the earnings per share; computed by dividing the market price of the stock by earnings per share. (p. 713).

**Profit margin** Measures the percentage of each dollar of sales that results in net income; computed by dividing net income by net sales. (p. 710).

**Profitability ratios** Measures of the income or operating success of an enterprise for a given period of time. (p. 710).

**Pro forma income** A measure of income that usually excludes items that a company thinks are unusual or nonrecurring. (p. 722).

**Quality of earnings** Indicates the level of full and transparent information provided to users of the financial statements (p. 721).

**Ratio** An expression of the mathematical relationship between one quantity and another. The relationship may be expressed either as a percentage, a rate, or a simple proportion. (p. 705).

**Ratio analysis** A technique for evaluating financial statements that expresses the relationship between selected financial statement data. (p. 705).

**Receivables turnover** A measure of the liquidity of receivables; computed by dividing net credit sales by average net receivables. (p. 708).

**Return on assets** An overall measure of profitability; computed by dividing net income by average assets. (p. 711).

**Return on common stockholders' equity** Measures the dollars of net income earned for each dollar invested by the owners; computed by dividing net income by average common stockholders' equity. (p. 711).

**Solvency ratios** Measures of the ability of the enterprise to survive over a long period of time. (p. 714).

**Times interest earned** Measures a company's ability to meet interest payments as they come due; computed by dividing income before interest expense and income taxes by interest expense. (p. 715).

**Trading on the equity** Borrowing money at a lower rate of interest than can be earned by using the borrowed money. (p. 712).

**Vertical analysis** A technique for evaluating financial statement data that expresses each item within a financial statement as a percent of a base amount. (p. 703).

---

## SELF-STUDY QUESTIONS

*Answers are at the end of the chapter.*

(SO 1) **1.** Comparisons of data within a company are an example of the following comparative basis:
  **a.** Industry averages.
  **b.** Intracompany.
  **c.** Intercompany.
  **d.** Both (b) and (c).

(SO 3) **2.** In horizontal analysis, each item is expressed as a percentage of the:
  **a.** net income amount.
  **b.** stockholders' equity amount.
  **c.** total assets amount.
  **d.** base year amount.

**3.** In vertical analysis, the base amount for depreciation expense is generally: (SO 4)
  **a.** net sales.
  **b.** depreciation expense in a previous year.
  **c.** gross profit.
  **d.** fixed assets.

**4.** The following schedule is a display of what type of analysis? (SO 4)

| | Amount | Percent |
|---|---|---|
| Current assets | $200,000 | 25% |
| Property, plant, and equipment | 600,000 | 75% |
| Total assets | $800,000 | |

a. Horizontal analysis.
b. Differential analysis.
c. Vertical analysis.
d. Ratio analysis.

(SO 3) **5.** Sammy Corporation reported net sales of $300,000, $330,000, and $360,000 in the years, 2006, 2007, and 2008, respectively. If 2006 is the base year, what is the trend percentage for 2008?
a. 77%.
b. 108%.
c. 120%.
d. 130%.

(SO 5) **6.** Which of the following measures is an evaluation of a firm's ability to pay current liabilities?
a. Acid-test ratio.
b. Current ratio.
c. Both (a) and (b).
d. None of the above.

(SO 5) **7.** A measure useful in evaluating the efficiency in managing inventories is:
a. inventory turnover.
b. average days to sell inventory.
c. Both (a) and (b).
d. None of the above.

(SO 6) **8.** In reporting discontinued operations, the income statement should show in a special section:

a. gains and losses on the disposal of the discontinued segment.
b. gains and losses from operations of the discontinued segment.
c. Both (a) and (b).
d. Neither (a) nor (b).

**9.** Scout Corporation has income before taxes of $400,000 (SO 6) and an extraordinary loss of $100,000. If the income tax rate is 25% on all items, the income statement should show income before extraordinary items and extraordinary items, respectively, of:
a. $325,000 and $100,000.
b. $325,000 and $75,000.
c. $300,000 and $100,000.
d. $300,000 and $75,000.

**10.** Which situation below might indicate a company has a (SO 7) low quality of earnings?
a. The same accounting principles are used each year.
b. Revenue is recognized when earned.
c. Maintenance costs are expensed as incurred.
d. The company is continually reporting pro forma income numbers.

Go to the book's website,
**www.wiley.com/college/weygandt**,
for Additional Self-Study questions.

 The Navigator

# QUESTIONS

**1.** (a) Juan Marichal believes that the analysis of financial statements is directed at two characteristics of a company: liquidity and profitability. Is Juan correct? Explain.
(b) Are short-term creditors, long-term creditors, and stockholders interested primarily in the same characteristics of a company? Explain.

**2.** (a) Distinguish among the following bases of comparison: (1) intracompany, (2) industry averages, and (3) intercompany.
(b) Give the principal value of using each of the three bases of comparison.

**3.** Two popular methods of financial statement analysis are horizontal analysis and vertical analysis. Explain the difference between these two methods.

**4.** (a) If Leonard Company had net income of $360,000 in 2008 and it experienced a 24.5% increase in net income for 2009, what is its net income for 2009?
(b) If six cents of every dollar of Leonard revenue is net income in 2008, what is the dollar amount of 2008 revenue?

**5.** What is a ratio? What are the different ways of expressing the relationship of two amounts? What information does a ratio provide?

**6.** Name the major ratios useful in assessing (a) liquidity and (b) solvency.

**7.** Raphael Ochoa is puzzled. His company had a profit margin of 10% in 2008. He feels that this is an indication that the company is doing well. Cindy Lore, his accountant, says that more information is needed to determine the firm's financial well-being. Who is correct? Why?

**8.** What do the following classes of ratios measure? (a) Liquidity ratios. (b) Profitability ratios. (c) Solvency ratios.

**9.** What is the difference between the current ratio and the acid-test ratio?

**10.** Donte Company, a retail store, has a receivables turnover of 4.5 times. The industry average is 12.5 times. Does Donte have a collection problem with its receivables?

**11.** Which ratios should be used to help answer the following questions?
(a) How efficient is a company in using its assets to produce sales?
(b) How near to sale is the inventory on hand?
(c) How many dollars of net income were earned for each dollar invested by the owners?
(d) How able is a company to meet interest charges as they fall due?

**12.** The price-earnings ratio of General Motors (automobile builder) was 8, and the price-earnings ratio of Microsoft (computer software) was 38. Which company did the stock market favor? Explain.

13. What is the formula for computing the payout ratio? Would you expect this ratio to be high or low for a growth company?

14. Holding all other factors constant, indicate whether each of the following changes generally signals good or bad news about a company.
    (a) Increase in profit margin.
    (b) Decrease in inventory turnover.
    (c) Increase in the current ratio.
    (d) Decrease in earnings per share.
    (e) Increase in price-earnings ratio.
    (f) Increase in debt to total assets ratio.
    (g) Decrease in times interest earned.

15. The return on assets for Tresh Corporation is 7.6%. During the same year Tresh's return on common stockholders' equity is 12.8%. What is the explanation for the difference in the two rates?

16. Which two ratios do you think should be of greatest interest to:
    (a) A pension fund considering the purchase of 20-year bonds?
    (b) A bank contemplating a short-term loan?
    (c) A common stockholder?

17. Why must preferred stock dividends be subtracted from net income in computing earnings per share?

18. (a) What is meant by trading on the equity?
    (b) How would you determine the profitability of trading on the equity?

19. Hillman Inc. has net income of $160,000, weighted average shares of common stock outstanding of 50,000, and pre-

ferred dividends for the period of $40,000. What is Hillman's earnings per share of common stock? Kate Hillman, the president of Hillman Inc., believes the computed EPS of the company is high. Comment.

20. Why is it important to report discontinued operations separately from income from continuing operations?

21. You are considering investing in Shawnee Transportation. The company reports 2008 earnings per share of $6.50 on income before extraordinary items and $4.75 on net income. Which EPS figure would you consider more relevant to your investment decision? Why?

22. STL Inc. reported 2007 earnings per share of $3.20 and had no extraordinary items. In 2008, EPS on income before extraordinary items was $2.99, and EPS on net income was $3.49. Is this a favorable trend?

23. Indicate which of the following items would be reported as an extraordinary item in Mordica Corporation's income statement.
    (a) Loss from damages caused by volcano eruption.
    (b) Loss from sale of short-term investments.
    (c) Loss attributable to a labor strike.
    (d) Loss caused when manufacture of a product was prohibited by the Food and Drug Administration.
    (e) Loss from flood damage. (The nearby Black River floods every 2 to 3 years.)
    (f) Write-down of obsolete inventory.
    (g) Expropriation of a factory by a foreign government.

24. Identify and explain factors that affect quality of earnings.

---

## BRIEF EXERCISES

*Follow the rounding procedures used in the chapter.*

**BE15-1**  You recently received a letter from your Uncle Frank. A portion of the letter is presented below.

*Discuss need for comparative analysis.*
(SO 1)

> You know that I have a significant amount of money I saved over the years. I am thinking about starting an investment program. I want to do the investing myself, based on my own research and analysis of financial statements. I know that you are studying accounting, so I have a couple of questions for you. I have heard that different users of financial statements are interested in different characteristics of companies. Is this true, and, if so, why? Also, some of my friends, who are already investing, have told me that comparisons involving a company's financial data can be made on a number of different bases. Can you explain these bases to me?

**Instructions**
Write a letter to your Uncle Frank which answers his questions.

**BE15-2**  Drew Carey Corporation reported the following amounts in 2007, 2008, and 2009.

*Identify and use tools of financial statement analysis.*
(SO 2, 3, 4, 5)

|                      | **2007**  | **2008**  | **2009**  |
|----------------------|-----------|-----------|-----------|
| Current assets       | $200,000  | $230,000  | $240,000  |
| Current liabilities  | $160,000  | $168,000  | $184,000  |
| Total assets         | $500,000  | $600,000  | $620,000  |

**Instructions**
(a) Identify and describe the three tools of financial statement analysis. (b) Perform each of the three types of analysis on Drew Carey's current assets.

*Prepare horizontal analysis.*
(SO 3)

**BE15-3** Using the following data from the comparative balance sheet of Rodenbeck Company, illustrate horizontal analysis.

|  | December 31, 2009 | December 31, 2008 |
|---|---|---|
| Accounts receivable | $ 520,000 | $ 400,000 |
| Inventory | $ 840,000 | $ 600,000 |
| Total assets | $ 3,000,000 | $2,500,000 |

*Prepare vertical analysis.*
(SO 4)

**BE15-4** Using the same data presented above in BE15-3 for Rodenbeck Company, illustrate vertical analysis.

*Calculate percentage of change.*
(SO 3)

**BE15-5** Net income was $500,000 in 2007, $450,000 in 2008, and $522,000 in 2009. What is the percentage of change from **(a)** 2007 to 2008 and **(b)** 2008 to 2009? Is the change an increase or a decrease?

*Calculate net income.*
(SO 3)

**BE15-6** If Soule Company had net income of $585,000 in 2009 and it experienced a 30% increase in net income over 2008, what was its 2008 net income?

*Calculate change in net income.*
(SO 3)

**BE15-7** Horizontal analysis (trend analysis) percentages for Epstein Company's sales, cost of goods sold, and expenses are shown below.

| Horizontal Analysis | 2009 | 2008 | 2007 |
|---|---|---|---|
| Sales | 96.2 | 106.8 | 100.0 |
| Cost of goods sold | 102.0 | 97.0 | 100.0 |
| Expenses | 109.6 | 98.4 | 100.0 |

Did Epstein's net income increase, decrease, or remain unchanged over the 3-year period?

*Calculate change in net income.*
(SO 4)

**BE15-8** Vertical analysis (common size) percentages for Charles Company's sales, cost of goods sold, and expenses are shown below.

| Vertical Analysis | 2009 | 2008 | 2007 |
|---|---|---|---|
| Sales | 100.0 | 100.0 | 100.0 |
| Cost of goods sold | 59.2 | 62.4 | 64.5 |
| Expenses | 25.0 | 25.6 | 27.5 |

Did Charles's net income as a percent of sales increase, decrease, or remain unchanged over the 3-year period? Provide numerical support for your answer.

*Calculate liquidity ratios.*
(SO 5)

**BE15-9** Selected condensed data taken from a recent balance sheet of Perkins Inc. are as follows.

### PERKINS INC.
#### Balance Sheet (partial)

| | |
|---|---|
| Cash | $ 8,041,000 |
| Short-term investments | 4,947,000 |
| Accounts receivable | 12,545,000 |
| Inventories | 14,814,000 |
| Other current assets | 5,571,000 |
| Total current assets | $45,918,000 |
| Total current liabilities | $40,644,000 |

What are the **(a)** working capital, **(b)** current ratio, and **(c)** acid-test ratio?

*Calculate profitability ratios.*
(SO 5)

**BE15-10** McLaren Corporation has net income of $11.44 million and net revenue of $80 million in 2008. Its assets are $14 million at the beginning of the year and $18 million at the end of the year. What are McLaren's **(a)** asset turnover and **(b)** profit margin?

**BE15-11**   The following data are taken from the financial statements of Morino Company.

| | 2009 | 2008 |
|---|---|---|
| Accounts receivable (net), end of year | $ 550,000 | $ 520,000 |
| Net sales on account | 3,960,000 | 3,100,000 |
| Terms for all sales are 1/10, n/60. | | |

*Evaluate collection of accounts receivable.*

*(SO 5)*

**(a)** Compute for each year (1) the receivables turnover and (2) the average collection period. At the end of 2007, accounts receivable (net) was $480,000.
**(b)** ━━━━▶ What conclusions about the management of accounts receivable can be drawn from these data?

**BE15-12**   The following data are from the income statements of Huntsinger Company.

| | 2009 | 2008 |
|---|---|---|
| Sales | $6,420,000 | $6,240,000 |
| Beginning inventory | 980,000 | 860,000 |
| Purchases | 4,340,000 | 4,661,000 |
| Ending inventory | 1,020,000 | 980,000 |

*Evaluate management of inventory.*

*(SO 5)*

**(a)** Compute for each year (1) the inventory turnover and (2) the average days to sell the inventory.
━━━━▶ **(b)** What conclusions concerning the management of the inventory can be drawn from these data?

**BE15-13**   Gladow Company has stockholders' equity of $400,000 and net income of $66,000. It has a payout ratio of 20% and a rate of return on assets of 15%. How much did Gladow pay in cash dividends, and what were its average assets?

*Calculate profitability ratios.*

*(SO 5)*

**BE15-14**   An inexperienced accountant for Ming Corporation showed the following in the income statement: income before income taxes and extraordinary item $400,000, and extraordinary loss from flood (before taxes) $70,000. The extraordinary loss and taxable income are both subject to a 30% tax rate. Prepare a correct income statement.

*Prepare income statement including extraordinary items.*

*(SO 6)*

**BE15-15**   On June 30, Reeves Corporation discontinued its operations in Mexico. During the year, the operating loss was $300,000 before taxes. On September 1, Reeves disposed of the Mexico facility at a pretax loss of $120,000. The applicable tax rate is 30%. Show the discontinued operations section of the income statement.

*Prepare discontinued operations section of income statement.*

*(SO 6)*

# EXERCISES ━━━━━━━━━━━━━━━━━━━━━━━━━━━━ WILEY PLUS

*Follow the rounding procedures used in the chapter.*

**E15-1**   Financial information for Blevins Inc. is presented below.

| | December 31, 2009 | December 31, 2008 |
|---|---|---|
| Current assets | $125,000 | $100,000 |
| Plant assets (net) | 396,000 | 330,000 |
| Current liabilities | 91,000 | 70,000 |
| Long-term liabilities | 133,000 | 95,000 |
| Common stock, $1 par | 161,000 | 115,000 |
| Retained earnings | 136,000 | 150,000 |

*Prepare horizontal analysis.*

*(SO 3)*

**Instructions**
Prepare a schedule showing a horizontal analysis for 2009 using 2008 as the base year.

**E15-2**   Operating data for Gallup Corporation are presented below.

| | 2009 | 2008 |
|---|---|---|
| Sales | $750,000 | $600,000 |
| Cost of goods sold | 465,000 | 390,000 |
| Selling expenses | 120,000 | 72,000 |
| Administrative expenses | 60,000 | 54,000 |
| Income tax expense | 33,000 | 24,000 |
| Net income | 72,000 | 60,000 |

*Prepare vertical analysis.*

*(SO 4)*

**Instructions**
Prepare a schedule showing a vertical analysis for 2009 and 2008.

*Prepare horizontal and vertical analyses.*

(SO 3, 4)

**E15-3** The comparative condensed balance sheets of Conard Corporation are presented below.

## CONARD CORPORATION
Comparative Condensed Balance Sheets
December 31

| | 2009 | 2008 |
|---|---|---|
| Assets | | |
| Current assets | $ 74,000 | $ 80,000 |
| Property, plant, and equipment (net) | 99,000 | 90,000 |
| Intangibles | 27,000 | 40,000 |
| Total assets | $200,000 | $210,000 |
| Liabilities and stockholders' equity | | |
| Current liabilities | $ 42,000 | $ 48,000 |
| Long-term liabilities | 143,000 | 150,000 |
| Stockholders' equity | 15,000 | 12,000 |
| Total liabilities and stockholders' equity | $200,000 | $210,000 |

**Instructions**

(a) Prepare a horizontal analysis of the balance sheet data for Conard Corporation using 2008 as a base.

(b) Prepare a vertical analysis of the balance sheet data for Conard Corporation in columnar form for 2009.

*Prepare horizontal and vertical analyses.*

(SO 3, 4)

**E15-4** The comparative condensed income statements of Hendi Corporation are shown below.

## HENDI CORPORATION
Comparative Condensed Income Statements
For the Years Ended December 31

| | 2009 | 2008 |
|---|---|---|
| Net sales | $600,000 | $500,000 |
| Cost of goods sold | 483,000 | 420,000 |
| Gross profit | 117,000 | 80,000 |
| Operating expenses | 57,200 | 44,000 |
| Net income | $ 59,800 | $ 36,000 |

**Instructions**

(a) Prepare a horizontal analysis of the income statement data for Hendi Corporation using 2008 as a base. (Show the amounts of increase or decrease.)

(b) Prepare a vertical analysis of the income statement data for Hendi Corporation in columnar form for both years.

*Compute liquidity ratios and compare results.*

(SO 5)

**E15-5** Nordstrom, Inc. operates department stores in numerous states. Selected financial statement data for the year ending January 29, 2005, are as follows.

## NORDSTROM, INC.
Balance Sheet (partial)

| (in millions) | End-of-Year | Beginning-of-Year |
|---|---|---|
| Cash and cash equivalents | $ 361 | $ 340 |
| Receivables (less allowance of 19 and 20) | 646 | 667 |
| Merchandise inventory | 917 | 902 |
| Prepaid expenses | 53 | 46 |
| Other current assets | 595 | 570 |
| Total current assets | $2,572 | $2,525 |
| Total current liabilities | $1,341 | $1,123 |

For the year, net sales were $7,131, and cost of goods sold was $4,559 (in millions).

**Instructions**

(a) Compute the four liquidity ratios at the end of the year.

(b) Using the data in the chapter, compare Nordstrom's liquidity with (1) that of J.C. Penney Company, and (2) the industry averages for department stores.

**E15-6**   Leach Incorporated had the following transactions occur involving current assets and current liabilities during February 2008.

*Perform current and acid-test ratio analysis.*

*(SO 5)*

| Feb. | 3 | Accounts receivable of $15,000 are collected. |
|---|---|---|
| | 7 | Equipment is purchased for $28,000 cash. |
| | 11 | Paid $3,000 for a 3-year insurance policy. |
| | 14 | Accounts payable of $12,000 are paid. |
| | 18 | Cash dividends of $5,000 are declared. |

Additional information:

1. As of February 1, 2008, current assets were $130,000, and current liabilities were $50,000.
2. As of February 1, 2008, current assets included $15,000 of inventory and $2,000 of prepaid expenses.

**Instructions**

(a) Compute the current ratio as of the beginning of the month and after each transaction.

(b) Compute the acid-test ratio as of the beginning of the month and after each transaction.

**E15-7**   Bennis Company has the following comparative balance sheet data.

*Compute selected ratios.*

*(SO 5)*

### BENNIS COMPANY
Balance Sheets
December 31

| | **2009** | **2008** |
|---|---|---|
| Cash | $ 15,000 | $ 30,000 |
| Receivables (net) | 70,000 | 60,000 |
| Inventories | 60,000 | 50,000 |
| Plant assets (net) | 200,000 | 180,000 |
| | $345,000 | $320,000 |
| | | |
| Accounts payable | $50,000 | $60,000 |
| Mortgage payable (15%) | 100,000 | 100,000 |
| Common stock, $10 par | 140,000 | 120,000 |
| Retained earnings | 55,000 | 40,000 |
| | $345,000 | $320,000 |

Additional information for 2009:

1. Net income was $25,000.
2. Sales on account were $410,000. Sales returns and allowances were $20,000.
3. Cost of goods sold was $198,000.

**Instructions**

Compute the following ratios at December 31, 2009.

(a) Current.

(b) Acid-test.

(c) Receivables turnover.

(d) Inventory turnover.

**E15-8**   Selected comparative statement data for Willingham Products Company are presented on the next page. All balance sheet data are as of December 31.

*Compute selected ratios.*

*(SO 5)*

|  | 2009 | 2008 |
|---|---|---|
| Net sales | $760,000 | $720,000 |
| Cost of goods sold | 480,000 | 440,000 |
| Interest expense | 7,000 | 5,000 |
| Net income | 50,000 | 42,000 |
| Accounts receivable | 120,000 | 100,000 |
| Inventory | 85,000 | 75,000 |
| Total assets | 580,000 | 500,000 |
| Total common stockholders' equity | 430,000 | 325,000 |

**Instructions**

Compute the following ratios for 2009.

**(a)** Profit margin.
**(b)** Asset turnover.
**(c)** Return on assets.
**(d)** Return on common stockholders' equity.

*Compute selected ratios.*
(SO 5)

**E15-9** The income statement for Christensen, Inc., appears below.

### CHRISTENSEN, INC.
Income Statement
For the Year Ended December 31, 2008

| | |
|---|---|
| Sales | $400,000 |
| Cost of goods sold | 230,000 |
| Gross profit | 170,000 |
| Expenses (including $16,000 interest and $24,000 income taxes) | 105,000 |
| Net income | $ 65,000 |

Additional information:

1. The weighted average common shares outstanding in 2008 were 30,000 shares.
2. The market price of Christensen, Inc. stock was $13 in 2008.
3. Cash dividends of $26,000 were paid, $5,000 of which were to preferred stockholders.

**Instructions**

Compute the following ratios for 2008.

**(a)** Earnings per share.
**(b)** Price-earnings.
**(c)** Payout.
**(d)** Times interest earned.

*Compute amounts from ratios.*
(SO 5)

**E15-10** Rees Corporation experienced a fire on December 31, 2009, in which its financial records were partially destroyed. It has been able to salvage some of the records and has ascertained the following balances.

|  | December 31, 2009 | December 31, 2008 |
|---|---|---|
| Cash | $ 30,000 | $ 10,000 |
| Receivables (net) | 72,500 | 126,000 |
| Inventory | 200,000 | 180,000 |
| Accounts payable | 50,000 | 90,000 |
| Notes payable | 30,000 | 60,000 |
| Common stock, $100 par | 400,000 | 400,000 |
| Retained earnings | 113,500 | 101,000 |

Additional information:

1. The inventory turnover is 3.5 times.
2. The return on common stockholders' equity is 24%. The company had no additional paid-in capital.
3. The receivables turnover is 8.8 times.
4. The return on assets is 20%.
5. Total assets at December 31, 2008, were $605,000.

**Instructions**
Compute the following for Rees Corporation.

**(a)** Cost of goods sold for 2009.
**(b)** Net sales (credit) for 2009.
**(c)** Net income for 2009.
**(d)** Total assets at December 31, 2009.

**E15-11**    Scully Corporation's comparative balance sheets are presented below.

*Compute ratios.*
(SO 5)

## SCULLY CORPORATION
### Balance Sheets
### December 31

|  | **2008** | **2007** |
|---|---|---|
| Cash | $ 4,300 | $ 3,700 |
| Accounts receivable | 21,200 | 23,400 |
| Inventory | 10,000 | 7,000 |
| Land | 20,000 | 26,000 |
| Building | 70,000 | 70,000 |
| Accumulated depreciation | (15,000) | (10,000) |
| Total | $110,500 | $120,100 |
| Accounts payable | $ 12,370 | $ 31,100 |
| Common stock | 75,000 | 69,000 |
| Retained earnings | 23,130 | 20,000 |
| Total | $110,500 | $120,100 |

Scully's 2008 income statement included net sales of $100,000, cost of goods sold of $60,000, and net income of $15,000.

**Instructions**
Compute the following ratios for 2008.

**(a)** Current ratio.
**(b)** Acid-test ratio.
**(c)** Receivables turnover.
**(d)** Inventory turnover.
**(e)** Profit margin.
**(f)** Asset turnover.
**(g)** Return on assets.
**(h)** Return on common stockholders' equity.
**(i)** Debt to total assets ratio.

**E15-12**    For its fiscal year ending October 31, 2008, Molini Corporation reports the following partial data.

*Prepare a correct income statement.*
(SO 6)

| | |
|---|---|
| Income before income taxes | $540,000 |
| Income tax expense (30% × $390,000) | 117,000 |
| Income before extraordinary items | 423,000 |
| Extraordinary loss from flood | 150,000 |
| Net income | $273,000 |

The flood loss is considered an extraordinary item. The income tax rate is 30% on all items.

**Instructions**
**(a)** Prepare a correct income statement, beginning with income before income taxes.
**(b)** ◄▬▬▬ Explain in memo form why the income statement data are misleading.

**E15-13**    Yadier Corporation has income from continuing operations of $290,000 for the year ended December 31, 2008. It also has the following items (before considering income taxes).

*Prepare income statement.*
(SO 6)

**1.** An extraordinary loss of $80,000.
**2.** A gain of $30,000 on the discontinuance of a division.

3. A correction of an error in last year's financial statements that resulted in a $20,000 under-
statement of 2007 net income.

Assume all items are subject to income taxes at a 30% tax rate.

**Instructions**
**(a)** Prepare an income statement, beginning with income from continuing operations.
**(b)** Indicate the statement presentation of any item not included in (a) above.

# EXERCISES: SET B

Visit the book's website at **www.wiley.com/college/weygandt**, and choose the Student
Companion site, to access Exercise Set B.

# PROBLEMS

*Follow the rounding procedures used in the chapter.*

*Prepare vertical analysis and comment on profitability.*

(SO 4, 5)

**P15-1**  Comparative statement data for Douglas Company and Maulder Company, two competitors, appear below. All balance sheet data are as of December 31, 2009, and December 31,
2008.

|  | **Douglas Company** | | **Maulder Company** | |
|---|---|---|---|---|
|  | **2009** | **2008** | **2009** | **2008** |
| Net sales | $1,549,035 | | $339,038 | |
| Cost of goods sold | 1,080,490 | | 241,000 | |
| Operating expenses | 302,275 | | 79,000 | |
| Interest expense | 8,980 | | 2,252 | |
| Income tax expense | 54,500 | | 6,650 | |
| Current assets | 325,975 | $312,410 | 83,336 | $ 79,467 |
| Plant assets (net) | 521,310 | 500,000 | 139,728 | 125,812 |
| Current liabilities | 65,325 | 75,815 | 35,348 | 30,281 |
| Long-term liabilities | 108,500 | 90,000 | 29,620 | 25,000 |
| Common stock, $10 par | 500,000 | 500,000 | 120,000 | 120,000 |
| Retained earnings | 173,460 | 146,595 | 38,096 | 29,998 |

*Unlike previous chapters, Chapter 15 has one set of problems in the book, not two. A second set appears at the Student Companion Site.*

(a) Net income (Douglas) 6.6%; (Maulder) 3.0%

**Instructions**
**(a)** Prepare a vertical analysis of the 2009 income statement data for Douglas Company and
Maulder Company in columnar form.
**(b)** ◖━━━▶ Comment on the relative profitability of the companies by computing the return
on assets and the return on common stockholders' equity ratios for both companies.

*Compute ratios from balance sheet and income statement.*

(SO 5)

**P15-2**  The comparative statements of Villa Tool Company are presented below.

## VILLA TOOL COMPANY
Income Statement
For the Year Ended December 31

|  | **2009** | **2008** |
|---|---|---|
| Net sales | $1,818,500 | $1,750,500 |
| Cost of goods sold | 1,011,500 | 996,000 |
| Gross profit | 807,000 | 754,500 |
| Selling and administrative expense | 516,000 | 479,000 |
| Income from operations | 291,000 | 275,500 |
| Other expenses and losses |  |  |
| Interest expense | 18,000 | 14,000 |
| Income before income taxes | 273,000 | 261,500 |
| Income tax expense | 81,000 | 77,000 |
| Net income | $ 192,000 | $ 184,500 |

## VILLA TOOL COMPANY
Balance Sheets
December 31

| Assets | 2009 | 2008 |
|---|---|---|
| Current assets | | |
| Cash | $ 60,100 | $ 64,200 |
| Short-term investments | 69,000 | 50,000 |
| Accounts receivable (net) | 117,800 | 102,800 |
| Inventory | 123,000 | 115,500 |
| Total current assets | 369,900 | 332,500 |
| Plant assets (net) | 600,300 | 520,300 |
| Total assets | $970,200 | $852,800 |
| **Liabilities and Stockholders' Equity** | | |
| Current liabilities | | |
| Accounts payable | $160,000 | $145,400 |
| Income taxes payable | 43,500 | 42,000 |
| Total current liabilities | 203,500 | 187,400 |
| Bonds payable | 200,000 | 200,000 |
| Total liabilities | 403,500 | 387,400 |
| Stockholders' equity | | |
| Common stock ($5 par) | 280,000 | 300,000 |
| Retained earnings | 286,700 | 165,400 |
| Total stockholders' equity | 566,700 | 465,400 |
| Total liabilities and stockholders' equity | $970,200 | $852,800 |

All sales were on account. The allowance for doubtful accounts was $3,200 on December 31, 2009, and $3,000 on December 31, 2008.

**Instructions**
Compute the following ratios for 2009. (Weighted-average-common shares in 2009 were 57,000.)

**(a)** Earnings per share.
**(b)** Return on common stockholders' equity.
**(c)** Return on assets.
**(d)** Current.
**(e)** Acid-test.

**(f)** Receivables turnover.
**(g)** Inventory turnover.
**(h)** Times interest earned.
**(i)** Asset turnover.
**(j)** Debt to total assets.

**P15-3**   Condensed balance sheet and income statement data for Kersenbrock Corporation appear below.

*Perform ratio analysis, and evaluate financial position and operating results.*

(SO 5)

## KERSENBROCK CORPORATION
Balance Sheets
December 31

| | 2009 | 2008 | 2007 |
|---|---|---|---|
| Cash | $ 25,000 | $ 20,000 | $ 18,000 |
| Receivables (net) | 50,000 | 45,000 | 48,000 |
| Other current assets | 90,000 | 95,000 | 64,000 |
| Investments | 75,000 | 70,000 | 45,000 |
| Plant and equipment (net) | 400,000 | 370,000 | 358,000 |
| | $640,000 | $600,000 | $533,000 |
| Current liabilities | $ 75,000 | $ 80,000 | $ 70,000 |
| Long-term debt | 80,000 | 85,000 | 50,000 |
| Common stock, $10 par | 340,000 | 310,000 | 300,000 |
| Retained earnings | 145,000 | 125,000 | 113,000 |
| | $640,000 | $600,000 | $533,000 |

## KERSENBROCK CORPORATION
### Income Statement
### For the Year Ended December 31

|  | 2009 | 2008 |
|---|---|---|
| Sales | $740,000 | $700,000 |
| Less: Sales returns and allowances | 40,000 | 50,000 |
| Net sales | 700,000 | 650,000 |
| Cost of goods sold | 420,000 | 400,000 |
| Gross profit | 280,000 | 250,000 |
| Operating expenses (including income taxes) | 235,000 | 220,000 |
| Net income | $ 45,000 | $ 30,000 |

Additional information:

1. The market price of Kersenbrock's common stock was $4.00, $5.00, and $8.00 for 2007, 2008, and 2009, respectively.
2. All dividends were paid in cash.

**Instructions**

(a) Compute the following ratios for 2008 and 2009.
   (1) Profit margin.
   (2) Asset turnover.
   (3) Earnings per share. (Weighted-average-common shares in 2009 were 32,000 and in 2008 were 31,000.)
   (4) Price-earnings.
   (5) Payout.
   (6) Debt to total assets.
(b) ▰◣▬▬▶ Based on the ratios calculated, discuss briefly the improvement or lack thereof in financial position and operating results from 2008 to 2009 of Kersenbrock Corporation.

*Compute ratios, and comment on overall liquidity and profitability.*

(SO 5)

**P15-4**    Financial information for Hanshew Company is presented below.

## HANSHEW COMPANY
### Balance Sheets
### December 31

| **Assets** | 2009 | 2008 |
|---|---|---|
| Cash | $ 70,000 | $ 65,000 |
| Short-term investments | 52,000 | 40,000 |
| Receivables (net) | 98,000 | 80,000 |
| Inventories | 125,000 | 135,000 |
| Prepaid expenses | 29,000 | 23,000 |
| Land | 130,000 | 130,000 |
| Building and equipment (net) | 180,000 | 175,000 |
|  | $684,000 | $648,000 |
| **Liabilities and Stockholders' Equity** |  |  |
| Notes payable | $100,000 | $100,000 |
| Accounts payable | 48,000 | 42,000 |
| Accrued liabilities | 50,000 | 40,000 |
| Bonds payable, due 2012 | 150,000 | 150,000 |
| Common stock, $10 par | 200,000 | 200,000 |
| Retained earnings | 136,000 | 116,000 |
|  | $684,000 | $648,000 |

## HANSHEW COMPANY
Income Statement
For the Years Ended December 31

|  | 2009 | 2008 |
|---|---|---|
| Sales | $850,000 | $790,000 |
| Cost of goods sold | 620,000 | 575,000 |
| Gross profit | 230,000 | 215,000 |
| Operating expenses | 187,000 | 173,000 |
| Net income | $ 43,000 | $ 42,000 |

Additional information:

1. Inventory at the beginning of 2008 was $118,000.
2. Receivables (net) at the beginning of 2008 were $88,000. The allowance for doubtful accounts was $4,000 at the end of 2009, $3,800 at the end of 2008, and $3,700 at the beginning of 2008.
3. Total assets at the beginning of 2008 were $630,000.
4. No common stock transactions occurred during 2008 or 2009.
5. All sales were on account.

### Instructions
**(a)** Indicate, by using ratios, the change in liquidity and profitability of Hanshew Company from 2008 to 2009. (*Note*: Not all profitability ratios can be computed.)
**(b)** Given below are three independent situations and a ratio that may be affected. For each situation, compute the affected ratio (1) as of December 31, 2009, and (2) as of December 31, 2010, after giving effect to the situation. Net income for 2010 was $50,000. Total assets on December 31, 2010, were $700,000.

| Situation | Ratio |
|---|---|
| (1) 18,000 shares of common stock were sold at par on July 1, 2010. | Return on common stockholders' equity |
| (2) All of the notes payable were paid in 2010. The only change in liabilities was that the notes payable were paid. | Debt to total assets |
| (3) Market price of common stock was $9 on December 31, 2009, and $12.80 on December 31, 2010. | Price-earnings ratio |

**P15-5** Selected financial data of Target and Wal-Mart for 2005 are presented here (in millions).

*Compute selected ratios, and compare liquidity, profitability, and solvency for two companies.*

(SO 5)

|  | Target Corporation | Wal-Mart Stores, Inc. |
|---|---|---|
|  | **Income Statement Data for Year** | |
| Net sales | $45,682 | $285,222 |
| Cost of goods sold | 31,445 | 219,793 |
| Selling and administrative expenses | 10,480 | 51,354 |
| Interest expense | 570 | 986 |
| Other income (expense) | 1,157 | 2,767 |
| Income tax expense | 1,146 | 5,589 |
| Net income | $ 3,198 | $ 10,267 |
|  | **Balance Sheet Data (End of Year)** | |
| Current assets | $13,922 | $ 38,491 |
| Noncurrent assets | 18,371 | 81,732 |
| Total assets | $32,293 | $120,223 |
| Current liabilities | $ 8,220 | $ 42,888 |
| Long-term debt | 11,044 | 27,939 |
| Total stockholders' equity | 13,029 | 49,396 |
| Total liabilities and stockholders' equity | $32,293 | $120,223 |

| | Beginning-of-Year Balances | |
|---|---|---|
| Total assets | $31,416 | $105,405 |
| Total stockholders' equity | 11,132 | 43,623 |
| Current liabilities | 8,314 | 40,364 |
| Total liabilities | 20,284 | 61,782 |
| | **Other Data** | |
| Average net receivables | $4,845 | $ 1,485 |
| Average inventory | 4,958 | 28,030 |
| Net cash provided by operating activities | 3,821 | 15,044 |

**Instructions**

**(a)** For each company, compute the following ratios.

| | |
|---|---|
| **(1)** Current. | **(7)** Asset turnover. |
| **(2)** Receivables turnover. | **(8)** Return on assets. |
| **(3)** Average collection period. | **(9)** Return on common stockholders' equity. |
| **(4)** Inventory turnover. | **(10)** Debt to total assets. |
| **(5)** Days in inventory. | **(11)** Times interest earned. |
| **(6)** Profit margin. | |

**(b)** Compare the liquidity, solvency, and profitability of the two companies.

*Compute numerous ratios.*
(SO 5)

**P15-6**  The comparative statements of Dillon Company are presented below.

## DILLON COMPANY
### Income Statement
### For Year Ended December 31

| | 2009 | 2008 |
|---|---|---|
| Net sales (all on account) | $600,000 | $520,000 |
| Expenses | | |
| Cost of goods sold | 415,000 | 354,000 |
| Selling and administrative | 120,800 | 114,800 |
| Interest expense | 7,800 | 6,000 |
| Income tax expense | 18,000 | 14,000 |
| Total expenses | 561,600 | 488,800 |
| Net income | $ 38,400 | $ 31,200 |

## DILLON COMPANY
### Balance Sheets
### December 31

| Assets | 2009 | 2008 |
|---|---|---|
| Current assets | | |
| Cash | $ 21,000 | $ 18,000 |
| Short-term investments | 18,000 | 15,000 |
| Accounts receivable (net) | 86,000 | 74,000 |
| Inventory | 90,000 | 70,000 |
| Total current assets | 215,000 | 177,000 |
| Plant assets (net) | 423,000 | 383,000 |
| Total assets | $638,000 | $560,000 |

**Liabilities and Stockholders' Equity**

| Current liabilities | | |
|---|---|---|
| Accounts payable | $122,000 | $110,000 |
| Income taxes payable | 23,000 | 20,000 |
| Total current liabilities | 145,000 | 130,000 |
| Long-term liabilities | | |
| Bonds payable | 120,000 | 80,000 |
| Total liabilities | 265,000 | 210,000 |
| Stockholders' equity | | |
| Common stock ($5 par) | 150,000 | 150,000 |
| Retained earnings | 223,000 | 200,000 |
| Total stockholders' equity | 373,000 | 350,000 |
| Total liabilities and stockholders' equity | $638,000 | $560,000 |

**Additional data:**

The common stock recently sold at $19.50 per share.

The year-end balance in the allowance for doubtful accounts was $3,000 for 2009 and $2,400 for 2008.

**Instructions**

Compute the following ratios for 2009.

(a) Current.
(b) Acid-test.
(c) Receivables turnover.
(d) Inventory turnover.
(e) Profit margin.
(f) Asset turnover.
(g) Return on assets.

(h) Return on common stockholders' equity.
(i) Earnings per share.
(j) Price-earnings.
(k) Payout.
(l) Debt to total assets.
(m) Times interest earned.

**P15-7** Presented below is an incomplete income statement and an incomplete comparative balance sheet of Cotte Corporation.

*Compute missing information given a set of ratios.*

(SO 5)

## COTTE CORPORATION
Income Statement
For the Year Ended December 31, 2009

| | |
|---|---|
| Sales | $11,000,000 |
| Cost of goods sold | ? |
| Gross profit | ? |
| Operating expenses | 1,665,000 |
| Income from operations | ? |
| Other expenses and losses | |
| Interest expense | ? |
| Income before income taxes | ? |
| Income tax expense | 560,000 |
| Net income | $ ? |

## COTTE CORPORATION
### Balance Sheets
### December 31

| Assets | 2009 | 2008 |
|---|---|---|
| **Current assets** | | |
| Cash | $ 450,000 | $ 375,000 |
| Accounts receivable (net) | ? | 950,000 |
| Inventory | ? | 1,720,000 |
| Total current assets | ? | 3,045,000 |
| Plant assets (net) | 4,620,000 | 3,955,000 |
| Total assets | $ ? | $7,000,000 |
| | | |
| **Liabilities and Stockholders' Equity** | | |
| Current liabilities | $ ? | $ 825,000 |
| Long-term notes payable | ? | 2,800,000 |
| Total liabilities | ? | 3,625,000 |
| Common stock, $1 par | 3,000,000 | 3,000,000 |
| Retained earnings | 400,000 | 375,000 |
| Total stockholders' equity | 3,400,000 | 3,375,000 |
| Total liabilities and stockholders' equity | $ ? | $7,000,000 |

**Additional information:**

1. The receivables turnover for 2009 is 10 times.
2. All sales are on account.
3. The profit margin for 2009 is 14.5%.
4. Return on assets is 22% for 2009.
5. The current ratio on December 31, 2009, is 3.0.
6. The inventory turnover for 2009 is 4.8 times.

**Instructions**

Compute the missing information given the ratios above. Show computations. (*Note*: Start with one ratio and derive as much information as possible from it before trying another ratio. List all missing amounts under the ratio used to find the information.)

*Prepare income statement with discontinued operations and extraordinary loss.*

(SO 6)

**P15-8** Cheaney Corporation owns a number of cruise ships and a chain of hotels. The hotels, which have not been profitable, were discontinued on September 1, 2008. The 2008 operating results for the company were as follows.

| | |
|---|---|
| Operating revenues | $12,850,000 |
| Operating expenses | 8,700,000 |
| Operating income | $ 4,150,000 |

Analysis discloses that these data include the operating results of the hotel chain, which were: operating revenues $2,000,000 and operating expenses $2,400,000. The hotels were sold at a gain of $200,000 before taxes. This gain is not included in the operating results. During the year, Cheaney suffered an extraordinary loss of $800,000 before taxes, which is not included in the operating results. In 2008, the company had other revenues and gains of $100,000, which are not included in the operating results. The corporation is in the 30% income tax bracket.

**Instructions**

*Net income $2,555,000*

Prepare a condensed income statement.

*Prepare income statement with nontypical items.*

(SO 6)

**P15-9** The ledger of LaRussa Corporation at December 31, 2008, contains the following summary data.

| | | | |
|---|---|---|---|
| Net sales | $1,700,000 | Cost of goods sold | $1,100,000 |
| Selling expenses | 120,000 | Administrative expenses | 150,000 |
| Other revenues and gains | 20,000 | Other expenses and losses | 28,000 |

Your analysis reveals the following additional information that is not included in the data on page 742.

1. The entire puzzles division was discontinued on August 31. The income from operations for this division before income taxes was $20,000. The puzzles division was sold at a loss of $90,000 before income taxes.
2. On May 15, company property was expropriated for an interstate highway. The settlement resulted in an extraordinary gain of $120,000 before income taxes.
3. The income tax rate on all items is 30%.

**Instructions**

Net income: $260,400

Prepare an income statement for the year ended December 31, 2008. Use the format illustrated in Demonstration Problem 2 (p. 726).

## PROBLEMS: SET B

Visit the book's website at **www.wiley.com/college/weygandt**, and choose the Student Companion site, to access Problem Set B.

## CONTINUING COOKIE CHRONICLE

(*Note:* This is a continuation of the Cookie Chronicle from Chapters 1–14.)

**CCC15**   Natalie and Curtis have comparative balance sheets and income statements for Cookie & Coffee Creations Inc. They have been told that they can use these financial statements to prepare horizontal and vertical analyses, and to calculate financial ratios, to analyze how their business is doing and to make some decisions they have been considering.

*Go to the book's website,*
**www.wiley.com/college/weygandt**,
*to see the completion of this problem.*

# BROADENING YOUR PERSPECTIVE

## FINANCIAL REPORTING AND ANALYSIS

# Financial Reporting Problem
## PepsiCo, Inc.

**BYP15-1**   Your parents are considering investing in PepsiCo, Inc. common stock. They ask you, as an accounting expert, to make an analysis of the company for them. Fortunately, excerpts from a current annual report of PepsiCo are presented in Appendix A of this textbook. Note that all dollar amounts are in millions.

**Instructions**

(Follow the approach in the chapter for rounding numbers.)

**(a)** Make a 5-year trend analysis, using 2001 as the base year, of (1) net sales and (2) net income. Comment on the significance of the trend results.
**(b)** Compute for 2005 and 2004 the (1) profit margin, (2) asset turnover, (3) return on assets, and (4) return on common stockholders' equity. How would you evaluate PepsiCo's profitability? Total assets at December 27, 2003, were $25,327, and total stockholders' equity at December 27, 2003, was $11,896.
**(c)** Compute for 2005 and 2004 the (1) debt to total assets and (2) times interest earned ratio. How would you evaluate PepsiCo's long-term solvency?
**(d)** What information outside the annual report may also be useful to your parents in making a decision about PepsiCo, Inc.?

## Comparative Analysis Problem

### PepsiCo, Inc. vs. The Coca-Cola Company

**BYP15-2** PepsiCo's financial statements are presented in Appendix A. The Coca-Cola Company's financial statements are presented in Appendix B.

**Instructions**

(a) Based on the information contained in these financial statements, determine each of the following for each company.

    (1) The percentage increase (decrease) in (i) net sales and (ii) net income from 2004 to 2005.

    (2) The percentage increase in (i) total assets and (ii) total common stockholders' (shareholders') equity from 2004 to 2005.

    (3) The basic earnings per share and price-earnings ratio for 2005. (For Coca-Cola, use the basic earnings per share.) Coca-Cola's common stock had a market price of $43.60 at the end of fiscal-year 2005.

(b) What conclusions concerning the two companies can be drawn from these data?

## Exploring the Web

**BYP15-3** The Management Discussion and Analysis section of an annual report addresses corporate performance for the year, and sometimes uses financial ratios to support its claims.

**Address: www.ibm.com/investor/tools/index.phtml** or go to **www.wiley.com/college/weygandt**

**Steps**

1. From IBM's Investor Tools, choose **Investment Guides**.
2. Choose **Guide to Annual Reports**.
3. Choose **Anatomy of an Annual Report**.

**Instructions**

Using the information from the above site, answer the following questions.

(a) What are the optional elements that are often included in an annual report?

(b) What are the elements of an annual report that are required by the SEC?

(c) Describe the contents of the Management Discussion.

(d) Describe the contents of the Auditors' Report.

(e) Describe the contents of the Selected Financial Data.

## CRITICAL THINKING

## Decision Making Across the Organization

**BYP15-4** As the CPA for Carismo Manufacturing Inc., you have been asked to develop some key ratios from the comparative financial statements. This information is to be used to convince creditors that the company is solvent and will continue as a going concern. The data requested and the computations developed from the financial statements follow.

|  | 2008 | 2007 |
|---|---|---|
| Current ratio | 3.1 times | 2.1 times |
| Acid-test ratio | .8 times | 1.4 times |
| Asset turnover | 2.8 times | 2.2 times |
| Net income | Up 32% | Down 8% |
| Earnings per share | $3.30 | $2.50 |
| Book value per share | Up 8% | Up 11% |

**Instructions**

With the class divided into groups, answer the following.

Carismo Manufacturing Inc. asks you to prepare a list of brief comments stating how each of these items supports the solvency and going-concern potential of the business. The company wishes to use these comments to support its presentation of data to its creditors. You are to prepare the comments as requested, giving the implications and the limitations of each item separately. Then prepare a collective inference that may be drawn from the individual items about Carismo's solvency and going-concern potential.

**BYP15-5**   General Dynamics develops, produces, and supports innovative, reliable, and highly sophisticated military and commercial products. In July of a recent year, the corporation announced that its Quincy Shipbuilding Division (Quincy) will be closed following the completion of the Maritime Prepositioning Ship construction program.

Prior to discontinuance, the operating results of Quincy were net sales $246.8 million, income from operations before income taxes $28.3 million, and income taxes $12.5 million. The corporation's loss on disposition of Quincy was $5.0 million, net of $4.3 million income tax benefits.

From its other operating activities, General Dynamics' financial results were net sales $8,163.8 million, cost of goods sold $6,958.8 million, and selling and administrative expenses $537.0 million. In addition, the corporation had interest expense of $17.2 million and interest revenue of $3.6 million. Income taxes were $282.9 million.

General Dynamics had an average of 42.3 million shares of common stock outstanding during the year.

**Instructions**

With the class divided into groups, answer the following.

**(a)** Prepare the income statement for the year, assuming that the year ended on December 31, 2008. Show earnings per share data on the income statement. All dollars should be stated in millions, except for per share amounts. (For example, $8 million would be shown as $8.0)

**(b)** In the preceding year, Quincy's earnings were $51.6 million before income taxes of $22.8 million. For comparative purposes, General Dynamics reported earnings per share of $0.61 from discontinued operations for Quincy in the preceding year.

   **(1)** What was the average number of common shares outstanding during the preceding year?

   **(2)** If earnings per share from continuing operations was $7.47, what was income from continuing operations during the preceding year? (Round to two decimals.)

# Communication Activity

**BYP15-6**   Beth Harlan is the CEO of Lafferty's Electronics. Harlan is an expert engineer but a novice in accounting. She asks you to explain (1) the bases for comparison in analyzing Lafferty's financial statements, and (2) the factors affecting quality of earnings.

**Instructions**

Write a letter to Beth Harlan that explains the bases for comparison and factors affecting quality of earnings.

# Ethics Case

**BYP15-7**   Jack McClintock, president of McClintock Industries, wishes to issue a press release to bolster his company's image and maybe even its stock price, which has been gradually falling. As controller, you have been asked to provide a list of twenty financial ratios along with some other operating statistics relative to McClintock Industries' first quarter financials and operations.

Two days after you provide the ratios and data requested, Jeremy Phelps, the public relations director of McClintock, asks you to prove the accuracy of the financial and operating data contained in the press release written by the president and edited by Jeremy. In the press release, the president highlights the sales increase of 25% over last year's first quarter and the positive change in the current ratio from 1.5:1 last year to 3:1 this year. He also emphasizes that production was up 50% over the prior year's first quarter.

You note that the press release contains only positive or improved ratios and none of the negative or deteriorated ratios. For instance, no mention is made that the debt to total assets ratio has increased from 35% to 55%, that inventories are up 89%, and that while the current ratio improved, the acid-test ratio fell from 1:1 to .5:1. Nor is there any mention that the reported profit for the quarter would have been a loss had not the estimated lives of McClintock's plant and machinery been increased by 30%. Jeremy emphasized, "The prez wants this release by early this afternoon."

**Instructions**
**(a)** Who are the stakeholders in this situation?
**(b)** Is there anything unethical in president McClintock's actions?
**(c)** Should you as controller remain silent? Does Jeremy have any responsibility?

 # "All About You" Activity

**BYP15-8** In this chapter you learned how to use many tools for performing a financial analysis of a company. When making personal investments, however, it is most likely that you won't be buying stocks and bonds in individual companies. Instead, when most people want to invest in stock, they buy mutual funds. By investing in a mutual fund, you reduce your risk because the fund diversifies by buying the stock of a variety of different companies, bonds, and other investments, depending on the stated goals of the fund.

Before you invest in a fund, you will need to decide what type of fund you want. For example, do you want a fund that has the potential of high growth (but also high risk), or are you looking for lower risk and a steady stream of income? Do you want a fund that invests only in U.S. companies, or do you want one that invests globally? Many resources are available to help you with these types of decisions.

**Instructions**
Go to **http://web.archive.org/web/20050210200843/http://www.cnb1.com/invallocmdl.htm** and complete the investment allocation questionnaire. Add up your total points to determine the type of investment fund that would be appropriate for you.

 ## Answers to Insight and Accounting Across the Organization Questions

**How to Manage the Current Ratio, p. 707**
Q: How might management influence the company's current ratio?
A: *Management can affect the current ratio by speeding up or withholding payments on accounts payable just before the balance sheet date. Management can alter the cash balance by increasing or decreasing long-term assets or long-term debt, or by issuing or purchasing equity shares.*

**Keeping Up to Date as an Investor, p. 715**
Q: If you want to keep current with the financial and operating developments of a company in which you own shares, what are some ways you can do so?
A: *You can obtain current information on your investments through a company's Web site, financial magazines and newspapers, CNBC television programs, investment letters, and a stockbroker.*

**What Is Extraordinary?, p. 720**
Q: If a company takes a large restructuring charge, what is the effect on the company's current income statement versus future ones?
A: *The current period's net income can be greatly diminished by a large restructuring charge, while the net income in future periods can be enhanced because they are relieved of costs (i.e., depreciation and labor expenses) that would have been charged to them.*

 ## Authors' Comments on *All About You: Should I Play the Market Yet?*, p. 723

For a number of reasons, it is probably a bad idea for Rachael to buy her employer's stock. First, if Rachael is going to invest in the stock market, she should diversify her investments across a number of different companies. Second, you should never have more than a small portion of your total investment portfolio invested in your employer. Suppose that your employer starts to do poorly, the stock price falls, and you get laid off. You lose on two counts: You don't have income, and your net worth has been affected adversely by the drop in the stock price. (This exact situation happened to thousands of Enron employees, who not only lost their jobs, but their retirement savings as well, as Enron's stock plummeted). Third, after purchasing her employer's stock, Rachael's liquidity would be negatively affected: She would have only $3,000 of remaining liquid assets.

If Rachel invests $7,000, she actually has only enough liquid assets to cover one month's worth of expenses. It is true that she could sell her stock, but if it has fallen in value, she will be reluctant to sell. In short, if she were to buy the stock, her financial flexibility would be very limited.

The bottom line is that we think that Rachael *should* invest in something that offers a higher return than her bank savings account, but we question whether she has enough liquidity to invest in individual stocks. We would recommend that she put some money in a stock mutual fund, some in a short-term CD, and the rest in a money-market fund.

## Answer to PepsiCo Review It Question 4, p. 705

PepsiCo presents horizontal analyses in its "Financial Highlights" section and its Management's Discussion and Analysis section. Vertical analysis is used in discussions presented in the Management's Discussion and Analysis section.

## Answers to Self-Study Questions

**1.** b  **2.** d  **3.** a  **4.** c  **5.** c  **6.** c  **7.** c  **8.** c  **9.** d  **10.** d

# SPECIMEN FINANCIAL STATEMENTS:
# PepsiCo, Inc.

## THE ANNUAL REPORT

Once each year a corporation communicates to its stockholders and other interested parties by issuing a complete set of audited financial statements. The **annual report**, as this communication is called, summarizes the financial results of the company's operations for the year and its plans for the future. Many annual reports are attractive, multicolored, glossy public relations pieces, containing pictures of corporate officers and directors as well as photos and descriptions of new products and new buildings. Yet the basic function of every annual report is to report financial information, almost all of which is a product of the corporation's accounting system.

The content and organization of corporate annual reports have become fairly standardized. Excluding the public relations part of the report (pictures, products, etc.), the following are the traditional financial portions of the annual report:

- Financial Highlights
- Letter to the Stockholders
- Management's Discussion and Analysis
- Financial Statements
- Notes to the Financial Statements
- Management's Report on Internal Control
- Management Certification of Financial Statements
- Auditor's Report
- Supplementary Financial Information

In this appendix we illustrate current financial reporting with a comprehensive set of corporate financial statements that are prepared in accordance with generally accepted accounting principles and audited by an international independent certified public accounting firm. We are grateful for permission to use the actual financial statements and other accompanying financial information from the annual report of a large, publicly held company, PepsiCo, Inc.

## FINANCIAL HIGHLIGHTS

Companies usually present the financial highlights section inside the front cover of the annual report or on its first two pages. This section generally reports the total or per share amounts for five to ten financial items for the current year and one or more previous years. Financial items from the income statement and the balance sheet that typically are presented are sales, income from continuing operations, net income, net income per share, net cash provided by operating activities, dividends per common share, and the amount of capital expenditures. The financial highlights section from PepsiCo's Annual Report is shown on page A-2.

---

The financial information herein is reprinted with permission from the PepsiCo, Inc. 2005 Annual Report. The complete financial statements are available through a link at the book's companion website.

## Financial Highlights

PepsiCo, Inc. and Subsidiaries
($ in millions except per share amounts; all per share amounts assume dilution)

**Net Revenue**
Total: $32,562

**Division Operating Profit**
Total: $6,710

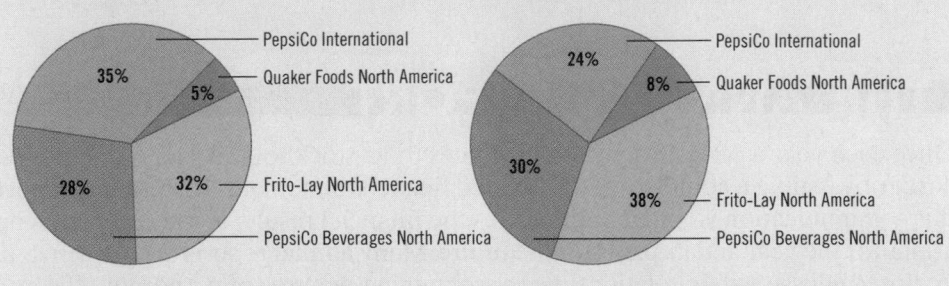

|  | 2005 | 2004 | % Chg(a) |
|---|---|---|---|
| **Summary of Operations** | | | |
| Total net revenue | $32,562 | $29,261 | 11 |
| Division operating profit | $6,710 | $6,098 | 10 |
| Total operating profit | $5,922 | $5,259 | 13 |
| Net income(b) | $4,536 | $4,004 | 13 |
| Earnings per share(b) | $2.66 | $2.32 | 15 |
| **Other Data** | | | |
| Management operating cash flow(c) | $4,204 | $3,705 | 13 |
| Net cash provided by operating activities | $5,852 | $5,054 | 16 |
| Capital spending | $1,736 | $1,387 | 25 |
| Common share repurchases | $3,012 | $3,028 | (0.5) |
| Dividends paid | $1,642 | $1,329 | 24 |
| Long-term debt | $2,313 | $2,397 | (3.5) |

(a) Percentage changes above and in text are based on unrounded amounts.

(b) In 2005, excludes the impact of AJCA tax charge, the 53rd week and restructuring charges. In 2004, excludes certain prior year tax benefits, and restructuring and impairment charges. See page 76 for reconciliation to net income and earnings per share on a GAAP basis.

(c) Includes the impact of net capital spending. Also, see "Our Liquidity, Capital Resources and Financial Position" in Management's Discussion and Analysis.

# LETTER TO THE STOCKHOLDERS

Nearly every annual report contains a letter to the stockholders from the chairman of the board or the president, or both. This letter typically discusses the company's accomplishments during the past year and highlights significant events such as mergers and acquisitions, new products, operating achievements, business philosophy, changes in officers or directors, financing commitments, expansion plans, and future prospects. The letter to the stockholders is signed by Steve Reinemund, Chairman of the Board and Chief Executive Officer, of PepsiCo.

Only a short summary of the letter is provided below. The full letter can be accessed at the book's companion website at **www.wiley.com/college/weygandt.**

---

## Dear Shareholders:

With profitable growth across all divisions, on every continent and across both convenient food and beverage categories, PepsiCo delivered a very strong 2005. The company's continued focus on health and wellness, and innovation — coupled with its efforts to build big, muscular brands and powerful go-to-market systems — generated industry leading results.

- Volume grew 7%.
- Net revenue grew 11%.
- Division operating profit grew 10%.
- Earnings per share grew 15%.
- Total return to shareholders was 15% compared with 5% for the S&P.
- Cash flow from operations was $5.9 billion and management operating cash flow was $4.2 billion.

**Steve Reinemund**
Chairman and Chief Executive Officer

## MANAGEMENT'S DISCUSSION AND ANALYSIS

The **management's discussion and analysis (MD&A)** section covers three financial aspects of a company: its results of operations, its ability to pay near-term obligations, and its ability to fund operations and expansion. Management must highlight favorable or unfavorable trends and identity significant events and uncertainties that affect these three factors. This discussion obviously involves a number of subjective estimates and opinions. In its MD&A section, PepsiCo breaks its discussion into three major headings: Our Business, Our Critical Accounting Policies, and Our Financial Results. PepsiCo's MD&A section is 22 pages long. You can access that section at **www.wiley.com/college/weygandt.**

## FINANCIAL STATEMENTS AND ACCOMPANYING NOTES

The standard set of financial statements consists of: (1) a comparative income statement for 3 years, (2) a comparative statement of cash flows for 3 years, (3) a comparative balance sheet for 2 years, (4) a statement of stockholders' equity for 3 years, and (5) a sct of accompanying notes that are considered an integral part of the financial statements. The auditor's report, unless stated otherwise, covers the financial statements and the accompanying notes. PepsiCo's financial statements and accompanying notes plus supplementary data and analyses follow.

# Consolidated Statement of Income

PepsiCo, Inc. and Subsidiaries
Fiscal years ended December 31, 2005, December 25, 2004 and December 27, 2003

| (in millions except per share amounts) | 2005 | 2004 | 2003 |
|---|---|---|---|
| Net Revenue | $32,562 | $29,261 | $26,971 |
| Cost of sales | 14,176 | 12,674 | 11,691 |
| Selling, general and administrative expenses | 12,314 | 11,031 | 10,148 |
| Amortization of intangible assets | 150 | 147 | 145 |
| Restructuring and impairment charges | – | 150 | 147 |
| Merger-related costs | – | – | 59 |
| Operating Profit | 5,922 | 5,259 | 4,781 |
| Bottling equity income | 557 | 380 | 323 |
| Interest expense | (256) | (167) | (163) |
| Interest income | 159 | 74 | 51 |
| Income from Continuing Operations before Income Taxes | 6,382 | 5,546 | 4,992 |
| Provision for Income Taxes | 2,304 | 1,372 | 1,424 |
| Income from Continuing Operations | 4,078 | 4,174 | 3,568 |
| Tax Benefit from Discontinued Operations | – | 38 | – |
| Net Income | $ 4,078 | $ 4,212 | $ 3,568 |
| Net Income per Common Share — Basic | | | |
| Continuing operations | $2.43 | $2.45 | $2.07 |
| Discontinued operations | – | 0.02 | – |
| Total | $2.43 | $2.47 | $2.07 |
| Net Income per Common Share — Diluted | | | |
| Continuing operations | $2.39 | $2.41 | $2.05 |
| Discontinued operations | – | 0.02 | – |
| Total | $2.39 | $2.44* | $2.05 |

\* Based on unrounded amounts.
See accompanying notes to consolidated financial statements.

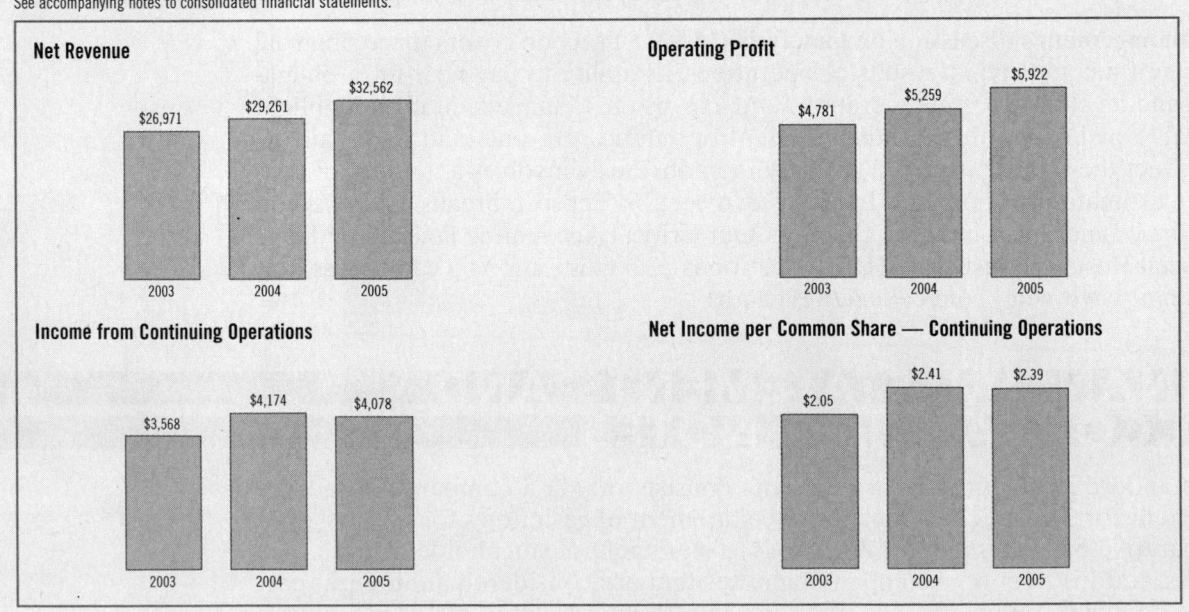

# Consolidated Statement of Cash Flows

PepsiCo, Inc. and Subsidiaries
Fiscal years ended December 31, 2005, December 25, 2004 and December 27, 2003

| (in millions) | 2005 | 2004 | 2003 |
|---|---|---|---|
| **Operating Activities** | | | |
| Net income | $ 4,078 | $ 4,212 | $ 3,568 |
| Adjustments to reconcile net income to net cash provided by operating activities | | | |
| Depreciation and amortization | 1,308 | 1,264 | 1,221 |
| Stock based compensation expense | 311 | 368 | 407 |
| Restructuring and impairment charges | – | 150 | 147 |
| Cash payments for merger-related costs and restructuring charges | (22) | (92) | (109) |
| Tax benefit from discontinued operations | – | (38) | – |
| Pension and retiree medical plan contributions | (877) | (534) | (605) |
| Pension and retiree medical plan expenses | 464 | 395 | 277 |
| Bottling equity income, net of dividends | (411) | (297) | (276) |
| Deferred income taxes and other tax charges and credits | 440 | (203) | (286) |
| Merger-related costs | – | – | 59 |
| Other non-cash charges and credits, net | 145 | 166 | 101 |
| Changes in operating working capital, excluding effects of acquisitions and divestitures | | | |
| Accounts and notes receivable | (272) | (130) | (220) |
| Inventories | (132) | (100) | (49) |
| Prepaid expenses and other current assets | (56) | (31) | 23 |
| Accounts payable and other current liabilities | 188 | 216 | (11) |
| Income taxes payable | 609 | (268) | 182 |
| Net change in operating working capital | 337 | (313) | (75) |
| Other | 79 | (24) | (101) |
| **Net Cash Provided by Operating Activities** | 5,852 | 5,054 | 4,328 |
| **Investing Activities** | | | |
| Snack Ventures Europe (SVE) minority interest acquisition | (750) | – | – |
| Capital spending | (1,736) | (1,387) | (1,345) |
| Sales of property, plant and equipment | 88 | 38 | 49 |
| Other acquisitions and investments in noncontrolled affiliates | (345) | (64) | (71) |
| Cash proceeds from sale of PBG stock | 214 | – | – |
| Divestitures | 3 | 52 | 46 |
| Short-term investments, by original maturity | | | |
| More than three months — purchases | (83) | (44) | (38) |
| More than three months — maturities | 84 | 38 | 28 |
| Three months or less, net | (992) | (963) | (940) |
| **Net Cash Used for Investing Activities** | (3,517) | (2,330) | (2,271) |
| **Financing Activities** | | | |
| Proceeds from issuances of long-term debt | 25 | 504 | 52 |
| Payments of long-term debt | (177) | (512) | (641) |
| Short-term borrowings, by original maturity | | | |
| More than three months — proceeds | 332 | 153 | 88 |
| More than three months — payments | (85) | (160) | (115) |
| Three months or less, net | 1,601 | 1,119 | 40 |
| Cash dividends paid | (1,642) | (1,329) | (1,070) |
| Share repurchases — common | (3,012) | (3,028) | (1,929) |
| Share repurchases — preferred | (19) | (27) | (16) |
| Proceeds from exercises of stock options | 1,099 | 965 | 689 |
| **Net Cash Used for Financing Activities** | (1,878) | (2,315) | (2,902) |
| Effect of exchange rate changes on cash and cash equivalents | (21) | 51 | 27 |
| **Net Increase/(Decrease) in Cash and Cash Equivalents** | 436 | 460 | (818) |
| **Cash and Cash Equivalents, Beginning of Year** | 1,280 | 820 | 1,638 |
| **Cash and Cash Equivalents, End of Year** | $ 1,716 | $ 1,280 | $ 820 |

See accompanying notes to consolidated financial statements.

# Consolidated Balance Sheet

PepsiCo, Inc. and Subsidiaries
December 31, 2005 and December 25, 2004

| (in millions except per share amounts) | 2005 | 2004 |
|---|---:|---:|
| **ASSETS** | | |
| **Current Assets** | | |
| Cash and cash equivalents | $ 1,716 | $ 1,280 |
| Short-term investments | 3,166 | 2,165 |
| | 4,882 | 3,445 |
| Accounts and notes receivable, net | 3,261 | 2,999 |
| Inventories | 1,693 | 1,541 |
| Prepaid expenses and other current assets | 618 | 654 |
| Total Current Assets | 10,454 | 8,639 |
| Property, Plant and Equipment, net | 8,681 | 8,149 |
| Amortizable Intangible Assets, net | 530 | 598 |
| Goodwill | 4,088 | 3,909 |
| Other nonamortizable intangible assets | 1,086 | 933 |
| Nonamortizable Intangible Assets | 5,174 | 4,842 |
| Investments in Noncontrolled Affiliates | 3,485 | 3,284 |
| Other Assets | 3,403 | 2,475 |
| Total Assets | $31,727 | $27,987 |
| **LIABILITIES AND SHAREHOLDERS' EQUITY** | | |
| **Current Liabilities** | | |
| Short-term obligations | $ 2,889 | $ 1,054 |
| Accounts payable and other current liabilities | 5,971 | 5,599 |
| Income taxes payable | 546 | 99 |
| Total Current Liabilities | 9,406 | 6,752 |
| Long-Term Debt Obligations | 2,313 | 2,397 |
| Other Liabilities | 4,323 | 4,099 |
| Deferred Income Taxes | 1,434 | 1,216 |
| Total Liabilities | 17,476 | 14,464 |
| Commitments and Contingencies | | |
| Preferred Stock, no par value | 41 | 41 |
| Repurchased Preferred Stock | (110) | (90) |
| **Common Shareholders' Equity** | | |
| Common stock, par value 1 2/3¢ per share (issued 1,782 shares) | 30 | 30 |
| Capital in excess of par value | 614 | 618 |
| Retained earnings | 21,116 | 18,730 |
| Accumulated other comprehensive loss | (1,053) | (886) |
| | 20,707 | 18,492 |
| Less: repurchased common stock, at cost (126 and 103 shares, respectively) | (6,387) | (4,920) |
| Total Common Shareholders' Equity | 14,320 | 13,572 |
| Total Liabilities and Shareholders' Equity | $31,727 | $27,987 |

See accompanying notes to consolidated financial statements.

# Consolidated Statement of Common Shareholders' Equity

PepsiCo, Inc. and Subsidiaries
Fiscal years ended December 31, 2005, December 25, 2004 and December 27, 2003

| (in millions) | 2005 Shares | 2005 Amount | 2004 Shares | 2004 Amount | 2003 Shares | 2003 Amount |
|---|---|---|---|---|---|---|
| **Common Stock** | 1,782 | $ 30 | 1,782 | $ 30 | 1,782 | $ 30 |
| **Capital in Excess of Par Value** | | | | | | |
| Balance, beginning of year | | 618 | | 548 | | 207 |
| Stock-based compensation expense | | 311 | | 368 | | 407 |
| Stock option exercises[a] | | (315) | | (298) | | (66) |
| Balance, end of year | | 614 | | 618 | | 548 |
| **Retained Earnings** | | | | | | |
| Balance, beginning of year | | 18,730 | | 15,961 | | 13,489 |
| Net income | | 4,078 | | 4,212 | | 3,568 |
| Cash dividends declared — common | | (1,684) | | (1,438) | | (1,082) |
| Cash dividends declared — preferred | | (3) | | (3) | | (3) |
| Cash dividends declared — RSUs | | (5) | | (2) | | – |
| Other | | – | | – | | (11) |
| Balance, end of year | | 21,116 | | 18,730 | | 15,961 |
| **Accumulated Other Comprehensive Loss** | | | | | | |
| Balance, beginning of year | | (886) | | (1,267) | | (1,672) |
| Currency translation adjustment | | (251) | | 401 | | 410 |
| Cash flow hedges, net of tax: | | | | | | |
| Net derivative gains/(losses) | | 54 | | (16) | | (11) |
| Reclassification of (gains)/losses to net income | | (8) | | 9 | | (1) |
| Minimum pension liability adjustment, net of tax | | 16 | | (19) | | 7 |
| Unrealized gain on securities, net of tax | | 24 | | 6 | | 1 |
| Other | | (2) | | – | | (1) |
| Balance, end of year | | (1,053) | | (886) | | (1,267) |
| **Repurchased Common Stock** | | | | | | |
| Balance, beginning of year | (103) | (4,920) | (77) | (3,376) | (60) | (2,524) |
| Share repurchases | (54) | (2,995) | (58) | (2,994) | (43) | (1,946) |
| Stock option exercises | 31 | 1,523 | 32 | 1,434 | 26 | 1,096 |
| Other | – | 5 | – | 16 | – | (2) |
| Balance, end of year | (126) | (6,387) | (103) | (4,920) | (77) | (3,376) |
| **Total Common Shareholders' Equity** | | $14,320 | | $13,572 | | $11,896 |

| | 2005 | 2004 | 2003 |
|---|---|---|---|
| **Comprehensive Income** | | | |
| Net income | $4,078 | $4,212 | $3,568 |
| Currency translation adjustment | (251) | 401 | 410 |
| Cash flow hedges, net of tax | 46 | (7) | (12) |
| Minimum pension liability adjustment, net of tax | 16 | (19) | 7 |
| Unrealized gain on securities, net of tax | 24 | 6 | 1 |
| Other | (2) | – | (1) |
| **Total Comprehensive Income** | $3,911 | $4,593 | $3,973 |

(a) Includes total tax benefit of $125 million in 2005, $183 million in 2004 and $340 million in 2003.
See accompanying notes to consolidated financial statements.

# Notes to Consolidated Financial Statements

## Note 1 — Basis of Presentation and Our Divisions

## Basis of Presentation

Our financial statements include the consolidated accounts of PepsiCo, Inc. and the affiliates that we control. In addition, we include our share of the results of certain other affiliates based on our economic ownership interest. We do not control these other affiliates, as our ownership in these other affiliates is generally less than 50%. Our share of the net income of noncontrolled bottling affiliates is reported in our income statement as bottling equity income. Bottling equity income also includes any changes in our ownership interests of these affiliates. In 2005, bottling equity income includes $126 million of pre-tax gains on our sales of PBG stock. See Note 8 for additional information on our noncontrolled bottling affiliates. Our share of other noncontrolled affiliates is included in division operating profit. Intercompany balances and transactions are eliminated. In 2005, we had an additional week of results (53rd week). Our fiscal year ends on the last Saturday of each December, resulting in an additional week of results every five or six years.

In connection with our ongoing BPT initiative, we aligned certain accounting policies across our divisions in 2005. We conformed our methodology for calculating our bad debt reserves and modified our policy for recognizing revenue for products shipped to customers by third-party carriers. Additionally, we conformed our method of accounting for certain costs, primarily warehouse and freight. These changes reduced our net revenue by $36 million and our operating profit by $60 million in 2005. We also made certain reclassifications on our Consolidated Statement of Income in the fourth quarter of 2005 from cost of sales to selling, general and administrative expenses in connection with our BPT initiative. These reclassifications resulted in reductions to cost of sales of $556 million through the third quarter of 2005, $732 million in the full year 2004 and $688 million in the full year 2003, with corresponding increases to selling, general and administrative expenses in those periods. These reclassifications had no net impact on operating profit and have been made to all periods presented for comparability.

The preparation of our consolidated financial statements in conformity with generally accepted accounting principles requires us to make estimates and assumptions that affect reported amounts of assets, liabilities, revenues, expenses and disclosure of contingent assets and liabilities. Estimates are used in determining, among other items, sales incentives accruals, future cash flows associated with impairment testing for perpetual brands and goodwill, useful lives for intangible assets, tax reserves, stock-based compensation and pension and retiree medical accruals. Actual results could differ from these estimates.

See "Our Divisions" below and for additional unaudited information on items affecting the comparability of our consolidated results, see "Items Affecting Comparability" in Management's Discussion and Analysis.

Tabular dollars are in millions, except per share amounts. All per share amounts reflect common per share amounts, assume dilution unless noted, and are based on unrounded amounts. Certain reclassifications were made to prior years' amounts to conform to the 2005 presentation.

## Our Divisions

We manufacture or use contract manufacturers, market and sell a variety of salty, sweet and grain-based snacks, carbonated and non-carbonated beverages, and foods through our North American and international business divisions. Our North American divisions include the United States and Canada. The accounting policies for the divisions are the same as those described in Note 2, except for certain allocation methodologies for stock-based compensation expense and pension and retiree medical expense, as described in the unaudited information in "Our Critical Accounting Policies." Additionally, begin-

ning in the fourth quarter of 2005, we began centrally managing commodity derivatives on behalf of our divisions. Certain of the commodity derivatives, primarily those related to the purchase of energy for use by our divisions, do not qualify for hedge accounting treatment. These derivatives hedge underlying commodity price risk and were not entered into for speculative purposes. Such derivatives are marked to market with the resulting gains and losses recognized as a component of corporate unallocated expense. These gains and losses are reflected in division results when the divisions take

delivery of the underlying commodity. Therefore, division results reflect the contract purchase price of the energy or other commodities.

Division results are based on how our Chairman and Chief Executive Officer evaluates our divisions. Division results exclude certain Corporate-initiated restructuring and impairment charges, merger-related costs and divested businesses. For additional unaudited information on our divisions, see "Our Operations" in Management's Discussion and Analysis.

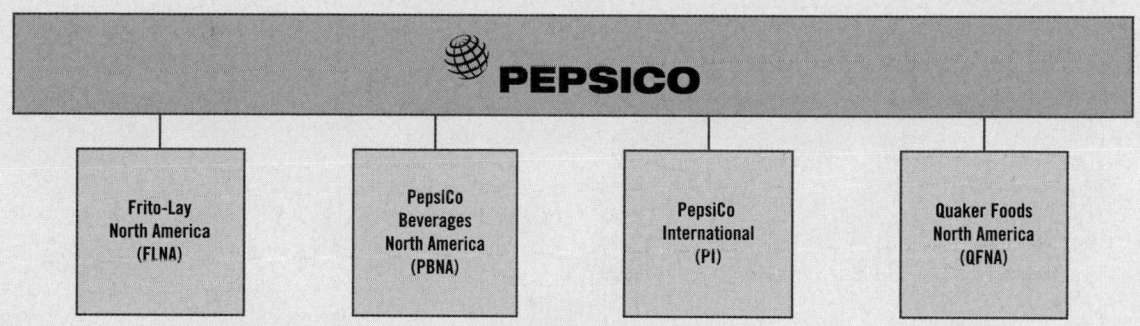

| | 2005 | 2004 | 2003 | 2005 | 2004 | 2003 |
|---|---|---|---|---|---|---|
| | Net Revenue | | | Operating Profit | | |
| FLNA | $10,322 | $ 9,560 | $ 9,091 | $2,529 | $2,389 | $2,242 |
| PBNA | 9,146 | 8,313 | 7,733 | 2,037 | 1,911 | 1,690 |
| PI | 11,376 | 9,862 | 8,678 | 1,607 | 1,323 | 1,061 |
| QFNA | 1,718 | 1,526 | 1,467 | 537 | 475 | 470 |
| Total division | 32,562 | 29,261 | 26,969 | 6,710 | 6,098 | 5,463 |
| Divested businesses | – | – | 2 | – | – | 26 |
| Corporate | – | – | – | (788) | (689) | (502) |
| | 32,562 | 29,261 | 26,971 | 5,922 | 5,409 | 4,987 |
| Restructuring and impairment charges | – | – | – | – | (150) | (147) |
| Merger-related costs | – | – | – | – | – | (59) |
| Total | $32,562 | $29,261 | $26,971 | $5,922 | $5,259 | $4,781 |

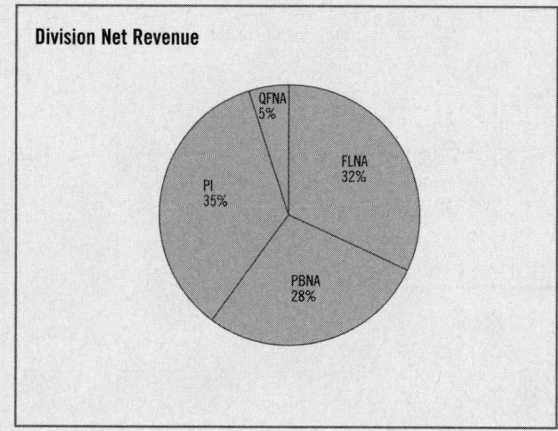

**Division Net Revenue**

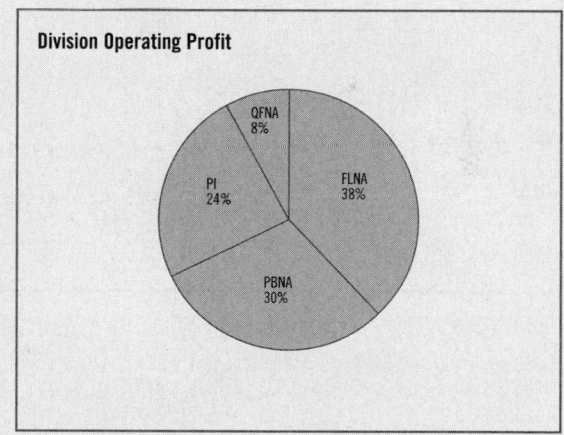

**Division Operating Profit**

**Divested Businesses**

During 2003, we sold our Quaker Foods North America Mission pasta business. The results of this business are reported as divested businesses.

**Corporate**

Corporate includes costs of our corporate headquarters, centrally managed initiatives, such as our BPT initiative, unallocated insurance and benefit programs, foreign exchange transaction gains and losses, and certain commodity derivative gains and losses, as well as profit-in-inventory elimination adjustments for our non-controlled bottling affiliates and certain other items.

**Restructuring and Impairment Charges and Merger-Related Costs** — See Note 3.

## Other Division Information

| | 2005 | 2004 | 2003 | 2005 | 2004 | 2003 |
|---|---|---|---|---|---|---|
| | **Total Assets** | | | **Capital Spending** | | |
| FLNA | $ 5,948 | $ 5,476 | $ 5,332 | $ 512 | $ 469 | $ 426 |
| PBNA | 6,316 | 6,048 | 5,856 | 320 | 265 | 332 |
| PI | 9,983 | 8,921 | 8,109 | 667 | 537 | 521 |
| QFNA | 989 | 978 | 995 | 31 | 33 | 32 |
| Total division | 23,236 | 21,423 | 20,292 | 1,530 | 1,304 | 1,311 |
| Corporate(a) | 5,331 | 3,569 | 2,384 | 206 | 83 | 34 |
| Investments in bottling affiliates | 3,160 | 2,995 | 2,651 | – | – | – |
| | $31,727 | $27,987 | $25,327 | $1,736 | $1,387 | $1,345 |

(a) Corporate assets consist principally of cash and cash equivalents, short-term investments, and property, plant and equipment.

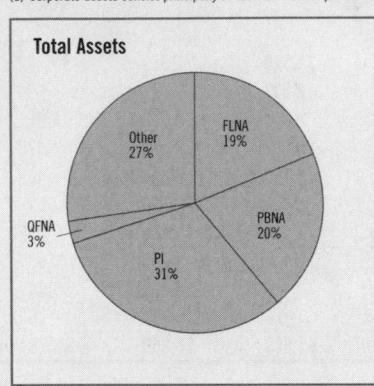

**Total Assets**

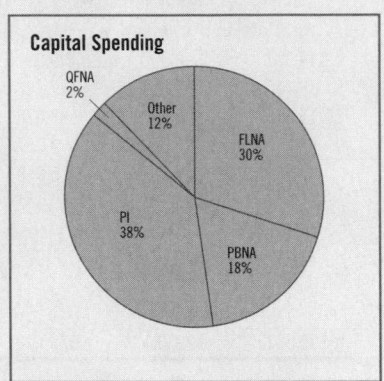

**Capital Spending**

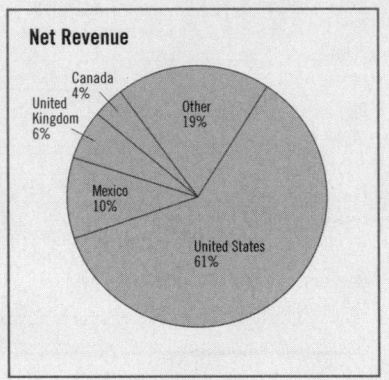

**Net Revenue**

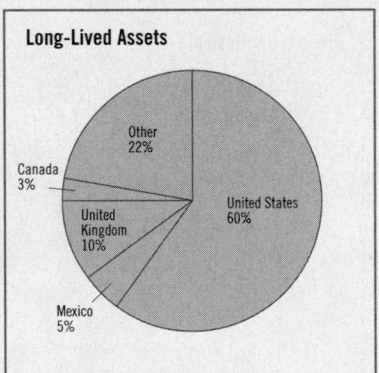

**Long-Lived Assets**

| | 2005 | 2004 | 2003 | 2005 | 2004 | 2003 |
|---|---|---|---|---|---|---|
| | **Amortization of Intangible Assets** | | | **Depreciation and Other Amortization** | | |
| FLNA | $ 3 | $ 3 | $ 3 | $ 419 | $ 420 | $ 416 |
| PBNA | 76 | 75 | 75 | 264 | 258 | 245 |
| PI | 71 | 68 | 66 | 420 | 382 | 350 |
| QFNA | – | 1 | 1 | 34 | 36 | 36 |
| Total division | 150 | 147 | 145 | 1,137 | 1,096 | 1,047 |
| Corporate | – | – | – | 21 | 21 | 29 |
| | $150 | $147 | $145 | $1,158 | $1,117 | $1,076 |

| | 2005 | 2004 | 2003 | 2005 | 2004 | 2003 |
|---|---|---|---|---|---|---|
| | **Net Revenue(a)** | | | **Long-Lived Assets(b)** | | |
| U.S. | $19,937 | $18,329 | $17,377 | $10,723 | $10,212 | $ 9,907 |
| Mexico | 3,095 | 2,724 | 2,642 | 902 | 878 | 869 |
| United Kingdom | 1,821 | 1,692 | 1,510 | 1,715 | 1,896 | 1,724 |
| Canada | 1,509 | 1,309 | 1,147 | 582 | 548 | 508 |
| All other countries | 6,200 | 5,207 | 4,295 | 3,948 | 3,339 | 3,123 |
| | $32,562 | $29,261 | $26,971 | $17,870 | $16,873 | $16,131 |

(a) Represents net revenue from businesses operating in these countries.

(b) Long-lived assets represent net property, plant and equipment, nonamortizable and net amortizable intangible assets and investments in noncontrolled affiliates. These assets are reported in the country where they are primarily used.

## Note 2 — Our Significant Accounting Policies

### Revenue Recognition

We recognize revenue upon shipment or delivery to our customers based on written sales terms that do not allow for a right of return. However, our policy for direct-store-delivery (DSD) and chilled products is to remove and replace damaged and out-of-date products from store shelves to ensure that our consumers receive the product quality and freshness that they expect. Similarly, our policy for warehouse distributed products is to replace damaged and out-of-date products. Based on our historical experience with this practice, we have reserved for anticipated damaged and out-of-date products. For additional unaudited information on our revenue recognition and related policies, including our policy on bad debts, see "Our Critical Accounting Policies" in Management's Discussion and Analysis. We are exposed to concentration of credit risk by our customers, Wal-Mart and PBG. Wal-Mart represents approximately 9% of our net revenue, including concentrate sales to our bottlers which are used in finished goods sold by them to Wal-Mart; and PBG represents approximately 10%. We have not experienced credit issues with these customers.

### Sales Incentives and Other Marketplace Spending

We offer sales incentives and discounts through various programs to our customers and consumers. Sales incentives and discounts are accounted for as a reduction of revenue and totaled $8.9 billion in 2005, $7.8 billion in 2004 and $7.1 billion in 2003. While most of these incentive arrangements have terms of no more than one year, certain arrangements extend beyond one year. For example, fountain pouring rights may extend up to 15 years. Costs incurred to obtain these arrangements are recognized over the contract period and the remaining balances of $321 million at December 31, 2005 and $337 million at December 25, 2004 are included in current assets and other assets in our Consolidated Balance Sheet. For additional unaudited information on our sales incentives, see "Our Critical Accounting Policies" in Management's Discussion and Analysis.

Other marketplace spending includes the costs of advertising and other marketing activities and is reported as selling, general and administrative expenses. Advertising expenses were $1.8 billion in 2005, $1.7 billion in 2004 and $1.6 billion in 2003. Deferred advertising costs are not expensed until the year first used and consist of:

- media and personal service prepayments,
- promotional materials in inventory, and
- production costs of future media advertising.

Deferred advertising costs of $202 million and $137 million at year-end 2005 and 2004, respectively, are classified as prepaid expenses in our Consolidated Balance Sheet.

### Distribution Costs

Distribution costs, including the costs of shipping and handling activities, are reported as selling, general and administrative expenses. Shipping and handling expenses were $4.1 billion in 2005, $3.9 billion in 2004 and $3.6 billion in 2003.

### Cash Equivalents

Cash equivalents are investments with original maturities of three months or less which we do not intend to rollover beyond three months.

### Software Costs

We capitalize certain computer software and software development costs incurred in connection with developing or obtaining computer software for internal use. Capitalized software costs are included in property, plant and equipment on our Consolidated Balance Sheet and amortized on a straight-line basis over the estimated useful lives of the software, which generally do not exceed 5 years. Net capitalized software and development costs were $327 million at December 31, 2005 and $181 million at December 25, 2004.

### Commitments and Contingencies

We are subject to various claims and contingencies related to lawsuits, taxes and environmental matters, as well as commitments under contractual and other commercial obligations. We recognize liabilities for contingencies and commitments when a loss is probable and estimable. For additional information on our commitments, see Note 9.

### Other Significant Accounting Policies

Our other significant accounting policies are disclosed as follows:

- *Property, Plant and Equipment and Intangible Assets* — Note 4 and, for additional unaudited information on brands and goodwill, see "Our Critical Accounting Policies" in Management's Discussion and Analysis.
- *Income Taxes* — Note 5 and, for additional unaudited information, see "Our Critical Accounting Policies" in Management's Discussion and Analysis.
- *Stock-Based Compensation Expense* — Note 6 and, for additional unaudited information, see "Our Critical Accounting Policies" in Management's Discussion and Analysis.
- *Pension, Retiree Medical and Savings Plans* — Note 7 and, for additional unaudited information, see "Our Critical Accounting Policies" in Management's Discussion and Analysis.
- *Risk Management* — Note 10 and, for additional unaudited information, see "Our Business Risks" in Management's Discussion and Analysis.

There have been no new accounting pronouncements issued or effective during 2005 that have had, or are expected to have, a material impact on our consolidated financial statements.

## Note 3 — Restructuring and Impairment Charges and Merger-Related Costs

**2005 Restructuring Charges**

In the fourth quarter of 2005, we incurred a charge of $83 million ($55 million after-tax or $0.03 per share) in conjunction with actions taken to reduce costs in our operations, principally through headcount reductions. Of this charge, $34 million related to FLNA, $21 million to PBNA, $16 million to PI and $12 million to Corporate (recorded in corporate unallocated expenses). Most of this charge related to the termination of approximately 700 employees. We expect the substantial portion of the cash payments related to this charge to be paid in 2006.

**2004 and 2003 Restructuring and Impairment Charges**

In the fourth quarter of 2004, we incurred a charge of $150 million ($96 million after-tax or $0.06 per share) in conjunction with the consolidation of FLNA's manufacturing network as part of its ongoing productivity program. Of this charge,

$93 million related to asset impairment, primarily reflecting the closure of four U.S. plants. Production from these plants was redeployed to other FLNA facilities in the U.S. The remaining $57 million included employee-related costs of $29 million, contract termination costs of $8 million and other exit costs of $20 million. Employee-related costs primarily reflect the termination costs for approximately 700 employees. Through December 31, 2005, we have paid $47 million and incurred non-cash charges of $10 million, leaving substantially no accrual.

In the fourth quarter of 2003, we incurred a charge of $147 million ($100 million after-tax or $0.06 per share) in conjunction with actions taken to streamline our North American divisions and PepsiCo International. These actions were taken to increase focus and eliminate redundancies at PBNA and PI and to improve the efficiency of the supply chain

at FLNA. Of this charge, $81 million related to asset impairment, reflecting $57 million for the closure of a snack plant in Kentucky, the retirement of snack manufacturing lines in Maryland and Arkansas and $24 million for the closure of a PBNA office building in Florida. The remaining $66 million included employee-related costs of $54 million and facility and other exit costs of $12 million. Employee-related costs primarily reflect the termination costs for approximately 850 sales, distribution, manufacturing, research and marketing employees. As of December 31, 2005, all terminations had occurred and substantially no accrual remains.

**Merger-Related Costs**

In connection with the Quaker merger in 2001, we recognized merger-related costs of $59 million ($42 million after-tax or $0.02 per share) in 2003.

## Note 4 — Property, Plant and Equipment and Intangible Assets

| | Average Useful Life | 2005 | 2004 | 2003 |
|---|---|---|---|---|
| **Property, plant and equipment, net** | | | | |
| Land and improvements | 10 – 30 yrs. | $ 685 | $ 646 | |
| Buildings and improvements | 20 – 44 | 3,736 | 3,605 | |
| Machinery and equipment, including fleet and software | 5 – 15 | 11,658 | 10,950 | |
| Construction in progress | | 1,066 | 729 | |
| | | 17,145 | 15,930 | |
| Accumulated depreciation | | (8,464) | (7,781) | |
| | | $ 8,681 | $ 8,149 | |
| Depreciation expense | | $1,103 | $1,062 | $1,020 |
| **Amortizable intangible assets, net** | | | | |
| Brands | 5 – 40 | $1,054 | $1,008 | |
| Other identifiable intangibles | 3 – 15 | 257 | 225 | |
| | | 1,311 | 1,233 | |
| Accumulated amortization | | (781) | (635) | |
| | | $ 530 | $ 598 | |
| Amortization expense | | $150 | $147 | $145 |

Depreciation and amortization are recognized on a straight-line basis over an asset's estimated useful life. Land is not depreciated and construction in progress is not depreciated until ready for service. Amortization of intangible assets for each of the next five years, based on average 2005 foreign exchange rates, is expected to be $152 million in 2006, $35 million in 2007, $35 million in 2008, $34 million in 2009 and $33 million in 2010.

Depreciable and amortizable assets are only evaluated for impairment upon a significant change in the operating or macroeconomic environment. In these circumstances, if an evaluation of the undiscounted cash flows indicates impairment, the asset is written down to its estimated fair value, which is based on discounted future cash flows. Useful lives are periodically evaluated to determine whether events or circumstances have occurred which indicate the need for revision. For additional unaudited information on our amortizable brand policies, see "Our Critical Accounting Policies" in Management's Discussion and Analysis.

**Nonamortizable Intangible Assets**

Perpetual brands and goodwill are assessed for impairment at least annually to ensure that discounted future cash flows continue to exceed the related book value. A perpetual brand is impaired if its book value exceeds its fair value. Goodwill is evaluated for impairment if the book value of its reporting unit exceeds its fair value. A reporting unit can be a division or business within a division. If the fair value of an evaluated asset is less than its book value, the asset is written down based on its discounted future cash flows to fair value. No impairment charges resulted from the required impairment evaluations. The change in the book value of nonamortizable intangible assets is as follows:

| | Balance. Beginning 2004 | Acquisition | Translation and Other | Balance. End of 2004 | Acquisition | Translation and Other | Balance. End of 2005 |
|---|---|---|---|---|---|---|---|
| **Frito-Lay North America** | | | | | | | |
| Goodwill | $ 130 | $ – | $ 8 | $ 138 | $ – | $ 7 | $ 145 |
| **PepsiCo Beverages North America** | | | | | | | |
| Goodwill | 2,157 | – | 4 | 2,161 | – | 3 | 2,164 |
| Brands | 59 | – | – | 59 | – | – | 59 |
| | 2,216 | – | 4 | 2,220 | – | 3 | 2,223 |
| **PepsiCo International** | | | | | | | |
| Goodwill | 1,334 | 29 | 72 | 1,435 | 278 | (109) | 1,604 |
| Brands | 808 | – | 61 | 869 | 263 | (106) | 1,026 |
| | 2,142 | 29 | 133 | 2,304 | 541 | (215) | 2,630 |
| **Quaker Foods North America** | | | | | | | |
| Goodwill | 175 | – | – | 175 | – | – | 175 |
| **Corporate** | | | | | | | |
| Pension intangible | 2 | – | 3 | 5 | – | (4) | 1 |
| Total goodwill | 3,796 | 29 | 84 | 3,909 | 278 | (99) | 4,088 |
| Total brands | 867 | – | 61 | 928 | 263 | (106) | 1,085 |
| Total pension intangible | 2 | – | 3 | 5 | – | (4) | 1 |
| | $4,665 | $29 | $148 | $4,842 | $541 | $(209) | $5,174 |

## Note 5 — Income Taxes

| | 2005 | 2004 | 2003 |
|---|---|---|---|
| **Income before income taxes — continuing operations** | | | |
| U.S. | $3,175 | $2,946 | $3,267 |
| Foreign | 3,207 | 2,600 | 1,725 |
| | $6,382 | $5,546 | $4,992 |
| **Provision for income taxes — continuing operations** | | | |
| Current:  U.S. Federal | $1,638 | $1,030 | $1,326 |
|          Foreign | 426 | 256 | 341 |
|          State | 118 | 69 | 80 |
| | 2,182 | 1,355 | 1,747 |
| Deferred: U.S. Federal | 137 | 11 | (274) |
|          Foreign | (26) | 5 | (47) |
|          State | 11 | 1 | (2) |
| | 122 | 17 | (323) |
| | $2,304 | $1,372 | $1,424 |
| **Tax rate reconciliation — continuing operations** | | | |
| U.S. Federal statutory tax rate | 35.0% | 35.0% | 35.0% |
| State income tax, net of U.S. Federal tax benefit | 1.4 | 0.8 | 1.0 |
| Taxes on AJCA repatriation | 7.0 | – | – |
| Lower taxes on foreign results | (6.5) | (5.4) | (5.5) |
| Settlement of prior years' audit | – | (4.8) | (2.2) |
| Other, net | (0.8) | (0.9) | 0.2 |
| Annual tax rate | 36.1% | 24.7% | 28.5% |
| **Deferred tax liabilities** | | | |
| Investments in noncontrolled affiliates | $ 993 | $ 850 | |
| Property, plant and equipment | 772 | 857 | |
| Pension benefits | 863 | 669 | |
| Intangible assets other than nondeductible goodwill | 135 | 153 | |
| Zero coupon notes | 35 | 46 | |
| Other | 169 | 157 | |
| Gross deferred tax liabilities | 2,967 | 2,732 | |
| **Deferred tax assets** | | | |
| Net carryforwards | 608 | 666 | |
| Stock-based compensation | 426 | 402 | |
| Retiree medical benefits | 400 | 402 | |
| Other employee-related benefits | 342 | 379 | |
| Other | 520 | 460 | |
| Gross deferred tax assets | 2,296 | 2,309 | |
| Valuation allowances | (532) | (564) | |
| Deferred tax assets, net | 1,764 | 1,745 | |
| Net deferred tax liabilities | $1,203 | $ 987 | |
| **Deferred taxes included within:** | | | |
| Prepaid expenses and other current assets | $231 | $229 | |
| Deferred income taxes | $1,434 | $1,216 | |
| **Analysis of valuation allowances** | | | |
| Balance, beginning of year | $564 | $438 | $487 |
| (Benefit)/provision | (28) | 118 | (52) |
| Other (deductions)/additions | (4) | 8 | 3 |
| Balance, end of year | $532 | $564 | $438 |

For additional unaudited information on our income tax policies, including our reserves for income taxes, see "Our Critical Accounting Policies" in Management's Discussion and Analysis.

**Carryforwards, Credits and Allowances**
Operating loss carryforwards totaling $5.1 billion at year-end 2005 are being carried forward in a number of foreign and state jurisdictions where we are permitted to use tax operating losses from prior periods to reduce future taxable income. These operating losses will expire as follows: $0.1 billion in 2006, $4.1 billion between 2007 and 2025 and $0.9 billion may be carried forward indefinitely. In addition, certain tax credits generated in prior periods of approximately $39.4 million are available to reduce certain foreign tax liabilities through 2011. We establish valuation allowances for our deferred tax assets when the amount of expected future taxable income is not likely to support the use of the deduction or credit.

**Undistributed International Earnings**
The AJCA created a one-time incentive for U.S. corporations to repatriate undistributed international earnings by providing an 85% dividends received deduction. As approved by our Board of Directors in July 2005, we repatriated approximately $7.5 billion in earnings previously considered indefinitely reinvested outside the U.S. in the fourth quarter of 2005. In 2005, we recorded income tax expense of $460 million associated with this repatriation. Other than the earnings repatriated, we intend to continue to reinvest earnings outside the U.S. for the foreseeable future and, therefore, have not recognized any U.S. tax expense on these earnings. At December 31, 2005, we had approximately $7.5 billion of undistributed international earnings.

**Reserves**
A number of years may elapse before a particular matter, for which we have established a reserve, is audited and finally resolved. The number of years with open tax audits varies depending on the tax jurisdiction. During 2004, we recognized $266 million of tax benefits related to the favorable resolution of certain open tax issues. In addition, in 2004, we recognized a tax benefit of $38 million upon agreement with the IRS on an open issue related to our discontinued restaurant operations. At the end of 2003, we entered into agreements with the IRS for open years through 1997. These agreements resulted in a tax benefit of $109 million in the fourth quarter of 2003. As part of these agreements, we also resolved the treatment of certain other issues related to future tax years.

The IRS has initiated their audits of our tax returns for the years 1998 through 2002. Our tax returns subsequent to 2002 have not yet been examined. While it is often difficult to predict the final outcome or the timing of resolution of any particular tax matter, we believe that our reserves reflect the probable outcome of known tax contingencies. Settlement of any particular issue would usually require the use of cash. Favorable resolution would be recognized as a reduction to our annual tax rate in the year of resolution. Our tax reserves, covering all federal, state and foreign jurisdictions, are presented in the balance sheet within other liabilities (see Note 14), except for any amounts relating to items we expect to pay in the coming year which are included in current income taxes payable. For further unaudited information on the impact of the resolution of open tax issues, see "Other Consolidated Results."

## Note 6 — Stock-Based Compensation

Our stock-based compensation program is a broad-based program designed to attract and retain employees while also aligning employees' interests with the interests of our shareholders. Employees at all levels participate in our stock-based compensation program. In addition, members of our Board of Directors participate in our stock-based compensation program in connection with their service on our Board. Stock options and RSUs are granted to employees under the shareholder-approved 2003 Long-Term Incentive Plan (LTIP), our only active stock-based plan. Stock-based compensation expense was $311 million in 2005, $368 million in 2004 and $407 million in 2003. Related income tax benefits recognized in earnings were $87 million in 2005, $103 million in 2004 and $114 million in 2003. At year-end 2005, 51 million shares were available for future executive and SharePower grants. For additional unaudited information on our stock-based compensation program, see "Our Critical Accounting Policies" in Management's Discussion and Analysis.

**SharePower Grants**
SharePower options are awarded under our LTIP to all eligible employees, based on job level or classification, and in the case of international employees, tenure as well. All stock option grants have an exercise price equal to the fair market value of our common stock on the day of grant and generally have a 10-year term with vesting after three years.

**Executive Grants**
All senior management and certain middle management are eligible for executive grants under our LTIP. All stock option grants have an exercise price equal to the fair market value of our common stock on the day of grant and generally have a 10-year term with vesting after three years. There have been no reductions to the exercise price of previously issued awards, and any repricing of awards would require approval of our shareholders.

Beginning in 2004, executives who are awarded long-term incentives based on their performance are offered the choice of stock options or RSUs. RSU expense is based on the fair value of PepsiCo stock on the date of grant and is amortized over the vesting period, generally three years. Each restricted stock unit can be settled in a share of our stock after the vesting period. Executives who elect RSUs receive one RSU for every four stock options that would have otherwise been granted. Senior officers do not have a choice and are granted 50% stock options and 50% RSUs. Vesting of RSU awards for senior officers is contingent upon the achievement of pre-established performance targets. We granted 3 million RSUs in both 2005 and 2004 with weighted-average intrinsic values of $53.83 and $47.28, respectively.

**Method of Accounting and Our Assumptions**

We account for our employee stock options under the fair value method of accounting using a Black-Scholes valuation model to measure stock-based compensation expense at the date of grant. We adopted SFAS 123R, *Share-Based Payment*, under the modified prospective method in the first quarter of 2006. We do not expect our adoption of SFAS 123R to materially impact our financial statements.

Our weighted-average Black-Scholes fair value assumptions include:

| | 2005 | 2004 | 2003 |
|---|---|---|---|
| Expected life | 6 yrs. | 6 yrs. | 6 yrs. |
| Risk free interest rate | 3.8% | 3.3% | 3.1% |
| Expected volatility | 23% | 26% | 27% |
| Expected dividend yield | 1.8% | 1.8% | 1.15% |

**Our Stock Option Activity(a)**

| | 2005 | | 2004 | | 2003 | |
|---|---|---|---|---|---|---|
| | Options | Average Price(b) | Options | Average Price(b) | Options | Average Price(b) |
| Outstanding at beginning of year | 174,261 | $40.05 | 198,173 | $38.12 | 190,432 | $36.45 |
| Granted | 12,328 | 53.82 | 14,137 | 47.47 | 41,630 | 39.89 |
| Exercised | (30,945) | 35.40 | (31,614) | 30.57 | (25,833) | 26.74 |
| Forfeited/expired | (5,495) | 43.31 | (6,435) | 43.82 | (8,056) | 43.56 |
| Outstanding at end of year | 150,149 | 42.03 | 174,261 | 40.05 | 198,173 | 38.12 |
| Exercisable at end of year | 89,652 | 40.52 | 94,643 | 36.41 | 97,663 | 32.56 |

**Stock options outstanding and exercisable at December 31, 2005(a)**

| | Options Outstanding | | | Options Exercisable | | |
|---|---|---|---|---|---|---|
| Range of Exercise Price | Options | Average Price(b) | Average Life(c) | Options | Average Price(b) | Average Life(c) |
| $14.40 to $21.54 | 905 | $20.01 | 3.56 yrs. | 905 | $20.01 | 3.56 yrs. |
| $23.00 to $33.75 | 14,559 | 30.46 | 3.07 | 14,398 | 30.50 | 3.05 |
| $34.00 to $43.50 | 82,410 | 39.44 | 5.34 | 48,921 | 39.19 | 4.10 |
| $43.75 to $56.75 | 52,275 | 49.77 | 7.17 | 25,428 | 49.48 | 6.09 |
| | 150,149 | 42.03 | 5.67 | 89,652 | 40.52 | 4.45 |

(a) Options are in thousands and include options previously granted under Quaker plans. No additional options or shares may be granted under the Quaker plans.

(b) Weighted-average exercise price.

(c) Weighted-average contractual life remaining.

**Our RSU Activity(a)**

| | 2005 | | | 2004 | | |
|---|---|---|---|---|---|---|
| | RSUs | Average Intrinsic Value(b) | Average Life(c) | RSUs | Average Intrinsic Value(b) | Average Life(c) |
| Outstanding at beginning of year | 2,922 | $47.30 | | – | $ – | |
| Granted | 3,097 | 53.83 | | 3,077 | 47.28 | |
| Converted | (91) | 48.73 | | (18) | 47.25 | |
| Forfeited/expired | (259) | 50.51 | | (137) | 47.25 | |
| Outstanding at end of year | 5,669 | 50.70 | 1.8 yrs. | 2,922 | 47.30 | 2.2 yrs. |

(a) RSUs are in thousands.

(b) Weighted-average intrinsic value.

(c) Weighted-average contractual life remaining.

**Other stock-based compensation data**

| | Stock Options | | | RSUs | |
|---|---|---|---|---|---|
| | 2005 | 2004 | 2003 | 2005 | 2004 |
| Weighted-average fair value of options granted | $13.45 | $12.04 | $11.21 | | |
| Total intrinsic value of options/RSUs exercised/converted(a) | $632,603 | $667,001 | $466,719 | $4,974 | $914 |
| Total intrinsic value of options/RSUs outstanding(a) | $2,553,594 | $2,062,153 | $1,641,505 | $334,931 | $151,760 |
| Total intrinsic value of options exercisable(a) | $1,662,198 | $1,464,926 | $1,348,658 | | |

(a) In thousands.

At December 31, 2005, there was $315 million of total unrecognized compensation cost related to nonvested share-based compensation grants. This unrecognized compensation is expected to be recognized over a weighted-average period of 1.6 years.

## Note 7 — Pension, Retiree Medical and Savings Plans

Our pension plans cover full-time employees in the U.S. and certain international employees. Benefits are determined based on either years of service or a combination of years of service and earnings. U.S. retirees are also eligible for medical and life insurance benefits (retiree medical) if they meet age and service requirements. Generally, our share of retiree medical costs is capped at specified dollar amounts, which vary based upon years of service, with retirees contributing the remainder of the costs. We use a September 30 measurement date and all plan assets and liabilities are generally reported as of that date. The cost or benefit of plan changes that increase or decrease benefits for prior employee service (prior service cost) is included in expense on a straight-line basis over the average remaining service period of employees expected to receive benefits.

The Medicare Act was signed into law in December 2003 and we applied the provisions of the Medicare Act to our plans in 2005 and 2004. The Medicare Act provides a subsidy for sponsors of retiree medical plans who offer drug benefits equivalent to those provided under Medicare. As a result of the Medicare Act, our 2005 and 2004 retiree medical costs were $11 million and $7 million lower, respectively, and our 2005 and 2004 liabilities were reduced by $136 million and $80 million, respectively. We expect our 2006 retiree medical costs to be approximately $18 million lower than they otherwise would have been as a result of the Medicare Act.

For additional unaudited information on our pension and retiree medical plans and related accounting policies and assumptions, see "Our Critical Accounting Policies" in Management's Discussion and Analysis.

| | Pension | | | | | | Retiree Medical | | |
|---|---|---|---|---|---|---|---|---|---|
| | **2005** | 2004 | 2003 | **2005** | 2004 | 2003 | **2005** | 2004 | 2003 |
| | | U.S. | | | International | | | | |
| **Weighted-average assumptions** | | | | | | | | | |
| Liability discount rate | **5.7%** | 6.1% | 6.1% | **5.1%** | 6.1% | 6.1% | **5.7%** | 6.1% | 6.1% |
| Expense discount rate | **6.1%** | 6.1% | 6.7% | **6.1%** | 6.1% | 6.4% | **6.1%** | 6.1% | 6.7% |
| Expected return on plan assets | **7.8%** | 7.8% | 8.3% | **8.0%** | 8.0% | 8.0% | – | – | – |
| Rate of compensation increases | **4.4%** | 4.5% | 4.5% | **4.1%** | 3.9% | 3.8% | – | – | – |
| | | | | | | | | | |
| **Components of benefit expense** | | | | | | | | | |
| Service cost | **$ 213** | $ 193 | $ 153 | **$ 32** | $ 27 | $ 24 | **$ 40** | $ 38 | $ 33 |
| Interest cost | **296** | 271 | 245 | **55** | 47 | 39 | **78** | 72 | 73 |
| Expected return on plan assets | **(344)** | (325) | (305) | **(69)** | (65) | (54) | – | – | – |
| Amortization of prior service cost/(benefit) | **3** | 6 | 6 | **1** | 1 | – | **(11)** | (8) | (3) |
| Amortization of experience loss | **106** | 81 | 44 | **15** | 9 | 5 | **26** | 19 | 13 |
| Benefit expense | **274** | 226 | 143 | **34** | 19 | 14 | **133** | 121 | 116 |
| Settlement/curtailment loss | – | 4 | – | – | 1 | – | – | – | – |
| Special termination benefits | **21** | 19 | 4 | – | 1 | – | **2** | 4 | – |
| Total | **$ 295** | $ 249 | $ 147 | **$ 34** | $ 21 | $ 14 | **$135** | $125 | $116 |

| | Pension | | | | Retiree Medical | |
|---|---|---|---|---|---|---|
| | **2005** | 2004 | **2005** | 2004 | **2005** | 2004 |
| | U.S. | | International | | | |
| **Change in projected benefit liability** | | | | | | |
| Liability at beginning of year | $4,968 | $4,456 | $ 952 | $758 | $1,319 | $1,264 |
| Service cost | 213 | 193 | 32 | 27 | 40 | 38 |
| Interest cost | 296 | 271 | 55 | 47 | 78 | 72 |
| Plan amendments | – | (17) | 3 | 1 | (8) | (41) |
| Participant contributions | – | – | 10 | 9 | – | – |
| Experience loss/(gain) | 517 | 261 | 203 | 73 | (45) | 58 |
| Benefit payments | (241) | (205) | (28) | (29) | (74) | (76) |
| Settlement/curtailment loss | – | (9) | – | (2) | – | – |
| Special termination benefits | 21 | 18 | – | 1 | 2 | 4 |
| Foreign currency adjustment | – | – | (68) | 67 | – | – |
| Other | (3) | – | 104 | – | – | – |
| Liability at end of year | $5,771 | $4,968 | $1,263 | $952 | $1,312 | $1,319 |
| Liability at end of year for service to date | $4,783 | $4,164 | $1,047 | $779 | | |
| **Change in fair value of plan assets** | | | | | | |
| Fair value at beginning of year | $4,152 | $3,558 | $ 838 | $687 | $ – | $ – |
| Actual return on plan assets | 477 | 392 | 142 | 77 | – | – |
| Employer contributions/funding | 699 | 416 | 104 | 37 | 74 | 76 |
| Participant contributions | – | – | 10 | 9 | – | – |
| Benefit payments | (241) | (205) | (28) | (29) | (74) | (76) |
| Settlement/curtailment loss | – | (9) | – | (2) | – | – |
| Foreign currency adjustment | – | – | (61) | 59 | – | – |
| Other | (1) | – | 94 | – | – | – |
| Fair value at end of year | $5,086 | $4,152 | $1,099 | $838 | $ – | $ – |
| **Funded status as recognized in our Consolidated Balance Sheet** | | | | | | |
| Funded status at end of year | $ (685) | $ (817) | $(164) | $(113) | $(1,312) | $(1,319) |
| Unrecognized prior service cost/(benefit) | 5 | 9 | 17 | 13 | (113) | (116) |
| Unrecognized experience loss | 2,288 | 2,013 | 474 | 380 | 402 | 473 |
| Fourth quarter benefit payments | 5 | 5 | 4 | 7 | 19 | 19 |
| Net amounts recognized | $1,613 | $1,210 | $ 331 | $ 287 | $(1,004) | $ (943) |
| **Net amounts as recognized in our Consolidated Balance Sheet** | | | | | | |
| Other assets | $2,068 | $1,572 | $367 | $294 | $ – | $ – |
| Intangible assets | – | – | 1 | 5 | – | – |
| Other liabilities | (479) | (387) | (41) | (37) | (1,004) | (943) |
| Accumulated other comprehensive loss | 24 | 25 | 4 | 25 | – | – |
| Net amounts recognized | $1,613 | $1,210 | $331 | $287 | $(1,004) | $(943) |
| **Components of increase in unrecognized experience loss** | | | | | | |
| Decrease in discount rate | $ 365 | $ – | $194 | $ 4 | $ 61 | $ – |
| Employee-related assumption changes | 57 | 196 | 2 | 65 | – | 109 |
| Liability-related experience different from assumptions | 95 | 65 | 7 | 4 | (54) | 31 |
| Actual asset return different from expected return | (133) | (67) | (73) | (12) | – | – |
| Amortization of losses | (106) | (81) | (15) | (9) | (26) | (19) |
| Other, including foreign currency adjustments and 2003 Medicare Act | (3) | (5) | (22) | 26 | (52) | (82) |
| Total | $ 275 | $108 | $ 93 | $ 78 | $(71) | $ 39 |
| **Selected information for plans with liability for service to date in excess of plan assets** | | | | | | |
| Liability for service to date | $(374) | $(320) | $(65) | $(191) | $(1,312) | $(1,319) |
| Projected benefit liability | $(815) | $(685) | $(84) | $(227) | $(1,312) | $(1,319) |
| Fair value of plan assets | $8 | $11 | $33 | $161 | $– | $– |

Of the total projected pension benefit liability at year-end 2005, $765 million relates to plans that we do not fund because the funding of such plans does not receive favorable tax treatment.

**Future Benefit Payments**
Our estimated future benefit payments are as follows:

| | 2006 | 2007 | 2008 | 2009 | 2010 | 2011-15 |
|---|---|---|---|---|---|---|
| Pension | $235 | $255 | $275 | $300 | $330 | $2,215 |
| Retiree medical | $85 | $90 | $90 | $95 | $100 | $545 |

These future benefits to beneficiaries include payments from both funded and unfunded pension plans.

**Pension Assets**
The expected return on pension plan assets is based on our historical experience, our pension plan investment guidelines, and our expectations for long-term rates of return. We use a market-related value method that recognizes each year's asset gain or loss over a five-year period. Therefore, it takes five years for the gain or loss from any one year to be fully included in the value of pension plan assets that is used to calculate the expected return. Our pension plan investment guidelines are established based upon an evaluation of market conditions, tolerance for risk and cash requirements for benefit payments. Our investment objective is to ensure that funds are available to meet the plans' benefit obligations when they are due. Our investment strategy is to prudently invest plan assets in high-quality and diversified equity and debt securities to achieve our long-term return expectation. Our target allocation and actual pension plan asset allocations for the plan years 2005 and 2004, are below.

Pension assets include approximately 5.5 million shares of PepsiCo common stock with a market value of $311 million in 2005, and 5.5 million shares with a market value of $267 million in 2004. Our investment policy limits the investment in PepsiCo stock at the time of investment to 10% of the fair value of plan assets.

| | | Actual Allocation | |
|---|---|---|---|
| Asset Category | Target Allocation | 2005 | 2004 |
| Equity securities | 60% | 60% | 60% |
| Debt securities | 40% | 39% | 39% |
| Other, primarily cash | – | 1% | 1% |
| Total | 100% | 100% | 100% |

**Retiree Medical Cost Trend Rates**
An average increase of 10% in the cost of covered retiree medical benefits is assumed for 2006. This average increase is then projected to decline gradually to 5% in 2010 and thereafter. These assumed health care cost trend rates have an impact on the retiree medical plan expense and liability. However, the cap on our share of retiree medical costs limits the impact. A 1 percentage point change in the assumed health care trend rate would have the following effects:

| | 1% Increase | 1% Decrease |
|---|---|---|
| 2005 service and interest cost components | $3 | $(2) |
| 2005 benefit liability | $38 | $(33) |

**Savings Plans**
Our U.S. employees are eligible to participate in 401(k) savings plans, which are voluntary defined contribution plans. The plans are designed to help employees accumulate additional savings for retirement. We make matching contributions on a portion of eligible pay based on years of service. In 2005 and 2004, our matching contributions were $52 million and $35 million, respectively.

## Note 8 — Noncontrolled Bottling Affiliates

Our most significant noncontrolled bottling affiliates are PBG and PAS. Approximately 10% of our net revenue in 2005, 2004 and 2003 reflects sales to PBG.

**The Pepsi Bottling Group**
In addition to approximately 41% and 42% of PBG's outstanding common stock that we own at year-end 2005 and 2004, respectively, we own 100% of PBG's class B common stock and approximately 7% of the equity of Bottling Group, LLC, PBG's principal operating subsidiary. This gives us economic ownership of approximately 45% and 46% of PBG's combined operations at year-end 2005 and 2004, respectively. In 2005, bottling equity income includes $126 million of pre-tax gains on our sales of PBG stock.

PBG's summarized financial information is as follows:

| | 2005 | 2004 | 2003 |
|---|---|---|---|
| Current assets | $ 2,412 | $ 2,183 | |
| Noncurrent assets | 9,112 | 8,754 | |
| Total assets | $11,524 | $10,937 | |
| Current liabilities | $2,598 | $1,725 | |
| Noncurrent liabilities | 6,387 | 6,818 | |
| Minority interest | 496 | 445 | |
| Total liabilities | $9,481 | $8,988 | |
| Our investment | $1,738 | $1,594 | |
| Net revenue | $11,885 | $10,906 | $10,265 |
| Gross profit | $5,632 | $5,250 | $5,050 |
| Operating profit | $1,023 | $976 | $956 |
| Net income | $466 | $457 | $416 |

Our investment in PBG, which includes the related goodwill, was $400 million and $321 million higher than our ownership interest in their net assets at year-end 2005 and 2004, respectively. Based upon the quoted closing price of PBG shares at year-end 2005 and 2004, the calculated market value of our shares in PBG, excluding our investment in Bottling Group, LLC, exceeded our investment balance by approximately $1.5 billion and $1.7 billion, respectively.

### PepsiAmericas

At year-end 2005 and 2004, we owned approximately 43% and 41% of PepsiAmericas, respectively, and their summarized financial information is as follows:

| | 2005 | 2004 | 2003 |
|---|---|---|---|
| Current assets | $ 598 | $ 530 | |
| Noncurrent assets | 3,456 | 3,000 | |
| Total assets | $4,054 | $3,530 | |
| Current liabilities | $ 722 | $ 521 | |
| Noncurrent liabilities | 1,763 | 1,386 | |
| Total liabilities | $2,485 | $1,907 | |
| Our investment | $968 | $924 | |
| Net revenue | $3,726 | $3,345 | $3,237 |
| Gross profit | $1,562 | $1,423 | $1,360 |
| Operating profit | $393 | $340 | $316 |
| Net income | $195 | $182 | $158 |

Our investment in PAS, which includes the related goodwill, was $292 million and $253 million higher than our ownership interest in their net assets at year-end 2005 and 2004, respectively. Based upon the quoted closing price of PAS shares at year-end 2005 and 2004, the calculated market value of our shares in PepsiAmericas exceeded our investment balance by approximately $364 million and $277 million, respectively.

In January 2005, PAS acquired a regional bottler, Central Investment Corporation. The table above includes the results of Central Investment Corporation from the transaction date forward.

### Related Party Transactions

Our significant related party transactions involve our noncontrolled bottling affiliates. We sell concentrate to these affiliates, which is used in the production of carbonated soft drinks and non-carbonated beverages. We also sell certain finished goods to these affiliates and we receive royalties for the use of our trademarks for certain products. Sales of concentrate and finished goods are reported net of bottler funding. For further unaudited information on these bottlers, see "Our Customers" in Management's Discussion and Analysis. These transactions with our bottling affiliates are reflected in our consolidated financial statements as follows:

| | 2005 | 2004 | 2003 |
|---|---|---|---|
| Net revenue | $4,633 | $4,170 | $3,699 |
| Selling, general and administrative expenses | $143 | $114 | $128 |
| Accounts and notes receivable | $178 | $157 | |
| Accounts payable and other current liabilities | $117 | $95 | |

Such amounts are settled on terms consistent with other trade receivables and payables. See Note 9 regarding our guarantee of certain PBG debt.

In addition, we coordinate, on an aggregate basis, the negotiation and purchase of sweeteners and other raw materials requirements for certain of our bottlers with suppliers. Once we have negotiated the contracts, the bottlers order and take delivery directly from the supplier and pay the suppliers directly. Consequently, these transactions are not reflected in our consolidated financial statements. As the contracting party, we could be liable to these suppliers in the event of any nonpayment by our bottlers, but we consider this exposure to be remote.

## Note 9 — Debt Obligations and Commitments

| | 2005 | 2004 |
|---|---|---|
| **Short-term debt obligations** | | |
| Current maturities of long-term debt | $ 143 | $ 160 |
| Commercial paper (3.3% and 1.6%) | 3,140 | 1,287 |
| Other borrowings (7.4% and 6.6%) | 356 | 357 |
| Amounts reclassified to long-term debt | (750) | (750) |
| | $2,889 | $1,054 |
| **Long-term debt obligations** | | |
| Short-term borrowings, reclassified | $ 750 | $ 750 |
| Notes due 2006-2026 (5.4% and 4.7%) | 1,161 | 1,274 |
| Zero coupon notes, $475 million due 2006-2012 (13.4%) | 312 | 321 |
| Other, due 2006-2014 (6.3% and 6.2%) | 233 | 212 |
| | 2,456 | 2,557 |
| Less: current maturities of long-term debt obligations | (143) | (160) |
| | $2,313 | $2,397 |

*The interest rates in the above table reflect weighted-average rates as of year-end.*

Short-term borrowings are reclassified to long-term when we have the intent and ability, through the existence of the unused lines of credit, to refinance these borrowings on a long-term basis. At year-end 2005, we maintained $2.1 billion in corporate lines of credit subject to normal banking terms and conditions. These credit facilities support short-term debt issuances and remained unused as of December 31, 2005. Of the $2.1 billion, $1.35 billion expires in May 2006 with the remaining $750 million expiring in June 2009.

In addition, $181 million of our debt was outstanding on various lines of credit maintained for our international divisions.

These lines of credit are subject to normal banking terms and conditions and are committed to the extent of our borrowings.

**Interest Rate Swaps**
We entered into interest rate swaps in 2004 to effectively convert the interest rate of a specific debt issuance from a fixed rate of 3.2% to a variable rate. The variable weighted-average interest rate that we pay is linked to LIBOR and is subject to change. The notional amount of the interest rate swaps outstanding at December 31, 2005 and December 25, 2004 was $500 million. The terms of the interest rate swaps match the terms of the debt they modify. The swaps mature in 2007.

At December 31, 2005, approximately 78% of total debt, after the impact of the associated interest rate swaps, was exposed to variable interest rates, compared to 67% at December 25, 2004. In addition to variable rate long-term debt, all debt with maturities of less than one year is categorized as variable for purposes of this measure.

**Cross Currency Interest Rate Swaps**
In 2004, we entered into a cross currency interest rate swap to hedge the currency exposure on U.S. dollar denominated debt of $50 million held by a foreign affiliate. The terms of this swap match the terms of the debt it modifies. The swap matures in 2008. The unrecognized gain related to this swap was less than $1 million at December 31, 2005, resulting in a U.S. dollar liability of $50 million. At December 25, 2004, the unrecognized loss related to this swap was $3 million, resulting in a U.S. dollar liability of $53 million. We have also entered into cross currency interest rate swaps to hedge the currency exposure on U.S. dollar denominated intercompany debt of $125 million. The terms of the swaps match the terms of the debt they modify. The swaps mature over the next two years. The net unrecognized gain related to these swaps was $5 million at December 31, 2005. The net unrecognized loss related to these swaps was less than $1 million at December 25, 2004.

**Long-Term Contractual Commitments**

| Payments Due by Period | Total | 2006 | 2007-2008 | 2009-2010 | 2011 and beyond |
|---|---|---|---|---|---|
| Long-term debt obligations[a] | $2,313 | $ – | $1,052 | $ 876 | $ 385 |
| Operating leases | 769 | 187 | 253 | 132 | 197 |
| Purchasing commitments[b] | 4,533 | 1,169 | 1,630 | 775 | 959 |
| Marketing commitments | 1,487 | 412 | 438 | 381 | 256 |
| Other commitments | 99 | 82 | 10 | 6 | 1 |
| | $9,201 | $1,850 | $3,383 | $2,170 | $1,798 |

(a) Excludes current maturities of long-term debt of $143 million which are classified within current liabilities.

(b) Includes approximately $13 million of long-term commitments which are reflected in other liabilities in our Consolidated Balance Sheet.

*The above table reflects non-cancelable commitments as of December 31, 2005 based on year-end foreign exchange rates.*

Most long-term contractual commitments, except for our long-term debt obligations, are not recorded in our Consolidated Balance Sheet. Non-cancelable operating leases primarily represent building leases. Non-cancelable purchasing commitments are primarily for oranges and orange juices to be used for our Tropicana brand beverages. Non-cancelable marketing commitments primarily are for sports marketing and with our fountain customers. Bottler funding is not reflected in our long-term contractual commitments as it is negotiated on an annual basis. See Note 7 regarding our pension and retiree medical obligations and discussion below regarding our commitments to noncontrolled bottling affiliates and former restaurant operations.

### Off-Balance Sheet Arrangements

It is not our business practice to enter into off-balance sheet arrangements, other than in the normal course of business, nor is it our policy to issue guarantees to our bottlers, noncontrolled affiliates or third parties. However, certain guarantees were necessary to facilitate the separation of our bottling and restaurant operations from us. In connection with these transactions, we have guaranteed $2.3 billion of Bottling Group, LLC's long-term debt through 2012 and $28 million of YUM! Brands, Inc. (YUM) outstanding obligations, primarily property leases, through 2020. The terms of our Bottling Group, LLC debt guarantee are intended to preserve the structure of PBG's separation from us and our payment obligation would be triggered if Bottling Group, LLC failed to perform under these debt obligations or the structure significantly changed. Our guarantees of certain obligations ensured YUM's continued use of certain properties. These guarantees would require our cash payment if YUM failed to perform under these lease obligations.

See "Our Liquidity, Capital Resources and Financial Position" in Management's Discussion and Analysis for further unaudited information on our borrowings.

## Note 10 — Risk Management

We are exposed to the risk of loss arising from adverse changes in:

- commodity prices, affecting the cost of our raw materials and energy,
- foreign exchange risks,
- interest rates,
- stock prices, and
- discount rates affecting the measurement of our pension and retiree medical liabilities.

In the normal course of business, we manage these risks through a variety of strategies, including the use of derivatives. Certain derivatives are designated as either cash flow or fair value hedges and qualify for hedge accounting treatment, while others do not qualify and are marked to market through earnings. See "Our Business Risks" in Management's Discussion and Analysis for further unaudited information on our business risks.

For cash flow hedges, changes in fair value are deferred in accumulated other comprehensive loss within shareholders' equity until the underlying hedged item is recognized in net income. For fair value hedges, changes in fair value are recognized immediately in earnings, consistent with the underlying hedged item. Hedging transactions are limited to an underlying exposure. As a result, any change in the value of our derivative instruments would be substantially offset by an opposite change in the value of the underlying hedged items. Hedging ineffectiveness and a net earnings impact occur when the change in the value of the hedge does not offset the change in the value of the underlying hedged item. If the derivative instrument is terminated, we continue to defer the related gain or loss and include it as a component of the cost of the underlying hedged item. Upon determination that the underlying hedged item will not be part of an actual transaction, we recognize the related gain or loss in net income in that period.

We also use derivatives that do not qualify for hedge accounting treatment. We account for such derivatives at market value with the resulting gains and losses reflected in our income statement. We do not use derivative instruments for trading or speculative purposes and we limit our exposure to individual counterparties to manage credit risk.

### Commodity Prices

We are subject to commodity price risk because our ability to recover increased costs through higher pricing may be limited in the competitive environment in which we operate. This risk is managed through the use of fixed-price purchase orders, pricing agreements, geographic diversity and derivatives. We use derivatives, with terms of no more than two years, to economically hedge price fluctuations related to a portion of our anticipated commodity purchases, primarily for natural gas and diesel fuel. For those derivatives that are designated as cash flow hedges, any ineffectiveness is recorded immediately. However, our commodity cash flow hedges have not had any significant ineffectiveness for all periods presented. We classify both the earnings and cash flow impact from these derivatives consistent with the underlying hedged item. During the next 12 months, we expect to reclassify gains of $24 million related to cash flow hedges from accumulated other comprehensive loss into net income.

### Foreign Exchange

Our operations outside of the U.S. generate over a third of our net revenue of which Mexico, the United Kingdom and Canada comprise nearly 20%. As a result, we are exposed to foreign currency risks from unforeseen economic changes and political unrest. On occasion, we enter into hedges, primarily forward contracts with terms of no more than two years, to reduce the effect of foreign exchange rates. Ineffectiveness on these hedges has not been material.

### Interest Rates

We centrally manage our debt and investment portfolios considering investment opportunities and risks, tax consequences and overall financing strategies. We may use interest rate and cross currency interest rate swaps to manage our overall interest expense and foreign exchange risk. These instruments effectively change the interest rate and currency of specific debt issuances. These swaps are entered into concurrently with the issuance of the debt that they are intended to modify. The notional amount, interest payment and maturity date of the swaps match the principal, interest payment and maturity date of the related debt. These swaps are entered into only with strong creditworthy counterparties, are settled on a net basis and are of relatively short duration.

**Stock Prices**

The portion of our deferred compensation liability that is based on certain market indices and on our stock price is subject to market risk. We hold mutual fund investments and prepaid forward contracts to manage this risk. Changes in the fair value of these investments and contracts are recognized immediately in earnings and are offset by changes in the related compensation liability.

**Fair Value**

All derivative instruments are recognized in our Consolidated Balance Sheet at fair value. The fair value of our derivative instruments is generally based on quoted market prices. Book and fair values of our derivative and financial instruments are as follows:

| | 2005 | | 2004 | |
|---|---|---|---|---|
| | Book Value | Fair Value | Book Value | Fair Value |
| **Assets** | | | | |
| Cash and cash equivalents(a) | $1,716 | $1,716 | $1,280 | $1,280 |
| Short-term investments(b) | $3,166 | $3,166 | $2,165 | $2,165 |
| Forward exchange contracts(c) | $19 | $19 | $8 | $8 |
| Commodity contracts(d) | $41 | $41 | $7 | $7 |
| Prepaid forward contract(e) | $107 | $107 | $120 | $120 |
| Cross currency interest rate swaps(f) | $6 | $6 | $— | $— |
| **Liabilities** | | | | |
| Forward exchange contracts(c) | $15 | $15 | $35 | $35 |
| Commodity contracts(d) | $3 | $3 | $8 | $8 |
| Debt obligations | $5,202 | $5,378 | $3,451 | $3,676 |
| Interest rate swaps(g) | $9 | $9 | $1 | $1 |
| Cross currency interest rate swaps(f) | $— | $— | $3 | $3 |

Included in our Consolidated Balance Sheet under the captions noted above or as indicated below. In addition, derivatives are designated as accounting hedges unless otherwise noted below.

(a) Book value approximates fair value due to the short maturity.

(b) Principally short-term time deposits and includes $124 million at December 31, 2005 and $118 million at December 25, 2004 of mutual fund investments used to manage a portion of market risk arising from our deferred compensation liability.

(c) 2005 asset includes $14 million related to derivatives not designated as accounting hedges. Assets are reported within current assets and other assets and liabilities are reported within current liabilities and other liabilities.

(d) 2005 asset includes $2 million related to derivatives not designated as accounting hedges and the liability relates entirely to derivatives not designated as accounting hedges. Assets are reported within current assets and other assets and liabilities are reported within current liabilities and other liabilities.

(e) Included in current assets and other assets.

(f) Asset included within other assets and liability included in long-term debt.

(g) Reported in other liabilities.

This table excludes guarantees, including our guarantee of $2.3 billion of Bottling Group, LLC's long-term debt. The guarantee had a fair value of $47 million at December 31, 2005 and $46 million at December 25, 2004 based on an external estimate of the cost to us of transferring the liability to an independent financial institution. See Note 9 for additional information on our guarantees.

## Note 11 — Net Income per Common Share from Continuing Operations

Basic net income per common share is net income available to common shareholders divided by the weighted average of common shares outstanding during the period. Diluted net income per common share is calculated using the weighted average of common shares outstanding adjusted to include the effect that would occur if in-the-money employee stock options were exercised and RSUs and preferred shares were converted into common shares. Options to purchase 3.0 million shares in 2005, 7.0 million shares in 2004 and 49.0 million shares in 2003 were not included in the calculation of diluted earnings per common share because these options were out-of-the-money. Out-of-the-money options had average exercise prices of $53.77 in 2005, $52.88 in 2004 and $48.27 in 2003.

The computations of basic and diluted net income per common share from continuing operations are as follows:

| | 2005 Income | 2005 Shares[a] | 2004 Income | 2004 Shares[a] | 2003 Income | 2003 Shares[a] |
|---|---|---|---|---|---|---|
| Net income | $4,078 | | $4,174 | | $3,568 | |
| Preferred shares: | | | | | | |
| Dividends | (2) | | (3) | | (3) | |
| Redemption premium | (16) | | (22) | | (12) | |
| Net income available for common shareholders | $4,060 | 1,669 | $4,149 | 1,696 | $3,553 | 1,718 |
| Basic net income per common share | $2.43 | | $2.45 | | $2.07 | |
| Net income available for common shareholders | $4,060 | 1,669 | $4,149 | 1,696 | $3,553 | 1,718 |
| Dilutive securities: | | | | | | |
| Stock options and RSUs | – | 35 | – | 31 | – | 17 |
| ESOP convertible preferred stock | 18 | 2 | 24 | 2 | 15 | 3 |
| Unvested stock awards | – | – | – | – | – | 1 |
| Diluted | $4,078 | 1,706 | $4,173 | 1,729 | $3,568 | 1,739 |
| Diluted net income per common share | $2.39 | | $2.41 | | $2.05 | |

(a) Weighted-average common shares outstanding.

## Note 12 — Preferred and Common Stock

As of December 31, 2005 and December 25, 2004, there were 3.6 billion shares of common stock and 3 million shares of convertible preferred stock authorized. The preferred stock was issued only for an employee stock ownership plan (ESOP) established by Quaker and these shares are redeemable for common stock by the ESOP participants. The preferred stock accrues dividends at an annual rate of $5.46 per share. At year-end 2005 and 2004, there were 803,953 preferred shares issued and 354,853 and 424,853 shares outstanding, respectively. Each share is convertible at the option of the holder into 4.9625 shares of common stock. The preferred shares may be called by us upon written notice at $78 per share plus accrued and unpaid dividends.

As of December 31, 2005, 0.3 million outstanding shares of preferred stock with a fair value of $104 million and 17 million shares of common stock were held in the accounts of ESOP participants. As of December 25, 2004, 0.4 million outstanding shares of preferred stock with a fair value of $110 million and 18 million shares of common stock were held in the accounts of ESOP participants. Quaker made the final award to its ESOP plan in June 2001.

| | 2005 Shares | 2005 Amount | 2004 Shares | 2004 Amount | 2003 Shares | 2003 Amount |
|---|---|---|---|---|---|---|
| Preferred stock | 0.8 | $41 | 0.8 | $41 | 0.8 | $41 |
| Repurchased preferred stock | | | | | | |
| Balance, beginning of year | 0.4 | $ 90 | 0.3 | $63 | 0.2 | $48 |
| Redemptions | 0.1 | 19 | 0.1 | 27 | 0.1 | 15 |
| Balance, end of year | 0.5 | $110* | 0.4 | $90 | 0.3 | $63 |

*Does not sum due to rounding.

## Note 13 — Accumulated Other Comprehensive Loss

Comprehensive income is a measure of income which includes both net income and other comprehensive income or loss. Other comprehensive loss results from items deferred on the balance sheet in shareholders' equity. Other comprehensive (loss)/income was $(167) million in 2005, $381 million in 2004, and $405 million in 2003. The accumulated balances for each component of other comprehensive loss were as follows:

| | 2005 | 2004 | 2003 |
|---|---|---|---|
| Currency translation adjustment | $ (971) | $(720) | $(1,121) |
| Cash flow hedges, net of tax[a] | 27 | (19) | (12) |
| Minimum pension liability adjustment[b] | (138) | (154) | (135) |
| Unrealized gain on securities, net of tax | 31 | 7 | 1 |
| Other | (2) | – | – |
| Accumulated other comprehensive loss | $(1,053) | $(886) | $(1,267) |

(a) Includes net commodity gains of $55 million in 2005. Also includes no impact in 2005, $6 million gain in 2004 and $8 million gain in 2003 for our share of our equity investees' accumulated derivative activity. Deferred gains/(losses) reclassified into earnings were $8 million in 2005, $(10) million in 2004 and no impact in 2003.

(b) Net of taxes of $72 million in 2005, $77 million in 2004 and $67 million in 2003. Also, includes $120 million in 2005, $121 million in 2004 and $110 million in 2003 for our share of our equity investees' minimum pension liability adjustments.

## Note 14 — Supplemental Financial Information

|  | 2005 | 2004 | 2003 |
|---|---|---|---|
| **Accounts receivable** |  |  |  |
| Trade receivables | $2,718 | $2,505 |  |
| Other receivables | 618 | 591 |  |
|  | 3,336 | 3,096 |  |
| Allowance, beginning of year | 97 | 105 | $116 |
| Net amounts (credited)/charged to expense | (1) | 18 | 32 |
| Deductions[a] | (22) | (25) | (43) |
| Other[b] | 1 | (1) | – |
| Allowance, end of year | 75 | 97 | $105 |
| Net receivables | $3,261 | $2,999 |  |
| **Inventory[c]** |  |  |  |
| Raw materials | $ 738 | $ 665 |  |
| Work-in-process | 112 | 156 |  |
| Finished goods | 843 | 720 |  |
|  | $1,693 | $1,541 |  |
| **Accounts payable and other current liabilities** |  |  |  |
| Accounts payable | $1,799 | $1,731 |  |
| Accrued marketplace spending | 1,383 | 1,285 |  |
| Accrued compensation and benefits | 1,062 | 961 |  |
| Dividends payable | 431 | 387 |  |
| Insurance accruals | 136 | 131 |  |
| Other current liabilities | 1,160 | 1,104 |  |
|  | $5,971 | $5,599 |  |
| **Other liabilities** |  |  |  |
| Reserves for income taxes | $1,884 | $1,567 |  |
| Other | 2,439 | 2,532 |  |
|  | $4,323 | $4,099 |  |
| **Other supplemental information** |  |  |  |
| Rent expense | $228 | $245 | $231 |
| Interest paid | $213 | $137 | $147 |
| Income taxes paid, net of refunds | $1,258 | $1,833 | $1,530 |
| Acquisitions[d] |  |  |  |
| Fair value of assets acquired | $ 1,089 | $ 78 | $178 |
| Cash paid and debt issued | (1,096) | (64) | (71) |
| SVE minority interest eliminated | 216 | – | – |
| Liabilities assumed | $ 209 | $ 14 | $107 |

(a) Includes accounts written off.

(b) Includes collections of previously written-off accounts and currency translation effects.

(c) Inventories are valued at the lower of cost or market. Cost is determined using the average, first-in, first-out (FIFO) or last-in, first-out (LIFO) methods. Approximately 17% in 2005 and 15% in 2004 of the inventory cost was computed using the LIFO method. The differences between LIFO and FIFO methods of valuing these inventories were not material.

(d) In 2005, these amounts include the impact of our acquisition of General Mills, Inc.'s 40.5% ownership interest in SVE for $750 million. The excess of our purchase price over the fair value of net assets acquired is $250 million and is included in goodwill. We also reacquired rights to distribute global brands for $263 million which is included in other nonamortizable intangible assets.

# ADDITIONAL INFORMATION

In addition to the financial statements and accompanying notes, companies are required to provide a report on internal control over financial reporting and to have an auditor's report on the financial statements. In addition, PepsiCo has provided a report indicating that financial reporting is management's responsibility. Finally, PepsiCo also provides selected financial data it believes is useful. The two required reports are further explained below.

## Management's Report on Internal Control over Financial Reporting

The Sarbanes-Oxley Act of 2002 requires managers of publicly traded companies to establish and maintain systems of internal control over the company's financial reporting processes. In addition, management must express its responsibility for financial reporting, and it must provide certifications regarding the accuracy of the financial statements.

## Auditor's Report

All publicly held corporations, as well as many other enterprises and organizations engage the services of independent certified public accountants for the purpose of obtaining an objective, expert report on their financial statements. Based on a comprehensive examination of the company's accounting system, accounting records, and the financial statements, the outside CPA issues the auditor's report.

The standard auditor's report identifies who and what was audited and indicates the responsibilities of management and the auditor relative to the financial statements. It states that the audit was conducted in accordance with generally accepted auditing standards and discusses the nature and limitations of the audit. It then expresses an informed opinion as to (1) the fairness of the financial statements and (2) their conformity with generally accepted accounting principles. It also expresses an opinion regarding the effectiveness of the company's internal controls. All of this additional information for PepsiCo is provided on the following pages.

## Management's Responsibility for Financial Reporting

**To Our Shareholders:**

At PepsiCo, our actions — the actions of all our associates — are governed by our Worldwide Code of Conduct. This code is clearly aligned with our stated values — a commitment to sustained growth, through empowered people, operating with responsibility and building trust. Both the code and our core values enable us to operate with integrity — both within the letter and the spirit of the law. Our code of conduct is reinforced consistently at all levels and in all countries. We have maintained strong governance policies and practices for many years.

The management of PepsiCo is responsible for the objectivity and integrity of our consolidated financial statements. The Audit Committee of the Board of Directors has engaged independent registered public accounting firm, KPMG LLP, to audit our consolidated financial statements and they have expressed an unqualified opinion.

We are committed to providing timely, accurate and understandable information to investors. Our commitment encompasses the following:

**Maintaining strong controls over financial reporting.** Our system of internal control is based on the control criteria framework of the Committee of Sponsoring Organizations of the Treadway Commission published in their report titled, *Internal Control — Integrated Framework.* The system is designed to provide reasonable assurance that transactions are executed as authorized and accurately recorded; that assets are safeguarded; and that accounting records are sufficiently reliable to permit the preparation of financial statements that conform in all material respects with accounting principles generally accepted in the U.S. We maintain disclosure controls and procedures designed to ensure that information required to be disclosed in reports under the Securities Exchange Act of 1934 is recorded, processed, summarized and reported within the specified time periods. We monitor these internal controls through self-assessments and an ongoing program of internal audits. Our internal controls are reinforced through our Worldwide Code of Conduct, which sets forth our commitment to conduct business with integrity, and within both the letter and the spirit of the law.

**Exerting rigorous oversight of the business.** We continuously review our business results and strategies. This encompasses financial discipline in our strategic and daily business decisions. Our Executive Committee is actively involved — from understanding strategies and alternatives to reviewing key initiatives and financial performance. The intent is to ensure we remain objective in our assessments, constructively challenge our approach to potential business opportunities and issues, and monitor results and controls.

**Engaging strong and effective Corporate Governance from our Board of Directors.** We have an active, capable and diligent Board that meets the required standards for independence, and we welcome the Board's oversight as a representative of our shareholders. Our

Audit Committee comprises independent directors with the financial literacy, knowledge and experience to provide appropriate oversight. We review our critical accounting policies, financial reporting and internal control matters with them and encourage their direct communication with KPMG LLP, with our General Auditor, and with our General Counsel. In 2005, we named a senior compliance officer to lead and coordinate our compliance policies and practices.

**Providing investors with financial results that are complete, transparent and understandable.** The consolidated financial statements and financial information included in this report are the responsibility of management. This includes preparing the financial statements in accordance with accounting principles generally accepted in the U.S., which require estimates based on management's best judgment.

**PepsiCo has a strong history of doing what's right.** We realize that great companies are built on trust, strong ethical standards and principles. Our financial results are delivered from that culture of accountability, and we take responsibility for the quality and accuracy of our financial reporting.

*Peter Bridgman*

Peter A. Bridgman
Senior Vice President and Controller

*Indra K Nooyi*

Indra K. Nooyi
President and Chief Financial Officer

*Steven S Reinemund*

Steven S Reinemund
Chairman of the Board
and Chief Executive Officer

## Management's Report on Internal Control over Financial Reporting

**To Our Shareholders:**

Our management is responsible for establishing and maintaining adequate internal control over financial reporting, as such term is defined in Rule 13a-15(f) of the Exchange Act. Under the supervision and with the participation of our management, including our Chief Executive Officer and Chief Financial Officer, we conducted an evaluation of the effectiveness of our internal control over financial reporting based upon the framework in *Internal Control — Integrated Framework* issued by the Committee of Sponsoring Organizations of the Treadway Commission. Based on that evaluation, our management concluded that our internal control over financial reporting is effective as of December 31, 2005.

KPMG LLP, an independent registered public accounting firm, has audited the consolidated financial statements included in this Annual Report and, as part of their audit, has issued their report, included herein, (1) on our management's assessment of the effectiveness of our internal controls over financial reporting and (2) on the effectiveness of our internal control over financial reporting.


Peter A. Bridgman
Senior Vice President and Controller


Indra K. Nooyi
President and Chief Financial Officer


Steven S Reinemund
Chairman of the Board
and Chief Executive Officer

## Report of Independent Registered Public Accounting Firm

**Board of Directors and Shareholders PepsiCo, Inc.:**

We have audited the accompanying Consolidated Balance Sheet of PepsiCo, Inc. and Subsidiaries as of December 31, 2005 and December 25, 2004 and the related Consolidated Statements of Income, Cash Flows and Common Shareholders' Equity for each of the years in the three-year period ended December 31, 2005. We have also audited management's assessment, included in Management's Report on Internal Control over Financial Reporting, that PepsiCo, Inc. and Subsidiaries maintained effective internal control over financial reporting as of December 31, 2005, based on criteria established in *Internal Control — Integrated Framework* issued by the Committee of Sponsoring Organizations of the Treadway Commission (COSO). PepsiCo, Inc.'s management is responsible for these consolidated financial statements, for maintaining effective internal control over financial reporting, and for its assessment of the effectiveness of internal control over financial reporting. Our responsibility is to express an opinion on these consolidated financial statements, an opinion on management's assessment, and an opinion on the effectiveness of PepsiCo, Inc.'s internal control over financial reporting based on our audits.

We conducted our audits in accordance with the standards of the Public Company Accounting Oversight Board (United States). Those standards require that we plan and perform the audits to obtain reasonable assurance about whether the financial statements are free of material misstatement and whether effective internal control over financial reporting was maintained in all material respects. Our audit of financial statements included examining, on a test basis, evidence supporting the amounts and disclosures in the financial statements, assessing the accounting principles used and significant estimates made by management, and evaluating the overall financial statement presentation. Our audit of internal control over financial reporting included obtaining an understanding of internal control over financial reporting, evaluating management's assessment, testing and evaluating the design and operating effectiveness of internal control, and performing such other procedures as we considered necessary in the circumstances. We believe that our audits provide a reasonable basis for our opinions.

A company's internal control over financial reporting is a process designed to provide reasonable assurance regarding the reliability of financial reporting and the preparation of financial statements for external purposes in accordance with generally accepted accounting principles. A company's internal control over financial reporting includes those policies and procedures that (1) pertain to the maintenance of records that, in reasonable detail, accurately and fairly reflect the transactions and dispositions of the assets of the company; (2) provide reasonable assurance that transactions are recorded as necessary to permit preparation of financial statements in accordance with generally accepted

accounting principles, and that receipts and expenditures of the company are being made only in accordance with authorizations of management and directors of the company; and (3) provide reasonable assurance regarding prevention or timely detection of unauthorized acquisition, use, or disposition of the company's assets that could have a material effect on the financial statements.

Because of its inherent limitations, internal control over financial reporting may not prevent or detect misstatements. Also, projections of any evaluation of effectiveness to future periods are subject to the risk that controls may become inadequate because of changes in conditions, or that the degree of compliance with the policies or procedures may deteriorate.

In our opinion, the consolidated financial statements referred to above present fairly, in all material respects, the financial position of PepsiCo, Inc. and Subsidiaries as of December 31, 2005 and December 25, 2004, and the results of their operations and their cash flows for each of the years in the three-year period ended December 31, 2005, in conformity with United States generally accepted accounting principles. Also, in our opinion, management's assessment that PepsiCo, Inc. maintained effective internal control over financial reporting as of December 31, 2005, is fairly stated, in all material respects, based on criteria established in *Internal Control — Integrated Framework* issued by COSO. Furthermore, in our opinion, PepsiCo, Inc. maintained, in all material respects, effective internal control over financial reporting as of December 31, 2005, based on criteria established in *Internal Control — Integrated Framework* issued by COSO.

*KPMG LLP*

KPMG LLP
New York, New York
February 24, 2006

## Selected Financial Data (in millions except per share amounts, unaudited)

| Quarterly | First Quarter | Second Quarter | Third Quarter | Fourth Quarter |
|---|---|---|---|---|
| Net revenue | | | | |
| 2005 | $6,585 | $7,697 | $8,184 | $10,096 |
| 2004 | $6,131 | $7,070 | $7,257 | $8,803 |
| Gross profit(a) | | | | |
| 2005 | $3,715 | $4,383 | $4,669 | $5,619 |
| 2004 | $3,466 | $4,039 | $4,139 | $4,943 |
| 2005 restructuring charges(b) | | | | |
| 2005 | – | – | – | $83 |
| 2004 restructuring and impairment charges(c) | | | | |
| 2004 | – | – | – | $150 |
| AJCA tax charge(d) | | | | |
| 2005 | – | – | $468 | $(8) |
| Net income(e) | | | | |
| 2005 | $912 | $1,194 | $864 | $1,108 |
| 2004 | $804 | $1,059 | $1,364 | $985 |
| Net income per common share — basic(e) | | | | |
| 2005 | $0.54 | $0.71 | $0.52 | $0.66 |
| 2004 | $0.47 | $0.62 | $0.80 | $0.58 |
| Net income per common share — diluted(e) | | | | |
| 2005 | $0.53 | $0.70 | $0.51 | $0.65 |
| 2004 | $0.46 | $0.61 | $0.79 | $0.58 |
| Cash dividends declared per common share | | | | |
| 2005 | $0.23 | $0.26 | $0.26 | $0.26 |
| 2004 | $0.16 | $0.23 | $0.23 | $0.23 |
| 2005 stock price per share(f) | | | | |
| High | $55.71 | $57.20 | $56.73 | $60.34 |
| Low | $51.34 | $51.78 | $52.07 | $53.55 |
| Close | $52.62 | $55.52 | $54.65 | $59.08 |
| 2004 stock price per share(f) | | | | |
| High | $53.00 | $55.48 | $55.71 | $53.00 |
| Low | $45.30 | $50.28 | $48.41 | $47.37 |
| Close | $50.93 | $54.95 | $50.84 | $51.94 |

The first, second, and third quarters consist of 12 weeks and the fourth quarter consists of 16 weeks in 2004 and 17 weeks in 2005.

(a) Reflects net reclassifications in all periods from cost of sales to selling, general and administrative expenses related to the alignment of certain accounting policies in connection with our ongoing BPT initiative. See Note 1.

(b) The 2005 restructuring charges were $83 million ($55 million or $0.03 per share after-tax). See Note 3.

(c) The 2004 restructuring and impairment charges were $150 million ($96 million or $0.06 per share after-tax). See Note 3.

(d) Represents income tax expense associated with the repatriation of earnings in connection with the AJCA. See Note 5.

(e) Fourth quarter 2004 net income reflects a tax benefit from discontinued operations of $38 million or $0.02 per share. See Note 5.

(f) Represents the composite high and low sales price and quarterly closing prices for one share of PepsiCo common stock.

| Five-Year Summary | 2005 | 2004 | 2003 |
|---|---|---|---|
| Net revenue | $32,562 | $29,261 | $26,971 |
| Income from continuing operations | $4,078 | $4,174 | $3,568 |
| Net income | $4,078 | $4,212 | $3,568 |
| Income per common share — basic, continuing operations | $2.43 | $2.45 | $2.07 |
| Income per common share — diluted, continuing operations | $2.39 | $2.41 | $2.05 |
| Cash dividends declared per common share | $1.01 | $0.850 | $0.630 |
| Total assets | $31,727 | $27,987 | $25,327 |
| Long-term debt | $2,313 | $2,397 | $1,702 |
| Return on invested capital(a) | 22.7% | 27.4% | 27.5% |

| Five-Year Summary (Cont.) | 2002 | 2001 |
|---|---|---|
| Net revenue | $25,112 | $23,512 |
| Net income | $3,000 | $2,400 |
| Income per common share — basic | $1.69 | $1.35 |
| Income per common share — diluted | $1.68 | $1.33 |
| Cash dividends declared per common share | $0.595 | $0.575 |
| Total assets | $23,474 | $21,695 |
| Long-term debt | $2,187 | $2,651 |
| Return on invested capital(a) | 25.7% | 22.1% |

(a) Return on invested capital is defined as adjusted net income divided by the sum of average shareholders' equity and average total debt. Adjusted net income is defined as net income plus net interest expense after tax. Net interest expense after tax was $62 million in 2005, $60 million in 2004, $72 million in 2003, $93 million in 2002, and $99 million in 2001.

• As a result of the adoption of SFAS 142, *Goodwill and Other Intangible Assets*, and the consolidation of SVE in 2002, the data provided above is not comparable.

• Includes restructuring and impairment charges of:

| | 2005 | 2004 | 2003 | 2001 |
|---|---|---|---|---|
| Pre-tax | $83 | $150 | $147 | $31 |
| After-tax | $55 | $96 | $100 | $19 |
| Per share | $0.03 | $0.06 | $0.06 | $0.01 |

• Includes Quaker merger-related costs of:

| | 2003 | 2002 | 2001 |
|---|---|---|---|
| Pre-tax | $59 | $224 | $356 |
| After-tax | $42 | $190 | $322 |
| Per share | $0.02 | $0.11 | $0.18 |

• The 2005 fiscal year consisted of fifty-three weeks compared to fifty-two weeks in our normal fiscal year. The 53rd week increased 2005 net revenue by an estimated $418 million and net income by an estimated $57 million or $0.03 per share.

• Cash dividends per common share in 2001 are those of pre-merger PepsiCo prior to the effective date of the merger.

• In the fourth quarter of 2004, we reached agreement with the IRS for an open issue related to our discontinued restaurant operations which resulted in a tax benefit of $38 million or $0.02 per share.

# SPECIMEN FINANCIAL STATEMENTS:
# The Coca-Cola Company

## THE COCA-COLA COMPANY AND SUBSIDIARIES
## CONSOLIDATED STATEMENTS OF INCOME

| Year Ended December 31, | 2005 | 2004 | 2003 |
|---|---|---|---|
| (In millions except per share data) | | | |
| **NET OPERATING REVENUES** | **$ 23,104** | $ 21,742 | $ 20,857 |
| Cost of goods sold | **8,195** | 7,674 | 7,776 |
| **GROSS PROFIT** | **14,909** | 14,068 | 13,081 |
| Selling, general and administrative expenses | **8,739** | 7,890 | 7,287 |
| Other operating charges | **85** | 480 | 573 |
| **OPERATING INCOME** | **6,085** | 5,698 | 5,221 |
| Interest income | **235** | 157 | 176 |
| Interest expense | **240** | 196 | 178 |
| Equity income — net | **680** | 621 | 406 |
| Other loss — net | **(93)** | (82) | (138) |
| Gains on issuances of stock by equity investees | **23** | 24 | 8 |
| **INCOME BEFORE INCOME TAXES** | **6,690** | 6,222 | 5,495 |
| Income taxes | **1,818** | 1,375 | 1,148 |
| **NET INCOME** | **$ 4,872** | $ 4,847 | $ 4,347 |
| **BASIC NET INCOME PER SHARE** | **$ 2.04** | $ 2.00 | $ 1.77 |
| **DILUTED NET INCOME PER SHARE** | **$ 2.04** | $ 2.00 | $ 1.77 |
| **AVERAGE SHARES OUTSTANDING** | **2,392** | 2,426 | 2,459 |
| Effect of dilutive securities | **1** | 3 | 3 |
| **AVERAGE SHARES OUTSTANDING ASSUMING DILUTION** | **2,393** | 2,429 | 2,462 |

Refer to Notes to Consolidated Financial Statements.

## THE COCA-COLA COMPANY AND SUBSIDIARIES
## CONSOLIDATED BALANCE SHEETS

| December 31,<br>(In millions except par value) | 2005 | 2004 |
|---|---:|---:|
| **ASSETS** | | |
| **CURRENT ASSETS** | | |
| Cash and cash equivalents | $ 4,701 | $ 6,707 |
| Marketable securities | 66 | 61 |
| Trade accounts receivable, less allowances of $72 and $69, respectively | 2,281 | 2,244 |
| Inventories | 1,424 | 1,420 |
| Prepaid expenses and other assets | 1,778 | 1,849 |
| **TOTAL CURRENT ASSETS** | 10,250 | 12,281 |
| **INVESTMENTS** | | |
| Equity method investments: | | |
| Coca-Cola Enterprises Inc. | 1,731 | 1,569 |
| Coca-Cola Hellenic Bottling Company S.A. | 1,039 | 1,067 |
| Coca-Cola FEMSA, S.A. de C.V. | 982 | 792 |
| Coca-Cola Amatil Limited | 748 | 736 |
| Other, principally bottling companies | 2,062 | 1,733 |
| Cost method investments, principally bottling companies | 360 | 355 |
| **TOTAL INVESTMENTS** | 6,922 | 6,252 |
| **OTHER ASSETS** | 2,648 | 2,981 |
| **PROPERTY, PLANT AND EQUIPMENT — net** | 5,786 | 6,091 |
| **TRADEMARKS WITH INDEFINITE LIVES** | 1,946 | 2,037 |
| **GOODWILL** | 1,047 | 1,097 |
| **OTHER INTANGIBLE ASSETS** | 828 | 702 |
| **TOTAL ASSETS** | $ 29,427 | $ 31,441 |
| **LIABILITIES AND SHAREOWNERS' EQUITY** | | |
| **CURRENT LIABILITIES** | | |
| Accounts payable and accrued expenses | $ 4,493 | $ 4,403 |
| Loans and notes payable | 4,518 | 4,531 |
| Current maturities of long-term debt | 28 | 1,490 |
| Accrued income taxes | 797 | 709 |
| **TOTAL CURRENT LIABILITIES** | 9,836 | 11,133 |
| **LONG-TERM DEBT** | 1,154 | 1,157 |
| **OTHER LIABILITIES** | 1,730 | 2,814 |
| **DEFERRED INCOME TAXES** | 352 | 402 |
| **SHAREOWNERS' EQUITY** | | |
| Common stock, $0.25 par value; Authorized — 5,600 shares; | | |
| Issued — 3,507 and 3,500 shares, respectively | 877 | 875 |
| Capital surplus | 5,492 | 4,928 |
| Reinvested earnings | 31,299 | 29,105 |
| Accumulated other comprehensive income (loss) | (1,669) | (1,348) |
| Treasury stock, at cost — 1,138 and 1,091 shares, respectively | (19,644) | (17,625) |
| **TOTAL SHAREOWNERS' EQUITY** | 16,355 | 15,935 |
| **TOTAL LIABILITIES AND SHAREOWNERS' EQUITY** | $ 29,427 | $ 31,441 |

Refer to Notes to Consolidated Financial Statements.

## THE COCA-COLA COMPANY AND SUBSIDIARIES
## CONSOLIDATED STATEMENTS OF CASH FLOWS

| Year Ended December 31,<br>(In millions) | 2005 | 2004 | 2003 |
|---|---|---|---|
| **OPERATING ACTIVITIES** | | | |
| Net income | $ **4,872** | $ 4,847 | $ 4,347 |
| Depreciation and amortization | **932** | 893 | 850 |
| Stock-based compensation expense | **324** | 345 | 422 |
| Deferred income taxes | **(88)** | 162 | (188) |
| Equity income or loss, net of dividends | **(446)** | (476) | (294) |
| Foreign currency adjustments | **47** | (59) | (79) |
| Gains on issuances of stock by equity investees | **(23)** | (24) | (8) |
| Gains on sales of assets, including bottling interests | **(9)** | (20) | (5) |
| Other operating charges | **85** | 480 | 330 |
| Other items | **299** | 437 | 249 |
| Net change in operating assets and liabilities | **430** | (617) | (168) |
| Net cash provided by operating activities | **6,423** | 5,968 | 5,456 |
| **INVESTING ACTIVITIES** | | | |
| Acquisitions and investments, principally trademarks and bottling companies | **(637)** | (267) | (359) |
| Purchases of investments and other assets | **(53)** | (46) | (177) |
| Proceeds from disposals of investments and other assets | **33** | 161 | 147 |
| Purchases of property, plant and equipment | **(899)** | (755) | (812) |
| Proceeds from disposals of property, plant and equipment | **88** | 341 | 87 |
| Other investing activities | **(28)** | 63 | 178 |
| Net cash used in investing activities | **(1,496)** | (503) | (936) |
| **FINANCING ACTIVITIES** | | | |
| Issuances of debt | **178** | 3,030 | 1,026 |
| Payments of debt | **(2,460)** | (1,316) | (1,119) |
| Issuances of stock | **230** | 193 | 98 |
| Purchases of stock for treasury | **(2,055)** | (1,739) | (1,440) |
| Dividends | **(2,678)** | (2,429) | (2,166) |
| Net cash used in financing activities | **(6,785)** | (2,261) | (3,601) |
| **EFFECT OF EXCHANGE RATE CHANGES ON CASH AND CASH EQUIVALENTS** | **(148)** | 141 | 183 |
| **CASH AND CASH EQUIVALENTS** | | | |
| Net increase (decrease) during the year | **(2,006)** | 3,345 | 1,102 |
| Balance at beginning of year | **6,707** | 3,362 | 2,260 |
| Balance at end of year | $ **4,701** | $ 6,707 | $ 3,362 |

Refer to Notes to Consolidated Financial Statements.

## THE COCA-COLA COMPANY AND SUBSIDIARIES
## CONSOLIDATED STATEMENTS OF SHAREOWNERS' EQUITY

| Year Ended December 31, | 2005 | 2004 | 2003 |
|---|---|---|---|
| (In millions except per share data) | | | |
| **NUMBER OF COMMON SHARES OUTSTANDING** | | | |
| Balance at beginning of year | 2,409 | 2,442 | 2,471 |
| Stock issued to employees exercising stock options | 7 | 5 | 4 |
| Purchases of stock for treasury[1] | (47) | (38) | (33) |
| Balance at end of year | 2,369 | 2,409 | 2,442 |
| **COMMON STOCK** | | | |
| Balance at beginning of year | $ 875 | $ 874 | $ 873 |
| Stock issued to employees exercising stock options | 2 | 1 | 1 |
| Balance at end of year | 877 | 875 | 874 |
| **CAPITAL SURPLUS** | | | |
| Balance at beginning of year | 4,928 | 4,395 | 3,857 |
| Stock issued to employees exercising stock options | 229 | 175 | 105 |
| Tax benefit from employees' stock option and restricted stock plans | 11 | 13 | 11 |
| Stock-based compensation | 324 | 345 | 422 |
| Balance at end of year | 5,492 | 4,928 | 4,395 |
| **REINVESTED EARNINGS** | | | |
| Balance at beginning of year | 29,105 | 26,687 | 24,506 |
| Net income | 4,872 | 4,847 | 4,347 |
| Dividends (per share — $1.12, $1.00 and $0.88 in 2005, 2004 and 2003, respectively) | (2,678) | (2,429) | (2,166) |
| Balance at end of year | 31,299 | 29,105 | 26,687 |
| **ACCUMULATED OTHER COMPREHENSIVE INCOME (LOSS)** | | | |
| Balance at beginning of year | (1,348) | (1,995) | (3,047) |
| Net foreign currency translation adjustment | (396) | 665 | 921 |
| Net gain (loss) on derivatives | 57 | (3) | (33) |
| Net change in unrealized gain on available-for-sale securities | 13 | 39 | 40 |
| Net change in minimum pension liability | 5 | (54) | 124 |
| Net other comprehensive income adjustments | (321) | 647 | 1,052 |
| Balance at end of year | (1,669) | (1,348) | (1,995) |
| **TREASURY STOCK** | | | |
| Balance at beginning of year | (17,625) | (15,871) | (14,389) |
| Purchases of treasury stock | (2,019) | (1,754) | (1,482) |
| Balance at end of year | (19,644) | (17,625) | (15,871) |
| **TOTAL SHAREOWNERS' EQUITY** | $ 16,355 | $ 15,935 | $ 14,090 |
| **COMPREHENSIVE INCOME** | | | |
| Net income | $ 4,872 | $ 4,847 | $ 4,347 |
| Net other comprehensive income adjustments | (321) | 647 | 1,052 |
| **TOTAL COMPREHENSIVE INCOME** | $ 4,551 | $ 5,494 | $ 5,399 |

[1] Common stock purchased from employees exercising stock options numbered 0.5 shares, 0.4 shares and 0.4 shares for the years ended December 31, 2005, 2004 and 2003, respectively.

Refer to Notes to Consolidated Financial Statements.

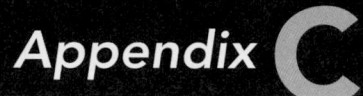
# Time Value of Money

Would you rather receive $1,000 today or a year from now? You should prefer to receive the $1,000 today because you can invest the $1,000 and earn interest on it. As a result, you will have more than $1,000 a year from now. What this example illustrates is the concept of the **time value of money**. Everyone prefers to receive money today rather than in the future because of the interest factor.

## THE NATURE OF INTEREST

**Interest** is payment for the use of another person's money. It is the difference between the amount borrowed or invested (called the **principal**) and the amount repaid or collected. The amount of interest to be paid or collected is usually stated as a **rate** over a specific period of time. The rate of interest is generally stated as an **annual rate**.

The amount of interest involved in any financing transaction is based on three elements:

1.  **Principal (p):** The original amount borrowed or invested.
2.  **Interest Rate (i):** An annual percentage of the principal.
3.  **Time (n):** The number of years that the principal is borrowed or invested.

### Simple Interest

**Simple interest** is computed on the principal amount only. It is the return on the principal for one period. Simple interest is usually expressed as shown in Illustration C-1 on the next page.

Illustration C-1
Interest computation

| Interest | = | Principal<br>$p$ | × | Rate<br>$i$ | × | Time<br>$n$ |
|---|---|---|---|---|---|---|

For example, if you borrowed $5,000 for 2 years at a simple interest rate of 12% annually, you would pay $1,200 in total interest computed as follows:

$$\text{Interest} = p \times i \times n$$
$$= \$5{,}000 \times .12 \times 2$$
$$= \$1{,}200$$

## Compound Interest

**Compound interest** is computed on principal **and** on any interest earned that has not been paid or withdrawn. It is the return on the principal for two or more time periods. Compounding computes interest not only on the principal but also on the interest earned to date on that principal, assuming the interest is left on deposit.

To illustrate the difference between simple and compound interest, assume that you deposit $1,000 in Bank Two, where it will earn *simple interest* of 9% per year, and you deposit another $1,000 in Citizens Bank, where it will earn compound interest of 9% per year *compounded annually*. Also assume that in both cases you will not withdraw any interest until three years from the date of deposit. Illustration C-2 shows the computation of interest you will receive and the accumulated year-end balances.

Illustration C-2
Simple versus compound interest

| **Bank Two** | | | | **Citizens Bank** | | |
|---|---|---|---|---|---|---|
| Simple Interest Calculation | Simple Interest | Accumulated Year-end Balance | | Compound Interest Calculation | Compound Interest | Accumulated Year-end Balance |
| Year 1  $1,000.00 × 9% | $    90.00 | $1,090.00 | | Year 1  $1,000.00 × 9% | $    90.00 | $1,090.00 |
| Year 2  $1,000.00 × 9% | 90.00 | $1,180.00 | | Year 2  $1,090.00 × 9% | 98.10 | $1,188.10 |
| Year 3  $1,000.00 × 9% | 90.00 | $1,270.00 | | Year 3  $1,188.10 × 9% | 106.93 | $1,295.03 |
| | $ 270.00 | | | | $ 295.03 | |

$25.03 Difference

Note in Illustration C-2 that simple interest uses the initial principal of $1,000 to compute the interest in all three years. Compound interest uses the accumulated balance (principal plus interest to date) at each year-end to compute interest in the succeeding year—which explains why your compound interest account is larger.

Obviously, if you had a choice between investing your money at simple interest or at compound interest, you would choose compound interest, all other things—especially risk—being equal. In the example, compounding provides $25.03 of additional interest income. For practical purposes, compounding assumes that unpaid interest earned becomes a part of the principal, and the accumulated balance at the end of each year becomes the new principal on which interest is earned during the next year.

Illustration C-2 indicates that you should invest your money at the bank that compounds interest annually. Most business situations use compound interest. Simple interest is generally applicable only to short-term situations of one year or less.

# SECTION 1 Future Value Concepts

## FUTURE VALUE OF A SINGLE AMOUNT

The **future value of a single amount** is the value at a future date of a given amount invested assuming compound interest. For example, in Illustration C-2, $1,295.03 is the future value of the $1,000 at the end of three years. The $1,295.03 could be determined more easily by using the following formula.

> **STUDY OBJECTIVE 2**
> Solve for future value of a single amount.

$$FV = p \times (1 + i)^n$$

**Illustration C-3**
Formula for future value

where:

$FV$ = future value of a single amount
$p$ = principal (or present value)
$i$ = interest rate for one period
$n$ = number of periods

The $1,295.03 is computed as follows.

$$FV = p \times (1 + i)^n$$
$$= \$1,000 \times (1 + i)^3$$
$$= \$1,000 \times 1.29503$$
$$= \$1,295.03$$

The 1.29503 is computed by multiplying $(1.09 \times 1.09 \times 1.09)$. The amounts in this example can be depicted in the following time diagram.

**Illustration C-4**
Time diagram

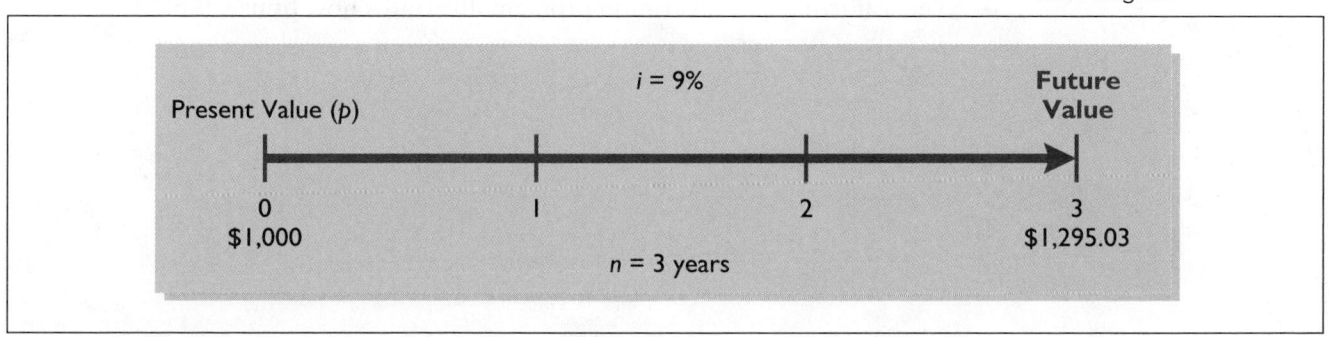

Present Value ($p$)        $i = 9\%$        Future Value

0        1        2        3
$1,000                            $1,295.03

$n = 3$ years

Another method that can be used to compute the future value of a single amount involves the use of a compound interest table. This table shows the future value of 1 for *n* periods. Table 1, shown below, is such a table.

## TABLE 1
### Future Value of 1

| (*n*) Periods | 4% | 5% | 6% | 8% | 9% | 10% | 11% | 12% | 15% |
|---|---|---|---|---|---|---|---|---|---|
| 1 | 1.04000 | 1.05000 | 1.06000 | 1.08000 | 1.09000 | 1.10000 | 1.11000 | 1.12000 | 1.15000 |
| 2 | 1.08160 | 1.10250 | 1.12360 | 1.16640 | 1.18810 | 1.21000 | 1.23210 | 1.25440 | 1.32250 |
| 3 | 1.12486 | 1.15763 | 1.19102 | 1.25971 | 1.29503 | 1.33100 | 1.36763 | 1.40493 | 1.52088 |
| 4 | 1.16986 | 1.21551 | 1.26248 | 1.36049 | 1.41158 | 1.46410 | 1.51807 | 1.57352 | 1.74901 |
| 5 | 1.21665 | 1.27628 | 1.33823 | 1.46933 | 1.53862 | 1.61051 | 1.68506 | 1.76234 | 2.01136 |
| 6 | 1.26532 | 1.34010 | 1.41852 | 1.58687 | 1.67710 | 1.77156 | 1.87041 | 1.97382 | 2.31306 |
| 7 | 1.31593 | 1.40710 | 1.50363 | 1.71382 | 1.82804 | 1.94872 | 2.07616 | 2.21068 | 2.66002 |
| 8 | 1.36857 | 1.47746 | 1.59385 | 1.85093 | 1.99256 | 2.14359 | 2.30454 | 2.47596 | 3.05902 |
| 9 | 1.42331 | 1.55133 | 1.68948 | 1.99900 | 2.17189 | 2.35795 | 2.55803 | 2.77308 | 3.51788 |
| 10 | 1.48024 | 1.62889 | 1.79085 | 2.15892 | 2.36736 | 2.59374 | 2.83942 | 3.10585 | 4.04556 |
| 11 | 1.53945 | 1.71034 | 1.89830 | 2.33164 | 2.58043 | 2.85312 | 3.15176 | 3.47855 | 4.65239 |
| 12 | 1.60103 | 1.79586 | 2.01220 | 2.51817 | 2.81267 | 3.13843 | 3.49845 | 3.89598 | 5.35025 |
| 13 | 1.66507 | 1.88565 | 2.13293 | 2.71962 | 3.06581 | 3.45227 | 3.88328 | 4.36349 | 6.15279 |
| 14 | 1.73168 | 1.97993 | 2.26090 | 2.93719 | 3.34173 | 3.79750 | 4.31044 | 4.88711 | 7.07571 |
| 15 | 1.80094 | 2.07893 | 2.39656 | 3.17217 | 3.64248 | 4.17725 | 4.78459 | 5.47357 | 8.13706 |
| 16 | 1.87298 | 2.18287 | 2.54035 | 3.42594 | 3.97031 | 4.59497 | 5.31089 | 6.13039 | 9.35762 |
| 17 | 1.94790 | 2.29202 | 2.69277 | 3.70002 | 4.32763 | 5.05447 | 5.89509 | 6.86604 | 10.76126 |
| 18 | 2.02582 | 2.40662 | 2.85434 | 3.99602 | 4.71712 | 5.55992 | 6.54355 | 7.68997 | 12.37545 |
| 19 | 2.10685 | 2.52695 | 3.02560 | 4.31570 | 5.14166 | 6.11591 | 7.26334 | 8.61276 | 14.23177 |
| 20 | 2.19112 | 2.65330 | 3.20714 | 4.66096 | 5.60441 | 6.72750 | 8.06231 | 9.64629 | 16.36654 |

In Table 1, *n* is the number of compounding periods, the percentages are the periodic interest rates, and the five-digit decimal numbers in the respective columns are the future value of 1 factors. In using Table 1, the principal amount is multiplied by the future value factor for the specified number of periods and interest rate. For example, the future value factor for two periods at 9% is 1.18810. Multiplying this factor by $1,000 equals $1,188.10, which is the accumulated balance at the end of year 2 in the Citizens Bank example in Illustration C-2. The $1,295.03 accumulated balance at the end of the third year can be calculated from Table 1 by multiplying the future value factor for three periods (1.29503) by the $1,000.

The following demonstration problem illustrates how to use Table 1.

John and Mary Rich invested $20,000 in a savings account paying 6% interest at the time their son, Mike, was born. The money is to be used by Mike for his college education. On his 18th birthday, Mike withdraws the money from his savings account. How much did Mike withdraw from his account?

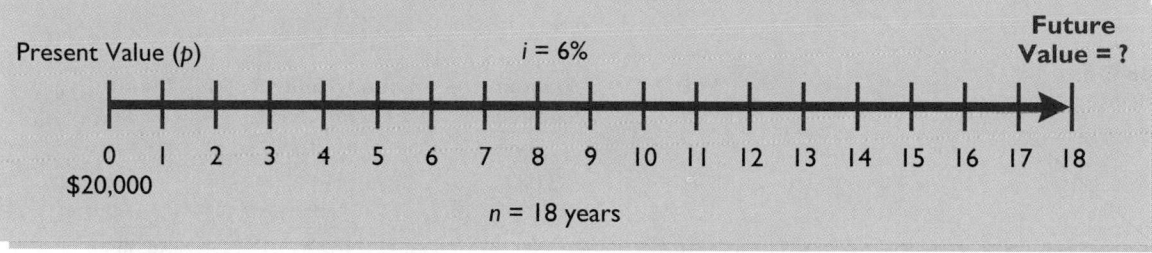

Present Value (*p*)    *i* = 6%    **Future Value = ?**

0  1  2  3  4  5  6  7  8  9  10  11  12  13  14  15  16  17  18
$20,000
*n* = 18 years

**Answer:** The future value factor from Table 1 is 2.85434 (18 periods at 6%). The future value of $20,000 earning 6% per year for 18 years is **$57,086.80** ($20,000 × 2.85434).

**Illustration C-5**
Demonstration Problem—
Using Table 1 for FV of 1

## FUTURE VALUE OF AN ANNUITY

The preceding discussion involved the accumulation of only a single principal sum. Individuals and businesses frequently encounter situations in which a series of equal dollar amounts are to be paid or received periodically, such as loans or lease (rental) contracts. Such payments or receipts of equal dollar amounts are referred to as **annuities**. The **future value of an annuity** is the sum of all the payments (receipts) plus the accumulated compound interest on them. In computing the future value of an annuity, it is necessary to know (1) the interest rate, (2) the number of compounding periods, and (3) the amount of the periodic payments or receipts.

To illustrate the computation of the future value of an annuity, assume that you invest $2,000 at the end of each year for three years at 5% interest compounded annually. This situation is depicted in the time diagram in Illustration C-6.

**STUDY OBJECTIVE 3**
Solve for future value of an annuity.

**Illustration C-6**
Time diagram for a three-year annuity

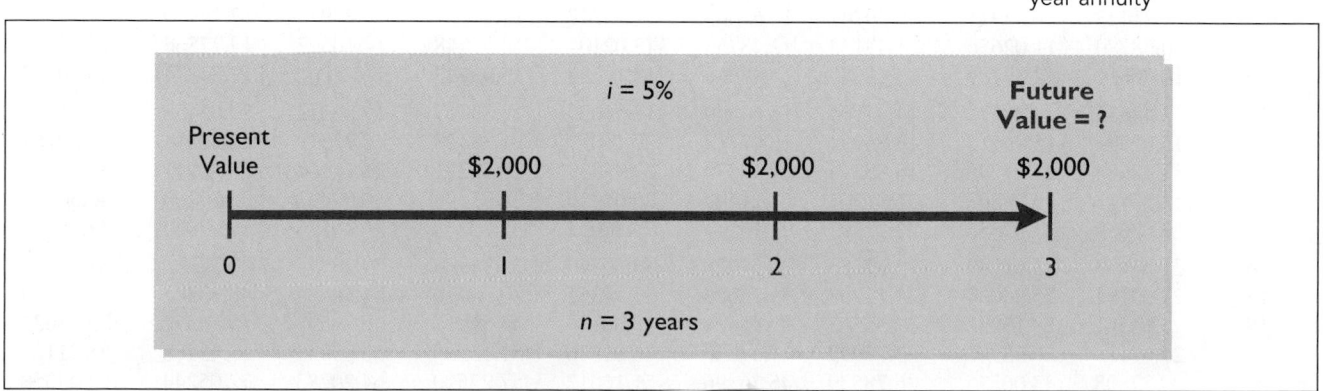

*i* = 5%    **Future Value = ?**

Present Value    $2,000    $2,000    $2,000

0    1    2    3

*n* = 3 years

As can be seen in Illustration C-6, the $2,000 invested at the end of year 1 will earn interest for two years (years 2 and 3), and the $2,000 invested at the end of year 2 will earn interest for one year (year 3). However, the last $2,000 investment (made at the end of year 3) will not earn any interest. The future value of these periodic payments could be computed using the future value factors from Table 1 as shown in Illustration C-7.

**Illustration C-7**
Future value of periodic payments

| Year Invested | Amount Invested | × | Future Value of 1 Factor at 5% | = | Future Value |
|---|---|---|---|---|---|
| 1 | $2,000 | × | 1.10250 | = | $2,205 |
| 2 | $2,000 | × | 1.05000 | = | 2,100 |
| 3 | $2,000 | × | 1.00000 | = | 2,000 |
| | | | 3.15250 | | $6,305 |

The first $2,000 investment is multiplied by the future value factor for two periods (1.1025) because two years' interest will accumulate on it (in years 2 and 3). The second $2,000 investment will earn only one year's interest (in year 3) and therefore is multiplied by the future value factor for one year (1.0500). The final $2,000 investment is made at the end of the third year and will not earn any interest. Consequently, the future value of the last $2,000 invested is only $2,000 since it does not accumulate any interest.

This method of calculation is required when the periodic payments or receipts are not equal in each period. However, when the periodic payments (receipts) are the same in each period, the future value can be computed by using a future value of an annuity of 1 table. Table 2, shown below, is such a table.

## TABLE 2
### Future Value of an Annuity of 1

| (n) Periods | 4% | 5% | 6% | 8% | 9% | 10% | 11% | 12% | 15% |
|---|---|---|---|---|---|---|---|---|---|
| 1 | 1.00000 | 1.00000 | 1.00000 | 1.00000 | 1.00000 | 1.00000 | 1.00000 | 1.00000 | 1.00000 |
| 2 | 2.04000 | 2.05000 | 2.06000 | 2.08000 | 2.09000 | 2.10000 | 2.11000 | 2.12000 | 2.15000 |
| 3 | 3.12160 | 3.15250 | 3.18360 | 3.24640 | 3.27810 | 3.31000 | 3.34210 | 3.37440 | 3.47250 |
| 4 | 4.24646 | 4.31013 | 4.37462 | 4.50611 | 4.57313 | 4.64100 | 4.70973 | 4.77933 | 4.99338 |
| 5 | 5.41632 | 5.52563 | 5.63709 | 5.86660 | 5.98471 | 6.10510 | 6.22780 | 6.35285 | 6.74238 |
| 6 | 6.63298 | 6.80191 | 6.97532 | 7.33592 | 7.52334 | 7.71561 | 7.91286 | 8.11519 | 8.75374 |
| 7 | 7.89829 | 8.14201 | 8.39384 | 8.92280 | 9.20044 | 9.48717 | 9.78327 | 10.08901 | 11.06680 |
| 8 | 9.21423 | 9.54911 | 9.89747 | 10.63663 | 11.02847 | 11.43589 | 11.85943 | 12.29969 | 13.72682 |
| 9 | 10.58280 | 11.02656 | 11.49132 | 12.48756 | 13.02104 | 13.57948 | 14.16397 | 14.77566 | 16.78584 |
| 10 | 12.00611 | 12.57789 | 13.18079 | 14.48656 | 15.19293 | 15.93743 | 16.72201 | 17.54874 | 20.30372 |
| 11 | 13.48635 | 14.20679 | 14.97164 | 16.64549 | 17.56029 | 18.53117 | 19.56143 | 20.65458 | 24.34928 |
| 12 | 15.02581 | 15.91713 | 16.86994 | 18.97713 | 20.14072 | 21.38428 | 22.71319 | 24.13313 | 29.00167 |
| 13 | 16.62684 | 17.71298 | 18.88214 | 21.49530 | 22.95339 | 24.52271 | 26.21164 | 28.02911 | 34.35192 |
| 14 | 18.29191 | 19.59863 | 21.01507 | 24.21492 | 26.01919 | 27.97498 | 30.09492 | 32.39260 | 40.50471 |
| 15 | 20.02359 | 21.57856 | 23.27597 | 27.15211 | 29.36092 | 31.77248 | 34.40536 | 37.27972 | 47.58041 |
| 16 | 21.82453 | 23.65749 | 25.67253 | 30.32428 | 33.00340 | 35.94973 | 39.18995 | 42.75328 | 55.71747 |
| 17 | 23.69751 | 25.84037 | 28.21288 | 33.75023 | 36.97351 | 40.54470 | 44.50084 | 48.88367 | 65.07509 |
| 18 | 25.64541 | 28.13238 | 30.90565 | 37.45024 | 41.30134 | 45.59917 | 50.39593 | 55.74972 | 75.83636 |
| 19 | 27.67123 | 30.53900 | 33.75999 | 41.44626 | 46.01846 | 51.15909 | 56.93949 | 63.43968 | 88.21181 |
| 20 | 29.77808 | 33.06595 | 36.78559 | 45.76196 | 51.16012 | 57.27500 | 64.20283 | 72.05244 | 102.44358 |

Table 2 shows the future value of 1 to be received periodically for a given number of periods. You can see from Table 2 that the future value of an annuity of 1 factor for three periods at 5% is 3.15250. The future value factor is the total of the three individual future value factors as shown in Illustration C-8. Multiplying this amount by the annual investment of $2,000 produces a future value of $6,305.

The demonstration problem in Illustration C-8 illustrates how to use Table 2.

**Illustration C-8**
**Demonstration Problem—**
Using Table 2 for FV of an annuity of 1

Henning Printing Company knows that in four years it must replace one of its existing printing presses with a new one. To insure that some funds are available to replace the machine in 4 years, the company is depositing $25,000 in a savings account at the end of each of the next four years (4 deposits in total). The savings account will earn 6% interest compounded annually. How much will be in the savings account at the end of 4 years when the new printing press is to be purchased?

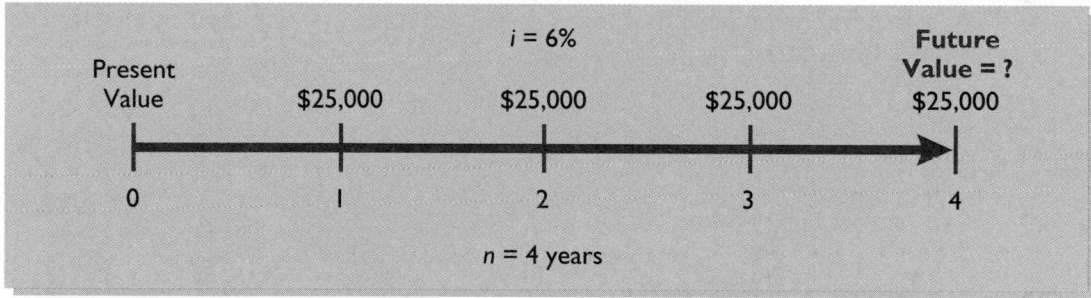

**Answer:** The future value factor from Table 2 is 4.37462 (4 periods at 6%). The future value of $25,000 invested at the end of each year for 4 years at 6% interest is **$109,365.50** ($25,000 × 4.37462).

# SECTION 2 **Present Value Concepts**

## PRESENT VALUE VARIABLES

The **present value** is the value now of a given amount to be paid or received in the future, assuming compound interest. The present value is based on three variables: (1) the dollar amount to be received (future amount), (2) the length of time until the amount is received (number of periods), and (3) the interest rate (the discount rate). The process of determining the present value is referred to as **discounting the future amount**.

> STUDY OBJECTIVE 4
> Identify the variables fundamental to solving present value problems.

In this textbook, we use present value computations in measuring several items. For example, Chapter 11 computed the present value of the principal and interest payments to determine the market price of a bond. In addition, determining the amount to be reported for notes payable involves present value computations.

# PRESENT VALUE OF A SINGLE AMOUNT

To illustrate present value, assume that you want to invest a sum of money that will yield $1,000 at the end of one year. What amount would you need to invest today to have $1,000 one year from now? Illustration C-9 shows the formula for calculating present value.

**Illustration C-9**
Formula for present value

$$\text{Present Value} = \text{Future Value} \div (1 + i)^n$$

Thus, if you want a 10% rate of return, you would compute the present value of $1,000 for one year as follows:

$$
\begin{aligned}
PV &= FV \div (1 + i)^n \\
&= \$1,000 \div (1 + .10)^1 \\
&= \$1,000 \div 1.10 \\
&= \$909.09
\end{aligned}
$$

We know the future amount ($1,000), the discount rate (10%), and the number of periods (one). These variables are depicted in the time diagram in Illustration C-10.

**Illustration C-10**
Finding present value if discounted for one period

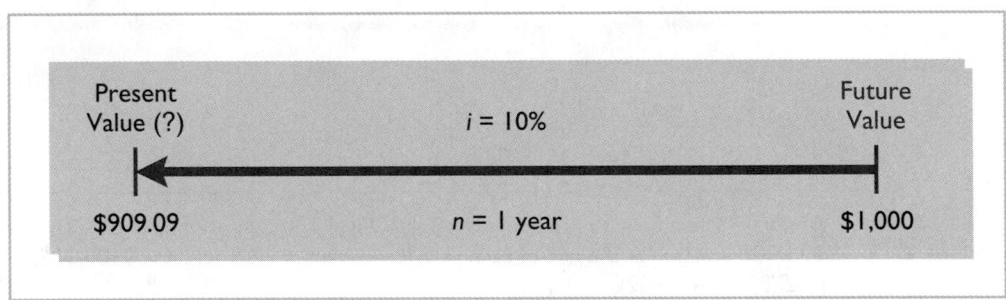

If you receive the single amount of $1,000 **in two years**, discounted at 10% $[PV = \$1,000 \div (1 + .10)^2]$, the present value of your $1,000 is $826.45 $[(\$1,000 \div 1.21)$, depicted as shown in Illustration C-11 below.

**Illustration C-11**
Finding present value if discounted for two periods

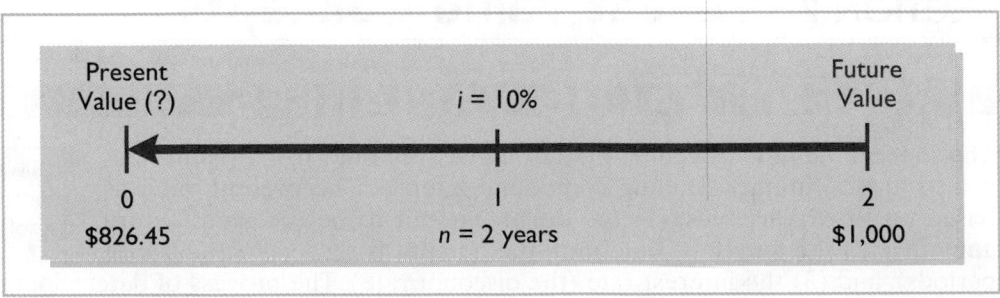

You also could find the present value of your amount through tables that show the present value of 1 for $n$ periods. In Table 3, on the next page, $n$ (represented in the table's rows) is the number of discounting periods involved. The percentages (represented in the table's columns) are the periodic interest rates or discount rates. The five-digit decimal numbers in the intersections of the rows and columns are called the **present value of 1 factors**.

When using Table 3 to determine present value, you multiply the future value by the present value factor specified at the intersection of the number of periods and the discount rate.

| **TABLE 3** Present Value of 1 | | | | | | | | | |
|---|---|---|---|---|---|---|---|---|---|
| (*n*) Periods | 4% | 5% | 6% | 8% | 9% | 10% | 11% | 12% | 15% |
| 1 | .96154 | .95238 | .94340 | .92593 | .91743 | .90909 | .90090 | .89286 | .86957 |
| 2 | .92456 | .90703 | .89000 | .85734 | .84168 | .82645 | .81162 | .79719 | .75614 |
| 3 | .88900 | .86384 | .83962 | .79383 | .77218 | .75132 | .73119 | .71178 | .65752 |
| 4 | .85480 | .82270 | .79209 | .73503 | .70843 | .68301 | .65873 | .63552 | .57175 |
| 5 | .82193 | .78353 | .74726 | .68058 | .64993 | .62092 | .59345 | .56743 | .49718 |
| 6 | .79031 | .74622 | .70496 | .63017 | .59627 | .56447 | .53464 | .50663 | .43233 |
| 7 | .75992 | .71068 | .66506 | .58349 | .54703 | .51316 | .48166 | .45235 | .37594 |
| 8 | .73069 | .67684 | .62741 | .54027 | .50187 | .46651 | .43393 | .40388 | .32690 |
| 9 | .70259 | .64461 | .59190 | .50025 | .46043 | .42410 | .39092 | .36061 | .28426 |
| 10 | .67556 | .61391 | .55839 | .46319 | .42241 | .38554 | .35218 | .32197 | .24719 |
| 11 | .64958 | .58468 | .52679 | .42888 | .38753 | .35049 | .31728 | .28748 | .21494 |
| 12 | .62460 | .55684 | .49697 | .39711 | .35554 | .31863 | .28584 | .25668 | .18691 |
| 13 | .60057 | .53032 | .46884 | .36770 | .32618 | .28966 | .25751 | .22917 | .16253 |
| 14 | .57748 | .50507 | .44230 | .34046 | .29925 | .26333 | .23199 | .20462 | .14133 |
| 15 | .55526 | .48102 | .41727 | .31524 | .27454 | .23939 | .20900 | .18270 | .12289 |
| 16 | .53391 | .45811 | .39365 | .29189 | .25187 | .21763 | .18829 | .16312 | .10687 |
| 17 | .51337 | .43630 | .37136 | .27027 | .23107 | .19785 | .16963 | .14564 | .09293 |
| 18 | .49363 | .41552 | .35034 | .25025 | .21199 | .17986 | .15282 | .13004 | .08081 |
| 19 | .47464 | .39573 | .33051 | .23171 | .19449 | .16351 | .13768 | .11611 | .07027 |
| 20 | .45639 | .37689 | .31180 | .21455 | .17843 | .14864 | .12403 | .10367 | .06110 |

For example, the present value factor for one period at a discount rate of 10% is .90909, which equals the $909.09 ($1,000 × .90909) computed in Illustration C-10. For two periods at a discount rate of 10%, the present value factor is .82645, which equals the $826.45 ($1,000 × .82645) computed previously.

Note that a higher discount rate produces a smaller present value. For example, using a 15% discount rate, the present value of $1,000 due one year from now is $869.57, versus $909.09 at 10%. Also note that the further removed from the present the future value is, the smaller the present value. For example, using the same discount rate of 10%, the present value of $1,000 due in **five years** is $620.92, versus the present value of $1,000 due in **one year**, which is $909.09.

The two demonstration problems on the next page (Illustrations C-12, C-13) illustrate how to use Table 3.

**Illustration C-12**
Demonstration problem—
Using Table 3 for *PV* of 1

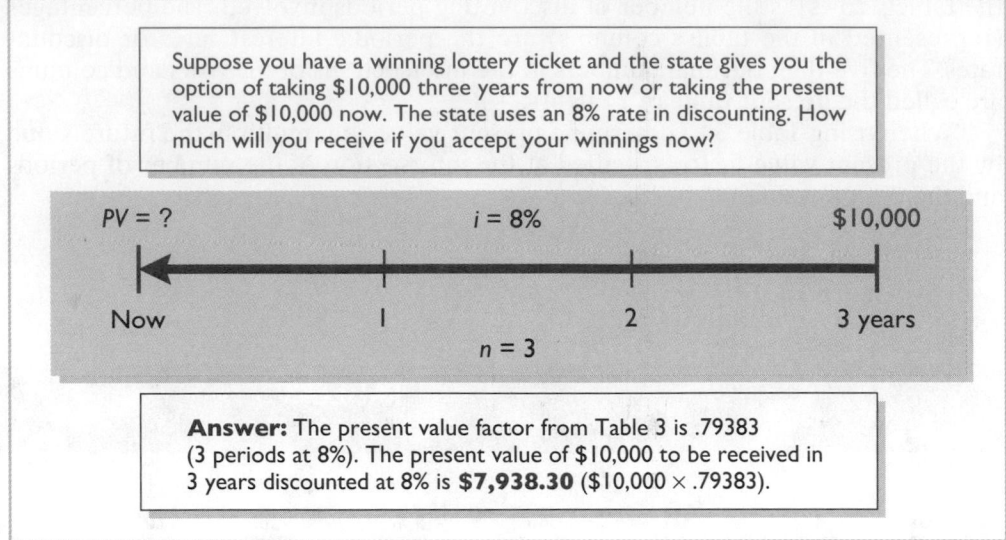

Suppose you have a winning lottery ticket and the state gives you the option of taking $10,000 three years from now or taking the present value of $10,000 now. The state uses an 8% rate in discounting. How much will you receive if you accept your winnings now?

PV = ?          i = 8%          $10,000

Now          1          2          3 years

n = 3

**Answer:** The present value factor from Table 3 is .79383 (3 periods at 8%). The present value of $10,000 to be received in 3 years discounted at 8% is **$7,938.30** ($10,000 × .79383).

**Illustration C-13**
Demonstration problem—
Using Table 3 for *PV* of 1

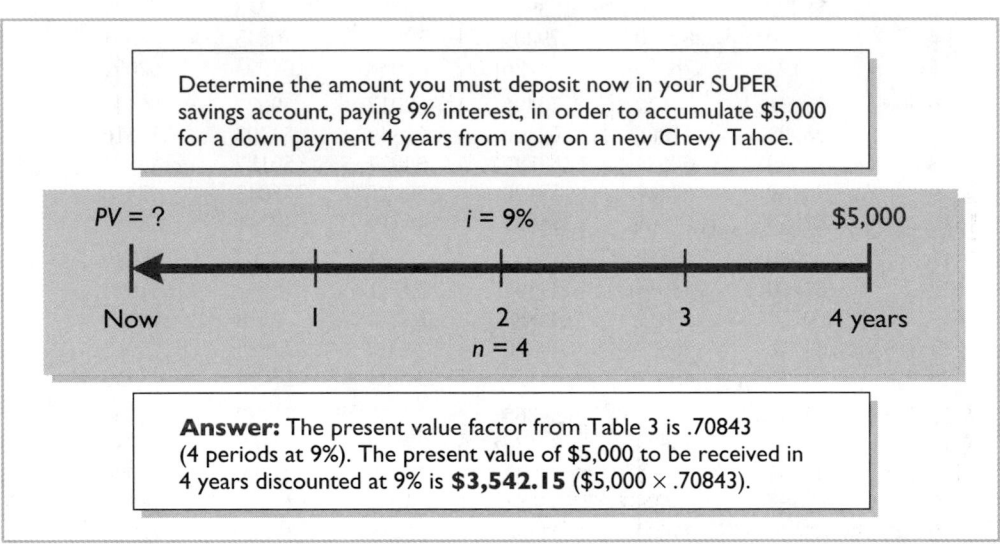

Determine the amount you must deposit now in your SUPER savings account, paying 9% interest, in order to accumulate $5,000 for a down payment 4 years from now on a new Chevy Tahoe.

PV = ?          i = 9%          $5,000

Now          1          2          3          4 years

n = 4

**Answer:** The present value factor from Table 3 is .70843 (4 periods at 9%). The present value of $5,000 to be received in 4 years discounted at 9% is **$3,542.15** ($5,000 × .70843).

# PRESENT VALUE OF AN ANNUITY

**STUDY OBJECTIVE 6**

Solve for present value of an annuity.

The preceding discussion involved the discounting of only a single future amount. Businesses and individuals frequently engage in transactions in which a *series* of equal dollar amounts are to be received or paid periodically. Examples of a series of periodic receipts or payments are loan agreements, installment sales, mortgage notes, lease (rental) contracts, and pension obligations. These periodic receipts or payments are **annuities**.

The **present value of an annuity** is the value now of a series of future receipts or payments, discounted assuming compound interest. In computing the present value of an annuity, you need to know: (1) the discount rate, (2) the number of discount periods, and (3) the amount of the periodic receipts or payments.

To illustrate how to compute the present value of an annuity, assume that you will receive $1,000 cash annually for three years at a time when the discount rate is 10%. Illustration C-14 depicts this situation, and Illustration C-15 shows the computation of its present value.

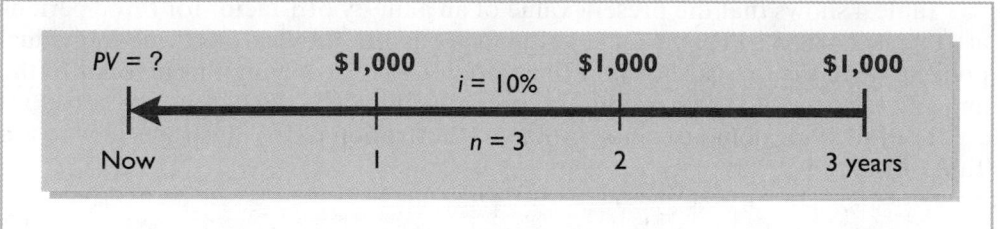

**Illustration C-14**
Time diagram for a three-year annuity

| Future Amount | × | Present Value of 1 Factor at 10% | = | Present Value |
|---|---|---|---|---|
| $1,000 (one year away) | | .90909 | | $ 909.09 |
| 1,000 (two years away) | | .82645 | | 826.45 |
| 1,000 (three years away) | | .75132 | | 751.32 |
| | | **2.48686** | | **$2,486.86** |

**Illustration C-15**
Present value of a series of future amounts computation

This method of calculation is required when the periodic cash flows are not uniform in each period. However, when the future receipts are the same in each period, there are two other ways to compute present value. First, you can multiply the annual cash flow by the sum of the three present value factors. In the previous example, $1,000 × 2.48686 equals $2,486.86. The second method is to use annuity tables. As illustrated in Table 4 below, these tables show the present value of 1 to be received periodically for a given number of periods.

## TABLE 4
### Present Value of an Annuity of 1

| (*n*) Periods | 4% | 5% | 6% | 8% | 9% | 10% | 11% | 12% | 15% |
|---|---|---|---|---|---|---|---|---|---|
| 1 | .96154 | .95238 | .94340 | .92593 | .91743 | .90909 | .90090 | .89286 | .86957 |
| 2 | 1.88609 | 1.85941 | 1.83339 | 1.78326 | 1.75911 | 1.73554 | 1.71252 | 1.69005 | 1.62571 |
| 3 | 2.77509 | 2.72325 | 2.67301 | 2.57710 | 2.53130 | 2.48685 | 2.44371 | 2.40183 | 2.28323 |
| 4 | 3.62990 | 3.54595 | 3.46511 | 3.31213 | 3.23972 | 3.16986 | 3.10245 | 3.03735 | 2.85498 |
| 5 | 4.45182 | 4.32948 | 4.21236 | 3.99271 | 3.88965 | 3.79079 | 3.69590 | 3.60478 | 3.35216 |
| 6 | 5.24214 | 5.07569 | 4.91732 | 4.62288 | 4.48592 | 4.35526 | 4.23054 | 4.11141 | 3.78448 |
| 7 | 6.00205 | 5.78637 | 5.58238 | 5.20637 | 5.03295 | 4.86842 | 4.71220 | 4.56376 | 4.16042 |
| 8 | 6.73274 | 6.46321 | 6.20979 | 5.74664 | 5.53482 | 5.33493 | 5.14612 | 4.96764 | 4.48732 |
| 9 | 7.43533 | 7.10782 | 6.80169 | 6.24689 | 5.99525 | 5.75902 | 5.53705 | 5.32825 | 4.77158 |
| 10 | 8.11090 | 7.72173 | 7.36009 | 6.71008 | 6.41766 | 6.14457 | 5.88923 | 5.65022 | 5.01877 |
| 11 | 8.76048 | 8.30641 | 7.88687 | 7.13896 | 6.80519 | 6.49506 | 6.20652 | 5.93770 | 5.23371 |
| 12 | 9.38507 | 8.86325 | 8.38384 | 7.53608 | 7.16073 | 6.81369 | 6.49236 | 6.19437 | 5.42062 |
| 13 | 9.98565 | 9.39357 | 8.85268 | 7.90378 | 7.48690 | 7.10336 | 6.74987 | 6.42355 | 5.58315 |
| 14 | 10.56312 | 9.89864 | 9.29498 | 8.24424 | 7.78615 | 7.36669 | 6.98187 | 6.62817 | 5.72448 |
| 15 | 11.11839 | 10.37966 | 9.71225 | 8.55948 | 8.06069 | 7.60608 | 7.19087 | 6.81086 | 5.84737 |
| 16 | 11.65230 | 10.83777 | 10.10590 | 8.85137 | 8.31256 | 7.82371 | 7.37916 | 6.97399 | 5.95424 |
| 17 | 12.16567 | 11.27407 | 10.47726 | 9.12164 | 8.54363 | 8.02155 | 7.54879 | 7.11963 | 6.04716 |
| 18 | 12.65930 | 11.68959 | 10.82760 | 9.37189 | 8.75563 | 8.20141 | 7.70162 | 7.24967 | 6.12797 |
| 19 | 13.13394 | 12.08532 | 11.15812 | 9.60360 | 8.95012 | 8.36492 | 7.83929 | 7.36578 | 6.19823 |
| 20 | 13.59033 | 12.46221 | 11.46992 | 9.81815 | 9.12855 | 8.51356 | 7.96333 | 7.46944 | 6.25933 |

Table 4 shows that the present value of an annuity of 1 factor for three periods at 10% is 2.48685.[1] (This present value factor is the total of the three individual present value factors, as shown in Illustration C-15.) Applying this amount to the annual cash flow of $1,000 produces a present value of $2,486.85.

The following demonstration problem (Illustration C-16) illustrates how to use Table 4.

**Illustration C-16**
Demonstration problem—
Using Table 4 for *PV* of an
annuity of 1

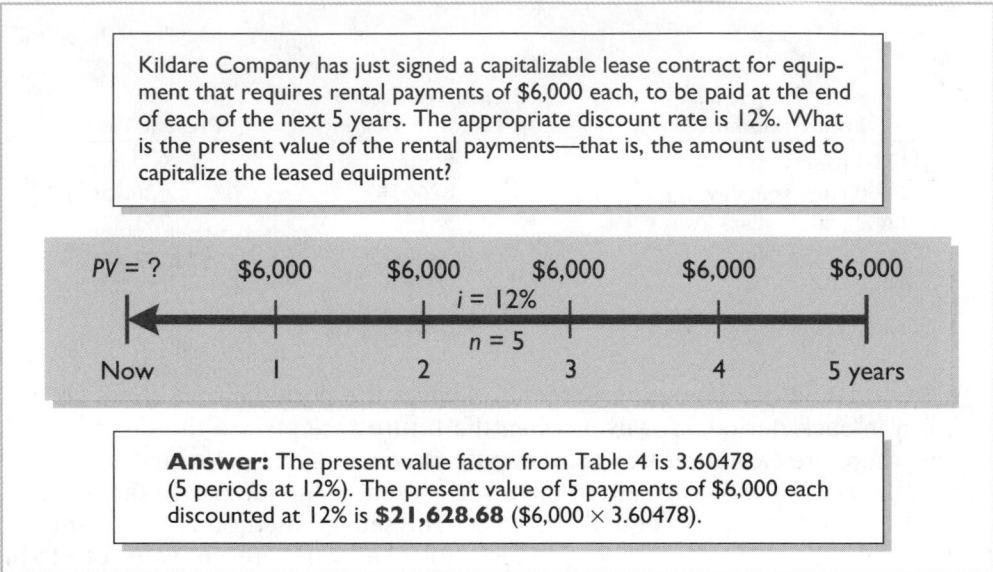

Kildare Company has just signed a capitalizable lease contract for equipment that requires rental payments of $6,000 each, to be paid at the end of each of the next 5 years. The appropriate discount rate is 12%. What is the present value of the rental payments—that is, the amount used to capitalize the leased equipment?

$PV = ?$    $6,000    $6,000    $6,000    $6,000    $6,000

$i = 12\%$

$n = 5$

Now    1    2    3    4    5 years

**Answer:** The present value factor from Table 4 is 3.60478 (5 periods at 12%). The present value of 5 payments of $6,000 each discounted at 12% is **$21,628.68** ($6,000 × 3.60478).

## TIME PERIODS AND DISCOUNTING

In the preceding calculations, the discounting was done on an *annual* basis using an *annual* interest rate. Discounting may also be done over shorter periods of time such as monthly, quarterly, or semiannually.

When the time frame is less than one year, you need to convert the annual interest rate to the applicable time frame. Assume, for example, that the investor in Illustration C-14 received $500 **semiannually** for three years instead of $1,000 annually. In this case, the number of periods becomes six (3 × 2), the discount rate is 5% (10% ÷ 2), the present value factor from Table 4 is 5.07569, and the present value of the future cash flows is $2,537.85 (5.07569 × $500). This amount is slightly higher than the $2,486.86 computed in Illustration C-15 because interest is paid twice during the same year; therefore interest is earned on the first half year's interest.

## COMPUTING THE PRESENT VALUE OF A LONG-TERM NOTE OR BOND

**STUDY OBJECTIVE 7**

Compute the present value of notes and bonds.

The present value (or market price) of a long-term note or bond is a function of three variables: (1) the payment amounts, (2) the length of time until the amounts are paid, and (3) the discount rate. Our illustration uses a five-year bond issue.

---

[1]The difference of .00001 between 2.48686 and 2.48685 is due to rounding.

The first variable—dollars to be paid—is made up of two elements: (1) a series of interest payments (an annuity), and (2) the principal amount (a single sum). To compute the present value of the bond, we must discount both the interest payments and the principal amount—two different computations. The time diagrams for a bond due in five years are shown in Illustration C-17.

**Illustration C-17**
Present value of a bond time diagram

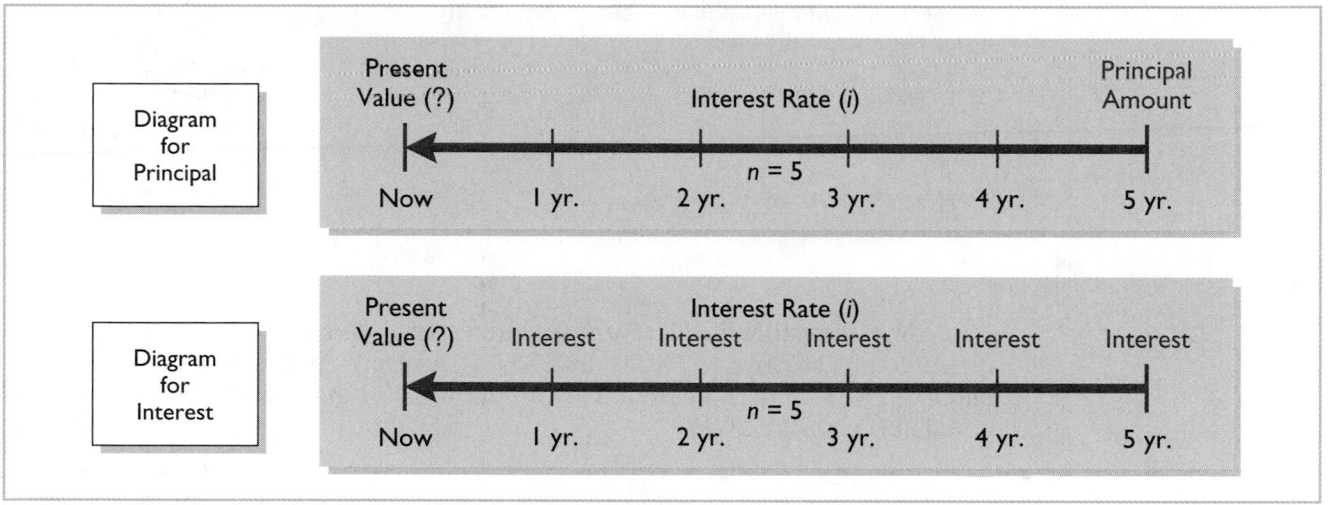

When the investor's market interest rate is equal to the bond's contractual interest rate, the present value of the bonds will *equal* the face value of the bonds. To illustrate, assume a bond issue of 10%, five-year bonds with a face value of $100,000 with interest payable **semiannually** on January 1 and July 1. If the discount rate is the same as the contractual rate, the bonds will sell at face value. In this case, the investor will receive the following: (1) $100,000 at maturity, and (2) a series of ten $5,000 interest payments [($100,000 × 10%) ÷ 2] over the term of the bonds. The length of time is expressed in terms of interest periods—in this case—10, and the discount rate per interest period, 5%. The following time diagram (Illustration C-18) depicts the variables involved in this discounting situation.

**Illustration C-18**
Time diagram for present value of a 10%, five-year bond paying interest semiannually

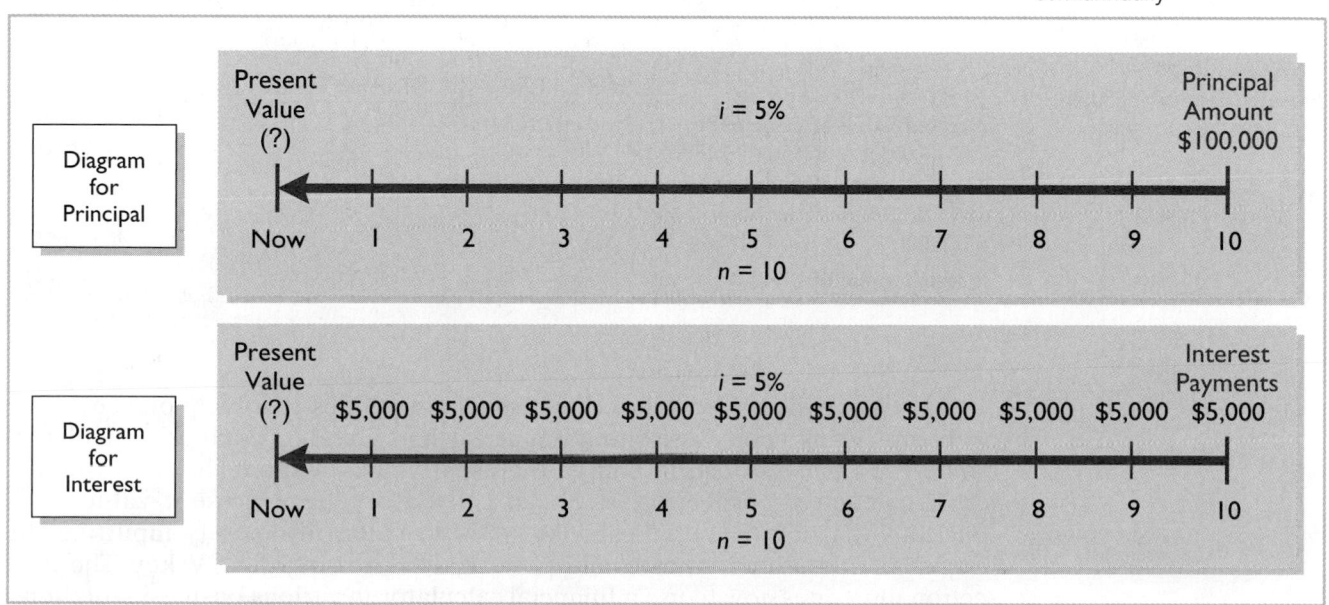

Illustration C-19 shows the computation of the present value of these bonds.

**Illustration C-19**
Present value of principal and interest—face value

| 10% Contractual Rate—10% Discount Rate | |
| --- | --- |
| **Present value of principal to be received at maturity** | |
| $100,000 × *PV* of 1 due in 10 periods at 5% | |
| $100,000 × .61391 (Table 3) | $ 61,391 |
| **Present value of interest to be received periodically over the term of the bonds** | |
| $5,000 × *PV* of 1 due periodically for 10 periods at 5% | |
| $5,000 × 7.72173 (Table 4) | 38,609* |
| **Present value of bonds** | **$100,000** |

*Rounded

Now assume that the investor's required rate of return is 12%, not 10%. The future amounts are again $100,000 and $5,000, respectively, but now a discount rate of 6% (12% ÷ 2) must be used. The present value of the bonds is $92,639, as computed in Illustration C-20.

**Illustration C-20**
Present value of principal and interest—discount

| 10% Contractual Rate—12% Discount Rate | |
| --- | --- |
| **Present value of principal to be received at maturity** | |
| $100,000 × .55839 (Table 3) | $55,839 |
| **Present value of interest to be received periodically over the term of the bonds** | |
| $5,000 × 7.36009 (Table 4) | 36,800 |
| **Present value of bonds** | **$92,639** |

Conversely, if the discount rate is 8% and the contractual rate is 10%, the present value of the bonds is $108,111, computed as shown in Illustration C-21.

**Illustration C-21**
Present value of principal and interest—premium

| 10% Contractual Rate—8% Discount Rate | |
| --- | --- |
| **Present value of principal to be received at maturity** | |
| $100,000 × .67556 (Table 3) | $ 67,556 |
| **Present value of interest to be received periodically over the term of the bonds** | |
| $5,000 × 8.11090 (Table 4) | 40,555 |
| **Present value of bonds** | **$108,111** |

The above discussion relies on present value tables in solving present value problems. Many people use spreadsheets such as Excel or Financial calculators (some even on websites) to compute present values, without the use of tables. Many calculators, especially financial calculators, have present value (*PV*) functions that allow you to calculate present values by merely inputting the proper amount, discount rate, and periods, and pressing the PV key. The next section illustrates how to use a financial calculator in various business situations.

## SECTION 3 Using Financial Calculators

Business professionals, once they have mastered the underlying concepts in sections 1 and 2, often use a financial (business) calculator to solve time value of money problems. In many cases, they must use calculators if interest rates or time periods do not correspond with the information provided in the compound interest tables.

> **STUDY OBJECTIVE 8**
>
> Use a financial calculator to solve time value of money problems.

To use financial calculators, you enter the time value of money variables into the calculator. Illustration C-22 shows the five most common keys used to solve time value of money problems.[2]

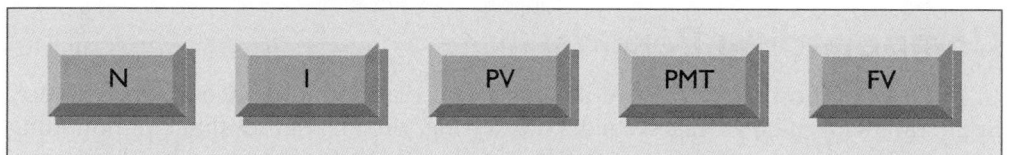

**Illustration C-22**
Financial calculator keys

where

| | |
|---|---|
| N | = number of periods |
| I | = interest rate per period (some calculators use I/YR or i) |
| PV | = present value (occurs at the beginning of the first period) |
| PMT | = payment (all payments are equal, and none are skipped) |
| FV | = future value (occurs at the end of the last period) |

In solving time value of money problems in this appendix, you will generally be given three of four variables and will have to solve for the remaining variable. The fifth key (the key not used) is given a value of zero to ensure that this variable is not used in the computation.

## PRESENT VALUE OF A SINGLE SUM

To illustrate how to solve a present value problem using a financial calculator, assume that you want to know the present value of $84,253 to be received in five years, discounted at 11% compounded annually. Illustration C-23 pictures this problem.

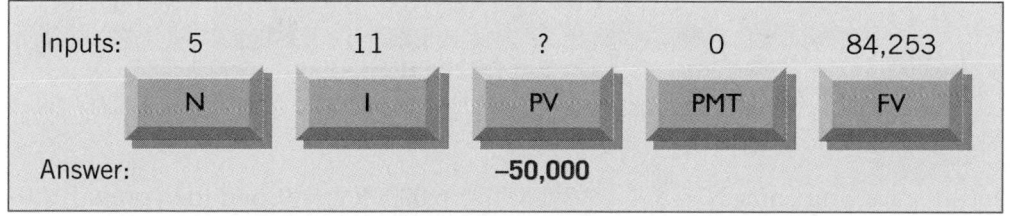

**Illustration C-23**
Calculator solution for present value of a single sum

The diagram shows you the information (inputs) to enter into the calculator: N = 5, I = 11, PMT = 0, and FV = 84,253. You then press PV for the answer: −$50,000. As indicated, the PMT key was given a value of zero because a series of payments did not occur in this problem.

---

[2]On many calculators, these keys are actual buttons on the face of the calculator; on others they appear on the display after the user accesses a present value menu.

## Plus and Minus

The use of plus and minus signs in time value of money problems with a financial calculator can be confusing. Most financial calculators are programmed so that the positive and negative cash flows in any problem offset each other. In the present value problem, we identified the $84,253 future value initial investment as a positive (inflow); the answer −$50,000 was shown as a negative amount, reflecting a cash outflow. If the 84,253 were entered as a negative, then the final answer would have been reported as a positive 50,000.

Hopefully, the sign convention will not cause confusion. If you understand what is required in a problem, you should be able to interpret a positive or negative amount in determining the solution to a problem.

## Compounding Periods

In the problem on page C15, we assumed that compounding occurs once a year. Some financial calculators have a default setting, which assumes that compounding occurs 12 times a year. You must determine what default period has been programmed into your calculator and change it as necessary to arrive at the proper compounding period.

## Rounding

Most financial calculators store and calculate using 12 decimal places. As a result, because compound interest tables generally have factors only up to 5 decimal places, a slight difference in the final answer can result. In most time value of money problems, the final answer will not include more than two decimal points.

# PRESENT VALUE OF AN ANNUITY

To illustrate how to solve a present value of an annuity problem using a financial calculator, assume that you are asked to determine the present value of rental receipts of $6,000 each to be received at the end of each of the next five years, when discounted at 12%, as pictured in Illustration C-24.

**Illustration C-24**
Calculator solution for present value of an annuity

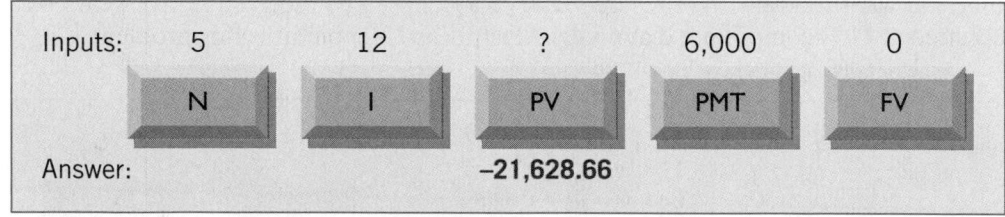

In this case, you enter N = 5, I = 12, PMT = 6,000, FV = 0, and then press PV to arrive at the answer of $21,628.66.

# USEFUL APPLICATIONS OF THE FINANCIAL CALCULATOR

With a financial calculator you can solve for any interest rate or for any number of periods in a time value of money problem. Here are some examples of these applications.

## Auto Loan

Assume you are financing a car with a three-year loan. The loan has a 9.5% nominal annual interest rate, compounded monthly. The price of the car is $6,000, and you want to determine the monthly payments, assuming that the payments start one month after the purchase. This problem is pictured in Illustration C-25.

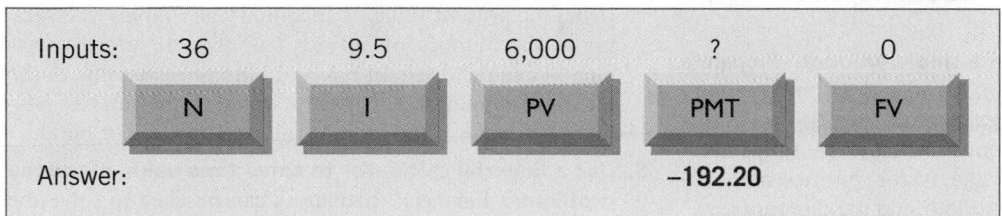

| Inputs: | 36 | 9.5 | 6,000 | ? | 0 |
|---------|-----|-----|-------|-----|-----|
| | N | I | PV | PMT | FV |
| Answer: | | | | −192.20 | |

**Illustration C-25**
Calculator solution for auto loan payments

To solve this problem, you enter N = 36 (12 × 3), I = 9.5, PV = 6,000, FV = 0, and then press PMT. You will find that the monthly payments will be $192.20. Note that the payment key is usually programmed for 12 payments per year. Thus, you must change the default (compounding period) if the payments are other than monthly.

## Mortgage Loan Amount

Let's say you are evaluating financing options for a loan on a house. You decide that the maximum mortgage payment you can afford is $700 per month. The annual interest rate is 8.4%. If you get a mortgage that requires you to make monthly payments over a 15-year period, what is the maximum purchase price you can afford? Illustration C-26 depicts this problem.

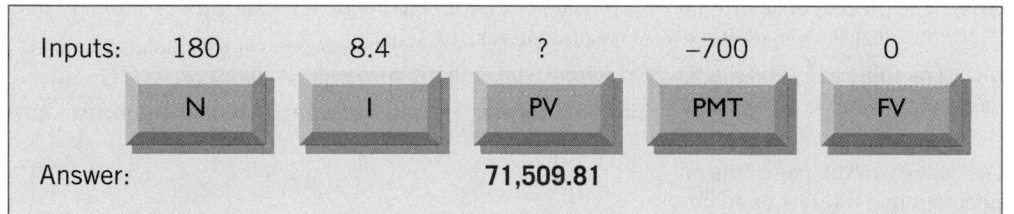

| Inputs: | 180 | 8.4 | ? | −700 | 0 |
|---------|-----|-----|-----|-------|-----|
| | N | I | PV | PMT | FV |
| Answer: | | | 71,509.81 | | |

**Illustration C-26**
Calculator solution for mortgage amount

You enter N = 180 (12 × 15 years), I = 8.4, PMT = −700, FV = 0, and press PV. With the payment-per-year key set at 12, you find a present value of $71,509.81—the maximum house price you can afford, given that you want to keep your mortgage payments at $700. Note that by changing any of the variables, you can quickly conduct "what-if" analyses for different situations.

## SUMMARY OF STUDY OBJECTIVES

1. **Distinguish between simple and compound interest.** Simple interest is computed on the principal only, whereas compound interest is computed on the principal and any interest earned that has not been withdrawn.

2. **Solve for future value of a single amount.** Prepare a time diagram of the problem. Identify the principal amount, the number of compounding periods, and the in-

terest rate. Using the future value of 1 table, multiply the principal amount by the future value factor specified at the intersection of the number of periods and the interest rate.

3. **Solve for future value of an annuity.** Prepare a time diagram of the problem. Identify the amount of the periodic payments, the number of compounding periods, and the

interest rate. Using the future value of an annuity of 1 table, multiply the amount of the payments by the future value factor specified at the intersection of the number of periods and the interest rate.

4. **Identify the variables fundamental to solving present value problems.** The following three variables are fundamental to solving present value problems: (1) the future amount, (2) the number of periods, and (3) the interest rate (the discount rate).

5. **Solve for present value of a single amount.** Prepare a time diagram of the problem. Identify the future amount, the number of discounting periods, and the discount (interest) rate. Using the present value of 1 table, multiply the future amount by the present value factor specified at the intersection of the number of periods and the discount rate.

6. **Solve for present value of an annuity.** Prepare a time diagram of the problem. Identify the future amounts (annuities), the number of discounting periods, and the discount (interest) rate. Using the present value of an annuity of 1 table, multiply the amount of the annuity by the present value factor specified at the intersection of the number of periods and the interest rate.

7. **Compute the present value of notes and bonds.** To determine the present value of the principal amount: Multiply the principal amount (a single future amount) by the present value factor (from the present value of 1 table) intersecting at the number of periods (number of interest payments) and the discount rate. To determine the present value of the series of interest payments: Multiply the amount of the interest payment by the present value factor (from the present value of an annuity of 1 table) intersecting at the number of periods (number of interest payments) and the discount rate. Add the present value of the principal amount to the present value of the interest payments to arrive at the present value of the note or bond.

8. **Use a financial calculator to solve time value of money problems.** Financial calculators can be used to solve the same and additional problems as those solved with time value of money tables. One enters into the financial calculator the amounts for all of the known elements of a time value of money problem (periods, interest rate, payments, future or present value) and solves for the unknown element. Particularly useful situations involve interest rates and compounding periods not presented in the tables.

## GLOSSARY

**Annuity** A series of equal dollar amounts to be paid or received periodically. (p. C5, C10)

**Compound interest** The interest computed on the principal and any interest earned that has not been paid or received. (p. C2)

**Discounting the future amount(s)** The process of determining present value. (p. C7)

**Future value of a single amount** The value at a future date of a given amount invested assuming compound interest. (p. C3)

**Future value of an annuity** The sum of all the payments or receipts plus the accumulated compound interest on them. (p. C5)

**Interest** Payment for the use of another's money. (p. C1)

**Present value** The value now of a given amount to be invested or received in the future assuming compound interest. (p. C7)

**Present value of an annuity** A series of future receipts or payments discounted to their value now assuming compound interest. (p. C10)

**Principal** The amount borrowed or invested. (p. C1)

**Simple interest** The interest computed on the principal only. (p. C1)

## BRIEF EXERCISES

Use tables to solve Brief Exercises 1-23.

*Compute the future value of a single amount.*
(SO 2)

**BEC-1** Russ Holub invested $4,000 at 5% annual interest, and left the money invested without withdrawing any of the interest for 10 years. At the end of the 10 years, Russ withdrew the accumulated amount of money.

**(a)** What amount did Russ withdraw assuming the investment earns simple interest?
**(b)** What amount did Russ withdraw assuming the investment earns interest compound annually?

*Use future value tables.*
(SO 2, 3)

**BEC-2** For each of the following cases, indicate (1) to what interest rate columns and (2) to what number of periods you would refer in looking up the future value factor.

**1.** In Table 1 (future value of 1):

| | Annual Rate | Number of Years Invested | Compounded |
|---|---|---|---|
| **(a)** | 8% | 5 | Annually |
| **(b)** | 5% | 3 | Semiannually |

**2.** In Table 2 (future value of an annuity of 1):

| | Annual Rate | Number of Years Invested | Compounded |
|---|---|---|---|
| (a) | 5% | 10 | Annually |
| (b) | 4% | 6 | Semiannually |

**BEC-3**   Racine Company signed a lease for an office building for a period of 10 years. Under the lease agreement, a security deposit of $10,000 is made. The deposit will be returned at the expiration of the lease with interest compounded at 4% per year. What amount will Racine receive at the time the lease expires?

*Compute the future value of a single amount.*
*(SO 2)*

**BEC-4**   Chaffee Company issued $1,000,000, 10-year bonds and agreed to make annual sinking fund deposits of $75,000. The deposits are made at the end of each year into an account paying 6% annual interest. What amount will be in the sinking fund at the end of 10 years?

*Compute the future value of an annuity.*
*(SO 3)*

**BEC-5**   Wayne and Brenda Anderson invested $5,000 in a savings account paying 5% compound annual interest when their daughter, Sue, was born. They also deposited $1,000 on each of her birthdays until she was 18 (including her 18th birthday). How much will be in the savings account on her 18th birthday (after the last deposit)?

*Compute the future value of a single amount and of an annuity.*
*(SO 2, 3)*

**BEC-6**   Ty Ngu borrowed $20,000 on July 1, 2002. This amount plus accrued interest at 6% compounded annually is to be repaid on July 1, 2008. How much will Ty have to repay on July 1, 2008?

*Compute the future value of a single amount.*
*(SO 2)*

**BEC-7**   For each of the following cases, indicate (a) to what interest rate columns and (b) to what number of periods you would refer in looking up the discount rate.

*Use present value tables.*
*(SO 5, 6)*

**1.** In Table 3 (present value of 1):

| | Annual Rate | Number of Years Involved | Discounts Per Year |
|---|---|---|---|
| (a) | 12% | 6 | Annually |
| (b) | 10% | 15 | Annually |
| (c) | 8% | 10 | Semiannually |

**2.** In Table 4 (present value of an annuity of 1):

| | Annual Rate | Number of Years Involved | Number of Payments Involved | Frequency of Payments |
|---|---|---|---|---|
| (a) | 8% | 20 | 20 | Annually |
| (b) | 10% | 5 | 5 | Annually |
| (c) | 12% | 4 | 8 | Semiannually |

**BEC-8**   (a) What is the present value of $20,000 due 8 periods from now, discounted at 8%? (b) What is the present value of $20,000 to be received at the end of each of 6 periods, discounted at 9%?

*Determine present values.*
*(SO 5, 6)*

**BEC-9**   Gonzalez Company is considering an investment that will return a lump sum of $500,000 5 years from now. What amount should Gonzalez Company pay for this investment in order to earn a 10% return?

*Compute the present value of a single-sum investment.*
*(SO 5)*

**BEC-10**   Lasorda Company earns 9% on an investment that will return $875,000 8 years from now. What is the amount Lasorda should invest now in order to earn this rate of return?

*Compute the present value of a single-sum investment.*
*(SO 5)*

**BEC-11**   Bosco Company is considering investing in an annuity contract that will return $30,000 annually at the end of each year for 15 years. What amount should Bosco Company pay for this investment if it earns a 6% return?

*Compute the present value of an annuity investment.*
*(SO 6)*

**BEC-12**   Modine Enterprises earns 11% on an investment that pays back $120,000 at the end of each of the next 4 years. What is the amount Modine Enterprises invested to earn the 11% rate of return?

*Compute the present value of an annuity investment.*
*(SO 6)*

**BEC-13**   Midwest Railroad Co. is about to issue $100,000 of 10-year bonds paying a 10% interest rate, with interest payable semiannually. The discount rate for such securities is 8%. How much can Midwest expect to receive from the sale of these bonds?

*Compute the present value of bonds.*
*(SO 5, 6, 7)*

*Compute the present value of bonds.*
(SO 5, 6, 7)

**BEC-14** Assume the same information as in BEC-13 except that the discount rate is 10% instead of 8%. In this case, how much can Midwest expect to receive from the sale of these bonds?

*Compute the present value of a note.*
(SO 5, 6, 7)

**BEC-15** Lounsbury Company receives a $50,000, 6-year note bearing interest of 8% (paid annually) from a customer at a time when the discount rate is 9%. What is the present value of the note received by Lounsbury Company?

*Compute the present value of bonds.*
(SO 5, 6, 7)

**BEC-16** Hartzler Enterprises issued 8%, 8-year, $2,000,000 par value bonds that pay interest semiannually on October 1 and April 1. The bonds are dated April 1, 2008, and are issued on that date. The discount rate of interest for such bonds on April 1, 2008, is 10%. What cash proceeds did Hartzler receive from issuance of the bonds?

*Compute the value of a machine for purposes of making a purchase decision.*
(SO 7)

**BEC-17** Vinny Carpino owns a garage and is contemplating purchasing a tire retreading machine for $16,280. After estimating costs and revenues, Vinny projects a net cash flow from the retreading machine of $3,000 annually for 8 years. Vinny hopes to earn a return of 11% on such investments. What is the present value of the retreading operation? Should Vinny Carpino purchase the retreading machine?

*Compute the present value of a note.*
(SO 5, 6)

**BEC-18** Rodriguez Company issues a 10%, 6-year mortgage note on January 1, 2008, to obtain financing for new equipment. Land is used as collateral for the note. The terms provide for semi-annual installment payments of $56,413. What were the cash proceeds received from the issuance of the note?

*Compute the maximum price to pay for the equipment.*
(SO 7)

**BEC-19** Goltra Company is considering purchasing equipment. The equipment will produce the following cash flows: Year 1, $30,000; Year 2, $40,000; Year 3, $50,000. Goltra requires a minimum rate of return of 12%. What is the maximum price Goltra should pay for this equipment?

*Compute the interest rate on a single sum.*
(SO 5)

**BEC-20** If Maria Sanchez invests $3,152 now, she will receive $10,000 at the end of 15 years. What annual rate of interest will Maria earn on her investment? (*Hint:* Use Table 3.)

*Compute the number of periods of a single sum.*
(SO 5)

**BEC-21** Lori Burke has been offered the opportunity of investing $42,410 now. The investment will earn 10% per year and at the end of that time will return Lori $100,000. How many years must Lori wait to receive $100,000? (*Hint:* Use Table 3.)

*Compute the interest rate on an annuity.*
(SO 6)

**BEC-22** Nancy Burns purchased an investment for $12,462.21. From this investment, she will receive $1,000 annually for the next 20 years, starting one year from now. What rate of interest will Nancy's investment be earning for her? (*Hint:* Use Table 4.)

*Compute the number of periods of an annuity.*
(SO 6)

**BEC-23** Betty Estes invests $7,536.08 now for a series of $1,000 annual returns, beginning one year from now. Betty will earn a return of 8% on the initial investment. How many annual payments of $1,000 will Betty receive? (*Hint:* Use Table 4.)

*Determine interest rate.*
(SO 8)

**BEC-24** Reba McEntire wishes to invest $19,000 on July 1, 2008, and have it accumulate to $49,000 by July 1, 2018.

**Instructions**
Use a financial calculator to determine at what exact annual rate of interest Reba must invest the $19,000.

*Determine interest rate.*
(SO 8)

**BEC-25** On July 17, 2008, Tim McGraw borrowed $42,000 from his grandfather to open a clothing store. Starting July 17, 2009, Tim has to make 10 equal annual payments of $6,500 each to repay the loan.

**Instructions**
Use a financial calculator to determine what interest rate Tim is paying.

*Determine interest rate.*
(SO 8)

**BEC-26** As the purchaser of a new house, Patty Loveless has signed a mortgage note to pay the Memphis National Bank and Trust Co. $14,000 every 6 months for 20 years, at the end of which time she will own the house. At the date the mortgage is signed the purchase price was $198,000, and Loveless made a down payment of $20,000. The first payment will be made 6 months after the date the mortgage is signed.

**Instructions**
Using a financial calculator, compute the exact rate of interest earned on the mortgage by the bank.

**BEC-27**    Using a financial calculator, solve for the unknowns in each of the following situations.

(a) On June 1, 2008, Shelley Long purchases lakefront property from her neighbor, Joey Brenner, and agrees to pay the purchase price in seven payments of $16,000 each, the first payment to be payable June 1, 2009. (Assume that interest compounded at an annual rate of 7.35% is implicit in the payments.) What is the purchase price of the property?

(b) On January 1, 2008, Cooke Corporation purchased 200 of the $1,000 face value, 8% coupon, 10-year bonds of Howe Inc. The bonds mature on January 1, 2018, and pay interest annually beginning January 1, 2009. Cooke purchased the bonds to yield 10.65%. How much did Cooke pay for the bonds?

**BEC-28**    Using a financial calculator, provide a solution to each of the following situations.

(a) Bill Schroeder owes a debt of $35,000 from the purchase of his new sport utility vehicle. The debt bears annual interest of 9.1% compounded monthly. Bill wishes to pay the debt and interest in equal monthly payments over 8 years, beginning one month hence. What equal monthly payments will pay off the debt and interest?

(b) On January 1, 2008, Sammy Sosa offers to buy Mark Grace's used snowmobile for $8,000, payable in five equal annual installments, which are to include 8.25% interest on the unpaid balance and a portion of the principal. If the first payment is to be made on December 31, 2008, how much will each payment be?

*Various time value of money situations.*
*(SO 8)*

*Various time value of money situations.*
*(SO 8)*

# Appendix D

# Payroll Accounting

## STUDY OBJECTIVE

*After studying this appendix, you should be able to:*

1. Discuss the objectives of internal control for payroll.
2. Compute and record the payroll for a pay period.
3. Describe and record employer payroll taxes.

Payroll and related fringe benefits often make up a large percentage of current liabilities. Employee compensation is often the most significant expense that a company incurs. For example, Costco recently reported total employees of 103,000 and labor and fringe benefits costs that approximated 70% of the company's total cost of operations.

Payroll accounting involves more than paying employees' wages. Companies are required by law to maintain payroll records for each employee, to file and pay payroll taxes, and to comply with numerous state and federal tax laws related to employee compensation. Accounting for payroll has become much more complex due to these regulations.

## PAYROLL DEFINED

The term "payroll" pertains to both salaries and wages. Managerial, administrative, and sales personnel are generally paid **salaries**. Salaries are often expressed in terms of a specified amount per month or per year rather than an hourly rate. Store clerks, factory employees, and manual laborers are normally paid **wages**. Wages are based on a rate per hour or on a piecework basis (such as per unit of product). Frequently, people use the terms "salaries" and "wages" interchangeably.

The term "payroll" does not apply to payments made for services of professionals such as certified public accountants, attorneys, and architects. Such professionals are independent contractors rather than salaried employees. Payments to them are called **fees**. This distinction is important because government regulations relating to the payment and reporting of payroll taxes apply only to employees.

## INTERNAL CONTROL OF PAYROLL

Chapter 8 introduced internal control. As applied to payrolls, the objectives of internal control are (1) to safeguard company assets against unauthorized payments of payroll and (2) to ensure the accuracy and reliability of the accounting records pertaining to payrolls.

> **STUDY OBJECTIVE 1**
> Discuss the objectives of internal control for payroll.

Irregularities often result if internal control is lax. Methods of theft involving payroll include overstating hours, using unauthorized pay rates, adding fictitious employees to the payroll, continuing terminated employees on the payroll, and distributing duplicate payroll checks. Moreover, inaccurate records will result in incorrect paychecks, financial statements, and payroll tax returns.

Payroll activities involve four functions: hiring employees, timekeeping, preparing the payroll, and paying the payroll. For effective internal control, the company should assign these four functions to different departments or individuals. To illustrate these functions, we will examine the case of Academy Company and one of its employees, Michael Jordan.

**Hiring Employees**

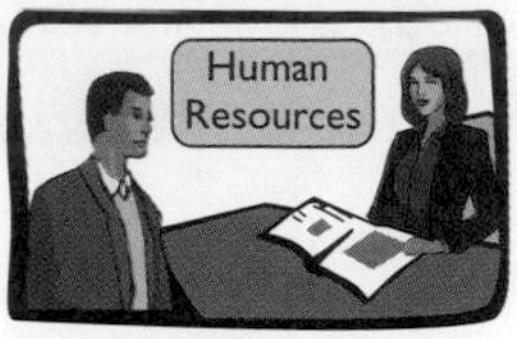


Human Resources department documents and authorizes employment.

## Hiring Employees

The human resources (personnel) department is responsible for posting job openings, screening and interviewing applicants, and hiring employees. From a control standpoint, this department provides significant documentation and authorization. When an employee is hired, the human resources department prepares an authorization form. The one used by Academy Company for Michael Jordan is shown in Illustration D-1.

**Illustration D-1**
Authorization form prepared by the human resources department

ACADEMY COMPANY

Employee Name: Jordan, (LAST) Michael (FIRST) (MI) — Starting Date: 9/01/06

Classification: Skilled-Level 10 — Social Security No.: 329-36-9547

Department: Shipping — Division: Entertainment

| | |
|---|---|
| **NEW HIRE** | Classification: Clerk — Salary Grade: Level 10 — Trans. from Temp. ☐<br>Rate $ 10.00 per hour — Bonus: N/A — Non-exempt ☒ Exempt ☐ |
| **RATE CHANGE** | New Rate $ 12.00 — Effective Date: 9/1/07<br>Present Rate $ 10.00<br>Merit ☒ Promotion ☐ Decrease ☐ Other ____<br>Previous Increase Date: None — Amount $ ____ per ____ Type ____ |
| **SEPARATION** | Resignation ☐ Discharge ☐ Retirement ☐ Reason ____<br>Leave of absence ☐ From ____ to ____ Type ____<br>Last Day Worked ____ |
| **APPROVALS** | BEW (BRANCH OR DEPT. MANAGER) — 9/1/07 (DATE) — EMW (DIVISION V.P.) — 9-1-07 (DATE)<br>James E. Speer (PERSONNEL DEPARTMENT) |

The human resources department sends the authorization form to the payroll department, where it is used to place the new employee on the payroll. A chief concern of the human resources department is ensuring the accuracy of this form. The reason is quite simple: One of the most common types of payroll frauds is adding fictitious employees to the payroll.

The human resources department is also responsible for authorizing changes in employment status. Specifically, they must authorize (1) changes in pay rates and (2) terminations of employment. Every authorization should be in writing, and a copy of the change in status should be sent to the payroll department. Notice in Illustration D-1 that Jordan received a pay increase of $2 per hour.

# Timekeeping

Another area in which internal control is important is timekeeping. Hourly employees are usually required to record time worked by "punching" a time clock. The employee inserts a **time card** into the clock, which automatically records the employee's arrival and departure times. Illustration D-2 shows Michael Jordan's time card.

Timekeeping

Supervisors monitor hours worked through time cards and time reports.

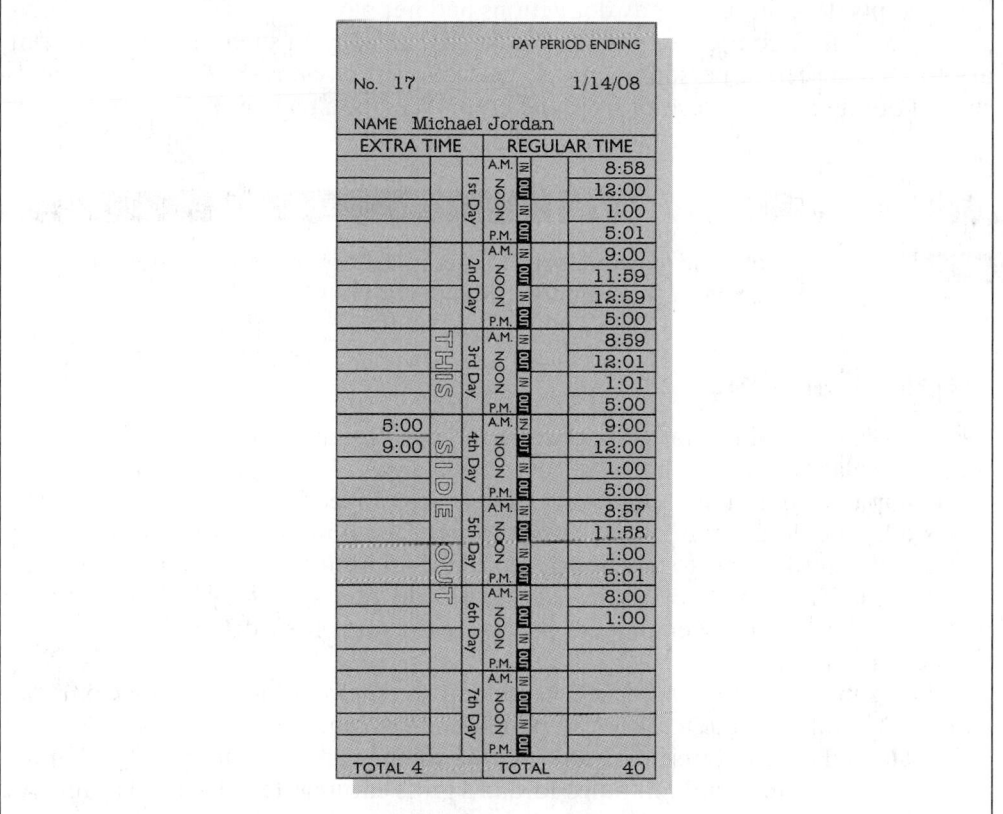

| | | | | | PAY PERIOD ENDING |
|---|---|---|---|---|---|
| No. 17 | | | | | 1/14/08 |

NAME Michael Jordan

| EXTRA TIME | | | | REGULAR TIME |
|---|---|---|---|---|
| | 1st Day | A.M. | IN | 8:58 |
| | | NOON | OUT | 12:00 |
| | | | IN | 1:00 |
| | | P.M. | OUT | 5:01 |
| | 2nd Day | A.M. | IN | 9:00 |
| | | NOON | OUT | 11:59 |
| | | | IN | 12:59 |
| | | P.M. | OUT | 5:00 |
| | 3rd Day | A.M. | IN | 8:59 |
| | | NOON | OUT | 12:01 |
| | | | IN | 1:01 |
| | | P.M. | OUT | 5:00 |
| 5:00 | 4th Day | A.M. | IN | 9:00 |
| 9:00 | | NOON | OUT | 12:00 |
| | | | IN | 1:00 |
| | | P.M. | OUT | 5:00 |
| | 5th Day | A.M. | IN | 8:57 |
| | | NOON | OUT | 11:58 |
| | | | IN | 1:00 |
| | | P.M. | OUT | 5:01 |
| | 6th Day | A.M. | IN | 8:00 |
| | | NOON | OUT | 1:00 |
| | | | IN | |
| | | P.M. | OUT | |
| | 7th Day | A.M. | IN | |
| | | NOON | OUT | |
| | | | IN | |
| | | P.M. | OUT | |
| TOTAL 4 | | TOTAL | | 40 |

THIS SIDE OUT

**Illustration D-2**
Time card

In large companies, time clock procedures are often monitored by a supervisor or security guard to make sure an employee punches only his or her own card. At the end of the pay period, each employee's supervisor approves the hours shown by signing the time card. When overtime hours are involved, approval by a supervisor is usually mandatory. This guards against unauthorized overtime. The approved time cards are then sent to the payroll department. For salaried employees, a manually prepared weekly or monthly time report kept by a supervisor may be used to record time worked.

# Preparing the Payroll

The payroll department prepares the payroll on the basis of two inputs: (1) human resources department authorizations and (2) approved time cards. Numerous calculations are involved in determining gross wages and payroll deductions. Therefore, a second payroll department employee, working independently, verifies all calculated amounts, and a payroll department supervisor then approves the payroll. The payroll department is also responsible for preparing (but not signing) payroll checks, maintaining payroll records, and preparing payroll tax returns.

**Preparing the Payroll**

Two (or more) employees verify payroll amounts; supervisor approves.

Paying the Payroll

Treasurer signs and distributes checks.

# Paying the Payroll

The treasurer's department pays the payroll. **Payment by check minimizes the risk of loss from theft, and the endorsed check provides proof of payment.** For good internal control, payroll checks should be prenumbered, and all checks should be accounted for. All checks must be signed by the treasurer (or a designated agent). Distribution of the payroll checks to employees should be controlled by the treasurer's department. Many employees have their pay credited electronically to their bank accounts. To control these disbursements, the company provides to employees receipts detailing gross pay deductions and net pay.

Occasionally companies pay the payroll in currency. In such cases it is customary to have a second person count the cash in each pay envelope. The paymaster should obtain a signed receipt from the employee upon payment.

# DETERMINING THE PAYROLL

**STUDY OBJECTIVE 2**

Compute and record the payroll for a pay period.

Determining the payroll involves computing three amounts: (1) gross earnings, (2) payroll deductions, and (3) net pay.

## Gross Earnings

Gross earnings is the total compensation earned by an employee. It consists of wages or salaries, plus any bonuses and commissions.

Companies determine total **wages** for an employee by multiplying the hours worked by the hourly rate of pay. In addition to the hourly pay rate, most companies are required by law to pay hourly workers a minimum of $1\frac{1}{2}$ times the regular hourly rate for overtime work in excess of eight hours per day or 40 hours per week. In addition, many employers pay overtime rates for work done at night, on weekends, and on holidays.

For example, assume that Michael Jordan, an employee of Academy Company, worked 44 hours for the weekly pay period ending January 14. His regular wage is $12 per hour. For any hours in excess of 40, the company pays at one-and-a-half times the regular rate. Academy computes Jordan's gross earnings (total wages) as follows.

**Illustration D-3**
Computation of total wages

| Type of Pay | Hours | × | Rate | = | Gross Earnings |
|---|---|---|---|---|---|
| Regular | 40 | × | $12 | = | $480 |
| Overtime | 4 | × | 18 | = | 72 |
| **Total wages** | | | | | **$552** |

**ETHICS NOTE**

Bonuses often reward outstanding individual performance, but successful corporations also need considerable teamwork. A challenge is to motivate individuals while preventing an unethical employee from taking another's idea for his or her own advantage.

This computation assumes that Jordan receives $1\frac{1}{2}$ times his regular hourly rate ($12 × 1.5) for his overtime hours. Union contracts often require that overtime rates be as much as twice the regular rates.

An employee's **salary** is generally based on a monthly or yearly rate. The company then prorates these rates to its payroll periods (e.g., biweekly or monthly). Most executive and administrative positions are salaried. Federal law does not require overtime pay for employees in such positions.

Many companies have **bonus** agreements for employees. One survey found that over 94% of the largest U.S. manufacturing companies offer annual bonuses to key executives. Bonus arrangements may be based on such factors as increased sales or net income. Companies may pay bonuses in cash and/or by granting employees the opportunity to acquire shares of company stock at favorable prices (called stock option plans).

## Payroll Deductions

As anyone who has received a paycheck knows, gross earnings are usually very different from the amount actually received. The difference is due to **payroll deductions**.

Payroll deductions may be mandatory or voluntary. Mandatory deductions are required by law and consist of FICA taxes and income taxes. Voluntary deductions are at the option of the employee. Illustration D-4 summarizes common types of payroll deductions. Such deductions do not result in payroll tax expense to the employer. The employer is merely a collection agent, and subsequently transfers the deducted amounts to the government and designated recipients.

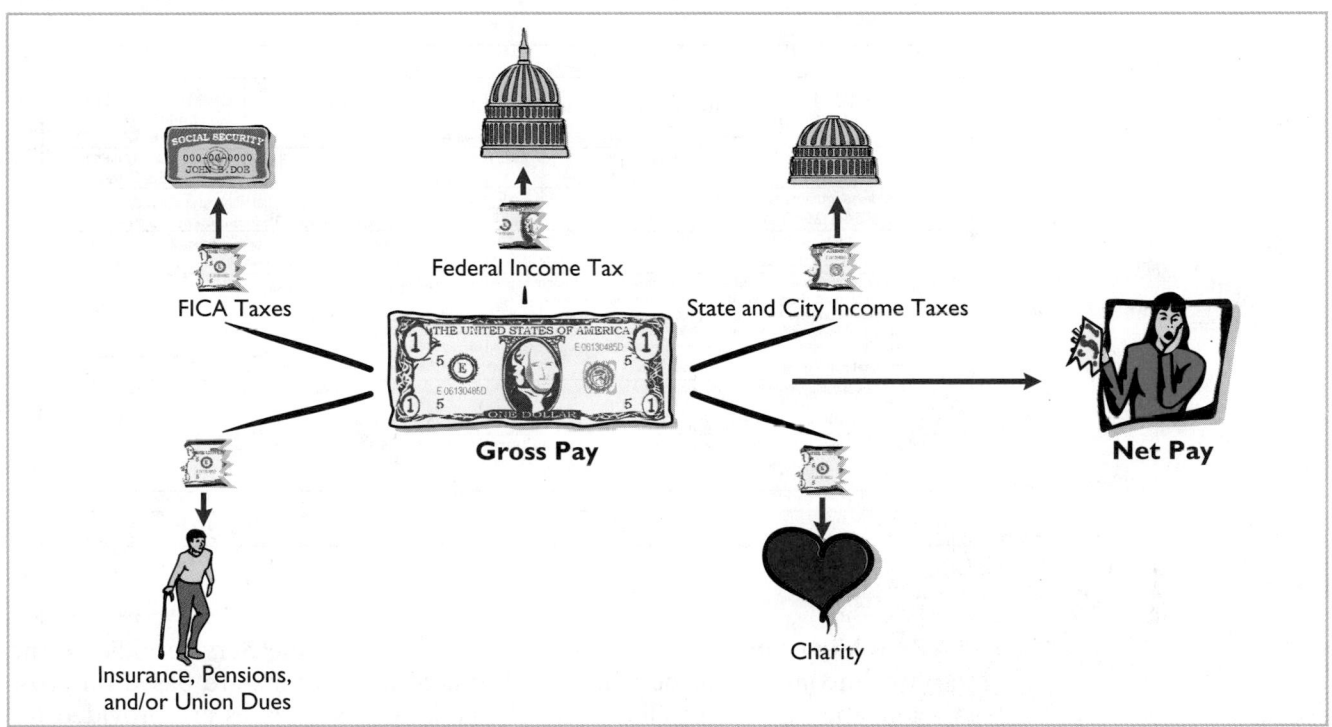

**Illustration D-4**
Payroll deductions

### FICA TAXES

In 1937 Congress enacted the Federal Insurance Contribution Act (FICA). **FICA taxes are designed to provide workers with supplemental retirement, employment disability, and medical benefits.** In 1965, Congress extended benefits to include Medicare for individuals over 65 years of age. The benefits are financed by a tax levied on employees' earnings. FICA taxes are commonly referred to as **Social Security taxes**.

Congress sets the tax rate and the tax base for FICA taxes. When FICA taxes were first imposed, the rate was 1% on the first $3,000 of gross earnings, or a maximum of $30 per year. The rate and base have changed dramatically since that time! In 2007, the rate was 7.65% (6.2% Social Security plus 1.45% Medicare) on the first $97,500 of gross earnings for each employee.[1] For purpose of illustration in this chapter, we will assume a rate of 8% on the first $97,500 of gross earnings, or a maximum of $7,800. Using the 8% rate, the FICA withholding for Jordan for the weekly pay period ending January 14 is $44.16 ($552 × 8%).

---

[1]The Medicare provision also includes a tax of 1.45% on gross earnings in excess of $97,500. In the interest of simplification, we ignore this 1.45% charge in our end-of-chapter assignment material. We assume zero FICA withholdings on gross earnings above $97,500.

### INCOME TAXES

Under the U.S. pay-as-you-go system of federal income taxes, employers are required to withhold income taxes from employees each pay period. Three variables determine the amount to be withheld: (1) the employee's gross earnings; (2) the number of allowances claimed by the employee; and (3) the length of the pay period.

The number of allowances claimed typically includes the employee, his or her spouse, and other dependents. **To indicate to the Internal Revenue Service the number of allowances claimed, the employee must complete an** Employee's Withholding Allowance Certificate (Form W-4). As shown in Illustration D-5, Michael Jordan claims two allowances on his W-4.

**Illustration D-5**
W-4 form

| Form **W-4**<br>Department of the Treasury<br>Internal Revenue Service | **Employee's Withholding Allowance Certificate**<br>► For Privacy Act and Paperwork Reduction Act Notice, see page 2. | OMB No. 1545-0010<br>20**08** |
|---|---|---|

1 Type or print your first name and middle initial    Michael     Last name    Jordan     2 Your social security number   329-36-9547

Home address (number and street or rural route)   2345 Mifflin Ave.

3 ☐ Single ☒ Married ☐ Married, but withhold at higher Single rate.
Note: *If married, but legally separated, or spouse is a nonresident alien, check the Single box.*

City or town, State, and ZIP code   Hampton, MI 48292

4 If your last name differs from that on your social security card, check here and call 1-800-772-1213 for a new card . . . . . . ► ☐

5 Total number of allowances you are claiming (from line H above or from the worksheet on page 2 if they apply) . . . . **5** 2
6 Additional amount, if any, you want withheld from each paycheck . . . . . . . . . . . . . . . **6** $
7 I claim exemption from withholding for 2006, and I certify that I meet BOTH of the following conditions for exemption:
  • Last year I had a right to a refund of ALL Federal income tax withheld because I had NO tax liability AND
  • This year I expect a refund of ALL Federal income tax withheld because I expect to have NO tax liability.
If you meet both conditions, enter "Exempt" here . . . . . . . . . . . . . . . ► **7**

Under penalties of perjury, I certify that I am entitled to the number of withholding allowances claimed on this certificate or entitled to claim exempt status.

Employee's signature ► *Michael Jordan*      Date ► September 1 , 20 08

8 Employer's name and address (Employer: Complete 8 and 10 only if sending to the IRS)    9 Office code (optional)    10 Employer identification number

Cat. No. 102200

Withholding tables furnished by the Internal Revenue Service indicate the amount of income tax to be withheld. Withholding amounts are based on gross wages and the number of allowances claimed. Separate tables are provided for weekly, biweekly, semimonthly, and monthly pay periods. Illustration D-6 (next page) shows the withholding tax table for Michael Jordan (assuming he earns $552 per week and claims two allowances). For a weekly salary of $552 with two allowances, the income tax to be withheld is $49.

In addition, most states (and some cities) require **employers** to withhold income taxes from employees' earnings. As a rule, the amounts withheld are a percentage (specified in the state revenue code) of the amount withheld for the federal income tax. Or they may be a specified percentage of the employee's earnings. For the sake of simplicity, we have assumed that Jordan's wages are subject to state income taxes of 2%, or $11.04 (2% × $552) per week.

There is no limit on the amount of gross earnings subject to income tax withholdings. In fact, under our progressive system of taxation, the higher the earnings, the higher the percentage of income withheld for taxes.

### OTHER DEDUCTIONS

Employees may voluntarily authorize withholdings for charitable, retirement, and other purposes. All voluntary deductions from gross earnings should be authorized in writing by the employee. The authorization(s) may be made individually or as part of a group plan. Deductions for charitable organizations, such as the United Way, or for financial arrangements, such as U.S. savings bonds and repayment of

**MARRIED** Persons — **WEEKLY** Payroll Period
(For Wages Paid in 2008)

| If the wages are — | | And the number of withholding allowances claimed is — | | | | | | | | | | |
|---|---|---|---|---|---|---|---|---|---|---|---|---|
| At least | But less than | 0 | 1 | 2 | 3 | 4 | 5 | 6 | 7 | 8 | 9 | 10 |
| | | The amount of income tax to be withheld is — | | | | | | | | | | |
| 490 | 500 | 56 | 48 | 40 | 32 | 24 | 17 | 9 | 1 | 0 | 0 | 0 |
| 500 | 510 | 57 | 49 | 42 | 34 | 26 | 18 | 10 | 3 | 0 | 0 | 0 |
| 510 | 520 | 59 | 51 | 43 | 35 | 27 | 20 | 12 | 4 | 0 | 0 | 0 |
| 520 | 530 | 60 | 52 | 45 | 37 | 29 | 21 | 13 | 6 | 0 | 0 | 0 |
| 530 | 540 | 62 | 54 | 46 | 38 | 30 | 23 | 15 | 7 | 0 | 0 | 0 |
| 540 | 550 | 63 | 55 | 48 | 40 | 32 | 24 | 16 | 9 | 1 | 0 | 0 |
| 550 | 560 | 65 | 57 | 49 | 41 | 33 | 26 | 18 | 10 | 2 | 0 | 0 |
| 560 | 570 | 66 | 58 | 51 | 43 | 35 | 27 | 19 | 12 | 4 | 0 | 0 |
| 570 | 580 | 68 | 60 | 52 | 44 | 36 | 29 | 21 | 13 | 5 | 0 | 0 |
| 580 | 590 | 69 | 61 | 54 | 46 | 38 | 30 | 22 | 15 | 7 | 0 | 0 |
| 590 | 600 | 71 | 63 | 55 | 47 | 39 | 32 | 24 | 16 | 8 | 1 | 0 |
| 600 | 610 | 72 | 64 | 57 | 49 | 41 | 33 | 25 | 18 | 10 | 2 | 0 |
| 610 | 620 | 74 | 66 | 58 | 50 | 42 | 35 | 27 | 19 | 11 | 4 | 0 |
| 620 | 630 | 75 | 67 | 60 | 52 | 44 | 36 | 28 | 21 | 13 | 5 | 0 |
| 630 | 640 | 77 | 69 | 61 | 53 | 45 | 38 | 30 | 22 | 14 | 7 | 0 |
| 640 | 650 | 78 | 70 | 63 | 55 | 47 | 39 | 31 | 24 | 16 | 8 | 0 |
| 650 | 660 | 80 | 72 | 64 | 56 | 48 | 41 | 33 | 25 | 17 | 10 | 2 |
| 660 | 670 | 81 | 73 | 66 | 58 | 50 | 42 | 34 | 27 | 19 | 11 | 3 |
| 670 | 680 | 83 | 75 | 67 | 59 | 51 | 44 | 36 | 28 | 20 | 13 | 5 |
| 680 | 690 | 84 | 76 | 69 | 61 | 53 | 45 | 37 | 30 | 22 | 14 | 6 |

loans from company credit unions, are made individually. Deductions for union dues, health and life insurance, and pension plans are often made on a group basis. We will assume that Jordan has weekly voluntary deductions of $10 for the United Way and $5 for union dues.

# Net Pay

**ALTERNATIVE TERMINOLOGY**

Net pay is also called *take-home pay.*

Academy Company determines **net pay** by subtracting payroll deductions from gross earnings. Illustration D-7 shows the computation of Jordan's net pay for the pay period.

| | | |
|---|---|---|
| Gross earnings | | $552.00 |
| Payroll deductions: | | |
| FICA taxes | $44.16 | |
| Federal income taxes | 49.00 | |
| State income taxes | 11.04 | |
| United Way | 10.00 | |
| Union dues | 5.00 | 119.20 |
| **Net pay** | | **$432.80** |

Assuming that Michael Jordan's wages for each week during the year are $552, total wages for the year are $28,704 (52 × $552). Thus, all of Jordan's wages are subject to FICA tax during the year. In comparison, let's assume that Jordan's department head earns $2,000 per week, or $104,000 for the year. Since only the first $97,500 is subject to FICA taxes, the maximum FICA withholdings on the department head's earnings would be $7,800 ($97,500 × 8%).

# RECORDING THE PAYROLL

Recording the payroll involves maintaining payroll department records, recognizing payroll expenses and liabilities, and recording payment of the payroll.

## Maintaining Payroll Department Records

To comply with state and federal laws, an employer must keep a cumulative record of each employee's gross earnings, deductions, and net pay during the year. The record that provides this information is the **employee earnings record**. Illustration D-8 shows Michael Jordan's employee earnings record.

**Illustration D-8**
Employee earnings record

| Academy Company.xls | | | | | | | | | | | | | |
|---|---|---|---|---|---|---|---|---|---|---|---|---|---|
| File Edit View Insert Format Tools Data Window Help | | | | | | | | | | | | | |
| A | B | C | D | E | F | G | H | I | J | K | L | M | N |

**ACADEMY COMPANY**
**Employee Earnings Record**
**For the Year 2008**

| Name | Michael Jordan | Address | 2345 Mifflin Ave. |
|---|---|---|---|
| Social Security Number | 329-36-9547 | | Hampton, Michigan 48292 |
| Date of Birth | December 24, 1962 | Telephone | 555-238-9051 |
| Date Employed | September 1, 2003 | Date Employment Ended | |
| Sex | Male | Exemptions | 2 |
| Single ___ | Married x | | |

| 2008 | | Gross Earnings | | | | Deductions | | | | | | Payment | |
|---|---|---|---|---|---|---|---|---|---|---|---|---|---|
| Period Ending | Total Hours | Regular | Overtime | Total | Cumulative | FICA | Fed. Inc. Tax | State Inc. Tax | United Way | Union Dues | Total | Net Amount | Check No. |
| 1/7 | 42 | 480.00 | 36.00 | 516.00 | 516.00 | 41.28 | 43.00 | 10.32 | 10.00 | 5.00 | 109.60 | 406.40 | 974 |
| **1/14** | **44** | **480.00** | **72.00** | **552.00** | **1,068.00** | **44.16** | **49.00** | **11.04** | **10.00** | **5.00** | **119.20** | **432.80** | **1028** |
| 1/21 | 43 | 480.00 | 54.00 | 534.00 | 1,602.00 | 42.72 | 46.00 | 10.68 | 10.00 | 5.00 | 114.40 | 419.60 | 1077 |
| 1/28 | 42 | 480.00 | 36.00 | 516.00 | 2,118.00 | 41.28 | 43.00 | 10.32 | 10.00 | 5.00 | 109.60 | 406.40 | 1133 |
| Jan. Total | | 1,920.00 | 198.00 | 2,118.00 | | 169.44 | 181.00 | 42.36 | 40.00 | 20.00 | 452.80 | 1,665.20 | |

Companies keep a separate earnings record for each employee, and update these records after each pay period. The employer uses the cumulative payroll data on the earnings record to: (1) determine when an employee has earned the maximum earnings subject to FICA taxes, (2) file state and federal payroll tax returns (as explained later), and (3) provide each employee with a statement of gross earnings and tax withholdings for the year. (Illustration D-12 on page D13 shows this statement.)

In addition to employee earnings records, many companies find it useful to prepare a **payroll register**. This record accumulates the gross earnings, deductions, and net pay by employee for each pay period. It provides the documentation for preparing a paycheck for each employee. Illustration D-9 (next page) presents Academy Company's payroll register. It shows the data for Michael Jordan in the wages section. In this example, Academy Company's total weekly payroll is $17,210, as shown in the gross earnings column.

Note that this record is a listing of each employee's payroll data for the pay period. In some companies, a payroll register is a journal or book of original entry;

**ACADEMY COMPANY**
**Payroll Register**
**For the Week Ending January 14, 2008**

| | Total Hours | Regular | Over-time | Gross | FICA | Federal Income Tax | State Income Tax | United Way | Union Dues | Total | Net Pay | Check No. | Office Salaries Expense | Wages Expense |
|---|---|---|---|---|---|---|---|---|---|---|---|---|---|---|
| | | Earnings | | | | Deductions | | | | | Paid | | Accounts Debited | |
| **Employee** | | | | | | | | | | | | | | |
| Office Salaries | | | | | | | | | | | | | | |
| Arnold, Patricia | 40 | 580.00 | | 580.00 | 46.40 | 61.00 | 11.60 | 15.00 | | 134.00 | 446.00 | 998 | 580.00 | |
| Canton, Matthew | 40 | 590.00 | | 590.00 | 47.20 | 63.00 | 11.80 | 20.00 | | 142.00 | 448.00 | 999 | 590.00 | |
| Mueller, William | 40 | 530.00 | | 530.00 | 42.40 | 54.00 | 10.60 | 11.00 | | 118.00 | 412.00 | 1000 | 530.00 | |
| Subtotal | | 5,200.00 | | 5,200.00 | 416.00 | 1,090.00 | 104.00 | 120.00 | | 1,730.00 | 3,470.00 | | 5,200.00 | |
| Wages | | | | | | | | | | | | | | |
| Bennett, Robin | 42 | 480.00 | 36.00 | 516.00 | 41.28 | 43.00 | 10.32 | 18.00 | 5.00 | 117.60 | 398.40 | 1025 | | 516.00 |
| **Jordan, Michael** | **44** | **480.00** | **72.00** | **552.00** | **44.16** | **49.00** | **11.04** | **10.00** | **5.00** | **119.20** | **432.80** | **1028** | | **552.00** |
| Milroy, Lee | 43 | 480.00 | 54.00 | 534.00 | 42.72 | 46.00 | 10.68 | 10.00 | 5.00 | 114.40 | 419.60 | 1029 | | 534.00 |
| Subtotal | | 11,000.00 | 1,010.00 | 12,010.00 | 960.80 | 2,400.00 | 240.20 | 301.50 | 115.00 | 4,017.50 | 7,992.50 | | | 12,010.00 |
| Total | | 16,200.00 | 1,010.00 | 17,210.00 | 1,376.80 | 3,490.00 | 344.20 | 421.50 | 115.00 | 5,747.50 | 11,462.50 | | 5,200.00 | 12,010.00 |

**Illustration D-9**
Payroll register

postings are made from the payroll register directly to ledger accounts. In other companies, the payroll register is a memorandum record that provides the data for a general journal entry and subsequent posting to the ledger accounts. At Academy Company, the latter procedure is followed.

## Recognizing Payroll Expenses and Liabilities

From the payroll register in Illustration D-9, Academy Company makes a journal entry to record the payroll. For the week ending January 14 the entry is:

| Jan. 14 | Office Salaries Expense | 5,200.00 | |
| | Wages Expense | 12,010.00 | |
| | FICA Taxes Payable | | 1,376.80 |
| | Federal Income Taxes Payable | | 3,490.00 |
| | State Income Taxes Payable | | 344.20 |
| | United Way Payable | | 421.50 |
| | Union Dues Payable | | 115.00 |
| | Salaries and Wages Payable | | 11,462.50 |
| | (To record payroll for the week ending January 14) | | |

A = L + SE
−5,200.00 Exp
−12,010.00 Exp
+1,376.80
+3,490.00
+344.20
+421.50
+115.00
+11,462.50

**Cash Flows**
no effect

The company credits specific liability accounts for the mandatory and voluntary deductions made during the pay period. In the example, Academy debits Office Salaries Expense for the gross earnings of salaried office workers, and it debits Wages Expense for the gross earnings of employees who are paid at an hourly rate. Other companies may debit other accounts such as Store Salaries or Sales Salaries. The amount credited to Salaries and Wages Payable is the sum of the individual checks the employees will receive.

# Recording Payment of the Payroll

A company makes payments by check (or electronic funds transfer) either from its regular bank account or a payroll bank account. Each paycheck is usually accompanied by a detachable **statement of earnings** document. This shows the employee's gross earnings, payroll deductions, and net pay, both for the period and for the year-to-date. Academy Company uses its regular bank account for payroll checks. Illustration D-10 shows the paycheck and statement of earnings for Michael Jordan.

**Illustration D-10**
Paycheck and statement of earnings

| **AC** | ACADEMY COMPANY | | | No. 1028 |
| | 19 Center St. | | | |
| | Hampton, MI 48291 | | *January 14*, 20 *08* | 62—1113 / 610 |

Pay to the order of _Michael Jordan_ ................................ $ _432.80_

_Four Hundred Thirty-two and 80/100_ _____ Dollars

City Bank & Trust
P.O. Box 3000
Hampton, MI 48291

For _Payroll_        _Randall E. Barnes_

⑆00324477⑆ 1028

- - - - - - - - - - - - - - - - - - - - - - - - - - - - - - - - - - - - - - - - - - - - -

DETACH AND RETAIN THIS PORTION FOR YOUR RECORDS

| NAME | | | | SOC. SEC. NO. | EMPL. NUMBER | NO. EXEMP | PAY PERIOD ENDING |
|---|---|---|---|---|---|---|---|
| Michael Jordan | | | | 329-36-9547 | | 2 | 1/14/08 |

| REG. HRS. | O.T. HRS. | OTH. HRS. (1) | OTH. HRS. (2) | REG. EARNINGS | O.T. EARNINGS | OTH. EARNINGS (1) | OTH. EARNINGS (2) | **GROSS** |
|---|---|---|---|---|---|---|---|---|
| 40 | 4 | | | 480.00 | 72.00 | | | **$552.00** |

| FED. W/H TAX | FICA | STATE TAX | LOCAL TAX | OTHER DEDUCTIONS | | | | **NET PAY** |
|---|---|---|---|---|---|---|---|---|
| 49.00 | 44.16 | 11.04 | | (1) 10.00 | (2) 5.00 | (3) | (4) | 432.80 |

| **YEAR TO DATE** | | | | | | | | |
|---|---|---|---|---|---|---|---|---|
| FED. W/H TAX | FICA | STATE TAX | LOCAL TAX | OTHER DEDUCTIONS | | | | **NET PAY** |
| 92.00 | 85.44 | 21.36 | | (1) 20.00 | (2) 10.00 | (3) | (4) | $839.20 |

**HELPFUL HINT**

Do any of the income tax liabilities result in payroll tax expense for the employer?

Answer: No. The employer is acting only as a collection agent for the government.

Following payment of the payroll, the company enters the check numbers in the payroll register. Academy Company records payment of the payroll as follows.

| A | = | L | + | OE |
|---|---|---|---|---|
| | | −11,462.50 | | |
| −11,462.50 | | | | |

**Cash Flows**
−11,462.50

| Jan. 14 | Salaries and Wages Payable | 11,462.50 | |
| | Cash | | 11,462.50 |
| | (To record payment of payroll) | | |

When a company uses currency in payment, it prepares one check for the payroll's total amount of net pay. The company cashes this check, and inserts the coins and currency in individual pay envelopes for disbursement to individual employees.

## Before You Go On...

**REVIEW IT**
1. Identify two internal control procedures that apply to each payroll function.
2. What are the primary sources of gross earnings?
3. What payroll deductions are (a) mandatory and (b) voluntary?
4. What account titles do companies use in recording a payroll, assuming only mandatory payroll deductions are involved?

### DO IT

Your cousin Stan is establishing a house-cleaning business and will have a number of employees working for him. He is aware that documentation procedures are an important part of internal control. But he is unsure about the difference between an employee earnings record and a payroll register. He asks you to explain the principal differences, because he wants to be sure that he sets up the proper payroll procedures.

**Action Plan**

■ Determine the earnings and deductions data that must be recorded and reported for each employee.

■ Design a record that will accumulate earnings and deductions data and will serve as a basis for journal entries to be prepared and posted to the general ledger accounts.

■ Explain the difference between the employee earnings record and the payroll register.

**Solution**   An employee earnings record is kept for *each* employee. It shows gross earnings, payroll deductions, and net pay for each pay period, as well as cumulative payroll data for that employee. In contrast, a payroll register is a listing of *all* employees' gross earnings, payroll deductions, and net pay for each pay period. It is the documentation for preparing paychecks and for recording the payroll. Of course, Stan will need to keep both documents.

*Related exercise material: BED-1, BED-3, and ED-1.*

# EMPLOYER PAYROLL TAXES

Payroll tax expense for businesses results from three taxes that governmental agencies levy **on employers**. These taxes are: (1) FICA, (2) federal unemployment tax, and (3) state unemployment tax. These taxes plus such items as paid vacations and pensions (discussed in the appendix to this chapter) are collectively referred to as **fringe benefits**. As indicated earlier, the cost of fringe benefits in many companies is substantial. The pie chart in the margin shows the pieces of the benefits "pie."

## FICA Taxes

Each employee must pay FICA taxes. In addition, employers must match each employee's FICA contribution. The matching contribution results in **payroll tax expense** to the employer. The employer's tax is subject to the same rate and maximum earnings as the employee's. The company uses the same account, FICA Taxes Payable, to record both the employee's and the employer's FICA contributions. For the January 14 payroll, Academy Company's FICA tax contribution is $1,376.80 ($17,210.00 × 8%).

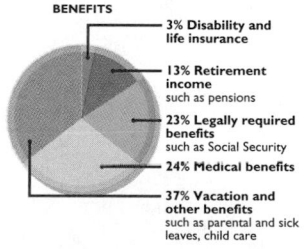

BENEFITS

- 3% Disability and life insurance
- 13% Retirement income such as pensions
- 23% Legally required benefits such as Social Security
- 24% Medical benefits
- 37% Vacation and other benefits such as parental and sick leaves, child care

## Federal Unemployment Taxes

The Federal Unemployment Tax Act (FUTA) is another feature of the federal Social Security program. Federal unemployment taxes provide benefits for a limited period of time to employees who lose their jobs through no fault of their own. The FUTA tax rate is 6.2% of taxable wages. The taxable wage base is the first $7,000 of wages paid to each employee in a calendar year. Employers who

**HELPFUL HINT**

Both the employer and employee pay FICA taxes. Federal unemployment taxes and (in most states) the state unemployment taxes are borne entirely by the employer.

pay the state unemployment tax on a timely basis will receive an offset credit of up to 5.4%. Therefore, the net federal tax rate is generally 0.8% (6.2%–5.4%). This rate would equate to a maximum of $56 of federal tax per employee per year (.008 × $7,000). State tax rates are based on state law.

The **employer** bears the entire federal unemployment tax. There is no deduction or withholding from employees. Companies use the account Federal Unemployment Taxes Payable to recognize this liability. The federal unemployment tax for Academy Company for the January 14 payroll is $137.68 ($17,210.00 × 0.8%).

## State Unemployment Taxes

All states have unemployment compensation programs under state unemployment tax acts (SUTA). Like federal unemployment taxes, **state unemployment taxes** provide benefits to employees who lose their jobs. These taxes are levied on employers.[2] The basic rate is usually 5.4% on the first $7,000 of wages paid to an employee during the year. The state adjusts the basic rate according to the employer's experience rating: Companies with a history of stable employment may pay less than 5.4%. Companies with a history of unstable employment may pay more than the basic rate. Regardless of the rate paid, the company's credit on the federal unemployment tax is still 5.4%.

Companies use the account State Unemployment Taxes Payable for this liability. The state unemployment tax for Academy Company for the January 14 payroll is $929.34 ($17,210.00 × 5.4%). Illustration D-11 summarizes the types of employer payroll taxes.

**Illustration D-11**
Employer payroll taxes

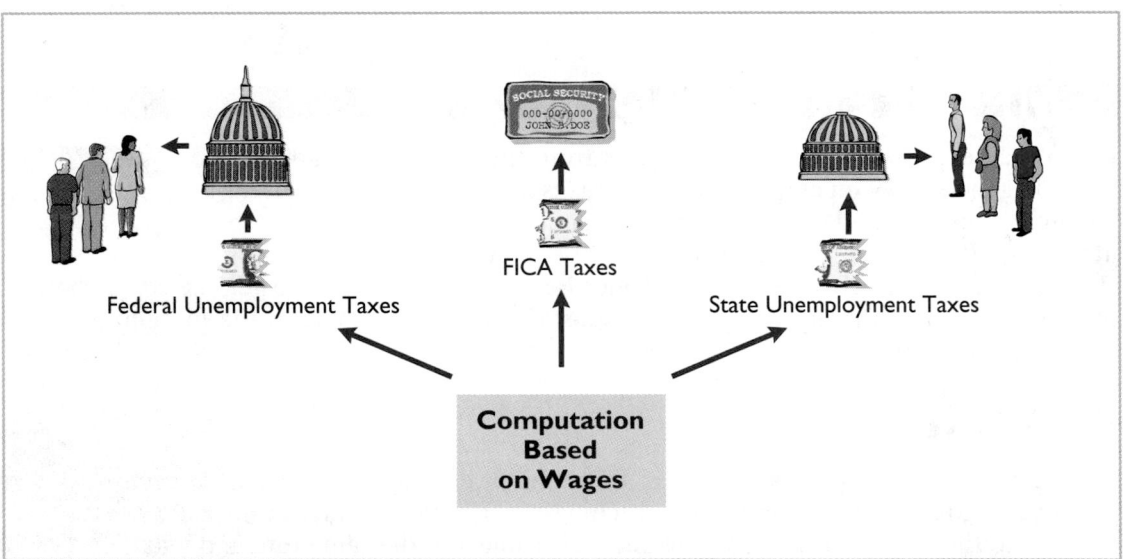

Federal Unemployment Taxes

FICA Taxes

State Unemployment Taxes

**Computation Based on Wages**

## Recording Employer Payroll Taxes

Companies usually record employer payroll taxes at the same time they record the payroll. The entire amount of gross pay ($17,210.00) shown in the payroll register in Illustration D-9 is subject to each of the three taxes mentioned above. Accordingly, Academy records the payroll tax expense associated with the January 14 payroll with the entry shown on page D13.

---

[2]In a few states, the employee is also required to make a contribution. *In this textbook, including the homework, we will assume that the tax is only on the employer.*

| Jan. 14 | Payroll Tax Expense | 2,443.82 | |
| | FICA Taxes Payable | | 1,376.80 |
| | Federal Unemployment Taxes Payable | | 137.68 |
| | State Unemployment Taxes Payable | | 929.34 |
| | (To record employer's payroll taxes on January 14 payroll) | | |

| A | = | L | + | SE |
|---|---|---|---|---|
| | | | | −2,443.82 Exp |
| | | +1,376.80 | | |
| | | +137.68 | | |
| | | +929.34 | | |

**Cash Flows**
no effect

Note that Academy uses separate liability accounts instead of a single credit to Payroll Taxes Payable. Why? Because these liabilities are payable to different taxing authorities at different dates. Companies classify the liability accounts in the balance sheet as current liabilities since they will be paid within the next year. They classify Payroll Tax Expense on the income statement as an operating expense.

## FILING AND REMITTING PAYROLL TAXES

Preparation of payroll tax returns is the responsibility of the payroll department. The treasurer's department makes the tax payment. Much of the information for the returns is obtained from employee earnings records.

For purposes of reporting and remitting to the IRS, the Company combines the FICA taxes and federal income taxes that it withheld. **Companies must report the taxes quarterly**, no later than one month following the close of each quarter. The remitting requirements depend on the amount of taxes withheld and the length of the pay period. Companies remit funds through deposits in either a Federal Reserve bank or an authorized commercial bank.

Companies generally file and remit federal unemployment taxes **annually** on or before January 31 of the subsequent year. Earlier payments are required when the tax exceeds a specified amount. Companies usually must file and pay state unemployment taxes by the **end of the month following each quarter**. When payroll taxes are paid, companies debit payroll liability accounts, and credit Cash.

Employers also must provide each employee with a **Wage and Tax Statement (Form W-2)** by January 31 following the end of a calendar year. This statement shows gross earnings, FICA taxes withheld, and income taxes withheld for the year. The required W-2 form for Michael Jordan, using assumed annual data, is shown in Illustration D-12. The employer must send a copy of each employee's

**Illustration D-12**
W-2 form

| Form **W-2 Wage and Tax Statement** | | | Calendar Year **2008** |
|---|---|---|---|
| 1 Control number | | OMB No. 1545-0008 | |

| 2 Employer's name, address and ZIP code | 3 Employer's identification number | 4 Employer's State number |
|---|---|---|
| Academy Company 19 Center St. Hampton, MI 48291 | 36-2167852 | |

| 5 Stat. employee | Deceased | Legal rep. | 942 emp. | Subtotal | Void |
|---|---|---|---|---|---|
| ☐ | ☐ | ☐ | ☐ | ☐ | ☐ |

| 6 Allocated tips | 7 Advance EIC payment |
|---|---|

| 8 Employee's social security number | 9 Federal income tax withheld | 10 Wages, tips, other compensation | 11 Social security tax withheld |
|---|---|---|---|
| 329-36-9547 | $2,248.00 | $26,300.00 | $2,104.00 |

| 12 Employee's name, address, and ZIP code | 13 Social security wages | 14 Social security tips |
|---|---|---|
| | $26,300.00 | |

| 16 | | |
|---|---|---|
| Michael Jordan 2345 Mifflin Ave. Hampton, MI 48292 | | |

| 17 State income tax | 18 State wages, tips, etc. | 19 Name of State |
|---|---|---|
| $526.00 | | Michigan |

| 20 Local income tax | 21 Local wages, tips, etc. | 22 Name of locality |
|---|---|---|

**HELPFUL HINT**

Employers generally transmit their W-2s to the government electronically. The taxing agencies store the information in their computer systems for subsequent comparison against earnings and taxes withheld reported on employees' income tax returns.

Wage and Tax Statement (Form W-2) to the Social Security Administration. This agency subsequently furnishes the Internal Revenue Service with the income data required.

## Before You Go On...

### REVIEW IT

1. What payroll taxes do governments levy on employers?
2. What accounts are involved in accruing employer payroll taxes?

### DO IT

In January, the payroll supervisor determines that gross earnings for Halo Company are $70,000. All earnings are subject to 8% FICA taxes, 5.4% state unemployment taxes, and 0.8% federal unemployment taxes. Halo asks you to record the employer's payroll taxes.

### Action Plan

- Compute the employer's payroll taxes on the period's gross earnings.
- Identify the expense account(s) to be debited.
- Identify the liability account(s) to be credited.

**Solution** The entry to record the employer's payroll taxes is:

| | | |
|---|---|---|
| Payroll Tax Expense | 9,940 | |
|   FICA Taxes Payable ($70,000 × 8%) | | 5,600 |
|   Federal Unemployment Taxes Payable ($70,000 × 0.8%) | | 560 |
|   State Unemployment Taxes Payable ($70,000 × 5.4%) | | 3,780 |
|     (To record employer's payroll taxes | | |
|     on January payroll) | | |

Related exercise material: *BED-2, BED-3, BED-4, ED-1, ED-2, ED-3, ED-4, and ED-5.*

## Demonstration Problem

Indiana Jones Company had the following selected transactions.

Feb. 1 Signs a $50,000, 6-month, 9%-interest-bearing note payable to CitiBank and receives $50,000 in cash.

   10 Cash register sales total $43,200, which includes an 8% sales tax.

   28 The payroll for the month consists of Sales Salaries $32,000 and Office Salaries $18,000. All wages are subject to 8% FICA taxes. A total of $8,900 federal income taxes are withheld. The salaries are paid on March 1.

   28 The following adjustment data are developed.

      1. Interest expense of $375 has been incurred on the note.

      2. Employer payroll taxes include 8% FICA taxes, a 5.4% state unemployment tax, and a 0.8% federal unemployment tax.

### Instructions

**(a)** Journalize the February transactions.
**(b)** Journalize the adjusting entries at February 28.

*Solution*

**action plan**

| | | | | |
|---|---|---|---|---|
| **(a)** Feb. 1 | Cash | | 50,000 | |
| | Notes Payable | | | 50,000 |
| | (Issued 6-month, 9%-interest-bearing note to CitiBank) | | | |
| 10 | Cash | | 43,200 | |
| | Sales ($43,200 ÷ 1.08) | | | 40,000 |
| | Sales Taxes Payable ($40,000 × 8%) | | | 3,200 |
| | (To record sales and sales taxes payable) | | | |
| 28 | Sales Salaries Expense | | 32,000 | |
| | Office Salaries Expense | | 18,000 | |
| | FICA Taxes Payable (8% × $50,000) | | | 4,000 |
| | Federal Income Taxes Payable | | | 8,900 |
| | Salaries Payable | | | 37,100 |
| | (To record February salaries) | | | |
| **(b)** Feb. 28 | Interest Expense | | 375 | |
| | Interest Payable | | | 375 |
| | (To record accrued interest for February) | | | |
| 28 | Payroll Tax Expense | | 7,100 | |
| | FICA Taxes Payable | | | 4,000 |
| | Federal Unemployment Taxes Payable (0.8% × $50,000) | | | 400 |
| | State Unemployment Taxes Payable (5.4% × $50,000) | | | 2,700 |
| | (To record employer's payroll taxes on February payroll) | | | |

✔ To determine sales, divide the cash register total by 100% plus the sales tax percentage.

✔ Base payroll taxes on gross earnings.

---

## SUMMARY OF STUDY OBJECTIVES

1 **Discuss the objectives of internal control for payroll.** The objectives of internal control for payroll are (1) to safeguard company assets against unauthorized payments of payrolls, and (2) to ensure the accuracy and reliability of the accounting records pertaining to payrolls.

2 **Compute and record the payroll for a pay period.** The computation of the payroll involves gross earnings, payroll deductions, and net pay. In recording the payroll, Salaries (or Wages) Expense is debited for gross earnings, individual tax and other liability accounts are credited for payroll deductions, and Salaries (Wages) Payable is credited for net pay. When the payroll is paid, Salaries and Wages Payable is debited, and Cash is credited.

3 **Describe and record employer payroll taxes.** Employer payroll taxes consist of FICA, federal unemployment taxes, and state unemployment taxes. The taxes are usually accrued at the time the payroll is recorded by debiting Payroll Tax Expense and crediting separate liability accounts for each type of tax.

---

## GLOSSARY

**Bonus** Compensation to management personnel and other employees, based on factors such as increased sales or the amount of net income. (p. D4).

**Employee earnings record** A cumulative record of each employee's gross earnings, deductions, and net pay during the year. (p. D8).

**Employee's Withholding Allowance Certificate (Form W-4)** An Internal Revenue Service form on which the employee indicates the number of allowances claimed for withholding federal income taxes. (p. D6).

**Federal unemployment taxes** Taxes imposed on the employer that provide benefits for a limited time period to employees who lose their jobs through no fault of their own. (p. D11).

**Fees** Payments made for the services of professionals. (p. D1).

**FICA taxes** Taxes designed to provide workers with supplemental retirement, employment disability, and medical benefits. (p. D5).

**Gross earnings** Total compensation earned by an employee. (p. D4).

**Net pay** Gross earnings less payroll deductions. (p. D7).

**Payroll deductions** Deductions from gross earnings to determine the amount of a paycheck. (p. D5).

**Payroll register** A payroll record that accumulates the gross earnings, deductions, and net pay by employee for each pay period. (p. D8).

**Salaries** Specified amount per month or per year paid to managerial, administrative, and sales personnel. (p. D1).

**Statement of earnings** A document attached to a paycheck that indicates the employee's gross earnings, payroll deductions, and net pay. (p. D10).

**State unemployment taxes** Taxes imposed on the employer that provide benefits to employees who lose their jobs. (p. D12).

**Wage and Tax Statement (Form W-2)** A form showing gross earnings, FICA taxes withheld, and income taxes withheld which is prepared annually by an employer for each employee. (p. D13).

**Wages** Amounts paid to employees based on a rate per hour or on a piece-work basis. (p. D1).

# SELF-STUDY QUESTIONS

*Answers are at the end of the appendix.*

(SO 1) **1.** The department that should pay the payroll is the:
  **a.** timekeeping department.
  **b.** human resources department.
  **c.** payroll department.
  **d.** treasurer's department.

(SO 2) **2.** J. Barr earns $14 per hour for a 40-hour week and $21 per hour for any overtime work. If Barr works 45 hours in a week, gross earnings are:
  **a.** $560.
  **b.** $630.
  **c.** $650.
  **d.** $665.

**3.** Employer payroll taxes do *not* include:  (SO 3)
  **a.** federal unemployment taxes.
  **b.** state unemployment taxes.
  **c.** federal income taxes.
  **d.** FICA taxes.

Go to the book's website,
**www.wiley.com/college/weygandt**,
for Additional Self-Study questions.

# QUESTIONS

**1.** You are a newly hired accountant with Schindlebeck Company. On your first day, the controller asks you to identify the main internal control objectives related to payroll accounting. How would you respond?

**2.** What are the four functions associated with payroll activities?

**3.** What is the difference between gross pay and net pay? Which amount should a company record as wages or salaries expense?

**4.** Which payroll tax is levied on both employers and employees?

**5.** Are the federal and state income taxes withheld from employee paychecks a payroll tax expense for the employer? Explain your answer.

**6.** What do the following acronyms stand for: FICA, FUTA, and SUTA?

**7.** What information is shown on a W-4 statement? On a W-2 statement?

**8.** Distinguish between the two types of payroll deductions and give examples of each.

**9.** What are the primary uses of the employee earnings record?

**10.** (a) Identify the three types of employer payroll taxes. (b) How are tax liability accounts and Payroll Tax Expense classified in the financial statements?

# BRIEF EXERCISES

*Identify payroll functions.*
(SO 1)

**BED-1** Hernandez Company has the following payroll procedures.
  **(a)** Supervisor approves overtime work.
  **(b)** The human resources department prepares hiring authorization forms for new hires.
  **(c)** A second payroll department employee verifies payroll calculations.
  **(d)** The treasurer's department pays employees.

Identify the payroll function to which each procedure pertains.

**BED-2** Sandy Teter's regular hourly wage rate is $16, and she receives an hourly rate of $24 for work in excess of 40 hours. During a January pay period, Sandy works 45 hours. Sandy's federal income tax withholding is $95, and she has no voluntary deductions. Compute Sandy Teter's gross earnings and net pay for the pay period.

*Compute gross earnings and net pay.*

*(SO 2)*

**BED-3** Data for Sandy Teter are presented in BED-2. Prepare the journal entries to record **(a)** Sandy's pay for the period and **(b)** the payment of Sandy's wages. Use January 15 for the end of the pay period and the payment date.

*Record a payroll and the payment of wages.*

*(SO 2)*

**BED-4** In January, gross earnings in Yoon Company totaled $90,000. All earnings are subject to 8% FICA taxes, 5.4% state unemployment taxes, and 0.8% federal unemployment taxes. Prepare the entry to record January payroll tax expense.

*Record employer payroll taxes.*

*(SO 3)*

# EXERCISES

**ED-1** Betty Williams' regular hourly wage rate is $14, and she receives a wage of 1½ times the regular hourly rate for work in excess of 40 hours. During a March weekly pay period Betty worked 42 hours. Her gross earnings prior to the current week were $6,000. Betty is married and claims three withholding allowances. Her only voluntary deduction is for group hospitalization insurance at $15 per week.

*Compute net pay and record pay for one employee.*

*(SO 2)*

**Instructions**
**(a)** Compute the following amounts for Betty's wages for the current week.
    **(1)** Gross earnings.
    **(2)** FICA taxes. (Assume an 8% rate on maximum of $97,500.)
    **(3)** Federal income taxes withheld. (Use the withholding table in the text, page D7.)
    **(4)** State income taxes withheld. (Assume a 2.0% rate.)
    **(5)** Net pay.
**(b)** Record Betty's pay, assuming she is an office computer operator.

**ED-2** Employee earnings records for Brantley Company reveal the following gross earnings for four employees through the pay period of December 15.

*Compute maximum FICA deductions.*

*(SO 2)*

| | | | |
|---|---|---|---|
| C. Mays | $83,500 | D. Delgado | $95,700 |
| L. Jeter | $95,200 | T. Rolen | $97,500 |

For the pay period ending December 31, each employee's gross earnings is $3,000. Employees are required to pay a FICA tax rate of 8% gross earnings of $97,500.

**Instructions**
Compute the FICA withholdings that should be made for each employee for the December 31 pay period. (Show computations.)

**ED-3** Piniella Company has the following data for the weekly payroll ending January 31.

*Prepare payroll register and record payroll and payroll tax expense.*

*(SO 2, 3)*

| | | | Hours | | | | Hourly | Federal Income Tax | Health |
|---|---|---|---|---|---|---|---|---|---|
| **Employee** | **M** | **T** | **W** | **T** | **F** | **S** | **Rate** | **Withholding** | **Insurance** |
| M. Hindi | 8 | 8 | 9 | 8 | 10 | 3 | $11 | $34 | $10 |
| E. Benson | 8 | 8 | 8 | 8 | 8 | 2 | 13 | 37 | 15 |
| K. Estes | 9 | 10 | 8 | 8 | 9 | 0 | 14 | 58 | 15 |

Employees are paid 1½ times the regular hourly rate for all hours worked in excess of 40 hours per week. FICA taxes are 8% on the first $97,500 of gross earnings. Piniella Company is subject to 5.4% state unemployment taxes on the first $9,800 and 0.8% federal unemployment taxes on the first $7,000 of gross earnings.

**Instructions**
**(a)** Prepare the payroll register for the weekly payroll.
**(b)** Prepare the journal entries to record the payroll and Piniella's payroll tax expense.

*Compute missing payroll amounts and record payroll.*

*(SO 2)*

**ED-4** Selected data from a February payroll register for Landmark Company are presented below. Some amounts are intentionally omitted.

| Gross earnings: | | State income taxes | $(3) |
|---|---|---|---|
| Regular | $8,900 | | |
| Overtime | (1) | Union dues | 100 |
| Total | (2) | Total deductions | (4) |
| Deductions: | | Net pay | $7,215 |
| FICA taxes | $ 760 | Accounts debited: | |
| Federal income taxes | 1,140 | Warehouse wages | (5) |
| | | Store wages | $4,000 |

FICA taxes are 8%. State income taxes are 3% of gross earnings.

**Instructions**
**(a)** Fill in the missing amounts.
**(b)** Journalize the February payroll and the payment of the payroll.

*Determine employer's payroll taxes; record payroll tax expense.*

*(SO 3)*

**ED-5** According to a payroll register summary of Cruz Company, the amount of employees' gross pay in December was $850,000, of which $70,000 was not subject to FICA tax and $760,000 was not subject to state and federal unemployment taxes.

**Instructions**
**(a)** Determine the employer's payroll tax expense for the month, using the following rates: FICA 8%, state unemployment 5.4%, federal unemployment 0.8%.
**(b)** Prepare the journal entry to record December payroll tax expense.

# EXERCISES: SET B

Visit the book's website at **www.wiley.com/college/weygandt**, and choose the Student Companion site, to access Exercise Set B.

# PROBLEMS: SET A

*Identify internal control weaknesses and make recommendations for improvement.*

*(SO 1)*

**PD-1A** The payroll procedures used by three different companies are described below.

1. In Brewer Company each employee is required to mark on a clock card the hours worked. At the end of each pay period, the employee must have this clock card approved by the department manager. The approved card is then given to the payroll department by the employee. Subsequently, the treasurer's department pays the employee by check.

2. In Hilyard Computer Company clock cards and time clocks are used. At the end of each pay period, the department manager initials the cards, indicates the rates of pay, and sends them to payroll. A payroll register is prepared from the cards by the payroll department. Cash equal to the total net pay in each department is given to the department manager, who pays the employees in cash.

3. In Hyun-chan Company employees are required to record hours worked by "punching" clock cards in a time clock. At the end of each pay period, the clock cards are collected by the department manager. The manager prepares a payroll register in duplicate and forwards the original to payroll. In payroll, the summaries are checked for mathematical accuracy, and a payroll supervisor pays each employee by check.

**Instructions**
**(a)** ━━━━▶ Indicate the weakness(es) in internal control in each company.
**(b)** For each weakness, describe the control procedure(s) that will provide effective internal control. Use the following format for your answer:

**(a) Weaknesses**  **(b) Recommended Procedures**

**PD-2A**    Graves Drug Store has four employees who are paid on an hourly basis plus time-and-a-half for all hours worked in excess of 40 a week. Payroll data for the week ended February 15, 2008, are presented below.

*Prepare payroll register and payroll entries.*

(SO 2, 3)

| Employees | Hours Worked | Hourly Rate | Federal Income Tax Withholdings | United Way |
|---|---|---|---|---|
| L. Leiss | 39 | $14.00 | $ ? | $–0– |
| S. Bjork | 42 | $12.00 | ? | 5.00 |
| M. Cape | 44 | $12.00 | 61 | 7.50 |
| L. Wild | 48 | $12.00 | 52 | 5.00 |

Leiss and Bjork are married. They claim 2 and 4 withholding allowances, respectively. The following tax rates are applicable: FICA 8%, state income taxes 3%, state unemployment taxes 5.4%, and federal unemployment 0.8%. The first three employees are sales clerks (store wages expense). The fourth employee performs administrative duties (office wages expense).

**Instructions**
**(a)** Prepare a payroll register for the weekly payroll. (Use the wage-bracket withholding table in the text for federal income tax withholdings.)
**(b)** Journalize the payroll on February 15, 2008, and the accrual of employer payroll taxes.
**(c)** Journalize the payment of the payroll on February 16, 2008.
**(d)** Journalize the deposit in a Federal Reserve bank on February 28, 2008, of the FICA and federal income taxes payable to the government.

(a) Net pay $1,786.32; Store wages expense $1,614.00

(b) Payroll tax expense $317.79

**PD-3A**    The following payroll liability accounts are included in the ledger of Eikleberry Company on January 1, 2008.

*Journalize payroll transactions and adjusting entries.*

(SO 2, 3)

| | |
|---|---|
| FICA Taxes Payable | $ 662.20 |
| Federal Income Taxes Payable | 1,254.60 |
| State Income Taxes Payable | 102.15 |
| Federal Unemployment Taxes Payable | 312.00 |
| State Unemployment Taxes Payable | 1,954.40 |
| Union Dues Payable | 250.00 |
| U.S. Savings Bonds Payable | 350.00 |

In January, the following transactions occurred.

Jan. 10    Sent check for $250.00 to union treasurer for union dues.
    12    Deposited check for $1,916.80 in Federal Reserve bank for FICA taxes and federal income taxes withheld.
    15    Purchased U.S. Savings Bonds for employees by writing check for $350.00.
    17    Paid state income taxes withheld from employees.
    20    Paid federal and state unemployment taxes.
    31    Completed monthly payroll register, which shows office salaries $17,600, store wages $27,400, FICA taxes withheld $3,600, federal income taxes payable $1,770, state income taxes payable $360, union dues payable $400, United Fund contributions payable $1,800, and net pay $37,070.
    31    Prepared payroll checks for the net pay and distributed checks to employees.

At January 31, the company also makes the following accrual for employer payroll taxes: FICA taxes 8%, state unemployment taxes 5.4%, and federal unemployment taxes 0.8%.

**Instructions**
**(a)** Journalize the January transactions.
**(b)** Journalize the adjustments pertaining to employee compensation at January 31.

(b) Payroll tax expense $6,390.00

*Prepare entries for payroll and payroll taxes; prepare W-2 data.*
(SO 2, 3)

**PD-4A** For the year ended December 31, 2008, R. Visnak Company reports the following summary payroll data.

| Gross earnings: | |
| --- | --- |
| Administrative salaries | $180,000 |
| Electricians' wages | 320,000 |
| Total | $500,000 |
| Deductions: | |
| FICA taxes | $ 35,200 |
| Federal income taxes withheld | 153,000 |
| State income taxes withheld (2.6%) | 13,000 |
| United Way contributions payable | 25,000 |
| *Hospital insurance premiums | 15,800 |
| Total | $242,000 |

R. Visnak Company's payroll taxes are: FICA 8%, state unemployment 2.5% (due to a stable employment record), and 0.8% federal unemployment. Gross earnings subject to FICA taxes total $440,000, and unemployment taxes total $110,000.

**Instructions**

(a) Wages Payable $258,000
(b) Payroll tax expense
   $38,830

**(a)** Prepare a summary journal entry at December 31 for the full year's payroll.
**(b)** Journalize the adjusting entry at December 31 to record the employer's payroll taxes.
**(c)** The W-2 Wage and Tax Statement requires the following dollar data.

| Wages, Tips, Other Compensation | Federal Income Tax Withheld | State Income Tax Withheld | FICA Wages | FICA Tax Withheld |
| --- | --- | --- | --- | --- |

Complete the required data for the following employees.

| Employee | Gross Earnings | Federal Income Tax Withheld |
| --- | --- | --- |
| R. Lopez | $60,000 | $27,500 |
| K. Kirk | 27,000 | 11,000 |

# PROBLEMS: SET B

*Identify internal control weaknesses and make recommendations for improvement.*
(SO 1)

**PD-1B** Selected payroll procedures of Wallace Company are described below.

1. Department managers interview applicants and on the basis of the interview either hire or reject the applicants. When an applicant is hired, the applicant fills out a W-4 form (Employee's Withholding Allowance Certificate). One copy of the form is sent to the human resources department, and one copy is sent to the payroll department as notice that the individual has been hired. On the copy of the W-4 sent to payroll, the managers manually indicate the hourly pay rate for the new hire.
2. The payroll checks are manually signed by the chief accountant and given to the department managers for distribution to employees in their department. The managers are responsible for seeing that any absent employees receive their checks.
3. There are two clerks in the payroll department. The payroll is divided alphabetically; one clerk has employees A to L and the other has employees M to Z. Each clerk computes the gross earnings, deductions, and net pay for employees in the section and posts the data to the employee earnings records.

**Instructions**
**(a)** ▬▬▶ Indicate the weaknesses in internal control.
**(b)** For each weakness, describe the control procedures that will provide effective internal control. Use the following format for your answer:

**(a) Weaknesses**      **(b) Recommended Procedures**

**PD-2B**   Lee Hardware has four employees who are paid on an hourly basis plus time-and-a half for all hours worked in excess of 40 a week. Payroll data for the week ended March 15, 2008, are presented below.

*Prepare payroll register and payroll entries.*
(SO 2, 3)

| Employee | Hours Worked | Hourly Rate | Federal Income Tax Withholdings | United Way |
|---|---|---|---|---|
| Joe Coomer | 40 | $15.00 | $? | $5.00 |
| Mary Walker | 42 | 13.00 | ? | 5.00 |
| Andy Dye | 44 | 13.00 | 60 | 8.00 |
| Kim Shen | 48 | 13.00 | 67 | 5.00 |

Coomer and Walker are married. They claim 0 and 4 withholding allowances, respectively. The following tax rates are applicable: FICA 8%, state income taxes 3%, state unemployment taxes 5.4%, and federal unemployment 0.8%. The first three employees are sales clerks (store wages expense). The fourth employee performs administrative duties (office wages expense).

**Instructions**

**(a)** Prepare a payroll register for the weekly payroll. (Use the wage-bracket withholding table in the text for federal income tax withholdings.)

**(b)** Journalize the payroll on March 15, 2008, and the accrual of employer payroll taxes.

**(c)** Journalize the payment of the payroll on March 16, 2008.

**(d)** Journalize the deposit in a Federal Reserve bank on March 31, 2008, of the FICA and federal income taxes payable to the government.

(a) Net pay $1,910.37; Store wages expense $1,757
(b) Payroll tax expense $345.48

**PD-3B**   The following payroll liability accounts are included in the ledger of Nordlund Company on January 1, 2008.

*Journalize payroll transactions and adjusting entries.*
(SO 2, 3)

| | |
|---|---|
| FICA Taxes Payable | $   760.00 |
| Federal Income Taxes Payable | 1,204.60 |
| State Income Taxes Payable | 108.95 |
| Federal Unemployment Taxes Payable | 288.95 |
| State Unemployment Taxes Payable | 1,954.40 |
| Union Dues Payable | 870.00 |
| U.S. Savings Bonds Payable | 360.00 |

In January, the following transactions occurred.

Jan. 10   Sent check for $870.00 to union treasurer for union dues.

12   Deposited check for $1,964.60 in Federal Reserve bank for FICA taxes and federal income taxes withheld.

15   Purchased U.S. Savings Bonds for employees by writing check for $360.00.

17   Paid state income taxes withheld from employees.

20   Paid federal and state unemployment taxes.

31   Completed monthly payroll register, which shows office salaries $21,600, store wages $28,400, FICA taxes withheld $4,000, federal income taxes payable $1,958, state income taxes payable $414, union dues payable $400, United Fund contributions payable $1,888, and net pay $41,340.

31   Prepared payroll checks for the net pay and distributed checks to employees.

At January 31, the company also makes the following accrued adjustment for employer payroll taxes: FICA taxes 8%, federal unemployment taxes 0.8%, and state unemployment taxes 5.4%.

**Instructions**

**(a)** Journalize the January transactions.

**(b)** Journalize the adjustments pertaining to employee compensation at January 31.

(b) Payroll tax expense $7,100

*Prepare entries for payroll and payroll taxes; prepare W-2 data.*

(SO 2, 3)

**PD-4B** For the year ended December 31, 2008, Niehaus Electrical Repair Company reports the following summary payroll data.

| Gross earnings: | |
| --- | --- |
| Administrative salaries | $180,000 |
| Electricians' wages | 370,000 |
| Total | $550,000 |

| Deductions: | |
| --- | --- |
| FICA taxes | $ 38,000 |
| Federal income taxes withheld | 168,000 |
| State income taxes withheld (2.6%) | 14,300 |
| United Way contributions payable | 27,500 |
| *Hospital insurance premiums | 17,200 |
| Total | $265,000 |

Niehaus Company's payroll taxes are: FICA 8%, state unemployment 2.5% (due to a stable employment record), and 0.8% federal unemployment. Gross earnings subject to FICA taxes total $475,000, and unemployment taxes total $125,000.

**Instructions**

(a) Wages payable $285,000

(b) Payroll tax expense $42,125

**(a)** Prepare a summary journal entry at December 31 for the full year's payroll.

**(b)** Journalize the adjusting entry at December 31 to record the employer's payroll taxes.

**(c)** The W-2 Wage and Tax Statement requires the following dollar data.

| Wages, Tips, Other Compensation | Federal Income Tax Withheld | State Income Tax Withheld | FICA Wages | FICA Tax Withheld |
| --- | --- | --- | --- | --- |

Complete the required data for the following employees.

| Employee | Gross Earnings | Federal Income Tax Withheld |
| --- | --- | --- |
| Anna Hashmi | $59,000 | $28,500 |
| Sharon Bishop | 26,000 | 10,200 |

# PROBLEMS: SET C

Visit the book's website at **www.wiley.com/college/weygandt**, and choose the Student Companion site, to access Problem Set C.

# BROADENING YOUR PERSPECTIVE

## FINANCIAL REPORTING AND ANALYSIS

## Exploring the Web

**BYPD-1** The Internal Revenue Service provides considerable information over the Internet. The following demonstrates how useful one of its sites is in answering payroll tax questions faced by employers.

**Address: www.irs.ustreas.gov/formspubs/index.html,** or go to **www.wiley.com/college/weygandt**

**Steps**

1. Go to the site shown above.
2. Choose **View Online, Tax Publications**.
3. Choose **Publication 15, Circular E, Employer's Tax Guide**.

**Instructions**

Answer each of the following questions.

**(a)** How does the government define "employees"?

**(b)** What are the special rules for Social Security and Medicare regarding children who are employed by their parents?

**(c)** How can an employee obtain a Social Security card if he or she doesn't have one?

**(d)** Must employees report to their employer tips received from customers? If so, what is the process?

**(e)** Where should the employer deposit Social Security taxes withheld or contributed?

## CRITICAL THINKING

# Decision Making Across the Organization

**BYPD-2** Summerville Processing Company provides word-processing services for business clients and students in a university community. The work for business clients is fairly steady throughout the year. The work for students peaks significantly in December and May as a result of term papers, research project reports, and dissertations.

Two years ago, the company attempted to meet the peak demand by hiring part-time help. However, this led to numerous errors and considerable customer dissatisfaction. A year ago, the company hired four experienced employees on a permanent basis instead of using part-time help. This proved to be much better in terms of productivity and customer satisfaction. But, it has caused an increase in annual payroll costs and a significant decline in annual net income.

Recently, Valarie Flynn, a sales representative of Davidson Services Inc., has made a proposal to the company. Under her plan, Davidson Services will provide up to four experienced workers at a daily rate of $80 per person for an 8-hour workday. Davidson workers are not available on an hourly basis. Summerville Processing would have to pay only the daily rate for the workers used.

The owner of Summerville Processing, Nancy Bell, asks you, as the company's accountant, to prepare a report on the expenses that are pertinent to the decision. If the Davidson plan is adopted, Nancy will terminate the employment of two permanent employees and will keep two permanent employees. At the moment, each employee earns an annual income of $22,000. Summerville Processing pays 8% FICA taxes, 0.8% federal unemployment taxes, and 5.4% state unemployment taxes. The unemployment taxes apply to only the first $7,000 of gross earnings. In addition, Summerville Processing pays $40 per month for each employee for medical and dental insurance.

Nancy indicates that if the Davidson Services plan is accepted, her needs for workers will be as follows.

| Months | Number | Working Days per Month |
|---|---|---|
| January–March | 2 | 20 |
| April–May | 3 | 25 |
| June–October | 2 | 18 |
| November–December | 3 | 23 |

**Instructions**

With the class divided into groups, answer the following.

**(a)** Prepare a report showing the comparative payroll expense of continuing to employ permanent workers compared to adopting the Davidson Services Inc. plan.

**(b)** What other factors should Nancy consider before finalizing her decision?

# Communication Activity

**BYPD-3** Ivan Blanco, president of the Blue Sky Company, has recently hired a number of additional employees. He recognizes that additional payroll taxes will be due as a result of this hiring, and that the company will serve as the collection agent for other taxes.

**Instructions**
In a memorandum to Ivan Blanco, explain each of the taxes, and identify the taxes that result in payroll tax expense to Blue Sky Company.

# Ethics Case

**BYPD-4** Johnny Fuller owns and manages Johnny's Restaurant, a 24-hour restaurant near the city's medical complex. Johnny employs 9 full-time employees and 16 part-time employees. He pays all of the full-time employees by check, the amounts of which are determined by Johnny's public accountant, Mary Lake. Johnny pays all of his part-time employees in cash. He computes their wages and withdraws the cash directly from his cash register.

Mary has repeatedly urged Johnny to pay all employees by check. But as Johnny has told his competitor and friend, Steve Hill, who owns the Greasy Diner, "First of all, my part-time employees prefer the cash over a check, and secondly I don't withhold or pay any taxes or workmen's compensation insurance on those wages because they go totally unrecorded and unnoticed."

**Instructions**
**(a)** Who are the stakeholders in this situation?
**(b)** What are the legal and ethical considerations regarding Johnny's handling of his payroll?
**(c)** Mary Lake is aware of Johnny's payment of the part-time payroll in cash. What are her ethical responsibilities in this case?
**(d)** What internal control principle is violated in this payroll process?

## Answers to Self-Study Questions
**1.** d   **2.** d   **3.** c

# Appendix E

# Subsidiary Ledgers and Special Journals

## STUDY OBJECTIVES

*After studying this appendix, you should be able to:*

1. Describe the nature and purpose of a subsidiary ledger.
2. Explain how companies use special journals in journalizing.
3. Indicate how companies post a multi-column journal.

## SECTION 1 Expanding the Ledger—Subsidiary Ledgers

## NATURE AND PURPOSE OF SUBSIDIARY LEDGERS

Imagine a business that has several thousand charge (credit) customers and shows the transactions with these customers in only one general ledger account—Accounts Receivable. It would be nearly impossible to determine the balance owed by an individual customer at any specific time. Similarly, the amount payable to one creditor would be difficult to locate quickly from a single Accounts Payable account in the general ledger.

> **STUDY OBJECTIVE 1**
>
> Describe the nature and purpose of a subsidiary ledger.

Instead, companies use subsidiary ledgers to keep track of individual balances. A **subsidiary ledger** is a group of accounts with a common characteristic (for example, all accounts receivable). It is an addition to, and an expansion of, the general ledger. The subsidiary ledger frees the general ledger from the details of individual balances.

Two common subsidiary ledgers are:

1. The **accounts receivable** (or **customers'**) **subsidiary ledger**, which collects transaction data of individual customers.

2. The **accounts payable** (or **creditors'**) **subsidiary ledger**, which collects transaction data of individual creditors.

In each of these subsidiary ledgers, companies usually arrange individual accounts in alphabetical order.

A general ledger account summarizes the detailed data from a subsidiary ledger. For example, the detailed data from the accounts receivable subsidiary ledger are summarized in Accounts Receivable in the general ledger. The general ledger account that summarizes subsidiary ledger data is called a **control account**. Illustration E-1 (page E2) presents an overview of the relationship of subsidiary ledgers to the general ledger. There, the general ledger control accounts and subsidiary ledger accounts are in green. Note that cash and owner's capital in this illustration are not control accounts because there are no subsidiary ledger accounts related to these accounts.

**At the end of an accounting period, each general ledger control account balance must equal the composite balance of the individual accounts in the related subsidiary ledger.** For example, the balance in Accounts Payable in Illustration E-1 must equal the total of the subsidiary balances of Creditors X + Y + Z.

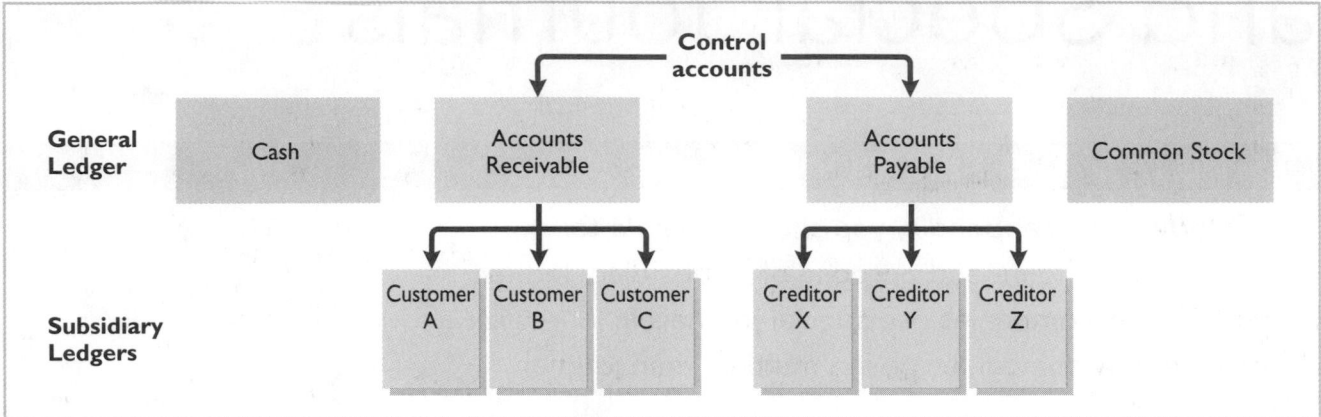

**Illustration E-1**
Relationship of general ledger and subsidiary ledgers

## Subsidiary Ledger Example

Illustration E-2 provides an example of a control account and subsidiary ledger for Pujols Enterprises. (Due to space considerations, the explanation column in these accounts is not shown in this and subsequent illustrations.) Illustration E-2 is based on the transactions listed in Illustration E-3 (next page).

**Illustration E-2**
Relationship between general and subsidiary ledgers

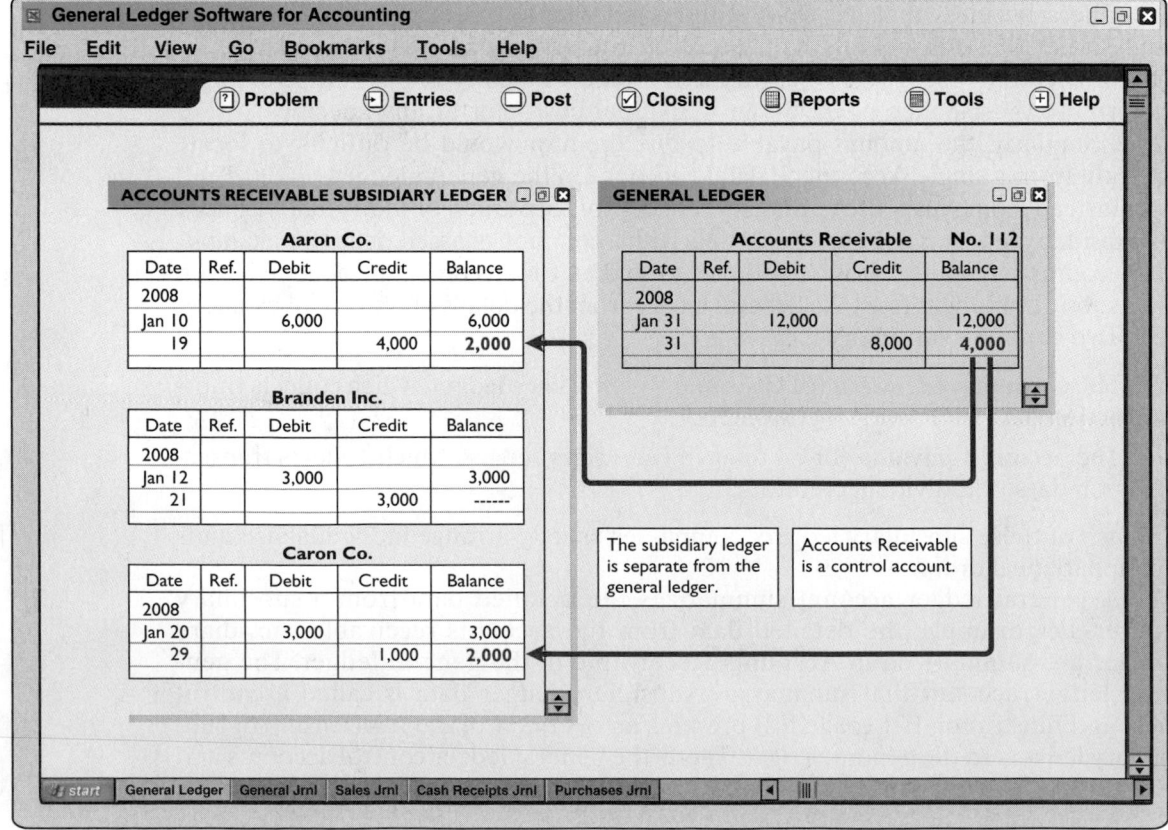

| Credit Sales | | | Collections on Account | | |
|---|---|---|---|---|---|
| Jan. 10 | Aaron Co. | $ 6,000 | Jan. 19 | Aaron Co. | $ 4,000 |
| 12 | Branden Inc. | 3,000 | 21 | Branden Inc. | 3,000 |
| 20 | Caron Co. | 3,000 | 29 | Caron Co. | 1,000 |
| | | $12,000 | | | $ 8,000 |

**Illustration E-3**
Sales and collection transactions

Pujols can reconcile the total debits ($12,000) and credits ($8,000) in Accounts Receivable in the general ledger to the detailed debits and credits in the subsidiary accounts. Also, the balance of $4,000 in the control account agrees with the total of the balances in the individual accounts (Aaron Co. $2,000 + Branden Inc. $0 + Caron Co. $2,000) in the subsidiary ledger.

As Illustration E-2 shows, companies make monthly postings to the control accounts in the general ledger. This practice allows them to prepare monthly financial statements. Companies post to the individual accounts in the subsidiary ledger daily. Daily posting ensures that account information is current. This enables the company to monitor credit limits, bill customers, and answer inquiries from customers about their account balances.

## Advantages of Subsidiary Ledgers

Subsidiary ledgers have several advantages:

1. **They show in a single account transactions affecting one customer or one creditor**, thus providing up-to-date information on specific account balances.
2. **They free the general ledger of excessive details.** As a result, a trial balance of the general ledger does not contain vast numbers of individual account balances.
3. **They help locate errors in individual accounts** by reducing the number of accounts in one ledger and by using control accounts.
4. **They make possible a division of labor** in posting. One employee can post to the general ledger while someone else posts to the subsidiary ledgers.

## Before You Go On...

### REVIEW IT

1. What is a subsidiary ledger, and what purpose does it serve?
2. What is a control account, and what purpose does it serve?
3. Name two general ledger accounts that may act as control accounts for a subsidiary ledger. Can you think of a third control account?

### DO IT

Presented below is information related to Sims Company for its first month of operations. Determine the balances that appear in the accounts payable subsidiary ledger. What Accounts Payable balance appears in the general ledger at the end of January?

| Credit Purchases | | | Cash Paid | | |
|---|---|---|---|---|---|
| Jan. 5 | Devon Co. | $11,000 | Jan. 9 | Devon Co. | $7,000 |
| 11 | Shelby Co. | 7,000 | 14 | Shelby Co. | 2,000 |
| 22 | Taylor Co. | 14,000 | 27 | Taylor Co. | 9,000 |

### Action Plan

- Subtract cash paid from credit purchases to determine the balances in the accounts payable subsidiary ledger.
- Sum the individual balances to determine the Accounts Payable balance.

**Solution** Subsidiary ledger balances:
Devon Co. $4,000 ($11,000 − $7,000)
Shelby Co. $5,000 ($7,000 − $2,000)
Taylor Co. $5,000 ($14,000 − $9,000).
General ledger Accounts Payable balance: $14,000 ($4,000 + $5,000 + $5,000).

Related exercise material: *BEE-4, BEE-5, EE-1, EE-2, EE-4, and EE-5.*

# SECTION 2 Expanding the Journal—Special Journals

**STUDY OBJECTIVE 2**

Explain how companies use special journals in journalizing.

So far you have learned to journalize transactions in a two-column general journal and post each entry to the general ledger. This procedure is satisfactory in only the very smallest companies. To expedite journalizing and posting, most companies use special journals **in addition to the general journal**.

Companies use special journals to record similar types of transactions. Examples are all sales of merchandise on account, or all cash receipts. The types of transactions that occur frequently in a company determine what special journals the company uses. Most merchandising enterprises record daily transactions using the journals shown in Illustration E-4.

**Illustration E-4**
Use of special journals and the general journal

| **Sales Journal** | **Cash Receipts Journal** | **Purchases Journal** | **Cash Payments Journal** | **General Journal** |
|---|---|---|---|---|
| Used for: | Used for: | Used for: | Used for: | Used for: |
| All sales of merchandise on account | All cash received (including cash sales) | All purchases of merchandise on account | All cash paid (including cash purchases) | Transactions that cannot be entered in a special journal, including correcting, adjusting, and closing entries |

**If a transaction cannot be recorded in a special journal, the company records it in the general journal.** For example, if a company had special journals for only the four types of transactions listed above, it would record purchase returns and allowances in the general journal. Similarly, **correcting, adjusting, and closing entries are recorded in the general journal**. In some situations, companies might use special journals other than those listed above. For example, when sales returns and allowances are frequent, a company might use a special journal to record these transactions.

Special journals **permit greater division of labor** because several people can record entries in different journals at the same time. For example, one employee may journalize all cash receipts, and another may journalize all credit sales. Also, the use of special journals **reduces the time needed to complete the posting process**. With special journals, companies may post some accounts monthly, instead of daily, as we will illustrate later in the chapter. On the following pages, we discuss the four special journals shown in Illustration E-4.

# SALES JOURNAL

In the **sales journal**, companies record **sales of merchandise on account**. Cash sales of merchandise go in the cash receipts journal. Credit sales of assets other than merchandise go in the general journal.

## Journalizing Credit Sales

To demonstrate use of a sales journal, we will use data for Karns Wholesale Supply, which uses a **perpetual inventory system**. Under this system, each entry in the sales journal results in one entry **at selling price** and another entry **at cost**. The entry at selling price is a debit to Accounts Receivable (a control account) and a credit of equal amount to Sales. The entry at cost is a debit to Cost of Goods Sold and a credit of equal amount to Merchandise Inventory (a control account). Using a sales journal with two amount columns, the company can show on only one line a sales transaction at both selling price and cost. Illustration E-5 shows this two-column sales journal of Karns Wholesale Supply, using assumed credit sales transactions (for sales invoices 101–107).

**HELPFUL HINT**

Postings are also made daily to individual ledger accounts in the inventory subsidiary ledger to maintain a perpetual inventory.

**Illustration E-5**
Journalizing the sales journal—perpetual inventory system

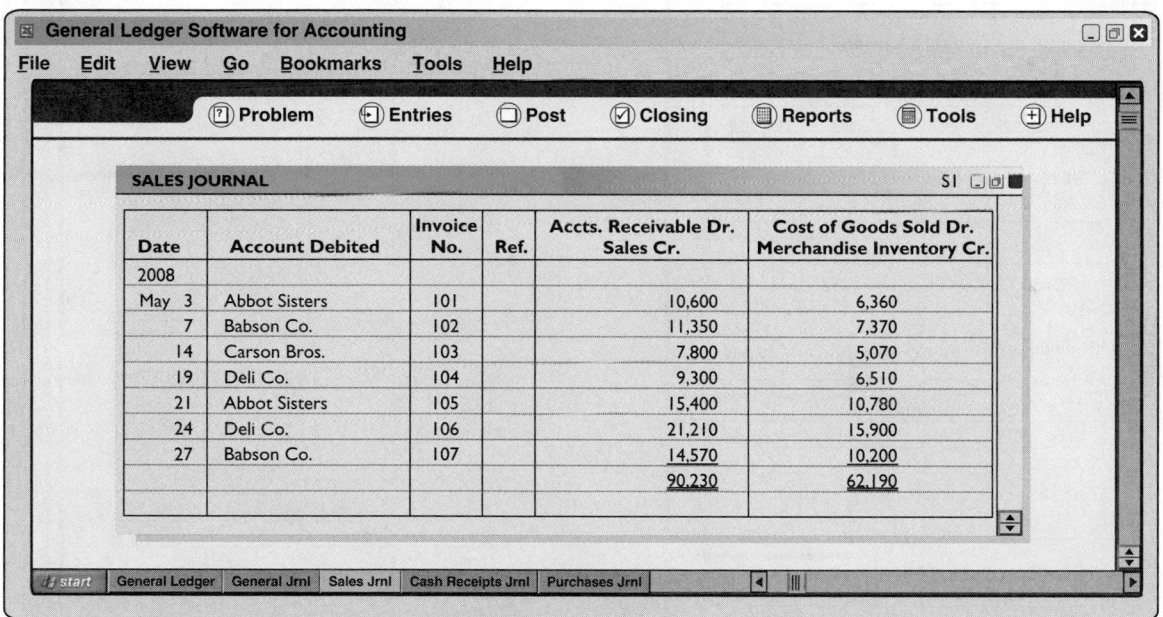

Note several points: Unlike the general journal, an explanation is not required for each entry in a special journal. Also, use of prenumbered invoices ensures that all invoices are journalized. Finally, the reference (Ref.) column is not used in journalizing. It is used in posting the sales journal, as explained next.

## Posting the Sales Journal

Companies make daily postings from the sales journal **to the individual accounts receivable** in the subsidiary ledger. Posting **to the general ledger** is done **monthly**. Illustration E-6 (page E6) shows both the daily and monthly postings.

A check mark (✓) is inserted in the reference posting column to indicate that the daily posting to the customer's account has been made. If the subsidiary ledger accounts were numbered, the account number would be entered in place of the check mark. At the end of the month, Karns posts the column totals of the sales

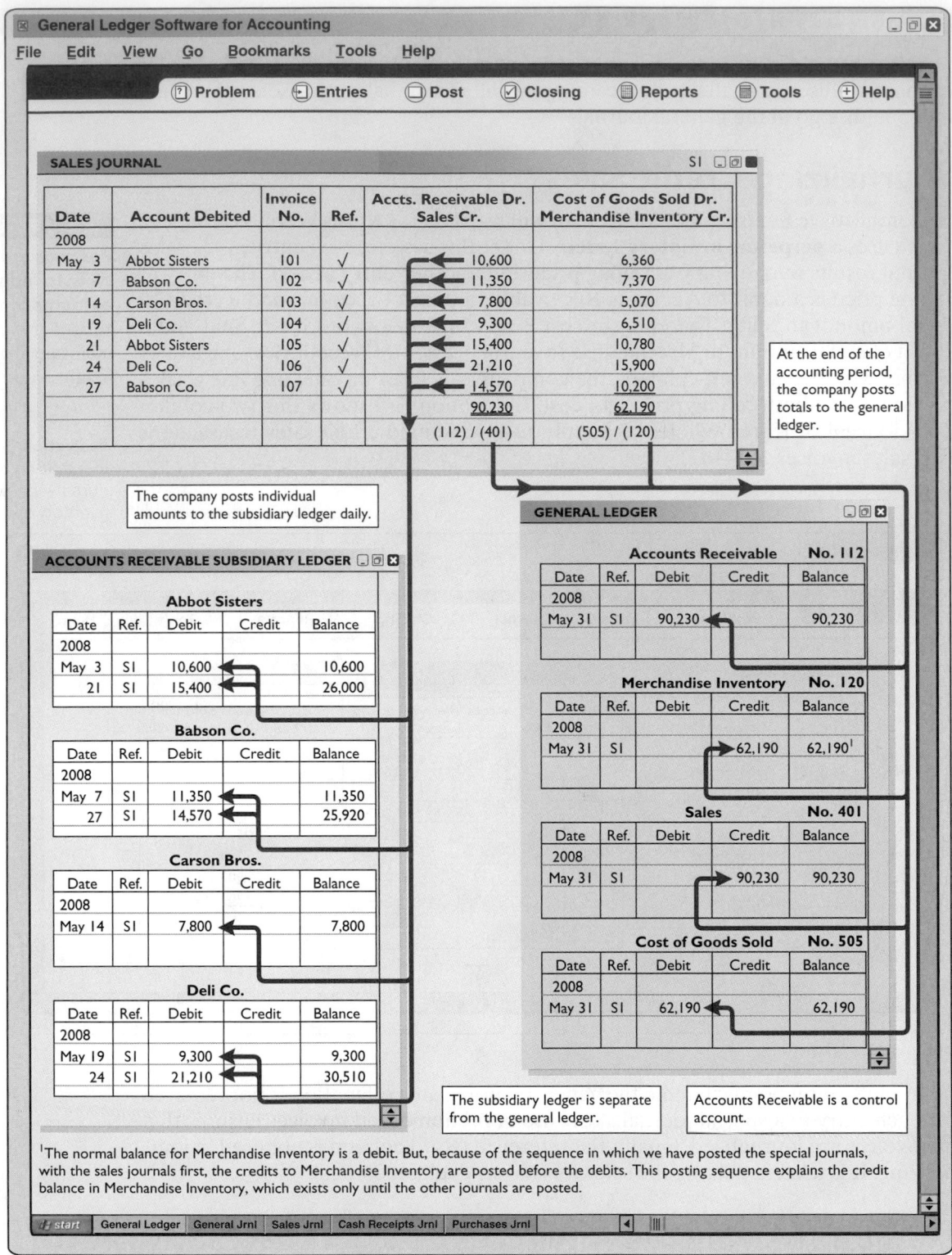

**Illustration E-6**
Posting the sales journal

journal to the general ledger. Here, the column totals are as follows: From the selling-price column, a debit of $90,230 to Accounts Receivable (account No. 112), and a credit of $90,230 to Sales (account No. 401). From the cost column, a debit of $62,190 to Cost of Goods Sold (account No. 505), and a credit of $62,190 to Merchandise Inventory (account No. 120). Karns inserts the account numbers below the column totals to indicate that the postings have been made. In both the general ledger and subsidiary ledger accounts, the reference **S1** indicates that the posting came from page 1 of the sales journal.

## Proving the Ledgers

The next step is to "prove" the ledgers. To do so, Karns must determine two things: (1) The total of the general ledger debit balances must equal the total of the general ledger credit balances. (2) The sum of the subsidiary ledger balances must equal the balance in the control account. Illustration E-7 shows the proof of the postings from the sales journal to the general and subsidiary ledger.

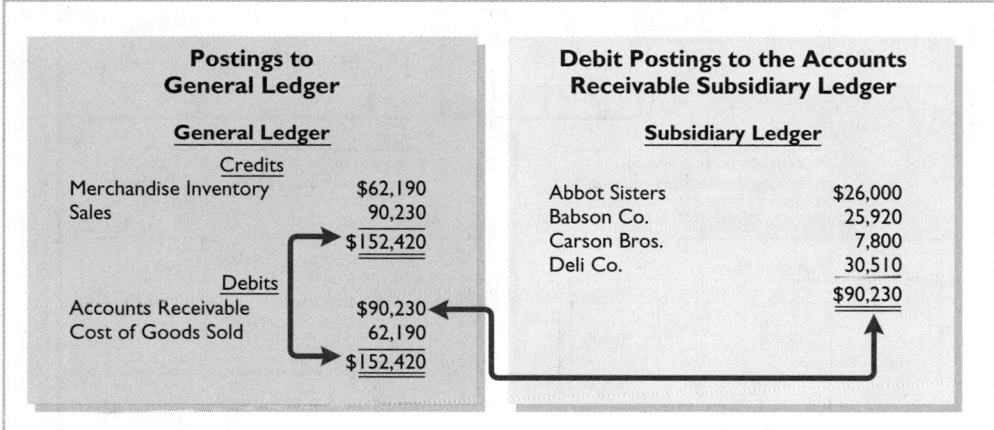

**Illustration E-7**
Proving the equality of the postings from the sales journal

## Advantages of the Sales Journal

Use of a special journal to record sales on account has several advantages. First, the one-line entry for each sales transaction saves time. In the sales journal, it is not necessary to write out the four account titles for each transaction. Second, only totals, rather than individual entries, are posted to the general ledger. This saves posting time and reduces the possibilities of posting errors. Finally, a division of labor results, because one individual can take responsibility for the sales journal.

## CASH RECEIPTS JOURNAL

In the **cash receipts journal**, companies record all receipts of cash. The most common types of cash receipts are cash sales of merchandise and collections of accounts receivable. Many other possibilities exist, such as receipt of money from bank loans and cash proceeds from disposal of equipment. A one- or two-column cash receipts journal would not have space enough for all possible cash receipt transactions. Therefore, companies use a multiple-column cash receipts journal.

Generally, a cash receipts journal includes the following columns: debit columns for Cash and Sales Discounts, and credit columns for Accounts Receivable, Sales, and "Other" accounts. Companies use the "Other Accounts" category when the cash receipt does not involve a cash sale or a collection of accounts receivable. Under a perpetual inventory system, each sales entry also is accompanied by an entry that debits Cost of Goods Sold and credits Merchandise Inventory for the cost of the merchandise sold. Illustration E-8 (page E8) shows a six-column cash receipts journal.

**Illustration E-8**
Journalizing and posting the
cash receipts journal

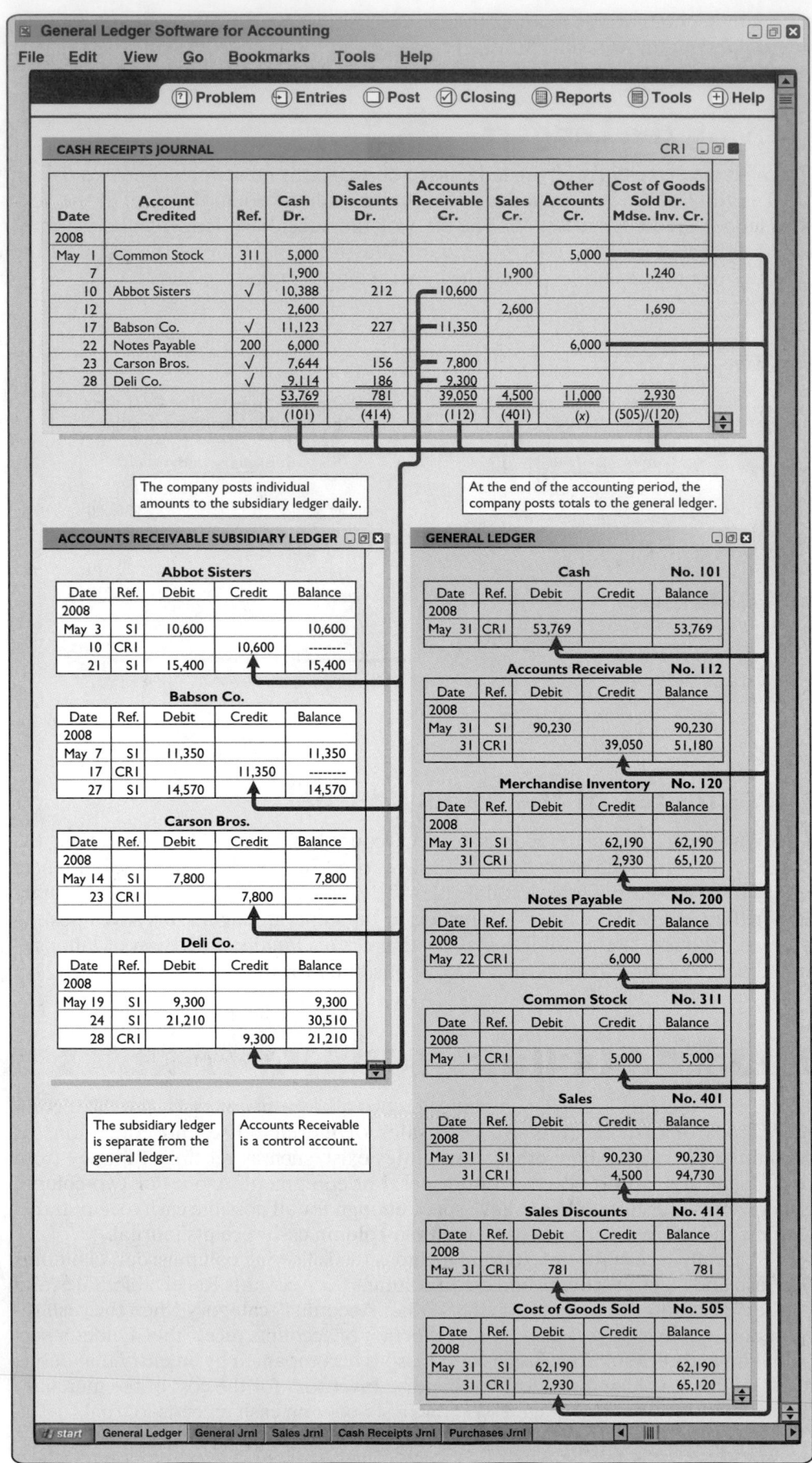

Companies may use additional credit columns if these columns significantly reduce postings to a specific account. For example, a loan company, such as Household International, receives thousands of cash collections from customers. Using separate credit columns for Loans Receivable and Interest Revenue, rather than the Other Accounts credit column, would reduce postings.

## Journalizing Cash Receipts Transactions

To illustrate the journalizing of cash receipts transactions, we will continue with the May transactions of Karns Wholesale Supply. Collections from customers relate to the entries recorded in the sales journal in Illustration E-5. The entries in the cash receipts journal are based on the following cash receipts.

May   1   Stockholders invested $5,000 in the business.
      7   Cash sales of merchandise total $1,900 (cost, $1,240).
     10   Received a check for $10,388 from Abbot Sisters in payment of invoice No. 101 for $10,600 less a 2% discount.
     12   Cash sales of merchandise total $2,600 (cost, $1,690).
     17   Received a check for $11,123 from Babson Co. in payment of invoice No. 102 for $11,350 less a 2% discount.
     22   Received cash by signing a note for $6,000.
     23   Received a check for $7,644 from Carson Bros. in full for invoice No. 103 for $7,800 less a 2% discount.
     28   Received a check for $9,114 from Deli Co. in full for invoice No. 104 for $9,300 less a 2% discount.

Further information about the columns in the cash receipts journal is listed below.

**Debit Columns:**

1. **Cash.** Karns enters in this column the amount of cash actually received in each transaction. The column total indicates the total cash receipts for the month.

2. **Sales Discounts.** Karns includes a Sales Discounts column in its cash receipts journal. By doing so, it does not need to enter sales discount items in the general journal. As a result, the cash receipts journal shows on one line the collection of an account receivable within the discount period.

**Credit Columns:**

3. **Accounts Receivable.** Karns uses the Accounts Receivable column to record cash collections on account. The amount entered here is the amount to be credited to the individual customer's account.

4. **Sales.** The Sales column records all cash sales of merchandise. Cash sales of other assets (plant assets, for example) are not reported in this column.

5. **Other Accounts.** Karns uses the Other Accounts column whenever the credit is other than to Accounts Receivable or Sales. For example, in the first entry, Karns enters $5,000 as a credit to Common Stock. This column is often referred to as the sundry accounts column.

**Debit and Credit Column:**

6. **Cost of Goods Sold and Merchandise Inventory.** This column records debits to Cost of Goods Sold and credits to Merchandise Inventory.

In a multi-column journal, generally only one line is needed for each entry. Debit and credit amounts for each line must be equal. When Karns journalizes the collection from Abbot Sisters on May 10, for example, three amounts are indicated. Note also that the Account Credited column identifies both general ledger and subsidiary ledger account titles. General ledger accounts are illustrated in the May 1

> **HELPFUL HINT**
>
> When is an account title entered in the "Account Credited" column of the cash receipts journal? Answer: A *subsidiary ledger* account is entered when the entry involves a collection of accounts receivable. A *general ledger* account is entered when the account is not shown in a special column (and an amount must be entered in the Other Accounts column). Otherwise, no account is shown in the "Account Credited" column.

and May 22 entries. A subsidiary account is illustrated in the May 10 entry for the collection from Abbot Sisters.

When Karns has finished journalizing a multi-column journal, it totals the amount columns and compares the totals to prove the equality of debits and credits. Illustration E-9 shows the proof of the equality of Karns's cash receipts journal.

**Illustration E-9**
Proving the equality of the cash receipts journal

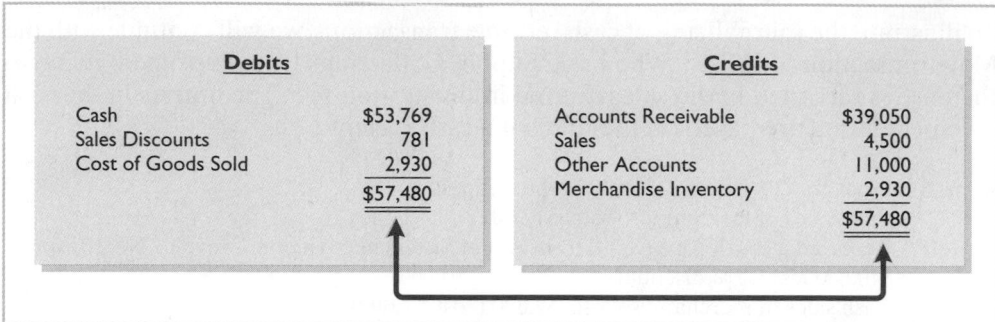

| **Debits** | | **Credits** | |
|---|---|---|---|
| Cash | $53,769 | Accounts Receivable | $39,050 |
| Sales Discounts | 781 | Sales | 4,500 |
| Cost of Goods Sold | 2,930 | Other Accounts | 11,000 |
| | $57,480 | Merchandise Inventory | 2,930 |
| | | | $57,480 |

Totaling the columns of a journal and proving the equality of the totals is called **footing** and **cross-footing** a journal.

## Posting the Cash Receipts Journal

Posting a multi-column journal involves the following steps.

1. **At the end of the month**, the company posts all column totals, except for the Other Accounts total, to the account title(s) specified in the column heading (such as Cash or Accounts Receivable). The company then enters account numbers below the column totals to show that they have been posted. For example, Karns has posted cash to account No. 101, accounts receivable to account No. 112, merchandise inventory to account No. 120, sales to account No. 401, sales discounts to account No. 414, and cost of goods sold to account No. 505.

2. The company **separately posts the individual amounts comprising the Other Accounts total** to the general ledger accounts specified in the Account Credited column. See, for example, the credit posting to Common Stock: The total amount of this column has not been posted. The symbol (X) is inserted below the total to this column to indicate that the amount has not been posted.

3. The individual amounts in a column, posted in total to a control account (Accounts Receivable, in this case), are posted **daily to the subsidiary ledger** account specified in the Account Credited column. See, for example, the credit posting of $10,600 to Abbot Sisters.

The symbol **CR**, used in both the subsidiary and general ledgers, identifies postings from the cash receipts journal.

## Proving the Ledgers

After posting of the cash receipts journal is completed, Karns proves the ledgers. As shown in Illustration E-10 (next page), the general ledger totals agree. Also, the sum of the subsidiary ledger balances equals the control account balance.

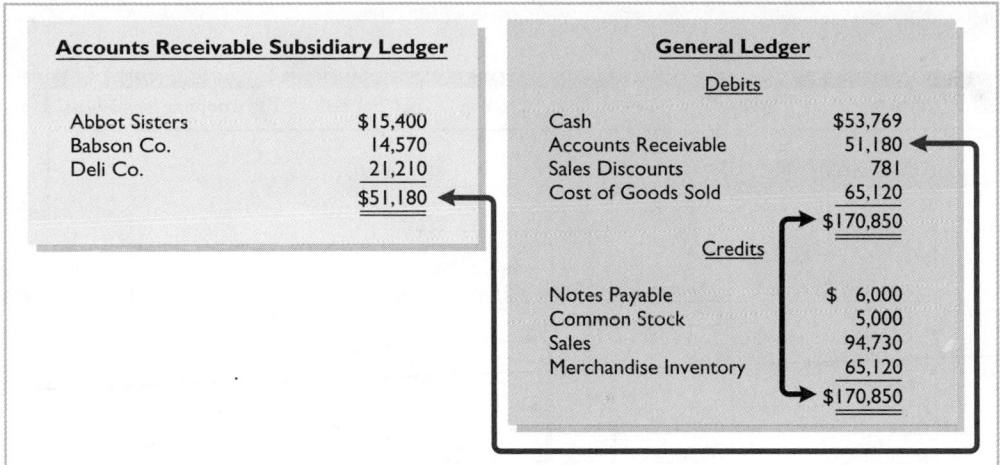

# PURCHASES JOURNAL

In the **purchases journal**, companies record all purchases of merchandise on account. Each entry in this journal results in a debit to Merchandise Inventory and a credit to Accounts Payable. Illustration E-11 (page E12) shows the purchases journal for Karns Wholesale Supply.

When using a one-column purchases journal (as in Illustration E-11), a company cannot journalize other types of purchases on account or cash purchases in it. For example, using the purchases journal shown in Illustration E-11, Karns would have to record credit purchases of equipment or supplies in the general journal. Likewise, all cash purchases would be entered in the cash payments journal. As illustrated later, companies that make numerous credit purchases for items other than merchandise often expand the purchases journal to a multi-column format. (See Illustration E-14 on page E13.)

## Journalizing Credit Purchases of Merchandise

The journalizing procedure is similar to that for a sales journal. Companies make entries in the purchases journal from purchase invoices. In contrast to the sales journal, the purchases journal may not have an invoice number column, because invoices received from different suppliers will not be in numerical sequence. To ensure that they record all purchase invoices, some companies consecutively number each invoice upon receipt and then use an internal document number column in the purchases journal. The entries for Karns Wholesale Supply are based on the assumed credit purchases listed in Illustration E-12 (page E12).

## Posting the Purchases Journal

The procedures for posting the purchases journal are similar to those for the sales journal. In this case, Karns makes **daily** postings to the **accounts payable ledger**; it makes **monthly** postings to Merchandise Inventory and Accounts Payable in the general ledger. In both ledgers, Karns uses **P1** in the reference column to show that the postings are from page 1 of the purchases journal.

Proof of the equality of the postings from the purchases journal to both ledgers is shown in Illustration E-13 (page E13).

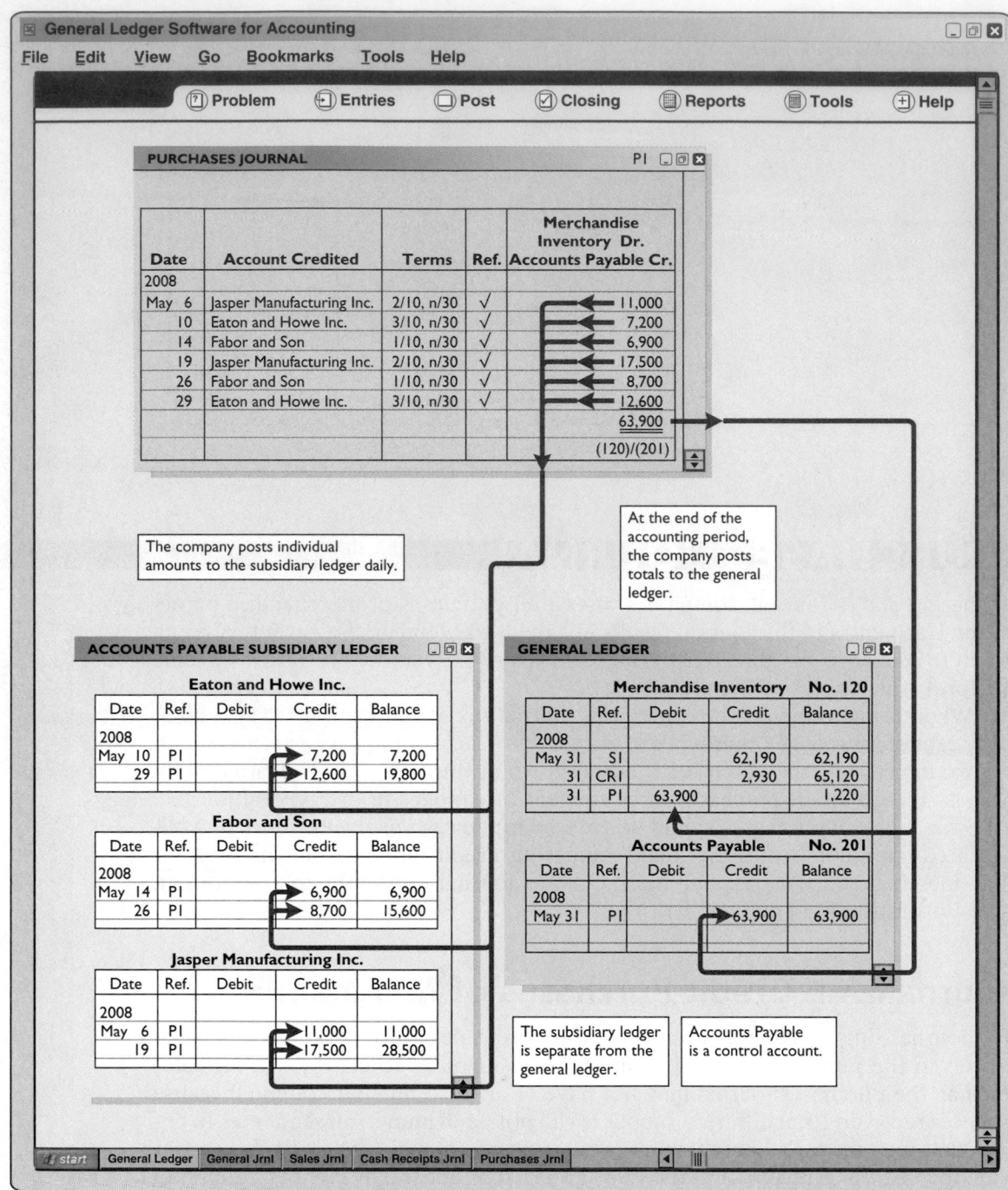

**Illustration E-11**
Journalizing and posting the purchases journal

**Illustration E-12**
Credit purchases transactions

| Date | Supplier | Amount |
|------|----------|--------|
| 5/6 | Jasper Manufacturing Inc. | $11,000 |
| 5/10 | Eaton and Howe Inc. | 7,200 |
| 5/14 | Fabor and Son | 6,900 |
| 5/19 | Jasper Manufacturing Inc. | 17,500 |
| 5/26 | Fabor and Son | 8,700 |
| 5/29 | Eaton and Howe Inc. | 12,600 |

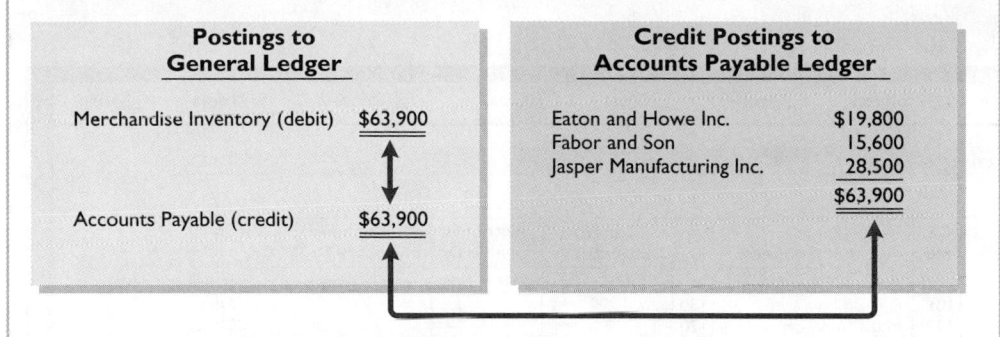

## Expanding the Purchases Journal

**HELPFUL HINT**

A single-column purchases
journal needs only to be
footed to prove the
equality of debits and
credits.

As noted earlier, some companies expand the purchases journal to include all types of purchases on account. Instead of one column for merchandise inventory and accounts payable, they use a multiple-column format. This format usually includes a credit column for Accounts Payable and debit columns for purchases of Merchandise Inventory, Office Supplies, Store Supplies, and Other Accounts. Illustration E-14 shows a multi-column purchases journal for Hanover Co. The posting procedures are similar to those shown earlier for posting the cash receipts journal.

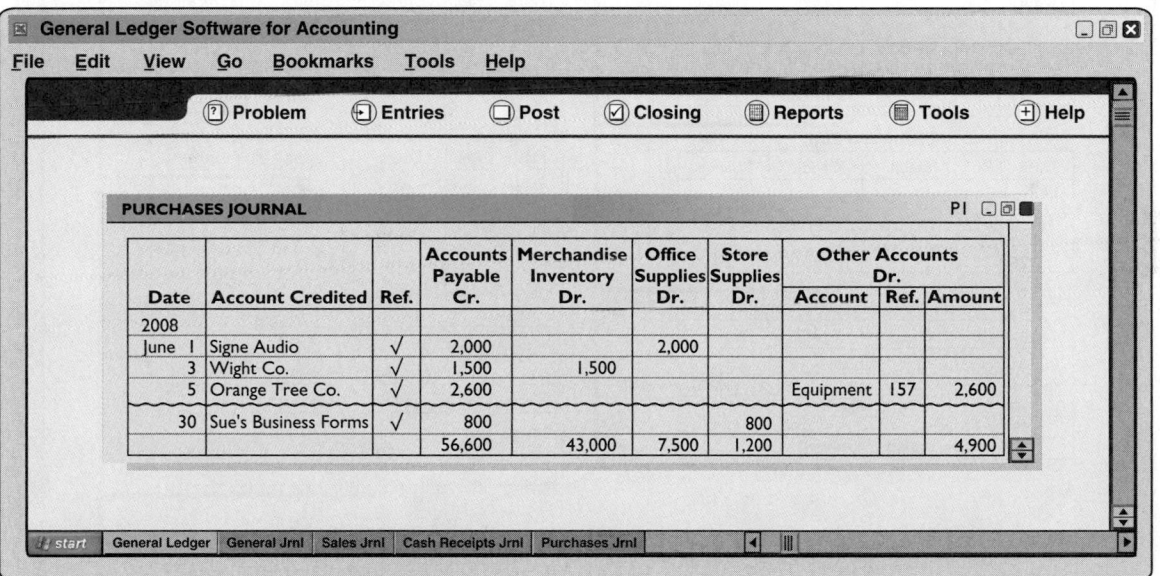

**CASH PAYMENTS JOURNAL**

In a **cash payments (cash disbursements) journal**, companies record all disbursements of cash. Entries are made from prenumbered checks. Because companies make cash payments for various purposes, the cash payments journal has multiple columns. Illustration E-15 (page E14) shows a four-column journal.

## Journalizing Cash Payments Transactions

The procedures for journalizing transactions in this journal are similar to those for the cash receipts journal. Karns records each transaction on one line, and for each line there must be equal debit and credit amounts. The entries in the cash payments

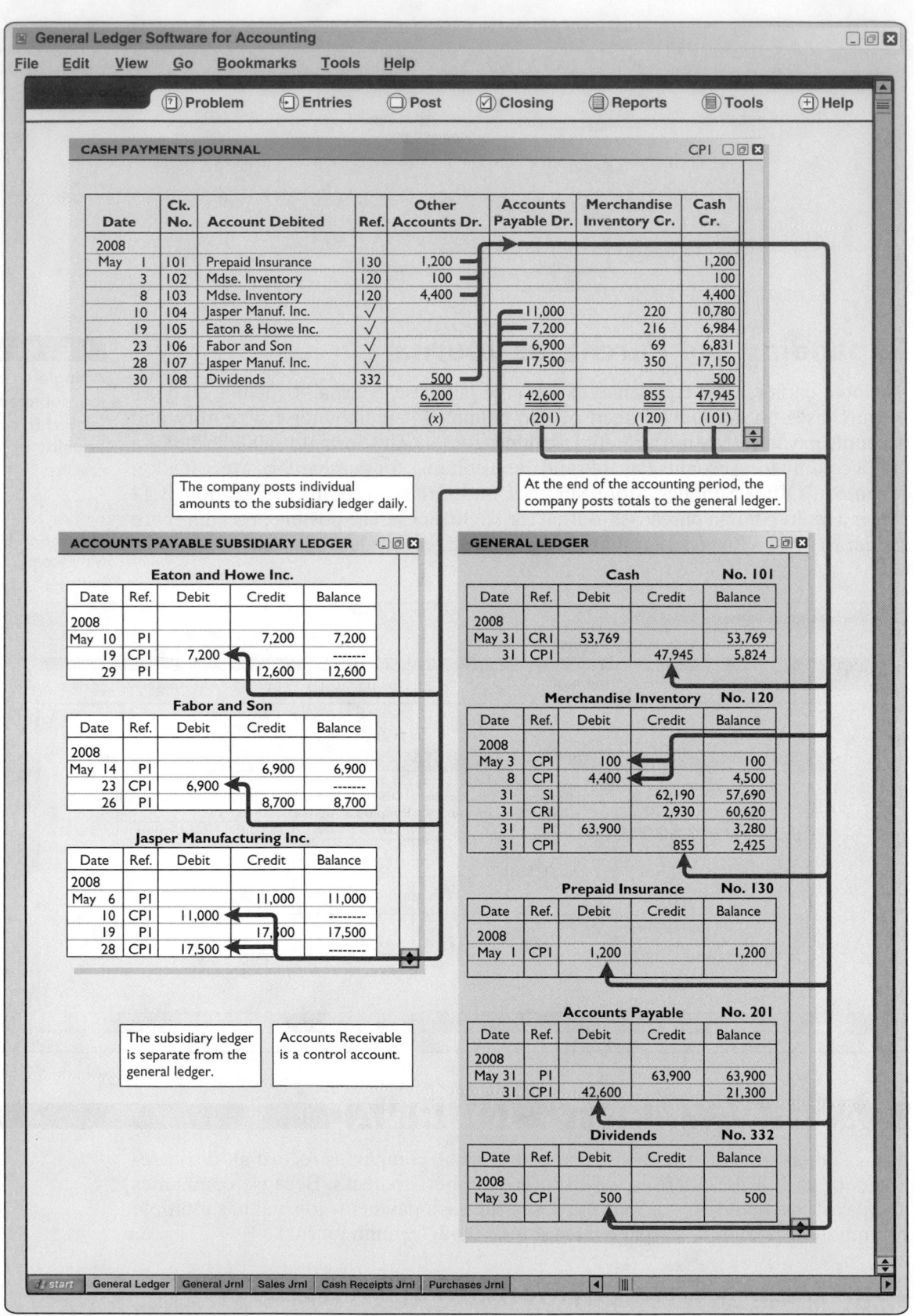

**Illustration E-15**
Journalizing and posting the
cash payments journal

journal in Illustration E-15 are based on the following transactions for Karns Wholesale Supply.

May  1  Issued check No. 101 for $1,200 for the annual premium on a fire insurance policy.
     3  Issued check No. 102 for $100 in payment of freight when terms were FOB shipping point.
     8  Issued check No. 103 for $4,400 for the purchase of merchandise.
    10  Sent check No. 104 for $10,780 to Jasper Manufacturing Inc. in payment of May 6 invoice for $11,000 less a 2% discount.
    19  Mailed check No. 105 for $6,984 to Eaton and Howe Inc. in payment of May 10 invoice for $7,200 less a 3% discount.
    23  Sent check No. 106 for $6,831 to Fabor and Son in payment of May 14 invoice for $6,900 less a 1% discount.
    28  Sent check No. 107 for $17,150 to Jasper Manufacturing Inc. in payment of May 19 invoice for $17,500 less a 2% discount.
    30  Issued check No. 108 for $500 to stockholders as a dividend.

Note that whenever Karns enters an amount in the Other Accounts column, it must identify a specific general ledger account in the Account Debited column. The entries for checks No. 101, 102, 103, and 108 illustrate this situation. Similarly, Karns must identify a subsidiary account in the Account Debited column whenever it enters an amount in the Accounts Payable column. See, for example, the entry for check No. 104.

After Karns journalizes the cash payments journal, it totals the columns. The totals are then balanced to prove the equality of debits and credits.

## Posting the Cash Payments Journal

The procedures for posting the cash payments journal are similar to those for the cash receipts journal. Karns posts the amounts recorded in the Accounts Payable column individually to the subsidiary ledger and in total to the control account. It posts Merchandise Inventory and Cash only in total at the end of the month. Transactions in the Other Accounts column are posted individually to the appropriate account(s) affected. The company does not post totals for the Other Accounts column.

Illustration E-15 shows the posting of the cash payments journal. Note that Karns uses the symbol **CP** as the posting reference. After postings are completed, the company proves the equality of the debit and credit balances in the general ledger. In addition, the control account balances should agree with the subsidiary ledger total balance. Illustration E-16 shows the agreement of these balances.

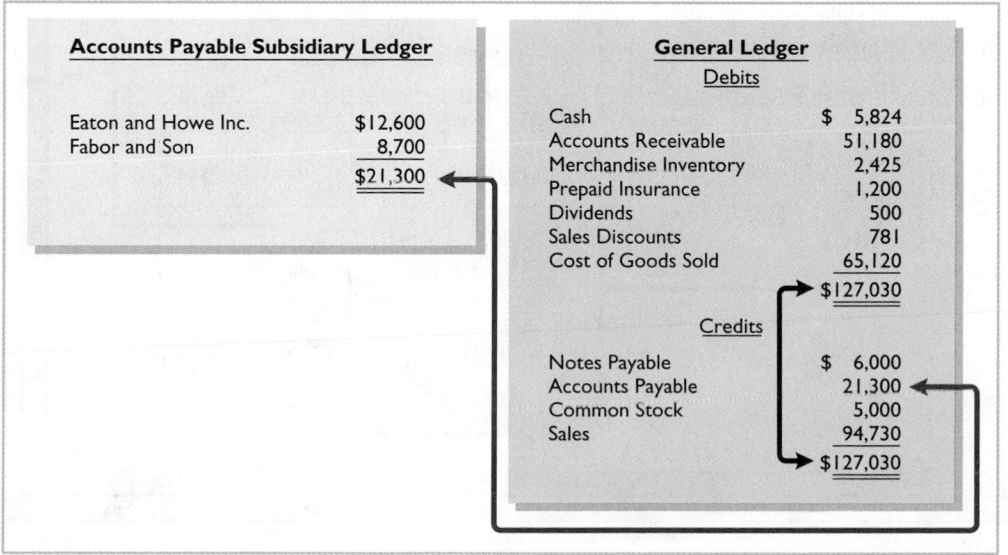

**Illustration E-16**
Proving the ledgers after postings from the sales, cash receipts, purchases, and cash payments journals

| Accounts Payable Subsidiary Ledger | |
| --- | --- |
| Eaton and Howe Inc. | $12,600 |
| Fabor and Son | 8,700 |
| | $21,300 |

| General Ledger | |
| --- | --- |
| **Debits** | |
| Cash | $ 5,824 |
| Accounts Receivable | 51,180 |
| Merchandise Inventory | 2,425 |
| Prepaid Insurance | 1,200 |
| Dividends | 500 |
| Sales Discounts | 781 |
| Cost of Goods Sold | 65,120 |
| | $127,030 |
| **Credits** | |
| Notes Payable | $ 6,000 |
| Accounts Payable | 21,300 |
| Common Stock | 5,000 |
| Sales | 94,730 |
| | $127,030 |

# EFFECTS OF SPECIAL JOURNALS ON THE GENERAL JOURNAL

Special journals for sales, purchases, and cash substantially reduce the number of entries that companies make in the general journal. **Only transactions that cannot be entered in a special journal are recorded in the general journal.** For example, a company may use the general journal to record such transactions as granting of credit to a customer for a sales return or allowance, granting of credit from a supplier for purchases returned, acceptance of a note receivable from a customer, and purchase of equipment by issuing a note payable. Also, **correcting, adjusting, and closing entries are made in the general journal**.

The general journal has columns for date, account title and explanation, reference, and debit and credit amounts. When control and subsidiary accounts are not involved, the procedures for journalizing and posting of transactions are the same as those described in earlier chapters. When control and subsidiary accounts *are* involved, companies make two changes from the earlier procedures:

1. In **journalizing**, they identify both the control and the subsidiary accounts.
2. In **posting**, there must be a **dual posting**: once to the control account and once to the subsidiary account.

**Illustration E-17**
Journalizing and posting the general journal

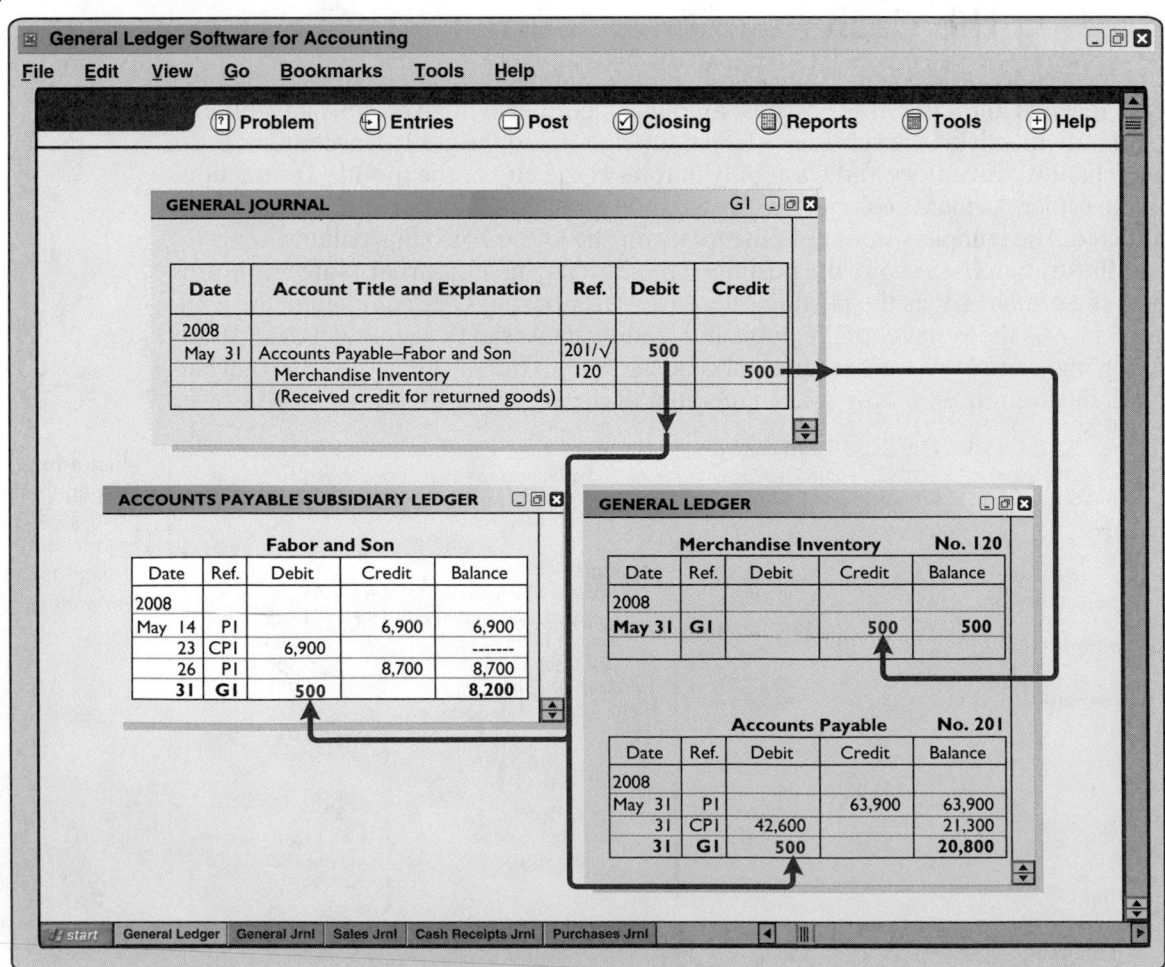

To illustrate, assume that on May 31, Karns Wholesale Supply returns $500 of merchandise for credit to Fabor and Son. Illustration E-17 shows the entry in the general journal and the posting of the entry. Note that if Karns receives cash instead of credit on this return, then it would record the transaction in the cash receipts journal.

Note that the general journal indicates two accounts (Accounts Payable, and Fabor and Son) for the debit, and two postings ("201/✓") in the reference column. One debit is posted to the control account and another debit to the creditor's account in the subsidiary ledger.

## Before You Go On...

### REVIEW IT

1. What types of special journals do companies frequently use to record transactions? Why do they use special journals?
2. Explain how companies post transactions recorded in the sales journal and the cash receipts journal.
3. Indicate the types of transactions that companies record in the general journal when they use special journals.

## Demonstration Problem

Cassandra Wilson Company uses a six-column cash receipts journal with the following columns:

| | |
|---|---|
| Cash (Dr.) | Other Accounts (Cr.) |
| Sales Discounts (Dr.) | Cost of Goods Sold (Dr.) and |
| Accounts Receivable (Cr.) |    Merchandise Inventory (Cr.) |
| Sales (Cr.) | |

Cash receipts transactions for the month of July 2008 are as follows.

July  3   Cash sales total $5,800 (cost, $3,480).
     5   Received a check for $6,370 from Jeltz Company in payment of an invoice dated June 26 for $6,500, terms 2/10, n/30.
     9   Stockholders made an additional investment of $5,000 cash in the business.
   10   Cash sales total $12,519 (cost, $7,511).
   12   Received a check for $7,275 from R. Eliot & Co. in payment of a $7,500 invoice dated July 3, terms 3/10, n/30.
   15   Received a customer advance of $700 cash for future sales.
   20   Cash sales total $15,472 (cost, $9,283).
   22   Received a check for $5,880 from Beck Company in payment of $6,000 invoice dated July 13, terms 2/10, n/30.
   29   Cash sales total $17,660 (cost, $10,596).
   31   Received cash of $200 on interest earned for July.

### Instructions

**(a)** Journalize the transactions in the cash receipts journal.
**(b)** Contrast the posting of the Accounts Receivable and Other Accounts columns.

### action plan

✔ Record all cash receipts in the cash receipts journal.

✔ The "account credited" indicates items posted individually to the subsidiary ledger or general ledger.

✔ Record cash sales in the cash receipts journal—not in the sales journal.

✔ The total debits must equal the total credits.

*Solution*

**(a)**

## CASSANDRA WILSON COMPANY

### Cash Receipts Journal

CR1

| Date | Account Credited | Ref. | Cash Dr. | Sales Discounts Dr. | Accounts Receivable Cr. | Sales Cr. | Other Accounts Cr. | Cost of Goods Sold Dr. Mdse. Inv. Cr. |
|---|---|---|---|---|---|---|---|---|
| 2008 | | | | | | | | |
| 7/3 | | | 5,800 | | | 5,800 | | 3,480 |
| 5 | Jeltz Company | | 6,370 | 130 | 6,500 | | | |
| 9 | Common Stock | | 5,000 | | | | 5,000 | |
| 10 | | | 12,519 | | | 12,519 | | 7,511 |
| 12 | R. Eliot & Co. | | 7,275 | 225 | 7,500 | | | |
| 15 | Unearned Revenue | | 700 | | | | 700 | |
| 20 | | | 15,472 | | | 15,472 | | 9,283 |
| 22 | Beck Company | | 5,880 | 120 | 6,000 | | | |
| 29 | | | 17,660 | | | 17,660 | | 10,596 |
| 31 | Interest Revenue | | 200 | | | | 200 | |
| | | | 76,876 | 475 | 20,000 | 51,451 | 5,900 | 30,870 |

**(b)** The Accounts Receivable column is posted as a credit to Accounts Receivable. The individual amounts are credited to the customers' accounts identified in the Account Credited column, which are maintained in the accounts receivable subsidiary ledger.

The amounts in the Other Accounts column are posted individually. They are credited to the account titles identified in the Account Credited column.

---

## SUMMARY OF STUDY OBJECTIVES

1 **Describe the nature and purpose of a subsidiary ledger.** A subsidiary ledger is a group of accounts with a common characteristic. It facilitates the recording process by freeing the general ledger from details of individual balances.

2 **Explain how companies use special journals in journalizing.** Companies use special journals to group similar types of transactions. In a special journal, generally only one line is used to record a complete transaction.

3 **Indicate how companies post a multi-column journal.** In posting a multi-column journal:
  **(a)** Companies post all column totals except for the Other Accounts column once at the end of the month to the account title specified in the column heading.

  **(b)** Companies do not post the total of the Other Accounts column. Instead, the individual amounts comprising the total are posted separately to the general ledger accounts specified in the Account Credited (Debited) column.

  **(c)** The individual amounts in a column posted in total to a control account are posted daily to the subsidiary ledger accounts specified in the Account Credited (Debited) column.

---

## GLOSSARY

**Accounts payable (creditors') subsidiary ledger** A subsidiary ledger that collects transaction data of individual creditors. (p. E1).

**Accounts receivable (customers') subsidiary ledger** A subsidiary ledger that collects transaction data of individual customers. (p. E1).

**Cash payments (disbursements) journal** A special journal that records all cash paid. (p. E13).

**Cash receipts journal** A special journal that records all cash received. (p. E7).

**Control account** An account in the general ledger that summarizes subsidiary ledger. (p. E1).

**Purchases journal**  A special journal that records all purchases of merchandise on account. (p. E11).

**Sales journal**  A special journal that records all sales of merchandise on account. (p. E5).

**Special journal**  A journal that records similar types of transactions, such as all credit sales. (p. E4).

**Subsidiary ledger**  A group of accounts with a common characteristic. (p. E1).

## SELF-STUDY QUESTIONS

*Answers are at the end of the chapter.*

(SO 1)  **1.** Which of the following is *incorrect* concerning subsidiary ledgers?
  **a.** The purchases ledger is a common subsidiary ledger for creditor accounts.
  **b.** The accounts receivable ledger is a subsidiary ledger.
  **c.** A subsidiary ledger is a group of accounts with a common characteristic.
  **d.** An advantage of the subsidiary ledger is that it permits a division of labor in posting.

(SO 2)  **2.** A sales journal will be used for:

| | Credit Sales | Cash Sales | Sales Discounts |
|---|---|---|---|
| **a.** | no | yes | yes |
| **b.** | yes | no | yes |
| **c.** | yes | no | no |
| **d.** | yes | yes | no |

(SO 2, 3)  **3.** Which of the following statements is *correct*?
  **a.** The sales discount column is included in the cash receipts journal.
  **b.** The purchases journal records all purchases of merchandise whether for cash or on account.
  **c.** The cash receipts journal records sales on account.
  **d.** Merchandise returned by the buyer is recorded by the seller in the purchases journal.

(SO 3)  **4.** Which of the following is *incorrect* concerning the posting of the cash receipts journal?
  **a.** The total of the Other Accounts column is not posted.
  **b.** All column totals except the total for the Other Accounts column are posted once at the end of the month to the account title(s) specified in the column heading.
  **c.** The totals of all columns are posted daily to the accounts specified in the column heading.
  **d.** The individual amounts in a column posted in total to a control account are posted daily to the subsidiary ledger account specified in the Account Credited column.

(SO 3)  **5.** Postings from the purchases journal to the subsidiary ledger are generally made:
  **a.** yearly.
  **b.** monthly.
  **c.** weekly.
  **d.** daily.

(SO 2)  **6.** Which statement is *incorrect* regarding the general journal?
  **a.** Only transactions that cannot be entered in a special journal are recorded in the general journal.
  **b.** Dual postings are always required in the general journal.
  **c.** The general journal may be used to record acceptance of a note receivable in payment of an account receivable.
  **d.** Correcting, adjusting, and closing entries are made in the general journal.

(SO 2)  **7.** When companies use special journals:
  **a.** they record all purchase transactions in the purchases journal.
  **b.** they record all cash received, except from cash sales, in the cash receipts journal.
  **c.** they record all cash disbursements in the cash payments journal.
  **d.** a general journal is not necessary.

(SO 2)  **8.** If a customer returns goods for credit, the selling company normally makes an entry in the:
  **a.** cash payments journal.
  **b.** sales journal.
  **c.** general journal.
  **d.** cash receipts journal.

Go to the book's website,
**www.wiley.com/college/weygandt**,
for Additional Self-Study questions.

## QUESTIONS

**1.** What are the advantages of using subsidiary ledgers?

**2.** (a) When do companies normally post to (1) the subsidiary accounts and (2) the general ledger control accounts? (b) Describe the relationship between a control account and a subsidiary ledger.

**3.** Identify and explain the four special journals discussed in the chapter. List an advantage of using each of these journals rather than using only a general journal.

**4.** Thogmartin Company uses special journals. It recorded in a sales journal a sale made on account to R. Peters for $435. A few days later, R. Peters returns $70 worth of merchandise for credit. Where should Thogmartin Company record the sales return? Why?

**5.** A $500 purchase of merchandise on account from Lore Company was properly recorded in the purchases journal. When posted, however, the amount recorded in the subsidiary ledger was $50. How might this error be discovered?

6. Why would special journals used in different businesses not be identical in format? What type of business would maintain a cash receipts journal but not include a column for accounts receivable?

7. The cash and the accounts receivable columns in the cash receipts journal were mistakenly overadded by $4,000 at the end of the month. (a) Will the customers' ledger agree with the Accounts Receivable control account? (b) Assuming no other errors, will the trial balance totals be equal?

8. One column total of a special journal is posted at month-end to only two general ledger accounts. One of these two accounts is Accounts Receivable. What is the name of this special journal? What is the other general ledger account to which that same month-end total is posted?

9. In what journal would the following transactions be recorded? (Assume that a two-column sales journal and a single-column purchases journal are used.)
   (a) Recording of depreciation expense for the year.
   (b) Credit given to a customer for merchandise purchased on credit and returned.
   (c) Sales of merchandise for cash.

(d) Sales of merchandise on account.
(e) Collection of cash on account from a customer.
(f) Purchase of office supplies on account.

10. In what journal would the following transactions be recorded? (Assume that a two-column sales journal and a single-column purchases journal are used.)
    (a) Cash received from signing a note payable.
    (b) Investment of cash by stockholders.
    (c) Closing of the expense accounts at the end of the year.
    (d) Purchase of merchandise on account.
    (e) Credit received for merchandise purchased and returned to supplier.
    (f) Payment of cash on account due a supplier.

11. What transactions might be included in a multiple-column purchases journal that would not be included in a single-column purchases journal?

12. Give an example of a transaction in the general journal that causes an entry to be posted twice (i.e., to two accounts), one in the general ledger, the other in the subsidiary ledger. Does this affect the debit/credit equality of the general ledger?

13. Give some examples of appropriate general journal transactions for an organization using special journals.

# BRIEF EXERCISES

**Identify subsidiary ledger balances.**

(SO 1)

**BEE-1**   Presented below is information related to Kienholz Company for its first month of operations. Identify the balances that appear in the accounts receivable subsidiary ledger and the accounts receivable balance that appears in the general ledger at the end of January.

| Credit Sales | | | Cash Collections | | |
|---|---|---|---|---|---|
| Jan. 7 | Agler Co. | $10,000 | Jan. 17 | Agler Co. | $7,000 |
| 15 | Barto Co. | 6,000 | 24 | Barto Co. | 4,000 |
| 23 | Maris Co. | 9,000 | 29 | Maris Co. | 9,000 |

**Identify subsidiary ledger accounts.**

(SO 1)

**BEE-2**   Identify in what ledger (general or subsidiary) each of the following accounts is shown.
1. Rent Expense
2. Accounts Receivable—Char
3. Notes Payable
4. Accounts Payable—Thebeau

**Identify special journals.**

(SO 2)

**BEE-3**   Identify the journal in which each of the following transactions is recorded.
1. Cash sales
2. Payment of dividends
3. Cash purchase of land
4. Credit sales
5. Purchase of merchandise on account
6. Receipt of cash for services performed

**Identify entries to cash receipts journal.**

(SO 2)

**BEE-4**   Indicate whether each of the following debits and credits is included in the cash receipts journal. (Use "Yes" or "No" to answer this question.)
1. Debit to Sales
2. Credit to Merchandise Inventory
3. Credit to Accounts Receivable
4. Debit to Accounts Payable

**Identify transactions for special journals.**

(SO 2)

**BEE-5**   Galindo Co. uses special journals and a general journal. Identify the journal in which each of the following transactions is recorded.
   (a) Purchased equipment on account.
   (b) Purchased merchandise on account.
   (c) Paid utility expense in cash.
   (d) Sold merchandise on account.

**BEE-6**   Identify the special journal(s) in which the following column headings appear.

1. Sales Discounts Dr.
2. Accounts Receivable Cr.
3. Cash Dr.
4. Sales Cr.
5. Merchandise Inventory Dr.

*Identify transactions for special journals.*

*(SO 2)*

**BEE-7**   Kidwell Computer Components Inc. uses a multi-column cash receipts journal. Indicate which column(s) is/are posted only in total, only daily, or both in total and daily.

1. Accounts Receivable
2. Sales Discounts
3. Cash
4. Other Accounts

*Indicate postings to cash receipts journal.*

*(SO 3)*

---

# EXERCISES

**EE-1**   Donahue Company uses both special journals and a general journal as described in this chapter. On June 30, after all monthly postings had been completed, the Accounts Receivable control account in the general ledger had a debit balance of $320,000; the Accounts Payable control account had a credit balance of $77,000.

*Determine control account balances, and explain posting of special journals.*

*(SO 1, 3)*

The July transactions recorded in the special journals are summarized below. No entries affecting accounts receivable and accounts payable were recorded in the general journal for July.

| | |
|---|---|
| Sales journal | Total sales $161,400 |
| Purchases journal | Total purchases $56,400 |
| Cash receipts journal | Accounts receivable column total $131,000 |
| Cash payments journal | Accounts payable column total $47,500 |

**Instructions**

(a) What is the balance of the Accounts Receivable control account after the monthly postings on July 31?
(b) What is the balance of the Accounts Payable control account after the monthly postings on July 31?
(c) To what account(s) is the column total of $161,400 in the sales journal posted?
(d) To what account(s) is the accounts receivable column total of $131,000 in the cash receipts journal posted?

**EE-2**   Presented below is the subsidiary accounts receivable account of Jeremy Dody.

*Explain postings to subsidiary ledger.*

*(SO 1)*

| Date | Ref. | Debit | Credit | Balance |
|---|---|---|---|---|
| 2008 | | | | |
| Sept. 2 | S31 | 61,000 | | 61,000 |
| 9 | G4 | | 14,000 | 47,000 |
| 27 | CR8 | | 47,000 | — |

**Instructions**

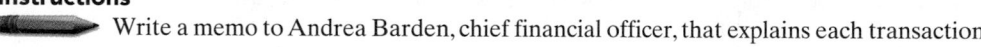 Write a memo to Andrea Barden, chief financial officer, that explains each transaction.

**EE-3**   On September 1 the balance of the Accounts Receivable control account in the general ledger of Seaver Company was $10,960. The customers' subsidiary ledger contained account balances as follows: Ruiz $1,440, Kingston $2,640, Bannister $2,060, Crampton $4,820. At the end of September the various journals contained the following information.

*Post various journals to control and subsidiary accounts.*

*(SO 1, 3)*

**Sales journal:** Sales to Crampton $800; to Ruiz $1,260; to Iman $1,330; to Bannister $1,100.
**Cash receipts journal:** Cash received from Bannister $1,310; from Crampton $2,300; from Iman $380; from Kingston $1,800; from Ruiz $1,240.
**General journal:** An allowance is granted to Crampton $220.

**Instructions**

(a) Set up control and subsidiary accounts and enter the beginning balances. Do not construct the journals.
(b) Post the various journals. Post the items as individual items or as totals, whichever would be the appropriate procedure. (No sales discounts given.)

(c) Prepare a list of customers and prove the agreement of the controlling account with the subsidiary ledger at September 30, 2008.

*Determine control and subsidiary ledger balances for accounts receivable.*
*(SO 1)*

**EE-4** Yu Suzuki Company has a balance in its Accounts Receivable control account of $11,000 on January 1, 2008. The subsidiary ledger contains three accounts: Smith Company, balance $4,000; Green Company, balance $2,500; and Koyan Company. During January, the following receivable-related transactions occurred.

|  | Credit Sales | Collections | Returns |
|---|---|---|---|
| Smith Company | $9,000 | $8,000 | $ -0- |
| Green Company | 7,000 | 2,500 | 3,000 |
| Koyan Company | 8,500 | 9,000 | -0- |

**Instructions**
(a) What is the January 1 balance in the Koyan Company subsidiary account?
(b) What is the January 31 balance in the control account?
(c) Compute the balances in the subsidiary accounts at the end of the month.
(d) Which January transaction would not be recorded in a special journal?

*Determine control and subsidiary ledger balances for accounts payable.*
*(SO 1)*

**EE-5** Nobo Uematsu Company has a balance in its Accounts Payable control account of $8,250 on January 1, 2008. The subsidiary ledger contains three accounts: Jones Company, balance $3,000; Brown Company, balance $1,875; and Aatski Company. During January, the following receivable-related transactions occurred.

|  | Purchases | Payments | Returns |
|---|---|---|---|
| Jones Company | $6,750 | $6,000 | $ -0- |
| Brown Company | 5,250 | 1,875 | 2,250 |
| Aatski Company | 6,375 | 6,750 | -0- |

**Instructions**
(a) What is the January 1 balance in the Aatski Company subsidiary account?
(b) What is the January 31 balance in the control account?
(c) Compute the balances in the subsidiary accounts at the end of the month.
(d) Which January transaction would not be recorded in a special journal?

*Record transactions in sales and purchases journal.*
*(SO 1, 2)*

**EE-6** Montalvo Company uses special journals and a general journal. The following transactions occurred during September 2008.

Sept.  2  Sold merchandise on account to T. Hossfeld, invoice no. 101, $720, terms n/30. The cost of the merchandise sold was $420.
  10  Purchased merchandise on account from L. Rincon $600, terms 2/10, n/30.
  12  Purchased office equipment on account from R. Press $6,500.
  21  Sold merchandise on account to P. Lowther, invoice no. 102 for $800, terms 2/10, n/30. The cost of the merchandise sold was $480.
  25  Purchased merchandise on account from W. Barone $860, terms n/30.
  27  Sold merchandise to S. Miller for $700 cash. The cost of the merchandise sold was $400.

**Instructions**
(a) Prepare a sales journal (see Illustration E-6) and a single-column purchase journal (see Illustration E-11). (Use page 1 for each journal.)
(b) Record the transaction(s) for September that should be journalized in the sales journal and the purchases journal.

*Record transactions in cash receipts and cash payments journal.*
*(SO 1, 2)*

**EE-7** Pherigo Co. uses special journals and a general journal. The following transactions occurred during May 2008.

May  1  I. Pherigo invested $50,000 cash in the business in exchange for common stock.
  2  Sold merchandise to B. Sherrick for $6,300 cash. The cost of the merchandise sold was $4,200.
  3  Purchased merchandise for $7,200 from J. DeLeon using check no. 101.
  14  Paid salary to H. Potter $700 by issuing check no. 102.

16  Sold merchandise on account to K. Kimbell for $900, terms n/30. The cost of the merchandise sold was $630.

22  A check of $9,000 is received from M. Moody in full for invoice 101; no discount given.

**Instructions**

**(a)** Prepare a multiple-column cash receipts journal (see Illustration E-8) and a multiple-column cash payments journal (see Illustration E-15). (Use page 1 for each journal.)

**(b)** Record the transaction(s) for May that should be journalized in the cash receipts journal and cash payments journal.

**EE-8**   Wick Company uses the columnar cash journals illustrated in the textbook. In April, the following selected cash transactions occurred.

*Explain journalizing in cash journals.*

*(SO 2)*

1. Made a refund to a customer for the return of damaged goods.
2. Received collection from customer within the 3% discount period.
3. Purchased merchandise for cash.
4. Paid a creditor within the 3% discount period.
5. Received collection from customer after the 3% discount period had expired.
6. Paid freight on merchandise purchased.
7. Paid cash for office equipment.
8. Received cash refund from supplier for merchandise returned.
9. Paid cash dividend to stockholders.
10. Made cash sales.

**Instructions**

Indicate **(a)** the journal, and **(b)** the columns in the journal that should be used in recording each transaction.

**EE-9**   Velasquez Company has the following selected transactions during March.

*Journalize transactions in general journal and post.*

*(SO 1, 3)*

Mar.  2  Purchased equipment costing $9,400 from Chang Company on account.
   5  Received credit of $410 from Lyden Company for merchandise damaged in shipment to Velasquez.
   7  Issued credit of $400 to Higley Company for merchandise the customer returned. The returned merchandise had a cost of $260.

Velasquez Company uses a one-column purchases journal, a sales journal, the columnar cash journals used in the text, and a general journal.

**Instructions**

**(a)** Journalize the transactions in the general journal.

**(b)** ◄━━━━━ In a brief memo to the president of Velasquez Company, explain the postings to the control and subsidiary accounts from each type of journal.

**EE-10**   Below are some typical transactions incurred by Kwun Company.

*Indicate journalizing in special journals.*

*(SO 2)*

1. Payment of creditors on account.
2. Return of merchandise sold for credit.
3. Collection on account from customers.
4. Sale of land for cash.
5. Sale of merchandise on account.
6. Sale of merchandise for cash.
7. Received credit for merchandise purchased on credit.
8. Sales discount taken on goods sold.
9. Payment of employee wages.
10. Payment of cash dividend to stockholders.
11. Depreciation on building.
12. Purchase of office supplies for cash.
13. Purchase of merchandise on account.

**Instructions**

For each transaction, indicate whether it would normally be recorded in a cash receipts journal, cash payments journal, sales journal, single-column purchases journal, or general journal.

**EE-11** The general ledger of Sanchez Company contained the following Accounts Payable control account (in T-account form). Also shown is the related subsidiary ledger.

## GENERAL LEDGER

### Accounts Payable

| | | | | | | |
|---|---|---|---|---|---|---|
| Feb. 15 | General journal | 1,400 | Feb. 1 | Balance | 26,025 |
| 28 | ? | ? | 5 | General journal | 265 |
| | | | 11 | General journal | 550 |
| | | | 28 | Purchases | 13,400 |
| | | | Feb. 28 | Balance | 9,500 |

## ACCOUNTS PAYABLE LEDGER

| **Perez** | | | **Tebbetts** | | |
|---|---|---|---|---|---|
| Feb. 28 | Bal. 4,600 | | Feb. 28 | Bal. ? |

| **Zerbe** | | |
|---|---|---|
| Feb. 28 | Bal. 2,300 |

**Instructions**

**(a)** Indicate the missing posting reference and amount in the control account, and the missing ending balance in the subsidiary ledger.

**(b)** Indicate the amounts in the control account that were dual-posted (i.e., posted to the control account and the subsidiary accounts).

**EE-12** Selected accounts from the ledgers of Lockhart Company at July 31 showed the following.

## GENERAL LEDGER

| | **Store Equipment** | | | | No. 153 |
|---|---|---|---|---|---|
| Date | Explanation | Ref. | Debit | Credit | Balance |
| July 1 | | G1 | 3,900 | | 3,900 |

| | **Accounts Payable** | | | | No. 201 |
|---|---|---|---|---|---|
| Date | Explanation | Ref. | Debit | Credit | Balance |
| July 1 | | G1 | | 3,900 | 3,900 |
| 15 | | G1 | | 400 | 4,300 |
| 18 | | G1 | 100 | | 4,200 |
| 25 | | G1 | 200 | | 4,000 |
| 31 | | P1 | | 8,300 | 12,300 |

| | **Merchandise Inventory** | | | | No. 120 |
|---|---|---|---|---|---|
| Date | Explanation | Ref. | Debit | Credit | Balance |
| July 15 | | G1 | 400 | | 400 |
| 18 | | G1 | | 100 | 300 |
| 25 | | G1 | | 200 | 100 |
| 31 | | P1 | 8,300 | | 8,400 |

## ACCOUNTS PAYABLE LEDGER

| | **Albin Equipment Co.** | | | | |
|---|---|---|---|---|---|
| Date | Explanation | Ref. | Debit | Credit | Balance |
| July 1 | | G1 | | 3,900 | 3,900 |

| | **Brian Co.** | | | | |
|---|---|---|---|---|---|
| Date | Explanation | Ref. | Debit | Credit | Balance |
| July 3 | | P1 | | 2,400 | 2,400 |
| 20 | | P1 | | 700 | 3,100 |

| | **Chacon Corp** | | | | |
|---|---|---|---|---|---|
| Date | Explanation | Ref. | Debit | Credit | Balance |
| July 17 | | P1 | | 1,400 | 1,400 |
| 18 | | G1 | 100 | | 1,300 |
| 29 | | P1 | | 1,600 | 2,900 |

| | **Drago Co.** | | | | |
|---|---|---|---|---|---|
| Date | Explanation | Ref. | Debit | Credit | Balance |
| July 14 | | P1 | | 1,100 | 1,100 |
| 25 | | G1 | 200 | | 900 |

| | **Erik Co.** | | | | |
|---|---|---|---|---|---|
| Date | Explanation | Ref. | Debit | Credit | Balance |
| July 12 | | P1 | | 500 | 500 |
| 21 | | P1 | | 600 | 1,100 |

| | **Heinen Inc.** | | | | |
|---|---|---|---|---|---|
| Date | Explanation | Ref. | Debit | Credit | Balance |
| July 15 | | G1 | | 400 | 400 |

**Instructions**
From the data prepare:
**(a)** the single-column purchases journal for July.
**(b)** the general journal entries for July.

**EE-13** Kansas Products uses both special journals and a general journal as described in this chapter. Kansas also posts customers' accounts in the accounts receivable subsidiary ledger. The postings for the most recent month are included in the subsidiary T accounts below.

*Determine correct posting amount to control account.*

*(SO 3)*

| | Bargo | | | | Leary | |
|---|---|---|---|---|---|---|
| Bal. | 340 | 250 | | Bal. | 150 | 150 |
| | 200 | | | | 240 | |

| | Carol | | | | Paul | |
|---|---|---|---|---|---|---|
| Bal. | –0– | 145 | | Bal. | 120 | 120 |
| | 145 | | | | 190 | |
| | | | | | 150 | |

**Instructions**
Determine the correct amount of the end-of-month posting from the sales journal to the Accounts Receivable control account.

**EE-14** Selected account balances for Matisyahu Company at January 1, 2008, are presented below.

*Compute balances in various accounts.*

*(SO 3)*

| | |
|---|---|
| Accounts Payable | $14,000 |
| Accounts Receivable | 22,000 |
| Cash | 17,000 |
| Inventory | 13,500 |

Matisyahu's sales journal for January shows a total of $100,000 in the selling price column, and its one-column purchases journal for January shows a total of $72,000.

The column totals in Matisyahu's cash receipts journal are: Cash Dr. $61,000; Sales Discounts Dr. $1,100; Accounts Receivable Cr. $45,000; Sales Cr. $6,000; and Other Accounts Cr. $11,100.

The column totals in Matisyahu's cash payments journal for January are: Cash Cr. $55,000; Inventory Cr. $1,000; Accounts Payable Dr. $46,000; and Other Accounts Dr. $10,000. Matisyahu's total cost of goods sold for January is $63,600.

Accounts Payable, Accounts Receivable, Cash, Inventory, and Sales are not involved in the "Other Accounts" column in either the cash receipts or cash payments journal, and are not involved in any general journal entries.

**Instructions**
Compute the January 31 balance for Matisyahu in the following accounts.
**(a)** Accounts Payable.
**(b)** Accounts Receivable.
**(c)** Cash.
**(d)** Inventory.
**(e)** Sales.

## EXERCISES: SET B

Visit the book's website at **www.wiley.com/college/weygandt**, and choose the Student Companion site, to access Exercise Set B.

## PROBLEMS: SET A

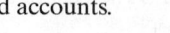

**PE-1A** Grider Company's chart of accounts includes the following selected accounts.

| | | | |
|---|---|---|---|
| 101 | Cash | 401 | Sales |
| 112 | Accounts Receivable | 414 | Sales Discounts |
| 120 | Merchandise Inventory | 505 | Cost of Goods Sold |
| 311 | Common Stock | | |

*Journalize transactions in cash receipts journal; post to control account and subsidiary ledger.*

*(SO 1, 2, 3)*

On April 1 the accounts receivable ledger of Grider Company showed the following balances: Ogden $1,550, Chelsea $1,200, Eggleston Co. $2,900, and Baez $1,800. The April transactions involving the receipt of cash were as follows.

Apr. 1 Stockholders invested $7,200 additional cash in the business, in exchange for common stock.
4 Received check for payment of account from Baez less 2% cash discount.
5 Received check for $920 in payment of invoice no. 307 from Eggleston Co.
8 Made cash sales of merchandise totaling $7,245. The cost of the merchandise sold was $4,347.
10 Received check for $600 in payment of invoice no. 309 from Ogden.
11 Received cash refund from a supplier for damaged merchandise $740.
23 Received check for $1,500 in payment of invoice no. 310 from Eggleston Co.
29 Received check for payment of account from Chelsea.

**Instructions**

*(a) Balancing totals $21,205*

**(a)** Journalize the transactions above in a six-column cash receipts journal with columns for Cash Dr., Sales Discounts Dr., Accounts Receivable Cr., Sales Cr., Other Accounts Cr., and Cost of Goods Sold Dr./Merchandise Inventory Cr. Foot and crossfoot the journal.

**(b)** Insert the beginning balances in the Accounts Receivable control and subsidiary accounts, and post the April transactions to these accounts.

*(c) Accounts Receivable $1,430*

**(c)** Prove the agreement of the control account and subsidiary account balances.

*Journalize transactions in cash payments journal; post to control account and subsidiary ledgers.*

*(SO 1, 2, 3)*

**PE-2A** Ming Company's chart of accounts includes the following selected accounts.

| | |
|---|---|
| 101 Cash | 201 Accounts Payable |
| 120 Merchandise Inventory | 332 Dividends |
| 130 Prepaid Insurance | 505 Cost of Goods Sold |
| 157 Equipment | |

On October 1 the accounts payable ledger of Ming Company showed the following balances: Bovary Company $2,700, Nyman Co. $2,500, Pyron Co. $1,800, and Sims Company $3,700. The October transactions involving the payment of cash were as follows.

Oct. 1 Purchased merchandise, check no. 63, $300.
3 Purchased equipment, check no. 64, $800.
5 Paid Bovary Company balance due of $2,700, less 2% discount, check no. 65, $2,646.
10 Purchased merchandise, check no. 66, $2,250.
15 Paid Pyron Co. balance due of $1,800, check no. 67.
16 Paid cash dividend of $400, check no. 68.
19 Paid Nyman Co. in full for invoice no. 610, $1,600 less 2% cash discount, check no. 69, $1,568.
29 Paid Sims Company in full for invoice no. 264, $2,500, check no. 70.

**Instructions**

*(a) Balancing totals $12,350*

**(a)** Journalize the transactions above in a four-column cash payments journal with columns for Other Accounts Dr., Accounts Payable Dr., Merchandise Inventory Cr., and Cash Cr. Foot and crossfoot the journal.

**(b)** Insert the beginning balances in the Accounts Payable control and subsidiary accounts, and post the October transactions to these accounts.

*(c) Accounts Payable $2,100*

**(c)** Prove the agreement of the control account and the subsidiary account balances.

*Journalize transactions in multi-column purchases journal; post to the general and subsidiary ledgers.*

*(SO 1, 2, 3)*

**PE-3A** The chart of accounts of Lopez Company includes the following selected accounts.

| | |
|---|---|
| 112 Accounts Receivable | 401 Sales |
| 120 Merchandise Inventory | 412 Sales Returns and Allowances |
| 126 Supplies | 505 Cost of Goods Sold |
| 157 Equipment | 610 Advertising Expense |
| 201 Accounts Payable | |

In July the following selected transactions were completed. All purchases and sales were on account. The cost of all merchandise sold was 70% of the sales price.

July 1 Purchased merchandise from Fritz Company $8,000.
2 Received freight bill from Wayward Shipping on Fritz purchase $400.
3 Made sales to Pinick Company $1,300, and to Wayne Bros. $1,500.

5  Purchased merchandise from Moon Company $3,200.
8  Received credit on merchandise returned to Moon Company $300.
13  Purchased store supplies from Cress Supply $720.
15  Purchased merchandise from Fritz Company $3,600 and from Anton Company $3,300.
16  Made sales to Sager Company $3,450 and to Wayne Bros. $1,570.
18  Received bill for advertising from Lynda Advertisements $600.
21  Made sales to Pinick Company $310 and to Haddad Company $2,800.
22  Granted allowance to Pinick Company for merchandise damaged in shipment $40.
24  Purchased merchandise from Moon Company $3,000.
26  Purchased equipment from Cress Supply $900.
28  Received freight bill from Wayward Shipping on Moon purchase of July 24, $380.
30  Made sales to Sager Company $5,600.

**Instructions**
(a) Journalize the transactions above in a purchases journal, a sales journal, and a general journal. The purchases journal should have the following column headings: Date, Account Credited (Debited), Ref., Accounts Payable Cr., Merchandise Inventory Dr., and Other Accounts Dr.
(b) Post to both the general and subsidiary ledger accounts. (Assume that all accounts have zero beginning balances.)
(c) Prove the agreement of the control and subsidiary accounts.

(a) Purchases journal—
Accounts Payable $24,100
Sales column total $16,530

(c) Accounts Receivable
$16,490
Accounts Payable
$23,800

**PE-4A**  Selected accounts from the chart of accounts of Boyden Company are shown below.

| 101 | Cash | 401 | Sales |
| 112 | Accounts Receivable | 412 | Sales Returns and Allowances |
| 120 | Merchandise Inventory | 414 | Sales Discounts |
| 126 | Supplies | 505 | Cost of Goods Sold |
| 157 | Equipment | 726 | Salaries Expense |
| 201 | Accounts Payable | | |

*Journalize transactions in special journals.*

(SO 1, 2, 3)

The cost of all merchandise sold was 60% of the sales price. During January, Boyden completed the following transactions.

Jan.  3  Purchased merchandise on account from Wortham Co. $10,000.
4  Purchased supplies for cash $80.
4  Sold merchandise on account to Milam $5,250, invoice no. 371, terms 1/10, n/30.
5  Returned $300 worth of damaged goods purchased on account from Wortham Co. on January 3.
6  Made cash sales for the week totaling $3,150.
8  Purchased merchandise on account from Noyes Co. $4,500.
9  Sold merchandise on account to Connor Corp. $6,400, invoice no. 372, terms 1/10, n/30.
11  Purchased merchandise on account from Betz Co. $3,700.
13  Paid in full Wortham Co. on account less a 2% discount.
13  Made cash sales for the week totaling $6,260.
15  Received payment from Connor Corp. for invoice no. 372.
15  Paid semi-monthly salaries of $14,300 to employees.
17  Received payment from Milam for invoice no. 371.
17  Sold merchandise on account to Bullock Co. $1,200, invoice no. 373, terms 1/10, n/30.
19  Purchased equipment on account from Murphy Corp. $5,500.
20  Cash sales for the week totaled $3,200.
20  Paid in full Noyes Co. on account less a 2% discount.
23  Purchased merchandise on account from Wortham Co. $7,800.
24  Purchased merchandise on account from Forgetta Corp. $5,100.
27  Made cash sales for the week totaling $4,230.
30  Received payment from Bullock Co. for invoice no. 373.
31  Paid semi-monthly salaries of $13,200 to employees.
31  Sold merchandise on account to Milam $9,330, invoice no. 374, terms 1/10, n/30.

Boyden Company uses the following journals.

1.  Sales journal.
2.  Single-column purchases journal.

3. Cash receipts journal with columns for Cash Dr., Sales Discounts Dr., Accounts Receivable Cr., Sales Cr., Other Accounts Cr., and Cost of Goods Sold Dr./Merchandise Inventory Cr.
4. Cash payments journal with columns for Other Accounts Dr., Accounts Payable Dr., Merchandise Inventory Cr., and Cash Cr.
5. General journal.

**Instructions**

Using the selected accounts provided:

**(a)** Record the January transactions in the appropriate journal noted.

**(b)** Foot and crossfoot all special journals.

**(c)** Show how postings would be made by placing ledger account numbers and checkmarks as needed in the journals. (Actual posting to ledger accounts is not required.)

(a) Sales journal $22,180
  Purchases journal $31,100
  Cash receipts journal
    balancing total $29,690
  Cash payments journal
    balancing total $41,780

*Journalize in sales and cash receipts journals; post; prepare a trial balance; prove control to subsidiary; prepare adjusting entries; prepare an adjusted trial balance.*

(SO 1, 2, 3)

GLS

**PE-5A** Presented below are the purchases and cash payments journals for Reyes Co. for its first month of operations.

## PURCHASES JOURNAL                 P1

| Date | Account Credited | Ref. | Merchandise Inventory Dr. Accounts Payable Cr. |
|------|------------------|------|-----------------------------------------------|
| July 4 | G. Clemens | | 6,800 |
| 5 | A. Ernst | | 8,100 |
| 11 | J. Happy | | 5,920 |
| 13 | C. Tabor | | 15,300 |
| 20 | M. Sneezy | | 7,900 |
| | | | 44,020 |

## CASH PAYMENTS JOURNAL                 CP1

| Date | Account Debited | Ref. | Other Accounts Dr. | Accounts Payable Dr. | Merchandise Inventory Cr. | Cash Cr. |
|------|-----------------|------|--------------------|----------------------|---------------------------|----------|
| July 4 | Store Supplies | | 600 | | | 600 |
| 10 | A. Ernst | | | 8,100 | 81 | 8,019 |
| 11 | Prepaid Rent | | 6,000 | | | 6,000 |
| 15 | G. Clemens | | | 6,800 | | 6,800 |
| 19 | Dividends | | 2,500 | | | 2,500 |
| 21 | C. Tabor | | | 15,300 | 153 | 15,147 |
| | | | 9,100 | 30,200 | 234 | 39,066 |

In addition, the following transactions have not been journalized for July. The cost of all merchandise sold was 65% of the sales price.

July 1 D. Reyes invested $80,000 in cash in exchange for common stock.
  6 Sold merchandise on account to Ewing Co. $6,200 terms 1/10, n/30.
  7 Made cash sales totaling $6,000.
  8 Sold merchandise on account to S. Beauty $3,600, terms 1/10, n/30.
  10 Sold merchandise on account to W. Pitts $4,900, terms 1/10, n/30.
  13 Received payment in full from S. Beauty.
  16 Received payment in full from W. Pitts.
  20 Received payment in full from Ewing Co.
  21 Sold merchandise on account to H. Prince $5,000, terms 1/10, n/30.
  29 Returned damaged goods to G. Clemens and received cash refund of $420.

**Instructions**

**(a)** Open the following accounts in the general ledger.

| | |
|---|---|
| 101 Cash | 127 Store Supplies |
| 112 Accounts Receivable | 131 Prepaid Rent |
| 120 Merchandise Inventory | 201 Accounts Payable |

311  Common Stock
332  Dividends
401  Sales
414  Sales Discounts

505  Cost of Goods Sold
631  Supplies Expense
729  Rent Expense

**(b)** Journalize the transactions that have not been journalized in the sales journal, the cash receipts journal (see Illustration E-8), and the general journal.

**(c)** Post to the accounts receivable and accounts payable subsidiary ledgers. Follow the sequence of transactions as shown in the problem.

**(d)** Post the individual entries and totals to the general ledger.

**(e)** Prepare a trial balance at July 31, 2008.

**(f)** Determine whether the subsidiary ledgers agree with the control accounts in the general ledger.

**(g)** The following adjustments at the end of July are necessary.

    **(1)** A count of supplies indicates that $140 is still on hand.

    **(2)** Recognize rent expense for July, $500.

    Prepare the necessary entries in the general journal. Post the entries to the general ledger.

**(h)** Prepare an adjusted trial balance at July 31, 2008.

*(b) Sales journal total*
*$19,700*
*Cash receipts journal*
*balancing totals $101,120*

*(e) Totals $119,520*
*(f) Accounts Receivable*
*$5,000*
*Accounts Payable $13,820*

*(h) Totals $119,520*

**PE-6A**    The post-closing trial balance for Cortez Co. is as follows.

*Journalize in special journals;*
*post; prepare a trial balance.*
*(SO 1, 2, 3)*

### CORTEZ CO.
Post-Closing Trial Balance
December 31, 2008

|                                       | Debit     | Credit    |
|---------------------------------------|-----------|-----------|
| Cash                                  | $ 41,500  |           |
| Accounts Receivable                   | 15,000    |           |
| Notes Receivable                      | 45,000    |           |
| Merchandise Inventory                 | 23,000    |           |
| Equipment                             | 6,450     |           |
| Accumulated Depreciation—Equipment    |           | $  1,500  |
| Accounts Payable                      |           | 43,000    |
| Common Stock                          |           | 86,450    |
|                                       | $130,950  | $130,950  |

    The subsidiary ledgers contain the following information: (1) accounts receivable—J. Anders $2,500, F. Cone $7,500, T. Dudley $5,000; (2) accounts payable—J. Feeney $10,000, D. Goodman $18,000, and K. Inwood $15,000. The cost of all merchandise sold was 60% of the sales price.

    The transactions for January 2009 are as follows.

Jan.  3  Sell merchandise to M. Rensing $5,000, terms 2/10, n/30.
     5  Purchase merchandise from E. Vietti $2,000, terms 2/10, n/30.
     7  Receive a check from T. Dudley $3,500.
   11  Pay freight on merchandise purchased $300.
   12  Pay rent of $1,000 for January.
   13  Receive payment in full from M. Rensing.
   14  Post all entries to the subsidiary ledgers. Issued credit of $300 to J. Aders for returned merchandise.
   15  Send K. Inwood a check for $14,850 in full payment of account, discount $150.
   17  Purchase merchandise from G. Marley $1,600, terms 2/10, n/30.
   18  Pay sales salaries of $2,800 and office salaries $2,000.
   20  Give D. Goodman a 60-day note for $18,000 in full payment of account payable.
   23  Total cash sales amount to $9,100.
   24  Post all entries to the subsidiary ledgers. Sell merchandise on account to F. Cone $7,400, terms 1/10, n/30.
   27  Send E. Vietti a check for $950.
   29  Receive payment on a note of $40,000 from B. Lemke.
   30  Post all entries to the subsidiary ledgers. Return merchandise of $300 to G. Marley for credit.

**Instructions**

**(a)** Open general and subsidiary ledger accounts for the following.

| | |
|---|---|
| 101 Cash | 311 Common Stock |
| 112 Accounts Receivable | 401 Sales |
| 115 Notes Receivable | 412 Sales Returns and Allowances |
| 120 Merchandise Inventory | 414 Sales Discounts |
| 157 Equipment | 505 Cost of Goods Sold |
| 158 Accumulated Depreciation—Equipment | 726 Sales Salaries Expense |
| 200 Notes Payable | 727 Office Salaries Expense |
| 201 Accounts Payable | 729 Rent Expense |

(b) Sales journal $12,400
Purchases journal $3,600
Cash receipts journal
(balancing) $57,600
Cash payments journal
(balancing) $22,050
(d) Totals $139,800
(e) Accounts Receivable
$18,600
Accounts Payable
$12,350

**(b)** Record the January transactions in a sales journal, a single-column purchases journal, a cash receipts journal (see Illustration E-8), a cash payments journal (see Illustration E-15), and a general journal.

**(c)** Post the appropriate amounts to the general ledger.

**(d)** Prepare a trial balance at January 31, 2009.

**(e)** Determine whether the subsidiary ledgers agree with controlling accounts in the general ledger.

# PROBLEMS: SET B

*Journalize transactions in cash receipts journal; post to control account and subsidiary ledger.*

*(SO 1, 2, 3)*

**GLS**

**PE-1B**    Darby Company's chart of accounts includes the following selected accounts.

| | |
|---|---|
| 101 Cash | 401 Sales |
| 112 Accounts Receivable | 414 Sales Discounts |
| 120 Merchandise Inventory | 505 Cost of Goods Sold |
| 311 Common Stock | |

On June 1 the accounts receivable ledger of Darby Company showed the following balances: Deering & Son $2,500, Farley Co. $1,900, Grinnell Bros. $1,600, and Lenninger Co. $1,300. The June transactions involving the receipt of cash were as follows.

June 1    Stockholders invested $10,000 additional cash in the business, in exchange for common stock.

3    Received check in full from Lenninger Co. less 2% cash discount.

6    Received check in full from Farley Co. less 2% cash discount.

7    Made cash sales of merchandise totaling $6,135. The cost of the merchandise sold was $4,090.

9    Received check in full from Deering & Son less 2% cash discount.

11    Received cash refund from a supplier for damaged merchandise $320.

15    Made cash sales of merchandise totaling $4,500. The cost of the merchandise sold was $3,000.

20    Received check in full from Grinnell Bros. $1,600.

**Instructions**

(a) Balancing totals $28,255

**(a)** Journalize the transactions above in a six-column cash receipts journal with columns for Cash Dr., Sales Discounts Dr., Accounts Receivable Cr., Sales Cr., Other Accounts Cr., and Cost of Goods Sold Dr./Merchandise Inventory Cr. Foot and crossfoot the journal.

**(b)** Insert the beginning balances in the Accounts Receivable control and subsidiary accounts, and post the June transactions to these accounts.

(c) Accounts Receivable $0

**(c)** Prove the agreement of the control account and subsidiary account balances.

*Journalize transactions in cash payments journal; post to the general and subsidiary ledgers.*

*(SO 1, 2, 3)*

**GLS**

**PE-2B**    Gonya Company's chart of accounts includes the following selected accounts.

| | |
|---|---|
| 101 Cash | 157 Equipment |
| 120 Merchandise Inventory | 201 Accounts Payable |
| 130 Prepaid Insurance | 332 Dividends |

On November 1 the accounts payable ledger of Gonya Company showed the following balances: A. Hess & Co. $4,500, C. Kimberlin $2,350, G. Ruttan $1,000, and Wex Bros. $1,500. The November transactions involving the payment of cash were as follows.

Nov. 1    Purchased merchandise, check no. 11, $1,140.

3    Purchased store equipment, check no. 12, $1,700.

5   Paid Wex Bros. balance due of $1,500, less 1% discount, check no. 13, $1,485.
11   Purchased merchandise, check no. 14, $2,000.
15   Paid G. Ruttan balance due of $1,000, less 3% discount, check no. 15, $970.
16   Paid cash dividend of $500, check no. 16.
19   Paid C. Kimberlin in full for invoice no. 1245, $1,150 less 2% discount, check no. 17, $1,127.
25   Paid premium due on one-year insurance policy, check no. 18, $3,000.
30   Paid A. Hess & Co. in full for invoice no. 832, $3,500, check no. 19.

**Instructions**
**(a)** Journalize the transactions above in a four-column cash payments journal with columns for Other Accounts Dr., Accounts Payable Dr., Merchandise Inventory Cr., and Cash Cr. Foot and crossfoot the journal.

*(a) Balancing totals $15,490*

**(b)** Insert the beginning balances in the Accounts Payable control and subsidiary accounts, and post the November transactions to these accounts.
**(c)** Prove the agreement of the control account and the subsidiary account balances.

*(c) Accounts Payable $2,200*

**PE-3B**   The chart of accounts of Emley Company includes the following selected accounts.

| | |
|---|---|
| 112  Accounts Receivable | 401  Sales |
| 120  Merchandise Inventory | 412  Sales Returns and Allowances |
| 126  Supplies | 505  Cost of Goods Sold |
| 157  Equipment | 610  Advertising Expense |
| 201  Accounts Payable | |

*Journalize transactions in multi-column purchases journal; post to the general and subsidiary ledgers.*

*(SO 1, 2, 3)*

In May the following selected transactions were completed. All purchases and sales were on account except as indicated. The cost of all merchandise sold was 65% of the sales price.

May   2   Purchased merchandise from Younger Company $7,500.
  3   Received freight bill from Ruden Freight on Younger purchase $360.
  5   Made sales to Ellie Company $1,980, DeShazer Bros. $2,700, and Liu Company $1,500.
  8   Purchased merchandise from Utley Company $8,000 and Zeider Company $8,700.
  10   Received credit on merchandise returned to Zeider Company $500.
  15   Purchased supplies from Rodriquez Supply $900.
  16   Purchased merchandise from Younger Company $4,500, and Utley Company $7,200.
  17   Returned supplies to Rodriquez Supply, receiving credit $100. (*Hint*: Credit Supplies.)
  18   Received freight bills on May 16 purchases from Ruden Freight $500.
  20   Returned merchandise to Younger Company receiving credit $300.
  23   Made sales to DeShazer Bros. $2,400 and to Liu Company $3,600.
  25   Received bill for advertising from Amster Advertising $900.
  26   Granted allowance to Liu Company for merchandise damaged in shipment $200.
  28   Purchased equipment from Rodriquez Supply $500.

**Instructions**
**(a)** Journalize the transactions above in a purchases journal, a sales journal, and a general journal. The purchases journal should have the following column headings: Date, Account Credited (Debited), Ref., Accounts Payable Cr., Merchandise Inventory Dr., and Other Accounts Dr.

*(a) Purchases journal—
Accounts Payable, Cr.
$39,060
Sales column total
$12,180*

**(b)** Post to both the general and subsidiary ledger accounts. (Assume that all accounts have zero beginning balances.)
**(c)** Prove the agreement of the control and subsidiary accounts.

*(c) Accounts Receivable
$11,980
Accounts Payable
$38,160*

**PE-4B**   Selected accounts from the chart of accounts of Litke Company are shown below.

| | |
|---|---|
| 101  Cash | 201  Accounts Payable |
| 112  Accounts Receivable | 401  Sales |
| 120  Merchandise Inventory | 414  Sales Discounts |
| 126  Supplies | 505  Cost of Goods Sold |
| 140  Land | 610  Advertising Expense |
| 145  Buildings | |

*Journalize transactions in special journals.*

*(SO 1, 2, 3)*

The cost of all merchandise sold was 70% of the sales price. During October, Litke Company completed the following transactions.

Oct. 2 Purchased merchandise on account from Camacho Company $16,500.
4 Sold merchandise on account to Enos Co. $7,700. Invoice no. 204, terms 2/10, n/30.
5 Purchased supplies for cash $80.
7 Made cash sales for the week totaling $9,160.
9 Paid in full the amount owed Camacho Company less a 2% discount.
10 Purchased merchandise on account from Finn Corp. $3,500.
12 Received payment from Enos Co. for invoice no. 204.
13 Returned $210 worth of damaged goods purchased on account from Finn Corp. on October 10.
14 Made cash sales for the week totaling $8,180.
16 Sold a parcel of land for $27,000 cash, the land's original cost.
17 Sold merchandise on account to G. Richter & Co. $5,350, invoice no. 205, terms 2/10, n/30.
18 Purchased merchandise for cash $2,125.
21 Made cash sales for the week totaling $8,200.
23 Paid in full the amount owed Finn Corp. for the goods kept (no discount).
25 Purchased supplies on account from Robinson Co. $260.
25 Sold merchandise on account to Hunt Corp. $5,220, invoice no. 206, terms 2/10, n/30.
25 Received payment from G. Richter & Co. for invoice no. 205.
26 Purchased for cash a small parcel of land and a building on the land to use as a storage facility. The total cost of $35,000 was allocated $21,000 to the land and $14,000 to the building.
27 Purchased merchandise on account from Kudro Co. $8,500.
28 Made cash sales for the week totaling $7,540.
30 Purchased merchandise on account from Camacho Company $14,000.
30 Paid advertising bill for the month from the *Gazette*, $400.
30 Sold merchandise on account to G. Richter & Co. $4,600, invoice no. 207, terms 2/10, n/30.

Litke Company uses the following journals.

1. Sales journal.
2. Single-column purchases journal.
3. Cash receipts journal with columns for Cash Dr., Sales Discounts Dr., Accounts Receivable Cr., Sales Cr., Other Accounts Cr., and Cost of Goods Sold Dr./Merchandise Inventory Cr.
4. Cash payments journal with columns for Other Accounts Dr., Accounts Payable Dr., Merchandise Inventory Cr., and Cash Cr.
5. General journal.

(b) Sales journal $22,870
   Purchases journal $42,500
   Cash receipts journal— Cash, Dr. $72,869
   Cash payments journal, Cash, Cr. $57,065

**Instructions**
Using the selected accounts provided:
(a) Record the October transactions in the appropriate journals.
(b) Foot and crossfoot all special journals.
(c) Show how postings would be made by placing ledger account numbers and check marks as needed in the journals. (Actual posting to ledger accounts is not required.)

*Journalize in purchases and cash payments journals; post; prepare a trial balance; prove control to subsidiary; prepare adjusting entries; prepare an adjusted trial balance.*

(SO 1, 2, 3)

**PE-5B** Presented below are the sales and cash receipts journals for Wyrick Co. for its first month of operations.

## SALES JOURNAL                                                                 S1

| Date | Account Debited | Ref. | Accounts Receivable Dr. Sales Cr. | Cost of Goods Sold Dr. Merchandise Inventory Cr. |
|------|-----------------|------|-----------------------------------|--------------------------------------------------|
| Feb. 3 | S. Arndt |  | 5,500 | 3,630 |
| 9 | C. Boyd |  | 6,500 | 4,290 |
| 12 | F. Catt |  | 8,000 | 5,280 |
| 26 | M. Didde |  | 7,000 | 4,620 |
|  |  |  | 27,000 | 17,820 |

## CASH RECEIPTS JOURNAL CR1

| Date | Account Credited | Ref. | Cash Dr. | Sales Discounts Dr. | Accounts Receivable Cr. | Sales Cr. | Other Accounts Cr. | Cost of Goods Sold Dr. Merchandise Inventory Cr. |
|------|------------------|------|----------|---------------------|-------------------------|-----------|--------------------|--------------------------------------------------|
| Feb. 1 | Common Stock | | 30,000 | | | | 30,000 | |
| 2 | | | 6,500 | | | 6,500 | | 4,290 |
| 13 | S. Arndt | | 5,445 | 55 | 5,500 | | | |
| 18 | Merchandise Inventory | | 150 | | | | 150 | |
| 26 | C. Boyd | | 6,500 | | 6,500 | | | |
| | | | 48,595 | 55 | 12,000 | 6,500 | 30,150 | 4,290 |

In addition, the following transactions have not been journalized for February 2008.

Feb. 2 Purchased merchandise on account from J. Vopat for $4,600, terms 2/10, n/30.
7 Purchased merchandise on account from P. Kneiser for $30,000, terms 1/10, n/30.
9 Paid cash of $1,250 for purchase of supplies.
12 Paid $4,508 to J. Vopat in payment for $4,600 invoice, less 2% discount.
15 Purchased equipment for $7,000 cash.
16 Purchased merchandise on account from J. Nunez $2,400, terms 2/10, n/30.
17 Paid $29,700 to P. Kneiser in payment of $30,000 invoice, less 1% discount.
20 Paid cash dividend of $1,100.
21 Purchased merchandise on account from G. Reedy for $7,800, terms 1/10, n/30.
28 Paid $2,400 to J. Nunez in payment of $2,400 invoice.

### Instructions

**(a)** Open the following accounts in the general ledger.

101 Cash      311 Common Stock
112 Accounts Receivable      332 Dividends
120 Merchandise Inventory      401 Sales
126 Supplies      414 Sales Discounts
157 Equipment      505 Cost of Goods Sold
158 Accumulated Depreciation—Equipment      631 Supplies Expense
201 Accounts Payable      711 Depreciation Expense

**(b)** Journalize the transactions that have not been journalized in a one-column purchases journal and the cash payments journal (see Illustration E-15).

*(b) Purchases journal total $44,800 Cash payments journal—Cash, Cr. $45,958*

**(c)** Post to the accounts receivable and accounts payable subsidiary ledgers. Follow the sequence of transactions as shown in the problem.

**(d)** Post the individual entries and totals to the general ledger.

**(e)** Prepare a trial balance at February 29, 2008.

*(e) Totals $71,300*

**(f)** Determine that the subsidiary ledgers agree with the control accounts in the general ledger.

*(f) Accounts Receivable $15,000 Accounts Payable $7,800*

**(g)** The following adjustments at the end of February are necessary.
   **(1)** A count of supplies indicates that $300 is still on hand.
   **(2)** Depreciation on equipment for February is $200.
   Prepare the adjusting entries and then post the adjusting entries to the general ledger.

**(h)** Prepare an adjusted trial balance at February 29, 2008.

*(h) Totals $71,500*

## PROBLEMS: SET C

Visit the book's website at **www.wiley.com/college/weygandt**, and choose the Student Companion site, to access Problem Set C.

## COMPREHENSIVE PROBLEM: CHAPTERS 3 TO 6 AND APPENDIX E

Packard Company has the following opening account balances in its general and subsidiary ledgers on January 1 and uses the periodic inventory system. All accounts have normal debit and credit balances.

## General Ledger

| Account Number | Account Title | January 1 Opening Balance |
|---|---|---|
| 101 | Cash | $33,750 |
| 112 | Accounts Receivable | 13,000 |
| 115 | Notes Receivable | 39,000 |
| 120 | Merchandise Inventory | 20,000 |
| 125 | Office Supplies | 1,000 |
| 130 | Prepaid Insurance | 2,000 |
| 157 | Equipment | 6,450 |
| 158 | Accumulated Depreciation | 1,500 |
| 201 | Accounts Payable | 35,000 |
| 311 | Common Stock | 70,000 |
| 320 | Retained Earnings | 8,700 |

## Accounts Receivable Subsidiary Ledger

| Customer | January 1 Opening Balance |
|---|---|
| R. Draves | $1,500 |
| B. Hachinski | 7,500 |
| S. Ingles | 4,000 |

## Accounts Payable Subsidiary Ledger

| Creditor | January 1 Opening Balance |
|---|---|
| S. Kosko | $ 9,000 |
| R. Mikush | 15,000 |
| D. Moreno | 11,000 |

Jan. 3 Sell merchandise on account to B. Remy $3,100, invoice no. 510, and J. Fine $1,800, invoice no. 511.
5 Purchase merchandise on account from S. Yost $3,000 and D. Laux $2,700.
7 Receive checks for $4,000 from S. Ingles and $2,000 from B. Hachinski.
8 Pay freight on merchandise purchased $180.
9 Send checks to S. Kosko for $9,000 and D. Moreno for $11,000.
9 Issue credit of $300 to J. Fine for merchandise returned.
10 Summary cash sales total $15,500.
11 Sell merchandise on account to R. Draves for $1,900, invoice no. 512, and to S. Ingles $900, invoice no. 513.
   Post all entries to the subsidiary ledgers.
12 Pay rent of $1,000 for January.
13 Receive payment in full from B. Remy and J. Fine.
15 Pay cash dividend of $800.
16 Purchase merchandise on account from D. Moreno for $15,000, from S. Kosko for $13,900, and from S. Yost for $1,500.
17 Pay $400 cash for office supplies.
18 Return $200 of merchandise to S. Kosko and receive credit.
20 Summary cash sales total $17,500.
21 Issue $15,000 note to R. Mikush in payment of balance due.
21 Receive payment in full from S. Ingles.
   Post all entries to the subsidiary ledgers.
22 Sell merchandise on account to B. Remy for $3,700, invoice no. 514, and to R. Draves for $800, invoice no. 515.
23 Send checks to D. Moreno and S. Kosko in full payment.
25 Sell merchandise on account to B. Hachinski for $3,500, invoice no. 516, and to J. Fine for $6,100, invoice no. 517.
27 Purchase merchandise on account from D. Moreno for $12,500, from D. Laux for $1,200, and from S. Yost for $2,800.
28 Pay $200 cash for office supplies.
31 Summary cash sales total $22,920.
31 Pay sales salaries of $4,300 and office salaries of $3,600.

**Instructions**

**(a)** Record the January transactions in the appropriate journal—sales, purchases, cash receipts, cash payments, and general.

**(b)** Post the journals to the general and subsidiary ledgers. Add and number new accounts in an orderly fashion as needed.

**(c)** Prepare a trial balance at January 31, 2008, using a worksheet. Complete the worksheet using the following additional information.

    **(1)** Office supplies at January 31 total $700.

    **(2)** Insurance coverage expires on October 31, 2008.

    **(3)** Annual depreciation on the equipment is $1,500.

    **(4)** Interest of $30 has accrued on the note payable.

    **(5)** Merchandise inventory at January 31 is $15,000.

**(d)** Prepare a multiple-step income statement and a retained earnings statement for January and a classified balance sheet at the end of January.

**(e)** Prepare and post the adjusting and closing entries.

**(f)** Prepare a post-closing trial balance, and determine whether the subsidiary ledgers agree with the control accounts in the general ledger.

(c) Trial balance totals
$196,820;
Adj. T/B totals $196,975

(d) Net income $9,685
Total assets $126,315

(f) Post-closing T/B totals
$127,940

# BROADENING YOUR PERSPECTIVE

## FINANCIAL REPORTING AND ANALYSIS

## Financial Reporting Problem—Mini Practice Set

**BYPE-1** **(You will need the working papers that accompany this textbook in order to work this mini practice set.)**    `GLS`

Bluma Co. uses a perpetual inventory system and both an accounts receivable and an accounts payable subsidiary ledger. Balances related to both the general ledger and the subsidiary ledger for Bluma are indicated in the working papers. Presented below are a series of transactions for Bluma Co. for the month of January. Credit sales terms are 2/10, n/30. The cost of all merchandise sold was 60% of the sales price.

Jan.  3   Sell merchandise on account to B. Richey $3,100, invoice no. 510, and to J. Forbes $1,800, invoice no. 511.

    5   Purchase merchandise from S. Vogel $5,000 and D. Lynch $2,200, terms n/30.

    7   Receive checks from S. LaDew $4,000 and B. Garcia $2,000 after discount period has lapsed.

    8   Pay freight on merchandise purchased $235.

    9   Send checks to S. Hoyt for $9,000 less 2% cash discount, and to D. Omara for $11,000 less 1% cash discount.

    9   Issue credit of $300 to J. Forbes for merchandise returned.

  10   Summary daily cash sales total $15,500.

  11   Sell merchandise on account to R. Dvorak $1,600, invoice no. 512, and to S. LaDew $900, invoice no. 513.

  12   Pay rent of $1,000 for January.

  13   Receive payment in full from B. Richey and J. Forbes less cash discounts.

  14   Pay an $800 cash dividend.

  15   Post all entries to the subsidiary ledgers.

  16   Purchase merchandise from D. Omara $18,000, terms 1/10, n/30; S. Hoyt $14,200, terms 2/10, n/30; and S. Vogel $1,500, terms n/30.

  17   Pay $400 cash for office supplies.

  18   Return $200 of merchandise to S. Hoyt and receive credit.

  20   Summary daily cash sales total $20,100.

  21   Issue $15,000 note, maturing in 90 days, to R. Moses in payment of balance due.

  21   Receive payment in full from S. LaDew less cash discount.

  22   Sell merchandise on account to B. Richey $2,700, invoice no. 514, and to R. Dvorak $1,300, invoice no. 515.

  22   Post all entries to the subsidiary ledgers.

> 23 Send checks to D. Omara and S. Hoyt in full payment less cash discounts.
> 25 Sell merchandise on account to B. Garcia $3,500, invoice no. 516, and to J. Forbes $6,100, invoice no. 517.
> 27 Purchase merchandise from D. Omara $14,500, terms 1/10, n/30; D. Lynch $1,200, terms n/30; and S. Vogel $5,400, terms n/30.
> 27 Post all entries to the subsidiary ledgers.
> 28 Pay $200 cash for office supplies.
> 31 Summary daily cash sales total $21,300.
> 31 Pay sales salaries $4,300 and office salaries $3,800.

**Instructions**

**(a)** Record the January transactions in a sales journal, a single-column purchases journal, a cash receipts journal as shown on page E8, a cash payments journal as shown on page E14, and a two-column general journal.

**(b)** Post the journals to the general ledger.

**(c)** Prepare a trial balance at January 31, 2008, in the trial balance columns of the worksheet. Complete the worksheet using the following additional information.
  **(1)** Office supplies at January 31 total $900.
  **(2)** Insurance coverage expires on October 31, 2008.
  **(3)** Annual depreciation on the equipment is $1,500.
  **(4)** Interest of $50 has accrued on the note payable.

**(d)** Prepare a multiple-step income statement and a retained earnings statement for January and a classified balance sheet at the end of January.

**(e)** Prepare and post adjusting and closing entries.

**(f)** Prepare a post-closing trial balance, and determine whether the subsidiary ledgers agree with the control accounts in the general ledger.

# Exploring the Web

**BYPE-2** Great Plains' Accounting is one of the leading accounting software packages. Information related to this package is found at its website.

**Address: www.microsoft.com/dynamics/gp/product/demos.mspx**, or go to **www.wiley.com/college/weygandt**

**Steps**
1. Go to the site shown above.
2. Choose **General Ledger**. Perform instruction (a).
3. Choose **Accounts Payable**. Perform instruction (b).

**Instructions**
**(a)** What are three key features of the general ledger module highlighted by the company?
**(b)** What are three key features of the payables management module highlighted by the company?

# CRITICAL THINKING

## Decision Making Across the Organization

**BYPE-3** Hughey & Payne is a wholesaler of small appliances and parts. Hughey & Payne is operated by two owners, Rich Hughey and Kristen Payne. In addition, the company has one employee, a repair specialist, who is on a fixed salary. Revenues are earned through the sale of appliances to retailers (approximately 75% of total revenues), appliance parts to do-it-yourselfers (10%), and the repair of appliances brought to the store (15%). Appliance sales are made on both a credit and cash basis. Customers are billed on prenumbered sales invoices. Credit terms are always net/30 days. All parts sales and repair work are cash only.

Merchandise is purchased on account from the manufacturers of both the appliances and the parts. Practically all suppliers offer cash discounts for prompt payments, and it is company policy to take all discounts. Most cash payments are made by check. Checks are most frequently issued to suppliers, to trucking companies for freight on merchandise purchases, and to newspapers, radio, and TV stations for advertising. All advertising bills are paid as received.

Rich and Kristen each make a monthly drawing in cash for personal living expenses. The salaried repairman is paid twice monthly. Hughey & Payne currently has a manual accounting system.

**Instructions**

With the class divided into groups, answer the following.

**(a)** Identify the special journals that Hughey & Payne should have in its manual system. List the column headings appropriate for each of the special journals.

**(b)** What control and subsidiary accounts should be included in Hughey & Payne manual system? Why?

# Communication Activity

**BYPE-4**  Barb Doane, a classmate, has a part-time bookkeeping job. She is concerned about the inefficiencies in journalizing and posting transactions. Jim Houser is the owner of the company where Barb works. In response to numerous complaints from Barb and others, Jim hired two additional bookkeepers a month ago. However, the inefficiencies have continued at an even higher rate. The accounting information system for the company has only a general journal and a general ledger. Jim refuses to install an electronic accounting system.

**Instructions**

Now that Barb is an expert in manual accounting information systems, she decides to send a letter to Jim Houser explaining (1) why the additional personnel did not help and (2) what changes should be made to improve the efficiency of the accounting department. Write the letter that you think Barb should send.

# Ethics Case

**BYPE-5**  Roniger Products Company operates three divisions, each with its own manufacturing plant and marketing/sales force. The corporate headquarters and central accounting office are in Roniger, and the plants are in Freeport, Rockport, and Bayport, all within 50 miles of Roniger. Corporate management treats each division as an independent profit center and encourages competition among them. They each have similar but different product lines. As a competitive incentive, bonuses are awarded each year to the employees of the fastest growing and most profitable division.

Jose Molina is the manager of Roniger's centralized computer accounting operation that enters the sales transactions and maintains the accounts receivable for all three divisions. Jose came up in the accounting ranks from the Bayport division where his wife, several relatives, and many friends still work.

As sales documents are entered into the computer, the originating division is identified by code. Most sales documents (95%) are coded, but some (5%) are not coded or are coded incorrectly. As the manager, Jose has instructed the data-entry personnel to assign the Bayport code to all uncoded and incorrectly coded sales documents. This is done he says, "in order to expedite processing and to keep the computer files current since they are updated daily." All receivables and cash collections for all three divisions are handled by Roniger as one subsidiary accounts receivable ledger.

**Instructions**

**(a)** Who are the stakeholders in this situation?

**(b)** What are the ethical issues in this case?

**(c)** How might the system be improved to prevent this situation?

## Answers to Self-Study Questions

**1.** a  **2.** c  **3.** a  **4.** c  **5.** d  **6.** b  **7.** c  **8.** c

# Other Significant Liabilities

## STUDY OBJECTIVE

*After studying this appendix, you should be able to:*

1. Describe the accounting and disclosure requirements for contingent liabilities.
2. Contrast the accounting for operating and capital leases.
3. Identify additional fringe benefits associated with employee compensation.

In addition to the current and long-term liabilities discussed in Chapter 11, several more types of liabilities may exist that could have a significant impact on a company's financial position and future cash flows. These other significant liabilities will be discussed in this appendix. They are: (a) contingent liabilities, (b) lease liabilities, and (c) additional liabilities for employee fringe benefits (paid absences and postretirement benefits).

## CONTINGENT LIABILITIES

With notes payable, interest payable, accounts payable, and sales taxes payable, we know that an obligation to make a payment exists. But suppose that your company is involved in a dispute with the Internal Revenue Service (IRS) over the amount of its income tax liability. Should you report the disputed amount as a liability on the balance sheet? Or suppose your company is involved in a lawsuit which, if you lose, might result in bankruptcy. How should you report this major contingency? The answers to these questions are difficult, because these liabilities are dependent—contingent—upon some future event. In other words, a **contingent liability** is a potential liability that may become an actual liability in the future.

> **STUDY OBJECTIVE 1**
> Describe the accounting and disclosure requirements for contingent liabilities.

How should companies report contingent liabilities? They use the following guidelines:

1. If the contingency is **probable** (if it is *likely* to occur) **and** the amount can be **reasonably estimated**, the liability should be recorded in the accounts.
2. If the contingency is only **reasonably possible** (if it *could* happen), then it needs to be disclosed only in the notes that accompany the financial statements.
3. If the contingency is **remote** (if it is *unlikely* to occur), it need not be recorded or disclosed.

## Recording a Contingent Liability

Product warranties are an example of a contingent liability that companies should record in the accounts. Warranty contracts result in future costs that companies may incur in replacing defective units or repairing malfunctioning units. Generally, a manufacturer, such as Black & Decker, knows that it will incur some warranty costs. From prior experience with the product, the company usually can reasonably estimate the anticipated cost of servicing (honoring) the warranty.

The accounting for warranty costs is based on the matching principle. **The estimated cost of honoring product warranty contracts should be recognized as an expense in the period in which the sale occurs.** To illustrate, assume that in 2008 Denson Manufacturing Company sells 10,000 washers and dryers at an average price of $600 each. The selling price includes a one-year warranty on parts. Denson expects that 500 units (5%) will be defective and that warranty repair costs will average $80 per unit. In 2008, the company honors warranty contracts on 300 units, at a total cost of $24,000.

At December 31, it is necessary to accrue the estimated warranty costs on the 2008 sales. Denson computes the estimated warranty liability as follows.

**Illustration F-1**
Computation of estimated product warranty liability

| | |
|---|---:|
| Number of units sold | 10,000 |
| Estimated rate of defective units | × 5% |
| Total estimated defective units | 500 |
| Average warranty repair cost | × $80 |
| **Estimated product warranty liability** | **$40,000** |

The company makes the following adjusting entry.

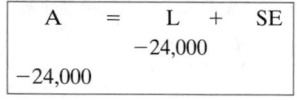

A = L + SE
     −40,000 Exp
+40,000

Cash Flows
no effect

| Dec. 31 | Warranty Expense | 40,000 | |
|---|---|---|---|
| | Estimated Warranty Liability | | 40,000 |
| | (To accrue estimated warranty costs) | | |

Denson records those repair costs incurred in 2008 to honor warranty contracts on 2008 sales as shown below.

A = L + SE
     −24,000
−24,000

Cash Flows
no effect

| Jan. 1– | Estimated Warranty Liability | 24,000 | |
|---|---|---|---|
| Dec. 31 | Repair Parts | | 24,000 |
| | (To record honoring of 300 warranty contracts on 2008 sales) | | |

The company reports warranty expense of $40,000 under selling expenses in the income statement. It classifies estimated warranty liability of $16,000 ($40,000 − $24,000) as a current liability on the balance sheet.

In the following year, Denson should debit to Estimated Warranty Liability all expenses incurred in honoring warranty contracts on 2008 sales. To illustrate, assume that the company replaces 20 defective units in January 2009, at an average cost of $80 in parts and labor. The summary entry for the month of January 2009 is:

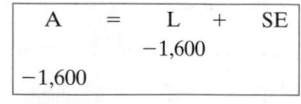

A = L + SE
     −1,600
−1,600

Cash Flows
no effect

| Jan. 31 | Estimated Warranty Liability | 1,600 | |
|---|---|---|---|
| | Repair Parts | | 1,600 |
| | (To record honoring of 20 warranty contracts on 2008 sales) | | |

## Disclosure of Contingent Liabilities

When it is probable that a company will incur a contingent liability but it cannot reasonably estimate the amount, or when the contingent liability is only reasonably possible, only disclosure of the contingency is required. Examples of contingencies that may require disclosure are pending or threatened lawsuits and assessment of additional income taxes pending an IRS audit of the tax return.

The disclosure should identify the nature of the item and, if known, the amount of the contingency and the expected outcome of the future event. Disclosure is usually accomplished through a note to the financial statements, as illustrated by the following.

| **YAHOO!** | **YAHOO! INC.** |
|---|---|
| | Notes to the Financial Statements |

**Contingencies**. From time to time, third parties assert patent infringement claims against the company. Currently the company is engaged in several lawsuits regarding patent issues and has been notified of a number of other potential patent disputes. In addition, from time to time the company is subject to other legal proceedings and claims in the ordinary course of business, including claims for infringement of trademarks, copyrights and other intellectual property rights.... The Company does not believe, based on current knowledge, that any of the foregoing legal proceedings or claims are likely to have a material adverse effect on the financial position, results of operations or cash flows.

**Illustration F-2**
Disclosure of contingent liability

The required disclosure for contingencies is a good example of the use of the full-disclosure principle. The **full-disclosure principle** requires that companies disclose all circumstances and events that would make a difference to financial statement users. Some important financial information, such as contingencies, is not easily reported in the financial statements. Reporting information on contingencies in the notes to the financial statements will help investors be aware of events that can affect the financial health of a company.

# LEASE LIABILITIES

A **lease** is a contractual arrangement between a lessor (owner of a property) and a lessee (renter of the property). It grants the right to use specific property for a period of time in return for cash payments. Leasing is big business. U.S. companies leased an estimated $125 billion of capital equipment in a recent year. This represents approximately one-third of equipment financed that year. The two most common types of leases are operating leases and capital leases.

**STUDY OBJECTIVE 2**
Contrast the accounting for operating and capital leases.

## Operating Leases

The renting of an apartment and the rental of a car at an airport are examples of **operating leases. In an** operating lease **the intent is temporary use of the property by the lessee, while the lessor continues to own the property.**

In an operating lease, the lessee records the lease (or rental) payments as an expense. The lessor records the payments as revenue. For example, assume that a sales representative for Western Inc. leases a car from Hertz Car Rental at the Los Angeles airport and that Hertz charges a total of $275. Western, the lessee, records the rental as follows:

| | | |
|---|---|---|
| Car Rental Expense | 275 | |
|    Cash | | 275 |
|      (To record payment of lease rental charge) | | |

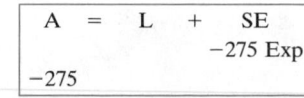

| A | = | L | + | SE |
|---|---|---|---|---|
| | | | | −275 Exp |
| −275 | | | | |

**Cash Flows**
−275

The lessee may incur other costs during the lease period. For example, in the case above, Western will generally incur costs for gas. Western would report these costs as an expense.

## Capital Leases

In most lease contracts, the lessee makes a periodic payment and records that payment in the income statement as rent expense. In some cases, however, the lease contract transfers to the lessee substantially all the benefits and risks of ownership. Such a lease is in effect a purchase of the property. This type of lease is a **capital lease**. Its name comes from the fact that the company capitalizes the present value of the cash payments for the lease and records that amount as an asset. Illustration F-3 indicates the major difference between operating and capital leases.

**Illustration F-3**
Types of leases

**HELPFUL HINT**

A capital lease situation is one that, although legally a rental case, is *in substance* an installment purchase by the lessee. Accounting standards require that substance over form be used in such a situation.

If **any one** of the following conditions exists, the lessee must record a lease **as an asset**—that is, as a capital lease:

1. **The lease transfers ownership of the property to the lessee.** *Rationale:* If during the lease term the lessee receives ownership of the asset, the lessee should report the leased asset as an asset on its books.

2. **The lease contains a bargain purchase option.** *Rationale:* If during the term of the lease the lessee can purchase the asset at a price substantially below its fair market value, the lessee will exercise this option. Thus, the lessee should report the lease as a leased asset on its books.

3. **The lease term is equal to 75% or more of the economic life of the leased property.** *Rationale:* If the lease term is for much of the asset's useful life, the lessee should report the asset as a leased asset on its books.

4. **The present value of the lease payments equals or exceeds 90% of the fair market value of the leased property.** *Rationale:* If the present value of the lease payments is equal to or almost equal to the fair market value of the asset, the lessee has essentially purchased the asset. As a result, the lessee should report the leased asset as an asset on its books.

To illustrate, assume that Gonzalez Company decides to lease new equipment. The lease period is four years; the economic life of the leased equipment is estimated to be five years. The present value of the lease payments is $190,000, which is equal to the fair market value of the equipment. There is no transfer of ownership during the lease term, nor is there any bargain purchase option.

In this example, Gonzalez has essentially purchased the equipment. Conditions 3 and 4 have been met. First, the lease term is 75% or more of the economic life of the asset. Second, the present value of cash payments is equal to the equipment's fair market value. Gonzalez records the transaction as follows.

| | | |
|---|---|---|
| Leased Asset—Equipment | 190,000 | |
|    Lease Liability | | 190,000 |
|      (To record leased asset and lease liability) | | |

| A | = | L | + | SE |
|---|---|---|---|---|
| +190,000 | | | | |
| | | | | +190,000 |

**Cash Flows**
no effect

The lessee reports a leased asset on the balance sheet under plant assets. It reports the lease liability on the balance sheet as a liability. **The portion of the lease liability expected to be paid in the next year is a current liability. The remainder is classified as a long-term liability.**

Most lessees do not like to report leases on their balance sheets. Why? Because the lease liability increases the company's total liabilities. This, in turn, may make it more difficult for the company to obtain needed funds from lenders. As a result, companies attempt to keep leased assets and lease liabilities off the balance sheet by structuring leases so as not to meet any of the four conditions mentioned on page F4. The practice of keeping liabilities off the balance sheet is referred to as **off-balance-sheet financing**.

**ETHICS NOTE**

Accounting standard setters are attempting to rewrite rules on lease accounting because of concerns that abuse of the current standards is reducing the usefulness of financial statements.

# ADDITIONAL LIABILITIES FOR EMPLOYEE FRINGE BENEFITS

**STUDY OBJECTIVE 3**

Identify additional fringe benefits associated with employee compensation.

In addition to the three payroll tax fringe benefits discussed in Appendix D (FICA taxes and state and federal unemployment taxes), employers incur other substantial fringe benefit costs. Indeed, fringe benefits have been growing faster than pay. In a recent year, benefits equaled 38 percent of wages and salaries. While vacations and other forms of paid leave still take the biggest bite out of the benefits pie, as shown in Illustration F-4, medical costs are the fastest-growing item.

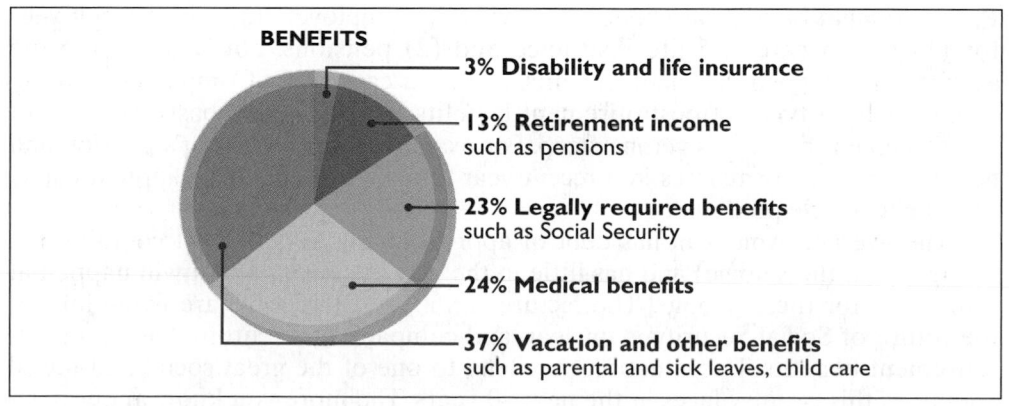

**Illustration F-4**
The fringe benefits pie

**BENEFITS**

- 3% Disability and life insurance
- 13% Retirement income such as pensions
- 23% Legally required benefits such as Social Security
- 24% Medical benefits
- 37% Vacation and other benefits such as parental and sick leaves, child care

We discuss two of the most important fringe benefits—paid absences and postretirement benefits—in this section.

## Paid Absences

Employees often are given rights to receive compensation for absences when certain conditions of employment are met. The compensation may be for paid vacations, sick pay benefits, and paid holidays. When the payment for such absences is **probable** and the amount can be **reasonably estimated**, a liability should be accrued for paid future absences. When the amount cannot be reasonably estimated, companies should instead disclose the potential liability. Ordinarily, vacation pay is the only paid absence that is accrued. The other types of paid absences are only disclosed.[1]

To illustrate, assume that Academy Company employees are entitled to one day's vacation for each month worked. If 30 employees earn an average of $110 per day in a given month, the accrual for vacation benefits in one month is $3,300. The liability is recognized at the end of the month by the following adjusting entry.

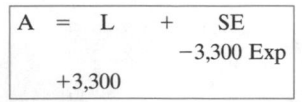

```
A = L + SE
        -3,300 Exp
   +3,300
```
Cash Flows
no effect

| | | | |
|---|---|---|---|
| Jan. 31 | Vacation Benefits Expense | 3,300 | |
| |     Vacation Benefits Payable | | 3,300 |
| |     (To accrue vacation benefits expense) | | |

This accrual is required by the matching principle. Academy would report Vacation Benefits Expense as an operating expense in the income statement, and Vacation Benefits Payable as a current liability in the balance sheet.

Later, when Academy pays vacation benefits, it debits Vacation Benefits Payable and credits Cash. For example, if the above benefits for 10 employees are paid in July, the entry is:

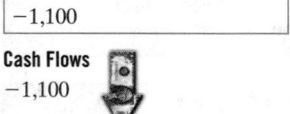

```
A  =  L  +  SE
     -1,100
-1,100
```
Cash Flows
-1,100

| | | | |
|---|---|---|---|
| July 31 | Vacation Benefits Payable | 1,100 | |
| |     Cash | | 1,100 |
| |     (To record payment of vacation benefits) | | |

The magnitude of unpaid absences has gained employers' attention. Consider the case of an assistant superintendent of schools who worked for 20 years and rarely took a vacation or sick day. A month or so before she retired, the school district discovered that she was due nearly $30,000 in accrued benefits. Yet the school district had never accrued the liability.

## Postretirement Benefits

**Postretirement benefits** are benefits provided by employers to retired employees for (1) health care and life insurance and (2) pensions. For many years the accounting for postretirement benefits was on a cash basis. Companies now account for both types of postretirement benefits on the accrual basis. The cost of postretirement benefits is getting steep. For example, General Motor's pension and health-care costs for retirees in a recent year totaled $6.2 billion, or approximately $1,784 per vehicle produced.

The average American has debt of approximately $10,000 (not counting the mortgage on their home) and has little in the way of savings. What will happen at retirement for these people? The picture is not pretty—people are living longer, the future of Social Security is unclear, and companies are cutting back on postretirement benefits. This situation may lead to one of the great social and moral dilemmas this country faces in the next 40 years. The more you know about post-

---

[1]The typical U.S. company provides an average of 12 days of paid vacation for its employees, at an average cost of 5% of gross earnings.

retirement benefits, the better you will understand the issues involved in this dilemma.

## POSTRETIREMENT HEALTH-CARE AND LIFE INSURANCE BENEFITS

Providing medical and related health-care benefits for retirees was at one time an inexpensive and highly effective way of generating employee goodwill. This practice has now turned into one of corporate America's most worrisome financial problems. Runaway medical costs, early retirement, and increased longevity are sending the liability for retiree health plans through the roof.

Many companies began offering retiree health-care coverage in the form of Medicare supplements in the 1960s. Almost all plans operated on a pay-as-you-go basis. The companies simply paid for the bills as they came in, rather than setting aside funds to meet the cost of future benefits. These plans were accounted for on the cash basis. But, the FASB concluded that shareholders and creditors should know the amount of the employer's obligations. As a result, employers must now use the **accrual basis** in accounting for postretirement health-care and life insurance benefits.

## PENSION PLANS

A **pension plan** is an agreement whereby an employer provides benefits (payments) to employees after they retire. Over 50 million workers currently participate in pension plans in the United States. The need for good accounting for pension plans becomes apparent when one appreciates the size of existing pension funds. Most pension plans are subject to the provisions of ERISA (Employee Retirement Income Security Act), a law enacted to curb abuses in the administration and funding of such plans.

Three parties are generally involved in a pension plan. The **employer** (company) sponsors the pension plan. The **plan administrator** receives the contributions from the employer, invests the pension assets, and makes the benefit payments to the **pension recipients** (retired employees). Illustration F-5 indicates the flow of cash among the three parties involved in a pension plan.

**Illustration F-5**
Parties in a pension plan

An employer-financed pension is part of the employees' compensation. ERISA establishes the minimum contribution that a company must make each year toward employee pensions. The most popular type of pension plan used is the 401(k) plan. A 401(k) plan works as follows: As an employee, you can contribute up to a certain percentage of your pay into a 401(k) plan, and your employer will match a percentage of your contribution. These contributions are then generally invested in stocks and bonds through mutual funds. These funds will grow without being taxed and can be withdrawn beginning at age 59-1/2. If you must access the funds earlier, you may be able to do so, but a penalty usually occurs along with a payment of tax on the proceeds. Any time you have the opportunity to be involved in a 401(k) plan, you should avail yourself of this benefit!

Companies record pension costs as an expense while the employees are working because that is when the company receives benefits from the employees' services. Generally the pension expense is reported as an operating expense in the company's income statement. Frequently, the amount contributed by the company to the pension plan is different from the amount of the pension expense. A **liability** is recognized when the pension expense to date is **more than** the company's contributions to date. An **asset** is recognized when the pension expense to date is **less than** the company's contributions to date. Further consideration of the accounting for pension plans is left for more advanced courses.

The two most common types of pension arrangements for providing benefits to employees after they retire are defined-contribution plans and defined-benefit plans.

**Defined-Contribution Plan.** In a defined-contribution plan, the plan defines the employer's contribution but not the benefit that the employee will receive at retirement. That is, the employer agrees to contribute a certain sum each period based on a formula. A 401(k) plan is typically a defined-contribution plan.

The accounting for a defined-contribution plan is straightforward: The employer simply makes a contribution each year based on the formula established in the plan. As a result, the employer's obligation is easily determined. It follows that the company reports **the amount of the contribution required each period as pension expense. The employer reports a liability only if it has not made the contribution in full.**

To illustrate, assume that Alba Office Interiors Corp. has a defined-contribution plan in which it contributes $200,000 each year to the pension fund for its employees. The entry to record this transaction is:

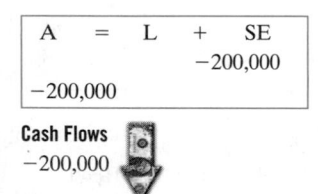

| A | = | L | + | SE |
|---|---|---|---|---|
| | | | | −200,000 |
| −200,000 | | | | |

**Cash Flows**
−200,000

| | | |
|---|---|---|
| Pension Expense | 200,000 | |
|    Cash | | 200,000 |
|      (To record pension expense and contribution to | | |
|      pension fund) | | |

To the extent that Alba did not contribute the $200,000 defined contribution, it would record a liability. Pension payments to retired employees are made from the pension fund by the plan administrator.

**Defined-Benefit Plan.** In a defined-benefit plan, the **benefits** that the employee will receive at the time of retirement are defined by the terms of the plan. Benefits are typically calculated using a formula that considers an employee's compensation level when he or she nears retirement and the employee's years of service. Because the benefits in this plan are defined in terms of uncertain future variables, an appropriate funding pattern is established to ensure that enough funds are available at retirement to meet the benefits promised. This funding level depends on a number of factors such as employee turnover, length of service, mortality, compensation levels, and investment earnings. **The proper accounting for these plans is complex and is considered in more advanced accounting courses.**

### POSTRETIREMENT BENEFITS AS LONG-TERM LIABILITIES

While part of the liability associated with (1) postretirement health-care and life-insurance benefits and (2) pension plans is generally a current liability, the greater portion of these liabilities extends many years into the future. Therefore, many companies are required to report significant amounts as long-term liabilities for postretirement benefits.

## Before You Go On...

**REVIEW IT**
1. What is a contingent liability?
2. How are contingent liabilities reported in financial statements?
3. What accounts are involved in accruing and paying vacation benefits?
4. What basis should be used in accounting for postretirement benefits?

## SUMMARY OF STUDY OBJECTIVES

**1 Describe the accounting and disclosure requirements for contingent liabilities.** If it is probable that the contingency will happen (if it is likely to occur) and the amount can be reasonably estimated, the liability should be recorded in the accounts. If the contingency is only reasonably possible (it could occur), then it should be disclosed only in the notes to the financial statements. If the possibility that the contingency will happen is remote (unlikely to occur), it need not be recorded or disclosed.

**2 Contrast the accounting for operating and capital leases.** For an operating lease, lease (or rental) payments are recorded as an expense by the lessee (renter). For a capital lease, the lessee records the asset and related obligation at the present value of the future lease payments.

**3 Identify additional fringe benefits associated with employee compensation.** Additional fringe benefits associated with wages are paid absences (paid vacations, sick pay benefits, and paid holidays), postretirement health care and life insurance, and pensions. The two most common types of pension arrangements are a defined-contribution plan and a defined-benefit plan.

## GLOSSARY

**Capital lease** A contractual arrangement that transfers substantially all the benefits and risks of ownership to the lessee so that the lease is in effect a purchase of the property. (p. F4).

**Contingent liability** A potential liability that may become an actual liability in the future. (p. F1).

**Defined-benefit plan** A pension plan in which the benefits that the employee will receive at retirement are defined by the terms of the plan. (p. F8).

**Defined-contribution plan** A pension plan in which the employer's contribution to the plan is defined by the terms of the plan. (p. F8).

**Lease** A contractual arrangement between a lessor (owner of a property) and a lessee (renter of the property). (p. F3).

**Operating lease** A contractual arrangement giving the lessee temporary use of the property, with continued ownership of the property by the lessor. (p. F3).

**Pension plan** An agreement whereby an employer provides benefits to employees after they retire. (p. F7).

**Postretirement benefits** Payments by employers to retired employees for health care, life insurance, and pensions. (p. F6).

## SELF-STUDY QUESTIONS

*Answers are at the end of the appendix.*

(SO 1) **1.** A contingency should be recorded in the accounts when:
   **a.** It is probable the contingency will happen but the amount cannot be reasonably estimated.
   **b.** It is reasonably possible the contingency will happen and the amount can be reasonably estimated.
   **c.** It is reasonably possible the contingency will happen but the amount cannot be reasonably estimated.
   **d.** It is probable the contingency will happen and the amount can be reasonably estimated.

**2.** At December 31, Anthony Company prepares an adjusting entry for a product warranty contract. Which of the following accounts are included in the entry? (SO 1)
   **a.** Warranty Expense.
   **b.** Estimated Warranty Liability.
   **c.** Repair Parts/Wages Payable.
   **d.** Both (a) and (b).

**3.** Lease A does not contain a bargain purchase option, but the lease term is equal to 90 percent of the estimated economic life of the leased property. Lease B does not (SO 2) transfer ownership of the property to the lessee by the end of the lease term, but the lease term is equal to 75 percent of the estimated economic life of the lease property. How should the lessee classify these leases?

| | Lease A | Lease B |
|---|---|---|
| a. | Operating lease | Capital lease |
| b. | Operating lease | Operating lease |
| c. | Capital lease | Capital lease |
| d. | Capital lease | Operating lease |

4. Which of the following is *not* an additional fringe benefit? (SO 3)
   a. Salaries.
   b. Paid absences.
   c. Paid vacations.
   d. Postretirement pensions.

# QUESTIONS

1. What is a contingent liability? Give an example of a contingent liability that is usually recorded in the accounts.

2. Under what circumstances is a contingent liability disclosed only in the notes to the financial statements? Under what circumstances is a contingent liability not recorded in the accounts nor disclosed in the notes to the financial statements?

3. (a) What is a lease agreement? (b) What are the two most common types of leases? (c) Distinguish between the two types of leases.

4. Orbison Company rents a warehouse on a month-to-month basis for the storage of its excess inventory. The company periodically must rent space when its production greatly exceeds actual sales. What is the nature of this type of lease agreement, and what accounting treatment should be accorded it?

5. Costello Company entered into an agreement to lease 12 computers from Estes Electronics Inc. The present value of the lease payments is $186,300. Assuming that this is a capital lease, what entry would Costello Company make on the date of the lease agreement?

6. Identify three additional types of fringe benefits associated with employees' compensation.

7. Often during job interviews, the candidate asks the potential employer about the firm's paid absences policy. What are paid absences? How are they accounted for?

8. What are the two types of postretirement benefits? During what years does the FASB advocate expensing the employer's costs of these postretirement benefits?

9. What basis of accounting for the employer's cost of postretirement health-care and life insurance benefits has been used by most companies, and what basis does the FASB advocate in the future? Explain the basic difference between these methods in recognizing postretirement benefit costs.

10. Identify the three parties in a pension plan. What role does each party have in the plan?

11. Brenna Ottare and Caitlin Wilkes are reviewing pension plans. They ask your help in distinguishing between a defined-contribution plan and a defined-benefit plan. Explain the principal difference to Brenna and Caitlin.

Go to the book's website,
**www.wiley.com/college/weygandt**,
for Additional Self-Study questions.

# BRIEF EXERCISES

*Prepare adjusting entry for warranty costs.*

(SO 1)

**BEF-1** On December 1, Vina Company introduces a new product that includes a 1-year warranty on parts. In December 1,000 units are sold. Management believes that 5% of the units will be defective and that the average warranty costs will be $60 per unit. Prepare the adjusting entry at December 31 to accrue the estimated warranty cost.

*Prepare entries for operating and capital leases.*

(SO 2)

**BEF-2** Prepare the journal entries that the lessee should make to record the following transactions.

1. The lessee makes a lease payment of $80,000 to the lessor in an operating lease transaction.
2. Zander Company leases a new building from Joel Construction, Inc. The present value of the lease payments is $900,000. The lease qualifies as a capital lease.

*Record estimated vacation benefits.*

(SO 3)

**BEF-3** In Alomar Company, employees are entitled to 1 day's vacation for each month worked. In January, 50 employees worked the full month. Record the vacation pay liability for January assuming the average daily pay for each employee is $120.

# EXERCISES

**EF-1**   Boone Company sells automatic can openers under a 75-day warranty for defective merchandise. Based on past experience, Boone Company estimates that 3% of the units sold will become defective during the warranty period. Management estimates that the average cost of replacing or repairing a defective unit is $15. The units sold and units defective that occurred during the last 2 months of 2006 are as follows.

*Record estimated liability and expense for warranties.*
*(SO 1)*

| Month | Units Sold | Units Defective Prior to December 31 |
|---|---|---|
| November | 30,000 | 600 |
| December | 32,000 | 400 |

**Instructions**
**(a)** Determine the estimated warranty liability at December 31 for the units sold in November and December.
**(b)** Prepare the journal entries to record the estimated liability for warranties and the costs (assume actual costs of $15,000) incurred in honoring 1,000 warranty claims.
**(c)** Give the entry to record the honoring of 500 warranty contracts in January at an average cost of $15.

**EF-2**   Larkin Online Company has the following liability accounts after posting adjusting entries: Accounts Payable $63,000, Unearned Ticket Revenue $24,000, Estimated Warranty Liability $18,000, Interest Payable $8,000, Mortgage Payable $120,000, Notes Payable $80,000, and Sales Taxes Payable $10,000. Assume the company's operating cycle is less than 1 year, ticket revenue will be earned within 1 year, warranty costs are expected to be incurred within 1 year, and the notes mature in 3 years.

*Prepare the current liabilities section of the balance sheet.*
*(SO 1)*

**Instructions**
**(a)** Prepare the current liabilities section of the balance sheet, assuming $40,000 of the mortgage is payable next year.
**(b)** Comment on Larkin Online Company's liquidity, assuming total current assets are $300,000.

**EF-3**   Presented below are two independent situations.
**1.**   Speedy Car Rental leased a car to Rundgren Company for 1 year. Terms of the operating lease agreement call for monthly payments of $500.
**2.**   On January 1, 2008, Miles Inc. entered into an agreement to lease 20 computers from Halo Electronics. The terms of the lease agreement require three annual rental payments of $40,000 (including 10% interest) beginning December 31, 2008. The present value of the three rental payments is $99,474. Miles considers this a capital lease.

*Prepare journal entries for operating lease and capital lease.*
*(SO 2)*

**Instructions**
**(a)** Prepare the appropriate journal entry to be made by Rundgren Company for the first lease payment.
**(b)** Prepare the journal entry to record the lease agreement on the books of Miles Inc. on January 1, 2008.

**EF-4**   Bunill Company has two fringe benefit plans for its employees:
**1.**   It grants employees 2 days' vacation for each month worked. Ten employees worked the entire month of March at an average daily wage of $80 per employee.
**2.**   It has a defined contribution pension plan in which the company contributes 10% of gross earnings. Gross earnings in March were $30,000. The payment to the pension fund has not been made.

*Prepare adjusting entries for fringe benefits.*
*(SO 3)*

**Instructions**
Prepare the adjusting entries at March 31.

# EXERCISES: SET B

Visit the book's website at **www.wiley.com/college/weygandt**, and choose the Student Companion site, to access Exercise Set B.

## PROBLEMS: SET A

*Prepare current liability entries, adjusting entries, and current liabilities section.*

*(SO 1)*

**PF-1A** On January 1, 2008, the ledger of Shumway Software Company contains the following liability accounts.

| | |
|---|---|
| Accounts Payable | $42,500 |
| Sales Taxes Payable | 5,800 |
| Unearned Service Revenue | 15,000 |

During January the following selected transactions occurred.

Jan. 1 Borrowed $15,000 in cash from Amsterdam Bank on a 4-month, 8%, $15,000 note.

 5 Sold merchandise for cash totaling $10,400 which includes 4% sales taxes.

 12 Provided services for customers who had made advance payments of $9,000. (Credit Service Revenue.)

 14 Paid state treasurer's department for sales taxes collected in December 2007 ($5,800).

 20 Sold 700 units of a new product on credit at $52 per unit, plus 4% sales tax. This new product is subject to a 1-year warranty.

 25 Sold merchandise for cash totaling $12,480, which includes 4% sales taxes.

**Instructions**

(a) Journalize the January transactions.

(b) Journalize the adjusting entries at January 31 for (1) the outstanding notes payable, and (2) estimated warranty liability, assuming warranty costs are expected to equal 5% of sales of the new product.

(c) Prepare the current liabilities section of the balance sheet at January 31, 2008. Assume no change in accounts payable.

*Analyze three different lease situations and prepare journal entries.*

*(SO 2)*

**PF-2A** Presented below are three different lease transactions in which Ortiz Enterprises engaged in 2008. Assume that all lease transactions start on January 1, 2008. In no case does Ortiz receive title to the properties leased during or at the end of the lease term.

| | Lessor | | |
|---|---|---|---|
| | **Schoen Inc.** | **Casey Co.** | **Lester Inc.** |
| Type of property | Bulldozer | Truck | Furniture |
| Bargain purchase option | None | None | None |
| Lease term | 4 years | 6 years | 3 years |
| Estimated economic life | 8 years | 7 years | 5 years |
| Yearly rental | $13,000 | $15,000 | $4,000 |
| Fair market value of leased asset | $80,000 | $72,000 | $27,500 |
| Present value of the lease rental payments | $48,000 | $62,000 | $12,000 |

**Instructions**

(a) Identify the leases above as operating or capital leases. Explain.

(b) How should the lease transaction with Casey Co. be recorded on January 1, 2008?

(c) How should the lease transactions for Lester Inc. be recorded in 2008?

## PROBLEMS: SET B

*Prepare current liability entries, adjusting entries, and current liabilities section.*

*(SO 1)*

**PF-1B** On January 1, 2008, the ledger of Zaur Company contains the following liability accounts.

| | |
|---|---|
| Accounts Payable | $52,000 |
| Sales Taxes Payable | 7,700 |
| Unearned Service Revenue | 16,000 |

During January the following selected transactions occurred.

Jan. 5 Sold merchandise for cash totaling $17,280, which includes 8% sales taxes.

 12 Provided services for customers who had made advance payments of $10,000. (Credit Service Revenue.)

14 Paid state revenue department for sales taxes collected in December 2007 ($7,700).

20 Sold 600 units of a new product on credit at $50 per unit, plus 8% sales tax. This new product is subject to a 1-year warranty.

21 Borrowed $18,000 from UCLA Bank on a 3-month, 9%, $18,000 note.

25 Sold merchandise for cash totaling $12,420, which includes 8% sales taxes.

**Instructions**

**(a)** Journalize the January transactions.

**(b)** Journalize the adjusting entries at January 31 for (1) the outstanding notes payable, and (2) estimated warranty liability, assuming warranty costs are expected to equal 7% of sales of the new product. (*Hint*: Use one-third of a month for the UCLA Bank note.)

**(c)** Prepare the current liabilities section of the balance sheet at January 31, 2008. Assume no change in accounts payable.

**PF-2B** Presented below are three different lease transactions that occurred for Milo Inc. in 2008. Assume that all lease contracts start on January 1, 2008. In no case does Milo receive title to the properties leased during or at the end of the lease term.

*Analyze three different lease situations and prepare journal entries.*

*(SO 2)*

| | Lessor | | |
| --- | --- | --- | --- |
| | **Gibson Delivery** | **Eller Co.** | **Louis Auto** |
| Type of property | Computer | Delivery equipment | Automobile |
| Yearly rental | $ 8,000 | $ 4,200 | $ 3,700 |
| Lease term | 6 years | 4 years | 2 years |
| Estimated economic life | 7 years | 7 years | 5 years |
| Fair market value of leased asset | $44,000 | $19,000 | $11,000 |
| Present value of the lease rental payments | $41,000 | $13,000 | $6,400 |
| Bargain purchase option | None | None | None |

**Instructions**

**(a)** Which of the leases above are operating leases and which are capital leases? Explain.

**(b)** How should the lease transaction with Eller Co. be recorded in 2008?

**(c)** How should the lease transaction for Gibson Delivery be recorded on January 1, 2008?

## PROBLEMS: SET C

Visit the book's website at **www.wiley.com/college/weygandt**, and choose the Student Companion site, to access Problem Set C.

# BROADENING YOUR PERSPECTIVE

## FINANCIAL REPORTING AND ANALYSIS

## Financial Reporting Problems

**BYPF-1** Refer to the financial statements of PepsiCo and the Notes to Consolidated Financial Statements in Appendix A to answer the following questions about contingent liabilities, lease liabilities, and pension costs.

**(a)** Where does PepsiCo report its contingent liabilities?

**(b)** What is management's opinion as to the ultimate effect of the "various claims and legal proceedings" pending against the company?

**(c)** Where did PepsiCo report the details of its lease obligations? What amount of rent expense from operating leases did PepsiCo incur in 2005? What was PepsiCo's total future minimum annual rental commitment under noncancelable operating leases as of December 31, 2005?

**(d)** What type of employee pension plan does PepsiCo have?

**(e)** What is the amount of postretirement benefit expense (other than pensions) for 2005?

**BYPF-2**  Presented below is the lease portion of the notes to the financial statements of CF Industries, Inc.

### CF INDUSTRIES, INC.
Notes to the Financial Statements

**Leases**   The present value of future minimum capital lease payments and the future minimum lease payments under noncancelable operating leases at December 31, 2006, are:

|  | (in millions) | |
| --- | --- | --- |
|  | **Capital Lease Payments** | **Operating Lease Payments** |
| 2007 | $ 7,733 | $3,067 |
| 2008 | 6,791 | 2,052 |
| 2009 | 6,730 | 1,056 |
| 2010 | 6,788 | 918 |
| 2011 | 6,785 | 86 |
| Thereafter | 13,441 | 6 |
| Future minimum lease payments | 48,268 | $7,185 |
| Less: Equivalent interest | 11,391 | |
| Present value | 36,877 | |
| Less: Current portion | 5,570 | |
|  | $31,307 | |

Rent expense for operating leases was $7.0 million for the year ended December 31, 2006, $5.3 million for 2005, and $5.6 million for 2004.

**Instructions**
What type of leases does CF Industries, Inc. use? What is the amount of the current portion of the capital lease obligation?

# CRITICAL THINKING

## Decision Making Across the Organization

**BYPF-3**  Presented below is the condensed balance sheet for Express, Inc. as of December 31, 2008.

### EXPRESS, INC.
Balance Sheet
December 31, 2008

| | | | |
| --- | --- | --- | --- |
| Current assets | $  800,000 | Current liabilities | $1,200,000 |
| Plant assets | 1,600,000 | Long-term liabilities | 700,000 |
| | | Common stock | 400,000 |
| | | Retained earnings | 100,000 |
| Total | $2,400,000 | Total | $2,400,000 |

Express has decided that it needs to purchase a new crane for its operations. The new crane costs $900,000 and has a useful life of 15 years. However, Express's bank has refused to provide any help in financing the purchase of the new equipment, even though Express is willing to pay an above-market interest rate for the financing.

The chief financial officer for Express, Lisa Colder, has discussed with the manufacturer of the crane the possibility of a lease agreement. After some negotiation, the crane manufacturer agrees to lease the crane to Express under the following terms: length of the lease 7 years; payments $100,000 per year. The present value of the lease payments is $548,732.

The board of directors at Express is delighted with this new lease. They reason they have the use of the crane for the next 7 years. In addition, Lisa Colder notes that this type of financing is a good deal because it will keep debt off the balance sheet.

**Instructions**

With the class divided into groups, answer the following.

**(a)** Why do you think the bank decided not to lend money to Express, Inc.?

**(b)** How should this lease transaction be reported in the financial statements?

**(c)** What did Lisa Colder mean when she said "leasing will keep debt off the balance sheet"?

**Answers to Self-Study Questions**

**1.** d    **2.** d    **3.** c    **4.** a

# PHOTO CREDITS

**Chapter 1**  Page 3: Dinodia Images/Alamy Limited. Page 9: Hai Wen China Tourism Press/Getty Images, Inc. Page 11: Brent Holland/iStockphoto. Page 23: iStockphoto.

**Chapter 2**  Page 47: NBAE/Getty Images. Page 56: Koichi Kamoshida/AsiaPac/Getty Images, Inc. Page 58: Mike Stewart/Corbis Sygma Page 70 PhotoDisc, Inc./Getty Images.

**Chapter 3**  Page 93: Witte Thomas E/Gamma Presse, Inc. Page 96: Kevin Winter/Getty Images, Inc. Page 100: Chris Weeks/Getty Images, Inc. Page 104: iStockphoto.

**Chapter 4**  Page 143: Brian Bahr/Getty Images, Inc. Page 155: M. Tcherevkoff/Getty Images, Inc. Page 160: Christian Lagereek/iStockphoto. Page 164: Digital Vision Page 164: Nikki Ward/iStockphoto. Page 165: Brand X/PictureArts. Page 166: iStockphoto. Page 166: iStockphoto.

**Chapter 5**  Page 195: Stone/Getty Images, Inc. Page 199: Courtesy Morrow Snowboards Inc. Page 205: iStockphoto. Page 213: Victor Prikhoddko/iStockphoto.

**Chapter 6**  Page 245: Pathaithai Chungyam/iStockphoto. Page 247: Bjorn Kindler/iStockphoto. Page 248: iStockphoto. Page 257: PhotoDisc, Inc./Getty Images. Page 262: Courtesy Samsung Electronics America.

**Chapter 7**  Page 293: image (c)2000 Artville, Inc. Page 301: iStockphoto. Page 302: Barbara Nessim/Stock Illustration Source/Images.com. Page 310: Steve Forney/SUPERSTOCK. Page 312: Olney Vasan/Stone/Getty Images.

**Chapter 8**  Page 339: Valerie Loiseleux/iStockphoto. Page 343: Gianni Dagli Orti/Corbis Images. Page 344: Terence John/Retna. Page 346: Nick Koudis/AFP/Getty Images. Page 357: Ingvald Kaldhussaeter/iStockphoto.

**Chapter 9**  Page 385: Jorg Greuel/AFP/Getty Images. Page 388: Alice Millikan/iStockphoto. Page 394: Joe Polillio/Getty Images, Inc. Page 397: Michael Braun/iStockphoto. Page 402: Jamie Evans/iStockphoto.

**Chapter 10**  Page 425: David Trood/Getty Images, Inc. Page 429: iStockphoto. Page 438: AFP/Getty Images. Page 445: Andy Lions/Photonica/Getty Images, Inc.

**Chapter 11**  Page 473: Cary Westfall/iStockphoto. Page 478: Catherine dee Auvil/iStockphoto. Page 486: iStockphoto. Page 494: Greg Nicholas/iStockphoto. Page 495: Corbis Stock Market.

**Chapter 12**  Page 533: David Young-Wolf/PhotoEdit. Page 537: Reuters NewMedia Inc/Corbis Images. Page 541: Brandon Laufenberg/iStockphoto. Page 548: Alex Fevzer/Corbis Images. Page 555 Tomasz Resiak/iStockphoto. Page 561: Arpad Benedek/iStockphoto.

**Chapter 13**  Page 595: Warner Bros. David James/The Kobal Collection, Ltd. Page 608: John Lamb/Stone/Getty Images, Inc.

**Chapter 14**  Page 637: Rudi Von Briel/PhotoEdit. Page 641: Elle Wagner and Lisa Gee/John Wiley & Sons. Page 644: Corbis Digital Stock. Page 655: PhotoDisc, Inc./Getty Images.

**Chapter 15**  Page 697: Jeremy Edwards/iStockphoto. Page 700. Don Wilkie/iStockphoto 700 Don Wilkie/iStockphoto. Page 707: Nora Good/Masterfile. Page 715: Royalty-Free/Corbis Images. Page 720: Martina Misar/iStockphoto. Page 724: iStockphoto. Page 724: iStockphoto.

# COMPANY INDEX

**A**
ABC, 445
Ace Hardware, 271
Adelphia, 10
Advanced Micro, 540
AIG, 8
Alcatel-Alsthom, 298
Alliance Atlantis Communications Inc., 676
Altria Group, 470, 603, 634
Aluminum Company of America
    (Alcoa), 581
Amazon.com, 560, 696
America Bank, 412
American Airlines, 102, 479
American Cancer Society, 534
American Eagle Outfitters, 350
American Express, 396, 473
American Standard, 707
America Online (AOL), 470, 595, 597
Anaheim Angels, 604
AOL Time Warner, 597
Apple Computer, 6, 115, 298, 443, 715
Arthur Andersen, 537
AT&T, 4, 603
Avis, 425, 431, 604

**B**
Babies "R" Us, 604
BankAmerica, 314
Bank of America, 11
Bank One Corporation, 70
Batten Ltd., 325–326
Baylor University, 514
Berkshire Hathaway, 470
Best Buy, 9, 104, 140
Bill and Melinda Gates Foundation, 29, 534
Black & Decker Manufacturing
    Company, 255
Boeing Capital Corporation, 429
Boeing Company, 440, 470, 485, 552, 710
Boise Cascade, 434
Book-of-the-Month Club, 595
Breyer, 470
Bristol-Myers Squibb, 215, 255, 722
Budget, 425

**C**
Cadbury-Schweppes, 10
Campbell Soup Company, 255, 433, 707
Capital Cities/ABC, Inc., 604
Cargill Inc., 535
Caterpillar Inc., 244–246, 257, 480, 481, 535
Caterpillar Logistics Services, Inc., 245
Cendant Corp., 314, 604
Century 21, 604
Chase, 70
Chevron, 434
Cisco Systems, 155, 193, 289, 404, 470, 722
Citibank, 409
Citigroup, 11
CNN, 595
Coca-Cola Amatil Limited, B2
The Coca-Cola Company, 3, 5, 10, 11, 42, 43,
    87, 100, 137, 163, 191, 215, 240, 243, 289, 333,
    381, 421, 468, 470, 480, 528, 589, 618, 632, 692,
    744, B1–B4
Coca-Cola Enterprises Inc., B2
Coca-Cola FEMSA, S.A. de C.V., B2
Coca-Cola Hellenic Bottling Company
    S.A., B2
Coldwell Banker, 604

Columbia Sportswear Company, 676
Computer Associates International, 106
ConAgra Foods, 212
Consolidated Edison, 711
Continental Bank, 429
Costco Wholesale Corp., 641, D1
Craig Consumer Electronics, 249
Crane Company, 551
Cypress Semiconductor Corporation, 676

**D**
DaimlerChrysler Corporation, 296, 491
Dairy Queen, 470
DeKalb Genetics Corporation, 626
Dell Computer, 60, 247, 298, 605
Dell Financial Services, 429
Delta Air Lines, 23, 45, 95, 102, 440
Discover, 395
Disney Company, *see* The Walt Disney
    Company
Disneyland, 604
DisneyWorld, 604
Dun & Bradstreet, 309, 699
Dunkin' Donuts, 23, 45
DuPont, 484, 485
Dynegy, Inc., 644, 694

**E**
EarthLink, 552
Eastman Kodak Company, 346, 363, 606, 638
eBay, 357
Enron, 8, 29, 213, 301, 314, 340, 537, 591,
    722, 746
ESPN, 445, 470, 604
Estée Lauder Companies, Inc., 724–725
ExxonMobil, 11, 296, 298, 470, 547

**F**
Fannie Mae, 70, 108
Fidelity Investments, 47, 48
First National Bank, 12
Florida Citrus Company, 718
Ford Motor Company, 4, 11, 198, 258, 296,
    532–536, 547
Frito-Lay, 315, A9, A10, A12, A13

**G**
GE, *see* General Electric
General Dynamics, 745
General Electric (GE), 7, 10, 204, 213, 298, 301,
    341, 470, 535, 597
General Mills, 433
General Motors (GM), 6–7, 11, 194, 296, 302,
    410, 538, 650, 695, 721, 728
Global Crossing, 301, 340
GM, *see* General Motors
Goldman Sachs, 11
Google, 29, 534, 540
Gulf Oil, 538

**H**
Harley-Davidson, 215
Harold's Club, 301, 335
HBO, 595
HealthSouth, 8
Hershey Foods Corp., 552
Hertz, 425, F3
Hewlett-Packard, 298
Hilton, 429
Home Depot, 4, 247, 271, 428
Howard Johnson, 604

**I**
IBM, 71, 213, 242, 298, 535, 539n.2
Imaginarium, 604
Intel Corporation, 325, 535, 555, 560
InterContinental, 429
International Harvester, 3
IT&T, 2

**J**
J. Crew, 350
J.C. Penney Company, Inc., 349, 387, 412–413,
    641, 698–700, 704–715
John Deere Capital Corporation, 429
Johnson & Johnson, 310, 325
J.P. Morgan Leasing, 429

**K**
Kellogg Company, 12, 29, 495, 560, 565, 566
Kids "R" Us, 604
Kmart, 196, 310, 699, 710, 717
Kodak, *see* Eastman Kodak Company
Kohl's Corporation, 641
KPMG LLP, A27, A29
Kraft Foods, Inc., 597, 603, 634
Krispy Kreme Doughnuts, 215
Kroger Stores, 198, 255, 310, 710, 711
K2, Inc., 164

**L**
Leslie Fay Cos., 248, 290
The Limited, 296
Limited Brands, 100
Little, Brown & Co., 595
L.L. Bean, 296
Lockheed Martin Corporation, 155, 440, 561
Long Beach City College, 334
Lotus, 71
Lucent Technologies, 314

**M**
McDonald's Corporation, 11, 443, 455, 470,
    493, 534
McKesson Corporation, 196, 290
Major League Baseball Players Association, 7
Marriott, 429, 433
Marshall Farms, 626
Massachusetts General Hospital, 11
MasterCard, 395–397, 412, 416
Merck, 310
Merrill Lynch, 11
Microsoft Corporation, 6, 11, 56, 89, 204, 295,
    302, 443, 470, 547, 555, 636–637, 655, 728
Mighty Ducks, 604
Minnesota Mining and Manufacturing Company,
    *see* 3M
Mitsubishi Motors, 402, 423
Moody's, 529, 699
Morgan Stanley, 608
Morrow Snowboards, Inc., 199
Motorola, 255, 325, 720

**N**
NationsBank, 314
NBC, 470
New York Stock Exchange, 609
Nike, Inc., 4, 100, 542, 552, 553, 558, 705–706
Nordstrom, Inc., 166, 397, 423, 732–733
Nortel Networks, 394, 715
North American Van Lines, 542
Northern Virginia Community College, 11
Northwest Airlines, 94, 166